The Cambridge Handbook of Intelligence

This volume provides the most comprehensive and up-to-date compendium of theory and research in the field of human intelligence. The 42 chapters are written by world-renowned experts, each in his or her respective field, and collectively, the chapters cover the full range of topics of contemporary interest in the study of intelligence. The handbook is divided into nine parts: Part I covers intelligence and its measurement; Part II deals with the development of intelligence; Part III discusses intelligence and group differences; Part IV concerns the biology of intelligence; Part V is about intelligence and information processing; Part VI discusses different kinds of intelligence; Part VII covers intelligence and society; Part VIII concerns intelligence in relation to allied constructs; and Part IX is the concluding chapter, which reflects on where the field is currently and where it still needs to go.

Robert J. Sternberg is provost and senior vice president and professor of psychology at Oklahoma State University. He was previously dean of the School of Arts and Sciences and professor of psychology and education at Tufts University. His PhD is from Stanford and he holds 11 honorary doctorates. Sternberg is president of the International Association for Cognitive Education and Psychology and president-elect of the Federation of Associations of Behavioral and Brain Sciences. He was the 2003 president of the American Psychological Association and was the president of the Eastern Psychological Association. The central focus of his research is on intelligence, creativity, and wisdom. He is the author of more than 1,200 journal articles, book chapters, and books; has received more than $20 million in government and other grants and contracts for his research; has won more than two dozen professional awards; and has been listed in the *APA Monitor on Psychology* as one of the top 100 psychologists of the 20th century. He is listed by the ISI as one of its most highly cited authors in psychology and psychiatry.

Scott Barry Kaufman is an adjunct assistant professor of psychology at New York University. He holds a PhD in cognitive psychology from Yale University; an M Phil in experimental psychology from King's College, University of Cambridge, where he was a Gates Cambridge Scholar; and a BS from Carnegie Mellon University. From 2009–2010, he was a postdoctoral Fellow at the Center Leo Apostel for Interdisciplinary Studies, Free University of Brussels. His research interests include the nature, identification, and development of human intelligence, creativity, imagination, and personality. In addition to publishing more than 25 book chapters and articles in professional journals such as *Cognition, Intelligence,* and *Journal of Creative Behavior,* he is co-editor of *The Psychology of Creative Writing* (2009) with James C. Kaufman. His work has been covered in media outlets such as *Scientific American Mind* and *Men's Health.* Additionally, he writes a blog for *Psychology Today* entitled "Beautiful Minds" and is a contributing writer for *The Huffington Post*. Kaufman is the recipient of the 2008 Frank X. Barron award from Division 10 of the American Psychological Association for his research on the psychology of aesthetics, creativity, and the arts.

The Cambridge Handbook of Intelligence

Edited by
ROBERT J. STERNBERG
Oklahoma State University
SCOTT BARRY KAUFMAN
New York University

CAMBRIDGE
UNIVERSITY PRESS

CAMBRIDGE UNIVERSITY PRESS
Cambridge, New York, Melbourne, Madrid, Cape Town,
Singapore, São Paulo, Delhi, Tokyo, Mexico City

Cambridge University Press
32 Avenue of the Americas, New York, NY 10013-2473, USA

www.cambridge.org
Information on this title: www.cambridge.org/9780521739115

First published 2011

Printed in the United States of America

A catalog record for this publication is available from the British Library.

Library of Congress Cataloging in Publication data

The Cambridge Handbook of Intelligence / [edited by] Robert J. Sternberg, Scott Barry Kaufman.
p. cm. – (Cambridge Handbooks in Psychology)
Includes bibliographical references and index.
ISBN 978-0-521-51806-2 – ISBN 978-0-521-73911-5 (pbk.)
1. Intellect. 2. Human information processing.
I. Sternberg, Robert J. (Robert Jeffrey), 1949– II. Kaufman, Scott Barry, 1979– III. Title. IV. Series.
BF431.C26837 2011
153.9–dc22 2010049730

ISBN 978-0-521-51806-2 Hardback
ISBN 978-0-521-73911-5 Paperback

This volume is dedicated to the memory of John L. Horn, foremost scholar, dedicated colleague, wonderful friend.

Contents

Contributors

PHILLIP L. ACKERMAN
Georgia Institute of Technology, USA

SOON ANG
Nanyang Technological University, Singapore

SUSAN M. BARNETT
Cornell University, USA

G. DAVID BATTY
Medical Research Council Social and Public Health Sciences Unit, Glasgow

ANNA S. BENINGER
Claremont McKenna College, USA

JILLIAN BRASS
Pace University, USA

MEGHAN M. BURKE
Vanderbilt University, USA

NANCY CANTOR
Syracuse University, USA

PRIYANKA B. CARR
Stanford University, USA

DAVID R. CARUSO
Yale University, USA

STEPHEN J. CECI
Cornell University, USA

LILLIA CHERKASSKIY
Yale University, USA

JOANNA CHRISTODOULOU
Harvard University, USA

ANDREW R. A. CONWAY
Princeton University, USA

CHRISTINE E. DALEY
Columbus Psychological Associates, USA

JANET E. DAVIDSON
Lewis & Clark College, USA

JIM DAVIES
Carleton University, Canada

KATIE DAVIS
Harvard University, USA

Ian J. Deary
University of Edinburgh, Scotland

Colin G. DeYoung
University of Minnesota, USA

Ron Dumont
Fairleigh Dickinson University, USA

Carol S. Dweck
Stanford University, USA

Linn Van Dyne
Michigan State University, USA

Pascale M. J. Engel de Abreu
University of Oxford, United Kingdom

Joseph F. Fagan
Case Western Reserve University, USA

David Henry Feldman
Tufts University, USA

Kurt W. Fischer
Harvard University, USA

Marisa H. Fisher
Vanderbilt University, USA

James R. Flynn
University of Otago, New Zealand

Liane Gabora
University of British Columbia, Canada

Howard Gardner
Harvard University, USA

Glenn Geher
State University of New York, New Paltz, USA

Sarah J. Getz
Princeton University, USA

Judith Glück
Alpen-Adria University Klagenfurt, Austria

Ashok K. Goel
Georgia Institute of Technology, USA

Megan M. Griffin
Vanderbilt University, USA

Elena L. Grigorenko
Columbia University, USA; Yale University, USA; and Moscow State University, Russia

Richard J. Haier
University of California, Irvine, USA

Diane F. Halpern
Claremont McKenna College, USA

Christopher Hertzog
Georgia Institute of Technology, USA

Robert M. Hodapp
Vanderbilt University, USA

Earl Hunt
The University of Washington, USA

Alan S. Kaufman
Yale University School of Medicine, USA

James C. Kaufman
California State University at San Bernardino, USA

Scott Barry Kaufman
New York University, USA

Iris A. Kemp
Lewis & Clark College, USA

John F. Kihlstrom
University of California, Berkeley, USA

Joni M. Lakin
The University of Iowa, USA

Christina S. Lee
Brown University, USA

David F. Lohman
The University of Iowa, USA

N. J. Mackintosh
University of Cambridge, United Kingdom

Brooke Macnamara
Princeton University, USA

Samuel D. Mandelman
Columbia University, USA

John D. Mayer
University of New Hampshire, USA

Richard E. Mayer
University of California, Santa Barbara, USA

Martha J. Morelock
Vanderbilt University, USA

Ted Nettelbeck
The University of Adelaide, USA

Raymond S. Nickerson
Tufts University, USA

Weihua Niu
Pace University, USA

Anthony J. Onwuegbuzie
Sam Houston State University, USA

Jonathan A. Plucker
Indiana University, USA

Sally M. Reis
The University of Connecticut, USA

Joseph S. Renzulli
The University of Connecticut, USA

Heiner Rindermann
Karl-Franzens-University Graz, Austria

L. Todd Rose
Harvard University, USA

Anne Russon
York University, Canada

Peter Salovey
Yale University, USA

Scott Seider
Boston University, USA

Ellen L. Short
Long Island University, USA

Keith E. Stanovich
University of Toronto, Canada

Ursula M. Staudinger
Jacobs University Bremen, Germany

Robert J. Sternberg
Oklahoma State University, USA

Carli A. Straight
Claremont Graduate University, USA

Lisa A. Suzuki
New York University, USA

Mei Ling Tan
Nanyang Technological University, Singapore

Maggie E. Toplak
York University, Canada

Susana Urbina
University of North Florida, USA

Richard K. Wagner
Florida State University, USA

Richard F. West
James Madison University, USA

Wendy M. Williams
Cornell University, USA

John O. Willis
Rivier College, USA

Thomas R. Zentall
University of Kentucky, USA

Preface

Suppose there were two identical twins stranded on a desert island. Because they have the same genes and are in the same environment, they adapt equally well to the rigorous demands of survival. Would the concept of intelligence ever arise? This conundrum was first posed by Quinn McNemar (1964) in his presidential address to the American Psychological Association. The conundrum raised the question of whether our concept of intelligence is based exclusively on individual differences. It also showed the extent to which in the earlier part of the 20th century, thinking about intelligence was very closely tied to the psychological study of individual differences, or "differential psychology." In those days, there were many different theories of intelligence but Edwin Boring's (1923) view of intelligence as whatever it is that intelligence tests measure seemed to be a starting point for much of this research. The factor-analytic theorists who belonged to the differential-psychology movement generally used such tests as the starting point for generating their theories. They still do.

As we start the second decade of the 21st century, approaches to the study of intelligence are far more varied and diverse than they were then. They still very much include the differentially based factor-analytic approach, but they include other approaches as well. Embracing such a diversity of approaches raises far more questions than were raised before about just what intelligence is. But there has never been much agreement on what intelligence is. Even in the early 20th century, when experts were asked what they believe intelligence to be, every expert gave a different answer ("Intelligence and Its Measurement," 1921). This situation leaves us with the Humpty Dumpty conundrum:

> *"I don't know what you mean by 'glory,'" Alice said. Humpty Dumpty smiled contemptuously. "Of course you don't – till I tell you. I meant 'there's a nice knock-down argument for you!'" "But 'glory' doesn't mean 'a nice knock-down argument,'" Alice objected. "When I use a word," Humpty Dumpty said, in rather a scornful tone, "it means just what I choose it*

> *to mean – neither more nor less." "The question is," said Alice, "whether you can make words mean so many different things." "The question is," said Humpty Dumpty, "which is to be master – that's all." (Lewis Carroll,* Through the Looking-Glass, *ch. VI)*

Does intelligence have any set meaning at all, or does it end up meaning what we want it to mean? Is it discovered, invented, or some combination of the two?

This handbook addresses the most basic questions about intelligence – such as how we come to conceive of it and what it means – and also addresses questions such as how to measure it, how it develops, and how it can be increased, if at all. The handbook is the culmination of a series of volumes, all published by Cambridge University Press. The first volume was published almost 30 years ago (Sternberg, 1982). That *Handbook of Human Intelligence* was the first comprehensive volume trying to set down and synthesize the entire field of human intelligence. The handbook was intended to guide research on intelligence for the remainder of the 20th century. The century ended and so the second volume was published 18 years later (Sternberg, 2000). The *Handbook of Intelligence* was broader than the original handbook and included material on animal intelligence as well – hence, the word "human" was dropped from the title. Four years later, the *International Handbook of Intelligence* (Sternberg, 2004) was published. The goal of that book was to present intelligence in a global way. How is intelligence conceived of, measured, and developed in countries around the world? The handbook revealed similarities but also great diversity in the ways in which intelligence is viewed around the world.

The field of intelligence has been moving forward at a much greater rate than ever before, and this explosion of knowledge is what has led to the publication of a new and even more comprehensive handbook only slightly more than a decade after the 2000 publication. This handbook is a joint effort between Sternberg and a collaborator and former student at Yale, Scott Barry Kaufman. The *Cambridge Handbook of Intelligence*, which you are now reading, is by far the most comprehensive single-volume work to present to readers the breadth and depth of work being done in recent years in the field of intelligence. The handbook is divided into nine parts.

Part I, "Intelligence and Its Measurement," contains four chapters that introduce the constructs. Chapter 1, "History of Theories and Measurement of Intelligence," by N. J. Mackintosh, reviews how our current theories and measurements of intelligence have come to be. Chapter 2, "Tests of Intelligence," by Susana Urbina, discusses the current state of intelligence tests and the issues confronting them. Chapter 3, "Factor-Analytic Models of Intelligence," by John O. Willis, Ron Dumont, and Alan S. Kaufman, reviews the differential approach to intelligence and the factor-analytic models that have arisen out of it. Chapter 4, "Contemporary Models of Intelligence," by Janet E. Davidson and Iris A. Kemp, surveys and evaluates some of the major contemporary models.

Part II deals with various aspects of the "Development of Intelligence." Chapter 5, "Intelligence: Genes, Environments, and Their Interactions," by Samuel D. Mandelman and Elena L. Grigorenko, reveals our current knowledge about how genes and environment interact to produce intelligence. Chapter 6, "Developing Intelligence through Instruction," by Raymond S. Nickerson, discusses what we have learned about how intelligence can be developed through instructional techniques. Chapter 7, "Intelligence in Infancy," by Joseph F. Fagan, analyzes what we know about intelligence in the earliest years of life. Chapter 8, "Intelligence in Childhood," by L. Todd Rose and Kurt W. Fischer, reviews the literature on how intelligence develops and manifests itself during the childhood and teenage years. Chapter 9, "Intelligence in Adulthood," by Christopher Hertzog, reviews our knowledge of how intelligence develops throughout the adult life span.

Part III deals with "Intelligence and Group Differences." Chapter 10,

"Intellectual Disabilities," by Robert M. Hodapp, Megan M. Griffin, Meghan M. Burke, and Marisa H. Fisher, discusses different intellectual disabilities, especially the intellectual disability formerly called mental retardation. Chapter 11, "Prodigies and Savants," by David Henry Feldman and Martha J. Morelock, presents our knowledge on extremely exceptional specific kinds of intelligence during childhood and, in some cases, adulthood as well. Chapter 12, "Intellectual Giftedness," by Sally M. Reis and Joseph S. Renzulli, portrays the development of children who have extraordinary intellectual gifts. Chapter 13, "Sex Differences in Intelligence," by Diane F. Halpern, Anna S. Beninger, and Carli A. Straight, summarizes and analyzes our knowledge about levels and patterns of differences between the sexes in intelligence. Chapter 14, "Racial and Ethnic Group Differences in Intelligence in the United States," by Lisa A. Suzuki, Ellen L. Short, and Christina S. Lee, discusses how different groups understand and display their intelligence in one society, the United States. Chapter 15, "Race and Intelligence," by Christine E. Daley and Anthony J. Onwuegbuzie, discusses the construct of race and reviews research on the existence and causes of race differences in intelligence.

Part IV is on the "Biology of Intelligence." Chapter 16, "Animal Intelligence," by Thomas R. Zentall, summarizes and integrates our knowledge about intelligence in animals other than humans. Chapter 17, "The Evolution of Intelligence," by Liane Gabora and Anne Russon, discusses how intelligence has evolved over time within but primarily across species boundaries. Chapter 18, "Biological Bases of Intelligence," by Richard J. Haier, evaluates our knowledge regarding biological bases, particularly as revealed by neurocognitive imaging.

Part V is about "Intelligence and Information Processing." Chapter 19, "Basic Processes of Intelligence," by Ted Nettelbeck, deals with the more basic attentional and perceptual processes that provide a foundation for intelligence. Chapter 20, "Working Memory and Intelligence," by Andrew R. A. Conway, Sarah J. Getz, Brooke Macnamara, and Pascale M. J. Engel de Abreu, points to interesting research that suggests that working memory and fluid intelligence are extremely closely related. Chapter 21, "Intelligence and Reasoning," by David F. Lohman and Joni M. Lakin, takes a more traditional approach, relating intelligence to reasoning and primarily inductive reasoning. Chapter 22, "Intelligence and the Cognitive Unconscious," by Scott Barry Kaufman, takes a look at interesting literature, some of it quite recent, suggesting that the cognitive unconscious may play more of a role in intelligence than many of us might think. Chapter 23, "Artificial Intelligence," by Ashok K. Goel and Jim Davies, provides a panorama of current views on artificial intelligence and how it relates to natural intelligence.

Part VI deals with "Kinds of Intelligence." Chapter 24, "The Theory of Multiple Intelligences," by Katie Davis, Joanna Christodoulou, Scott Seider, and Howard Gardner, presents the widely known and utilized theory of multiple intelligences originally presented by Howard Gardner. Chapter 25, "The Theory of Successful Intelligence," by Robert J. Sternberg, summarizes the (triarchic) theory of successful intelligence and the empirical evidence supporting it. Chapter 26, "Emotional Intelligence," by John D. Mayer, Peter Salovey, David R. Caruso, and Lillia Cherkasskiy, reviews a literature that has shown explosive growth during the last two decades or so, that on emotional intelligence. Chapter 27. "Practical Intelligence," by Richard K. Wagner, highlights our understanding of practical intelligence, or how people use their intelligence in their everyday lives. Chapter 28, "Social Intelligence," by John F. Kihlstrom and Nancy Cantor, discusses how social intelligence, or intelligence as exhibited in our interactions with people, can make a difference to people's lives. Chapter 29, "Cultural Intelligence," by Soon Ang, Linn Van Dyne, and Mei Ling Tan, discusses cultural intelligence, or how we can adapt to different cultural contexts. Finally, Chapter 30,

"Mating Intelligence," by Glenn Geher and Scott Barry Kaufman, presents the intriguing notion that intelligence may be in large part an evolutionary adaptation to increase our ability to attract the mates we want.

Part VII covers "Intelligence and Society." Chapter 31, "Intelligence in Worldwide Perspective, " by Weihua Niu and Jillian Brass, provides an overview of intelligence as it exists in a wide variety of cultures. Chapter 32, "Secular Changes in Intelligence," by James R. Flynn, discusses the astonishing finding, by Flynn himself, that levels of intelligence as measured by intelligence tests increased by about three points per decade during the 20th century. Chapter 33, "Society and Intelligence," by Susan M. Barnett, Heiner Rindermann, Wendy M. Williams, and Stephen J. Ceci, deals with the relationship between IQ test scores and outcomes in society that are viewed as more or less successful in the contexts of various societies. Chapter 34, "Intelligence as a Predictor of Health, Illness, and Death," by Ian J. Deary and G. David Batty, reviews results analyzed by Deary and others, especially of the Scottish Mental Surveys, linking intelligence to issues of longevity and health during one's life span.

Part VIII is entitled "Intelligence in Relation to Allied Constructs." Chapter 35, "Intelligence and Personality," by Colin G. DeYoung, surveys the ever-growing literature on how intelligence relates to personality as captured by different theories, especially five-factor theory. Chapter 36, "Intelligence and Achievement," by Richard E. Mayer, summarizes what we know about how measured levels of intelligence predict school and other types of achievement. Chapter 37, "Intelligence and Motivation," by Priyanka B. Carr and Carol S. Dweck, shows that people's attitudes toward their intelligence, and especially its modifiability, may be key in their ability to acquire new knowledge and to succeed in learning, both in school and elsewhere. Chapter 38, "Intelligence and Creativity," by James C. Kaufman and Jonathan A. Plucker, reviews the widely dispersed literature on the relationship of intelligence to creativity, a relationship whose nature has been in dispute for many years and continues to be. Chapter 39, "Intelligence and Rationality," by Keith E. Stanovich, Richard F. West, and Maggie E. Toplak, reviews the literature on intelligence and rationality, suggesting that although they may be related, they are by no means the same. Chapter 40, "Intelligence and Wisdom," by Ursula M. Staudinger and Judith Glück, shows that understanding wisdom can help us better understand how intelligence can play either a positive or a negative role in society. Chapter 41, "Intelligence and Expertise," by Phillip L. Ackerman, discusses how intelligence matters in the acquisition and manifestation of expertise in its various phases.

Finally, Part IX is called "Moving Forward." In the final chapter of the book, Chapter 42, "Where Are We? Where Are We Going? Reflections on the Current and Future States of Research on Intelligence," Earl Hunt, one of the pioneers of the cognitive approach to intelligence, discusses both where the field is and where it is going and should be going.

We hope you enjoy the book and find it profitable. The book has been a labor of love for both of us. But most of all, it has been a labor for all the authors involved and we are grateful to them for taking the time and putting in the effort to make this volume possible. We wish to thank our editors at Cambridge University Press, Simina Calin and Jeanie Lee, for their support of this project, as well as our copy editor Patterson Lamb for her patience and hard work and Ken Karpinski for his help with production. We also want to thank Cambridge University Press for its support of the entire endeavor in its publication of all the successive handbooks of which this one is a culmination.

RJS and SBK
February 2011

References

Boring, E. G. (1923, June 6). Intelligence as the tests test it. *New Republic*, 35–37.

Caroll, Lewis. (year). *Through the looking-glass*. City: Publisher.
"Intelligence and its measurement": A symposium (1921). *Journal of Educational Psychology*, **12**, 123–147, 195–216, 271–275.
McNemar, Q. (1964). Lost: Our intelligence? Why? *American Psychologist*, 19, 871–882.
Sternberg, R. J. (Ed.). (1982). *Handbook of human intelligence*. New York: Cambridge University Press.
Sternberg, R. J. (Ed.). (2000). *Handbook of intelligence*. New York: Cambridge University Press.
Sternberg, R. J. (Ed.). (2004). *International handbook of intelligence*. New York: Cambridge University Press.

Part I

INTELLIGENCE AND ITS MEASUREMENT

CHAPTER 1

History of Theories and Measurement of Intelligence

N. J. Mackintosh

It would be difficult to start measuring "intelligence" without at least some implicit or intuitive theory of what intelligence is, and from the earliest Greek philosophers to the present day, many writers have enunciated their ideas about the nature of intelligence (see Sternberg, 1990). For Plato, it was the love of learning – and the love of truth; St. Augustine, on the other hand, believed that superior intelligence might lead people away from God. Thomas Hobbes in *Leviathan* went into more detail, arguing that superior intelligence involved a quick wit and the ability to see similarities between different things, and differences between similar things (ideas that have certainly found their way into some modern intelligence tests).

Measurement, however, implies something further: No one would be interested in *measuring* people's intelligence unless they believed that people differ in intelligence. Many early writers did of course believe this. Homer's Odysseus, in contrast to the other heroes of the *Iliad* and *Odyssey*, is often described as clever, resourceful, wily, and quick-witted. But not all theorists shared this belief. Adam Smith in *The Wealth of Nations* argued that the division of labor was responsible not only for that wealth but also for the apparent differences in the talents of a philosopher and a street porter. And when Francis Galton published *Hereditary Genius* in 1869, in which he sought to prove that people differed in their natural abilities, his cousin Charles Darwin wrote to him: "You have made a convert of an opponent . . . for I have always maintained that, excepting fools, men do not differ in intellect, only in zeal and hard work" (Galton, 1908, p. 290).

Measuring Intelligence

Galton

Francis Galton had no doubt on this score.

> *I have no patience with the hypothesis occasionally expressed, and often implied, especially in tales written to teach children to be good, that babies are born pretty much alike, and that the sole agencies in creating differences between boy and boy, and man and man, are steady application and*

> *moral effort. It is in the most unqualified manner that I object to pretensions of natural equality. The experiences of the nursery, the school, the University, and of professional careers, are a chain of proofs to the contrary. (Galton, 1869, p. 12)*

The results of public examinations, he claimed, confirmed his belief. Even among undergraduates of Cambridge University, for example, there was an enormous range in the number of marks awarded in the honor examinations in mathematics, from less than 250 to over 7,500 in one particular two-year period. As a first (not entirely convincing) step in the development of his argument that this wide range of marks arose from variations in natural ability, he established that these scores (like other physical measurements) were normally distributed, the majority of candidates obtaining scores close to the average, with a regular and predictable decline in the proportion obtaining scores further away from the average.

Allied to an almost compulsive desire to measure anything and everything, it was perhaps inevitable that Galton should wish to provide a direct measure of such differences in natural ability. But what measures would succeed in doing this? In 1884, at the International Health Exhibition held in London, he set up an Anthropometric Laboratory, where for a small fee visitors could be measured for their keenness of sight and hearing, color vision, reaction time, manual strength, breathing power, height, weight and so on. He could hardly have supposed that these were all interchangeable measures of intelligence, and some were surely there simply because they could be measured. But Galton was a follower of the British empiricist philosophers and argued that if all knowledge comes through the senses, then a "larger," more intelligent mind must be one capable of finer sensory discrimination and thus able to store and act upon more sensory information. Hence the relation between intelligence and discrimination – which we will come across again.

J. McK. Cattell

A more systematic attempt to measure differences in mental abilities was proposed by James McKeen Cattell (1890), who published a detailed list of 10 "mental tests" (plus another 40 in brief outline); they included measures of two-point tactile threshold, just noticeable difference for weights, judgment of temporal intervals, reaction time, and letter span. Cattell did not claim that this rather heterogeneous collection of tests would provide a good measure of intelligence – indeed the word "intelligence" does not even appear in his paper. Once again, it seems clear that the tests were chosen largely because the techniques required were already available. These were the standard experimental paradigms of the new experimental psychology being developed in Germany, and whatever it was that they were measuring, at least one could hope that they were measuring it accurately. Although no doubt unfair, it is hard to resist the analogy with the man who has lost his keys when out at night, and confines his search to an area underneath a street lamp, not because he thinks that is where he lost them, but because at least he can see there.

As a measure of intelligence, indeed, Cattell's tests did not last long. Their demise came from a study conducted in his laboratory by Wissler (1901), who administered the tests to undergraduates at Columbia University and reported two seemingly devastating findings. First, although the students did indeed differ in their performance on many of the tests, there was virtually no correlation between their performance on one and their performance on another. Even the correlations between different measures of speed, for example, averaged less than .20. If one test, therefore, was succeeding in measuring differences in intelligence, the others could not be. But which was the successful one? The second finding suggested that none of them were, for there was essentially no correlation between any of the tests and the students' college grades, which did in fact tend to correlate with one another, and which, following Galton, presumably were reflecting differences in intellectual ability between the students.

Binet

It was the Frenchman, Alfred Binet, who solved the problem of devising an apparently satisfactory measure of intelligence. Although he and his colleague, Victor Henri, had made earlier attempts to measure differences in intelligence, they had not been spectacularly successful (Binet & Henri, 1896), and it was a commission from the French Ministry of Education that revived their efforts. The introduction of (nearly) universal primary education had brought into elementary schools a number of children of apparently below average intelligence, who would never had attended school before. They did not seem to be profiting from normal classroom teaching and were deemed to be in need of special education. The problem was to devise a quick and inexpensive way of identifying such children. Binet had little time for the new experimental psychology coming from Wundt's laboratory in Leipzig, and although much less hostile to the associationist tradition of British empiricism, he did not believe that associationism could answer all questions. Above all, he thought it nonsense to suppose that intelligence could be reduced to simple sensory function or reaction time. Observation of his own young daughters had convinced him that they were just as good as adults at making fine sensory discriminations, and although their average reaction time might be longer than that of an adult, this was not because they could never respond rapidly but rather because they occasionally responded very slowly – a failure Binet attributed (perhaps rather presciently as I shall show later) to lapses of attention.

For Binet, "intelligence" consisted in a multiplicity of different abilities and depended on a variety of "higher" psychological faculties – attention, memory, imagination, common sense, judgment, abstraction. Even more important, it involved coping successfully with the world and would thus be best measured by tests that required young children to show they were capable of coping with everyday problems. Could they follow simple instructions such as pointing to their nose and mouth? Did they understand the difference between morning and afternoon, and know what a fork is used for? Could they count the number of items in a display, and name the months of the year (in correct order)? And so on. Were these adequate measures of intelligence? Binet's critical insight was that as young children become more intellectually competent as they grow older, a good measure of intelligence would be one that older children found easier than younger ones; this was particularly relevant for his main task of identifying children who were mildly or perhaps more seriously retarded: The difference between "normal" and retarded children was that the former passed his tests at a younger age than the latter.

The validity of a particular item as a measure of intelligence in 6-year-old children, then, was that most children of this age could pass it, while essentially all 8-year-olds, but many fewer 4-year-olds, could. Thus Binet and his later collaborator Theodore Simon devised a series of different tests of increasing difficulty, for 4-, 6-, 8-, and 10-year-old children, all based on this empirical insight and extensive trial and error (Binet & Simon, 1908). They acknowledged that there was no abrupt cutoff to most children's performance. A normal 6-year-old would probably answer nearly all the items in the 4-year test, most of those in the 6-year test, but quite possibly also manage one or two in the 8-year test. It was only with some reluctance and in a later paper (Binet & Simon, 1911) that he was prepared to assign any precise score (a mental age) to an individual child.Stern (1912) later introduced the concept of the intelligence quotient or IQ, defined as mental age divided by chronological age, but he seems to have set little store by the innovation that has guaranteed his place in so many textbooks. He does not so much as mention it in his autobiography (Stern 1930). Binet's reluctance to provide any precise measurement of a child's intelligence arose partly from his important observation that different children might get exactly the same total number of items in each test correct, but with quite different patterns of correct and incorrect answers. This simply confirmed his belief that "intelligence" involved a number of more or less independent faculties.

Spearman and the Theory of General Intelligence

Faculty psychology was Charles Spearman's bête noire. He abhorred the program that would separate the mind into a loose confederation of independent faculties of learning, memory, attention, and so on. What was needed was to understand its operations as a whole. Without knowing about Wissler's experiment, he repeated something very like it with a group of young children in a village school (Spearman, 1904; he later admitted that had he been aware of Wissler's results he would probably never have run his own study). He obtained independent ratings of each child's "cleverness in school" (from their teacher) and "sharpness and common sense out of school" (from two older children), and also measured their performance on three sensory tasks. Unlike Wissler, he did observe modest positive correlations between all his measures: the average correlation between the three ratings of intelligence was .55; that between the three sensory measures was .25, and that between the intelligence and sensory measures was .38. These were certainly more encouraging than Wissler's results – perhaps because the obvious restriction of range in students at Columbia University lowered Wissler's correlations. But they were still rather modest. Undaunted, Spearman argued that this was because his measures were *unreliable*, and a correction for attenuation had to be applied. The true correlation between two tests was the observed correlation between them divided by the square root of the product of their reliabilities. This is of course a standard formula for "disattenuating" correlations between two tests, but in modern test theory, the reliability of a test is measured by the correlation between performance on the test on separate occasions, or performance on one half of the test versus the other. Spearman had no such information and instead assumed that the reliability of his three measures of intelligence was the observed correlation between them, and similarly for the three sensory measures. Armed with this assumption, he was able to calculate the "true" correlation between intelligence and sensory discrimination:

$$r(\text{true}) = .38/\sqrt{(.55 \times .25)} = 1.01.$$

Of course, correlations cannot actually be greater than 1.0, but Spearman assumed that this was a minor error and confidently asserted that he had shown that general intelligence was general sensory discrimination.

In fact, Spearman later acknowledged that these measures of reliability were inappropriate, and he did not pursue the argument about the identity of intelligence and sensory discrimination. A much more important observation was one he made in data collected in another school, where he obtained somewhat more objective measures of academic performance, namely, each child's rank order in class for each of four different subjects, as well as measures of pitch discrimination and musical ability as rated by their music teacher. Interestingly, he anticipated Binet's appreciation of the importance of age by making an allowance for a pupil's age in adjusting their class ranking. The correlation matrix he reported between all these six measures is shown in Table 1.1. As can be seen, the correlations form what Spearman called a "hierarchy"; with one small exception, the correlations decrease as one goes down each column or across each row of the matrix. What was the meaning of this? Spearman's "Two Factor" theory provided the proposed answer. Each test measures its own specific factor, but also, to a greater or lesser extent, a general factor that is common to *all* the tests in the battery. It is this general factor, which Spearman labeled *g* for general intelligence,

Table 1.1. Spearman's reported correlations between six different measures of school attainment and musical performance. The figures comes from Spearman (1904) – although Fancher (1985), going back to Spearman's raw data, has shown that they are not, alas, perfectly accurate

	Classics	*French*	*English*	*Maths*	*Pitch*	*Music*
Classics	–					
French	.83	–				
English	.78	.67	–			
Maths	.70	.67	.64	–		
Pitch	.66	.65	.54	.45	–	
Music	.63	.57	.51	.51	.40	

that was said to explain why all tests correlated with one another. That this was a sufficient explanation of the observed correlation matrix, Spearman argued, was proved by the application of his "tetrad equation." If $r_{1.2}$ stands for the observed correlation between tests 1 and 2 and so on, then the tetrad equation was as follows:

$$r_{1.2} \times r_{3.4} = r_{1.3} \times r_{2.4} \qquad (1)$$

Substitute the appropriate numbers from Table 1.1 into this equation, and you have $.83 \times .64 = .53$, and $.78 \times .67 = .52$, as close as one could reasonably ask – and much the same will hold for any other two pairs of correlations in the table. Why should this be? Spearman's explanation was straightforward: The reason that tests 1 and 2 correlate is because both measure *g*. The observed correlation between the two tests is simply a product of each test's separate correlation with *g*:

$$r_{1.2} = r_{1.g} \times r_{2.g} \qquad (2)$$

And because this is true of all other pairs of tests, equation 1 can be rewritten as follows:

$$r_{1.g} \times r_{2.g} \times r_{3.g} \times r_{4.g} = r_{1.g} \times r_{3.g} \times r_{2.g} \times r_{4.g} \qquad (3)$$

which is clearly true. When the correlation matrix of a battery of tests forms a hierarchy such as that seen in Table 1.1, to which the tetrad equation applies, the explanation, said Spearman, is because the correlations between all tests are entirely due to each test's correlation with the single general factor, *g*.

It is worth remarking that the development of Spearman's two-factor theory was not based on the results of anything that could properly be called an intelligence test. But that theory allowed Spearman later to argue that Binet's tests, without Binet's knowing it, had in fact succeeded in providing a good measure of general intelligence. Every item in Binet's tests measured its own specific factor as well as the general factor. Over the test as a whole, however, the specific factors would, so to say, cancel each other out, leaving the general factor to shine strongly through. This was the principle of "the indifference of the indicator." More or less any mental test battery, witheringly referred to as any "hotchpotch of multitudinous measurements" (Spearman, 1930, p. 324), would end up measuring general intelligence, provided only that it was sufficiently large and sufficiently diverse.

What was the explanation of the general factor? At different times, Spearman came up with two quite different explanations. One was couched in terms of his "noegenetic" laws, which asserted that the three fundaments of general intelligence were the apprehension of one's own experience, the eduction of relations and the eduction of correlates (Spearman, 1930). The second was that *g* was "something of the nature of an "energy" or "power" that serves in common the whole cortex" (Spearman, 1923, p. 5). Two of the noegenetic laws bore fruit in that their emphasis on the importance of the perception of relations between superficially dissimilar items, otherwise known as analogical reasoning, provided the impetus for the construction of Raven's Matrices (Penrose & Raven, 1936). The second perhaps bears some passing resemblance to more modern ideas, discussed below, that speed of information processing is the basis of *g* (Anderson, 1992; Jensen, 1998).

The Divorce between Theory and Practice

Binet's tests were introduced into the United States by Henry Goddard, the director of research at the Vineland Training School in New Jersey, an institution for individuals with developmental disabilities. These tests later formed the initial basis for Lewis Terman's greatly improved version, the Stanford-Binet test (Terman, 1916), now in its fifth edition (Roid, 2003). Terman and Goddard then joined the committee set up by Robert Yerkes to devise the U.S. Army Alpha and Beta tests used to screen some 1.75 million draftees in World War I. The apparent success of these tests and the wide publicity they attracted after the war led to a proliferation of new test construction – with many new tests based on the Army tests themselves but most designed for use in schools, where they were often used to assign children to different tracks or classes. The first on the scene was the National Intelligence Test developed by Yerkes and Brigham, but later tests included the Henmon-Nelson tests, and the Otis "Quick Scoring Mental Ability Tests." For such tests to be economically viable, it was important that they could be administered to relatively large numbers of people in a relatively short time. In other words, they needed to be group tests, and as the name of the Otis test implies, one desideratum was that they could be rapidly and reliably scored. Hence the introduction of the multiple-choice question format. Brigham also developed tests for the College Entrance Exam Board, which were the forerunners of the Scholastic Aptitude Test (SAT). Eventually more individual tests were devised, including the first individual test of adult intelligence, the Wechsler-Bellevue test, the forerunner of the Wechsler Adult Intelligence Scale (WAIS), but which also borrowed and adapted many items from the Army tests. Wechsler also introduced the concept of the "deviation IQ." IQ defined as mental age divided by chronological age might work for children up to the age of 16 or so, but because 40-year-old adults do not obtain mental age scores twice those of 20-year-olds, mental ages will not work for adults. Wechsler's solution was to compare an individual's test score with the average score obtained by people of the same age.

Both Goddard and Terman had stressed the practical *usefulness* of Binet's test and Terman's revision of it. Goddard argued that the tests identified not only those referred to at that time as "idiots" and "imbeciles" – those severely disabled with an IQ score below 50 – but also, and even more important because they were not so easy to diagnose by other methods, the mildly disabled or "feebleminded" (for whom Goddard coined the term "moron"). Goddard (1914) had no doubt that it was in society's best interests to curb the reproduction of such individuals – and in this echoing eugenic views that were commonplace at the time (see Kevles, 1985) – but this association has served to give IQ tests a bad name ever since (e.g., Murdoch, 2007). Terman (1916), in his introduction to the Stanford-Binet test, also spent much time extolling the test's practical value, not only for identifying the "feebleminded" but also in schools, where much time would be saved by identifying the more and the less able. Later test constructors also stressed the value of identifying intellectually gifted children. The important point for the test constructors was to establish the predictive validity of their tests. Test scores would not only identify the disabled but also predict who would do well at school, who would therefore profitably continue on to college and university, and thereafter who would be suitable for what job. Many organizations, including, for example, the military and the police, routinely gave all applicants an IQ test and imposed a lower cutoff score as a minimum admission requirement.

In sharp contrast to Binet, who regarded his tests as simply providing an estimate of a child's present level of intellectual functioning, Spearman, Burt, Goddard, Terman, and Yerkes were also united in their conviction that their tests "were originally intended, and are now definitely known, to measure native intellectual ability" (Yoakum & Yerkes, 1920, p. 27). It hardly needs to be said that they had not a shred of real evidence for this conviction. But it too did little to endear other psychologists to the psychometric tradition – especially when this hereditarian bias was combined with one that saw differences in average native ability between different social or racial groups.

All this contributed to the independent development of IQ tests as a technology, divorced from mainstream psychology, and, it is commonly assumed, without any theoretical understanding of the nature of the intelligence they were supposed to be measuring. But Galton and Binet both had theories of intelligence, and both supposed that a successful measure of intelligence would be guided by their theory. Wissler's results suggested that Galton's theory was wrong, while the success of Binet's test perhaps implies that his theory was right. The trouble was that although it was indeed based on some empirical observation of his children, it was a rather commonsensical theory that owed little to the experimental psychology of his day. Galton's and especially Cattell's ideas were indeed based on contemporary experimental psychology – but that psychology, in the shape of Wissler's data, had apparently shown they were wrong. This concatenation of events is often blamed for the development of the two separate disciplines of psychology, the experimental and the correlational, so famously lamented by Cronbach (1957).

This must be at least a large part of the story – but perhaps not quite all. In his autobiography, Spearman (1930, p. 326) had referred to the division between what he called general and individual psychology as "among the worst evils in modern psychology." He was not talking about Wissler's data in this context. The truth of the matter is surely that for much of the 20th century, and certainly in the early years of the century, experimental psychology had no worthwhile theory of intelligence or cognition to offer. Intelligence tests could not be based on a psychological theory of intelligence because there was no such theory. Neither Binet's nor Spearman's "theories" could really be said to provide a satisfactory explanation of what it is to be more or less intelligent. Any rapprochement between experimental and correlational psychology had to wait on the development of theory in cognitive psychology – and that did not happen until the final quarter of the century.

Factor Analysis

In the meantime, what was left for psychometricians to do? The answer was that they developed new intelligence tests and explored the relationships between them. One impetus for this was, as implied above, to cash in on the popularity of any measure that seemed to promise the practical advantages held out by Terman, Yerkes, and Brigham. A theoretically much more important rationale was to assess the adequacy of Spearman's two-factor theory: Would all test batteries yield a "hierarchy" consistent with the idea that all correlations between tests could be explained by postulating a single general factor? This was of course a theoretical question, and to that extent test developers were exploring theories of intelligence. The question was soon answered in the negative: A correlation matrix that reveals clusters of high correlations between some tests separated by lower correlations between these tests and another cluster of high correlations will disconfirm the tetrad equation. Burt (1917) claimed to find evidence of a cluster of high correlations between different "verbal" tests while El Koussy (1935) found a similar cluster of high correlations between a variety of "spatial" tests. New techniques of factor analysis made clear the need to postulate additional "group factors" in addition to *g*. Then Thurstone (1938) argued that a different procedure for factor analysis (rotation to simple structure) eliminated the need for any *g* at all: Instead, there were a number of independent "primary mental abilities," suspiciously akin to Spearman's detested faculties. Thurstone identified seven in all, including verbal comprehension, verbal fluency, number, spatial visualization, inductive reasoning, memory, and possibly perceptual speed, and designed a series of tests, his Primary Mental Abilities (PMA) tests, that were intended to provide measures of each distinct ability.

In a separate development, Raymond Cattell proposed that Spearman's *g* should be divided into two distinct but correlated factors, fluid and crystallized intelligence, Gf and Gc, the former reflecting the ability to solve problems such as Raven's Matrices, the latter measured by tests of knowledge, such as vocabulary (Cattell, 1971; Horn & Cattell, 1966). In Cattell's original account, Gf was seen as the biological basis of intelligence, and Gc as the expression of that ability in the accumulated knowledge acquired as a result of exposure to a particular culture. That particular formulation of the theory was abandoned by Horn, who argued (surely correctly) that the ability to solve the analogical reasoning and series completion tasks that measure Gf are just as dependent on past learning (even if not explicitly taught in school) as are the tests of vocabulary or general knowledge that define Gc (see Horn & Hofer, 1992). Nevertheless, most modern accounts of the structure of intelligence have acknowledged the importance of the distinction between Gf and Gc. More to the point, at least one modern test battery, the W-J III (Woodcock-Johnson test) has been designed in part to provide separate measures of Gc and Gf – as well as of other components of intelligence identified by the theory.

It soon became apparent, and was acknowledged by Thurstone himself, that his primary mental abilities were not in fact wholly independent. The pervasive "positive manifold" reflected the fact that performance on any one test was correlated with performance on all other tests, and *g* reappeared to account for the correlation between Thurstone's primary abilities. As early as 1938, Holzinger and Harman (1938) had proposed one way of doing this, but the preferred method was later introduced by Schmid and Leiman (1957) in their "orthogonalized hierarchical" solution. In his magisterial survey of 20th century factorial studies, Carroll (1993) concluded that the structure of intellectual abilities revealed by factor analysis included a general factor, *g*, at a third "stratum," some half dozen or more broad group factors, including Gf and Gc at a second stratum, as well as factors of visuospatial abilities (Gv), retrieval (Gr), and processing speed (Gs), and a large, perhaps indefinite number of specific factors at a first stratum. This is now sometimes referred to as the Carroll-Horn-Cattell (or CHC) model and could be seen as a reconciliation between, or amalgamation of, Spearman's and Thurstone's accounts, the first and third strata corresponding to Spearman's general and specific factors, the second stratum to Thurstone's primary mental abilities.

The story does not, of course, end here. Other factorists, most famously Guilford (1967, 1985, 1988), in his structure-of-intellect model, postulated a far larger number of abilities than Thurstone had ever dreamed of. He started with 120, moved to 150 and ended up with 180; the novel feature of his account was that these abilities were derived from theoretical first principles: particular abilities were said to consist of five different kinds of operation, applied to five different types of content, expressed in terms of one of six different products (this produced the 150 number). Although initially skeptical of the need to postulate a higher order general factor, later versions of the model did include a general factor. Guilford's abilities should be seen as corresponding to the numerous specific first stratum abilities in the CHC model. One of the virtues of his approach is that he included measures of creativity and social intelligence that have not commonly appeared in traditional IQ test batteries. Suss and Beauducel (2005) have provided a sympathetic account, and Brody a rather less sympathetic one which concluded that "Guilford's theory is without empirical support" (Brody, 1992, p. 34). There also remain those, such as Gould (1997) and Gardner (1993), who have disputed whether there is any general factor at all. Without going as far as Guilford, Gardner believes that there are eight or possibly more distinct intelligences, most of them not measured by IQ tests at all. He is surely right to suppose that traditional IQ tests fail to measure important aspects of human intelligence. But it seems merely perverse to deny, or seek to explain away, the fact that a general factor will be revealed by analysis of most batteries of mental tests. The pervasive positive manifold guarantees that a significant general factor will emerge from factor analysis of virtually any battery of cognitive tests – and this applies as strongly to tests of most of Gardner's intelligences as it does to traditional IQ test batteries (Visser, Ashton, & Vernon, 2006).

Within the more traditional mainstream, Johnson and Bouchard (2005) have rejected the factorial structure proposed by Carroll and Horn and Cattell in favor of one advanced by Vernon (1950), in which *g* sits above two group factors, *v:ed* and *k:m*, the former verbal-educational, the latter spatial and mechanical. They claimed that Vernon's structure, slightly modified, provided a better fit to two large datasets they analyzed than either Carroll's account or Horn and Cattell's Gf-Gc theory. In the Vernon model, fluid reasoning is part of *g* rather than identified as Gf, while *k:m* refers to perceptual and spatial abilities rather than more general reasoning. Vernon's *v:ed* is a specifically verbal ability, as opposed to Gc, which can include figural knowledge. It is surely too soon to pass judgment on this dispute.

Factor analysis has clearly had important implications for theories of human intelligence. Spearman and Thurstone initially held diametrically opposed views about the structure of abilities, and factor analysis of different test batteries eventually forced them both to acknowledge that their original theories had been wrong – even if each had also been partly right. So it would be quite wrong to claim that mainstream research on human intelligence was, for most of the 20th century, conducted in a theoretical void. But the theories in question were theories about the structure of human abilities and the relationship between different aspects or components of intelligence, not about the nature of the operations, processes, or mechanisms underlying these abilities. Factor analysis was never going to answer these questions.

What is *g*?

Although most intelligence researchers today probably accept that the general factor is here to stay, they remain sharply divided on its explanation. These disagreements go well beyond a rejection of Spearman's specific suggestions that *g* is either mental energy or the eduction of relations and correlates.

One of the earliest scholars to raise a much wider issue and to question the *logic* of Spearman's account of *g* was Thomson (1916), who argued that the positive manifold arises, not because all tests measure a single psychological or neurobiological process, as Spearman supposed, but because each test taps a subset of a very large number of elementary processes or operations, and there will almost necessarily be some overlap between the processes engaged by one test and those engaged by another. In general, if tests 1 and 2 each engage a proportion, P_1 and P_2, of the mind's elementary operations, the correlation between the two tests will be $\sqrt{P_1 \times P_2}$. There is no doubt that Thomson's argument is valid – although it has not been taken up in the form he presented it. But Ceci (1990) pointed out that the fact that three tests, 1, 2, and 3, all correlate with one another does not necessarily imply that there is any process common to all three. If each test depended on two processes, test 1 on a and b, test 2 on b and c, and test 3 on a and c, then all tests will correlate without there being any process common to all three.

Thurstone also advanced a principled objection to Spearman's emphasis on the importance of *g*. His argument was that even if the positive manifold guaranteed that it would always be possible to extract a general factor from factor analysis of any IQ test battery, the nature of that general factor would vary from one test battery to another, depending on the nature of the tests included in the battery. In principle, his argument seems valid: The general factor of a test battery, such as the earlier versions of the Stanford-Binet or Wechsler scales, with a preponderance of measures of Gc, will surely be different from that extracted from a battery of tests focusing on measures of Gf or Gv. And as a matter of fact, researchers have often appeared to assume without question, and without evidence, that *g* is always one and the same. Thus Rushton (1999) asked whether the rise in test scores over the course of the 20th century, known as the Flynn effect (Flynn, 2007), was a rise in *g* – since if it was not, then it could not really be regarded as a genuine rise in intelligence. Analyzing data from the WAIS, he was able to show that the magnitude of the increase in scores on the individual tests comprising the scale was actually negatively correlated with those tests' loading on the general factor of the WAIS, and he concluded that the Flynn effect did not represent any increase in *g*. In fact, Rushton's findings are unsurprising, since it has always been clear that the rise in test scores has been far more pronounced on tests of Gf than on most tests of Gc – and on the Performance half of the old WAIS than on the Verbal half (Flynn, 2007). But the WAIS tests with the highest loading on WAIS *g* are the Verbal tests. Theorists such as Carroll (1993) have argued that Gf is closer to *g* than is any other second stratum factor; indeed some, such as Gustafsson (1988), have argued that Gf and *g* are indistinguishable. It would follow from this argument, then, that the Flynn effect has indeed been a rise in *g*. More important, WAIS *g* is *not* Gf, and probably not the same *g* as that extracted from other test batteries.

Given the potential importance of Thurstone's argument, it is remarkable that there have been so few attempts to undertake the experiment needed to test its validity. What is needed is quite simple: Administer two or more large and diverse, but independent, test batteries, with no overlap in the actual tests included in each battery, to a large and reasonably representative sample of participants, factor analyze the resulting correlation matrices of these batteries, and see if the *g* extracted from one is, or is not, the same as the *g* extracted from the others. The experiment has now been done twice, by Johnson, Bouchard, Krueger, McGue, and Gottesman (2004) and by Johnson, te Nijenhuis, and Bouchard (2008). In the first study, the correlations between the general factors of each of their three batteries were .99, .99 and 1.00 – effective identity. In the second study, with five rather more diverse test batteries, the correlations between pairs of four of them ranged from .95 to 1.00. The fifth test battery consisted of Cattell's Culture Fair tests, a measure of Gf. The correlations between the general factor of the Cattell tests and those of the other four batteries were .77, .79, .88, and .96. With this exception, the results of these two studies are strikingly clear: The *g* of one large and diverse test battery is exactly the same as that of another. They would thus seem to provide strong support for the view that *g* is not just a statistical phenomenon, which necessarily arises from the pervasive positive correlation between all measures of intelligence. Some researchers will want to conclude that *g* must be something real – appropriately labeled "general intelligence," although others will argue that this hardly proves that there is any unitary process of general intelligence – or even that performance on all IQ tests must depend on the same set of processes. It is worth adding that the lower correlations between the general factor extracted from the Cattell tests and those of the other test batteries in the Johnson et al. (2008) study must count as evidence that Gf is not the same as *g*.

The Explanation of *g*

Spearman saw that he needed to provide a psychological or (better still) a neurobiological explanation of *g*. His psychological explanation, in terms of the eduction of relations and correlates, could be said to provide a redescription of what is involved in analogical reasoning (i.e., of part of what is measured by tests of Gf) and contributed to the attempt by Sternberg (1977) and Pellegrino (1986) to understand the "cognitive components" of analogical reasoning or fluid intelligence. Analogies take the form: A is to B as C is to ? Their procedure involved presenting participants with a series of simple analogies – for example, simple line drawings of people, where A might be a picture of a smiley man wearing a top hat, B a glum-looking woman with a pointed hat, C the same smiley man, but now smaller, and the answer would be a small glum woman in a pointed hat. The problems were sufficiently simple that errors were rare, and the measure of performance taken was reaction time.

Their analysis argued that the following processes were involved in solving such analogies: encoding the attributes of each of the terms of the analogy; inferring the relation between the A and B terms (which amounted to listing the transformations that turned A into B; mapping the relation between A and C (again a matter of listing the transformations that turned A into C); applying the A:B transform to C; producing the correct response. These are, of course, the operations that must be performed to solve such analogies – although a critic such as Kline (1991) would argue that this does not turn the account into a *theory* of analogical reasoning. But studies did find significant correlations between the times taken to perform inference, mapping, and application operations and participants' scores on conventional measures of Gf (Sternberg & Gardner, 1983). Perhaps, however, this is a case where correlations should be interpreted cautiously. There must surely remain some doubt (expressed indeed later by Sternberg, 1990, himself), whether the speed with which people solve such simple analogies really tells one much about the reasons some people can, and others cannot, solve the sort of difficult analogies or series completion tasks that appear in Raven's Matrices. One finding that cast doubt on the premise that speed of operations was an important ingredient of successful intelligence was that older children, who were better at analogical reasoning than younger ones, actually spent *more* time encoding the terms of the analogies (Sternberg & Rifkin, 1979).

What became of Spearman's concept of *g* as "mental energy"? It was never clear how this idea might be operationalized, but perhaps the nearest parallel is with the idea that the speed and efficiency of information processing by the brain was the basis of general intelligence (Anderson, 1992; Eysenck, 1982; Jensen, 1998). Anderson (1992), for example, proposed that the nervous system consists of a series of relatively independent and specialized modules for dealing with different types of problem – verbal/propositional or visuospatial, for example – but that the outputs of these modules fed into a single central processor, whose speed and efficiency of operation formed the basis of *g*. What would count as evidence for such a theory? According to Anderson:

> *General intelligence cannot, by definition, be specific to any domain of knowledge. Thus it must be either a function of a cognitive control process that is involved in all domains or a non-cognitive physiological property of the brain. In either case it should be possible to find correlates of general intelligence in tasks that are relatively* knowledge-free. *(Anderson, 1992, p. 27, italics in original)*

The search was on for "elementary cognitive tasks" (ECTs) that would satisfy this requirement.

Inspection Time and Reaction Time

The two favorite paradigms for this program of research were inspection time (IT) and choice reaction time (RT). In the former, the participant's task is typically to decide which of two very briefly presented lines is the longer. In the latter (as in Wissler's original experiments), the task is to respond as rapidly as possible to the appropriate button when one of several possible lights turns on. Contrary to Wissler's own data, there is no doubt that both IT and RT correlate significantly with measures of intelligence. Indeed, in one early experiment, Nettelbeck and Lalley (1976) reported an astonishing raw correlation of –.92 between IT and performance scores on the WAIS (the correlation is negative because high IQ is associated with short inspection time). When such behavioral data were complemented by neurobiological results suggesting a correlation of the same order of magnitude between IQ and measures of event-related potentials (ERPs) to briefly presented stimuli (Hendrickson, 1982), it seemed to some that the Holy Grail had been found. Eysenck, for example, announced "the astonishing conclusion that the best tests of individual differences in cognitive ability are non-cognitive in nature!" (Eysenck, 1982, p. 9).

Sadly, the conclusion was premature. There is evidence that some components of ERPs to briefly presented stimuli may correlate with IQ under some circumstances (Deary, 2000), but attempts to replicate Hendrickson's results have had distinctly mixed success: The largest single study reported correlations with IQ ranging from –.087 to +.035 (Vogel, Kruger, Schalt, Schnobel, & Hassling, 1987).

In the case of RT and IT, it is clear that performance on both tasks does correlate with IQ, but the correlations are distinctly more modest than some early small studies had suggested, and probably no more than about –.20 to –.50. This might still seem surprisingly large, but it is surely far too small to provide any strong support for Eysenck's, Jensen's, or Anderson's position. As Detterman (2002) has perhaps rather sternly argued, that would require correlations on the order of .80 or higher. Whatever else *g* may or may not be, it cannot be *reduced* to speed of information processing by the nervous system – if that speed is at all satisfactorily measured by these two tasks. Perhaps even more important, there is reason to believe that Binet was quite right when he opined that young children respond more slowly on average than adults on RT tasks, not because they *cannot* respond rapidly but because occasional lapses of attention cause them sometimes to respond very slowly. There is good evidence that this forms a significant part of the explanation for the association between low IQ and slow RT or IT performance (e.g., Carlson, Jensen, & Widaman, 1983). There is not only a correlation between average RT or IT and IQ; there is an equally strong correlation between IQ and the trial-to-trial *variability* of RT and IT: Juhel (1993) and Larson and Alderton (1990) showed this for RT, while Fox, Roring, and Mitchum (2009) reported that the correlation between scores on Raven's Matrices and mean IT was –.25, but that between Raven's scores and the standard deviation of IT scores was –.34.

It is clear that the correlation between IQ and RT or IT does not arise because the higher people's IQ, the faster they are capable of responding or detecting small stimulus differences. It is because they make fewer slow responses. This hardly supports the idea that RT or IT is a direct measure of the speed or accuracy with which information is transmitted through the nervous system, let alone that differences in this speed are the cause of differences in *g*.

Cognitive Psychology to the Rescue?

Research on the relationship between IQ test scores and RT or IT was undertaken by psychologists whose primary allegiance was to psychometrics rather than experimental or cognitive psychology. At about the same time, however, several other psychologists started programs of research designed to demonstrate whether performance on other ECTs, in particular some of the simpler paradigms of the relatively new cognitive psychology, might be associated with differences in intelligence. Here too, the measure of performance often taken was reaction time, but the stimuli to which participants were required to respond were not the simple lights and auditory signals of traditional RT studies.

Hunt (1978) employed variants on the letter matching task devised by Posner and Mitchell (1967). On each trial, participants have to choose between a "same" and a "different" response, but different versions of the task differ in what counts as same or different. In the physical identity (PI) version, "same" means two physically identical letters, A – A, or a – a, while "different" means an upper and a lower case letter, A-a. In letter name identity (NI), two As still count as the same, even if shown in different type face, A-a. The stimuli for other versions are words. Again, physical identity is a matter of whether two words are exactly the same – for example, DEER – DEER. In the homonym identity condition, two words that merely sound alike are still to be judged the same, such as DEER – DEAR; while in categorical identity, two words from the same category – DEER – ELK – count as the same, even if different in all other respects. Reaction times on all these tasks correlate with IQ scores (particularly with measures of Gc), and these correlations increase in size as one progresses through the list. But they are rarely greater than −.30.

Hunt, Davidson, and Landsman (1981) employed the sentence verification task, initially devised by Clark and Chase (1972). This task requires the participant to decide whether a given sentence provides a true or false description of a simple diagram – for example, of a star placed above a cross. Once again, RT is the measure taken, and once again performance correlates about −.30 with measures of Gc. While these correlations may be mildly encouraging, like those reported for simple RT and IT they are simply not high enough to justify any claim to have found a simple basis for crystallized intelligence. Another finding with the sentence verification paradigm is perhaps more illuminating. Clark and Chase had also looked at the differences in participants' RTs as a function of whether the sentence was true or false, and affirmative or negative, and developed a model of participants' strategy to account for the pattern they observed. McLeod, Hunt, and Mathews (1978) reported similar results for the majority of their participants, but a relatively small minority yielded a quite different pattern of RTs. The interesting finding was that for the majority, overall RTs were correlated with scores on a test of Gc; for the minority, however, overall RTs correlated with their scores on a test of Gv or spatial ability, not Gc. The surely important implication is that different people employ different strategies, either propositional or visuospatial to solve what is intended to be exactly the same problem.

Breaching the .30 Barrier

Reviewing much of this evidence, Hunt came to a somewhat pessimistic conclusion:

> *Keele ... has summarized the situation nicely by referring to the "0.3 barrier"; no single information processing task seems able to account for more than 10 percent of the variance in a general intelligence test. (Hunt, 1980, p. 455)*

Until evidence was found of correlations between IQ scores and some more tractable and better understood measures of cognitive processes reliably in excess of .30, this "cognitive correlates" approach to intelligence could not be said to have made any dramatic impact on theories of intelligence. Rather presciently, Hunt argued that one way through the barrier might be to look at "dual task performance," where participants are given a distractor task to perform at the same time as a primary task. Almost immediately, a number of studies began to appear that seemed to solve the problem. Daneman and Carpenter (1980) and Daneman and Green (1986) devised a "reading span" task, in which students were required to read aloud a series of sentences, visually presented one at a time, and then required to recall the last word of each sentence in the correct order. They observed correlations ranging from just below .50 to nearly .60 between reading span scores and students' scores on a vocabulary test and on the

Verbal SAT. There were even higher correlations, ranging from .70 to .85, between students' reading span scores and their ability to answer factual questions about the contents of a passage of prose they had just read (a reading comprehension test).

Working Memory

The reading span test is an example of what Baddeley has called "working memory" tasks (Baddeley & Hitch, 1974; Baddeley, 2007). A simple immediate memory span task, such as the digit span test that appeared in the Stanford-Binet and Wechsler tests, presents a list of digits and requires the testee to recall the list in the correct order. A working memory task requires participants to remember this sort of information while simultaneously processing some other information. In the reading span task, you must try to remember the last word of the preceding sentence(s) while reading a new sentence. Numerous other tests of working memory have since been devised: a meta-analysis by Ackerman, Beier, and Boyle (2005) listed some 50 different procedures, divided into 9 different categories. They summarized results from 86 separate samples and nearly 10,000 participants. The precise magnitude of the correlation between working memory and IQ test performance clearly depends on the nature both of the working memory paradigm and the IQ test, but it has rarely dropped below the .30 barrier. For the first time, a moderately strong correlation has been reliably established between scores on a variety of different IQ tests and performance on a relatively straightforward and tractable (even if, for the participants, a surprisingly difficult) experimental paradigm.

Getting Together Again?

Research on working memory began within mainstream experimental or cognitive psychology (Baddeley & Hitch, 1974), and only later did researchers begin to study individual differences. The Baddeley and Hitch model, with a "central executive" aided by two temporary stores, the "phonological loop" and the "visuospatial sketchpad," now updated with an "episodic buffer" (Baddeley, 2007), is still perhaps the modal model of working memory. But different cognitive psychologists have proposed many others (see Miyake & Shah, 1999). Now there are a number of different models designed to account for the association between working memory and intelligence: see, for example, the books edited by Wilhelm and Engle (2005) and Conway, Jarrold, Kane, Miyake, and Towse (2007). The point is that psychometricians and cognitive psychologists have joined forces to work together on the same problem – perhaps to the mutual benefit of both. The divorce between the two traditions of psychology, which Spearman saw as the great evil afflicting psychology at the beginning of the 20th century, may be ending in a more or less happy reconciliation. Certainly one happy consequence has been that, aided by the new technologies of brain imaging, research on intelligence, working memory, and other so-called executive functions has begun to point to some of the brain structures common to them all (Kane, 2005).

References

Ackerman, P. L., Beier, M. E., & Boyle, M. O. (2005). Working memory and intelligence: The same or different constructs? *Psychological Bulletin*, **131**, 30–60.

Anderson, M. (1992). *Intelligence and development: A cognitive theory*. Oxford, UK: Blackwell.

Baddeley, A. D. (2007). *Working memory, thought, and action*. Oxford, UK: Oxford University Press.

Baddeley, A. D., & Hitch, G. (1974). Working memory. In G. A. Bower (Ed.), *Recent advances in learning and motivation* (Vol. 8). New York, NY: Academic Press.

Binet, A., & Henri, V. (1896). La psychologie individuelle. *L'Année Psychologique*, **2**, 411–465.

Binet, A., & Simon, T. (1908). Le développement de l'intelligence chez les enfants. *L'Année Psychologique*, **14**,1–94.

Binet, A., & Simon, T. (1911). *A method of measuring the development of the intelligence of young children*. Lincoln, IL: Courier.
Brody, N. (1992). *Intelligence* (2nd ed.). San Diego, CA: Academic Press.
Burt, C. L. (1917). *The distribution and relations of educational abilities*. London, UK: County Council.
Carlson, J. S., Jensen, C. M., & Widaman, K. F. (1983). Reaction time, intelligence and attention. *Intelligence, 7*, 329–344.
Carroll, J. B. (1993). *Human cognitive abilities*. Cambridge, UK: Cambridge University Press.
Cattell, J. M. (1890). Mental tests and measurements. *Mind, 15*, 373–381.
Cattell, R. B. (1971). *Abilities: Their structure, growth and action*. Boston, MA: Houghton Mifflin.
Ceci, S. J. (1990). *On intelligence . . . more or less. A bio-ecological treatise on intellectual development*. Englewood Cliffs, NJ: Prentice Hall.
Clark, H. H., & Chase, W. G. (1972). On the process of comparing sentences against pictures. *Cognitive Psychology, 3*, 472–517.
Conway, A. R. A., Jarrold, C., Kane, M. J., & Towse, J. N. (2007). *Variation in working memory*. New York, NY: Oxford University Press.
Cronbach, L. J. (1957). The two disciplines of scientific psychology. *American Psychologist, 12*, 671–684
Daneman, M., & Carpenter, P. A. (1980). Individual differences in working memory and reading. *Journal of Verbal Learning and Verbal Behavior, 19*, 450–466.
Daneman, M., & Green, I. (1986). Individual differences in comprehending and producing words in context. *Journal of Memory and Language, 25*, 1–18.
Deary, I. J. (2000). *Looking down on human intelligence*. New York, NY: Oxford University Press.
Detterman, D. K. (2002). General intelligence: Cognitive and biological explanations. In R. J. Sternberg & E. L. Grigorenko (Eds.), *The general factor of intelligence: How general is it?* Mahwah, NJ: Erlbaum.
El Koussy, A. A. H. (1935). The visual perception of space. *British Journal of Psychology, 20* (Monograph Supplement).
Eysenck, H. J. (Ed.). (1982). *A model for intelligence*. New York, NY: Springer-Verlag.
Fancher, R. E. (1985). Spearman's original computation of *g*: A model for Burt? *British Journal of Psychology, 76*, 341–352.
Fox, M. C., Roring, R. W., & Mitchum, A. L. (2009). Reversing the speed-IQ correlation: Intra-individual variability and attentional control in the inspection time paradigm. *Intelligence, 37*, 76–80.
Flynn, J. R. (2007). *What is intelligence?* New York, NY: Cambridge University Press.
Galton, F. (1869). *Hereditary genius: An inquiry into its laws and consequences*. London, UK: MacMillan.
Galton, F. (1908). *Memories of my life*. London, UK: Methuen
Gardner, H. (1993). *Frames of mind* (2nd ed.). New York, NY: Basic Books.
Goddard, H. H. (1914). *Feeble-mindedness: Its causes and consequences*. New York, NY: MacMillan.
Gould, S. J. (1997). *The mismeasure of man* (2nd ed.). London, UK: Penguin Books.
Guilford, J. P. (1967). *The nature of human intelligence*. New York, NY: McGraw-Hill.
Guilford, J. P. (1985). The structure-of-intellect model. In B. B. Wolman (Ed.), *Handbook of intelligence: Theories, measurements, and applications*. New York, NY: John Wiley.
Guilford, J. P. (1988). Some changes in the structure-or-intellect model. *Educational and Psychological Measurement, 48*, 1–4.
Gustafsson, J.-E. (1988). Hierarchical models of individual differences in cognitive abilities. In R. J. Sternberg (Ed.), *Advances in the psychology of human intelligence* (Vol. 4). Hillsdale, NJ: Erlbaum.
Hendrickson, D. E. (1982). The biological basis of intelligence. Part II: Measurement. In H. J. Eysenck (Ed.), *A model for intelligence*. New York, NY: Springer-Verlag.
Holzinger, K. J., & Harman, H. H. (1938). Comparison of two factorial analyses. *Psychometrika, 3*, 45–60.
Horn, J. L., & Cattell, R. B. (1966). Refinement and test of the theory of fluid and crystallized intelligence. *Journal of Educational Psychology, 57*, 253–270.
Horn, J. L., & Hofer, S. M. (1992). Major abilities and development in the adult period. In R. J. Sternberg & C. A. Berg (Eds.), *Intellectual development*. New York, NY: Cambridge University Press.
Hunt, E. (1978). Mechanics of verbal ability. *Psychological Review, 85*, 109–130.
Hunt, E. (1980). Intelligence as an information processing concept. *British Journal of Psychology, 71*, 449–474.

Hunt, E., Davidson, J., & Lansman, M. (1981). Individual differences in long-term memory access. *Memory and Cognition*, 9, 599–608.

Jensen, A. R. (1998). *The g factor: The science of mental ability*. London, UK: Westport.

Johnson, W., & Bouchard, T. J., Jr. (2005). The structure of human intelligence: It is verbal, perceptual, and image rotation (VPR), not fluid and crystallized. *Intelligence*, 33, 393–416.

Johnson, W., Bouchard, T. J., Jr., Krueger, R. F., McGue, M., & Gottesman, I. I. (2004). Just one *g*: Consistent results from three test batteries. *Intelligence*, 32, 95–107.

Johnson, W., te Nijenhuis, J., & Bouchard, T. J., Jr. (2008). Still just 1 *g*: Consistent results from five test batteries. *Intelligence*, 36, 81–95.

Juhel, J. (1993). Should we take the shape of the reaction time distribution into account when studying the relationship between RT and psychometric intelligence? *Personality and Individual Differences*, 15, 357–360.

Kane, M. J. (2005). Full frontal fluidity. In O. Wilhelm, & R. W. Engle (Eds.), *Handbook of understanding and measuring intelligence*. Thousand Oaks, CA: Sage.

Kevles, D. J. (1985). *In the name of eugenics: Genetics and the uses of human heredity*. New York, NY: Knopf.

Kline, P. (1991). *Intelligence: The psychometric view*. London, UK: Routledge.

Larson, G. E., & Alderton, D. L. (1990). Reaction time variability and intelligence: "Worst performance" analysis of individual differences. *Intelligence*, 14, 309–325.

Miyake, A., and Shah, P. (1999). *Models of working memory: Mechanisms of active maintenance and executive control*. New York, NY: Cambridge University Press.

Murdoch, S. (2007). *IQ: The brilliant idea that failed*. Hoboken, N J: John Wiley.

Nettelbeck, T., & Lalley, M. (1976). Inspection time and measured intelligence. *British Journal of Psychology*, 67, 17–22.

Pellegrino, J. W. (1986). Deductive reasoning ability. In R. J. Sternberg (Ed.), *Human abilities: An information-processing approach*. New York, NY: W. H. Freeman.

Penrose, L. S., & Raven, J. C. (1936). A new series of perceptual tests: Preliminary communication. *British Journal of Medical Psychology*, 16, 97–104.

Posner, M., & Mitchell, R. (1967). Chronometric analysis of classification. *Psychological Review*, 74, 392–409.

Roid, G. H. (2003). Stanford-Binet Intelligence Scales (5th ed.). *Technical manual*. Itasca, IL: Riverside.

Rushton, J. P. (1999). Secular gains in IQ not related to the g factor and inbreeding depression – unlike black-white differences: A reply to Flynn. *Personality and Individual Differences*, 26, 381–389.

Schmid, J., & Leiman, J. M. (1957). The development of hierarchical factorial solutions. *Psychometrika*, 22, 53–61.

Spearman, C. (1904). General intelligence, objectively determined and measured. *American Journal of Psychology*, 15, 201–293.

Spearman, C. (1923). *The nature of intelligence and the principles of cognition*. London, UK: Macmillan.

Spearman, C. (1930). Autobiography. In C. Murchison (Ed.), *A history of psychology in autobiography* (Vol. 1). Worcester, MA: Clark University Press.

Stern, W. (1912). *Die psychologische methoden der intelligenzprüfung*. Leipzig: Barth.

Stern, W. (1930). Autobiography. In C. Murchison (Ed.), *A history of psychology in autobiography* (Vol. 1). Worcester, MA: Clark University Press.

Sternberg, R. J. (1977). *Intelligence, information processing and analogical reasoning: The componential analysis of human abilities*. Hillsdale, NJ: Erlbaum.

Sternberg, R. J., & Gardner, M. K. (1983). Unities in inductive reasoning. *Journal of Experimental Psychology: General*, 112, 80–116.

Sternberg, R.J., & Rifkin, B. (1979). The development of analogical reasoning processes. *Journal of Experimental Child Psychology*, 27, 195–232.

Suss, H.-M., & Beauducel, A. (2005). Faceted models of intelligence. In O. Wilhelm & R. W. Engle (Eds.), *Handbook of understanding and measuring intelligence*. Thousand Oaks, CA: Sage.

Terman, L. M. (1916). *The measurement of intelligence*. Boston, MA: Houghton Mifflin.

Thomson, G. H. (1916). A hierarchy without a general factor. *British Journal of Psychology*, 8, 271–281.

Thurstone, L. L. (1938). *Primary mental abilities*. Chicago, IL: University of Chicago Press.

Vernon, P. E. (1950). *The structure of human abilities*. London, UK: Methuen.

Visser, B. A., Ashton, M. C., & Vernon, P. A. (2006). Beyond g: Putting multiple intelligences theory to the test. *Intelligence*, 34, 487–502.

Vogel, F., Kruger, J., Schalt, E., Schnobel, R., & Hassling. L. (1987). No consistent relationships between oscillations and latencies of visual evoked EEG potentials and measures of mental performance. *Human Neurobiology*, 6, 173–182.

Wissler, C. (1901). The correlation of mental and physical tests. *Psychological Review Monograph Supplement*, 3, no. 6.

Yoakum, L. S., & Yerkes, R. M. (1920). *Army mental tests*. New York, NY: Holt.

CHAPTER 2

Tests of Intelligence

Susana Urbina

There are many ways of approaching the topic of intelligence tests. This chapter deals with just two of them. One approach centers on what intelligence tests measure and is tied to the issue of defining what intelligence is. The close connection between those two questions can be seen in E. G. Boring's (1923) definition of intelligence as that which intelligence tests measure. Most readers will probably agree that this definition, while easy to remember, is thoroughly unsatisfactory because of its circular nature and limited utility. More substantial and satisfying definitions can be found later in this chapter and in many other sources (e.g., Sternberg & Detterman, 1986; Urbina, 1993). Boring's definition, such as it is, does provide us with a reason to examine what the multiplicity of intelligence tests do measure and thus understand what some of the basic aspects of the construct of intelligence are, at least in the cultures that gave rise to those tests.

The second way to approach the topic of intelligence tests is far more pragmatic. It concerns the issue of why these tests exist or the purposes for which they are employed. In an interesting but not altogether surprising coincidence, both ways of approaching intelligence tests – clarifying what they measure and what kinds of practical purposes they can serve – date back to the beginning of the 20th century.

This chapter reviews the basic elements of both approaches by examining intelligence tests in some detail. In particular, it poses and attempts to answer the following questions:

- What are intelligence tests?
- When and how did intelligence tests come to be?
- Do intelligence tests really measure intelligence?
- What do intelligence tests actually do?
- What functions or purposes do intelligence tests serve?
- Do intelligence tests have a future?

What Are Intelligence Tests?

The latest edition of the *Tests in Print* (TIP) series (Murphy, Spies, & Plake, 2006) lists

202 tests in the "Intelligence and General Aptitude" category. Of these, only 27 tests use the term *intelligence* in their titles. This number has not changed since the previous edition of TIP. By and large, the tests published in the past few decades avoid using intelligence in their titles, whereas the older tests continue to do so, even in their new editions, in order to provide continuity and because their names are well established.[1] In addition, the traditional intelligence tests – especially the Wechsler scales and the Stanford-Binet–also have been the most widely used and studied (Camara, Nathan, & Puente, 2000). If one examines the items and manuals of the tests within the TIP category of "Intelligence and General Aptitude," one finds striking similarities of both form and purpose among them, whether or not they have the word intelligence in their titles.

The truth about IQ tests. Although the phrase "IQ test" is frequently used to refer to intelligence tests, the two terms are not at all equivalent. The confusion between them stems from the fact that the earliest intelligence tests, such as the Stanford-Binet, used a score called the *intelligence quotient* or IQ for short. Originally, the IQ was an actual quotient obtained by dividing a number labeled Mental Age (MA) – which reflected a person's performance on the test and was expressed in years and months – by the person's Chronological Age (CA) and multiplying the result by 100 to eliminate the decimals. If performance on the test or MA matched the person's CA exactly, the IQ would be 100. Hence that number became known as the "normal" or average intelligence level. Numbers above and below 100 indicated that performance on the test had exceeded or fallen short of the levels expected at a given CA and became associated with above and below average intelligence, respectively. Eventually it became clear that, for a variety of reasons, this way of obtaining intelligence test scores did not work well – especially in adulthood when mental development levels off so that increases in CA cannot be matched by corresponding increases in MA. Thus, a new way of arriving at IQ scores was devised.[2]

The newer measure, known as the *deviation IQ*, is the type of score currently in use by the major tests that still use the IQ. In spite of the label, the deviation IQ is no longer a quotient. Instead, IQs are now derived by comparing a person's performance or raw score on a test of intellectual abilities to norms established by the performance of a representative group – known as a *normative* or *standardization sample* – of people in the person's age range. Raw scores for each normative age group are converted into standard scores with a mean of 100 and a standard deviation (SD) typically set at 15. The difference between a person's score and the average score of her or his age group – in SD units – determines the person's IQ. Thus, deviation IQ scores of 85 and 115 are 1 SD unit away from the mean and both reflect performance that deviates equally from the average performance of a comparable age group sample, but in opposite directions. Since test scores obtained from representative samples produce distributions resembling the normal curve model, they can be made to fit into the normal curve parameters so that *approximately* 68% of the scores are within ±1 SD from the average, 95% are within ±2 SD, and 99% are within ±3 SD. This is just one of the reasons to be suspicious of reported IQ scores much higher than 160, which – if the SD is set at 15 – is a number that would represent performance at 4 SDs above the average and thus in the top one-tenth of 1% of the age group norm. IQ scores much higher than 160 cannot be obtained in most of the current tests of this type.

As of now, the TIP lists barely more than a dozen tests that produce IQ scores. These include the current versions of the oldest traditional intelligence test batteries,

1 Tests within the cited TIP category that were published since the 1970s or 1980s tend to use terms such as *cognitive abilities*, *general ability*, or simply *aptitude* in their titles.

2 For a more complete history of the IQ score, see Murdoch (2007).

such as the Stanford-Binet Intelligence Scale (SB), the Slosson Full-Range Intelligence Test (S-FRIT), the Wechsler Adult Intelligence Scale (WAIS), the Wechsler Intelligence Scale for Children (WISC), and the Wechsler Preschool and Primary Scale of Intelligence (WPPSI). Some test batteries of more recent vintage also yield IQ scores, notably the Kaufman Adolescent and Adult Intelligence Test (KAIT), but most of the newly developed tests that yield IQ scores are either abbreviated versions of other tests, such as the Wechsler Abbreviated Scale of Intelligence (WASI) and the Kaufman Brief Intelligence Test (K-BIT), or tests limited to nonverbal content, such as the Universal Nonverbal Intelligence Test (UNIT), the Leiter International Performance Scale-Revised (Leiter-R), or the General Ability Measure of Adults (GAMA). Due to the controversies surrounding IQ scores and to the excessive and unjustified meanings that the IQ label has acquired, the use of IQs in scoring intelligence or general aptitude tests is rapidly being abandoned, replaced by terms such as *General Ability Score* or *Standard Age Score*. In keeping with tradition, however, most of these scores are derived in the same way as deviation IQs and have a mean set at 100 and SDs of 15 or 16.

When and How Did Intelligence Tests Come to Be?

The origins of intelligence testing are inextricably linked to Francis Galton and Alfred Binet. Of course there were others – both before and after them – who contributed to the development of intelligence tests in significant ways, but these two men, who had very different goals, set the stage for most of the positive and negative consequences that would follow. Accounts of the history of intelligence testing and of the leading figures in that history, as well as of the controversies they generated, can be found in many sources. Among the most interesting and readable ones are those provided by Fancher (1985), Sokal (1987), and Zenderland (1998).

Among psychologists, Francis Galton is most often remembered as the originator of the so-called "nature-nurture" controversy that has been such a crucial point of debate in the social sciences. Galton's desire to devise a way to measure intelligence stemmed from his interest in giftedness and genius and his eugenicist notion that the intellectual caliber of society would be improved by identifying highly intelligent young men and women and encouraging them to procreate early and profusely. This idea, in turn, arose from his conviction that intelligence is an inherited and unitary trait rooted in physiology. Using the theory of evolution developed by his cousin Charles Darwin as a source of inspiration, Galton investigated the extent of resemblance in terms of intellectual achievement among people with different degrees of familial ties. Even though his findings were insufficient to prove his argument conclusively, Galton nevertheless proceeded to develop a series of measures of reaction time, sensory acuity, and such, which he believed were indices of one's natural inherited ability associated with functions of the central nervous system. Although Galton collected such data on thousands of individuals at his Anthropometric Laboratory in England, it was left to an American psychologist named James McKeen Cattell – who was influenced by Galton – to continue this line of work in the United States and to see the premises on which it was based discredited. Cattell coined the term *mental tests* to refer to a series of tasks involving primarily psychomotor and sensory measures along the lines of those suggested by Galton's theory and he proceeded to collect data using these measures at Columbia University. Unfortunately for the theory, a study by one of Cattell's own students (Wissler, 1901) indicated that there was practically no relationship among the mental tests or between them and the indices of academic achievement used as a criterion of mental ability.

Whereas Galton, as well as Cattell, failed in his endeavor to create a device for assessing intellectual abilities, their French contemporary Alfred Binet succeeded admirably. Unlike Galton, Binet worked with children and was interested in identifying intellectual retardation rather than giftedness. He got involved in this effort in 1904 when he was appointed by the French government to a commission whose task was to implement the new law requiring public education for all children. Identifying individuals who, due to mental retardation, would be unable to attend ordinary schools and would require special education was an essential aspect of this mandate. Due to a variety of circumstances in his personal and professional life, Binet was at that point particularly well prepared for the job he undertook (Wolf, 1973). He and his collaborator Theodore Simon were able, by 1905, to develop and publish a scale consisting of 30 simple tasks of increasing difficulty that could distinguish among children with different levels of intellectual capacity. Binet and Simon used their experiences with this first scale to extend and refine it, concentrating on those items that had proved most useful in discriminating among children of different ages and mental capacity levels. They realized that by tapping a variety of cognitive tasks – such as memory, attention, verbal comprehension, and reasoning – at different levels of difficulty and organizing the items according to the age levels at which children of normal intellectual functioning were likely to succeed, they could produce a scale that would classify children's levels of mental functioning based on the number of items they passed at the various levels. In 1908 and 1911 Binet and Simon published considerably improved revisions of their scale, which quickly gained in popularity, especially in the United States where the scales were almost immediately translated, used, and distributed at the Training School for the Feebleminded in Vineland, New Jersey, by its director of research, Henry H. Goddard.

In fact, after Binet's death in 1911, the main center of research and test development on intelligence shifted from Europe to the United States where several other adaptations of the Binet-Simon scale were being tried out, culminating with the publication, in 1916, of the Stanford Revision of the Binet-Simon Intelligence Scale developed by Lewis Terman and his graduate students at Stanford University. This scale, which became known as the Stanford-Binet (SB), was considerably expanded and was adapted for and standardized on children from the United States. In addition, Terman decided to use the IQ formula – MA/CA times 100 – to express scores on the SB scale. In spite of the fact that the SB was primarily suitable for children, this scale dominated the field of individual intelligence testing for the next few decades. The SB was singularly responsible for popularizing the IQ score, which became synonymous with intelligence and was adopted by several other tests of abilities, some of which are still in use today. In fact, when David Wechsler published each of his series of enormously successful intelligence tests, starting in 1939 with the Wechsler-Bellevue Intelligence Scale, he chose to keep the term *IQ* to designate the scores on those scales. As mentioned earlier, Wechsler's deviation IQs, were very different from the SB IQs in that they were no longer quotients and could be meaningfully applied to people of all age groups.

Group intelligence tests. Whereas Binet and Wechsler are famous for their overwhelming impact on the field of individual intelligence tests, the person most responsible for the development of group tests, Arthur S. Otis, is not as well known. Otis studied with Lewis Terman at Stanford University in the years prior to World War I and became intrigued by the possibility of adapting some of the tasks of the Binet scale for use with groups in a paper-and-pencil test format. One of the most significant innovations that Otis devised was the multiple-choice type of item format. This innovation, in turn, was instrumental in the development of the first group test of mental ability, namely, the Army's Group Examination Alpha also known as the Army Alpha, which was used in the selection and classification of Army personnel during the First World War.

The success of the Army Alpha spawned the rapid development of many other paper-and-pencil tests of cognitive abilities. Otis himself developed the Otis Group Intelligence Scale, published in 1918, which was the first American group test of mental ability specifically designed for use in educational institutions. Otis developed other tests of mental ability and contributed several innovations and refinements that made the scoring and administration of group tests more practical and efficient (Robertson, 1972). The Otis-Lennon School Ability Test, Eighth Edition (OLSAT8), which is the current version of the Group Intelligence Scale, is still widely used to evaluate cognitive abilities related to success in school from kindergarten to 12th grade. Another contemporary group test designed for the same purpose and population is the Cognitive Abilities Test, Form 6 (CogAT-6). At the higher education level, the College Board's SAT Reasoning Test and the Graduate Record Examination General Test are the prime examples of group tests used to screen applicants in terms of their level of cognitive abilities.

In addition to the Army Alpha, which no longer is used, a variety of other group tests have been developed and used – though not always wisely or effectively – by military and civilian organizations to select and classify personnel. Some of these tests, such as the Wonderlic Personnel Test (WPT) – originally adapted from the Otis Self-Administering Tests of Mental Ability – attempt to get a general estimate of cognitive ability, whereas others are aimed at evaluating specific skills required for performance in a given occupation, such as clerical or mechanical abilities.

Do Intelligence Tests Really Measure Intelligence?

The short and simple answer to this question is no. Given that semantics play a large part in this answer, a review of the meaning of the terms in the question may clarify the answer. The meaning of *measure* is clear: to measure something is to assign numbers or labels to objects, events, or people according to some established method or rules (see Kirk, 1999, e.g.). Based on this definition, we can establish that intelligence tests do measure something. After all, they produce numbers that are assigned to the responses of test takers on the behavior samples that make up each test, and those numbers are assigned according to designated standards or rules.

Whether what intelligence tests measure is intelligence, on the other hand, is far more complicated as even a casual perusal of the field should reveal. Although many people assume that since intelligence tests exist, it must be possible for intelligence to be measured, the fact is that intelligence is an abstraction, a construct we infer based on the data at our disposal and our own criteria. As such, it is not something everyone can agree on or quantify objectively.[3] Thus, even among psychologists there is a wide variety of opinion about the meaning of intelligence, depending on the perspective from which they approach the topic.

Neither Galton nor Binet ever really defined intelligence. In fact, Galton seldom even used the term. Nevertheless, Galton's observations led him to believe that intelligence or general mental ability is a single hereditary, biological trait that is largely responsible for outstanding achievements in any field of endeavor. Although he recognized the existence of additional special aptitudes for certain fields, such as music and art, Galton believed that in order for these abilities to reach expression in extraordinary accomplishments, they had to be paired with an innate and superior level of general ability (Jensen, 1998).

The closest Binet came to defining intelligence was in an article he co-authored with

3 One of the many reasons the question of which of the two sexes is more intelligent cannot be answered is that most intelligence tests are deliberately constructed in a way that will result in no overall sex difference by balancing tasks that favor females and those that favor males.

Simon (1904) in which they equate intelligence with judgment or common sense, adding that "to judge well, to comprehend well, to reason well" (p. 197) are the essential *activities* of intelligence. Unlike Galton, Binet believed that intelligence consists of a complex set of abilities – such as attention, memory, and reasoning – that are fluid and shaped by environmental and cultural influences. Binet was also far less inclined than Galton to believe that intelligence could be reliably or precisely measured. He thought that to the extent that his scale captured some of the essential aspects of intellectual functioning, it would prove more serviceable in evaluating those at the subnormal range rather than at the superior levels of intellectual functioning that were Galton's primary concern.

Although it was Binet who succeeded in producing a practical method for estimating mental ability and in providing a useful solution to the problem of identifying children at the lower end of the ability spectrum, his notions about the nature of what his method was actually tapping were not, by any means, universally adopted. On the contrary, Binet's successful technique and the great variety of tests that proliferated following his lead provided additional means for other investigators to carry on research programs influenced by Galton's ideas. In particular, Charles Spearman's application of factor analysis to data derived from mental tests led him to believe that though numerous *specific* (*s*) factors are involved in the performance of tasks requiring specialized abilities, there is an overarching *general* (*g*) factor that is implicated to a greater or lesser extent in *all* intellectual activities (Spearman, 1927). Although Spearman himself thought of the *g* factor as a mathematical abstraction and did not equate it with intelligence, many others did and continue to do so (see, e.g., Gottfredson, 2009). In opposition to this, other theorists propagated views that were more in line with Binet's. L. L. Thurstone, for example, also applied factor analytic techniques to mental test data but, unlike Spearman, he argued that there are several distinct and *independent* group factors, such as verbal comprehension, numerical reasoning, memory, and such involved in intellectual activities (Thurstone, 1934). Much of the disagreement between those who supported Spearman's emphasis on the singular role of the *g* factor and those who favored multiple factors was based on different ways of conducting factor analyses on ability test data, as well as on the number and types of tests included in the analyses.

Aside from Binet, the other towering figure in the history of intelligence testing is David Wechsler. The test series that Wechsler developed starting in the 1930s, much like the scales originated by Binet in an earlier time, became the most widely used instruments for the individual assessment of intelligence and have been, for several decades, the standard against which other such tests are compared. Unlike Binet, however, Wechsler did provide a carefully crafted definition of intelligence which he modified somewhat over time. In the final version of that definition, Wechsler stated that intelligence is "the aggregate or global capacity of the individual to act purposefully, to think rationally and to deal effectively with his [*sic*] environment" (1958, p. 7).

Wechsler studied with Cattell and Spearman as well as with E. L. Thorndike, a psychologist whose views of intelligence differed considerably from Spearman's. Based on this training, he developed a position on intelligence that encompassed aspects of each of their viewpoints. In addition, Wechsler had been directly involved in administering and helping to develop intelligence tests since the time of World War I. As a result, when he started his own work on test development, Wechsler was uniquely qualified to address the topic of intelligence and its measurement. Near the end of his life, hoping to facilitate consensus about how to assess intelligence, Wechsler (1975) wrote an article in which he clearly aimed to debunk some of the common assumptions about the nature and meaning of intelligence that had led to the many conflicting views of it. Among the more interesting points Wechsler made in this article, were the following:

- intelligence is not a quality of mind, but an aspect of behavior;
- intelligence can neither be defined in absolute terms nor equated with cognitive ability;
- intelligent behavior requires nonintellectual capabilities, such as drive and persistence, as well as the ability to perceive and respond to social and aesthetic values; and
- intelligent behavior must not only be rational and purposeful; it must also be esteemed.

In this article, Wechsler quite sensibly admitted that intelligence is a relative concept. When it comes to intelligence tests, Wechsler stated his belief that they are valid and useful and that a competent examiner can do much better at evaluating intelligence with them than without them. Considering that he was keenly aware that his reputation would rest on the intelligence scales bearing his name, this is not surprising. In the final paragraph of the article, however, Wechsler came up with this puzzling conclusion:

> *What we measure with tests is not what tests measure – not information, not spatial perception, not reasoning ability. These are only means to an end. What intelligence tests measure, what we hope they measure, is something much more important: the capacity of an individual to understand the world about him and his resourcefulness to cope with its challenges. (Wechsler, 1975, p. 139)*

Such a conclusion might be tenable if Wechsler had said that intelligence tests allow us to *infer* an individual's capacity to understand the world and to cope with its challenges. However, as stated, his conclusion is puzzling in that it negates the possibility that tests measure some fairly well-defined and clear-cut constructs while suggesting that they can measure an infinitely more complex one. For who can doubt that what Wechsler meant by "the capacity . . . to understand the world" and the "resourcefulness to cope with its challenges" was anything other than intelligence itself?

What Do Intelligence Tests Actually Do?

Notwithstanding Wechsler, all intelligence tests – indeed all psychological tests of any kind – measure nothing more or less than samples of behavior. In the case of intelligence tests, the behavior samples are relevant to cognitive abilities of one sort or another and these abilities, in turn, have a very significant impact in various life outcomes, such as educational and occupational success. For example, many intelligence tests sample test takers' knowledge of vocabulary by asking them to define words at various difficulty levels, ranging from simple words used in everyday speech to more difficult and obscure ones. Test takers' scores depend on the number and difficulty of the words they are able to define and on how well that compares to what others in their age group can do. To a large extent, performance on vocabulary tests depends on the amount of reading people do and – all other things being equal – people who read more tend to acquire a larger fund of knowledge, understand verbal communications better, and do better in academic work than people who read less. Thus, while all that is measured by a vocabulary test – provided the words have been correctly scaled in terms of difficulty and provided the age group used for comparison is appropriate – is the level of a test taker's vocabulary compared to her or his age peers, what we can *infer* based on that measure is much more than that. Intelligence tests rely for their validity on the demonstrable relationships between the samples of behavior they tap and what can be justifiably inferred from those samples in terms of general ability. In addition to vocabulary, which is typically a reliable indicator of a person's general intellectual ability, intelligence tests include behavior samples that require quantitative, verbal, and visual-spatial reasoning skills as well as processing speed and various kinds of memory.

The question of validity. If we agree with Wechsler's argument, reiterated by Anne Anastasi years later, that "intelligence is . . . a quality of behavior" and that intelligent behavior is displayed in "effective ways of coping with the demands of a changing environment" (Anastasi, 1986, pp. 19–20), it follows that intelligence cannot be measured or encompassed by a single number. Nevertheless, for approximately the first half of the 20th century, from the time of the original Binet-Simon scales until the Wechsler scales for adults and children took over the preeminent role in intelligence testing, many – if not most – psychologists and educators as well as the general public assumed that the IQ was just such a number. This erroneous assumption was due in part to the enormous influence of the Stanford-Binet, which for much of its history yielded a single global IQ score that generally seemed to correctly classify people at the extreme levels of intellectual functioning. Unfortunately, however, this led to a proliferation of so-called "IQ tests" and to some egregious misuses which have been pointed out by critics from several perspectives throughout the history of these instruments (see, e.g., Gould, 1996; Stanovich, 2009).

In spite of the oftentimes virulent critiques to which intelligence tests have been subjected as a result of their misapplications, several of the traditional ones, such as the Stanford-Binet and Wechsler scales, continue to be used and new ones continue to arise. Furthermore, as discussed in a later section, the older scales have been repeatedly revised – and improved – as they have confronted new generations of instruments that apply advances from cognitive and psychometric theory in their development. A good part of the continued popularity of intelligence tests is due to the renewed ascendance of Spearman's notion of *g*. This, in turn, results from the accumulation of decades of factor analytic research confirming the existence of a theoretical construct that accounts for a large portion of the variance in the performance of intellectual tasks, namely, the *g* factor (Carroll, 1993; Jensen, 1998). Although it must not be assumed that the *g* factor and intelligence are the same, or that an IQ score is a direct measure of *g*, the major comprehensive intelligence test batteries are made up of subtests which, for the most part, have high loadings on *g*, as shown by factor analyses of their intercorrelations. In addition to the findings of numerous factor analytic studies, the major arguments for the validity of intelligence tests are based on (a) their high levels of reliability, as demonstrated by internal consistency and temporal stability coefficients that are typically in the .90s range for the total scores and global indices; (b) the extremely high correlations – in the .80s and .90s range – between the global scores produced by most of the major intelligence tests; and (c) the marked differences in the scores that various special populations, such as individuals with different levels of mental retardation or various learning disabilities, obtain (see, e.g., Flanagan & Harrison, 2005; Kaufman & Lichtenberger, 2006).

The latest version of the *Testing Standards* (American Educational Research Association, American Psychological Association, & National Council on Measurement in Education, 1999) defines validity as "the degree to which evidence and theory support the interpretations of test scores entailed by proposed uses of tests" (p. 9). With this definition, the burden of determining whether a particular application of intelligence test scores is valid is placed entirely on the person or institution responsible for the selection and administration of the test, for the interpretation of the scores, and for any decisions or actions taken on the basis of those scores.

Varieties of intelligence tests. There are, at least, four basic ways in which intelligence tests may be classified: (a) by administration mode, that is, individual versus group tests; (b) by the population for which they are intended, such as tests aimed at children or adults, or at other specific groups; (c) by type of content, such as verbal and nonverbal tests; and (d) by whether they are full-length batteries or abbreviated versions. Although this classification of tests is based on those that carry the term intelligence in their title, it could just as well apply to those that use different labels, such as general or cognitive ability tests.

A thorough discussion of all the varieties of intelligence tests is beyond the scope of this chapter. Nevertheless, a few critical points about these distinctions are necessary in order to understand the field even in the most general terms.

Mode of administration. Individual tests are those administered one-on-one, by a highly trained examiner to a single examinee. The need for thorough training of examiners is critical in this type of test administration because the procedures for presenting items, scoring responses, and handling the test stimulus materials and timing the tasks need to be strictly followed to comply with standardization requirements. When tests of this type are properly used, they provide the examiner with the opportunity to observe the examinee in the process of responding to challenging tasks presented in a highly structured format that is uniform for all examinees. Thus, in addition to scores, these tests yield a wealth of information that can prove extremely useful in clinical assessment. By the same token, it follows that when individual tests are not administered or scored according to standardized procedures, the reliability of results obtained comes into question. *Group tests*, on the other hand, can be administered safely to large numbers of people by almost anyone familiar with some very simple procedures and can be scored objectively. Thus, what is lost in terms of the type of information that can be gathered about the test taker with individual tests is made up in terms of efficiency and economy by group tests. Which type of test should be used depends on the purpose of the assessment and the available resources with which to do it.

Target population. The population for whom tests are intended is critical in at least two ways. It is crucial to remember that all normative scores, such as deviation IQs, indicate only the position or rank of a person's performance when compared to the specific group of individuals who comprise the norms for the test, not how intelligent a person is in any more basic sense. For example, if a test is to be used with adults over the age of 70, it is important to know if normative data were gathered from individuals who represent that population adequately, not only in terms of age and demographic characteristics but also with regard to variables such as living arrangements and health status. Average performance gauged in comparison to institutionalized older adults in nursing homes would be very different from average performance compared to people of the same age living independently.

The Flynn effect. The relative nature of the normative scores employed by intelligence tests is pointedly exemplified by the so-called Flynn effect. Starting in the 1980s, Flynn (1984, 1987) documented a trend that was interpreted as a general rise in the IQ of populations based on the observation that when tests like the Wechsler scales and the Raven's Progressive Matrices Test were revised and updated, successive normative samples set higher standards of performance than the groups employed in earlier versions. Naturally, this finding gave rise to questions regarding the possible reasons for this phenomenon as well as questions about why intelligence test performance would be rising while scores on tests such as the SAT, as well as other indices of academic achievement were not (Neisser, 1998). The changes that Flynn noted have been attributed to a variety of biological and environmental causes – such as better nutrition, medical advances, technological developments, and familiarity with the types of items of intelligence tests – but have never been satisfactorily explained. In fact, some studies have pointed out that the trend for ever-increasing standards in intelligence test performance is slowing or even reversing, at least in developed countries (Sundet, Barlaug, & Torjussen, 2004; Teasdale & Owen, 2005). Regardless of what cause(s) may be responsible for the fluctuations in intelligence test scores known as the Flynn effect, it is clear that they reflect *relative* changes in the performance of people from different generations on some of the cognitive abilities that the intelligence tests assess rather than in the more comprehensive view of intelligence as a quality of behavior that allows individuals to cope effectively with their environment. In particular, the rise in intelligence test performance standards is more pronounced in tasks that demand *fluid intelligence*, which involves the processing of new information and the solution of novel types of problems, as opposed to those that require *crystallized intelligence*, which entails the application of consolidated knowledge typically acquired in academic settings (Horn & Cattell, 1966).

Test content. The Flynn effect highlights another aspect of intelligence tests that has important consequences for their results, namely, the content of the tests. The most obvious distinction in this regard is between verbal and nonverbal test content, that is, between tests that require the use of receptive and expressive language and those that do not. In general, nonverbal tests of abilities, such as the Raven's Progressive Matrices and the Performance subtests of the Wechsler scales, rely on figural stimuli and visual-spatial reasoning tasks and tend to show larger gains in performance across successive generations than tests that rely on language (Flynn, 1987). Nonverbal tests also are generally considered to be less susceptible to the influence of culture. The verbal-nonverbal test content distinction has an impact both in deciding which type of test is appropriate for a given population and in determining the meaning and significance of test results. Nonverbal tests have been used with ethnically, linguistically, or otherwise culturally diverse populations based on the premise that by removing the influence of language such tests are less culture-laden and thus fairer. By instituting this limitation in content, however, the nature of the construct that is assessed may also be limited and the capacity of intelligence test scores to predict future performance in many academic or occupational endeavors that require verbal abilities may consequently be reduced.

Test length. A similar caveat, in terms of interpretability, applies to intelligence tests that differ in length from their original prototypes, such as the WASI or the K-BIT, which are short tests from the Wechsler and Kaufman series, respectively. When validity information for such brief tests is presented in the form of very high and positive correlations with longer versions or with each other, it simply means that the rank order positions of test takers' scores on both tests is substantially the same. High as those validity coefficients may be, however, they clearly do not mean that the results of the shorter tests are comparable to those of the full batteries either in terms of the range of abilities they tap or in the amount of information about a person's cognitive functioning they provide. See Homack and Reynolds's (2007) *Essentials of Assessment with Brief Intelligence Tests* for a useful and compact introduction to the subject featuring four of the most prominent examples of this type of instrument.

What Functions or Purposes Do Intelligence Tests Serve?

For the purpose of the discussion that follows, the term *intelligence tests* refers only to the full-length comprehensive batteries – based on large and representative samples of children or adults in the United States population – that are individually administered, regardless of whether their titles include the word intelligence. The major current examples of this type of test batteries – besides the Stanford-Binet, Fifth Edition (SB5; Roid, 2003) and the Wechsler scales (WAIS-IV, WISC-IV, & WPPSI-III; Wechsler, 2008, 2003, 2002) – are the Cognitive Assessment System (CAS; Naglieri & Das, 1997), the Differential Ability Scales (DAS-II: Elliott, 2007), the Kaufman Adolescent and Adult Intelligence Scale

(KAIT; Kaufman & Kaufman, 1993), the Kaufman Assessment Battery for Children, Second Edition (KABC-II; Kaufman & Kaufman, 2004), the Reynolds Intellectual Assessment Scales (RIAS; Reynolds & Kamphaus, 2003), and the Woodcock-Johnson III Test of Cognitive Abilities (WJ III; Woodcock, McGrew, & Mather, 2001). Although some group tests, brief tests, or tests that sample only nonverbal content are often used for the same purposes as the comprehensive intelligence tests, their limitations in length, content, or mode of administration are such that they cannot provide the same wealth of information that intelligence test batteries do.

The impact that intelligence tests have had on both the professional and lay notions of what intelligence is, and on the almost complete identification of intelligence with the IQ score, cannot be overestimated. In order to understand this, it helps to review the makeup of those tests, starting with the Stanford-Binet. From the beginning, the Binet scales were age-based in their organization and in the way their results were interpreted. As Binet figured out, by including items in his scale that tapped a variety of cognitive functions – such as verbal comprehension, logical reasoning, and memory – at different levels of difficulty, he could assess children's levels of mental development. So for the better part of its history, until the Stanford-Binet, Fourth Edition, was published (Thorndike, Hagen, & Sattler, 1986), the Binet scales were organized according to age levels, with a heterogeneous mixture of item types for each chronological age level covered by the scales. Thus, the examiner first had to establish a basal age; this was the age level at which all items were passed and before the level at which the first failure occurred. To begin testing, the examiner estimated the age level at which the examinee was likely to succeed with some effort, based on the examinee's chronological age and background. The examiner would then proceed by administering all of the various types of items designated for that age level. At the younger age levels, appropriate for preschool children, items would include simple performance tasks, such as stringing beads, sorting buttons, or tying knots as well as some verbal tasks such as naming objects or repeating series of two or three digits. As the age levels progressed, items would naturally be more difficult and would rely heavily on verbal comprehension and reasoning tasks, such as word definitions and explaining the meaning of proverbs. Depending on how many items were passed at levels subsequent to the basal age, testing would continue until a ceiling age was reached. The procedures for establishing a basal and a ceiling age were quite important as it was critical to determine reliably the age level below which it could be safely assumed that all items would be passed (basal age) or above which all further items would be failed (ceiling age). The mental age (MA) score on the SB was obtained by adding to the basal age credit in years and months for the items the examinee had passed above her or his basal age. Although the specific bases for determining the SB IQ varied somewhat over time, until the fourth edition, the IQ score hinged on the relationship between the MA and the CA of the examinee.

The advent of the Wechsler scales brought many changes that would have significant consequences for the way in which intelligence is assessed. Most of these changes stemmed from the fact that Wechsler intended to develop an instrument suitable for adults. As a result, Wechsler adopted the use of a point scale, rather than an age scale like the one employed by the SB. Thus, in all of the Wechsler intelligence scales, starting with the original Wechsler-Bellevue, items of the same type are arranged in order of difficulty and organized into 10 or more subtests of homogeneous content. Examinees are presented with one subtest at a time and earn points based on how many items they pass on each subtest. In addition, subtest scores can be grouped in a variety of ways. The traditional Verbal and Performance subscale categories, for example, grouped subtests based on whether their content was primarily verbal or not. Subtests such as Information, Vocabulary, Comprehension, and

Similarities made up the Verbal subscale whereas Block Design, Picture Completion, Picture Arrangement, and Object Assembly were among the subtests making up the Performance subscale. The Wechsler scales originally yielded Verbal and Performance IQs (VIQs and PIQs), based on the respective subscales, as well as a Full Scale IQ (FSIQ) based on a combination of the full range of subtest scores.[4] More recently, subtests have been grouped into index scores – namely, Verbal Comprehension, Perceptual Reasoning, Working Memory, and Processing Speed – that are empirically derived on the basis of factor analyses of subtest data. As mentioned earlier, Wechsler also adopted and popularized the use of deviation IQs based on the extent to which examinees' raw scores differ from the mean of their corresponding age group in the standardization sample. Because one's performance is compared to that of the most closely similar age group, IQs obtained in this fashion make sense in that they indicate whether that performance is at, above, or below average – regardless of the age of the examinee.

Even though, from the beginning, the Wechsler scales produced scores on a variety of subtests besides the IQs, for most practical purposes their interpretation was limited to classifying test takers in terms of their general level of intellectual functioning, based on the FSIQ. As time went by, however, the Wechsler scales acquired an overwhelming popularity compared to the SB, especially among clinical psychologists who realized that the variety of scores the Wechsler scales yielded afforded the opportunity to develop diagnostically significant interpretive hypothesis based on particular aspects of an examinee's performance. For example, according to traditional theories of brain organization – which aligned the left hemisphere with language functions and the right hemisphere with spatial skills – differences in the Wechsler Verbal IQ (VIQ) and Performance IQ (PIQ), if present and sufficiently large, were interpreted as indications of dysfunction in either the left or right cerebral hemispheres, depending on whether the PIQ was larger than the VIQ or vice versa. An excellent summary of the research on neuropsychological correlates of VIQ-PIQ discrepancies provided by Kaufman and Lichtenberger (2006), however, leads to the conclusion that whereas right hemisphere and bilateral brain damage often is reflected in a VIQ>PIQ pattern, left hemisphere damage does not show a PIQ>VIQ discrepancy consistently enough to be of diagnostic benefit.

The practice of analyzing the pattern of responses to items and subtests of the Wechsler scales to extract information about test takers' cognitive abilities and psychological functioning beyond that provided by a single summary score was given impetus by Rapaport, Gill, and Schafer (1945, 1946) who proposed a system that was adopted by many psychologists and was augmented over the next few decades. This practice, which became known as profile analysis, was largely based on the observations of clinicians and their experiences with various types of patients. By the 1990s, profile analysis of Wechsler subtest data came under serious criticism, notably by McDermott, Fantuzzo, and Glutting (1990) who pointed out that such analyses as commonly applied for diagnostic purposes suffered from inadequate reliability and validity data and could thus lead to too many incorrect inferences.

Even before disagreement with the traditional ways of analyzing and interpreting intelligence test score profiles was voiced, there were indications of dissatisfaction with the Stanford-Binet and Wechsler scales. This dissatisfaction stemmed from two sources. One was the increasing emphasis the testing professions started to place on the need for multiple sources of validity evidence (see, e.g., American Psychological Association, 1974; American Educational Research Association, American Psychological Association, & National Council on Measurement

4 Verbal and Performance IQs have been abandoned in favor of index scores in all the current versions of the Wechsler intelligence scales except for the WPPSI-III.

in Education, 1985). In this regard, for example, it now seems remarkable that the manual for the WISC, published in 1949, did not mention validity at all and even the WAIS-R, published in 1981, dealt with the topic in three short paragraphs, basically asserting that the validity of the WAIS-R stemmed from its close connection with the Wechsler-Bellevue, which in turn was correlated with other intelligence tests of that time. Thus, over time, simply demonstrating that the scores on intelligence tests were highly correlated with each other came to be perceived as a clearly insufficient basis for establishing their validity for diagnostic purposes.

Another significant source of discontent with the Binet and Wechsler scales stemmed from the fact that theories of intelligence had continued to evolve in the decades following the creation of those tests. One of the main driving forces in the theorizing about intelligence was the continuous and voluminous accumulation of factor analytic research on human cognitive abilities, best summarized by Carroll's (1993) encyclopedic survey of studies on that topic. This research, in turn, led to a useful model of cognitive trait organization.

As a consequence of the changes just described, simple global estimates of general ability or *g*, while useful in projecting the likelihood of success in academic and job settings (see, e.g., Neisser et al., 1996), were increasingly seen as not providing enough clinically useful information about a person's cognitive functioning to justify the cost and time involved in the administration, scoring, and interpretation of a full-length comprehensive individual intelligence test. Furthermore, as theoretical views of intelligence evolved, and advances in neuroscience provided new information about the role of the brain in cognition, it became clear that the comprehensive instruments for the assessment of cognitive abilities could and should be grounded on these more firm theoretical and empirical bases.

One of the first significant steps in the development of a new generation of intelligence tests was the publication of the Kaufman Assessment Battery for Children (K-ABC; Kaufman & Kaufman, 1983). In developing this instrument, Alan and Nadine Kaufman used the differentiation between sequential and simultaneous types of cognitive processing, based on the theories of the Russian neuropsychologist A. R. Luria, as one of the organizing principles in their battery. Prior to developing the K-ABC, Alan Kaufman – who had had a major role in the revision of the original Wechsler Intelligence Scale for Children – published an influential book (Kaufman, 1979) that proposed a more sophisticated method for analyzing and interpreting WISC-R data. Kaufman's *intelligent testing* system was grounded on cognitive theories as well as factor analytic research. It started with the assumption that the FSIQ is inadequate as an explanation of a child's intellectual functioning and it used the reliability indices as well as the variety of measures provided by the WISC-R to generate more informative interpretive hypotheses to be supported or discarded in light of information derived from the test battery and from additional sources of data about the child.

The ideas that had been percolating for some time concerning the limitations of the traditional scales, as well as the possibility of developing intelligence tests that would reflect advances in theories of cognitive trait organization and that would apply the information collected in over six decades of factor analytic research on measures of cognitive abilities, gave impetus to the development of new and improved tests of intelligence.[5] In fact, some of these advances even began to be applied to the SB and the Wechsler scales with each successive revision. For example, the SB Fourth Edition (Thorndike, Hagen, & Sattler, 1986) used a model of cognitive abilities that incorporated the theory of fluid (*Gf*) and crystallized (*Gc*) intelligence (Horn & Cattell, 1966) as the middle level of a hierarchy with the *g* factor above it

5 It should be noted that group tests of abilities had been applying factor analytic findings in their development well before the 1970s.

and with four group factors – namely, verbal, quantitative, and abstract-visual reasoning as well as short-term memory – below it.[6] Similarly, after the death of David Wechsler in 1981, the scales that still bear his name started to explicitly incorporate a multifactor structure for grouping subtests in order to devise interpretive strategies rooted more firmly on an empirically defensible basis. The Wechsler scales published after 1990 have added new subtests as needed to shore up and clarify the factorial structure of the scales (see, e.g., Wechsler, 1991, 1997, 2003, and 2008). Thus, besides the Full Scale IQ, the other four major scores derived from the WISC-IV and the WAIS-IV, namely the Verbal Comprehension, Perceptual Reasoning, Working Memory, and Processing Speed composites, are based on groupings of subtest scores arrived at through factor analyses.

In addition to the structural revisions made by the traditional intelligence test batteries, a number of completely new instruments – with new scales and novel types of items – have also been appearing in the past few decades. Most of these make use to some extent or another of what has come to be known as the Cattell-Horn-Carroll (CHC) model of cognitive abilities. This model epitomizes the psychometric approach to intelligence pioneered by Spearman (1904, 1927) and pursued by many other investigators specializing in factor analysis of cognitive test data and in theories of cognitive trait organization. It consists of a hierarchical three-stratum arrangement devised by Carroll (1993) that serves to organize the massive amount of factor analytic research on human cognitive abilities accumulated over six or seven decades. The full model includes about 70 narrow abilities in the first or lowest stratum, approximately eight broad factors – including fluid and crystallized intelligence– in the second or middle stratum, and the general (*g*) intelligence factor in the third or highest stratum.

6 The Stanford-Binet 5th edition (Roid, 2003) uses a modified five-factor hierarchical model.

The Woodcock-Johnson III Test of Cognitive Abilities (WJ III; Woodcock, McGrew, & Mather, 2001), which is the current version of a test battery originally published in 1978, is one of the tests that has used the CHC model of cognitive abilities most extensively in its design, incorporating as it does seven of the CHC broad factors and over 20 of the narrow abilities in that model. Two other recent test batteries that use some aspects of the CHC model for their interpretive schemes are the Reynolds Intellectual Assessment Scales (RIAS; Reynolds & Kamphaus, 2003) and the second edition of the Differential Ability Scales (DAS-II; Elliott, 2007). In addition, the theory and research behind the CHC model, along with the intelligent testing method pioneered by Kaufman (1979, 1994), have been used to develop the *cross battery assessment* approach (XBA; Flanagan & McGrew, 1997; Flanagan, Ortiz, & Alfonso, 2007). This approach, as the name implies, offers guidance on how to design cognitive assessments using one of the comprehensive intelligence test batteries and supplementing it with additional tests from another intelligence or achievement battery, as may be required in light of the unique referral question to be addressed. Kaufman's intelligent testing provides an ideal basis for the utilization of the CHC. His method is geared toward understanding an examinee's pattern of cognitive strengths and weakness through the application of clinical and psychometric methods in a flexible and individualized fashion. The cross-battery approach is especially geared toward the evaluation of learning disabilities and toward the assessment of individuals from culturally or linguistically diverse backgrounds.

Developers of the new generation of intelligence tests have also employed the functional theory of brain organization developed by A. R. Luria and mentioned previously in connection with the K-ABC. This theory makes a distinction among functional units of the brain devoted primarily to attention, to planning, and to the successive and simultaneous processing of information.

Table 2.1. Major Examples of Current Intelligence Tests

Test Title and Acronym	*Author(s) and Date of Publication*	*Primary Theoretical/Empirical Rationale*
Cognitive Assessment System (CAS)	J. A. Naglieri & J. P. Das (1997)	PASS theory of cognitive functioning: Planning, Attention, Simultaneous, & Sequential Processing (Das, Naglieri, & Kirby, 1994)
Differential Ability Scales-Second Edition (DAS-II)	C. D. Elliott (2007)	Cattell-Horn-Carroll (CHC) model – Stratum II: Broad abilities (Carroll, 1993)
Kaufman Adolescent and Adult Intelligence Test (KAIT)	A. S. Kaufman & N. L. Kaufman (1993)	Horn and Cattell's (1966) model of Fluid (Gf) and Crystallized (Gc) intelligence & Luria's (1973, 1980) neuropsychological theory
Kaufman Assessment Battery for Children-Second Edition (KABC-II)	A. S. Kaufman & N. L. Kaufman (2004)	Luria's (1973, 1980) neuropsychological theory & Cattell-Horn-Carroll (CHC) model (Carroll, 1993)
Reynolds Intellectual Assessment Scales (RIAS)	C. R. Reynolds & R. W. Kamphaus (2003)	Cattell-Horn-Carroll (CHC) model – Stratum III: *g* & Stratum II: Broad abilities (Carroll, 1993)
Stanford-Binet Intelligence Scales-Fifth Edition (SB5)	G. H. Roid (2003)	Cattell-Horn-Carroll (CHC) model (Carroll, 1993) and factor analyses
Wechsler Adult Intelligence Scale-Fourth Edition (WAIS-IV), Wechsler Intelligence Scale for Children-Fourth Edition (WISC-IV)	D. Wechsler (2008, 2003)	Factor analytically derived composites: Verbal Comprehension, Perceptual Reasoning, Working Memory, & Processing Speed
Woodcock-Johnson III Test of Cognitive Abilities (WJ III)	R. W. Woodcock, K. S. McGrew, & N. Mather (2001)	Cattell-Horn-Carroll (CHC) model-Stratum III, II, & I: *g* plus broad and narrow abilities (Carroll, 1993)

Successive processing involves serial or temporal sequencing of information whereas simultaneous processing involves synthesizing or organizing material as a whole and at once. As elaborated by J. P. Das and others (Das, Naglieri, & Kirby, 1994), Luria's conceptualizations were the foundation of the PASS theory of intelligence used as the primary basis for the development of the Cognitive Assessment System (CAS), an intelligence test battery authored by Das and Naglieri (1997). Alan and Nadine Kaufman, meanwhile, have also continued to use aspects of Luria's theory and of the Horn-Cattell model of *Gf* and *Gc* in developing the Kaufman Adolescent and Adult Intelligence Test (KAIT; Kaufman & Kaufman, 1993) and the second edition of the Kaufman Assessment Battery for Children (KABC-II; Kaufman & Kaufman, 2004). Table 2.1 lists the major examples of current intelligence test batteries, along with their authors and the theoretical or empirical rationale on which they are based.

Do Intelligence Tests Have a Future?

Here the short answer is, most likely, yes. As far as group tests of intelligence and general aptitude are concerned, most of those listed in TIP can produce good estimates of general intellectual ability or *g*, provided their content is appropriate for the age, culture, educational background, and any special characteristics or disabilities of the examinee. They can also produce such estimates at low cost and without the need of extensive apparatus. With regard to the individually administered comprehensive intelligence test batteries that have been discussed here, the situation is somewhat different. To be sure, most of them can also provide good estimates of general intellectual ability and fulfill the original purpose for which the Binet and the Wechsler scales were developed. If that were all they could do, however, their cost and the extensive training required to properly administer them, score them, and interpret their results would not be justified.

The reason that individual intelligence tests are likely to endure is tied to their versatility and clinical usefulness. They essentially provide a standardized and structured interview script that the well-trained user can employ for gathering a broad sample of behavioral data relevant to cognitive functioning while observing stylistic variations that can also reveal clinically significant personality data. In the survey published by Camara et al. (2000), for example, out of the top 20 most frequently used tests, the WAIS-R was ranked in first place by clinical psychologists and in second place by neuropsychologists.[7] Not only have the traditional scales evolved and been improved with regard to their composition, psychometric properties, and normative bases, but a number of new ones have been published which expand the range of cognitive tasks that can be sampled and the array of empirical and theoretical evidence that can be adduced to support their validity. Thus, the utility of the tests for the assessment of adaptive/functional behavior, intellectual development, learning difficulties, neuropsychological and psychiatric problems, as well as for rehabilitation or remedial planning, has been greatly increased. Already, the procedures of some intelligence test batteries, notably the WISC-IV Integrated (Kaplan et al., 2004), have been modified so as to take advantage of the one-on-one administration mode to gather additional dynamic information on examinees' problem-solving processes and to contribute more directly to remediation planning. Furthermore, as Goldstein (2008) points out, recent advances in neuroimaging, such as the functional MRI, offer exciting possibilities for applying the more sophisticated and well-validated tasks of current tests to neurodiagnosis and to extending knowledge of brain-behavior relationships.

In a sense, nearly all of human behavior involves cognitive abilities as these encompass processes that include attention, perception, comprehension, judgment, decision making, reasoning, intuition, and memory, among others. Not all of these are tapped by intelligence tests (see, e.g., Stanovich, 2009). Nevertheless, the fact that the term *cognitive abilities* is increasingly used instead of intelligence – even in the titles of tests that might have been called "intelligence" tests in another era – is helpful because cognitive processes are more easily defined, grasped, and assessed and are not as emotionally laden as "intelligence" is. When the cognitive abilities tapped by intelligence tests are used in performing mental tasks or in problem solving, it is reasonable to assume that the one who is performing those tasks or solving those problems is displaying intelligent behavior. However, it also seems clear that not all intelligent behavior is simply a function of the cognitive abilities measured by the tests. What the tests do not measure, namely, characteristics such as motivation, flexibility, leadership ability, persistence, conscientiousness, and creativity, are as important as – or even more so than – the cognitive abilities the tests *do* measure in allowing individuals to behave intelligently and to cope with the challenges that life presents.

7 The MMPI, which was reported in the survey as the most frequently used instrument for personality assessment, was ranked in first place by neuropsychologists and in second place by clinical psychologists.

References

American Educational Research Association, American Psychological Association, & National Council on Measurement in Education. (1999). *Standards for educational and psychological testing*. Washington, DC: American Educational Research Association.

American Educational Research Association, American Psychological Association, & National Council on Measurement in Education. (1985). *Standards for educational and psychological testing*. Washington, DC: American Psychological Association.

American Psychological Association. (1974). *Standards for educational and psychological tests*. Washington, DC: Author.

Anastasi, A. (1986). Intelligence as a quality of behavior. In R. J. Sternberg & D. K. Detterman (Eds.), *What is intelligence? Contemporary viewpoints on its nature and definitions* (pp. 19–21). Norwood, NJ: Ablex.

Binet, A., & Simon, Th. (1904). Méthodes nouvelles pour le diagnostic du niveau intellectuel des anormaux. *L'Année Psychologique*, **11**, 191–244. Retrieved from http://www.persee.fr/web/revues/home/prescript/issue/psy_0003-5033_1904_num_11_1.

Boring, E. G. (1923, June 6). Intelligence as the tests test it. *New Republic*, **35**, 35–37.

Camara, W. J., Nathan, J. S., & Puente, A. E. (2000). Psychological test usage: Implications in professional psychology. *Professional Psychology: Research and Practice*, **31**, 141–154.

Carroll, J. B. (1993). *Human cognitive abilities: A survey of factor-analytic studies*. New York, NY: Cambridge University Press.

Das, J. P., Naglieri, J. A., & Kirby, J. R. (1994). *Assessment of cognitive processes: The PASS theory of intelligence*. Boston, MA: Allyn & Bacon.

Elliott, C. D. (2007). *DAS-II administration and scoring manual*. San Antonio, TX: PsychCorp.

Fancher, R. E. (1985). *The intelligence men: Makers of the IQ controversy*. New York, NY: W.W. Norton.

Flanagan, D. P., & Harrison, P. L. (Eds.). (2005). *Contemporary intellectual assessment: Theories, tests, and issues* (2nd ed.). New York, NY: Guilford Press.

Flanagan, D. P., & McGrew, K. S. (1997). A cross-battery approach to assessing and interpreting cognitive abilities: Narrowing the gap between practice and cognitive science. In D. P. Flanagan, J. L. Genshaft, & P. L. Harrison (Eds.), *Contemporary intellectual assessment: Theories, tests, and issues* (pp. 314–325). New York, NY: Guilford Press.

Flanagan, D. P., Ortiz, S. O., & Alfonso, V. C. (2007). *Essentials of cross-battery assessment* (2nd ed.). Hoboken, NJ: Wiley.

Flynn, J. R. (1984). The mean IQ of Americans: Massive gains 1932 to 1978. *Psychological Bulletin*, **95**, 29–51.

Flynn, J. R. (1987). Massive IQ gains in 14 nations: What IQ tests really measure. *Psychological Bulletin*, **101**, 171–191.

Goldstein, G. (2008). Intellectual assessment. In M. Hersen & A. M. Gross (Eds.), *Handbook of clinical psychology* (Vol. 1, pp. 395–421). Hoboken, NJ: Wiley.

Gottfredson, L. S. (2009). Logical fallacies used to dismiss the evidence on intelligence testing. In R. P. Phelps (Ed.), *Correcting fallacies about educational and psychological testing* (pp. 11–65). Washington, DC: American Psychological Association.

Gould, S. J. (1996). *The mismeasure of man* (Rev. ed.). New York, NY: W. W. Norton.

Homack, S. R., & Reynolds, C. R. (2007). *Essentials of assessment with brief intelligence tests*. Hoboken, NJ: Wiley.

Horn, J. L., & Cattell, R. B. (1966). Refinement and test of the theory of fluid and crystallized intelligence. *Journal of Educational Psychology*, **57**, 253–270.

Jensen, A. R. (1998). *The g factor: The science of mental ability*. Westport, CT: Praeger.

Kaplan, E., Fein, D., Kramer, J., Morris, R., Delis, D., & Maerlender, A. (2004). *WISC-IV Integrated: Technical and interpretive manual*. San Antonio, TX: PsychCorp.

Kaufman, A. S. (1979). *Intelligent testing with the WISC-R*. New York, NY: Wiley.

Kaufman, A. S. (1994). *Intelligent testing with the WISC-III*. New York, NY: Wiley.

Kaufman, A. S., & Kaufman, N. L. (1983). *Kaufman Assessment Battery for Children: Interpretive manual*. Circle Pines, MN: American Guidance Service.

Kaufman, A. S., & Kaufman, N. L. (1993). *Manual for the Kaufman Adolescent & Adult Intelligence Test (KAIT)*. Circle Pines, MN: American Guidance Service.

Kaufman, A. S., & Kaufman, N. L. (2004). *Manual for the Kaufman Assessment Battery for Children – Second Edition (KABC-II): Comprehensive Form*. Circle Pines, MN: American Guidance Service.

Kaufman, A. S., & Lichtenberger, E. O. (2006). *Assessing adolescent and adult intelligence* (3rd ed.). Hoboken, NJ: Wiley.
Kirk, R. E. (1999). *Statistics: An introduction* (4th ed.). Fort Worth, TX: Harcourt Brace.
Luria, A. R. (1973). *The working brain: An introduction to neuropsychology*. New York: Basic Books.
Luria, A. R. (1980). *Higher cortical functions in man* (2nd ed.). New York, NY: Basic Books.
McDermott, P. A., Fantuzzo, J. W., & Glutting, J. J. (1990). Just say no to subtest analysis: A critique of Wechsler theory and practice. *Journal of Psychoeducational Assessment*, 8, 290–302.
Murdoch, S. (2007). *IQ: A smart history of a failed idea*. Hoboken, NJ: Wiley.
Murphy, L. L., Spies, R. A., & Plake, B. S. (Eds.). (2006). *Tests in Print VII*. Lincoln, NE: Buros Institute of Mental Measurements.
Naglieri, J. A., & Das, J. P. (1997). *Das-Naglieri Cognitive Assessment System*. Chicago, IL: Riverside.
Neisser, U. (Ed.). (1998). *The rising curve: Long-term gains in IQ and related measures*. Washington, DC: American Psychological Association.
Neisser, U., Boodoo, G., Bouchard, T. J., Boykin, A. W., Brody, N., Ceci, S. J., Halpern, D. F., Loehlin, J. C., Perloff, R., Sternberg, R. J., & Urbina, S. (1996). Intelligence: Knowns and unknowns. *American Psychologist*, **51**, 77–101.
Rapaport, D., Gill, M., & Schafer, R. (1945). *Diagnostic psychological testing* (Vol. 1). Chicago, IL: Year Book.
Rapaport, D., Gill, M., & Schafer, R. (1946). *Diagnostic psychological testing: The theory, statistical evaluation, and diagnostic application of a battery of tests* (Vol. 2). Chicago, IL: Year Book.
Reynolds, C. R., & Kamphaus, R. W. (2003). *Reynolds Intellectual Assessment Scales*. Lutz, FL: Psychological Assessment Resources.
Robertson, G. J. (1972). Development of the first group mental ability test. In G. H. Bracht, K. D. Hopkins, & J. C. Stanley (Eds.), *Perspectives in educational and psychological measurement* (pp. 183–190). Englewood Cliffs, NJ: Prentice-Hall.
Roid, G. H. (2003). *Stanford-Binet Intelligence Scales, Fifth Edition: Technical manual*. Itasca, IL: Riverside.
Society for Industrial and Organizational Psychology. (2003). *Principles for the validation and use of personnel selection procedures*. Retrieved from http://www.siop.org/_Principles/principles.pdf.
Sokal, M. M. (Ed.). (1987). *Psychological testing and American society: 1890–1930*. New Brunswick, NJ: Rutgers University Press.
Spearman, C. (1904). "General intelligence," objectively determined and measured. *American Journal of Psychology*, **15**, 201–293.
Spearman, C. (1927). *The abilities of man*. New York, NY: Macmillan.
Stanovich, K. E. (2009). *What intelligence tests miss: The psychology of rational thought*. New Haven, CT: Yale University Press.
Sternberg, R. J., & Detterman, D. K. (Eds.). (1986). *What is intelligence?* Norwood, NJ: Ablex.
Sundet, J. M., Barlaug, D. G., & Torjussen, T. M. (2004). The end of the Flynn effect? A study of secular trends in mean intelligence scores of Norwegian conscripts during half a century. *Intelligence*, **32**, 349–362.
Teasdale, T. W., & Owen, D. R. (2005). A long-term rise and recent decline in intelligence test performance: The Flynn effect in reverse. *Personality and Individual Differences*, **39**, 837–843.
Thorndike, R. L., Hagen, E. P., & Sattler, J. M. (1986). *The Stanford-Binet Intelligence Scale: Fourth Edition, Guide for administering and scoring*. Chicago, IL: Riverside.
Thurstone, L. L. (1934). The vectors of mind. *Psychological Review*, **41**, 1–32.
Urbina, S. (1993). Intelligence: Definition and theoretical models. In F. N. Magill (Ed.), *Survey of social science: Psychology*. Pasadena, CA: Salem Press.
Wechsler, D. (1958). *The measurement and appraisal of adult intelligence* (4th ed.). Baltimore, MD: Williams & Wilkins.
Wechsler, D. (1975). Intelligence defined and undefined: A relativistic appraisal. *American Psychologist*, **30**, 135–139.
Wechsler, D. (1991). *Wechsler Intelligence Scale for Children – Third Edition*. San Antonio, TX: Psychological Corporation.
Wechsler, D. (1997). *Wechsler Adult Intelligence Scale – Third Edition*. San Antonio, TX: Psychological Corporation.
Wechsler, D. (2002). *Wechsler Preschool and Primary Scale of Intelligence – Third Edition*. San Antonio, TX: Harcourt Assessment.
Wechsler, D. (2003). *Wechsler Intelligence Scale for Children – Fourth Edition*. San Antonio, TX: Psychological Corporation.

Wechsler, D. (2008). *Wechsler Adult Intelligence Scale – Fourth Edition*. San Antonio, TX: Pearson.

Wissler, C. (1901). The correlation of mental and physical tests. *Psychological Monographs*, 3(6), 1–62.

Wolf, T. H. (1973). *Alfred Binet*. Chicago, IL: University of Chicago Press.

Woodcock, R. W., McGrew, K. S., & Mather, N. (2001). *Woodcock-Johnson III*. Itasca, IL: Riverside.

Zenderland, L. (1998). *Measuring minds: Henry Herbert Goddard and the origins of American intelligence testing*. New York, NY: Cambridge University Press.

CHAPTER 3

Factor-Analytic Models of Intelligence

John O. Willis, Ron Dumont, and Alan S. Kaufman

The great tragedy of Science – the slaying of a beautiful hypothesis by an ugly fact.

*Thomas Huxley**

Get your facts first, and then you can distort them as much as you please.

Attributed to Mark Twain†

Clearly, there are many ways to define intelligence. Wasserman and Tulsky (2005, p. 15) list 11 definitions provided by psychologists who responded in 1921 to a survey regarding their opinions about the definition of the term intelligence. Sternberg and Detterman (1986) provided an updated symposium with more definitions and some overlap of components. Sattler (2008, p. 223) provided an additional list of 19 different definitions that have been suggested over the years by several of the major experts in the field of psychology. Although intelligence, like Freud's "ego," is probably best thought of as a process, it is treated in much of the literature and often in professional practice as a "thing." The lack of a single, accepted definition of intelligence contributes to disagreements about how to assess it. Without agreement on the definition of intelligence – and even on whether IQ exists – it is difficult to reach agreement on how to measure intelligence. For information about the major theories of intelligence that have influenced testing, see Carroll (1993, chapter 2); Daniel (1997); Flanagan and Harrison, (2005); Kaufman (2009); McGrew and Flanagan (1998, chapter 1), Sattler (2008, chapter 7); Sternberg (2000); and Woodcock (1990). And for some of the many disputes about the construct and measurement of intelligence, see Eysenck versus Kamin (1981); Gould (1981); Herrnstein and Murray (1994); and Jacoby and Glauberman (1995), among a great many, many other sources (it is a contentious field).

* Presidential address at the British Association, "Biogenesis and abiogenesis" (1870); later published in *Collected Essays*, Vol. 8, p. 229. London, UK: Macmillan and Co., 1894. [Elibron Classics Replica Edition, Chestnut Hill, MA: Adamant Media, 2001.]

† Commonly quoted as: "First get your facts, then you can distort them at your leisure." Rudyard Kipling, An interview with Mark Twain, p. 180, From *Sea to sea: Letters of travel*, 1899, Doubleday & McClure.

Global Intellectual Ability Versus Separate Abilities

A persistent and unresolved question in both professional theories and lay conceptualizations of intelligence has been whether an individual has one, overall level of "intelligence" or, instead, what we call "intelligence" is actually a set of several separate abilities. These theorists could be characterized respectively as "lumpers" and "splitters" (McKusick, 1969). Although apparently dichotomous, this fundamental question has spawned continua of hotly debated theories.

At one end, there is the extreme lumper position that each person has a single level of cognitive ability (often referred to as *g*, as discussed later in the chapter; e.g., Jensen, 1998; Spearman, 1904). The *expression* of this intelligence may vary with different tasks, and as a function of education, sensory and motor abilities, and other influences, but the individual has one, single level of reasoning ability that will be seen on a wide variety of intelligence tests. This theoretical perspective matches the common observation that among our friends and acquaintances, some individuals are consistently pretty smart about almost everything and some are consistently incompetent and clueless. Most of us can categorize the people we know as "smart," "dumb," or something in between. Theorists and practitioners who adhere to this position tend to consider the total score on an intelligence test an approximation of the individual's overall level of intelligence, although scores will vary somewhat on different tests.

The opposite extreme, the splitter end of this continuum, is the position that there is a set of several higher order cognitive abilities that are more or less independent of each other (e.g., Cattell, 1941; Horn & Blankson, 2005; Horn & Cattell, 1966; Guilford, 1967; Thorndike, 1927; Thurstone, 1938). A person might demonstrate, for example, a high level of verbal knowledge, vocabulary, and verbal reasoning ability but be weak in visual-spatial thinking and unable to read a map or to "see" how a decorator's floor plan would translate into the actual layout of furniture in the real room. Most of us can think of acquaintances who may be terribly clever in some ways and notably incompetent in others. Theorists and practitioners who adhere to this extreme splitter position tend to ignore or deemphasize total scores on intelligence tests and focus on patterns of strengths and weaknesses.

Other splitter theorists focus their attention on different mental *processes* (rather than a set of discrete *abilities*) such as planning; attention; and dealing with information in a step-by-step, sequential process or in an all-at-once, holistic approach (e.g., Kaufman, Kaufman, Kaufman-Singer, & Kaufman, 2005; Luria, 1980; Naglieri & Das, 2005). Again, this theoretical perspective is mirrored in popular psychology. People often characterize themselves and others as, for example, either sequential (successive, auditory/sequential) or holistic (simultaneous, visual/spatial) thinkers (e.g., Kaufman, Kaufman, & Goldsmith, 1984; Silverman, 2000).

Still other splitter theorists (e.g., Gardner, 1983, 2003; Stanovich, 2009; Sternberg, 1982, 2005) object to the narrow scope of intelligence as it is measured by most existing intelligence tests. They note that the oral question-and-answer, paper-and-pencil, and picture-and-puzzle intelligence tests deemphasize or entirely omit such essential capacities as practical intelligence, creativity, artistic and musical abilities, and rational thinking.

General Intelligence – Spearman's g

British psychologist Charles Spearman (1904) proposed a conception of intelligence perhaps most widely (though by no means universally) accepted by authors and users of intelligence tests. His idea was that each person has a certain general level of intellectual ability, which the person can demonstrate in most areas of endeavor, although it will be expressed differently under different circumstances. This general intelligence is commonly referred to by the single italicized letter, *g*.

As noted above, Spearman's general ability theory is appealing on a commonsense level. One finds, for example, that some colleagues are generally pretty smart at most things while others have a lack of ability that seems to extend with equally broad application to many endeavors. There is also, as Spearman showed, statistical support for the general ability theory. Using the statistical techniques of factor analysis to examine a number of mental aptitude tests, he observed that people who performed well on one cognitive test tended to perform well on other tests, while those who scored badly on one test tended to score badly on others. Spearman demonstrated that measures of different mental abilities correlated substantially with each other. People with high verbal abilities are likely also to have high spatial and quantitative abilities, and so on. (Persons with higher IQs apparently are also likely to be taller and have more body symmetry than persons with lower ability scores – Silventoinen, Posthuma, van Beijsterveldt, Bartels, & Boomsma, 2006; Prokosch, Yeo, & Miller, 2005.) Spearman postulated that those positive correlations across different tests indicated that there must be a general function or "pool" of mental energy, which he named the general factor, or *g* (Spearman, 1904, 1927). Spearman also acknowledged specific factors(s) representing particular tests or subtests, but not generalized across tests.

Karl Holzinger and colleagues (Holzinger & Harman, 1938; Holzinger & Swineford, 1937) developed the Bi-factor theory, which, in its simplest form . . . is merely an extension of Spearman's Two-factor pattern to the case of group factors. The Spearman pattern is a theoretical frame of reference consisting of a general factor running through all variables and uncorrelated factors present in each variable. The Bi-factor pattern is also a theoretical frame of reference in which a general factor is assumed to run through all variables with specific factors in each variable, but in addition a number of uncorrelated group factors, each through two or more variables, are also included. The minimum number of factors of these three types for *n* variables may then be briefly summarized as follows: one general factor, *n* specific factors and *q* group factors where *q* is usually much smaller than *n*. In the modified pattern some of the group factors may overlap. (Holzinger & Swineford, 1937, p. 41)

Louis (Eliyahu) Guttman (1954, 1971), among many contributions to statistics and social sciences, applied his Radex model, an alternative to traditional factor analysis, to psychological tests (Levy, 1994). The Radex model includes a linear dimension of increasing task complexity from recall through application to inference of rules (simplex) and a circular dimension (circumplex) of correlation between tasks in numerical, figural, and verbal material sectors. Two similar tests of low complexity would be close together toward the periphery of the plane. Two tests of high complexity would be near the center, which essentially corresponds to *g*.

Most intelligence tests in use today are based, at least in part, on the general ability theory. Critics (e.g., Gould, 1981) assert that correlations with older tests based on the *g* theory are used to justify new tests based on the same theory, which, they claim, adds more circular and artificial support to the construct of *g*.

It has long been recognized that many immediate or enduring, nonintellectual influences can affect the expression of *g* (e.g., Wechsler, 1926). For instance, a math "phobia," lack of training in higher math, or an interacting combination of the two forces could prevent the successful expression of a person's full *g* in the area of mathematics.

Some problems require more than *g* for their solution. For instance, solving problems in engineering, housekeeping, teaching, farming, mechanics, and medicine usually requires specialized knowledge, skills, and ways of thinking. Further, emotions and intellect often interact, sometimes aiding and sometimes interfering with one another in solving problems, including IQ-test items (e.g., Daleiden, Drabman, & Benton, 2002; Glutting, Youngstrom, Oakland, & Watkins,

1996; Oakland, Glutting, & Watkins, 2005; Stanovich, 2009; Wechsler, 1943, 1950). For example, frustration tolerance, impulsiveness, and persistence are important components of test performance.

The *g* theory of intelligence is not necessarily linked to theories of either hereditary or environmental influences on intelligence (e.g., Eysenck vs. Kamin, 1981). The idea necessary for acceptance of the *g* theory is that intelligence operates primarily as a single capacity.

Brain damage, disease, deprivation, and disturbance are, of course, known to affect some expressions of intelligence differentially. For example, a stroke may impair one function, such as speech, while sparing others, such as drawing. Sacks (1970) offers many highly readable examples of differential effects of diseases and injuries. Springer and Deutsch (1993), Sauerwein and Lassonde (1997), and others discuss split-brain studies. Hale and Fiorello (2004), Lezak, Howieson, and Loring (2004), and Miller (2007, 2010) provide detailed textbooks on neuropsychological assessment. General ability theorists might hold that it is the expression of intelligence that is affected, and that intelligence itself is still mostly unitary, even though its application is unevenly handicapped.

For more than three-quarters of a century, Spearman's *g* theory was the only one that mattered for practical assessment of intelligence. Indeed, Spearman's *g* was at the root of Terman's (1916) Stanford-Binet adaptation of Binet's test (Binet & Simon, 1916/1980) in the United States, forming the foundation for offering only a single score, the global IQ (Kaufman, 2009). Until 1939, intelligence tests generally offered only a total score to be taken as an approximation of *g*. David Wechsler's (1939) Wechsler-Bellevue Intelligence Scale offered two IQs (Verbal and Performance) in addition to the Full Scale IQ or proxy for *g*, which inspired an industry of profile analysis as clinicians and researchers interpreted various patterns of subtest scores from diverse perspectives (e.g., Kaufman, 1979, 1994; Rapaport, Gill, & Schafer, 1945–1946; Zimmerman & Woo-Sam, 1973). Ultimately, another industry was formed dedicated to condemnation of the practice of profile interpretation – for example, McDermott, Fantuzzo, and Glutting (1990), who proclaimed, "Just say no to subtest analysis: A critique on Wechsler theory and practice." That debate continues to the present day (Flanagan & Kaufman, 2009; Lichtenberger & Kaufman, 2009; Watkins, Glutting, & Youngstrom, 2005). Ironically, Wechsler provided clinicians with a profile of IQs and subtest scaled scores to interpret – and he championed the interpretation of subtest profiles for diagnosis of brain damage and psychopathology (Wechsler, 1958) – but he always considered the Wechsler-Bellevue and all his subsequent intelligence scales to be measures of global intellectual ability, measures of *g*.

Thurstone's Primary Mental Abilities

Other theorists (e.g., Edward L. Thorndike, 1927; Thomson, 1916) have historically placed more importance on separate areas of intelligence and argued that *g* and specific factors (referred to as "*s*" by Spearman) interact to determine the expression of intelligence in different situations. The opponents of Spearman's *g* did not deny that cognitive tests tend to correlate positively (sometimes called "a condition of positive manifold"; Horn & Blankson, 2005, p. 61). Instead, they maintained that a positive manifold can occur for a variety of reasons that have nothing to do with a common factor. Nearly a century ago – the same year that Terman (1916) published the Stanford-Binet – Thomson articulated this anti-*g* argument cogently. Thomson (1916) maintained that the emergence of *g* "was a consequence of the overlap existing among discrete elements that are used to solve various intellectual tasks. Thus, the positive manifold is a consequence of relationships among discrete elements combined according to the laws of chance" (Brody, 2000, p. 30).

There are many different conceptions of the specific mental factors. In 1938, Louis L. Thurstone, an outspoken opponent of Spearman's *g*, offered a differing theory of intelligence. Thurstone, who had developed methods for scaling psychological measures, assessing attitudes, and testing theory, developed new factor analytic techniques to determine the number and nature of latent constructs within a set of observed variables. Using his new methods, Thurstone argued that Spearman's *g* resulted from a statistical artifact based upon the mathematical procedures that Spearman had used. Thurstone believed that human intelligence should not be regarded as a single unitary trait, and in its place, he proposed the theory of Primary Mental Abilities (1938), a model of human intelligence that challenged Spearman's unitary conception of intelligence. Holzinger and Harry H. Harman applied Holzinger's Bi-factor method to Thurstone's (1936) factor analysis and found "striking agreement" (Holzinger & Harman, 1938, p. 45) between Thurstone's results and their own.

Thurstone's early theory, based upon an analysis of mental test data from samples composed of people with similar overall IQs, suggested that intelligent behavior does not arise from a general factor but instead emerges from different "primary mental abilities" (Thurstone, 1938). The abilities that he described were verbal comprehension, inductive reasoning, perceptual speed, numerical ability, verbal fluency, associative memory, and spatial visualization.

British psychologist P. E. Vernon (1950) proposed a hierarchical group factor theory of the structure of human intellectual abilities, based upon factor analysis. His proposed intellectual structure had at the highest level General ability (*g*) with major, minor, and specific factors tiered below *g*. Major factors were Verbal-educational and Spatial-mechanical, while the minor group included such factors as Verbal Fluency, Numerical, and Psychomotor abilities. Specific factors (lowest in the hierarchy) referred to narrow ranges of behavior. Because Vernon's theory included both a general factor and group factors, it may be viewed as something of a compromise between Spearman's two-factor theory (which was composed of *g* and *s*, but did not include group factors) and Thurstone's multiple-factor theory (which did not have a general factor).

Guilford's Structure of Intellect Model

One prominent multifactor theorist was J. P. Guilford (1967, 1975, 1988), who devised the Structure of the Intellect (SOI) model. Guilford's theory laid out, in a three-dimensional model, five different mental operations needed to solve problems (such as *Convergent Production* or *Divergent Production*) on four different contents (such as *Symbolic* or *Figural*), yielding six kinds of products (such as *Classes* or *Relations*) for a total of 120 ($5 \times 4 \times 6 = 120$) possible intellectual factors. Guilford's model, because of the huge number of intellectual abilities it posited, was the most dramatic contrast to Spearman's unitary *g* theory.

Despite the clear distinction between Spearman's single-factor model and Guilford's multidimensional model, both suffered from a similar problem. As Kaufman (2009) notes, "If one ability was too few to build a theory on, then 120 was just as clearly too many. And Guilford did not stop at 120. He kept refining the theory, adding to its complexity. He decided that one Figural content was not enough, so he split it into figural-auditory and figural-visual (Guilford, 1975). Nor was a single memory operation adequate, so he subdivided it into memory recording (long-term) and memory retention (short-term) (Guilford, 1988). The revised and expanded SOI model now included 180 types of intelligence!" (p. 52). Guilford's model, although influential, particularly in special education and education of gifted children (e.g., Meeker, 1969), was widely and sometimes harshly criticized for lack of solid empirical support for the separate abilities (e.g., Carroll, 1968; Horn & Knapp, 1973, 1974; Vernon, 1979; Thorndike, 1963). In particular, "these researchers claimed that there wasn't enough evidence to support the existence of the independent abilities that Guilford had described" (Kaufman, 2009, p. 51). For example, "the factor analytic results that have been presented as evidence for the theory do not provide convincing support because they are based upon methods that permit very little opportunity to reject hypotheses" (Horn & Knapp, 1973, p. 33).

One Influential Synthesis – Cattell, Horn, and Carroll

Spearman (1904) had originally insisted that the separate, *s*, factors were limited to their particular tests or subtests. Eventually, though, he recognized that some *s* factors were common to multiple measures but, unlike *g*, they were not common to all measures (Spearman, 1927). The final version of Spearman's theory with the two factors, one *g* and various *s* factors (some of which applied to groups of tests), was closer to Thurstone's formulation than his original theory had been.

At the other end of our continuum, when Thurstone administered his tests to an intellectually heterogeneous group of children, he found that his seven primary abilities were *not* entirely separate; instead he found evidence of a second-order factor that he theorized might be related to *g* (Sattler, 2008). According to Ruzgis (1994), the final version of Thurstone's theory, which accounted for the presence of both a general factor and the seven specific abilities, helped lay the groundwork for future researchers who proposed hierarchical theories and theories of multiple intelligences. Thurstone's final formulation was closer than his original theoretical framework to Spearman's model. In the end, the two extremes of the lumper-splitter continuum (Spearman and Thurstone) each gravitated a bit toward the center.

Cattell and Horn's Gf-Gc Model

Probably the best known and most widely accepted theories of intellectual factors derive from the model of Raymond B. Cattell (1941) and his student, John L. Horn (1965). Cattell first proposed two types of intelligence: *Gf* and *Gc*, which refer, respectively, to "fluid intelligence" and "crystallized intelligence" (Cattell, 1963). Cattell and Horn and colleagues (e.g., Cattell & Horn, 1978; Horn, 1985; Horn & Blankson, 2005; Horn & Cattell 1966; Horn & Noll, 1997) – drawing on factor analytic studies and evidence from "neurological damage and aging" and "genetic, environmental, biological, and developmental variables" (Horn & Blankson, 2005, p. 45) – gradually expanded this initial bifurcation of *g* into eight or nine primary abilities. Horn (1985, 1994) argued unyieldingly against the reality of a single general ability factor (*g*), because he did not believe that research supported a unitary theory.

Gf, fluid intelligence, refers to inductive, deductive, and quantitative reasoning with materials and processes that are new to the person doing the reasoning. Fluid abilities allow an individual to think and act quickly, solve novel problems, and encode short-term memories. The vast majority of fluid reasoning tasks on intelligence tests use nonverbal, relatively culture-free stimuli, but require an integration of verbal and nonverbal thinking.

Gc, crystallized intelligence, refers to the application of acquired knowledge and learned skills to answering questions and solving problems presenting at least broadly familiar materials and processes. It is reflected in tests of knowledge, general information, use of language (vocabulary), and a wide variety of acquired skills (Horn & Cattell, 1966). Most verbal subtests of intelligence scales are classified primarily as measuring crystallized intelligence, However, some such subtests, like Wechsler's Similarities, clearly require fluid reasoning as well as crystallized knowledge to earn high scaled scores.

Carroll's Three-Stratum Hierarchy

John B. Carroll (1993) undertook a truly staggering reanalysis of all of the usable correlational studies of mental test data that he could find. He winnowed a collection of about 1,500 studies down to a set of 461 datasets that met four technical criteria (Carroll, 1993, pp. 78–80, 116) and then subjected the data from those studies to a uniform process of reanalysis by exploratory factor analysis (pp. 80–91). Carroll noted that this massive project was "in a sense an outcome of work I started in 1939, when . . . I became aware of L. L. Thurstone's research on what he called 'primary mental abilities' and undertook, in my doctoral dissertation, to apply his factor-analytic techniques to the study of abilities in the domain of language" (1993, p. vii; see also Carroll, 1943). As a result of his reanalysis of the 461 data sets, Carroll presented extensive data in the domains of Language, Reasoning, Memory and Learning, Visual Perception, Auditory Reception, Idea Production, Cognitive Speed, Knowledge and Achievement, Psychomotor Abilities, Miscellaneous Domains of Ability and Personal Characteristics, and Higher-Order Factors of Cognitive Ability (1993, p. 5). Based on his data, Carroll (1993, pp. 631–655) presented "A Theory of Cognitive Abilities: The Three-Stratum Theory" with "*narrow* (stratum I), *broad* (stratum II), and *general* (stratum III)" (p. 633) abilities. See also Carroll (1997/2005) for further discussion.

Integration of Horn-Cattell and Carroll Models to Form CHC Theory

The remarkable similarity between Carroll's *broad* stratum II abilities and Cattell and Horn's expanded *Gf-Gc* abilities suddenly became apparent at a meeting in March 1996 convened by the publisher of the Woodcock-Johnson Psycho-Educational Battery (Woodcock & Johnson, 1977) to begin the process of developing the Woodcock-Johnson – Revised (Woodcock & Johnson, 1989). Kevin McGrew (2005) describes this "fortuitous" meeting that included Richard Woodcock, John Horn, and John Carroll, among other important figures in test theory and development, including McGrew. McGrew considers that meeting the "flash point that resulted in *all* subsequent theory-to-practice bridging events leading to today's CHC theory and related assessment developments" (p. 144).

"CHC" stands for "Cattell-Horn-Carroll," a synthesis of the work of Cattell and Horn with that of Carroll. McGrew (2005, p. 148) believes that the term and abbreviation "Cattell-Horn-Carroll theory" and "CHC" were first published in Flanagan, McGrew, and Ortiz (2000) and first formally defined in print in his and Woodcock's technical manual for the third edition of the Woodcock-Johnson battery (McGrew & Woodcock, 2001). CHC theory synthesizes two of the most widely recognized theories of intellectual abilities (McGrew, 2005; Sternberg & Kaufman, 1998).

Although Horn and Carroll agreed to the use of the term Cattell-Horn-Carroll (McGrew, 2005, p. 149), Horn and Carroll always disagreed sharply about *g* or the general stratum III (McGrew, 2005, p. 174). Horn, like Thurstone in his earlier formulations, consistently and adamantly maintained that there was no single *g*. Carroll always considered *g* or stratum III essential to his hierarchical, three-stratum theory.

Carroll (1993, 1997) stated that "there are a fairly large number of distinct individual differences in cognitive ability, and that the relationships among them can be derived by classifying them into three different strata: stratum I, 'narrow' abilities; stratum II, 'broad' abilities; and stratum III, consisting of a single 'general' ability" (Carroll, 1997, p. 122). Carroll's model, although similar to that proposed by Cattell and Horn, differs in several substantial ways. First, as noted, Carroll included at stratum III the general intelligence factor (*g*) because he believed that the evidence for such a factor was overwhelming. Second, where Cattell and Horn differentiate Quantitative knowledge as a separate Gf-Gc factor, in this case G*q*, Carroll believed quantitative ability was best subsumed as a narrow G*f* ability. Third, while the Cattell-Horn model included measures of Reading and Writing as a combined, separate factor (G*rw*), Carroll believed these to be narrow abilities subsumed in the G*c* factor.

Applications of CHC Theory – Cross-Battery Assessment and Test Development

CHC theory provided the basis for the McGrew, Flanagan, and Ortiz integrated Cross-Battery Approach to assessment (see, for example, Flanagan & McGrew, 1997; Flanagan, McGrew, & Ortiz, 2000; Flanagan, Ortiz, & Alfonso, 2007; Flanagan, Ortiz, Alfonso, & Mascolo, 2006; McGrew, 1997; and McGrew & Flanagan, 1998). These authors attempted – on the basis of factor analytic studies, especially Carroll's (1993) massive effort, and on the basis of expert judgments of newer tests for which factor analytic data were lacking – to characterize each of a great many subtests from cognitive ability scales (and achievement tests) as assessing one or more narrow (stratum I) and broad (stratum II) CHC abilities. They provided detailed guidelines for using a core cognitive ability scale along with subtests from one or more additional instruments to assess all of the CHC broad abilities with measures of at least two different narrow abilities. Additional testing would be required if the scores on the two narrow ability measures within a broad ability differed significantly from each other, raising the possibility of different levels of capacity on narrow abilities, rather than a unitary level of skill on the broad ability.

Although the CHC Cross-Battery Approach quickly gained many adherents among evaluators, it does not meet with universal approval. There was, for example, a lively debate in the journal *Communiqué*: Floyd (2002) offered "recommendations for school psychologists" for using the CHC Cross-Battery Approach. Watkins, Youngstrom, & Glutting, 2002) responded with "Some cautions concerning cross-battery assessment," to which Ortiz & Flanagan (2002a, 2002b) replied with their own "cautions concerning 'some cautions.'" Watkins, Glutting, and Youngstrom (2002) were "still concerned."

Watkins, Youngstrom, and Glutting wrote that the CHC Cross-Battery Approach was "well articulated and noteworthy in many respects" (2002, p. 16), but raised eight concerns, including among others, whether scores from different tests with different norming samples and other variations were comparable with one another; the effects of taking subtests out of their usual context and sequence, differential practice and other effects; the lack of factor analytic studies of batteries of many cognitive tests given to large; representative, national samples and the consequent use of an expert consensus process to assign narrow and broad abilities to subtests of new instruments; ipsative interpretation using differences between scores and the examinee's own mean score rather than strictly normative scores; and the lack of attention to *g* in the CHC Cross-Battery assessment model.

The CHC Cross-Battery advocates contended that modern standards and practices for test norming (including varying the administration order of subtests on some tests) and the use of only recently normed tests; reliance on Carroll's (1993) and other factor analytic studies; and high levels of interscorer reliability among judgments by their panels of experts obviated the concerns. They noted that the CHC Cross-Battery Approach uses normative, not ipsative scores, although ipsative comparisons are mentioned in some publications on the CHC Cross-Battery Approach.

CHC theory also, to varying degrees, contributed to the structure of many recent tests of cognitive ability. The Woodcock-Johnson Psycho-Educational Battery – Revised (WJ-R; Woodcock & Johnson, 1989; see also Woodcock, 1990, 1993, 1997) and Woodcock-Johnson III (WJ III; Woodcock, McGrew, & Mather, 2001) are explicitly based on CHC theory, and the WJ III attempts to measure the nine most commonly agreed upon CHC broad (stratum II) abilities. Some other cognitive ability tests with very explicit CHC foundations include the Kaufman Assessment Battery for Children, second edition (KABC-II; Kaufman & Kaufman, 2004) and Stanford-Binet Intelligence Scale, fifth edition (SB 5; Roid, 2003). CHC abilities are cited in the test manuals to help explain and describe scales and subtests for many tests, including the Differential Ability Scales, second edition (DAS-II: Elliott, 2007), the Leiter International Performance Scale – Revised (LIPS-R; Roid & Miller, 1997), the Reynolds Intellectual Assessment Scales (RIAS; Reynolds & Kamphaus, 2003), and recent editions of the Wechsler intelligence scales, such as the Wechsler Adult Intelligence Scale – fourth edition (WAIS-IV; Wechsler, 2008), Wechsler Intelligence Scale for Children – fourth edition (WISC-IV; Wechsler, 2003), and Wechsler Preschool and Primary Scale of Intelligence – third edition (WPPSI-III; Wechsler, 2002). There is a growing body of research showing relationships between various CHC factors and different aspects of school achievement (e.g., Evans, Floyd, McGrew, & Leforgee, 2002; Floyd, Evans, & McGrew, 2003; Hale, Fiorello, Dumont, Willis, Rackley, & Elliott, 2008; Hale, Fiorello, Kavanagh, Hoeppner, & Gaitherer, 2001).

Cognitive Abilities – What's in a Name?

CHC theory continues to evolve. Complete agreement has not quite been reached on the broad (stratum II) abilities, and the narrow (stratum I) abilities within each broad ability are occasionally redefined. Current formulations can be found in Flanagan, Ortiz, Alfonso, and Mascolo (2006) and Flanagan, Ortiz, and Alfonso (2007). Those books, and others cited earlier, classify a great many intelligence and achievement test subtests by broad (stratum II) and narrow (stratum I) CHC abilities on the basis of factor analytic research and surveys of expert opinion. The names and the abbreviations or symbols for the abilities are taken, with alterations, from Carroll, 1993, who observed (p. 644), "The naming of a factor in terms of a process, or the assertion that a given process or component of mental architecture is involved in a factor, can be based only on inferences and makes little if any contribution to explaining or accounting for that process unless clear criteria exist for defining and identifying processes."

Even more broadly, we need to be careful not to confuse verbal names for factors with the factor analytic bases for them. For example, *Gv* has been referred to as, among other things, "visual-spatial thinking," which sounds like a high-level cognitive process, and "visual perception," which sounds much more physiological than intellectual. By either name, it is the same *Gv*, defined by loadings of various subtests on the same factor, and we should not be distracted, biased, or misled by the verbal name assigned by an author. For example, when Cohen (1959) made a tremendous contribution to the field by publishing his factor analysis of the Wechsler Intelligence Scale for Children (WISC; Wechsler, 1949), he also, we believe, inadvertently caused decades of misunderstanding by assigning the name "freedom from distractibility" to a factor consisting of the Arithmetic, Digit Span, and Coding subtests. Generations of psychologists and educators consequently persisted in the misguided belief that those subtests were definitively diagnostic of attention deficit disorder. Kaufman (1979) tried to resolve this confusion by neutrally calling his derived score for those three subtests simply "the third factor," but in our personal experience, the misunderstanding remained robust. This cautionary tale might inspire us to take advantage of the more-or-less implication-free abbreviations and symbols offered by current formulations of CHC theory. The following discussion draws heavily on presentations in Carroll (1993); Flanagan and McGrew (1997); Flanagan, McGrew, and Ortiz (2000); Flanagan, Ortiz, and Alfonso, 2007; Flanagan, Ortiz, Alfonso, and Mascolo (2006); McGrew, 1997; and McGrew and Flanagan (1998).

Definitions of CHC Abilities

Fluid and crystallized intelligence, described earlier, were the original Cattell-Horn *Gf-Gc* factors. As noted, over the years, the original dichotomous *Gf-Gc* theory was expanded to include additional abilities. These additional broad (stratum II) abilities are defined here.

Gv, or *visual-spatial thinking*, involves a range of visual processes, ranging from fairly simple visual perceptual tasks to higher level, visual, cognitive processes. Woodcock and Mather (1989) define *Gv* in part: "In Horn-Cattell theory, 'broad visualization' requires fluent thinking with stimuli that are visual in the mind's eye." Although *Gf* tasks are also often nonverbal (e.g., matrix tests), *Gv* does not include the aspect of dealing with novel stimuli or applying novel mental processes that characterize *Gf* tasks. Many writers seem to consider *Gv* a relatively low-level cognitive ability, more perceptual than intellectual. However, the "fluent thinking with stimuli that are visual in the mind's eye" may well be a higher level intellectual process on a par with *Gc* and *Gf* (see, for example, Johnson & Bouchard, 2005, and Johnson, te Nijenhuis, & Bouchard, 2007, who differentiate perceptual from image rotation abilities). Engineers, auto mechanics, architects, nuclear physicists, sculptors, carpenters, and parts department managers all use *Gv* to deal with the demands of their jobs. Elliott (2007), for example, made two subtests each of *Gf*, *Gc*, and *Gv* abilities the Core subtests for the General Conceptual Ability summary score for the School-Age and Upper Early Years levels of the Differential Ability Scales, second edition. Other CHC abilities are included among the Diagnostic subtests, but are not counted in the General Conceptual Ability score.

Ga, *auditory processing*, involves tasks such as recognizing similarities and differences between sounds; recognizing degraded spoken words, such as words with sounds omitted or separated (e.g., "tel – own" and /t/ ĕ /l/ ĕ /f/ ō /n/ both as "telephone"); and mentally manipulating sounds in spoken words (e.g., "say *blend* without the /l/ sound" or "change the ĕ in *blend* to ĭ"). Phonemic awareness skills, terribly important for acquisition of reading skills (Rath, 2001), are *Ga* tasks.

Gs, *processing speed* or attentional speediness, refers to measures of clerical speed and accuracy, especially when there is pressure to maintain focused attention and concentration.

Gt, *decision/reaction time or speed*, reflects the immediacy (quickness) with which an individual can react and make a decision (decision speed) to typically simple stimuli. It can be difficult to distinguish between *Gs* tasks, which are relatively common on intelligence tests, and *Gt* tasks, which are more often found on computerized neuropsychological measures of vigilance and reaction time. *Gs* tasks generally require a sustained effort over at least two or three minutes and simply measure the number of simple items completed (or number right minus number wrong) for the entire span of time. *Gt* tasks are more likely to measure response speed to each item or a few items.

Gsm, *short-term or immediate memory*, refers to the ability to take in and hold information in immediate memory and then to use it within a few seconds. Given the relatively small amount of information that can be held in short-term memory, information is typically retained for only a short period of time before it is lost. When additional tasks are required that tax an individual's short-term memory abilities, information in short-term memory is either lost or transferred and stored as acquired knowledge through the use of long-term storage and retrieval (*Glr*). *Gsm* is divided in current CHC formulations into memory span (MS) and working memory (MW) with a distinction between simple recall (MS) (e.g., repeating increasing long series of dictated digits) and mental manipulation of material held in short-term memory (MW) (e.g., repeating the dictated series in reversed sequence). This is another example of the difficulty with verbal labels for abilities, since "working memory" is used by many authors to mean not MW, but MS, particularly with reference to brief retention on the way to long-term storage. The different meanings of the terms can cause considerable confusion. Factor analyses have indicated that short-term visual memory (such as recognizing in a group of pictures the one picture that had been seen earlier) is a narrow ability within *Gv* rather than *Gsm*.

Glr, *long-term storage and retrieval*, involves memory storage and retrieval over longer periods of time than *Gsm*. How much longer varies from task to task. It is important to note that *Glr* is referring to the *efficiency* of what is stored, not *what* is stored. *Glr* is usually measured with controlled learning tasks in which the efficiency of learning – for example, rebus symbols for words – is assessed during the learning, and then, on some tests, retention is assessed with a delayed recall measure.

Grw includes reading and writing abilities, which were part of *Gc* in Carroll's formulation. The narrow, stratum I abilities within *Grw* may not be sufficiently detailed to satisfy educators specializing in literacy.

Gq, knowledge, is distinct from the quantitative reasoning that is a narrow ability within *Gf*.

The last two broad abilities raise the question of the distinction between "ability" and "achievement." Carroll (1993, p. 510, emphasis in the original) discusses this problem: "It is hard to draw the line between factors of cognitive abilities and factors of achievement. Some will argue that *all* cognitive abilities are in reality learned achievements of one kind or another." Carroll suggests that we "conceptualize a continuum that extends from the most general abilities to the most specialized types of knowledges." Flanagan, Ortiz, Alfonso, and Mascolo (2002, p. 21) quote Carroll (1993, p. 510) and then also Horn (1988, p. 655), "Cognitive abilities are measures of achievements, and measures of achievements are just as surely measures of cognitive ability." They reach the same conclusion as Carroll: "Thus, rather than conceiving of cognitive abilities and academic achievements as mutually exclusive, they may be better thought of as lying on an *ability continuum* that has the most general types of abilities at one end and the most specialized types of knowledge at the other" (Carroll, 1993).

Other Formulations

Although they are slightly or substantially outside the factor analytic focus of this chapter, there are other important theories and models that bear mention.

Planning, Attention, Simultaneous, Successive (PASS)

Building on the work of Russian psychologist, A. R. Luria (1966, 1973, 1990), J. P. Das, Jack Naglieri, and colleagues (e.g., Das, Kirby, & Jarman, 1979; Naglieri & Das, 2002; 2005); have developed the Planning, Attention, Simultaneous, Successive (PASS) theory of intelligence. Luria posited three functional units or "blocks": arousal and attention (the Attention in PASS), representing Luria's Block 1; taking in, processing, and storing information (the Simultaneous and Successive processes in PASS), or Block 2 coding processes; and synthesizing information and regulating behavior (the Planning in PASS), which are the executive functions associated with Block 3.

The Kaufman Assessment Battery for Children (K-ABC; Kaufman & Kaufman, 1983; Kaufman, Kaufman, & Goldsmith, 1984) was a pioneering test based on Simultaneous versus Sequential (Successive) processing, the components of Luria's second processing unit (Block 2). The second edition of the Kaufman Assessment Battery for Children (KABC-II; Kaufman & Kaufman, 2004; Kaufman, Kaufman, Kaufman-Singer, & Kaufman, 2005) is uniquely designed to permit interpretation on the basis of four Luria-based processes or on the basis of five CHC factors: Sequential processing or *Gsm*, Simultaneous processing or *Gv*, Learning or *Glr*, Planning or *Gf*, and *Gc*.

Naglieri and Das's (1997) Cognitive Assessment System (CAS) "is built strictly on the Planning, Attention, Simultaneous, and Successive (PASS) theory" (Naglieri, 2005, p. 441). There are three Planning, three Attention, three Simultaneous, and four Successive subtests.

As with CHC theory, there is evidence of correlations of PASS measures with different aspects of educational achievement. There is also evidence of the utility of PASS profiles for planning instruction (e.g., Naglieri & Johnson, 2000). Differences between scores of African American and Euro-American students are notably smaller on the PASS-based CAS and

KABC-II than on other comprehensive cognitive ability tests in current use (Kaufman & Kaufman, 2004; Naglieri & Das, 1997).

Triarchic Theory

Many experts (e.g., Robert Sternberg, 1982, 1985; 2003, 2005; Howard Gardner, 1983, 1999); and Keith Stanovich, 2009) (also see Stanovich, this volume) argue that none of the theories discussed earlier goes far enough. Sternberg argues for recognition of "successful intelligence [which] is (1) the use of an integrated set of abilities needed to attain success in life, however an individual defines it, within his or her sociocultural context. People are successfully intelligent by virtue of (2) recognizing their strengths and making the most of them, at the same time that they recognize their weaknesses and find ways to correct or compensate for them. Successfully intelligent people (3) adapt to, shape, and select environments through (4) finding a balance in their use of analytical, creative, and practical abilities (Sternberg, 1997, 1999)" (Sternberg, 2005, p. 104). Although not strictly speaking a factor analytic theory of intelligence, Sternberg's theory is supported by studies showing the "factorial separability of analytic, creative, and practical abilities" (Sternberg, 2005, pp. 104–105). Sternberg and the Rainbow Project Collaborators (2006) investigated the use of the multiple-choice Sternberg Triarchic Abilities Test (STAT; Sternberg, 1993; Sternberg & Clinkenbeard, 1995; Sternberg, Ferrari, Clinkenbeard, & Grigorenko, 1996) and several other measures of the same domains (open-ended, performance measures of creativity and performance measures of practical skills) to improve prediction of college grade-point averages (GPA) above the prediction based on SAT scores and high school GPA alone. "The triarchic measures predict an additional 8.9% to college GPA beyond the initial 15.6% contributed by the SAT and high school GPA. These findings, combined with the substantial reduction of between-ethnicity differences, made a compelling case for furthering the study of the measurement of analytical, creative, and practical skills for predicting success in college" (Sternberg & the Rainbow Project Collaborators, 2006, p. 344). The authors pointed out several relatively minor methodological limitations in their study and anticipated that "Over time, still better measures perhaps will be created" (Sternberg & the Rainbow Project Collaborators, 2006, p. 347). Sternberg also points to evidence of effective instructional interventions based on the theory. The triarchic theory of successful human intelligence expands considerably the domain of "intelligence" beyond what is measured by most current tests. We believe that Sternberg's theory comes much closer to Wechsler's famous definition of intelligence ["the aggregate or global capacity of the individual to act purposefully, to think rationally and to deal effectively with his environment" (Wechsler, 1958, p. 7)] than do any of any of Wechsler's own intelligence tests.

Multiple Intelligences

Gardner argues for the existence of at least eight "intelligences," including linguistic, logical-mathematical, musical, spatial, bodily-kinesthetic, naturalistic, interpersonal, and intrapersonal, each meeting the requisite two biological, two developmental psychological, two traditional psychological, and two logical criteria to qualify as *intelligences* (Gardner, 1993). "The identification of intelligences is based on empirical evidence and can be revised on the basis of new empirical findings" (Gardner, 1994, 2003), quoted in Chen and Gardner (2005, p. 79). Gardner's multiple intelligences are difficult to measure, especially as Gardner insists on measuring various aspects of each intelligence; using a variety of media, including physical and social activities, that are suited to the various intelligences; engaging the child in meaningful activities and learning; assuring comfortable familiarity of the child with the materials and activities; putting the activities into contexts that have ecological validity and relevance for instruction; and creating complete profiles of intelligences that can be used to support teaching and learning (Chen & Gardner, 2005, pp. 82–85). Nonetheless, several assessment programs have been created, including the Spectrum Assessment System (Chen, Isberg, & Krechevsky, 1998; Chen, Krechevsky, & Viens, 1998; Krechevsky, 1991, 1998) and Bridging: Assessment for Teaching (McNamee & Chen, 2004). These observational assessment systems include focus on activities as well as children and yield detailed reports. There is evidence that individual children do perform at different levels in the various domains and that performance improves with instruction (e.g., Chen & Gardner, 2005) and that at least six of the multiple intelligences do not correlate highly with each other (Adams, 1993), a finding that support's Gardner's formulation. However, it appears to be difficult to directly assess the validity of Gardner's eight aptitudes as intelligences (e.g., Sternberg, 1991).

Rationality

Stanovich (2009) agrees with Sternberg and Gardner that the aspects of intelligence measured by traditional tests, which he terms "MAMBIT (to stand for the mental abilities measured by intelligence tests)" (p. 13), are too narrow. He focuses particularly on the absence of measures of rational thinking (e.g., Sternberg, 2002). However, rather than including rational thinking and other abilities in a definition of "intelligence," Stanovich argues for separating MAMBIT from other abilities, such as rational decision making, Sternberg's three components of successful intelligence, and Gardner's eight intelligences. He suggests that calling abilities other than MAMBIT "intelligence" increases the power of the traditional conception of intelligence in the popular mind and that rational thinking and other important abilities should receive greater attention as a result of narrowing, not broadening, the popular conception of "intelligence" or MAMBIT. Although the term, MAMBIT, seems unlikely to catch on, the argument has some appeal.

A Parting Thought

Factor-based theories of intelligence have proliferated since Spearman (1904) started the ball rolling more than a century ago. The once-extreme "lumper-splitter" dichotomy has became less extreme and the pendulum has rested somewhere between the two ends, though decidedly closer to the Thurstone than the Spearman end. The uneasy balance between *g* and multiple abilities is probably best reflected by CHC theory, which reflects an integration of the life's work of John Carroll (a believer in *g*) and John Horn (a devout nonbeliever), and forms the foundation of most contemporary "IQ tests." We believe that CHC theory has important positive features and merits a key role in the assessment of intelligence. But, however well researched CHC theory may be, it reflects only one-third of Sternberg's theory, and perhaps a similar portion of Gardner's theory – but, as Stanovich aptly points out, MAMBIT is too narrow. At present, CHC theory and, to a lesser extent, Luria's neuropsychological theory, provide the theoretical basis of virtually all major tests of cognitive abilities. It is time for that status quo to change. The time has come for developers of individual clinical tests of intelligence to broaden their basis of test construction beyond the analytic dimension of Sternberg's triarchic theory and to begin to embrace the assessment of both practical intelligence and creativity.

References

Adams, M. (1993). *An empirical investigation of domain-specific theories of preschool children's cognitive abilities*. Unpublished doctoral dissertation, Tufts University.

Binet, A., & Simon, T. (1916/1980). *The development of intelligence in children*, with marginal notes by Lewis M. Terman and preface by Lloyd M. Dunn. Translated by Elizabeth S. Kite with an introduction by Henry Goddard. Facsimile limited edition issued by Lloyd M. Dunn. Nashville, TN: Williams.

Brody, N. (2000). History of theories and measurements of intelligence. In R. J. Sternberg

(Ed.), *Handbook of intelligence* (pp. 16–33). New York, NY: Cambridge University Press.

Carroll, J. N. (1968). Review of the nature of human intelligence by J. P. Guilford. *American Educational Research Journal, 73*, 105–112.

Carroll, J. B. (1985). Exploratory factor analysis: A tutorial. In D. K. Detterman (Ed.), *Current topics in human intelligence* (Vol. 1, pp. 25–58). Norwood, NJ: Ablex.

Carroll, J. B. (1993). *Human cognitive abilities: A survey of factor-analytic studies*. Cambridge, UK: Cambridge University Press.

Carroll, J. B. (1997). The three-stratum theory of cognitive abilities. In D. P. Flanagan, J. L. Genshaft, & P. L. Harrison (Eds.), *Contemporary intellectual assessment: Theories, tests, and issues* (pp. 122–130). New York, NY: Guilford Press.

Cattell, R. B. (1941). Some theoretical issues in adult intelligence testing. *Psychological Bulletin, 38*, 592.

Cattell, R. B. (1963). Theory of fluid and crystallized intelligence: A critical experiment. *Journal of Educational Psychology, 54*, 1–22.

Cattell, R. B., & Horn, J. L. (1978). A check on the theory of fluid and crystallized intelligence with description of new subtest designs. *Journal of Educational Measurement, 15*, 139–164.

Chen, J-Q., & Gardner, H. (2005). Assessment based on multiple-intelligence theories. In D. P. Flanagan, J. L. Genshaft, & P. L. Harrison (Eds.), *Contemporary intellectual assessment: Theories, tests, and issues* (pp. 77–102). New York, NY: Guilford Press.

Chen, J. Q., Isberg, E., & Krechevsky, M. (Eds.). (1998). *Project Spectrum: Early learning activities*. New York, NY: Teachers College Press.

Chen, J. Q., Krechevsky, M., & Viens, J. (1998). *Building on children's strengths: The experience of Project Spectrum*. New York. NY: Teachers College Press.

Daleiden, E., Drabman, R. S., & Benton, J. (2002). The guide to the assessment of test session behavior: Validity in relation to cognitive testing and parent-reported behavior problems in a clinical sample. *Journal of Clinical Child Psychology, 31*, 263–271.

Daniel, M. H. (1997). Intelligence testing: Status and trends. *American Psychologist, 52*(10), 1038–1045.

Das, J. P., Kirby, J. R., & Jarman, R. F. (1979). *Simultaneous and successive cognitive processes*. New York, NY: Academic Press.

Elliott, C. D. (2007). *Differential Ability Scales – second edition*. San Antonio, TX: Psychological Corporation.

Evans, J. J., Floyd, R. G., McGrew, K. S., & Leforgee, M. H. (2002). The relations between measures of Cattell-Horn-Carroll (CHC) cognitive abilities and reading achievement during childhood and adolescence. *School Psychology Review, 31*, 246–262.

Eysenck, H. J., vs. Kamin, L. J. (1981). *The intelligence controversy*. Hoboken, NJ: Wiley-Interscience.

Flanagan, D. P., & Harrison, P. L. (Eds.). (2005). *Contemporary intellectual assessment: Theories, tests and issues* (2nd ed.). New York, NY: Guilford Press.

Flanagan, D. P., & Kaufman, A. S. (2009). *Essentials of WISC-IV assessment* (2nd ed.). Hoboken, NJ: Wiley.

Flanagan, D. P., & McGrew, K. S. (1997). A cross-battery approach to assessing and interpreting cognitive abilities: Narrowing the gap between practice and cognitive science. In D. P. Flanagan, J. L. Genshaft, & P. L. Harrison (Eds.), *Contemporary intellectual assessment* (ch. 17, pp. 314–325). New York: Guilford Press.

Flanagan, D. P, McGrew, K. S., & Ortiz, S. O. (2000). *The Wechsler Intelligence Scales and Gf-Gc theory: A contemporary approach to interpretation*. Boston: Allyn & Bacon.

Flanagan, D. P., Ortiz, S. O., & Alfonso, V. (2007). *Essentials of cross-battery assessment* (2nd ed.). Hoboken, NJ: Wiley.

Flanagan, D. P., Ortiz, S. O., Alfonso, V. & Mascolo, J. T. (2002). *The achievement test desk reference: Comprehensive assessment of learning disabilities*. Boston, MA: Allyn & Bacon.

Flanagan, D. P., Ortiz, S. O., Alfonso, V., & Mascolo, J. T. (2006). *Achievement test desk reference (ATDR-II): A guide to learning disability identification (2nd ed.)*. Hoboken, NJ: Wiley.

Floyd, R. (2002). The Cattell-Horn-Carroll (CHC) Cross-Battery Approach: Recommendations for school psychologists. *Communiqué, 30*(5), 10–14.

Floyd, R. G., Evans, J. J., & McGrew, K. S. (2003). Relations between measures of Cattell-Horn-Carroll (CHC) cognitive abilities and mathematics achievement across the school-age years. *Psychology in the Schools, 60*(2), 155–171.

Gardner, H. (1983). *Frames of mind*. New York, NY: Basic Books.

Gardner, H. (1993). *Frames of mind: The theory of multiple intelligences* (10th anniversary ed.). New York, NY: Basic Books.

Gardner, H. (1994). Multiple intelligences theory. In R. J. Sternberg (Ed.), *Encyclopedia of human intelligence* (pp. 740–742). New York, NY: Macmillan.

Gardner, H. (1999). *Intelligence reframed: Multiple intelligences for the 21st century*. New York, NY: Basic Books.

Gardner, H. (2003, April). *Multiple intelligences after twenty years*. Paper presented at the annual meeting of the American Education Research Association, Chicago, IL.

Glutting, J. J., Youngstrom, E. A., Oakland, T., & Watkins, M. W. (1996). Situational specificity of generality of test behaviors for examples of normal and referred children. *School Psychology Review, 25*, 64–107.

Gould, S. J. (1981). *The mismeasure of man*. New York, NY: Norton.

Guilford, J. P. (1967). *The nature of human intelligence*. New York, NY: McGraw-Hill.

Guilford, J. P. (1975). Varieties of creative giftedness, their measurement and development. *Gifted Child Quarterly, 19*, 107–121.

Guilford, J. P. (1988). Some changes in the structure-of-intellect model. *Educational and Psychological Measurement, 48*, 1–4.

Guttman, L. (1954). A new approach to factor analysis: The radix. In P. F. Lazarfeld (Ed.), *Mathematical thinking in the social sciences*. New York, NY: Free Press.

Guttman, L. (1971). Measurement as structural theory. *Psychometrika, 36*, 329–347.

Hale, J. B., & Fiorello, C. A. (2004). *School neuropsychology: A practitioner's handbook*. New York, NY: Guilford Press.

Hale, J. B, Fiorello, C. A., Dumont, R., Willis, J. O., Rackley, C., & Elliott, C. (2008). Differential Ability Scales-Second Edition (neuro)psychological predictors of math performance for typical children and children with math disabilities. *Psychology in the Schools, 45*(9), 838–858.

Hale, J. B., Fiorello, C. A., Kavanagh, J. A., Hoeppner, J. B., & Gaitherer, R. A. (2001). WISC-III predictors of academic achievement for children with learning disabilities: Are global and factor scores comparable? *School Psychology Quarterly, 16*(1), 31–35.

Herrnstein, R. J., & Murray, C. (1994). *The bell curve: Intelligence and class structure in American life*. New York, NY: Simon & Schuster (Free Press Paperbacks).

Holzinger, K. J., & Harman, H. H. (1938). Comparison of two factorial analyses. *Psychometrika, 3*, 45–60.

Holzinger, K. J., & Swineford, F. (1937). The bifactor method. *Psychometrika, 2*, 41–54.

Horn, J. L. (1965). *Fluid and crystallized intelligence: A factor analytic study of the structure among primary mental abilities*. Unpublished doctoral dissertation, University of Illinois.

Horn, J. L. (1985). Remodeling old models of intelligence. In B. B. Wolman (Ed.), *Handbook of intelligence: Theories, measurements, and applications* (pp. 267–300). Hoboken, NJ: Wiley.

Horn, J. L. (1988). Thinking about human abilities. In J. R. Nesselroade & R. B. Cattell (Eds.), *Handbook of multivariate psychology* (rev. ed., pp. 645–685). New York, NY: Academic Press.

Horn, J. L. (1994). The theory of fluid and crystallized intelligence. In R. J. Sternberg (Ed.), *Encyclopedia of human intelligence* (pp. 433–451). New York, NY: Macmillan.

Horn, J. L., & Blankson, B. (2005). Foundations for better understanding of cognitive abilities. In D. P. Flanagan & P. L. Harrison (Eds.), *Contemporary intellectual assessment* (2nd ed., pp. 41–68). New York, NY: Guilford Press.

Horn, J. L., & Cattell, R. B. (1966). Refinement and test of the theory of fluid and crystallized general intelligences. *Journal of Educational Psychology, 57*, 253–270

Horn, J. L., & Knapp, J. R. (1973). On the subjective character of the empirical base of Guilford's structure of intellect model. *Psychological Bulletin, 80*, 33–43.

Horn, J. L., & Knapp, J. R. (1974). Thirty wrongs do not make a right. *Psychological Bulletin, 81*, 502–504.

Horn, J. L., & Noll, J. (1997). Human cognitive capabilities: Gf-Gc theory. In D. P. Flanagan, J. L. Genshaft, & P. L. Harrison (Eds.), *Contemporary intellectual assessment: Theories, tests, and issues* (pp. 53–91). New York, NY: Guilford Press.

Jacoby, R., & Glauberman, N. (Eds.). (1995). *The Bell Curve debate*. New York, NY: Times Books.

Jensen, A. R. (1998). *The g factor: The science of mental ability*. Westport, CT: Praeger.

Johnson, W., & Bouchard, T. J. (2005). The structure of human intelligence: It is verbal, perceptual, and image rotation (VPR), not fluid and crystallized. *Intelligence, 33*, 393–416.

Johnson, W., te Nijenhuis, J., & Bouchard, T.J. (2007). Replication of the hierarchical visual-perceptual-image rotation model in de Wolff and Buiten's (1963) battery of 46 tests of mental ability. *Intelligence*, 35, 69–81.

Kamphaus, R. W., Winsor, A. P., Rowe, E. W., & Kim, S. (2005). A history of intelligence assessment. In D. P. Flanagan & P. L. Harrison (Eds.), *Contemporary intellectual assessment: Theories, tests and issues* (2nd ed., pp. 23–38). New York, NY: Guilford Press.

Kaufman, A. S. (1979). *Intelligent testing with the WISC-R*. New York, NY: Wiley.

Kaufman, A. S. (1994). *Intelligent testing with the WISC-III*. New York, NY: Wiley.

Kaufman, A. S. (2009). *IQ Testing 101*. New York, NY: Springer.

Kaufman, A. S., & Kaufman, N. L. (1983). *The Kaufman Assessment Battery for Children*. Circle Pines, MN: American Guidance Service.

Kaufman, A. S., & Kaufman, N. L. (2004). *The Kaufman Assessment Battery for Children* (2nd ed.). Circle Pines, MN: American Guidance Service.

Kaufman, A. S., Kaufman, N. L., & Goldsmith, B. Z. (1984). *Kaufman Sequential or Simultaneous (K-SOS)?* Circle Pines, MN: American Guidance Service.

Kaufman, J. C., Kaufman, A. S., Kaufman-Singer, J., & Kaufman, N. L. (2005). The Kaufman Assessment Battery for Children – Second Edition. In D. P. Flanagan & P. L. Harrison (Eds.), *Contemporary intellectual assessment: Theories, tests and issues* (2nd ed., pp. 344–370). New York, NY: Guilford Press.

Krechevsky, M. (1991). Project Spectrum: An innovative assessment alternative. *Educational Leadership*, **2**, 43–48.

Krechevsky, M. (1998). *Project Spectrum preschool assessment handbook*. New York, NY: Teachers College Press.

Levy, S. (Ed.). (1994). *Louis Guttman on theory and methodology: Selected writings*. Aldershot, UK: Dartmouth.

Lezak, M. D., Howieson, D. B., & Loring, D. W. (2004). *Neuropsychological assessment* (4th ed.). New York, NY: Oxford University Press.

Lichtenberger, E. O., & Kaufman, A. S. (2009). *Essentials of WAIS-IV assessment*. Hoboken, NJ: Wiley.

Luria, A. R. (1966). *Human brain and psychological processes*. New York, NY: Harper & Row.

Luria, A. R. (1973). *The working brain*. New York, NY: Basic Books.

Luria, A. R. (1980). *Higher cortical functions in man* (2nd ed.). New York, NY: Basic Books.

McDermott, P. A., Fantuzzo, J. W., & Glutting, J. J. (1990). Just say no to subtest analysis: A critique on Wechsler theory and practice. *Journal of Psychoeducational Assessment*, 8, 290–302.

McGrew, K. S. (1997). Analysis of the major intelligence batteries according to a proposed comprehensive Gf-Gc framework. In D. P. Flanagan, J. L. Genshaft, & P. L. Harrison (Eds.), *Contemporary intellectual assessment* (pp. 151–179). New York: Guilford Press.

McGrew, K. S. (2005). The Cattell-Horn-Carroll theory of cognitive abilities. In D. P. Flanagan & P. L. Harrison (Eds.), *Contemporary intellectual assessment: Theories, tests and issues* (2nd ed., pp. 136–181). New York, NY: Guilford Press.

McGrew, K. S., & Flanagan, D. P. (1998). *The intelligence test desk reference (ITDR): Gf-Gc Cross-Battery Assessment*. Boston, MA: Allyn & Bacon.

McGrew, K. S., & Woodcock, R. W. (2001). Technical manual. *Woodcock-Johnson III*. Itasca, IL: Riverside Publishing.

McKusick, V. A. (1969). On lumpers and splitters, or the nosology of genetic disease. *Perspectives in Biology and Medicine*, **12**(2), 298–312.

McNamee, G., & Chen, J. Q. (2004, August). *Assessing diverse cognitive abilities in young children's learning*. Paper presented at the 27th International Congress of the International Association for Cross-Cultural Psychology, Xi'an, China.

Meeker, M. N. (1969). *The structure of intellect: Its interpretation and uses*. Columbus, OH: Merrill.

Miller, D. C. (2007). *Essentials of neuropsychological assessment*. Hoboken, NJ: Wiley.

Miller, D. C. (Ed.). (2010). *Best practices in school neuropsychology*. Hoboken, NJ: Wiley.

Naglieri, J. A. (2005). The cognitive assessment system. In D. P. Flanagan & P. L. Harrison (Eds.), *Contemporary intellectual assessment: Theories, tests and issues* (2nd ed., pp. 441–460). New York, NY: Guilford Press.

Naglieri, J. A., & Das, J. P. (1997). *Das-Naglieri Cognitive Assessment System*. Itasca, IL: Riverside Publishing.

Naglieri, J. A., & Das, J. P. (2002). Practical implications of general intelligence and PASS cognitive processes. In R. J. Sternberg & E. L. Grigorenko (Eds.), *The general factor of intelligence: How general is it?* (pp. 855–884). New York, NY: Erlbaum.

Naglieri, J. A., & Das, J. P. (2005). Planning, attention, simultaneous, successive (PASS) theory. In D. P. Flanagan & P. L. Harrison (Eds.), *Contemporary intellectual assessment: Theories, tests and issues* (2nd ed., pp. 120–135). New York, NY: Guilford Press.

Naglieri, J. A., & Johnson, D. (2000). Effectiveness of a cognitive strategy intervention to improve math calculation based on the PASS theory. *Journal of Learning Disabilities, 33*, 591–597.

Oakland, T., Glutting, J., & Watkins, M. W. (2005). Assessment of test behaviors with the WISC-IV. In A. Prifitera, D. H. Saklofske, & L. G. Weiss (Eds.), *WISC-IV clinical use and interpretation: Scientist-practitioner perspectives*. Burlington, MA: Elsevier Academic Press.

Ortiz, S. O., & Flanagan, D. P. (2002a). Cross-Battery Assessment revisited: Some cautions concerning "Some Cautions" (Part I). *Communiqué*, 30(7), 32–34.

Ortiz, S. O., & Flanagan, D. P. (2002b). Cross-Battery Assessment revisited: Some cautions concerning "Some Cautions" (Part II). *Communiqué*, 30(8), 36–38.

Prokosch, M. D., Yeo, R. A., & Miller, G. F. (2005). Intelligence tests with higher g-loadings show higher correlations with body symmetry: Evidence for a general fitness factor mediated by developmental stability. *Intelligence, 33*, 203–213.

Rapaport, D., Gill, M., & Schafer, R. (1945–1946). *Diagnostic psychological testing* (2 vols.). Chicago, IL: Year Book Medical.

Rath, L. K. (2001). Phonemic awareness: Segmenting and blending the sounds of language. In S. Brody (Ed.), *Teaching reading: Language, letters, and thought* (2nd ed.). Milford, NH: LARC Publishing.

Reynolds, C. R., & Kamphaus, R. W. (2003). *Reynolds Intellectual Assessment Scales*. Lutz, FL: Psychological Assessment Resources.

Roid, G. H. (2003). *Stanford-Binet Intelligence Scales* (5th ed.). Itasca, IL: Riverside Publishing.

Roid, G. H., & Miller, L. J. (1997). *Leiter International Performance Scale – Revised*. Wood Dale, IL: Stoelting.

Ruzgis, P. (1994). Thurstone, L. L. (1887–1955). In R. J. Sternberg (Ed.), *Encyclopedia of human intelligence* (pp. 1081–1084). New York, NY: Macmillan.

Sattler, J. M. (2008). *Assessment of children: Cognitive foundations* (5th ed.) San Diego, CA: Jerome M. Sattler.

Sacks, O. (1970). *The man who mistook his wife for a hat and other clinical tales*. New York, NY: Simon & Schuster. Paperback edition Harper & Row (Perennial Library), 1987.

Sauerwein, H. C., & Lassonde, M. (1997). Neuropsychological alterations after split-brain surgery. *Journal of Neurosurgical Sciences*, 41(1), 59–66.

Silventoinen, K., Posthuma, D., van Beijsterveldt, T., Bartels, M., & Boomsma, D. I. (2006). Genetic contributions to the association between height and intelligence: Evidence from Dutch twin data from childhood to middle age. *Genes, Brain & Behavior*, 5(8), 585–595.

Silverman, L. K. (2000). Identifying visual-spatial and auditory-sequential learners: A validation study. In N. Colangelo & S. G. Assouline (Eds.), *Talent development V: Proceedings from the 2000 Henry B. and Jocelyn Wallace National Research Symposium on Talent Development*. Scottsdale, AZ: Gifted Psychology Press.

Spearman, C. (1904). "General intelligence," objectively determined and measured. *American Journal of Psychology, 15*, 201–293.

Spearman, C. (1927). *The abilities of man: Their nature and measurement*. New York, NY: Macmillan.

Springer, S. P., & Deutsch, G. (1993) *Left brain, right brain* (4th ed.). San Francisco, CA: Freeman.

Stanovich, K. E. (2009). *What intelligence tests miss: The psychology of rational thought*. New Haven, CT: Yale University Press.

Sternberg, R. J. (1982). Reasoning, problem solving, and intelligence. In R. J. Sternberg (Ed.), *Handbook of human intelligence* (pp. 225–307). New York, NY: Cambridge University Press.

Sternberg, R. J. (1985). *Beyond IQ: A triarchic theory of human intelligence*. New York, NY: Cambridge University Press.

Sternberg, R. J. (1991). Death, taxes, and bad intelligence tests. *Intelligence, 15*, 257–270.

Sternberg, R. J. (1993). *Sternberg Triarchic Abilities Test*. Unpublished test.

Sternberg, R. J. (1997). *Successful intelligence*. New York, NY: Plume.

Sternberg, R. J. (1999). The theory of successful intelligence. *Review of General Psychology, 3*, 292–316.

Sternberg, R. J. (Ed.). (2000). *Handbook of intelligence*. Cambridge, UK: Cambridge University Press.

Sternberg, R. J. (2002). *Why smart people can be so stupid*. New Haven, CT: Yale University Press.

Sternberg, R. J. (2003). Construct validity of the theory of successful intelligence. In R. J. Sternberg, J. Lautrey, & T. I. Lubart (Eds.), *Models of intelligence: International perspectives* (pp. 55–80). Washington, DC: American Psychological Association.

Sternberg, R. J. (2005). *The triarchic theory of successful intelligence*. In D. P. Flanagan & P. L. Harrison (Eds.), *Contemporary intellectual assessment: Theories, tests and issues* (2nd ed., pp. 103–119). New York, NY: Guilford Press.

Sternberg, R. J., & Clinkenbeard, P. R. (1995). A triarchic model applied to identifying, teaching, and assessing gifted children. *Roeper Review*, *17*(4), 255–260.

Sternberg, R. J., & Detterman D. K. (1986). *What is intelligence? Contemporary viewpoints on its nature and definition*. Norwood, NJ: Ablex.

Sternberg, R. J., Ferrari, M., Clinkenbeard, P. R., & Grigorenko, E. L. (1996). Identification, instruction, and assessment of gifted children: A construct validation of a triarchic model. *Gifted Child Quarterly*, *40*, 129–137.

Sternberg, R. J., & Kaufman, J. C. (1998). Human abilities. *Annual Review of Psychology*, *49*, 1134–1139.

Sternberg, R. J., & the Rainbow Project Collaborators. (2006). The Rainbow Project: Enhancing the SAT through assessments of analytical, practical, and creative skills. *Intelligence*, *34*, 321–350.

Terman, L. M. (1916). *The measurement of intelligence*. Boston, MA: Houghton Mifflin.

Thomson, G. A. (1916). A hierarchy without a general factor. *British Journal of Psychology*, *8*, 271–281.

Thorndike, E. L. (1927). *The measurement of intelligence*. New York, NY: Bureau of Publications, Teachers College, Columbia University.

Thorndike, R. L. (1963). Some methodological issues in the study of creativity. In *Proceedings of the 1962 invitational conference on testing problems*. Princeton, NJ: Educational Testing Service.

Thurstone, L. L. (1936). The factorial isolation of primary abilities. *Psychometrika*, *1*, 175–182.

Thurstone, L. L. (1938). *Primary mental abilities*. Chicago, IL: University of Chicago Press.

Vernon, P. E. (1950). *The structure of human abilities*. London, UK: Methuen.

Vernon, P. E. (1979). *Intelligence: Heredity and environment*. San Francisco, CA: Freeman.

Wasserman, J. D., & Tulsky, D. S. (2005). A history of intelligence assessment. In D. P. Flanagan & P. L. Harrison (Eds.), *Contemporary intellectual assessment: Theories, tests and issues* (2nd ed., pp. 3–22). New York, NY: Guilford Press.

Watkins, M. W., Glutting, J., & Youngstrom. E. (2002). Cross-battery cognitive assessment: Still concerned. *Communiqué*, *31*(2), 42–44.

Watkins, M. W., Glutting, J. J., & Youngstrom, E. A. (2005). Issues in subtest profile analysis. In D. P. Flanagan & P. L. Harrison (Eds.), *Contemporary intellectual assessment: Theories, tests and issues* (2nd ed., pp. 251–268). New York, NY: Guilford Press.

Watkins, M. W., Youngstrom, E. A., & Glutting, J. J. (2002). Some cautions regarding Cross-Battery Assessment. *Communiqué*, *30*(5), 16–20.

Wechsler, D. (1926). On the influence of education on intelligence as measured by the Binet-Simon tests. *Journal of Educational Psychology*, *17*, 248–257.

Wechsler, D. (1939). *The measurement of adult intelligence*. Baltimore, MD: Williams & Wilkins.

Wechsler, D. (1943). Nonintellective factors in general intelligence. *Journal of Abnormal and Social Psychology*, 38, 101–103.

Wechsler, D. (1949). *Wechsler Intelligence Scale for Children*. New York, NY: Psychological Corporation.

Wechsler, D. (1950). Cognitive, conative, and non-intellective intelligence. *American Psychologist*, *5*, 78–83

Wechsler, D. (1958). *The measurement and appraisal of adult intelligence*. Baltimore, MD: Williams & Wilkins.

Wechsler, D. (2002). *Wechsler Preschool and Primary Scale of Intelligence Scale – Third Edition*. San Antonio, TX: Psychological Corporation.

Wechsler, D. (2003). *Wechsler Intelligence Scale for Children – Fourth Edition*. San Antonio, TX: Psychological Corporation.

Wechsler, D. (2008). *Wechsler Adult Intelligence Scale – Fourth Edition*. San Antonio, TX: Psychological Corporation.

Woodcock, R. W. (1990). Theoretical foundations of the WJ-R measures of cognitive ability. *Journal of Psychoeducational Assessment*, *8*, 231–258.

Woodcock, R. W., & Johnson, M. B. (1977). *Woodcock-Johnson Psycho-Educational Battery*. Chicago, IL: Riverside Publishing.

Woodcock, R. W., & Johnson, M. B. (1989). *Woodcock-Johnson Psycho-Educational Battery-Revised.* Chicago IL: Riverside Publishing.

Woodcock, R. W., McGrew, K. S., & Mather, N. (2001). *Woodcock-Johnson III.* Itasca, IL: Riverside Publishing.

Woodcock, R. W., & Mather, N. (1989). WJ-R Tests of Cognitive Ability – Standard and Supplemental Batteries: Examiner's manual. In R. W. Woodcock & M. B. Johnson, *Woodcock-Johnson Psychoeducational Battery-Revised.* Chicago, IL: Riverside Publishing.

Zimmerman, I. L., & Woo-Sam, J. M. (1973). *Clinical interpretation of the Wechsler Adult Intelligence Scale.* New York, NY: Grune & Stratton.

CHAPTER 4

Contemporary Models of Intelligence

Janet E. Davidson and Iris A. Kemp

Few constructs are as mysterious and controversial as human intelligence. One mystery is why, even though the concept has existed for centuries, there is still little consensus on exactly what it means for someone to be intelligent or for one person to be more intelligent than another. Oddly enough, the heterogeneity among views of intelligence seems to have increased over time rather than decreased (Stanovich, 2009). This lack of agreement fuels unresolved controversies, such as whether intelligence is comprised of one main component or many, and it results in claims that intelligence is too imprecise a term to be useful (Jensen, 1998). A related mystery is why the field has generated relatively few new models of intelligence in the past 20 years. Is this scarcity due to a perceived futility? Will it eventually result in the field's demise? Or has scientific progress been sufficient enough to make the pursuit of new directions unnecessary?

The existence of the first mystery is understandable and perhaps inevitable, given that intelligence is currently defined, assessed, and studied on at least three different levels: psychometric, physiological, and social (Eysenck, 1988; Flynn, 2007). Each level has its own organizing concepts, hypotheses, research methodologies, and conclusions that can limit comparison and consensus. For example, the physiological approach typically employs advanced technology to examine indices of intelligence in the brain, whereas the social (or societal usefulness) approach uses performance on "real-world" tasks to study intellectual skills in context. Fortunately, there has been some recent cross-fertilization between levels, which bodes well for future agreement on what it means to be intelligent (Flynn, 2007).

Why are the mysteries surrounding intelligence important ones to solve? Even though the construct is difficult to define, assess, and explain, the goal is a worthy one. If humans continue to live among each other and differ in their abilities to learn and adapt, the concept of intelligence is going to endure socially and scientifically. Fully and indisputably understanding this elusive construct means that cultures can fairly identify and cultivate it (Nisbett, 2009). Scientific knowledge about the workings of the human mind would also be advanced. In short, a deep understanding of intelligence would benefit individuals, societies as a whole, and science.

The most promising method for fulfilling this mission is through theory-based models that describe, explain, and predict intelligence, allowing generalization from the known to the unknown. However, these models must meet certain criteria in order to be useful to individuals, societies, and science. Bad models, such as phrenology and eugenics, damage human lives and the field. Therefore, models of intelligence must be held to the high standards in the following list. These criteria are similar to those cited in the literature on theories (Davidson, 1990; Hempel, 1966; Kaplan, 1964).

- First, the models must be based on relevant assumptions, build on previous knowledge, and have appropriate empirical support. Obviously, they should avoid any mistakes from models that came before them.
- Second, all components and the mechanisms by which they interact should be well specified, internally consistent, and testable. If a model of intelligence is inconsistent, impossible to falsify, or difficult to compare with other models then it is useless and potentially harmful.
- Third, the models should contain only relevant and comprehensible components. Put another way, they should be as economical as possible and understandable to a reasonably competent person.
- Fourth, they must describe, explain, and predict intelligent behavior across time and place. Ideally, contemporary models should address how and why the properties of intelligence develop and change, or remain stable, throughout the life span. The effects of culture should also be taken into consideration.
- Fifth, the models should generate and guide new research that advances the field.
- Finally, and perhaps most important, the models should have the potential to foster high-quality applications and provide practical guidance about intelligence and how societies can identify and cultivate it.

With these criteria in mind, this chapter will describe frequently cited contemporary models of intelligence for each of the three levels mentioned earlier: psychometric, physiological, and social. Whenever possible, each view's assumptions, empirical support, perspective on the development of intellectual abilities, and applications will be reviewed. In the fourth section, models that bridge more than one level will be examined. At the end of each section, we will return to the questions: Does this work fit the criteria for an intelligent model of intelligence? Does this type of model advance the field? Finally, conclusions will be drawn and recommendations will be made for the future.

The Psychometric Level and Its Models

This approach is older than the other two levels covered in this chapter and it has been more prolific in terms of research quantity and practical applications (Neisser et al., 1996). Basically, psychometric models systematically focus on individual differences in performance on mental ability tests. The main underlying assumption is that the resulting interrelationship of test scores reveals the overall structure of intelligence. These models are typically developed by first administering a range of mental tasks to large numbers of individuals and then statistically reducing the correlations among test scores to identify the latent sources, or "factors," of intelligence. However, it should be noted that many contemporary psychometric models are developed somewhat differently from those of the past. Currently, confirmatory analyses are used more than exploratory ones; the structural analysis of test items is more important than the structural analysis of variables; and models are often based on item response theory (Embretson & McCollam, 2000).

Despite these new trends in statistical methods, widely cited contemporary psychometric models can best be understood in terms of a discrepancy between two earlier models, which began the controversy over whether intelligence comprises one main component or many. More specifically, Charles Spearman (1927) found one general factor (*g*) pervaded performance on all mental ability tests and Louis Thurstone (1938) did not. Spearman also found what he considered to be less important test-specific factors (e.g., arithmetic computations, vocabulary). In contrast, Thurstone's results revealed seven broad factors, or primary mental abilities, which could be psychologically interpreted as comprising intelligence. Example primary abilities are Verbal Comprehension and Number Facility. (However, it should be noted that Thurstone and Thurstone (1941) did find evidence for *g*, in addition to the primary mental abilities, when they later tested a more representative sample of children.)

Current psychometric models of intelligence have helped resolve some of the discrepancies and issues raised by Spearman's and Thurstone's original models. These newer models typically propose a hierarchical structure that places one or more broad factors, which represent general abilities, at the top stratum and more specific factors, representing increasingly specialized abilities, at lower strata. Three hierarchical models will briefly be reviewed here: the extended theory of fluid and crystallized intelligence (*Gf-Gc* theory), three-stratum theory, and the Cattell-Horn-Carroll (CHC) Theory of Cognitive Abilities. The first two widely cited theories have been in existence for several years. However, recent additions and applications warrant their inclusion here. Furthermore, both of these theories are incorporated into the third one to be described.

Extended Gf-Gc *Theory*

The original *Gf-Gc* theory received its name when Raymond Cattell (1943; 1963) divided Spearman's factor of general intelligence into two broad, independent ones: fluid intelligence (*Gf*) and crystallized intelligence (*Gc*). The purpose of this separation was to account for individuals' cognitive development in adolescence and adulthood. *Gf* involves mentally working well with novel information and it is dependent on the efficient functioning of the central nervous system. In contrast, *Gc* is dependent on education and other forms of acculturation. *Gc* consists of the set of skills and information that individuals acquire and retain in memory throughout their lives. Cattell (1941) proposed that *Gf* is derived from genetic and biological effects, while *Gc* primarily reflects environmental influences, such as amount of education and socioeconomic status.

Providentially, Cattell had a graduate student, John Horn, who concluded that there was more to intelligence than just *Gf* and *Gc*. Today's version of this model is sometimes referred to as extended *Gf-Gc* theory because other broad, second-order factors joined *Gf* and *Gc* at the top level (Stratum II) of its hierarchical structure (Horn & Blankson, 2005). For example, Quantitative Knowledge, Speed of Thinking Abilities, and Abilities of Long-term Memory Storage and Retrieval are among the nine Stratum II factors. Their addition was based on five types of evidence: structural (psychometric), developmental, neurocognitive, achievement prediction, and behavioral genetic (Horn, 1986). Over 80 first-order factors, which include Thurstone's (1938) primary mental abilities, are at the lower stratum (Stratum I). These intercorrelated factors represent specialized abilities that are highly associated with the broad, second-order abilities.

Developmental perspectives. Extended *Gf-Gc* theory has been useful in explaining and predicting intellectual change, especially in adulthood (Horn, 1994; Horn & Blankson, 2005; Horn & Donaldson, 1976). Some abilities, unfortunately, are susceptible to decline in adulthood due to the accumulation of injuries to the central nervous system. These abilities tend to be related to *Gf*, speed of thinking, and short-term (or working) memory. When individuals are around age 20, for example, *Gf* tends to reach its peak and then subsequently begins a slow decline (Horn, Donaldson, & Engstrom, 1981). Other abilities, such as *Gc*, retrieval from long-term memory, and quantitative knowledge are less affected by the central nervous system. They improve during childhood and increase or remain stable throughout adulthood (Horn & Blankson, 2005).

The good news about getting older, according to extended *Gf*-*Gc* theory, is that adults often channel their knowledge and intellectual abilities into specific areas of expertise. Extensive, well-structured practice in these domains helps them develop cognitive abilities related to their proficiency (Ericsson, 1996; Ericsson & Charness, 1994). In particular, experts develop wide-span memory that can be used in their areas of specialty (Horn & Blankson, 2005). This form of memory allows them to bring relatively large amounts of information into immediate memory and hold it there for several minutes. It also allows them to reason deductively at a higher level than do non-experts, who tend to rely primarily on *Gf*. Furthermore, the attainment of high levels of proficiency is related to the development of cognitive speed ability in one's domain of expertise. (Horn & Blankson, 2005; Krampe & Ericsson, 1996). In other words, the growth of expertise-related abilities offsets declines in the vulnerable abilities (i.e., *Gf*, speed of thinking, and short-term memory), although the two types are structurally and developmentally independent of each other.

Horn and Blankson (2005) argue that these expertise-related abilities, which do not reach fruition until some time in adulthood, represent the highest form of intellectual capacity. These abilities allow individuals to make major contributions to their societies and they help explain why intellectual leaders in various fields often are well over age 40. Regrettably, expertise-related abilities are not typically captured by standard intelligence tests because current measures of *Gc* do not assess in-depth knowledge and reasoning.

Applications. The extended *Gf*-*Gc* theory has been widely used in the formation and interpretation of standardized intelligence tests. For example, it influenced the development of the Woodcock-Johnson Psycho-educational Battery-Revised (WJ-R), the Kaufman Adolescent and Adult Intelligence Test, and the Stanford-Binet IV (Kaufman, 2000; Robinson, 1992). In addition, the theory has been instrumental in the development and evaluation of cognitive training programs for older adults (e.g., Baltes, Staudinger, & Lindenberger, 1999).

The Three-stratum Theory

Unlike the two-stratum *Gf*-*Gc* model, John Carroll's (1993) three-stratum theory portrays the structure of intelligence as a pyramid. Stratum III, the apex of the pyramid, consists solely of the conceptual equivalent of Spearman's *g*. Although Carroll does not support Spearman's (1927) interpretation of *g* as representing mental energy, he agrees that it underlies all intellectual activity and has a high degree of heritability. Stratum II, the middle of the pyramid, represents eight broad abilities that are differentially influenced by *g*. Fluid intelligence is the factor most related to *g*, while processing speed is the least related. The eight factors, which are similar to the second-order ones in the *Gf*-*Gc* theory, correspond to individuals' traits that can influence their performance in a given domain. Stratum I, the base of the pyramid, consists of 69 specialized abilities, such as quantitative reasoning and spelling. As in the *Gf*-*Gc* model, a subset of these factors represents Thurstone's (1938) primary mental abilities. Each factor at Stratum I is highly related to at least one of the eight broad abilities that comprise Stratum II.

The three-stratum model is well supported by evidence because it is based on Carroll's comprehensive meta-analysis of 461 diverse datasets meeting specific criteria. Carroll (1993) is careful to emphasize that abilities in each stratum merely reflect their levels of generality in governing a range of cognitive abilities; intermediate strata may exist between the three he identified. It should be noted that recent confirmatory factor analyses have found that four strata models are the best fit for some data (Bickley, Keith, & Wolfe, 1995; Johnson & Bouchard, 2005).

Developmental perspectives. Unlike *Gf-Gc* theory, Carroll's model was not created to account for human intellectual development. Although the two models have similar broad factors at their second strata, the three-stratum theory does not include the developmental trajectories that are connected with *Gf-Gc* theory. However, Carroll's model has been empirically examined in light of age differentiation. For example, Bickley et al. (1995) tested the three-stratum model using confirmatory factor analysis on the mental test scores of over 6,000 participants between the ages of 2 and 90 years. No significant developmental changes in the organization of cognitive abilities were found, which supports Carroll's (1993) claim that the structure of mental abilities, as defined by the three strata in his model, does not vary with age.

Applications. The three-stratum theory's potential contributions to the fields of intelligence, education, and applied psychometrics should not be underestimated. This model, which integrates and extends previous psychometric views, provides an empirically based framework and taxonomy to guide research and assessment of individual differences. For example, the three-stratum nomenclature draws attention to a frequently overlooked critical distinction between speed factors and degree of mastery factors (Burns, 1994).

Currently, the three-stratum theory is not widely employed in education, although the suggestion has been made that it should be more fully considered (Plucker, 2001). As will be described in more detail later in the chapter, the theory has been useful in guiding research on cognitive abilities and the construction and interpretation of mental abilities tests (Flanagan & McGrew, 1997; McGrew, 1997).

The Cattell-Horn-Carroll (CHC) Theory

The CHC theory is an integration of the *Gf-Gc* and three-stratum theories described earlier. Interestingly, this synthesis occurred for pragmatic reasons. The goal was to provide a bridge between theory and practice by creating a common framework for use in the development, interpretation, and revision of mental abilities tests (McGrew, 2005, 2009). In particular, a single taxonomy was needed for classifying the narrow, specialized abilities measured by batteries of individually administered intelligence tests.

As the name indicates, CHC theory captures the numerous similarities between Cattell and Horn's *Gf-Gc* theory and Carroll's three-stratum model, while reconciling the discrepancies. The four main differences are that (1) the three-stratum model strongly endorses *g* but the extended *Gf-Gc* model does not include it; (2) the three-stratum theory does not have a distinct factor for quantitative knowledge, whereas *Gf-Gc* theory does; (3) the three-stratum theory incorporates reading and writing abilities under *Gc*, while some versions of *Gf-Gc* (McGrew, Werder, & Woodcock, 1991; Woodcock, 1994) include them as a separate broad factor; and (4) the three-stratum model combines short- and long-term memory into one "general memory and learning" factor, whereas they are separate second-order factors in *Gf-Gc* theory (McGrew, 2009). There are also some minor discrepancies in factor names between the two views.

The ways that CHC theory handles these differences has changed markedly since its conception in 1997 (McGrew, 1997). Earlier versions involved a two-stratum model; the *g* factor was omitted or questioned because of its irrelevance to the construction and evaluation of mental ability tests (McGrew, 1997, 2005; McGrew & Flanagan, 1998). For example, *g* does not help with (a) assessment and interpretation across batteries of tests or (b) the selection of diagnostic tools for students suspected of having learning disabilities. Nine or sometimes 10 broad factors comprised Stratum II. These represented abilities that were good fits with those found in the two theories on which the model was based. Where there are discrepancies between the second-order factors in the three-stratum and *Gf-Gc* theories, CHC tended to adopt those found in *Gf-Gc*. Over 70 primary or specialized cognitive abilities (e.g., phonetic coding, reading speed) were placed at Stratum I and Carroll's (1993) taxonomy was used to establish a common nomenclature for them.

Surprisingly, the most recent version of CHC has three strata (McGrew, 2009). As in Carroll's three-stratum theory, Stratum III consists solely of *g*. However, it is emphasized that this factor may have only an indirect effect on performance because it is mediated by some of the broad and narrow abilities at the other two strata. Stratum II is still viewed as the most relevant level, and it is now comprised of 16 broad, second-order abilities. The first nine match those found in earlier versions of the CHC model. The remaining second-order factors are "tentatively identified Stratum II ability domains" and, for the most part, they pertain to olfactory, tactile, and kinesthetic abilities (p. 3). These additions reflect the view that a complete taxonomic model of mental abilities should include all sensory modalities. The number of narrow factors at Stratum I has increased accordingly.

CHC is relatively new compared to the models on which it is based; revisions are expected and encouraged (McGrew, 2009). Even so, CHC has already generated a great deal of research in a variety of areas, ranging from school-based assessment of children who are deaf (Miller, 2008) to the acquisition of current events knowledge (Hambrick, Pink, Meinz, Pettibone, & Oswald, 2008).

Developmental perspectives. Like the three-stratum theory, the CHC model was not specifically created to account for human development. However, CHC theory does incorporate the developmental evidence that helped with the selection of broad ability factors for the extended *Gf-Gc* theory and it has been used to examine age differences in cognitive abilities (e.g., Kaufman, Johnson, & Liu, 2008).

Applications. CHC theory is increasingly used to construct and revise mental ability tests. For example, it was foundational in the development of the CHC cross-battery approach to assessment (McGrew & Flanagan, 1998), which allows practitioners to select appropriate measures for their purposes. In addition, the theory has been influential in revisions to several intelligence tests and assessment batteries (Alfonso, Flanagan, & Radwan, 2005).

Critique of the Psychometric Level and Its Models

The three psychometric theories just described meet several of our criteria for models of intelligence. First, all three build on previous research and help reconcile some of the earlier psychometric findings. In addition, the extended *Gf-Gc* theory incorporates prior research on expertise (Ericsson, 1996; Ericsson & Charness, 1994), while the CHC theory goes even further by integrating two previous psychometric models. Second, the theories embody a large amount of empirical evidence in support of their well-specified, hierarchical structures of intelligence. There is also considerable and reassuring overlap in the broad factors that have been proposed and tested by various psychometric researchers. CHC capitalizes on this overlap and provides a common terminology for it. Third, these hierarchical theories describe, explain, and predict performance over time and across a wide range of problems. The extended *Gf-Gc* model, in particular, provides constructive explanations and predictions about intellectual development across the life span. Finally, these theories have generated a great deal of research on human intelligence and its assessment. Some of this work has resulted in new and revised measures of cognitive abilities (Alfonso et al., 2005) and practical programs for fostering these abilities (Baltes et al., 1999). The psychometric approach has also influenced other models that will be discussed later in this chapter.

However, the psychometric approach and its models seem to have at least two shortcomings. The first has to do with our criterion that models be based on relevant assumptions. It is not clear that psychometric theories meet this requirement; they rest on the supposition that analyses of scores, from tests taken once, reveal the true structure of intelligence. Test taking occupies a relatively small part of most people's lives and it does not necessarily reflect their intelligent behavior in daily problem-solving situations. Even though the scores are moderately predictive of school achievement and work success (Flynn, 2007), they fall short of capturing many aspects of what is considered intelligence. For example, as Horn and Blankson (2005) note, standard tests of *Gc* do not measure the depth of knowledge and reasoning required for expertise in a domain. Mental ability tests will probably always exist and we are not advocating their demise. However, it might be too much to assume that they can tell us all that we would like to know about the structure of intelligence.

The second shortcoming has to do with the criterion that models should contain only relevant and comprehensible components. Unfortunately, *g* and its role in intelligence are not well understood. For example, the *Gf-Gc* theory does not propose *g* as a latent source of individual differences in intelligence, while Carroll's three-stratum theory does. Partly because of these hierarchical models, *g* remains a controversial and pervasive issue for contemporary theories of intelligence.

At one time we thought that the meaning of *g* needed to be resolved before intelligence could fully be understood (Davidson & Downing, 2000). Perhaps it is time to consider that this might never occur. Is *g* a useful construct if there is never consensus on what it represents? Earlier versions of the CHC model omitted *g* because of its irrelevance to the development, interpretation, selection, and revision of intelligence tests. In contrast, patterns of broad and narrow abilities are relevant (McGrew & Flanagan, 1998) and some of these abilities explain school achievement beyond the effects of *g* (McGrew, 2009). Given that a single factor does not account for all individual differences in intellectual performance and little consensus has been reached on *g*'s meaning, it seems unlikely that correlations between g and scores on mental ability tests will ever capture the full story of intelligence. This point brings us to the next section on the physiological approach to intelligence.

The Physiological Level and its Models

Everyone we have met believes that the brain plays a central role in intelligence, and no one we have met knows exactly what this role entails. Fortunately, this lack of knowledge is likely to change because of the physiological level's focus on the relationship between brain activity and mental ability. The primary goal of this level is to determine the neural basis of intelligence. Recent theories, hypotheses, and empirical results related to this goal will be reviewed in this section.

Brain Efficiency and the Parieto-Frontal Integration Theory (P-FIT)

The parieto-frontal integration theory identifies a network of discrete brain regions related to individual differences in general intelligence and reasoning (Jung & Haier, 2007). As the theory's name implies, these areas are primarily located in the parietal and frontal lobes, and one of their main functions is to integrate information among various parts of the brain. Many of the P-FIT regions are related to basic cognitive processes, such as attention and working memory. In other words, the attributes of general intelligence are not associated with one central part of the brain but with a network of structures and functions distributed throughout the cortex. According to Jung and Haier's theory, highly intelligent people have cortical networks that operate more accurately and quickly than those of less intelligent individuals.

The argument for brain efficiency is not new. Studies using positron emission tomography (PET) found that individuals who obtained high IQ scores had brains that expended less energy, and consequently consumed less glucose, than the brains of individuals with lower IQ scores (Haier et al., 1988). Similarly, research employing electroencephalography (EEG) mapping methods discovered that highly intelligent participants exhibited more focused cortical activation, and less overall brain activation, than did their lower ability counterparts (Neubauer & Fink, 2005). P-FIT builds on this earlier work and extends the neural efficiency hypothesis by specifying where in the cortex this neural efficiency occurs.

More specifically, P-FIT is based on converging evidence from 37 cognitive neuroimaging studies that varied in their operational definitions of intelligence and their methods of assessing it (Jung & Haier, 2007). Despite procedural differences, there was reassuring consistency across studies in the brain regions associated with individual differences in performance on general intelligence and reasoning tasks. The underlying theoretical assumptions tying the data together are that (a) regions within the occipital and temporal lobes help humans begin processing relevant visual and auditory information from their environments; (b) the results from this early sensory processing are sent to areas in the parietal cortex for more in-depth processing; (c) the parietal cortex then interacts with regions in the frontal cortex that perform hypothesis testing on solutions to a known problem; (d) after an optimal solution is reached, the anterior cingulate constrains response selection and inhibits competing responses; and (e) the underlying white matter facilitates efficient transmission of data from the posterior to frontal regions of the brain. According to Jung and Haier (2007), regions of the brain that are not part of the P-FIT network contribute minimally to individual differences in intelligence; their role is to ensure the reliability of basic brain functions common to all humans. In contrast, regions within the P-FIT network set no limits on potential variations between individuals and can differ in terms of their blood flow, volume, and chemical composition.

P-FIT accounts for a range of empirical findings on individual differences in intelligence and reasoning (e.g., Colom et al., 2009; Jung & Haier, 2007; Schmithorst, 2009), However, the theory is not without its critics. For example, several researchers (Blair, 2007; Lee, Choi, & Gray, 2007; Roring, Nandagopal, & Ericsson, 2007) claim that the P-FIT network focuses primarily on fluid intelligence and working memory rather than on the broader construct of intelligence.

Developmental perspectives. It is not yet clear how P-FIT addresses systematic changes in intelligence across the life span. In their comparison of P-FIT with a model of cognitive development, Demetriou and Mouyi (2007) found areas of agreement and a few shortcomings. As Jung and Haier (2007) note, more empirical work and revision of P-FIT need to occur to account for development.

Applications. After extensive testing and modification, P-FIT will most likely have practical implications for societal issues. According to Jung and Haier (2007), for example, the model might eventually be useful in developing treatments for mental retardation and other neurological conditions.

The Neural Plasticity Model of Intelligence

The ability to adapt to a wide range of circumstances is central to many definitions of intelligence (Binet & Simon, 1916; Neisser et al., 1996; Sternberg, 1985). Dennis Garlick's (2002, 2003) neural plasticity model of intelligence imports adaptability to the physiological level. According to this model, intelligent individuals have brains that productively change in response to their surrounding environments.

A great deal of empirical research has shown that neural plasticity allows synaptic connections between neurons to develop, change, and reorganize in response to environmental stimulation (Hebb, 1949; Rosenzweig, 2003). For example, enlarged hippocampi were commonly found in London taxi drivers, who heavily relied on this area of their brains to navigate the city (Maguire et al., 2000). In short, the environment shapes specialized neural connections that are required for different cognitive abilities (Garlick, 2002, 2003).

On the surface, the plasticity and specialization of neural connections in response to environmental stimuli implies that a highly genetic general factor of intelligence (*g*) does not underlie all mental activities. Instead, individual differences in intelligence would be due to individual differences in environments and to the specialized synaptic connections these environments create. However, through the use of computer simulations and neurophysiological data, Garlick (2002) demonstrates that some human brains may be more "plastic" than others and, therefore, better able to adapt to a range of circumstances. According to Garlick, this capacity for neural adaptation is dependent, in large part, on a variety of neural substrates encoded in the genes. Moreover, the brain's overall ability for neural plasticity would be reflected in a general factor of intelligence.

Garlick's model also explains individual differences in neural efficiency. Individuals who have neural networks that are shaped and organized to fit a variety of task demands are better able to process information quickly and accurately. In addition, only task-appropriate regions of their brains are activated, which limits the amount of glucose needing to be metabolized.

Two recent theoretical views are related in many respects to Garlick's model of neural plasticity. The first explains fluid intelligence as the product of a flexible, adaptive neural system. More specifically, Newman and Just (2005) propose that intelligent individuals have dynamic neural networks that alter their composition in order to accommodate task demands, and cortical regions that work in synchrony to perform a specific function. In support of this theory, results from neuroimaging studies have found that neural synchrony becomes more precise when tasks become more difficult. In addition, this synchrony is positively related to task performance and scores on intelligence tests (Newman & Just, 2005; Stankov, 2005).

Recently, Eduardo Mercado III (2008, 2009) refined the neural plasticity model of intelligence by focusing on cortical modules. In short, these modules are specific, vertical columns of interconnected neurons located in different areas of the cerebral cortex. According to Mercado, the capacity to learn (i.e., cognitive plasticity) is directly related to the availability, reconfigurability, and customizability of the cortical modules. In other words, the neural modules and their flexibility provide the structural basis for acquiring knowledge and improving skills. Individual differences in intelligence are a product of the number and diversity of available cortical modules.

Developmental perspective. According to Garlick (2002), intellectual development and its time frame are due to a "long-term process whereby the brain gradually alters its connections to allow for the processing of more complex environmental stimuli" (p. 120). In addition, he emphasizes critical periods for neural plasticity in different regions of the brain. These periods influence the development of intelligence. Fortunately, some plasticity has been found to occur throughout the life span (Kaas, 1991).

Applications. Models of neural plasticity highlight the importance of being exposed to stimulating environments. According to Mercado (2009), research on the relationship between cognitive and neural plasticity has relevant implications for education and other societal practices.

Critique of the Physiological Level and Its Model

The physiological level and its models are appealing for a variety of reasons. From a scientific standpoint, this approach provides a potentially uncomplicated, parsimonious view of intelligence as a biological phenomenon. Furthermore, recent advances in neuroimaging techniques make it possible to examine the brain regions associated with intelligence, reducing the need to make inferences about the brain from behavioral measures. From a practical standpoint, neurological measurements provide a glimmer of hope for future "culture-fair" measurement of intelligence. For example, physiological measures are less likely to penalize individuals for poor test-taking skills. Similarly, understanding the relationship between the brain and intelligent behavior could result in interventions and treatments that foster both brain development and cognitive abilities.

Unfortunately, fully understanding the neural basis of intelligence will probably not occur any time soon. Even though the physiological models meet our criteria of building on previous knowledge and generating new research that advances the field, they are faced with some difficult problems. One methodological concern involves the inconsistency of neuroimaging results across studies. For example, not all empirical results support the neural efficiency hypothesis. Rypma and Prabhakaran (2009) propose that replication failures are due to differences in cognitive tasks and analysis techniques. They propose that neuroimaging studies need to separate individual differences in processing speed from individual variations in processing capacity.

Another common problem for the physiological models is that the empirical support tends to be based on the questionable assumption that intelligence quotients (IQ) and related tests are sufficient standards of comparison for the physiological measurements. As noted in this chapter and elsewhere (Gardner, 1983; Kaufman, 2009; Sternberg, 1985), there is persuasive evidence that IQ is an incomplete measure of intelligence. Dempster (1991) and Kaufman (2009), for example, note that the ability appropriately to resist task-irrelevant information plays a crucial role in intelligence that is frequently overlooked on most standardized tests. Furthermore, extensive work still needs to be done cross-culturally to determine whether the relationship between performance on the neurological measures and the tasks of intelligence is universal.

Finally, the physiological models are not yet fully explanatory. The mechanisms causing neural efficiency and neural plasticity in the brain still need to be established. Similarly, the direction of causality is not known. For example, it is tempting to conclude that brain efficiency is the underlying cause of high intelligence. However, as implied by the work on neural plasticity, some neurological responses may be reacting to behavioral responses rather than causing them. Another possibility is that neurological functions and cognitive performance are reflections of some other aspect of physiological or psychological functioning that has yet to be discovered. Unfortunately, correlational studies cannot explain causation. Different types of experiments will need to clarify the relationship between the brain's activity and an individual's intelligent behavior.

In short, the physiological models have shortcomings but tremendous heuristic value. Current empirical support is primarily positive and the physiological approach will undoubtedly continue to generate a great deal of intriguing research.

The Social Level and Its Models

Our third approach focuses on the social usefulness of intelligence and takes into account individuals' functional abilities and skills that make significant contributions to their societies (Flynn, 2007). Consequently, the resulting models view intelligence as a complex dynamic system involving interactions between mental processes, contextual influences, and multiple abilities that may or may not be recognized in an academic setting. Although the following three models have been in existence for some time, their recent applications, additions, and clarifications merit inclusion in this chapter.

The Triarchic Theory of Successful Intelligence and Beyond

Robert Sternberg's theories have an admirable history of building upon themselves. His componential theory (Sternberg,

1977) was foundational to his triarchic theory of intelligence (Sternberg, 1985), which was then modified to account for successful intelligence (Sternberg, 1997). Currently, his theory of wisdom, intelligence, and creativity synthesized (WICS; Sternberg, 2003a) explains how successful intelligence lays the foundation for creativity and wisdom. Sternberg's triarchic theory of successful intelligence will briefly be described next, followed by his WICS model.

According to Sternberg (1997; 2005), three interacting aspects contribute to the successful application of intelligence within a society. The first consists of the analytical skills that help individuals evaluate, judge, or critique information. The second involves practical abilities that create an optimal match between individuals' skills and their external environments, allowing these individuals to apply and implement ideas in the "real" world. The third is creative intelligence, which involves maximizing experiences in order to generate new products, solve relatively novel problems, and quickly automatize procedures.

These three aspects of intelligence are fairly independent from each other; individuals who are strong in one are not necessarily strong in the others. The one commonality among the aspects is that each relies on the same set of interdependent mental processes that allow individuals to (a) plan, execute, and monitor their performance (i.e., metacomponents), (b) implement the metacomponents' instructions (i.e., performance components), and (c) learn new skills and information (i.e., knowledge-acquisition components). Sternberg proposes that these mental processes are domain general and they are an essential part of all intelligent behavior worldwide. However, what is considered an intelligent instantiation of them may differ across cultures because cultural values and problems often vary.

According to Sternberg's view (1997), successful intelligence occurs in all cultures when individuals achieve their life goals by capitalizing on their strengths and compensating for their weaknesses. To accomplish this, they must adapt to, shape, or select their environments by effectively combining the three aspects of intelligence.

Developmental perspectives. The triarchic model of successful intelligence provides a general foundation for Sternberg's theory of developing expertise (Birney & Sternberg, 2006; Sternberg, 1999). Like the extended *Gf-Gc* theory, Sternberg's theory proposes that intelligence can be specifically conceptualized as "the acquisition and consolidation of a set of skills needed for a high level of mastery in one or more domains of life performance" (Sternberg, 1999, p. 359). Sternberg's view of developing expertise involves five interactive elements, most of which correspond to components of the triarchic model. *Motivation* refers to a person's drive to accomplish tasks. It affects *metacognitive skills*, which can be equated with the triarchic metacomponents. Metacognitive skills, in part, drive *learning skills* (knowledge acquisition components) and *thinking skills* (performance components). Thinking and learning skills, in turn, influence metacognitive skills, and also lead to declarative and procedural *knowledge*. Finally, context can influence the way in which all five components contribute to an individual's performance. This entire cycle of interactions can occur repeatedly for one individual in one particular domain, as he or she reaches increasingly higher levels of proficiency. According to this model, analytical, practical, and creative abilities constitute types of developing expertise.

Applications. Taken together, Sternberg's triarchic model of successful intelligence and subsequent theory of developing expertise carry implications for testing and education at all levels. According to Sternberg (1999), conventional ability and achievement tests often focus narrowly on the form of developing expertise most valued by the testing culture. Thus, the intelligence of some individuals will go unrecognized if their areas of developing expertise fall outside this range. One test that shows promise as a broader identifier of intelligence is the Sternberg Triarchic Abilities Test (STAT; Sternberg, 1993).

Perhaps most important, the STAT shows relatively high ethnic and socioeconomic diversity among high scorers in the practical and creative categories, especially when compared to such widely used tests as the SAT and Advanced Placement (AP) assessments (Sternberg, 2008). If the triarchic model were utilized in standard academic assessments, Sternberg posits, selective colleges might admit a more diverse population of students.

The STAT appears to carry considerable predictive power for academic achievement. In one summer college immersion program for high school students, the STAT correctly predicted high achievement on a final assessment for students who scored high in analytic, practical, or creative ability (as cited in Sternberg, 2008). In a separate study, the STAT actually outperformed the standard college admissions benchmark (the SAT) as a predictor of first-year college grades (Sternberg & the Rainbow Project Collaborators, 2006).

The models of successful intelligence and developing expertise also carry ramifications for the classroom. At the elementary level, greater teacher recognition of creative and practical abilities can lead to higher self-esteem for a wide range of children (Uszajnska-Jarmoc, 2007). Evidence also suggests that high school students perform better on a final assessment when the teaching style matches their analytic, creative, or practical strengths (Sternberg, 2008). In general, Sternberg (1999) urges teachers to recognize students' particular areas of developing expertise and teach to all three patterns of intelligence.

Beyond triarchic intelligence: The WICS model. Sternberg asserts that intelligence, as defined by the triarchic model, forms the basis for creativity and, at an even higher level, wisdom. To be creative, individuals must achieve a balance of all three aspects of intelligence. That is, they must be able to *creatively* generate ideas, *analytically* separate good ideas from bad ones, and *practically* transform ideas into accomplishments that can be "sold" high by convincing others of their worth (Sternberg, 2003b, 2005). Wisdom, in turn, relies on the application of both intelligence and creativity. In particular, individuals must use practical intelligence to acquire tacit or implicit knowledge about themselves, others, and situational contexts (Sternberg, 2004a). Wise individuals use their intelligence and creativity to work for the common good, balancing their own needs with those of others and their social or environmental context. They achieve their goals by constructively selecting, adapting to, and changing environments for themselves and for others (Sternberg, 1998, 2003b). The triarchic model of successful intelligence, therefore, provides an explanatory foundation not only for intelligence, but also for the hierarchical organization of other desirable traits.

Although intelligence and creativity are certainly important, Sternberg suggests that wisdom may be the most valuable trait for a society to seek and foster in individuals. Fortunately, the WICS theory has applications for the selection and training of leaders (Sternberg, 2007) and for education in general (Sternberg, 2004b).

The Theory of Multiple Intelligences

Like Sternberg, Howard Gardner rejects the conception of intelligence as a unitary ability. However, Gardner's theory of multiple intelligences (MI) focuses more on domains of intelligence and less on mental processes than does the triarchic theory of successful intelligence.

According to Gardner (2006a), all humans possess at least eight distinct intelligences, which exist in a particular proportional blend unique to each individual (Gardner, 2006b). An intelligence is defined as "the ability to solve problems, or to create products, that are valued within one or more cultural settings" (Gardner, 1993, p. x). To qualify as part of the MI model, a candidate intelligence must (a) be isolable in the case of brain damage, (b) have the potential for evolutionary history, (c) involve an identifiable core or set of core operations, (d) be amenable to a system of symbolic representation, (e) have a developmental history with the potential for expert performance, (f) be evident in the existence of exceptional individuals, such as savants, (g) have evidence from experimental psychology, and (h) be supported by psychometric research (Gardner, 1999). Each of the intelligences evolves through interactions between one's biological predispositions and the opportunities provided by one's environment. While recognizing that every individual has a unique combination of intelligences, Gardner also describes two basic types of intelligence profile. Individuals with a dramatic spike in one or two intelligences are said to have *laser profiles*, while those with a broader distribution are described as *searchlight profiles* (Gardner, 2006b).

Three of the intelligences – linguistic, logical-mathematical, and spatial – are similar to abilities measured by conventional intelligence tests. They are also represented by some of the Stratum II broad abilities found in the three psychometric models described earlier. The remaining five types are valued in most cultures, even though they are not measured by conventional intelligence tests. Musical intelligence includes sensitivity to various musical properties and the ability to appreciate, produce, and combine pitch, tones, and rhythms. Bodily kinesthetic intelligence is the skillful use of one's body. Intrapersonal intelligence reflects the understanding of one's own motives, emotions, strengths, and weaknesses, while interpersonal intelligence requires the understanding of, and sensitivity to, other people's motives, behaviors, and emotions. Naturalist intelligence involves the skilled discrimination and categorization of natural patterns or material goods (Gardner, 2006a).

Gardner has addressed the possibility of additional intelligences, including existential, spiritualist, and moral intelligence. However, MI theory does not allow for the favoring of a specific moral code or religion, or the requirement of phenomenological experiences, which would seem necessary components of the latter two possibilities. Gardner therefore grants partial acceptance only to existential intelligence, which involves the addressing of cosmic or existential questions (Gardner, 1999). Even this intelligence deviates substantially from the other eight, leading to more recent conceptualizations of MI theory as a set of "8 ½ intelligences" (Gardner, 2006a, p. 91).

Developmental perspectives. One of Gardner's eight criteria for intelligences involves the existence of a distinct developmental history with potential end-state expertise (1999). Given this stipulation and the widespread acclaim for MI theory in the field of education, it is somewhat surprising that more attention is not paid to the possible developmental perspectives provided by the model. Perhaps the next step in Gardner's research will be to investigate the relationship between his theory and cognitive development. At present, however, Gardner seems to provide only a few initial nods toward prior theories of development in his original publication of MI theory (1983). For example, he notes that MI theory often dovetails closely with the cognitive developmental sequence outlined by Jean Piaget. In his description of bodily kinesthetic intelligence, Gardner refers to the circular activities of infants and toddlers in the sensorimotor stage, the gradual piecing together of simple acts to achieve goals, and the subsequent abstract use of tools. Logical-mathematical, spatial, and both personal intelligences similarly follow a Piagetian pattern.

Applications. Although not originally developed as an educational framework, MI theory has had an enormous international impact on education. Applications of MI theory can be found in schools on six continents (Kornhaber, 2004). According to one report, schools implementing an MI-based curriculum noted particular improvements in student behavior, standardized test scores, and parental participation, and in the effort, motivation, social involvement, and learning of children with learning disabilities (Kornhaber & Krechevsky, as cited in Kornhaber, 2004). Research has particularly highlighted the use of MI theory in educational interventions for individuals with attention deficit hyperactivity disorder, with the argument that the MI approach provides a positive emphasis on these students' strengths (Schirduan & Case, 2004).

MI theory has not only been incorporated into elementary and secondary school curricula, but also implemented in adult literacy education, where it appears to encourage the development of effective individual learning strategies (Kallenbach & Viens, 2004). In addition, research conducted with second language students revealed that students taught using MI theory outperformed controls on assessments of oral and written language proficiency (Haley, 2004).

Until fairly recently, Gardner has shown a decided lack of involvement in the practical interpretation of MI theory. However, following some dubious implementations of his work – including a curriculum based on the supposed intelligences of different ethnic groups – he has begun to offer specific support or disapproval of certain MI-based educational practices (Gardner, 2006b). While MI theory does not necessarily condone teaching every lesson via all eight intelligences, it does emphasize the importance of presenting a topic in a variety of relevant ways. MI theory also encourages the adoption of a personalized approach to each student and the careful cultivation of socially valued skills (Gardner, 2006b; Kornhaber, 2004).

According to Gardner, multiple intelligences cannot be properly assessed with traditional paper-and-pencil psychometrics. However, MI theory lends itself to various progressive methods of school assessment. Spectrum classroom assessments, in which young children are observed in their interactions with a wide range of materials, can provide educators with clear individual intelligence profiles (Gardner, 1999). "Bridging" assessments, which are organized by school subject rather than by Gardner's intelligences, nevertheless emphasize the individualized perspective encouraged by MI theory (Chen & Gardner, 2005). Educators participate in various activities with a child, with the motives of deducing the child's unique learning process, and setting individualized rather than norm-based goals for progress.

Beyond multiple intelligences: Multiple minds. Sternberg's and Gardner's views might be moving closer together. Recently, Gardner (2006c) described five kinds of minds (or cognitive abilities) that will be important for citizens, leaders, and employees in our changing world. These five types are disciplined, synthesizing, creating, respectful, and ethical. The disciplined mind is able to master knowledge within the major disciplines of thought. The synthesizing mind integrates the relevant aspects of this knowledge into a coherent story. The creative mind takes risks, discovers new problems, and thinks about material in new ways. The respectful mind is attentive to, and appreciative of, differences between people. Finally, the ethical mind meets responsibilities and works toward the common good. According to Gardner, educators will play a crucial role in cultivating these abilities in their students.

Models of Emotional Intelligence

Gardner's (1983) intra- and interpersonal intelligences are related to the multifaceted construct of emotional intelligence (EI). There are specific models of EI that will be reviewed elsewhere in this volume. What they have in common is a focus on the abilities that allow some individuals to use emotions effectively in their daily lives. These capacities include being able to perceive and convey emotions, understand and reason with emotions, and regulate emotions in one's self and others (Roberts, Zeidner, & Matthews, 2007).

It has been argued (Mayer, Caruso, & Salovey, 2000) that EI meets the criteria for a legitimate intelligence because the abilities comprising it (a) can be operationalized as a unified set, (b) are related to each other and to preexisting intelligences, while showing unique variance, and (c) develop with experience and age. Moreover, the field of EI is confronted with many of the same problems faced by intelligence researchers in general. For example, EI is viewed as an elusive construct that is difficult to define, conceptualize, and measure. There is debate over whether EI has a general factor (*g*) and the possibility has even been raised of incorporating EI into Carroll's three-stratum theory (Matthews, Zeidner, & Roberts, 2007).

Another issue under debate is the relationship between emotion and cognition (Matthews et al., 2007). Two EI abilities – emotional facilitation of thinking and regulation of emotions – seem particularly predictive of scores on traditional measures of intelligence. According to Salovey and Pizarro (2003), individuals high in emotional intelligence use their emotions productively when solving different types of problems. For example, happy moods have been found to facilitate creativity and inductive reasoning, while sad affect fosters attention to detail and deductive reasoning. Given that individuals have a range of emotional experience to draw from, matching mood with problem type can improve task performance. Similarly, the ability to regulate emotions helps individuals reduce an emotion, such as test-taking anxiety, if it is perceived as maladaptive to a situation (Lopes & Salovey, 2004). Moreover, preschoolers who were able to delay emotional gratification had higher attentional and cognitive competencies in adolescence than did preschoolers who could not regulate their emotions and, therefore, acted impulsively (Shoda, Mischel, & Peake, 1990).

Developmental perspectives. Three aspects of human development have been found to be particularly relevant to individual differences in EI (Zeidner, Matthew, Roberts, & MacCann, 2003). These are (a) temperament, which has a strong genetic component that can be modified by interactions with the environment; (b) the acquisition of emotional display rules and other language-dependent skills; and (c) engagement in the self-reflective regulation of emotions. In addition, early development of emotion knowledge (e.g., accurately identifying and labeling emotions) contributes to later academic and social competence (Izard, Trentacosta, King, Morgan, & Diaz, 2007).

Applications. EI assessment and training programs have been implemented in a wide range of settings, including businesses, schools, and clinical practices. However, as with implementations of MI theory in the classroom, these programs vary dramatically in their quality and effectiveness (Mathews et al., 2007).

Critique of the Social Level and Its Models

These three views highlight the potential range and complexity of intelligence. One of the greatest strengths of the social level is that it focuses on intelligent behaviors that occur in a variety of settings and are valued by most societies. More specifically, these models meet our criterion of describing, explaining, and predicting intelligent behaviors across time and place. In addition, all three fulfill the requirement of building on previous knowledge and research. The wide range of evidence they incorporate takes advantage of different subfields of psychology (e.g., biological, emotional, psychometric, developmental, information processing, and cross-cultural). It is especially commendable that Sternberg's and Gardner's newer models build on their older ones. In addition, Sternberg shows how intelligence is central to creativity and wisdom. Finally, these social views have generated new research and practical applications.

However, these social models also raise three concerns. One has to do with our criterion of falsifiability. Social theories are often complex and difficult to test in their entirety. Although Sternberg, in particular, has extensively subjected his theory of successful intelligence to internal and external validation (e.g., Sternberg, 2003), research at the social level tends to be missing in studies across labs that try to replicate and extend each other's work. In contrast, knowledge at the psychometric and physiological levels has been moved forward by cross-lab discrepancies. For some reason, researchers at the social level are not empirically scrutinizing each other's theories to the same degree. We suspect that this difference arises because the social theories are more complex and less concrete than those at the other levels.

The second concern is general and it has to do with how we will know when to stop expanding the construct of intelligence's scope. These three types of social models present compelling cases for extending our views of intelligence to include a variety of domains and processes. We are not criticizing these particular models for going beyond IQ in the ways that they do. However, Stanovich (2009, p. 221) notes, "if we concatenate all of the broad theories that have been proposed by various theorists – with all of their different 'intelligences'– under the umbrella term intelligence, we will have encompassed virtually all of mental life. Intelligence will be 'everything the brain does' – a vacuous concept." Even though the field has not yet reached consensus on exactly what intelligence is, perhaps it is time for a clear and accepted definition of what it is not.

Our final concern has to do with the risks and responsibilities that come with calling something an intelligence. The social views have been highly popular in education and other areas of society. Unfortunately, this popularity has resulted in some dubious applications of the MI and emotional intelligence theories. It is not clear that these practices can be stopped, but perhaps guidelines and more oversight need to be associated with theories of intelligence to increase the chances that the theories will be used wisely.

Models that Bridge Levels

According to Flynn (2007), it will be a long time before findings from the psychometric, physiological, and social levels can be integrated into a comprehensive theory of intelligence. Meanwhile, models forming a bridge between levels help direct the field toward this integration by challenging each approach's assumptions and broadening its perspectives. Three such models will be reviewed here.

PASS Theory

The Planning, Attention, Simultaneous, and Successive (PASS) model of intelligence (Das, Naglieri, & Kirby, 1994) builds on Luria's physiologically based description of intelligence as a collection of functional units that provide the capability for specific actions (as cited in Naglieri & Kaufman, 2001). Unlike some of the psychometric models, PASS's emphasis is on the modularity of brain function and the strength of its individual processing units, rather than on *g* (Naglieri & Das, 2005).

According to the PASS model, there are three distinct processing units and each is associated with specific areas of the brain (Das et al., 1994; Naglieri & Kaufman, 2001). The first unit involves *arousal* and *attention*, and is primarily attributed to the brainstem, diencephalon, and medial cortical regions of the brain, although Das et al. (1994) note that the frontal lobe is likely also important for the conscious direction of attention. According to Das et al., arousal is a necessary predecessor to voluntarily focused selective and divided attention. The second unit consists of *simultaneous and successive* processing (Naglieri & Kaufman, 2001). Simultaneous processing allows for the holistic integration of related pieces of information – an essential component of basic academic tasks such as reading comprehension. In contrast, successive processing involves the serial organization of information, which is important for rounding numbers and understanding the phonetic construction of words. The functions of simultaneous and successive processing are broadly attributed to the occipital, parietal, and posterior temporal lobes. The third unit, *planning*, enables individuals to generate solutions to problems, choose and apply the best solutions, and evaluate their problem-solving strategies. This unit is linked to the brain's frontal lobes. While certain tasks are primarily the domain of one functional unit, many tasks require the activation of all three units, with emphasis shifting from one unit to another as various subgoals are addressed.

Although the bulk of PASS theory is devoted to the three main processing units, its authors acknowledge additional components to the model (Das et al., 1994; Jarman & Das, 1996). According to PASS theory, cognitive functioning can be affected by *input* deficiencies such as auditory or visual processing problems. Problems with *output* may similarly impact an individual's measured cognitive ability; here, Das et al. refer specifically to individuals with mental retardation or brain damage who may have difficulty with motor tasks. Finally, the PASS processes function within the context of an individual's *knowledge base and cognitive tools*. In other words, a child's inability to comprehend the phonetic structure of a foreign language likely reflects his or her lack of experience with that language rather than a deficit in the child's abilities of planning, attention, or simultaneous or successive processing (Naglieri & Das, 2005).

Developmental perspectives. Standardized PASS-based measures of intelligence show a progression of scores across age categories (Fein & Day, 2004), indicating that at least some of the PASS units develop and lead to increasing intelligence with age. Attention, in particular, may develop as children learn mechanisms of self-regulation; the authors of PASS theory argue that this functional unit reaches its optimum capacity in late childhood (Das et al., 1994). However, it has been noted that the value and definition of self-regulation vary between cultures, so this developmental perspective may in fact depend upon cultural context (Naglieri & Das, 2005).

Applications. The PASS model provides the theoretical basis for the Cognitive Assessment System (CAS; Naglieri & Das, 1997). This measure, which yields one subscore each for planning, attention, successive processing, and simultaneous processing, as well as a cumulative full-scale score, shows promise as an effective tool for the identification of gifted and creative children (Naglieri & Kaufman, 2001). Furthermore, in a young adult population, the CAS full-scale score was a significant predictor of skill and knowledge acquisition, skill retention, and skill transfer (Fein & Day, 2004). Perhaps because of the model's lack of emphasis on acquired knowledge, the CAS full-scale score shows smaller differences between ethnic populations than those found on traditional intelligence tests (Naglieri & Kaufman, 2001). However, the simultaneous and successive processing subscales tend to yield scores comparable to those obtained by traditional intelligence tests.

PASS theory also provides a useful framework for the qualitative definition of mental retardation (Jarman & Das, 1996). Individuals with mental retardation often show particular deficits in regulation of attention, performance of successive processing tasks, planning, the use of an effective base of practical social knowledge, and possibly input and output of information. In general, the PASS model suggests a number of interventions based on these specifically defined areas. For example, the PASS Reading Enhancement Program (PREP) is often used in the classroom to help children who have reading difficulties (Das, 1999).

The Theory of the Minimal Cognitive Architecture

To some extent, the theory of the minimal cognitive architecture underlying intelligence and development (Anderson, 1992) bridges the psychometric and social approaches. This theory builds on Fodor's (1983) distinction between central thought processes and dedicated processing modules. More specifically, Anderson (1999) asserts that *g* is a function of a basic central processing mechanism, the speed of which determines the acquisition of knowledge through thinking. The basic processing mechanism comprises a verbal processor and a spatial processor. These two processors each have a distinct latent power; these latent levels are uncorrelated with each other and are normally distributed throughout the population. The human range of intelligence thus results from individual differences in both the speed (or neural efficiency) of the basic processing mechanism and the latent power of the two specific processors.

While the basic processing mechanism accounts for most measurements of *g*, it is only one component of the minimal cognitive architecture. There also exist dedicated processing systems, or modules, that operate independently of the basic mechanism. These modules may incorporate skills and knowledge that are unaffected by basic processing speed or latent visual or spatial power. Rather than reflecting individual differences, the specific modules are manifest in between-age differences in reasoning ability (Davis & Anderson, 1999). Deficits in these modules are hypothesized to be the source of some specific pervasive developmental disorders and learning differences. For instance, a deficient theory of mind module could result in symptoms of autism, while a deficient phonological processing module could contribute to dyslexia (Anderson, 2008).

Developmental perspectives. The minimal cognitive architecture theory acknowledges development with distinct components for between-age and within-age differences (Davis & Anderson, 1999). Under this model, basic processing speed does not change with age. This constancy accounts for resilient differences in individual reasoning ability. However, specific modules do mature with age. For instance, phonological encoding and theory of mind seem to develop as children grow older, leading to between-age differences in reasoning ability. Thus, some aspects of intelligence are a function of developmental age, while others result from consistent individual differences in processing speed.

Applications. Little research exists on the application of the theory of the minimal cognitive architecture. Indeed, few authors other than Anderson seem to have addressed this model in their work. However, Anderson has recently suggested that his theory holds explanatory power for such diverse disorders as autism and learning differences (Anderson, 2008). Perhaps other researchers will offer tests of, and feedback for, this hypothesis, and work with Anderson to develop strategies for its possible application in educational and clinical settings.

The Dual Process Theory of Human Intelligence

According to the dual process (DP) theory (Kaufman, 2009), intelligent behavior can be explained through a hierarchical structure of directed and spontaneous mental processes. (Only part of this structure will be described here.) At the top of the hierarchy are two broad forms of cognition: controlled and autonomous. Controlled cognition is intentional and serial in its processing, which means that it is relatively effortful and slow. This form of thought allows individuals to think about their thinking (metacognition), process abstract information, and plan for the future. Directly below controlled cognition in the hierarchy are central executive functioning and reflective engagement, which are independent sources of variance. Central executive functioning is associated with the next level's abilities to update working memory, inhibit irrelevant responses, and think flexibly. At the level below these three executive functions is explicit cognitive ability (ECA), which involves the ability to solve complex, well-structured problems. According to DP theory, ECA is essentially the same as *g*. Intellectual engagement, which is the drive to engage in academic pursuits, is directly below reflective engagement and at the same hierarchical level as ECA.

In contrast to controlled cognition, autonomous cognition is unintentional, fast (due to parallel distributed processing), and context dependent. This form of cognition allows individuals to acquire information automatically. Directly below autonomous cognition's position at the top of the hierarchy are autonomous information acquisition abilities and autonomous engagement. Information acquisition abilities are associated with implicit learning (i.e., learning without being consciously aware of it) and latent inhibition (i.e., the ability to ignore irrelevant stimuli), while autonomous engagement is related to affective engagement (i.e., the desire for emotional engagement), aesthetic engagement (i.e., the desire to use creative processes), and fantasy engagement. The model's inclusion of the different types of engagement for controlled and autonomous cognition reflect the assumptions that individuals engage in activities they are good at and, in turn, this engagement improves their abilities in these areas.

Importantly, autonomous cognition explains a variety of intelligent behaviors beyond the effects of controlled cognition's ECA (or *g*). For example, research with college student participants found that implicit learning was positively related to processing speed, verbal analogical reasoning, language learning achievement, and aspects of emotional intelligence and personality. Similarly, reduced latent inhibition (an inability to screen out irrelevant stimuli) was positively correlated with creative achievement in the arts and self-reported faith in affective intuition. Important to the divergent validity of the DP theory was the finding that implicit learning and latent inhibition were not significantly correlated with ECA. In addition, differential patterns of correlations were found between cognitive ability measures and measures of the various types of engagement for controlled and autonomous cognition. In general, empirical results support the DP theory and the role of autonomous cognition in intelligence (Kaufman, 2009). More specifically, intelligent individuals flexibly switch back and forth between controlled and autonomous cognition, using the form of cognition that works best for a particular task's demands.

Developmental perspectives. Currently, DP theory does not specifically account for human intellectual development.

Applications. The DP theory is quite recent and, therefore, its practical applications have not yet been established. However, it has been suggested that interactions between individual differences in controlled and autonomous cognition could provide insight into schizophrenia and other mental disorders (Kaufman, 2009).

Critique of the Bridge Models

These models take the field of intelligence down some intriguing paths related to the processing of various types of information. For example, the theory of the minimal cognitive architecture and the dual process theory help break new ground by proposing two interactive systems of thought underlying human intelligence. These models retain the notion of *g* but go well beyond it through their inclusion of automatic, unintentional processes. The PASS model, in contrast, rejects *g* but includes many of the same mental processes addressed by the other two models. In a sense, the three theories use cognitive hypotheses to address psychometric, physiological, and social issues.

These theories meet many of our criteria for models of intelligence. In particular, they build on previous knowledge and have appropriate empirical support. Furthermore, the models' components are well specified and relevant. Even the name of Anderson's model, the theory of the minimal cognitive architecture, seems to promote parsimony. (We do not yet know if all parts of DP's hierarchical structure are relevant but Kaufman (2009) builds a good case for them.) Finally, the models describe, explain, and predict intelligent behavior across time and place to some extent. Anderson's minimal cognitive architecture theory explicitly incorporates development, while the other two do so only indirectly. All three theories have the potential to account for abnormal, as well as normal, developmental outcomes.

For some reason, the minimal cognitive architecture and PASS theories are not as widely cited as the other ones reviewed in this chapter. (DP theory has not existed long enough for frequent citation.) PASS theory is currently the only one of the three to have practical applications. As with models at the social level, perhaps those that bridge levels would benefit from future cross-lab empirical studies.

Conclusions and Implications

The Latin root for the word intelligence roughly translates as "to understand." Do the contemporary models reviewed in this chapter help us understand what it means for one person to be more intelligent than another? Not exactly, in that each level of research has its own answer to the question. According to the psychometric level and its models, one person is more intelligent than another due to higher test scores that reflect greater amounts of one or more broad mental abilities. The physiological models claim that neural efficiency in the brain's parietal and frontal lobes as well as neural plasticity are responsible for individual differences in intelligence. In contrast, the social level's answer includes a range of processes and domains that are relevant to everyday life within a culture. Finally, the models that bridge levels propose that one person is more intelligent than another due to differences in intentional and unintentional cognitive processes.

Oddly enough, four types of answers to the same question might be a promising sign for future understanding of intelligence. According to Eysenck (1998), intelligence is threefold in nature, with psychometric (IQ), biological, and social comprising its three parts. These three parts are well represented by the contemporary models reviewed here. However, no one part can explain or dominate the entire construct. Instead, the three levels will need to come together as equal partners before consensus can be reached about the nature of intelligence. Models that bridge levels are the first step toward this merger. A second step is to examine commonalities across models in order to find constructive clues for how to transform the four answers into one.

One such clue involves the ability to adapt. All four types of models emphasize adaptability of mental processing as an important aspect of intelligence. For example, the psychometric models incorporate fluid intelligence, which involves the ability to adjust to novel information. The physiological models are based on neural adaptability to task demands and the brain's ability to reorganize neural connections in response to experience. The social models explain intelligence, or intelligences, as adapting potential abilities to the values and demands of one's culture. Finally, the models that bridge levels propose that interactions between parallel and sequential processing allow successful adaptation to environmental demands and constraints.

This emphasis on adaptability means that most contemporary models view intelligence as dynamic in nature. They acknowledge that intelligent behaviors and neural connections often change when environmental conditions change, which explains why human intellectual performance can be high in some contexts and low in others. Through their dynamic focus, the models advance the field of intelligence beyond a narrow, static conception of intelligence. As a result, interactive assessment of cognitive abilities has become more common, and new environmental programs are designed to foster intelligence.

Another commonality among some of the models is the view that intelligence is the ongoing development of expertise in one or more domains. For example, extended *Gf-Gc* theory, Sternberg's theory of developing expertise, the DP theory, and Anderson's theory of the minimal cognitive architecture have mechanisms for deliberate practice and the continual refinement of abilities. Similarly, the potential for expertise is a criterion for the domains in Gardner's theory of multiple intelligences. Unfortunately, traditional intelligence tests measure very few expertise-related abilities.

Both automaticity of mental processes and neural efficiency are integral to expertise because they free cognitive and physiological resources for other mental pursuits, such as mastery of a domain or creativity. Sternberg's triarchic theory, the models bridging levels, and the neural efficiency model relate automaticity, efficiency, and availability of cerebral resources to intelligence.

Capitalizing on the commonalities among current models could help solve some of the mysteries surrounding intelligence. Rather than expanding the construct's scope even farther by identifying more intelligences, it would be useful for the field to focus on areas of potential agreement within and between levels of research. Most contemporary models, and the research methods on which they are based, are not mutually exclusive of each other. For example, Sternberg notes (1997) that his analytic, practical, and creative aspects of intelligence could be applied to Gardner's domains of intelligences. Similarly, neuroimaging studies could examine areas of the brain that are activated before, during, and after the acquisition of expertise (Roring, Nandagopal, & Ericsson, 2007).

The psychometric, physiological, and social levels and their current models have headed the field of intelligence down three productive paths. Perhaps the time has come for these paths to converge into one.

References

Alfonso, V. C., Flanagan, D. P., & Radwan, S. (2005). The impact of the Cattell-Horn-Carroll theory on test development and interpretation of cognitive and academic abilities. In D.P. Flanagan & P.L. Harrison (Eds.), *Contemporary intellectual assessment: Theories, tests, and issues* (2nd ed., pp. 185–202). New York, NY: Guilford Press.

Anderson, M. (1992). *Intelligence and development: A cognitive theory*. Malden, MA: Blackwell.

Anderson, M. (1999). Project development – The shape of things to come. In M. Anderson, (Ed.), *The development of intelligence* (pp. 3–15). Hove, UK: Psychology Press/Taylor & Francis (UK).

Anderson, M. (2008). What can autism and dyslexia tell us about intelligence? *Quarterly Journal of Experimental Psychology*, 61(1), 116–128.

Baltes, P. B., Staudinger, U. M., & Lindenberger, U. (1999). Lifespan psychology: Theory and application to intellectual functioning. *Annual Review of Psychology*, 50, 471–507.

Bickley, P. G., Keith, T. Z., & Wolfe, L. M. (1995). The three-stratum theory of cognitive agilities: Test of the structure of intelligence across the lifespan. *Intelligence*, 20, 309–328.

Binet, A., & Simon, T. (1916). *The development of intelligence in children* (E. S. Kite, Trans.). Baltimore, MD: Williams & Wilkins.

Birney, D. P., & Sternberg, R. J. (2006). Intelligence and cognitive abilities as competencies in development. In E. Bialystok & F. I. M. Craik (Eds.), *Lifespan cognition: Mechanisms of change* (pp. 315–330). New York, NY: Oxford University Press.

Blair, C. (2007). Open peer commentary: Inherent limits on the identification of a neural basis for general intelligence. *Behavioral and Brain Sciences*, 30, 154–155.

Burns, R. B. (1994). Surveying the cognitive terrain. *Educational Researcher*, 23 (3), 35–37.

Carroll, J. B. (1993). *Human cognitive abilities: A survey of factor-analytic studies*. Cambridge, UK: Cambridge University Press.

Cattell, R. B. (1941). Some theoretical issues in adult intelligence testing. *Psychological Bulletin*, 38, 592.

Cattell, R. B. (1943). The measurement of adult intelligence. *Psychological Bulletin*, 40, 153–193.

Cattell, R. B. (1963). Theory of fluid and crystallized intelligence: A critical experiment. *Journal of Educational Psychology*, 54, 1–22.

Chen, J. Q., & Gardner, H. (2005). Assessment based on multiple-intelligences theory. In D. P. Flanagan, & P. L. Harrison (Eds.), *Contemporary intellectual assessment: Theories, tests, and issues* (2nd ed., pp. 77–102). New York, NY: Guilford Press.

Colom, R., Haier, R. J., Head, K., Alvarez-Linera, J., Quiroga, M. A., Shih, P. C., et al. (2009). Gray matter correlates of fluid, crystallized, and spatial intelligence: Testing the P-FIT model. *Intelligence*, 37, 124–135.

Das, J. P. (1999). *PASS Reading Enhancement Program*. Deal, NJ: Sarka Educational Resources.

Das, J. P., Naglieri, J. A., & Kirby, J. R. (1994). *Assessment of cognitive processes: The PASS theory of intelligence*. Boston, MA: Allyn & Bacon.

Davidson, J. E. (1990). Intelligence recreated. *Educational Psychologist*, 25 (3&4), 337–354.

Davidson, J. E., & Downing, C. L. (2000). Contemporary models of intelligence. In R. J. Sternberg (Ed.), *Handbook of intelligence* (pp. 34–52). New York, NY: Cambridge University Press.

Davis, H., & Anderson, M. (1999). Individual differences and development – One dimension or two? In M. Anderson (Ed.), *The development of intelligence* (pp. 161–191). Hove, UK: Psychology Press/Taylor & Francis (UK).

Demetriou, A., & Mouyi, A. (2007). Peer commentary: A roadmap for integrating the brain with mind maps. *Behavioral and Brain Sciences, 30*, 156–158.

Dempster, F. N. (1991). Inhibitory processes: A neglected dimension of intelligence. *Intelligence, 15*, 157–173.

Embretson, S. E., & McCollam, S. S. (2000). Psychometric approaches to understanding and measuring intelligence. In R. J. Sternberg (Ed.), *Handbook of intelligence* (pp. 423–444). New York, NY: Cambridge University Press.

Ericsson, K. A. (1996). The acquisition of expert performance. In K. A. Ericsson (Ed.), *The road to excellence* (pp. 1–50). Mahwah, NJ: Erlbaum.

Ericsson, K. A., & Charness, N. (1994). Expert performance. *American Psychologist, 49*, 725–747.

Eysenck, H. J. (1988). The concept of "intelligence": Useful or useless? *Intelligence, 12*, 1–16.

Fein, E. C., & Day, E. A. (2004). The PASS theory of intelligence and the acquisition of a complex skill: A criterion-related validation study of Cognitive Assessment System scores. *Personality and Individual Differences, 37*, 1123–1136.

Flanagan, D. P., & McGrew, K. S. (1997). A cross-battery approach to assessing and interpreting cognitive abilities: Narrowing the gap between practice and cognitive science. In D. P. Flanagan, J. L. Genshaft, & P. L. Harrison (Eds.), *Contemporary intellectual assessment: Theories, tests, and issues* (pp. 314–325). New York, NY: Guilford Press.

Flynn, J. R. (2007). *What is intelligence? Beyond the Flynn effect.* New York, NY: Cambridge University Press.

Fodor, J. A. (1983). *The modularity of mind.* Cambridge, MA: MIT Press.

Gardner, H. (1983). *Frames of mind: The theory of multiple intelligences.* New York, NY: Basic Books.

Gardner, H. (1993). *Frames of mind: The theory of multiple intelligences* (10th anniversary edition). New York, NY: Basic Books.

Gardner, H. (1999). *Intelligence reframed: Multiple intelligences for the 21st century.* New York, NY: Basic Books.

Gardner, H. (2006a). *The development and education of the mind.* New York, NY: Routledge Taylor and Francis Group.

Gardner, H. (2006b). *Multiple intelligences: New horizons.* New York, NY: Basic Books.

Gardner, H. (2006c). *Five minds for the future.* Boston, MA: Harvard Business School Press.

Garlick, D. (2002). Understanding the nature of the general factor of intelligence: The role of individual differences in neural plasticity as an explanatory mechanism. *Psychological Review, 109*(1), 116–136.

Garlick, D. (2003). Integrating brain science research with intelligence research. *Current Directions in Psychological Science, 12*(5), 185–189.

Haier, R. J., Siegel, B. V., Jr., Nuechterlein, K. H., Hazlet, E., Wu, J. C., Paek, J., et al. (1988). Cortical glucose metabolic rate correlates of abstract reasoning and attention studied with positron emission tomography. *Intelligence, 12*, 199–217.

Haley, M. H. (2004). Learner-centered instruction and the theory of multiple intelligences with second language learners. *Teachers College Record, 106*(1), 163–180.

Hambrick, D. Z., Pink, J. E., Meinz, E. J., Pettibone, J. C., & Oswald, F. L. (2008). The roles of ability, personality, and interests in acquiring current events knowledge: A longitudinal study. *Intelligence, 36*, 261–278.

Hebb, D. O. (1949). *The organization of behavior: A neuropsychological theory.* New York, NY: Wiley.

Hempel, C. G. (1966). *The philosophy of natural science.* Englewood Cliffs, NJ: Prentice-Hall.

Horn, J. L. (1986). Intellectual ability concepts. In R. J. Sternberg (Ed.), *Advances in the psychology of human intelligence* (Vol. 3, pp. 35–77). Hillsdale, NJ: Erlbaum.

Horn, J. L. (1994). Theory of fluid and crystallized intelligence. In R. J. Sternberg (Ed.), *Encyclopedia of human intelligence* (pp. 443–451). New York, NY: Macmillan.

Horn, J. L., & Blankson, N. (2005). Foundations for better understanding of cognitive abilities. In D. P. Flanagan & P. L. Harrison (Eds.), *Contemporary intellectual assessment: Theories, tests, and issues* (2nd ed., pp. 41–76). New York, NY: Guilford Press.

Horn, J. L., & Donaldson, G. (1976). On the myth of intellectual decline in adulthood. *American Psychologist, 31*, 701–719.

Horn, J. L., Donaldson, G., & Engstrom, R. (1981). Apprehension, memory, and fluid intelligence decline in adulthood. *Research on Aging, 3*, 33–84.

Izard, C., Trentacosta, C., King, K., Morgan, J., & Diaz, M. (2007). Emotions, emotionality, and intelligence in the development of adaptive behavior. In R. D. Roberts, M. Zeidner, & G. Matthews (Eds.), *The science of emotional intelligence: Knowns and unknowns* (pp. 127–150). Oxford, UK: Oxford University Press.

Jarman, R. F., & Das, J. P. (1996). A new look at intelligence and mental retardation. *Developmental Disabilities Bulletin*, *24*(1), 3–17.

Jensen, A. R. (1998). *The g factor: The science of mental ability*. Westport, CT: Praeger.

Johnson, W., & Bouchard, T. J. (2005). The structure of human intelligence: It is verbal, perceptual, and image rotation (VPR), not fluid and crystallized intelligence. *Intelligence*, *33*(4), 393–416.

Jung, R. E., & Haier, R. J. (2007). The parieto-frontal integration theory (P-FIT) of intelligence: Converging neuroimaging evidence. *Behavioral and Brain Sciences*, *30*, 135–187.

Kaas, J. H. (1991). Plasticity of sensory and motor maps in adult mammals. *Annual Review of Neuroscience*, *14*, 137–167.

Kallenbach, S., & Viens, J. (2004). Open to interpretation: Multiple intelligences theory in adult literacy education. *Teachers College Record*, *106*(1), 58–66.

Kaplan, A. (1964). *The conduct of inquiry: Methodology for behavioral science*. San Francisco, CA: Chandler.

Kaufman, A. S. (2000). Tests of intelligence. In R. J. Sternberg (Ed.), *Handbook of intelligence* (pp. 445–476). New York, NY: Cambridge University Press.

Kaufman, A. S., Johnson, C. K., & Liu, X. (2008). A CHC theory-based analysis of age differences on cognitive abilities and academic skills at ages 22 to 90 years. *Journal of Psychoeducational Assessment*, *26*(4), 350–381.

Kaufman, S. B. (2009). *Beyond general intelligence: The dual-process theory of human intelligence*. Unpublished doctoral dissertation, Yale University.

Kornhaber, M. (2004). Multiple intelligences: From the ivory tower to the dusty classroom – but why? *Teachers College Record*, *106*(1), 67–76.

Krampe, R. T., & Ericsson, K. A. (1996). Maintaining excellence: Deliberate practice and elite performance in young and older pianists. *Journal of Experimental Psychology: General*, *125*, 331–359.

Lee, K. H., Choi, Y. Y., & Gray, J. R. (2007). Open peer commentary: What about the neural basis of crystallized intelligence? *Behavioral and Brain Sciences*, *30*, 159–161.

Lopes, P. N., & Salovey, P. S. (2004). Toward a broader education: Social, emotional, and practical skills. In J. E. Zins, R. P. Weissberg, M. C. Wang, & H. J. Walberg (Eds.), *Building school success on social and emotional learning: What does the research say?* (pp. 76–93). New York, NY: Teachers College Press.

Maguire, E. A., Gadian, D. G., Johnsrude, I. S., Good, C. D., Ashburner, J., Frackowiak, R. S. J., et al. (2000). Navigation-related structural change in the hippocampi of taxi drivers. *Proceedings of the National Academy of Sciences*, *97*, 4398–4403.

Matthews, G., Zeidner, M., & Roberts, R. D. (2007). Emotional intelligence: Consensus, controversies, and questions. In R. D. Roberts, M. Zeidner, & G. Matthews (Eds.), *The science of emotional intelligence: Knowns and unknowns* (pp. 1–46). Oxford, UK: Oxford University Press.

Mayer, J. D., Caruso, D. R., & Salovey, P. S. (2000). Emotional intelligence meets traditional standards for an intelligence. *Intelligence*, *27*(4), 267–298.

Mercado, E. III (2008). Neural and cognitive plasticity: From maps to minds. *Psychological Bulletin*, *134*, 109–137.

Mercado, E. III (2009). Cognitive plasticity and cortical modules. *Current Directions in Psychological Science*, *18*, 153–158.

McGrew, K. S. (1997). Analysis of the major intelligence batteries according to a proposed comprehensive Gf-Gc framework. In D. P. Flanagan, J. L. Genshaft, & P. L. Harrison (Eds.), *Contemporary intellectual assessment: Theories, tests, and issues* (pp. 151–179). New York, NY: Guilford Press.

McGrew, K. S. (2005). CHC theory of cognitive abilities. In D. P. Flanagan & P. L. Harrison (Eds.), *Contemporary intellectual assessment: Theories, tests, and issues* (2nd ed., pp. 136–181). New York, NY: Guilford Press.

McGrew, K. S. (2009). CHC theory and the human cognitive abilities: Standing on the shoulders of the giants of psychometric intelligence research. *Intelligence*, *37*, 1–10.

McGrew, K. S., & Flanagan, D. P. (1998). *The intelligence test desk reference (ITDR): Gf-Gc cross-battery assessment*. Boston, MA: Allyn & Bacon.

McGrew, K. S., Werder, J. K., & Woodcock, R. W. (1991). *The WJ-R technical manual*. Chicago, IL: Riverside.

Miller, B. B. (2008). Cattell-Horn-Carroll (CHC) theory-based assessment with deaf and hard of hearing children in the school setting. *American Annals of the Deaf*, *152*(5), 459–466.

Naglieri, J. A., & Das, J. P. (1997). *Cognitive assessment system*. Itasca, IL: Riverside Publishing.

Naglieri, J. A., & Das, J. P. (2005). Planning, Attention, Simultaneous, Successive (PASS) theory: A revision of the concept of intelligence. In D. P. Flanagan & P. L. Harrison (Eds.), *Contemporary intellectual assessment: Theories, tests, and issues* (2nd ed., pp. 120–135). New York, NY: Guilford Press.

Naglieri, J. A., & Kaufman, J. C. (2001). Understanding intelligence, giftedness and creativity using PASS theory. *Roeper Review, 23*(3), 151–156.

Neisser, U., et al. (1996). Intelligence: Knowns and unknowns. *American Psychologist, 51*, 77–101.

Newman, S. D., & Just, M. A. (2005). The neural basis of intelligence: A perspective based on functional neuroimaging. In R. J. Sternberg & J. E. Pretz (Eds.), *Cognition and intelligence: Identifying the mechanisms of the mind* (pp. 88–103). New York, NY: Cambridge University Press.

Neubauer, A. C., & Fink, A. (2005). Basic information processing and the psychophysiology of intelligence. In R. J. Sternberg & J. E. Pretz (Eds.), *Cognition & intelligence: Identifying the mechanisms of the mind* (pp. 68–87). New York, NY: Cambridge University Press.

Nisbett, R. E. (2009). *Intelligence and how to get it*. New York, NY: W.W. Norton.

Plucker, J. A. (2001). Intelligence theories on gifted education. *Roeper Review, 23*(3), 124–125.

Roberts, R. D., Zeidner, M., & Matthews, G. (2007). Emotional intelligence: Knowns and unknowns. In R. D. Roberts, M. Zeidner, & G. Matthews (Eds.), *The science of emotional intelligence: Knowns and unknowns* (pp. 419–474). Oxford, UK: Oxford University Press.

Robinson, N. (1992). Stanford-Binet IV, of course! Time marches on. *Roeper Review, 15*(1), 32–34.

Roring, R. W., Nandagopal, K., & Ericsson, K. A. (2007). Open peer commentary: Can the parieto-frontal integration theory be extended to account for individual differences in skilled and expert performance in everyday life? *Behavioral and Brain Sciences, 30*, 168–169.

Rosenzweig, M. R. (2003). Effects of differential experience on the brain and behavior. *Developmental Neuropsychology, 24*(2&3), 523–540.

Rypma, B., & Prabhakaran, V. (2009). When less is more and when more is more: The mediating roles of capacity and speed in brain-behavior efficiency. *Intelligence, 37*, 207–222.

Salovey, P. S., & Pizarro, D. A. (2003). The value of emotional intelligence. In R. J. Sternberg, J. Lautrey, & T. I. Lubart (Eds.), *Models of intelligence: International perspectives* (pp. 263–278). Washington, DC: American Psychological Association.

Schirduan, V., & Case, K. (2004). Mindful curriculum leadership for students with attention deficit hyperactivity disorder: Leading in elementary schools by using multiple intelligences theory (SUMIT). *Teachers College Record, 106*(1), 87–95.

Schmithorst, V. J. (2009). Developmental sex differences in the relation of neuroanatomical connectivity to intelligence. *Intelligence, 37*, 164–173.

Shoda, Y., Mischel, W., & Peake, P. K. (1990). Predicting adolescent cognitive and self-regulatory competencies from preschool delay of gratification: Identifying diagnostic conditions. *Developmental Psychology, 26*(6), 978–986.

Spearman, C. (1927). *The abilities of man*. New York, NY: Macmillan.

Stankov, L. (2005). Reductionism versus charting: Ways of examining the role of lower-order cognitive processes in intelligence. In R. J. Sternberg & J. E. Pretz (Eds.), *Cognition and intelligence: Identifying the mechanisms of the mind* (pp. 51–67). New York, NY: Cambridge University Press.

Stanovich, K.E. (2009). *What intelligence tests miss: The psychology of rational thought*. New Haven, CT: Yale University Press.

Sternberg, R. J. (1977). *Intelligence, information processing, and analogical reasoning: The componential analysis of human abilities*. Hillsdale, NJ: Erlbaum.

Sternberg, R. J. (1985). *Beyond IQ: A triarchic theory of human intelligence*. New York, NY: Cambridge University Press.

Sternberg, R. J. (1993). *Sternberg Triarchic Abilities Test*. Unpublished test.

Sternberg, R. J. (1997). *Successful intelligence*. New York, NY: Plume.

Sternberg, R. J. (1998). A balance theory of wisdom. *Review of General Psychology, 2*(4), 347–365.

Sternberg, R. J. (1999). Intelligence as developing expertise. *Contemporary Educational Psychology, 24*, 359–375.

Sternberg, R. J. (2003a). *Wisdom, intelligence, and creativity synthesized.* New York, NY: Cambridge University Press.

Sternberg, R. J. (2003b). EICS as a model of giftedness. *High Ability Studies, 14*(2), 109–137.

Sternberg, R. J. (2004a). Introduction to definitions and conceptions of giftedness. In R. J. Sternberg & S. M. Reis (Eds.), *Definitions and conceptions of giftedness*. Thousand Oaks, CA: Sage.

Sternberg, R. J. (2004b). Teaching for wisdom: What matters is not what students know, but how they use it. In D. R. Walling (Ed.), *Public education, democracy, and the common good* (pp. 121–132). Bloomington, IN: Phi Delta Kappan.

Sternberg, R. J. (2005). The WICS model of giftedness. In R. J. Sternberg & J. E. Davidson (Eds.), *Conceptions of giftedness* (2nd ed., pp. 327–342). New York, NY: Cambridge University Press.

Sternberg, R. J. (2007). A systems model of leadership: WICS. *American Psychologist, 62*(1), 34–42.

Sternberg, R. (2008). Applying psychological theories to educational practice. *American Educational Research Journal, 45*(1), 150–165.

Sternberg, R. J., & Rainbow Project Collaborators. (2006). The Rainbow Project: Enhancing the SAT through assessments of analytical, practical, and creative skills. *Intelligence, 34*, 321–350.

Thurstone, L. L. (1938). *Primary mental abilities.* Chicago, IL: University of Chicago Press.

Thurstone, L. L., & Thurstone, T. G. (1941). *Factorial studies of intelligence.* Chicago, IL: University of Chicago Press.

Uszynska-Jarmoc, J. (2007). Self-esteem and different forms of thinking in seven and nine year olds. *Early Child Development and Care, 117*(4), 337–348.

Woodcock, R. W. (1994). Extending Gf-Gc into practice. In J. C. McArdle & R. W. Woodcock (Eds.), *Human abilities in theory and practice* (pp. 137–156). Mahwah, NJ: Erlbaum.

Zeidner, M., Matthews, G., Roberts, R. D., & MacCann, C. (2003). Development of emotional intelligence: Towards a multi-level investment model. *Human Development, 46*, 69–96.

Part II

DEVELOPMENT OF INTELLIGENCE

CHAPTER 5

Intelligence

Genes, Environments, and Their Interactions

Samuel D. Mandelman and Elena L. Grigorenko

"In China, DNA tests on kids ID genetic gifts, careers" (*http://edition.cnn.com/2009/WORLD/asiapcf/08/03/china.dna.children.ability/index.html*) This CNN.com/Asia entry could certainly catch readers' attention! And it does, for at least two reasons. First, it concerns competition and high achievement. For the Chinese authorities who support this initiative, it is about identifying "DNA prodigies" as early as possible and coming up with a specialized developmental plan for them. This initiative is somewhat disconcerting; the use of genetics for societal stratification purposes has a long and controversial history and seeing its resurgence, in yet another shape and form, triggers all kinds of ethical concerns. Second, it raises some important questions concerning the scientific validity of such practices, specifically: How much scientific evidence underlies this initiative? What kinds of data might be generated by this initiative, and with what kind of certainty can they then be interpreted?

This chapter focuses primarily on the these questions, which seek to scientifically establish the connection between *genetics* and *intelligence*, the terms so easily linked by CNN, while in reality the etiological bases of intellectual abilities and disabilities have formed a central and not uncontroversial query within the sciences of psychology, philosophy, and education since the inception of these fields. The answers to this query have been highly variable, changing over time and cultures, and appear to be bracketed by two extreme positions.

A major proponent of the first polar position, Sir Francis Galton, advocated the genetic underpinning of human abilities (Galton, 1869). A major proponent of the second position, Dr. John Watson, argued for the overarching powers of environmental

Preparation of this chapter was supported in part by the following research grants from the National Institutes of Health: R01 DC007665 and PO HD052120. Grantees undertaking such projects are encouraged to express their professional judgment freely. Therefore, this article does not necessarily reflect the position or policies of the National Institutes of Health, and no official endorsement should be inferred. The content of this chapter partially overlaps with the content in Grigorenko (2009). We are thankful to Ms. Mei Tan for her editorial assistance.

influences (Watson, 1924). The positions gathered between these two extremes are all the colors and shades of Newton's sevenfold rainbow, with the most balanced points of view acknowledging that both forces matter. Contemplating the etiology of human abilities and disabilities, one might first question its importance and, second, wonder why its pursuit has taken so much time. In this chapter, we attempt to broadly outline the current understanding of the etiology of intelligence and intelligence-related processes. First, we briefly describe the major concepts that have primarily guided studies of the etiological bases of intellectual abilities and disabilities. Second, we summarize the state of the field's understanding of cases of intellectual abilities and disabilities. Finally, we provide a point of view on the Chinese initiative as presented in the CNN electronic publication, the reference that opened this chapter.

Vocabulary Prep: Terms and Concepts

In this section we will describe the major concepts that have been and are used to explore the connection between the genes and intelligence. We provide this brief overview to ensure that the content discussion presented in the section that follows is as clear as possible. Heritability is a statistic that describes the proportion of a given trait's variation (i.e., phenotypic[1] variation) within a population that is attributable to variation in the genes. Higher heritability indicates higher levels of covariation between genetic and phenotypic variation; lower heritability indicates higher levels of covariation between environmental and phenotypic variation. As discussed in the following section of the chapter, heritability studies have, so far, dominated the field of studies connecting genes and intelligence. Generally speaking, heritability estimates of the majority of intellectual abilities fall in the range of 40% to 60%. Heritability estimates for intellectual abilities and disabilities have been estimated through numerous twin, adoption, and family studies.

Twin studies examine the genetic contribution to a trait by comparing monozygotic (MZ) twins who are, in terms of the structural variation in the genome,[2] almost genetically identical, and dizygotic (DZ) twins who are approximately 50% genetically similar. MZ and DZ twins' performance on cognitive (intelligence, achievement, cognitive-processes-based) assessments are compared to each other to examine the similarity of performance between respective twins in each twin pair. For the overwhelming majority of cognitive indicators, MZ twins tend to score more similarly to each other than do DZ twins, thus indicating that their genetic similarity accounts for their similar performance on ability-related tasks and clearly highlighting the genetic contribution to intelligence. When twin methods are used in studies of intelligence, the heritability of intelligence can be estimated through the "quick and dirty" method of doubling the differences between MZ and DZ correlations (Ignat'ev, 1934) or through sophisticated statistical approaches to decomposing variance (e.g., Neale, 2009; Posthuma, 2009).

Adoption studies are used to separate genetic and environmental influences on intelligence. Adoption studies allow the measurement of genetic effects on a phenotype by comparing twins (or siblings or other family members) who are genetically similar, but have been raised in different environments. This procedure allows one to eliminate the environmental contribution to a phenotype and capture the purely genetic influence. Adoption studies can also be used to study the environmental effects on a phenotype by comparing nonbiological siblings who share an environment; this procedure allows one to examine the purely (or predominantly, with the exception of interactive effects) environmental contribution to phenotypes. Similar to the twin

1 Phenotype: An observable trait or characteristic.

2 Genome: The entire set of genetic instructions found in a cell.

methodology, there are quick and also there are sophisticated ways of generating hypotheses with regard to the roles of genes. To be quick and, possibly, imprecise, one might appraise the magnitude of genetic influences by looking at the correlations between biological relatives living apart and then, to evaluate the role of environments, consider the correlations between adoptive relatives living together. To be substantially more involved but more precise, one can apply various modeling approaches (e.g., Neale, 2009; Posthuma, 2009).

In addition to twin and adoption studies, family studies can also be used to examine the genetic and environmental contributions to a phenotype. Family studies often include a nontwin sibling as well as the parents in the study. Recently, studies on the children of twins have been conducted to carry out even more comprehensive explorations of the genetic contribution to intelligence (e.g., Iacono, Carlson, Taylor, Elkins, & McGue, 1999). Family studies do not permit a quick way to estimate heritability. Yet, there are various approaches utilizing variance component analyses and Markov Chain Monte Carlo (MCMC) approaches that can estimate heritability based on data from family units of different structures (e.g., Naples, Chang, Katz, & Grigorenko, 2009).

Heritability estimates, however, represent only one type of statistic that may be used to estimate the degree of genetic endowment associated with a complex trait. Researchers have developed an impressive variety of relevant methodologies, designs, and statistics. One such statistic, for example, is the relative risk statistic[3] (Risch, 1990). This indicator can be estimated for different pairs of relatives (e.g., sibling pairs, or parent-offspring pairs) and has been particularly informative in studies of clinical phenotypes.

In addition, there are methods of investigating patterns of familial transmission of a particular trait from generation to generation. These types of investigations are referred to as segregation analyses. Once again, there are varieties of statistics and approaches associated with such analyses. In some approaches (e.g., MCMC) these types of statistics might include not only estimates of main (genetic and environmental) and interactive (e.g., gene-gene) effects, but may also gauge the magnitudes of the effect sizes of these various effects, as well as the number of genes involved and the percent-variance each gene might contribute to the overall genetic variance of the trait (e.g., Naples et al., 2009). Various investigations into the familial transmission of characteristics of intellectual functioning suggest that multiple genes are involved in the substrate of this transmission, and that the patterns of this transmission are rather complex (i.e., far from following simple Mendelian laws).

Heritability estimates, genetic risk ratios, and parameters of segregation analyses are all methodologies that capitalize on the availability of behavioral data only (i.e., indicators of a trait of interest collected from different types of relatives and the correlations between these indicators). Lately, however, much more interest has been given to combining these behavior indicators with measured genotypic information (i.e., genotypes as they are captured by structural variation in the DNA; for a review, see Frazer, Murray, Schork, & Topol, 2009). If information on genotypes (or genotyping information) is available, then this information is, broadly speaking, correlated with behavioral information. Two major data designs and analytic strategies are used for these purposes: linkage analyses and association analyses.

Linkage studies allow researchers to track the patterns of inheritance exhibited by specific genetic variants or larger chunks of genetic material (e.g., chromosomal pieces or regions) within families. Linkage studies examine genetically related people only, that is, members from extended or nuclear families, or pairs of any degree of relatedness (parents and children, siblings, cousins, and so on). These studies suggest linkage

3 Relative risk statistic: A statistic that is used to calculate the amount of risk in one population in relation to the risk in a different population.

between a disorder or trait (i.e., a phenotype) and a particular location in the genome that may subsequently be investigated for an association with specific genes harbored in this location.

Association studies allow researchers to investigate connections between particular variants in particular genes (e.g., a variant that alters the production of a particular protein) and a disorder or trait of interest by detecting a statistical correlation between the two. Both related and unrelated people can be used in association studies. For related individuals, a popular design includes nuclear families (or trios – a proband[4] and his or her parents). What is investigated here is the degree of the association (or overtransmission) between a particular genetic risk variant and the phenotype of interest (e.g., a disorder). Unrelated people used in association studies are referred to as cases (people with the phenotype of interest) and controls (people who are matched to the cases on a number of important parameters, e.g., ethnicity, gender, age, exposure to a particular type of environment, but do not have the phenotype of interest).

Both linkage and association genetic studies have been carried out in the field; these studies are relatively novel, however slowly but surely they are decreasing the accent on heritability studies of intellectual functioning.

Intelligence and the Genome

In this main portion of the chapter, we discuss the evidence pertaining to observations that the genome is a major source of the variations in individuals' intellectual abilities and disabilities. In this section, we refer to the concepts and methods presented earlier.

There are almost 300 monogenetic disorders that include symptoms of mental retardation (Flint, 1999; Inlow & Restifo, 2004). These disorders are rather diverse, but they have four common features: (1) They are caused by disruptions of single genes (thus, the reference to *mono*genic disorders); (2) their presentation is typically severe, with a limited range of phenotypic variability and mental functioning that constitutes moderate to profound retardation; (3) when considered individually they are rare (most at .01%), but together they account for a considerable portion of developmental disabilities; and (4) they are highly pleiotropic, meaning that the disrupted gene appears to impact many brain-related pathways, and these affected pathways in turn cause large deviations from normative development.

The important question here with regard to the literature on the genetic bases of mental retardation is whether there are any findings or insights in this literature that can be brought to bear on the etiological bases of individual differences in intelligence as they are distributed in the general population. The answer to this question is still pending. The general conclusion of the field right now suggests that genes, in which mutations causing mental retardation have been identified, might not be directly related to individual differences in intelligence but might be involved in pathways (i.e., gene networks) that involve genes related to variation in intelligence.

There is a substantial body of literature dedicated to studies of the genetic bases of intelligence in the general population, that is, literature that draws on samples of individuals that are representative of their cultures and societies. As there is no single definition of intelligence, there is no single assessment that is used for its measurement (e.g., Cianciolo & Sternberg, 2004; Sternberg, 1996). In fact, there are probably hundreds of different assessments of intelligence, its different types and its facets, all sharing some common aspects and all characterized by some specific features.

The fact that diverse cognitive abilities correlate among each other at a variety of values, ranging from low to high depending on the particulars of those abilities, has led to the formulation of the concept of the *g* factor, Spearman's *g* (Spearman, 1904).

4 Proband: An affected individual.

Whereas nobody argues that these correlations, although estimated at the moderate value of ~.30 (Carroll, 1993) or slightly higher (Jensen, 1998) are present, a variety of theoretical approaches attempt to explain these correlations. These explanations range from statements that the correlations are, indeed, driven by the *g* factor, which is genetic in nature and manifestation (Rijsdijk, Vernon, & Boomsma, 2002), to the view that the interdependency between cognitive abilities can be explained by the developmental, temporal, and functional (but not etiological!) dependencies of these abilities on each other (van der Maas et al., 2006).

Also of interest is that regardless of the particular instrument or instruments used for the purposes of assessing intelligence or the intellectual quotient, IQ, and the language in which such assessment is carried out, the findings on heritability, or the statistical estimate of the contributions of genetic variability to individual variability in intelligence, are quite consistent. Specifically, when summarized in reviews or meta-analyzed, the data suggest that IQ's heritability is ~.50 (Deary, Spinath, & Bates, 2006; Devlin, Daniels, & Roeder, 1997; Plomin & Spinath, 2004).

In fact, there have been so many studies on the heritability of intelligence that the flow of "generic" studies on the heritability of IQ, similar to those included in the meta-analyses and reviews mentioned above, has noticeably decreased. What is at the center of genetic and genomic studies of intelligence now are (1) studies that differentiate heritability patterns by some other third variables (e.g., age or environment); (2) studies that investigate the heritability of various intelligence-related componential cognitive processes that are correlated with intelligence but cannot substitute it; and (3) studies that attempt to "translate" the heritability of intelligence into the identification of specific genes that contribute to or form the genetic foundation of intelligence as it is captured in the concept of heritability. The next portion of the chapter is structured around these topics.

Differentiating Heritability Estimates

It has been convincingly demonstrated by many studies that levels of heritability are not static – they differ throughout the life span and in different environmental conditions. While it would be logical to assume that heritability would decrease with age due to accumulated life experience, thus minimizing the importance of the role of genetics, something rather different has been found. In fact, heritability in infancy is estimated to be as low as 20%, while in adulthood it can be as high as 80%, though it does seem to decrease again in the later years of life. Based on results from twin (E. G. Bishop et al., 2003; Bouchard & McGue, 2003; Cardon & Fulker, 1993; McGue, Bouchard, Iacono, & Lykken, 1993; Patrick, 2000; Price et al., 2000; Reznick, Corley, & Robinson, 1997) and adoption (Petrill et al., 2004) studies, it appears that from birth onward, genetic variance becomes increasingly important in explaining individual differences in verbal and nonverbal intellectual abilities. Moreover, genetic influences appear not only to increase in their magnitude but also to form the genetic foundation for the stability of intelligence across different stages of the life span (Bartels, Rietveld, Van Baal, & Boomsma, 2002; Polderman et al., 2006; Rietveld, Dolan, van Baal, & Boomsma, 2003). It seems that genetic variance in intelligence stabilizes in postadolescence and remains relatively high and constant until later in life (Brant et al., 2009; van der Sluis, Willemsen, de Geus, Boomsma, & Posthuma, 2008). It also appears, however, that the dynamics change again in later life (from ~65 years of age on), indicating decreasing genetic and increasing nonshared environmental variations as an individual ages (Reynolds et al., 2005). These dynamics of heritability estimates across the life span have been of substantial interest to the field; their etiology is unknown, but they are, indeed, quite curious.

Similarly, there are studies indicating that heritability estimates differ substantially when they are sampled from different environments, emphasizing the importance of considering gene-environment interactions. For example, researchers (van Leeuwen, van den Berg, & Boomsma, 2008) carried out a study of families of twins, considering not only the heritability of IQ but also the indicators of assortative mating[5] occurring between parents. The results still indicated that the main source of variance in IQ was genetic (estimated at 67%). Yet, gene-environment interaction appeared to account for 9% of additional variance. These results suggested that environmental effects are larger for children with a genetic predisposition for low IQ, thus indicating that environmental influences do not affect all siblings uniformly.

The presence of gene-environment effects was also indicated by studies of differential heritabilities in families of different socioeconomic status (SES) (Harden, Turkheimer, & Loehlin, 2007). Shared environmental influences were reported to be more powerful for adolescents from families with low SES, while genetic influences were reported to be more powerful for adolescents from high SES. Similarly, environmental influences were reported to be greater on reading skills of children whose parents had less education, compared with children whose parents had higher levels of education (Friend, DeFries, & Olson, 2008).

Thus, the field has moved from obtaining heritability estimates for intelligence and related skills per se to looking for "other" factors that differentiate these estimates.

Dissecting Intelligence into Its Componential Processes

Another "movement" in the research on understanding the etiology of individual differences in intelligence and its related processes is associated with the direction from molar to molecular, that is, from intelligence as a holistic construct to its components. A central question here investigates the presence and magnitude of genetic factors that influence *all* intelligence-related processes as opposed to genetic factors that influence only *some* of such processes.

Electrophysiological Measures

Since early in the history of the field of intelligence, researchers have looked for ways to register and measure the brain's activity while it is engaged in intellectual tasks. One of the major lines of inquiry in this domain is related to the utilization of electrophysiological indicators obtained by scale-recording.

Electroencephalography (EEG) is the measurement of the electrical activity produced by the brain at rest, when the brain, arguably, is not engaged in responding to any particular stimulus. The EEG is typically described through components of its rhythmic activity, divided into bands by frequency. EEG patterns also differ in their preferential registration location and in the activities that are associated with these locations. In general, states of low arousal are associated with a relatively high amount of slow activity; states of high arousal are indicated by faster activity. For example, the α-wave's frequency range is 8–12Hz; it is typically registered in a condition of relaxation, with eyes closed. The β-wave frequency range is 12–30Hz, and it is associated with active engagement in cognitive processing. The γ-wave frequency range is 30–100Hz, and it is registered when the brain is performing certain cognitive and motor operations.

There is a history of research relating various EEG waves to various cognitive components, with a great amount of discussion regarding whether these measures do or do not relate to *g* (Deary, 2000; Ertl, 1971). There is also a substantial body of research investigating heritability estimates for different EEG peaks. This research has repeatedly reported moderate to high heritability estimates for different EEG peak frequencies (e.g., Posthuma, Neale, Boomsma, & de Geus, 2001), as well as for EEG coherence (i.e., the squared cross-correlation between

5 Assortative mating: Nonrandom mating in which people choose mates who are similar to themselves (in this case, of similar intelligence).

two EEG signals at different scalp locations which is regarded as an index indicator of brain interconnectivity; van Beijsterveldt, Molenaar, de Geus, & Boomsma, 1998a). Yet, there is a substantial amount of variability between these estimates, depending on the age of the subject and the part of the brain being registered.

For example, in a longitudinal investigation of stability and change in genetic and environmental influences on EEG coherence in children ages 5 to 7 years, researchers (van Baal, Boomsma, & de Geus, 2001) reported moderate heritability estimates for EEG coherence across all ages (the average value was at .58), but registered an increase in heritability for occipito-cortical connections of the right hemisphere and a decrease in heritability in the prefronto-cortical connections in the left hemisphere. Modeling the continuity of genetic variance, they reported the presence of both stable (i.e., age-general) and novel (age-specific) genetic influences.

The heritability of α-peaks was also reported to be moderate-high (e.g., .66; Posthuma et al., 2001). It is notable that when this genetic variance was co-modeled with the genetic variance in IQ (as represented through verbal comprehension, working memory, perceptual organization, and processing speed, derived from the WAIS-IIIR), there was no evidence of shared genetic variance between the α-peak frequency and any of the four WAIS dimensions (Posthuma et al., 2001).

Methodologies that are based on *event-related potentials* (ERPs) record stereotyped electrophysiological responses to external (e.g., a stimulus) or internal (e.g., thought) events. ERPs reflect fluctuations in the pattern and/or amplitude of an EEG. Needless to say, these fluctuations are very small and, correspondingly, can be extrapolated from the background activity only (or mostly) within the framework of repeated measures, that is, the recordings of many trials presenting the same stimulus or stimuli. When dissected into its components, ERPs are typically classified into two broad categories – exogenous (auditory, visual, somatosensory EPs, N100, P200) and endogenous (P300, N400, P600/SPS) structural units (Fabiani, Gratton, & Federmeier, 2007). Early exogenous components are typically used to study information processing by primary sensory cortices (e.g., selective attention, early object recognition), whereas later endogenous components are utilized to investigate higher order cognitive processes (e.g., working memory, executive control; for a review, see de Geus, Wright, Martin, & Boomsma, 2001; Winterer & Goldman, 2003b).

There have been numerous studies using different ERP units, particularly P300, which have been carried out in studies employing genetically informative designs. For example, it has been observed that both the amplitude and the latency of P300 are moderately heritable (e.g., Katsanis, Iacono, McGue, & Carlson, 1997; van Baal, van Beijsterveldt, Molenaar, Boomsma, & de Geus, 2001), although there are fluctuations in these estimates that have been attributed to task conditions (Winterer & Goldman, 2003b), gender (van Beijsterveldt, Molenaar, de Geus, & Boomsma, 1998b), and age (van Baal, van Beijsterveldt, et al., 2001). Yet, the heritability of the amplitude and latency of P200 was reported to be relatively low (van Beijsterveldt & Boomsma, 1994). There is also some evidence of shared genetic variance among slow wave ERP units and working memory, but the amount of this variance appears to fluctuate regionally (e.g., ~35–37% at the prefrontal site and ~51–52% at the parietal site), and, most curiously, the sites showed no evidence of common genetic variance (Hansell et al., 2001).

Speed of Information Processing

Studies of various indicators of information processing speed have been prominent in the field of intelligence due to the observation that these indicators reliably (although not necessarily substantially) correlate with various aspects of intelligence, especially, with the *g* factor (Deary, 2000). Correspondingly, many researchers have attempted to estimate heritability coefficients for these indicators. Here we will briefly summarize this work, but, prior to this summary, it is important to make the following comments.

First, the magnitudes of correlations differ between various types of indicators of speed of information processing obtained from different mental chronometric tasks. For example, correlations between *g* and reaction time were reported to be ~.3, whereas correlations between *g* and perceptual discrimination speed were reported to be ~.5 (Winterer & Goldman, 2003b). Second, it is thought that there might be age- and gender-related differentiation in correlations between mental chronometric tasks and *g* (Beaujean, 2005). Both of these bits of information/hypotheses are important for interpreting the findings regarding the heritability estimated for various indicators of speed of information processing.

In a recent meta-analytic study (Beaujean, 2005), a variety of indicators of performance differences in mental chronometric tasks were obtained within the context of genetically informative designs (i.e., designs that allow estimates of heritability). The results demonstrated that heritability estimates vary broadly (from ~30% to ~ 50%) and that they are somewhat dependent on task difficulty (i.e., increased task complexity is associated with higher heritability estimates). That is, heritability estimates of chronometric tasks are differentiated by their levels of difficulty. They are also differentiated by the age at which they are estimated: As information processing becomes more efficient in children, heritability estimates go up.

Researchers have also estimated the genetic overlap, or shared genetic variance, between various chronometric tasks, and then among these tasks and other intelligence-related indicators. For example, looking at the genetic overlap between IQ and indicators of inspection time and reaction time, researchers (Luciano et al., 2004) completed a series of model-fitting exercises using twin data. Results were interpreted as revealing the insufficiency of a unitary factor model for capturing the relationship between cognitive speed measures and all IQ subtests. Although there was some sharing of genetic variance, independent genetic effects were needed in the model to explain the associations between chronometric tasks and the various subtests of the utilized intelligence assessment. Based on these results, it is not surprising that different speed indicators show different amounts of genetic overlap (i.e., genetic correlations of different magnitude) with different intelligence-related indicators. For example, in one study, the overlapping genetic variance (a) between inspection time and Performance IQ was ~30% and (b) between inspection time and Verbal IQ was ~7% (Edmonds et al., 2008). In yet another study, the average amount of shared genetic variance between three different choice reaction time tasks and (a) IQ was ~33% and between these reaction time tasks and (b) a working memory indicator was ~18% (Luciano et al., 2001). Regardless, it appears that genetic variance in chronometric tasks (which is not highly shared) explains a moderate, although respectable amount of variance in intelligence and intelligence-related processes (Luciano et al., 2005). Yet, substantial specific and separate genetic factors appear to operate differently within different chronometric and intelligence tasks (Singer, MacGregor, Cherkas, & Spector, 2006).

Other Cognitive Processes

There are two large groups of cognitive processes that are often studied in conjunction with indicators of intelligence. These processes are captured by indicators of executive functioning and academic achievement.

Executive functioning is an umbrella term for several related cognitive functions like selective and sustained attention, working memory, and inhibition. These processes are also related to intelligence (Friedman et al., 2006), although when they were first introduced as a concept, they were thought to account for the variance in cognitive performance that could not be explained by intelligence. Executive functioning is not a unidimensional construct and the processes (functions) that contribute to it are not homogeneous. Correspondingly, the literature contains differential heritability estimates for different executive functions. There is also evidence that there are different amounts of genetic variance shared between indicators of intelligence, the *g* factor, and various executive functions. Specifically, it has been reported that genetic variance appears to be substantial and dominant in explaining individual differences in executive functioning in early and middle childhood (Polderman et al., 2007). When multiple executive functions (i.e., inhibiting dominant responses, updating working memory representations, and shifting between task sets) were considered in a twin study simultaneously, it was shown that behavioral correlations between these functions were attributable to the presence of a highly heritable common factor. Yet, each of these functions also appeared to be associated with a unique, substantial, function-specific genetic factor (Friedman et al., 2008). The literature also contains evidence of shared genetic variance between short-term memory and executive functions; yet, it appeared that each of the investigated functions was also associated with its own source of genetic variance (Ando, Ono, & Wright, 2001).

Indicators of academic achievement are also often considered alongside indicators of intelligence in studies of twins. The consensus in the field is that indicators of achievement and intelligence share common genetic variance (e.g., Luciano et al., 2003). Yet, once again, the reports on the specifics of this sharing vary widely (Hart, Petrill, Thompson, & Plomin, 2009). For example, when academic achievement in reading and math as well as the *g* factor were evaluated through Internet tools, heritabilities were 0.38 for reading, 0.49 for mathematics, and 0.44 for *g*. Multivariate genetic analysis showed substantial genetic correlations between learning abilities: 0.57 between reading and mathematics, 0.61 between reading and *g*, and 0.75 between mathematics and *g* (Davis et al., 2008). Yet the degree of these genetic correlations and the traits' heritability estimates vary depending on a number of factors. For example, depending on whether the same or different teachers assess both members of a twin pair, a decrease in the heritability estimates by ~33% to 42% is observed (Walker, Petrill, Spinath, & Plomin, 2004). Similarly, heritability estimates depend on how broadly or narrowly the trait of interest is conceived and measured; a wider sampling net typically results in more variation among heritability estimates and lower values of shared genetic variance (Kremen et al., 2007).

Of note also are repeated references to the presence of achievement-specific genetic factors. For example, when a set of reading achievement indicators was considered alongside indicators from the WAIS-R in adolescent and young adult twins, the resulting model supported one genetic general factor and three genetic group factors (verbal, performance, and reading). The genetic general factor accounted for 13% to 20% of reading performance, whereas "other" nongeneral factors accounted for the majority of the genetic variance, with specific reading factors explaining as much as or more variance (~21%) than any of the other factors (Wainwright et al., 2004). Consistently, it appears that the observed phenotypic covariation between indicators of achievement and intelligence is primarily due to common genetic influence, but that the variance in the measure of academic achievement itself cannot be fully (or even mostly) explained by that common genetic factor (Wainwright, Wright, Geffen, Luciano, & Martin, 2005).

In summary, the results of quantitative genetic (or biometrical or behavior-genetic) research on the etiology of intelligence and related processes rule out the possibility of a single gene being behind the corresponding individual differences. Unlike mental retardation, there are no few genes of major effect that are responsible for individual differences in intelligence. However the quest for the number of genes involved (if they are at all countable), whether they contribute to all intelligence and intelligence-related traits or whether there are some *general* and *specific* genes, and the magnitudes of effect these genes have, is still unfolding (e.g., Butcher, Kennedy, & Plomin, 2006; Naples et al., 2009).

Grounding the Heritability of IQ

For the last two decades or so, researchers have been engaged in a search for the specific genes that are involved in the etiology of intelligence and intellectual abilities and disabilities (for a review, see Deary, Johnson, & Houlihan, 2009). Such searches usually unfold in one of two ways: as exploratory whole-genome investigations/screens (often also referred to as "scans"), or as hypothesis-driven studies of candidate regions in the genome or candidate genes[6] (see the brief descriptions of both methodologies earlier).

Up until this chapter was written, there have been six genome-wide scans for genes contributing to intelligence and cognition (Butcher, Davis, Craig, & Plomin, 2008; Buyske et al., 2006; Dick et al., 2006; Luciano et al., 2006; Posthuma et al., 2005; Wainwright et al., 2006). The results of these scans are quite variable, but there are interesting partial overlaps. Specifically, the findings coincide in regions on chromosomes 2q (for 4 out 6 studies), 6p (for 5 out of 6 studies), and 14q (for 3 out of 6 studies). These overlapping regions have been putatively interpreted as indicative of the presence of genes that could explain some of the variance in IQ.

A number of observations can be derived from this work. Consider them in turn.

The first observation pertains to the variety of the measures used in these studies. In fact, only one study (Butcher et al., 2008) utilizes an indicator that was referred to as the general factor of intelligence, the *g* factor. The remaining studies used a range of indicators of both achievement and abilities and generated a wide spectrum of findings, allegedly implicating 13 (out of 22) autosomal[7] chromosomes, five of which, reportedly, demonstrated signals on both arms, short (p) and long (q). Thus, between all of these phenotypes and all of these regions, the resulting picture is rather difficult to interpret.

Second, the magnitudes of the presented statistics and *p*-values are rather modest. Although they are not indicative of the associated effect sizes, it is notable, that when such effect sizes are estimated (e.g., as in Butcher et al., 2008), they are reported to be very low (topping out at .4%).

Third, these studies are not independent of each other. These studies are collectively presented by four groups (two of whom, the Dutch and the Australian group, have also published on samples together; Posthuma et al., 2005), and it appears that there is a substantial overlap in the samples (e.g., Buyske et al., 2006; Dick et al., 2006, and Luciano et al., 2006; Posthuma et al., 2005; Wainwright et al., 2006). Given that the presentations are split based on the availability of a complete (semicomplete) IQ battery versus the availability of specific subtests from IQ tests and/or other cognitive tests, and different inclusion/exclusion criteria (e.g., as in Buyske et al., 2006; Dick et al., 2006, and as in Luciano et al., 2006; Wainwright et al., 2006), the question arises as to whether any of the reported signals would survive if a conservative but traditional approach to correcting for multiple comparisons were applied.

Fourth, these studies used a variety of designs and methodologies, analyzing both pooled DNAs for groups of individuals and individual DNAs, recruiting family members and singletons, and covering the genome with genetic markers at highly variable densities. All of these "differences and similarities" need to be carefully taken into account when considering the patterns of consistencies and inconsistencies in these findings. Fifth, none of these studies were specifically built to investigate the genetic

6 Candidate gene: A gene whose function may be associated with a trait.

7 Autosomal: Any chromosome besides the sex chromosomes of X and Y.

bases of intelligence, however defined. In fact, the same genetic data were used to investigate linkage/association with multiple other phenotypes in different subsamples of the same samples. At this point, the impact of such reutilization of data on inferential statistics has not been carefully appraised, but there have been concerns in the literature regarding the impact of such reutilization on *p*-values, the definition of replicability, and the generalizability of the results (e.g., McCarthy et al., 2008).

In summary, although these scans present interesting data, the reported findings need to be interpreted with caution. In general, we tend to be somewhat less optimistic about the promise, stability, and replicability of these results as compared to what is present in the literature (Posthuma & de Geus, 2006) but consider them as interesting enough to argue that further investigations on the genetic bases of intelligence (broadly defined!) are warranted.

Although these particular scans have not generated specific candidate genes for intelligence, there have been other types of studies implicating specific genetic regions or specific genes. For example, some earlier studies of the *g* factor focused on specific chromosomes; however, although promising *p*-values were presented, they have not resulted in the suggestion of candidate genes. Other studies utilized the information for investigations of mild mental retardation (Butcher, Meaburn, Dale, et al., 2005; Butcher, Meaburn, Knight, et al., 2005) and investigated a set of associated single-nucleotide polymorphisms (SNPs)[8] from these studies in a longitudinal community sample of British twins aged 2–10 (Arden, Harlaar, & Plomin, 2007). Although interesting age- and gender-dependent results were presented, these results, once again, are difficult to interpret. The associated genetic markers, SNPs rs9916849 (2q33.3),[10] rs4128492 (6q25.3), rs2382591 (7q11.21), rs1136141 (11q24.1), and rs726523 (18q22.1), do not reside in coding regions[11] and four of these SNPs are located in regions that do not harbor any known genes. Of interest, perhaps, is that rs1136141 is located in the untranslated region[12] of the heat-shock cognate protein 8 gene (*HSPA8*, a gene that has been studied as a candidate gene for intelligence), and that rs2382591 is located in a region that comparative genetics has shown to be not evolutionarily conserved. It is also noteworthy that none of these SNPs featured in the latest screen for the *g* factor conducted on DNAs from the same study (see earlier and Butcher et al., 2008). Yet, there are some at least partial regional overlaps among these SNPs and those are the "suggestive" regions identified in genome-scans mentioned earlier, with the two closest SNPs on 2q ~2.5 million base pairs apart). Similar to the SNPs discussed above, the Butcher et al.'s SNPs are also located either in intronic[13] or intergenic[14] regions; thus, their functional relatedness to intelligence is difficult to hypothesize. Yet, when considered together as an aggregated set, these SNPs demonstrated a correlation of .11 at $p < 10^{-7}$. Although these might be helpful in the future, at this stage such findings simply contribute to the treasury of data on the connection between intelligence and the genome without triggering any particular hypotheses.

Note, however, that there are "luckier" outcomes for scans for specific, intelligence-associated, cognitive processes. Specifically, in a whole-genome association study of memory that screened more than

8 Single-nucleotide polymorphisms: A variation in the genetic sequence that involves the mutation of a single base pair (A,T,G,C) and can cause a change in the amino acid sequence.

9 rs: reference SNP id.

10 For each chromosomal location, the number indicates the number of the chromosome, the following letter indicates the arm (p for short and q for long arms), and the final number indicates the chromosomal band.

11 Coding region: A region in the gene that codes for a amino acids.

12 Untranslated region: A region of the gene that is not translated.

13 Intronic: A DNA sequence that is within a gene, but does not code for amino acids as opposed to an exonic region that codes for amino acids.

14 Intergenic: Between genes.

500,000 SNPs (Papassotiropoulos et al., 2006), the results revealed the potential effects of an SNP in the *KIBRA* gene. This gene is located at 5q35 and encodes a neuronal protein. The *KIBRA* association has been replicated with it present with some, but not all memory measures in some studies (Bates et al., 2009; Nacmias et al., 2008; Rodriguez-Rodriguez et al., 2009; Schaper, Kolsch, Popp, Wagner, & Jessen, 1123) and not replicated in others (Need et al., 2008). However, this association has already been interpreted rather broadly that this gene exerts potential effect on cognition (note, not memory only!).

The fact that none of the genome scans has resulted in identifying specific genes for intelligence does not mean that there are no candidate genes for intelligence. To the contrary, numerous studies have investigated associations between intelligence, its various facets, and specific genes that were selected to be tested for such association for one reason or another. Some of these investigations are directly related to the scans discussed earlier and capitalize on the findings from those scans (e.g., Comings et al., 2003; Dick et al., 2007; Gosso, van Belzen, et al., 2006; Jones et al., 2004 for association with the cholinergic muscarinic 2 receptor gene, CHRM2, at 7q33), whereas the majority of these candidate gene studies are totally unrelated to the scans, although they may come from the same research groups (e.g., Gosso, de Geus, et al., 2006; Gosso et al., 2008 for association with the synaptosomal-associated protein of 25 kDa gene, SNAP-25, at 20p12).

Here we briefly summarize the pattern of findings resulting from such investigations in general and discuss studies of only a number of selected genes in particular. In general, there have been numerous studies of a variety of candidate genes (for reviews, see Deary et al., 2009; Deary et al., 2006; Grigorenko, 2009; Payton, 2006; Polderman et al., 2006; Shaw, 2007). This list of genes is inclusive of but not limited to (a) neurotransmitters and genes related to their metabolism (e.g., catechol-O-methyl transferase, *COMT* located at 22q11; monoamine oxidase A gene, *MAOA* at Xp11; cholinergic muscarinic 2 receptor, *CHRM2* at 7q33; dopamine D2 receptor, *DRD2* at 11q23; serotonin receptor 2A, *HTR2A* at 13q13; the serotonin transporter gene, *SLC6A4*, at 17q11.2; metabotrophic glutamate receptor, *GRM3* at 7q21; the glutathione transferase zeta 1 gene, *GSTz1*, at 14q24.3; the tryptophan hydroxylase 1 gene, *TPH1*, at 11p15.1; the tryptophan hydroxylase 2 gene, *TPH2*, at 12q21.1; the synapsin III gene, *SYN3*, at 22q12.3l and the adrenergic alpha 2A receptor gene, *ADRA2A* at 10q25); (b) genes related to developmental processes, broadly defined (e.g., cathepsin D, *CTSD* at 11p15; succinic semialdehyde dehydrogenase, *ALDH5A1* at 6p22; type-I membrane protein related to beta-glucosidases, *klotho* at 13q13; brain-derived neurotrophic factor, *BDNF*, at 11p14; muscle segment homeobox 1, *MSX1* at 4p16; synaptosomal-associated protein 25, *SNAP25*, at 20p12; androgen receptor, *AR*, also known as *NR3C4*, at Xq11–12); and (c) genes of variable functions (e.g., heat-shock 70kDa protein 8, *HSPA8* at 11q24; insulin-like growth factor 2 receptor, *IGF2R* at 6q25; prion protein, *PRNP* at 20p13; dystrobrevin binding protein 1 or dysbinding-1, *DTNBP1* at 6p22; apolipoprotein E, *APOE* at 19q13; cystathionine-beta-synthase, *CBS* at 21q22; MHC class II antigen or Major Histocompatibility Complex, class II, DR beta 1 gene, *HLA-DRB1* at 6p21). It is important to note, however, that in many of these studies of genes and cognition, the behavioral variables of interest are defined beyond IQ. In fact, they encompass a whole gamut of characteristics of intelligence and even cognition (e.g., executive functioning, creativity, working memory, and IQ itself). And although replication of the findings from some of these studies has never been attempted or the findings have failed to be replicated, there is a certain amount of consistency in the findings for selected genes. We view establishing these specific associations between genes and intelligence (or cognition, however broadly defined) as a fundamental breakthrough, a switch from the hypothetical decomposition of variance that was characteristic of earlier heritability studies to a firm "grounding" of these heritabilities in the genome. The hope is that by understanding the functions of these genes and their interactive protein networks, the field will gain some additional understanding of how the general biological (and the specific genetic) machinery of intelligence works.

To exemplify this line of work, here we present brief comments on research on three particular genes, *APOE*, *COMT*, and *BDNF*, which are relevant to research on both brain structure and intelligence.

The apolipoprotein E gene (*APOE*) is located on chromosome 19q13 and is responsible for the production of an apoprotein that is essential for the normal catabolism of triglyceride-rich lipoprotein components. This gene has been long studied in the context of research on neuronal development and repair; this research, in turn, is directly related to work on Alzheimer's disease (AD) (Blackman, Worley, & Strittmatter, 2005; Buttini et al., 1999; Rapoport et al., 2008; Teasdale, Murray, & Nicoll, 2005; Teter & Ashford, 2002). The gene is polymorphic,[15] and there are three variants of *APOE* that have been studied extensively: *ApoE2*, *ApoE3*, and *ApoE4*. These variants are responsible for the production of three different isoforms (Apo-ε2, Apo-ε3, and Apo-ε4)[16] of the protein that differ only by single amino acid substitutions, but these substitutions have been shown to be associated with dramatic physiological outcomes. Of these three isoforms, ApoE-ε3 is associated with a normal protein, whereas Apo-ε2 and Apo-ε4 are related to abnormal proteins.

In the context of this discussion, the *ApoE4* allele[17] is of particular interest because it has been associated with atherosclerosis, AD, reduced neurite outgrowth, and impaired cognitive function. To illustrate, a meta-analysis of dozens of studies combining the data from ~20,000 individuals established that possession of the *ApoE4* allele in older people is associated with poorer performance on tests of global cognitive function, episodic memory, and executive function (Small, Rosnick, Fratiglioni, & Backman, 2004). Moreover, it has been shown that young healthy adults who carry the *ApoE4* allele demonstrate altered patterns of brain activity both at rest and during cognitive challenges (Scarmeas & Stern, 2006).

In a pediatric cohort, carrying the *ApoE4* allele was related to having a thinned cortex in the region of the brain, the so-called entorhinal region, where the earliest AD-associated changes are typically registered (Shaw et al., 2007). However, an attempt to find an association between these polymorphisms and the *g* factor in a case control sample of 101 high *g* and 101 average *g* children did not yield positive results (Turic, Fisher, Plomin, & Owen, 2001). Similarly, there are some studies that report a differential pattern of associations for the *ApoE4* allele in young adults. In particular, it has been reported that *ApoE4*, compared to both *ApoE2* and *ApoE3*, is associated with better episodic memory and a smaller neural investment (i.e., "economical" brain activity) in learning and retrieval (Mondadori et al., 2007).

There is also some evidence that the *ApoE2* allele may be protective; however the mechanisms of this differential action of the variants in the *APOE* gene are not understood (Deary et al., 2002; Smith, 2002; Sundstrom et al., 2007). Also, it appears that even in familial AD only a relatively small portion of variation in memory is attributable to *APOE* (Lee, Flaquer, Stern, Tycko, & Mayeux, 2004). Thus, there are many unanswered questions with regard to the connections between the variation in this gene and differences in performance on memory and other cognitive tasks. It has been proposed that when by itself, the *ApoE4* allele does not influence any cognitive domains. Yet, when

15 Polymorphic: A locus with two or more alternative forms.

16 These three allelic variants differ at two single-base variations located in exon 4 at codon positions 112 and 158. The T and C alleles of *APOE* 112T>C (rs429358) and *APOE* 158C>T (rs7412) encode arginine and cysteine, respectively. The variants differ such that *ApoE2* has a T allele at both positions 112 and 158; *ApoE3* has T and C alleles at positions 112 and 158, respectively; and *ApoE4* has C at both positions.

17 Allele: An alternative form of a gene at a locus.

this allele co-occurs with other risk alleles,[18] such as, for example, the risk allele (allele T in the functional exon 2 polymorphism) in the Cathepsin D gene (*CTSD*), the carriers of the two alleles demonstrate scores on cognitive tasks that are substantially lower than when either of the polymorphisms is considered independently (Payton et al., 2006). Thus, understanding this variation and its connection to individual differences in cognition and, subsequently, to the acquisition of AD or not, is of great interest to researchers in a variety of fields.

Likewise, the connections between a protein and its respective isoforms, brain structure, and cognition are of great interest to researchers studying the gene for catechol-O-methyl transferase (COMT). Among the polymorphisms in this gene, there is a single nucleotide substitution (G-to-A), which in turn leads to a valine-to-methionine substitution at codon 158.[19] This polymorphism is typically signified in the literature as the Val158Met variant. The function of this polymorphism is well studied: the Met allele results in a fourfold decrease in enzymatic activity in the prefrontal cortex (Lachman et al., 1996). This functional property of the Met allele results in slower inactivation of dopamine in the prefrontal cortex (Tunbridge, Bannerman, Sharp, & Harrison, 2004; Winterer & Goldman, 2003a).

It has been hypothesized, based on a number of findings in the literature, that slower inactivation of dopamine in the prefrontal cortex and, correspondingly, the possession of the Met allele, may confer a greater efficiency in prefrontal cortical processing (Winterer & Goldman, 2003a) and thus higher IQ and raised functioning of a number of other cognitive processes, including memory and executive functions (Barnett et al., 2007; Shashi et al., 2006; Tunbridge, Harrison, & Weinberger, 2006). Although, in general, the literature seems to be consistent in supporting this general hypothesis, it presents many complexities for the field's understanding of the role of this polymorphism in cognition.

First, there are other polymorphisms in the *COMT* gene that affect dopamine metabolism (e.g., Palmatier et al., 2004). Second, the *COMT* is not the only gene that affects this turnover (i.e., metabolism); in fact, there is evidence indicating the importance of gene-gene interactions in this turnover (e.g., the role of polymorphisms in the DRD2, dopamine receptor D2, gene; Reuter et al., 2005). Third, there are interesting studies showing the differential (in some cases differentially advantageous, in others disadvantageous) impacts of Val and Met on a variety of psychological functions (Stein, Newman, Savitz, & Ramesar, 2006). Fourth, there are inconsistencies with regard to the differential impacts of Val and Mat alleles on brain activation versus behavior patterns (S. J. Bishop, Fossella, Croucher, & Duncan, 2008). Moreover, it appears that not all cognitive tasks are equally sensitive to dopaminergic modulation and, correspondingly, not all cognitive tasks are expected to show the advantage of the Met allele (MacDonald, Carter, Flory, Ferrell, & Manuck, 2007; H.-Y. Tan et al., 2007). And, fifth, there are mixed reports regarding the connection between the Val158Met polymorphism and cognition across the life span (de Frias et al., 2005; Harris et al., 2005).

Likewise, there is an intriguing story involving another Val to Met substitution (Val66Met), in yet a different gene, the brain-derived neurotrophic factor gene, *BDNF*. The BDNF protein is found in the central and peripheral nervous systems; it is engaged in both the survival of existing neurons and synapses as well as the growth and differentiation of new ones. In the brain, it is expressed widely and is notably present in the hippocampus, cortex, and basal forebrain. The Val66Met polymorphism alters the activity-dependent secretion of BDNF. This polymorphism has been reported to be associated with cognitive functioning, again, broadly defined. Yet, the pattern of the results is curiously inconsistent. Specifically, a substantial portion of the reports indicate

18 Risk allele: An alternate form of a gene that is associated with risk.

19 Codon: A sequence of three base pairs coding for a single amino acid.

that the Met allele, which is associated with a reduced secretion of BDNF, affects long-term memory via its influence on the presence of BDNF in the hippocampus but has little impact on working memory or other cognitive processes or IQ (Egan et al., 2003). The impact of the Met allele on long-term memory has been reasserted by a number of studies (Dempster et al., 2005; Echeverria et al., 2005; Hariri et al., 2003; Y. L. Tan et al., 2005) and has failed to be reproduced in only one study (Strauss et al., 2004). Thus, there is a growing impression that the Met allele exerts a domain-specific effect impacting the hippocampus (Hansell et al., 2007). Yet, this impression has been challenged by studies showing that the Met allele may be associated with a decrease in performance on not only long-term memory tasks but also short-term memory (Echeverria et al., 2005; Rybakowski, Borkowska, Czerski, Skibinska, & Hauser, 2003; Rybakowski et al., 2006), IQ-related tasks (Tsai, Hong, Yu, & Chen, 2004), and indicators of fluid intelligence and processing speed (Miyajima et al., 2008). In addition, it has been shown that the Met allele significantly reduces hippocampal and cerebral neocortex volume and that these effects appear to be independent of age and gender (Bueller et al., 2006; Frodl et al., 2007; Pezawas et al., 2004). In contrast, other studies have indicated that Met homozygotes[20] score significantly higher than heterozygotes[21] and Val homozygotes on a set of cognitive tasks, including the Raven's matrices, an essential measure of *g* (e.g., Harris et al., 2006). Yet, it has been shown that the Met allele appears to be playing a protective role in certain neurological conditions and is associated with improved nonverbal reasoning skills in the elderly (Oroszi et al., 2006; Zivadinov et al., 2007).

In summary, there is a lot to sort out here. Although the importance of genetic factors to the development of intelligence and intelligence-related cognitive processing is widely acknowledged, and the field appears to be accepting of the role of specific genes such as *APOE*, *COMT*, and *BDNF*, the specific neurocognitive processes underlying their involvement continue to be a matter of debate. There could be multiple reasons for such a state of affairs.

First confirmation of the specific genes that form these genetic factors has proven difficult. While positive evidence of association has been reported for several interesting genes, thus far there has not been widespread success in replicating reported associations. Even though there are publications that present findings at borderline levels of *p*-values (e.g., $p = .048$), these evaporate when corrections for multiple comparisons are introduced (e.g., Younger et al., 2005). In general, it is assumed that the effect sizes of specific genes involved in complex human traits are small (Greenwood & Parasuraman, 2003). Correspondingly, special attention needs to be given to designing powerful studies with a large N that displays as much genetic homogeneity as possible. Second, there are sometimes contradictory results with regard to an association of a particular gene/gene variant and cognition, albeit with different intelligence-related processes, as reported by the same or related groups of investigators (e.g., Reuter, Ott, Vaitl, & Hennig, 2007; Reuter et al., 2005). This suggests that findings might be presented partially, and such partiality might, once again, affect the corresponding *p*-values. Third, looking at such a diverse picture of findings, it has been rather difficult to systematically distinguish between false positive findings, pleiotropic effects of genes on multiple cognitive processes, and the role of the *g*-factor (Starr, Fox, Harris, Deary, & Whalley, 2008). As mentioned above, very few studies actually limit themselves as "true" indicators of the *g* factor (i.e., some kind of summative indicator of multiple intelligence-related measures). Most studies employ and analyze a variety of intelligence-related indicators. Thus, similar to the findings obtained from genome scans, the field unequivocally supports the

20 Homozygote: A combination of same alleles on both (maternal and paternal) chromosomes at a given locus.

21 Heterozygotes: A combination of different alleles on both chromosomes at a given locus.

idea of the involvement of genetic factors in the development of intelligence and abilities, but it is far from able to generate a cohesive picture of the genetic machinery behind these factors.

In Place of Conclusion

In view of the lack of cohesiveness in our understanding of the genetic machinery of intelligence and intelligence-related processes, what can be said regarding the Chinese initiative described by CNN? Our answer to this question is that such an initiative is premature. Not only is it premature because there is no diagnostic tool to identify the DNA profile predisposing for intellectual giftedness, it is also premature because even if there were such a profile, it is unclear what kinds of environments should be formed for the individuals possessing such a profile. Most important, however, it is premature for the very reason that we continue to value and study individual differences in cognitive functions in humans – to celebrate and promote human diversity, not to control or constrain it.

References

Ando, J., Ono, Y., & Wright, M. J. (2001). Genetic structure of spatial and verbal working memory. *Behavior Genetics*, 31, 615–624.

Arden, R., Harlaar, N., & Plomin, R. (2007). Sex differences in childhood associations between DNA markers and general cognitive ability. *Journal of Individual Differences*, 28, 161–164.

Barnett, J. H., Heron, J., Ring, S. M., Golding, J., Goldman, D., Xu, K., et al. (2007). Gender-specific effects of the catechol-O-methyltransferase Val(108)/(158)Met polymorphism on cognitive function in children. *American Journal of Psychiatry*, 164, 142–149.

Bartels, M., Rietveld, M. J. H., Van Baal, G. C. M., & Boomsma, D. I. (2002). Genetic and environmental influences on the development of intelligence. *Behavior Genetics*, 32, 237–249.

Bates, T. C., Price, J. F., Harris, S. E., Marioni, R. E., Fowkes, F. G., Stewart, M. C., et al. (2009). Association of KIBRA and memory. *Neuroscience Letters*, 458, 140–143.

Beaujean, A. A. (2005). Heritability of cognitive abilities as measured by mental chronometric tasks: A meta-analysis. *Intelligence*, 33, 187–201.

Bishop, E. G., Cherny, S. S., Corley, R., Plomin, R., DeFries, J. C., & Hewitt, J. K. (2003). Development genetic analysis of general cognitive ability from 1 to 12 years in a sample of adoptees, biological siblings, and twins. *Intelligence*, 31, 31–49.

Bishop, S. J., Fossella, J., Croucher, C. J., & Duncan, J. (2008). COMT val158met genotype affects recruitment of neural mechanisms supporting fluid intelligence. *Cerebral Cortex*, 18, 2132–2140.

Blackman, J. A., Worley, G., & Strittmatter, W. J. (2005). Apolipoprotein E and brain injury: Implications for children. *Developmental Medicine & Child Neurology*, 47, 64–70.

Bouchard, T. J., Jr., & McGue, M. (2003). Genetic and environmental influences on human psychological differences. *Journal of Neurobiology*, 54, 4–45.

Brant, A., Haberstick, B., Corley, R., Wadsworth, S., DeFries, J. C., & Hewitt, J. K. (2009). The developmental etiology of high IQ. *Behavior Genetics*, 39, 393–405.

Bueller, J. A., Aftab, M., Sen, S., Gomez-Hassan, D., Burmeister, M., & Zubieta, J. K. (2006). BDNF Val66Met allele is associated with reduced hippocampal volume in healthy subjects. *Biological Psychiatry*, 59, 812–815.

Butcher, L. M., Davis, O. S. P., Craig, I. W., & Plomin, R. (2008). Genome-wide quantitative trait locus association scan of general cognitive ability using pooled DNA and 500K single nucleotide polymorphism microarrays. *Genes, Brain and Behavior* 7, 435–446.

Butcher, L. M., Kennedy, J. K., & Plomin, R. (2006). Generalist genes and cognitive neuroscience. *Current Opinion in Neurobiology*, 16, 145–151.

Butcher, L. M., Meaburn, E., Dale, P. S., Sham, P., Schalkwyk, L., Craig, I. W., et al. (2005). Association analysis of mild mental impairment using DNA pooling to screen 432 brain-expressed SNPs. *Molecular Psychiatry*, 10, 384–392.

Butcher, L. M., Meaburn, E., Knight, J., Sham, P. C., Schalkwyk, L. C., Craig, I. W., et al. (2005). SNPs, microarrays, and pooled DNA: Identification of four loci associated with mild mental impairment in a sample of 6,000 children. *Human Molecular Genetics*, 14, 1315–1325.

Buttini, M., Orth, M., Bellosta, S., Akeefe, H., Pitas, R. E., Wyss-Coray, T., et al. (1999). Expression of human apolipoprotein E3 or E4 in the brains of Apoe-/- mice: Isoform-specific effects on neurodegeneration. *Journal of Neuroscience*, *19*, 4867–4880.

Buyske, S., Bates, M. E., Gharani, N., Matise, T. C., Tischfield, J. A., & Manowitz, P. (2006). Cognitive traits link to human chromosomal regions. *Behavior Genetics*, *36*, 65–76.

Cardon, L. R., & Fulker, D. W. (1993). Genetics of specific cognitive abilities. In R. Plomin & G. E. McClearn (Eds.), *Nature, nurture and psychology* (pp. 99–120). Washington, DC: American Psychological Association.

Carroll, J. B. (1993). *Human cognitive abilities*. New York, NY: Cambridge University Press.

Cianciolo, A. T., & Sternberg, R. J. (2004). *A brief history of intelligence*. Malden, MA: Blackwell.

Comings, D. E., Wu, S., Rostamkhani, M., McGue, M., Iacono, W. G., Cheng, L. S., et al. (2003). Role of the cholinergic muscarinic 2 receptor (CHRM2) gene in cognition. *Molecular Psychiatry*, *8*, 10–13.

Davis, O. S. P., Kovas, Y., Harlaar, N., Busfield, P., McMillan, A., Frances, J., et al. (2008). Generalist genes and the Internet generation: Etiology of learning abilities by web testing at age 10. *Genes, Brain and Behavior*, *7*, 455–462.

de Frias, C. M., Annerbrink, K., Westberg, L., Eriksson, E., Adolfsson, R., & Nilsson, L.-G. (2005). Catechol-O-Methyltransferase Val158Met polymorphism is associated with cognitive performance in nondemented adults. *Journal of Cognitive Neuroscience*, *17*, 1018–1025.

de Geus, E., Wright, M., Martin, N., & Boomsma, D. (2001). Editorial: Genetics of brain function and cognition. *Behavior Genetics*, *31*(6), 489–495.

Deary, I. J. (2000). *Looking down on human intelligence: From psychometrics to the brain*. Oxford, UK: Oxford University Press.

Deary, I. J., Johnson, W., & Houlihan, L. (2009). Genetic foundations of human intelligence. *Human Genetics*, *126*, 215–232.

Deary, I. J., Spinath, F. M., & Bates, T. C. (2006). Genetics of intelligence. *European Journal of Human Genetics*, *14*, 690–700.

Deary, I. J., Whiteman, M. C., Pattie, A., Starr, J. M., Hayward, C., Wright, A. F., et al. (2002). Cognitive change and the APOE epsilon 4 allele. *Nature*, *481*, 932.

Dempster, E., Toulopoulou, T., McDonald, C., Bramon, E., Walshe, M., Filbey, F., et al. (2005). Association between BDNF val66 met genotype and episodic memory. *American Journal of Medical Genetics. Neuropsychiatric Genetics* *134*, 73–75.

Devlin, B., Daniels, M., & Roeder, K. (1997). The heritability of IQ. *Nature*, *388*, 468–471.

Dick, D. M., Aliev, F., Bierut, L., Goate, A., Rice, J., Hinrichs, A., et al. (2006). Linkage analyses of IQ in the collaborative study on the genetics of alcoholism (COGA) sample. *Behavior Genetics*, *36*, 77–86.

Dick, D. M., Aliev, F., Kramer, J., Wang, J. C., Hinrichs, A., Bertelsen, S., et al. (2007). Association of CHRM2 with IQ: Converging evidence for a gene influencing intelligence. *Behavior Genetics*, *37*, 265–272.

Echeverria, D., Woods, J. S., Heyer, N. J., Rohlman, D. S., Farin, F. M., Bittner, A. C. J., et al. (2005). Chronic low level mercury exposure, BDNF polymorphism, and associations with cognitive and motor function. *Neurotoxicology and Teratology*, *27*, 781–796.

Edmonds, C. J., Isaacs, E. B., Visscher, P. M., Rogers, M., Lanigan, J., Singhal, A., et al. (2008). Inspection time and cognitive abilities in twins aged 7 to 17 years: Age-related changes, heritability and genetic covariance. *Intelligence*, *36*, 210–225.

Egan, M. F., Kojima, M., Callicott, J. H., Goldberg, T. E., Kolachana, B. S., Bertolino, A., et al. (2003). The BDNF val66met polymorphism affects activity-dependent secretion of BDNF and human memory and hippocampal function. *Cell*, *112*, 257–269.

Ertl, J. P. (1971). Fourier analysis of evoked potentials and human intelligence. *Nature*, *230*, 525–526.

Fabiani, M., Gratton, G., & Federmeier, K. D. (2007). Event-related brain potentials: Methods, theory, and applications. In J. T. Cacioppo, L. G. Tassinary & G. G. Berntson (Eds.), *Handbook of psychophysiology* (3rd ed., pp. 85–119). New York, NY: Cambridge University Press.

Flint, J. (1999). The genetic basis of cognition. *Brain*, *122*, 2015–2031.

Frazer, K. A., Murray, S. S., Schork, N. J., & Topol, E. J. (2009). Human genetic variation and its contribution to complex traits. *Nature Reviews Genetics*, *10*, 241–251.

Friedman, N. P., Miyake, A., Corley, R. P., Young, S. E., DeFries, J. C., & Hewitt, J. K. (2006). Not all executive functions are related to intelligence. *Psychological Science*, *17*, 172–179.

Friedman, N. P., Miyake, A., Young, S. E., DeFries, J. C., Corley, R. P., & Hewitt, J. K. (2008). Individual differences in executive functions are almost entirely genetic in origin. *Journal of Experimental Psychology*, *137*, 201–225.

Friend, A., DeFries, J. C., & Olson, R. K. (2008). Parental education moderates genetic influences on reading disability. *Psychological Science*, *19*, 1–7.

Frodl, T., Schule, C., Schmitt, G., Born, C., Baghai, T., Zill, P., et al. (2007). Association of the brain-derived neurotrophic factor Val66Met polymorphism with reduced hippocampal volumes in major depression. *Archives of General Psychiatry*, *64*, 410–416.

Galton, F. (1869). *Hereditary genius. An inquiry into its laws and consequences*. London, England: Macmillan.

Gosso, M. F., de Geus, E. J., van Belzen, M. J., Polderman, T. J., Heutink, P., Boomsma, D. I., et al. (2006). The SNAP-25 gene is associated with cognitive ability: Evidence from a family-based study in two independent Dutch cohorts. *Molecular Psychiatry*, *11*, 878–886.

Gosso, M. F., de Geus, E. J. C., Polderman, T. J. C., Boomsma, D. I., Heutink, P., & Posthuma, D. (2008). Common variants underlying cognitive ability: Further evidence for association between the SNAP-25 gene and cognition using a family-based study in two independent Dutch cohorts. *Genes, Brain, & Behavior*, *7*, 355–364.

Gosso, M. F., van Belzen, M., de Geus, E. J., Polderman, J. C., Heutink, P., Boomsma, D. I., et al. (2006). Association between the CHRM2 gene and intelligence in a sample of 304 Dutch families. *Genes, Brain, and Behavior*, *5*, 577–584.

Greenwood, P. M., & Parasuraman, R. (2003). Normal genetic variation, cognition, and aging. *Behavioral & Cognitive Neuroscience Reviews*, *2*, 278–306.

Grigorenko, E. L. (2009). What is so stylish about styles? Comments on the genetic etiology of intellectual style. In L.-F. Zhang & R. J. Sternberg (Eds.), *Perspectives on the nature of intellectual styles* (pp. 233–252). New York, NY: Springer.

Hansell, N. K., James, M. R., Duffy, D. L., Birley, A. J., Luciano, M., Geffen, G. M., et al. (2007). Effect of the BDNF V166M polymorphism on working memory in healthy adolescents. *Genes, Brain, & Behavior*, *6*, 260–268.

Hansell, N. K., Wright, M. J., Geffen, G. M., Geffen, L. B., Smith, G. A., & Martin, N. G. (2001). Genetic influence on ERP slow wave measures of working memory. *Behavior Genetics*, *31*, 603–614.

Harden, K. P., Turkheimer, E., & Loehlin, J. C. (2007). Genotype by environment interaction in adolescent's cognitive aptitude. *Behavior Genetics*, *37*, 273–283.

Hariri, A. R., Goldberg, T. E., Mattay, V. S., Kolachana, B. S., Callicott, J. H., Egan, M. F., et al. (2003). Brain-derived neurotrophic factor val66met polymorphism affects human memory related hippocampal activity and predicts memory performance. *Journal of Neuroscience*, *23*, 6690–6694.

Harris, S. E., Fox, H., Wright, A. F., Hayward, C., Starr, J. M., Whalley, L. J., et al. (2006). The brain-derived neurotrophic factor Val66Met polymorphism is associated with age-related change in reasoning skills. *Molecular Psychiatry*, *11*, 505–513.

Harris, S. E., Wright, A. F., Hayward, C., Starr, J. M., Whalley, L. J., & Deary, I. J. (2005). The functional COMT polymorphism, Val 158 Met, is associated with logical memory and the personality trait intellect/imagination in a cohort of healthy 79 year olds. *Neuroscience Letters*, *385*, 1–6.

Hart, S. A., Petrill, S. A., Thompson, L. A., & Plomin, R. (2009). The ABCs of math: A genetic analysis of mathematics and its links with reading ability and general cognitive ability. *Journal of Educational Psychology*, *101*, 388–402.

Iacono, W. G., Carlson, S. R., Taylor, J., Elkins, I. J., & McGue, M. (1999). Behavioral disinhibition and the development of substance use disorders: Findings from the Minnesota Twin Family Study. *Development and Psychopathology*, *11*, 869–900.

Ignat'ev, M. V. (1934). Opredelinie genotipicheskoi i paratipichskoi obuslovlennostyi pomoshchi bliznetsovogo metoda [The measurement of geneotypic and paratypic influences on continuous characteristics by means of the twin method]. In S. G. Levit (Ed.), *Trudy mediko-biologicheskogo instituta* (pp. 18–31). Moscow: Biomedgiz.

Inlow, J. K., & Restifo, L. L. (2004). Molecular and comparative genetics of mental retardation. *Genetics*, *166*, 835–881.

Jensen, A. R. (1998). *The g factor: The science of mental ability*. New York, NY: Praeger.

Jones, K. A., Porjesz, B., Almasy, L., Bierut, L., Goate, A., Wang, J. C., et al. (2004). Linkage and linkage disequilibrium of evoked EEG oscillations with CHRM2 receptor gene polymorphisms: Implications for human brain dynamics and cognition. *International Journal of Psychophysiology*, 53, 75–90.

Katsanis, J., Iacono, W. G., McGue, M. K., & Carlson, S. R. (1997). P300 event-related potential heritability in monozygotic and dizygotic twins. *Psychophysiology*, 34, 47–58.

Kremen, W. S., Jacobsen, K., Xian, H., Eisen, S. A., Eaves, L. J., Tsuang, M. T., et al. (2007). Genetics of verbal working memory processes: A twin study of middle-aged men. *Neuropsychology*, **21**, 569–580.

Lachman, H. M., Papolos, D. F., Saito, T., Yu, Y. M., Szumlanski, C. L., & Weinshilboum, R. M. (1996). Human catechol-O-methyltransferase pharmacogenetics: Description of a functional polymorphism and its potential application to neuropsychiatric disorders. *Pharmacogenetics*, 6, 243–250.

Lee, J. H., Flaquer, A., Stern, Y., Tycko, B., & Mayeux, R. (2004). Genetic influences on memory performance in familial Alzheimer disease. *Neurology*, 62, 414–421.

Luciano, M., Posthuma, D., Wright, M. J., de Geus, E. J. C., Smith, G. A., Geffen, G. M., et al. (2005). Perceptual speed does not cause intelligence, and intelligence does not cause perceptual speed. *Biological Psychology*, 70, 1–8.

Luciano, M., Wright, M. J., Duffy, D. L., Wainwright, M. A., Zhu, G., Evans, D. M., et al. (2006). Genome-wide scan of IQ finds significant linkage to a quantitative trait locus on 2q. *Behavior Genetics*, 36, 45–55.

Luciano, M., Wright, M. J., Geffen, G. M., Geffen, L. B., Smith, G. A., Evans, D. M., et al. (2003). A genetic two-factor model of the covariation among a subset of Multidimensional Aptitude Battery and Wechsler Adult Intelligence Scale–Revised subtests. *Intelligence*, **31**, 589–605.

Luciano, M., Wright, M. J., Geffen, G. M., Geffen, L. B., Smith, G. A., & Martin, N. G. (2004). A genetic investigation of the covariation among inspection time, choice reaction time, and IQ subtest scores. *Behavior Genetics*, 34, 41–50.

Luciano, M., Wright, M. J., Smith, G. A., Geffen, G. M., Geffen, L. B., & Martin, N. G. (2001). Genetic covariance among measures of information processing speed, working memory, and IQ. *Behavior Genetics*, **31**, 581–592.

MacDonald III, A. W., Carter, C. S., Flory, J. D., Ferrell, R. E., & Manuck, S. B. (2007). COMT val158Met and executive control: A test of the benefit of specific deficits to translational research. *Journal of Abnormal Psychology*, **116**, 306–312.

McCarthy, M. I., Abecasis, G. R., Cardon, L. R., Goldstein, D. B., Little, J., Ioannidis, J. P., et al. (2008). Genome-wide association studies for complex traits: Consensus, uncertainty and challenges. *Nature Reviews Genetics*, 9, 356–369.

McGue, M., Bouchard, T. J., Jr., Iacono, W. G., & Lykken, D. T. (1993). Behavioral genetics of cognitive ability: A life-span perspective. In R. Plomin & G. E. McClearn (Eds.), *Nature, nurture, and psychology* (pp. 59–76). Washington, DC: American Psychological Association.

Mondadori, C. R. A., de Quervain, D. J.-F., Buchmann, A., Mustovic, H., Wollmer, M. A., Schmidt, C. F., et al. (2007). Better memory and neural efficiency in young Apolipoprotein E e4 carriers. *Cerebral Cortex*, 17, 1934–1947.

Nacmias, B., Bessi, V., Bagnoli, S., Tedde, A., Cellini, E., Piccini, C., et al. (2008). KIBRA gene variants are associated with episodic memory performance in subjective memory complaints. *Neuroscience Letters*, 436, 145–147.

Naples, A. J., Chang, J. T., Katz, L., & Grigorenko, E. L. (2009). Same or different? Insights into the etiology of phonological awareness and rapid naming. *Biological Psychology*, 80, 226–239.

Need, A. C., Attix, D. K., McEvoy, J. M., Cirulli, E. T., Linney, K. N., Wagoner, A. P., et al. (2008). Failure to replicate effect of Kibra on human memory in two large cohorts of European origin. *American Journal of Medical Genetics, Part B, Neuropsychiatric Genetics*, ***147B***, 667–668.

Neale, M. C. (2009). Biometrical models in behavioral genetics. In Y.-K. Kim (Ed.), *Handbook of behavior genetics* (pp. 15–33). New York, NY: Springer.

Oroszi, G., Lapteva, L., Davis, E., Yarboro, C. H., Weickert, T., Roebuck-Spencer, T., et al. (2006). The Met66 allele of the functional Val66Met polymorphism in the brain-derived neurotrophic factor gene confers protection against neurocognitive dysfunction in systemic lupus erythematosus. *Annals of the Rheumatic Diseases*, 65, 1330–1335.

Palmatier, M. A., Pakstis, A. J., Speed, W., Paschou, P., Goldman, D., Odunsi, A., et al. (2004). COMT haplotypes suggest P2 promoter region relevance for schizophrenia. *Molecular Psychiatry*, 9, 1359–4184.

Papassotiropoulos, A., Stephan, D. A., Huentelman, M. J., Hoerndli, F. J., Craig, D. W., Pearson, J. V., et al. (2006). Common Kibra alleles are associated with human memory performance. *Science*, 314, 475–478.

Patrick, C. L. (2000). Genetic and environmental influences on the development of cognitive abilities: Evidence from the field of developmental behavior genetics. *Journal of School Psychology*, 38, 79–108.

Payton, A. (2006). Investigating cognitive genetics and its implications for the treatment of cognitive deficit. *Genes, Brain, & Behavior*, 5 Suppl 1, 44–53.

Payton, A., Van Den Boogerd, E., Davidson, Y., Gibbons, L., Ollier, W., Rabbitt, P., et al. (2006). Influence and interactions of cathepsin D, HLA-DRB1 and APOE on cognitive abilities in an older non-demented population. *Genes, Brain & Behavior*, 5, 23–31.

Petrill, S. A., Lipton, P. A., Hewitt, J. K., Plomin, R., Cherny, S. S., Corley, R., et al. (2004). Genetic and environmental contributions to general cognitive ability through the first 16 years of life. *Developmental Psychology*, 40, 805–812.

Pezawas, L., Verchinski, B. A., Mattay, V. S., Callicott, J. H., Kolachana, B. S., Straub, R. E., et al. (2004). The brain-derived neurotrophic factor val66met polymorphism and variation in human cortical morphology. *Journal of Neuroscience*, 24, 10099–10102.

Plomin, R., & Spinath, F. M. (2004). Intelligence: genetics, genes, and genomics. *Journal of Personality & Social Psychology*, 86, 112–129.

Polderman, T. J. C., Gosso, M. F., Posthuma, D., Van Beijsterveldt, T. C. E. M., Heutink, P., Verhulst, F. C., et al. (2006). A longitudinal twin study on IQ, executive functioning, and attention problems during childhood and early adolescence. *Acta Neurologica Belgica*, 106, 191–207.

Polderman, T. J. C., Posthuma, D., De Sonneville, L. M. J., Stins, J. F., Verhulst, F. C., & Boomsma, D. I. (2007). Genetic analyses of the stability of executive functioning during childhood. *Biological Psychology*, 76, 11–20.

Posthuma, D. (2009). Multivariate genetic analysis. In Y.-K. Kim (Ed.), *Handbook of behavior genetics* (pp. 47–59). New York, NY: Springer.

Posthuma, D., & de Geus, E. J. C. (2006). Progress in the molecular genetic study of intelligence. *Current Directions in Psychological Science*, 15, 151–155.

Posthuma, D., Luciano, M., Geus, E. J., Wright, M. J., Slagboom, P. E., Montgomery, G. W., et al. (2005). A genomewide scan for intelligence identifies quantitative trait loci on 2q and 6p. *American Journal of Human Genetics*, 77, 318–326.

Posthuma, D., Neale, M. C., Boomsma, D. I., & de Geus, E. J. C. (2001). Are smarter brains running faster? Heritability of alpha peak frequency, IQ, and their interrelation. *Behavior Genetics*, 31, 567–579.

Price, T. S., Eley, T. C., Dale, P. S., Stevenson, J., Saudino, K., & Plomin, R. (2000). Genetic and environmental covariation between verbal and nonverbal cognitive development in infancy. *Child Development*, 71, 948–959.

Rapoport, M., Wolf, U., Herrmann, N., Kiss, A., Shammi, P., Reis, M., et al. (2008). Traumatic brain injury, Apolipoprotein E-epsilon4, and cognition in older adults: A two-year longitudinal study. *Journal of Neuropsychiatry & Clinical Neurosciences*, 20, 68–73.

Reuter, M., Ott, U., Vaitl, D., & Hennig, J. (2007). Impaired executive control is associated with a variation in the promoter region of the Tryptophan Hydroxylase 2 gene. *Journal of Cognitive Neuroscience*, 19, 401–408.

Reuter, M., Peters, K., Schroeter, K., Koebke, W., Lenardon, D., Bloch, B., et al. (2005). The influence of the dopaminergic system on cognitive functioning: A molecular genetic approach. *Behavioural Brain Research*, 164, 93–99.

Reynolds, C. A., Finkel, D., McArdle, J. J., Gatz, M., Berg, S., & Pedersen, N. L. (2005). Quantitative genetic analysis of latent growth curve models of cognitive abilities in adulthood. *Developmental Psychology*, 41, 3–16.

Reznick, J. S., Corley, R., & Robinson, J. A. (1997). A longitudinal twin study of intelligence in the second year. *Monographs of the Society for Research in Child Development, serial no.* 249, 62(1).

Rietveld, M. J. H., Dolan, C. V., van Baal, G. C. M., & Boomsma, D. I. (2003). A twin study of differentiation of cognitive abilities in childhood. *Behavior Genetics*, 33, 367–381.

Rijsdijk, F. V., Vernon, P. A., & Boomsma, D. I. (2002). Application of hierarchical genetic models to Raven and WAIS subtests: A Dutch twin study. *Behavior Genetics*, 32, 199–210.

Risch, N. (1990). Linkage strategies for genetically complex traits. II. The power of affected relative pairs. *American Journal of Human Genetics*, *46*(2), 229–241.

Rodriguez-Rodriguez, E., Infante, J., Llorca, J., Mateo, I., Sanchez-Quintana, C., Garcia-Gorostiaga, I., et al. (2009). Age-dependent association of KIBRA genetic variation and Alzheimer's disease risk. *Neurobiology of Aging*, *30*, 322–324.

Rybakowski, J. K., Borkowska, A., Czerski, P. M., Skibinska, M., & Hauser, J. (2003). Polymorphism of the brain-derived neurotrophic factor gene and performance on a cognitive prefrontal test in bipolar patients. *Bipolar Disorders*, *5*, 468–472.

Rybakowski, J. K., Borkowska, A., Skibinska, M., Szczepankiewicz, A., Kapelski, P., Leszczynska-Rodziewicz, A., et al. (2006). Prefrontal cognition in schizophrenia and bipolar illness in relation to Val66Met polymorphism of the brain-derived neurotrophic factor gene. *Psychiatry & Clinical Neurosciences*, *60*, 70–76.

Scarmeas, N., & Stern, Y. (2006). Imaging studies and APOE genotype in persons at risk for Alzheimer's disease. *Current Psychiatry Reports*, *8*, 11–17.

Schaper, K., Kolsch, H., Popp, J., Wagner, M., & Jessen, F. (1123). KIBRA gene variants are associated with episodic memory in healthy elderly. *Neurobiology of Aging*, *29*, 1123–1125.

Shashi, V., Keshavan, M. S., Howard, T. D., Berry, M. N., Basehore, M. J., Lewandowski, E., et al. (2006). Cognitive correlates of a functional COMT polymorphism in children with 22q11.2 deletion syndrome. *Clinical Genetics*, *69*, 234–238.

Shaw, P. (2007). Intelligence and the developing human brain. *Bioessays*, *29*, 962–973.

Shaw, P., Lerch, J. P., Pruessner, J. C., Taylor, K. N., Rose, A. B., Greenstein, D., et al. (2007). Cortical morphology in children and adolescents with different apolipoprotein E gene polymorphisms: an observational study. *Lancet Neurology*, *6*, 494–500.

Singer, J. J., MacGregor, A. J., Cherkas, L. F., & Spector, T. D. (2006). Genetic influences on cognitive function using the Cambridge Neuropsychological Test Automated Battery. *Intelligence*, *34*, 421–428.

Small, B. J., Rosnick, C. B., Fratiglioni, L., & Backman, L. (2004). Apolipoprotein E and cognitive performance: A meta-analysis. *Psychology & Aging*, *14*, 592–600.

Smith, J. D. (2002). Apolipoprotiens and aging: emerging mechanisms. *Ageing Research Reviews*, *1*, 345–365.

Spearman, C. (1904). General intelligence, objectively determined and measured. *American Journal of Psychology*, *15*, 201–292.

Starr, J. M., Fox, H., Harris, S. E., Deary, I. J., & Whalley, L. J. (2008). GSTz1 genotype and cognitive ability. *Psychiatric Genetics*, *18*, 211–212.

Stein, D. J., Newman, T. K., Savitz, J., & Ramesar, R. (2006). Warriors versus worriers: The role of COMT gene variants. *Cns Spectrums*, *11*, 745–758.

Sternberg, R. J. (1996). *Successful intelligence*. New York, NY: Simon & Schuster.

Strauss, J., Barr, C. L., George, C. J., Ryan, C. M., King, N., Shaikh, S., et al. (2004). BDNF and COMT polymorphisms: Relation to memory phenotypes in young adults with childhood-onset mood disorder. *NeuroMolecular Medicine*, *5*, 181–192.

Sundstrom, A., Nilsson, L. G., Cruts, M., Adolfsson, R., Van Broeckhoven, C., & Nyberg, L. (2007). Fatigue before and after mild traumatic brain injury: Pre-post-injury comparisons in relation to Apolipoprotein E. *Brain Injury*, *21*, 1049–1054.

Tan, H.-Y., Chen, Q., Goldberg, T. E., Mattay, V. S., Meyer-Lindenberg, A., Weinberger, D. R., et al. (2007). Catechol-O-methyltransferase Val158Met modulation of prefrontal-parietal-striatal brain systems during arithmetic and temporal transformations in working memory. *Journal of Neuroscience*, *27*, 13393–13401.

Tan, Y. L., Zhou, D. F., Cao, L. Y., Zou, Y. Z., Wu, G. Y., & Zhang, X. Y. (2005). Effect of the BDNF Val66Met genotype on episodic memory in schizophrenia. *Schizophrenia Research*, *77*, 355–356.

Teasdale, G. M., Murray, G. D., & Nicoll, J. A. (2005). The association between APOE epsilon4, age and outcome after head injury: A prospective cohort study. *Brain*, *128*, 2556–2561.

Teter, B., & Ashford, J. W. (2002). Neuroplasticity in Alzheimer's disease. *Journal of Neuroscience Research*, *70*, 402–437.

Tsai, S. J., Hong, C. J., Yu, Y. W., & Chen, T. J. (2004). Association study of a brain-derived neurotrophic factor (BDNF) Val66Met polymorphism and personality trait and intelligence in healthy young females. *Neuropsychobiology*, *49*, 13–16.

Tunbridge, E. M., Bannerman, D. M., Sharp, T., & Harrison, P. J. (2004). Catechol-O-methyltransferase inhibition improves set-shifting performance and elevates stimulated dopamine release in the rat prefrontal cortex. *Journal of Neuroscience, 24*, 5331–5335.

Tunbridge, E. M., Harrison, P. J., & Weinberger, D. R. (2006). Catechol-o-methyltransferase, cognition, and psychosis: Val158Met and beyond. *Biological Psychiatry, 60*, 141–151.

Turic, D., Fisher, P. J., Plomin, R., & Owen, M. J. (2001). No association between apolipoprotein E polymorphisms and general cognitive ability in children. *Neuroscience Letters, 299*, 97–100.

van Baal, G. C. M., Boomsma, D. I., & de Geus, E. J. C. (2001). Longitudinal genetic analysis of EEG coherence in young twins. *Behavior Genetics, 31*, 637–651.

van Baal, G. C. M., van Beijsterveldt, C. E. M., Molenaar, P. C. M., Boomsma, D. I., & de Geus, E. J. C. (2001). A genetic perspective on the developing brain: Electrophysiological indices of neural functioning in young and adolescent twins. *European Psychologist, 6*, 254–263.

van Beijsterveldt, C. E., & Boomsma, D. I. (1994). Genetics of the human electroencephalogram (EEG) and event-related brain potentials (ERPs): A review. *Human Genetics, 94*, 319–330.

van Beijsterveldt, C. E., Molenaar, P. C., de Geus, E. J., & Boomsma, D. I. (1998a). Genetic and environmental influences on EEG coherence. *Behavior Genetics, 28*, 443–453.

van Beijsterveldt, C. E., Molenaar, P. C., de Geus, E. J., & Boomsma, D. I. (1998b). Individual differences in P300 amplitude: A genetic study in adolescent twins. *Biological Psychology, 47*, 97–120.

Van Der Maas, H. L. J., Dolan, C. V., Grasman, R. P. P. P., Wicherts, J. M., Huizenga, H. M., & Raijmakers, M. E. J. (2006). A dynamical model of general intelligence: The positive manifold of intelligence by mutualism. *Psychological Review, 113*, 842–861.

Van Der Sluis, S., Willemsen, G., de Geus, E. J. C., Boomsma, D. I., & Posthuma, D. (2008). Gene-environment interaction in adults' IQ scores: Measure of past and present environment. *Behavior Genetics, 38*, 348–360.

van Leeuwen, M., van den Berg, S. M., & Boomsma, D. I. (2008). A twin-family study of general IQ. *Learning and Individual Differences 18*, 76–88.

Wainwright, M. A., Wright, M. J., Geffen, G., Luciano, M., & Martin, N. (2005). The genetic basis of academic achievement on the Queensland Core Skills Test and its shared genetic variance with IQ. *Behavior Genetics*, 35(2), 133–145.

Wainwright, M. A., Wright, M. J., Geffen, G. M., Geffen, L. B., Luciano, M., & Martin, N. G. (2004). Genetic and environmental sources of covariance between reading tests used in neuropsychological assessment and IQ subtests. *Behavior Genetics, 34*, 365–376.

Wainwright, M. A., Wright, M. J., Luciano, M., Montgomery, G. W., Geffen, G. M., & Martin, N. G. (2006). A linkage study of academic skills defined by the Queensland Core Skills Test. *Behavior Genetics, 36*, 56–64.

Walker, S. O., Petrill, S. A., Spinath, F. M., & Plomin, R. (2004). Nature, nurture and academic achievement: A twin study of teacher assessments of 7-year-olds. *British Journal of Educational Psychology, 74*, 323–342.

Watson, J. B. (1924). *Behaviorism*. Chicago: University of Chicago Press.

Winterer, G., & Goldman, D. (2003a). Genetics of human prefrontal function. *Brain Research Reviews, 43*, 134–163.

Winterer, G., & Goldman, D. (2003b). Genetics of human prefrontal function. *Brain Research Reviews, 43*, 134–163.

Younger, W. Y. Y., Shih-Jen, T., Chen-Jee, H., Ming-Chao, C., Chih-Wei, Y., & Tai-Jui, C. (2005). Association study of a functional MAOA-uVNTR gene polymorphism and cognitive function in healthy females. *Neuropsychobiology, 52*, 77–82.

Zivadinov, R., Weinstock-Guttman, B., Benedict, R., Tamano-Blanco, M., Hussein, S., Abdelrahman, N., et al. (2007). Preservation of gray matter volume in multiple sclerosis patients with the Met allele of the rs6265 (Val66Met) SNP of brain-derived neurotrophic factor. *Human Molecular Genetics, 16*, 2659–2668.

CHAPTER 6

Developing Intelligence through Instruction

Raymond S. Nickerson

Few topics in psychology have motivated more commentary and controversy than "intelligence." What is it? What determines it? How should it be measured? What uses should be made of its assessment in practical decision making? Among these and numerous closely related questions that have generated debate, none has evoked more passion than that of whether intelligence can be modified intentionally, say through instruction. That this should generate keen interest is not surprising in view of the prevailing assumption that one's level of intelligence limits what one can be expected to achieve in life and of the role that intelligence assessment has come to play in determining educational and career opportunities. The question of whether intelligence can be modified through instruction is the focus of this chapter.

The chapter begins with a brief consideration of what intelligence is taken to be for present purposes. There follows a discussion of reasons for believing intelligence, so conceptualized, to be malleable. Some organized efforts to develop intelligence through instruction are noted and briefly described. Specific teaching objectives of efforts to enhance intelligence – or intelligent behavior – through instruction are suggested. The conclusion that is drawn is that enhancing intelligence through instruction is an ambitious, but attainable, goal. How best to pursue that goal is a continuing challenge for research.

What Is Intelligence and What Determines It?

Numerous answers have been proposed to the question of what intelligence is, and debate on the matter continues. Many adjectives have been used to modify *intelligence*, among them *general* (Spearman, 1904), *social* (Thorndike, 1920), *fluid* and *crystallized* (Catell, 1963), *academic* and *practical* (Sternberg & Wagner, 1986), *interactional* and *analytic* (Levinson, 1995), *neural, experiential,* and *reflective* (Perkins, 1995), *creative* (Sternberg, 1999), *emotional* (Mayer, 1999), *verbal* and *perceptual* (Kaufman, 2000), and *visual-spatial, bodily-kinesthetic, musical, interpersonal, intrapersonal, linguistic* and *logical-mathematical* (Gardner, 2006). It is not always clear whether such modifiers are intended to be taken as indicative of different types of intelligence, of different ways in which an integral ability manifests itself to suit different demands, or something else.

In short, intelligence is a vexed concept; moreover, it seems likely to remain so. For purposes of this chapter, I shall take as a working definition of intelligence the ability to learn, to reason well, to solve novel problems, and to deal effectively with the challenges – often unpredictable – that confront one in daily life. This is consistent with an increased interest in recent years of studying intelligence, or cognition more generally, in the context of performing meaningful tasks rather than studying it only in the psychological laboratory with tasks of little intrinsic interest to those asked to perform them.

IQ, Rationality and Expertise

One would like to believe that a high IQ is a guarantor of a high level of intellectual performance, or at least an antidote to irrational thinking and behavior, but empirical support for such a belief is not strong. In a series of experiments, Stanovich and West (2008) found the prevalence of myside bias and a preference for one-sided (as distinct from balanced) arguments to be independent of general cognitive ability as indicated by SAT scores. Other investigators have found that cognitive ability does not insulate one from the false consensus effect (see Ross, Greene, & House, 1977) and overconfidence (Krueger, 2000), among other cognitive infelicities. Nor does having a high IQ assure ethical and socially acceptable behavior. History is replete with examples of people who quite probably would have scored very well on an IQ test but who did despicable things. In *The Mask of Sanity*, Cleckley (1941/1988) documents many cases of exceptionally bright sociopaths.

Stanovich (1994) describes rationality as less a matter of capability than of a *disposition* to shape one's beliefs by evidence and to strive to maintain consistency among those beliefs. He argues that standard methods for assessing intelligence do not assess such dispositions, and that examples of a lack of the disposition for rationality among people who perform well on tests of intellectual capacity are so common as to be grounds for recognition of *dysrationalia*, which he defines as "the inability to think and behave rationally, despite adequate intelligence" (p. 11).

Conversely poor showing on an IQ test guarantees neither poor performance on other cognitively demanding tasks nor antisocial behavior.

If proof is needed that IQ is not always an accurate predictor in individual cases, one is provided an observation by the historian of mathematics Eric Temple Bell (1937) regarding Henri Poincaré. Renowned as a mathematician, theoretical physicist, and philosopher/popularizer of science, Poincaré was a man of unquestioned brilliance, a polymath whose published works included contributions to the special theory of relativity and quantum mechanics. According to Bell, Poincaré "submitted to the Binet tests and made such a disgraceful showing that, had he been judged as a child instead of as the famous mathematician he was, he would have been rated – by the tests – as an imbecile" (p. 532). To be sure, IQ tests have evolved considerably since the days of Binet's early experimentation, but using IQ scores to predict the cognitive performance of individuals is still chancy business. That the ability to perform complicated mathematical tasks does not necessarily rest on unusually high intelligence, as measured by IQ tests, gets support from a study by Ceci and Liker (1986) of the performance of harness-racing handicappers, as well as from studies of mathematical creativity among unschooled children who would be unlikely to do well on standardized tests of intelligence (Nuñes, Schliemann, & Carraher, 1993; Saxe, 1988).

Nature plus Nurture

The results of research bear out the commonsense assumption that intelligence, however defined, is the product of genetic and environmental factors in combination. Recognition of this has focused much attention on the question of the relative importance of genetics and environment and on the ways in which the two types of causal factors interact. There have been, and continue to be, strong advocates for opposing points of view. Defenders of the assumption that intelligence is largely inherited include Eysenck (1973), Jensen (1998), and Harris (1998). Proponents of the greater importance of environmental factors include Perkins (1995), Sternberg (1999), and Nisbett (2009).

Teasing apart the two types of influence has proved to be very difficult. Anastasi (1988) notes several factors that contribute to this difficulty, among them the fact that monozygotic twins share a more closely similar environment than do dizygotic twins (Anastasi, 1958; Koch, 1966), while siblings reared together can experience very different psychological environments (Daniels & Plomin, 1985). She recognizes the importance of both heredity and environmental factors as determinants of intelligence, and expressly acknowledges its amenability to modification by environmental interventions.

That the interaction of genetics with environmental factors has yet to be fully understood is demonstrated by the finding by Turkheimer, Haley, Waldron, D'Onofrio, and Gottesman (2003) of a relationship between socioeconomic status and the amount of IQ variance that can be attributed to genetics. The analysis that these researchers performed indicates that for children from high socioeconomic families (as indicated by parental education, occupation, and income) genetics accounted for a relatively large percentage of IQ variation, whereas for children from low socioeconomic families, the shared family environment was the more important factor. The importance of the early home environment as a contributor to shaping the character and capabilities of people who have achieved eminence as adults is well documented (Goertzel, Goertzel, & Goertzel, 1978).

Nisbett (2009) argues that estimates of heritability based on the correlation between the IQs of identical twins raised apart rest on the false assumption that such twins were placed in environments at random. How similar the environments are in which identical twins are placed is unknown, but there are reasons to assume that they are more similar than they would be if random placement were the rule, which means that results from twin studies that have been attributed to genetic variables may have been influenced by environmental factors to an unknown degree. Following an extensive review of work on the factors that affect intelligence, Nisbett concludes that the extent to which intelligence is determined by genetics varies from one population to another and that for any given population, it depends on the circumstances in which that population lives. If the environment is relatively the same for all members of a population and favorable to the growth of intelligence, as it is for upper middle-class families in developed countries, then the heritability of intelligence is likely to be quite high – "perhaps as high as 70 percent" – but if the environment differs greatly for families within a population, as it generally does for the poor, then the environment will play a larger role than genetics as a determinant of differences in intelligence among individuals. He estimates that in the aggregate, the maximum contribution of genetics is probably about 50%, and that the remaining variation is largely due to environmental factors.

The American Psychological Association (APA) Task Force on Intelligence – convened as a result of the debate generated by publication of *The Bell Curve* (Herrnstein & Murray, 1994) – agreed that both genetics and environmental factors contribute substantially to intelligence but did not attempt to quantify the relative contributions (Neisser et al., 1996).

The role of heredity as a determinant of intelligence continues to be an active area of research. For present purposes, the main points to be gleaned from the results of such research to date are these: (1) While the evidence that heredity is an important determinant of intelligence is compelling, (2) the extent to which heredity determines intelligence is unknown, and (3) most estimates of the extent to which heredity determines intelligence leave considerable room for the influence of nonhereditary factors.

Reasons to Believe that Intelligence Is Malleable

The focus of this chapter is on the influence of environmental factors – especially instruction – and it will be apparent that I believe them to be very substantial. In this section I want to consider what appear to me to be some of the more compelling reasons for believing that intelligence is changeable as a consequence of environmental factors.

Effects of Experience on the Central Nervous System

Although the human fetus is assumed to have nearly a full complement of cortical neurons by about six months following conception, the brain continues to develop in several ways for many years, possibly over the entire life span. Experimentation has shown that the neurological development of animals is affected by the richness of the sensory stimulation they receive early in life (Diamond, 1988). The extent to which the results of these studies can be generalized to human infants is debatable, but the importance of children's care and experiences during their early years for their future cognitive development is well established (Zigler, Finn-Stevenson, & Hall, 2002).

Over the first 15 years or so of life, a child's brain appears to grow in several spurts (Epstein, 1978). This has invited speculation that the brain growth that occurs during these spurts provides the neurobiological basis for changes in cognitive functioning of the type hypothesized by stage theories of cognitive development. An extreme form of the view that there are periods during a child's development that are especially conducive to the acquisition of new cognitive abilities holds that if a specific ability is not acquired during the optimal time window, its later acquisition will be more difficult (Hensch, 2004). If critical cognitive abilities form a progression in which the abilities that are acquired earlier are prerequisites to the acquisition of more complicated abilities that normally are acquired later, interruptions of the normal developmental sequence would have cumulative effects. The idea of critical periods has been challenged (Bruer, 1999), but that early experience affects later development seems not to be in question.

Not only does the brain add tissue during the first few years of life, but interconnections among neurons are formed. The specifics of the developing neuronal interconnectedness vary considerably among individuals and are influenced by experience (Draganski, Gaser, Busch, Schuierer, Bogdahn, & May, 2004; Huttenlocher & Dabholkar, 1997). "London taxi drivers have a bigger hippocampus – the center for remembered navigation – than the rest of us; violinists have bigger motor centers associated with the fingers of the left hand" (Kaplan & Kaplan, 2006, p. 297; see also Maguire, Gadian, Johnsrude, Good, Ashburner, Frackowiak, & Frith, 2000).

Until recently it was believed that unlike other organs, adult brains lack the ability to generate new cells to compensate for cells lost by disease or physical trauma. Evidence obtained beginning in the latter half of the 20th century indicates that this belief was wrong. The adult brain does have generative – and regenerative – ability; the extent of this ability and the conditions under which new brain tissue (neurons and glial cells) and connections can be produced are active areas of research (Gage, 2003; Nottebohm, 2002). It is generally acknowledged that young brains evidence greater plasticity than do older brains, but it appears that older brains have a greater ability to continue development than previously thought (Greenwood, 2007; Park & Reuter-Lorenz, 2009).

That the production of neural growth – neurogenesis – can be stimulated by the administration of drugs, such as epidermal growth factor and fibroblast growth factor, is of great interest for obvious reasons. Gage (2003) cautions that much remains to be learned before such drugs can be used routinely for therapeutic purposes inasmuch as indiscriminate use could have disruptive effects as well as beneficial ones. Of particular interest for present purposes is the finding that neurogenesis appears to be facilitated by mental activity, which suggests the importance of lifestyle factors in maintaining brain function.

About half of the human brain is composed of white cells, which are clustered beneath a two-millimeter thick canopy of gray cells. The myelin that covers the neurons in the white matter and gives it its white color is laid down over a period perhaps as long as the first 25 years or so of life. Myelin affects the speed at which impulses travel across neurons – myelinated fibers conduct faster than unmyelinated ones (prompting speculation that the relative lack of myelin, especially in the forebrain, may help account for why teenagers lack adult decision-making abilities; Fields, 2008).

The gray cells – the cortex – long believed to play the star role in underlying the cognitive functions that most distinguish humans from other species, have attracted more attention from researchers than the white cells. The latter were generally regarded as primarily transmission lines between different areas of the brain. Attitudes about the role of the white matter appear to be changing, however, as studies using new imaging techniques are beginning to reveal their involvement in learning and other cognitive functions. Researchers have found that changes in the white matter occur when an individual – especially a young individual – learns a complex skill like playing a musical instrument (Bengtsson, Nagy, Skare, Forsman, Forssberg, & Ullén, 2005; Schmithorst & Wilke, 2002). Fields (2008) concludes from studies like those mentioned and others that "there is no doubt that myelin responds to the environment and participates in learning skills" (p. 59). This is why, at least in part, he argues, that it is much easier for children whose brains are still myelinating to acquire new skills than for their grandparents to do so, which is not to say that the grandparents can learn no new skills.

Changes in Average Intelligence over Time

Average scores on standardized intelligence tests increased regularly around the world at the rate of about a point approximately every three years, at least over most of the 20th century. This is generally known as the "Flynn effect," named for James Flynn, who published widely cited articles about it (Flynn, 1984, 1987). How to account for this increase and, in particular, whether it represents a real increase in intelligence as opposed to an effect of changing assessment materials and procedures have been matters of debate (Neisser, 1997, 1998). A surprising aspect of the data is that among the greater increases in test scores have been those on the Raven's Progressive Matrices (Flynn, 2007), which are generally considered to be indicants of fluid intelligence (reasoning ability that is believed to be relatively independent of experience). Given these data, it is hard to escape the conclusion that average intelligence, as assessed by performance on conventional standardized tests, has been increasing worldwide for several decades.

Changes in Individuals' IQ over Time

Many studies have shown that IQ test scores obtained at one time in individuals' lives typically correlate highly with those obtained from the same individuals at other times, especially during the school years (Bradway, Thompson, & Cravens, 1958; McCall, Appelbaum, & Hogarty, 1973). The correlation is far from perfect, however, and investigators have documented many cases of large increases or decreases in measured IQ – some as large as 50 points (Honzik, Macfarlane, & Allen, 1948). Over the period of the primary and secondary school years, the IQs of 59% of the children studied by Honzik et al. changed by 15 or more points, and

9% by 30 or more. According to Anastasi (1988), studies attempting to identify possible causes of such shifts have revealed close associations between the shifts, up or down, "with the cultural milieu and emotional climate in which the child was reared" (p. 340). Analysis of the data of McCall, Applebaum, and Hogarty (1973) showed a relationship between rising IQ and deliberate early parental training of the child in mental and motor skills.

Citing specific "natural experiments" – involving adoptions of children into families that differ with respect to the favorability of the conditions for cognitive development – Nisbett (2009) concludes that "being raised under conditions highly favorable to intelligence has a huge effect on IQ" (p. 32). A comparable effect is seen on school achievement. It appears from the cited studies that adoption alone has a substantial positive effect, and that its magnitude varies with the socioeconomic status of the adoptive family. "The crucial implication of these findings is that the low IQs expected for children born to lower-class parents can be greatly increased if their environment is sufficiently rich cognitively" (p. 35).

That school attendance has a substantial effect on IQ scores is well established (Ceci, 1991; Ceci & Williams, 1997). Put in negative terms, extended absence from school pretty much assures a drop in IQ, with the extent of the drop proportional to the duration of the absence.

Effects of Beliefs about Intelligence

Beliefs, especially about intelligence, can have large effects – both beneficial and detrimental – on cognitive performance (Baron, 1991; D'Andrade, 1981; Schoenfeld, 1987). People who believe that intelligence is malleable are more likely to attempt to improve their problem-solving capabilities than are those who believe it to be innate and fixed; the latter are more susceptible to a feeling of helplessness in the face of difficult cognitive challenges (Dweck, 1999; Heyman & Dweck, 1998). Beliefs about the causes of success and failure on cognitively demanding tasks can affect performance on such tasks (Andrews & Debus, 1978; Deci & Ryan, 1985). Fortunately there is evidence that beliefs about the nature of intelligence – in particular the belief that it is immutable – can be changed through instruction and in ways that can translate into improved performance (Hong, Chiu, Dweck, Lin, & Wan, 1999).

Expectations (of teachers and of students) can affect performance either positively or negatively. Perhaps the most widely cited case of a positive effect of expectations is what has been called the *Pygmalion effect* (Rosenthal & Jacobsen, 1968/1992): when teachers were led to expect superior performance from their students, that is what they got. That beliefs that affect performance negatively can be acquired is reflected in the concept of *learned helplessness* (Gentile & Monaco, 1986; Seligman, 1975). Numerous illustrations of negative effects of expectations have also been documented under the rubric of *stereotype threat*. These effects have been observed especially among members of stigmatized groups, who characteristically perform below the level of their capabilities when reminded that members of their group are expected to perform poorly (Good, Aronson, & Inzlicht, 2003; Steele & Aronson, 1995). *Stereotype lift* has also been reported, whereby people do better when reminded that they belong to a group that is expected to do well than when they are not given such a reminder (Shih, Pittinsky, & Ambady, 1999; Spencer Steele, & Quinn, 1999).

Motivation and Intelligence

Presumably few people would contend that motivation plays no role in achievement; however, one might expect to find a range of opinions regarding how important motivation is relative to intelligence. Data obtained by Duckworth and Seligman (2005) suggest that indicators of motivation may do at least as well as IQ in predicting course grades. That students from East Asia (Japan, South Korea, Taiwan, Hong Kong, Singapore, and mainland China) outperform

American students in educational achievement, especially in mathematics, has been a matter of concern to American educators and educational researchers for some time (Geary, 1996; Stevenson, Chen, & Lee, 1993; Stevenson, Lee, & Stigler, 1986). The differences in achievement appear not to reflect differences in intelligence; factors that have been identified as probably contributory include motivation, beliefs about the dependence of success on effort, and the relatively high value that Asian parents place on academic achievement (Caplan, Choy, & Whitmore, 1992; Chen & Stevenson, 1995; Tsang, 1988). In a review of the role of practice in the development of expertise, Ericsson, Krampe, and Tesch-Römer (1993) note that the most frequently cited condition among those identified as necessary to optimize learning and improve performance is "motivation to attend to the task and exert effort to improve performance" (p. 367).

One of the ways in which beliefs affect performance is via their effects on motivation. If one believes that one's intelligence is unchangeable one may have little reason to make the effort that is necessary to acquire the expertise that is within one's reach, whereas the contrary belief that one's cognitive capabilities can be enhanced through learning can motivate that effort (Dweck & Eliott, 1983; Torgeson & Licht, 1983).

Intelligence and the Malleability of Working Memory

Many researchers have identified working memory capacity as a factor that limits performance on cognitively demanding tasks (Jonides, 1995). Theoretical accounts of reasoning generally put considerable stress on the role of working-memory capacity, whether they assume that reasoning is based on a mental logic (Rips, 1994, 1995) or on mental models (Johnson-Laird, 1983; Johnson-Laird & Byrne, 1991). The prevailing opinion seems to be that the larger one's working memory capacity is, the more effectively one can deal with cognitive challenges. Some researchers argue that many of the common reasoning errors that people make and that are often attributed to biases could arise because of limitations of working memory (Houdé, 2000; Houdé & Moutier, 1996). Working memory capacity is believed to increase spontaneously during adolescence, which may account for the increasing likelihood that conditional assertions will be interpreted as conditionals rather than as conjunctives over those years (Barrouillet & Lecas, 1999). So the question of whether one's working memory capacity can be increased through instruction becomes important to considerations of whether, or how, intelligence might be increased. It has been known at least since Miller's (1956) classic article on the magical number 7 that one can increase the number of items that one can repeat immediately after a single hearing by learning to encode items in small groups or "chunks." What the standard or typical working memory capacity is when chunking is prevented is currently a focus of research, but there are advocates for the position that it is quite low – perhaps not more than three or four items (Cowan, Nugent, Elliott, Ponomarev, & Saults, 1999).

Can practice increase working memory capacity? The results of some studies suggest that it can (Jaeggi, Buschkuehl, Jonides, & Perring, 2008; Thorell, Lindqvist, Bergman, Bholin, & Klingberg, 2008; Verhaeghen, Cerella & Basak, 2004; Westerberg & Klingberg, 2007). Whether this reflects an increase in working memory capacity or development of a more efficient encoding technique is a matter of interpretation, but what is important from a practical point of view is that training can produce improvements in memory-dependent performance.

Age and Intelligence

Mean IQ scores tend to change systematically over the life span, rising from adolescence until the mid-twenties and then falling regularly, perhaps by as much as 25% to 30% over the next 50 years (Wechsler, 1981). According to Cattell (1987), the decline occurs primarily in fluid intelligence, whereas crystallized intelligence tends to continue to increase, or at least not decline, over most of the life span. The good news is that age-related trends are more apparent in cross-sectional comparisons (IQs of one age cohort compared with those of a different age cohort) than in longitudinal comparisons (IQs of the same individuals measured at different times in their lives) (Schaie & Srother, 1968). This invites the thought that the trends seen in the cross-sectional data could reflect intergenerational differences, at least in part. But still the general picture is one of cognitive function declining with advancing age. Specific aspects of cognitive function that have been identified as declining with age include working memory capacity (Hultsch, Herzog, Dixon, & Small, 1998), speed of information processing (Li, Huxhold, & Schmiedek, 2004; Salthouse, 1996) and the rate at which new skills can be acquired (Li et al., 2008).

One would like to know whether anything can be done to stop, postpone, or slow this decline. Is there any truth in the old "use-it-or-lose-it" adage? Does regularly exercising one's mind – keeping it active with challenging problems – help extend its useful life? Does a daily dose of crossword puzzles, sudokus, kenkens, and the like help keep the neurons alive and firing? Can the aging brain benefit from instruction in reasoning, problem solving, and decision making? Is it the case that any stimulus to active thought is beneficial? Is physical exercise cognitively beneficial? Such questions are of considerable general interest, given that most people presumably hope to live to advanced age.

Studies have shown a connection between mental activity throughout the life span and the retention of cognitive function. The incidence of Alzheimer's disease and other forms of dementia varies inversely, for example, with people's level of education and with their habitual engagement in cognitively challenging activities (Hultsch, Hertzog, Small, & Dixon, 1999; Ott et al., 1999; Scarmeas, Levy, Tang, Manly, & Stern, 2001). Higher frequency of participation in cognitive leisure activities has been shown to be associated with lower risk of cognitive impairment due to vascular problems (Verghese, Wang, Katz, Sanders, & Lipton, 2009), and with a slower rate of decline with age more generally (Hertzog, Kramer, Wilson, & Lindenberger, 2009). The data are mostly correlational, and the degree to which there is a cause-effect relationship as well as the question of the direction in which it may go is a focus of continuing study (Gatz, 2005). Neverthless, the available evidence generally supports the idea that living in a mentally stimulating environment is beneficial to the maintenance of cognitive function in later life. Based on an extensive review of research on the question of whether the functional capacity of older adults can be preserved and enhanced, Hertzog, Kramer, Wilson, and Lindenberger (2009) conclude that the evidence favors the view that the answer is yes: "a considerable number of studies indicate that maintaining a lifestyle that is intellectually stimulating predicts better maintenance of cognitive skills and is associated with a reduced risk of developing Alzheimer's disease in late life" (p. 1).

Organized Attempts to Increase Intelligence

There are, in short, many evidences that intelligence is malleable and that it is so pretty much throughout the entire life span. This being the case, it is only natural to expect there to be organized efforts to increase intelligence – or, if one prefers, to improve people's performance on cognitively demanding tasks. And there have been many such efforts. Here I will briefly describe three of them in which instruction has played a leading role.

Head Start

The largest and probably best-known project aimed at facilitating the cognitive and social development of preschool children is Head Start (Payne, Mercer, Payne, & Davison, 1973). Established by the U.S. government in 1965 and still functioning, this program aims to promote school readiness of disadvantaged preschoolers – mostly 3- and 4-year olds – by helping them develop early reading and mathematics skills that will contribute to their later success in school. In 1995, the program was extended, with the establishment of Early Head Start, to include children from birth to age 3. The program is administered by the Office of Head Start, within the Administration for Children and Families, U.S. Department of Health and Human Services.

Head Start functions as an umbrella entity under which numerous local projects exist – mostly in preschool classrooms – throughout the United States. Parental involvement is strongly encouraged. Funding has increased from approximately $200 million for its first full year (1966) to approximately $6.9 billion for fiscal year 2008. As of the end of fiscal year 2007, the program claimed a total enrollment of 908,412 (39.7% White, 34.7% Hispanic, 30% Black/African American) in 49,400 classrooms at an average annual cost per child of approximately $7,500 (http://www.acf.hhs.gov/programs/ohs/about/fy2008.html).

Since the beginning there have been issues concerning objectives (what should the precise goals of the project be) and evaluation (how should the success or failure be assessed). Early in the project's history, a panel of experts tasked with defining social competency identified 29 components that could serve as goals for the project (Anderson & Messick, 1974). There appears to have been general agreement that assessment should not focus primarily on effects of the program on IQ scores (Lewis, 1973; Sigel, 1973).

Published assessments of the effectiveness of Head Start are mixed, ranging from severely critical (Herrnstein & Murray, 1994; Hood, 1992) to strongly positive (Barnett, 2002; Zigler & Muenchow, 1992). Barnett (2002), who is the director of the National Institute for Early Education Research, claims that Head Start is effective and produces substantial educational benefits but argues that it could be even more effective with more funds and better trained teachers – only one in three Head Start teachers has a four-year college degree.

Among the more thought-provoking outcomes of assessment efforts is the finding that although substantial gains in performance are realized while the children are participating in the program, the gains appear to diminish, if not disappear, after participation in the program is over and the children have entered school (McKey et al., 1985; Ramey, Bryant, & Suarez, 1985). The postparticipation fading of the positive effects has been blamed by some on the low quality of the schools that most Head Start participants enter (Lee & Loeb, 1994). Assessment of long-term effects has been lacking.

The Carolina Abecedarian Project

The Carolina Abecedarian Project was established in 1972 to address the needs of preschoolers and schoolchildren, considered to be at risk for delayed development and school failure, through the first three years of elementary school. Participants were low income, mostly from African American (98%) and single female parent families (85%). Parents' average age was 20 and their average IQ 85. The preschool program was a day-care service that provided, for children from 6 weeks of age until entry to kindergarten, nutritional supplements, pediatric care, social work services and, of special interest in the present context, an environment intended to enhance cognitive and linguistic development. For children 3 years old and older, this environment included structured curricula designed to become increasingly similar to what a child would experience upon entering public school. The program for school-age children provided a resource teacher for each child, who served as an intermediary between the classroom teachers and parents, facilitating communication both ways and engaging parents in home activities with children to support and complement what was being taught in the classroom. Resource teachers made frequent visits both to their students' schools and homes.

Evaluation of the program involved a controlled study in which participants were assigned to intervention and control groups. Performance data on a variety of intelligence and abilities tests were collected at various times during the intervention and at regular intervals for several years later (from former participants at ages ranging from 8 to 21 years). Results of evaluation studies are documented in a series of publications (Burchinal, Lee, & Ramey, 1989; Horacek, Ramey, Campbell, Hoffmann, & Fletcher, 1987; Martin, Ramey, & Ramey, 1990; Ramey & Campbell, 1984, 1994). Longer term results are reported by Campbell and Ramey (1994, 1995), Clarke and Campbell (1998), and Campbell, Ramey, Pungello, Sparling, and Miller-Johnson (2002). In brief, scores on assessment tests were higher for children in the intervention group than for those in the control group over the entire span of the assessment period; academic achievement of the children in the intervention group was also enhanced. Evidence of positive effects on the subsequent education and employment of parents of participating children was also obtained. That at least some of the assessment data are open to conflicting interpretations is illustrated by the exchange of views on the topic by Spitz (1992, 1993a, 1993b) and Ramey (1992, 1993).

Project Intelligence

Project Intelligence is the label that was given to a project undertaken in Venezuela in the early 1980s. The idea for the project originated with Luis Alberto Machado, then Venezuelan Minister of State for the Development of Human Intelligence, a post created at his suggestion to make possible the establishment of a variety of innovative projects aimed at improving the educational opportunities and accomplishments of Venezuelan youth. Machado was a firm believer that intelligence is determined, to a large extent, by experience, especially by events in early childhood. A visionary and activist, he had aggressively promoted the idea that the state has an obligation to see that every child has the opportunity to develop his or her potential intelligence to the fullest, and he had expressed his views and vision in several publications, notably *The Right to Be Intelligent*, which appeared in 1980, shortly after creation of the ministerial post that he occupied.

Project Intelligence was undertaken, at Minister Machado's request, as a collaboration among researchers at Harvard University, Bolt Beranek and Newman Inc. (BBN), and teachers in Venezuela. It is described in several publications (Adams, 1989; Chance, 1986; Nickerson, 1986, 1994a; Nickerson, Perkins, & Smith, 1985; Perkins, 1995) and most completely in the project's final report submitted to the government of Venezuela (Harvard University, 1983) and in Herrnstein, Nickerson, Sanchez, and Swets (1986).

The project's objectives were to develop and evaluate materials and methods for teaching cognitive skills in seventh-grade classrooms in Venezuela. A one-year course intended to engage students in discussion and thought-provoking classroom activities was designed and implemented in several Venezuelan schools. Course materials and activities focused on specific capabilities such as observation and classification, critical and careful use of language, reasoning, problem solving, inventive thinking, and decision making. Development of the materials was a collaborative effort among members of the Harvard/BBN team in consultation with several experienced Venezuelan teachers who were to prepare a larger group of Venezuelan teachers to use the materials in a planned year-long evaluation.

The evaluation matched experimental and control groups in six public schools in Barquisimeto, Venezuela – 24 classes, four from each school; the four classes from three of the schools serving as the experimental classes and the four from the other three serving as controls. Each class had approximately 30 to 40 students. Control classes were matched, insofar as was possible, with experimental classes. The experimental classes, which were taught by regular Venezuelan middle school teachers who had volunteered to participate in the project, met for about 45 minutes a day, 4 days a week. Tests that were used for evaluation purposes were the Otis-Lennon School Ability Test (Olsat) (Otis & Lennon, 1977), the Cattell Culture-Fair Intelligence Test (Cattell & Cattell, 1961), and a group of General Abilities Tests (Manuel, 1962a, b). In addition, about 500 special test items were constructed to assess competence with respect to the specific skills the course was intended to enhance.

The standardized general-abilities tests and the target-abilities tests were administered to experimental and control groups before and after the teaching of the course. Both groups improved their scores on both types of test over the period of the course. The effectiveness of the course was judged by comparing the magnitudes of the gains realized by the two groups. Details of test administration and test results are reported in Herrnstein, Nickerson, Sánchez, and Swets (1986) and Swets, Herrnstein, Nickerson, and Getty, 1988). Gains on both types of test were significantly greater for the experimental students than for the controls. The gains realized by the students in the experimental classes were 121%, 146%, 168%, and 217% of those realized by the controls on the Cattell, the Olsat, the GAT, and the Target Abilities battery, respectively. Further analyses showed the magnitude of the gains to have been relatively independent of the initial ability levels of the students as indicated by pretest scores. Unfortunately, data regarding long-term effects of the intervention are not available. Presumably, whether gains realized in any limited-time project of this sort are maintained and amplified following completion of the project will depend greatly on the extent to which subsequent educational experiences build upon them. A brief update on Project Intelligence and related Venezuelan projects is provided by de Capdevielle (2003).

Others

There have been many other organized programs to improve cognitive performance. Several of these are described in Nickerson, Perkins, and Smith (1985), including the Instrumental Enrichment Program (Feuerstein, Rand, Hoffman & Miller, 1980), the Structure of Intellect Program (Meeker, 1969), Science a Process Approach (Gagne, 1967; Klausmeier, 1980), Thinkabout (Sanders & Sonnad, 1982), Basics (Ehrenberg & Ehrenberg, 1982), Patterns of Problem Solving (Rubenstein, 1975), Schoenfeld's (1985) approach to teaching Mathematical Problem Solving, the Productive Thinking Program (Covington, Crutchfield, Davies, & Olton, 1974), among others. Some are also described in Nickerson (1988/1989, 1994b) and in Perkins (1995).

The Philosophy for Children program, with its emphasis on making classrooms "communities of inquiry," was developed in the 1970s by Matthew Lipman and soon formalized in the establishment of the Institute for the Advancement of Philosophy for Children; it has been adapted for use in a variety of countries and contexts (Fisher, 2003; Lipman, 2003; Maughn, 2008; Sasseville, 1999). Its international appeal is evidenced by the establishment in 1985 of the International Council for Philosophical Inquiry with Children, which sponsors an international conference every other year.

America's Foundation for Chess has been exploring the possibility of using the teaching of chess to second- and third-graders as a means of improving children's thinking skills (Fischer, 2006), and some encouraging data have been obtained showing higher educational achievement scores by students who received chess instruction than by those who did not receive such instruction (Smith & Cage, 2000). The arts have been promoted also as a vehicle for teaching thinking (Grotzer, Howick, Tishman, & Wise, 2002).

Active Learning Practice for Schools (ALPS) is a Worldwide-Web based system developed by Project Zero of the Harvard School of Graduate Education for the purpose of making a range of educational resources widely available electronically (Andrade, 1999). The Thinking Classroom is a "region" within ALPS that focuses on the teaching of critical and creative thinking.

Details are available at http://learnweb.harvard.edu/alps/thinking/intro.cfm.

The National Center for the Teaching of Thinking was established as a nonprofit organization in 1992, having begun three years earlier as a federally funded three-year education laboratory. The philosophy of the center is articulated by its director (Swartz) and colleagues in Swartz, Costa, Beyer, Regan, and Kallick (2008) and in several lesson and lesson-design books. Details of the center's offerings and activities are available at http://www.nctt.net/.

Several programs have been designed to provide remedial help for college students to develop the cognitive (or metacognitive, self-management) skills needed to do well with conventional college work. Examples are described in Nickerson, Perkins, and Smith (1985). The offering of such programs reflects recognition of the need for remedial training for many students entering college that has been well documented in numerous reports, including, notably *A Nation at Risk* (National Commission on Excellence in Education, 1983). Unfortunately, evaluative data regarding the effectiveness of the various efforts to address this problem are less plentiful and conclusive than one would like.

Many books have been published over the last couple of decades that offer ideas for promoting thinking in the classroom. Examples include Kruse (1988), Collins & Mangieri (1992), Swartz & Parks (1994), Bean (1996), Sternberg and Spear-Swerling (1996), and Beyer (1997). Cotton (1991) provides a review and annotated bibliography of work preceding 1991. Collections of reports of more recent work have been compiled by Costa (2001) and Costa and Kallick (2000).

What Can Be Taught to Increase One's Ability to Perform Cognitively Demanding Tasks?

The question of whether IQ can be increased by instruction or any other environmental means is an interesting one, but not the most important one to ask. Imagine that it were possible by instruction either (1) to raise one's IQ score or (2) to enhance one's ability to learn, to reason well, to solve novel problems, and to deal effectively with the challenges of daily life, but not to do both. Surely there can be no question about the preference for the second objective over the first. It might be argued that raising one's IQ score is tantamount to enhancing one's ability to learn, to reason well, and so on, but this argument effectively acknowledges that the enhanced ability is the ultimate objective and the raised IQ is of interest only as an (imprecise) indicant of the degree to which that objective has been realized.

The fallibility of IQ as an indicator of cognitive performance or academic achievement was noted at the beginning of this chapter. It is also evidenced by the results of educational interventions that have yielded little or no increase in measured IQ but have produced substantial improvements in school grades and other indicators of academic achievement and, in some cases, postschool success. Several such programs are summarized by Nisbett (2009), among them the Perry Preschool Program (Schweinhart et al., 2005), the Milwaukee Project (Garber, 1988), and the Abecedarian Project (mentioned earlier) and some replications. Nisbett's conclusion:

> *Early childhood intervention for disadvantaged and minority children works – when it is strenuous and well conducted. Many different programs get high gains in IQ by the time they end. These gains generally fade over the course of elementary school, but there is some evidence that this is less true if children are placed in high-quality elementary schools. Much more important are the achievement gains that are possible: lower percentage of children assigned to special education, less grade repetition, higher achievement on standardized tests, better rates of high school completion and college attendance, less delinquency, higher incomes, and less dependence on welfare. And these changes can be very large. (p. 130)*

Barnett (1993, 1998) argues that the appearance of fadeout has often been a statistical artifact of assessment procedures and that assessments that consider a variety of factors generally yield a more favorable picture than do those that focus on IQ scores.

Many of the available assessments have been performed by entities that have a vested interest in a program's continuation and presented in documents that are not widely available, but some also have been published in peer-reviewed journals. Examples of the latter include Hale, Seitz, and Zigler (1990), Bryant (1994), Whitehurst (1994), Lee (1998), Ramey (1999), Arnold (2002) and Kaminski (2002). Assessments often focus on one or more specific consequences from a particular program, making general conclusions difficult concerning the cost-effectiveness of the program as a whole. In a critical review of several programs to teach thinking, Ellis (2005) points out that reports of assessments can be difficult to interpret because of the use of imprecise language (What is a thinking skill? A thinking disposition?).

Assuming that one wants to enhance the cognitive performance of people, and one is not concerned with whether in doing so one also increases their IQ scores, what might one do? I believe the evidence indicates that much can be taught that can be effective in realizing that goal. Among the possibilities are the following, most of which I have discussed elsewhere (Nickerson, 1988/1989, 1994b, 2004).

- *Knowledge*. The importance of domain-specific knowledge to effective problem solving in specific domains has been emphasized by many researchers (Hunter, 1986; Larkin, McDermott, Simon, & Simon, 1980b). Knowledge about cognition, and especially about how human reasoning commonly goes astray (e.g., confirmation bias, myside bias, gambler's fallacy, rationalizing versus reasoning, effects of preferences on beliefs, overconfidence in one's own judgments, weighting irrelevancies in argument evaluation, and so on) has also been stressed (Evans, 1989; Nickerson, 1998; Piattelli-Palmarini, 1994; Stanovich, 1999).
- *Logic (both formal and – perhaps more important – informal)*. The teaching of formal logic as a means of enhancing cognitive performance is not promoted by most psychologists and educators. Some argue that it has little to do with the way people actually think (Cheng & Holyoak, 1985; Evans, 1989). Despite this, I lean toward believing that neglecting it is a bad idea; and there is some empirical evidence to support this view (Dickstein, 1975; Rips & Conrad, 1983). Familiarity with informal logic – with techniques commonly used to persuade and/or win arguments – strikes me as an important requirement for intelligent living in modern society.
- *Statistics*. Much of the problem solving and decision making that people do in their daily lives is done under conditions of uncertainty. Judging the likelihoods of possible events, assessing the risks associated with specific courses of action, estimating costs and benefits of possible consequences of decisions are things we all do frequently, either explicitly or implicitly. Dealing with situations that require probabilistic or statistical thinking is improved by training in probability or statistics (Fong, Krantz, & Nisbett, 1986; Kosonen & Winne, 1995).
- *Specific cognitive skills*. Increasingly in recent years researchers have been exploring the effectiveness of efforts to train people – especially elderly people – on specific cognitive skills. Target skills include methods to improve attention control, memory (mnemonic systems), visual search, reasoning, and performance on other tasks of the types that are found on tests of intelligence. The results of such efforts have been mixed – and transfer of positive results to tasks other than those on which training is focused has been limited – but, on balance, the results have been sufficiently promising to motivate further research. Hertzog, Kramer, Wilson, and Lindenberger (2009) point out that most training studies in this

arena are of very short duration relative to the time it typically takes in the normal course of life to acquire or hone cognitive skills; it remains to be seen what can be accomplished with much longer training regimens.

- *Stategies/heuristics*. Strategies for learning are teachable (Jones, Palincsar, Ogle, & Carr, 1987; Paris, Lipson, & Wixson, 1983), as are strategies for problem solving (Bransford & Stein, 1984; Wickelgren, 1974) and for decision making (Beyth-Marom, Fischhoff, Quadrel, & Furby, 1991). Some strategies are general, not specific to subject matter or problem type; these include breaking the problem down into manageable bites, finding a similar (but easier or more familiar) problem, finding a helpful way of representing the problem (a figure, a table, a flowchart), working backward (from where one wants to be – at the solution – to where one is), considering extreme cases, and so on. Specific disciplines and problem domains have heuristics and "tricks-of-the-trade" that are teachable and useful for people who work in those areas. Domain-specific heuristics are typically more effective than the more general ones for problems in the relevant domains but are less likely to be useful across domains.
- *Self- management and other metacognitive skills and knowledge*. The effectiveness of self-monitoring and self-management skills and knowledge is well documented (Batha & Carroll, 2007; Flavell, 1981; Weinert, 1987). Among other important aspects of metacognition are knowledge of one's own strengths and weaknesses and acceptance of responsibility for one's own learning.
- *Habits of thought – thoughtful habits*. Often poor performance on cognitively challenging tasks is due to inattentiveness, carelessness, or failure to check one's work. Hasty and careless reading of instructions can result in misunderstanding of the problem(s) one is trying to solve. Mechanical application of problem-solving procedures or failure to check the results of one's work can yield nonsensical "solutions." I am not aware of data-based estimates of the percentage of errors that are made on ability or achievement tests that are due to carelessness and that could be avoided by reflection, but I suspect that it is not negligible.
- *Attitudes and beliefs conducive to learning and thinking*. Fostering an attitude of carefulness and reflectiveness regarding one's work has been promoted as an eminently worthwhile goal (Ennis, 1986; Resnick, 1987). Other attitudes of importance include inquisitiveness (Dillon, 1988; Millar, 1992) and fair-mindedness (Baron, 1988). I noted in a preceding section that beliefs about intelligence can have large effects on cognitive performance. Beliefs about whether one has any control over the retention of skills, or the learning of new ones, during one's later years can help determine how well one does in this regard (Bandura, 1997; Seeman, McAvay, Merrill, Albert, & Rodin, 1996).
- *Other*. This list of things that can be taught in the interest of enhancing cognitive performance could easily be extended to include *principles of good reasoning, outlooks that motivate effort* (seeing the world as an incredibly interesting place and learning as not only important for practical reasons but intrinsically rewarding), *counterfactual thinking* (the usefulness of imagining alternative possibilities), *perspective taking* (looking at things from different points of view), and numerous other principles, practices, and perspectives that are conducive to a thoughtful approach to problems and life more generally.

What Should the Goal Be?

There is an assumption implicit in many discussions of the possibility of increasing intelligence through instruction or other environmental interventions. That assumption is that techniques that prove to be effective in increasing the intelligence of people whose intelligence is now relatively low will not also increase the intelligence, conceivably by the same amount or more, of those whose intelligence is now relatively high. The same observation holds when "intelligence" is replaced with "achievement." This assumption is suggested by the use of "closing-the-gap" terminology when the gap that is to be closed is between people (typically students) who score high and those who score low on tests of either intelligence or academic achievement.

The distribution of intelligence, however measured, is well represented at the present by the famous (or infamous) bell curve. One can imagine several ways in which the distribution might change as a consequence of the development and application of effective educational interventions aimed at enhancing intelligence. The entire distribution might move to the right by a constant, its mean increasing but its variability, as indicated by its standard deviation, remaining about the same. (Something close to this appears to have been happening over the last century or so; Flynn, 1987; Neisser, 1997.) The lower end of the distribution might move to the right more than the upper end, with the resulting distribution having a higher mean but a smaller standard deviation; this would reflect a shrinking of the intelligence range. A third possibility is that the higher end of the distribution would move to the right more than the lower end, yielding a distribution with a higher mean and a larger standard deviation – greater variability. There are other possibilities, but consideration of these three suffices to make the point that developing and applying effective ways to enhance intelligence could have a variety of possible outcomes, not all of which would close, or even narrow, the gap between the more highly intelligent and the less so.

It seems to me likely that any novel effective intelligence- or achievement-enhancing techniques that are forthcoming will benefit people at the high end of the intelligence (or achievement) continuum as well as those at the low end. A counterargument might be that those at the high end are already benefiting from the best that the environment has to offer and the challenge is to see that those at the low end get the same environmental advantages that those at the high end already have.

That is a strong argument, and it has the force of equity on its side. Clearly there are great inequities in the degree to which individuals live under conditions that are conducive to the development of their cognitive potential, and addressing those inequities should be a major goal of any civilized society. But how intelligence would be distributed if all children lived under conditions that are maximally conducive to the realization of their full potential – whether the distribution would be less or more variable than it now is – is an open question.

Concluding Comments

There is considerable agreement among many – I believe most – researchers on intelligence that both nature and nurture play major roles in determining intelligence and cognitive performance, despite differences of opinion regarding the relative contributions of the two types of factors. Herrnstein and Murray (1994), who are widely held to be among the stauncher proponents of the idea that intelligence is inherited, estimate that genetics accounts for only about 60% of intelligence (as represented by IQ scores) and attribute the remaining 40% to environmental factors. Not surprisingly, theorists who emphasize the role of environmental factors judge their contribution to be much greater. The obvious conclusion is that those who aspire to increase intelligence or to enhance people's ability to perform cognitively demanding tasks, by instruction or other environmental means, are not tilting at windmills but are pursuing a reasonable goal. Efforts to develop procedures and programs to help realize this goal have produced sufficiently positive results to justify its continued vigorous pursuit, but the results to date also make it clear that the goal is an ambitious one and the question of how best to pursue it remains a challenge for research.

References

Adams, M. J. (1989). Thinking skills curricula: Their promise and progress. *Educational Psychologist, 24*, 25–77.

Anastasi, A. (1958). *Differential psychology* (3rd ed.). New York, NY: Macmillan.

Anastasi, A. (1988). *Psychological testing* (6th ed.). New York, NY: Macmillan.

Anderson, S. B., & Messick, S. (1974). Social competency in young children. *Developmental Psychology, 10*, 282–293.

Andrade, A. (1999). ALPS *The thinking classroom*. Retrieved 8/24/09 from http://learnweb.harvard.edu/alps/thinking/index.cfm.

Andrews, G. R., & Debus, R. I. (1978). Persistence and the causal perception of failure: Modifying cognitive attributions. *Journal of Educational Psychology, 70*, 154–166.

Arnold, D. H. (2002). Accelerating math development in Head Start classrooms. *Journal of Educational Psychology., 94*, 762–770.

Bandura, A. (1997). *Self efficacy: The exercise of control*. New York, NY: Freeman.

Barnett, W. S. (1993, May 19). Does Head Start fade out? *Education Week*, p. 40.

Barnett, W. S. (1998). Long-term effects on cognitive development and school success. In W. S. Barnett & S. S. Boocock (Eds.), *Early care and education for children in poverty: Promises, programs, and long-term outcomes* (pp. 11–44). Buffalo: SUNY Press.

Barnett, W. S. (2002). *The battle over Head Start: What the research shows*. Paper presented at a congressional Science and Public Policy briefing on the impact of Head Start on September 13, 2002. Retrieved 8/26/08 from http://nieer.org/resources/research/BattleHeadStart.

Baron, J. (1988). *Thinking and deciding*. New York, NY: Cambridge University Press.

Baron, J. (1991). Beliefs about thinking. In J. F. Voss, D. N. Perkins, & J. W. Segal (Eds.), *Informal reasoning and education* (pp. 169–186). Hillsdale, NJ: Erlbaum.

Barrouillet, P., & Lecas, J.-F. (1999). Mental models in conditional reasoning and working memory. *Thinking and reasoning, 5*, 289–302.

Batha, K., & Carroll, M. (2007). Metacognitive training aids decision making. *Australian Journal of Psychology, 59*, 64–69.

Bean, J. C. (1996). *Engaging ideas: The professor's guide to integrating writing, critical thinking, and active learning in the classroom*. San Francisco, CA: Jossey-Bass.

Bell, E. T. (1937). *Men of mathematics: The lives and achievements of the great mathematicians from Zeno to Poincare*. New York, NY: Dover.

Bengtsson, S. L., Nagy, Z., Skare, S., Forsman, L., Forssberg, H., & Ullén, F. (2005). Extensive piano practicing has regionally specific effects on white matter development. *Nature Neuroscience, 8*, 1148–1150.

Beyer, B. (1997). *Improving student thinking: A comprehensive approach*. Boston, MA: Allyn & Bacon.

Beyth-Marom, R., Fischhoff, B., Quadrel, M. J., & Furby, L. (1991). Teaching adolescents decision making: A critical review. In J. Baron & R. V. Brown (Eds.), *Teaching decision making to adolescents* (pp. 19–59). Hillsdale, NJ: Erlbaum.

Bradway, K. P., Thompson, C. W., & Cravens, R. B. (1958). Preschool IQs after twenty-five years. *Journal of Educational Psychology, 49*, 278–281.

Bransford, J. D., & Stein, B. S. (1984). *The ideal problem solver: A guide for improving thinking, learning, and creativity*. New York, NY: Freeman.

Bruer, J. T. (1999). *The myth of the first three years: A new understanding of early brain development and lifelong learning*. New York, NY: Free Press.

Bryant, D. (1994). Family and classroom correlates of Head Start children's development. *Early Childhood Research Quarterly, 9*, 289–309.

Burchinal, M., Lee, M., & Ramey, C. T. (1989) Type of daycare and preschool intellectual development in disadvantaged children. *Child Development, 60*, 128–137

Campbell, F. A., & Ramey, C. T. (1994). Effects of early intervention on intellectual and academic achievement: A follow-up study of children from low-income families. *Child Development, 65*, 684–698.

Campbell, F. A., & Ramey, C. T. (1995). Cognitive and school outcomes for high-risk African-American students at middle adolescence: Positive effects of early intervention. *American Educational Research Journal, 32*, 743–772.

Campbell, F. A., Ramey, C. T., Pungello, E., Sparling, J., & Miller-Johnson, S. (2002). Early childhood education: Young adult outcomes from the Abecedarian Project. *Applied Developmental Science, 6*, 42–57.

Caplan, N., Choy, M. H., & Whitemore, J. K. (1992). Indochinese refugee families and academic achievement. *Scientific American, 266*(2), 36–42.

Cattell, R. B. (1963). Theory of fluid and crystallized intelligence: A critical experiment. *Journal of Educational Psychology, 54*, 1–22.

Cattell, R. B. (1987). *Intelligence: Its structure, growth and action*. Amsterdam: North-Holland.

Cattell, R. B., & Cattell, A. K. S. (1961). *Culture Fair Intelligence Test* (Scale 2, Forms A & B). Champaign, IL: Institute for Personality and Ability Testing.

Ceci, S. J. (1991). How much does schooling influence general intelligence and its cognitive components? A reassessment of the evidence. *Developmental Psychology, 27*, 703–722.

Ceci, S. J., & Liker, J. K. (1986b). A day at the races: A study of IQ, expertise, and cognitive complexity. *Journal of Experimental Psychology: General, 115*, 255–266.

Ceci, S. J., & Williams, W. M. (1997). Schooling, intelligence and income. *American Psychologist, 52*, 1051–1058.

Chance, P. (1986). *Thinking in the classroom*. New York, NY: Teachers College Press.

Cheng, P. W., & Holyoak, K. J. (1985). Pragmatic reasoning schemas. *Cognitive Psychology, 17*, 391–416.

Chen, C., & Stevenson, H. W. (1995). Motivation and mathematics achievement: A comparative study of Asian-American, Caucasian-American and East Asian high school students. *Child Development, 66*, 1215–1234.

Clarke, S. H., & Campbell, F. A. (1998). Can intervention early prevent crime later? The Abecedarian Project compared with other programs. *Early Childhood Research Quarterly, 13*, 319–343.

Cleckley, H. (1988). *The mask of sanity* (5th ed.). Emily S. Cleckley. (Original published in 1941)

Collins, C., & Mangieri, J. N. (Eds.). (1992). *Teaching thinking: An agenda for the 21st century*. Hillsdale, NJ: Erlbaum.

Costa, A. (Ed.). (2001). *Developing minds: A resource book for teaching thinking* (3rd ed.). Alexandria, VA: Association for Supervision and Curriculum Development.

Costa, A., & Kallick, B. (Eds.). (2000). *Discovering and exploring habits of mind*. Alexandria, VA: Association for Supervision and Curriculum Development.

Cotton, K. (1991). Close-up #11: Teaching thinking skills. Retrieved 8/10/09, from Northwest Regional Educational Laboratory's School Improvement Research Series Web site: http://www.nwrel.org/scpd/sirs/6/cu11.html.

Covington, M. V., Crutchfield, R. S., Davies L., & Olton, R. M. (1974). *The productive thinking program: A course in learning to think*. Columbus, OH: Merrill.

Cowan, N., Nugent, L. D., Elliott, E. M., Ponomarev, I., & Saults, J. S. (1999). The role of attention in the development of short-term memory: Age differences in the verbal span of apprehension. *Child Development, 70*, 1082–1097.

D'Andrade, R. G. (1981). The cultural part of cognition. *Cognitive Science, 5*, 179–195.

Daniels, D., & Plomin, R. (1985). Differential experience of siblings in the same family. *Developmental Psychology, 21*, 747–760.

Davis, R. B., & McKnight, C. (1980). The influence of semantic content on algorithmic behavior. *Journal of Mathematical Behavior, 3*, 39–87.

de Capdevielle, B. C. (2003). Update from the Venezuelan Intelligence Project. *New Horizons for Learning Online Journal*, 9(4). Retrieved 8/10/09 from http://www.newhorizons.org/trans/international/capdevielle.htm.

Deci, E. L., & Ryan, R. M. (1985). *Intrinsic motivation and self-determination in human behavior*. New York, NY: Plenum Press.

Diamond, M. (1988). *Enriching heredity: The impact of the environment on the anatomy of the brain*. London, UK: Collier Macmillan.

Dickstein, L. S. (1975). Effects of instructions and premise ordering errors in syllogistic reasoning. *Journal of Experimental Psychology: Human Learning and Memory, 104*, 376–384.

Dillon, J. T. (1988). The remedial status of student questioning. *Journal of Curriculum Studies, 20*, 197–210.

Draganski, B., Gaser, C., Busch, V., Schuierer, G., Bogdahn, U., & May, A. (2004). Changes in grey matter induced by training. *Nature, 427*, 311–312.

Duckworth, A. L., & Seligman, M. E. P. (2005). Self-discipline outdoes IQ in predicting academic performance of adolescents. *Psychological Science, 16*, 939–944.

Dweck, C. S. (1999). *Self-theories: Their role in motivation, personality and development*. Philadelphia, PA: Psychology Press.

Dweck, C. S., & Eliott, E. S. (1983). Achievement motivation. In P. H. Mussen (Ed.), *Handbook of child psychology* (Vol. 4). New York, NY: Wiley.

Ehrenberg, S. D., & Ehrenberg, L. M. (1982). *BASICS: Building and applying strategies for intellectual competencies in students*. Coshocton, OH: Institute for Curriculum and Instruction.

Ellis, A. K. (2005). *Research on educational innovations* (4th ed.). Larchmont, NY: Eye on Education.

Ennis, R. H. (1986). A taxonomy of critical thinking dispositions and abilities. In J. B. Baron & R. S. Sternberg (Eds.), *Teaching thinking skills: Theory and practice* (pp. 9–26). New York, NY: Freeman.

Epstein, H. T. (1978). Growth spurts during brain development: Implications for educational policy and practice. In J. Chall (Ed.), *Education and the brain: National Society for the Study of Education 79th yearbook, part II* (pp. 343–370). Chicago, IL: University of Chicago Press.

Ericsson, K. A., Krampe, R. T., & Tesch-Römer, C. (1993). The role of deliberate practice in the acquisition of expert performance. *Psychological Review*, **100**, 363–406.

Evans, J. St. B. T. (1989). *Bias in human reasoning: Causes and consequences*. Hillsdale, NJ: Erlbaum.

Eysenck, H. J. (1973). *The inequality of man*. London, UK: Temple Smith.

Feuerstein, R., Rand,, Y., Hoffman, M., & Miller, R. (1980). *Instrumental enrichment*. Baltimore, MD: University Park Press.

Fields, R. D. (2008). White matter matters. *Scientific American*, **298**(3), 54–61.

Fischer, W. (2006). The educational value of chess. *New Horizons for Learning*. Retrieved 8/24/09 from http://www.newhorizons.org; info@newhorizons.org.

Fisher, R. (2003). *Teaching thinking: Philosophical enquiry in the classroom* (2nd ed.). London, UK: Continuum.

Flavell, J. H. (1981). Cognitive monitoring. In W. P. Dickson (Ed.), *Children's oral communication skills*. New York, NY: Academic Press.

Flynn, J. R. (1984). The mean IQ of Americans: Massive gains 1932 to 1978. *Psychological Bulletin*, **95**, 29–51.

Flynn, J. R. (1987). Massive IQ gains in 14 nations: What IQ tests really measure. *Psychological Bulletin*, **101**, 171–191.

Flynn, J. R. (2007). *What is intelligence? Beyond the Flynn effect*. New York, NY: Cambridge University Press.

Fong, G. T., Krantz, D. H., & Nisbett, R. E. (1986). The effects of statistical training on thinking about everyday problems. *Cognitive Psychology*, **18**, 235–292.

Gage, F. H. (2003). Brain, repair yourself. *Scientific American*, **289**(3), 46–53.

Gagne, R. M. (1967). *Science – A process approach: Purposes, accomplishments, expectations*. Washington, DC: American Association for the Advancement of Science.

Garber, H. L. (1988). *The Milwaukee Project: Preventing mental retardation in children at risk*. Washington, DC: American Association on Mental Retardation.

Gardner, H. (2006). *Multiple intelligences: New horizons*. New York: Basic Books.

Gardner, H., Krechevsky, M., Sternberg, R. J., & Okagaki, L. (1994). Intelligence in context: Enhancing students' practical intelligence for school. In K. McGilly (Ed.), *Classroom lessons: Integrating cognitive theory and classroom practice* (pp. 105–127). Cambridge, MA: MIT Press.

Gatz, M. (2005). Educating the brain to avoid dementia: Can mental exercise prevent Alzheimer disease? *PLoS Med* **2**(1), e7.

Geary, D. C. (1996). Biology, culture, and cross-national differences in mathematical ability. In R. J. Sternberg & T. Ben-Zeev (Eds.), *The nature of mathematical thinking* (pp. 145–171). Mahwah, NJ: Erlbaum.

Gentile, J. R., & Monaco, N. M. (1986). Learned helplessness in mathematics: What educators should know. *Journal of Mathematical Behavior*, **5**, 159–178.

Goertzel, M. G., Goertzel, V., & Goertzel, T. G. (1978). *Three hundred eminent personalities*. San Francisco, CA: Jossey-Bass.

Good, C., Aronson, J., & Inzlicht, M. (2003). Improving adolescents' standardized test performance: An intervention to reduce the effects of stereotype threat. *Applied Developmental Psychology*, **24**, 645–662.

Greenwood, P. M. (2007). Functional plasticity in cognitive aging: Review and hypothesis. *Neuropsychology*, **21**, 657–673.

Grotzer, T., Howick, L., Tishman, S., & Wise, D. (Eds.). (2002). *Art works for schools: A curriculum for teaching thinking in and through the arts*. Lincoln, MA: DeCordova Museum and Sculpture Park.

Hale, B., Seitz, V., & Zigler, E. (1990). Health service and Head Start: A forgotten formula. *Journal of Applied Developmental Psychology*, **11**, 447–58.

Harris, J. R. (1998). *The nurture assumption: Why children turn out the way they do*. New York, NY: Touchstone.

Harvard University. (1983, October). *Project Intelligence: The development of procedures to enhance thinking skills*. Final Report, submitted to the Minister for the Development of Human Intelligence, Republic of Venezuela.

Hensch, T. K. (2004). Critical period regulation. *Annual Review of Neuroscience*, 27, 549–579.

Herrnstein, R., & Murray, C. (1994). *The bell curve*. New York, NY: Simon & Schuster.

Herrnstein, R. J., Nickerson, R. S., Sanchez, M., & Swets, J. A. (1986). Teaching thinking skills. *American Psychologist*, 41, 1279–1289.

Hertzog, C., Kramer, A. F., Wilson, R. S., & Lindenberg, U. (2009). Enrichment effects on adult cognitive development. *Psychological Science in the Public Interest*, 9, 1–65.

Heyman, G. D., & Dweck, C. S. (1998). Children's thinking about traits: Implications for judgments of the self and others. *Child Development*, 64, 391–403.

Hong, Y. Y., Chiu, C., Dweck, C. S., Lin, D., & Wan, W. (1999). Implicit theories, attributions, and coping: A meaning system approach. *Journal of Personality and Social Psychology*, 77, 588–599.

Honzik, M. P., Macfarlane, J. W., & Allen, L. (1948). The stability of mental test performance between two and eighteen years. *Journal of Experimental Education*, 17, 309–324.

Hood, J. (1992). *Caveat emptor: the Head Start scam*. Policy Analysis, 187. Washington, DC: Cato Institute.

Horacek, H. J., Ramey, C. T., Campbell, F. A., Hoffmann, K., & Fletcher, R. H. (1987). Predicting school failure and assessing early intervention with high-risk children. *American Academy of Child and Adolescent Psychiatry*, 26, 1987, 758–763.

Houdé, O. (2000). Inhibition and cognitive development: Object, number, categorization, and reasoning. *Cognitive Development*, 15, 63–73.

Houdé, O., & Moutier, S. (1996). Deductive reasoning and experimental inhibition, training: The case of the matching bias. *Current Psychology of Cognition*, 15, 409–434.

Hultsch, D. F., Hertzog, C., Dixon, R. A., & Small, B. J. (1998). *Memory change in the aged*. New York: Cambridge University Press.

Hultsch, D. F., Hertzog, C., Small, B. J., & Dixon, R. A. (1999) Use it or lose it: Engaged lifestyle as a buffer of cognitive decline in aging? *Psychology of Aging*, 14, 245–263.

Hunter, J. E. (1986). Cognitive ability, cognitive aptitudes, job knowledge, and job performance. *Journal of Vocational Behavior*, 29, 340–362.

Huttenlocher, P. R., & Dabholkar, A. S. (1997). Regional differences in synaptogenesis in human cerebral cortex. *Journal of Comparative Neurology*, 387, 167–178.

Jaeggi, S. M., Buschkuehl, M., Jonides, J., & Perrig, W. J. (2008). Improving fluid intelligence with training on working memory. *Proceedings of the National Academy of Sciences of the United States of America*, 105, 6829–6833.

Jensen, A. R. (1998). *The g factor*. Westport, CT: Praeger.

Johnson-Laird, P. N. (1983). *Mental models*. Cambridge, MA: Harvard University Press.

Johnson-Laird, P. N., & Byrne, R. M. J. (1991). *Deduction*. Hove, UK: Erlbaum.

Jones, B. F., Palincsar, A. S., Ogle, D. S., & Carr, E. G. (1987). Learning and thinking. In B. F. Jones, A. S. Palincsar, D. S. Ogle, & E. G. Carr (Eds.), *Strategic teaching and learning: Cognitive instruction in the content areas* (pp. 3–32). Alexandria, VA: Association for Supervision and Curriculum Development.

Jonides, J. (1995). Working memory and thinking. In E. E. Smith & D. N. Osherson (Eds.), *Thinking: An invitation to cognitive science* (2nd ed., Vol. 3, pp. 215–265). Cambridge, MA: MIT Press.

Kaminski, R. A. (2002). Prevention of substance abuse with rural Head Start children and families. *Psychology of Addictive Behaviors*, 16, 11–22.

Kaplan, M., & Kaplan, E. (2006). *Chances are... Adventures in probability*. New York, NY: Penguin Books.

Kaufman, A. S. (2000). Tests of intelligence. In R. J. Sternberg (Ed.), *Handbook of intelligence* (pp. 445–476). New York, NY: Cambridge University Press.

Klausmeier, H. J. (1980). *Learning and teaching concepts – A strategy for testing applications of theory*. New York, NY: Academic Press.

Koch, H. L. (1966). *Twins and twin relations*. Chicago, IL: University of Chicago Press.

Kosonen, P., & Winne, P. H. (1995). Effects of teaching statistical laws on reasoning about everyday problems. *Journal of Educational Psychology*, 87, 33–46.

Krueger, J. (2000). Individual differences and Pearson's *r*: Rationality revealed? *Behavioral and Brain Sciences*, 23, 684–685.

Kruse, J. (1988). *Classroom activities in thinking skills*. Philadelphia, PA: Research for Better Schools.

Larkin, J. H., McDermott, J., Simon, D. P., & Simon, H. A. (1980a). Expert and novice performance in solving physics problems. *Science, 208*, 1335–1342.

Lee, V. E. (1998) Does Head Start really work? A 1 year follow-up comparison of disadvantaged children attending Head Start, no preschool, and other preschool programs. *Developmental Psychology, 24*, 210–222.

Lee, V. E., & Loeb, S. (1994). *Where do Head Start attendees end up? One reason why preschool effects fade out* (Report No. ED368510). Available from the Education Resources Information Center (ERIC).

Levinson, S. C. (1995). *Interactional biases in human thinking*. In E. Goody (Ed.), New York, NY: Cambridge University Press.

Lewis, M. (1973). Infant intelligence tests: Their use and misuse. *Human Development, 16*, 108–118.

Lipman, M. (2003). *Thinking in education*, Cambridge, UK: Cambridge University Press.

Li, S.-C., Huxhold, O., & Schmiedek, F. (2004). Aging and attenuated processing robustness: Evidence from cognitive and sensorimotor functioning. *Gerontology, 50*, 28–34.

Li, S.-C., Schmiedek, F., Huxhold, O., Röcke, C., Smith, J., & Lindenberger, U. (2008). Working memory plasticity in old age: Transfer and maintenance. *Psychology and Aging, 23*, 731–742.

Machado, L. A. (1980). *The right to be intelligent*. New York, NY: Pergamon Press.

Maguire, E. A., Gadian, D. G., Johnsrude, I. S., Good, C. D., Ashburner, J., Frackowiak, R. S. J., & Frith, C. D. (2000). Navigation-related structural changes in the hippocampi of taxi drivers. *Proceedings of the National Academy of Sciences, 97*, 4398–4403.

Manuel, H. T. (1962a). *Tests of General Ability: Inter-American Series* (Spanish, Level 4, Forms A & B). San Antonio, TX: Guidance Testing Associates.

Manuel, H. T. (1962b). *Tests of Reading: Inter-American Series* (Spanish, Levels 3 & 4, Forms A & B). San Antonio, TX: Guidance Testing Associates.

Martin, S. L., Ramey, C. T., & Ramey, S. (1990). The prevention of intellectual impairment in children of impoverished families: Findings of a randomized trial of educational day care. *American Journal of Public Health, 80*, 844–847.

Maughn, G. (2008). *Philosophy for children: Practitioner handbook*. Montclair State University, NJ: Institute for the Advancement of Philosophy for Children.

Mayer, J. D. (1999). Emotional intelligence: Popular or scientific psychology? *APA Monitor, 30*, 50.

McCall, R. B., Appelbaum, M. I., & Hogarty, P. S. (1973). Developmental changes in mental performance. *Monographs of the Society for Research in Child Development, 42*(3, Serial No. 150).

McKey, R., Condelli, L., Ganson, H., Barrett, B., McConkey, C., & Plantz, M. (1985). *The impact of Head Start on children, families, and communities. Final report of the Head Start Evaluation, Synthesis, and Utilization Project.* Washington, DC: U.S. Department of Health and Human Services.

Meeker, M. N. (1969). *The structure of intellect: Its interpretation and uses*. Columbus, OH: Charles E. Merrill.

Millar, G. (1992). *Developing student questioning skills – A handbook of tips and strategies for teachers*. Bensenville, IL: Scholastic Testing Service.

Miller, G. A. (1956). The magical number seven, plus or minus two: Some limits on our capacity for processing information. *Psychological Review, 63*, 81–97.

National Commission on Excellence in Education. (1983). *A nation at risk: The imperative for educational reform*. Washington, DC: U.S. Government Printing Office.

Neisser, U. (1997). Rising scores on intelligence tests. *American Scientist, 85*, 440–447.

Neisser, U. (Ed.). (1998). *The rising curve: Long-term gains in IQ and related measures*. Washington, DC: American Psychological Association.

Neisser, U., Boodoo, G., Bouchard, T. J., Boykin, A. W., Brody, N., Ceci, S. J., Halpern, D. F., Loehlin, J. C., Perloff, R., Sterberg, R. J., & Urgina, S. (1996). Intelligence: Knowns and unknowns. *American Psychologist, 51*, 77–101.

Nickerson, R. S. (1986). Project Intelligence: An account and some reflections. In M. Schwebel & C. A. Maher (Eds.), *Facilitating cognitive development: International perspectives, programs, and practices* (pp. 83–102). New York, NY: Hayworth Press.

Nickerson, R. S. (1988/1989). On improving thinking through instruction. In E. Z. Rothkopf (Ed.), *Review of research in education* (Vol. 15, pp. 3–58). Washington, DC: American Educational Research Association.

Nickerson, R. S. (1994a). Project Intelligence. In R. J. Sternberg, S. J. Ceci, J. Horn, E. Hunt, J. D. Matarazzo, & S. Scarr (Eds.),

Encyclopedia of intelligence (pp. 857–860). New York, NY: MacMillan.

Nickerson, R. S. (1994b). The teaching of thinking and problem solving. In R. J. Sternberg (Ed.), *Thinking and problem solving*. Volume 12 of E. C. Carterette & M. Friedman (Eds.), *Handbook of perception and cognition* (pp. 409–449). San Diego, CA: Academic Press.

Nickerson, R. S. (1998). Confirmation bias: A ubiquitous phenomenon in many guises. *Review of General Psychology*, **2**, 175–220.

Nickerson, R. S. (2004). Teaching reasoning. In J. P. Leighton & R.J. Sternberg (Eds.), *The nature of reasoning* (pp. 410–442). New York, NY: Cambridge University Press.

Nickerson, R. S., Perkins, D. N., & Smith, E. E. (1985). *The teaching of thinking*. Hillsdale, NJ: Erlbaum.

Nisbett, R. E. (2009). *Intelligence and how to get it: Why schools and cultures count*. New York, NY: W. W. Norton.

Nottebohm, F. (2002). Why are some neurons replaced in adult brains? *Journal of Neuroscience*, **22**, 624–628.

Nunes, T., Schliemann, A. D., & Carraher, D. W. (1993). *Street mathematics and school mathematics*. Cambridge, UK: Cambridge University Press.

Otis, A. S., & Lennon, R. T. (1977). *Otis-Lennon School Ability Test* (Intermediate Level 1, Form R). New York, NY: Harcourt Brace Jovanovich.

Ott, A., van Rossum, C. T., van Harskamp, F., van de Mheen, H., Hofman, A., & Breteler, M. M. (1999). Education and the incidence of dementia in a large population-based study: The Rotterdam study. *Neurology*, **52**, 663–666.

Paris, S. G., Lipson, M. Y., & Wixson, K. K. (1983). Becoming a strategic reader. *Contemporary Educational Psychology*, 8, 293–316.

Park, D. C., & Reuter-Lorenz, P. (2009). The adaptive brain: Aging and neurocognitive scaffolding. *Annual Review of Psychology*, 60, 173–196.

Payne, J. E., Mercer, C. D., Payne, A., & Davison, R. G. (1973). *Head Start: A tragicomedy with epilogue*. New York, NY: Behavioral Publications.

Perkins, D. N. (1995). *Outsmarting IQ: The emerging science of learnable intelligence*. New York, NY: Free Press.

Piattelli-Palmarini, M. (1994). *Inevitable illusions: How mistakes of reason rule our minds*. New York, NY: Wiley.

Ramey, C. T. (1992). High-risk children and IQ: Altering intergenerational patterns. *Intelligence*, **16**, 239–256.

Ramey, C. (1993). A rejoinder to Spitz's critique of the Abecedarian Experiment. *Intelligence*, **17**, 25–30.

Ramey, C. T., Bryant, D. M., & Suarez, T. M. (1985). Preschool compensatory education and the modifiability of intelligence: A critical review. In D. Detterman (Ed.), *Current topics in human intelligence* (pp. 247–296). Norwood, NJ: Ablex.

Ramey, C. T., & Campbell, F. A. (1984). Preventive education for high-risk children: Cognitive consequences of the Carolina Abecedarian Project. *American Journal of Mental Deficiency*, 88, 515–523.

Ramey, C. T., & Campbell, F. A. (1994). Poverty, early childhood education, and academic competence: The Abecedarian experiment. In A. C. Huston (Ed.), *Children in poverty: Child development and public policy* (pp. 190–221). New York, NY: Cambridge University Press.

Ramey, S. L. (1999). Head Start and preschool education: Toward continued improvement. *American Psychologist*, **54**, 344–346.

Resnick, L. B. (1987). *Education and learning to think*. Washington, DC: National Academy Press.

Rips, L. J. (1994). *The psychology of proof*. Cambridge, MA: MIT Press.

Rips, L. J. (1995). Deduction and cognition. In E. E. Smith & D. N. Osherson (Eds.), *Thinking: An invitation to cognitive science* (2nd ed., Vol. 3, pp. 297–343). Cambridge, MA: <MIT Press.

Rips, L. J., & Conrad, F. G. (1983). Individual differences in deduction. *Cognition and Brain Theory*, 6, 259–285.

Rosenthal, R., & Jacobson, L. (1992). *Pygmalion in the classroom* (Expanded ed.). New York, NY: Irvington. (Originally published in 1968)

Ross, L., Greene, D., & House, P. (1977). The false consensus phenomenon: An attributional bias in self-perception and social perception processes. *Journal of Experimental Social Psychology*, **13**, 279–301.

Rubenstein, M. F. (1975). *Patterns of problem solving*. Englewood Cliffs, NJ: Prentice-Hall.

Salthouse, T. A. (1996). The processing-speed theory of adult age differences in cognition. *Psychological Review*, **103**, 403–428.

Sanders, J. R., & Sonnad, S. R. (1982, January). Research on the introduction, use and impact of the *ThinkAbout* instructional television series: Executive summary. Bloomington, IN: Agency for Instructional Television.

Sasseville, M. (1999). The state of international cooperation in philosophy for children. *Critical and Creative Thinking: The Australasian Journal of Philosophy for Children*, 7, 57–79.

Saxe, G. B. (1988). The mathematics of child street vendors. *Child Development*, 59, 1415–1425.

Scarmeas, N., Levy, G., Tang, M. X., Manly, J., & Stern, Y. (2001). Influence of leisure activity on the incidence of Alzheimer's disease. *Neurology* 57, 2236–2242.

Schaie, K. W., & Strother, C. R. (1968). A cross-sequential study of age changes in cognitive behavior. *Psychological Bulletin*, 70, 671–680.

Schmithorst, V. J., & Wilke,, M. (2002). Differences in white matter architecture between musicians and non-musicians: A diffusion tensor imaging study. *Neuroscience Letters*, 2002, 321, 57–60.

Schoenfeld, A. H. (1985). *Mathematical problem solving*. New York, NY: Academic Press.

Schoenfeld, A. H. (1987). What's all the fuss about metacognition? In A. H. Schoenfeld (Ed.), *Cognitive science and mathematics education* (pp. 189–215). Hillsdale, NJ: Erlbaum.

Schweinhart, L. J., Montie, J., Xiang, Z., Barnett, W. S., Belfield, C. R., & Nores, M. (2005). *Lifetime effects: The High/Scope Perry Preschool Study through age 40*. Ypsilanti, MI: High/Scope Foundation.

Seeman, T. E., McAvay, G., Merrill, S., Albert, M., & Rodin, J. (1996). Self-efficacy beliefs and changes in cognitive performance: MacArthur studies of successful aging. *Psychology and Aging*, 11, 538–551.

Seligman, M.E.P. (1975). *Helplessness: On depression, development, and death*. San Francisco: Freeman.

Shih, M., Pittinsky, T. L., & Ambady, N. (1999). Stereotype susceptibility: Identity salience and shifts in quantitative performance. *Psychological Science*, 10, 80–83.

Sigel, I. E. (1973). Where is preschool education going: Or are we en route without a road map? *Proceedings of the 1972 Invitational Conference on Testing Problems: Assessment in a pluralistic society* (pp. 99–116). Princeton, NJ: Educational Testing Service.

Smith, J. P., & Cage, B. N. (2000). The effects of chess instruction on the mathematics achievements of southern, rural, black secondary students. *Research in the Schools*, 7, 19–26.

Spearman, C. (1904). "General intelligence" objectively determined and measured. *American Journal of Psychology*, 15, 201–293.

Spencer, S. J., Steele, C. M., & Quinn, D. M. (1999). Stereotype threat and women's math performance. *Journal of Experimental Social Psychology*, 35, 4–28.

Spitz, H. H. (1992). Does the Carolina Abecedarian Early Intervention Project prevent sociocultural mental retardation? *Intelligence*, 16, 225–237.

Spitz, H. H. (1993a). Spitz's reply to Ramey's response to Spitz's first reply to Ramey's first response to Spitz's critique of the Abecedarian project. *Intelligence*, 17, 31–35.

Spitz, H. H. (1993b). When prophecy fails: On Ramey's response to Spitz's critique of the Abecedarian Project. *Intelligence*, 17, 17–23.

Stanovich, K. E. (1994). Reconceptualizing intelligence: Dysrationalia as an intuition pump. *Educational Researcher*, 23, 11–22.

Stanovich, K. E. (1999). *Who is rational? Studies of individual differences in reasoning*. Mahwah, NJ: Erlbaum.

Stanovich, K. E., & West, R. (2008). On the failure of cognitive ability to predict myside bias and one-sided thinking biases. *Thinking and Reasoning*, 14, 129–167.

Steele, C. M., & Aronson, J. (1995). Stereotype threat and the intellectual test performance of African Americans. *Journal of Personality and Social Psychology*, 69, 797–811.

Sternberg, R. J. (1999). The theory of successful intelligence. *Review of General Psychology*, 3, 292–316.

Sternberg, R. J., & Spear-Swerling, L. C. (1996). *Teaching for thinking*. Washington, DC: American Psychological Association.

Sternberg, R. J., & Wagner, R. K. (Eds.). (1986). *Practical intelligence: Nature and origins of competence in the everyday world*. Cambridge, UK: Cambridge University Press.

Stevenson, H. W., Chen, C., & Lee, S-Y. (1993). Mathematics achievement of Chinese, Japanese, and American children: Ten years later. *Science*, 259, 53–58.

Stevenson, H. W., Lee, S. Y., & Stigler, J. W. (1986). Mathematics achievement of Chinese, Japanese, and American children. *Science*, 231, 693–699.

Swartz, R. J., Costa, A. L., Beyer, B. K., Regan, R., & Kallick, B. (2008). *Thinking-based learning: Activating students' potential.* Norwood, MA: Christopher-Gordon.

Swartz, R., & Parks, S. (1994). *Infusing critical and creative thinking into elementary instruction: A lesson design handbook.* Pacific Grove, CA: Critical Thinking Books and Software.

Swets, J. A., Herrnstein, R. J., Nickerson, R. S., & Getty, D. J. (1988). Design and evaluation issues in an experiment on teaching thinking skills. *American Psychologist, 43*, 600–602.

Thorell, L. B., Lindqvist, S., Bergman, S., Bholin, G., & Klingberg, T. (2008). Training and transfer effects of executive functions in preschool children. *Developmental Science, 11*, 969–976.

Thorndike, E. L. (1920). Intelligence and its uses. *Harper's Magazine, 140*, 227–235.

Torgeson, J. K., & Licht, B. G. (1983). The LD child as an inactive learner: Retrospects and prospects. In K. D. Gadow & I. Bialer (Eds.), *Advances in learning and behavioral disabilities.* Greenwich, CT: JAI Press.

Tsang, S. L. (1988). The mathematics achievement characteristics of Asian-American students. In R. R. Cocking & J. P. Mestre (Eds.), *Linguistic and cultural influences on learning mathematics* (pp. 123–136). Hillsdale, NJ: Erlbaum.

Turkheimer, E., Haley, A., Waldron, M., D'Onofrio, B., & Gottesman, I. I. (2003). Socioeconomic status modifies heritability of IQ in young children. *Psychological Science, 14*, 623–628.

Verghese, J., Wang, C., Katz, M. J., Sanders, A., & Lipton, R. B. (2009). Leisure activities and risk of vascular cognitive impairment in older Adults. *Journal of Geriatric Psychiatry and Neurology, 22*, 110–118.

Verhaeghen, P., Cerella, J., & Basak, C. (2004). A working memory workout: How to expand the focus of serial attention from one to four items in 10 hours or less. *Journal of Experimental Psychology: Learning, Memory, & Cognition, 30*, 1322–1337.

Wechsler, D. (1981). *WAIS-R manual: Wechsler Adult Intelligence Scale – Revised.* San Antonio, TX: Psychological Corporation.

Weinert, F. E. (1987). Introduction and overview: Metacognition and motivation as determinants of effective learning and understanding. In F. Weinert & R. Kluwe (Eds.), *Metacognition, motivation, and understanding* (pp. 1–16). Hillsdale, NJ: Erlbaum.

Westerberg, H., & Klingberg, T. (2007). Changes in cortical activity after training of working memory – a single-subject analysis. *Physiology and Behavior, 92*, 186–192.

Whitehurst, G. L. (1994). Outcomes of an emergent literacy intervention in Head Start. *Journal of Educational Psychology, 86*, 542–555.

Wickelgren, W. A. (1974). *How to solve problems.* San Francisco, CA: W. H. Freeman.

Zigler, E. F., Finn-Stevenson, M., & Hall, N. W. (2002). *The first three years and beyond: Brain development and social policy.* New Haven, CT: Yale University Press.

Zigler, E., & Muenchow, S. (1992). *Head Start: The inside story of American's most successful educational experiment.* New York: Basic Books.

CHAPTER 7

Intelligence in Infancy

Joseph F. Fagan

Overview

Many tasks have been developed to estimate the infant's ability to take in and to retain information. Such tasks provide a means for investigating classic theoretical issues as to whether intelligence is continuous or takes different forms with development, how to approach the question of whether there is one or there are many forms of intelligence early in life, the origins of the genetic and environmental determinants of intelligence, and the study of the initial neurological bases of intelligence. Practically, the study of how infants gain knowledge allows the identification of infants most in need, can reveal intellectual strength masked by other handicaps, and aids in the discovery of the causes early in life of intellectual disability.

Theory

Chen and Siegler (2000) list three major historical approaches to the understanding of intelligence. The developmental approach of Piaget (1952) emphasizes differences with development in the kinds of thinking that children use to solve problems. The psychometric or individual differences approach focuses upon analyses within and among intelligence tests to provide clues as to the nature of intelligence. The psychometric approach has led some theorists to conclude that there is a single intelligence (Jensen, 1998) and other theorists to conclude that there are multiple intelligences (Sternberg, 1997a, 1997b). The third approach, which recognizes developmental considerations as well as aspects of both psychometric approaches, emphasizes information-processing ability as a definition of intelligence (Ackerman, 1996; Fagan 1992, 2000) while pointing to additional influences on the knowledge one ultimately attains.

A common thread running through these theories is the sense that some basic learning abilities, however defined, underlie intelligent functioning. Piaget, for example, believed that certain processes, which operated throughout development, characterized intelligence. One process is called assimilation, which, in simple terms, is the taking in of information. The second is accommodation which is the change in knowledge when new information is taken in. Jensen holds that there is a general factor in intelligence explainable, in part, as the speed or efficiency of information processing. Sternberg's (1997a, 1997b, 2000a, 2000b) concept of multiple intelligences emphasizes, as fundamental, elementary learning abilities underlying intelligence, processes remaining the same across cultural contexts, and he advocates testing procedures designed to quantify such basic learning ability in new situations (Grigorenko & Sternberg, 1998). Ackerman's (1996) theory posits intelligence as information-processing abilities interacting with personality and with interests to result in intelligence as knowledge. Fagan (1992, 2000) assumes that a set of mental activities which are influenced by genetic mechanisms and by biophysical influences on the brain operate on information provided by the culture to result in knowledge. These mental activities would include sensing and perceiving, selective attention to old or new aspects of received information, and association leading to the accommodation of newly acquired information to what is already known.

The assumption that basic learning and memory abilities may underlie intelligence has made it possible to approach a century's worth of questions and controversies as to the developmental origins and nature of intelligence. Does intelligence begin in infancy? Can we obtain accurate estimates of the initial influences of genetics and of the environment on intelligence? What are the early neurological underpinnings of intelligence? Can we find, and prevent, early life causes of intellectual disability? Can we spot normal thinking in otherwise handicapped infants? Are sociocultural differences in intelligence present during infancy? Ceci (2000, p. 242) notes that viewing intelligence in terms of processing abilities "is a provocative proposal" and that "its promise is so important for society that future research could be very fruitful."

The Origins of Cognition

Theories developed in the 1950s and 1960s by Berlyne (1960), Gibson (1969), and Zeaman and House (1963) focused on the construct of selective attention as the basis of perceptual and discriminative learning and provided a conceptual rationale for the assessment of such abilities in infants. Terms used by Berlyne (1960) such as *attention, novelty, habituation, surprise, anticipatory responses*, and *oddity* in summarizing and explaining his own and related work on the determinants of what he called *stimulus selection* would be quite familiar to all current students of the infant's ability to know the world. Gibson (1969), summarizing decades of her work, pointed out that perceptual learning goes on via *selective attention* to *distinctive features, invariant relations, structure or rules*, and *affordances*, all of which are readily available in the environment. Zeaman and House (1963) developed an *attention* theory of discrimination learning, which linked *selective attention to relevant dimensions* as the essential determinant of differences among children in discrimination learning and intelligence.

A method that allowed these theoretical notions about the role of attention in cognition to be investigated during infancy was the visual interest test developed by Fantz (1956). Fantz reasoned that if infants look more at some things than at others, they must be able to distinguish among them. Fantz (1961) found many visual preferences present from birth. One such visual preference (Caron & Caron, 1968; Fagan, 1970; Fantz, 1964) is selective attention to novelty, a behavior indicative of recognition memory. Infants tend to look differentially at something new rather than at something they have seen, thus indicating that they have acquired knowledge about what they have seen. A typical way to measure selective attention to novelty during infancy (Fagan, 1970) is to expose an infant to a picture for a standard period of time. When the standard study time has been reached, the tester withdraws the picture from the infant's view and then pairs the previously seen picture with a new one for a brief time. Infants typically average about 60% of their time looking at the new picture. Pairing a new with an old target and measuring attention is only one example of a task used to measure knowledge acquisition early in life. Students of the mind of the infant have used additional tasks to discover what infants know and to test the validity of such measures for the prediction of later cognitive functioning. Among these are tasks that measure the infant's decreased responding in the presence of a repeated signal (e.g., Ashmead & Davis, 1996; Pancratz & Cohen, 1970), measures of the infant's duration of first look at a novel stimulus (Arterberry, Midgett, Putnick, & Bornstein, 2007), observations of infants learning to act in a certain way to get a reward (e.g., Rovee-Collier, 1997), and measures of the speed of an infant's eye movements that anticipate where a display will be following the observation of a regular sequence of events (Dougherty & Haith, 1997).

The Intelligent Infant

Theoretically, infants acquire knowledge. Does this early ability to take in and retain information bear any relationship to IQ scores at a later age? The answer is yes. Studies in the late 1970s and early 1980s by Fagan (1984), Fagan and McGrath (1981), Fagan and Singer (1983), Lewis and Brooks-Gunn (1981), and Yarrow, Klein, Lomonaco, and Morgan (1975) found significant associations (mean *r* of .42) between selective attention during infancy and later IQ measured at various points from 2 to 7 years. Since that time, numerous studies have found average correlations of about .36 to .40 between infants' learning abilities and the later IQs of those children (see reviews by Anastasi & Urbina, 1997; Bornstein et al., 2006; Bornstein & Sigman, 1986; Chen & Siegler, 2000; Deary, 2000; Domsch, Lohaus, & Thomas, in press; Fagan & Detterman, 1992; Fagan & Singer, 1983; Fagan, Holland, & Wheeler, 2007; Hetherington, Parke, Gauvain, & Locke, 2006; Kavsek, 2004; McCall & Carriger, 1993; Rose, Feldman, & Jankowski, 2009; Rose, Feldman, Jankowski, & Van Rossem, 2008; Sternberg, Grigorenko, & Bundy, 2001).

In the majority of studies, continuity in intellectual functioning is usually examined from infancy to childhood. Sigman, Cohen, and Beckwith (1997), who tested simple visual attention to abstract patterns in preterm newborns seen at date of term birth, did find a relationship between individual differences in infants' attention and intelligence at 18 years at $r = .36$. A study by Fagan, Holland, and Wheeler (2007) asked if measures of selective attention to novelty on the part of 6- to 12-month-old infants would predict their later IQ at 21 years as well as their academic achievement (years of education completed). Information-processing ability during infancy was predictive of adult IQ and of academic achievement with coefficients of .34 and .32, and coefficients corrected for unreliability, of .59 and .53, respectively.

McCall and Carriger (1993) estimated that correlation coefficients between cognitive abilities during infancy and IQ during childhood (2–8 years) are consistent at about $r = .36$, a conclusion similar to that of Kavsek (2004), who put the value at .37. McCall and Carriger call such consistency "provocative" (p. 76) and note that longitudinal prediction typically declines with age. The level of prediction to later IQ found in the Fagan, Holland, and Wheeler study, an *r* of .34, is consistent with the average value of .36 noted by McCall and Carriger in their meta-analysis and is identical to the value reported by Sigman, Cohen, and Beckwith for prediction from early tests of attention to IQ at 18 years. Moreover, predictions from infancy to either IQ at 21 years or to academic accomplishment by 21 years in the Fagan, Holland, and Wheeler study were virtually identical at *r*s of .34 and .32, or *R*s (coefficients corrected for unreliability) of .59 and .53, respectively.

To put into perspective the correlations of about .36 to .40 between infant learning and memory abilities and later IQ, summarized earlier, note that typically brief (10–20 minute) sessions involving from 1 to 10 items on which to base a score for an infant yield predictive validity coefficients of .36 to .40. Such coefficients are identical to those reported for extensive studies of the predictive validities obtained between SAT tests (taking hours to complete and comprising more than 100 items) and subsequent college GPAs (Zwick, 2002).

In summary, there appears to be a substantial relationship between how well infants process the information they are given to think about and how high their scores on an intelligence test will be later in life as well as to what levels of education they will reach by early adulthood. The fact that later intelligence and achievement can be predicted from infancy has theoretical implications that will now be considered.

Implications for Theory: Single Versus Multiple Intelligences

A classic issue in the study of intelligence is whether there is a single, general intelligence (Jensen, 1998) or whether there are multiple intelligences (Gardner, 1993; Sternberg, 1997b). Each camp assumes that everyone (of the same age and speaking the same language) taking an intelligence test has had equal opportunity for exposure to the information necessary to achieve success on the test. Given the equal opportunity for exposure assumption, if the correlations among the subtests of an IQ test are high, the *g* theorists assert that the same intelligence is being applied to each subtest. If the correlations among the subtests are low, than the multiple intelligences theorists claim vindication for their view that performance on each subtest relies on a different kind of intelligence.

How can work on the origins of intelligence in infancy aid in clarifying the single versus multiple intelligences controversy? Many paradigms have now been developed to measure cognition in infants, paradigms that experimentally ensure that exposure to the information to be acquired has been made commonly available to all infants undergoing testing. Among these paradigms are the following: decreased responding in the presence of a repeated signal (assuming such a procedure is done properly – see Cohen, 2004), the surprise an infant displays when an anticipated event does not occur (Baillargeon, 2004; Hespos & Baillargeon, 2008), the infant's knowledge of faces in the context of actions (Bahrick & Newell, 2008), the infant's knowledge of facial affect (Flom & Bahrick, 2007) and of face-voice relations (Bahrick, Hernandez-Reif, & Flom (2005), the infant's ability to understand the intentions of others (Woodward, 2009), the infant's ability to perform basic mathematical operations (McCrink & Wynn, 2007), long-term recognition (Bornstein, Arterberry, & Mash, 2004) and recall abilities of infants (Bauer, 2007), early language abilities (Estes, Evans, Alibali, & Saffran, 2007; Maye, Weiss, & Aslin, 2008; Saffran, 2003; Saffran, Pollak, Seibel, & Shkolnik, 2007; Saffran & Wilson, 2003; Teinonen, Aslin, Alku, & Csibra, 2008), object perception (Amso & Johnson, 2006, Mash, Arterberry, & Bornstein, 2007; Needham, 2009), object individuation (Wilcox, Woods, Chapa, & McCurry, 2007), understanding of solids and liquids (Hespos, Ferry, & Rips, 2009), visual statistical learning (Kirkham, Slemmer, & Johnson, 2002; Kirkham, Slemmer, Richardson, & Johnson, 2007), imitation skills (Demiris & Meltzoff, 2008; Legerstee & Markova, 2008, Meltzoff & Moore, 2002), and the infant's ability to categorize (Arterberry & Bornstein, 2002; Bornstein & Arterberry, 2003; Oakes, Horst, Kovack-Lesh, & Perone 2009).

Consider each of these paradigms as diverse subtests of a test of intelligence for infants. Assume also that the items on each subtest have been shown to be not too easy or too difficult for normal infants of that age to solve. If such a test could be given, at the same ages, to a large number of infants representing a normative demographic spread, the question of the scope of the developmental origins of a general factor of intelligence or of multiple intelligences could be addressed. The beginnings of such an approach are contained in a recent study by Rose, Feldman, and Jankowski (in press), who posit a general relationship among at least a small number of measures of information processing from the first through the third years of life.

Implications for Theory: Continuity Versus Discontinuity

The debate as to whether the nature of intelligence is continuous or discontinuous over age has a long history in the field of developmental psychology. Many years ago people developed "intelligence" tests for infants based on the infant's ability to perform various sensory or motor feats. At what age would a baby's eyes first follow a moving object? How soon would a baby roll over? When does the baby first sit alone? At what age does the baby walk? Age norms were developed for such physical accomplishments. Testing instruments were developed to measure the age at which infants could succeed at such sensorimotor tasks. Scores on these tests of sensorimotor development were widely assumed to be measures of intelligence. However, as early as the mid 1950s, people realized that the attempt to predict later IQ from sensorimotor accomplishments during infancy was not going to be successful. For example, Nancy Bayley noted in 1955 that later intelligence could not be predicted from tests of physical milestones made during infancy. In succeeding years, a variety of investigators confirmed that scores based on early sensorimotor functioning have no significant value in predicting how much a child knows on an IQ test later in life. Fagan and Singer (1983) reviewed the results of 101 studies published to that time in which attempts had been made to predict IQs in childhood from tests of sensorimotor functioning given during the first year of life. They found that the average correlations between widely used tests of infant sensorimotor development given during the first year of life and later IQ scores obtained between 3 and 6 (or more) years of age for 50 groups of normal infants and 51 groups of infants expected to be at risk for later mental retardation (due to various circumstances at birth) were .14 and .21, respectively. The results indicated that tests of sensorimotor functioning have little validity for the prediction of later IQ. Similar reviews by Anastasi and Urbina (1997), Chen and Siegler (2000), Hetherington et al. (2006), and Sternberg, Grigorenko, and Bundy (2001) have come to the same conclusion.

Why do these tests of sensorimotor functioning have little power in predicting later IQ? Bayley (1955) and other theorists (see also McCall, Hogarty, & Hurlburt, 1972) interpreted the predictive shortcomings of the sensorimotor tests for infants as reflecting a fundamental change in the nature of intelligence over age. They assumed that the growth of intelligence was a "discontinuous" process. You have one kind of intelligence as an infant and another kind of intelligence as a child. This idea of "discontinuity" in intelligence was conceptually appealing because it corresponded with, and was influenced by, a similar view of intelligence held by Piaget (1952), who saw intelligence as a progression, with age, through a series of stages, each characterized by its own unique type of intelligence (see Miller, 2002, for a complete exposition of Piaget's theory). Piaget, in fact, labeled the first stage of intelligence, the stage during infancy, as "sensorimotor" intelligence.

In effect, by assuming that intelligence is what anything called an "intelligence test" measures, theorists concluded that the failure to predict later IQ scores from early tests of sensorimotor functioning during infancy meant that the very nature of intelligence changes with age. Bayley went on, in fact, to publish an intelligence test for infants in 1969. Bayley's test was based on sensorimotor functioning. She noted, in her test manual, that her scales had "limited value as predictors of later abilities." Given the notion that it is the nature of intelligence that changes with age, however, she justified the use of her scales as providing "the basis for establishing a child's current status" (Bayley, 1969, p. 4).

There is, however, an obvious alternative to the discontinuity explanation for why tests of infant sensorimotor functioning do not predict later IQ. Quite simply, sensorimotor skills are not intellectual skills, so why should tests of sensorimotor functioning be predictive of later IQ? On intelligence tests, which do predict how well one does in school, children are asked to discriminate, to categorize, to retrieve previously learned information, and so on. Infants faced with novel and previously exposed information also evidence such intellectual skills, skills predictive of later IQ. Thus, the findings that the infant's ability to acquire and retain information predicts later IQ means that the discontinuity theory of intellectual development is not well supported. Rather, the findings support theories that assume the continuity of intelligence over age.

If the basic elements of the acquisition of knowledge are present from infancy, what is it that changes with age? What changes with development is a person's state of knowledge. Courage and Howe (2002) reviewed data indicating what appear to be shifts in ability at the end of the second year of life. They came to the conclusion that the findings, in fact, are much more indicative of continuity than of discontinuity. They also emphasized that such continuity in development is driven by basic underlying processes that are themselves continuous. They note that their review supports models that assume cognitive development as a continuous process. In the same vein, Quinn (2008), in a reply to Kagan (2008), provides a strong argument for what he calls core competencies of infants as underlying continuity in cognitive processing marked by quantitative but not by qualitative change.

In a recent theoretical and empirical review as to how adult memory evolves from the memory abilities of infants, Rovee-Collier and Cuevas (2009) conclude that the basic abilities of infants and adults to learn and remember remain the same although what is learned about the world grows with age. Wagner and Lakusta (2009) go further in a recent theoretical article, in which they argue that the infant's ability to represent objects and actions and to realize how events are related may involve the same mechanisms that underlie knowledge of semantic structures in language. They argued that studies on the infant's understanding of language can aid in resolving questions about the infant's ability to represent objects, actions, and relations among events. It is also possible that the reverse is true. We can also resolve questions about language development by knowing how the infant represents actions and events. With regard to the question of the bases of the continuity of intelligence from infancy to adulthood, the suggestion in the present chapter is that what can be learned about common mechanisms underlying language and nonlinguistic representations may also aid in discovering the nature of some of the basic cognitive processes underlying intelligence.

Finally, note that arguments about the influence of basic cognitive processes relative to the importance of what might be considered more advanced or more complex, high-level cognitive functioning are not unique to developmental psychologists. Barrouillet, Lepine, and Camos (2008), for example, showed that the influence of working memory on high-level cognition in adults is itself mediated by more basic cognitive processes. Thus, findings as to the validity of selective attention and other measures of early cognitive functioning for the long-term prediction of intelligence and of academic achievement support the view that intelligence is continuous over age and, theoretically, that the cause of such continuity lies in basic cognitive abilities.

Implications for Theory: Genetic and Environmental Influences on Intelligence

A fuller understanding of the processes underlying performance on learning and memory tasks during infancy may, ultimately, allow the identification of the fundamental units of intelligence and the genetic and environmental factors that influence them. Conclusions regarding the influence of heritability or the influence of environment on intelligence are invariably linked to how intelligence is theoretically and operationally defined. The fact that later IQ can be predicted from measures of basic cognitive abilities taken during infancy supports the suggestion of Fagan and Holland (2002) that more accurate estimates of the genetic and environmental contributions to intelligence must involve the application of behavior genetic models to measures of information processing where equal opportunity for exposure to information has been experimentally assured. Following such a course is in line with current views on the importance of investigating a "process" as opposed to a "state" analysis of intellectual functioning (Grigorenko, 2000) and an emphasis on how genes and environments may interact in producing particular outcomes (Champagne, 2009). Such an approach might allow us to explain, for example, why socioeconomic status (SES) modifies heritability estimates of IQ. Turkheimer, Haley, Waldron, D'Onofrio, and Gottesman (2003) analyzed data from a national sample of twins and found that the IQs of poor children were primarily influenced by the environment, while the IQs of children from affluent families were largely determined by genetics. Would such findings emerge from a similar study where intelligence was measured by cognitive processing abilities rather than by the IQ score? That is, does SES make a difference in the processing of information? Or does SES more likely reflect differences in access to information?

Smith, Fagan, and Ulvund (2002) investigated the influences of recognition memory ability at 7 and 12 months of age and parental socioeconomic status on later intellectual functioning at 8 years of age in a study conducted in Norway. Measures of a parent's socioeconomic status such as education and occupation give a rough estimate of the cultural environment of a young child and parental socioeconomic status predicts the later IQ of a child. Does socioeconomic status have an effect on IQ because children from upper class homes are better information processors than children from lower class homes? Tests of selective attention predicted the later IQs of the children. The level of their parents' socioeconomic status also was a strong predictor of the child's IQ. But the infants' ability to remember what they had seen bore no relation to the parents' socioeconomic status. Infants from lower SES families processed information as well as infants from upper SES families. Most important, stepwise multiple regression analyses indicated that early selective attention to novelty made a significant contribution to the prediction of later IQ, a contribution independent of the prediction made by parental SES.

Smith et al. (2002) noted that their understanding of the relations between SES and memory ability during infancy in determining later IQ was based on a limited sample from one culture and called for replication. In fact, the study by Fagan, Holland, and Wheeler (2007), noted earlier, allowed a comparison to the findings of Smith et al. Partial correlations indicated that selective attention to novelty during infancy predicted later adult IQ and adult academic achievement independently of any effect of parental educational level. Thus, the Smith et al. finding that information-processing ability during infancy and variations in SES each contributed significant independent variance to the prediction of later IQ in a Norwegian sample were replicated in the study by Fagan, Holland, and Wheeler in America.

Loehlin (2000) points out that any changes in group differences in achievement will only come about when their causes are understood. Sternberg and Grigorenko (2004) emphasize the need to explore the cultural context to understand group differences in intellectual development. As noted, IQ scores later in life are due to both early information-processing abilities and to the circumstances in life that determine what children have been taught by their culture. Studies of the relative influences of cognitive ability and cultural effects on IQ have been further elucidated by studies examining differences in IQ between children differing in race, where measures of their memory ability during infancy are also available. The question is whether group differences in the ability to process information during infancy accompany group differences in later IQ. If groups of infants do not differ in how well they process information, differences in later IQ between the groups must be due to differences in the information they have subsequently been given to process.

Studies by Fagan et al. (1991) and by Park-Choi, Roo, Iian, and Fagan (1994) compared culturally and racially diverse groups on a test of intelligence based on selective attention to novelty developed for infants (Fagan & Detterman, 1992). The infants tested included White Americans, African Americans, African Ugandans, Bahrainians, Laotians, and Koreans. The main finding from these studies was that infants from widely different cultural backgrounds did equally well. Fagan (2000) noted studies involving samples of American children who, as infants, were tested for selective attention to novelty and, as children, on standard IQ tests. In an initial sample of 299 American children, 35 were African American and 264 were White. All came from middle-class, suburban homes. The second sample, drawn from a multisite, national study in the United States, included 70 infants at risk for later IQ deficit (34 Whites and 36 African Americans) from predominantly lower class families. The results from both samples were quite clear. Whites had higher IQ scores than African Americans. Early attention to novelty, however, was the same for African Americans as it was for Whites. A parsimonious explanation for the findings is that later differences in IQ between different racial-ethnic groups may spring from differences in cultural exposure to information past infancy, not from group differences in the basic ability to process information.

Implications for Practice: The Physically Compromised Infant

Tests of memory abilities can be used to provide an assessment of the intelligence of physically compromised infants. In some cases, intelligence is not impaired despite debilitating circumstances. Drotar, Mortimer, Shepherd, and Fagan (1989), for example, tested selective attention to novelty on the part of an infant paralyzed in both arms and both legs at birth. The infant's recognition memory ability was normal despite severe physical handicap and a life spent in a hospital. The infant, who had been having feeding problems, fed much better once he was viewed by his caretakers as intellectually normal and was given appropriate social contact during feeding sessions. The results of the testing also influenced a decision to place the child in a nursing home for physically impaired children who were intellectually intact. Dutch investigators (De Moor & Hendriksen, 1994) have also used selective attention to novelty to determine that a 12-month-old infant with severe physical limitations and spastic quadriplegia was, nevertheless, developing normally intellectually.

Implications for Practice: Causes of Disordered Intellectual Functioning

Intervention to relieve or to prevent intellectual disability will not come about until we know the causes of such disabilities. Investigators are measuring recognition memory ability during infancy to investigate the effect that exposure to particular chemical agents may have on early and later intellectual development. Chemical agents explored include PCBs and alcohol (see review by Jacobson, 2006) and cocaine (e.g., Chiriboga, Kuhn, & Wasserman, 2007; Gaultney, Gingras, Martin, & DeBrule, 2005; Singer et al., 2005). Tests of selective attention to novelty have also been used to explore the processing ability of HIV-infected infants (Drotar et al., 1997; Drotar et al., 1999). HIV-infected infants, despite progressive sensorimotor deterioration over the first year of life, appear to be capable of age-appropriate memory functioning during the first year of life. Thus, on a positive note, infants with HIV appear able to profit from what they are being taught by their caretakers even though the infants are ill and are delayed in their motor development.

A further positive note comes from a study by Colombo et al. (2004), who explored maternal docosahexaenoic acid (DHA) levels in mother's milk at birth and the subsequent development of infant attention. Infants of mothers with higher DHA when the baby was born showed more advanced development of attention based on habituation measures of information processing during the first year.

Implications for Practice: Genetic Factors in Early Intellectual Disability

One approach to understanding the biochemical bases of disordered intellectual functioning early in life is to study the effects of the common bodily biochemicals on cognitive functioning in populations with known neurological dysfunction. Such was the purpose of a study of children with Down syndrome undertaken in Norway by Nygaard, Reichelt, and Fagan (2001). The purpose of the Nygaard et al. study was to see if there is a relationship between the ability of Down syndrome children to attend to novelty and the child's levels of urine peptide or levels of serum antibodies to food proteins. The assumption was that certain peptides derived from gluten that can cross the blood-brain barrier may affect the development of the central nervous system. A computer-based version of the Fagan Test of Infant Intelligence adapted for use with children was employed in the testing of 55 Down syndrome children who ranged in age from 4 to 11 years. The Down syndrome children had a mean Stanford-Binet IQ of 51.9. Correspondingly, their mean score on the Fagan test was quite low, at 54%, on immediate tests of attention to novelty and 50.8% on delayed tests of attention to novelty. Blood samples of IgG and IgA antibodies to food proteins were also measured by Nygaard et al. The most important results of the Nygaard et al. study centered on highly statistically significant negative correlations ranging from −.44 to −.51 between IgG and IgA activity to gliadin and gluten and immediate tests of recognition memory. In other words, higher IgG and IgA activity to gliadin and gluten resulted in poorer selective attention to novelty. Such negative correlations between antibodies to gliadin/gluten and Stanford-Binet IQ scores were also obtained (*rs* of −.27 to −.33) but were not as predictive as those found with the test based on selective attention. Thus the Nygaard et al. study found a strong relationship between levels of antibodies to gluten and a basic ability to process information. Any causal link between these two factors, of course, remains to be established, but the findings call for further investigation since gluten is a commonly ingested food protein.

Later cognitive developmental disabilities based on possible genetic influences may also be identified by the use of tests of recognition memory ability during infancy. The dopamine system, for example, is implicated in attention deficit hyperactivity disorder (commonly known as ADHD). ADHD is associated with the dopamine D4 receptor (called DRD4). More specifically, the seven-repeat allele (7-DRD4) is more frequent in children with ADHD. In a recent study (Auerbach, Benjamin, Faroy, Geller, & Ebstein, 2001), a team of Israeli investigators found that 12-month-old infants at risk for ADHD who were carrying the 7-D4DR allele were less attentive to visual novelty.

Understanding the Neurological Bases of Infant Cognition

Colombo (2002) notes the emergence of an emphasis on an understanding of the neurological bases of the infant's cognitive abilities. Quinn, Westerland, and Nelson (2006) report distinct event-related potentials corresponding to the infant's familiarization to examples from a common category and the infant's responses to an example from a novel category. Ackles (2007) finds that Nc event-related potentials of greater amplitude are made to novel stimuli on the part of 6- to 7-month-olds. Lepage and Theoret (2007) and Bertenthal and Longo (2007) note evidence for possible involvement of the mirror neuron system in the infant's ability to imitate the actions of others. The search for the neurological bases of the mechanisms that may underlie intelligent behavior during infancy can also be related to an extensive body of research across various species that employs an organism's attention to or reactions to stimulus novelty as a means of imputing the neurological bases of the learning and memory abilities of that organism. Recent reviews of such research involving species as disparate as humans, monkeys, rodents, and flies can be found in Kumaran and Maguire (2007), Bachevalier and Nemanic (2008), Dere, Huston, and Silva (2007), and van Swinderen (2007), respectively.

The hope of all this activity is that the use of tests of cognitive functioning early in life, and across species, will lead to the discovery of some of the causes of intellectual disabilities due to neurological dysfunction, perhaps due to environmental causes that can be altered. Once causes are found, programs of treatment or prevention can be initiated. The discovery of any of the causes of intellectual or learning disabilities and the prevention of those causes would be of enormous economic and social benefit.

Summary

The use of measures of learning and memory in infancy has allowed persistent controversies as to the nature of intelligence to be addressed. Is there continuity in intelligence from age to age? Yes. Individual differences in how well infants can acquire and retain information predict how much they know later in childhood and in early adulthood. Is there a genetic basis to racial or socioeconomic status differences in IQ? Evidence presented here says that infants from different racial or SES groups do not differ in how well they process information. Such equality implies that current estimates of the influence of genetics on intelligence based on standard IQ scores may not be as accurate as would estimates based on individual differences in information-processing abilities. More broadly, the study of basic learning and memory abilities in various species based on paradigms used to study the origins of intelligence in infancy is currently a focus of scientists in many areas of psychology, neurology, and microbiology. Such a focus creates the possibility of a unified, multidisciplinary, and comprehensive understanding of the basic components of intelligence from the psychological to the molecular level. Practically, the study of information processing in the infant allows the identification of normal intelligence in otherwise handicapped individuals and facilitates the search for the causes of intellectual disability. In brief, the study of the origins of intelligence in infancy by measures of early cognitive functioning may aid in clarifying theoretical issues, contribute to a methodologically integrated study of intelligence across a number of scientific disciplines, and, eventually, aid in reducing the incidence of intellectual disability.

Acknowledgments

The preparation of this chapter was supported, in part, by a Leffingwell Professorship.

References

Ackles, P. K. (2008). Stimulus novelty and the cognitive-related ERP components of the infant brain. *Perceptual and Motor Skills*, **106**, 3–20.

Ackerman, P. L. (1996). A theory of adult intellectual development: Process, personality, interests, and knowledge. *Intelligence*, **22**, 227–257.

Amso, D., & Johnson, S. P. (2006). Learning by selection: Visual search and object perception in young infants. *Developmental Psychology*, **42**, 1236–1245.

Anastasi, A., & Urbina, S. (1997). *Psychological testing*. Upper Saddle River NJ: Prentice-Hall.

Arterberry, M. E., & Bornstein, M. H. (2002). Variability and its sources in infant categorization. *Infant Behavior and Development*, **25**, 515–528.

Arterberry, M. E., Midgett, C., Putnick, D. L., & Bornstein, M. H. (2007). Early attention and

literary experiences predict adaptive communication. *First Language*, 27, 175–189.
Ashmead, D. H., & Davis, D. L. (1996). Measuring habituation in infants: An approach using regression analysis. *Child Development*, 67, 2677–2690.
Auerbach, J. G., Benjamin, J., Faroy, M., Geller, V., & Ebstein, R. (2001). DRD4 related to infant attention and information processing: A developmental link to ADHD? *Psychiatric Genetics*, 11, 31–35.
Bachevalier, J., & Nemanic, S. (2008). Memory for spatial location and object-place associations are differentially processed by the hippocampal formation, parahippocampal areas TH/TF and perirhinal cortex. *Hippocampus*, 18, 64–80.
Bahrick, L. E., Hernandez-Reif, M., & Flom, R. (2005). The development of infant learning about specific face-voice relations. *Developmental Psychology*, 41, 541–552.
Bahrick, L. E., & Newell, L. C. (2008). Infant discrimination of faces in naturalistic events: Actions are more salient than faces. *Developmental Psychology*, 44, 983–996.
Baillargeon, R. (2004). Infants' physical world. *Current Directions in Psychological Science*, 13, 89–94.
Barrouillet, P., Lepine, R., & Camos, V. (2008). Is the influence of working memory capacity on high-level cognition mediated by complexity or resource-dependent elementary processes? *Psychonomic Bulletin and Review*, 15, 528–534.
Bauer, P.J. (2007). Recall in infancy: A neurodevelopmental account. *Current Directions in Psychological Science*, 16, 142–146.
Bayley, N. (1955). On the growth of intelligence. *American Psychologist*, 10, 805–818.
Bayley, N. (1969). *The Bayley Scales of Infant Development*. New York, NY: Psychological Corporation.
Berlyne, D. E. (1960). *Conflict, arousal, and curiosity*. New York, NY: McGraw-Hill.
Bertenthal, B. J., & Longo, M. R. (2007). Is there evidence for a mirror system from birth? *Developmental Science*, 10, 526–529.
Bornstein, M. H., & Arterberry, M. E. (2003). Recognition, discrimination and categorization of smiling by 5-month-old infants. *Developmental Science*, 6, 585–599.
Bornstein, M. H., & Arterberry, M. E. (2004). Long-term memory for an emotional interpersonal interaction occurring at 5 months of age. *Infancy*, 6, 407–416.
Bornstein, M. H., & Sigman, M. D. (1986). Continuity in mental development from infancy. *Child Development*, 57, 251–274.
Bornstein, M. H., Hahn, C., Bell, C., Haynes, O. M., Slater, A., Golding, J., Wolke, D., & ALSPAC Study Team. (2006). Stability in cognition across early childhood: A developmental cascade. *Psychological Science*, 17, 151–158.
Caron, R. F., & Caron, A. J. (1968). The effects of repeated exposure and stimulus complexity on visual fixation in infants. *Psychonomic Science*, 10, 207–208.
Ceci, S. J. (2000). So near and yet so far: Lingering questions about the use of measures of general intelligence for college admission and employment screening. *Psychology, Public Policy, and Law*, 6, 233–252.
Champagne, F. A. (2009). Beyond nature vs. nurture: Philosophical insights from molecular biology. *Observer*, 22(4), 27–28.
Chen, Z., & Siegler, R. (2000). Intellectual development in childhood. In R. J. Sternberg (Ed.), *Handbook of intelligence*. New York, NY: Cambridge University Press.
Chiriboga, C. A., Kuhn, L., & Wasserman, G. A. (2007). Prenatal cocaine exposures and dose related cocaine effects on infant tone and behavior. *Neurotoxicology and Teratology*, 29, 323–330.
Cohen, L. B. (2004). Uses and misuses of habituation and related preference paradigms. *Infant and Child Development*, 13, 349–352.
Colombo, J. (2002). Infant attention grows up: The emergence of a developmental cognitive neurological perspective. *Current Directions in Psychological Science*, 11, 196–2000.
Colombo, J., Kannass, K. N., Shaddy, D. J., Kundurthi, S., Maikranz, J. M., Anderson, C. J., Blaga, O. M., & Carlson, S. E. (2004). Maternal DHA and the development of attention in infancy and toddlerhood. *Child Development*, 75, 1254–1267.
Courage, M. L., & Howe, M. L. (2002). From infant to child: The dynamics of cognitive change in the second year of life. *Psychological Bulletin*, 128, 250–277.
Deary, I. (2000). Simple information processing and intelligence. In R. J. Sternberg (Ed.), *Handbook of intelligence*. New York, NY: Cambridge University Press.
Demiris, Y., & Meltzoff, A. (2008). The robot in the crib: A developmental analysis of imitation skills in infants and robots. *Infant and Child Development*, 17, 43–53.

De Moor, J. M. H., & Hendriksen, J. G. M. (1994). Cognitieve ontwikkelingssbeoordeling met de Fagan-test van een jong kind met spastische tetraparese. *Tijdschr Kindergeneeskd*, *62*, 14–17.

Dere, E., Huston, J. P., & De Souza Silva, M. A. The pharmachology, neuroanatomy and neurogenetics of one-trial object recognition in rodents. *Neuroscience and Biobehavioral Reviews*, *31*, 673–704.

Domsch, H., Lohaus, A., & Thomas, H. (in press). Prediction of childhood cognitive abilities from a set of early indicators of information processing capabilities. *Infant Behavior and Development*.

Dougherty, T. M., & Haith, M. (1997). Infant expectations and reaction time as predictors of childhood speed of processing and IQ. *Developmental Psychology*, *33*, 146–155.

Drotar, D., Mortimer, J., Shepherd, P. A., & Fagan, J. F. (1989). Recognition memory as a method of assessing intelligence of an infant with quadriplegia. *Developmental Medicine and Child Neurology*, *31*, 391–397.

Drotar, D., Olness, K., Wiznitzer, M., Guay, L., Marum, L., Svilar, G., Hom, D., Fagan, J. F., Ndugwa, C., & Kiziri-Mayengo, R. (1997). Neurodevelopmental outcomes of Ugandan infants with human immunodeficiency virus type 1 infection. *Pediatrics*, *100*, e1–e7.

Drotar, D., Olness, K., Wiznitzer, M., Schatschneider, C., Marum, L., Guay, L., Fagan, J. F., Hom, D., Svilar, G., Ndugwa, C., & Kiziri-Mayengo, R. (1999). Neurodevelopmental outcomes of Ugandan infants with HIV infection: An application of growth curve analysis. *Health Psychology*, *18*, 114–121.

Estes, K. G., Evans, J. L., Alibali, M. W., & Saffran, J. R. (2007). Can infants map meaning to newly segmented words? Statistical segmentation and word learning. *Psychological Science*, *18*, 254–260.

Fagan, J. F. (1970). Memory in the infant. *Journal of Experimental Child Psychology*, *9*, 217– 226.

Fagan, J. F. (1984). The relationship of novelty preferences during infancy to later intelligence and later recognition memory. *Intelligence*, *8*, 339–346.

Fagan, J. F. (1992). Intelligence: A theoretical viewpoint. *Current Directions in Psychological Science*, *1*, 82–86.

Fagan, J. F. (2000). A theory of intelligence as processing: Implications for society. *Psychology, Public Policy, and Law*, *6*, 168–179.

Fagan, J. F., & Detterman, D. K. (1992). The Fagan Test of Infant Intelligence: A technical summary. *Journal of Applied Developmental Psychology*, *13*, 173–193.

Fagan, J. F., Drotar, D., Berkoff, K., Peterson, N., Kiziri-Mayengo, R., Guay, C., & Zaidan, S. (1991). The Fagan Test of Infant Intelligence: Cross-cultural and racial comparisons. *Journal of Developmental and Behavioral Pediatrics*, *12*, 168.

Fagan, J. F., & Holland, C. R. (2002). Equal opportunity and racial differences in IQ. *Intelligence*, *30*, 361–387.

Fagan, J. F., Holland, C. R., & Wheeler, K. (2007). The prediction, from infancy, of adult IQ and achievement. *Intelligence*, *35*, 225–231.

Fagan, J. F., & McGrath, S. K. (1981). Infant recognition memory and later intelligence. *Intelligence*, *5*, 239–243.

Fagan, J. F., & Singer, L. T. (1983). Infant recognition memory as a measure of intelligence. In L. P. Lipsitt (Ed.), *Advances in infancy research* (Vol. 2). New York, NY: Ablex.

Fantz, R. L. (1956). A method for studying early visual development. *Perceptual and Motor Skills*, *6*, 13–15.

Fantz, R. L. (1961). The origin of form perception. *Scientific American*, *204*, 66–72.

Fantz, R. L. (1964). Visual experience in infants: Decreased attention to familiar patterns relative to novel ones. *Science*, *146*, 668–670.

Flom, R., & Bahrick, L. E. (2007). The development of infant discrimination of affect in multimodal and unimodal stimulation: The role of intersensory redundancy, *Developmental Psychology*, *43*, 238–252.

Gardner, H. (1993). *Multiple intelligence: The theory in practice*. New York, NY: Basic Books.

Gaultney, J. F., Gingras, J. L., Martin, M., & DeBrule, D. (2005). Prenatal cocaine exposure and infants' preference for novelty and distractibility. *Journal of Genetic Psychology*, *166*, 385–406.

Gibson, E. J. (1969). *Principles of perceptual learning and development*. New York, NY: Appleton- Century-Crofts.

Grigorenko, E. L. (2000). Heritability and intelligence. In R. J. Sternberg (Ed.), *Handbook of intelligence*. New York, NY: Cambridge University Press.

Grigorenko, E. L., & Sternberg, R. J. (1998). Dynamic testing. *Psychological Bulletin*, *124*, 75–111.

Hespos, S. J., & Baillargeon, R. (2008). Young infants' actions reveal their developing knowledge of support variables: Converging evidence for violation-of-expectation findings. *Cognition*, 107, 304–316.

Hespos, S. J., Ferry, A. L., & Rips, L. J. (2009). Five-month-old infants have different expectations for solids and liquids. *Psychological Science*, 20, 603–611.

Hetherington, E. M., Parke, R. D., Gauvain, M., & Locke, V. O. (2006). *Childhood psychology: A contemporary viewpoint* (6th ed.). Boston, MA: McGraw-Hill.

Jacobson, S. W. (2006). Specificity of neurobehavioral outcomes associated with prenatal alcohol exposure. *Alcoholism: Clinical and Experimental Research*, 22, 313–320.

Jensen, A. R. (1998). *The g factor*. Westport, CT: Praeger.

Kagan, J. (2008). In defense of qualitative changes in development. *Child Development*, 79, 1606–1624.

Kavsek, M. (2004). Predicting later IQ from infant visual habituation and dishabituation: A meta-analysis. *Journal of Applied Developmental Psychology*, 25, 369–393.

Kirkham, N. Z., Slemmer, J. A., & Johnson, S. P. (2002). Visual statistical learning in infancy: Evidence for a domain general learning mechanism. *Cognition*, 83, B35–B42.

Kirkham, N. Z., Slemmer, J. A., Richardson, D. C., & Johnson, S. P. (2007). Location, location, location: Development of spatiotemporal sequence learning in infancy. *Child Development*, 78, 1559–1571.

Kumaran, D., & Maguire, E. A. (2007). Match-mismatch processes underlie human hippocampal responses to associative novelty. *Journal of Neuroscience*, 27, 8517–8524.

Legerstee, M., & Markova, G. (2008). Variations in 10-month-old infant imitation of people and things. *Infant Behavior & Development*, 31, 81–91.

Lepage, J-F, & Theoret, H. (2007). The mirror neuron system: Grasping others' intentions from birth? *Developmental Science*, 10, 513–523.

Lewis, M., & Brooks-Gunn, J. (1981). Visual attention at three months as a predictor of cognitive functioning at two years of age. *Intelligence*, 5, 131–140.

Loehlin, J. C. (2000). Group differences in intelligence. In R. J. Sternberg (Ed.), *Handbook of intelligence*. New York, NY: Cambridge University Press.

Mash, C., Arterberry, M. E., & Bornstein, M. H. (2007). Mechanisms of visual object recognition in infancy: Five-month-olds generalize beyond the interpolation of familiar views. *Infancy*, 12, 31–43.

Maye, J., Weiss, D. J., & Aslin, R. N. (2008). Statistical phonetic learning in infants: Facilitation and feature generalization. *Developmental Science*, 11, 122–134.

McCall, R. B., & Carriger, M. S. (1993). A meta-analysis of infant habituation and recognition memory performance as predictors of later IQ. *Child Development*, 64, 57–79.

McCall, R. B., Hogarty, P., & Hurlburt, N. (1972). Transitions in infant sensorimotor development and prediction of childhood IQ. *American Psychologist*, 27, 728–748.

McCrink, K., & Wynn, K. (2007). Ratio abstraction by 6-month-old infants. *Psychological Science*, 18, 740–745.

Meltzoff, A. N., & Moore, M. K. (2002). Imitation, memory, and the representation of persons. *Infant Behavior & Development*, 25, 39–61.

Miller, P. H. (2002). *Theories of developmental psychology*. New York, NY: Worth.

Needham, A. (2009). Learning in infants' object perception, object-directed action, and tool use. In A. Woodward & A. Needham (Eds.), *Learning and the infant mind*. New York, NY: Oxford University Press.

Nygaard, E., Rreichelt, K. L., & Fagan, J. F. (2001). The relation between the psychological functioning of children with Down syndrome and their urine peptide levels and levels of serum antibodies to food proteins. *Down Syndrome: Research and Practice*, 6, 139–145.

Oakes, L. M., Horst, J. S., Kovack-Lesh, K. L., & Perone, S. (2009). How infants learn categories. In A. Woodward & A. Needham (Eds.), *Learning and the infant mind*. New York, NY: Oxford University Press.

Pancratz, C. N., & Cohen, L. B. (1970). Recovery of habituation in infants. *Journal of Experimental Child Psychology*, 9, 208–216.

Park-Choi, H., Roo, H., Iian, Y., & Fagan, J. F. (1994). Study of the utility of the Fagan Test of Infant Intelligence (FTII) with Korean full-term and premature infants. Poster given at the International Conference on Infant Studies, Paris.

Piaget, J. (1952). *The origins of intelligence in children* (M. Cook, Trans.). New York, NY: W. W. Norton.

Quinn, P. C. (2008). In defense of core competencies, quantitative change, and continuity. *Child Development*, 79, 1633–1638.

Quinn, P. C., Westerlund, A., & Nelson, C. A. (2006). Neural markers of categorization in

6-month-old infants. *Psychological Science*, **17**, 59–66.
Rose, S. A., Feldman, J. F., & Jankowski, J. J. (2009). A cognitive approach to the development of early language. *Child Development*, **80**, 134–150.
Rose, S. A., Feldman, J. F., & Jankowski, J. J. (in press). Information processing in toddlers: Continuity from infancy and persistence of preterm deficits. *Intelligence*.
Rose, S. A., Feldman, J. F., Jankowski, J. J., & Van Rossem, R. (2008). A cognitive cascade in infancy: Pathways from prematurity to later mental development. *Intelligence*, **36**, 367–378.
Rovee-Collier, C. (1997). Dissociations in infant memory: Rethinking the development of implicit and explicit memory. *Psychological Review*, **104**, 467–498.
Rovee-Collier, C., & Cuevas, K. (2009). Multiple memory systems are unnecessary to account for infant memory development: An ecological model. *Developmental Psychology*, **45**, 160–174.
Saffran, J. R. (2003). Statistical language learning: Mechanisms and constraints. *Current Directions in Psychological Science*, **12**, 110–114.
Saffran, J. R., Pollak, S. D., Seibel, R. L., & Shkolnik, A. (2007). *Cognition*, **105**, 669–680.
Saffran, J. R., & Wilson, D. P. (2003). From syllables to syntax: Multilevel statistical learning by 12-month-old infants. *Infancy*, **4**, 273–284.
Sigman, M., Cohen, S. E., & Beckwith, L. (1997). Why does infant attention predict adolescent intelligence? *Infant Behavior and Development*, **20**, 133–140.
Singer, L. T., Eisengart, L. J., Minnes, S., Noland, J., Jey, A., Lane, C.. & Min, M. O. (2005). Prenatal cocaine exposure and infant cognition. *Infant Behavior and Development*, **28**, 432–444.
Smith, L., Fagan, J. F., & Ulvund, S. E. (2002). The relation of recognition memory in infancy and parental socioeconomic status to later intellectual competence. *Intelligence*, **30**, 247–259.
Sternberg, R. J. (1997a). The concept of intelligence and its role in lifelong learning and success. *American Psychologist*, **52**, 1030–1037.
Sternberg, R. J. (1997b). *Successful intelligence*. New York, NY: Plume.
Sternberg, R. J. (2000a). The concept of intelligence. In R. J. Sternberg (Ed.), *Handbook of intelligence*. New York, NY: Cambridge University Press.
Sternberg, R. J. (2000b). Implicit theories of intelligence as exemplar stories of success: Why intelligence test validity is in the eye of the beholder. *Psychology, Public Policy, and Law*, **6**, 159–167.
Sternberg, R. J., & Grigorenko, E. L. (2004). Why we need to explore development in its cultural context. *Merrill-Palmer Quarterly*, **50**, 369–386.
Sternberg, R. J., Grigorenko, E. L., & Bundy, D. A. (2001). The predictive value of IQ. *Merrill- Palmer Quarterly*, **47**, 1–41.
Sternberg, R. J., Grigorenko, E. L., & Kidd, K. K. (2005). Intelligence, race, and genetics. *American Psychologist*, **60**, 46–59.
Teinonen, T., Aslin, R. N., Alku, P., & Csibra, G. (2008). Visual speech contributes to phonetic learning in 6-month-old infants. *Cognition*, **108**, 850–855.
Turkheimer, E., Haley, A., Waldron, M., D'Onofrio, B., & Gottesman, I. I. (2003). Socioeconomic status modifies heritability of IQ in young children. *Psychological Science*, **14**, 623–628.
van Swinderen, B. (2007). Attention-like processes in *drosophila* require short-term memory genes. *Science*, **315**, 1590–1593.
Wagner, L., & Lakusta, L. (2009). Using language to navigate the infant mind. *Perspectives on Psychological Science*, **4**, 177–184.
Wilcox, T., Woods, R., Chapa, C., & McCurry, S. (2007). Multisensory exploration and object individuation in infancy. *Developmental Psychology*, **43**, 479–495.
Woodward, A. L. (2009). Infants' grasp of others' intentions. *Current Directions in Psychological Science*, **18**, 53–57.
Yarrow, L. J., Klein, R. P., Lomonaco, S., & Morgan, G. A. (1975). Cognitive and motivational development in early childhood. In B. X. Freidlander, G. M. Sterritt, & G. E. Kirk (Eds.), *Exceptional infant* (Vol. 3). New York: Brunner/Mazel.
Zeaman, D., & House, B. J. (1963). The role of attention in retardate discrimination learning. In N. R. Ellis (Ed.), *Handbook of mental deficiency*. New York, NY: McGraw-Hill.
Zwick, R. (2002). *Fair game? The use of standardized admissions tests in higher education*. New York, NY: RoutledgeFalmer.

CHAPTER 8

Intelligence in Childhood

L. Todd Rose and Kurt W. Fischer

As parents and teachers know, a child's behavior is incredibly variable. Regardless of age and across all cultures, the maturity of a child's thoughts and actions changes dramatically depending on context, task demands, and with different people. For example, Parisa, a sixth-grader, can easily solve a logical puzzle her teacher gave her in class, but she struggles with the same puzzle at home on her own. Similarly, David, a third-grader, has no trouble doing a difficult math problem about the cost of oranges with his father's help, but he has considerable difficulty doing the same problem in class the next day. On the other hand, if given a similar problem about the cost of video games, David can easily solve the problem. Such rapid fluctuations in competence can be a source of frustration for teachers, parents, and students alike, but they are normal. The fact is that variability is a natural part of all childhood behavior, intelligent or not.

The notion that variation is fundamental to behavior is hardly controversial. It does, however, present a serious challenge for classical models of intelligence, which focus almost exclusively on stability and ignore or *explain away* variability in behavior despite its pervasiveness (for example, Chomsky, 1965; Horn, 1976; Piaget, 1983). While these theories have their usefulness, to the extent that they fail to capture the complexity of real behavior they offer at best a one-dimensional view of intelligence. At worst they lead to distorted simplifications being put forward as explanations and give the impression that something as complex as intelligence is simple. It is not.

Behavior always functions in multiple parts, and as a result there are many ways to think and act, all of which are profoundly influenced by an individual's biology, culture, and immediate context. This view of behavior means that intelligence is difficult to pin down with a single number on a test, or even a group of numbers – behavior is simply more interesting than that!

The challenge facing contemporary research on childhood intelligence is to explain patterns of both variability and stability *together* in children's behavior (Fischer & Bidell, 2006; Mascolo & Fischer, 2010;

Overton, 2006; van Geert, 1998). To accomplish this requires an alternative framework to replace traditional models of behavior as the basis for research and interpretation. Classic models are static and so can characterize regularities in the organization of behavior, but they struggle to account for the variability that underpins such stability. In recent years, advancements have been made in the concepts, methods, and tools available to scholars seeking a dynamic analysis of intelligence – advancements grounded in dynamic systems theory. In this chapter we draw on these advancements and put forward a developmental framework – dynamic skill theory – that is capable of reconciling the tensions between order and variability in behavior, and in this way advancing the study of intelligence.

The chapter is organized as follows: We begin by discussing a core problem that has plagued the study of intelligence for decades – the complexity of behavior. We then outline the central tenets of dynamic systems, which underpin efforts to analyze the organization and development of behavior in its complexity, keeping person and context connected and treating variability as the starting point for analysis. Next, we review classic approaches to intelligence – psychometric, Piagetian, nativist, and dynamic/constructivist – and show how disputes between them have illuminated learning sequences, resolved important questions, and paved the way for a dynamic approach to intelligence.

We introduce the dynamic skill theory framework, emphasizing its conceptual origins in dynamic systems, ways that it has advanced understanding variability and consistency in intelligence, and its relevance to understanding childhood intelligence. We close by considering several important areas where dynamic systems concepts and models have generated usable knowledge directly relevant to intelligence, learning, and the practice of education. The take-home point from this chapter is that a dynamic approach to behavior is advancing understanding of the core nature of intelligence in childhood and beyond. Variability in behavior is vast, and analyzing it dynamically provides a firm grounding for both finding stabilities and understanding the scope and range of variations that children routinely demonstrate in their intelligent behavior

Framing Childhood Intelligence

The hallmark of the dynamic nature of behavior is that it is both organized and variable: It both changes systematically over time and fluctuates moment-to-moment depending on multiple characteristics of the person and context. Classical models of intelligence have proven capable of explaining certain stable aspects of children's behavior and have generated a body of data that has shaped research and practice for decades. This chapter focuses on areas where classic models have fallen short, but note that these criticisms are possible, in part, because of the success of classic research and theory. The power of the classic models is that by focusing on normative data they have been able to construct descriptions of global regularities in children's intelligent behavior, such as the difference between problem solving in 4-year-olds versus 14-year-olds. This work has had a lasting impact on theory and research and has influenced the practice of education.

However, the power of classical models is also their limitation: Although they account elegantly for stability, they offer little explanation for the pervasive variability that children show in their behavior. Static models can offer valuable summaries of normative changes, but in learning contexts such as schools, being effective in shaping learning requires understanding variation and diversity. Normative findings are not sufficient. The development of intelligence is complex, involving many interdependent components that must be coordinated to produce skilled activity. To understand the nature of childhood intelligence, researchers must be able to detect and analyze patterns in the development of children's behavior, even when they are variable and complex.

In recent years, a number of scholars have emphasized the importance of variability (Fischer & Bidell, 2006; Mascolo & Fischer, 2010; Overton, 2006; Siegler, 2007; van Geert, 1998) and have sought to explain stability and diversity in behavior over time. In order to capture the richness and complexity of children's intelligence, these researchers have increasingly adopted concepts, methods, and tools from dynamic systems theory. In doing so, they follow in the footsteps of developmental science, which recently underwent a similar shift – catalyzed by dynamic systems – where classic, static models are giving way to dynamic ones that emphasize variability in developmental processes as well as moment-to-moment behavior. The fields of intelligence and development are obviously not the same. However, to the extent that they share a focus on complex behavior and struggle with the same *crisis of variability* (Fischer & Bidell, 2006; Rose & Fischer, 2009a), recent advancements in developmental science are relevant to the contemporary study of childhood intelligence. Here we provide a brief overview of the central tenets of dynamic systems, as applied to the study of behavior and development. This framework will set the stage for an in-depth discussion of dynamic skill theory.

Dynamics of Intelligent Behavior

The field of development is undergoing a conceptual shift that is dramatically reorienting theory and research. At the heart of this shift is *dynamic systems theory* – a flexible set of concepts and powerful nonlinear mathematical models uniquely suited to the study of complex phenomena, such as action, thought, and emotion (Rose & Fischer, 2009b). A full treatment of dynamic systems theory is beyond the scope of this chapter (for a thorough review, see Abraham & Shaw, 2005; Damon & Lerner, 2006; Thelen & Smith, 1994; van Geert, 1991, 1998). Here we limit discussion to two essential dynamic systems concepts – person-in-context and variability-as-information – and the mathematical models that serve as a powerful tool for understanding the richness and complexity of childhood intelligence.

Dynamic Concepts

From a dynamic systems perspective, it is not possible to analyze behavior outside of the context in which it occurs. Behavior is not something that a person "has"; it emerges from interactions between person and context. Performance in sports provides a good illustration of this principle. Even the relatively simple act of throwing a baseball is not a fixed action that happens identically every time. Context matters! In the moment, a pitcher throws differently depending on multiple factors working together: temperature, crowd noise, lighting, fatigue, a runner on base, or the catcher's skill (to name a few). Understanding a pitcher's performance, including its natural variation, depends on analyzing how such factors function in the immediate context, which includes the characteristics of the person throwing the ball, of course. Such dynamic processes are part of all behaviors, not just throwing a baseball.

Because the dynamic systems approach assumes that behavior is actively organized and context-specific, variability obviously should be expected as a natural outcome. In contrast to traditional models of intelligence, which assume that a child has a relatively fixed level of ability, the dynamic systems approach starts by assuming that children vary in their actions and seeks to identify stable patterns within that variability. This assumption represents an important difference from other approaches to behavior, and it has important conceptual and methodological consequences for the study of intelligence. If variability is systematically ignored, intelligence becomes synonymous with statistical averages, and researchers lose the ability to account for the very processes that underpin the behavior they seek to explain. Variability is the essence of adaptive behavior.

Dynamic Models

Dynamic systems concepts have already influenced the way scientists think about children's behavior and development. Yet simply changing concepts is not sufficient to produce meaningful results. Indeed, a danger inherent in applying systems concepts to behavior is a tendency to adopt vaguely a new label – such as contextualized behavior – without specifying exactly *how* it functions. Full realization of the potential of dynamic systems requires more than changing labels for processes of behavior and development. We must build explicit mathematical models of those processes. Vague concepts can be useful for a time, but eventually they must be pinned down as models with clearly defined parameters. Only then can researchers determine whether the processes they hypothesize actually produce the patterns of intelligent behavior they expect (Fischer & Kennedy, 1997; van der Maas & Molenaar, 1992; van Geert, 1998; van Geert & van Dijk, 2002). Realizing the power of the dynamic systems approach to behavior and development requires using mathematical models that go beyond conjecture to make dynamic concepts testable and falsifiable, and therefore scientific.

Educational scholars have historically shown an aversion to mathematical modeling. This reluctance was not entirely unwarranted early on, as scientists were basically forcing static, linear models onto behavior. Given how complex children's behavior is known to be, a static model – where something like intelligence is assumed to progress in the same way for all children – makes no sense. Fortunately, dynamic systems theory provides powerful *nonlinear* models that allow scholars to study children's behavior in its complexity, without separating the child from his or her environment. One reason for the growing interest in using dynamic models is their increased accessibility to anyone who can use a computer. In fact, any spreadsheet program such as Excel can be used to build nonlinear, dynamic models. In addition, modeling programs have been designed and books written specifically for building such models (for example, Abraham & Shaw, 2005; van Geert 1994, 1998).

Dynamic modeling of children's behavior and development is still young, but it has genuine potential. For example, biologists have had success creating models of interacting species in an ecosystem, such as predatory/prey models that easily capture patterns of variation in, for example, rabbits and foxes in the wild. Meteorologists have successfully modeled changes in weather systems, making it possible to predict the paths of hurricanes or thunderstorms. Similarly, scientists interested in intelligence can move toward a richer analysis of children developing skills that have many components and are influenced by many different factors. Nonlinear dynamic modeling has the potential to transform the field of intelligence from a body of rich but loosely formulated descriptions of behavior to explicit dynamic models that are rigorously grounded in empirically testable data (Fischer & Bidell, 2006; Thelen & Smith, 1994; Stein, Dawson, & Fischer, in press; van Geert, 1998; van Geert & Fischer, 2009). This is the promise of a dynamic approach to studying children's behavior and development.

Beyond Concepts and Models

Dynamic systems models provide the first real opportunity to analyze children's behavior with its complexity intact – to move beyond static explanations of intelligence, where oversimplification is often the rule. However, it is important to recognize that dynamic systems theory is not a theory of intelligence. It simply provides concepts and tools that enable the analysis of complex systems. Even by themselves, dynamic models can provide insights about intelligent behavior, such as the importance of feedback from the context in shaping learning and development (van Geert, 1998). Yet to advance the field, dynamic concepts must be grounded in a framework for specifying the relevant parameters affecting the interacting components that create behavior and shape its development. Later in the chapter, we will outline a framework for dynamic analysis of learning and development. But first to understand some of the parameters and components of intelligence, we begin with reviewing classical approaches.

Classical Approaches to Intelligence

There are many different approaches to conceptualizing intelligence, each with its own strengths and weaknesses, and we cannot discuss all of them in this chapter. (For a full treatment of different theories and their underlying metaphors, see Sternberg, 1997 and Lerner, 2002, as well as various chapters in this book.) Instead, we focus on approaches that have contributed substantially to dynamic analysis of intelligence – psychometric, Piagetian, and nativist approaches, and the dynamic approach that integrates their insights. Building on fundamental concepts from these approaches, we will discuss how dynamic systems analysis unifies seemingly disparate frameworks to explain both the variability and the stability of intelligence.

Psychometric Approach: Factors of Intelligence

Over the past century the most dominant of the classic approaches to intelligence has been the psychometric. Originating with the work of Charles Spearman (1904, 1923), the psychometric approach has focused mainly on using the statistical tools of factor analysis to identify and define the latent factors underpinning individual differences in mental abilities, as they are measured by standardized tests based in psychometric analysis (Neisser et al., 1996). This structural approach to intelligence has proven successful at generating many factorial theories (models of factors of intelligence), as well as a considerable body of empirical research that spans multiple decades (described in many other chapters in this book). It continues to serve as the foundation for tests of intelligence that are commonly used in educational settings such as the Stanford-Binet (Terman & Merrill, 1973), the Wechsler (1939) Intelligence Scales, and Raven's Progressive Matrices (Raven, Raven, & Court, 2003).

Although scientists and educators widely acknowledge now that intelligence is not a single entity (Gardner, 1983; Sternberg, 1985), considerable debate continues among researchers about the number and nature of factors of intelligence. In his seminal work, Spearman (1904, 1927) argued for a two-factor theory: a general factor that is common to all tests, and specific factors unique to the particular test being administered. Spearman's idea that a general ability underpins performance on all intelligence tests came from his observation of the so-called positive manifold – the finding that various measures of intelligence tend to correlate positively. This general factor represents the theoretical basis for the postulate that intelligence can be measured with a single IQ score (Ardila, 1999).

While the positive manifold is one of the most robust and replicable findings in the field of intelligence (Carroll, 1993), Spearman's interpretation has generated considerable debate and criticism from the beginning (Thurstone, 1938). The result has been a wide variety of alternative theories that have influenced both research and practice, with the number of factors for different models varying from two or three to several hundred (e.g., Cattell, 1971; Eysenck, 1986; Gardner, 1983; Guilford, 1967; Jensen, 1987; Sternberg, 1985; Vernon, 1950).

One particularly influential factorial theory that relates to development of intelligence is the theory of fluid and crystallized intelligence (Cattell, 1971; Horn, 1976; Horn & Cattell, 1967), which defines two factors that show different patterns of development with age during adulthood. Both fluid and crystallized intelligence increase sharply throughout childhood. Then the pattern shifts in adulthood: The abilities called crystallized intelligence increase slowly, continuing well into old age so long as the person remains healthy and active. The abilities in fluid intelligence, on the other hand, begin to decline by early or middle adulthood.

Crystallized intelligence is often characterized as knowledge and skill based in a person's regular experience, such as vocabulary that people use commonly and problems that are part of people's everyday life. Fluid intelligence, in contrast, involves unfamiliar tasks and experiences, which people do not commonly experience. For example, most people seldom encounter visual-spatial puzzles and analogies, such as those in Raven's Progressive Matrices (Raven, Raven, & Court, 2003), which therefore involve fluid intelligence. Sometimes fluid intelligence is said to be connected to creativity, because on fluid tasks people solve problems that are unfamiliar or novel. (Note, however, that people who are famous for creativity usually demonstrate it in tasks that are highly familiar for them, such as Mozart with music and Darwin with biology; Simonton, 1999.)

A key problem with the psychometric approach is that despite many decades of often contentious debate, different procedures for analysis lead to not one but many models of the structure of intelligence. This variability of intelligence needs to be faced directly, and factor models remain static. Even the model of fluid and crystallized intelligence, which is based in patterns of change with development, portrays these factors as fixed, while in fact they are dynamic. For example, when a person practices working with visual-spatial problems over many months, such as training to be an architect, tasks that began as indicators of fluid intelligence become crystallized. They shift from being novel and unfamiliar to being highly practiced and familiar, and their pattern of growth in adulthood shifts accordingly. Dynamic effects of this kind need to be included in models of intelligence. Psychometric models treat factors of intelligence as largely stable. They provide almost no account of the dynamics of development and the constructive processes by which people produce intelligent behavior (Jencks, 1992; Fischer & Bidell, 2006). This limitation of the psychometric approach is fundamental, particularly in the context of education, where knowledge and learning are so obviously affected by the dynamics of motivation, emotion, context, and task specifics.

Piagetian Approach: Logic and Constructivism

In the 1960s and 1970s, Piaget's (1983; Piaget & Inhelder, 1966) framework became the dominant approach to cognitive development and intelligence. Piaget moved beyond the associative learning principles that dominated the psychometric and behavioral approaches and analyzed the mind as actively constructing and interpreting the environment. He and his colleagues searched for the structure of the mind, defined by its underlying logic and a set of experience-dependent universals. In specifying how logic shaped the mind, Piaget (1983) postulated several stages of cognitive development, characterized as the logic of action in infancy, the faulty half-logic (egocentrism) of representations in the preschool years, the logic of concrete operations in childhood, and the logic of formal operations in adolescence.

Piaget's framework and research agenda still define many of the central research questions for today's researchers and educators, and his detailed, insightful observations of children's cognitive activities remain the source of many ideas for current research and theory (Rose & Fischer, 2009a). His focus on constructivism has fared well, but his emphasis on universal logical structures of the mind has not.

A major criticism of Piagetian theory is the overwhelming evidence for asynchrony in children's development, which he called "décalage," meaning unevenness (Fischer, 1980). Piaget predicted that when a new logic emerged in the mind (such as the logic of concrete operations), it would catalyze the whole mind into a new kind of intelligence, but research has not supported this prediction. To the contrary, children consistently show décalage instead of monolithic transformation, even with logically equivalent tasks. Piaget and his colleagues recognized this fact, acknowledging, for example, that the conservation of number (how many stones or dolls) develops on average around age 5 or 6 years, but conservation of amount of liquid (water or orange juice) appears a year or two later at 7 or 8, and conservation of volume several years later still (Piaget, 1983; Piaget & Inhelder, 1966). Research shows that skills for different kinds of conservation develop along separate pathways, not synchronously (Halford, 1989). This unevenness is difficult to reconcile with a concept of strong stages: If the mind is governed by underlying logical structures, why would they manifest themselves at one age in some contexts, but not until later ages in others? Piaget (1972) acknowledged this source of variability, but he never explained it.

The limitations of the theory of logical stages became evident with a tidal wave of empirical research starting in the 1960s and continuing to the present, revealing remarkable variability in every aspect of cognitive development (Siegler, 1994). Researchers have shown repeatedly that changes in Piaget's tasks and procedures led to clear departures from the stability predicted by stage theory. Demonstrably, décalage is the norm in cognitive development, not the exception. This evidence rendered untenable the hypothesis that universal forms of mental logic created stages of development (Fischer & Bidell, 2006; Rose & Fischer, 2009a). On the other hand, the constructivism of Piaget's theory continues to be supported by a broad array of research, from neuroscience (Battro, 2000; Immordino-Yang & Damasio, 2007; Singer, 1995), cognitive development (Case & Edelstein, 1993; Griffin & Case, 1997; Halford, 1989), and emotional development (Ayoub et al., 2006; Damasio, 2003; Fischer, Shaver, & Carnochan, 1990). Children build knowledge actively based on their experiences.

Nativist Approach: Early Competences

One of the major themes of research challenging Piaget's theory was that it seriously underestimated the competence of infants and young children (Carey & Gelman, 1991; Spelke et al., 1992). A movement of neo-nativism in the 1970s surged forth to demonstrate many ways that infants and young children showed surprising abilities in prominent domains such as concepts of number, space, and object as well as language. Nativist researchers worked tirelessly to show that Piagetian tasks can mask the real abilities of children (Halford, 1989). The goal of this research is to find "essential" knowledge, stripping away as much support for process and performance as possible to get at the underlying "competence." Researchers have simplified the questions, instructions, scoring criteria, and procedural details in assessment tasks, and in the process they have developed new versions of Piaget's classic tasks that sometimes demonstrate surprising competences in infants and toddlers.

Consider for example object permanence, the notion that an object continues to exist even when an infant cannot perceive it. Piaget used successful retrieval of a hidden object to assess object permanence and found that it emerged in infants around 8 months of age when infants began to search for an object that they had seen disappear under a cloth or screen (Piaget, 1954). Nativists, in contrast, have used surprise as the criterion for object permanence – for example, does an infant show surprise when an object is not present upon removal of a screen behind which it had disappeared? Infants show surprise as early as 3 to 4 months of age, and some researchers have used these findings to argue that Piaget was wrong about the development of object knowledge (Baillargeon, 1987; Spelke et al., 1992).

Such discrepancies raise the important question: What explains the origin of this early knowledge? Nativists typically reply that the knowledge is innate – precocious knowledge, an inborn, genetically determined competence module about, for example, objects. They say that sensorimotor limitations such as difficulty grasping an object prevent infants from demonstrating what they "know" in most experimental paradigms. This *argument from precocity*

(Fischer & Bidell, 1991) has been used to claim innate determination for a wide range of concepts beyond object permanence, including space, number, language, and theory of mind (Carey & Spelke, 1994; Saxe, Carey, & Kanwisher, 2004).

The argument has a fundamental problem: The first glimmer of infant behavior related to a domain such as object permanence is taken to show a general competence – knowledge of the permanence of objects. How does this glimmer prove general knowledge of object permanence even though infants fail every aspect of such knowledge except one (showing mild surprise at the disappearance of an object). The first glimmer is only a small beginning. From that beginning, children build a sequence of skills that eventually create broad knowledge of object permanence (Fischer & Bidell, 2006). A glimmer does not indicate full competence.

Knowledge needs to be taken as contextually influenced and variable, not fixed based on one task that infants can do. Knowledge varies across tasks based on their complexity, familiarity, and other factors; and within a domain children develop skills in a learning sequence, an ordering of tasks along a developmental pathway. Nativist research has selectively focused on downward variation in age of onset for concepts like object permanence, and it has ignored the complementary and widely observed upward variation in age for other tasks and conditions (Pinard, 1981). For a theory of development to be useful, it cannot simply opt out of explaining change, growth, and variability. Explanation is required! A major starting point for explanation is defining knowledge not as fixed but as varying along learning sequences.

Learning sequences describe how concepts of an object involve many skills arrayed along strands in a developmental web, as shown in Figure 8.1. The web begins with the abilities of young infants that nativists have uncovered and moves toward complex, diverse knowledge and action. Gradually over time children build knowledge along multiple strands for each domain.

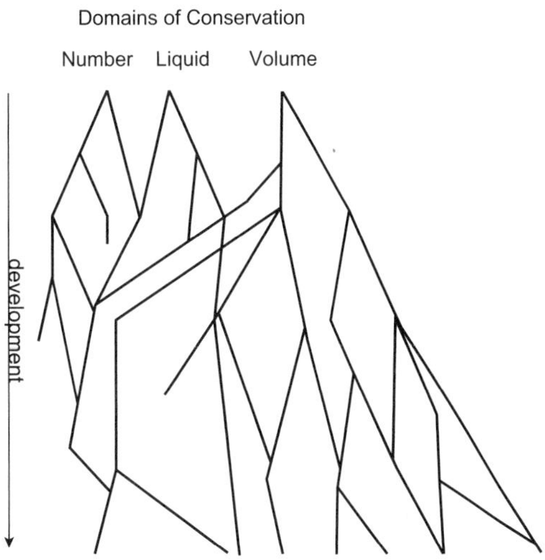

Figure 8.1. A constructive web of development.

Toward Dynamics: Building Knowledge Step by Step

The arguments between nativist and neo-Piagetian researchers about early knowledge have led to new research on how children build knowledge. Research on literacy (Snow, Griffin, & Burns, 2005) and mathematics has made some of the greatest advances. We will focus on the development of arithmetic in the early years, where (sometimes to their own surprise) researchers and educators have discovered learning sequences for the construction of basic mathematical knowledge and shown how educators can facilitate learning by helping children move through those sequences. With number, for example, children construct the number line as they develop, especially when they receive experience and instruction to facilitate their understanding.

Before the number line, infants demonstrate two kinds of simple numerical knowledge (Dehaene, 1997; Spelke et al., 1992) – subitizing for enumeration of small numbers (1 or 2 or 3) and number sense for judging relative magnitude (proportionate comparison of sets of objects such as many versus few buttons). These elementary number skills form a foundation for understanding arithmetic, but they are not sufficient by

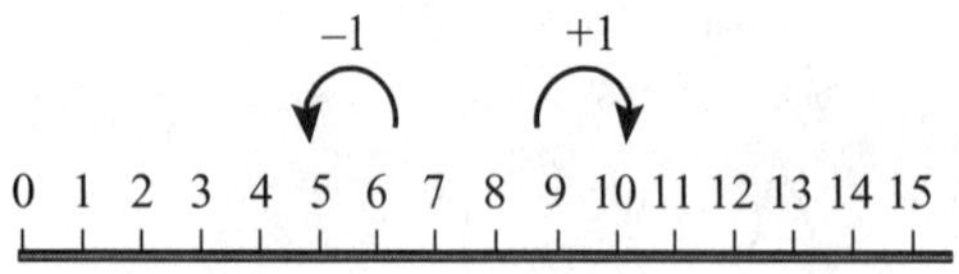

The number line forms the foundation for understanding the basics of number. For this simple version, adding 1 makes the number higher to the right. Subtracting 1 makes it lower to the left.

Figure 8.2. Central conceptual structure for the number line. The number line forms the foundation for understanding the basics of number. For this simple version, adding 1 makes the number higher to the right. Subtracting 1 makes it lower to the left.

themselves. Children need specific experience about numbers to support their building the complex knowledge for elementary number.

An important breakthrough in understanding children's building of early number skills is the discovery by Case, Griffin, Siegler, and their colleagues that children construct a *central conceptual structure* for number, which when effectively taught shows powerful generalization across tasks (Case et al., 1996; Griffin, Case, & Siegler, 1994; Griffin & Case, 1997). Children construct the number line to represent the ways that numbers move up and down along a line or scale, as in Figure 8.2. In this central conceptual structure, numbers vary along the line, increasing one unit at a time in one direction (2 to 3, or 6 to 7) and decreasing in the other direction.

The number line goes far beyond the two infant systems for number (subitizing and number sense), and its construction depends on experience with a number line. Games with number lines built into them, such as Chutes and Ladders (an ancient game) and many other board games, are particularly effective at teaching the number line. The curriculum program called Number Worlds for early arithmetic focuses on teaching the number line, with games where children move objects or themselves along a number line, forward and backward. Such programs have been shown to powerfully enhance mathematics learning with as little as 10 weeks of training, especially in children from educationally disadvantaged homes (Case et al., 1996; Griffin & Case, 1997). Children develop a central conceptual structure for the number line, and that knowledge facilitates reasoning across a wide range of tasks that differ greatly except for their focus on number, such as doing arithmetic problems in school, telling time with a clock, and counting birthday presents at home. The power of the number line construct is evident in the huge size of the effects, explaining as much as 50% of the variance in performance over time, much larger than the effects of most curricula.

Interestingly, researchers taking a nativist approach discovered how children between 2 and 4 years of age construct the number line gradually (Carey, 2009; Le Corre et al., 2006). Starting with an initial hypothesis that young children would use a number line spontaneously, they discovered instead that the children gradually built it one digit at a time between 2 and 4 years of age. These children grew up in environments that supported learning the number line at home or in preschool. Still, as Case and Griffin had hypothesized, it took them several years to build this central conceptual structure.

Children sat at a table with a number of similar toys spread out on it, such as an array of dinosaurs. An interviewer asked a child to give her a particular number of objects, for example "3 dinosaurs" or "1 dinosaur." In performing this task the children built the number line one digit at a time. First, they used 1 as a true number (1 and only 1 dinosaur), but treated other numbers as meaning "many" dinosaurs. A few months later, they added 2 as a true number, with 3 and 4 meaning "many." After a few more months they added 3 as a number, and then still later 4. At about age 3.5, a few months after they understood 1, 2, 3, and 4, they generalized their knowledge to a number line, starting with 1, 2, 3, and 4. This knowledge included understanding that the number of objects can be determined by counting: The last number counted is the number of dinosaurs. This is the beginning of the number-line framework that becomes the foundation of arithmetic and mathematics.

Progress from Research

In this way, research is often the arbiter in debates such as those between nativism and neo-Piagetian constructivism. The learning sequence for understanding number came from bringing together nativist with neo-Piagetian research. The nativist approach predicted that understanding the number line would spontaneously develop in young children, such as 2-year-olds. Research showed, however, that young children build the number line gradually one digit at a time. The learning sequence for number knowledge begins with infants' capacities for subitizing and number sense, but the central conceptual structure of the number line takes several years to build, laying the foundation for much more elaborate construction of mathematical concepts to follow. Understanding the development of intelligence requires explaining how children build these kinds of learning sequences out of the variability that they routinely show in action and thought.

Dynamic Skill Theory

Dynamic skill theory is an approach to studying children's behavior that integrates dynamic systems concepts and tools within a robust developmental framework to explain learning and development. Emerging from the broader neo-Piagetian movement in developmental science, dynamic skill theory has made significant contributions to modern developmental research by providing a framework for reconciling long-standing tensions that plagued the field for decades. For example, it reconciles the evidence for commonalities in developmental sequences and achievements with the pervasive variability that underpins all development and learning. The power of the framework, and a principal reason for its impact on the field of developmental science, is that it simultaneously describes the large-scale changes of development and at the same time the incremental, daily, even minute-to-minute dynamics of learning and short-term variability (Fischer & Bidell, 2006; Fischer & Yan, 2002).

In this section we provide an overview of dynamic skill theory as it applies to the study of children's intelligence. Obviously, a complete account of the framework is beyond the scope of the chapter (for a thorough review, see Fischer & Bidell, 2006, and Mascolo & Fischer, 2010). Here we focus on its conceptual foundations, and on findings and methodological advancements from the framework. We begin by outlining two concepts at the heart of skill theory: the construct of *dynamic skill* and the metaphor of a *constructive web*. Then we show examples of how the dynamic analysis of skills can predict and explain both long-term macrodevelopmental changes and patterns of variability that are commonly observed in children's behavior but have eluded traditional models of intelligence.

Webs of Skill: Conceptual Foundations

In science, concepts and models (or constructs and metaphors) play a major role in shaping the scope and direction of a field: The constructs and metaphors scientists choose provide a structure for illuminating certain dimensions of a problem, determine the questions researchers are able to ask, and shape the development of methods and tools for addressing those questions. Conversely, metaphors and constructs can also blind scientists to alternative dimensions or explanations, rule out questions that should be asked, and limit the development of methods and tools that appear unrelated to the questions generated by the dominant metaphor (Hanson, 1961; Kuhn, 1970; Lakoff, 1987). The influence of metaphors and constructs is particularly salient in the field of intelligence, where contentious arguments historically have often derived from different underlying metaphors (Lakoff & Johnson, 1980; Lerner, 2002; Overton, 2006; Sternberg et al., 2003), which essentially means that by definition, they are not resolvable empirically because they ask different questions.

To move toward a dynamic view of intelligence, it is critical to adopt constructs that embody dynamics and to ground these constructs in models and metaphors that promote a more dynamic perspective. These constructs and models then foster development of tools for addressing the variability and complexity of behavior in context. There will not be only one right metaphor or construct for this purpose, since many different concepts, from a range of disciplines, can be based in dynamic systems theory (Abraham & Shaw, 1992–2005; Vallacher & Nowak, 1998; van der Maas & Molenaar, 1992; van Geert, 1998). The key is to think critically about whether a construct or metaphor that underpins a model of intelligence captures the essential characteristics of dynamic systems. In this spirit, we will discuss the ways that skill theory embodies dynamic systems in its core construct (dynamic skill) and one of its dominant metaphors (constructive web), before we outline advancements made in research and theory.

Dynamic Skills

An essential starting point for the dynamic analysis of intelligence is *dynamic skill*, which integrates many characteristics of dynamic systems into a single idea (Fischer, 1980). A skill is the capacity for acting in an organized way in a specific context – skills are, therefore, both task-specific and context-dependent (Fischer & Bidell, 1998, 2006; van Geert, 1991). Importantly, children do not have skills that are totally abstract, applying across all domains. Instead they have skills for specific contexts: a skill for playing chess, another for writing poetry, and yet another for interacting with their friends. These skills do not spring up full-grown; they are *constructed* when the children do real activities in real contexts over long time periods. Only gradually can children extend them to new contexts (Detterman & Sternberg, 1993; Fischer & Farrar, 1987; Salomon & Perkins, 1989; Willingham, 2007).

The skill construct also helps to frame relationships among the psychological, biological, and sociocultural processes that contribute to action, thought, and emotion. Consider an 8-year-old girl's skill for storytelling. It depends on her coordination of many different skills, including pretending, understanding of emotions and social reciprocity, understanding of cultural scripts and social roles, and her ability to plan and remember the story. All of these skills must work in concert with each other for her to tell an organized story to specific people in a specific context. The construct of dynamic skill helps facilitate the study of such relations among different skills and the patterns of variation they produce.

Constructive Webs

A dynamic representation of intelligence requires metaphors that promote analysis of the complexities and dynamic variations in children's behavior. Most classic metaphors for intelligence do not capture the full richness and complexity of behavior: Either they are profoundly static (such as the metaphor for development moving along a static geography; Waddington, 1966), or they focus too narrowly on stable process at the expense of variability in behavior (such as the computational metaphor; Atkinson & Shiffrin, 1968; Schacter, 1999). The problem is that these metaphors offer no mechanism for variability, and overly simple accounts of how behavior changes over time.

An alternative metaphor, one that captures both variability and stability in behavior, is the *constructive web* (Fischer & Bidell, 1998; Fischer et al., 1997). Figure 8.1 depicts a small-scale version of the web, where strands represent skills being developed, the connections between strands represent connections/integrations between skills, and forks represent differentiations of skills. The web provides a metaphor for constructing behavior that facilitates reconceptualizing children's intelligence in dynamic terms. Unlike traditional metaphors, the web highlights integration, specificity by domain, multiple pathways, active construction, and other central properties of behavior and development (Bidell & Fischer, 1992).

People are always constructing multiple strands (skills) of their web simultaneously, and strands interweave as progression is made toward more complex skills. Strands in a web start in many different places (organized by domain and context), are not confined to a particular direction, and end up at a range of points. While there is substantial variation in the development of webs, there is also a great deal of order: Children commonly show similar separations and integrations of strands, as well as similar beginning and ending points. The metaphor is useful for dynamic models because it supports thinking about active skill construction in a variety of contexts with multiple components, and it promotes an awareness of variability.

Order from Variation

Of course, the ultimate test of usefulness is that researchers can identify and analyze patterns of variability in children's behavior, not just pay homage to them. Skill theory offers powerful methods to detect such naturally occurring patterns of variability – some of which are general tools from dynamic systems theory and others of which are tools specifically derived from skill analysis (for relevant reviews, see Epstein, 1997; Fischer, Pipp, & Bullock, 1984; Fischer & Bidell, 2006; Mascolo & Fischer, 2010; Singer & Willett, 2003; Thelen & Smith, 1994; van Geert, 1998). Building on concepts, methods, and tools of skill theory, scholars have made exciting new discoveries about ordered variation in children's (and adults') behavior, discoveries that are relevant to analyzing intelligence. Here we focus on three kinds of variation: (1) developmental or learning pathways, (2) developmental range, and (3) skill levels. In each case, the goal is to show how the characteristics of skills, including the web-like process of skill construction, can predict and explain patterns of variability in children's behavior that have eluded classical models of intelligence.

Developmental Pathways

An important concept in skill theory is that while one child may develop according to the web in Figure 8.1, another child will develop along a different web. It will have important similarities, but it will be different. That is, children can and do construct skilled behavior along different developmental pathways. In addition, they can take multiple pathways to the same intelligent behaviors. Even when the outcome looks identical between two children, such as their scores on a measure of verbal concepts on the Wechsler Intelligence Scale for Children, individual webs will show unique sequences, with different sets of branches and distinct integration patterns. The notion of variability in the development of behavior is not new: Educators have argued for years that children routinely show variable patterns of performance (Dewey, 1963; Rose & Meyer, 2002; Schneps & Sadler, 1988; Siegler, 2007; Vygotsky, 1978). However, research within the skill framework shows how a focus on variability in pathways leads to discovery of new kinds of order in learning and development. This insight has implications for research and practice, especially in areas where normative approaches have not been effective. The development of single-word reading illustrates how order can be discovered from variability.

Without a doubt, the act of reading is a complex process with multiple components influencing whether a child will be successful (LaBerge & Samuels, 1974; Snow, Burns, & Griffin, 1998). In one study of pathways for reading single English words, Knight and Fischer (1992) used the concepts and methods of skill theory to study reading in first-, second-, and third-grade students. Classic models assume that skillful reading depends on early integration of sound-analysis

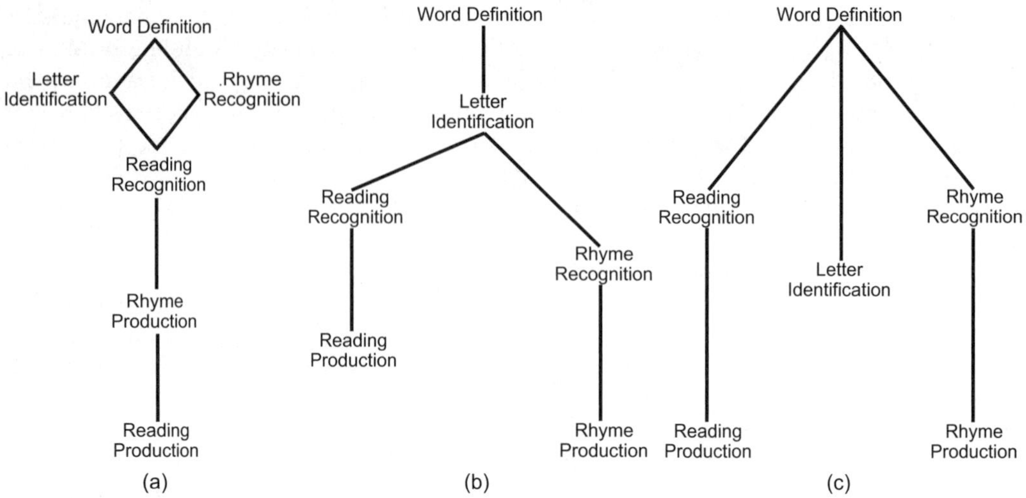

Figure 8.3. (a) Pathway A: A normative pathway for reading single words. (b) Pathway B: Independence of reading and rhyming. (c) Pathway C: Independence of reading, letter identification, and rhyming

and visual-graphic skills (Goswami, 2002; Torgesen, Wagner, & Rashotte, 1994; Wolf & Bowers, 1999). This prototypical model, shown in Figure 8.3a, begins with word definition (a child must know the word before being able to use it). To begin with, sound analysis (assessed by rhyming words) and visual-graphic skills (assessed by letter identification or spelling) are independent. An early step in reading is that students learn to integrate sight and sound on their way to proficient reading.

For many children in this study, the findings supported the classic model. Not only did it account for the learning web of a majority of the children, but it was strongly associated with good reading skills. However, not all students followed the prototypical pathway. Were these students simply delayed relative to their peers? Dynamic methods for detecting patterns in the variation uncovered evidence that the students were progressing along two alternative pathways (Figures 8.3b and 8.3c), both notable for their lack of integration. For pathway B (Figure 8.3b), letter identification led development, but reading and rhyming continued as independent strands. Interestingly, while this pathway characterized many struggling readers, some students following this path had strong reading skills! In contrast, pathway C (Figure 8.3c) was marked by a three-strand web, with reading, letter identification, and rhyming developing independently of one another. This path characterized most children with profound reading impairments. Remarkably, all 120 students in the study showed one of these three developmental pathways – there were no ambiguous cases!

The detection of alternative pathways for early reading is a powerful example of the natural variability inherent in complex behaviors. It also speaks against the assumption – built into many standardized assessments and research methodologies – that all children construct behaviors in exactly the same way. They do not. Normative data can make children seem similar when passing (or failing) assessments. In the study of reading pathways, standard statistical tests including all 120 students led to the conclusion that there was one pathway, the predicted, normative one (Figure 8.3a). But many of the children took different pathways, based on different strengths and weaknesses, as evidenced by Figures 8.3b and 8.3c. When this kind of ordered variability is ignored, children can end up characterized as "delayed" or "less intelligent" because they are not moving along an idealized pathway (Ayoub et al., 2006; Fischer et al., 1997).

In these cases, children are learning along distinctive pathways, but researchers use concepts and tools that cannot detect the differences. This serious misconception has profound consequences, severely underestimating the intelligence of many children. It can inadvertently misguide intervention strategies for children who struggle academically. For example, recent research on dyslexia (difficulty learning to read) indicates that many students with dyslexia have developed a different visual system (as well as a different auditory system), which gives them not only visual deficits but also specific visual talents (Schneps, Rose, & Fischer, 2007; von Károlyi, Winner, Gray, & Sherman, 2003).

By removing conceptual and methodological restrictions that come with normative models of behavior, skill theory allows scholars to detect and analyze ordered variability in developmental pathways. This is important because it puts the emphasis on *how* children actually construct intelligent behavior and offers ways for educators to support children progressing along non-normative pathways. This kind of work is already bearing fruits for children with normative abilities and those with learning disabilities (Case & Edelstein, 1993; Fischer, Bernstein, & Immordino-Yang, 2007; Fischer, Rose, & Rose, 2007; Rosc & Mcycr, 2002) as well as maltreated children (Ayoub et al., 2006; Fischer et al, 1997; Kupersmidt & Dodge, 2004; Watson, Fischer, Andreas, & Smith, 2004). Yet it is not limited to such groups: Many factors influence developmental pathways, including social, cultural, and biological processes. All of these have the potential to contribute to alternative pathways, and it is imperative that researchers use methods that reflect this variation instead of assessing only in terms of normative behavior.

Developmental Range

Beyond developmental pathways, children also vary considerably in their level of skilled behavior from moment to moment, depending on context and individual state. This fact runs counter to classical accounts of intelligence that, explicitly or implicitly, assume children's behavior is relatively fixed within a given domain, such as receptive vocabulary or spatial reasoning. This assumption is not tenable: A child's level of ability fluctuates routinely over time in response to different contexts, people, and problems. For example, a child may come to school one day – after a night's rest, having been well fed, and feeling secure – and do well on a set of tasks (such as receptive vocabulary). Yet the same child may come to school the next day – having missed breakfast, or having heard her parents argue the night before – and perform significantly worse on the exact same tasks. This change is not simply error; it is natural variability, and it represents a change in the relationship between strands of the web that must be coordinated for this set of tasks. Skilled teachers understand this kind of variation intuitively, and they are skeptical of claims that students have fixed levels of ability that are easily measured with one test, administered one time, in one context.

An important source of variability is contextual support: With the priming of key ideas or actions by an adult or a well-designed artifact (such as a book, a digital environment, or even a videogame), a child can perform at a higher level but cannot sustain that performance without support (Rose & Fischer, 2009a). For example, a first grader might be able to sound out and suggest rhymes for words, but only if his or her teacher helps by providing a choice of words that rhyme, or by modeling the skill of sounding out (Fischer & Rose, 2001; Knight & Fischer, 1992). Such differences between supported and unsupported contexts – which we call the *developmental range* – have been documented across many domains, such as mathematics Fischer & Kenny, 1986), critical thinking (Fischer & Pruyne, 2002; Kitchener, Lynch, Fischer, & Wood, 1993), and social skills (Rappolt-Schlichtmann et al., 2009; Watson & Fischer, 1980).

There is widespread evidence for the importance of contextual support, but in the field of intelligence it has been mostly ignored. When studied through the lens of

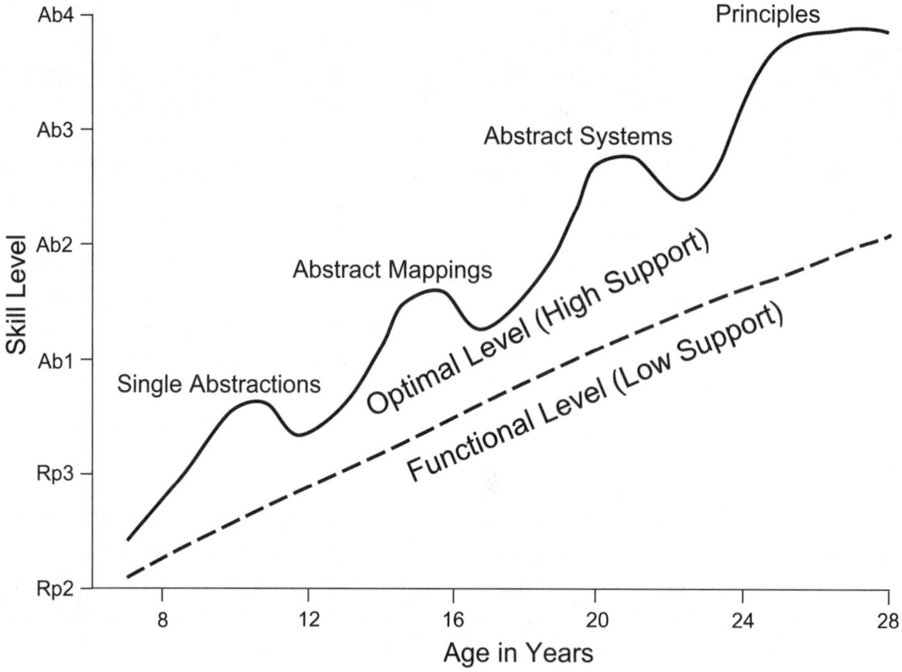

Figure 8.4. Different growth curves for optimal and functional levels. High support conditions evoke optimal level performance, which shows spurts when a new skill level emerges. Low support conditions evoke functional level performance, which commonly demonstrates smooth growth.

skill theory, variability is analyzed instead of ignored. A fundamental fact about behavior is that children's performance is not at all fixed but varies *systematically* between two upper limits (Figure 8.4). At their *functional level,* they produce their best performance without support, and at their (higher) *optimal level,* they perform at their best with explicit support (Fischer & Bidell, 2006).

This range demonstrates the fundamental importance of analyzing variability. There is not one level of performance even when looking at the upper limit of skill in one domain. Children (and adults too) show two different upper limits. Over time a child slowly builds toward automatic performance even of complex skills, and the need for support drops away. For example, a teenager learning to drive a car requires both undivided attention and (usually) some explicit guidance, but over time and with practice this ability becomes relatively automatic, and she or he becomes increasingly capable of driving skillfully on different roads, in different situations (such as rain), and with different people in the car.

A powerful illustration of ordered variation due to contextual support – of optimal and functional levels – comes from a study on the development of understanding arithmetic operations (addition, subtraction, multiplication, division) in 7- to 20-year olds (Fischer & Kenny, 1986). In one set of tasks students had to explain each operation in general (abstract) terms, and in another set how pairs of operations related to each other (for example, addition and subtraction, addition and multiplication).

To investigate the effect of support, students were assessed under two conditions: In the low-support condition (functional level) students explained the operation or the relation between two operations. In the high-support condition (optimal) the interviewer primed the key ideas by showing the student a prototypical good answer. Each student had to explain the ideas in his or her own words and apply them to a few

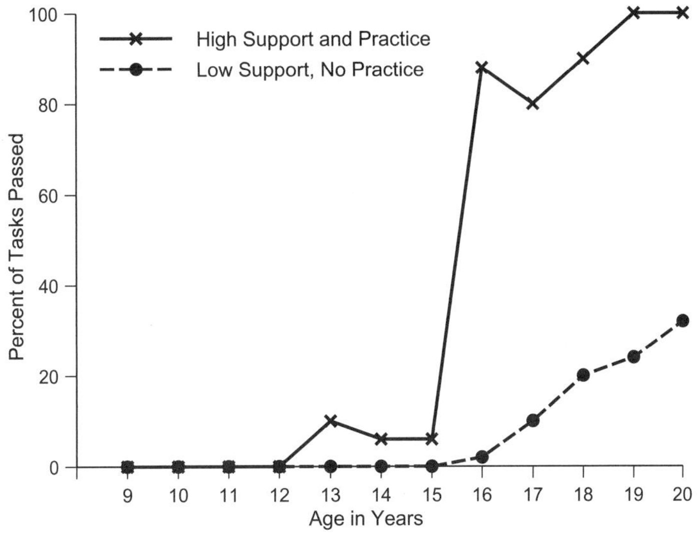

Figure 8.5. Development of mappings of arithmetic operations.

specific arithmetic problems (9 − 2 = 7, 7 + 2 = 9). To demonstrate the level of single abstractions, students had to move beyond concrete, problem-specific answers (addition and subtraction relate because 9 − 2 = 7 and 7 + 2 = 9) and generate an abstract explanation (addition is combining two numbers to get a bigger number). For the next level of abstract mappings, they had to explain the general relation between two operations (addition and subtraction are opposites: Addition puts numbers together, subtraction takes them apart).

Different contextual support produced strikingly different growth patterns. Low-support performance improved gradually with age, but never climbed very high (Figure 8.5). High-support performance, on the other hand, showed a sharp jump between 15 and 16 years of age for every student. This spurt in optimal-level knowledge was dramatic: Whereas no student understood more than one abstract mapping at age 15 (even with support), *every* student understood most of them at age 16. For low-support, this jump did not occur: Only one 16-year-old understood one of eight relations. Similar spurts in optimal-level ability have been documented in several domains and age ranges across different cultures, such as reflective judgment (Kitchener, Lynch, Fischer, & Wood, 1993), moral reasoning (Dawson & Garielian, 2003), self-understanding (Fischer & Kennedy, 1997), and vocabulary knowledge (Ruhland & van Geert, 1998).

The systematic effect of contextual support on "ability" shows that children possess not a single level of skilled behavior within a domain but a range within which their ability typically varies. This developmental range holds too for domains like those tapped in intelligence tests, such as working memory and understanding concepts. Children have a range of abilities – characterized by their functional and optimal levels – reflecting the underlying dynamics of real behavior. This range of variation suggests that intelligence needs to be measured differently, and that testing information needs to be used differently in schools and more generally. Behavior is too complex – and too interesting – to be captured by a single test, under one condition. At best, this kind of assessment method offers a limited snapshot of children's intelligence. At worst, it paints a misleading picture that can misshape and distort in profound ways children's learning and conceptions of self. Measuring children's intelligence requires more than a point estimate – it requires, at least, measuring the full range of their abilities.

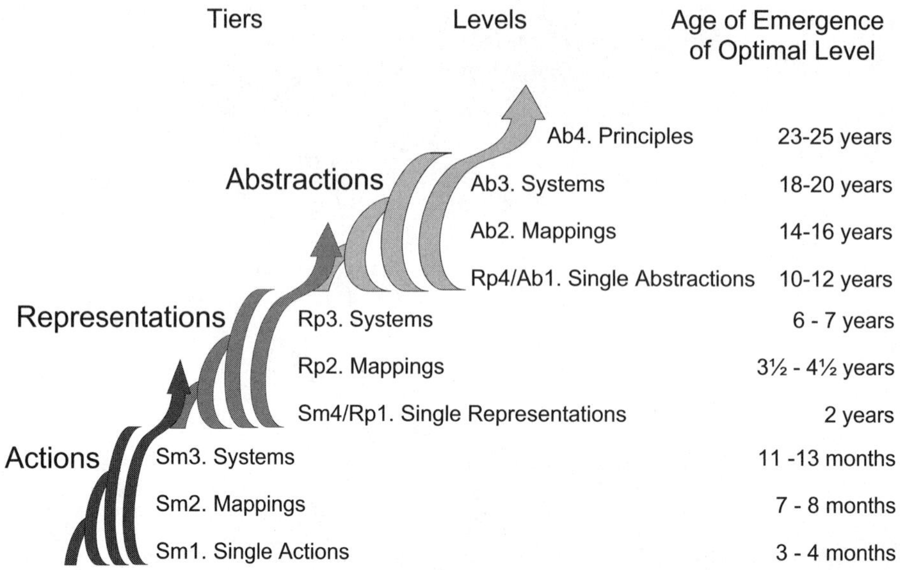

Figure 8.6. Developmental scale of levels and tiers.

Attending to the range has provided important insights about the processes of learning and development, leading to new ways of measuring how children learn. Particularly informative is the optimal performance when children act with high support: Optimal level performance shows clear-cut spurts and other kinds of discontinuities that led to the discovery of a fundamental scale underlying learning and development.

Developmental Levels: Universal Scale Across Domains

When people construct skills, the construction process follows a universal scale, moving systematically through a series of levels based on complexity and hierarchical integration and differentiation, as shown in Figure 8.6. Cognitive development has been marked by unproductive debates about whether stages exist or not, typically oversimplified into claims and counterclaims: "Development occurs in stages." "No, development takes place continuously." "No, it follows stages." "No, it develops continuously."

Fortunately, the debates have been resolved resoundingly by research analyzing when development and learning demonstrate stage-like change and when they do not, as illustrated in Figure 8.5 from the study of arithmetic. Studies searching for discontinuities (spurts, drops, reorganizations) uncovered a common scale of skill complexity that captures a central dimension of long-term growth as well as short-term learning (Dawson & Wilson, 2004; Fischer 1980; Fischer & Bidell, 2006; Mascolo & Fischer, 2010. Analysis of growth curves shows sudden changes (Fischer & Rose, 1994; van Geert, 1998; van der Maas & Molenaar, 1992), and Rasch (1980) scaling of test and interview performances demonstrates consistent evidence of clusters and gaps with the same patterns of discontinuity on the same scale (Dawson, 2003; Dawson, Xie, & Wilson, 2003).

An essential point is that performance is not fixed for an age but instead varies dynamically depending on contextual support, emotional/motivational state, familiarity, and many other factors. For example, an 11-year-old can perform not only at the level of single abstractions (the usual upper limit at that age) but when she encounters a novel problem, such as explaining an unfamiliar gadget or learning to speak a new language, she can move down to low levels typical of infants (Fischer & Granott,

1995; Granott, 2002). This dynamic variation provides important information about the processes underlying learning and development.

The skill scale relates approximately to the stages that Piaget (1983) outlined, but the levels are better grounded empirically, there are more of them than he usually described, and they form subscales with fractal properties. The scale shows similarities to most other developmental analyses (because it is universal!), including those of Case (1985), Biggs and Collis (1982), Halford (1982), Kohlberg (Colby, Kohlberg, Gibbs, & Lieberman, 1983), and many others (Fischer & Silvern, 1985). In addition, findings on brain development suggest straightforward connections between brain growth patterns and the emergence of cognitive levels (Fischer, 2008).

Development and learning move along a scale of at least 10 levels of hierarchical complexity (Figure 8.6), all involving control of actions, thoughts, and emotions. The scale begins with sensorimotor actions, which a person (infant, child, or adult) coordinates to form more and more complex coordinations of actions at successive levels to eventually form representations. In turn, the person coordinates ever more complex relations of representations at successive levels to eventually form abstractions. Ultimately, coordination of abstractions leads to ever more complex levels that eventuate in principles that organize relations of abstractions. The scale thus moves through three larger growth cycles called tiers – actions, then representations, then abstractions. Clusters of discontinuities (spurts, drops, reorganizations) mark emergence of each level in development across all tiers. The right column in Figure 8.6 indicates the ages when skills first emerge under optimal conditions for each level.

Figure 8.7 shows the characteristic skill structure for each level within a tier (actions, representations, or abstractions). At the first level a person controls single actions, representations, or abstractions. He or she coordinates and differentiates these skills to form the second and third levels – first mappings, then systems. At the fourth level the person forms systems of systems, building a new kind of unit that starts the next tier – a new kind of single set: Actions form representations, representations form abstractions, abstractions form principles.

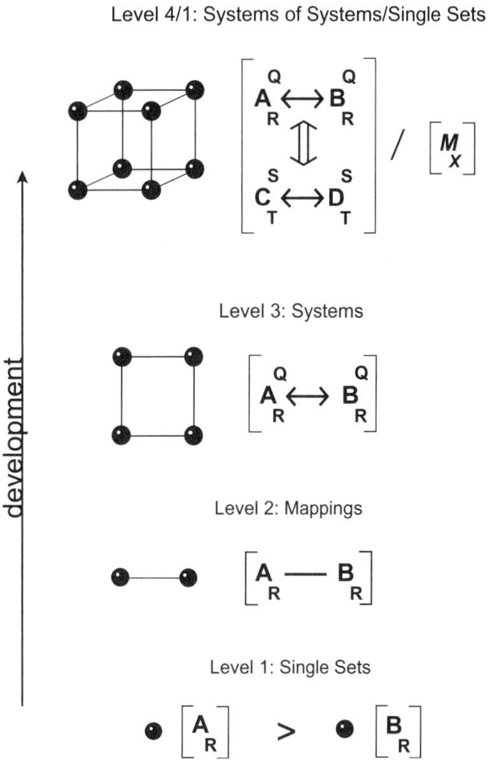

Figure 8.7. Cycles of levels in a tier: Cube models and skill diagrams. Brackets demarcate a skill structure. Each letter indicates a skill component, with subscripts and superscripts marking subsets. A line connecting sets denotes a mapping. A single-line arrow marks a system. A double-line vertical arrow indicates a system of systems. A greater than symbol (>) shows a shift between skills without integration.

A Case of Emotional Behavior

Building and maintaining skills requires both self-regulation and coordination with other people. Human beings are intensely social and emotional, and many skills are devoted to social-emotional interaction and knowledge (Tomasello et al., 2005). Susan at age 5 has developed representations of positive and negative social interactions with her

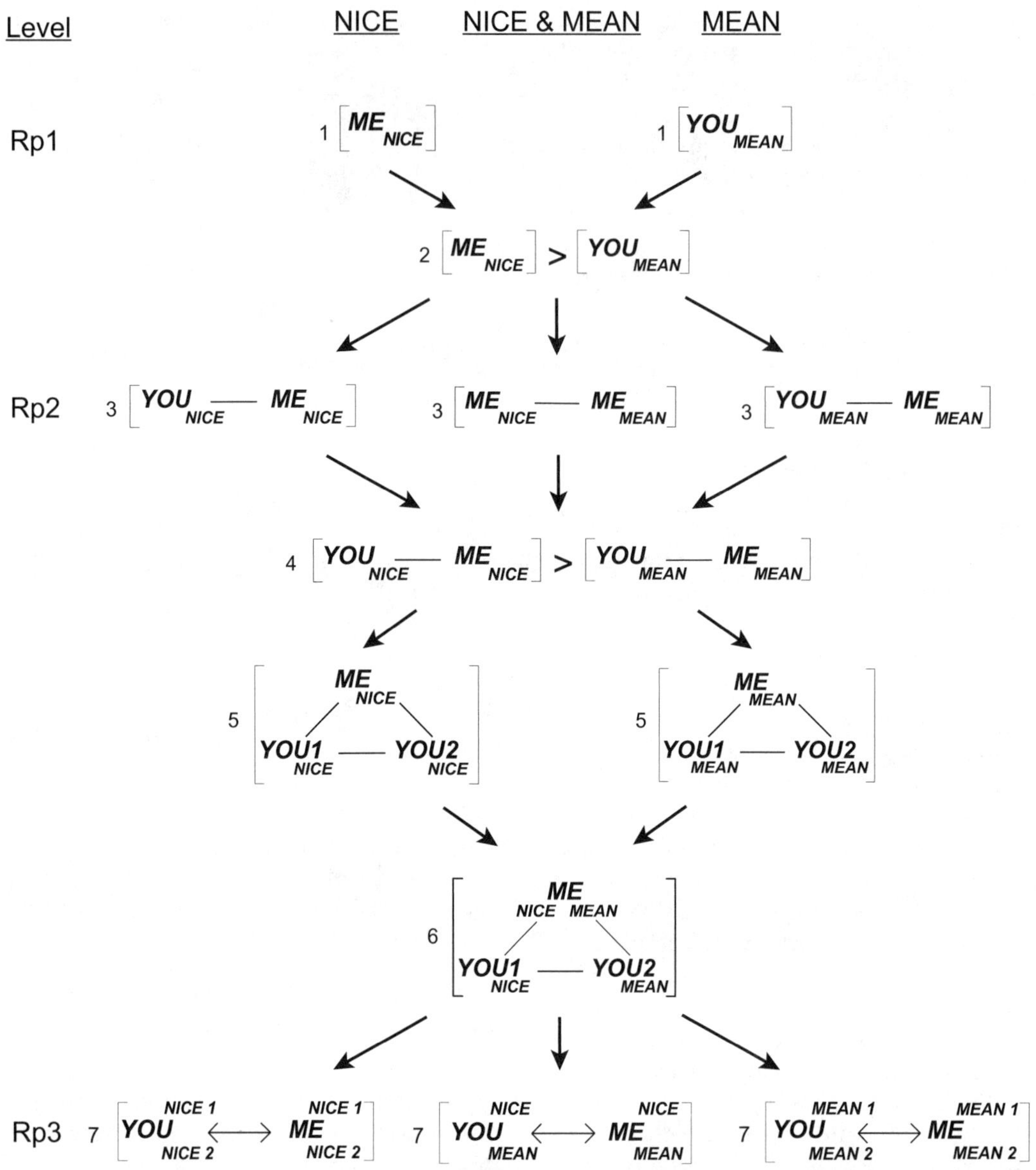

Figure 8.8. Developmental web for nice and mean social interactions. Numbers to the left of brackets denote step in complexity ordering. The words inside brackets indicate skill structures. The left column marks a skill level. Brackets demarcate a skill structure. Each letter indicates a skill component, with subscripts and superscripts marking subsets. A line connecting sets denotes a mapping. A single-line arrow marks a system. A double-line vertical arrow indicates a system of systems. A greater than symbol (>) shows a shift between skills without integration.

father, and they illustrate the natural variations in complexity and emotional organization that characterize people in general (Ayoub et al., 2006; Fischer & Ayoub, 1994) (see Figure 8.8). Her interviewer acts out a pretend story with dolls, in which a child doll called Susan gives her father a drawing of their family that she has just made. The interviewer makes the Susan doll say, "Daddy, here's a present for you. I love you," and the father doll hugs her, saying "I love you too, and thanks for the pretty picture." Giving her a toy, he says, "Here's a present for you too, Susan." When the interviewer asks Susan to tell a story after this high-support modeling, she likewise shows positive social reciprocity, with Daddy being nice to Susan because she has been nice to him.

After 10 minutes of play, the interviewer asks Susan to show the best story she can with people being nice to each other, like the one she showed earlier. Susan acts out a story much simpler than the one before, having the Daddy doll give the Susan doll several presents but showing no reciprocal interaction.

After several minutes Susan changes spontaneously to stories about fighting, continuing even when the interviewer demonstrates another nice story between father and daughter. Susan does not follow the modeled story but changes the content to negative and aggressive. The girl doll slugs the father, and he screams at her, "Don't you hit me," slapping her face and shoving her hard – a kind of violent story that many children often show, and especially those who have been maltreated. The Susan doll screams and cries, saying that she is afraid of being hit. While Susan has shifted to strong negative emotion, she still shows social reciprocity. The father doll hits the girl doll because she first hit him. Similarly, she is afraid as a result of his hitting her.

Susan becomes upset, running around yelling and throwing toys. The interviewer attempts to shift her attention back to storytelling, asking her to tell the best story she can, but she has the dolls push and hit each other haphazardly, showing no social reciprocity (just everyone hitting everyone) and providing no explanation. The complex negative stories that she told before have disappeared, replaced by simple social categories of acting mean.

Web of Representations for the Case

Is there one "real" story for Susan? Does she see her relationship with her father as positive or negative? Can she represent reciprocal interaction, or not? Researchers and practitioners often ask questions like these, but they make no sense, because they assume that children's representations are overly simple. Instead, Susan clearly demonstrates four distinct skills in her stories – (a) positive reciprocal interaction, (b) simple positive action without reciprocity, (c) negative reciprocal interaction, and (d) simple negative action without reciprocity. Over time she shifts both emotional valence and skill level, changing her "abilities" depending on her emotional state, the immediate context, and the kinds of support she receives from the interviewer. Susan's and her father's nice or mean actions shape the other's actions. That is the way that skills work. They are not fixed, static abilities but adaptive, regulated structures for activities (actions, thoughts, and feelings). By coordinating actions together, people create new systems of skills that affect and build on each other.

As people learn and develop, they organize their skills into hierarchies that follow the scale in Figures 8.6 and 8.7. Susan showed this process when she built stories about social interactions that were shaped by emotions and coordinated diverse actions into social categories (father, daughter, nice, mean, etc.) and reciprocal interactions (mean reciprocity or nice reciprocity). She embedded individual actions of pretending (Sm3 systems of actions) in social categories (Rp1 single representations), and she then embedded the categories in socially reciprocal activities between the Susan doll and the father doll (Rp2 representational mappings). When she integrated the component skills, she could still use the components by themselves – for example, dropping back to simpler action categories when she had less contextual support or was upset emotionally. Stories like this illustrate how skills both develop over many years (macrodevelopment or ontogenesis) and vary from one moment to the next (microdevelopment).

Development occurs in a constructive web, as shown in Figure 8.1. Stories about mean and nice social interactions illustrate key dynamic properties of the web. Each strand of the web represents a different learning sequence (a domain), with strands potentially differentiating or becoming coordinated. Strands in Figure 8.8 cluster into domains, such as those for nice, mean, and the combination of nice and mean. The universal skill scale captures the processes of skill growth in each strand, but the skills in each strand are independent. Being at the same level means that they are the same complexity, not that they are the same skill.

Figure 8.8 shows a developmental web for nice and mean stories, based on research with American children from a wide range of ethnic groups and social classes (Ayoub et al., 2006; Fischer & Ayoub, 1994). In their play, children routinely act nice sometimes and mean other times, like Susan. The web has three separate strands (domains) organized by emotional valence – nice on the left, mean on the right, and the coordination of nice and mean in the center. Emotions shape human behavior in this way, defining separate domains based on types of feelings, and positive/negative has one of the most powerful shaping effects (Fischer, Shaver, & Carnochan, 1990). (Environmental contexts also shape domains.) Vertically in the figure the tasks are ordered by skill complexity, with steps of the same complexity shown at the same point horizontally in the web. The numbers next to each skill structure also show the ordering. People readily use multiple steps at the same level in separate strands (or learning sequences).

The variations in Susan's stories show how a developmental web relates to variations in action, thought, and feeling. When Susan feels good (positive, nice) and when the interviewer supports her story by prompting key components (telling her a brief story), she organizes a complex story about having a nice interaction with her father. She shows a story that fits Step 3 under Nice in Figure 8.8: Dad is nice to Susan because she was nice to him.

After several minutes pass and the interviewer asks for another story, Susan has become stressed and produces not a positive story but a complex negative one, supported by the interviewer's prompting of reciprocity. On the other hand, without support from the interviewer, Susan creates only simple positive or negative stories, with individuals being mean (or nice) but no clear reciprocity. She falls back to her functional level instead of producing her optimal level for this content domain. Note that the form of her narrative has been shaped by her family and culture. People develop narrative forms based on their own experience, shaped by the culture they live in. Susan's stories belong to her cultural community and do not fit the narrative forms of many other families or communities.

For the research on which Figure 8.8 is based, interviewers told 2- to 9-year-old children stories about two or three people playing together, and each story belonged to one of the three strands in the figure (Nice, Mean, or Nice with Mean). Sometimes all the dolls were children, and then each child chose one doll to have his or her name, and then gave names for the other two dolls. Sometimes the dolls were adults and children, and they were given the names of the child and his or her caregivers (usually mother and father). Scaling techniques provided statistical tests of the orderings along strands (Ayoub et al., 2006).

For example, Step 3 includes two reciprocity stories, mapping nice to nice or mean to mean. One doll acted nice (or mean) because the other one had acted that way. If you are mean to me, I will be mean to you. This structure fits some of the stories that Susan told about her interactions with her father. The skill formulas in Figure 8.8 include the central components that children need to control: roles (you or me), emotional valence (nice or mean), and connections between roles (mappings, systems, shifts without coordination). Of course, every component in the diagram subsumes hierarchically organized component actions, perceptions, feelings, expectations, and goals.

At times people misunderstand this developmental web to mean that each strand represents a different kind of child. To the contrary, all children develop at the same time along each strand, for example, simultaneously building understandings about nice, mean, and the combination. In

Figure 8.8 the three strands are all closely parallel, but when children experience a strong affective state such as joy or anger, that emotion shifts the web. When people are angry, for example, the mean strand becomes prominent, and the web tilts to move the nice strands further down the web – harder to produce. Child abuse commonly produces a general bias toward the negative, going beyond effects of short-term mood fluctuations (Ayoub et al., 2006; Fischer et al., 1997; Westen, 1994). Webs thus capture variations in developmental pathways that relate to domains defined by both context and emotional state.

In summary, we discovered the universal skill scale by analyzing discontinuities and clusters in developmental assessments and other tests. The scale provides powerful tools for analyzing developmental webs, with skills built along independent strands that follow the same scale of learning sequences even though the skills are independent. This scale makes possible the creation of many tools for analyzing and measuring learning and development and thus has important implications for assessment, especially in educational settings and learning environments.

From Research to Usable Knowledge: Dynamic Assessment

Thus far we have largely focused on implications of dynamic systems for theory and research on children's behavior and intelligence. But research within dynamic systems and skill theory has relevance for education as well. Indeed, because skill theory analyzes the variability of real behavior in real contexts, research findings from within this framework are often relevant to educational practice and policy. Dynamic models of behavior and development are particularly well suited to generating *usable knowledge*.

Although the field is young, dynamic concepts and findings have already challenged long-standing assumptions about the nature of learning. The concept of contextualized behavior and the findings of alternative pathways have led to changes in concepts of learning ability and disability (Rose & Meyer, 2002; Schneps, Rose, & Fischer, 2007). This research fundamentally shifts the emphasis from a child *having* a learning disability to the contributions of context and child in creating abilities and disabilities. Applying the dynamic approach to developmental dyslexia, for example, has led to discovering that the same behavioral/neurological variability that impairs reading for people with dyslexia confers a selective visual strength for some dyslexics: A talent at integration of peripheral visual information is highly advantageous in visually intensive domains of science such as astrophysics (Schneps, Rose, & Fischer, 2007).

Dynamic concepts and research are reshaping the landscape of teaching and learning in many ways. One particularly important area is assessing what a child knows and understands – a central topic for both the study of intelligence and the practice of education. Assessment of students' learning is a natural part of educational settings (Fischer, 2009; Stein, Dawson, & Fischer, in press). Teachers use informal assessment frequently in their classrooms as they work with students, and they occasionally use formal assessments when they give quizzes, have students write essays, do projects, answer questions. Students as well regularly assess their own learning and the state of their knowledge to shape what they learn in school and in life. Assessment is thus a natural part of learning and education, like a conversation between teacher, student, and curriculum.

However, testing has come to be dominated by complex standardized testing infrastructures that strongly shape educational systems. So many people take so many tests! Now is the time to ask fundamental questions about what today's tests measure and how they are used in learning environments. Important questions to ask include these: *What are the tests measuring? What is worth measuring? What are the functions of the tests? Are important functions being neglected?*

Most standardized testing has become isolated from research about learning, with an emphasis on using tests as sorting mechanisms. In the words of Mislevy (1993, p. 19) the current testing infrastructure involves "the application of 20th century statistics to 19th century psychology." Many schools and teachers attempt to shape their teaching to these high-stakes assessments, which can be likened to preparing students for life as a set of multiple-choice questions (Stein, Dawson, & Fischer, in press; but see Boudett, City, & Murnane, 2005).

Assessments can be used productively to enhance learning and teaching. In classrooms and other learning environments teachers and students assess the progress of learning every day, both informally and with specific assignments. Unfortunately, most standardized tests omit the use of assessment to shape and improve learning. They focus on sorting students and schools and neglect the many ways that tests can serve as aids to learning and education for students and teachers.

The universal scale for learning and a set of methods that build upon it make possible the creation of new kinds of tests that guide learning and teaching (Stein, Dawson, & Fischer, in press). The new tests build upon the newest findings from learning science, and they can use the latest computer technology to facilitate usability. With dynamic skill theory and the developmental assessment system built upon it, called the *Lectical Assessment System* (Dawson & Stein, 2008; Fischer & Bidell, 2006), we are creating DiscoTests based in assessing students' actions and explanations (*www.discotest.org*). That is, we analyze the same actions and explanations that students use in classroom discussions, essays, and class projects. Based in analysis of the content and complexity of students' explanations and arguments, DiscoTests provide assessments that are as rigorous and quantitative as standard high-stakes tests, while simultaneously providing feedback that students and teachers can use to guide and improve their own learning and teaching. This new kind of test moves beyond merely sorting students or schools toward aiding learning and education.

Tests should be built around research into how students learn (NRC, 2001). The methods of dynamic skill theory and Lectical Assessment provide for systematic construction of learning sequences for important educational domains, such as how energy works in bouncing balls or what caused World War II. The learning sequences include characterization of the range of possible conceptions for a topic – the steps from simple to complex understanding (illustrated in Figure 8.8). Both teacher and student can see a specific performance in relation to the range of possible performances, providing information about what a student understands currently and what he or she is likely to benefit from learning next. The empirically grounded learning sequences can also be directly related to curricula about for example concepts of energy.

With these new tools based on students' own answers and explanations, we can meet the demand for rigorous measurement while fitting the assessment naturally with the learning environment. The assessment addresses questions such as these: What concepts is this student working with? How does she understand these concepts? What is her line of reasoning? How well does she explain her thinking? Here are some examples of questions and student responses about the nature of energy in balls that bounce or roll or sit still.

Questions about Energy in a Bouncing Ball and One Student's Answers

Question 1. What happens to the energy of a ball as it falls to the floor?

Student Answer. "As it falls, some of the energy is, hmm, released?"

Question 2. What happens to the energy of a ball as it hits the floor?

Student Answer. "Some of the energy is transferred to the floor and the other energy is staying with the ball as it rebounds upward."

Question 3. What happens to the energy of a ball right after it hits the floor?

Student Answer. "Good question, some of the energy remains with the ball. Does it move the ball? I don't know?"

From data of this kind, we infer learning sequences using Rasch scaling, content analysis, and the skill scale (Dawson & Stein, 2008; Stein, Dawson, & Fischer, in press), capturing patterns of learning for a specific topic or domain. A learning sequence describes reasoning along a thematic strand as concepts develop across a subset of skill levels. Because of the connection with the natural learning environment, students and teachers can readily use the learning sequences to assess their own learning and to guide themselves to learn more effectively. Based on the database of other students' responses, we can create activities, hints, and suggestions to facilitate learning depending on a student's location in a common learning sequence for a topic such as energy in a bouncing ball.

The tests are built around a psychometrically sophisticated metric (the skill scale), which serves as a standardized measure of student performance that can be compared across different contents (energy, World War II, analysis of a Shakespeare sonnet). The goals of the DiscoTest effort are to create standardized tests that (a) are built around research into how students learn in particular domains, (b) can be customized to different curricula for teaching in those domains, and provide both (c) psychometrically reliable scores assessing learning and (d) rich feedback to students and teachers to improve learning and education.

Broadly, the objectives of this work are to facilitate the creation of optimal learning environments through assessments that promote learning through rich educative feedback. These assessments show students and teachers each student's location (range) along his or her learning trajectory and how student and teacher can facilitate movement toward the next step for mastery. In other words, they combine the functions of formative and standardized (summative) assessments, creating what could be called standardized formative assessments (Stein, Dawson, & Fischer, in press).

Conclusion: Analyzing Variability and Stability to Illuminate Intelligence

Children's behavior varies widely in its complexity and content, both across development and moment-to-moment, depending on multiple characteristics of the child and context. Classic models of intelligence focus on stable dimensions of normative behavior but offer little explanation for variability and alternative learning patterns. According to the psychometric approach, intelligence forms several distinct types, which are treated as stable entities. For the Piagetian approach, intelligence develops from one type of logic to another as infants become children and then children become adults. Each logic is treated as a separate stable entity. For the nativist approach, the foundations of knowledge are sought in early childhood, and development and variability in intelligence are mostly ignored.

In contrast, the dynamic approach *begins* with an account of the diversity in children's behavior and analyzes variability to find patterns of order within the variation. Viewing intelligence through the lens of dynamic systems, as with dynamic skill theory, elucidates patterns of ordered variability in children's behavior that have eluded classic models of intelligence. For example, behavior varies naturally within a range of complexity – from a lower functional level of ordinary performance without support to a higher optimal level evoked by high contextual support. Analysis of such variability has led to discovery of various important phenomena in development and learning, including a general complexity scale that can be used to analyze learning in any domain.

Starting with a focus on variability leads to new, elegant explanations for the richness of children's behavior, including models and methods for assessing the dynamic organization of intelligence in educational settings. These tools help more closely to align theory, research, and practice. As a result, we can now analyze how children learn in actual learning environments such as classrooms and video games. The joint focus on both stability and variation in behavior shifts the understanding of intelligence beyond static abilities toward continual real-time interactions between child and context in specific settings. Integrating flexible metaphors with new assessment tools and precise mathematical models for variability leads toward powerful ways of understanding how children learn and develop.

Acknowledgment

Work on this chapter was supported by funds from the Center for Applied Special Technology, Harvard Graduate School of Education, and the Ross Institute.

References

Abraham, R. H., & Shaw, C. D. (2005). *Dynamics: The geometry of behavior* (4th ed.). Santa Cruz, CA: Aerial Press.

Ardila, A. (1999). A neuropsychological approach to intelligence. *Neuropsychological Review, 9*(3), 117–136.

Atkinson, R. C., & Shiffrin, R. M. (1968). Human memory: A proposed system and its control processes. In K. W. Spence & J. T. Spence (Eds.), *The psychology of learning and motivation: Advances in research and theory* (Vol. 2, pp. 89–195). New York, NY: Academic Press.

Ayoub, C. C., Rogosh, F., Toth, S. L., O'Connor, E., Cicchetti, D., Rappolt-Schlichtmann, G., & Fischer, K.W. (2006). Cognitive and emotional differences in young maltreated children: A translational application of dynamic skill theory. *Development and Psychopathology, 18*, 670–706.

Baillargeon, R. (1987). Object permanence in 31/2- and 41/2-month-old infants. *Developmental Psychology, 23*, 655–664.

Battro, A. (2000). *Half a brain is enough: The story of Nico*. Cambridge, UK: Cambridge University Press.

Bidell, T. R., & Fischer, K. W. (1992). Beyond the stage debate: Action, structure, and variability in Piagetian theory and research. In R. J. Sternberg & C. A. Berg (Eds.), *Intellectual development* (pp. 100–140). New York, NY: Cambridge University Press.

Biggs, J., & Collis, K. (1982). *Evaluating the quality of learning: The SOLO taxonomy (structure of the observed learning outcome)*. New York, NY: Academic Press.

Boudett, K. P., City, E., & Murnane, R. (2005). *Data wise: A step-by-step guide to using assessment results to improve teaching and learning.* Cambridge, MA: Harvard Education Publishing.

Carey, S. (2009). *The origin of concepts*. New York, NY: Oxford University Press.

Carey, S., & Gelman, R. (Eds.). (1991). *The epigenesis of mind: Essays on biology and knowledge*. Hillsdale, NJ: Erlbaum.

Carey, S., & Spelke, E. (1994). Domain-specific knowledge and conceptual change. In L. A. Hirschfeld & S. A. Gelman (Eds.), *Mapping the mind: Domain specificity in cognition and culture* (pp. 169–200). Cambridge, UK: Cambridge University Press.

Carroll, J. B. (1993). *Human cognitive abilities: A survey of factor-analytic studies*. New York, NY: Cambridge University Press.

Case, R. (1985). *Intellectual development: Birth to adulthood*. New York, NY: Academic Press.

Case, R., Okamoto, Y., with Griffin, S., McKeough, A., Bleiker, C., Henderson, B., et al. (1996). The role of central conceptual structures in the development of children's thought. *Monographs of the Society for Research in Child Development, 61*(5–6, Serial No. 246).

Case, R., & Edelstein, W. (1993). The new structuralism in cognitive development: Theory and research on individual pathways. *Contributions to human development* (Vol. 23, pp. x, 123). Basel, Switzerland: S. Karger, AG.

Cattell, R. B. (1971). *Abilities: Their structure, growth, and action*. Boston, MA: Houghton Mifflin.

Chomsky, N. (1965). *Aspects of the theory of syntax*. Cambridge, MA: MIT Press.

Colby, A., Kohlberg, L., Gibbs, J., & Lieberman, M. (1983). A longitudinal study of moral judgement. *Monographs of the Society for Research in Child Development, 48*(1, Serial no. 200).

Damasio, A. R. (2003). *Looking for Spinoza: Joy, sorrow, and the feeling brain*. New York, NY: Harcourt/Harvest.

Damon, W., & Lerner, R. M. (Eds.). (2006). *Handbook of child psychology: Theoretical models of human development* (Vol. 1, 6th ed.). New York, NY: Wiley.

Dawson, T., & Wilson, M. (2004). The LAAS: A computerizable scoring system for small- and large-scale developmental assessments. *Educational Assessment, 9*, 153–191.

Dawson, T. L. (2003). A stage is a stage is a stage: A direct comparison of two scoring systems. *Journal of Genetic Psychology, 164*, 335–364.

Dawson, T. L., & Gabrielian, S. (2003). Developing conceptions of authority and contract across the lifespan: Two perspectives. *Developmental Review*, 23, 162–218.

Dawson, T. L., & Stein, Z. (2008). Cycles of research and application in science education: Learning pathways for energy concepts. *Mind, Brain, and Education*, 2, 89–102.

Dawson, T. L., Xie, Y., & Wilson, J. (2003). Domain-general and domain-specific developmental assessments: Do they measure the same thing? *Cognitive Development*, 18(2003), 61–78.

Dehaene, S. (1997). *The number sense: How the mind creates mathematics*. New York, NY: Oxford.

Detterman, D. K., & Sternberg, R. J. (1993). *Transfer on trial: Intelligence, cognition, and instruction*. Norwood, NJ: Ablex.

Dewey, J. (1963). *Experience and education*. New York, NY: Macmillan.

Epstein, J. M. (1997). *Nonlinear dynamics, mathematical biology, and social science* (Vol. 4). Cambridge, MA: Perseus Press.

Eysenck, H. J. (1986). The theory of intelligence and the psychophysiology of cognition. In R. J. Sternberg (Ed.), *Advances in the psychology of human intelligence* (Vol. 3, pp. 1 – 34). Hillsdale, NJ: Erlbaum.

Fischer, K. W. (1980). A theory of cognitive development: The control and construction of hierarchies of skills. *Psychological Review*, 87, 477–531.

Fischer, K. W. (2008). Dynamic cycles of cognitive and brain development: Measuring growth in mind, brain, and education. In A. M. Battro, K. W. Fischer, & P. Léna (Eds.), *The educated brain* (pp. 127–150). Cambridge, UK: Cambridge University Press.

Fischer, K. W. (2009). Mind, brain, and education: Building a scientific groundwork for learning and teaching. *Mind, Brain, and Education*, 3, 2–15.

Fischer, K. W., & Bidell, T. (1991). Constraining nativist inferences about cognitive capacities. In S. Carey & R. Gelman (Eds.), *The epigenesis of mind: Essays on biology and cognition. The Jean Piaget Symposium series* (pp. 199–235). Hillsdale, NJ: Erlbaum.

Fischer, K. W., & Ayoub, C. (1994). Affective splitting and dissociation in normal and maltreated children: Developmental pathways for self in relationships. In D. Cicchetti & S. L. Toth (Eds.), *Disorders and dysfunctions of the self* (Vol. 5, pp. 149–222). Rochester, NY: Rochester University Press.

Fischer, K. W., Ayoub, C. C., Noam, G. G., Singh, I., Maraganore, A., & Raya, P. (1997). Psychopathology as adaptive development along distinctive pathways. *Development and Psychopathology*, 9, 751–781.

Fischer, K. W., Bernstein, J. H., & Immordino-Yang, M. H. (Eds.). (2007). *Mind, brain, and education in reading disorders*. Cambridge, UK: Cambridge University Press.

Fischer, K. W., & Bidell, T. R. (1998). Dynamic development of psychological structures in action and thought. In R. M. Lerner (Ed.), *Theoretical models of human development* (5th ed., Vol. 1, pp. 467–561). New York, NY: Wiley.

Fischer, K. W., & Bidell, T. R. (2006). Dynamic development of action and thought. In W. Damon & R. M. Lerner (Eds.), *Theoretical models of human development. Handbook of child psychology* (6th ed., Vol. 1, pp. 313–399). New York, NY: Wiley.

Fischer, K. W., & Farrar, M. J. (1987). Generalizations about generalization: How a theory of skill development explains both generality and specificity. Special Issue: The neo-Piagetian theories of cognitive development: Toward an integration. *International Journal of Psychology*, 22(5–6), 643–677.

Fischer, K. W., Goswami, U., Geake, J., & Panel on the Future of Educational Neuroscience. (in press). The future of educational neuroscience. *Mind, Brain, and Education*.

Fischer, K. W., & Granott, N. (1995). Beyond one-dimensional change: Parallel, concurrent, socially distributed processes in learning and development. *Human Development*, 38, 302–314.

Fischer, K. W., & Kennedy, B. (1997). Tools for analyzing the many shapes of development: The case of self-in-relationships in Korea. In E. Amsel & K. A. Renninger (Eds.), *Change and development: Issues of theory, method, and application* (pp. 117–152). Mahwah, NJ: Erlbaum.

Fischer, K. W., & Kenny, S. L. (1986). The environmental conditions for discontinuities in the development of abstractions. In R. Mines & K. Kitchener (Eds.), *Adult cognitive development: Methods and models* (pp. 57–75). New York, NY: Praeger.

Fischer, K. W., Pipp, S. L., & Bullock, D. (1984). Detecting discontinuities in development: Method and measurement. In R. Emde & R. Harmon (Eds.), *Continuities and discontinuities in development* (pp. 95–121). New York, NY: Plenum.

Fischer, K. W., & Pruyne, E. (2002). Reflective thinking in adulthood: Emergence, development, and variation. In J. Demick & C. Andreoletti (Eds.), *Handbook of adult development* (pp. 169–197). New York: Plenum.

Fischer, K. W., & Rose, L. T. (2001). Webs of skill: How students learn. *Educational Leadership, 59*(3), 6–12.

Fischer, K.W., Rose, L.T., & Rose, S.P. (2007). Growth cycles of mind and brain: Analyzing developmental pathways of learning disorders. In K.W. Fischer, J. H. Bernstein, & M. H. Immordino-Yang (Eds.), *Mind, brain, and education in reading disorders*. Cambridge, UK: Cambridge University Press.

Fischer, K. W., & Rose, S. P. (1994). Dynamic development of coordination of components in brain and behavior: A framework for theory and research. In G. Dawson & K. W. Fischer (Eds.), *Human behavior and the developing brain* (pp. 3–66). New York, NY: Guilford Press.

Fischer, K. W., Shaver, P. R., & Carnochan, P. (1990). How emotions develop and how they organise development. *Cognition & Emotion, 4*(2), 81–127.

Fischer, K. W., & Silvern, L. (1985). Stages and individual differences in cognitive development. *Annual Review of Psychology, 36*, 613–648.

Fischer, K. W., & Yan, Z. (2002). Development of dynamic skill theory. In R. Lickliter & D. Lewkowicz (Eds.), *Conceptions of development: Lessons from the laboratory* (pp. 279–312). Hove, UK: Psychology Press.

Goswami, U. (2002). Phonology, reading development and dyslexia: A cross-linguistic perspective. *Annals of Dyslexia, 52*, 1–23.

Gardner, H. (1983). *Frames of mind: The theory of multiple intelligences*. New York: Basic Books.

Granott, N. (2002). How microdevelopment creates macrodevelopment: Reiterated sequences, backward transitions, and the zone of current development. In N. Granott & J. Parziale (Eds.), *Microdevelopment: Transition processes in development and learning* (pp. 213–242). Cambridge, UK: Cambridge University Press.

Griffin, S., & Case, R. (1997). Rethinking the primary school math curriculum. *Issues in Education: Contributions from Educational Psychology, 3*(1), 1–49.

Griffin, S. A., Case, R., & Siegler, R. S. (1994). Rightstart: Providing the central conceptual prerequisites for first formal learning of arithmetic to students at risk for school failure. In K. McGilly (Ed.), *Classroom lessons: Integrating cognitive theory and classroom practice* (pp. 25–49). Cambridge, MA: MIT Press.

Guilford, J. P. (1967). *The nature of human intelligence*. New York, NY: McGraw-Hill.

Halford, G. S. (1982). *The development of thought*. Hillsdale, NJ: Erlbaum.

Halford, G. S. (1989). Reflections on 25 years of Piagetian cognitive developmental psychology, 1963–1988. *Human Development, 32*, 325–357.

Hanson, N. R. (1961). *Patterns of discovery*. Cambridge, UK: Cambridge University Press.

Horn, J. L. (1976). Human abilities: A review of research and theory in the early 1970s. *Annual Review of Psychology, 27*, 437–486.

Horn, J. L., & Cattell, R. B. (1967). Age differences in fluid and crystallized intelligence. *Acta Psychologica, 26*, 107–129.

Immordino-Yang, M. H., & Damasio, A. (2007). We feel, therefore we learn: The relevance of affective and social neuroscience to education. *Mind, Brain, and Education, 1*(1), 3–10.

Jencks, C. (1992). *Rethinking social policy: Race, poverty, and the underclass*. Cambridge, MA: Harvard University Press.

Jensen, A. R. (1987). Further evidence for Spearman's hypothesis concerning black-white differences on psychometric tests. *Behavioral and Brain Sciences, 10*, 512–519.

Kitchener, K. S., Lynch, C. L., Fischer, K. W., & Wood, P. K. (1993). Developmental range of reflective judgment: The effect of contextual support and practice on developmental stage. *Developmental Psychology, 29*, 893–906.

Knight, C. C., & Fischer, K. W. (1992). Learning to read words: Individual differences in developmental sequences. *Journal of Applied Developmental Psychology, 13*, 377–404.

Kuhn, T. (1970). *The structure of scientific revolutions* (2nd ed.). Chicago, IL: University of Chicago.

Kupersmidt, J. B., & Dodge, K. A. (Eds.). (2004). *Children's peer relations: From development to intervention*. Washington, DC: American Psychological Association.

LaBerge, D., & Samuels, S. J. (1974). Toward a theory of automatic information processing in reading. *Cognitive Psychology, 6*, 293–323.

Lakoff, G. (1987). *Women, fire, and dangerous things: What categories reveal about the mind*. Chicago, IL: University of Chicago Press.

Lakoff, G., & Johnson, M. (1980). *Metaphors we live by*. Chicago, IL: University of Chicago Press.

Le Corre, M., Van de Walle, G., Brannon, E. M., & Carey, S. (2006). Re-visiting the competence/performance debate in the acquisition of counting as a representation of the positive integers. *Cognitive Psychology*, *52*, 130–169.

Lerner, R. M. (2002). *Concepts and theories of human development* (3rd ed.). Mahwah, NJ: Erlbaum.

Mascolo, M. F., & Fischer, K. W. (2010). The dynamic development of thinking, feeling, and acting over the lifespan. In R. M. Lerner & W. F. Overton (Eds.), *Handbook of life-span development. Vol. 1: Biology, cognition, and methods across the lifespan*. Hoboken, NJ: Wiley.

Mislevy, R. J. (1993). Foundations of a new test theory. In N. Frederiksen, R. J. Mislevy, & I. I. Bejar (Eds.), *Test theory of a new generation of tests* (pp. 19–39). Hillsdale, NJ: Erlbaum.

National Research Council. (2001). *Knowing what students know: The science and design of educational assessment*. Washington, DC: National Academy Press.

Neisser, U., Boodoo, G., Bouchard, T. J., Boykin, A. W., Brody, N., Ceci, S. J., Halpern, D. F., Loehlin, J. C., Perloff, R., Sternberg, R. J., and Urbina, S. (1996). Intelligence: Knowns and unknowns. *American Psychologist*, *51*, 77–101.

Overton, W. F. (2006). Developmental psychology: Philosophy, concepts, methodology. In W. Damon & R. M. Lerner (Eds.), *Theoretical models of human development. Handbook of child psychology* (6th ed., Vol. 1, pp. 20–88). New York, NY: Wiley.

Piaget, J. (1954). *The construction of reality in the child* (M. Cook, Trans.). New York, NY: Basic Books.

Piaget, J. (1972). Intellectual evolution from adolescence to adulthood. *Human Development*, *15*, 1–12.

Piaget, J., & Inhelder, B. (1966). *The psychology of the child*. New York, NY: Basic Books.

Piaget, J. (1972). Intellectual evolution from adolescence to adulthood. *Human Development*, *15*, 1–12.

Piaget, J. (1983). Piaget's theory. In W. Kessen (Ed.), *History, theory, and methods* (Vol. 1, pp. 103–126). New York, NY: Wiley.

Piaget, J., & Inhelder, B. (1966). *The psychology of the child*. New York, NY: Basic Books.

Pinard, A. (1981). *The concept of conservation*. Chicago, IL: University of Chicago Press.

Rappolt-Schlichtmann, G., Willett, J. B., Ayoub, C. C., Lindsley, R., Hulette, A. C., & Fischer, K. W. (2009). Poverty, relationship conflict, and the regulation of cortisol in small and large group contexts at child care. *Mind, Brain, and Education*, *3*, 131–142.

Rasch, G. (1980). *Probabilistic model for some intelligence and attainment tests*. Chicago, IL: University of Chicago Press.

Raven, J., Raven, J. C., & Court, J. H. (2003). *Manual for Raven's Progressive Matrices and Vocabulary Scales. Section 1: General Overview*. San Antonio, TX: Harcourt Assessment.

Rose, D., & Meyer, A. (2002). *Teaching every student in the digital age*. Alexandria, VA: American Association for Supervision & Curriculum Development.

Rose, L. T., & Fischer, K. W. (2009a). Dynamic development: A neo-Piagetian approach. In U. Mueller, J. I. M. Carpendale & L. Smith (Eds.), *Cambridge companion to Piaget*. Cambridge, UK: Cambridge University Press.

Rose, L. T., & Fischer, K. W. (2009b). Dynamic systems theory. In R. A. S. and T. Bidell (Ed.), *Chicago companion to the child*. Chicago, IL: University of Chicago Press.

Ruhland, R., & van Geert, P. (1998). Jumping into syntax: Transitions in the development of closed class words. *British Journal of Developmental Psychology*, *16*(Pt 1), 65–95.

Salomon, G., & Perkins, D. N. (1989). Rocky roads to transfer: Rethinking mechanisms of a neglected phenomenon. *Educational Psychologist*, *24*, 185–221.

Saxe, R., Carey, S., & Kanwisher, N. (2004). Understanding other minds: Linking developmental psychology and functional neuroimaging. *Annual Review of Psychology*, *55*, 87–124.

Schacter, D. L. (1999). The seven sins of memory: Insights from psychology and cognitive neuroscience. *American Psychologist*, *54*, 182–203.

Schneps, M., H., & Sadler, Phillip M. (Writer). (1988). *A private universe [video]*. Santa Monica, CA: Pyramid Films.

Schneps, M. H., Rose, L. T., & Fischer, K. W. (2007). Visual learning and the brain: Implications for dyslexia. *Mind, Brain, and Education*, *1*(3), 128–139.

Siegler, R. S. (1994). Cognitive variability: A key to understanding cognitive development. *Current Directions in Psychological Science*, *3*, 1–5.

Siegler, R. S. (2007). Cognitive variability. *Developmental Science*, *10*, 104–109.

Simonton, D. K. (1999). Talent and its development: An emergenic and epigenetic model. *Psychological Review*, *106*, 435–457.

Singer, J. D., & Willett, J. B. (2003). *Applied longitudinal data analysis: Modeling change and event occurrence*. New York, NY: Oxford University Press.

Singer, W. (1995). Development and plasticity of cortical processing architectures. *Science, 270*, 758–764.

Snow, C. E., Griffin, P., & Burns, M. S. (2005). *Knowledge to support the teaching of reading: Preparing teachers for a changing world*. San Francisco, CA: Jossey-Bass.

Snow, C. E., Burns, M. S., & Griffin, P. (Eds.). (1998). *Preventing reading difficulties in young children*. Washington, DC: National Academy Press.

Spearman, C. E. (1904). "General intelligence" objectively determined and measured. *American Journal of Psychology, 15*, 201–293.

Spearman, C. (1923). *The nature of 'intelligence' and the principles of cognition*. London, UK: Macmillan.

Spearman, C. (1927). *The abilities of man*. New York, NY: Macmillan.

Spelke, E. S., Breinlinger, K., Macomber, J., & Jacabson, K. (1992). Origins of knowledge. *Psychological Review, 99*, 605–632.

Stein, Z., Dawson, T., & Fischer, K. W. (in press). Redesigning testing: Operationalizing the new science of learning. In M. S. Khine & I. M. Saleh (Eds.), *New science of learning: Cognition, computers, and collaboration in education*. New York, NY: Springer.

Sternberg, R. J. (1985). *Beyond IQ: A triarchic theory of intelligence*. New York, NY: Cambridge University Press.

Sternberg, R. J. (1997). The concept of intelligence and its role in life-long learning and success. *American Psychologist, 52*, 1030–1037.

Sternberg, R. J., Lautrey, J., & Lubart, T. I. (Eds.). (2003). *Models on intelligence: International perspectives*. Washington, DC: American Psychological Association.

Terman, L. M., & Merrill, M. A. (1973). *Stanford-Binet intelligence scale: Manual for the third revision*. Boston, MA: Houghton Mifflin.

Thelen, E., & Smith, L. B. (1994). *A dynamic systems approach to the development of cognition and action*. Cambridge, MA: MIT Press.

Thurstone, L. L. (1938). *Primary mental abilities*. Chicago, IL: University of Chicago Press.

Tomasello, M., Carpenter, M., Call, J., Behne, T., & Moll, H. (2005). Understanding and sharing intentions: The origins of cultural cognition. *Behavioral and Brain Sciences, 28*, 675–735.

Torgesen, J., Wagner, R., & Rashotte, C. (1994). Longitudinal studies of phonological processes of reading. *Journal of Learning Disabilities, 27*, 276–286.

Vallacher, R., & Nowak, A. (1998). The emergence of dynamical social psychology. *Psychological Inquiry, 8*(2), 73–99.

Van Der Maas, H., & Molenaar, P. (1992). A catastrophe-theoretical approach to cognitive development. *Psychological Review, 99*, 395–417.

van Geert, P. (1991). A dynamic systems model of cognitive and language growth. *Psychological Review, 98*, 3–53.

van Geert, P. (1994). A dynamic systems model of cognitive growth: Competition and support under limited resource conditions. In L. Smith & E. Thelen (Eds.), *A dynamical systems approach to development: Applications* (pp. 265–331). Cambridge, MA: MIT Press.

van Geert, P. (1998). A dynamic systems model of basic developmental mechanisms: Piaget, Vygotsky, and beyond. *Psychological Review, 105*, 634–677.

van Geert, P., & Fischer, K. W. (2009). Dynamic systems and the quest for individual-based models of change and development. In J. P. Spencer, M. S. C. Thomas, & J. L. McClelland (Eds.), *Toward a unified theory of development: Connectionism and dynamic systems theory reconsidered* (pp. 313–336). Oxford, UK: Oxford University Press.

van Geert, P., & van Dijk, M. (2002). Focus on variability: New tools to study intra-individual variability in developmental data. *Infant Behavior & Development, 25*(4), 340–374.

Vernon, P. E. (1950). *The structure of human abilities*. New York, NY: Wiley.

von Károlyi, C., Winner, E., Gray, W., & Sherman, G. F. (2003). Dyslexia linked to talent: Global visual-spatial ability. *Brain & Language, 85*, 427–431.

Vygotsky, L. (1978). *Mind in society: The development of higher psychological processes* (M. Cole, V. John-Steiner, S. Scribner, & E. Souberman, Trans.). Cambridge, MA: Harvard University Press.

Waddington, C. H. (1966). *Principles of development and differentiation*. New York, NY: Macmillan.

Watson, M. W., & Fischer, K. W. (1980). Development of social roles in elicited and spontaneous behavior during the preschool years. *Developmental Psychology, 16*, 484–494.

Watson, M. W., Fischer, K. W., Andreas, J. B., & Smith, K. W. (2004). Pathways to aggression in children and adolescents. *Harvard Educational Review, 74*, 404–430.

Wechsler, David (1939). *The measurement of adult intelligence*. Baltimore, MD: Williams & Wilkins.

Westen, D. (1994). The impact of sexual abuse on self structure. In D. Cicchetti & S. L. Toth (Eds.), *Disorders and dysfunctions of the self* (Vol. 5, pp. 223–250). Rochester, NY: University of Rochester Press.

Willingham, D. T. (2007). Critical thinking: Why is it so hard to teach? *American Educator, 31*(2), 8–19.

Wolf, M., & Bowers, P. (1999). The "double-deficit hypothesis" for the developmental dyslexias. *Journal of Educational Psychology, 91*, 1–24.

CHAPTER 9

Intelligence in Adulthood

Christopher Hertzog

The field of gerontology – the scientific study of aging – emerged as a major scientific discipline in the 20th century (e.g., Birren, 1964). Research on intelligence and intellectual development played a major role in shaping the field of psychological gerontology (e.g., Botwinick, 1977). This chapter reviews what is known and not yet known about adult intellectual development after decades of research on the topic. Most of the information we have available concerns aspects of what Sternberg (1985) has defined as academic intelligence (based on traditional psychometric tests of human abilities). This chapter focuses on what is known about these types of human abilities and their correlates, although I also briefly treat other aspects of intellect, such as practical intelligence and tacit knowledge.

Descriptive Research on Adult Age Differences

Early studies of psychometric intelligence prior to 1940 determined that there were large differences in performance on general tests of intellectual aptitude (see Salthouse, 1982 for an excellent summary and review). Wechsler (1939) characterized the performance tests on the Wechsler Adult Intelligence Scale (WAIS) as "don't-hold" tests because of the lower performance on those subscales (e.g., WAIS Block Design) by older adults in his cross-sectional norming studies of the test. Conversely, Wechsler found that tests like WAIS vocabulary were typically shown to have much smaller age differences, causing them to be characterized as "hold" tests. This basic idea, that one class of intellectual ability tests manifests age decline whereas others do not, has been widely replicated and studied across a variety of intelligence tests, and today represents a virtual "truism" about aging and intelligence. These findings mirrored outcomes of studies using other tests to evaluate age differences in human abilities, studies that spanned much of the 20th century (Salthouse, 1982).

The concept of contrasting maintenance of knowledge and verbal abilities, relative to other types of human abilities, has therefore figured prominently in theoretical treatment of how aging affects intelligence. Cattell (1971) developed the theory of fluid and crystallized intelligence, arguing that this basic pattern reflected two prototypic classes of intellectual abilities. Fluid intelligence was seen as the fundamental ability to think, reason, and process information, and prone to adult age decline as a function of biological aging processes (Horn & Cattell, 1967; Horn & Hofer, 1992). Crystallized intelligence, on the other hand was seen as determined by investment of fluid intelligence in knowledge acquisition, which was largely maintained or even improved into old age (Horn & Cattell, 1967).

Baltes and his colleagues characterized the distinction as involving a decline in basic information-processing mechanisms labeled the mechanics of cognition (e.g., Baltes, 1997). In contrast, experience with a culture leads to acquisition of a broad class of declarative and procedural knowledge and skills about how to achieve goals in a cultural context, labeled the pragmatics of intelligence. Although Baltes' conceptualization emphasized mechanisms that influence observed abilities, similar arguments were being made by Horn (e.g., Horn & Hofer, 1992) in extended versions of fluid-crystallized theory. As a consequence, the differences between these theoretical viewpoints are subtle at best.

Can a two-curve model actually account for most of the age-related variance in adult intellectual development? If so, it would be surprising, for several reasons. First, theories of psychometric abilities generally acknowledge that a large number of intellectual abilities exist. Theoretical approaches based on the work by Thurstone on primary mental abilities (e.g., Thurstone, 1938) typically argue for 30 or more primary abilities (Carroll, 1993; Horn & Hofer, 1992). It would be surprising if all these abilities declined at the same rate in adulthood. Second, contemporary hierarchical models of abilities typically acknowledge that fluid and crystallized intelligence are distinct from other higher order ability factors. Horn (1985; Horn & Hofer, 1992) argued that, for example, general visualization abilities, general auditory abilities, speediness, and secondary memory are all empirically distinct from fluid intelligence. To the extent that these second-order factors are indeed differentiable from fluid intelligence, one might expect their developmental curves in adulthood to also differ. Third, theories of biological aging identify a large number of potential biological clocks, operating at different levels of basic physiology, that appear to be associated with rates of biological aging.

What do the empirical data tell us? The cross-sectional age curves for episodic memory, spatial visualization, and measures of fluid intelligence and general processing speed vary somewhat as a function of issues like how the tests are constructed and scaled, their processing requirements, and the like. Yet there is surprising similarity in the curves across these different classes of abilities. Certainly the ability that is typically found to have the largest cross-sectional age differences is speed of processing, such as identified by the Perceptual Speed factor (Carroll, 1993). Salthouse (1996) has evaluated Perceptual Speed in a plethora of studies, typically finding the largest cross-sectional age differences for that factor (see also Schaie, 1989). However, fluid intelligence shows considerable similarity in magnitude of estimated decline to measures of episodic memory, working memory, and spatial visualization (e.g., Hertzog, 1989; Hultsch, Hertzog, Dixon, & Small, 1998; Park et al., 1996; Salthouse, Pink, & Tucker-Drob, 2008). No one study has examined all the relevant abilities in a truly representative sample of the adult population, and most observe at least some variation in cross-sectional age slopes across abilities. Nevertheless, the available cross-sectional evidence on the mechanics of cognition is more or less consistent with the argument that abilities emphasizing cognitive mechanics decline in adulthood. There are important exceptions – not all processing mechanisms decline, and not all aspects of pragmatics are maintained (see Hertzog, 2008). Also, cross-sectional data disagree as to whether the cross-sectional curves are linear or curvilinear – accelerating the magnitude of estimated decline in old age (e.g., compare Hultsch et al., 1998, with Park et al., 1996, regarding episodic memory). Nevertheless, the negative correlation of age with fluid intelligence, working memory, spatial visualization, and the like from early adulthood to old age is about −.4.

There is evidence that the cross-sectional age curves for crystallized intelligence may differ as a function of the type of knowledge being assessed. Work by Ackerman and colleagues has focused on tracking domain-specific knowledge that may occur during and after the time that young adults begin to specialize vocational and personal interests, crystallizing them into a pattern of preferences for information sought, acquired, digested, and assimilated into existing knowledge structures (e.g., Ackerman, 2000; Beier & Ackerman, 2005). Ackerman's argument is that crystallized intelligence, as manifested in general cultural knowledge tests (like WAIS Information) or in recognition vocabulary tests, underestimate acquisition of new knowledge during adulthood. Thus, although the existing psychometric data suggesting long-term stability in verbal abilities and cultural knowledge diverges from the pattern of negative age differences seen with fluid intelligence and other human abilities, it may not capture the lifelong learning that occurs in the specific domains in which people invest time and effort to acquire knowledge. Even within the domain of vocabulary, there may be activity-dependent differences in the types of word knowledge that are acquired. Frequent crossword puzzle players show major cross-sectional age differences in esoteric vocabulary terms that are correctly recognized, probably as a direct function of actual experience with encountering these terms while solving puzzles (Hambrick, Meinz, & Salthouse, 1999). Be that as it may, there is little question that abilities that reflect specific knowledge acquisition are maintained or improved, at least into the 60s.

Beier and Ackerman's (2005) work on specificity of knowledge acquisition resonates with other evidence that people of different ages also differ in historical life contexts that produce cohort differences in knowledge-based abilities. Schaie (2005) has studied adult intellectual development for over 50 years, using hybrid cross-sectional and longitudinal designs known as sequential strategies, enabling an evaluation of age changes across different birth cohorts and epochs of historical time. One of Schaie's findings is that there are large cohort differences in vocabulary, which helps to explain why studies of age and cognition that use older vocabulary tests – particularly with "advanced" and perhaps dated items – tend to find that older adults perform better than younger adults. Such age differences probably reflect a combination of improvement with experience in the older adults, but lower knowledge of esoteric word meanings in younger generations. By the same token, it is likely to be true that younger adults have more word knowledge in domains they commonly employ, such as technical terms and jargon associated with advanced technology (older adults are less likely to use new technology such as iPhones or iPods; Czaja et al., 2006). Schaie (2005) has also shown that there are cohort differences favoring earlier born generations in simple mental calculations such as two-column addition. One could view this effect as being a societal consequence of the use of computers and calculators, slowing the efficiency of mental arithmetic in more recent cohorts apt to rely on technological support.

In sum, the distinction in developmental functions between knowledge and experience-based abilities, on the one hand, and fluid-like abilities, on the other hand, is consistent with a large body of cross-sectional evidence.

Longitudinal Evidence Regarding Levels of Adult Intellectual Development

As noted earlier, Schaie and colleagues (e.g., Schaie, 2005) have assembled the largest extant database with combined longitudinal and cross-sectional intelligence test data. A reasonable question to ask, then, is whether these data produce radically different conclusions regarding age changes in adult intellectual development, relative to the cross-sectional data.

On the one hand, Schaie's (2005) data clearly indicate that cohort differences are not confined to aspects of knowledge and crystallized intelligence. He also observes substantial generational differences on a tests of fluid reasoning and spatial relations. Others have noted the changes during the 20th century in performance on tests of reasoning and fluid intelligence, as manifested in the so-called Flynn effect (Flynn, 2007; Raven, 2000). The impact of these cohort effects is primarily in attenuating the estimated changes in intelligence from ages 20 to 50, but they also reduce the magnitude of estimated age change in late life as well (Zelinski, Kennison, Watts, & Lewis, 2009).

Certainly the STAMAT Verbal Meaning test shows a prolonged period of maintenance, relative to the other abilities, but it too manifests evidence of longitudinal decline in old age. Separate evidence, however, suggests that this pattern of apparent decline is an artifact of the speeded properties of the STAMAT Verbal Meaning test (e.g., Hertzog, 1989). In fact, all of the STAMAT tests are substantially influenced by speed of processing, in part because of limited item difficulty, even for the Letter Series and Space tests.

The pattern of mean ability changes based on sequential data can be separated into three parts. The first is the similarity of age changes across different aspects of cognitive mechanics. The second is the conclusion that meaningful age-related changes in cognitive mechanics occur after mid-life and accelerate in magnitude in late life. The third is the presence of substantial cohort effects on variables measuring different aspects of cognitive mechanics that inflate estimates of age changes made from cross-sectional data.

Regarding cohort effects, there is broad agreement across studies that there are few cohort effects in general information-processing speed, including the Perceptual Speed factor identified by psychometric tests (e.g., Hultsch et al., 1998; Schaie, 1990). However, the limited available data from studies other than Schaie's Seattle Longitudinal Study confirm substantial cohort effects on tests of reasoning (Raven, 2000; Zelinski & Kennison, 2007; Rönnlund & Nilsson, 2008) and visuospatial ability (Rönnlund & Nilsson, 2008; Zelinski & Kennison, 2007). These effects attenuate estimated age changes in cognition. For example, Zelinski and Kennison (2007) found that six-year effect sizes in reasoning, spatial ability, and episodic memory were reduced in old age by between 0.2 and 0.3 standard deviations (SD) by controlling on cohort differences. Interestingly, some studies report few cohort effects on crystallized intelligence while finding larger effects on abilities more related to cognitive mechanics (see Zelinski et al., 2009; cf. Alwin, 2009).

The conclusion that declines in cognitive mechanics are subtle before age 50 and accelerating thereafter is broadly consistent with reported results from a number of other longitudinal studies of cognition and intellectual abilities in adulthood, including the Long Beach Longitudinal Study (Zelinski & Kennison, 2007), the Victoria Longitudinal Study (Hultsch et al., 1998), and the Betula Longitudinal Study (Rönnlund, Nyberg, Bäckman, & Nilsson, 2005). These studies all suggest curvilinear patterns of average age changes from the period of mid-life through old age, with an acceleration in the rate of aging effects on fluid intelligence, episodic memory, and spatial visualization and other fluid-like abilities after age 65.

Salthouse (2009) has argued that the type of longitudinal gradients produced by Schaie (2005) are contaminated by practice effects on the tests, an internal validity threat (Shadish, Cook, & Campell, 2002) that is problematic for longitudinal designs (Schaie, 1977). Because individuals are repeatedly given the same tests, they may show some savings in generating problem answers. If it were the case that younger adults manifest larger practice effects (an age X practice interaction), perhaps due to retention of prior test answers, then the contamination by practice would produce shallower age slopes. One way to address the problem of practice effects has been to incorporate effects of number of occasions of measurement as a proxy for exposure that would benefit from practice. Models that use this approach also tend to increase the magnitude of age-related decline and estimate an earlier onset of reliable age-related decline (e.g., Ferrer, Salthouse, Stewart, & Schwartz, 2004; Rabbitt, Diggle, Holland, & McInnes, 2004).

However, this modeling approach is controversial (see the exchange between Salthouse, 2009, Schaie, 2009, and Nilsson, Sternäng, Rönnlund, & Nyberg, 2009). A model that uses all available data in a standard longitudinal panel and then jointly estimates age changes and practice effects (under the convergence assumption – see McArdle & Bell, 2001) confounds the estimates of practice effects with other influences that are not modeled, including historical period (time), experimental mortality (attrition), and selection X period interactions. Sliwinski, Hoffman, and Hofer (2010) argue that such models inevitably assign within-person changes that deviate from cross-sectional trends to estimates of practice, morphing the estimated age effects away from within-person change toward between-person differences. As pointed out by Nilsson et al. (2009), studies that use an independent samples comparison group to estimate practice effects report far less impressive practice adjustments than studies like Ferrer et al. (2004).

Age Changes in the Factor Structure of Intelligence Tests

Another important question about aging is whether it influences the underlying factor structure of human abilities. A leading developmental hypothesis has been the dedifferentiation hypothesis (deFrias, Lövdén, Lindenberger, & Nilsson, 2007). It states that shared causes of age effects across different kinds of human abilities will produce increased correlations among ability factors. In the extreme, such changes could lead to a reduced number of distinct human abilities.

Factor analytic questions of this type cannot be separated from issues of how broadly or narrowly tests are selected. A unifying perspective on this issue derives from hierarchical models of abilities, such as in Carroll (1993). This view suggests that one can evaluate factor structure at a relatively narrow level (how different tests define primary abilities, such as inductive reasoning or working memory), at a second-order level (how different primary abilities define higher order factors like fluid intelligence, general speed of processing, or spatial visualization), or at the highest levels (how second-order factors define a highest order general intelligence factor). At the primary ability or second-order level, one can also evaluate the correlations among ability factors, treating these correlations as an index of differentiation. In addressing these questions one can run into difficulty separating measurement invariance and suboptimal measurement properties of tests from changes in relationships among constructs. For example, use of speeded tests of intelligence may produce a substantial degree of dedifferentiation that is attributable to the global effects of speed of processing on test performance, rather than because the underlying ability constructs are becoming more correlated (Hertzog & Bleckley, 2001).

The best available evidence suggests that the factor structure of intelligence is not materially affected by aging. A large number of confirmatory factor analytic studies, using both cross-sectional and longitudinal data, indicate that the same human abilities can be identified in young adulthood, middle age, and old age (e.g., Anstey, Hofer, & Luszcz, 2003; Hertzog & Schaie, 1986; Hertzog, Dixon, Hultsch, & MacDonald, 2003; Hultsch et al., 1998; Brickley, Keith, & Wolfe, 1995; Lane & Zelinski, 2003; Schaie et al., 1998). In all cases, the hypothesis of configural invariance (i.e., that the same variables load on the same factors at all ages; Meredith & Horn, 2001) has been supported. In most cases, the evidence supports the stronger hypothesis of metric invariance, that the unstandardized factor pattern weights, or factor loadings (Meredith & Horn, 2001), are equivalent across time in longitudinal studies or are equivalent across age groups. This is a broad generalization, and there are some interesting exceptions. Nevertheless, the developmental changes that occur in adulthood do not appear to radically alter the underlying nature of human abilities.

On the other hand, the evidence regarding whether adult development results in increasing correlations among human ability factors is mixed. Some studies have not found such effects (e.g., Zelinski et al, 2009; Bickley et al., 1995), whereas other studies have (deFrias et al., 2007; Hertzog & Bleckley, 2001; Hertzog et al., 2003; Hultsch et al., 1998; Schaie et al., 1998; Verhaeghen & Salthouse, 1997). However, major increases in factor correlations may be restricted to old age (deFrias et al., 2007; Schaie et al., 1998).

One methodological concern with age-comparative factor analysis is that aggregation over long epochs of age is often needed to generate sufficient sample sizes for factor analysis of cross-sectional data. For example, one might pool data from people within the ages of 20 and 39, 40 and 59, 60 and 79 to create "young," "middle aged," and "old" age groups. Aggregation over wide age spans (such as 20 years) can create spurious increases in factor correlations because of the inflating influence of age-heterogeneity on variable correlations (Hofer, Flaherty, & Hoffman, 2006). Given greater average age change after age 60 that is similar across variables, factor correlations in the oldest group would be inflated. Forming narrower age spans, if possible given the sample size, avoids this effect.

In sum, factor analytic evidence indicates subtle changes, if any, in the factor structure of human abilities. Thus, quantitative comparisons of ability test scores may not be compromised by age-related changes in the measurement properties of the tests (Baltes & Nesselroade, 1970).

Individual Differences in Cognitive Change

One of the remarkable features of human intelligence is its relative stability of individual differences over years, even decades. When longitudinal data are collected on the same person over time, it is possible to compute correlations of ability test scores across that interval. These correlations can be remarkably high. For example, Ian Deary and colleagues discovered large sample data on a general ability test for cohorts of Scottish schoolchildren in multiple cohorts, and readministered the test over 60 years later to those who could be located. Test-retest correlations were approximately .65 across the different cohorts (e.g., Deary et al., 2004). Similar findings have been reported in long-term longitudinal studies using a wider range and variety of intelligence test and cognitive tasks (e.g., Schaie, 2005). Moreover, when statistical corrections are possible to correct for attenuation of the stability estimates for measurement error, the correlations are even higher. Hertzog and Schaie (1986) reported that the latent seven-year stability of a general intelligence factor formed from primary ability tests was about .9. Hence it is reasonable to conclude that individual differences in abilities are to a reasonable degree preserved as a function of aging. Those individuals who perform well in a particular domain are likely to continue to do so across their adult lives.

Longitudinal studies may overestimate the stability of individual differences. Selective attrition has been universally demonstrated in longitudinal studies of human abilities – those individuals who return for testing performed higher at the inception of the study than those who fail to return (e.g., Ghisletta, McArdle, & Lindenberger, 2006; Schaie, 2005). Selective attrition and population mortality are also likely to upwardly bias estimates of stability of individual differences in intelligence.

Nevertheless, even in positively selected samples, the stability observed still implies that there are reliable individual differences in rates of change. When growth curve analyses or latent difference score analyses are performed on longitudinal cognitive data, it is generally the case that there are reliable variances in the slopes of the growth curves (e.g., deFrias et al., 2007; Ghisletta et al. 2006; McArdle et al., 2002). Not all individuals are changing at the same rate; some decline faster than others, and some even show improvements. Schaie (2005) has argued that, although the modal pattern of individual change is one of relative stability in mid-life, one can identify also individuals who reliably decline or who reliably improve, even on abilities related to cognitive mechanics. Data on six-year stability from the Victoria Longitudinal Study (VLS) on a number of different cognitive variables, including working memory, episodic memory, fluid intelligence, ideational fluency, verbal comprehension, and speed of processing show reliable variances in latent difference scores (Hertzog et al., 2003), despite corrected stabilities that were typically in the 0.8 to 0.9 range. As pointed out by deFrias et al. (2007), these individual differences in cognitive changes may be more pronounced in old age than in middle age.

The existence of individual differences in change on different human abilities raises an intriguing question. Are these changes related to each other? Rabbitt (1993) once framed the question this way: Does it all go together when it goes? There is good evidence that changes across variables are not independent but are instead correlated. Given the extended measurement batteries in studies like the Betula Longitudinal Study and the VLS, we probably know the most about associations in age-related changes in different aspects of memory. In the case of the VLS, analyses in two different six-year longitudinal samples show that individual differences in changes in working memory are correlated with changes in episodic memory (measured by free recall of word lists and narrative text content) and in a measure of semantic memory (fact recall). In addition, changes in working memory also correlate with changes in other abilities, including ideational fluency, inductive reasoning, and speed of processing (Hultsch et al., 1998; Hertzog et al., 2003). Betula study data indicates correlations among different aspects of episodic memory and processing speed (Lövdén et al., 2004). Hertzog et al. (2003) showed that one could fit a higher order general factor of change to the latent change factors for multiple cognitive abilities. This latent variable was defined principally by working memory but also had substantial loadings on most other variables, with the exception of changes in vocabulary.

One interesting feature of the VLS data was the strong association of changes in fact recall with changes in working memory. The fact recall measure assessed cultural knowledge (e.g., "who is the cartoon character who gets his strength from eating spinach?"). Cross-sectionally, the fact recall measure behaves like a measure of crystallized intelligence, as one would expect (Hultsch et al., 1998). Longitudinally, it dissociates from verbal comprehension. Instead, changes in fact recall are more highly correlated with changes in working memory and episodic memory. Such a pattern suggests late life changes in retrieval or access to information held in semantic memory that are shared across episodic and semantic memory tasks.

One typically observes high correlations of measures of inductive reasoning and working memory. The strong association of working memory and reasoning has been observed in a number of individual differences studies (e.g., Kane & Engle, 2002; Salthouse et al., 2008). Kyllonen and Chrystal (1990) once remarked that reasoning might not be, in fact, differentiable from working memory. Yet working memory changes and reasoning changes are only moderately correlated in the VLS data (Hertzog et al., 2003); instead, changes in working memory are more highly correlated with changes in fact recall than with changes in reasoning. The influences that drive age changes may not be the same influences that determine the factor structure of abilities in young adulthood.

Perhaps the most interesting aspect of the VLS change factor is that there is reliable

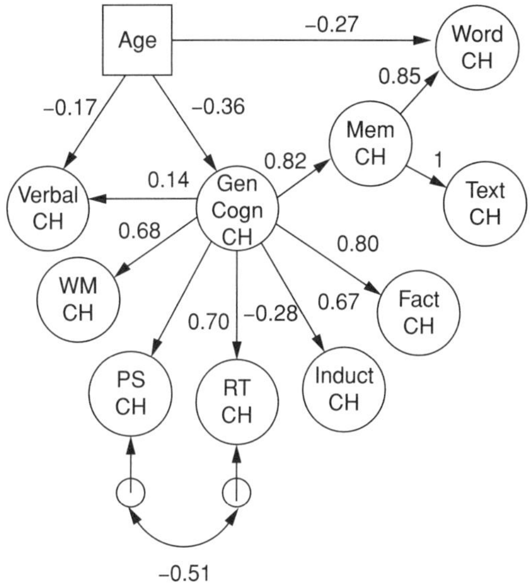

Figure 9.1. A structural equation model for general cognitive change from 6-year longitudinal data from the VLS (from Hertzog et al., 2003). Published by the American Psychological Association. Reprinted with permission.

change variance in almost all human abilities that is unique to each variable. Figure 9.1, taken from Hertzog et al. (2003), shows the results of a model where a higher order factor of general cognitive change is used to account for the correlations of change among the different cognitive variables. The general change factor has moderate to strong relationships to change in most of the cognitive variables. Thus there is a coherence to the individual differences in rates of cognitive change in later life. Nevertheless, changes in the latent variables do not correlate up to the limit defined by the variance of their changes. Cognitive change is both common and unique, in the factor analytic sense of those terms. There are certainly shared aspects of change, but different human abilities change independent of each other. The answer to Rabbitt's (1993) question, it seems, is not that everything goes together, but that, when working memory goes, a lot of other abilities seem to go too, to at least a degree.

These results are therefore divergent from the similarity of average age trends in fluid intelligence and other aspects of cognitive mechanics. The coherence to cognitive change – as manifested in moderate correlations of longitudinal changes across variables obscures the fact that variables are changing independently, such that people will have different profiles of change across a set of cognitive variables. Unlike the inferences about the dimensions of change from cross-sectional data (e.g., Salthouse et al., 2008), such findings indicate that a potentially large number of causes influence age-related changes in cognition.

Why the discrepancy between cross-sectional and longitudinal results? Certainly, there are potential issues with the validity of the longitudinal estimates of correlated change. For instance, Ferrer et al. (2005) noted that differential practice effects across variables could distort the estimated longitudinal change correlations. It is difficult to believe, however, that such effects could produce artifactual variable-specific change variance of the type observed in the VLS data, given that the VLS uses rotating alternate forms to measure word recall, text recall, and fact recall with different items at each occasion of measurement.

To my mind the difference arises essentially because the question cannot be adequately addressed by statistical models of cross-sectional data (Hofer et al., 2006; Lindenberger et al., 2009). Cross-sectional analyses can only estimate, in effect, correlations among cross-sectional age curves by testing for whether cognitive variables have a partial correlation with age, controlling on other cognitive variables. This approach can reveal whether average age trends differ between variables (e.g., Horn, Donaldson, & Engstrom, 1981). Failing to detect different shapes of cross-sectional curves neither implies that the variables in question change in lockstep nor that their changes have the same underlying causes. To actually assess individual differences in change, one must repeatedly measure the same people (Baltes & Nesselroade, 1979).

In sum, there is a high degree of stability in human abilities across the adult life course, but at the same time there are individual differences in cognitive changes, particularly in old age. A critical question, then, is what determines these individual differences in cognitive trajectories.

Influences on Adult Cognitive Development

The individual differences in cognitive change just reviewed could in principle reflect a number of different influences. Cognitive psychologists tend to focus on processing mechanisms that are associated with changes in complex cognition. As noted earlier, resources like working memory, processing speed, and inhibitory aspects of attention are often cited as causes of age changes in intelligence (see Hertzog, 2008; Salthouse, 1996; Verhaeghen & Salthouse, 1997). Even if one emphasizes a componential approach to human intelligence, the question remains as to what determines age-related changes in fundamental processing mechanisms.

One important influence is individual differences in genetically programmed biological aging – often termed senescence. In essence, the idea is that our biological aging clocks may be ticking in different metrics of time. Newer research derived from insights into the human genomic code indicates that genetic polymorphisms associated with neurotransmitters, neurotrophins, and related hormones influence adult cognitive development (e.g., Harris et al., 2006; Lindenberger et al., 2008). Behavioral genetic studies indicate a considerable degree of heritability in cognitive change in late life (Reynolds, 2008). However, genetic predispositions interact with social and psychological mechanisms to produce cognitive phenotypes.

When we organize our data by chronological age, we are not measuring individual differences in rates of biological aging. The effects of age revealed in group mean changes or in individual differences in change reflect variation in cognition that is systematically correlated with how old people are. But there are many contextual variables that are correlated with chronological age as well, including age-graded events like retirement, experience, and shrinkage of one's social network. Furthermore, non-normative, negative life events are correlated with age, such as risks for contracting different kinds of chronic disease that can impact cognition, either directly through influences on the brain or indirectly through psychological effects of medications used to treat them (Birren, 1964). The longitudinal studies that generate the data in question may measure physical health but typically cannot control on disease by only assessing disease-free older adults. The average older adult has three or more chronic health conditions, including arthritis, vascular disease, Type II diabetes, reduced hormonal secretion, pulmonary or renal disease, and declining sensory and perceptual function (e.g., macular degeneration; see Spiro & Brady, 2008). There is also a host of brain pathologies that are correlated with age and which may have impact on cognition before they are clinically detected, including different forms of dementia and Parkinson's disease). Lifestyles also change as people grow older, sometimes as a consequence of limitations produced by chronic disease, in other cases as a function of changing patterns of behavior that have psychological and social origins.

Certainly, structural features in the brain undergo changes that are correlated with cognition. For instance, Raz et al. (2008) analyzed a longitudinal sample that had been measured with structural magnetic resonance imaging to evaluate changes in gray matter volume in the cerebral cortex. Individual differences in the structural changes in dorsolateral prefrontal cortex and hippocampal areas of the brain were correlated with changes in fluid intelligence.

Disease and brain pathology. The findings of Raz et al. (2008) do not necessarily imply that neurobiological aging in the brain drives cognitive changes. The morphological changes in the brain can also be caused by disease, such as cardiovascular disease and dementia. Sliwinski et al. (2003) conducted a fascinating study in this regard, using data from the Bronx Longitudinal Study (Sliwinski & Buschke, 2004). The study involved a prospective design of the incidence of dementing illnesses in a nondemented control group collected as part of a larger study of Alzheimer's disease and related disorders. Individuals in this group were measured cognitively at regular intervals, but they were also assessed for dementia. Over time some of the participants were clinically diagnosed as having dementia, and this allowed Sliwinski and colleagues to compare cognitive change in the preclinical phase with change in those individuals who did not convert to dementia. As might be expected, individuals who had not yet been diagnosed with dementia (but undoubtedly had contracted the disease) showed greater change in episodic memory during their preclinical phase, compared to individuals who did not later receive a dementia diagnosis. Even more interesting, however, was the fact that the aggregate control sample manifested individual differences in cognitive change, as well as correlations of changes across cognitive variables. However, the magnitude of individual differences was reduced by controlling on later dementia diagnosis, as were the correlations of change among different variables. Furthermore, within the dementia group, organizing the time scale by point of diagnosis rather than chronological age eliminated the individual differences in rates of cognitive change.

What does this pattern imply? It would appear that in this sample, the presence of preclinical dementia was a major source of individual differences in change. Because people vary in the age at which the disease is contracted and later diagnosed, organizing the data by age (without knowledge of the disease and its progression) produces larger individual differences in rates of change. Given that other prospective studies of Alzheimer's disease, vascular dementia, and other dementing illnesses indicate a fairly long preclinical period in which cognition may be affected (e.g., Bäckman & Small, 2007), it would appear that a major influence on individual differences in cognitive change in old age is the presence or absence of dementia. Furthermore, a number of studies have directly linked magnitudes of longitudinal changes in cognitive abilities to different kinds of disease, including cardiovascular and cerebrovascular disease, late-onset diabetes, and their precursors, or risk factors, such as obesity, hypertension, poor cholesterol profiles, and the like (Spiro & Brady, 2008).

Disease and terminal decline. A focus on disease effects on cognition raises an additional set of important questions about aging and intellectual development. To what extent are the average curves for cognitive abilities and age misleading, in the sense that they are not representative of the actual developmental trajectories of individuals? Means, even if generated from longitudinal data, are simply best guesses as to the level of function, on average, at a particular age. We link the means of different ages with a line (or fit a curve to the data), but this does not imply that the developmental pathways of individuals have the shape implied by the shape of the aggregate mean curve.

The population of adults might be quite heterogeneous in nature, with the major changes in psychological functioning, including cognition, occurring during a period of decline preceding death (e.g., Berg, 1996; Bosworth, Schaie, & Willis, 1999). Indeed, time to death may be a more important way of indexing cognitive loss in old age than chronological age (Singer et al. 2003). Some new and impressive data on this score come from models of longitudinal data that jointly use time to death and age to organize the data (Ram et al., 2010). The modeling approach is fairly complex, requiring estimation of a change point (Hall, Sliwinski, Stewart, & Lipton, 2000), at which the slope of decline prior to a change point is lower than the slope immediately prior to death. Thorvaldsson et al. (2008) used this method to demonstrate accelerated cognitive decline occurring about seven years before death in the Swedish Goteborg Longitudinal Study data. Wilson, Beck, Bienias, and Bennett (2007) found evidence for a shorter period of terminal decline of about four years. Terminal decline was associated

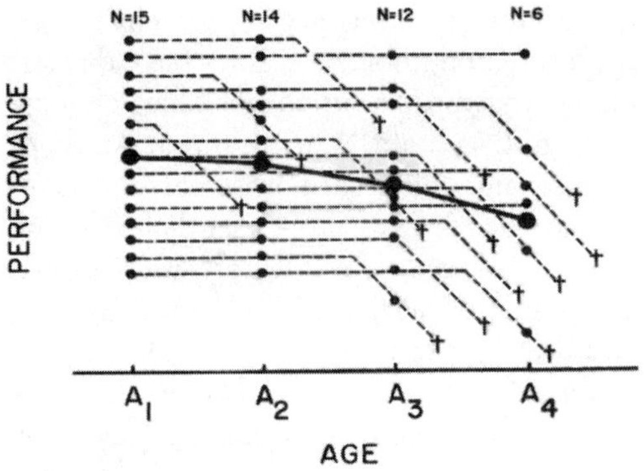

Figure 9.2. Demonstration of how aggregating over persons conforming to a pattern of stability, followed by terminal decline, would produce a mean curvilinear change given (1) an age-related increase in the risk of terminal decline and (2) mortality-related attrition from the sample. From Baltes and Labouvie (1973). Published by the American Psychological Association. Reprinted with permission.

with the apolipoprotein E ε4 allele, a genetic polymorphism thought to be associated with risk for Alzheimer's disease (AD). Laukka, MacDonald, and Backman (2008) also concluded that a substantial proportion of the variance in terminal cognitive decline might be due to emergence of dementia, but there was evidence of decline in individuals who did not develop AD. Undoubtedly future research will clarify the extent to which other disease factors play a role in terminal cognitive decline, including vascular disease and organ failure (e.g., renal dysfunction, see Buchman et al., 2009).

In light of the evidence for terminal decline effects, the possibility exists that the curvilinear age trends for cognitive function in late life are actually an artifact of aggregation over individuals with different functions. This idea was nicely illustrated by Baltes and Labouvie (1973), who showed that a combination of (1) a change point function of stable level of cognition, followed by terminal decline, and (2) a variable onset of the terminal decline that was correlated with advancing age could produce aggregate curvilinear functions that did not capture the functional form of individual change (see Figure 9.2). The aggregate function could be influenced by the increasing risk of terminal decline, with its curvature reflecting an averaging of persons in terminal decline with persons who are still stable.

Exercise and an engaged life style. A critical question regarding adult intellectual development is whether health-promoting behaviors such as exercise, nutrition, and an active lifestyle promote better developmental outcomes (Hertzog, Kramer, Wilson, & Lindenberger, 2009). Over the last decade, compelling evidence has emerged that aerobic exercise in middle age and old age promotes enhanced cognitive function in older adults. Colcombe and Kramer's (2003) meta-analysis evaluated aerobic exercise intervention studies in older adults and compared exercise groups' cognitive performance to performance in a groups doing toning and stretching only. Short-term aerobic exercise resulted in substantial improvements in tasks assessing executive functioning and controlled attention (domains highly correlated with fluid intelligence; Salthouse et al., 2008). The data are broadly consistent with cross-sectional studies suggesting an association of self-reported exercise with human abilities (e.g., Eggermont et al., 2009), but the intervention effects help to argue for a causal influence of exercise on cognition. Unfortunately, there are at present no longitudinal studies that contrast longer term adherence with exercise regimens and degree of cognitive change in adulthood.

Does engaging in intellectually stimulating activities also promote better cognitive outcomes? Salthouse (2006) expressed skepticism on this score, given that his cross-sectional data on self-reported activities have failed to observe age X activity interactions (see Hertzog et al., 2009, for a critique of this argument). Certainly, simple cross-sectional correlations of activities and intelligence are insufficient grounds for arguing that activities help preserve cognitive functioning, because individuals with high intelligence tend to manifest higher levels of intellectual engagement in early adulthood (Ackerman & Heggestad, 1997). However, longitudinal evidence is needed, given the potential lack of sensitivity of cross-sectional data to change alluded to earlier. Longitudinal studies have often found relationships of self-reported intellectual engagement with cognition (e.g., Schooler, Mulatu, & Oates, 1999; Wilson et al., 2003; see Hertzog et al., 2009 for a review). However, as noted by Hultsch, Hertzog, Small, and Dixon (1999), longitudinal correlations of activities with cognitive change could still be due to late-life cognitive changes leading to curtailed activity (MacKinnon et al., 2003).

There are fewer intervention studies with activities, but there is at least some indication that encouraging older adults to engage in stimulating activities may have cognitive benefits (Carlson et al., 2009; Stine-Morrow et al., 2007; Tranter & Koutstaal, 2008). In one recent study, participation in a complex videogame environment led to short-term improvements in attentional control and executive function (Basak, Boot, Voss, & Kramer, 2008). This outcome is consistent with intervention studies that target executive control (Hertzog et al., 2009), producing more transfer of training than is typically observed when training focuses on teaching specific processing strategies (e.g., Ball et al., 2002). The evidence favors an impact of activities on cognitive function, but there is still some disagreement and controversy on this point.

Functional Aspects of Adult Intelligence

Given that there are, on average, adult age changes in cognitive abilities, what are the practical consequences of these changes? Evidence is beginning to emerge that there are fewer practical implications for cognitive functioning in everyday life than some might have supposed.

For example, older workers, even those with intellectually demanding jobs, function well on the job even into old age (e.g., Ng & Feldman, 2008). Work by Colonia-Willner (1998) may suggest a reason for this maintenance; experience on the job (which correlates with age) brings with it increases in tacit knowledge (Cianciolo et al., 2006) about how to perform effectively on the job. Colonia-Willner studied bankers of different ages in Brazil. Although her cross-sectional sample showed typical age differences in fluid intelligence, expert ratings of tacit knowledge about hypothetical banking situations indicated age-related improvements in this domain.

Such effects can be observed in intellectually demanding game situations as well. Masunaga and Horn (2001) studied the relationship of fluid intelligence to performance on the Japanese game of Go, a cognitively demanding task with some resemblance to chess. Go performance was less correlated with standard measures of fluid intelligence and working memory than with measures of reasoning that directly represented reasoning about Go moves. In a similar vein, Charness and colleagues have demonstrated good memory retention for chess positions by older chess experts, relative to their impaired episodic memory for chess pieces placed in random positions on the chess board (e.g., Charness, 1981). Hershey, Jacobs-Lawson, and Walsh (2003) reported sound simulated financial decision making by older adults who had prior experience in investing or gained it through structured task experience. Performance in familiar environmental contexts is associated with beneficial effects of pragmatic knowledge about typical scripts and scenarios, common decisions and choice points, and intact access to effective strategies for performance that help older adults preserve effective cognitive functioning, even in the face of decline in fluid ability (Hertzog, 2008).

Older adults may also be effective at using strategies that enhance cognition in everyday life, such as through the use of external aids or behavioral routines that support timely remembering of what to do and when to do it. For instance, older adults are sometimes better at remembering to take medications than middle-aged and younger adults, despite age deficits in standard tests of reasoning and episodic memory (Park et al., 1999). In general, older adults do well in everyday prospective memory tasks relative to laboratory tasks (Phillips, Henry, & Martin, 2008), probably because of a more active use of strategies to promote remembering.

Conclusions

The study of adult cognitive and intellectual development is entering a vibrant new phase, one in which the advances in statistical methods for modeling individual differences are being integrated with designs and measures that permit a subtle understanding of individual differences in cognitive change. The next decades are likely to see an expanded understanding of how social and psychological forces interact with biological and genetic influences to shape individual trajectories of adult cognitive development, at the level of both brain structure and behavior.

References

Ackerman, P. L. (2000). Domain-specific knowledge as the "dark matter" of adult intelligence: Gf/Gc personality and interest correlates. *Journal of Gerontology: Psychological Sciences*, **55**, P69–P84.

Ackerman, P. L., & Heggestad, E. D. (1997). Intelligence, personality, and interests: Evidence for overlapping traits. *Psychological Bulletin*, **121**, 219–245.

Alwin, D. F. (2009). History, cohorts, and patterns of cognitive aging. In H. B. Bosworth & C. Hertzog (Eds.), Aging and cognition: *Research methodologies and empirical advances* (pp. 9–38). Washington, DC: American Psychological Association.

Anstey, K. J., Hofer, S. M., & Luszcz, M. A. (2003). Cross-sectional and longitudinal patterns of dedifferentiation in late-life cognitive and sensory function: The effects of age, ability, attrition, and occasion of measurement. *Journal of Experimental Psychology: General*, **132**, 470–487.

Bäckman, L., & Small, B. J. (2007). Cognitive deficits in preclinical Alzheimer's disease and vascular dementia: Patterns of findings from the Kungsholmen project. *Physiology and Behavior*, **92**, 80–86.

Ball, K., Berch, D. B., Helmer, K. F., Jobe, J. B., Leveck, M. D., Marsiske, M., et al. (2002). Effects of cognitive training interventions with older adults: A randomized controlled trial. *Journal of the American Medical Association*, **288**, 2271–2281.

Baltes, P. B. (1997). On the incomplete architecture of human ontogeny: Selection, optimization, and compensation as a foundation for developmental theory. *American Psychologist*, **52**, 366–380.

Baltes, P. B., & Labouvie, G. V. (1973). Adult development of intellectual performance: Description, explanation, and modification. In C. Eisdorfer & M. P. Lawton (Eds.), *The psychology of adult development and aging* (pp. 157–219). Washington, DC: American Psychological Association.

Baltes, P. B., & Nesselroade, J. R. (1970). Multivariate longitudinal and cross-sectional sequences for analyzing ontogenetic and generational change: A methodological note. *Developmental Psychology*, **2**, 163–168.

Baltes, P. B., & Nesselroade, J. R. (1979). History and rationale of longitudinal research. In J. R. Nesselroade & P. B. Baltes (Eds.), *Longitudinal research in the study of behavior and development*. New York, NY: Academic Press.

Baltes, P. B., Reese, H. W., & Nesselroade, J. R. (1988). *Life-span developmental psychology: Introduction to research methods*. Hillsdale, NJ: Erlbaum.

Baltes, P. B., Staudinger, U. M., & Lindenberger, U. (1999). Lifespan psychology: Theory and application to intellectual functioning. *Annual Review of Psychology*, **50**, 471–507.

Basak, C., Boot, W. R., Voss, M. W., & Kramer, A. F. (2008). Can training in a real-time strategy videogame attenuate cognitive decline in older adults? *Psychology and Aging*, **23**, 765–777.

Beier, M., & Ackerman, P. L. (2005). Age, ability, and the role of prior knowledge on the acquisition of new domain knowledge: Promising results in a real-world learning environment. *Psychology and Aging*, **20**, 341–355.

Berg, S. (1996). Aging, behavior, and terminal decline. In J. E. Birren & K. W. Schaie (Eds.), *Handbook of the psychology of aging* (4th ed., pp. 323–337). San Diego, CA: Academic Press.

Birren, J.E. (1964). *The psychology of aging*. Englewood Cliffs, NJ: Prentice-Hall.

Bosworth, H. B., Schaie, K. W., & Willis, S. L. (1999). Cognitive and sociodemographic risk factors for mortality in the Seattle Longitudinal Study. *Journal of Gerontology: Psychological Sciences, 54*, P273–P282.

Botwinick, J. (1977). Intellectual abilities. In J. E. Birren & K. W. Schaie (Eds.), *Handbook of the psychology of aging* (pp. 580–605). New York, NY: Van Nostrand Reinhold.

Brickley, P. G., Keith, T. Z., & Wolfle, L. M. (1995). The three-stratum theory of cognitive abilities: Test of the structure of intellect across the adult life span. *Intelligence, 20*, 309–328.

Buchman, A. S., Tanne, D., Boyle, P. A., Shah, R. C., Leurgans, S. E., & Bennett, D. A. (2009). Kidney function is associated with the rate of cognitive decline in the elderly. *Neurology, 73*, 920–927.

Carlson, M. C., Saczynski, J. S., Rebok, G. W., McGill, S., Tielsch, J., Glass, T. A., et al. (in press). Exploring the effects of an everyday activity program on executive function and memory in older adults: Experience Corps. *Gerontologist.*

Carroll, J. B. (1993). *Human cognitive abilities: A survey of factor analytic studies*. Cambridge, UK: Cambridge University Press.

Cattell, R. B. (1971). *Abilities: Their structure, growth, and action*. Boston, MA: Houghton Mifflin.

Charness, N. (1981). Aging and skilled problem solving. *Journal of Experimental Psychology: General, 110*, 21–38.

Cianciolo, A. T., Grigorenko, E. L., Jarvin, L., Gil, G., Drebot, M. E., & Sternberg, R. J. (2006). Practical intelligence and tacit knowledge: Advancements in the measurement of developing expertise. *Learning and Individual Differences, 16*, 235–253.

Colcombe, S., & Kramer, A.F. (2003). Fitness effects on the cognitive function of older adults: A meta-analytic study. *Psychological Science, 14*, 125–130.

Colonia-Willner, R. (1998). Practical intelligence at work: Relationships between aging and cognitive efficiency among managers in a bank environment. *Psychology and Aging, 13*, 45–57.

Czaja, S., Charness, N., Fisk, A. D., Hertzog, C., Nair, S., Rogers, W. A., & Sharit, J. (2006). Factors predicting the use of technology: Findings from the Center for Research and Education on Aging and Technology Enhancement (CREATE). *Psychology and Aging, 21*, 333–352.

Deary, I. J., Whiteman, M. C., Starr, J. M., Whalley, L. J., & Fox, H. C. (2004). The impact of childhood intelligence on later life: Following up the Scottish Mental Surveys of 1932 and 1947. *Journal of Personality and Social Psychology, 86*, 130–147.

deFrias, C. M., Lövdén, M., Lindenberger, & Nilsson, L.-G. (2007). Revisiting the dedifferentiation hypothesis with longitudinal multi-cohort data. *Intelligence, 35*, 381–392.

Eggermont, L. H. P., Milberg, W. P., Lipsitz, L. A., Scherder, E. J. A., & Leveille, S. G. (2009). Physical activity and executive function in aging: The MOBILIZE Boston study. *Journal of the American Geriatric Society, 57*, 1750–1756.

Ferrer, E., Salthouse, T. A., Stewart, W. F., & Schwartz, B. S. (2004). Modeling age and retest processes in longitudinal studies of cognitive abilities. *Psychology and Aging, 19*, 243–249.

Ferrer, E., Salthouse, T. A. McArdle, J. J., Stewart, W. F., & Schwartz, B. S. (2005). Multivariate modeling of age and retest in longitudinal studies of cognitive abilities. *Psychology and Aging, 20*, 412–422.

Flynn, J. R. (2007). *What is intelligence? Beyond the Flynn effect*. Cambridge, UK: Cambridge University Press.

Ghisletta, P., McArdle, J. J., & Lindenberger, U. (2006). Longitudinal cognition-survival relations in old and very old age: 13-year data from the Berlin Aging Study. *European Psychologist, 11*, 204–223.

Hall, C. B., Lipton, R. B., Sliwinski, M., & Stewart, W. F. (2000). A change point model for estimating the onset of cognitive decline in preclinical Alzheimer's disease. *Statistics in Medicine, 19*, 1555–1566.

Hambrick, D. Z., Meinz, E. J., & Salthouse, T. A. (1999). Predictors of crossword puzzle proficiency and moderators of age-cognition relations. *Journal of Experimental Psychology: General, 128*, 131–164.

Harris, S. E., Fox, H., Wright, A. F., Hayward, C., Starr, J. M., Whalley, L. J., Deary, I, J. (2006). The brain-derived neurotrophic factor Val66Met polymorphism is associated with age-related change in reasoning skills. *Molecular Psychiatry, 11*, 505–513.

Hershey, D. A., Jacobs-Lawson, J. M., & Walsh, D. A. (2003). Influences of age and training on script development. *Aging, Neuropsychology, and Cognition, 10*, 1–19.

Hertzog, C. (1989). The influence of cognitive slowing on age differences in intelligence. *Developmental Psychology, 25*, 636–651.

Hertzog, C. (2008). Theoretical approaches to the study of cognitive aging: An individual-differences perspective. In S. M. Hofer & D. F. Alwin (Eds.), *Handbook of cognitive aging: Interdisciplinary perspectives* (pp. 34–49). Thousand Oaks, CA: Sage.

Hertzog, C. (2009). Use it or lose it: An old hypothesis, new evidence, and an ongoing controversy. In H. Bosworth & C. Hertzog (Eds.), *Cognition and aging: Research methodologies and empirical advances* (pp. 161–179). Washington, DC: American Psychological Association.

Hertzog, C., & Bleckley, M. K. (2001). Age differences in the structure of intelligence: Influences of information processing speed. *Intelligence, 29*, 191–217.

Hertzog, C., Dixon, R. A., Hultsch, D. F., & MacDonald, S. W. S. (2003). Latent change models of adult cognition: Are changes in processing speed and working memory associated with changes in episodic memory? *Psychology and Aging, 18*, 755–769.

Hertzog, C., Kramer, A. F., Wilson, R. S., & Lindenberger, U. (2009). Enrichment effects on adult cognitive development: Can the functional capacity of older adults be preserved and enhanced? *Psychological Science in the Public Interest* (Vol. 9, Whole No. 1). Washington, D C: Association for Psychological Science.

Hertzog, C., & Schaie, K. W. (1986). Stability and change in adult intelligence: 1. Analysis of longitudinal covariance structures. *Psychology and Aging, 1*, 159–171.

Hofer, S. M., Flaherty, B. P., & Hoffman, L. (2006). Cross-sectional analysis of time-dependent data: Mean-induced association in age-heterogeneous samples and an alternative method based on sequential narrow age-cohort samples. *Multivariate Behavioral Research, 41*, 165–187.

Horn, J. L. (1985). Remodeling old models of intelligence: Gf – Gc theory. In B. B. Wolman (Ed.), *Handbook of intelligence* (pp. 267–300). New York, NY: Wiley.

Horn, J. L., & Cattell, R. B. (1967). Age differences in fluid and crystallized intelligence. *Acta Psychologica, 26*, 107–129.

Horn, J. L., Donaldson, G., & Engstrom, R. (1981). Apprehension, memory, and fluid intelligence decline in adulthood. *Research on Aging, 3*, 33–84.

Horn, J. L., & Hofer, S. M. (1992). Major abilities and development in the adult period. In R. J. Sternberg & C. A. Berg (Eds.), *Intellectual development* (pp. 44–99). New York, NY: Cambridge University Press.

Hultsch, D. F., Hertzog, C., Dixon, R. A., & Small, B. J. (1998). *Memory change in the aged.* New York, NY: Cambridge University Press.

Hultsch, D. F., Small, B. J., Hertzog, C., & Dixon, R. A. (1999). Use it or lose it: Engaged lifestyle as a buffer of cognitive decline in aging. *Psychology and Aging, 14*, 245–263.

Kane, M. J., & Engle, R. W. (2002). The role of prefrontal cortex in working-memory capacity, executive attention, and general fluid intelligence: An individual differences perspective. *Psychonomic Bulletin & Review, 9*, 637–671.

Kyllonen, P. C., & Chrystal, R. E. (1990). Reasoning ability is (little more than) working-memory capacity? *Intelligence, 14*, 389–433.

Lane, C. J., & Zelinski, E. M. (2003). Longitudinal hierarchical linear models of the Memory Functioning Questionnaire. *Psychology and Aging, 18*, 38–53.

Laukka, E., J., MacDonald, S. M. S., & Bäckman, L. (2008). Terminal-decline effects for select cognitive tasks after controlling for preclinical dementia. *American Journal of Geriatric Psychiatry, 16*, 355–365.

Lindenberger, U., Nagel, I. E., Chicherio, C., Li, S-C., Heekeren, H. R., & Bäckman, L. (2008). Age-related decline in brain resources modulates genetic effects on cognitive functioning. *Frontiers in Neuroscience, 2*, 234–244.

Lindenberger, U., von Oertzen, T., Ghisletta, P., & Hertzog, C. (2009). *Cross-sectional age variance extraction: What's change got to do with it?* Unpublished manuscript.

Lövdén, M., Rönnlund, M., Wahlin, A., Bäckman, L., Nyberg, L., & Goran-Nilsson, L. (2004). The extent of stability and change in episodic and semantic memory in old age: Demographic predictors of stability and change. *Journal of Gerontology: Psychological Sciences, 59B*, P130–P134.

Mackinnon, A., Christensen, H., Hofer, S. M., Korten, A. E., & Jorm, A. F. (2003). Use it and still lose it? The association between activity and cognitive performance established using latent growth techniques in a community sample. *Aging Neuropsychology and Cognition, 10*, 215–222.

Masunaga, H., & Horn, J. L. (2001). Expertise and age-related changes in components of intelligence. *Psychology and Aging, 16*, 293–311.

McArdle, J. J., & Bell, R. Q. (2001). An introduction to latent growth models for developmental data analysis. In T. D. Little & K. U. Schabel (Eds.), *Modeling longitudinal and multi-level data: Practical issues, applied approaches, and specific examples* (pp. 69–81). Mahwah, NJ: Erlbaum.

McArdle, J. J., Ferrer-Caja, E., Hamagami, F., & Woodcock, R. W. (2002). Comparative longitudinal structural analyses of the growth and decline of multiple intellectual abilities over the life span. *Developmental Psychology, 38*, 115–142.

Meredith, W., & Horn, J. L. (2001). The role of factorial invariance in modeling growth and change. In L. M. Collins & A. G. Sayer (Eds.), *New methods for the analysis of change* (pp. 203–240). Washington, DC: American Psychological Association.

Ng, T. W. H., & Feldman, D. C. (2008). The relationship of age to ten dimensions of job performance. *Journal of Applied Psychology, 93*, 392–423.

Nilsson, L.-G., Sternäng, O., Rönnlund, M., & Nyberg, L. (2009). Challenging the notion of an early onset of cognitive decline. *Neurobiology of Aging, 30*, 521–524.

Park, D. C., Smith, A. D., Lautenschlager, G., Earles, J. L., Frieske, D., Zwahr, M., & Gaines, C. L. (1996). Mediators of long-term memory performance across the life span. *Psychology and Aging, 11*, 621–637.

Park, D.C., Hertzog, C., Leventhal, H., Morrell, R.W., Leventhal, E., Birchmore, D., et al. (1999). Medication adherence in rheumatoid arthritis patients: Older is wiser. *Journal of the American Geriatrics Society, 47*, 172–183.

Phillips, L. H., Henry, J. D., & Martin, M. (2008). Adult aging and prospective memory: The importance of ecological validity. In M. Kliegel, M. A. McDaniel, & G. O. Einstein (Eds.), *Prospective memory: Cognitive, neuroscience, developmental, and applied perspectives* (pp. 161–185). New York, NY: Taylor and Francis.

Rabbitt, P. M. A. (1993). Does it all go together when it goes? The nineteenth Bartlett memorial lecture. *Quarterly Journal of Experimental Psychology, 46A*, 385–434.

Rabbitt, P., Diggle, P., Holland, F., & McInnes, L. (2004). Practice and drop-out effects during a 17-year longitudinal study of cognitive aging. *Journal of Gerontology: Psychological Sciences and Social Sciences, 59B*, P84–P97.

Ram, N., Gerstorf, D., Fauth, E., Zarit, S., & Malmberg, B. (2010). Aging, disablement, and dying: Using time-as-process and time-as-resources metrics to chart late-life change. *Research on Human Development, 7*, 27–44.

Raven, J. (2000). The Raven's Progressive Matrices: Change and stability over culture and time. *Cognitive Psychology, 41*, 1–48.

Raz, N. Lindenberger, U., Ghisletta, P., Rodrigue, K. M., Kennedy, K. M., & Acker, J. M. (2008). Neuroanatomical correlates of fluid intelligence in healthy adults and persons with vascular risk factors. *Cerebral Cortex, 18*, 718–726.

Reynolds, C. A. (2008). Genetic and environmental influences on cognitive change. In S. M. Hofer & D. F. Alwin (Eds.), *Handbook of cognitive aging: Interdisciplinary perspectives* (pp. 557–574). Thousand Oaks, CA: Sage.

Rönnlund, M, Nyberg, L., Bäckman, L., & Nilsson, L.-G. (2005). Stability, growth, and decline in adult life span development of declarative memory: Data from a population-based study. *Psychology and Aging, 20*, 3–18.

Rönnlund, M., & Nilsson, L.-G. (2008). The magnitude, generality, and determinants of Flynn effects on forms of declarative memory and visuospatial ability: Time-sequential analyses of data from a Swedish cohort study. *Intelligence, 36*, 192–209.

Salthouse, T. A. (1982). *Adult cognition: An experimental psychology of human aging*. New York, NY: Springer-Verlag.

Salthouse, T. A. (1996). The processing-speed theory of adult age differences in cognition. *Psychological Review, 103*, 403–428.

Salthouse, T. A. (2006). Mental exercise and mental aging: Evaluating the validity of the "use it or lose it" hypothesis. *Perspectives on Psychological Science, 1*, 68–87.

Salthouse, T. A. (2009). When does age-related cognitive decline begin? *Neurobiology of Aging, 30*, 507–514.

Salthouse, T. A., Pink, J. E., & Tucker-Drob, E. M. (2008). Contextual analysis of fluid intelligence. *Intelligence, 36*, 464–486.

Schaie, K. W. (1977). Quasi-experimental designs in the psychology of aging. In J. E. Birren & K. W. Schaie (Eds.), *Handbook of the psychology of aging* (pp. 39–58). New York: Van Nostrand Reinhold.

Schaie, K. W. (1989). Perceptual speed in adulthood: Cross-sectional and longitudinal studies. *Psychology and Aging, 4*, 443–453.

Schaie, K. W. (2005). *Developmental influences on adult intelligence: The Seattle Longitudinal Study*. New York, NY: Oxford University Press.

Schaie, K. W. (2009). "When does age-related cognitive decline begin?": Salthouse again reifies the "cross-sectional fallacy." *Neurobiology of Aging, 30*, 528–529.

Schaie, K. W., Maitland, S. B., Willis, S. L, & Intrieri, R. C. (1998). Longitudinal invariance of adult psychometric ability factor structures across 7 years. *Psychology and Aging, 13*, 8–20.

Schooler, C., Mulatu, M. S., & Oates, G. (1999). The continuing effects of substantively complex work on the intellectual functioning of older workers. *Psychology and Aging, 14*, 483–506.

Shadish, W., Cook, T. D., & Campbell, D. T. (2002). *Experimental and quasi-experimental designs for generalized causal inference*. Boston, MA: Houghton Mifflin.

Singer, T., Verhaeghen, P., Ghisletta, P., Lindenberger, U., & Baltes, P.B. (2003). The fate of cognition in very old age: Six-year longitudinal findings in the Berlin Aging Study (BASE). *Psychology and Aging, 18*, 318–331.

Sliwinski, M. & Buschke, H. (2004). Modeling intraindividual cognitive change in aging adults: Results from the Einstein Aging Studies. *Aging, Neuropsychology and Cognition, 11*, 196–211.

Sliwinski, M. J., Hofer, S. M., Hall, C., Bushke, H., & Lipton, R. B. (2003). Modeling memory decline in older adults: The importance of preclinical dementia, attrition and chronological age. *Psychology and Aging, 18*, 658–671.

Sliwinski, M. J., Hoffman, L., & Hofer, S. M. (2010). Evaluating convergence of within-person change and between-person differences in age-heterogeneous longitudinal studies. *Research on Human Development, 7*, 45–60

Spiro, A. III, & Brady, C. B. (2008). Integrating health into cognitive aging research and theory: Quo vadis? In S. M. Hofer & D. F. Alwin (Eds.), *Handbook of cognitive aging: Interdisciplinary perspectives* (pp. 260–283). Thousand Oaks, CA: Sage.

Sternberg, R. J. (1985). *Beyond IQ: A triarchic theory of human intelligence*. Cambridge, UK: Cambridge University Press.

Stine-Morrow, A. L., Parisi, J. M., Morrow, D. G., Greene, J., & Park, D. C. (2007). The senior odyssey project: A model of intellectual and social engagement. *Journal of Gerontology: Psychological Sciences, 62B*, P62–P69.

Thorvaldsson, V., Hofer, S. M., Berg, S., Skoog, I., Sacuiu, S., & Johansson, B. (2008). Onset of terminal decline in cognitive abilities in individuals without dementia. *Neurology, 71*, 882–887.

Thurstone, L. L. (1938). Primary mental abilities. *Psychological Monographs* (Whole No. 1).

Tranter, L. J., & Koutstaal, W. (2008). Age and flexible thinking: An experimental demonstration of the beneficial effects of increased cognitively stimulating activity on fluid intelligence in healthy older adults. *Aging, Neuropsychology, and Cognition, 15*, 184–207.

Verhaeghen, P., & Salthouse, T. A. (1997). Meta-analyses of age-cognition relations in adulthood: Estimates of linear and non-linear age effects and structural models. *Psychological Bulletin, 122*, 231–249.

Wechsler, D. (1939). *Measurement of adult intelligence*. Baltimore, MD: Williams & Wilkins.

Wilson, R. S., Bennett, D. A., Bienias, J. L., Mendes de Leon, C. F., Morris, M. C., & Evans, D. A. (2003). Cognitive activity and cognitive decline in a biracial community population. *Neurology, 61*, 812–816.

Wilson, R. S., Beck, T. L., Bienias, J. L., & Bennett, D. A. (2007). Terminal cognitive decline: Accelerated loss of cognition in the last years of life. *Psychosomatic Medicine, 69*, 131–137.

Zelinski, E. M., & Kennison, R. F. (2007). Not your father's test scores: Cohort reduces psychometric aging effects. *Psychology and Aging, 22*, 546–557.

Zelinski, E. M., Kennison, R. F., Watts, A., & Lewis, K. L. (2009). Convergence between cross-sectional and longitudinal studies: Cohort matters. In H. B. Bosworth & C. Hertzog (Eds.), *Aging and cognition: Research methodologies and empirical advances* (pp. 101–118). Washington, DC: American Psychological Association.

Part III

INTELLIGENCE AND GROUP DIFFERENCES

CHAPTER 10

Intellectual Disabilities

Robert M. Hodapp, Megan M. Griffin, Meghan M. Burke, and Marisa H. Fisher

Intellectual Disabilities

The field of intellectual disabilities (formerly referred to as "mental retardation") has a long and complicated relationship to the field of intelligence. Yet to many intelligence researchers – and even to researchers in other branches of psychology and social science – those with intellectual disabilities present a fairly straightforward problem. To these researchers, children with intellectual disabilities develop at a slower rate and as adults they show intellectual performances that fall below those of others. End of story.

But to us, the intelligence-intellectual disabilities story has scarcely begun. Simply put, the field of intellectual disabilities is on the cusp of connecting its findings to the field of intelligence. For example, we have barely begun to illustrate the ways that individuals with intellectual disabilities show specific profiles of strengths and weaknesses that inform us about how human intelligence is structured, and the ties of these strengths-weaknesses to brain functioning are increasingly being examined. Such individuals show changes in development and critical (or sensitive) periods that inform us about the effects of experience at different times. When their disabilities are caused by certain genetic conditions, children and adults often display specific cognitive, linguistic, adaptive, and maladaptive profiles. To the field of intelligence, then, individuals with intellectual disabilities increasingly serve as "natural experiments." Such information, in turn, guides clinicians, teachers, and interventionists.

In this chapter, we highlight the most interesting work relating to intelligence in persons with intellectual disabilities. Such work informs theoretical and practical concerns and makes salient how the life success of individuals is only partially dependent on intelligence per se. Such findings also bring to the fore other issues related to the nature, timing, and effects of educational interventions.

In discussing these issues, it is important to provide perspectives relating to the field's past, present, and future. We therefore begin by providing a quick overview of history and basic issues before we present the current state of the intellectual disabilities field. We end this chapter with a quick look into the future, the ways in which the decades ahead will witness expanding, evolving connections between the fields of intellectual disabilities and intelligence.

History and Background

Three issues dominate the history of intellectual disabilities vis-à-vis intelligence. The first pertains to the developmental-difference controversy; the second to undifferentiated versus differentiated approaches to intellectual disabilities; and the third to motivation, different life experiences, and other nonintellectual concerns.

Developmental-Difference Debate

Looked at in purely psychological terms, what causes intellectual disabilities? Is the child with intellectual disabilities developing at a slower rate – as implied by the term "mental retardation" (i.e., retarded development of mental abilities) – or, instead, are specific "defects" present? Historically, developmental theorists have examined children with intellectual disabilities to determine whether these children were developing in the usual or normative sequences of development ("similar sequence hypothesis") and were achieving levels across different domains that were roughly equivalent ("similar structure hypothesis"; Zigler & Hodapp, 1986). More recently, such researchers have examined the influences of etiological differences on various developments and interconnections (Hodapp & Dykens, 2006). Defect theorists, in contrast, have hypothesized that the lower IQs of all children with intellectual disabilities are due to a single, core defect. Historically, different researchers emphasized different core defects, including such characteristics as cognitive rigidity, or particular impairments in memory processes, discrimination learning, and attention-retention capabilities (for a review, see Burack, 1990).

By now, the developmental-difference approach has somewhat devolved into a debate about how to perform studies. On one side are the defect or difference theorists, who argue that children with intellectual disabilities should be compared to children of the same chronological age (Ellis & Cavalier, 1982). Adherents of this approach compare children with intellectual disabilities to typically developing children of the same chronological age (i.e., CA-matches).

On the other side are those researchers who argue that only comparisons using overall mental age (MA) should be used to identify areas of performance deficits. The idea is that only by comparing the child with intellectual disabilities to an MA-matched child without disabilities can one identify an area of deficit over and above the overall delays in development of the child with intellectual disability. As Cicchetti and Pogge-Hesse (1982) noted, we already know that children with intellectual disabilities function below children of the same chronological age in most areas of cognition, but "*the important and challenging research questions concern the developmental processes*" (p. 279, italics in original). Such processes can only be determined by comparing children with intellectual disabilities to typically developing controls of the same level of mental functioning (i.e., so-called mental-age, or MA-matched, controls).

Although issues concerning appropriate control-contrast groups have become more complicated over the years (Hodapp & Dykens, 2001), the intellectual disabilities field seems mostly agreed to use MA-matched designs to examine intellectual performance in children with intellectual disabilities. Extensions of MA-matching designs are also widely used, by comparing groups with and without intellectual disabilities who are matched on age-equivalent functioning in such areas as language (e.g., Mean Length of Utterance) or adaptive behavior (Vineland Adaptive Behavior Scales; Sparrow, Balla, & Cicchetti, 2005). Capitalizing on the norming process of intelligence, adaptive, language, and other psychometric instruments, one might even have no control group whatsoever, examining strengths and weaknesses by comparing an individual's scores across different domains or subdomains (i.e., "using subjects as their own controls").

Although such level-of-functioning designs are currently used in most intellectual disability research, there is one area in which comparisons based on chronological age (CA) are common. This situation occurs when researchers examine whether a specific domain of functioning might be "spared" (i.e., at age-appropriate levels) among children who have a specific intellectual-disability condition. For instance, to test whether children with Williams syndrome might be spared in their language abilities, comparisons have been made to typically developing children of the same chronological age (e.g., Bishop, 1999; Mervis, Morris, Bertrand, & Robinson, 1999). Usually, however, MA-comparisons are the rule in most research examining intellectual profiles in individuals with intellectual disabilities.

From One Undifferentiated Group, to Two Groups, to Multiple Groups

A second historical issue concerns whether individuals with different causes of their intellectual disabilities behave differently. From the early 20th century, a few researchers have differentiated individuals based on each individual's cause of intellectual disabilities (see Burack, 1990), but most researchers have not. To these researchers, the reason the child has intellectual disabilities is irrelevant. As a main proponent of this undifferentiated view proclaimed, "rarely have behavioral differences characterized different etiological groups" (Ellis, 1969).

In contrast, Zigler (1967, 1969) has long championed the so-called two-group approach to intellectual disabilities. Two groups of individuals are hypothesized, those with "cultural-familial" intellectual disabilities and those with "organic" causes. The first group consists of persons who show no identifiable cause for their intellectual disabilities. Such individuals are generally more mildly impaired and tend to blend in with other persons who do not have disabilities. Hypothesized causes range from polygenetic inheritance to environmental deprivation, and different persons may have different polygenic or environmental causes or there may be an interplay between the two (Hodapp, 1994).

In contrast, individuals in the second, "organic" group show a clear organic cause for their intellectual disabilities. Such causes include hundreds of organic insults that can occur pre-, peri-, or postnatally. Prenatal causes include all of the 1,000+ genetic disorders, fetal alcohol syndrome (FAS), fetal alcohol exposure (FAE), rubella, as well as all accidents in utero. Perinatal causes include prematurity, anoxia at birth, and other birth-related complications. Postnatal causes range from sicknesses (meningitis) to head trauma. Those with organic causes are more likely to show greater degrees of intellectual impairments; as IQ levels decrease, higher percentages of persons show an identifiable organic cause (Stromme & Hagberg, 2000).

Beginning in the early 1990s, this two-group approach itself began to be updated, moving from a focus on a heterogeneous organic group to one focusing on individual (usually genetic) causes (Burack, Hodapp, & Zigler, 1988; Hodapp & Dykens, 1994). This more differentiated etiological approach also reflects recent biomedical advances. In contrast to earlier years – when little was known about causes – over 1,000 genetic anomalies have now been linked to intellectual disabilities (King, Hodapp, & Dykens, 2009). For most such disorders, we can now go back and forth between the beginning point – the genetic anomaly itself – and the end points – the behavioral, physical, or medical characteristics that are predisposed by having that anomaly. Recent studies of intelligence focus heavily on children and adults who have different genetic causes for their intellectual disabilities.

Role of Nonintellectual Factors

For many decades, professionals in intellectual disabilities have appreciated that the functioning of individuals with intellectual disabilities is not dependent on intelligence alone. Such thinking led to Edgar Doll's (1953) work on the construct of adaptive behavior, the idea that everyday adaptive behavior is to some extent separable from one's intelligence. Such thinking has also led to changes in how intellectual disabilities are diagnosed, as well as the growth of a subfield designed to study nonintellectual issues among individuals with intellectual disabilities.

Nonintellectual factors operate in several ways. First, for persons with intellectual disabilities, intelligence comprises only one among several variables related to ultimate life outcomes. As we detail later in the chapter, the relations between one's levels of intelligence and adaptive behavior are fairly complicated. Beyond researchers who examine formal adaptive behavior, a small but active subdiscipline studies motivation and other nonintellectual factors that affect behavioral performance (Zigler, 1971; Switzky, 2006a, b). While it may seem obvious that life outcomes are not totally explained by one's level of intelligence, for persons with intellectual disabilities, it seems especially important to highlight such nonintellectual factors.

Second, one must also pay attention to these individuals' external environments and experiences. Specifically, persons with intellectual disabilities experience higher than normal levels of poverty (Emerson, 2007; Parish, Rose, Grinstein-Weiss, Richman, & Andrews, 2008) as well as higher rates of single-parent and minority households (Fujiura & Yamaki, 2000). Other negative events also seem more common, including higher rates of maladaptive behavior-psychopathology (Dykens, 2000), health problems (Walsh, 2008), and child abuse (Fisher, Hodapp, & Dykens, 2008). Beyond lower levels of intelligence, individuals with intellectual disabilities are also more likely to experience other problems that strongly impact their life outcomes.

Current State of the Art: Basic Issues

Defining Intellectual Disability

Despite advances in our understandings of the causes and correlates of intellectual disabilities, the field continues to debate the appropriate way to define an intellectual disability. But at least in principle, the definition of intellectual disabilities has remained relatively stable over time. Thus, in the early 1980s, Grossman (1983) noted that intellectual disability (then called "mental retardation") pertained to individuals who have "significantly subaverage intellectual functioning resulting in or associated with impairments in adaptive behavior and manifested during the developmental period" (p. 11).

For over two decades, the field has been guided by this "three factor" definition of intellectual disabilities. First, in order for a diagnosis of intellectual disabilities to be warranted, the individual must have "subaverage intellectual functioning." To most researchers and practitioners, subaverage intellectual functioning is operationalized as the individual scoring at IQ 70 or below on an appropriately standardized, individually administered IQ test.

Second, individuals must show impairments in everyday adaptive behavior. This second criterion relates to the idea that intellectual disabilities should not involve intellectual deficits alone but also concurrent deficits in everyday functioning. To be diagnosed with intellectual disabilities, then, children or adults must also display impaired adaptive behavior (as measured, for example, by the Vineland Adaptive Behavior Scales; Sparrow, Balla, & Cicchetti, 2005).

Third, to be diagnosed with intellectual disabilities, individuals must also show deficits in intellectual and adaptive behaviors prior to the age of 18 years. "Intellectual disabilities" is not considered to be the appropriate diagnosis for individuals showing deficits related to accidents, illnesses, or aging that occur during the adult years.

While most would agree with these three criteria, controversy abounds regarding how each is operationalized. With respect to lower intelligence, several major court decisions, especially the Larry P. case in California (*Larry P. v. Riles*, 1979), have questioned the legitimacy of IQ testing for minority students. The judge in the Larry P. case (Judge Peckham) cited inherent cultural biases in psychological tests, and concerns have also been expressed about variations in any child's exact IQ score from one testing to another and errors of measurement that make one's score only an approximation of one's "true" IQ (Grossman, 1983). Similarly, in adaptive behavior, professionals debate which specific skills should be considered as adaptive behavior, with the field's major organization changing in its numbers and names of adaptive domains in subsequent definitional manuals (American Association on Mental Retardation, 1992, 2002). Concerns also exist regarding appropriate measures of adaptive behavior, the relation between adaptive skills and cognition, and the potentially limited opportunities that certain individuals have to develop adaptive skills.

Mental Retardation Versus Intellectual Disability

Beyond exact definitional criteria, professionals and advocates have also debated the best term to refer to these individuals. In Great Britain, for example, professionals use the term "learning disability" to describe individuals with intellectual disabilities. In contrast, other countries, along with the International Association for the Scientific Study of Intellectual Disabilities (IASSID), use the term "intellectual disability." Within the United States, we have evolved from using a variety of now-derogatory terms ("feeble-minded," "mentally deficient," "idiocy"), to the term "mental retardation," to the current terms "intellectual disabilities" and "intellectual and developmental disabilities."

One way to track this change in terminology is by examining changes in the title of what is today the American Association on Intellectual and Developmental Disabilities. Founded as the Association of Medical Officers of American Institutions for Idiotic and Feeble Minded Persons in 1876, the name changed to American Association for the Study of the Feeble Minded in 1906, to the American Association on Mental Deficiency in 1933, and to American Association on Mental Retardation (AAMR) in 1987, before the organization assumed its current title as the American Association on Intellectual and Developmental Disabilities (AAIDD) in 2007 (Schalock, 2002). The changing terms for intellectual disability are reflected by changes in the name of the field's oldest and most prestigious professional organization. Following this new terminology, Rosa's Law was recently enacted, officially replacing the term "mental retardation" with "intellectual disability" in most federal statutes.

Theoretical Issues

However one diagnoses or refers to persons with intellectual disabilities, the intellectual functioning of this group increasingly ties to several important issues within the field of intelligence. These ties run in two directions. First, many issues relate to the intellectual profiles of persons with a specific cause – or etiology – of intellectual disabilities. Second, everyday adaptive functioning of persons with intellectual disabilities highlights the difficulties inherent in connecting intelligence with real-life functioning and problems.

Etiology-Related Profiles

With the increasing realization that children and adults with specific genetic conditions differ in their behaviors, much attention has been paid to profiles of intellectual strengths and weaknesses in different etiological groups. We now focus on two such etiological groups, Down syndrome and Williams syndrome.

Down syndrome. Occurring in 1 per 800 to 1,000 live births, Down syndrome is the most common genetic-chromosomal disorder involving intellectual disability. Most children with Down syndrome deficit score in the moderate range of intelligence (IQ 40 to 54), although IQ scores vary widely from one child to another. These children usually display their highest IQ scores in the earlier years, with gradually decreasing IQs as time goes on (Hodapp, Evans, & Gray, 1999). Even during the earliest years, infants and young children with Down syndrome slow in their development as they get older (Dunst, 1990).

Young children with Down syndrome also show an etiology-related profile of strengths and weaknesses. Across the preschool period, most children with Down syndrome show a profile in which abilities in receptive language are advanced over the child's expressive abilities (and over the child's overall MA). Such discrepancies become more pronounced – for increasing numbers of children – as children develop over the preschool period (Miller, 1999). This pattern of receptive-over-expressive language abilities may also relate to the high rates of articulation problems among children with Down syndrome (Kumin, 1994), as well as these children's marked problems in linguistic grammar (Abbeduto, Warren, & Connors, 2007; Chapman & Hesketh, 2000).

Conversely, as a group, children with Down syndrome are considered by others to have strengths in social skills. Compared to children without disabilities of the same MAs, toddlers with Down syndrome look to others (as opposed to objects) much more often (Kasari, Mundy, Yirmiya, & Sigman, 1990) and, while performing problem-solving tasks at later ages, these children tend to look to adults and engage in social behaviors (Kasari & Freeman, 2001; Pitcairn & Wishart, 1994). At the same time, however, children with Down syndrome do not perform well on higher level social tasks. For example, most children perform poorly on tasks of emotion-recognition (Kasari, Freeman, & Hughes, 2001) and their levels on theory-of-mind tasks are no better than their overall mental abilities (Abbeduto et al., 2006). In short, while even infants and young children with Down syndrome are oriented toward others, their "sociability" may be confined to the lower levels of social skills.

Recent work examines the development of these intellectual and personality profiles by combining cognitive-linguistic weaknesses with infant-toddler sociability. By examining the early development of infant cognitive skills and infant behaviors during mother-child interactions, Fidler, Philofsky, Hepburn, and Rogers (2005) found that infants with Down syndrome show particular difficulties in means-ends thinking, or tasks that involve using objects (e.g., stick, stool) as a means for obtaining desired objects. Such deficits seem to relate to these children's increased amounts of looking to others for solutions to difficult problems. Eventually, "the coupling of poor strategic thinking [i.e., means-ends thinking] and strengths in social relatedness is hypothesized to lead to the less persistent and overly social personality-motivational orientation observed in this population" (Fidler, 2006, p. 147).

Williams syndrome. Occurring in approximately 1 per 10,000 live births, Williams syndrome is caused by a microdeletion on chromosome 7 that contains approximately 25 genes. Children and adults with this disorder have a particular facial appearance, with a small "pug" nose. Cardiac abnormalities (especially supravalvular aortic stenosis) are present in about 80% of children with Williams syndrome. Behaviorally, most children with Williams syndrome score in the mild range of intellectual disabilities (IQ = 55 to 69; Howlin et al., 1998), and these scores remain stable throughout adulthood (Searcy et al., 2004). In addition to having friendly – even overly friendly – personalities, most children with Williams syndrome are anxious and have many fears (Dykens, 2003; Einfeld, Tonge, & Florio, 1997).

Most striking, however, are the relatively strong language abilities and weak visuospatial abilities of many children with Williams syndrome. Indeed, early researchers argued that children with Williams syndrome might have near-normal or "spared" levels of language. Although such spared language occurs in only a few persons with Williams syndrome (Bishop, 1999), these children's levels in language and communication do appear higher than their overall mental abilities. Conversely, visuospatial processing skills appear particularly weak. Children with Williams syndrome have extreme difficulty in drawing pictures, in distinguishing left from right, and in performing other visuospatial tasks (Bellugi, Wang, & Jernigan, 1994; Dykens, Rosner, & Ly, 2000).

As in Down syndrome, development over the early years allows for glimmerings of the later emerging phenotype. In addition to work documenting infants' delays in pointing, showing, and other communicative gestures (see Mervis & Becerra, 2007), studies also document keen interests in faces and aberrant facial gaze in toddlers with Williams syndrome (Laing et al., 2002). The connections of communication-language and cognitive measures are also being examined, and the early development of infants-toddlers with Williams syndrome is rapidly being understood.

From this thumbnail sketch of intellectual profiles of only two conditions, several themes emerge. A first, obvious theme relates to the structure of intelligence. Although the "true" structure of intelligence is a perennial – maybe irreconcilable – issue within the intelligence field, individuals with specific genetic disorders do show specific strengths and weaknesses that may inform this controversy. Indeed, the early findings depicting children with Williams syndrome as having "language without thought" were considered as evidence of the "modularity of intelligence" (Fodor, 1983), and it may indeed be the case that different genetic syndromes can help point out connections and dis-connections across different domains of intelligence.

A second, related issue concerns the development of such profiles. As is becoming increasingly apparent, etiology-related characteristics – also called "behavioral phenotypes" – do not arise fully formed at birth. Instead, most young children with one or another genetic disorder show a particular propensity, which then becomes more pronounced over time. Most young children with Down syndrome do look to others and have difficulty in means-ends thinking; repeatedly combining these two characteristics over time may make them more likely to rely on others (as opposed to themselves) for later problem solving. Similarly, even during infancy, children with Williams syndrome may experience particular difficulties on visuospatial compared to linguistic tasks, possibly leading to these children's later profile of language over visuospatial skills.

Finally, current work examines both the trajectories of such profiles and their brain correlates. Jarrold, Baddeley, Hewes, and Phillips (2001) examined adolescents with Williams syndrome multiple times over a four-year period to identify developmental trajectories in vocabulary (a relative strength in this syndrome) and in visuospatial skills (a relative weakness). For these adolescents, vocabulary skills developed much more quickly over time than did visuospatial skills. Such divergent trajectories allowed an already existing strength in vocabulary to become gradually "stronger" (vs. visuospatial skills) over the course of the four-year period. Conversely, as visuospatial skills developed much more slowly, a relative weakness became even weaker over time. The brain correlates of such relative strengths and weaknesses are gradually being examined via functional magnetic resonance imaging (MRI), event-related potential (ERP), and other technologies (Schaer & Eliez, 2007).

Granted, such work is in its infancy. To date, few definitive connections have been made between the functioning of children and adults with a specific genetic condition and the field of intelligence. But we know already that individuals with several genetic syndromes show etiology-related profiles, trajectories of development over time, and brain correlates. In the years ahead, such findings should tell us much about intelligence, its structure, and its development.

IQ Versus Adaptive Functioning

When most people think of a person with intellectual disabilities, they generally consider a person who is low functioning and totally dependent upon others for support. This sense of intellectual disabilities is false. In fact, most individuals with intellectual disabilities have a mild intellectual disability and are able to function rather independently within society. These individuals blend well within society and are often married, employed, and living independently (Zigler & Hodapp, 1986).

But since not all individuals with mild intellectual disabilities function well in society, the question arises: What differentiates persons who are and are not able to function independently, especially if both groups have identical IQs? The answer relates to adaptive functioning, or the second part of the definition of intellectual disabilities.

In the 1970s, researchers in Sweden were able to examine the difference between individuals with mild intellectual disabilities who were functioning independently and those who required more extensive supports (Granat & Granat, 1973, 1975, 1978). In Sweden, unless diagnosed with intellectual disabilities or other medical problem, all males are required to enlist for military service at the age of 19. Upon enrollment, all individuals who have enlisted are administered an intelligence test and an interview with a psychologist (Granat & Granat, 1973). Upon examining the IQ scores of the men who enlisted, it was discovered that a proportion of the enrolled men attained an IQ score below 84, indicating they had a mild or a borderline intellectual disability. In short, some proportion of 19-year-old men had lower IQs but had never been diagnosed as having intellectual disabilities during their school years.

Granat and Granat (1973) then compared the men who were not diagnosed during the school years to those with identical IQs who had previously received a diagnosis of intellectual disabilities. Differences were related to the degree of social competence, such that the previously unidentified group showed no impairment in social adaptation. In a follow-up study, Granat and Granat (1978) investigated the adjustment of those men who scored below 84 on the IQ test upon enrollment. These men fit into one of four groups: a well-adjusted group; a personal problem group; a crime group; and a work-problem group. Of the total sample, 50% were well adjusted and 50% were poorly adjusted. Those whose poor adjustment showed up in the workplace had also had problems in school, and those who had problems with crime and problems in the workplace were more likely in the future to be labeled with an intellectual disability.

More than 30 years later, Greenspan (2006) and others are still examining the connections between IQ and the adaptive functioning in individuals with mild intellectual disabilities. Similar to Zigler's (1967, 1969) two-group approach, those with intellectual disabilities can be divided into two distinct groups. The first, smaller group comprises individuals with severe intellectual disabilities. Such individuals are more easily recognized as having intellectual disabilities, more often show a clear organic cause, and are usually diagnosed at younger ages. In this first group, IQ scores more closely relate to adaptive "quotient" scores ("overall adaptive quotient" on the Vineland; Sparrow, Balla, & Cicchetti, 2005).

In the second group (akin to Zigler's familial or cultural-familial group), individuals show more mild impairments, often do not have a clear genetic or biological basis for their intellectual impairments, and are often diagnosed only at later ages. For this second group, IQ and adaptive behavior are less often in synch. Thus, while an adult with mild intellectual disabilities may be capable of functioning within society (working a full-time job, living independently, and even marrying and having children), that same individual may still require supports in certain areas (remembering to take care of hygiene, budgeting money). Unfortunately, supports are not always available for individuals who appear to be functioning independently within society.

Relation of Adaptive Behavior to Adverse Life Outcomes

Also related to adaptive behavior are certain specific situations that may prove especially difficult for individuals with mild intellectual disabilities. For example, while a person with mild intellectual disabilities may be able to live independently and cook his own food, this same individual could have great difficulty discerning social cues and relating to others. This social difficulty, in turn, could lead to instances of social exploitation. Some have postulated that because people with mild intellectual disabilities do not appear to have a disability, they are more at risk of certain forms of exploitation (Greenspan, 2006). At the same time, these individuals are less able to discern that they are being taken advantage of, thus perpetuating an abusive cycle.

In fact, throughout their lives, individuals with mild intellectual disabilities are at increased risk of abuse and exploitation (Nettelbeck & Wilson, 2002; Petersilia, 2001; Sullivan & Knutson, 2000). During childhood, children with (versus without) disabilities are 4 to 10 times more likely to experience physical and sexual abuse and neglect (Ammerman & Baladerian, 1993). And, compared to children who show severe disabilities, children with more mild disabilities are at greater risk of child abuse. Verdugo, Bermejo, and Fuertes (1995) concluded that children with "less obvious" disabilities were more likely to experience abuse, similar to adults with disabilities who experience exploitation.

A similar phenomenon occurs during adulthood. Older individuals with intellectual disabilities are twice as likely to experience crimes against the person (physical assault, sexual assault, robbery, and personal theft) and 1.5 times more likely to experience such property crimes as breaking and entering and household property theft (Wilson & Brewer, 1992). Adults with intellectual disabilities are also likely to experience minor abuses such as being teased or cheated out of money (Halpern, Close, & Nelson, 1986). Again, individuals who display vulnerable behaviors, such as acting gullible or not taking precautions, may encourage perpetrators (Greenspan, Loughlin, & Black, 2001). Individuals with poor perspective-taking and poor personal/social achievement also seem to be at increased risk of victimization (Doren, Bullis, & Benz, 1996), as these traits could make it difficult for them to recognize nonverbal and contextual cues that identify a situation as deceptive or manipulative (Wilson, Seaman, & Nettlebeck, 1996).

Ultimately, while a low IQ score is often used as a main reason that individuals are diagnosed with intellectual disabilities, it is apparent that intellectual disability is related to far more than just one's IQ. Individuals with mild intellectual disabilities are able to function within society and often go unrecognized. Unfortunately, even those who are not diagnosed often have trouble with the more subtle issues of social adaptation. They often need support handling money as well as training in social skills and relating to others. As they are less able to recognize signs of abuse, and perpetrators often view them as easy targets, individuals with mild intellectual disabilities are at much higher risk of experiencing abuse and exploitation. For these reasons, while they may be relatively independent, individuals with disabilities still need supports within society.

In a theoretical sense, then, the functioning of persons with intellectual disabilities connects to the field of intelligence in two ways. First, particularly for children and adults with different genetic conditions, there seem to be specific, etiology-related profiles of intellectual strengths and weaknesses. Such profiles shed light on how intelligence is structured, how profiles develop, how profiles become more pronounced over time, and how such profiles correlate to specific genetic anomalies and to brain functioning (so-called gene-brain-behavior relations). Second, individuals with mild intellectual disabilities show us the complicated ways that formal intelligence (i.e., IQ) and everyday adaptive behavior relate; these individuals also illustrate the degree to which slightly higher IQ scores may be inadequate to defend against exploitation, abuse, and being taken advantage of more generally.

Implications for Intervention

Apart from such theoretical issues, recent research also provides clues concerning more practical, applied interventions. As before, some of these intervention ideas relate to developing better ways to intervene with children and adults with intellectual disabilities (or with specific etiologies); others hint at the characteristics and limits of intervention itself.

Inclusive Schooling for Children with Intellectual Disabilities

Students with intellectual disabilities are increasingly being included in general education classrooms. This positive trend is largely a response to the Individuals with Disabilities Education Act (IDEA), which requires that students with disabilities be educated in the least restrictive environment (Katsiyannis, Zhang, & Archwamety, 2002). Indeed, the 1997 and 2004 Amendments to IDEA mandate that individualized supports and services be provided to ensure that students with disabilities can access the general curriculum (Wehmeyer, 2006).

Beyond this legal mandate, the inclusion of students with intellectual disabilities in general education classrooms is supported by educational research. A review of academic and social outcomes for students with intellectual disabilities reveals that inclusion produces more positive results than segregated instruction (Freeman & Alkin, 2000). When students with intellectual disabilities in inclusive settings were compared to those in special education settings, the students who participated in inclusive education achieved higher levels of academic and social competence.

What Should Children with Intellectual Disabilities Be Taught?

Although studies have predominantly focused on teaching functional (as opposed to academic) skills to students with intellectual disabilities, several studies reveal that most of these students are capable of learning specific academic content and skills in reading, mathematics, and science (Browder, Spooner, Wakeman, Trela, & Baker, 2006). Of all academic areas, reading instruction has been researched the most thoroughly. Particularly, interventions that use systematic prompting and support – then fading (gradually lessening) that support – have been found to be effective in teaching sight words to students with intellectual disabilities. These instructional developments have been critical to advancing the literacy of students with intellectual disabilities. To give one example, students with Down syndrome historically were not considered capable of learning to read. However, given the opportunity and appropriate instruction, these students can acquire literacy skills (Buckley & Bird, 2002). Advances in instructional strategies, coupled with the recent trend toward inclusive education, have helped advance the ability of students with Down syndrome to read, and have furthered their integration into the community (Bochner, Outhred, & Pieterse, 2001).

In What Ways Can Teaching Be Optimized for All Children?

Although reading is critical for accessing the curriculum used in general education for all students, students lacking literacy skills may still be capable of accessing the general curriculum with appropriate accommodations and supports. One of these supports involves using the principles of so-called universal design (Browder et al., 2006). These principles, adapted from universal design concepts originating in architecture, are applied to instructional materials and activities. Just as universal design in architecture allows accessibility to a building (e.g., curb-cuts that are accessible to wheelchairs, strollers, and pedestrians), universal design fosters access to the general education curriculum for students of all ability levels.

Universal design is a way of designing instruction so that students with diverse strengths and limitations can access the material in their required or preferred modality (Wehmeyer, 2006). Three qualities characterize universally designed instruction. First, universally designed instruction presents academic content in flexible and varied formats (Wehmeyer, 2006). Traditionally, academic content is provided to students in the form of written text; however, students with limited reading skills are less able to access this material. Fortunately, recent advances in technology afford many different ways to offer material in more accessible formats. For example, some software programs offer assistance in guiding the reader with highlighted words and offering definitions of unfamiliar words. For students who cannot read, other assistive technology can read electronic text aloud; these students might also benefit from alternate representations of text-based materials (e.g., pictorial or video formats).

Second, universally designed instruction offers students various ways to express themselves (Wehmeyer, 2006). Traditionally accepted forms of student expression typically involve writing. For students who struggle with writing, this format does not afford them the opportunity to express their understanding of the material. Students should have access to various options through which they may communicate in assigned work and assessments. Different forms of technology (e.g., photographs and video) allow variety in student expression. However, technology is not necessary to offer students an alternative form of expression; for example, a student who struggles with writing could answer questions verbally rather than in a traditional essay.

Third, universally designed curriculum presents diverse opportunities for student engagement (Wehmeyer, 2006). Just as students benefit from flexibility and variety in presentation and expression, universal design also involves various options for engaging with academic material. Again, technological advances have made many options available for students through audio, video, and other media. By offering students a variety of options for classroom engagement, universally designed instruction may also increase student motivation and participation.

While critical to helping students with intellectual disabilities access the K–12 general education curriculum, universally designed curriculum also promises to help these students access more advanced content in postsecondary settings. Recent decades have seen a trend toward offering students inclusive postsecondary education opportunities on college campuses (Neubert, Moon, Grigal, & Redd, 2001). The idea is that adolescents and young adults with intellectual disabilities should be afforded experiences that are as "college-like" as possible. Similar to inclusive education at the primary and secondary levels, postsecondary education offers students with intellectual disabilities the opportunity to learn academic material, expand social networks, and develop independence alongside typical peers.

Looking to the Future

Although one could cite additional ties, we feel that the following three questions will lead to the most interesting studies in the years ahead.

1. *What do etiology-related profiles tell us about the domains of intelligence, their development, and their effects on psychological functioning?*

Although individuals with certain genetic syndromes show etiology-related profiles of intellectual abilities, the implications of such profiles remain mostly unexplored. A first, major question relates to the nature of intelligence. Although various researchers disagree as to the domains of intelligence, children and adults do show etiology-related profiles that may indicate how best to cut the intellectual pie. Visuospatial abilities seem especially delayed in Williams syndrome, and grammar and articulation are especially delayed (even compared to other areas of language) in Down syndrome. What do such findings tell us about separable domains of intelligence or language?

Ongoing studies are also charting the emergence and expansion of such etiology-related profiles. At what ages do relative strengths enter in and why do some children with a specific condition show more or less of a specific relative strength? Ultimately, even profiles that are especially common in a specific condition – for example, the special problems in grammar in Down syndrome – are not seen by every individual. Note, for example, the case of Francoise, a young woman with Down syndrome who nevertheless has unimpaired grammar (Rondal, 1995).

Similarly, what does the presence of etiology-based profiles mean to the everyday existence of children with one or another condition? To give one example, Rosner, Hodapp, Fidler, Sagun, and Dykens (2004) examined the everyday leisure activities of three groups of children: those with Williams syndrome, Prader-Willi syndrome (who are especially high in visuospatial skills), and Down syndrome. Using parent-reports of leisure-time behavior from Achenbach's (1991) Child Behavior Checklist, behaviors were grouped into those involving music, reading, visual-motor activities, athletics, pretend play, and focused interests. Findings mostly reflected etiology-related strengths and weaknesses. In line with their visuospatial weaknesses, for example, only 31% of individuals with Williams syndrome participated in any visual-motor activities, compared to 76% and 60% of persons with Prader-Willi and Down syndromes, respectively. Specific behaviors like arts-and-crafts activities were listed in 35% of the group with Down syndrome and in 30% of individuals with Prader-Willi syndrome, but in only 7% of those with Williams syndrome. Persons with Williams syndrome (or their parents) seem to avoid activities that they find difficult to perform.

Although we do not yet know for certain, genetic etiologies may predispose children to particular cognitive-linguistic profiles, but these profiles may then become more pronounced due to the child's ongoing experiences. For most syndromes, the degree of difference between levels of "strong" versus "weak" areas is probably relatively small during the early years. But as children more often perform activities in strong areas and avoid activities in weaker areas, increasing discrepancies may arise. A snowball effect may thus result from the interplay of the child's etiology-related propensities and the child's ongoing transactions with the environment.

2. *What are the relations among IQ and adaptive behavior and everyday competence?*

A second question relates to the connections of IQ and adaptive behavior. Although impaired functioning in both areas has long characterized definitions of intellectual disabilities, the exact connections among the two areas are difficult to pinpoint. Why are IQ and adaptive levels closely related for children and adults at lower functioning levels, but much less closely tied at higher levels of functioning? This issue pertains as well to issues of gullibility, suggestibility, and being taken advantage of. Or, to put a more basic cast on this question, are many skills of everyday living more related to intelligence – possibly with the term encompassing more than IQ alone (Greenspan et al., 2001; Sternberg, 1988) – or to other skills, abilities, or personality variables? At this point, we really do not know.

3. *What are the possibilities and limitations of intervention?*

The final question relates to intervention and to environments more generally. On one level, this question relates to etiology-related profiles and the degree to which special education and other interventions might be tailored to fit with etiology-based strengths and weaknesses (Fidler, Philofsky, & Hepburn, 2007; Hodapp & Fidler, 1999).

But the question of interventions may go beyond etiology per se, to instead address the limits of different intervention practices. Consider universally designed learning, the idea that interventions will be optimally beneficial when they use flexible, varied contexts, allow students to express themselves, and provide maximal, diverse opportunities for student engagement. Although such ideas seem helpful, specific effects of such practices are yet to be explored. Will such practices benefit all students at all or even most levels of ability? Might instead there be certain ages of the learner, or propensities in the learner, that make universal design more or less effective? Are all academic contents equally easy to adapt to a universal design framework, or might certain topics or subjects be more amenable to drawn, written, computer, tactile, musical, or other modalities? Again, such fine-grained connections, this time between specific interventions and specific characteristics of persons with intellectual disabilities, have only begun to be examined.

Conclusion

To many researchers, persons with intellectual disabilities simply display lower levels of intelligence and offer few ties to their specific fields. But as we hope we have demonstrated, these children and adults do show specific intellectual strengths-weaknesses, ties to adaptive and everyday functioning, and ties to educational and other interventions. Granted, the fields of intelligence and intellectual disabilities continue to function somewhat independently, and only a handful of researchers interested in intelligence are also interested in intelligence as it pertains to persons with disabilities. But given the many continuing controversies – and the findings of specific profiles and brain correlates arising from persons with different types of intellectual disabilities – it is our hope that this state of affairs might be changing. To us – and, we hope, to the intelligence field as well – the connections between those with intellectual disabilities and those interested in intelligence constitute an incomplete story, one that we expect will increasingly be fleshed out over the years ahead.

References

Abbeduto, L., Murphy, M. M., Richmond, E. K., Amman, A., Beth, P., Weissman, M. D., Kim, J. S., Cawthon, S. W., & Daradottir, S. (2006). Collaboration in referential communication: Comparison of youth with Down syndrome or fragile X syndrome. *American Journal on Mental Retardation, 111*, 170–183.

Abbeduto, L., Warren, S. F., & Connors, F. A. (2007). Language development in Down syndrome: From the prelinguistic period to the acquisition of literacy. *Mental Retardation and Developmental Disabilities Research Reviews, 13*, 247–261.

Achenbach, T. M. (1991). *Manual for the Child Behavior Checklist/4–18 and 1991 Profile.* Burlington: University of Vermont, Department of Psychiatry.

American Association on Mental Retardation. (1992). *Mental retardation: Definition, classification, and systems of supports.* Washington, DC: Author.

American Association on Mental Retardation. (2002). *Mental retardation: Definition, classification, and systems of supports* (10th ed.) Washington, DC: Author.

Ammerman, R. T. & Baladerian, N. J. (1993). *Maltreatment of children with disabilities.* Chicago, IL: Nashville Committee to Prevent Child Abuse.

Bellugi, U., Wang, P., & Jernigan, T. (1994). Williams syndrome: An unusual neuropsychological profile. In S. H. Broman & J. Grafman (Eds.), *Atypical cognitive deficits in developmental disorders* (pp. 23–56). Hillsdale, NJ: Erlbaum.

Bishop, D. V. M. (1999). An innate basis for language? *Science*, *286*, 2283–2284.

Bochner, S., Outhred, L., & Pieterse, M. (2001). A study of functional literacy skills in young adults with Down syndrome. *International Journal of Disability, Development and Education*, *48*, 67–90.

Browder, D. M., Spooner, F., Wakeman, S., Trela, K., & Baker, J. N. (2006). Aligning instruction with academic content standards: Finding the link. *Research and Practice for Persons with Severe Disabilities*, *31*, 309–321.

Buckley, S., & Bird, G. (2002). Cognitive development and education: Perspectives on Down syndrome from a twenty-year research programme. In M. Cuskally, A. Jobling, & S. Buckley (Eds.), *Down syndrome across the life span* (pp. 66–80). London, UK: Whurr.

Burack, J. A. (1990). Differentiating mental retardation: The two-group approach and beyond. In R. M. Hodapp, J. A. Burack, & E. Zigler (Eds.), *Issues in the developmental approach to mental retardation* (pp. 27–48). New York, NY: Cambridge University Press.

Burack, J. A., Hodapp, R. M., & Zigler, E. (1988). Issues in the classification of mental retardation: Differentiating among organic etiologies. *Journal of Child Psychology and Psychiatry*, *29*, 765–779.

Chapman, R. S., & Hesketh, L. J. (2000). Behavioral phenotype of individuals with Down syndrome. *Mental Retardation and Developmental Disabilities Research Reviews*, *6*, 84–95.

Cicchetti, D., & Pogge-Hesse, P. (1982). Possible contributions of the study of organically retarded persons to developmental theory. In E. Zigler & D. Balla (Eds.), *Mental retardation: The developmental-difference controversy* (pp. 277–318). Hillsdale, NJ: Erlbaum.

Developmental Disabilities Act and Amendments of 1984, P.L. 98–527.

Doll, E. A. (1953). *Measurement of social competence: A manual for the Vineland Social Maturity Scale*. Circle Pines, MN: American Guidance Services.

Doren, B., Bullis, M., & Benz, M. R. (1996). Predictors of victimization experiences of adolescents with disabilities in transition. *Exceptional Children*, *63*, 7–18.

Dunst, C. J. (1990). Sensorimotor development of infants with Down syndrome. In D. Cicchetti & M. Beeghly (Eds.), *Children with Down syndrome: A developmental perspective* (pp. 180–230). New York, NY: Cambridge University Press.

Dykens, E. M. (2000). Psychopathology in children with intellectual disability. *Journal of Child Psychology and Psychiatry*, *41*, 407–417.

Dykens, E. M. (2003). Anxiety, fears, and phobias in persons with Williams syndrome. *Developmental Neuropsychology*, *23*(1–2), 291–316.

Dykens, E. M., Rosner, B. A., & Ly, T. M. (2001). Drawings by individuals with Williams syndrome: Are people different from shapes? *American Journal of Mental Retardation*, *106*(1), 94–107.

Einfeld, S. L., Tonge, B. J., & Florio, T. (1997). Behavioral and emotional disturbance in individuals with Williams syndrome. *American Journal of Mental Retardation*, *102*, 45–53.

Ellis, N. R. (1969). A behavioral research strategy in mental retardation: Defense and critique. *American Journal of Mental Deficiency*, *73*, 557–566.

Ellis, N. R., & Cavalier, A. R. (1982). Research perspectives in mental retardation. In E. Zigler & D. Balla (Eds.), *Mental retardation: The developmental-difference controversy*. Hillsdale, NJ: Erlbaum.

Emerson, E. (2007). Poverty and people with intellectual disabilities. *Mental Retardation and Developmental Disabilities Research Reviews*, *13*, 107–113.

Fidler, D. J. (2006). The emergence of a syndrome-specific personality profile in young children with Down syndrome. *Down Syndrome Research and Practice*, *10*, 53–60.

Fidler, D. J., Philofsky, A., & Hepburn, S. L. (2007). Language phenotypes and intervention planning: Bridging research and practice. *Mental Retardation and Developmental Disabilities Research Reviews*, *13*, 47–57.

Fidler, D. J., Philofsky, A., Hepburn, S. L., & Rogers, S. J. (2005). Nonverbal requesting and problem-solving by toddlers with Down syndrome. *American Journal of Mental Retardation*, *110*, 312–322.

Fisher, M. H., Hodapp, R. M., & Dykens, E. M. (2008). Child abuse among children with disabilities: What we know and what we need to know. *International Review of Research in Mental Retardation*, *35*, 251–289.

Fodor, J. (1983). *Modularity of mind: An essay on faculty psychology*. Cambridge, MA: MIT Press.

Freeman, S. F. N., & Alkin, M. C. (2000). Academic and social attainments of children with mental retardation in general education and special education settings. *Remedial and Special Education*, *21*, 3–26.

Fujiura, G. T., & Yamaki, K. (2000). Trends in demography of childhood poverty and disability. *Exceptional Children, 66,* 187–199.

Granat, K., & Granat, S. (1973). Below-average intelligence and mental retardation. *American Journal of Mental Deficiency, 78,* 27–32.

Granat, K., & Granat, S. (1975). Generalizability of patterns of intellectual performance from institutionalised to non-labeled intellectually subaverage adults. *Journal of Mental Deficiency Research, 19,* 43–55.

Granat, K., & Granat, S. (1978). Adjustment of intellectually below-average men not identified as mentally retarded. *Scandinavian Journal of Psychology, 19,* 41–51.

Greenspan, S. (2006). Functional concepts in mental retardation: Finding the natural essence of an artificial category. *Exceptionality, 14,* 205–224.

Greenspan, S., Loughlin, G., &. Black, R. S. (2001). Credulity and gullibility in people with developmental disorders: A framework for future research. In L. M. Glidden (Ed.), *International Review of Research in Mental Retardation, 24,* 101–135.

Grossman, H. J. (1983). *Classification in mental retardation.* Washington DC: American Association on Mental Deficiency.

Halpern, A., Close, D. W., & Nelson, D. J. (1986). *On my own: The impact of semi-independent living programs for adults with mental retardation.* Baltimore, MD: Paul Brookes.

Hodapp, R. M. (1994). Cultural-familial mental retardation. In R. Sternberg (Ed.), *Encyclopedia of intelligence* (pp. 711–717). New York, NY: Macmillan.

Hodapp, R. M., & Dykens, E. M. (1994). The two cultures of behavioral research in mental retardation. *American Journal on Mental Retardation, 97,* 675–687.

Hodapp, R. M., & Dykens, E. M. (2001). Strengthening behavioral research on genetic mental retardation disorders. *American Journal on Mental Retardation, 106,* 4–15.

Hodapp, R. M., & Dykens, E. M. (2006). Mental retardation. In I. Sigel & A. Renninger (Eds.), Vol. 4. *Research to Practice* (pp. 453–496), of W. Damon & R. Lerner (overall editors), *Handbook of Child Psychology.* New York, NY: Wiley.

Hodapp, R. M., Evans, D. W., & Gray, F. L. (1999). Intellectual development in children with Down syndrome. In J. Rondal, J. Perera, & L. Nadel (Eds.), *Down syndrome: A review of current knowledge* (pp. 124–132). London, UK: Whurr.

Hodapp, R. M., & Fidler, D. J. (1999). Special education and genetics: Connections for the 21st century. *Journal of Special Education, 33,* 130–137.

Howlin, P., Davies, M., & Udwin, O. (1998). Syndrome specific characteristics in Williams syndrome: To what extent do early behavioural patterns persist into adult life? *Journal of Applied Research in Intellectual Disabilities, 11*(3), 207–226.

Individuals with Disabilities Education Act of 2004, 20 U.S.C. 1400 et seq.

Jarrold, C., Baddeley, A. D., Hewes, A. K., & Phillips, C. (2001). A longitudinal assessment of diverging verbal and non-verbal abilities in the Williams syndrome phenotype. *Cortex, 37,* 423–431.

Kasari, C., & Freeman, S. F. N. (2001). Task-related social behavior in children with Down syndrome. *American Journal on Mental Retardation, 106,* 253–264.

Kasari, C., Freeman, S. F. N., & Hughes, M. A. (2001). Emotion recognition by children with Down syndrome. *American Journal on Mental Retardation, 106,* 59–72.

Kasari, C., Mundy, P., Yirmiya, N., & Sigman, M. (1990). Affect and attention in children with Down syndrome. *American Journal of Mental Retardation, 95,* 55–67.

Katsiyannis, A., Zhang, D., & Archwamety, T. (2002). Placement and exit patterns for students with mental retardation: An analysis of national trends. *Education and Training in Mental Retardation and Developmental Disabilities, 37,* 134–145.

Kavale, K. A., & Forness, S. R. (1999). *Efficacy of special education and related services.* Washington, DC: American Association on Mental Retardation.

King, B. H., Hodapp, R. M., & Dykens, E. M. (2009). Intellectual disability. In B. J. Sadock & V. A. Sadock (Eds.), *Kaplan and Sadock's comprehensive textbook of psychiatry* (9th ed., pp. 3444–3474). Philadelphia, PA: Lippincott Williams & Wilkins.

Kumin, L. (1994). Intelligibility of speech in children with Down syndrome in natural settings: Parents' perspective. *Perceptual and Motor Skills, 78,* 307–313.

Laing, E., Butterworth, G., Ansari, D., Gsodl, M., Longhi, E., Panagiotaki, G., Paterson, S., & Karmiloff-Smith, A. (2002). Atypical development of language and social communication in toddlers with Williams syndrome. *Developmental Science*, 5, 233–246.

Larry P. v. Riles, 343 F. Supp. 1306 (9th Circuit 1979).

Mervis, C. B, & Becerra, A. M. (2007). Language and communicative development in Williams syndrome. *Mental Retardation Development and Disability Research Review*, 13, 3–15.

Mervis, C. B., Morris, C. A., Bertrand, J., & Robinson, B. F. (1999). Williams syndrome: Findings from an integrated program of research. In H. Tager-Flusberg (Ed.), *Neurodevelopmental disorders* (pp. 65–110). Cambridge, MA: MIT Press.

Miller, J. (1999). Profiles of language development in children with Down syndrome. In J. F. Miller, M. Leddy, & L. A. Leavitt (Eds.), *Improving the communication of people with Down syndrome* (pp. 11–39). Baltimore, MD: Paul H. Brookes.

Nettelbeck, T., & Wilson, C. (2002). Personal vulnerability to victimization of people with mental retardation. *Trauma, Violence, & Abuse*, 3, 289–306.

Neubert, D. A., Moon, M. S., Grigal, M., & Redd, V. (2001). Post-secondary educational practices for individuals with mental retardation and other significant disabilities: A review of the literature. *Journal of Vocational Rehabilitation*, 16, 155–168.

Parish, S. L., Rose, R. A., Grinstein-Weiss, M., Richman, E. L., & Andrews, M. E. (2008). Material hardship in U.S. families raising children with disabilities. *Exceptional Children*, 75, 71–92.

Petersilia, J. R. (2001). Crime victims with developmental disabilities. *Criminal Justice and Behavior*, 28, 655–694.

Pitcairn, T. K., & Wishart, J. G. (1994). Reactions of young children with Down syndrome to an impossible task. *British Journal of Developmental Psychology*, 12, 485–489.

Rondal, J. (1995). *Exceptional language development in Down syndrome*. New York, NY: Cambridge University Press.

Rosa's Law of 2010, P.L. 111–256.

Rosner, B. A., Hodapp, R. M., Fidler, D. J., Sagun, J. N., & Dykens, E. M. (2004). Social competence in persons with Prader-Willi, Williams, and Down syndromes. *Journal of Applied Research in Intellectual Disabilities*, 17, 209–217.

Schaer, M., & Eliez, S. (2007). From genes to brain: Understanding brain development in neurogenetic disorders using neuroimaging techniques. *Child and Adolescent Psychiatric Clinics of North America*, 16, 557–579.

Schalock, R. L. (2002). What's in a name? *Mental Retardation*, 40, 59–61.

Searcy, Y. M., Lincoln, A. J., Rose, F. E., Kilma, E. S., Bavar, N., Korenberg, J. R. (2004). The relationship between age and IQ in adults with Williams syndrome. *American Journal on Mental Retardation*, 109(3), 231–236.

Sparrow, S. S., Balla, D. A., & Cicchetti, D. V. (2005). *Vineland Adaptive Behavior Scales-II*. Upper Saddle River, NJ: Pearson Education.

Sternberg, R. J. (1988). *The triarchic mind: A new theory of human intelligence*. New York, NY: Viking.

Stromme, P., & Hagberg, G. (2000). Aetiology in severe and mild mental retardation: A population-based study of Norwegian children. *Developmental Medicine and Child Neurology*, 42, 76–86.

Sullivan, P. M. & Knutson, J. F. (2000). Maltreatment and disabilities: A population-based epidemiological study. *Child Abuse & Neglect*, 24, 1257–1273.

Switzky, H. N. (Ed.). (2006a). Mental retardation, personality, and motivational systems. *International Review of Research in Mental Retardation*, 31, 1–339.

Switzky, H. N. (2006b). The importance of cognitive-motivational variables in understanding the outcome performance of persons with mental retardation: A personal view from the early twenty-first century. *International Review of Research in Mental Retardation*, 31, 1–30.

Verdugo, M. A., Bermejo, B. G., & Fuertes, J. (1995). The maltreatment of intellectually handicapped children and adolescents. *Child Abuse and Neglect*, 19, 205–215.

Walsh, P. N. (2008). Health indicators and intellectual disability. *Current Opinion in Psychiatry*, 21, 474–478.

Wehmeyer, M. L. (2006). Universal design for learning, access to the general education curriculum and students with mild mental retardation. *Exceptionality*, 14, 225–235.

Wilson, C., & Brewer, N. (1992). The incidence of criminal victimization of individuals with an intellectual disability. *Australian Psychologist*, 27, 114–117.

Wilson, C., Seaman, L., & Nettlebeck, T. (1996). Vulnerability to criminal exploitation: Influence of interpersonal competence differences among people with mental retardation. *Journal of Intellectual Disability Research, 40,* 8–16.

Zigler, E. (1967). Familial mental retardation: A continuing dilemma. *Science, 155,* 292–298.

Zigler, E. (1971). The retarded child as a whole person. In H. E. Adams & W. K. Boardman (Eds.), *Advances in experimental clinical psychology* (pp. 47–121). Oxford, UK: Pergamon.

Zigler, E. (1969). Developmental versus difference theories of retardation and the problem of motivation. *American Journal of Mental Deficiency,* 73, 536–556.

Zigler, E., & Hodapp, R. M. (Eds.), (1986). *Understanding mental retardation.* New York, NY: Cambridge University Press.

CHAPTER 11

Prodigies and Savants

David Henry Feldman and Martha J. Morelock

A chapter on intelligence in prodigies and savants would at first glance appear to be straightforward: Prodigies may be examples of extreme high intelligence, while savants may be examples of extreme low intelligence. On this interpretation, prodigies are children able to perform at amazingly proficient levels in very demanding fields because of their exceptionally high IQs. Savants are suppressed in their performance in all but a single area because of a general deficiency in IQ. Although straightforward, this way of looking at savants and prodigies is limited. For neither savants nor prodigies does the IQ distribution account for the very specific areas of performance that mark them. IQ is a broad index of general intellectual ability to deal with logic, reflection, reason, and abstract concepts, while the prodigy and the savant are marked by their remarkable capabilities in very specific domains like music, art, mathematics, chess, or memory. In an earlier publication on savants and prodigies (Morelock & Feldman, 1993), we reviewed what was known about these two extreme kinds of cases in order to reconsider the issue of general versus specific intelligence (cf. Gardner, Kornhaber, & Wake, 1996). In this chapter, we will continue this theme but will do so in the context of more recent work.

Because prodigies and savants have rarely been studied together, we will review each literature separately, attempting to provide a current summary of what is known and understood about each of the two sets of manifestations of extreme behavior. For example, prodigies appear in a wider array of fields than savants, and there are some areas where the two do not overlap; there are no calendar prodigies and there are no savants in chess. After the summary of each research field of inquiry, we will attempt to provide a view of prodigies and of savants as distinctive and remarkable manifestations of diversity in human intellectual functioning. We will also attempt to provide a framework for joint study of the two phenomena that may shed light on each as well as on their possible relationships to each other. We will make suggestions for particularly promising areas of future research and conclude with a proposed resolution to the long-standing issue of general versus specific forms of intelligence.

Before turning to the task at hand, we should note that the two subfields of research that deal with savants and prodigies are different in several ways, and that these differences influence how much is known and how confident we can be in research findings to date. For savants, there is a research tradition that goes back more than a century and is part of the medical field (Treffert, 1989, 2000, 2006, 2008, 2009). The techniques for doing research tend to reflect the deficit/remediation preoccupations of a medical approach. Over the years there has been a sustained interest in and commitment to research that may provide intervention to or relief for some of the burdens that most savants carry. For prodigies, research stretches back almost as long but has been sporadic and relatively uncommon. Although there were a small number of studies in the early decades of the previous century (e.g., Baumgarten, 1930; Revesz, 1925), the empirical base of knowledge about prodigies is not large, and almost all of it is based on case studies by psychologists. Prodigies are generally assumed to be blessed with greater gifts than most. They are typically not seen as requiring resources to ameliorate their "condition," and they are not seen as a burden to society. Consequently, research support for the study of prodigies has been minimal.

Defining Prodigies and Savants

There is relative consensus on how to define a savant but less agreement on the definition of a child prodigy. A savant (formerly referred to as an "idiot savant") is a person (not necessarily a child) who displays an island of exceptional mental performance in a sea of disability (Miller, 1989, 1999; Treffert, 1989; 2000, 2006, 2008, 2009). The syndrome can be either congenital or acquired by a normal person after injury or disease to the central nervous system. The skills can appear – and disappear – suddenly and inexplicably. The area of exceptionality for savants can be simply remarkable in contrast to their generally low level of functioning in other areas (i.e., "talented savant"), or it can be so extreme as to be spectacular even if it had been viewed in a normal person (i.e., "prodigious savant"; Treffert, 1989, 2000). For example, a calculating savant may be able to multiply numbers of many digits by other numbers of many digits in his or her head as quickly as a computer. Or a calendar savant may be able to produce the day or the week for any day in the past or the future with only a few seconds' delay, with uncanny (if not perfect) accuracy. There have been artistic savants whose works are considered to be of professional quality. In spite of such exceptionalities, most savants are unable to live independently and require major support from family and/or society to survive.

Unlike research into the savant, prodigy research has generated a fair amount of disagreement over definitional issues. Until late in the last century, there was no scientific or technical definition of the child prodigy. Dictionary definitions referred to the origin of the word "prodigy" as an omen or portent, an event out of the usual course of nature (Webster's *Third New International Dictionary*, 1961). The earliest definitions of prodigies were not limited to children but rather referred to an event that was cause for wonder and/or for impending changes that were not necessarily welcome. During the decades when psychometric definitions of intelligence were dominant, prodigies were defined as exceptionally high-IQ children (cf. Hollingworth, 1942; Tannenbaum, 1993). For Hollingworth, an IQ exceeding 180 put the child in the range of what would be required to be considered a prodigy.

In recent decades, an effort to provide a more technical definition of the child prodigy for purposes of research has stimulated both the desired research and some disagreement over just what constitutes a prodigy (Ruthsatz & Detterman, 2003; Hulbert, 2005; Edmunds & Noel, 2003;

Morelock & Feldman, 1993, 2003; Shavinina, 1999). The definition proposed in Feldman (with Goldsmith, 1986) posited that a prodigy is a child younger than 10 years of age who performs at an adult professional level in a highly demanding field. This definition was intended to guide research and, at the same time, to be explicit and precise enough to be tested empirically. For example, if further research revealed that children, although performing extraordinarily well for children, still did not reach adult professional levels of performance until well after 10 years of age, that finding would tend to weaken the part of the definition that is age specific. For the most part, research on child prodigies has used the 1986 definition either as a guide or as a foil for revision (e.g., Kenneson, 1998; McPherson, 2006, 2007; Radford, 1990; Shavinina, 1999).[1] For the purposes of this chapter, we will use a variation of the definition proposed in 1986, recognizing that there is some disagreement as to its adequacy. A prodigy is defined as a child who, at a very young age (typically younger than 10 years old), performs at an adult professional level in a highly demanding, culturally recognized field of endeavor. A prodigy's performance is ultimately assessed as being of a professional level through critiques based on standards of the field as well as the reaction of the buying audience, reflected, for example, in sales of paintings and positive reviews of performances.

Although both prodigies and savants are very rare, there are no solid estimates of the frequencies of their occurrence in the general population. Most identified savants are males, although there have certainly been exceptions (e.g., Selfe, 1977). It has been estimated that savant syndrome occurs six times as often in males as in females (Hill, 1977). Traditionally, most prodigies have been males as well, although that has changed dramatically in the past 30 years (Feldman, with Goldsmith, 1986; Goldsmith, 1987).

Recent Research on Child Prodigies

The contemporary field of research with child prodigies began with the publication of a study of six boys under the age of 10 in the fields of music, chess, and writing (and a child, labeled an "omnibus prodigy," who had not yet settled into a specific area) (Feldman, with Goldsmith, 1986). The boys were between 3 and 8 when first studied, and were followed for as many as 10 years. The study focused on each child's specific and general abilities, experiences with their teachers and their families, and development in their specific field in the context of their more general development. This is the study that proposed the working definition described in the previous section. The findings most frequently cited from this research are that a child prodigy has a mix of child and adult-like qualities; that prodigies require the sustained efforts of at least one parent, teachers, and others to support the development of their talent; that the process requires several years even in the most extreme cases; that the talents of prodigies are at least partly natural and inborn (the more extreme the case, the more nearly completely inborn the talents are likely to be); and that prodigies' talents tend to be domain specific and require above average but not extreme intelligence.

One study of eight prodigies (as defined above) in chess explored the extent to which proficiency at the level of a professional tournament player as a child predicted how well these chess players performed as young adults (Howard, 2008). The research was intended to shed light on the issue of natural talent as well as the role of practice in achieving world-class levels of performance. The study also dealt with an issue that often is cited as a reason to be skeptical of the prodigy phenomenon: the fact that relatively few child prodigies become

1 There have also been several books written by journalists, critics and historians, or the individuals themselves about child prodigy lives. These works have added valuable information about specific cases but are not social science research as such. Examples of works in this tradition are Conway and Siegelman, (2005); Kanigel, (1991); Rolfe, 1978); Wallace (1986); Weiner (1953) and the many books about Mozart (e.g., Hildesheimer, 1982/1977).

successful adult performers in their original field of endeavor. In chess, at least, the child performers were highly likely to become successful adult performers in the same domain.

The results of this study support the importance of natural talent in the field of chess as a critical ingredient in success and that a prodigy is difficult to explain without recourse to a substantial natural talent base from which to work (Feldman, 1995, 2008; Winner, 1996). Most of the children have achieved a high level of international success in spite of the fact that they are not likely to have practiced as long as many players who have performed less well. On a number of measures, the child prodigy chess players exceeded in skill other high-level players in chess. For example, they needed fewer games to reach master levels, required fewer years to achieve grandmaster status, and were younger when they received grandmaster ratings. One of the eight became a world champion, although other known world champions were not necessarily identified as child prodigies under the present definition.

Another study (Ruthsatz & Detterman, 2003) explored the importance of general intellectual ability (IQ) in the performance of a piano prodigy, arguing that IQ contributes significantly to the 6-year-old's ability to perform at a high, professional concert level in his chosen domain. Along with "domain-specific skills," a well above average IQ (an attained score in what would typically be considered the gifted range) was found to contribute to the child's overall performance. Most striking was the child's general and specific musical memory capabilities. The study tended to discount the most common alternative explanation for the child's exceptional level of performance, namely, practice (Ericsson, Krampe, & Tesch-Romer, 1993), inasmuch as the child had not yet received formal training in music. Overall, this study points to a combination of elevated IQ, domain-specific natural abilities, and practice as implicated in high-level performance within the field of music, a conclusion that we will affirm at the end of this chapter when we summarize the state of current knowledge and theorizing about prodigies and savants.

A case study in another domain (writing) was carried out by Edmunds and Noel (2003). The study focused on the writing that their subject produced during a period of about 12 months, from about age 5 in 1999 to about age 6. This child (Geoffrey) was interested in math and science and much of his writing reflected these interests, although his first 30-page work was based on the then-popular *Pokemon* cartoon books and was written for Geoffrey's younger brother. The authors report that this work was done very quickly and in a "rush of creative energy" (Edmunds & Noel, 2003, p. 188), which was to become Geoffrey's way of writing.

All told, Geoffrey wrote 129 works during this brief period, totaling more than 1,500 handwritten pages. Reproduced here is part of the final work, a letter to one of his mentors, which communicates his astonishing levels of understanding of math and science concepts and a remarkable ability to communicate them in writing, as well as some childish playfulness:

> Dear Jim,
>
> I am into math but also science. Here's the math part. I know addition, addition with tens and ones, multiplication, multiplication with tens and ones, division, and division by zero!! Here's how that works. 5 [divided by] 0 = undefined, or, the answer is undefined. I can do algebra, addition with tens, ones, hundreds, thousands, and millions up to infinity. . . . I also have a bunch of questions. What is calculus? . . . How do you get –0 if it exists?
>
> Now, some science. I do theoretical physics just like you. I am working on a unified theory. Are you? And if you're not, what's the theory you're working on anyways? . . . My unified theory is broken up into many parts, each part the size of special relativity . . . E = sp, meaning energy = speed of light pulses. It is the theoretical answer to why Pikachuic electricity is so fast. . . . I really know my geometry, even though I'm in grade 1!

I know that a rhombicosidodecahedron has 240 forces. A rhombicosidodecahedron is the largest known polyhedron. It is huge!

XOX
Geoffrey

Edmunds and Noel (2003) analyzed examples of Geoffrey's writing over the year-long period in which his work was studied and noted areas of major change in style and sophistication. Using standard measures of language, Geoffrey's level exceeded high school students' norms, and showed tendencies toward transformation and innovation in language that are unusual at any age.

As to the question of intelligence in the traditional psychometric sense, Geoffrey had been given a WISC-III test and scored "moderate-to-high," with an IQ of 128. On the Raven's, he scored higher, above the 99th percentile for age 13 (Edmunds & Noel, 2003, p. 192). Informally, the authors noted an unusual memory ability that allowed Geoffrey to recall, in detail, work that he had done several months prior to the interviews. Overall, the authors found that the most striking quality that Geoffrey displayed was a "dogged persistence" to learn. This persistence is what Kevin Kearney, father of Michael, who graduated from college at age 10, called a "rage to learn" (Kearney & Kearney, 1998; Morelock, 1995). It appears in the most extreme cases of prodigious achievement. Geoffrey used his writing to organize and consolidate what he had learned – to affirm that he understood what he had read in fiction and nonfiction books – qualities also noted by other scholars who have studied prodigies (e.g. Goldsmith, 2000).

Edmunds and Noel (2003) preferred the term "precocity" to prodigy, emphasizing rapid early mastery of knowledge and focusing less on the mysterious and elusive qualities of the child himself and the difficulties in defining a prodigy precisely. Terminology and emphasis notwithstanding, their case study adds significantly to the existing literature on prodigies. Writing prodigies are rare even among the range of prodigies, and the approach that Edmunds and Noel have taken to understanding Geoffrey's abilities in the context of his domain of expertise and his development adds richness and detail to the small body of knowledge in the scholarly literature.

Theoretical Interpretations

There has been a small number of more interpretive or theoretical efforts to try to comprehend and make sense of the prodigy phenomenon. This is a welcome development; prodigies have fascinated and inspired awe and wonder for millennia, but there has been little advance in explanation beyond divine inspiration, reincarnation, or magical incantation. Some of the more conceptual/theoretical work has centered on definitional issues, such as in the Edmunds and Noel (2003) study just described. The term "prodigy" continues to carry powerful associations stemming from its ancient meaning as something "out of the usual course of nature" or a "portent" (Webster's *Third New International Dictionary*, 1961). Consequently, there is considerable aversion to the term both within and outside the scholarly community (Radford, 1990).

One response to the definitional issue was simply to place the prodigy within the range of IQs from lowest to highest, with the child prodigy at the highest extreme of the distribution (i.e., above 180 IQ), as Leta Hollingworth (1942) did in her classic work on extremely high IQ. By placing the prodigy under the umbrella of IQ, its many complexities and associations with nonscientific traditions could be wiped away. It also put prodigies squarely into the psychometric IQ tradition. Unfortunately, the prodigy did not fit well under this definition; an IQ of 180 (or even several standard deviations lower) was not required for a child to become a prodigy, and the astonishing performance of children in specific domains could not be explained by high general intelligence alone.

Feldman proposed a revised definition of the prodigy, placing the phenomenon within an evolutionary and cultural historical framework (Feldman, with Goldsmith, 1986), which he then termed "co-incidence." The construct of co-incidence was intended to acknowledge the mysterious nature of the prodigy phenomenon and to recognize that interpretations that seem irrational and unscientific, such as reincarnation and astrology, are understandable in the face of the baffling reality that the prodigy represents. Reducing the prodigy to extreme high IQ, Feldman argued, diminishes its complexity, ignores the fact that prodigies occur only in a small number of domains, and tends to discourage further research. It also was unsupported by empirical data: only one of the six cases in the study would have qualified using Hollingworth's definition (above 180 IQ).

It is assumed in this framework that child prodigies are naturally endowed with extraordinary talent. Even the most extreme talent, however, cannot fully account for the prodigy. The child's family (particularly a parent who is totally devoted to the development of the child's talent), his or her teachers (who must balance the astonishing capability of the child with the need to guide and direct the child's mastery of critical skills and knowledge, in proper sequence); the current state of the child's chosen domain (as it is claimed that domains, as well as children, undergo developmental transitions and transformations); the broader social/cultural context in which a field channels resources, sets standards, responds to pressures from inside and outside, and confers status that can increase or decrease the likelihood that a prodigy's talent will be recognized and celebrated; and the period of history in which all of the other forces interact (a war, pestilence, or a great economic boom can have profound influences on opportunities or the lack of them; Simonton, 1994).

A number of scholars have criticized the co-incidence framework, and in doing so, have added some important additional conceptual distinctions and possible areas of further research (Edmunds & Noel, 2003; Ruthsatz & Detterman, 2003; Shavanina, 1999). Edmunds and Noel, for example, believe that precocity is a better designation than child prodigy to avoid the issues that tend to come along with the term. The advantage of the focus on precocity is that it invites close attention to the specific behavior of the child in relation to what is normative for the domain, for age peers, or in relation to more advanced students of the domain. Psychologist and educator Julian Stanley promoted the term "precocity" in advocating accelerated education for intellectually *precocious* youth, including youths who could reason exceptionally well mathematically or verbally, and those showing exceptional spatial and mechanical talent (Brody & Stanley, 2005; Lubinski, Benbow, & Morelock, 2000; Lubinski, Webb, Morelock, & Benbow, 2001; Stanley, 1996, 2000).

Ruthsatz and Detterman (2003) found that co-incidence tends to diminish the importance of psychometric intelligence in accounting for the prodigy's achievements; in their case study of a 6-year-old musical prodigy, they found that the child scored IQ 132 on the 1985 version of the Stanford-Binet Intelligence Test, although his pattern of scores was idiosyncratic, with a range from 114 (abstract reasoning) to 158 (short-term memory). The argument that general intelligence as traditionally assessed – that is, through an IQ test – is implicated in this child's superior performance in music is consistent with data from other studies (e.g., Feldman, with Goldsmith, 1986; Simonton, 1999). For a child prodigy (as contrasted with a calculating savant, for example), an IQ in the above-normal range seems to be necessary.

Shavinina (1999) comes at co-incidence from a different angle, finding it inadequate in its ability to explain the actual mental and emotional processes of development and experience that are distinctive to the gifted and to the prodigy. Shavanina's proposed addition to the set of considerations when trying to comprehend the reality of the prodigy is a function of a phenomenon called "age sensitivity," which in turn is involved with "sensitive periods" in the child's development. These notions are adapted from research and theory done by Leites (1960, 1996), with use of terms somewhat different from Western scholarly research. "Sensitive periods" (Bornstein & Krasnegor, 1989; Thompson & Nelson, 2001), for example, refer to universal processes that help explain why children during a period of years are particularly receptive to and particularly adept at learning languages, much less so thereafter. Sensitive periods as used in Western psychological studies do not refer to individual differences between and among children, but this is how Shavinina (1999) uses the term.

Terminology aside, Shavinina's emphasis on the distinctive cognitive and emotional qualities and experiences that may be involved in producing a prodigy is a welcome one. It is a fair criticism that the coincidence framework gives relatively little emphasis to the specific processes that may be involved with and help explain why a child would engage in deep, sustained activity in a domain that most children will ignore or only afford a modest involvement. This is one of the perennial mysteries of the prodigy phenomenon. In Shavinina's terminology, for the prodigy, a "sensitive period" of intense involvement with a domain changes from a more typical "developmental" sensitive period to an "individual" one. In other words, for the prodigy, the often intense but fleeting passions of growing children may transform into a lifelong career, as in the case of a child who was fascinated by birds and became a highly renowned ornithologist as an adult (Shavinina, 1999).

Brain Imaging Research on Prodigies

Although it would seem like an obvious choice for research, there have been few studies of brain function and/or brain development in prodigies. With the availability of powerful imaging techniques like functional magnetic resonance imaging (fMRI), positron emission tomography (PET), and others, prodigy cases may be able to shed light on some of the most enduring issues in the study of intelligence. Questions of both anatomical and functional differences between prodigy brains and more typical brains appear to be compelling areas of research. Since its beginning more than a century ago, the question of one versus more than one form of intelligence has remained controversial. Given that the prodigy tends to be a child with extreme ability in a single field, knowing what brain areas tend to be implicated compared with those of brains in less gifted children might help address the domain general versus domain specific question. Are prodigies' brains anatomically distinct in any detectable ways? Are the distinctive areas different for different prodigy fields – for example, for music, for chess, for visual art?

As compelling as these questions may be, we know of no research directly addressing them. There are, however, some studies on related topics that may be relevant to prodigies. A number of studies examined mathematically gifted students as compared with less gifted ones (e.g., O'Boyle, 2008a, b; Singh & O'Boyle, 2004). In these studies, the brains of mathematically precocious children and adolescents were studied morphologically, developmentally, and functionally. Distinctive processes and patterns of activation were found for the mathematically talented children, as well as evidence of enhanced development of the right cerebral hemisphere and possible enhanced connectivity and integrative exchange between right and left hemispheres (Singh & O'Boyle, 2004). It is reasonable to expect that similar, and perhaps more pronounced, differences between mathematical prodigies and others would be likely to occur.

A related area of research has been carried out with calculating "prodigies," one of the traditional areas in which astonishing performance has been observed going back several centuries (Smith, 1983). That these calculating savants were called prodigies has led to some confusion about the phenomenon. For most of the history of Western mathematics, arithmetic was a major activity. In more recent centuries, complex mathematical reasoning has become increasingly more central to the field. Thus, centuries ago a calculating savant (who, for example, could divide or multiply large sums rapidly) was called a "mathematics prodigy," where today such a child or adult would be labeled a "calculating savant."

An article reviewing research on Rudiger Gamm, in which he is called a "calculating prodigy," illustrates the problem. The title of the article (Butterworth, 2001) is "What Makes a Prodigy?" when it perhaps should have been "What Makes a Savant?" As the article says, "Gamm is remarkable in that he is able (for example) to calculate 9th powers and 5th roots with great accuracy, and he can find the quotient of 2 primes to 60 decimal places" (Butterworth, 2001, p. 11). The analysis of Gamm's brain activation as compared with six nonexpert calculators revealed (using PET scan procedures) distinctly different patterns. The problem is that by contemporary standards, Gamm is a calculating savant, not a child prodigy, particularly because he did not begin his calculating efforts until he was 20.

There have also been brain imaging studies of trained musicians versus less trained or untrained individuals, revealing reliable differences between and among the various levels of training and experience (e.g., Schlaug, Jancke, Huang, & Steinmetz, 1995a,b), showing that trained musicians have a larger than average corpus callosum (as was true of the mathematically precocious children) as well as other differences in brain morphology and activation. Studies of the effects of musical training on cortical development also have shown that training affects organization and reorganization of brain circuitry without resolving the question of plasticity and/or inborn susceptibility to training effects as the main source of the change (Baeck, 2002).

General and Specific Abilities in Prodigies

A small number of studies of child prodigies in the fields of art and music have been carried out by scholars with a background in the specific field rather than in social science research. One such study (Kenneson, 1998) of musical prodigies was done by Claude Kenneson, a professor of music at the University of Alberta in Canada. Kenneson did not consider his subjects' academic intelligence as a separate topic, but it can be indirectly accessed from his account of their experiences. For example, Canadian cellist Shauna Rolston received bachelor's and master's degrees in music history and music performance with distinction from Yale University and later became a professor of cello at the University of Toronto. Academic achievements of this sort are unlikely without substantial academic ability, and we can assume with confidence that Shauna Rolston possessed such abilities. Similarly, cellist Yo Yo Ma studied at Columbia and Harvard. As Kenneson writes: "It was at Harvard, where he [Ma] distinguished himself studying the humanities, that he realized that music has as much to do with philosophy, history, psychology, and anthropology as it has to do with playing an instrument well" (Kenneson, 1998, p. 330).

The advantages are significant when a study is carried out by someone who is deeply involved and highly accomplished in a field where prodigies are found. One of the very few additional examples in the literature of a study by a scholar with training and experience in *both* the domain of interest and in social science research is that of Milbrath (1998), who studied visual art.

Milbrath's study bears directly on issues of intelligence and talent, although not in the traditional psychometric sense. Milbrath studied several highly talented drawing prodigies over several years, giving her the opportunity to analyze change over time and the contributions of various aspects of intellectual functioning to the drawings that children produced. Examples of drawings by one of Milbrath's subjects are shown in Figures 11.1–4 below.

A question that interested Milbrath was the role that natural talent plays in the development of exceptionally talented visual artists. Taking Piaget's notions of figurative

Figure 11.1. Drawing by 2-year-old Peregrine. (Figure 3.7b in Milbrath, 1998)

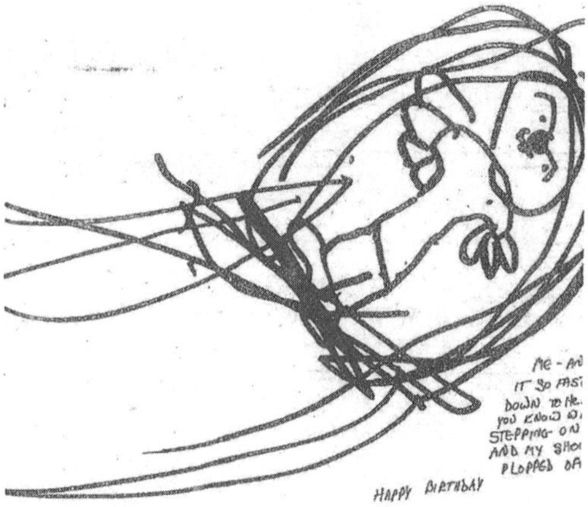

Figure 11.2. Drawing by 2-year-old Peregrine. (Figure 3.7a in Milbrath, 1998)

and operative knowledge as a starting point, Milbrath asked if these processes might help explain how her very young subjects could possibly have produced drawings as sophisticated as they did.

In Piaget's theory of intelligence, figurative and operative knowing are reciprocal processes that, together, provide the basis for construction of knowledge (Feldman, 2000), functioning similarly in all people. As an artist, Milbrath wondered if figurative and operative knowing might vary from person to person, with future artists tending to have more acute figurative processes (sharper perceptions, a more acute sense of color, etc.) while at the same time being less controlled than others by operative processes of ordering, categorizing, and discerning logical relationships. The other way in which Milbrath thought artistic prodigies might differ from others less talented is in their continued emphasis on sensorimotor intelligence even as other children move toward more advanced (in the

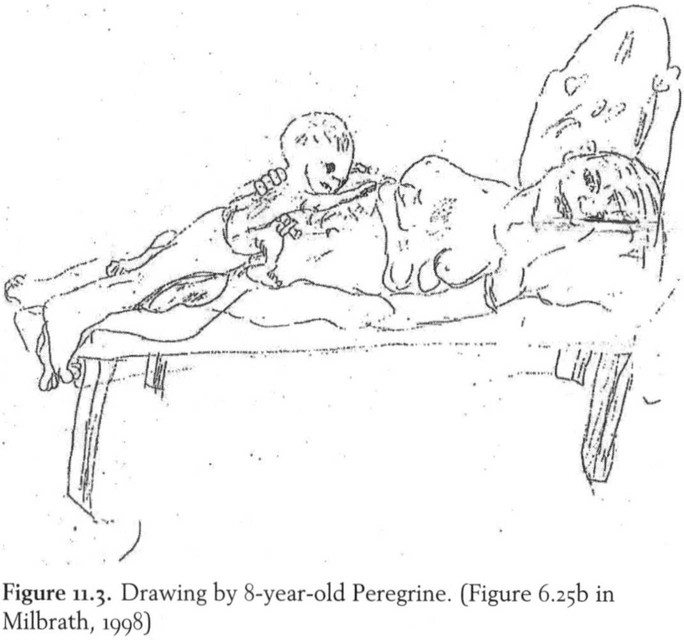

Figure 11.3. Drawing by 8-year-old Peregrine. (Figure 6.25b in Milbrath, 1998)

Figure 11.4. Drawing by 11-year-old Peregrine. (Figure 4.10b in Milbrath, 1998)

Piagetian sense) cognitive developmental processes.

Milbrath found support for her hypotheses and shed light on one of the current controversies in the field. A number of scholars who have studied high-level performance in several fields (sports, music, visual arts, chess, and others) claim that "deliberate practice" is the best explanation for differences in levels of expertise (Ericsson, 1996; Howe, Davidson, & Sloboda, 1998). These scholars argue that about 10,000 hours of well-planned and guided practice is the variable that separates exceptional from less exceptional performers. For Milbrath, the age and quality of her subjects' work would make deliberate practice an unlikely source of explanation for their work (although, to be sure, her subjects spent a great deal of time practicing their craft).

Milbrath found that the developmental course of talented children's drawing is qualitatively distinct from that of less talented children, with the difference primarily in attentiveness, awareness, and preoccupation of the talented children to the figural qualities of objects. Talented children are also less controlled by the conceptual structures that constrain less talented children, leading them to emphasize what they "know" more than what they "see."

Savants and Intelligence

According to Darold Treffert (2008), a physician and one of the leading scholars of savant syndrome, the first case of savant syndrome was reported in the scientific literature more almost 160 years ago, although it was about 120 years ago that Dr. J. Langdon Down described savant syndrome as a distinct condition. As compared with research on child prodigies, there has been a great deal more work done over more than a century of activity. The vast majority of savant studies have come from the medical research community, although a significant number of studies have also been reported by psychologists. More recently, brain studies have begun to appear in the scientific literature.

There is a sufficiently large base of research on savant syndrome, as it tends to be labeled since Treffert's 1989 book (it had been originally labeled "idiot savant"), to divide this review into subsections: calendar calculation, music, mathematics, art (primarily drawing), and memory. There are also occasional cases in other areas, such as sensory sensitivity, mechanical aptitude, and language (Miller, 1999). There has been a good deal of interest in savant cases as they relate to both general psychometric intelligence and more specific cognitive processes, There are also several films that have portrayed the savant, from the 1988 commercial film *Rain Man*, starring Dustin Hoffman, to a documentary called *A Real Rainman*, based on the late Richard Wawro, an autistic savant who was a remarkable visual artist (Zimmerman, 1989). The life of Kim Peek, the savant who was actually a real-life inspiration for the character Dustin Hoffman played in *Rain Man*, has also been documented in two fascinating accounts by his father, Fran Peek (1997, 2007).

General and Specific Abilities in Savants

From the earliest studies, savants have been described as severely lacking in general intellectual abilities, with an area of superior ability that stands out relative to their overall low functioning, or more rarely, stands out relative to the broad population. It is the latter kind of case that has drawn the most attention from the research community (and, not surprisingly, from the media). In recent decades, the degree of severity of the overall intellectual deficit appears often to be less than was originally believed (in IQ terms, savant cases were originally thought to have IQs around 20–40, but several studies have shown savants with IQs near or even above normal; Treffert, 2009); the appearance of Daniel Tammet (2006, 2009) in the literature has further supported the possibility of both high IQ and extreme savant skills appearing in the same person.

Savant research has also shed light on the question of the viability of theories of multiple intelligences (e.g., Gardner, 1983; Sternberg, 1985). Treffert (2009), for example, believes there is evidence among some savants that supports the existence of several intelligences in the areas where savants appear: music, mathematics, visual art, mnemonics, and perhaps others. Although Treffert acknowledges that most savants are known have low IQ scores, he finds that fact to be of limited value in explaining the remarkable ways that "intelligence" sometimes manifests itself in savants. For example, Treffert describes a concert by Leslie Lemke, a blind, autistic musical savant whose IQ measures in the 35–55 range:

> *At this particular concert Leslie was asked to play a piece he had never heard before with the other pianist, rather than waiting for the piece to conclude and then play it back as he usually does. The other pianist began playing. Leslie waited about three seconds and then did indeed play the piece with the other pianist, separated only by those three seconds.... Leslie was parallel processing, just as some very intelligent, but rare, interpreters are able to translate what a speaker is saying into another language simultaneously.... That would not be possible if the level of IQ of 35–55 was an accurate barometer of his over-all intelligence. He exceeds that level by far... which signals that more than a single "intelligence" was at work during that complex performance. (Treffert, 2008, pp. 2–3)*

Brain researcher Allan Snyder (2009) proposes that all individuals have savant skills, but most of us have inhibited these skills through adoption of and preference for the reasoning and abstract thinking that is adaptive in our highly technological and rationalized environments. Thus, we normally respond to our experience not in terms of the stream of information and sensory details bombarding us but, rather in terms of conceptual mind-sets. Using magnetic techniques to "turn off" higher mental processes of the brain, he and his coworkers have demonstrated that savant-like abilities are sometimes latent in normal subjects.

Robyn Young (1995) investigated the talents and family backgrounds of 51 savants recruited throughout Australia and the United States. The selection of savants included prodigious and talented savants as well as those with "splinter skills" – levels of interest and competence only marginally above the level of general functioning. Young found the parents and siblings of the savant participants to be exceptionally able, with above-average IQ and frequency of high-level skills, though not necessarily the same skills as those displayed by the savants. In addition, there was a family predisposition toward high achievement, possibly genetically predisposed and/or part of a tradition, which provided encouragement and reinforcement for savant skills. The researcher concluded that savants have an underlying biological predisposition toward high general ability that is tempered by neurological impairment. The resultant savant skills are encouraged through familial support.

Research on Savants' Intelligence and Related Topics

Young, incorporating psychometric measures into the study, found peaks and valleys in the WAIS profiles of the savant sample. The researcher consequently took exception to the widely held notion that savants manifest islands of extreme capability showcased against a backdrop of *overall severely deficient intellect*. Among the 51 savants, 16 had a subtest score at least one standard deviation above the population mean, and 60% had at least 1 subtest one standard deviation above the full-scale score. Highest scores were revealed in Block Design, Object Assembly, and Digit Span; lowest scores were found on Comprehension, Coding, and Vocabulary. These patterns are compatible with strengths and weaknesses of savant functioning documented in the literature (i.e., verbal/conceptual weaknesses and perceptual strengths). In addition, the level of precocity exhibited by the savants (i.e., prodigious or talented) was found to be positively correlated with the level of general cognitive ability, as indexed by IQ.

The idea that savant cognition is best described as islands of extreme capability showcased against a backdrop of overall severely deficient intellect emerged from the earliest writings on savants. A case study by Scheerer, Rothmann, and Goldstein (1945) was the first to document features of savant functioning that thereafter were repeatedly observed. These include (1) minimal abstract reasoning ability and almost exclusive reliance on concrete and literal patterns of expression and thought, (2) lack of metacognition, (3) extraordinary memory, (4) flattened affect, and (4) limited creativity. Elaboration and examples of each of these follow.

Scheerer, Rothman, and Goldstein (1945) wrote of one savant who memorized and sang operas in several languages yet had no comprehension of the conceptual and symbolic meaning of the words. Still, the question of abstract reasoning in savants is a complex one. Studies show that savants have an immediate, seemingly intuitive access to the underlying structural rules and regularities of their domain, whether it be music (Miller, 1989; Treffert, 1989), mathematical calculation (O'Connor & Hermelin, 1984; Hermelin & O'Connor, 1986), or art (O'Connor & Hermelin, 1987). Furthermore, these are the same rules and regularities as those applied by practitioners of normal or high reasoning ability who are skilled in the same area.

It appears, therefore, that even though most savants can't reason conceptually, they can abstract to a degree – at least in circumscribed and domain-specific areas (O'Connor, 1989; Miller, 1999). Miller (1999) suggests that what is missing in savants is a conceptual system that can reconstrue domain-specific knowledge, transferring it into a more generalized framework, affording a decontextualized representation containing less perceptual detail but better adapted to varied application (see Karmiloff-Smith, 1992).

Savants appear to be incapable of metacognition. They cannot reflect upon their internal thinking processes or explain how they arrived at correct responses to posed questions (Scheerer et al., 1945). When asked to account for how they can do whatever it is that they do, they frequently respond with something irrelevant. O'Connor (1989) reports that one calendar calculator who was able to render remarkably fast responses to date questions was, nevertheless, usually unable to add or subtract without pencil and paper. Yet, when asked how he managed his calendar feats (e.g., giving the correct answer to a question such as "On what day of the week did September 1744, fall?"), he responded simply "I make all sorts of mathematical calculations, don't I?" Some savants are able to articulate rule-based strategies. Those who do so tend to have higher IQs than do their counterparts (Hermelin & O'Connor, 1986). Savant Daniel Tammet, who reports having a measured IQ of 150 on the WAIS (top 1% of the population on that measure), has an exceptional ability to describe what he sees in his head and to reflect on his cognitive processes (Tammet, 2009). This has prompted Allan Snyder's comment that Tammet "could be the Rosetta Stone" in terms of what we can learn from him about savant cognition (Johnson, 2005)

All savants have extraordinary memories. Savant mnemonists are notable solely for their impressive memory for miscellaneous or mundane happenings (e.g., some savants have been known to remember weather conditions for each day of most of their lives). In other savants, it is the norm for their incredibly powerful memories to be limited to their domains of achievement.

Savants exhibit a restricted range of emotion, precluding the experience of heightened passion, excitement, or sentiment (Treffert, 1989, 2000). In the case of musical savants, for example, this usually comes across in performance as shallow imitative expressiveness lacking subtlety or innuendo. However, there have been some cases of musical savants demonstrating emotional connection with the music they were performing (Viscott, 1970; Miller, 1989). In one such case (Viscott, 1970), the savant exhibited more expanded verbal abilities than is commonly the case with savants and this ability may have allowed for an interpretive response to the music. As another possible explanation, emotional response to music can be, to some extent, the direct result of the physiological changes it evokes (Winner, 1982). Music has been found to affect pulse, respiration, blood pressure, and the electrical resistance of the skin, while also delaying the onset of fatigue (Mursell, 1937). These types of changes also occur during emotional experience. The question is whether the emotional response seen in musical savants is more a straightforward reflection of specific physiological effect than is the case with musicians more conceptually and interpretively involved in the performance of their music.

Earlier research findings suggested that savants are incapable of being creative in the sense of producing original work. Treffert (1989) concluded that while musical savants might imitate, improvise, or embellish based on preestablished constraining musical rules, they are generally incapable of composing. Sacks (1995) later distinguished between two different kinds of creativity, acknowledging as creative the individuality of savant ability based on perceptual talent while recognizing that even the prodigious savant does not achieve a higher order of creativity involving the invention of new ideas and new ways of seeing things. Daniel Tammet appears to be an exception once again. In his recent (2009) book, he brings together research on the brain and neuroscience, concluding with a theory of "hyperconnectivity" to account for autistic functioning as well as creativity. In addition, he describes an original language which he has been creating since childhood called "Mänti" based on the lexical and grammatical structures of Baltic and Scandinavian languages.

Supporting Sacks's observation is evidence that musical savants with more highly developed language capacities are more likely to compose music. One musical savant, "L.L.," studied by Miller (1989), developed more complex language over a period of months, with capacities evolving from simple monosyllabic or echolalic responses to conversational generation of requests, comments, and more sophisticated responses to questions. At the beginning of this period, L.L. remained musically confined to renditions of songs and melodies written by others, with little inclination to improvise or compose. At the end of the study, however, L.L. announced and played an original composition. This concordance of the development of expanded language skills with the onset of musical creativity led Miller to speculate that music and language are not mutually exclusive (see also Patel, 2008).

More Recent Research and Interpretation of the Savant Phenomenon

Research has intensified and increased greatly during recent years, with some important new findings and interpretations of savant skills and how they develop. There have been advances in two areas that bear directly on savants and intelligence. One of these is of general interest and deals with all savants; this work tends to show that previously assumed constraints on IQ and other capabilities do not always hold for savants – that there is more diversity and greater plasticity in savant development than was previously believed (Miller, 1999; Treffert,

1989, 2000, 2006, 2008, 2009). The other advance is specific to calendar savants; there are now plausible explanations for how calendar savants are able to achieve their remarkable results (Thioux, Stark, Klaiman, & Schultz, 2006) as well as some research on the ways that general intellectual level may interact with savant capabilities over the course of development (Cowan, Stainthorp, Kapnogianni, & Anastasiou, 2004). We will review these recent areas of research for what they may tell us about savants and intelligence.

Plasticity and Diversity in Savants

While, in general, it remains true that savants tend to be impaired in most areas other than their special skill, it is less true than was believed until quite recently. In a review of research, Miller (1999, 2005) found considerable variation among savant cases within a skill area as well as variation from specialty to specialty. Treffert (2006, 2008, 2009) reported similar findings. Nonetheless, there do seem to be certain abilities that are implicated in each specific savant domain. These tend to be present in all cases, whether of the more profound sort, with performance comparable to that of a person not afflicted with disabilities, to more "splinter" skills that are exceptional in relation to the other areas of functioning of the savant but not necessarily exceptional when compared with the best performers in that field.

Miller (2005) reports that among musical savants, component skills preestablished of absolute pitch, aural melody retention, aptitude for harmonic analysis, and ability to reproduce what is heard tend to be present. For drawing savants, visual memory for detail, awareness of perspective, and an ability to depict what is seen are the common skills. Among calendar savants, event memory and attribution of personal meaning to date and numerical information are typically found.

Along with the typical strengths, there are typical weaknesses: recognition of previously seen figure drawings was no better among drawing savants than for other mentally impaired individuals (O'Connor & Hermelin, 1987). Musical savants have difficulty with same versus different judgments, even with musical notes that they can identify perfectly. And savants rarely have general intellectual abilities above normal. For calendar calculation in particular, there appears to be a relationship between the development of calendar calculation knowledge and IQ, with higher IQ associated with more extensive and more accurate calendar calculating skills (O'Connor, Cowan, & Samella, 2000 cited in Miller, 2005).

In a study of two young calendar savants aged 5 and 6 years, Cowan, Stainthorp, Kapnogianni, and Anastasiou (2004) explored the relationship of general intellectual ability (IQ) to calendar calculation development. As children, the two boys were remarkable in their skills, but not as adept or as accurate as most adult calendar savants. When retested two years later, neither boy had improved in calendar calculation, and the hypothesized reason for their lack of improvement (indeed, their diminished interest in calendar calculation) was attributed to their normal and exceptional IQs (scored on the Wechsler III – UK edition); one child had a full scale IQ of 105, the other, 141. These robust scores on a standard IQ appeared to give the boys options to pursue other interests typically not available to a savant. The early stimulus for calendar activity was probably a physical limitation that isolated the boys (one had a hearing problem, the other a visual one). Both boys had become more social and were pursuing activities more typical of boys their age. Although these results are from only a single study of two boys, they suggest that lower IQ or general intellectual ability of the sort assessed on an IQ test may constrain development in other areas.

Miller (1999), summarizing studies of calendar savants by Hermelin and O'Connor (1986; O'Connor & Hermelin,1987) and others, reports some evidence for IQ-related differences (range 50–114), with higher IQ associated with better performance: a wider range of calendar knowledge and better application of rules in other tasks. The finding was particularly robust when based on the Performance subscale of the Wechsler Adult Intelligence scale (WAIS).

In a study of one of the most impressive young calendar calculating savants, Thioux, Stark, Klaiman, and Schultz (2006) tried to account for the child's performance with a series of studies that led to an explanatory model for his behavior. The model includes three components: memory of 14 calendars stored in the form of 14 verbal associative networks; processes that access these 14 calendars through "anchoring years" close to the present; finally, simple arithmetic operations based on calendar rules to match past and future with a year already associated with a calendar. Here is how Thioux et al. describe their findings:

> *Our working hypothesis is that the appearance of savant skills is determined not only by the presence of circumscribed interests but also by a specific profile of neuropsychological abilities including, in the case of calendar skills, strong rote memory and good elementary calculation ability.... The model presented here suggests that calendar skills may rely mostly on parietal areas of the brain because this region is important both for simple calculation (addition and subtraction) and for rote verbal memorization of multiplication facts, which we believe is a process quite similar to memorizing date-weekday association.... In summary, we propose that two conditions are necessary and probably sufficient for the development of savant skills: (a) the presence of circumscribed foci of interests with a predilection for repeating behaviors and (b) the relative preservation of parietal lobe learning abilities. (pp. 1167–1168)*

Two other areas where savant syndrome research has influenced the field of intelligence are the venerable issue of one versus several intelligences, typically described as "g" versus "s" theories of intelligence; and the related question of the existence of distinct "modules" that are innately available and that are designed to respond to and process specific kinds of information (e.g., musical, linguistic, spatial, social, etc.). Within the savant syndrome research community, there has been growing consensus that an adequate theory of intelligence needs to be able to account for the reality of savant behavior, and this consensus leads to a tendency to embrace one or another form of "multiple intelligence" theory (Gardner, 1983; Miller, 1999, 2005; Treffert, 1989, 2006, 2008, 2009).

Miller (1999) concludes an extensive review of the savant research literature with the argument that the existence of savants supports multiple-intelligence frameworks:

> *The traditional notion that savants represent exceptionality in the context of general mental retardation has been modified in recent definitions. The consistent finding of at least some intact component skills in savants stands in contrast to the inconsistent evidence for special motivational conditions or tutoring. This suggests that modular explanations of savant behavior are likely to fare better than those stressing more generic factors in skill acquisition.... [T]he types of skills found in savants... are at best loosely congruent with current modular models (e.g., Gardner, 1983). (p. 36)*

Taking this conclusion more cautiously, Treffert, whose career has been spent studying and working with savants, sees the general versus specific theories of intelligence issue as far from resolved: Arguing for comparative studies involving prodigies, genius, and savants, Treffert (2009) calls for such research:

> *since the interface between genius, prodigies and savants is an important, and in some ways a very narrow one, those persons should be included also in the multidisciplinary, multimodality compare and contrast studies. Such studies can shed light on the debate regarding general intelligence versus separate intelligences. (p. 1355)*

On the other hand, in describing the more extreme "prodigious" cases of savant abilities, Treffert (1989) leaves little doubt that a theory that includes separate intelligences as well as general intelligence is necessary:

> *In the prodigious savant . . . the skills are so spectacular, and the inherent access to the rules and "language" behind those skills so extensive, that there must be, at least as part of the reason, a genetic endowment that somehow is preserved apart from, and that exists separately from, overall intelligence. (p. 222)*

These recent efforts calling for a theory that transcends the either/or debate over one versus more than one intelligence appear to be moving toward a more nuanced view (see Chapter 22, Intelligence and the Cognitive Unconscious, this volume). Based on both prodigy and savant research, the existence of relatively isolated, relatively specific natural abilities seems likely to be confirmed. The existence of at least some domain-general abilities is also likely to be affirmed. The questions become more about how the specific and the more general abilities interact, influence each other, and explain the range and diversity of intellectual profiles found in our species.

The related topic of modules (Fodor, 1983) and/or modularization (Karmiloff-Smith, 1992) of functions has tended to play itself out largely around the topic of language development, an area of deficit in virtually all savant cases. For this reason, much of the work on modules is only indirectly relevant to savants. There have been only a few language savants, however, and these have been controversial and closely studied because of their potential direct relevance to the modularity issue.

The case of "Christopher" has been at the center of the discussion in recent years. Christopher is a remarkable language savant who can read, write, and translate between and among more than a dozen languages. Smith and Tsimpli (1995) wrote a book about Christopher, in which they claim that his abilities provide compelling evidence for a "language module" that functions quite independently from general intelligence. Follow-up work (Tsimpli & Smith, 1999) responds to criticism of their claims that Christopher proves by his amazing abilities the existence of such a language module. The disputed evidence turns on whether Christopher is sufficiently impaired in general intelligence to support the claim that his language abilities (which are indeed protean) function independently of "cognitive prerequisites" associated with a mental age of about five years.

When Christopher's intelligence was tested, his performance IQ was consistently lower than his verbal intelligence (Bates, 1997), with scores on nonverbal tests ranging from 42 to 76 and verbal scores all above average. The question is what specifically are the prerequisites of cognitive development that may underlie first-language acquisition, and there is no clear consensus on this question. If Smith and Tsimpli (1995) are right, Christopher functions in language areas substantially independent of general cognitive development, thus supporting the modularity claim. If not, then his first language acquisition was enabled normally, that is, bootstrapped off general cognitive functions available between 3 and 5 years of age in normal developing children.

A key issue is that Christopher's abilities in his first language (English) are unremarkable; what is remarkable is his ability to learn second languages. It may be that the same abilities are involved with both processes or that there are differences between them. At the least, learning a first language is (logically) prerequisite to learning the second, and so on. The arguments are complex and technical, but the conclusions reached at this point seem tentative. There is evidence that some functions of language are independent of more general cognitive development and general intelligence, and there is some evidence that learning one's first language depends at least in part on at least some of the functions attributed to general cognitive development. Tsimpli and Smith

(1998) offered a reasonable summary of the current situation:

> *Language is only partially modular. It also belongs in the central system. This is not just vague anarchic agnosticism; we have made explicit suggestions about which parts of language belong in which domain. (p. 213)*

Although the questions of specific versus general functions and modules versus general intelligence are not fully resolved, research with savants has helped to sharpen the issues and provide important data that bear directly on the issues.

Brain Studies of Savants

Because savants are often in institutional care, they are frequently the responsibility of the medical community. The desire to learn about the source of the savant's abilities and disabilities has led to studies of brain function, morphology, and development. Although not many studies exist, there is a sufficient number to offer some provisional interpretations of brain and central nervous system involvement in savants.

Current imaging technologies provide clear views of savant brain architecture, allowing comparisons to be made with normal brains. Brain function, however, has been more difficult to access because most technologies require that subjects remain immobile during the procedure (e.g., computed tomography [CT], magnetic resonance imaging [MRI]). Some newer techniques (e.g., positron emission tomography [PET], functional magnetic resonance imaging [fMRI], and single photon emission computed tomography-computed tomography [SPECT-CT]) allow activity (e.g., drawing) during the imaging procedure. The newest ones (e.g., diffusion tensor imaging, diffusion tensor tracking) provide information about brain connectivity between hemispheres and other parts of the brain, as well as images of brain fibers, that is, the "wiring" of the brain. Near infrared spectroscopy allows the subject to perform music or paint while wearing an infrared cap (Treffert, 2009).

Young's (1995) previously referenced work was the largest study of savants to date and included 51 cases (12 "prodigious," 20 "talented," and 19 with "splinter" skills). All had neurological impairments but preserved neurological capacity for information processing in their specific area of skill. A process of atypical brain development may account for some savants, that is, left brain dysfunction (language, abstract reasoning, reflection) with right brain compensation. This applies to both congenital and acquired savant skills. Comparable compensatory brain functioning has been found in other populations, as well. Miller and colleagues (Miller et al., 1998; Miller, Boone, Cummings, & Mishkin, 2000) and Hou and colleagues (2000), studying fronto-temporal dementia patients, found that this condition generally involved loss of function in the left temporal lobe with enhanced functioning of the posterior neocortex (Treffert, 2009).

There is also growing acknowledgment of greater than previously believed plasticity in brain development and function. As has been found in studies of brain development in normal subjects (cf. Thompson & Nelson, 2001), savants appear to recruit and reassign brain materials for the specialized purposes of their skill (Treffert, 2009). The ability of the brain to recruit resources from areas that are not usually devoted to the functions that savants develop appears in both congenital and acquired cases. These findings, should they be confirmed by future studies, have implications for our understanding of intelligence and how its more general and more specific forms are developed.

General Conclusions

The past few decades have seen significant progress in research with prodigies and savants. The field of prodigy studies has been revived and, although not large, has produced a steady flow of research and some important new findings and interpretations. The area of savant studies has seen a marked increase in activity, stimulated in part by the availability of new technologies for brain imaging that include the possibility of studying savants while they are actively engaged with their skill area. In this concluding section, we summarize some of the noteworthy advances in each area of study and put forward some provisional generalizations about the ways in which more general and more specific kinds of intelligence interact, placing what appear to be opposite extremes within a single interpretive framework.

Progress in Prodigies Research

For prodigies, there is considerable evidence that extremely high IQ is not a prerequisite for prodigious achievement. The more likely relationship between IQ and child prodigies is that IQ in the average range sets the lower boundary between prodigy and savant. For some domains (e.g., mathematics, physics), an IQ much higher than average is probably a necessary prerequisite for prodigious achievement (cf. Simonton, 1999), while for visual art an extremely high IQ may be an impediment to the emphasis on the figurative aspects of knowledge essential for that kind of endeavor (cf. Milbrath, 1998).[2]

Recent research tends to affirm that child prodigies can be found among girls, in some fields more frequently than boys. There were few girls found in research studies before the 1980s, although there have been some famous girl prodigies in the public eye for centuries (cf., Goldsmith, 1987). In the visual arts, though no cases had been documented in scientific case studies before 1980 (there were autistic girl artists like Nadia; see Selfe, 1977), artists like Wang Yani (Ho, 1989) and the cases in Milbrath (1998) are mostly girls.

There has been progress in distinguishing between mathematical prodigies and calculating savants (sometimes called calculating prodigies). Historically (cf. Smith 1983), calendar calculators and arithmetic calculators were called prodigies. Since diagnostic procedures were not available to determine how many such cases were also autistic, mentally impaired, or both, there is no way to be sure, but recent child prodigy studies have found no cases of individuals younger than 10 years old that would meet the definition of adult professional performance in the domain of mathematics as it is now practiced. It appears likely that the widely held belief that there have been mathematics prodigies is inaccurate, and that the cases so labeled were actually calculating savants of various IQ levels (see later discussion on IQ and savant skill development) or even high-IQ individuals with apparent savant-like skills.

This labeling dilemma is worth pondering in more depth. As a case for definitional discussion, consider George Parker Bidder (1806–1878), one of the most brilliant 19th-century English civil engineers. Bidder is recorded as having been able, by the age of 10, to solve calculations such as dividing 468,592,413,563 by 9,076 (Campbell, 2005). The question arises: Was Bidder a savant, a high-IQ savant (autistic or autistic), a prodigy, or a high-IQ individual with savant-like skills?

It is clear from the level of his adult achievement that Bidder possessed sufficient general cognitive ability to be considered a "prodigy" or even a high-IQ savant rather than either a talented or prodigious savant, as classically defined. Bidder's later achievements in engineering, debate, and politics, with all that implies in the sense of complex professional and social demands (Clark & Linfoot, 1983), rules out the classical savant possessing extraordinary skills standing in stark contrast to overall handicap, or even the notion of his being a high-IQ autistic savant like Daniel Tammet, since such would imply considerable social deficits.

Was he a nonautistic savant? In 1856, Bidder made a presentation to the Institution of Civil Engineers, carefully laying

2 Although Milbrath's interpretation of the interplay between figurative and operative processes seems plausible, a case like Leonardo da Vinci seems to contradict it. A man of immense intelligence as well as an artist of great stature, Leonardo may be an exception that proves the rule.

out the principal operations and algorithms involved in his mental computation. As a very simple example, he reported that to multiply two 3-digit numbers, he started from the left, multiplying first the hundreds together, and adding each successive product to the total so as to hold as few intermediate sums in his head during the calculation as possible (Clark & Linfoot, 1983). He carried in his head key results from earlier calculations, learned to use successive approximations, and deduced new rules as he went along. Unlike Tammet and other savants, whose numerical abilities are largely intuitive and unconscious, Bidder's calculations were conscious and explicitly logical. He was capable of analyzing them and explicating them, and even believed that his methods could be taught to children to improve their mental arithmetic. Bidder also reported that he visualized numbers as shapes in his mind, a predilection that he attributed to the fact that he began to calculate before he learned to write (Clark & Linfoot, 1983). Daniel Tammet also reports that numbers appear in three-dimensional shapes in his mind. Unlike Bidder, however, Tammet reports that these shapes spontaneously chunk together to generate a mathematical solution. He then reads off the "numerical landscape," a process typical of savant skills (Snyder, 2009).

Was Bidder, then, a prodigy? The deciding rule of thumb would be whether at that time, arithmetic calculation was considered a culturally recognized domain of achievement ripe for prodigies, with associated standards for professional-level performance. While Bidder, as a child, developed a national reputation as a "calculating boy" who performed at local fairs and even, at one point, for the queen, calculating alone failed to parlay itself into a professional path. Bidder required a viable profession, such as engineering, for him to use his calculating skills productively and to contribute to society.

Ultimately, what we can conclude is that Bidder was a high-IQ individual with savant-like domain specific skills. His introspective reports and later professional achievement leave no doubt that his skills reflected robust executive functioning and extraordinary conscious analytical and logical skills harnessed in the process of calculation. Nevertheless, his childhood domain of achievement did not allow for the emergence of a prodigy whose level of performance could be assessed as equal to that of an adult professional, since standards for "adult professionals" did not exist – nor did adult professionals exist in the field of mathematical calculation at that point in history.

Availability of appropriate resources, technologies, instruction, and opportunities for recognition enable or constrain the expression of prodigy possibilities, as do broader cultural and historical contexts that may impact opportunities and possibilities. In the extreme, a war on home soil is certain to constrain organized development and recognition of exceptional performance in all prodigy fields. On the other hand, the same conditions may make the appearance of prodigious achievement more likely in other domains; Joan of Arc may be an example from history of a prodigy in military leadership (Feldman, with Goldsmith, 1986).

Research on prodigies bears on the general versus specific intelligence issue, although it does not support an either/or resolution. The prodigy reveals a complex relationship between more general and more specific aspects of intelligence (as does the savant, as we discuss later). For the prodigy, an IQ in the average range (minimally about 90–110) seems necessary as a contributor to the amazing performance that is the hallmark of the child prodigy. The general intelligence aspect of prodigy performance seems to give the child access to the social, cultural, and specific traditions of the domain, to allow for generalization and reflection, as well as give the child access to the social, emotional, and pedagogical dimensions of the field. These broader aspects of the knowledge domain and its context provide access to and a basis for the child's progress in reaching the higher levels of his or her domain.

The more specific aspects of intelligence help determine which domain the child will engage, and which specific areas the child will pursue (e.g., in music, instrument choice, musical genre, pedagogical tradition, performance venues, and the like). Specific talents for particular kinds of activities (e.g., chess versus visual art) are related to but not determined by general intellectual abilities. It is in the interplay between more general abilities and more specific talents that the child prodigy's area of achievement will crystallize. Both general as well as specific aspects of intelligence are involved in the choice of domain, the kind of activity within that domain, and the level of achievement ultimately reached through their sustained interplay.

Progress in Research With Savants

Savants are now seen more as a source of knowledge about brain and cognitive functions and less as anomalies (Treffert, 1989, 2006). Whereas most research on child prodigies remains based on single or small case studies, savant research now includes larger samples, some experimental studies, and several sustained research centers with systematic programs of research. What has emerged from this heightened activity is a better understanding of savant syndrome, recognition that the constraints on savant performance are not as severe as once believed, and an understanding that general intelligence is likely to be a moderating variable that helps determine how and why a savant does what he (or occasionally, she) does.

Perhaps the greatest advances in understanding of the savant mind have been with calendar savants (and calendar "prodigies" and "calculators," who tend to have higher IQs). It now seems likely that the severity of the disabilities that accompany the specific talents of the savant, as well as the degree of general intellectual impairment, largely determine the initial involvement in calendar activity, the degree of skill, and the range of the savant's capabilities, as well as the likelihood that a savant will continue his or her preoccupation with the activity into adulthood (cf. Cowan, Stainthorp, Kapnogianni, & Anastiou, 2004).

The main reasons for continuing to pursue savant-like activities are that they provide a sense of competence and that they are recognized and admired in the (typically) institutional context (Miller, 1999; Treffert, 2000, 2006). If a savant at some point is able to function in the wider community, the likelihood of sustaining and enhancing the specific savant skills diminishes (Cowan et al., 2004). The greater the constraints from other limitations and/or impairments, the greater the likelihood that the savant will sustain and continue to pursue greater achievements in the circumscribed domain in which he or she can succeed.

A second advance, also with calendar savants, is in research that has led to a plausible framework to account for their amazing abilities. In a series of elegant studies, Thioux, Stark, Klaiman, and Schultz (2006) were able to construct a relatively straightforward cognitive model to explain how "Donny" (one of the fastest and most accurate calendar savants on record) was able to perform his feats. For Donny, 14 calendar types were stored in long-term memory; these types were accessed through a set of anchoring years close to the present, and a few simple arithmetic calculations link the 14 models with any past or future year. An overall IQ that is not severely retarded, and at least nominal access to the knowledge domain, complete the picture. The model does not demean or lessen the remarkable achievement of the savant, but it does go a long way toward demystifying how and why that achievement occurs.

Finally, brain imaging studies have provided important information on the likely source of savant abilities. Specific areas of the brain that have known functions and that are influenced by various anatomical and/or developmental variations have been found. The picture that is emerging is one that provides a plausible set of possible brain compensation and regeneration processes for savant syndrome and some of its more specific manifestations.

Savant syndrome is often associated with left brain dysfunction (specifically left anterior temporal lobe or LATL), which leads to right brain compensation. The conditions can appear very early, even prenatally, or they can appear later as in cases of frontemporal dementia (FTD) when the functions of a normal brain deteriorate as part of the aging process. In most right-handed individuals, this part of the brain is responsible for language and semantic processing, symbolic representation, and reflection. For the savant, the absence, diminishing, or deterioration of these functions is associated with the kinds of activity characteristic of the savant, particularly the autistic savant.

One way to test whether this interpretation of brain functions (LATL) involved in savant syndrome may be correct is to artificially suppress normal brain functioning through repetitive transcranial magnetic stimulation (rTMS; Snyder, Mulcahy, Taylor, Mitchell, Sachdev, & Gandevia, 2003) of the suspected areas. Results from such studies have shown that savant skill-related capabilities often increased under these conditions (Snyder, 2009).

Although the number of studies of brain functioning and brain-related events in savant behavior is still small compared with research into other aspects of intelligence, the techniques and technologies are promising and advancing rapidly, making it likely that more results will be forthcoming. We should know a great deal more about the brains of savants and others with savant-like skills in the not too distant future (Treffert, 2009).

The Interplay of General and Specific Intellectual Abilities: Transcending the General Versus Specific Intelligence Issue

Given these findings, it appears that a picture of the way in which various degrees and varieties of intelligence interact to produce both prodigies and savants is emerging. In this respect, research with extreme cases has shed light on the long-standing debate between advocates of a more general interpretation of intelligence (typically IQ), and those who favor a more multiple intelligence–oriented view (e.g., Gardner's [1983] multiple intelligences, Sternberg's [1985] triarchic theory). In this final section, we summarize how more general and more specific forms of intelligence jointly contribute to the appearance of the kinds of individuals we have called prodigies and savants.

If we assume that human evolution of intellectual abilities has had variations and redundancies built into the system over time, as is true of other species, it seems likely that our brains include more than one way to respond to the challenges of our environments (Snyder, 2009). Most of our primate ancestors were specialized to habitat (although importantly not all; cf. Bruner, 1971). For humans, however, a distinctive feature of our evolution has been that it has equipped us to adapt to and thrive in highly varied environments. What we call general intelligence seems to be one of the main sources of this distinctly human capability (Feldman, 2003).

The tendency of evolution to "hedge its bets" with many variations and combinations of general and specific abilities helps explain humanity's selective advantage over its competitors for resources (Feldman, with Goldsmith, 1986). The extreme examples of specific ability without general support from IQ (savants) is an example of "niche" evolution that produced people capable of keeping track of the calendar, of telling the time, of remembering names and locations, of calculating sums in important transactions, of carrying and sharing cultural traditions such as stories, songs and poems, and no doubt many other narrowly circumscribed and specific abilities. A savant may be anachronistic given modern technologies for doing the things that they were uniquely able to do historically, but they point to a natural source of specialized talent.

A picture is emerging of intelligences as varying along a continuum of general to specific, with numerous possibilities for combinations that reveal how these combinations may have evolved and how they have been utilized through history. Physical evolution appears to have produced both general (IQ-like) and highly specific (savant-like) abilities; in some individuals a given individual may possess one or the other kind of intelligence and others may be blessed with substantial doses of both. Perhaps an extremely high-IQ individual with no specific talents might tend to function primarily using general, abstract, logical reasoning, while the most constrained savants (e.g., those who can say the day of the week of any date on the calendar) reflect a tendency to evolve highly specific cognitive skills. Depending upon their strength, the degree of general versus specific abilities, and their interaction, a prediction can be made about the possible outcome for a given person, especially at the extremes (Feldman, 1999, 2003).

For individuals who have low (30–50 IQ or so) general ability, but who have a powerful specific ability in a particular area (e.g., music), the probability of a musical savant is likely (given availability of appropriate technology and exposure), but more creative musical ability may prove difficult if not impossible. For individuals with moderate impairment of general ability (50–80 IQ or so), a musical savant, with appropriate encouragement and support (Treffert, 2009), may be capable of improvisation and creative expression comparable to that of a professional musician. For individuals whose general abilities are in the average range (80–110 IQ or so), the kinds of achievements that are associated with prodigies may be possible in some fields (like music and visual art). For individuals whose general abilities (IQ 120–150) are exceptional, along with strong interests and abilities in certain areas (e.g., physics, mathematics), the probabilities of becoming notable achievers in those fields are substantial (Simonton, 1999).

Inspired by the study of prodigies and savants and the ways in which general and specific intelligences are involved in their amazing accomplishments, a coherent interpretation of human abilities has begun to emerge. The issue of general versus specific ability can now be transcended and replaced by an integrated view that turns on the interplay among general and specific intelligences as they express themselves in social, cultural, historical, and evolutionary contexts.

References

Baeck, E. (2002). The neural networks of music. *European Journal of Neurology*, 9(5), 449–460.

Bates, E. (1997). On language savants and the structure of the mind. *International Journal of Bilingualism*, 1(2), 163–186.

Baumgarten, F. (1930). *Wunderkinder psychologische untersuchungen*. Leipzig: Johann Ambrosious Barth. (untranslated)

Bidder, G. P. (1856, February 19 and 26). On mental calculation. Minutes of the proceedings of the Institution of Civil Engineers, Vol. 15, session 1855–56.

Bornstein, M. H., & Krasnegor, N. A. (Eds.). (1989). *Stability and continuity in mental development: Behavioral and biological perspectives*. Hillsdale, NJ: Erlbaum.

Brody, L. E. & Stanley, J. C. (2005). Youths who reason exceptionally well mathematically and/or verbally: Using the MVCT: 4 Model to develop their talents. In R. J. Sternberg & J. E. Davidson (Eds.), *Conceptions of giftedness* (2nd ed., pp. 20–37). New York, NY: Cambridge University Press.

Bruner, J. (1971). The nature and uses of immaturity. *American Psychologist*, 27, 1–22.

Butterworth, B. (2001). What makes a prodigy? *Nature Neuroscience*, 4(1), 11–12.

Campbell, J. I. D. (2005). *Handbook of mathematical cognition*. New York, NY: Psychology Press.

Clark, E. F., & Linfoot, J. J. (1983). George Parker Bidder: The calculating prodigy. *Institute of Mathematics and Its Applications*, 23, 68–71.

Conway, F., & Siegelman, J. (2005). *Dark hero of the information age: In search of Norbert Wiener, the father of cybernetics*. New York, NY: Basic Books.

Cowan, R., Stainthorp, R., Kapnogianni, S., & Anastasiou, M. (2004). The development of calendrical skills. *Cognitive Development*, 19(2), 169–178.

Edmunds, A. L., & Noel, K. A. (2003). Literary precocity: An exceptional case among exceptional cases. *Roeper Review*, 25(4), 185–194.

Ericsson, K. A. (Ed.). (1996). *The road to excellence: The acquisition of expert performance in the arts and sciences, sports and games*. Mahwah, NJ: Erlbaum.

Ericsson, K. A., Krampe, R. T., & Tesch-Romer, C. (1993). The role of deliberate practice in the acquisition of expert performance. *Psychological Review*, 100(3), 363–406.

Feldman, D. H., with Goldsmith, L. T. (1986). *Nature's gambit: Child prodigies and the development of human potential*. New York, NY: Basic Books.

Feldman, D. H. (1995). Intelligence in prodigies. In R. Sternberg (Ed.), *Encyclopedia of intelligence* (pp. 845–850). New York, NY: Macmillan.

Feldman, D. H. (1999). A developmental, evolutionary perspective on gifts and talents. *Journal for the Education of the Gifted*, 22(2), 159–167.

Feldman, D. H. (2000). Figurative and operative processes in the development of artistic talent. *Human Development*, 43, 60–64.

Feldman, D. H. (2003). A developmental, evolutionary perspective on gifts and talents. In J. Borland (Ed.), *Rethinking gifted education* (pp. 9–33). New York, NY: Teachers College Press.

Feldman, D. H. (2008). *Prodigies*. In J. Plucker & C. Callahan (Eds.), *Critical issues and practices in gifted education* (pp. 501–512). Waco, TX: Prufrock Press.

Fodor, J. (1983). *The modularity of mind*. Cambridge, MA: MIT Press.

Gardner, H. (1983). *Frames of mind*. New York, NY: Basic Books.

Gardner, H., Kornhaber, M., & Wake, W. (1996). *Intelligence: Multiple perspectives*. Fort Worth, TX: Holt, Rinehart and Winston.

Goldsmith, L. T. (1987). Girl prodigies: Some evidence and some speculations. *Roeper Review*, 10(2), 74–82.

Goldsmith, L. T. (2000). Tracking trajectories of talent: Child prodigies growing up. In R. C. Friedman & B. M. Shore (Eds.), *Talents unfolding: Cognition and development* (pp. 89–118). Washington: American Psychological Association.

Hermelin, B., & O'Connor, N. (1986). Idiot savant calendrical calculators: Rules and regularities. *Psychological Medicine*, 16, 1–9.

Hildesheimer, W. (1982/1977). *Mozart*. New York, NY: Vintage Books.

Hill, A. L. (1977). Idiots-savants: Rate of incidence. *Perceptual and Motor Skills*, 44, 161–162.

Ho, W. (Ed.). (1989). *Yani: The brush of innocence*. New York: Hudson Hills Press.

Hou, C., Miller, B., Cummings, J., Goldberg, M., Mychack, P., Bottino, B., & Benson, F. (2000). Artistic savants. *Neuropsychiatry*, 13, 29–38.

Hollingworth, L. (1942). *Children above 180 IQ*. Yonkers-on-Hudson, NY: World Book. (Reprinted by Arno Press, 1975)

Howard, R. W. (2008). Linking extreme precocity and adult eminence: A study of eight prodigies at international chess. *High Ability Studies*, 19(2), 117–130.

Howe, M. J. A., Davidson, J. W., & Sloboda, J. A. (1998). Innate talents: Reality or myth? *Behavioral and Brain Sciences*, 21, 399–406.

Hulbert, A. (2005, November 30). The prodigy puzzle. *New York Times Magazine*, 64–71.

Johnson, R. (2005, February 12). *A genius explains*. Retrieved July 19, 2009, from http://www.guardian.co.uk/the guardian/2005/feb/12/weekend7.weekend2.

Kanigel, R. (1991). *The man who knew infinity: A life of the genius Ramanujan*. New York, NY: Washington Square Press.

Karmiloff-Smith, A. (1992). *Beyond modularity: A developmental perspective on cognitive science*. Cambridge, MA: MIT Press.

Kearney, K., & Kearney, C. (1998). *Accidental genius*. Juneau, AK: Woodshed Press.

Kenneson, C. (1998). *Musical prodigies: Perilous journeys, remarkable lives*. Portland, OR: Amadeus Press.

Leites, N. S. (1960). *Intellectual giftedness*. Moscow: APN Press.

Leites, N. S. (Ed.). (1996). *Psychology of giftedness of children and adolescents*. Moscow: Academia.

Lubinski, D., & Benbow, C. P. (2006). Study of mathematically precocious youth after 35 years: Uncovering antecedents for the development of math-science expertise. *Perspectives on Psychological Science*, 1(4), 316–345.

Lubinski, D., Benbow, C. P., & Morelock, M. J. (2000). Gender differences in engineering and physical sciences among the gifted: An inorganic-organic distinction. In K. Heller, F. Mönks, R. Sternberg, & R. Subotnik (Eds.), *International handbook of giftedness and talent* (2nd ed., pp. 633–648). New York, NY: Pergamon Press.

Lubinski, D., Webb, R. M., Morelock, M. J., & Benbow, C. P. (2001). 1 in 10,000: A longitudinal study of the profoundly gifted. *Journal of Applied Psychology*, 86, 718–729.

McPherson, G. E. (Ed.). (2006). *The child as musician: A handbook of musical development*. Oxford, UK: Oxford University Press.
McPherson, G. E. (2007). Diary of a child prodigy musician. In A. Williamson & D. Coimbra (Eds.), *Proceedings of the International Symposium on Performance Science 2007* (pp. 213–218). Porto, Portugal: Association of European Conservatories.
Milbrath, C. (1998). *Patterns of artistic development in children: Comparative studies of talent*. New York, NY: Cambridge University Press.
Miller, B. L., Cummings, J., Mishkin, F., Boone, K., Prince, F., Ponton, M., & Cotman, C. (1998). Emergence of artistic talent in frontotemporal dementia. *Neurology, 51*, 978–982.
Miller, B. L., Boone, K., Cummings, L. R., & Mishkin, F. (2000). Functional correlates of musical and visual ability in frontempora dementia. *British Journal of Psychiatry, 176*, 458–463.
Miller, L. K. (1989). *Musical savants: Exceptional skill in the mentally retarded*. Hillsdale, NJ: Erlbaum.
Miller, L. K. (1999). The savant syndrome: Intellectual impairment and exceptional skill. *Psychological Bulletin, 125*(1), 31–46.
Miller, L. K. (2005). What the savant syndrome can tell us about the nature and nurture of talent. *Journal for the Education of the Gifted*, 28(3–4), 361–374.
Morelock, M. J. (1995). *The profoundly gifted child in family context*. Unpublished doctoral dissertation, Tufts University, Medford, MA.
Morelock, M. J. & Feldman, D. H. (1993). Prodigies and savants: What they have to tell us about giftedness and human cognition. In K. A. Heller, F. J. Monks, & A. H. Passow (Eds.), *International handbook of research and development of giftedness and talent* (pp. 161–181). Oxford: Pergamon Press.
Morelock, M. J., & Feldman, D. H. (1999). Prodigies. In M. Runco & S. Pritzker (Eds.), *Encyclopedia of creativity* (pp. 1303–1320). San Diego, CA: Academic Press.
Morelock, M. J., & Feldman, D. H. (2003). Extreme precocity: Prodigies, savants, and children of extraordinarily high IQ. In N. Colangelo & G. A. Davis (Eds.), *Handbook of gifted education* (3rd ed., pp. 455–469). Boston, MA: Allyn & Bacon.
Morelock, M. J., & Feldman, D. H. (2003). Prodigies, savants and Williams Syndrome: Windows into talent and cognition. In F. J. Monks, K. A. Heller, R. J. Sternberg, & R. Subotnik (Eds.), *International handbook for research on giftedness and talent* (2nd ed., pp. 455–469). Oxford, UK: Pergamon Press.
Mursell, J. (1937). *The psychology of music*. New York: W. W. Norton.
O'Boyle, M. (2008a). Adolescent psychopathology and the developing brain. *Journal of Youth and Adolescence, 37*, 481–483.
O'Boyle, M. (2008b). Mathematically gifted children: Developmental brain characteristics and their prognosis for well-being. *Roeper Review, 30*, 181–186.
O'Connor, N. (1989). The performance of the "idiot savant": Implicit and explicit. *British Journal of Disorders of Communication, 24*, 1–20.
O'Connor, N., & Hermelin, B. (1984). Idiot savant calendrical calculators: Math or memory? *Psychological Medicine, 14*, 801–806.
O'Connor, N., & Hermelin, B. (1987). Visual and graphic abilities of the idiot savant artist. *Psychological Medicine, 17*, 79–80.
Patel, A. D. (2008). *Music, language and the brain*. New York: Oxford University Press.
Peek, F. (1997). *The real Rain Man. Salt Lake City*, UT: Harkness.
Peek, F. with Hanson, L. L (2007). *The life and message of the real Rain Main: The journey of a mega-savant*. Port Chester, NY: Dude Publishing/National Professional Resources.
Radford, J. (1990). *Child prodigies and exceptional early achievers*. New York, NY: Free Press.
Revesz, G. (1925/1970). *The psychology of a musical prodigy*. Freeport, NY: Books for Libraries Press.
Rolfe, L. (1978). *The Menuhins: A family odyssey*. San Francisco, CA: Panjandrum Books.
Ruthsatz, J., & Detterman, D. K. (2003). An extraordinary memory: The case study of a musical prodigy. *Intelligence, 31*, 509–518.
Sacks, O. (1995). *An anthropologist on Mars*. New York, NY: Alfred A. Knopf.
Scheerer, M., Rothman, E., & Goldstein, K. (1945). A case of "idiot savant": An experimental study of personality organization. *Psychology Monograph, 58*, 1–63.
Schlaug, G., Jancke, L., Huang, Y., & Steinmetz, H. (1995a). In vivo evidence of structural brain assymetry in musicians. *Science, 267*, 699–701.
Schlaug, G., Jancke, L., Huang, Y., & Steinmetz, H. (1995b). Increased corpus callosum size in musicians. *Neuropsychologica, 33*, 1047–1055.
Selfe, L. (1977). *Nadia: A case of extraordinary drawing ability in an autistic child*. New York, NY: Academic Press.

Shavinina, L. (1999). The psychological essence of the child prodigy phenomenon: Sensitive periods and cognitive experience. *Gifted Child Quarterly*, 43(1), 25–38.

Simonton, D. K. (1994). *Greatness: Why makes history and why*. New York, NY: Guilford Press.

Simonton, D. K. (1999). Talent and its development: An emergenic and epigenetic model. *Psychological Review*, 106(3), 435–457.

Singh, H., & O'Boyle, M. W. (2004). Interhemispheric interaction during global-local processing in mathematically gifted adolescents, average-abillity youth, and college students. *Neuropsychology*, 18(2), 371–377.

Smith, N. V., & Tsimpli, I. (1995). *The mind of a savant: language learning and modularity*. Cambridge, MA: Blackwell.

Smith, S. B. (1983). *The great mental calculators: The psychology, methods, and lives of calculating prodigies past and present*. New York, NY: Columbia University Press.

Snyder, A. (2009). Explaining and inducing savant skills: Privileged access to lower level, less processed information. *Philosophical Transactions of the Royal Society*, 364, 1399–1405.

Snyder, A., Mulcahy, E., Taylor, J., Mitchell, D., Sachdev, P., & Gandevia, S. (2003). Savant-like skills exposed in normal people by suppressing the left fronto-temporal lobe. *Journal of Integrative Neuroscience*, 2, 149–158.

Stanley, J. C. (1996). SMPY in the beginning. In C. P. Benbow & D. Lubinski (Eds.), *Intellectual talent: Psychometric and social issues* (pp. 225–235). Baltimore, MD: Johns Hopkins University Press.

Stanley, J. C. (2000). Helping students learn only what they don't already know. *Psychology, Public Policy, and Law*, 6, 216–222.

Sternberg, R. (1985). *Beyond IQ: A triarchic theory of human intelligence*. New York, NY: Cambridge University Press.

Tammet, D. (2006). *Born on a blue day: Inside the extraordinary mind of an autistic savant*. New York, NY: Free Press.

Tammet, D. (2009). *Embracing the wide sky: A tour across the horizons of the mind*. New York, NY: Free Press.

Tannenbaum, A. (1993). History of giftedness and "gifted education" in world perspective. In K. A. Heller, F. J. Monks, & A. H. Passow (Eds.), *International handbook of research and development of giftedness and talent* (pp. 3–27). Oxford, UK: Pergamon Press.

Thioux, M., Stark, D. E., Klaiman, C., & Schultz, R. T. (2006). The day of the week when you were born in 700 ms: Calendar computation in an autistic savant. *Journal of Experimental Psychology: Human Perception and Performance*, 32(5), 1155–1168.

Thompson, R., & Nelson, C. (2001). Developmental science and the media. *American Psychologist*, 56(1), 5–15.

Treffert, D. (1989). *Extraordinary people: Understanding "idiot savants."* New York: Harper & Row.

Treffert, D. (2000). *Extraordinary people: Understanding savant syndrome*. Lincoln, NE: iuniverse.com.

Treffert, D. (2006). *Extraordinary people: Understanding savant syndrome*. Omaha, NE: iuniverse.

Treffert, D. (2008). *Myths that persist: Savant syndrome* 2008. Retrieved from http://www.wisconsinmedicalsociety.org/savant_syndrome/savant_articles/myths_that_persist.

Treffert, D. (2009). The savant syndrome: An extraordinary condition. A synopsis: Past, present, future. *Philosophical Transactions of the Royal Society*, 364, 1351–1357.

Tsimpli, I., & Smith, N. (1999). Modules and quasi-modules: Language and theory of mind in a polyglot savant. *Learning and Individual Differences*, 10(3), 193–215.

Viscott, D. S. (1970). A musical idiot savant. *Psychiatry*, 33, 494–515.

Wallace, A. (1986). *The prodigy: A biography of William James Sidis, America's greatest child prodigy*. New York, NY: Dutton.

Wiener, N. (1953). *Ex-prodigy: My childhood and youth*. Cambridge, MA: MIT Press.

Winner, E. (1982). *Invented worlds*. Cambridge, MA: Harvard University Press.

Winner, E. (1996). The rage to master: The decisive role of talent in the visual arts. In K. A. Ericsson (Ed.), *The road to excellence: The acquisition of expert performance in the arts and sciences, sports and games* (pp. 271–301). Mahwah, NJ: Erlbaum.

Young, R. (1995). *Savant syndrome: Processes underlying extraordinary abilities*. Unpublished doctoral dissertation, University of Adelaide, South Australia.

Zimmerman, R. (Writer) (1989). A Real Rainman [VHS Film]. U.S.A.: Simitar Entertainment.

CHAPTER 12

Intellectual Giftedness

Sally M. Reis and Joseph S. Renzulli

The study of gifts and talents and how innate abilities interact with one's environment, personality, educational opportunities, family support, and life experiences has fascinated psychologists, educators, and parents for decades. Why is it that one child with remarkably high potential born into a particular family in a particular environment grows up to become a neurosurgeon while a child of similar intellectual potential who lives in the same community and attends the same schools, decides to drop out of high school? What have researchers and scholars learned in the last few decades about the nature of talent development and intellectual giftedness? What general concepts are widely accepted about intellectual giftedness? How is it defined and can it be developed? What combinations of genetic abilities and talents interact with one's environment and personality to result in the development of intellectual giftedness?

In this chapter, these questions, none of which can be answered simply, are discussed and current research about intellectual giftedness is summarized. As the research points out, one of the core concepts that has emerged about intellectual giftedness in the last few decades relates to its diversity, for there is no more varied group of people than those labeled intellectually gifted (Neihart, Reis, Robinson, & Moon, 2002). Those labeled gifted as children and/or adults are found in every ethnic and socioeconomic group and in every culture (Sternberg, 2004). They exhibit an unlimited range of personal and learning characteristics and differ in effort, temperament, educational and vocational attainment, productivity, creativity, risk taking, introversion, and extraversion (Renzulli & Reis, 2003; Renzulli & Park, 2002). They have variable abilities to self-regulate and sustain the effort needed to achieve personally, academically, and in their careers (Housand & Reis, 2009). And despite the label that this diverse population has been given, within the population some do and some do not demonstrate high levels of accomplishment in their education or their chosen professions and work (Reis & McCoach, 2000; Renzulli & Park, 2002).

Despite this broad diversity, however, several common themes about intellectual giftedness and the conditions for its development exist. We begin our review of the research related to intellectual giftedness with a discussion of these themes, summarizing highlights about research on intellectual giftedness in the United States, including the seminal work of Lewis Terman, and presenting an overview of what we believe to be some interesting and potentially important American theories to date. We conclude the chapter with some interesting research-based trends related to new ideas in defining and developing academic gifts and talents. It is important to understand, however, that there is no agreed-upon consensus about who is gifted and no final answers about our evolving understandings of how intellectual giftedness develops and the characteristics that help us to identify and nurture intellectual gifts and talents. To introduce the challenge associated with both defining and identifying giftedness in students, four brief case studies are introduced below.

Four Case Studies

Dwayne

Dwayne was identified as a gifted student in first grade. Highly verbal and the son of two university professors, he read at age 4, was exceptionally analytical, and excelled in nursery school and first grade, particularly in his verbal skills. His energy and enthusiasm for learning were noted by all of his teachers and both his kindergarten and first grade teacher referred him for the gifted program in his school despite the fact that formal identification for most students did not usually occur until fourth grade. Dwayne excelled in the primary grades, but with each year that passed, he struggled more with schoolwork that depended upon his ability to write. In fourth grade, despite very high abilities, he had begun to express his difficulties in writing. At this point, his classroom teacher suspected that Dwayne might have a learning disability and discussed dysgraphia with his parents for the first time. Dysgraphia, a learning disability connected to the graphomotor aspect of writing, is often identified by examining and evaluating writing samples for word and letter spacing, that is, how and if the letters fit on the line and the quality of what is written. Students with dysgraphia often struggle with holding pencils and writing for long periods of time. Dwayne's teachers also described him as shaking his hands and constantly stretching and rubbing his hands, wrists, or fingers while writing. Dwayne began to use overly simplistic language and very short sentences in his minimal writing. When questioned orally, he responded with fluency and insight, but when he had to write in class, his work resulted in short stilted responses with limited description. As Dwayne matured, his lack of attention in class and academic struggles intensified, despite his scores at the 99th percentile in IQ assessments in both verbal and figural areas. His fourth grade teacher and the special education teacher suggested a series of academic recommendations in both special and gifted education as part of an individual education plan for Dwayne.

Lily was in second grade when her teachers recommended her for participation in the gifted program. She was highly verbal and read at approximately the seventh grade level, excelling in every aspect of her academic work. Gifted program participation in her school was not dependent upon scores on IQ tests, and Lily was identified based on her achievement tests (99th percentile in all academic areas), teacher nominations, leadership and creativity, and classroom work. Lily was a high-achieving student throughout elementary and secondary school and graduated in the top three of her class, earning entrance to an Ivy League university.

However, prior to her freshman year in high school, her parents moved and she transferred to a new school district that required an IQ test for formal identification as gifted. Her score was 119, well below the cutoff for gifted program entrance in the new school district. Despite being a star in the gifted program in her former district, she was denied entrance to the program in her new district. Lily, however, excelled in all of her AP and Honors courses, scored over 700 on each of her SATs, completed a complex and highly evaluated senior year project, and ultimately entered and made the dean's list at her highly prestigious university.

Kendra

Kendra was a shy, quiet fifth-grader who had been identified as gifted in second grade in a school in which a 130 cutoff score on an individually administered IQ test was used to determine which students qualified for the gifted program. An avid reader and introvert, she displayed few characteristics related to most traditional notions of giftedness. Although she loved to read, she did not initially appear to display verbal precocity. Her current teachers had not observed any indications of problem solving, reasoning, insight, or other commonly acknowledged characteristics of academic giftedness. Kendra was primarily known for being quiet, kind, and an advanced reader who did not like to discuss or share what she was reading, perhaps due to her shyness. As she grew up, she remained a quiet and passive learner who despite her intelligence rarely spoke in class and achieved well but was not outstanding in any one particular area.

Patrick

Patrick was identified as gifted in third grade; however his ensuing schoolwork frustrated both his parents and teachers for years following his identification and placement in a gifted program. Always a child of very high potential, Patrick's grades fluctuated in elementary, middle, and senior high school. To qualify as gifted in his district, Patrick had to achieve an IQ score above 130 on an aptitude assessment in addition to demonstrating high achievement in the classroom. He enjoyed discussing his ideas with others and was highly verbal, but he had poor work habits in required subjects. As the years progressed, Patrick's work became less and less impressive, and his teachers questioned his identification as gifted. His writing was considered below average and the only class in which he consistently excelled was math.

Patrick disliked reading anything that was unrelated to his interests. His grades varied, from top marks in math and technology to failing grades in subjects that did not interest him. Although he took advanced math classes in middle and high school and achieved a near-perfect score on the math section of the SAT, during his junior year of high school, Patrick's teachers and parents labeled him an "underachiever" because of his fluctuating performance in and attitudes about school. He rarely displayed characteristics of a gifted student in classes in which he did not have an interest. His technology and math teachers realized his potential and saw his talents in problem solving, persistence, and creativity. Few other teachers noted any positive characteristics and he continued to underachieve in school, attaining below average grades.

Common Themes Related to Intellectual Giftedness

As these brief case studies illustrate, despite decades of attempts to study and identify a standard pattern of intellectual giftedness among high-potential children and individuals, no clear pathway has been identified and no specific formula exists regarding the "right" combination of genes, personality, and environment needed to produce intellectual giftedness. In other words, we do not know which combinations of genes and environment interact to produce a desired outcome, such as a specific talent or gift (Bronfenbrenner & Ceci, 1994). We know, for example, that a child who has high scientific aptitude, who likes science, and whose parents are scientists will have more opportunities, resources, and encouragement in science than a child with the same cognitive aptitude who does not like science and whose parents do not have similar patterns of education and interest in this area. The child with interest in and parental support for science is, of course, more likely to seek a college degree and perhaps a career in this area. However, the nuances related to the development of intellectual giftedness are many and varied, and the child with high aptitude, interest, and parental support may subsequently encounter negative school experiences in science, deflating his interests and derailing him from the science pipeline. If positive elementary and secondary school experiences continue to enhance scientific interests, negative college experiences (i.e., a first low grade in organic chemistry or an understanding of the struggles associated with earning a Ph.D. and finding work in research in this field) may also change aspirations and careers choices. Gifts and talents emerge in conjunction with a series of environmental events and personality variables – and of course chance factors (Tannenbaum, 1991). Any discussion of intellectual giftedness must acknowledge the importance of these factors in the development of this construct. This is even true in persons of the highest levels of cognitive ability, as suggested by Lubinski, Webb, Morelock, and Benbow (2001), who found variability in the accomplishments of this group. Lubinski and colleagues (2001) investigated the patterns of those in the top 1% or higher of cognitive abilities and identified some variation in both development trajectories and important life accomplishments. They found that the likelihood of earning a doctorate, earning exceptional compensation, publishing novels, securing patents, and earning tenure at a top university varied as a function of the individual differences in childhood cognitive abilities assessed decades earlier, suggesting the need to study the importance of both genetic and environmental origins of exceptional abilities, a finding also noted by Terman decades earlier (1925).

In this review of research on intellectual giftedness, several important themes emerged. The first is that giftedness is comprised of an open, dynamic, intentional system that is capable of building increasingly complex behaviors through self-organization and self-direction (Dai & Renzulli, 2008; Renzulli, 2005). Themes that guide this chapter also include the many ways in which intellectual giftedness develops; the ways in which cultures define and influence giftedness; the presence and importance of nonintellectual components of intellectual giftedness; the many ways used to assess intellectual giftedness which, according to Sternberg (2000), are too often validated almost exclusively against the societally approved criteria and thus provide an appearance of validity that may not exist within a specific sociocultural group (Sternberg, 2000); and the importance of understanding that there is no right or wrong way to define intellectual giftedness. Some theorists believe that we can identify gifted individuals across domains, even children at a young age, as if there is a golden chromosome that enables one to be identified with the right assessment tools. Others believe that giftedness occurs within a domain, such as those who are scientifically or mathematically gifted. Different conceptions of giftedness across cultures (Phillipson & McCann, 2007) suggest emerging research and understandings of the ways in which languages and cultures influence and contribute to giftedness in Western, Chinese, Japanese, Australian Aboriginal, and Malaysian cultures, for example, suggesting that creativity and problem solving are important attributes of giftedness across these cultures.

The themes that appear across many contemporary conceptions of giftedness are briefly discussed next. They illustrate the difficulties of defining giftedness and identifying intellectually gifted individuals, for as our own research has found, giftedness is manifested in certain individuals, at certain times, and under certain circumstances (Renzulli, 1986; Renzulli & Reis, 2003).

Intellectual Giftedness Is Developmental

Over three decades ago, Renzulli summarized research suggesting that giftedness existed in certain people, at certain times, and under certain circumstances (Renzulli, 1978, 1986, 2005). This notion of giftedness argues against considering giftedness as a trait such as eye color or something that a child has or does not possess. Currently, many other researchers also support developmental constructs of giftedness. For example, Gagne's (2000) Differentiated Model of Giftedness and Talent (DMGT) is another developmental theory that distinguishes giftedness from talent and discusses how outstanding natural abilities (gifts) can develop into specific expert skills (talents). Gagne believes that those labeled as gifted have the potential for extraordinary work and that those who are subsequently identified as talented develop their inherent potential for contributions. He identifies six components that interact in multiple ways to foster the transition of moving from having natural abilities (giftedness) to systematically developed skills (Gagne, 2000). These components include the gift itself, chance, environmental catalysts, intrapersonal catalysts, learning/practice, and the outcome of talent (Gagne, 2000).

Many of the chapter authors in two seminal books on conceptions of giftedness edited by Sternberg and Davidson (1986, 2005) identify similar themes related to the developmental nature of intellectual giftedness. Simonton (2005), for example, proposed a model of giftedness in which talents result from the coming together of genetic components that develop on individual trajectories. These genetic components would include any and all characteristics needed to develop a particular gift, such as superior visual spatial skills or a high degree of mathematical creativity in gifted mathematicians. Simonton suggested further that the absence or late development of a key trait would prevent or delay the development of a given talent. This model provides an explanation for why individuals begin to demonstrate talents at different times, and why certain types of talents emerge earlier while others emerge later in life. In another publication, Subotnik and Jarvin (2005) proposed that giftedness can be equated to high performance. In this model, superior abilities must be transformed into competencies, then expertise, and, in rare cases, finally to "elite talent" (p. 343). This is a process that occurs through practice, environmental factors, and maturation, with timelines varying across individuals and gifts.

The Multidimensional Aspects of Intellectual Giftedness

Few, if any, researchers or theorists who have studied intelligence or intellectual giftedness continue to believe that giftedness is unidimensional rather than multidimensional. Similar to psychologists who believe in the multidimensional aspects of intelligence (Carroll, 1993; Gustafsson & Undheim, 1996), theorists who study intellectual giftedness (Gagne, 2000; Gardner, 1993; Renzulli, 1986, 2005; Sternberg, 1997) agree that we must look beyond the traditional early notions stating that intellectual giftedness can be equated with a high score on one assessment such as an IQ test. In fact, recent research on assessment has found that large, significant discrepancies among verbal, figural, and quantitative reasoning abilities as measured by standardized IQ tests are more common among high- and low-ability students than among average-ability students (Lohman, Gambrell, & Lakin, 2008; Shavinia, 2001; Sternberg, 2000). Lohman, Gambrell, and Lakin, for example, examined the score profiles of students obtaining stanine scores of 9 on at least two batteries of a standardized achievement test. They found that the percentage of these highly able students demonstrating an "extreme" or significant weakness in at least one of the three tested areas – verbal, spatial, or quantitative reasoning – was equal to the percentage of students with more even profiles. They noted that this finding suggests that gifted programs using a single composite IQ score for identification may miss many highly able students whose scores are brought down by a single area of relative weakness.

Several multiple conceptions of intellectual giftedness have been suggested by many researchers; these range from general, broad, and overarching characterizations to more specific definitions of giftedness identified by *specific* actions, products, or abilities within certain domains (Sternberg & Davidson, 2005). This research, generally conducted during the last few decades, supports a more broad-based conception of giftedness as a combination of multiple qualities, in addition to intellectual potential, which includes nonintellectual traits such as motivation and creativity (Renzulli, 1978, 2005; Sternberg & Lubart, 1995) and positive beliefs in self (Reis, 2005).

Diverse Patterns in Intellectual Giftedness

As illustrated by the case studies and earlier discussion, those labeled intellectually gifted are a varied group with differing cognitive profiles, learning disabilities, attention deficits, varied learning styles, issues related to procrastination and perfectionism, and faster or slower processing speeds. They may demonstrate asynchronous (uneven) development, cognitive and/or academic relative strengths and weaknesses, or learning disabilities (Reis, Neu, & McGuire, 1997). Sternberg's (1997) work suggests that many different patterns of giftedness may exist and change over time.

Culture, Gender, and Environment Influence Intellectual Giftedness

The notion of intellectual giftedness itself has and will continue to have different meanings for different people, and discussions and debates about these meanings are often influenced by the culture, environment, and context in which the gifts emerge as well as the values associated with each (Simonton, 1998). Not surprisingly, within different cultures, contexts, and environments, the outcomes of intellectual giftedness vary. Cultural influences can negatively or positively affect the choices and products that emanate from one's gifts, and the ability to select, shape, and/or adapt one's environment (Sternberg, 1996; Sternberg & Grigorenko, 2000). Gender also has an impact on giftedness, as little doubt exists that gifted males in many cultures far surpass gifted women in accomplishment and professional attainments (Reis, 1998).

Reis explored the paths leading to female talent realization in women in a study of 22 American women who gained eminence in diverse fields over a decade (Reis, 1998). Each eminent woman was recognized as a major contributor in her field, and several achieved the distinction of being the first or one of the first women in her respective domain, such as theater, politics, academe, literature and poetry, science, musical composition, government, business, environmental sciences, art, education, and other fields.

Reis proposed a theory of talent development in women (Reis, 2002, 2005) that includes abilities (intelligence and special talents), personality traits, environmental factors, and personal perceptions, such as the social importance of the use of one's talents to make a positive difference in the world. Underlying this theory is the belief that talent is developed in women of high potential through systematic work, active choices, and individual, sustained effort (Dweck, 1999, 2006; Renzulli, 1978, 1986). Most of these women made difficult choices about their personal lives in order for their creative productivity to emerge, including whether to divorce or refrain from marrying, to forgo having children or to have fewer children than they might otherwise have had, to live alone, or any combination of these (Reis, 1998). These decisions were usually consciously made to support a lifestyle conducive to the production of highly challenging work. Within multicultural societies, it is usually the views held by the dominant culture and gender that guide the ways that giftedness is defined and measured, and research summarized in this chapter shows the links among culture, environment, and gender and the development of intellectual giftedness.

Noncognitive Aspects of Intellectual Giftedness

In addition to cognitive contributors to the development of high performance, a number of other factors referred to by Renzulli (2005) as "intelligences outside the normal curve" have also been found to play a role in the accomplishments of intellectually gifted young people and adults. Factors such as creativity, motivation, courage, optimism, sense of power to change things, empathy, and physical and mental energy are aspects of the gifts that we respect in the work of people such as Rachel Carson, Nelson Mandela, Mother Teresa, and Martin Luther King, Jr. (Renzulli, 2005). Combined with other noncognitive skills such as collaboration, leadership, organization, planning, and self-efficacy, what emerges is a picture of giftedness that extends far beyond the "golden chromosome" theory that would lead us to believe that some people are preordained to be gifted (Renzulli, 2005).

Important American Contributions to Research on Intellectual Giftedness

Four seminal theoretical contributions related to research on intellectual giftedness are summarized in this section on the historical work of Lewis Terman, and the recent work of Joseph Renzulli, Howard Gardner, and Robert Sternberg.

Genetic Studies of Genius: Terman's Early Contributions

Lewis M. Terman edited five volumes in a series entitled *Genetic Studies of Genius* between 1925 and 1959, resulting in a body of work that is widely acknowledged to be a seminal contribution to the field of intellectual giftedness. The background of the use of the word "genius" in the title stems from his publication in 1916 of the Stanford-Binet Intelligence Scale, based on the work of Alfred Binet, who devised a scale commissioned by the French government to identify children who needed help in school. Terman conducted longitudinal research on a sample of over 1,500 boys and girls who usually scored over 140 on the Stanford-Binet Intelligence Scale. Terman and his colleagues tested students who had been nominated by their teachers, and some researchers have suggested that these teachers may have nominated those students who performed well academically in the classroom. This procedure for selection illustrates a continuing debate related to the study of intellectual giftedness, which is how intellectual giftedness is defined and measured by various scales and tests.

Terman's research resulted in several important findings. The high-IQ children he studied longitudinally were physically and emotionally healthy, and most did well in school and college and had successful professional careers. But as Renzulli (1978) pointed out over 30 years ago, the longitudinal findings of Terman's work also produced some interesting results that raise questions about how potential translates into actualized giftedness. During the period in which Terman's research was conducted, most women became homemakers rather than pursuing full-time careers and achieving college degrees, resulting in different career profiles from those of the men in his study. Also, almost one-third of the men in the sample did not realize their expected potential and might even have been labeled underachievers, as they did not complete the level of education or attain the career goals that might have been expected in their professional lives. Few in the sample would later be labeled geniuses but many did achieve eminence across various fields and domains.

Three-Ring Conception of Giftedness: Joseph Renzulli

For many years following the publications of Terman's work, psychologists and educators continued to equate intellectual giftedness with high scores on an intelligence or IQ test. It is important to remember that pioneers in intelligence assessment such as Binet believed that both genetic and environmental factors contributed to intellectual ability and would not have supported the subsequent practice of Terman, who equated intelligence with a number achieved on one intellectual assessment. Intelligence and measurement theory were developed simultaneously and often conflated, meaning that scores on standardized measurements of intellectual ability were widely interpreted as also measuring intelligence in the decades following Terman's work.

Renzulli's (1978) definition helped to move the focus of previous discussions from an examination of gifted individuals to an examination of gifted behaviors and suggested the inclusion of nonintellectual components in giftedness. He defined giftedness as reflecting an interaction among three basic clusters (popularly known as the three-ring conception of giftedness) of human traits – above-average ability, high levels of task commitment, and high levels of creativity – stating that individuals capable of developing gifted behavior are those possessing or capable of developing this composite set of traits and applying them to any potentially valuable area of human performance. He also distinguished between schoolhouse or high academic giftedness and creative productive giftedness, arguing that many individuals who excel in school and are labeled gifted do not make creative contributions as adults because they lack both creativity and task commitment for creative productive giftedness (Renzulli, 1986). His definition became widely used and adapted by some states and school districts across the country.

Most recently, Renzulli (2002) continued the work on his three-ring conception by examining personality and environmental factors that contribute to socially constructive behaviors reflected in the works of people who have made contributions to the greater good in all walks of life. These interactive factors are depicted by the houndstooth background of his three ring conception (see Figure 12.1).

Renzulli identified six variables contributing to giftedness that will form the basis for his newest research on how these specific traits are manifested, the extent to which they exist, and the ways they interact with one another. He believes that these variables, coupled with abilities, creativity, and task commitment, are the key to both explaining and nurturing the kind of genius that has been used for the betterment of mankind. The first of the six variables is optimism, defined as the belief that the future holds good outcomes. Optimism can be considered an attitude associated with expectations of a future that is socially desirable, to the individual's advantage, or to the advantage of others. It is characterized by a sense of hope and a willingness to work long hours for a cause. The second variable is courage, the ability to face difficulty or danger while overcoming physical, psychological, or moral fears. Courage is characterized by integrity and strength of character, the most salient marks of those creative people who actually increase social capital. The third is romance with a topic or discipline that occurs when an individual is passionate about a topic or discipline. The passion of this romance often becomes an image of the future in young people and provides the motivation for a long-term commitment to a course of action. The fourth is sensitivity to human concerns, a trait that encompasses one's abilities to comprehend another's world and to accurately and sensitively communicate such understanding through action. Altruism and empathy also characterize this trait. The fifth is physical/mental energy, or the amount of energy an individual is willing and able to invest in the achievement of a goal, a crucial issue in high levels of accomplishment. In the case of eminent individuals, this energy investment is a major contributor to task commitment. Charisma and curiosity are frequent correlates of high physical and

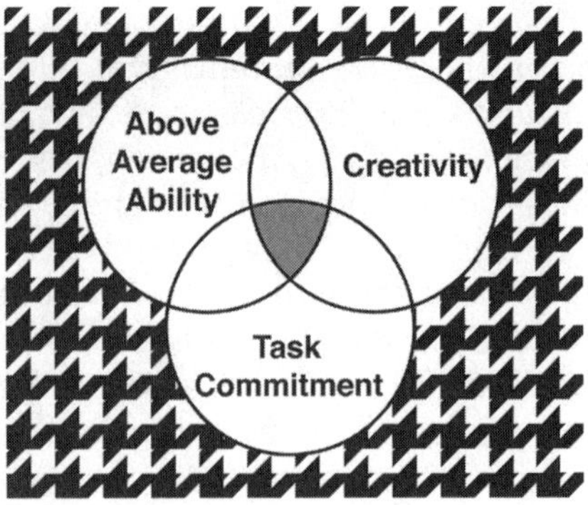

Figure 12.1. Three-ring conception of giftedness with houndstooth background.

mental energy. The last trait Renzulli identified is vision/sense of destiny, which although complex and difficult to define, may best be described by a variety of interrelated concepts, such as internal locus of control, motivation, volition, and self-efficacy. When an individual has a vision or sense of destiny about future activities, events, and involvements, this vision serves to stimulate planning and becomes an incentive for present behavior.

Application of Multiple Intelligence to Gifted Contributors: Howard Gardner

Gardner's (1983) theory of multiple intelligences (MI) proposes seven relatively autonomous but interactive intelligences. Gardner developed his theory based on his work with individuals exhibiting extreme cognitive abilities (or deficits) in particular areas, such as music or math, but not general cognitive superiority. The seven intelligences initially proposed by Gardner were linguistic, logical-mathematical, musical, spatial, bodily-kinesthetic, interpersonal, and intrapersonal.

Linguistic intelligence relates to a person's ability to read, write, and speak, and along with logical-mathematical intelligence composes the traditional conception of intelligence. Musical intelligence is related to one's ability to create, communicate, and understand sound, whereas spatial intelligence is revealed through perceiving, manipulating, and recreating visual and spatial objects. Gardner's idea of bodily-kinesthetic intelligence refers to the use of the body's strength, agility, balance, grace, and control of movements in persons such as Jackie Joyner Kersey, a well-known Olympic athlete. Interpersonal and Intrapersonal intelligence both involve social skills relating to understanding emotions regarding others and the self, respectively. Naturalist intelligence, or the ability to care for and nurture living things in nature, has since been added to Gardner's theory, but has yet to be as widely accepted as the original components of MI theory (Gardner, 1995; 2006).

How does Gardner define intellectual giftedness? Gardner (1993) applied his MI theory to an analysis of the intelligences of creative leaders of the 20th century, explaining that outstanding performance emanated from a particular intelligence. Gardner, for example, believed that Mahatma Gandhi excelled in intrapersonal intelligence and Einstein in logical-mathematical intelligence. Although these individuals excelled in one particular intelligence, Gardner theorized that most individuals exhibit some balance across levels of the various intelligences (Gardner, 2006).

Triarchic Theory Applied to Cognitive Giftedness: Robert Sternberg

Robert Sternberg developed his own multidimensional conception of intelligence, the triarchic theory of intelligence (1985). According to this theory, intelligence is the interplay between analytical, creative, and practical abilities in a given sociocultural environment. Analytical abilities are those most traditionally associated with intelligence and involve evaluating and analyzing information. Creative and practical abilities differ from traditional conceptions of intelligence as they are more associated with generating new ideas and applying knowledge in a given context. Recently, Sternberg adapted his conception to focus on a theory of successful intelligence expressing how individuals can optimize their different strengths while compensating for their relative weaknesses. Successful intelligence shifts away from ability or aptitude measurement and relies on individualized assessments of achievement. In his theory of successful intelligence, intelligence can be transformed into the development of expert performance in a given field and is measured by how a person develops her or his abilities by adapting, shaping, and selecting different environments.

Sternberg is one of the few cognitive psychologists who have conducted research on the ways in which his theory of intelligence applies to cognitive giftedness (Sternberg, 2005). Gifted individuals, according to Sternberg, demonstrate three common attributes that comprise his definition of intelligence (Sternberg, 1985, 1997). These include analytical giftedness, demonstrated by an ability to analyze and evaluate one's own ideas and those of others; creative giftedness, an ability to generate one or more major ideas that are novel and of high quality; and practical giftedness, an ability to convince people of the value and practicality of ideas.

According to other work by Sternberg (1997), individuals have patterns of strengths and weaknesses by which they can be classified. People may exhibit certain patterns, although their patterns may change over time. But the fact that many tasks require all three kinds of thinking does not mean that people, in general, or gifted people, in particular, are equally adept at all three kinds of thinking. Rather, gifted individuals capitalize on their strengths and compensate for or correct their weaknesses. (Sternberg, 1996). People may show different patterns of skills, in general, and of giftedness, in particular periods over the course of their lives.

Sternberg (1997) identified seven patterns of giftedness based on his triarchic theory of intelligence, each involving a different combination of analytical, creative, and practical abilities. The seven patterns are the Analyzer, the Creator, the Practitioner, the Analytical Creator, the Analytical Practitioner, the Creative Practitioner, and the Consummate Balancer. Because gifted individuals are rarely a pure case of any one pattern of giftedness, an additional pattern of balanced giftedness has also been added, which includes people who are high in all three aspects of intelligence (Sternberg, 2003).

Interesting Directions in Research on Intellectual Giftedness

Contributions and the "10,000 Hours" Necessary: Simonton and Ericsson

Simonton (1999) has spent his career studying the creative accomplishments of persons from various domains and disciplines, as well as the ages at which different persons make significant contributions. His research found that mathematicians and physicists tend to make their most significant contributions early in their careers (by their late 20s), that psychologists achieve their greatest contributions in midlife, and historians make their greatest contributions in their 60s or later. Simonton's contributions can help to focus attention to the need for time in order to develop high levels of expertise, an area in which Ericsson has argued for a "10,000 hour" threshold, suggesting that the practice time of experts reveals the importance of years of practice in those with demonstrated potential in an area. Ericsson and his collaborators have focused their research on the amount of time and practice involved in developing high levels of expertise (Ericsson, 1996). A fascinating aspect of both Simonton's and Ericsson's work involves the roles and debates about innate talents and gifts and the subsequent development of high levels of expertise as a consideration across different domains.

Talent Development in Young People

Research on the development of intellectual giftedness has demonstrated how talents develop across multiple domains. This research suggests that talents develop over time with the right combination of innate talent, parental support, expert teaching, and the desire of the individual to apply the effort necessary to develop the innate talent (Bloom, 1985; Csikszentmihalyi, Rathunde, & Whalen, 1993; Renzulli, 1978). Some studies examine the childhoods and backgrounds of highly accomplished individuals across different domains to identify common features that contribute to their talent development. Across this research, high levels of talent development appear to require constant attention, nurturing, and focused effort and task commitment. Whether or not a talent ultimately develops seems to depend upon many factors, including abilities, creativity, effort, motivation to achieve, societal support and appreciation of the talent area, environmental support and opportunities, and chance or luck (Bloom, 1985; Csikszentmihalyi et al., 1993). Research also suggests that supportive experiences at school, in the community, and at home are critical forces in transforming potential into fully developed talents (Bloom, 1985; Csikszentmihalyi et al., 1993). For example, Csikszentmihalyi and his colleagues (1993) studied intellectually talented teens, identifying a variety of factors that contribute to the development of their talents, including enjoyment of classes and activities, having adults help them establish both short- and long-term goals, and encouraging student engagement and commitment to their talent areas during critical periods of development, such as adolescence. Talent development research conducted by Bloom (1985) and Csikszentmihalyi et al. (1993) demonstrates that outstanding talent is developed by individuals over long periods of time and is influenced by a variety of factors, such as the personal characteristics of the talented person and an individual's support systems.

Bloom (1985), in collaboration with colleagues, studied musicians, athletes, and scholars who achieved high-level public recognition, focusing on the significant factors in the development of talent and the contributions of home and school. A positive family environment as well as support and encouragement from parents or family members with a personal interest in the talent field were found to be essential in the development of exceptional accomplishment in a talent area.

Bloom found that talented individuals across domains demonstrate certain qualities such as a strong interest and emotional commitment to a particular talent field, a desire to reach a high level of attainment in the talent field, and a willingness to put in the great amounts of time, and the effort needed to reach very high levels of achievement in the talent field. The psychological factors involved in the development of outstanding talent often occur over a long time period and are influenced by a variety of individuals and factors, including the personal characteristics of the talented person and a strong support system. Parents instill the value of working hard during the early years. In the second phase (the precision phase), a master coach or teacher helps the talented individual to master the long-term systematic skills necessary to hone the talent. The focus is on technical mastery, technique, and excellence in skill development. Finally, in the third phase (the elite years), the individual continues to work with a master teacher and practice many hours each day to turn training and technical skills into personalized performance excellence. During this phase there is a realization that the activity has become very significant in one's life.

Csikszentmihalyi, Rathunde, and Whalen (1993) examined, in a five-year longitudinal study, the experiences of 200 talented teenagers in athletics, art, music, and science to identify similarities and differences between teens who developed and used their talents in adulthood, as opposed to those who drifted away from their talents to pursue work that required only average skills. The researchers described the need for talented teenagers to acquire a set of "metaskills" that allowed them to work with intense concentration and curiosity in order to develop their talents. Talent, these researchers learned, was developmental and affected by contextual factors in the environment. Talent was nurtured by the acquisition of knowledge of the domain, motivation provided by the family and persons in the specialized field of talent, and discipline created by a set of habits resulting in long-term concentrated study and superior performance.

The talented teenagers studied had personal characteristics, including the ability to concentrate, which led to both achievement and endurance, and an awareness of experience, enhancing understanding. They experienced flow, a "state in which people are so involved in an activity that nothing else seems to matter; the experience itself is so enjoyable that people will do it even at great cost, for the sheer sake of doing it" (p. 4). When immersed in pleasurable work, these teenagers pursued work as a reward in itself.

Csikszentmihalyi and his colleagues also found that teens with little family support spent large amounts of time with peers instead of working on their talents and subsequently failed to develop their abilities, suggesting the need for careful parental monitoring of talent development. They also found that children must first be recognized as talented to develop that talent, and therefore must have skills considered useful in their cultures. These researchers also found that talents can be developed if the process produces optimal, enjoyable experiences, and if the memories of peak moments will continue to motivate students.

Fixed Versus Malleable Traits: Carol Dweck

Other new and promising work may also have an impact in the future in the development of gifts and talents. Carol Dweck (2006) and colleagues (Dweck, Chiu, & Hong, 1995) have posited a theory related to cognitive ability that, although not a formal theory of intellectual giftedness, may contribute to research about the developmental nature of intellectual giftedness in the future. Dweck's discussion of an entity view of intelligence as opposed to an incremental (malleable) view of intelligence may contribute to our understanding of why some high-potential children are more willing than others to expend effort to be successful. If a child believes that intelligence is a fixed trait, (e.g., I can't do this because I am not smart enough), she may fail or even refuse to try to complete a challenging task simply because she believes she does not have the capacity to succeed. If the same person believes that her abilities can improve, that is, that they are malleable, she will have more of a chance at being successful. In other words, a belief that one's performance can improve is a key to success on cognitive tasks. Dweck's research about how beliefs influence cognitive ability and whether or not a student's view of intelligence is a fixed or malleable ability may eventually be recognized as an interesting addition to current research on intellectual giftedness. This positive belief about intelligence as malleable can strongly influence the ways in which people both perform on cognitive tasks and interact with their environment. Her research also suggests that students who are praised for intelligence are more likely to consider intelligence a fixed trait than children who are praised for effort, who are more likely to consider intelligence as malleable and developmental.

Multiplier Effects

Ceci, Barnett, and Kanaya (2003) investigated the importance of a "multiplier effect," hypothesizing this as one mechanism that may transform the development of childhood abilities into adult accomplishment. These studies of a multiplier effect may eventually develop into a theory that contributes to our knowledge of how intellectual giftedness may develop over time. A multiplier effect, according to these researchers, occurs when a single impetus that may appear to be quite small sets into motion a chain reaction of events that can result in a stronger growth of some measurable outcome. Multiplier effects, Ceci and his colleagues explain, are not a new idea, as they have been used across various domains to explain a wide range of outcomes in psychological and behavioral development. These effects explain how small changes that affect an individual can serve as a trigger or impetus for a series of actions or interactions between individuals and their environment that subsequently encourage higher levels of gifts and talents to emerge. A highly demanding new piano teacher may, for example, set into motion a multiplier effect (more practice, interaction with other talented students taught by the new teacher, new environment, new practice piano) that may result in dramatic positive changes in musical performance.

Where Things Stand Today

In the last two decades, a consensus seems to have been reached that giftedness cannot be expressed in a unitary manner, suggesting a wider acceptance of more multifaceted approaches to intellectual giftedness. Research conducted in the last few decades has provided support for multiple components of intellectual giftedness. This is particularly evident in two different volumes related to conceptions of giftedness by Sternberg and Davidson (1986, 2005). The distinct conceptions of giftedness presented in both volumes are interrelated in several ways. Most of the researchers define giftedness in terms of multiple qualities and most extend beyond unitary views of intellectual giftedness. Most also believe that IQ scores alone are inadequate measures of intellectual giftedness, and that motivation, high self-concept, and creativity are key qualities in many of these broader conceptions of giftedness (Sternberg & Davidson, 1986; 2005).

The realization that many students demonstrate traits of intellectual giftedness and still fail to achieve in school or life is also an increasing concern for parents, psychologists, and educators. Why, for example, do some extremely smart children fail to realize their promise and potential (Reis, Hébert, Díaz, Maxfield, & Ratley, 1995; Reis & McCoach, 2000; Renzulli & Park, 2002)? Why is it that some prodigies grow up to be average performers in the very fields in which they showed such promise when they were children (Feldman & Goldsmith, 1991)? Why do other traits, described by Renzulli (2002) as co-cognitive traits, appear to be so important in the process of talent development and intellectual giftedness? This chapter has summarized some important research about intellectually gifted and talented individuals but much remains to be learned. Some researchers who have studied talent development have contributed to this line of inquiry, identifying trends and findings that can help us as we consider the types of experiences needed to maximize any developmental considerations related to intellectual giftedness. However, a consensus has not and probably will not be reached about how to define and develop intellectual giftedness. This lack of consensus may be completely appropriate, as the complexities surrounding this construct continue to both intrigue and challenge researchers.

Current Federal Definition

When a task force of psychologists, educational psychologists, educational researchers, and teachers worked for a year to draft a new federal definition, healthy debate and discussion resulted. The current federal definition that emerged from this committee and is widely used by many states and school districts is as follows:

> *Children and youth with outstanding talent perform or show the potential for performing at remarkably high levels of accomplishment when compared with others of their age, experience, or environment. These children and youth exhibit high performance capability in intellectual, creative, and/or artistic areas, possess an unusual leadership capacity, or excel in specific academic fields. They require services or activities not ordinarily provided by the schools. Outstanding talents are present in children and youth from all cultural groups, across all economic strata, and in all areas of human endeavor. (U.S. Department of Education, 1993, p. 26)*

Characteristics of Individuals With High Intellectual Ability or Potential

Some consensus also exists about the characteristics of these students. In an extensive review of research about identified gifted and high-potential students from diverse backgrounds, Frasier and Passow (1994) identified "general/common attributes of giftedness" – traits, aptitudes, and behaviors consistently identified by researchers as common to all gifted students. They found that the following basic elements of giftedness are similar across cultures (though each is not displayed by every student): motivation, advanced interests, communication skills, problem-solving ability, well-developed memory, inquiry, insight, reasoning, imagination/creativity, sense of humor, and an advanced ability to deal with symbol systems. Each of these common characteristics may be manifested in different ways in different students and we should be especially careful in attempting to identify these characteristics in students from diverse backgrounds since behavioral manifestations of the characteristics may vary with context,. By this we mean that motivation may be manifested differently by a Hispanic urban student who speaks English as a second language than by a student who lives in an upper-socioeconomic neighborhood and is from a majority culture.

Interventions and Programs for Gifted and High Potential Students

The need for and types of interventions required by high-potential and gifted and talented students suggest several important points. First, research has consistently demonstrated that the needs of these students are generally not met in American classrooms where the focus is most often on struggling learners and where most classroom teachers have not had the training necessary to meet the needs of gifted and students (Archambault et al., 1993; Reis et al., 2004; Westberg, Archambault, Dobyns, & Salvin, 1993). Second, research documents the benefits of grouping gifted students together for instruction in order to increase achievement for gifted students, and in some cases, also for students who are achieving at average and below-average levels (Gentry & Owen, 1999; Kulik, 1993). Grouping students, however, without changing the curriculum after the grouping has occurred results in far fewer benefits, and so curriculum changes, such as including different advanced or accelerated content, adding more depth to the content, or offering differentiated enrichment possibilities based on interests should be offered to students (Rogers, 1991; Kulik, 1993; Renzulli & Reis, 1997).

Relating to interventions for this population, a strong research base also demonstrates that the use of acceleration results in higher achievement for gifted and talented learners (Colangelo et al., 2004). Acceleration of various types as described in *A Nation at Risk* (Colangelo et al., 2004), such as grade skipping, accelerated content such as giving fifth grade reading to an advanced third grade reader, is usually warranted when students are very high academic achievers who require advanced content to keep them engaged and challenged. Enrichment, including interest-based projects, opportunities for independent study, or opportunities to learn related topics of interest that extend beyond the regular curriculum should also be considered for these students, and for students with advanced interests or creativity (Renzulli & Reis, 1997). Whenever possible, we recommend a combination of enrichment and acceleration to engage and challenge gifted and high-potential students.

Research on the use of enrichment and curriculum enhancement resulted in higher achievement for gifted and talented learners as well as other students (Gavin et al., 2007; Gentry & Owen, 1999; Kulik, 1993; Reis et al., 2007; Gubbins et al., 2007; Rogers, 1991; Tieso, 2002). Gifted programs and strategies have been found effective at serving gifted and high-ability students in a variety of educational settings (Colangelo et al., 2004; Gavin et al., 2007; Reis et al., 2007), high-ability students with learning disabilities (Baum, 1988), students who attend schools that serve diverse ethnic and socioeconomic populations (Hébert, & Reis, 1999; Reis & Diaz, 1999), and also in reversing underachievement (Baum, Renzulli, & Hebert, 1995). Gifted education programs and strategies have also been found to benefit gifted and talented students longitudinally, helping students increase aspirations for college and careers, determine postsecondary and career plans, develop creativity and motivation that is applied to later work, and achieve more advanced degrees (Colangelo et al., 2004; Delcourt, 1993; Hébert, 1993; Taylor, 1992; Lubinski, Webb, Morelock, & Benbow, 2001).

To challenge these learners, educators should develop a continuum of services in each school, as suggested by the Schoolwide Enrichment Model (SEM) (Renzulli & Reis,

1997). This continuum of services should challenge the diverse learning and affective needs of gifted and talented students. Services should be targeted for gifted and high-potential students across all grade levels, and a broad range of services should be defined to ensure that children have access to areas such as curriculum and instructional differentiation. A broad range of enrichment and acceleration opportunities should be offered to meet the needs of rapid, advanced learners; opportunities for advanced content should be delivered so that students can continue to make progress in all content areas; and opportunities should be made available for individualized research for students who are highly creative and want the chance to pursue appropriate interests. For students who are underachieving or who have gifts and talents but also learning disabilities, counseling and other services are recommended to address these special affective needs. The SEM includes specific strategies for implementing the model in a variety of schools with students of different ages and demographic backgrounds. The model, based on more than 30 years of research and development, is a comprehensive system for infusing "high-end learning" and enrichment opportunities for all children while simultaneously challenging high-achieving students. Specific strategies in the SEM include the development of total talent portfolios, curriculum modification techniques, and enrichment teaching and learning opportunities that expose children to new topics and issues, provide them with opportunities for thinking skills and training in specific areas of interest, and time to pursue areas of interest as well as problems in which they have a personal interest. The SEM also provides opportunities for highly creative children who are not outstanding at taking tests to be included in a talent pool for which they are recommended by their teachers or for which they can even nominate themselves and therefore become eligible for participation in a continuum of services (Renzulli & Reis, 1997).

Our schools and nation must be cautious that we do not squander the intellectual opportunities of all of our students and we do not cause underachievement in our most academically able children. As many as half of our urban high-poverty gifted and talented students underachieve by the time they reach high school (Reis et al., 1995), and although psychologists differ on exactly how we should define giftedness, a consensus exists that we must try harder to develop it by understanding how personal variables, family influences, and school and other environmental factors can be enhanced to achieve what Gruber (1986) argued for, over two decades ago – that significant amounts of time and effort are required to make a contribution and to begin the process of "self-constructing the extraordinary."

References

Archambault, F. X., Jr., Westberg, K. L., Brown, S., Hallmark, B. W., Emmons, C., & Zhang, W. (1993). *Regular classroom practices with gifted students: Results of a national survey of classroom teachers* (RM93102). Storrs: National Research Center on the Gifted and Talented, University of Connecticut.

Baum, S. M. (1988). An enrichment program for gifted learning disabled students. *Gifted Child Quarterly*, **32**, 226–230.

Baum, S. M., Renzulli, J. S., & Hébert, T. P. (1995). Reversing underachievement: Creative productivity as a systematic intervention. *Gifted Child Quarterly*, **39**, 224–235.

Bloom, B. S. (Ed.). (1985). *Developing talent in young people*. New York, NY: Ballantine Books.

Bronfenbrenner, U., & Ceci, S. J. (1994). Nature-nurture reconceptualized in developmental perspective: A bioecological model. *Psychological Review*, **101**, 568–586.

Carroll, J. B. (1993). *Human cognitive abilities: A survey of factor-analytic studies*. New York, NY: Cambridge University Press.

Ceci, S. J., Barnett, S. M., & Kanaya, T. (2003). Developing childhood proclivities into adult competencies: The overlooked multiplier effect. In R. J. Sternberg & E. L. Grigorenko (Eds.), *The psychology of abilities, competencies, and expertise* (pp. 70–92). Cambridge, UK: Cambridge University Press.

Colangelo, N., Assouline, S., & Gross, M. (Eds.). (2004). *A nation deceived: How schools hold back America's brightest students* (pp. 109–117). Iowa City: University of Iowa.

Csikszentmihalyi, M., Rathunde, K., & Whalen, S. (1993). *Talented teenagers: A longitudinal study of their development.* New York, NY: Cambridge University Press.

Dai, D. Y., & Renzulli, J. S. (2008). Snowflakes, living systems, and the mystery of giftedness. *Gifted Child Quarterly, 52*, 114–130.

Delcourt, M. A. B. (1993). Creative productivity among secondary school students: Combining energy, interest, and imagination. *Gifted Child Quarterly, 37*, 23–31.

Dweck, C. S. (1999). *Self theories: Their role in motivation, personality and development.* Philadelphia, PA: Psychology Press.

Dweck, C. S. (2006). *Mindset: The new psychology of success.* New York, NY: Random House.

Dweck. C. S., Chiu, C., & Hong. Y. (1995). Implicit theories and their role in judgments and reactions: A world from two perspectives. *Psychological Inquiry, 6*, 267–285.

Ericsson, K. A. (1996). The acquisition of expert performance: An introduction to some of the issues. In K. A. Ericsson (Ed.), *The road to excellence: The acquisition of expert performance in the arts and sciences, sports, and games* (pp. 1–50). Mahwah, NJ: Erlbaum.

Ericsson K. A., & Charness, N. (1994). Expert performance: Its structure and acquisition. *American Psychologist, 49*, 725–747.

Feldman, D. H., & Goldsmith, L. T. (1991). *Nature's gambit: Child prodigies and the development of human potential.* New York, NY: Teachers College Press.

Frasier, M., & Passow, A. (1994). *Toward a new paradigm for identifying talent potential.* Storrs: National Research Center on the Gifted and Talented, University of Connecticut.

Gagne, F. (2000). Understanding the complex choreography of talent development. In K. A. Heller, F. J. Monks, R. J. Sternberg, & R. F. Subotnik (Eds.), *International handbook of giftedness and talent* (pp. 67–79). Amsterdam, the Netherlands: Elsevier.

Gardner, H. (1983). *Frames of mind: The theory of multiple intelligences.* Needham Heights, MA: Allyn & Bacon.

Gardner, H. (1993). *Multiple intelligences: The theory in practice.* New York, NY: Basic Books.

Gardner, H. (1995). Reflections on multiple intelligences: Myths and messages. *Phi Delta Kappan, 77*(3), 200–209.

Gardner, H. (2006). *Multiple intelligences: New horizons.* New York, NY: Basic Books.

Gavin, M. K., Casa, T. M., Adelson, J. L., Carroll, S. R., Sheffield, L. J., & Spinelli, A. M. (2007). Project M3: Mentoring mathematical minds: Challenging curriculum for talented elementary students. *Journal of Advanced Academics, 18*, 566–585.

Gentry, M. L., & Owen, S. V. (1999). An investigation of the effects of total school flexible cluster grouping on identification, achievement, and classroom practices. *Gifted Child Quarterly, 43*, 224–243.

Gruber, H. E. (1986). The self-construction of the extraordinary. In R. J. Sternberg & J. E. Davidson (Eds.), *Conceptions of giftedness* (pp. 247–263). New York, NY: Cambridge University Press.

Gubbins, E. J., Housand, B., Oliver, M., Schader, R., & De Wet, C. (2007). *Unclogging the mathematics pipeline through access to algebraic understanding: University of Connecticut site.* Storrs: National Research Center on the Gifted and Talented, University of Connecticut.

Gustafsson, J., & Undheim, J. O. (1996). Individual differences in cognitive functions. In D. C. Berliner & R. C. Calfee (Eds.), *Handbook of educational psychology* (pp. 186–242). New York, NY: Macmillan.

Hébert, T. P. (1993). Reflections at graduation: The long-term impact of elementary school experiences in creative productivity. *Roeper Review, 16*, 22–28.

Hébert, T. H., & Reis, S. M. (1999). Culturally diverse high-achieving students in an urban high school. *Urban Education, 34*, 428–457.

Housand, A., & Reis, S. M. (2009). Self-regulated learning in reading: Gifted pedagogy and instructional settings. *Journal of Advanced Academics, 20*, 108–136.

Kulik, J. A. (1993). *An analysis of the research on ability grouping: Historical and contemporary perspectives* (RBDM 9204). Storrs: National Research Center on the Gifted and Talented, University of Connecticut.

Kulik, C. L. C., & Kulik, J. A. (1982). Effects of ability grouping on secondary school students: A meta-analysis of evaluation findings. *American Educational Research Journal, 19*, 415–428.

Lohman, D. F., Gambrell, J., & Lakin, J. (2008). The commonality of extreme discrepancies in the ability profiles of academically gifted students. *Psychology Science Quarterly, 50*, 269–282.

Lubinski, D., Webb, R. M., Morelock, M. J., & Benbow, C. P. (2001). Top 1 in 10,000: A 10 year follow-up of the profoundly gifted. *Journal of Applied Psychology, 4*, 718–729.

Neihart, M., Reis, S. M., Robinson, N. M., & Moon, S. M. (Eds.). (2002). *The social and emotional development of gifted children: What do we know?* Waco, TX: Prufrock Press.

Phillipson, S. N., & McCann, M. (2007). *Conceptions of giftedness: Sociocultural perspectives*. Mahwah, NJ: Erlbaum.

Reis, S. M. (1998). *Work left undone: Compromises and challenges of talented females*. Mansfield Center, CT: Creative Learning Press.

Reis, S. M. (2002). Toward a theory of creativity in diverse creative women. *Creativity Research Journal, 14*, 305–316.

Reis, S. M. (2005). Feminist perspectives on talent development: A research based conception of giftedness in women. In R. J. Sternberg & J. Davidson (Eds.), *Conceptions of giftedness* (2nd ed., pp. 217–245). Boston, MA: Cambridge University Press.

Reis, S. M., & Diaz, E. I. (1999). Economically disadvantaged urban female students who achieve in school. *Urban Review, 31*, 31–54.

Reis, S. M., Gubbins, E. J., Briggs, C., Schreiber, F. R., Richards, S., & Jacobs, J. (2004). Reading instruction for talented readers: Case studies documenting few opportunities for continuous progress. *Gifted Child Quarterly, 48*, 309–338.

Reis, S. M., Hébert, T. P., Díaz, E. I., Maxfield, L. R., & Ratley, M. E. (1995). *Case studies of talented students who achieve and underachieve in an urban high school* (Research Monograph No. 95120). Storrs: National Research Center on the Gifted and Talented, University of Connecticut.

Reis, S. M., & McCoach, D. B. (2000). The underachievement of gifted students: What do we know and where do we go? *Gifted Child Quarterly, 44*, 152–170.

Reis, S. M., McCoach, D. B., Coyne, M., Schreiber, F. J., Eckert, R. D., & Gubbins, E. J. (2007). Using planned enrichment strategies with direct instruction to improve reading fluency, comprehension, and attitude toward reading: An evidence-based study. *Elementary School Journal, 108*, 3–24.

Reis, S. M., Neu, T. W., & McGuire, J. M. (1997). Case studies of high ability students with learning disabilities who have achieved. *Exceptional Children, 63*, 463–479.

Renzulli, J. S. (1978). What makes giftedness: Reexamining a definition. *Phi Delta Kappan, 00*, 180–184.

Renzulli, J. S. (1986). The three ring conception of giftedness: A developmental model for creative productivity. In R. J. Sternberg & J. Davidson (Eds.), *Conceptions of giftedness* (246–279). New York, NY: Cambridge University Press.

Renzulli, J. S. (2002). Expanding the conception of giftedness to include co-cognitive traits and to promote social capital. *Phi Delta Kappan, 84*(1), 33–40, 57–58.

Renzulli, J. S. (2005). The three-ring conception of giftedness: A developmental model for promoting creative productivity. In R. J. Sternberg & J. Davidson (Eds.), Conceptions of giftedness (2nd ed., pp. 217–245). Boston, MA: Cambridge University Press.

Renzulli, J. S., & Park, S. (2002). *Giftedness and high school dropouts: Personal, family, and school related factors*. Storrs: National Research Center on the Gifted and Talented, University of Connecticut.

Renzulli, J. S., & Reis, S. M. (1997). *The schoolwide enrichment model: A comprehensive plan for educational excellence*. Mansfield Center, CT: Creative Learning Press.

Renzulli, J. S., & Reis, S. M. (2003). Conception of giftedness and its relation to the development of social capital. In N. Colangelo & G. A. Davis (Eds.), *Handbook of gifted education* (3rd ed., pp. 75–87). Boston, MA: Allyn & Bacon.

Rogers, K. B. (1991). *The relationship of grouping practices to the education of the gifted and talented learner* (RBDM 9102). Storrs: National Research Center on the Gifted and Talented, University of Connecticut.

Shavinia, L. V. (2001). Beyond IQ: A new perspective on the psychological assessment of intellectual abilities. *New Ideas in Psychology, 19*(1), 27–47.

Simonton, D. K. (1998). Creativity, genius, and talent development. *Roeper Review 21*(1), 86–87.

Simonton, D. K. (1999). Talent and its development: An emergenic and epigenetic model. *Psychological Review, 106*, 435–457.

Simonton, D. K. (2005). Genetics of giftedness: The implications of an emergenic-epigenetic model of giftedness. In R. J. Sternberg & J. E. Davidson (Eds.), *Conceptions of giftedness* (2nd ed., pp. 312–326). Boston, MA: Cambridge University Press.

Sternberg, R. J. (1985). *Beyond IQ: A triarchic theory of human intelligence*. New York, NY: Cambridge University Press.

Sternberg, R. J. (1996). *Successful intelligence: how practical and creative intelligence determine success in life*. New York, NY: Simon & Schuster.

Sternberg, R. J (1997). *Successful intelligence*. New York, NY: Plume.

Sternberg, R. J. (2000). Implicit theories of intelligence as exemplar stories of success: Why intelligence test validity is in the eye of the beholder. *Psychology, Public Policy, and Law*, 6(1), 159–167.

Sternberg, R. J. (2003). WICS as a model of giftedness. *High Ability Studies*, 14(2), 109–137.

Sternberg, R. J. (2004). Culture and intelligence. *American Psychologist*, 59, 325–338.

Sternberg, R. J. (2005). The WISC model of giftedness. In R. J. Sternberg & J. Davidson (Eds.), *Conceptions of giftedness* (2nd ed., pp. 327–342). Boston, MA: Cambridge University Press.

Sternberg, R. J., & Davidson, J. (Eds.). (1986). *Conceptions of giftedness*. New York, NY: Cambridge University Press.

Sternberg, R. J., & Davidson, J. (Eds.). (2005). *Conceptions of giftedness* (2nd ed.). Boston, MA: Cambridge University Press.

Sternberg, R. J., Ferrari, M., Clinkenbeard, P. R., & Grigorenko, E. L. (1996). Identification, instruction, and assessment of gifted children: A construct validation of a triarchic model. *Gifted Child Quarterly*, 40, 129–137.

Sternberg R. J., & Grigorenko, E. L. (2000). *Teaching for successful intelligence. To increase student learning and achievement*. Arlington Heights, IL: Merrill-Prentice Hall.

Sternberg, R. J., Grigorenko, E. L., Ferrari, M., & Clinkenbeard, P. (1999). A triarchic analysis of an aptitude-treatment interaction. *European Journal of Psychological Assessment*, 15(1), 1–11.

Sternberg, R. J., & Lubart, T. I. (1995). *Defying the crowd: Cultivating creativity in a culture of conformity*. New York, NY: Free Press.

Subotnik, R. F., & Arnold, K. D. (Eds.). (1994). *Beyond Terman: Contemporary longitudinal studies of giftedness and talent*. Norwood, NJ: Ablex.

Subotnik, R. F., & Jarvin, L. (2005). Beyond expertise: Conceptions of giftedness as great performance. In R. J. Sternberg & J. Davidson (Eds.), *Conceptions of giftedness* (2nd ed., pp. 343–357). Boston, MA: Cambridge University Press.

Tannenbaum, A. J. (1991). The social psychology of giftedness. In N. Colangelo & G. A. Davis (Eds.), *Handbook of gifted education* (pp, 27–44). Boston, MA: Allyn & Bacon.

Taylor, L. A. (1992). *The effects of the Secondary Enrichment Triad Model and a career counseling component on the career development of vocational-technical school students*. Storrs: National Research Center on the Gifted and Talented, University of Connecticut.

Terman, L. M. (1925–1959). *Genetic studies of genius* (5 vols.). Stanford, CA: Stanford University Press.

Terman, L. M. (1926). *Genetic studies of genius: Mental and physical traits of a thousand gifted children* (Vol. I, 2nd ed.). Stanford, CA: Stanford University Press.

Tieso, C. L. (2002). The effects of grouping and curricular practices on intermediate students' math achievement (RM02154). Storrs: National Research Center on the Gifted and Talented, University of Connecticut.

United States Department of Education, Office of Educational Research and Improvement. (1993). *National excellence: A case for developing America's talent*. Washington, DC: U.S. Government Printing Office.

Westberg, K. L., Archambault, F. X., Jr., Dobyns, S. M., & Salvin, T. J. (1993). *An observational study of instructional and curricular practices used with gifted and talented students in regular classrooms*. (RM93104). Storrs: National Research Center on the Gifted and Talented, University of Connecticut.

CHAPTER 13

Sex Differences in Intelligence

Diane F. Halpern, Anna S. Beninger, and Carli A. Straight

Questions about whether, why, and how much females and males differ in intelligence have engendered heated debates in contemporary psychology. The way researchers answer these questions has implications for public policy decisions as well as the way people think about education, career choices, and "natural" roles for males and females. For example, less than two decades ago, research was released proclaiming that girls are being "shortchanged" in schools (e.g., American Association of University Women, 1992; Sadker & Sadker, 1995). This conclusion was soon met with counterclaims that schools are biased against boys (Sommers, 2000). This controversy has continued unabated with no signs of weakening or either side calling for a truce. Claims about biases for and against girls and boys in school were interpreted in the context of international comparisons that document the overall low achievement of both boys and girls in the United States, relative to students in other countries, especially in science and math (National Science Board, 2006) and low high school graduation rates for both sexes, but especially for low-income males (Greene & Winters, 2006). These proclamations about biases in education soon took on a political tone about the causes of and cure for sex differences in intelligence.

Although most education pundits agree that education in the United States is in need of serious reform, some politicians and educators used the available data to argue that girls and boys learn differently and thus need single-sex schooling that would cater to these differences. The No Child Left Behind Act of 2001 authorized school districts to use funding to offer single-sex schools and classrooms at public expense, as long as this arrangement was consistent with applicable laws. An October 2006 amendment to Title IX, which mandates that educational institutions not discriminate on the basis of sex, was reinterpreted to allow single-sex schooling at public expense. According to the National Association for Single-Sex Public Education, research supports the superiority of single-sex schools (see www.singlesexschools.org). Advocates for single-sex schooling maintain this position even though an extensive review conducted by the U. S. Department of Education found that the majority of studies comparing single-sex with coeducational schooling report either no difference or mixed results (U. S. Department of Education, 2005). Other reviews report a host of negative consequences associated with single-sex education, including increased sex-role stereotyping, which harms both boys and girls (Karpiak, Buchanan, Hosey, & Smith, 2007). Challenges to the reinterpretation of Title IX to allow single-sex classes (in public education) are moving from the laboratory to the courthouse, where research findings will be scrutinized by lawyers, judges, news reporters, and the general public, all of whom will be asking these questions: What are the sex differences in intelligence? Are the brains of females and males so dissimilar that they justify the conclusion that males and females need separate educational experiences tailored to "the way they learn?" Should empirical research inform political decisions about how to educate boys and girls?

In this chapter, we explore the ways in which the sexes are similar and different in their cognitive abilities. Obviously, there are differences in the relative roles that men and women play in reproduction, but these have few, if any, implications for intellectual functioning. In this chapter, we present a balanced overview of the current findings in the research literature on sex differences in intelligence.

The Smarter Sex

Which is the smarter sex – males or females? This may seem like an easy question to answer because it would be a simple task to compare the average scores of large samples of females and males on intelligence tests. However, this obvious strategy will not work because tests of intelligence are carefully written so that there will be no average overall difference between the sexes (Brody, 1992). Questions that favor either sex are either eliminated from the test or matched with questions that favor the other sex to the same degree. Although some researchers report a small advantage for males on tests that were standardized to show no sex differences (Nyborg, 2005), most studies do not (Colom, Juan-Espinosa, Abad, & García, 2000; Spinath, Spinath, & Plomin, 2008). In a recent review of this question, Dykiert, Gale, and Deary (2008) found that reported sex differences on intelligence tests can be explained by the use of samples that are not representative of females and males, in general, and thus reflect errors in the methods used to study this question. This conclusion was confirmed by Hunt and Madhyastha (2008), who provided a model of the subject-selection problem that occurred in studies that report sex differences in intelligence. Researchers vary in the extent to which they stress either similarities or differences. In a comprehensive review of the sex differences literature, Hyde (2005) concluded that males and females are more similar than different. By contrast, Irwing and Lynn (2005) focused their discourse on differences. The reality is far more nuanced, with some tests and measurements showing consistent findings that favor one sex over the other and many others that show little or no differences.

One set of findings that has been replicated many times is that females, on average, score higher on some tests of verbal abilities, especially those that require rapid access to and use of phonological and semantic information in long-term memory, production and comprehension of complex prose, and perceptual speed (Hedges & Nowell, 1995; Jensen, 1998; Kimura, 1993; Torres, Gómez-Gil, Vidal, Puig, Boget, & Salamero, 2006). Males, on the other hand, score higher on some tasks that require transformations in visual-spatial working memory, motor skills involved in aiming, spatiotemporal responding, and fluid reasoning, especially in abstract mathematical and scientific domains (Hedges & Nowell, 1995; Hyde, 2005; Torres et al., 2006). Results with tasks that require generating an image and maintaining it in memory while "working" on it vary depending on the complexity of the image to be generated and the specific nature of the task, with observed differences favoring males that range between $d = .63$ and $d = .77$ (Loring-Meier & Halpern, 1999). Kaufman (2007) investigated whether sex differences in visuospatial ability could result from differences in spatial working memory. He found sex differences favoring males on spatial working memory and that these differences could explain a portion of the sex differences in mental rotation and other spatial tasks.

Jensen (1998) addressed the question of female-male differences in intelligence by analyzing tests that "load heavily on *g*," but were not normed to eliminate sex differences. He concluded, "No evidence was found for sex differences in the mean level of *g* or in the variability of *g*. . . . Males, on average, excel on some factors; females on others" (pp. 531–532). The distinction among cognitive tasks that favor either females or males has led to a recent model of intelligence (often denoted as *g*, which stands for general intelligence) that is comprised of three subcomponents – verbal, perceptual, and visuospatial – with females showing an advantage for verbal and perceptual and males showing an advantage for visuospatial (Johnson & Bouchard, 2006). Because much of the research literature has focused on sex differences in these components of intelligence, we frequently use the term "cognitive abilities" instead of the more global term "intelligence" when discussing sex differences.

Although sex differences in mathematics have received widespread attention as a possible reason for the underrepresentation of women in math-intensive careers, these differences depend on the portion of the distribution examined and the data that are used to support a particular conclusion. There are many more mentally retarded males than females, suggesting an X-linked genetic locus for many categories of mental retardation. A review of the literature placed the ratio of males to females at 3.6:1 across several categories of mental retardation (Volkman, Szatmari, & Sparrow, 1993). Some tests of quantitative and visuospatial abilities also show more males at the high end of the distribution and miss the greater number of males at the low end because the mentally retarded are rarely included in tests that are administered in school settings. These data support the generally accepted conclusion that males are more variable in quantitative and visuospatial abilities, with more males at both high- and low-ability ends of test scores. In a large-scale study of sex differences in variability, Johnson, Carothers, and Deary (2008) found that males are more variable, with greater variability at the low end of the distribution than at the high end, which reflects a greater incidence of mental retardation among males. These authors conclude that sex differences at the high end of the distribution of intelligence scores cannot account for sex differences in high-level achievement.

Sex differences in variability in intelligence emerge in individuals as young as 3 years of age, even though girls obtain higher mean scores and it is girls who are overrepresented at the high-ability tail at ages 2, 3, and 4 (Arden & Plomin, 2006). By age 10 boys are overrepresented at the high-ability tail, as would be expected given their greater variability. These data suggest that sex differences in variability emerge before preschool and are not shaped by educational experiences. Data from the Study of Mathematically Precocious Youth (2006) can help us understand the fact that more boys achieve scores at the high end of the distribution on tests that presumably reflect mathematical ability. In the early 1980s, Benbow and Stanley observed sex differences in mathematical reasoning ability among tens of thousands of intellectually talented 12- to 14-year-olds who had taken the SAT several years before the typical age achieved by high school seniors. Among this elite group, no significant sex differences were found on the verbal section of the SAT, but the math section revealed sex differences favoring boys. There were twice as many boys as girls with math scores of 500 or higher (out of a possible score of 800), four times as many boys with scores of at least 600, and 13 times as many boys with scores of at least 700 (putting these test takers in the top 0.01% of the 12- to 14-year-olds nationwide). These data were widely reported in the popular press. Although it has drawn little media coverage, dramatic changes have been occurring among these junior math wizards over the last two decades: The relative number of girls among them has been soaring. The ratio of boys to girls has been dropping steadily and is now only approximately 3 to 1, while the gender ratio of high verbal scores remains close to 1 to 1 (Blackburn, 2004). A recent analysis based on the 1.6 million seventh-grade students who took the SAT and ACT as part of the screening process to identify academically precocious youth found that the ratio of boys to girls in the high-ability tail of the math and science portions of these exams has remained steady at between 3:1 to 4:1 since the early 1990s (Wai, Cacchio, Putzllaz, & Makel, 2010). The time period during which the number of girls has risen among the ranks of the mathematically precocious coincides with a trend of special programs and mentoring to encourage girls to take higher level math and science courses, and with girls participating in high school calculus classes at approximately the same rate as boys (Snyder, Dillow, & Hoffman, 2009).

Sex Differences Across the Life Span

Sex differences in cognitive abilities vary throughout the life span. For example, among young children (ages 4 to 10 years), girls and boys perform similarly on tests of primary mathematical reasoning abilities (Spelke, 2005). During or shortly after elementary school, however, when quantitative tests become more complex and more visuospatial in nature, sex differences emerge and continue to grow thereafter (Beilstein & Wilson, 2000). By the end of their secondary schooling (12th grade), males demonstrate significantly higher achievement than females in the areas of number properties and operations as well as measurement and geometry (Rampey, Dion, & Donahue, 2009). This trend has remained steady since 1973. Interestingly, females get higher grades than males in school in all subjects, including math, at all grade levels (Kimball, 1989; Snyder, Dillow, & Hoffman, 2009; Willingham & Cole, 1997) and do slightly better on international tests of algebra (National Center for Education Statistics, 2005). But when males and females are compared on tests that reflect content learned in school, such as statewide assessment tests, the differences disappear. However, it should be noted that these tests tend to evaluate lower level skills and leave open the possibility of sex differences if higher order skills were assessed (Hyde, Lindberg, Linn, Ellis, & Williams, 2008). Math differences favoring males are larger and more commonly found on tests that are not directly tied to the curriculum, such as the SATs, which may reflect novel problem-solving skills. On average, males taking the SATs have consistently scored about a third of a standard deviation higher than girls over the last 25 years (data from College Entrance Examination Board, 2004; see Halpern et al., 2007, for a review). However, these values can be misleading because many more females than males take the SATs; lower average scores for females may therefore reflect the greater range of levels of female abilities, especially toward the lower region of the distribution (Hyde et al., 2008).

Spatial abilities are often categorized into three broad areas – spatial perception (ability to determine spatial relationships with respect to the orientation of one's own body, such as indicating the water level in a tilted glass); spatial visualization (ability to engage in multistep manipulations of spatial information, such as finding figures embedded in borders of larger figures; and mental rotation (ability to imagine what a complex figure would look like if it were in another orientation). Sex differences are smaller for spatial perception ($d = .04$ to $.84$) and spatial visualization ($d = .24$ to $.50$) than for mental rotation ($d = .50$ to $.96$; Linn & Petersen, 1985). Given these results, most of the research in cognitive sex differences has focused on mental rotation tasks. For mental rotation, a visuospatial skill that is related to some types of mathematics such as geometry and topology, boys demonstrate an advantage across the life span, especially when figures are three dimensional. A male advantage in mental rotation, a task that requires participants to imagine what a complex figure would look like if it were rotated in space, is found as early as 3 to 5 months of age (Moore & Johnson, 2008; Quinn & Liben, 2008). In a review of the preschool literature on sex differences in spatial skills, researchers found that, on average, preschool boys are more accurate than girls at spatial tasks that measure accuracy of spatial transformations ($d = .31$) and score higher on the Mazes subtest of the Wechsler Preschool and Primary Scale of Intelligence ($d = .30$; Levine, Huttenlocher, Taylor, & Langrock, 1999). Although this very early difference in the ability to visualize an object that is rotated in space suggests a strong biological basis for the large sex differences in mental rotation, there is also evidence for a large sociocultural/learning contribution. For example, in one study, female and male college students were trained with computer games that required the use of spatial visualization skills (with appropriate controls for prior experience and other types of games; Feng, Spence, & Pratt, 2007). As the researchers predicted, this intervention reduced the gap between male and female performance; however, it was not completely eliminated.

Sex differences in mental rotation have been studied for over 25 years and findings have been summarized in several meta-analytic reviews. A recent review of the sex-differences literature on mental rotation found that male performance exceeds that of females across all age ranges, with the size of the between-sex difference ranging between $d = 0.52$ to 1.49, and the size of the difference increasing slightly across the life span (Geiser, Lehmann, & Eid, 2008).

Girls begin talking somewhat earlier than boys and have a greater vocabulary at 2 years of age (Lutchamaya, Baron-Cohen, & Raggatt, 2002). Girls also show better language skills in preschool (e.g., Blair, Granger, & Razzam, 2005). Based on a review of 24 large datasets (including several large representative samples of U.S. students, working adults, and military personnel), Willingham and Cole (1997) concluded that differences are small in the elementary school grades, with only writing, language use, and reading favoring females at fourth grade, $d > 0.2$. In the United States, by the end of high school, the largest differences, again favoring females, are found for writing (d between 0.5 and 0.6) and language usage (d between 0.4 and 0.5). Another report on writing proficiency for children in grades 4, 8, and 11 in 1984, 1988, and 1990 showed that girls were better writers in each of the nine comparison groups (U.S. Department of Education, 1997). More recently, the 2007 *Nation's Report Card* reports that females are 20 points ahead of males in writing in eighth grade and 18 points ahead in 12th grade (National Assessment of Educational Progress, 2008). After a comprehensive review of the literature on writing skills, Hedges and Nowell concluded: "The large sex differences in writing . . . are alarming. These data imply that males are, on average, at a rather profound disadvantage in the performance of this basic skill" (1995, p. 45).

In a study of sex differences across the adult life span, Maitland and colleagues analyzed data from the Seattle Longitudinal Study (Maitland, Intrieri, Schaie, & Willis, 2000). These researchers grouped participants into three age categories at the start of the study: younger (22–49), middle-aged (50–63), and older (64–87). They then tracked their performance on six cognitive ability tests over seven years. Women in the younger and middle-aged groups performed better than men on processing speed. Across all age groups, women performed better than men on verbal recall and men performed better than women on spatial orientation. There were no sex differences in inductive reasoning, verbal comprehension, or numerical facility. Research that looks at elderly populations generally finds that all cognitive abilities decline with age (e.g., Gerstorf, Herlitz, & Smith, 2006; Read et al., 2006). Some findings indicate that cognitive abilities decline at a faster rate for females (Read et al., 2006), whereas others do not find differences in the rate of decline (Barnes et al., 2003; Gerstorf et al., 2006). Interestingly, there is evidence that, among individuals aged 85 and older, females perform better on tests of cognitive speed and memory (van Exel et al., 2001).

Sex Differences Over Time

There has been speculation over the possibility that sex differences in cognitive abilities are decreasing, possibly as a result of decreased pressure to conform to sex-role stereotypes (e.g., Baker & Jones, 1992; Corbett, Hill, & St. Rose, 2008; Hyde, Fennema, & Lamon, 1990). In an extensive meta-analytic review of tests of reading, writing, math, and science, Hedges and Nowell (1995) concluded, "Contrary to the findings of small scale studies, these average differences do not appear to be decreasing, but are relatively stable across the 32-year period investigated" (p. 45). Often the basis of claims that sex differences are decreasing over time comes from evidence of more flexible sex-role stereotypes and socialization practices. However, a meta-analysis of parents' sex-role socialization practices found that parenting has not become less sex differentiated (Lytton & Romney, 1991). Other researchers have found that despite changes in sex roles and attitudes over a 17-year period of study (1974 to 1991), perceptions of sex-typed personality traits actually increased (Lueptow, Garovich, & Lueptow, 1995). Numerous other researchers share this conclusion, although some reviewers note that there may be some exceptions (e.g., Masters & Sanders, 1993; Stumpf & Stanley, 1996).

Why?

Evolutionary Perspectives

For evolutionary psychologists, the answer to the "why" questions of sex differences lies in the division of labor in hunter-gatherer societies (Buss, 1995; Eals & Silverman, 1994; Geary, 2007). Proponents of this perspective base their claims on evidence that males in early human societies roamed over large areas in their hunt for the animals that provided protein for the community, whereas females gathered crops and traveled shorter distances because much of their adult lives were spent in pregnancy, nursing, and child care. Through the evolutionary pressures of adaptations, males developed brain structures that supported the cognitive and motor skills needed in navigating large areas and killing animals.

Geary (1996) made a distinction between those skills that are primary, skills that were shaped by evolutionary pressures and therefore would be found across cultures and developed universally in children's play, and those that are secondary, skills found only in technologically complex societies (i.e., skills such as reading and spelling that are important in school but would not have evolved in hunter-gatherer societies). Most of the cognitive skills that we can observe today are thought to be built upon earlier adaptive solutions for functioning in a specific cultural context rather than directly resulting from evolution (Geary, 1996, 2007).

Although theories that posit evolutionary origins for complex human behaviors offer interesting alternatives to nature-nurture dichotomies, they are untestable and ignore large bodies of data that do not conform to these explanatory frameworks. Virtually any finding can be explained by hypothesizing how that difference might have been advantageous to hunter-gatherers. For example, evolutionary theorists criticized Hyde's (2005) analysis of the relationship between psychosocial variables and sex differences for not considering the larger picture. They also used her findings as evidence for their own theories by arguing that social mores exert selection pressures for sex-typed traits, resulting in observed sex differences (e.g., Davies & Sheckelford, 2006). Evolutionary theories ignore the fact that women have always engaged in spatial tasks and they have often had to travel long distances to gather food because plants ripen in different locations in different seasons. Additionally, there is archaeological evidence that women played significant roles in hunting and warfare (Adler, 1993). Typical "women's work" like basket weaving and cloth- and shelter-making work are spatial tasks that were very important to the survival of a community because success at gathering depended on the quantity and strength of the baskets, and the protections afforded by clothing and shelters was critical. In addition, the visual-spatial tasks that show the largest sex differences favoring males, such as mental rotation, are performed in small arenas of functioning (paper-and-pencil tasks), which are qualitatively different from finding one's way over miles of territory.

Biological Perspectives

Researchers have identified three mutually influencing biological systems that could account for cognitive sex differences: (1) chromosomal or genetic determinants of sex; (2) sex hormones secreted from endocrine glands and other systems; and (3) structure, organization, and function of the brain (Halpern, in press). Each of these systems and its effects are the topic of large bodies of research and introduce a few of the possibilities for sex differences as a result of biological processes. First, it is important to note that because these systems are interrelated in most individuals, it is difficult to isolate the relative influence of each. For example, chromosomes determine the type of sex hormones that are secreted. Sex hormones then influence brain development and the development of internal reproductive organs and external genitalia (Halpern, in press).

Genes, Hormones, and Brains

Genetic theories emphasize that males and females both inherit intelligence (Schmidt & Hunter, 2004) and possess separate mental capacities related to verbal and spatial abilities (Shah & Miyake, 1996). Genetic studies of sex differences in intelligence seek out links between the X and Y chromosomes (males are XY, females are XX) and cognitive abilities. It is well established that some types of mental retardation are linked to the sex chromosomes, which explains the disproportionate numbers of males who are mentally retarded (Skuse, 2005). Recently, Johnson, Carothers, and Deary (in press) proposed an X-linked basis for high intelligence. The hypothesized relationship between genes that are responsible for high intelligence and their location on the sex chromosomes is purely speculative, with good evidence supporting the notion that high intelligence must result from the simultaneous influences of many, perhaps hundreds, of genes that are located on many chromosomes (Turkheimer & Halpern, in press).

Three sex hormones – estrogen, progesterone, and testosterone – have primarily been investigated with respect to their influence on sex differences in cognitive abilities (e.g., Neave, Menaged, & Weightman, 1999; Sherwin, 2003). Females, in general, possess much higher concentrations of estrogen and progesterone, whereas males possess higher concentrations of androgens, the most common of which is testosterone. In addition, these hormones convert from one to another via chemical processes in the brain. At various stages of life, sex hormones play an important role in brain development and subsequent cognition and behavior (e.g., Halpern & Tan, 2001; Kimura, 1996).

In normal humans, the genetic code determines whether the undifferentiated gonads will become ovaries or testes. If development is in the male direction, approximately seven weeks after conception, the newly formed testes will secrete androgens, primarily testosterone and dihydrotestosterone. If ovaries are formed, they will develop approximately 12 weeks following conception and secrete estrogens (e.g., estradiol) and progestins (e.g., progesterone). Although these hormones are commonly referred to as male and female hormones, all three are found in both females and males (Collaer & Hines, 1995). As these hormones circulate through the bloodstream, they are converted by enzymes into chemical structures that are important in the formation of the brain and internal and external sex organs.

Brain structure, organization, and function are complicated and greatly influenced by hormones. Broadly, there is some evidence that different areas of the brain are activated for males and females during cognitive tasks, and that the overall size and shape of some portions of the brain are different between the sexes (Giedd, Castellanos, Rajapakse, Vaituzis, & Rapoport, 1997). In general, females have a higher percentage of gray matter brain tissue, areas with closely packed neurons and fast blood flow, whereas males have a higher volume of connecting white matter tissue, nerve fibers that are insulated by a white fatty protein called myelin (Gur et al., 1999). Furthermore, men tend to have a higher percentage of gray matter in the left hemisphere compared to the right, whereas no such asymmetries are significant in females. A variety of experimental techniques has shown that numerous areas of the brain that are not involved in reproduction are sexually dimorphic (e.g., hippocampus, amygdala, and thickness or proportions of the cortex; see Collaer & Hines, 1995, for a review). Although each of these differences has been the subject of intense disagreement among researchers, many now agree that there are sex differences in the shape, and probably the volume, of some portions of the corpus callosum, with females in general, having a larger and more bulbous structure (Allen, Richey, Chai, & Gorski, 1991; Steinmetz, Staiger, Schluag, Huang, & Jancke, 1995). The difference in the shape of the corpus callosum, which is the largest fiber track in the brain, implies better connectivity between the two cerebral hemispheres, on average, for females (Innocenti, 1994), and also supports the theory that female brains are more bilaterally organized in their representation of cognitive functions (Jancke & Steinmetz, 1994).

Exciting advances in brain imagery have shown that there are also different patterns of activity in male and female brains when they are engaged in some cognitive tasks. Imaging studies assessing brain function support the notion that females perform better on tasks such as language processing that call on more symmetric activation of brain hemispheres, whereas males excel in tasks requiring activation of one hemisphere, typically the left, for the same language tasks (Shaywitz et al., 1995). The same pattern of symmetric activation for females and asymmetric activation for males appears to be associated with stronger performance by males on spatial tasks (Gur et al., 2000). As the complexity of spatial tasks increases, females tend to use more distributed and bilateral recruitment of brain regions than males (Kucian, Loenneker, Dietrich, Martin, & von Aster, 2005). It is important to emphasize, though, that finding sex differences in brain structures and functions does not suggest these are the cause of observed cognitive differences between males and females. Because the brain reflects learning and other experiences, it is possible that sex differences in the brain are influenced by the differences in life experiences that are typical for women and men.

Causal links between prenatal hormones and sex differences in brain structures and organization have been determined in several different ways, including experimental manipulations with nonhuman mammals (e.g., administering testosterone, estrogens, or both, prenatally and perinatally and removing naturally occurring hormones from the prenatal and perinatal environment). For example, a recent study tested the effect of prenatal androgen exposure in rhesus monkeys on spatial memory and strategy use (Herman & Wallen, 2007). Surprisingly, these researchers found that females performed better than males regardless of prenatal treatment or the availability of landmarks. Another study treated postmenopausal women with estrogen, an estrogen-progesterone combination, or no hormone substitution. When performing a verbal task, the women in the estrogen-only group showed enhanced activity in the right hemisphere (Bayer & Erdmann, 2008).

Individuals with various diseases that cause over- or underproduction of gonadal hormones either prenatally or later in life show cognitive patterns that are in the direction predicted by the data from normal individuals. For example, girls exposed to high levels of prenatal androgens (congenital adrenal hyperplasia) are raised as girls from birth and have normal female hormones starting at birth, yet they tend to show male-typical cognitive patterns and other male-typical behaviors such as preferences for "boys' toys," rough play, and an increased incidence of sexual orientation toward females (Berenbaum, Korman, & Leveroni, 1995). Females exposed to high levels of prenatal androgens perform at high levels on visuospatial tasks; their performance is comparable to that of same-aged males and better than the performance of control females (Mueller et al., 2008). These findings show that prenatal sex hormones manifest long-lasting changes in cognitive functioning. Imperato-McGinley and colleagues compared individuals with complete androgen insensitivity syndrome (AI) to control male and female family members on the Wechsler Adult Intelligence Scale (WAIS). Results showed that control males and females performed better than their androgen insensitive counterparts on visuospatial subtests, but that males, overall, still performed better on these tests than females; however, there were no group differences in Full Scale I.Q. (Imperato-McGinley, Pichardo, Gautier, Voyer, & Bryden, 1991).

One of the most fascinating areas of recent research has shown that testosterone and estrogen continue to play critical roles in sex-typical cognitive abilities throughout the life span in normal populations. Highly publicized studies have shown that women's cognitive abilities and fine motor skills fluctuate in a reciprocal fashion across the menstrual cycle (Hampson, 1990; Hampson & Kimura, 1988). Males also show cyclical patterns of hormone concentrations and the correlated rise and fall of specific cognitive abilities. The spatial-skills performance of normal males fluctuates in concert with daily variations in testosterone (e.g., higher testosterone concentrations in early morning than later in the day; Moffat & Hampson, 1996) and season variations (e.g., in North America, testosterone levels are higher in autumn than in spring; Kimura & Hampson, 1994). Killgore and Killgore (2007) examined the correlation between morningness-eveningness and verbal ability and found a stronger relationship for females than males. Similarly, regardless of gender, intellectually gifted children between the ages of 6 and 9 exhibited lower salivary testosterone levels than nongifted children (Ostatníková, Laznibatová, Putz, Mataseje, Dohnányiová, & Pastor, 2000). To complicate matters even more, researchers have discovered a negative U-shaped relationship between testosterone levels and performance on spatial tasks for males and a positive U-shaped relationship for females (Ostatníková, Dohnányiová, Laznibatová, Putz, & Celec, 2001). Thus, although we can conclude that sex hormones play a role in adult cognition, it is more difficult to specify the effects of each hormone separately or as it interacts with other factors.

Steroidal hormones influence performance on tests of cognitive abilities throughout adulthood and well into old age. Large numbers of postmenopausal women and comparably aged men are treated with various sex hormones for a wide range of possible benefits including better sexual responsivity and cognitive enhancement. Although initial data strongly suggested positive effects on cognition for hormone replacement therapies, more recent studies present a mixed picture. For example, Ryan, Carriere, Scali, Ritchie, and Ancelin (2009) concluded that "the results also suggest that current hormone therapy may be beneficial for a number of cognitive domains," (p. 287) and LeBlanc, Janowsky, Chan, and Nelson (2001) concluded that hormone replace therapy is associated with a decreased risk of dementia. However, other researchers have found negative effects for hormone replacement therapy, with at least one study reporting an increased risk of dementia (see Low & Ansley, 2006, for a review). It is likely that the effects of hormone therapies on cognition depend on multiple variables including age, type and dosage of hormones, timing of hormone therapy (i.e., soon after menopause or decades after menopause), and different cognitive assessments (Luine, 2008). Much more research is needed to untangle the multiple variables that determine the effect of hormone therapy on intelligence. Hormone levels also respond to environmental factors, which blurs the distinction between biological and environmental variables.

Intensive exercise, stress, disease, nutrition, and many other variables cause changes in hormones, which in turn affect behavior and emotions, creating continuous feedback loops between hormone levels and life events. Brain structures also change over the life span in response to both hormonal and environmental events, and the response properties of neurons are modified through experience, even in adulthood (Innocenti, 1994). Numerous chemicals in the environment mimic the action of gonadal hormones. Studies have shown alarming changes in the genitals of male alligators that live in water that is polluted with pesticides (Begley, 1994). Similar effects on human reproductive organs and cognitive functions that are linked to pesticide exposure have been hypothesized (e.g., Straube et al., 1999).

Sociocultural Perspectives

"Math class is tough"; "I love dressing up"; "Do you want to braid my hair?" (Teen-Talk Barbie's first words). "Attack the Cobra Squad with heavy fire power"; "When I give the orders, listen or get captured" (GI Joe, as cited in Viner, 1994). Males and females face multiple and pervasive differences in their life experiences (Baenninger & Newcombe, 1989). The massive literature on observational learning (Bandura, 1977), social reinforcement (Lott & Maluso, 1993), and the ubiquitous influence of sex-role stereotypes (Jost & Kay, 2005) shows that males and females still receive sex-differentiated messages, models, rewards, and punishments. From this perspective, it is the sex-typed practices of the socializing community that are most important in creating and understanding nonreproductive differences between the sexes.

Social learning theories are more difficult to test than those involving hormone chemistry and brain structures because the experimental control needed to infer causality is virtually impossible to achieve. There is also the problem of causal-arrow ambiguity when psychologists study messy, real-world variables. Consider, for example, the finding that participation in spatial activities is important in the development of spatial activities, and females engage in fewer spatial activities than males (Baenninger & Newcombe, 1989). This sort of finding still leaves open the question of why females engage in fewer spatial activities. It could be because they have been socialized to participate in other activities or because they have less spatial ability than males, on average, and therefore less interest. Of course, both are possible. In this case, an initially small sex difference could be widened by societal practices that magnify differences through differential experiences (Reinisch & Sanders, 1992). Dickens and Flynn (2001) devised a mathematical model that can explain how events in the environment interact with heritability to produce large changes in intelligence.

It is also possible that differences are reduced by education and training. In an experimental test of these possibilities, Sorby and Baartmans (1996) targeted improvement in visuospatial skills. All first-year engineering students at their university with low scores on a test of visuospatial ability were encouraged to enroll in a course designed to teach these skills. Enrollment resulted in improved performance in subsequent graphics courses by these students and better retention in engineering programs, which suggests that the effects persisted over time and were of at least some practical significance for both women and men. Terlecki (2005) examined the impact of training and practice on performance on mental rotation tasks and found that both men and women improved. Training produced more improvement than simple repetition of the task. However, her findings show that neither practice nor training was enough to reduce gender gaps in mental rotation, as both men and women improved equally. Cherney (2008) measured the effect of training using 3-D and 2-D computer games on tests of mental rotation. She found that training, in general, improved mental rotation scores, but women's gains were much greater than men's in this study. Virtually everyone can improve on cognitive tests if they receive appropriate instruction. These are all learnable skills. Education is one of the most potent variables in predicting level of achievement in a cognitive domain (assuming at least an educable range of mental functioning; Ceci, 1990).

There are substantial differences in the values, attitudes, and interests of contemporary males and females, which may help to explain cognitive sex differences. This conclusion is based on studies that have used the Allport-Vernon-Lindzey Study of Values (1970) assessment instrument (Lubinski, Schmidt, & Benbow, 1996) over many decades. "Masculine-typical" and "feminine-typical" patterns emerge from the Study of Values instrument, even when intelligence is held constant. Further support was found in a survey of college freshmen. Astin, Sax, Korn, and Mahoney (1995) found that college men spent much more time exercising, partying, watching television, and playing video games (37% spent one or more hour per week on video games compared with 7% of the women). The college women spent much more time on household and child care, reading for pleasure, studying, and volunteer work. On average, women and men live systematically different lives.

One of the most successful models of social learning has incorporated expectancies and motivation as a means for understanding the life choices that people make (Eccles, 1987). The attributions that people make for their successes and failures, expectations of success, individual aptitudes, strategies, and socialized beliefs work in concert to determine how hard they are willing to work at certain tasks and which tasks they select from the environment. Oswald (2008) demonstrated how the model works when she tested the influence of gender stereotypes (beliefs about groups of people) on women's liking for and perceived ability in masculine- and feminine-typed occupations. She found that strongly gender-identified women who were primed with traditional gender stereotypes showed more liking for feminine-typed occupations than controls. Similarly, another set of researchers hypothesized that the level of control and values would affect gender differences in emotions related to mathematics, even when controlling for prior achievement (Frenzel, Pekrun, & Goetz, 2007). These authors found that even though girls and boys had received similar grades in mathematics, girls reported significantly less enjoyment and pride than boys.They explain their findings in that the emotions described by the females could be attributed to the girls' low competence beliefs and domain value of mathematics, combined with their high subjective values of achievement in mathematics. This is a strong model that links values to achievement-related outcomes. It opens many educational routes for changing the status quo.

Two new approaches to studying the effects of stereotypes have been proposed. The significance of these new paradigms lies in the way they demonstrate the unconscious, automatic, and powerful influences that stereotypes have on thought and performance. Steele and Aronson (1995) investigated stereotype threat in African Americans. Their study was based on the notion that "when negative stereotypes targeting a social identity provide a framework for interpreting behavior in a given domain, the risk of being judged by, or treated in terms of, those negative stereotypes can evoke a disruptive state among stigmatized individuals" (Davies, Spencer, & Steele, 2005, p. 276). In their studies, they manipulated testing conditions so that instructions described a college-entrance-type test as either a test of intelligence or an investigation of a research problem. When African Americans were told that their intelligence was being tested, they performed significantly worse than when they were given other instructions. This difference was not found for the White students.

Steele and Aronson's (1995) findings regarding stereotypes of African Americans easily translate to a wide range of stereotypes and were confirmed in a study of female and male differences on a difficult math test (Steele, 1997). Females scored more poorly on a math test when they were told that the test produced gender differences than when the test was described as being insensitive to gender differences. The participants were not conscious of the effect of these instructions on their performance, but activating their knowledge of negative stereotypes prior to the tests had a substantial negative effect. In another study, women's attitudes toward the sex-stereotyped domains of the arts and mathematics were manipulated through subtle reminders of their gender identity. In both cases, those who were primed of their standing as female demonstrated more negative attitudes toward math and more positive attitudes toward the arts than females in the control condition (Steele & Ambady, 2006).

Banaji and her colleagues (Banaji & Hardin, 1996; Blair & Banaji, 1996; Greenwald & Banaji, 1995) used a different experimental paradigm that also revealed strong effects for stereotype knowledge on how people think. Banaji was primarily interested in understanding the automatic activation of sex-role stereotypes that underlie society's thoughts about females and males. The experimental procedure was varied, but all used tasks in which a prime word was flashed on a screen very quickly (about 0.25 seconds) followed by a target word. Participants had to respond quickly and accurately in making a judgment about the target word. The prime and target words were either consistent with regard to sex role stereotypes (e.g., soft-woman), inconsistent with sex role stereotypes (e.g., soft-man), or neutral. In general, participants responded more quickly and accurately when the target was consistent with the prime than when it was not. Sex-role stereotypes were affecting how the participants decoded simple words, yet the participants were unaware of this powerful influence. Together, these two new types of investigations show that expectancies and group-level beliefs can have effects that are unknown even to the participants. A study of female undergraduates enrolled in a college-level calculus class examined the effects of gender identification and implicit and explicit stereotypes on a math aptitude test (Kiefer & Sekaquaptewa, 2007). These authors found that women with low gender identification and low implicit stereotyping scored best on the math aptitude test and women who scored high on both measures were least inclined to pursue math careers.

An international study of implicit stereotypes that associate science and math abilities with being male has found a linear relationship between implicit stereotyping and the size of the male-female gap in science performance in the countries that participated in the Third International Math and Science Study (TIMSS; Nosek et al., 2009). Explicitly stated stereotypes were unrelated to the gender gap across countries. These data suggest that implicit stereotypes can exert powerful effects on the achievement of girls and boys in multiple countries.

Peer group socialization is another explanatory concept that has taken center stage among social learning theories. These theories show that parents and other adults may be less influential in the socialization of children than the children's own peer groups. In a review of the literature, Harris (1995) reached the unorthodox and unpopular conclusion that "parental behaviors have no effect on the psychological characteristics their children will have as adults" (p. 458). She raised the classical problem of causal-arrow ambiguity in her argument that parents and other adults respond to differences in children rather than causing the differences by their actions. Of course, children who read well grow up in homes with many books, but, according to Harris, the parents provide these children with books because they are good readers. This is an example of a child-driven effect in which the genetically determined disposition of the child caused the correlated behavior in the parents. She also posited relationship-drive effects in which the dispositions of the child match or fail to match the dispositions of the parents, resulting in correlations between dispositions in families and that of the child that do not support causal inferences.

If parents and other adults have little effect on the social and cognitive development of children, then what does affect this development? Harris (1995) believes that the answer lies in the peer group, specifically in those processes that create and maintain in-group favoritism, out-group hostilities, and between-group contrasts. Sex-typed behaviors are fostered through these peer group pressures. The sexual composition of the child's peer group is always important, with sex segregation especially critical in middle childhood. Harris reported that even infants can correctly classify females and males. Children are often more concerned about maintaining sex-typed behaviors than their parents because assimilation into the sex-segregated peer groups requires children to conform to group norms, a theory supported by Lytton and Romney's (1991) conclusion that parents engage in surprisingly few sex-differentiated socialization practices. Studies of peer group influence in childhood find that children's math grades are correlated with the average verbal and math skills of children in their peer groups (Kurdek & Sinclair, 2000). Children also appear to stereotype mathematics as masculine. As early as the fourth grade, girls and boys tend to select mostly boys as the best mathematics pupils in their classrooms (Räty, Kasanen, Kiiskinen, & Nykky, 2004). By middle adolescence, girls generally receive less peer support for science activities than boys (Stake & Nickens, 2005).

Biopsychosocial Model

A biopsychosocial model based on the inextricable links between the biological bases of intelligence and environmental events is an alternative to the nature-nurture dichotomy. Research and debate about the origins of sex differences are grounded in the belief that the nonreproductive differences between men and women originate from sex-differentiated biological mechanisms (nature; e.g., "sex" hormones), socialization practices (nurture; e.g., girls are expected to perform poorly on tests of advanced mathematics), and their interaction. A biopsychosocial model offers an alternative conceptualization: It is based on the idea that some variables are both biological and social and therefore cannot be classified into one of these two categories. Consider, for example, the role of learning in creating and maintaining an average difference between females and males. Learning is both a socially mediated event and a biological process. Individuals are predisposed to learn some topics more readily than others. A predisposition to learn some behaviors or concepts more easily than others is determined by prior learning experiences, the neurochemical processes that allow learning to occur (release of neurotransmitters), and change in response to learning (e.g., long-term potentiation and changes in areas of the brain that are active during performance of a task; Posner & Raichle, 1994). Thus, learning depends on what is already known and on the neural structures and processes that undergird learning. Of course, psychological variables such as interest and expectancy are also important in determining how readily information is learned, but interest and expectancy are also affected by prior learning. The biopsychosocial model is predicated on an integral conceptualization of nature and nurture that cannot be broken into nature or nurture subcomponents. Neural structures change in response to environmental events; environmental events are selected from the environment on the basis of, in part, predilections and expectancies; and the biological and socially mediated underpinnings of learning help to create the predilections and expectancies that guide future learning.

It is true that multiple psychological and social factors play a part in determining career direction. People's individual expectations for success are shaped by their perception of their own skills. One factor in forming our self-perception is how authority figures such as teachers perceive and respond to males and females. Jussim and Eccles (1992) found that the level at which teachers rated a student's mathematical talent early in the school year predicted later test scores – even when objective measures of ability were at odds with the teacher's perception. A study of London cab drivers found that they had enlarged portions of their right posterior hippocampus relative to a control group of adults. The cab drivers demonstrated a positive correlation between the size of the hippocampus that is activated during recall of complex routes and the number of years they had worked in this occupation, thus showing a "dose-size relationship" that is indicative of environmental influences (Maguire, Frackowiak, & Frith, 1997; Maguire et al., 2000).

Where We Go From Here

Understanding sex differences in intelligence is crucial to understanding cognition in general and the joint effects of nature and nurture on cognition. The truth about sex differences in intelligence depends on the nature of the cognitive task being assessed, the range of ability that is tested, the age and education of the participants, and numerous other modifying variables. There are intellectual areas in which females, on average, excel and others in which males, on average, excel. Psychological, social, and biological factors explain these differences. However, it does not seem that biology is limiting intelligence in any way because biology alone cannot explain the vast improvement of female performance on certain measures such as the increasing numbers of females scoring at the highest end on the SAT Math test (Blackburn, 2004).

Data showing differences between men and women in intelligence do not support the notion of a smarter sex, nor do they imply that the differences are immutable. There is direct evidence showing that specifically targeted training on cognitive tasks boosts performance for both men and women. Thus, the application of good learning principles in education can improve intellectual performance for all students. There are no cognitive reasons to support sex-segregated education, especially given the large amount of overlap in test scores for girls and boys on all tests of cognitive ability. The finding that girls get higher grades in school has been linked, at least in part, to better self-regulation and self-discipline, which allows them to delay gratification and behave in ways that are rewarded in classrooms (Duckworth & Seligman, 2006). Self-discipline has been used to explain many outcomes in life because it is critical to learning, especially when the material is complex and requires extended effort. Thus, the ability to self-regulate is rewarded in school grades and necessary for advanced learning. The fact that girls get better grades in every subject in school shows that they are learning at least as well as boys, and the fact that boys score higher on some standardized measures of achievement shows that they are learning at least as well as girls. For those concerned with increasing the number of females in math and science, the problem lies in convincing more females that "math counts" and making academic and career choices that are "mathwise."

The data on intelligence show that both sexes, on average, have their strengths and weaknesses. Nevertheless, the research argues that much can be done to try to help more women excel in science and encourage them to choose it as a profession. The challenges are many, requiring innovations in education, targeted mentoring and career guidance, and a commitment to uncover and root out bias, discrimination, and inequality. In the end, tackling these issues will benefit women, men, the economy, and science itself.

References

Adler, L. L. (Ed.). (1993). *International handbook on gender roles*. Westport, CT: Greenwood.

Allen, L. S., Richey, M. F., Chai, Y. M., & Gorski, R. A. (1991). Sex differences in the corpus callosum of the living human being. *Journal of Neuroscience, 11*, 933–942.

Allport, G. W., Vernon, P. E., & Lindzey, G. (1970). *Manual for the study of values* (3rd ed.). Boston, MA: Houghton Mifflin.

American Association of University Women. (1992). *The AAUW Report: How schools shortchange girls*. New York, NY: Marlowe.

Arden, R., & Plomin, R. (2006). Sex differences in variance of intelligence across childhood. *Personality and Individual Differences, 41*, 39–48.

Astin, A., Sax, L., Korn, W., & Mahoney, K. (1995). *The American freshman: National norms for fall 1995*. Los Angeles, CA: Higher Education Research Institute.

Baenninger, M., & Newcombe, N. (1989). The role of experience in spatial test performance: A meta-analysis. *Sex Roles, 20*, 327–344.

Baker, D. P., & Jones, D. P. (1992). *Opportunity and performance: A sociological explanation for gender differences in academic mathematics*. In J. Wrigley (Ed.), Education and gender equality (pp. 193–206). London, UK: Falmer Press.

Banaji, M. R., & Hardin, C. D. (1996). Automatic stereotyping. *Psychological Science, 7*, 136–141.

Bandura, A. (1977). *Social learning theory*. Englewood Cliffs, NJ: Prentice-Hall.

Barnes, L. L., Wilson, R. S., Schneider, J. A., Bienas, J. L., Evans, D. A., & Bennett, D. A. (2003). Gender, cognitive decline, and risk of AD in older persons. *Neurology, 60*, 1777–1781.

Bayer, U., & Erdmann, G. (2008). The influence of sex hormones on functional cerebral asymmetries in postmenopausal women. *Brain and Cognition, 67*, 140–149.

Begley, S. (1994, March 21). The estrogen complex. *Newsweek*, pp. 76–77.

Beilstein, C. D., & Wilson, J. F. (2000). Landmarks in route learning by girls and boys. *Perceptual & Motor Skills, 91*, 877–882.

Benbow, C. P., & Stanley, J. C. (1983). Sex differences in mathematical reasoning ability: More facts. *Science, 222*, 1029–1030.

Berenbaum, S. A., Korman, K., & Leveroni, C. (1995). Early hormones and sex differences in cognitive abilities [Special issue]. *Learning and Individual Differences, 7*, 303–321.

Blackburn, C. C. (2004, May). *Developing exceptional talent: Descriptive characteristics of highly precocious mathematical and verbal reasoners*. Paper presented at the Seventh Biennial Henry B. & Joycelyn Wallace National Research Symposium on Talent Development, University of Iowa, Iowa City.

Blair, C., Granger, D., & Razzam R. P. (2005). Cortisol reactivity is positively related to executive function in preschool children attending Head Start. *Child Development, 76*, 554–567.

Blair, I. V., & Banaji, M. R. (1996). Automatic controlled processes in stereotype priming. *Journal of Personality and Social Psychology, 70*, 1142–1163.

Brody, N. (1992). *Intelligence* (2nd ed.). New York, NY: Academic Press.

Buss, D. M. (1995). Psychological sex differences: Origins through sexual selection. *American Psychologist, 50*, 164–168.

Ceci, S. J. (1990). *On intelligence . . . more or less. A bio-ecological treatise on intellectual development*. Englewood Cliffs, NJ: Prentice-Hall.

Cherney, I. D. (2008). Mom, let me play more computer games: They improve my mental rotation skills. *Sex Roles, 59*, 776–786.

Collaer, M. L., & Hines, M. (1995). Human behavioral sex differences: A role for gonadal hormones during early development? *Psychological Bulletin, 118*, 55–107.

College Entrance Examination Board. (2004). *2004 college-bound seniors: A profile of SAT program test takers*. Retrieved June 21, 2009, from http://professionals.collegeboard.com/data-reports-research/sat/archived/2004.

Colom, R., Juan-Espinosa, M., Abad, F. & García, L. F. (2000). Negligible sex differences in general intelligence, *Intelligence, 28*, 57–68.

Corbett, C., Hill, C., & St. Rose, A. (2008). *Where the girls are: The facts about gender equity in education*. Washington, DC: American Association of University Women.

Davies, A. P. C., & Sheckelford, T. K. (2006, September). An evolutionary psychological perspective on gender similarities and differences. *American Psychologist*, 640–641.

Davies, P. G., Spencer, S. J., & Steele, C. M. (2005). Clearing the air: Identity safety moderates the effects of stereotype threat on women's leadership aspirations. *Journal of Personality and Social Psychology*, 88, 276–287.

Dickens, W. T., & Flynn, J. R. (2001). Heritability estimates versus large environmental effcts: The IQ paradox. *Psychological Review, 108*, 346–369.

Duckworth, A. L., & Seligman, M. E. P. (2006). Self-discipline gives girls the edge: Gender in self-discipline, grades, and achievement test scores. *Journal of Educational Psychology, 98*, 198–208.

Dykiert, D., Gale, C. R., & Deary, I. J. (2008). Are apparent sex differences in mean IQ scores created in part by sample restriction and increased male variance? *Intelligence*, *37*, 42–47.

Eals, M., & Silverman, I. (1994). The hunter-gatherer theory of spatial sex differences: Proximate factors mediating the female advantage in recall of object arrays. *Ethology and Sociobiology*, *15*, 95–105.

Eccles, J. S. (1987). Gender roles and women's achievement-related decisions. *Psychology of Women Quarterly*, *11*, 135–172.

Feng, J., Spence, I., & Pratt, J. (2007). Playing an action video game reduces gender differences in spatial cognition. *Psychological Science*, *18*, 850–855.

Frenzel, A. C., Pekrun, R., & Goetz, T. (2007). Girls and mathematics – A "hopeless" issue? A control-value approach to gender differences in emotions towards mathematics. *European Journal of Psychology of Education*, *22*, 497–514.

Geary, D. C. (1996). Sexual selection and sex differences in mathematical abilities. *Behavioral and Brain Sciences*, *19*, 229–284.

Geary, D. C. (2007). Educating the evolved mind: Conceptual foundations for an evolutionary educational psychology. In J. S. Carlson & J. R. Levin (Eds.), *Educating the evolved mind* (pp. 1–100). Greenwich, CT: Information Age.

Geiser, C., Lehmann, W., & Eid, M. (2008). A note on sex differences in mental rotation in different age groups. *Intelligence*, *36*, 556–563.

Gerstorf, D., Herlitz, A., & Smith, J. (2006). Stability of sex differences in cognition in advanced old age: The role of education and attrition. *Journal of Gerontology: Psychological Sciences and Social Sciences*, *61*, 245–249.

Giedd, J. N., Castellanos, F. X., Rajapakse, J. C., Vaituzis, A. C., & Rapoport, J. L. (1997). Sexual dimorphism of the developing human brain. *Progress in Neuropsychopharmacology & Biological Psychiatry*, *21*, 1185–1901.

Greene, J. P., & Winters, M. A. (2006). *Leaving boys behind: Public high school graduation rates* (Civic Report 48). Retrieved June 7, 2009, from http://www.manhattan-institute.org/html/cr_48.htm.

Greenwald, A. G., & Banaji, M. R. (1995). Implicit social cognition: Attitudes, self-esteem, and stereotypes. *Psychological Review*, *102*, 4–27.

Gur, R. C., Alsop, D., Glahn, D., Petty, R., Swanson, C. L., Maldjian, J. A., et al. (2000). An fMRI study of sex differences in regional activation to a verbal and a spatial task. *Brain and Language*, *74*, 157–170.

Gur, R. C., Turetsky, B. I., Matsui, M., Yan, M., Bilker, W., Hughett, P., & Gur, R. E. (1999). Sex differences in brain gray and white matter in healthy young adults: Correlations with cognitive performance. *Journal of Neuroscience*, *19*, 4065–4072.

Halpern, D. F. (in press). *Sex differences in cognitive abilities* (4th ed.). New York, NY: Psychology Press.

Halpern, D. F., Benbow, C., Geary, D., Gur, D., Hyde, J., & Gernsbacher, M. A. (2007). The science of sex-differences in science and mathematics. *Psychological Science in the Public Interest*, 8, 1–52.

Halpern, D. F., & Tan, U. (2001). Stereotypes and steroids: Using a psychobiosocial model to understand cognitive sex differences. *Brain and Cognition*, *45*, 392–414.

Hampson, E. (1990). Estrogen-related variations in human spatial and articulatory-motor skills. *Psychoneuroendocrinology*, *15*, 97–111.

Hampson, E., & Kimura, D. (1988). Reciprocal effects of hormonal fluctuations on human motor and perceptual-spatial skills. *Behavioral Neuroscience*, *102*, 456–459.

Harris, J. R. (1995). Where is the child's environment? A group socialization theory of development. *Psychological Review*, *102*, 458–489.

Hedges, L. V., & Nowell, A. (1995). Sex differences in mental test scores, variability, and numbers of high-scoring individuals. *Science*, *269*, 41–45.

Herman, R. A., & Wallen, K. (2007). Cognitive performance in rhesus monkeys varies by sex and prenatal androgen exposure. *Hormones and Behavior*, *51*, 496–507.

Hunt, E., & Madhyastha, T. (2008). Recruitment modeling: An analysis and an application to the study of male-female differences in intelligence. *Intelligence*, *36*, 653–663.

Hyde, J. S. (2005). The gender similarity hypothesis. *American Psychologist*, *60*, 581–592.

Hyde, J. S., Fennema, E., & Lamon, S. J. (1990). Gender differences in mathematics performance: A meta-analysis. *Psychological Bulletin*, *107*, 139–155.

Hyde, J. S., Lindberg, S. M., Linn, M. C., Ellis, A. B., & Williams, C. C. (2008). Gender similarities characterize math performance. *Science*, *321*, 494–495.

Imperato-McGinley, J., Pichardo, M., Gautier, T., Voyer, D., & Bryden, M. P. (1991). Cognitive abilities in androgen insensitive subjects – Comparison with control males and females from the same kindred. *Clinical Endocrinology*, 34, 341–347.

Innocenti, G. M. (1994). Some new trends in the study of the corpus callosum. *Behavioral and Brain Research*, 64, 1–8.

Irwing, P., & Lynn, R. (2005). Intelligence: Is there a difference in IQ scores? *Nature*, 438, 31–32.

Jancke, L., & Steinmetz, H. (1994). Interhemispheric-transfer time and corpus callosum size. *Neuroreport*, 5, 2385–2388.

Jensen, A. R. (1998). *The g factor: The science of mental ability*. New York, NY: Praeger.

Johnson, W., & Bouchard, T. J. (2006). Sex differences in mental abilities: g masks the dimensions on which they lie. *Intelligence*, 35, 23–59.

Johnson, W., Carothers, A., & Deary, I. J. (2008). Sex differences in variability in general intelligence: A new look at an old question. *Perspectives on Psychological Science*, 3, 518–531.

Johnson, W., Carothers, A., & Deary, I. J. (2009). A role for the X chromosome in sex differences in variability in general intelligence? *Perspectives in Psychological Science*, 4, 598–611.

Jost, J. T., & Kay, A. C. (2005). Exposure to benevolent sexism and complementary gender stereotypes: Consequences for specific and diffuse forms of system justification. *Journal of Personality and Social Psychology*, 88, 498–509.

Jussim, L., & Eccles, J. S. (1992). Teacher expectations: II. Construction and reflection of student achievement. *Journal of Personality and Social Psychology*, 63, 947–961.

Karpiak, C. P., Buchanan, J. P., Hosey, M., & Smith., A. (2007). University students from single-sex and coeducational high schools: Differences in majors and attitudes at a Catholic university. *Psychology of Women Quarterly*, 31, 282–289.

Kaufman, S. B. (2007). Sex differences in mental rotation and spatial visualization ability: Can they be accounted for by differences in working memory capacity? *Intelligence*, 35, 211–223.

Kiefer, A. K., & Sekaquaptewa, D. (2007). Implicit stereotypes, gender identification, and math-related outcomes: A prospective study of female college students. *Psychological Science*, 18, 13–18.

Killgore, W. D., & Killgore, D. B. (2007). Morningness-eveningness correlates with verbal ability in women but not men. *Perceptual and Motor Skills*, 104, 33–338.

Kimball, M. M. (1989). A new perspective on women's mathematics achievement. *Psychological Bulletin*, 105, 198–214.

Kimura, D. (1993). *Neuromotor mechanisms in human communication*. New York, NY: Oxford University Press.

Kimura, D. (1996). Sex, sexual orientation and sex hormones influence human cognitive function. *Current Opinion in Neurobiology*, 6, 259–263.

Kimura, D., & Hampson, E. (1994). Cognitive pattern in men and women is influenced by fluctuations in sex hormones. *Psychological Science*, 3, 57–61.

Kucian, K., Loenneker, T., Dietrich, T., Martin, E., & von Aster, M. (2005). Gender differences in brain activation patterns during mental rotation and number related cognitive tasks. *Psychology Science*, 47, 112–131.

Kurdek, L. A., & Sinclair, R. J. (2000). Psychological, family, and peer predictors of academic outcomes in first- through fifth-grade children. *Journal of Educational Psychology*, 92, 449–457.

LeBlanc, E. S., Janowsky, J., Chan, B. K., & Nelson, H. D. (2001). Hormone replacement therapy and cognition: Systematic review and metaanalysis. *Journal of American Medical Association*, 285, 1489–1499.

Levine, S. C., Huttenlocher, J., Tayler, A., & Langrock, A. (1999). Early sex differences in spatial skill. *Developmental Psychology*, 35, 940–949.

Linn, M. C., & Petersen, A. C. (1985). Emergence and characterization of sex differences in spatial ability: A meta-analysis. *Child Development*, 56, 1479–1498.

Loring-Meier, S., & Halpern, D. F. (1999). Sex differences in visual-spatial working memory: Components of cognitive processing. *Psychonomic Bulletin & Review*, 6, 464–471.

Lott, B., & Maluso, D. (1993). The social learning of gender. In A. E. Beall & R. Sternberg (Eds.), *The psychology of gender* (pp. 99–123). New York, NY: Guilford Press.

Low, L.-F., & Ansley, K. J. (2006). Hormone replacement therapy and cognitive performance in postmenopausal women – a review by cognitive domain. *Neuroscience and Biobehavioral Reviews*, 30, 66–84.

Lubinski, D., Schmidt, D. B., & Benbow, C. P. (1996). A 20-year stability analysis of the Study of Values for intellectually gifted individuals from adolescence to adulthood. *Journal of Applied Psychology*, 81, 443–451.

Lueptow, L. B., Garovich, L., & Lueptow, M. B. (1995). The persistence of gender stereotypes in the face of changing sex roles: Evidence contrary to the sociocultural model. *Ethology & Sociobiology*, *16*, 509–530.

Luine, V. N. (2008). Sex steroids and cognitive function. *Journal of Neuroendocrinology*, *20*, 866–872.

Lutchamaya, S., Baron-Cohen, S., & Raggatt, P. (2002). Foetal testosterone and vocabulary size in 18- and 24-month-old infants. *Infant Behavior and Development*, *24*, 418–424.

Lytton, H., & Romney, D. M. (1991). Parents' differential socialization of boys and girls: A meta-analysis. *Psychological Bulletin*, *109*, 267–296.

Maguire, E. A., Frackowiak, R. S. J., & Frith, C. D. (1997). Recalling routes around London: Activation of the right hippocampus in taxi drivers. *Journal of Neuroscience*, *17*, 7103–7110.

Maguire, E. A., Gadian, D. G., Johnsrude, I. S., Ashburner, C. D., Frackowiak, R. S. J., & Frith, C. D. (2000). Navigation-related structural change in the hippocampi of taxi drivers. *Proceedings of the National Academy of Science, USA*, *97*, 4398–4403.

Maitland, S. B., Intrieri, R. C., Schaie, K. W., & Willis, S. L. (2000). Gender differences and changes in cognitive abilities across the adult life span. *Aging, Neuropsychology, and Cognition*, *7*, 32–53.

Masters, M. S., & Sanders, B. (1993). Is the gender difference in mental rotation disappearing? *Behavior Genetics*, *23*, 337–341.

Moffat, S. D., & Hampson, E. (1996). A curvilinear relationship between testosterone and spatial cognition in humans: Possible influence of hand preference. *Psychoneuroendocrinology*, *21*, 323–337.

Moore, D. S., & Johnson, S. P. (2008). Mental rotation in human infants: A sex difference. *Psychological Science*, *19*, 1063–1066.

Mueller, S. C., Temple, V., Oh, E., VanRyzin, C., Williams, A., Cornwell, B., Grillon, C., Pine, D. S., Ernst, D. S. & Merke, D. P. (2008). Early androgen exposure modulates spatial cognition in congenital adrenal hyperplasia. *Psychoneuroendocrinology*, *33*, 973–980.

National Assessment of Educational Progress. (2008). *The nation's report card: Writing 2007*. Retrieved May 27, 2009, from http://nces.ed.gov/nationsreportcard/.

National Center for Education Statistics. (2005). *Highlights for the Trends in International Mathematics and Science Study (TIMSS,) 2003*. Retrieved May 27, 2009, from http://nces.ed.gov/pubs2005/timss03.

National Science Board. (2006). *New formulas for America's workforce 2: Girls in science and engineering* (NSF 06–60). Retrieved June 21, 2009, from http://www.nsf.gov/publications/.

Neave, N., Menaged, M., & Weightman, D. R. (1999). Sex differences in cognition: The role of testosterone and sexual orientation. *Brain and Cognition*, *41*, 245–262.

Nosek, B. A., et al. (2009). National differences in gender-science stereotypes predict national sex differences in science and math achievement. *Proceedings of the National Academy of Science*, *106*, 10593–10597.

Nyborg, H. (2005). Sex-related differences in general intelligence g, brain size, and social status. *Personality and Individual Differences*, *39*, 497–509.

Ostatníková, D., Dohnányiová, M., Laznibatová, J., Putz, Z., & Celec, P. (2001). Fluctuations of salivary testosterone level in relation to cognitive performance. *Homeostasis in Health and Disease*, *41*, 51–53.

Ostatníková, D., Laznibatová, J., Putz, Z., Mataseje, A., Dohnányiová, M., & Pastor, K. (2000). Salivary testosterone levels in intellectually gifted and non-intellectually gifted preadolescents: An exploratory study. *High Ability Studies*, *11*, 41–54.

Oswald, D. L. (2008). Gender stereotypes and women's reports of liking and ability in traditionally masculine and feminine occupations. *Psychology of Women Quarterly*, *32*, 196–203.

Posner, M. I., & Raichle, M. E. (1994). *Images of mind*. New York, NY: Freeman.

Quinn, P. C., & Liben, L. S. (2008). A sex difference in mental rotation in young infants. *Psychological Science*, *19*, 1067–1070.

Rampey, B. D., Dion, G. S., & Donahue, P. L. (2009). *NAEP trends in academic progress* (NCES 2009–479). National Center for Education Statistics, Institute of Education Sciences, U.S. Department of Education, Washington, DC.

Räty, H., Kasanen, K., Kiiskinen, J., & Nykky, M. (2004). Learning intelligence: Children's choices of the best pupils in the mother tongue and mathematics. *Social Behavior and Personality*, *32*, 303–312.

Read, S., Pedersen, N. L., Gatz, M., Berg, S., Vuoksimaa, E., Malmberg, B., Johansson, B., & McClearn, G. E. (2006). Sex differences after all those years? Heritability of cognitive abilities in old age. *Journals of Gerontology, 61*, 137–143.

Reinisch, J. M., & Sanders, S. A. (1992). Prenatal hormonal contributions to sex differences in cognitive and personality development. In A. A. Gerall, H. Moltz, & I. I. Ward (Eds.), *Sexual differentiation: Vol. 11. Handbook of behavioral neurobiology* (pp. 221–243). New York, NY: Plenum.

Ryan, J., Carriere, I., Scali, J., Ritchie, K., & Ancelin, M-L. (2009). Life-time estrogen exposure and cognitive functioning in later life. *Psychoneuroendocrinology, 34*, 287–298.

Sadker, M., & Sadker, D. (1995). *Failing at fairness: How our schools cheat girls*. New York, NY: Touchstone.

Schmidt, F. L., & Hunter, J. (2004). General mental ability in the world of work: Occupational attainment and job performance. *Journal of Personality and Social Psychology, 86*, 162–173.

Shah, P., & Miyake, A. (1996). The separability of working memory resources for spatial thinking and language processing: An individual differences approach. *Journal of Experimental Psychology, 125*, 4–27.

Shaywitz, B. A., Shaywitz, S. E., Pugh, K. R., Constable, R. T., Skudlarski, P., Fulbright, R. K., Bronen, R. A., Fletcher, J. M., Shankweller, D. P., Katz, L., & Gore, J. C. (1995). Sex differences in the functional organization of the brain for language. *Nature, 373*, 607–609.

Sherwin, B. (2003). Estrogen and cognitive functioning in women. *Endocrine Reviews, 24*, 133–151.

Skuse, D. (2005). X-linked genes and mental functioning. *Human Molecular Genetics, 14*, R27–R32.

Snyder, T. D., Dillow, S. A., & Hoffman, C. M. (2009). *Digest of Education Statistics 2008* (NCES 2009–020). National Center for Education Statistics, Institute of Educational Sciences, U. S. Department of Education. Washington, DC. Table 149.

Sommers, C. H. (2000, May). The war against boys. *Atlantic*. Retrieved June 11, 2009, from http://www.theatlantic.com/doc/200005/war-against-boys.

Sorby, S. J., & Baartmans, B. J. (1996). The development and assessment of a course for enhancing the 3-D spatial visualization skills of first year engineering students. *Engineering Design Graphics Journal, 60*, 13–20.

Spelke, E. S. (2005). Sex difference in intrinsic aptitude for mathematics and science? A critical review. *American Psychologist, 60*, 950–958.

Spinath, F. M., Spinath, B., & Plomin, R. (2008). The nature and nurture of intelligence and motivation in the origins of sex differences in elementary school achievement. *European Journal of Personality, 22*, 211–229.

Stake, J. E., & Nickens, S. D. (2005). Adolescent girls' and boys' science peer relationships and perceptions of the possible self as scientist. *Sex Roles, 52*, 1–12.

Steele, C. M. (1997). A threat in the air: How stereotypes shape intellectual identity and performance. *American Psychologist, 52*, 613–629.

Steele, J. R., & Ambady, N. (2006). "Math is hard!" The effect of gender priming on women's attitudes. *Journal of Experimental Social Psychology, 42*, 428–436.

Steele, C. M., & Aronson, J. (1995). Stereotype threat and the intellectual test performance of African Americans. *Journal of Personality and Social Psychology, 69*, 797–811.

Steinmetz, H., Staiger, J. F., Schluag, G., Huang, Y., & Jancke, L. (1995). Corpus callosum and brain volume in women and men. *Neuroreport, 6*, 1002–1004.

Straube, E., Straube, W., Krüger, E., Bradatsch, M., Jacob-Meisel, M., & Rose, H. (1999). Disruption of male sex hormones with regard to pesticides: Pathophysiology and regulatory aspects. *Toxicology Letters, 107*, 225–231.

Stumpf, H., & Stanley, J. C. (1996). Gender-related differences on the College Board's advanced placement and achievement tests, 1982–1992. *Journal of Educational Psychology, 88*, 353–364.

Study of Mathematically Precocious Youth. (2006). Retrieved June 23, 2009, from http://www.vanderbilt.edu/Peabody/SMPY/PsychScience2006.pdf.

Terlecki, M. S. (2005). The effects of long-term practice and training on mental rotation. *Dissertation Abstracts International, 65*(10-B), 5434.

Torres, A., Gómez-Gil, E., Vidal, A., Puig, O., Boget, T., & Salamero, M. (2006). Gender differences in cognitive functions and the influence of sexhormones. *Actas Españolas de Psyiquiatria, 34*, 408–415.

Turkheimer, E., & Halpern, D. F. (in press). Sex differences in variability for cognitive measures: Do the ends justify the genes? *Perspectives in Psychological Science*.

U. S. Department of Education. (1997). *National assessment of educational progress* (Indicator 32: Writing Proficiency; prepared by the Educational Testing Service). Retrieved May 27, 2009, from http://www.ed.gov/nces.

U. S. Department of Education, Office of Planning, Evaluation and Policy Development, Policy and Program Studies Research. (2005). *Single-sex versus coeducational schooling: A systematic review*. Washington, DC: Author.

van Exel, E., Gussekloo, J., de Craen, A. J. M., Bootsma-van der Wiel, A., Houx, P., Knook, D. L., & Westendorp, R. G. J. (2001). Cognitive function in the oldest old: Women perform better than men. *Journal of Neurology, Neurosurgery, & Psychiatry*, 71, 29–32.

Viner, K. (1994). Issues. *Cosmopolitan*, p. 105.

Volkman, F., Szatmari, P., & Sparrow, S. (1993). Sex differences in pervasive developmental disabilities. *Journal of Autism and Developmental Disabilities*, 23, 579–591.

Wai, J., Cacchio, M., Putallaz, M., & Makel, M. C. (2010). Sex differences in the right tail of cognitive abilities: A 30-year examination. *Intelligence*, 38, 412–423.

Willingham, W. W., & Cole, N. S. (1997). *Gender and fair assessment*. Mahwah, NJ: Erlbaum.

CHAPTER 14

Racial and Ethnic Group Differences in Intelligence in the United States

Multicultural Perspectives

Lisa A. Suzuki, Ellen L. Short, and Christina S. Lee

The relationship between culture and intelligence is complex and characterized by a lack of consensus regarding the definition and operationalization of each construct. One can find thousands of publications with "culture" in the title and be overwhelmed by the range of indicators designed to measure its components (e.g., acculturation, racial identity, ethnic identity, cultural intelligence). By the same token, it is a misperception to assume that simply because numerous intelligence tests exist and have gained global popularity that the construct is unambiguous.

Understanding the relationship between culture and intelligence has real-world implications for members of the racially and ethnically diverse communities that reside in the United States and abroad. This chapter will address multicultural perspectives of intelligence in the United States; the reader is referred to Chapter 31, Intelligence in Worldwide Perspective, this volume, for a discussion of work that has been done internationally. We will focus our attention on the following: definitions of relevant concepts; environment, social location, and cultural context; measures of intelligence; and outcome implications in testing ethnocultural populations.

Defining the Relevant Concepts

The multiple definitions of culture and intelligence have made it difficult to achieve consensus on these constructs. In the following sections we highlight the definitions of terms that will serve as the foundation of our discussion in this chapter. Our caveat to the reader is that we are aware that in selecting a limited set of definitions we exclude other perspectives.

Culture

"Culture is emerging as one of the most important and perhaps one of the most misunderstood constructs in contemporary theories of psychology" (Pedersen, 1999, p. 3). While hundreds of definitions of culture are found in the literature (Kroeber & Kluckhohn, 1963), one of the most frequently cited definitions in the social sciences literature comes from Geertz's (1973) text *The Interpretation of Cultures* (1973).

> *[Culture] denotes a historically transmitted pattern of meanings embodied in symbols, a system of inherited conceptions expressed in symbolic forms by means of which men communicate, perpetuate, and develop their knowledge about and attitudes toward life. (p. 89)*

Serpell (2000) elaborates further by stating:

> *Culture consists of a set of practices (constituted by a particular pattern of recurrent activities with associated artifacts) that are informed by a system of meanings (encoded in language and other symbols) and maintained by a set of institutions over time. (p. 549)*

Pedersen (1999) identifies multiculturalism as the fourth force or dimension in psychology, placing it among the other three major theories of humanism, behaviorism, and psychodynamism. Despite its prominence, however, there are numerous challenges in multicultural understanding given the complex nature of cultures that are so often dynamic and not static; that is, cultures change and evolve over time (e.g., López & Guarnaccia, 2000). In addition, individuals often belong to different cultures and possess multiple intersecting identities over their lifetime. For example, Goldberger and Veroff (1995) define culture as a common set of experiences related to a variety of variables, such as geographic boundaries, language, race, ethnicity, religious belief, social class, gender, sexual orientation, age, and ability status.

Overall, most definitions converge on one important point: culture provides a context in which people develop and learn. Therefore, it is difficult to define intelligence without first understanding the individual's sociocultural context.

Intelligence

Most definitions of intelligence contain reference to cognitively based abilities such as abstract thinking, reasoning, problem solving, and acquisition of knowledge (Snyderman & Rothman, 1988). In 1994, the *Wall Street Journal* published an article entitled "Mainstream Science on Intelligence," promoting the following definition:

> *A very general mental capability that, among other things, involves the ability to reason, plan, solve problems, think abstractly, comprehend complex ideas, learn quickly and learn from experience. (p. A18)*

What is missing from this definition of intelligence is an understanding of the pervasive role of culture. As Sternberg and Kaufman (1998) note:

> *Cultures designate as "intelligent" the cognitive, social and behavioral attributes that they value as adaptive to the requirements of living in those cultures. To the extent that there is overlap in these attributes across cultures, there will be overlap in the cultures' conceptions of intelligence. Although, conceptions of intelligence may vary across cultures, the underlying cognitive attributes probably do not. There may be some variation in social and behavioral attributes. As a result, there is probably a common core of cognitive skills that underlies intelligence in all cultures, with the cognitive skills having different manifestations across the cultures. (p. 497)*

It is important to note that there are a number of intelligences (e.g., Ceci, 1996; Gardner, 1983; Sternberg, 1996), among which conventionally measured cognitive abilities and skills are only one component. Definitions of intelligence are "value laden," given their focus on "concepts of appropriateness, competence, and potential" (Serpell, 2000, p. 549). Within the last decade more attention has been focused on cultural intelligence that refers to skills that enable an individual to operate socially in multiple cultural contexts, transferring the skills learned in one context to other contexts effectively (Brislin, Worthley, & Macnab, 2006).

Fagan and Holland (2006) investigated definitions of intelligence based on information processing focusing on racial equality in intelligence. They hypothesized that racial differences in intelligence scores were due to differences in individuals' intellectual ability or to differences in their exposure to information. In other words, the IQ score was a measure of an individual's knowledge based upon the person's information-processing ability and the information given to the individual by the culture. The authors suggest that all individuals have not had equal opportunity of exposure to information presented in standardized tests of intelligence.

One of the measures based upon an information processing model is the Cognitive Assessment System (CAS; Naglieri & Das, 1997). The CAS was developed to focus on planning, attention, and simultaneous and successive processing. A study comparing this measure with a traditional intelligence test yielded a reduction in group differences between matched samples of Hispanic and non-Hispanic students (Naglieri, Rojahn, & Matto, 2007). The authors reported similar findings with a Black sample and, in addition, noted that fewer Black students were classified as mentally retarded using the CAS than with the Wechsler Intelligence Scale for Children-III. Thus, the information-processing model appears promising.

Heritability

One of the most heated debates about intelligence and race exists at the intersection of genetics, heritability, and culture. Heritability itself is an elusive construct and estimates of this construct are generally obtained "for particular populations at particular times. They can vary in different populations or at different times" (Rushton & Jensen, 2005, p. 239).

> *Heritability describes* what *is the genetic contribution to individual differences in a particular population at a particular time, not* what could be. *If either the genetic or the environmental influences change (e.g., due to migration, greater educational opportunity, better nutrition), then the relative impact of genes and environment will change. (p. 239)*

Rushton and Jensen (2005) published a review of 30 years of research on racial differences in cognitive ability. After discussion of research underlying 10 categories of evidence, they conclude that a "genetic component" exists underlying the differences between Blacks and Whites. Since this article's publication, a number of scholars have critiqued their conclusions that favor a hereditarian explanation that they identify as 50% genetic–50% environmental. For example, Rushton and Jensen (2005) cite decades of research on high correlations of intelligence test scores between identical twins reared apart to support their hereditarian perspective. Nisbett (2009) provides a contrasting argument, noting that the high correlation among twins reared apart "reflects not just the fact that their genes are identical but also the fact that their environments are highly similar" (p. 26). Thus, it is unlikely that identical twins would be raised in diametrically different environments.

Helms (1992) notes that the biological and environmental explanations that have been used to explain racial and ethnic group differences in Cognitive Ability Test (CAT) performance have not been "operationally defined adequately enough to permit valid interpretations of racial and ethnic group differences in CAT performance nor to justify the extensive use of such measures across racial and ethnic groups other than for research purposes" (p. 1083). Moreover, Helms states that neither perspective employs culture-specific models, principles, or definitions that can be used to examine the influence of culture upon the content of the CAT and in the performance of test takers. She proposes application of the culturalist perspective, which encourages "consideration of the idea that many intact cultures can exist within the same national (e.g., U.S.) environment," and may offer "the rudiments of a framework for formulating testable hypotheses concerning the impact of the test constructors' cultural orientations on the content of their products" (p. 1091). She notes that the culturalist perspective may also "suggest different explanations for what are ostensibly racial or ethnic group differences in CAT performance, but may be cultural differences in actuality" (p. 1091).

Environment, Poverty, and Home Environment

Culture and environment are intimately linked as culture impacts the meaning assigned to perception of one's environment. This relationship is evident even in early phases of child development.

> *Children appear effortlessly to detect, abstract, and internalize culturally based rules of performance and systems of meaning. As an organizer of the environment, thus, culture assures that key meaning systems are elaborated in appropriate ways at different stages of development, and that learning occurs across behavioral domains and various scales of time. (Harkness, Super, Barry, Zeitlin, & Long, 2009, p. 138)*

The culture of poverty produces a number of environmental factors that have been related to lower intelligence. Nisbett (2009) summarizes these as the presence of lead (e.g., in substandard housing), usage of alcohol by pregnant women, health concerns leading to impediments in learning, health issues (e.g., poorer dental health, higher numbers of asthma cases, poorer vision, poorer hearing), more exposure to smoke and pollution, mothers less likely to breastfeed, poorer medical care, less exposure to reading material, and less exposure to language (i.e., fewer words spoken to them by parents). The list goes on for those experiencing a lack of resources, including vitamin and mineral deficiencies, emotional trauma, poor schools, poor neighborhoods, a less desirable peer group, frequent moving, and disruption of education. In their study of environmental risk factors and the impact of these on 4-year-old children's verbal IQ scores, Sameroff, Seifer, Barocas, Zax, and Greenspan (1987) concluded:

> *The multiple pressures of environmental context in terms of amount of stress from the environment, the family's resources for coping with that stress, the number of children that must share those resources, and the parents' flexibility in understanding and dealing with their children all play a role in fostering or hindering of child intellectual and social competencies. (p. 349)*

Valencia and Suzuki (2001) reviewed studies related to learning experiences in the home environment and intelligence. The research on minority families indicates a positive correlation between measures of home environment and children's intelligence. The authors caution, however, that there may be "variations [in home environment] across racial/ethnic groups" that impact these overall findings (p. 110). In addition, their work points to the importance of home environment measures as being a potentially better predictor of children's measured intelligence than socioeconomic status. Therefore, "it is possible for parents to modify their behavior by acquiring knowledge about how to structure an intellectually stimulating home environment for their children" taking into consideration cultural variations (p. 110).

These findings do not negate the relationship between lower socioeconomic status and lower measured intelligence. Sattler (2008) reports, "Poverty in and of itself is not necessary nor sufficient to produce intellectual deficits, especially if nutrition and the home environment are adequate" (p. 137). In many instances, however, children are exposed to

> *low level parental education, poor nutrition and health care, substandard housing, family disorganization, inconsistent discipline, diminished sense of personal worth, low expectations, frustrated aspirations, physical violence in their neighborhoods, and other environmental pressures. (Sattler, 2008, pp. 137–138)*

While they do not automatically produce intellectual deficits, these conditions are often associated with lower performance on intelligence measures.

Due to limited or nonexistent health care, particular racial and ethnic groups are at greater risk for sensory loss and other health problems that may lower their performance on intelligence measures – for example, higher blood lead levels leading to cognitive deficits or untreated ear infections resulting in auditory losses. Other characteristics of the sociocultural context include these:

- **Education**: Years of education are related to intelligence test performance, with more educated individuals obtaining higher scores. However, what is unclear is whether more intelligent individuals just stay in school longer or whether people score higher on intelligence tests because they are in school longer (Kaufman, 1990). Kaufman reported that college graduates score 32.5 points higher on the Wechsler Adult Intelligence Scale than those who have been in school seven years or fewer.
- **Residence:** Children residing in isolated communities may obtain lower scores on intelligence tests due to a lack of familiarity with the test materials and a lack of understanding of test-taking strategies. However, this issue may be moot given that urban versus rural and regional differences have decreased over time. Access to technology, input from the media, and improved educational practices appear to account for this change (Kaufman, 1990).
- **Language:** Fluency in English may impact verbal test scores, as familiarity with the dominant culture upon which the test is based impacts performance. Large discrepancies are noted between children with limited English proficiency and those students who have mastery of English (Puente & Puente, 2009).
- **Acculturation:** Acculturation is "a dynamic process of change and adaptation that individuals undergo as a result of contact with members of different cultures" (Rivera, 2008, p. 76). The process of acculturation involves the environment as well as characteristics of the individual. Acculturation impacts attitudes, beliefs, values, affect, and behavior. Razani, Murcia, Tabares, and Wong (2007) noted that acculturation accounted for a significant amount of variance on a verbal measure of intelligence among an ethnically diverse sample. In addition, a formal measure of acculturation was a better predictor of performance on a verbal measure than length of residence in the United States that is often used as a proxy for acculturation. Some researchers have indicated that "level of acculturation is one of the most important variables that affects test performance" (Mpofu & Ortiz, 2009).
- **Other Contextual Variables:** Acculturation is often linked to contextual variables such as language proficiency and familiarity with a testing situation, which in turn influence performance on intelligence tests (Mpofu & Ortiz, 2009). While attitude of the examiner toward the test taker, the ethnicity of the examiner, and the language of the test administration have been identified as potentially influencing performance on cognitive assessments (Okazaki & Sue, 2002), results regarding their impact are inconclusive. For example, in a review of 29 studies examining the impact of Euro-American examiners on intelligence test scores of African American children, 25 of the studies indicated no significant relationship between the race of the examiner and test scores (Sattler & Gwynne, 1982). The relationship may be based on more specific characteristics of the examinee and the test. Frisby (1999) reports that examiner familiarity was most positive for African American participants from low socioeconomic backgrounds in comparison with Whites, especially when the tests were difficult and the examiner had known the examinee for a substantial period of time.

Measures of Intelligence

While "test use is universal" (Oakland, 2009, p. 2), most test development occurs "in countries that emphasize individualism and favor meritocracy (i.e., the belief that persons should be rewarded based upon their accomplishments) rather than collectivism and egalitarianism (i.e., the belief that all people are equal and should have equal access to resources and opportunities)" (Oakland, 2009, p. 4). In addition, as Serpell (2000) notes, "Assessment of intelligence as a distinct, formally structured activity, is a product of very particular cultural arrangements" (p. 555) that are found in Western contexts. In other words, people coming from cultures where achievement on standardized tests is not a valued or prioritized method of assessment may not perform as well on these measures.

g Factor

In 1927, Spearman hypothesized that intelligence consists of a general factor (*g*) and two specific factors, verbal ability and fluency. His work in the development of factor analysis led to the operationalization of *g* as the first unrotated factor of an orthogonal factor analysis. Tests with high *g* loadings included those focusing on "reasoning, comprehension, deductive operations, eduction of relations (determining the relationship between or among two or more ideas), eduction of correlates (finding a second idea associated with a previously stated one), and hypothesis-testing tasks" (Valencia & Suzuki, 2001, p. 31). In contrast, tests with low *g* loadings are those that focus on visual-motor ability, speed, recognition, and recall. Spearman hypothesized that racial and ethnic group differences in intelligence exist because levels of *g* differ between groups. Jensen's (1998) review supported this hypothesis. The concept of a general intelligence factor continues, and most intelligence tests will provide an indicator of the level of *g* identified with various subtests that comprise the measure.

Test Bias

Test bias often refers to the existence of systematic error in the measurement of a construct or variable, in this case, intelligence.

> *The discussion of bias in psychological testing as a* scientific *issue should concern only the statistical meaning: whether or not there is systematic error in the measurement of a psychological attribute as a function of membership in one or another cultural or racial subgroup. (Reynolds, 1982a,1982b, cited in Reynolds & Lowe, 2009, p. 333)*

Reynolds and Lowe (2009) report the following as possible sources of test bias: inappropriate content, inappropriate standardization samples, examiner bias, language bias, inequitable social consequences, measurement of different constructs, differential predictive validity, and qualitatively distinct minority and majority aptitude and personality. Serpell (2000) cites work distinguishing among various forms of bias, including outcome bias, predictive bias, and sampling bias. Some scholars hypothesize that lower mean scores of Black/African American students reflect outcome bias resulting from discrimination against members of this group by society at large (e.g., Helms, 2006). This perspective has spurred controversy with opponents of this view arguing that discrepancies are not necessarily indicative of discrimination but rather the presence of other societal differences (e.g., home environment). Predictive bias focuses on intelligence tests as they predict "future performance in educational settings" (Serpell, 2000, p. 563). Sampling bias occurs when a standardized test of intelligence is "biased in favor of a range of skills, styles, and attitudes valued by the majority culture (and promoted within the developmental niche that it informs" (p. 563). Helms (2004) cites problems with existing definitions of test bias: "evidence of test-score validity and lack of bias, as those terms are currently construed in the literature, does not mean that test scores are fair for African American test takers and other people of color" (p. 481). She argues that African American, Latino/Latina, Asian American, and Native American "test takers are competing with White test takers whose racial socialization experiences are either irrelevant to their test performance or give them an undeserved advantage" (Helms, 2006, p. 855).

Valencia, Suzuki, and Salinas (2001) note, "Test bias in the context of race/ethnicity often is referred to as cultural bias" (p. 115). In a review of 62 empirical studies of cultural bias with cognitive ability tests, the majority (71%) detected no significant evidence of bias, while the remainder (29%) indicated bias or mixed findings (Valencia, Suzuki, & Salinas, 2001). It appears that the findings on test bias with respect to cognitive ability testing remains inconclusive.

In order to address the potential of cultural (i.e., race/ethnicity) bias, most state-of-the-art intelligence tests are standardized based upon representative census data with respect to gender, race and/or ethnicity, region of the country, urban or rural status, parental occupation, socioeconomic status, and educational level (Valencia & Suzuki, 2001). In addition, test developers employ expert reviewers to examine item content and statisticians to perform analyses to determine differential item functioning (e.g., Mantel-Haenszel statistic). Numerous reliability (e.g., split-half, test-retest, internal consistency) and validity studies (e.g., factor analytic studies, external validity) are often conducted and may employ the Rasch model of item response theory to assess the fit of subtest items to the ability area being assessed. Some test developers also engage in racial and ethnic oversampling to address potential test bias issues.

Cultural Loading

Cultural loading refers to the degree of cultural specificity contained within a particular measure. All tests are culturally loaded, as their content and format reflect what is important in the cultural context of the community for which it was developed. Cultural loading has important implications for understanding cultural bias.

> *For an intelligence test to be deemed culturally biased, it must be culturally loaded. A culturally loaded test does not, however, necessarily mean that such a test is culturally biased. In other words, cultural loading on an intelligence test is a necessary, but not a sufficient, condition for the existence of cultural bias. (Valencia, Suzuki, & Salinas, 2001, p. 114)*

If there is a match or "congruence" between tasks required on an intelligence test and the cultural background of the test taker, then the cultural loading is "minimized" (p. 114). If there is "little or no congruence" between the content of the test and the cultural background of the test taker, then cultural loading is increased. "As congruence increases, cultural loading decreases" (Valencia, Suzuki, & Salinas, 2001, p. 114). Given that all forms of measurement are developed within a cultural context, it is difficult to ascertain a fundamental cognitive task that would not be impacted by cultural loading.

Test Fairness

Cultural equivalence, cultural bias, test fairness, and the impact of individual difference variables and their relationship to the racial/ethnic group ordering of intelligence test scores has been a focus of the literature in the past two decades (Helms, 1992, 2004, 2006). The racial/ethnic hierarchy of intelligence refers to the ordering of different minority groups based upon their average intelligence test score. As noted earlier, test bias refers to systematic error in the measurement of intelligence for a particular group. Helms (2006) provides input into the complexity of addressing error that may be due to factors unrelated to intelligence (e.g., internalized racial or cultural experiences and environmental socialization). She hypothesizes that these factors may have a greater impact on the test performance of members of racial and ethnic minority groups relative to nonminority group members. More research is needed to examine these proposed factors.

Neuroscience implications. Researchers have also looked to the neurosciences to explain racial and ethnic differences in cognitive assessment. Chan, Yeung, et al. (2002) reported findings suggesting that neurocognitive networks mediating the use of English and Chinese differ. They hypothesized that speaking and thinking in Chinese involved more bilateral brain areas than did speaking and thinking in English, which were more lateralized to the left brain hemisphere. This finding suggests that early language experiences can influence how the brain processes information. Language structure can lead to cultural variations in performance on basic cognitive tasks (Cheung & Kemper, 1993; Chincotta & Underwood, 1997; Hedden et al., 2002). Hwa-Froelich and Matsuo (2005) examined how quickly bilingual (Vietnamese-English) preschool children were able to "fast map," or learn the meaning of a new word by associating it with a sound or image, after hearing the word. They found that regardless of exposure to English or Vietnamese, children were more likely to produce sound patterns that were more familiar to them, even when the stimuli presented to them were new. This finding emphasizes the importance of cultural exposure to words and images in determining learning style and cognitive performance among new immigrants.

In addition, relationships have been identified between information-processing efficiency and psychophysiological measures (i.e., task-evoked pupillary dilation response) used to examine how culture may relate to cognitive ability testing. In one study by Verney, Granholm, Marshall, Malcarne, and Saccuzzo (2005), pupillary responses (a marker of mental effort) and detection accuracy scores on a visual backward-masking task were both related to performance on an intelligence test (i.e., WAIS-R) for a Caucasian American student sample but not to a comparable sample of Mexican American students. Thus, the authors conclude that the "differential validityin prediction suggests that the WAIS-R test may contain cultural influences that reduce the validity of the WAIS-R as a measure of cognitive ability for Mexican American students (Verney et al., 2005, p. 303).

Alternative Assessment Practices

A number of alternative assessment practices have emerged in recent years in part to address criticisms of the usage of intelligence tests with members of racial and ethnic minority groups. These assessments address concerns related to the limited impact of intelligence testing on actual instruction and intervention. We provide a brief discussion of the major areas and types of assessment that are currently used.

Nonverbal tests. A number of nonverbal measures have been developed and are often referred to as culturally reduced measures of abilities. The researchers hoped that by "reducing the emphasis on verbal skills or removing language altogether from the testing process, they can minimize the impact of culturally based linguistic differences on assessment results and outcomes" (Harris, Reynolds, & Koegel, 1996, p. 223). Current nonverbal measures include the Test of Nonverbal-Intelligence (TONI-3; Brown, Sherbenou, & Johnson, 1997); Raven's Advanced Progressive Matrices (Raven, 1998); Leiter International Performance Scale-Revised (Roid & Miller, 1997); Naglieri Nonverbal Ability Test (Naglieri, 1997); and the Universal Nonverbal Intelligence Test – 2 (UNIT; Bracken, Keith, & Walker, 1998). All tests, however, involve some form of language and communication. Therefore, nonverbal tests "are not entirely devoid of cultural content" (Mpofu & Ortiz, 2009, p. 65). Nonverbal tests also assess a more limited range of ability areas including "visual processing, short-term memory, and processing speed" (p. 65). Differences in performance by racial and ethnic minority groups are decreased on these measures. For example, in a comparison study of White, African American, Hispanic, and Asian children on the Naglieri Nonverbal Ability Test, differences between matched samples from the standardization sample revealed minimal or small discrepancies between groups (Naglieri & Ronning, 2000).

Dynamic assessment. Intelligence tests have been criticized as having limited if any impact on educational instruction and intervention. A number of dynamic assessment procedures have been developed to provide more relevant data about students to inform educational planning. Dynamic assessment is an active form of informal assessment and often involves the examiner engaging in a test-teach-test procedure (Meller & Ohr, 1996). The focus of the assessment is on the process. Dynamic assessment enables evaluators to observe the processes of learning for an individual as they provide feedback to the examinee to improve performance. This is an important assessment tool, as it provides opportunities for an individual to demonstrate learning of material that he or she may not have been exposed to in the past (Sternberg, 2004). The focus on process has implications for culturally diverse individuals, as they are provided with feedback and the opportunity to demonstrate learning.

Curriculum-based assessment. Curriculum-based assessment (CBA) measures were designed to address concerns regarding norm-based measures like intelligence tests (Hintze, 2009) in response to concerns that "published tests have played too large a role in educational and psychological decision making, not just with students from diverse backgrounds" (Shinn & Baker 1996, p. 186). Shinn and Baker (1996) note that CBA involves the use of curriculum as testing materials ranging from "generally widespread approaches such as informal reading inventories (IRIs) to more specific testing and decision making practices" (p. 187). CBA examines behavior in a natural context, focuses on what is being taught in the classroom, leads to purposeful interventions in the classroom, and is useful in formative and idiographic (i.e., within-student) evaluation of progress (Hintze, 2009). "CBA can be used in screening, determining eligibility for special education, setting goals, evaluating programs, and developing interventions" (Hintze, 2009, p. 398).

Response to intervention. Response to intervention (RTI) "is a data-based process to establish, implement, and evaluate interventions that are designed to improve human services outcomes" (Reschly & Bergstrom, 2009, p. 434). RTI involves a series of tiered interventions taking into consideration the prior knowledge of the individual learner. "RTI systems emphasize instructional and behavioral programs and interventions that have empirically validated significant benefits to children and youth" (Reschly & Bergstrom, 2009, p. 438). This approach has the potential of eliminating the use of tests that have been accused of being biased against particular racial and ethnic groups.

The Gf-Gc Cross-Battery Assessment Model (XBA; Flanagan, Ortiz, & Alfonso, 2007). The XBA is a method of intelligence assessment that enables evaluators to measure a wider range of cognitive abilities by selecting from a range of potential tests (assessing broad and narrow ability areas) rather than relying upon any one intelligence battery (McGrew& Flanagan, 1998). As part of this assessment model, McGrew and Flanagan provide information regarding the cultural content and linguistic demands of various measures in the Culture-Language Test Classifications (C-LTC). The C-LTC is based upon an analysis of the degree of cultural loading (e.g., cultural specificity) and degree of linguistic demand (e.g., verbal versus nonverbal, receptive language, expressive language) for each measure. The classification of measures is based upon examination of empirical data available on the particular test and expert consensus procedures in the absence of data. The Culture-Language Interpretive Matrix (C-LIM) represents an extension of this classification system. On the C-LIM, tests are placed in a matrix based upon their degree of cultural loading and linguistic demand along with the scores obtained on the tests. The matrix serves to assist clinicians in interpreting test score patterns. Both the C-LTC and the C-LIM represent systematic guides for test selection and interpretation when standardized measures are deemed appropriate for use (Ortiz & Ochoa, 2005). They also take into consideration the potential impact of acculturation and language proficiency in examining the test performance of individuals from diverse racial and ethnic backgrounds.

The Multidimensional Assessment Model for Bilingual Individuals (MAMBI; Ortiz & Ochoa, 2005). The MAMBI takes into consideration the unique features of each testing case based upon the designated referral question. The evaluator must make decisions regarding the methods and approaches to be used to assess the student to obtain the most relevant and accurate information.

> *Comprehensive nondiscriminatory assessment involves the collection of multiple sources of data under the direction of a broad, systemic framework that uses the individual's cultural and linguistic history as the ultimate and most appropriate context from which to derive meaning and conclusions. (Rhodes, Ochoa, & Ortiz, 2005, p. 169)*

The MAMBI integrates three areas: language (i.e., preproduction, early production, speech-emergence, and intermediate fluency; development of cognitive academic language proficiency), instructional programming/history (i.e., type of bilingual instruction impacts cognitive and linguistic development) and current grade level (i.e., level of formal schooling impacts language development). The complexities of assessing linguistically diverse persons are emphasized, given the issues surrounding language proficiency. Understanding these three areas enables the evaluator to select the most appropriate assessment modality (i.e., nonverbal assessment, assessment primarily in the native language, assessment primarily in English, and bilingual assessment).

Outcome Implications for Multicultural Populations

A number of controversies surround the use of intelligence measures centering on findings of a racial and ethnic group hierarchy of scores. Overall estimates of group scores based upon a mean of 100 and standard deviation of 15 are as follows: Whites 100; Blacks (African Americans), 85; Hispanics, midway between Whites and Blacks; and Asians and Jews, above 100 ("Mainstream Science on Intelligence," 1994). Research indicates that American Indians score at approximately 90 (McShane, 1980). The ordering of racial and ethnic groups by average intelligence test scores has been consistent across various measures. Despite these overall differences in racial and ethnic group averages in measured intelligence,

> *there is always more within-group variability than between-group variability in performance on psychological tests, whether one considers race, ethnicity, gender, or socioeconomic status (SES). The differences are, nevertheless, real ones and are unquestionably complex. (Reynolds & Jensen, 1983; cited in Reynolds and Lowe, 2009, p. 333)*

Tests as Gatekeepers

Despite the growing number of alternatives readily available to substitute for traditional intelligence tests, the traditional tests continue to play a role in educational placement. In particular, intelligence tests play a role in admission to services (i.e., special education, giftedness).

One concern when attempting to evaluate the appropriateness of a test for a given population is that many test developers do not include average scores by race and ethnic group. This absence of data may be a result of concerns about how these data are interpreted. Weiss et al. (2006) note that people often automatically assume that group differences imply test bias. They suggest that this is often not the case and that the scores reflect societal differences tied to the current practices in test development – that is, stratified norming taking into consideration age, gender, region of the country, parental education, and socioeconomic status. The authors note that the "sampling methodology accurately reflects each population as it exists in society, [but] it exaggerates the differences between the mean IQ of groups because the SES levels of the various racial/ethnic samples are not equal"

(p. 31). If test developers equated the percentages for all groups, then the discrepancies between the groups would be minimized but not eliminated. Thus, SES level accounts only partially for group differences. Other variables may also play a role, including home environment factors that may differ even within comparable SES levels.

In addition to examining the impact of these stratification variables, Weiss et al. (2006) also reported that parental expectations were assessed by asking parents how likely they believed their child would be to get good grades, graduate from high school, attend college, and graduate from college. Interestingly, parental expectations accounted for approximately 31% of the variance in Full Scale IQ. Thus, the researchers conclude that parental expectations account for more variance than parent education and income combined.

The Black-White test score gap has decreased and scores for the African American group increased from 88.6 (low average) on the WISC-III to 91.7 (average) on the WISC-IV, a gain of 3 score points based on the standardization sample (Weiss et al., 2006). However, once again, the same ordering or pattern of group differences on IQ tests remains consistent on the most recently revised intelligence measures (Sattler, 2008).

What is most salient about this ordering is that it does reflect the sociocultural contexts for particular racial and ethnic minority groups in the United States, and these scores have significant implications. Intelligence tests are used to determine eligibility for special services and classifications of learning disabilities, mental retardation, and other intellectual impairments. Table 14.1 presents the percentages of students by racial and ethnic group for the major classifications, including specific learning disabilities, speech or language impairments, mental retardation, emotional disturbances, and multiple disabilities (U.S. Department of Education, 2005). As Serpell (2000) reports, because there are "striking differences in diagnostic rates of MR-ID across ethnic groups, the general public understandably became suspicious that some type of measurement bias might be distorting the pattern of diagnosis and referral" (p. 560). Table 14.1 also includes data indicating the overall racial and ethnic group percentages for school-age children (ages 5–17) in 2000 and 2007 (U.S. Census Bureau, 2007) to allow for comparison. It is interesting to note the increase in the proportion of Hispanic students from 16% in 2000 and 20% in 2007. Whites are clearly underrepresented in mental retardation. Asian/Pacific Islanders are underrepresented in all categories, while Blacks continue to be overrepresented in all categories with the exception of speech-language impaired. Learning disabilities and mental retardation classifications are of concern. It should be noted that while the gap between Blacks and Whites on the WISC-IV standardization sample have decreased, this may not be reflected here, given that many of these students may not have been tested on this new version. In addition, current school practices no longer require that students' intellectual functioning be retested every three years; therefore, a number of these students may not be tested on newer versions (e.g., WISC-IV) or alternate assessments (e.g., nonverbal tests).

Black-White Test Score Gap: Intelligence

"Differences between African Americans and Whites on IQ measures in the United States have received extensive investigation over the past 100 years" (Reynolds & Lowe, 2009, p. 333). It should be noted that the IQ difference between Black and White 12-year-olds has dropped 5.5 points (i.e., 9.5 points from 15 points) over the past three decades (Nisbett, 2009). In addition, when socioeconomic status is taken into account the differences between groups is reduced. For example, the mean difference between Blacks and Whites in the United States drops from 1 standard deviation to 0.5 to 0.7 standard deviations (Reynolds & Lowe, 2009). Despite the lowered discrepancy between Black and White children on this standardized IQ test, and an understanding of the

Table 14.1. Placements of Racial and Ethnic Minority Students in Special Education Ages 6–21

Disability	*White*	*Black*	*Hispanic*	*Asian/ Pacific Islander*	*Native American*
Percentage of Resident Population Ages 5–17* (Note 2000–2007)	62%–58.5%	16%–15.5%	16%–20%	5%–4%	1%–1%
Specific Learning Disabilities**	1,639,042 58.07%	553,520 19.61%	534,911 18.95%	46,267 1.64%	48,908 1.73%
Speech or Language Impairments**	173,677 64.55%	176,353 15.77%	173,677 15.53%	32,071 2.87%	1,170 1.29%
Mental Retardation**	284,596 49.83%	198,909 34.83%	70,037 12.26%	10,853 1.90%	6,765 1.18%
Emotional Disturbance**	283,693 58.67%	138,547 28.65%	48,457 10.02%	5,635 1.17%	7,212 1.49%
Multiple Disabilities**	81,939 62.34%	26,853 20.43%	17,612 13.40%	3,208 2.44%	1,832 1.39%

* *Source:* U.S. Census Bureau. (2007). *Annual Estimates of the Population by Race, Hispanic Origin, Sex and Age for the United States: April 1, 2000 to July 1, 2007* (NC-EST2007–04; release date: May 1, 2009.

** *Source:* U.S. Department of Education. (2005). *27th Annual Report to Congress on the Implementation of the Individuals with Disabilities Education Act, 2005* (Vol. 2, pp. 116). Data updated as of July 31, 2004.

role of SES, researchers, scholars, and other professionals continue to struggle with the complexities inherent in the understanding of intelligence and racial difference.

Historically, the discussion of intelligence among Black/African American populations has been ongoing in both educational and academic research environments. Franklin (2007) reviewed publications appearing in the *Journal of Negro Education* (*JNE*) since 1932 focusing on the intelligence testing of African Americans. He notes that social scientists contributing to the *JNE* have, for many decades, attempted to identify and clarify what the tests were measuring and to emphasize the culturally biased processes involved in the standardization of these measures (i.e., favoring White middle-class populations). The *JNE* "participated in laying the educational and legal ground work for the U.S. Supreme Court's *Brown v. Board of Education* decision" in 1954 and published literature concerning the impact of the Brown decision throughout the 1950s and 1960s (p. 11). Additionally, in the late 1960s, the Association of Black Psychologists (ABPsi) submitted a petition of concerns to the American Psychological Association calling for a "moratorium of testing of all Black children until appropriate and culturally sensitive tests were developed" (Franklin, 2007, p. 11). These calls for better assessment measures for African Americans also came in response to research that was conducted in the late 1960s and early 1970s by Jensen, in which he focused on the heritability of intelligence.

Stereotype threat. Steele and Aronson's (1995) seminal article about the effect of stereotype threat on the test-taking performance of African American students included a series of four experiments that revealed depressed standardized test performance among African American participants relative to White participants, when the African American students were made vulnerable to judgment by negative stereotypes. Stereotype threat has been defined as a phenomenon that occurs when an individual recognizes that negative stereotypes about a group to which they belong are applicable to themselves, in a particular context or situation (Steele, 1998). When conditions were designed to alleviate stereotype threat, African American participants' test performance improved. Steele and Aronson concluded that although stereotype threat was not the sole explanation for the gap in scores, it did appear to cause an "inefficiency of processing much like that caused by other evaluative pressures" among the African American participants (p. 809).

In the last 14 years since the publication of the Steele and Aronson (1995) article, there has been much debate about stereotype threat as an explanation for the Black-White test score gap. Critical analyses of the research conducted by Steele and Aronson (1995) have included concerns about internal validity of empirical studies of stereotype threat, specifically, perceptions of face validity and test-taking motivation among African American participants (Whaley, 1998). Additional criticisms of the study identified alleged "misinterpretation of research" and questioned the generalizability of stereotype threat in applied testing sessions (Sackett, Hardison, & Cullen, 2004, p. 11). Relationships between stereotype threat and gender have also been explored (e.g., Spencer, Steele, & Quinn, 1999) and greater specificity in the construct has been identified in terms of stereotype specific (e.g., threat that results directly from the testing environment) and stereotype general (e.g., based on a global sense of threat that is pervasive in a variety of contexts/situations) (Mayer & Hanges, 2003). A number of studies have been conducted to address the level of contribution of stereotype threat to the test score gap (e.g., Brown & Day, 2006; Cohen & Sherman, 2005; Helms, 2005; Steele, 1998; Steele & Aronson, 2004; Wicherts, 2005). The validity of stereotype threat and its impact on test-taking performance continues to be debated in the literature.

Racial identity. Helms's (1995) racial identity theory posits identity statuses, some of which are characterized by self-denial and others by self-affirmation regarding one's socioracial group. Each racial identity status is related to distinct affects, behaviors, and cognitions concerning one's understanding of race and racism. These statuses comprise individual difference variables that have been linked to Black student performance on cognitive ability tests (Helms, 2002, 2004). Data indicate that higher levels of Black idealization (i.e., idealization of an individual's Blackness and Black culture) were associated with lower SAT scores, and higher SAT scores were related to lower levels of Black idealization (Helms, 2002).

Higher Intelligence Test Scores for Asians

Asians and Asian Americans have often obtained the highest group averages on standardized intelligence tests, with high scores reported in particular on subtests measuring numerical and spatial reasoning abilities. What accounts for this difference has been the focus of speculation for decades. Some believe that the higher scores are due to perseverance and not to innate intellectual aptitude. As Nisbett (2009) writes:

> *What is not in dispute is that Asian Americans achieve at a level far in excess of what their measured IQ suggests they would be likely to attain. Asian intellectual accomplishment is due more to sweat than to exceptional gray matter. (p. 154)*

In a related vein, the "model minority myth" portrays Asian students as being, on average, more perfectionistic, self-controlled, cooperative, academically successful, and with fewer behavioral problems than other students (e.g., Chang & Sue, 2003; Loo & Rappaport, 1998). Chang and Demyan (2007) examined the content of teachers' race-related stereotypes. Their findings indicated that Asian students were noted to be significantly more industrious, intelligent, and less athletic and sociable compared with African and European American students. Similar results were found for ethnic minority teachers. The authors note that the implications of these findings are that real learning needs, such as weaknesses in math or science, are overlooked.

Studies on the intelligence of Asian Americans note that there has been little published data on the reliability and validity of the most frequently used intelligence measures (i.e., Wechsler Scales) with Asian samples in the United States alone (Okazaki & Sue, 2000). Most of the published studies in the past decade have focusing on non-U.S. Asian samples (e.g., Chinese internationals). Okazaki and Sue hypothesize that Asians were not often included in studies to standardize cognitive or personality assessments because of a lack of clinicians proficient in the native language of the particular Asian group, difficulties locating Asian participants who may be more geographically scattered, and difficulties in recruitment as a result of Asian cultural attitudes toward testing. Asian Americans may be less likely to seek testing because of potential stigma associated with learning disabilities (Okazaki & Sue, 2000; Uba, 1994), especially in contrast to a community emphasis on achievement.

In addition, major intelligence tests like the Wechsler scales have been exported to other Asian countries, normed, and restandardized. The WAIS has been translated and standardized in China, Hong Kong, India, Japan, Korea, Taiwan, Thailand, and Vietnam (Cheung, Leong, & Ben-Porath, 2003). The restandardized norms developed in an Asian country may not be applicable to someone living in the United States. First, norms may be outdated. Second, U.S. immigrant Asian groups are more heterogeneous relative to their overseas counterparts (Okazaki & Sue, 2000). Chinese immigrants in the United States, for example, may represent diverse population clusters from China and speak different dialects compared with a sample of Chinese individuals living in Hong Kong. Therefore, applying norms based on one Asian ethnic group to interpret the test results of an individual from a different ethnic group may be misleading. Yet another source of heterogeneity among U.S. immigrants is that they are exposed to American values and are considered a minority group here in the United States (Okazaki & Sue, 2000). Future research should compare the validity of overseas Asian norms to Asian Americans and vice versa, to determine whether U.S. Asians need to be normed as a separate stand-alone sample.

Intelligence From an American Indian/Native American Perspective

Suzuki, Jordan, Vraniak, Short, Aguiar, and Kubo (2003) conducted a preliminary meta-analysis of Wechsler studies conducted between 1986 and 2003 on American Indian cognitive abilities. A total of 63 empirical studies were identified representing a number of tribal groups. The most frequently cited groups were Navajo, Papago, Ojibwa, Inuit, and Eskimo. All studies indicated that the American Indian samples scored consistently higher on nonverbal spatial reasoning measures with specific strengths noted on Object Assembly and Block Design and relative weaknesses on Vocabulary and Information subtests. The average standard score difference between Verbal IQ and Performance IQ was 17 points (SD 8.92), range 3.4–31.3. Interpretation of these findings often focuses on the Verbal IQ as lower due to linguistic and cultural factors rather than intelligence, with attention to the Performance IQ as more indicative of an individual's true abilities. It should be noted that contextual variables were often not reported (e.g., reservation and referral status). In addition, important demographic and health information was often not provided (e.g., socioeconomic status, presence of ear infections, primary language spoken in the home).

Test bias was examined on the Bayley Scales of Infant Development and the WISC-III, with findings indicating that the performance of American Indian students may be impacted by "poverty, remoteness, access to resources, and health care" (Hagie, Gallip, & Svien, 2003, p. 15). Hagie and colleagues note that these widely used tests "in most areas fail to reflect the local and cultural experiences of American Indian students and, subsequently, present a skewed picture of their true ability and performance" (p. 23). Many American Indian children learn problem solving through collaborative effort that is not represented in traditional testing practices. The authors also note that limited health care on the reservations may also impact test performance.

Estimates of Hispanic and Latino/a Intelligence in Context

Obtaining an accurate reading of the intelligence of Hispanic/Latino/as involves a number of challenges. This diverse group is notably the "fastest growing and possibly the most disenfranchised group in the United States today" (Puente & Puente, 2009, p. 418). One must attend to issues of limited educational opportunities, low socioeconomic status, and language. A number of diverse subgroups comprise the category of Hispanics. Each group has different histories of immigration and cultural traditions. There is growing emphasis on the need to examine ethnic group differences instead of grouping individuals under one "Hispanic" label. Nevertheless, a large percentage of Hispanics has limited English proficiency and has not fared well in the American educational system (Puente & Puente, 2009).

Puente and Puente (2009) also note that most tests that are published in the United States do not have Spanish translations. Tests that have been translated into Spanish are often not normed on American samples but rather on samples from Spanish-speaking countries abroad. This is an issue because "subcultures of Hispanic heritage may be as dissimilar with each other as they are to the U.S. culture" (Puente & Puente, 2009, p. 424). The complexities of translation are also evident given issues of equivalence; linguistic or language equivalence does not ensure cognitive equivalence, which focuses on meaning.

Among Hispanic samples, a consistent discrepancy between the verbal and performance abilities on the Wechsler scales is often identified, indicating the potentially important role of language in cognitive assessment (DiCerbo & Barona, 2000).

> *The assessment of Hispanic children continues to be very complex and difficult to address. One cannot simply assume that all Hispanic children are ESL (English as a Second Language) or LEP (Limited English Proficient), nor can one assume they are English proficient. For this reason, it is imperative that Hispanic children's language be formally and informally assessed. Even after language has been assessed, it is often difficult to determine how much performance may be been affected (positively or negatively) by the use of other languages. (DiCerbo & Barona, 2000, p. 351)*

Despite these concerns, recent data on the Spanish version of the Wechsler Adult Intelligence Scale (WAIS-III) with a sample of American, urban, and Spanish-speaking Hispanics indicated satisfactory internal consistency indicators for subtests, with the exception of the Letter Number Sequencing subtest (Renteria, Tinsley Li, & Pliskin, 2007). Convergent and divergent validity of the Spanish version was deemed similar to the North American normative sample. The Spanish version of the WASI-III was normed and validated in Spain. The study sample included a majority of participants indicating a low level of acculturation (69%) to the American culture. Eighteen percent viewed themselves as equally competent in both cultures, and 13% reported a high level of acculturation. Interestingly, the subtest judged to have inadequate internal consistency was Letter Number Sequencing. In addition, potential bias was reported in item ordering. Many individuals missed earlier items on the Similarities and Information subtests indicating that the "easy" items might have been more difficult due to the ethnic origin of the sample. Given these findings the authors recommend that the Letter Number Sequencing subtest be omitted or interpreted with caution given that it may underestimate working memory ability. In addition, items on the Information and Similarities subtests may be biased given a focus on knowledge that would be gained through the educational system in Spain.

With the growing numbers of Hispanic individuals in the United States, particularly school-age children and adolescents, the need to develop adequate instruments to address their cognitive skills is imperative. The task is not an easy one because of the linguistic and cultural complexities of this population.

Conclusions

Understanding intelligence through a multicultural lens is an arduous task. As presented in this chapter, difficulties of interpretation and operationalization of relevant constructs; complexities of environmental context (e.g., home and community); and availability of instruments and methods of assessment are only a few of the challenges.

In terms of environmental factors, the importance of parental expectations, support of academic pursuits in the home, higher socioeconomic status, and familiarity with testing procedures are just some of the variables that have been found to impact the measurement of intelligence. The evaluator is presented with a menu of potential instruments with which to assess cognitive functioning, some based upon relatively newer theories (e.g., information processing). In addition, a number of approaches to assessment have evolved focusing on the integration of cultural variables into the assessment process (cultural loading and linguistic demands) and methods to guide the selection of the most appropriate methods (e.g., MAMBI, XBA, C-LTC, C-LIM).

Despite the availability of these new measures, the concerns that have historically plagued the intelligence literature remain (e.g., the racial/ethnic ordering of intelligence test scores remains intact though there is evidence that the discrepancies are growing smaller; Weiss et al., 2006). Given the major role that intelligence tests continue to play in the classification of individuals (e.g., special education), the discrepancies between groups and the disproportionately high representation of African American/ Black students in classifications pertaining to cognitive deficits (i.e., specific learning disability and mental retardation) are of great importance.

The limited impact of intelligence test scores on instructional intervention has led to a number of promising alternative assessment processes (e.g., Dynamic Assessment, CBM, RTI) that in many ways do not call into focus the issues of cultural bias and test fairness as they are based upon learning curriculum models (e.g., test – teach – test). Despite their appearance on the assessment scene, they have not been able to unseat the usage of intelligence tests.

The stronghold of intelligence has persisted despite blistering criticisms from members of the minority community for decades. Indeed, the most popular tests have been transported, renormed, and restandardized globally. It appears that intelligence tests are here for the long haul and therefore the search should perhaps not be on how to replace them but on how to determine their appropriate role in helping practitioners understand the abilities of individuals from diverse cultural contexts.

References

Bracken, B. A., Keith, L. K., & Walker, C. (1998). *Universal Nonverbal Intelligence Test.* Itasca, IL: Riverside.

Brislin, R., Worthley, R., & Macnab, B. (2006). Cultural intelligence: Understanding behaviors that serve people's goals. *Group and Organizational Management, 31*(1), 40–55.

Brown, R. P., & Day, E. (2006). The difference isn't Black and White: Stereotype threat and the race gap on Raven's Advanced Progressive Matrices. *Journal of Applied Psychology, 91*(4), 979–985.

Brown, L., Sherbenou, R. J., & Johnson, S. K. (1997). *Test of Nonverbal Intelligence-Third Edition (TONI-3).* Los Angeles, CA: Western Psychological Services.

Ceci, S. J. (1996). *On intelligence . . . more or less: A bioecological treatise on intellectual development.* Englewood Cliffs, NJ: Prentice-Hall.

Chan, A., Yeung, D., Chan, Y. L., He, W. J., Cheung, M. C., Lam, J., et al. (2002, February). *Different neurocognitive semantic processes for alphabetic and logographic languages.* Abstract presented at the 30th Annual Meeting of the International Neuropsychological Society, Toronto, Canada.

Chang, D. F., & Demyan, A. (2007). Teachers' stereotypes of Asians, Blacks, and White students. *School Psychology Quarterly*, 22(2), 91–114.

Chang, D. F., & Sue, S. (2003). The effects of race and problem type on teachers' assessment of student behavior. *Journal of Consulting and Clinical Psychology*, 71, 235–242.

Cheung, H., & Kemper, S. (1993). Recall and articulation of English and Chinese words by Chinese English bilinguals. *Memory & Cognition*, 21(5), 666–670.

Cheung, F. M., Leong, F. T. L., & Ben-Porath, Y. S. (2003). Psychological assessment in Asia: Introduction to the special section. *Psychological Assessment*, 15, 243–247.

Chincotta, D., & Underwood, G. (1997). Digit span and articulatory suppression: A cross-linguistic comparison. *European Journal of Cognitive Psychology*, 9(1), 89–96.

Cohen, G. L., & Sherman, D. K. (2005). Stereotype threat and the social and scientific contexts of the race achievement gap. *American Psychologist*, 60(3), 270–271.

DiCerbo, K. E., & Barona, A. (2000). A convergent validity study on the Differential Ability Scales and the Wechsler Intelligence Scale for Children-Third Edition with Hispanic children. *Journal of Psychoeducational Assessment*, 18, 344–352.

Fagan, J. F., & Holland, C. R. (2006). Racial equality in intelligence: Predictions from a theory of intelligence as processing. *Intelligence*, 35(4), 319–334.

Flanagan, D. P., Ortiz, S. O., & Alfonso, V. C. (2007). *Essentials of cross-battery assessment* (2nd ed.). San Francisco, CA: Wiley.

Franklin, V. P. (2007). The tests are written for the dogs: The *Journal of Negro Education*, African American children, and the intelligence testing movement in historical perspective. *Journal of Negro Education*, 76(3), 216–231.

Frisby, C. L. (1999). Culture and test session behavior: Part II. *School Psychology Quarterly*, 14(3), 281–303.

Gardner, H. (1983). *Frames of mind: The theory of multiple intelligences*. New York, NY: Basic Books.

Geertz, C. (1973). *The interpretation of cultures: Selected essays by Clifford Geertz*. New York, NY: Basic Books.

Goldberger, N. R., & Veroff, J. B. (Eds.). (1995). *The culture and psychology reader*. New York: New York University Press.

Hagie, M. U., Gallipo, P. L., & Svien, L. (2003). Traditional culture versus traditional assessment for American Indian students: An investigation of potential test item bias. *Assessment for Effective Intervention*, 29(1), 15–25.

Harkness, S., Super, C. M., Barry, O., Zeitlin, M., & Long, J. (2009). Assessing the environment of children's learning: The developmental niche in Africa. In E. L. Grigorenko (Ed.), *Multicultural psychoeducational assessment* (pp. 133–155). New York, NY: Springer.

Harris, A. M., Reynolds, M. A., & Koegel, H. M. (1996). Nonverbal assessment: Multicultural perspectives. In L. A. Suzuki, P. J. Meller, & J. G. Ponterotto (Eds.), *Handbook of multicultural assessment: Clinical, psychological, and educational applications* (pp. 223–252). San Francisco, CA: Jossey-Bass.

Hedden, T., Park, D. C., Nisbett, R., Ji, L. J., Jing, Q., & Jiao, S. (2002). Cultural variation in verbal versus spatial neuropsychological function across the life span. *Neuropsychology*, 16(1), 65–73.

Helms, J. E. (1992). Why is there no study of cultural equivalence in standardized cognitive ability testing? *American Psychologist*, 47(9), 1083–1101.

Helms, J. E. (1995). An update of Helms' White and People of Color Racial Identity models. In J. G. Ponterotto, J. M. Casas, L. A. Suzuki, & C. M. Alexander (Eds.), *Handbook of multicultural counseling* (pp. 181–198). Thousand Oaks, CA: Sage.

Helms, J. E. (2002). A remedy for the Black-White score disparity. *American Psychologist*, 57(4), 303–305.

Helms, J. E. (2004). The 2003 Leona Tyler Award Address: Making race a matter of individual differences within groups. *Counseling Psychologist*, 32(3), 473–483.

Helms, J. E. (2005). Stereotype threat might explain the black-white test score difference. *American Psychologist*, 60(3), 269–270.

Helms, J. E. (2006). Fairness is not validity or cultural bias in racial-group assessment: A quantitative perspective. *American Psychologist*, 61(88), 845–859.

Hintze, J. M. (2009). Curriculum-based assessment. In T. B. Gutkin & C. R. Reynolds (Eds.), *The handbook of school psychology* (4th ed., pp. 397–409). Hoboken, NJ: Wiley.

Hwa-Froelich, D. A., & Matsuo, H. (2005). Vietnamese children and language-based processing tasks. *Language, Speech and Hearing Services in Schools*, 36(3), 230–243.

Jensen, A. R. (1998). *The g factor: The science of mental ability*. Westport, CT: Praeger.

Kaufman, A. S. (1990). *Assessing adolescent and adult intelligence*. Boston, MA: Allyn & Bacon.

Kroeber, A. L., & Kluckhohn, C. (1963). *Culture: A critical review of concepts and definitions*. Cambridge, MA: Harvard University Press.

Loo, S. K., & Rappaport, M. D. (1998). Ethnic variations in children's problem behaviors: A cross-sectional, developmental study of Hawaii school children. *Journal of Child Psychology and Psychiatry and Allied Disciplines*, 39, 567–575.

López, S. R., & Guarnaccia, P. J. J. (2000). Cultural psychopathology: Uncovering the social world of mental illness. *Annual Review of Psychology*, **51**, 571–598.

Mainstream science on intelligence. (1994, December 13). *Wall Street Journal*, p. A18.

Mayer, D. M., & Hanges, P. J. (2003). Understanding stereotype threat effect with "culture-free" tests: An examination of its mediators and measurement. *Human Performance*, 16(3), 207–230.

McShane, D. (1980). A review of scores of American Indian children on the Wechsler Intelligence Scale. *White Cloud Journal*, 2, 18–22.

McGrew, K. S., & Flanagan, D. P. (1998). *The intelligence test desk reference (ITDR): Gf-Gc Cross Battery Assessment*. Boston, MA: Allyn & Bacon.

Meller, P. J., & Ohr, P. S. (1996). The assessment of culturally diverse infants and preschoolers. In L. A. Suzuki, P. J. Meller, & J. G. Ponterotto (Eds.), *Handbook of multicultural assessment: Clinical, psychological and educational applications* (pp. 561–610). San Francisco, CA: Jossey-Bass.

Mpofu, E., & Ortiz, S. O. (2009). Equitable assessment practices in diverse contexts. In E. L. Grigorenko (Ed.), *Multicultural psychoeducational assessment* (pp. 41–76). New York, NY: Springer.

Naglieri, J. A. (1997). *Naglieri Nonverbal Ability Test*. San Antonio, TX: Psychological Corporation.

Naglieri, J. A., & Das, J. P. (1997). *Cognitive Assessment System: Administration and scoring manual*. Itasca, IL: Riverside.

Naglieri, J. A., Rojahn, J., & Matto, H. C. (2007). Hispanic and non-Hispanic children's performance on PASS cognitive processes and achievement. *Intelligence*, 35, 568–579.

Naglieri, J. A., & Ronning, M. E. (2000). Comparison of White, African American, Hispanic, and Asian children on the Naglieri Nonverbal Ability Test. *Psychological Assessment*, **12**(3), 328–334.

Nisbett, R. E. (2009). *Intelligence and how to get it: Why schools and cultures count*. New York, NY: Norton.

Oakland, T. (2009). How universal are test development and use? In E. L. Grigorenko (Ed.), *Multicultural psychoeducational assessment* (pp. 1–40). New York, NY: Springer.

Okazaki, S., & Sue, S. (2000). Implications of test revisions for assessment with Asian Americans. *Psychological Assessment*, **12**(30, 272–280.

Ortiz, S. O., & Ochoa, S. H. (2005). Advances in cognitive assessment of culturally linguistically diverse individuals. In D. P. Flanagan & P. L. Harrison (Eds.), *Contemporary intellectual assessment: Theories, tests and issues* (2nd ed., pp. 234–250). New York, NY: Guilford Press.

Pedersen, P. (Ed.). (1999). Culture-centered interventions as a fourth dimension of psychology. In P. Pedersen (Ed.), *Multiculturalism as a fourth force* (pp. 3–18). New York, NY: Sage.

Puente, A. E., & Puente, A. N. (2009). The challenge of meaning, abilities and competence in Hispanic/Latinos. In E. L. Grigorenko (Ed.), *Multicultural psychoeducational assessment* (pp. 417–441). New York, NY: Springer.

Razani, J., Murcia, G., Tabares, J., & Wong, J. (2007). The effects of culture on WASi test performance in ethnically diverse individuals. *Clinical Neuropsychologist*, **21**(5), 776–788.

Raven, J. C. (1999). *Raven's Advanced Progressive Matrices*. San Antonio, TX: Pearson.

Renteria, L., Tinsley Li, S., & Pliskin, N. H. (2007). Reliability and validity of the Spanish Language Wechsler Adult Intelligence Scale (3rd Edition) in a sample of American, urban, Spanish-speaking Hispanics. *Clinical Neuropsychologist*, **22**(3), 455–470.

Reschly, D. J., & Bergstrom, M. K. Response to intervention. In T. B. Gutkin & C. R. Reynolds (Eds.), *The handbook of school psychology* (4th ed., pp. 434–460). Hoboken, NJ: Wiley.

Reynolds, C. R., & Lowe, P. A. (2009). The problem of bias in psychological assessment. In

T. B. Gutkin & C. R. Reynolds (Eds.), *The handbook of school psychology* (4th ed., pp. 332–374). Hoboken, NJ: Wiley.

Rhodes, R. L., Ochoa, S. H., & Ortiz, S. O. (2005). *Assessing culturally and linguistically diverse students: A. practical guide*. New York, NY: Guilford Press.

Rivera, L. M. (2008). Acculturation and multicultural assessment: Issues, trends, and practice. In L. A. Suzuki & J. G. Ponterotto (Eds.), *Handbook of multicultural assessment* (3rd ed., pp. 73–91). San Francisco, CA: Jossey-Bass.

Roid, G. H., & Miller, L. J. (1997). *Leiter International Performance Scale-Revised*. Wood Dale, IL: Stoelting.

Rushton, J. P., & Jensen, A. R. (2005). Thirty years of research on race differences in cognitive ability. *Psychology, Public Policy, and Law*, 11(2), 235–294.

Sackett, P. R., Hardison, C. M., & Cullen, M. J. (2004). On interpreting stereotype threat as accounting for African American-White differences on cognitive tests. *American Psychologist*, 59(1), 7–13.

Sameroff, A. J., Seifer, R., Barocas, R., Zax, M., & Greenspan, S. (1987). Intelligence quotient scores of 4-year-old children: Social-environmental risk factors. *Pediatrics*, 79(3), 343–350.

Sattler, J. M. (2008). *Assessment of children: Cognitive foundations* (5th ed.). San Diego, CA: Jerome M. Sattler.

Sattler, J. M., & Gwynne, J. (1982). White examiners generally do not impede the intelligence test performance of black children: To debunk a myth. *Journal of Consulting and Clinical Psychology*, 50, 196–208.

Serpell, R. (2000). Intelligence and culture. In R. J. Sternberg (Ed.), *Handbook of Intelligence* (pp. 549–577). New York, NY: Cambridge University Press.

Shinn, M. R., & Baker, S. K. (1996). The use of curriculum-based measurement with diverse learners. In L. A. Suzuki, P. J. Meller, & J. G. Ponterotto (Eds.), *Handbook of multicultural assessment: Clinical, psychological, and educational applications* (pp. 179–222). San Francisco, CA: Jossey-Bass.

Snyderman, M., & Rothman, S. (1988). *The IQ controversy: The media and public policy*. New Brunswick, NJ: Transaction Books.

Spearman, C. (1927). *The abilities of man*. New York, NY: Macmillan.

Spencer, S. J., Steele, C. M., & Quinn, D. M. (1999). Stereotype threat and women's math performance. *Journal of Experimental Social Psychology*, 35, 4–28.

Steele, C. M. (1998). Stereotyping and its threat are real. *American Psychologist*, 53, 680–681.

Steele, C. M., & Aronson, J. (1995). Stereotype threat and the intellectual test performance of African Americans. *Journal of Personality and Social Psychology*, 69(5), 787–811.

Steele, C. M., & Aronson, J. (2004). Stereotype threat does not live by Steele and Aronson alone. *American Psychologist*, 59(1), 47–48.

Sternberg, R. J. (1996). *Successful intelligence: How practical and creative intelligences determine success in life*. New York, NY: Simon & Schuster.

Sternberg, R. J. (2004). APA presidential address: Culture and intelligence. *American Psychologist*, 59(5), 325–338.

Sternberg, R. J., & Kaufman, J. C. (1998). Human abilities. *Annual Review of Psychology*, 49, 479–502.

Suzuki, L. A., Jordan, T., Vraniak, D., Short, E. L., Aguiar, L., & Mogami, T. (2003, August). *Meta-analysis of Wechsler studies conducted on American Indian cognitive abilities*. Poster session II presented at the 111th American Psychological Association Convention, Toronto, Canada.

Uba, L. (1994). *Asian Americans: Personality patterns, identity, and mental health*. New York, NY: Guilford Press.

U.S. Census Bureau. (2007). *Annual estimates of the population by race, Hispanic origin, sex and age for the United States: April 1, 2000 to July 1, 2007* (NC-EST2007–04; release date: May 1, 2009). Retrieved December 9, 2009, from www.census.gov/popest/national/asrh/NC-EST2007-asrh.html.

U.S. Department of Education. (2005). *27th annual report to Congress on the implementation of the Individuals with Disabilities Education Act, 2005* (Vol. 2, pp. 116). Data updated as of July 31, 2004. Retrieved December 5, 2009, from www.ed.gov/about/reports/annual/osep/2005/index.html.

Valencia, R. R., & Suzuki, L. A. (2001). *Intelligence testing and minority students: Foundations, performance factors, and assessment issues*. Thousand Oaks, CA: Sage.

Valencia, R. R., Suzuki, L. A., & Salinas, M. F. (2001). Test bias. In R. R. Valencia & L. A. Suzuki (Eds.), *Intelligence testing and minority students: Foundations, performance factors, and assessment issues* (pp. 111–150). Thousand Oaks, CA: Sage.

Verney, S. P., Granholm, E., Marshall, S. P., Malcarne, V. L., & Saccuzzo, D. P. (2005). Culture-fair cognitive ability assessment: Information processing and psychophysiological approaches. *Assessment*, 12(3), 303–319.

Weiss, L. G., Harris, J. G., Prifitera, A., Courville, T., Rolthus, E., Saklofske, D. H., & Holdneck, J. A. (2006) WISC-IV interpretation in a societal context. In L. G. Weiss, D. H. Saklofske, A. Prifitera, & J. A. Holdnack (Eds.), *Wechsler Intelligence Scale for Children – IV: Advanced clinical interpretation* (pp. 1–56). San Diego, CA: Academic Press.

Whaley, A. L. (1998). Issues of validity in empirical tests of stereotype threat theory. *American Psychologist*, 53, 679–680.

Wicherts, J. M. (2005). Stereotype threat research and the assumptions underlying analysis of covariance. *American Psychologist*, 60(3), 267–269.

CHAPTER 15

Race and Intelligence

Christine E. Daley and Anthony J. Onwuegbuzie

The debate over racial differences in intelligence remains one of the most hotly contested issues in the social sciences today, with the preponderance of the literature and subsequent media attention focusing heavily upon the alleged disparity between the cognitive abilities of Blacks and Whites. From the earliest suggestion of such discrepancies (e.g., Galton, 1892) to more sophisticated modern-day reviews and analyses such as those of Hunt and Carlson (2007a), Hocutt and Levin (1999), and Sternberg, Grigorenko, and Kidd (2005), the topic evokes no less emotional response. Indeed, if there were any doubt about the degree to which this controversy ignites sentiments in the scientific community to the point of absurdity one need only examine the case of James Watson.

Watson, one of the most famous scientists alive today, whose pioneering work provided us with the molecular structure of DNA, in 2007 was pilloried by his peers and forced to resign his position as chair of Cold Spring Harbor Laboratory because of unfortunate words uttered in his characteristically brash and uncensored style. The substance of his comments regarding contributory causes for slow economic development in southern Africa was the suggestion that social policies tend to be predicated upon the assumption that Blacks and Whites are equal in intelligence, whereas testing suggests this is not the case (Ceci & Williams, 2009).

The firestorm surrounding the Black-White intelligence debate was elevated to particularly colossal heights following the 1994 publication of Herrnstein and Murray's controversial book, *The Bell Curve*. What made this event such a sensation was the fact that the text was not limited in its distribution to the predominantly scientific community but was released to the public in the popular press. Needless to say, its circulation engendered fierce disputes in both the professional and lay populations, resulting in responses ranging from thoughtful consideration to acrimonious accusation. Indeed, even the present authors jumped into the fray (Onwuegbuzie & Daley, 1996, 2001). In essence, the book supported the hereditarian assumptions that intelligence is substantially genetic in origin, that the environment plays little or no role in its determination, and that IQ tests, which purport to measure it and yield a Black-White differential of fully one standard deviation, are equally valid across racial groups. Let us first examine the *fuzzy* constructs of race and intelligence.

Race as a Construct

The concept of race itself is intensely debated in the social and behavioral sciences, with some subscribing to the notion that it represents a biological fact. Those who hold this view believe that human beings can be divided into a specific number of genetically determined groups possessing similar physical characteristics such as skin color, facial features, and hair texture. For example, Rushton (2000) argues for the existence of distinct groups classified as Mongoloid (those whose ancestors were born in East Asia), Caucasoid (those of European ancestry), and Negroid (those whose origins can be traced to sub-Saharan Africa). There are a number of difficulties with this reasoning. First, most anthropologists abandoned the notion of race nearly a half a century ago, arguing that *all* human beings belong to a single genus and species (i.e., Homo sapiens) and that we are all descended from an evolutionary line of humans originating in Africa approximately 200,000 years ago (Fish, 2002). Second, although there is little doubt that groups of people share common genetically transmitted physical traits, the biological perspective ignores the role of migration in the development of regional differences in these physical characteristics. Adding to the confusion is the considerable interbreeding among the so-called races in industrialized societies. According to Schaefer (1988), "Given frequent migration, exploration, and invasion, pure gene frequencies have not existed for some time, if they ever did" (p. 12). In fact, as noted by Pearson (1995),

> *The vast majority of blacks harbor some degree of European as well as black African ancestry, and 40 percent harbor Native American ancestry too (and some white Americans, southerners in particular, harbor black African ancestry), further complicating any attempt to draw a definitive correlation between race and intelligence. (pp. 166–167)*

Further, this racial intermixing compromises virtually every inferential statistical test that compares races because the samples cannot be considered independent (Wilson & Williams, 1998).

Third, there seems to be no rationale for the selection of certain physical features to determine race and not others. Why skin color and not eye color? Fourth, the fact that scientists have postulated the existence of anywhere from 3 to 200 races (Schaefer, 1988) sheds considerable light on the lack of agreement as to the criteria used to delineate categories. In reality, there are more similarities than differences among groups and more differences within racial groups than among them (Littlefield, Lieberman, & Reynolds, 1982). In fact, in a comprehensive study, Rosenberg et al. (2002) found that 94% of the variation in the human genome is due not to population-specific genetic material but to the variation among unrelated individuals within the *same* subgroup.

Throughout the literature, race is alternately defined as a biological feature; a local geographic population; a group linked by common descent or origin; a population connected by a shared history, nationality, or geographic distribution; a subspecies; and a social construct; and the term is used interchangeably with *ethnicity*, *ancestry*, *culture*, *color*, *national origin*, and even *religion* (Hoffman, 2006). The majority of anthropologists today contend that *race* is nothing more than a sociopolitical phenomenon (e.g., Smedley & Smedley, 2005) based on phenotypic differences and too often used to perpetuate caste-like stratification. Furthermore, subjective self-identification is probably the most common specification of race when it comes to classification of participants for scientific research.

Yet there are sometimes significant discrepancies between researcher identification and participant self-identification of race. For example, in one national study, 6% of self-identified African Americans, 29% of self-identified Asian Pacific Islanders, 62% of self-identified Native Americans, and 80% of participants who identified themselves with another race were categorized by the researcher as White (Massey, 1980) – representing a fatal flaw in terms of measurement. The fact is, there simply is no scientific basis for the concept of race (Sternberg et al., 2005), yet being labeled a member of a specific racial group has pervasive and indelible consequences psychologically, educationally, socially, and politically.

Intelligence as a Construct

As with race, there is no universally accepted definition of intelligence. Some examples include the following:

> *Judgment, otherwise called good sense, practical sense, initiative, the faculty of adapting one's self to circumstances. To judge well, to comprehend well, to reason well, these are the essential activities of intelligence. (Binet & Simon, 1916, pp. 42–43)*

> *The ability to undertake activities that are characterized by (1) difficulty, (2) complexity, (3) abstractness, (4) economy, (5) adaptiveness to a goal, (6) social value, and (7) the emergence of originals, and to maintain such activities under conditions that demand a concentration of energy and a resistance to emotional forces. (Stoddard, 1943, p. 4)*

> *The aggregate or global capacity of the individual to act purposefully, to think rationally, and to deal effectively with his environment. (Wechsler, 1958, p. 7)*

> *A human intellectual competence must entail a set of skills of problem solving – enabling the individual to resolve genuine problems or difficulties that he or she encounters, and, when appropriate, to create an effective product – and must also entail the potential for finding or creating problems – thereby laying the groundwork for the acquisition of new knowledge. (Gardner, 1983, pp. 60–61)*

The question thus arises, How does one purport to measure a construct for which there is no consensus explanation? Despite the obvious conundrum, researchers and test publishers throughout the years have continued in their efforts to unearth the Holy Grail of assessment instruments capable of capturing the elusive concept of intelligence. The extent to which this undertaking has been successful depends on whether one is willing to accept as evidence the rather significant degree of correlation among scores generated by these assorted measures and, even more fundamentally, whether one is willing to accept the equivalency of *intelligence* and *IQ*.

Whence the term IQ?

IQ was an expression coined in the early part of the 20th century to refer to the quotient obtained when one multiplied by 100 the ratio of mental age (a concept developed by Alfred Binet and Theodore Simon in France in 1905) to chronological age. Examples of early tests of mental ability, that is, *IQ*, included the U.S. Army's Alpha and Beta Tests used to classify and assign large numbers of recruits prior to World War I. By 1916, Lewis Terman at Stanford University had adapted the work of Binet and Simon for use in the U.S. school system, and within a few years, the term *IQ* had become part of the popular vernacular. It remains today a convenient, albeit unfortunate, synonym for intelligence, to which James Watson owes his demise.

Admittedly, intelligence testing has come a long way in the past 100 years. Developers of modern tests of cognitive ability have attempted to achieve culture neutrality and tap a broader spectrum of underlying skills, and IQ has become a far more psychometrically sophisticated concept. Examples include the Wechsler Scales

(Wechsler, 2002, 2003, 2008) and the Stanford-Binet Intelligence Scales (Roid, 2003), which yield a *Full Scale IQ*; the Kaufman Assessment Battery for Children (Kaufman & Kaufman, 2004), generating a *Mental Processing Index* (Luria model) or a *Fluid-Crystallized Index* (Cattell-Horn model); the Woodcock-Johnson Tests of Cognitive Abilities (Woodcock, McGrew, & Mather, 2007), yielding a *General Intellectual Ability Score*; and the Das-Naglieri Cognitive Assessment System (Naglieri & Das,1997), producing a *Full Scale Standard Score*. Despite what one chooses to call them, however, what these summary scores capture at best is a narrow set of cognitive abilities represented by a unitary construct identified by researchers as *Spearman's g* or simply, *g*, and bearing little resemblance to the definitions of intelligence found throughout the literature. That is, although these measures come in many forms and comprise a variety of subtests evaluating, for instance, an individual's facility with verbal or symbolic reasoning, pattern recognition, detecting similarities or details, or processing information quickly, their scores tend to be highly intercorrelated, suggesting some overarching factor common to all of them but independent of their specific subject matter. This factor, *g*, is argued by some (e.g., Jensen, 1969, 1998) to represent the essence of human intellectual ability.

The validity of *g* as a singular estimator of intelligence has long been contested (e.g., Gould, 1996; Kamin, 1997). Critics of this view contend that key cognitive abilities are poorly evaluated or left entirely untapped by traditional intelligence tests. Sternberg (1997a), for example, has posited a triarchic model of intelligence in which analytical abilities (in essence, *g*) are equally weighted against practical abilities (pragmatic and social skills) and creativity (the ability to generate novel solutions to problems). Thus, *intelligence* becomes a *system* in which the *internal* and *external* worlds of individuals are mediated by their experiences (Sternberg, 1997b). An even broader approach is that taken by Gardner (2006), who proposes the existence of at least nine types of intelligence: linguistic, logical-mathematical, spatial, musical, bodily-kinesthetic, naturalistic, interpersonal, intrapersonal, and (at least provisionally) existential. According to Gardner, those who endorse the primacy of *g* confuse intelligence with a highly specific type of scholastic aptitude, what others (e.g., Fagan, 1992, 2000) contend is *knowledge* acquired in a cultural context. And herein lies the conundrum, for traditional *g*-saturated tests of intelligence have been found, in general, to be very good predictors of performance in the educational environment for both Blacks and Whites (e.g., McCardle, 1998; Rushton, Skuy, & Fridjohn, 2003). This phenomenon, referred to in the literature as *positive manifold*, derives from the observation that individuals who perform well on one domain measure will perform equally well on other measures in the same or similar domains (Neisser, 1998). According to Onwuegbuzie (2003), this presents a threat to validity such that the resulting correlations, in this case between scores on IQ tests and scores on measures of educational performance, might result in incorrect inferences.

Whereas there are fewer data on IQ as a predictor of achievement in the workplace (Hunt & Carlson, 2007a), one must consider syllogistically that if IQ scores between Blacks and Whites differ on average by 15 points (i.e., one standard deviation), and if IQ scores are equally predictive of educational success for both Blacks and Whites (positive manifold), then Whites have a decided advantage in situations where ability scores are used to determine access to higher education. Proceeding with this logic, it follows that higher education would provide access to more prestigious and lucrative employment opportunities for Whites. If one then considers the reported correlations between socioeconomic status (SES) and childhood IQ (e.g., Gottfried, Gottfried, Bathurst, Guerin, & Parramore, 2003; Liaw & Brooks-Gunn, 1994; Smith, Brooks-Gunn, & Klebanov, 1997) and the fact that Blacks in the United States tend to be disproportionately represented in the lower socioeconomic classes, one encounters a classic example of circular reasoning. Or as Layzer (1995) observed, "intelligence is what is measured by tests that successfully predict success in enterprises whose success is commonly believed to depend strongly on what is measured by tests that successfully predict success in enterprises whose success is commonly believed to depend strongly on . . ." (p. 669).

Thus, it would appear that the practice of equating intelligence with an IQ score helps to perpetuate – and even exacerbate – the continuing disparity between success rates of Blacks and Whites in the United States. However, with all due respect to Boring (1923), intelligence is *not* simply whatever it is that IQ tests measure.

A Question of Validity

A particular difficulty with IQ instruments is that, historically, they have not been subjected to comprehensive and rigorous score validation. Onwuegbuzie, Daniel, and Collins (2009), in an extension of Messick's (1989, 1995) theory, have provided a comprehensive framework that can be used to assess the fidelity of IQ tests. This *meta-validation model*, presented in Table 15.1, suggests that content-, criterion-, and construct-related validity each can be further partitioned into validity subtypes.

It might be argued that the validity evidence for IQ tests is at least reasonable with respect to criterion-related validity (i.e., both concurrent and predictive validity). For example, as noted previously, IQ scores have been found to forecast an array of educational, occupational, and financial outcomes. Further, it might be contended that at least moderate evidence has been documented for three elements of construct-related validity – namely, convergent validity, divergent validity, and structural validity.

Convergent validity appears to be the most strongly substantiated, with scores from the target intelligence scale often being highly correlated with scores from one or more other intelligence scales (e.g., Jazayeri & Poorshahbaz, 2003). Similarly, evidence of divergent validity is routinely provided for measures of IQ by demonstrating a low correlation with variables deemed to have an irrelevant relationship (e.g., Kolar, 2001). Evidence of structural validity has been provided by researchers who have documented the existence of *g* via factor analysis, although others have expressed concern about the instability of the extracted factors and the inconsistency in the number and nature of factors (e.g., Carroll, 1993; Caruso & Cliff, 1998; Frank, 1983; Geary & Whitworth, 1988; Kamphaus, Benson, Hutchison, & Platt, 1994; O'Grady, 1989, 1990). Even if one accepts the existing support for structural validity, sufficient evidence appears to be lacking with regard to the remaining construct-related validity types: substantive validity, discriminant validity, outcome validity, and generalizability.

In the context of IQ tests, substantive validity refers to the extent that the nature of the IQ testing process is consistent with the construct (i.e., intelligence) being measured. Unfortunately, because knowledge is limited with regard to the range of cognitive processes involved as individuals respond to items on an IQ test, it is difficult to claim that researchers have provided sufficient evidence of substantive validity regarding IQ scores. Some have attempted to develop IQ measures based on tested models of cognitive processing – in particular, the Cognitive Assessment System (CAS; Naglieri & Das, 1997). However, as noted by Telzrow (1990), "the degree to which the CAS meets the authors' stated objectives of providing diversity in content and mode of presentation varies among the [Planning Attention Simultaneous and Successive processing] PASS domains" (p. 344). A further criticism of IQ tests relative to substantive validity is that they focus more on acquired knowledge than on the ability to learn (Kolar, 2001).

As noted earlier, discriminant validity of IQ tests is questionable due to positive manifold. Thus, it is not unusual for scores generated from the target IQ test to be significantly related to scores from

Table 15.1. Areas of Validity Evidence

Validity Type	*Description*
Criterion-Related:	
Concurrent Validity	Assesses the extent to which scores on an instrument are related to scores on another, already established instrument administered approximately simultaneously or to a measurement of some other criterion that is available at the same point in time as the scores on the instrument of interest
Predictive Validity	Assesses the extent to which scores on an instrument are related to scores on another, already established instrument administered in the future or to a measurement of some other criterion that is available at a future point in time as the scores on the instrument of interest
Content-Related:	
Face Validity	Assesses the extent to which the items appear relevant, important, and interesting to the respondent
Item Validity	Assesses the extent to which the specific items represent measurement in the intended content area
Sampling Validity	Assesses the extent to which the full set of items samples the total content area
Construct-Related:	
Substantive Validity	Assesses evidence regarding the theoretical and empirical analysis of the knowledge, skills, and processes hypothesized to underlie respondents' scores
Structural Validity	Assesses how well the scoring structure of the instrument corresponds to the construct domain
Convergent Validity	Assesses the extent to which scores yielded from the instrument of interest are highly correlated with scores from other instruments that measure the same construct
Discriminant Validity	Assesses the extent to which scores generated from the instrument of interest are slightly but not significantly related to scores from instruments that measure concepts theoretically and empirically related to but not the same as the construct of interest
Divergent Validity	Assesses the extent to which scores yielded from the instrument of interest are not correlated with measures of constructs antithetical to the construct of interest
Outcome Validity	Assesses the meaning of scores and the intended and unintended consequences of using the instrument
Generalizability	Assesses the extent that meaning and use associated with a set of scores can be generalized to other populations

Reproduced from A. J. Onwuegbuzie, L. G. Daniel, & K. M. T. Collins (2009), with kind permission from Springer Science+Business Media.

instruments that measure concepts theoretically and empirically related to, but not the same as, the construct of interest (e.g., educational performance). Outcome validity, or what Messick (1989, 1995) termed *consequential aspects*, involves the assessment of the meaning of scores and the intended and unintended consequences of assessment use. Evidence of outcome validity related to IQ tests is particularly inadequate because of the widespread disagreement as to how IQ scores should be interpreted.

Generalizability data provide perhaps the weakest evidence of IQ score validity simply because intelligence is so inextricably embedded in culture. Indeed, Greenfield (1998) observed that (1) "cultures define intelligence by what is adaptive in their particular ecocultural niche" (p. 83) and (2) "definitions of intelligence are as much cultural ideals as scientific statements" (p. 83). Furthermore, as noted by Gould (1996),

> *Facts are not pure and unsullied bits of information; culture also influences what we see and how we see it. Theories, moreover, are not inexorable inductions from facts. The most creative theories are often imaginative visions imposed upon facts; the source of the imagination is also strongly cultural. (p. 54)*

Even IQ tests designed expressly to be *culture fair*, such as Raven's Progressive Matrices (Raven, Raven, & Court, 1995), necessitate conventional knowledge that is culture specific, such as the "ordinal relationship among the columns and among the rows as well as specific knowledge concerning what mental operations are relevant to perform on the test matrix" (Greenfield, 1998, p. 106).

Finally, there is insufficient evidence of content-related validity with regard to IQ tests – specifically, face validity, item validity, and sampling validity. Face validity is questionable because items on IQ tests are not relevant, important, or interesting for many test takers. Indeed, negative attitudes can adversely affect the score validity of IQ tests (Steele & Aronson, 1995). Further, because IQ tests are so influenced by culture, the item content selected for IQ tests for one cultural group – even if psychometrically sound for that cultural group – likely is inappropriate for other cultural groups, thereby threatening both item validity and sampling validity.

Table 15.2 summarizes the quality of validity evidence pertaining to IQ tests extracted from the extant literature using Onwuegbuzie et al.'s (2009) meta-validation model. It can be seen from this table that inadequate validity evidence has been provided for IQ tests for the majority of validity types.

Table 15.2. Interpretation of Quality of Validity Evidence for IQ Tests Using Onwuegbuzie et al.'s Meta-Validation Model

Validity Type	*Evidence*
Criterion-Related:	
Concurrent Validity	Strong
Predictive Validity	Strong
Content-Related:	
Face Validity	Inadequate
Item Validity	Weak
Sampling Validity	Weak
Construct-Related:	
Substantive Validity	Weak
Structural Validity	Adequate
Convergent Validity	Strong
Discriminant Validity	Inadequate
Divergent Validity	Adequate
Outcome Validity	Weak
Generalizability	Weak

Socioeconomic Status (SES) and IQ

But let us for a moment suspend belief and assume that intelligence tests are psychometrically flawless. What of the relationship between SES and IQ? Much of the criticism of Herrnstein and Murray (1994) centered around their quick dismissal of SES as a mitigating factor in the difference between Blacks and Whites on measures of IQ (e.g., Gardner, 1995; Lind, 1995; Nisbett, 1995). Yet SES has been found to be associated with a number of IQ correlates, including achievement test scores (Brooks-Gunn, Guo, & Furstenberg, 1993), grade retentions, and functional literacy (Baydar, Brooks-Gunn, & Furstenberg, 1993). More recently, Noble, Norman, and Farah (2005) found that SES differences were associated with specific disparities in cognitive performance involving the brain's language and executive function systems.

Other factors that vary systematically with SES and likely play a role in creating the SES disparity in ability and achievement include physical health, home environment, neighborhood characteristics, and early education (Bornstein & Bradley, 2003). For example, SES is an important predictor of an array of health and illness outcomes (e.g., Adler & Ostrove, 1999; Anderson & Armstead, 1995), with research consistently documenting a strong SES gradient (i.e., lower SES corresponding to poorer health and vice versa) for cardiovascular disease, tuberculosis, chronic respiratory disease, gastrointestinal disease, arthritis, diabetes, metabolic syndrome, and adverse birth outcomes (Cantwell, Mckenna, McCray, & Onorato, 1998; Cunningham & Kelsey, 1984; Kaplan & Keil, 1993; Matthews, Kelsey, Meilahn, Kuller, & Wing, 1989; O'Campo, Xue, Wang, & Caughy, 1997; Pamuk, Makuc, Heck, Reuben, & Lochner, 1998; Robbins, Vaccarino, Zhang, & Kasl, 2001). SES also has been found to be positively related to perceptions of access and safety for physical activity, as well as to physical activity behaviors (Wilson, Kirtland, Ainsworth, & Addy, 2004), and, most recently, Jokela, Elovainio, Singh-Manoux, and Kivimäki (2009) found that SES largely explains the relationship between low IQ and early mortality in the United States. Furthermore, the relationships between SES and prenatal care (e.g., Lia-Hoagberg et al., 1990) and SES and nutrition (e.g., Brown & Pollitt, 1996) are well documented.

Home environment factors include number of siblings (Blake, 1989); the presence of two parents (Amato & Keith, 1991); home literacy or disciplinary style (Jackson, Brooks-Gunn, Huang, & Glassman, 2000); household resources such as books, computers, and a study room, as well as availability of after-school and summer educational services (Eccles, Lord, & Midgley, 1991; Entwisle & Astone, 1994; McLoyd, 1998); and cognitive stimulation and emotional stress levels (Noble et al., 2005).

In addition to home resources, SES, which is a primary determinant in the location of a child's neighborhood and school, also provides what Coleman (1988) refers to as *social capital*, the supportive relationships among individuals and institutions that promote the sharing of social norms and values necessary to school success. Furthermore, according to the National Research Council (1999), SES is the most important determinant of school financing in the United States, because nearly one half of all public school funding is based on local property taxes. Research comparing low-SES and higher SES schools found significant differences in instructional arrangements, materials, teacher experience, teacher retention, and teacher-student ratio (Wenglinsky, 1998) as well as poorer quality relationships between school personnel and parents (Watkins, 1997). Children who live in poor school districts also have to contend with the stressors of limited social services, more violence, homelessness, and illicit drug activity (Wilson, 1987).

Although it has been argued that the benefits of early childhood education dissipate soon after termination of the program (e.g., Haskins, 1989; Herrnstein & Murray, 1994), Brooks-Gunn et al. (1994) demonstrated that the positive effects of intervention on verbal ability and reasoning skills were still evident two years after the end of their randomized control trial. Furthermore, a meta-analysis of the long-term benefits of early childhood education programs led to the conclusion that these interventions produce persistent, cost-effective effects on academic achievement (Barnett, 1998).

Nature Versus Nurture

The relationship between IQ and SES (and its many correlates) is only one argument challenging hereditarian assumptions about the largely genetic nature of intelligence. Bouchard, Lykken, McGue, Segal, and Tellegen (1990) found that the IQs of individuals correlated more highly with their monozygotic twins, siblings, and parents if they grew up together (.86, .47, .42, respectively) than if they did not (.72, .24, .22, respectively). This suggests that family environment (e.g., child-rearing practices) plays at least some role in the acquisition of intelligence. A number of other environmental factors have been identified in the literature as having either a favorable or unfavorable impact on IQ. These include exposure to toxins or hazards; diet; illness; schooling; prenatal variables such as mother's use of cigarettes, drugs, or alcohol; even duration of breastfeeding, not to mention the variety of random individual life experiences that are impossible to quantify or control (Toga & Thompson, 2005). There also appears to be some evidence that environment can determine the relative impact of genetic variation. Turkheimer, Haley, Waldron, D'Onofrio, and Gottesman (2003), in a study of 320 pairs of twins tested at age 7, found that environmental factors had a far more significant impact on childhood IQ in poor families (heritability = .10) than in wealthier families (heritability = .72). This suggests that *nature* may be more important at the higher end of the socioeconomic spectrum and *nurture* may be more important at the lower end (Toga & Thompson, 2005).

Still more evidence for the impact of environment on IQ is the observation of population-level increases in IQ scores over generations, a phenomenon known as the Flynn effect. This occurrence has been detected across tests and groups and in more than a dozen countries (Flynn, 1987). Noted increases have been attributed to improvements in education, nutrition, and health care; advancements in technology; and improved access to information via television and the Internet.

Other research has focused on gene-environment correlations. For example, it has been posited that more intelligent individuals tend to seek out more stimulating or challenging mental activities or may, in fact, create or evoke situations that further enhance their intellectual prowess (Plomin & Kosslyn, 2001; Ridley, 2003). Whereas there is ample documentation of the impact of heredity on intelligence (e.g., Jensen, 1998; Herrnstein & Murray, 1994), the evidence has been misconstrued to imply that IQ is static and intelligence immutable. As the forgoing arguments suggest, this is simply not the case. Furthermore, we must remember that heritability estimates are *population* statistics and cannot be applied to individuals or their IQ scores. Nor can we infer that the proportion of IQ variance explained by heredity *within* groups is equivalent to the proportion of IQ variance it explains *between* groups. Indeed, this is one of the most grievous errors of generalization made when interpreting findings on heritability. By way of illustration, Lewontin (1982) and others (Tishkoff & Kidd, 2004; Rosenberg et al., 2002) have demonstrated that approximately 85% of genetic variation in a given trait occurs between any two individuals *within* a socially defined racial group and only 6% to 7% occurs *between* socially defined racial groups.

Summary and Conclusions

So, what we have is a strong relationship between two weak phenomena (race and intelligence), one of which – intelligence – is reported to be measurable with IQ tests that happen to correlate with socioeconomic status and that represent a narrowly defined set of cognitive skills which, not surprisingly, predict similarly defined academic skills and therefore, occupational success and wealth, which in turn predict intelligence as represented by an IQ score. Flawed constructs, flawed instruments, and flawed relationships yield flawed inferences and flawed educational and social policies.

What's to be done? Race appears to be a phenomenon of our human tendency to classify, perhaps driven by a need to impose order on nature (Sternberg et al., 2005). The fact is, we have been socialized to label ourselves, and we will probably continue to do so. The problem arises when those in the scientific community reify social conceptions such that they are presented as biological certainties, thereby perpetuating erroneous beliefs about between-group differences. When these beliefs are used in an attempt to advance dubious political agendas, scientists risk becoming instruments of those who would attempt to stifle the progress of minorities in the United States and elsewhere. These authors agree with the position taken by Hunt and Carlson (2007b) that studies with immediate social relevance, such as those investigating group differences, be held to higher technical and methodological standards than those examining purely scientific issues, and that risk-benefit trade-offs be considered in making decisions to publish.

We need to be clear that *IQ* is not synonymous with *intelligence* and to continue in our efforts to reach a consensus on the substance of this elusive construct. In this regard, the authors are impressed with the work of Fagan and Holland (2002, 2007, 2009) who argue that intelligence is information processing and that cultural differences in the provision of information appear to account for observed racial differences in IQ. Specifically, what Fagan and Holland's research demonstrates is that differences in knowledge between Blacks and Whites for intelligence test items can be erased when equal opportunity is provided for exposure to the information to be tested. Other studies have yielded similar findings. For example, Bridgeman and Buttram (1975) found that training in verbal strategies eliminated the differences between Black and White schoolchildren on nonverbal analogy tests; Sternberg et al. (2002) demonstrated that teaching cognitive skills and strategies to Tanzanian children increased their scores relative to nontrained peers on tests of syllogisms, sorting, and 20 questions; and Skuy et al. (2002) reported that Black South African college students benefited more from a mediated learning experience on matrices tasks than did their White counterparts.

Fagan and Holland (2002) state:

> *We believe that the failure to develop tests of intelligence that can be fairly applied across racial groups stems from a theoretical bias to equate the IQ score with intelligence rather than with knowledge. If we define intelligence as information processing and the IQ score as knowledge, the possibility of culture-fair tests of intelligence based on estimates of information processing arises.* (p. 385)

There is little doubt that valid, unbiased measures of intellectual ability would be useful for the processes of selection, recruitment, and promotion of individuals to positions in which they can function most effectively, both in the educational and occupational arenas. However, we must remember that intelligence is only one of many collinear variables that determine success or failure in society; that what is considered *intelligent* behavior in one context may not be relevant or valued in another; and that even conceptions of success vary from culture to culture. Furthermore, as Sternberg (2000) notes, by confusing intelligence with what society says is intelligent, we risk overlooking or giving up on individuals who have valuable skills and abilities to contribute.

In conclusion, continued research on race and intelligence is important, particularly with regard to the etiology of differences in IQ scores. In conducting studies of this nature, however, investigators must be objective, comprehensive, and cautious, given the potential for divisiveness and far-reaching sociopolitical implications. For this reason, all such explorations should be subjected to rigorous peer review, regardless of the distinction of the authors involved. It is only by holding such research to the highest standards that we can hope to make constructive and meaningful contributions to the field.

References

Adler, N. E., & Ostrove, J. M. (1999). Socioeconomic status and health: What we know and what we don't. In N. E. Adler, M. Marmot, B. S. McEwen, & J. Stewart (Eds.), *Socioeconomic status and health in industrial nations; Social, psychological, and biological pathways.* Annals of the New York Academy of Sciences (Vol. 896, pp. 3–15). New York: New York Academy of Sciences.

Amato, P. R., & Keith, B. (1991). Parental divorce and adult well-being: A meta-analysis. *Journal of Marriage and the Family*, 53, 43–58.

Anderson, N. B., & Armstead, C. A. (1995). Toward understanding the association of socioeconomic status and health: A new challenge for the biopsychosocial approach. *Psychosomatic Medicine*, 57, 213–225.

Barnett, W. S. (1998). Long-term cognitive and academic effects of early childhood education on children in poverty. *Preventive Medicine*, 27, 204–207.

Baydar, N., Brooks-Gunn, J., & Furstenberg, F. (1993). Early warning signs of functional illiteracy: Predictors in childhood and adolescence. *Child Development*, 64, 815–829.

Binet, A., & Simon, T. (1916). *The development of intelligence in children* (E. S. Kite, Trans.). Baltimore, MD: Williams & Wilkins.

Blake, J. (1989). Number of siblings and educational attainment. *Science*, 245, 32–37.

Boring, E. G. (1923, June 6). Intelligence as the tests test it. *New Republic*, 35–37.

Bornstein, M. H., & Bradley, R. H. (2003). *Socioeconomic status, parenting, and child development*. Mahwah, NJ: Erlbaum.

Bouchard, T. J., Lykken, D. T., McGue, M., Segal, N. L., & Tellegen, A. (1990). Sources of human psychological differences: The Minnesota Study of Twins Reared Apart. *Science*, 250, 223–228.

Bridgeman, B., & Buttram, J. (1975). Race differences on nonverbal analogy test performance as a function of verbal strategy training. *Journal of Educational Psychology*, 67, 586–590.

Brooks-Gunn, J., Guo, G., & Furstenberg, F. (1993). Who drops out of and who continues beyond high school? *Journal of Research on Adolescence*, 3, 271–294.

Brooks-Gunn, J., McCarton, C., Casey, P., McCormick, M., Bauer, C., Bernbaum, J., & Tyson, J. (1994). Early intervention in low birthweight, premature infants. *Journal of the American Medical Association*, 272, 1257–1262.

Brown, J. L., & Pollitt, E. (1996, February). Malnutrition, poverty, and intellectual development. *Scientific American*, 38–43.

Cantwell, M. F., Mckenna, M. T., McCray, E., & Onorato, I. M. (1998). Tuberculosis and race/ethnicity in the United States: Impact of socioeconomic status. *American Journal of Respiratory and Critical Care Medicine*, 157, 1016–1020.

Carroll, J. B. (1993). *Human cognitive abilities. A survey of factor-analytic studies*. Cambridge, UK: Cambridge University Press.

Caruso, J. C., & Cliff, N. (1998). The factor structure of the WAIS-R: Replicability across age-groups. *Multivariate Behavioral Research*, 33, 273–293.

Ceci, S., & Williams, W. (2009). Darwin 200: Should scientists study race and IQ? YES: The scientific truth must be pursued. *Nature*, 457, 788–789.

Coleman, J. S. (1988). Social capital in the creation of human capital. *American Journal of Sociology*, 94, S95–S120.

Cunningham, L. S., & Kelsey, J. L. (1984). Epidemiology of musculoskeletal impairments and associated disability. *Journal of Public Health*, 74, 574–579.

Eccles, J. S., Lord, S., & Midgley, C. (1991). What are we doing to early adolescents? The impact of educational context on early adolescents. *American Journal of Education*, 99, 521–542.

Entwisle, D. R., & Astone, N. M. (1994). Some practical guidelines for measuring youth's race/ethnicity and socioeconomic status. *Child Development*, 65, 1521–1540.

Fagan, J. F. (1992). Intelligence: A theoretical viewpoint. *Current Directions in Psychological Science*, 1, 82–86.

Fagan, J. F. (2000). A theory of intelligence as processing: Implications for society. *Psychology, Public Policy, and Law*, 6, 168–179.

Fagan, J., & Holland, C. (2002). Equal opportunity and racial differences in IQ. *Intelligence*, 30, 361–387.

Fagan, J., & Holland, C. (2007). Racial equality in intelligence: Predictions from a theory of intelligence as processing. *Intelligence*, 35, 319–334.

Fagan, J., & Holland, C. (2009). Culture-fair prediction of academic achievement. *Intelligence*, 37, 62–67.

Fish, J. M. (2002). A scientific approach to understanding race and intelligence. In J. M. Fish (Ed.), *Race and intelligence: Separating science from myth* (pp. 1–28). Mahwah, NJ: Erlbaum.

Flynn, J. R. (1987). Massive IQ gains in 4 nations: What IQ tests really measure. *Psychological Bulletin*, 101, 171–191.

Frank, G. (1983). *The Wechsler enterprise: An assessment of the development, structure, and use of the Wechsler test of intelligence*. New York, NY: Pergamon Press.

Galton, F. (1892). *Hereditary genius*. London, UK: Macmillan.

Gardner, H. (1983). *Frames of mind: The theory of multiple intelligences*. New York, NY: BasicBooks.

Gardner, H. (1995). Cracking open the IQ box. In S. Fraser (Ed.), *The bell curve wars: Race, intelligence, and the future of America* (pp. 23–35). New York, NY: BasicBooks.

Gardner, H. (2006). *Multiple intelligences: New horizons*. New York, NY: BasicBooks.

Geary, D. C., & Whitworth, R. H. (1988). Dimensional structure of the WAIS-R: A simultaneous multi-sample analysis. *Educational and Psychological Measurement*, 48, 945–956.

Gottfried, A. W., Gottfried, A. E., Bathurst, K., Guerin, D. W., & Parramore, M. M. (2003). Socioeconomic status in children's development and family environment: Infancy through adolescence. In M. H. Bornstein & R. H. Bradley (Eds.), *Socioeconomic status, parenting and child development* (pp. 189–207). Mahwah, NJ: Erlbaum.

Gould, S. J. (1996). *The mismeasure of man*. New York, NY: W. W. Norton.

Greenfield, P. M. (1998). The cultural evolution of IQ. In U. Neisser (Ed.), *The rising curve* (pp. 81–124). Washington, DC: American Psychological Association.

Haskins, R. (1989). Beyond metaphor: The efficacy of early childhood education. *American Psychologist*, 44, 274–282.

Herrnstein, R. J., & Murray, C. (1994). *The bell curve*. New York, NY: Simon & Schuster.

Hocutt, M., & Levin, M. (1999). The *bell curve* case for heredity. *Philosophy of the Social Sciences*, 29, 389–415.

Hoffman, S. (2006). "Racially tailored" medicine unraveled. *American University Law Review*, 55, 395–452.

Hunt, E., & Carlson, J. (2007a). Considerations relating to the study of group differences in intelligence. *Perspectives on Psychological Science*, 2, 194–213.

Hunt, E., & Carlson, J. (2007b). The standards for conducting research on topics of immediate social relevance. *Intelligence*, 35, 393–399.

Jackson, A. P., Brooks-Gunn, J. Huang, C., & Glassman, M. (2000). Single mothers in low-wage jobs: Financial strain, parenting and preschoolers' outcomes. *Child Development*, 71, 1409–1423.

Jazayeri, A. R., & Poorshahbaz, A. (2003). Reliability and validity of Wechsler Intelligence Scale for Children-Third Edition (WISC-III) in Iran. *Journal of Medical Education*, 2, 75–80.

Jensen, A. R. (1969). How much can we boost I.Q. and scholastic achievement? *Harvard Educational Review*, 39(1), 1–123.

Jensen, A. R. (1998). *The g factor: The science of mental ability*. Westport, CT: Praeger.

Jokela, M., Elovainio, M., Singh-Manoux, A., & Kivimäki, M. (2009). IQ, socioeconomic status, and early death: The US National Longitudinal Survey of Youth. *Psychosomatic Medicine*, 71, 322–328.

Kamin, L. J. (1997). Twin studies, heritability, and intelligence. *Science*, 278, 1385.

Kamphaus, R. W., Benson, J., Hutchison, S., & Platt, I. O. (1994). Identification of factor models for the WISC-III. *Educational and Psychological Measurement*, 54, 174–186.

Kaplan, G. A., & Keil, J. E. (1993). Socioeconomic factors and cardiovascular disease: A review of the literature. *Circulation*, 88, 1973–1998.

Kaufman, A. S., & Kaufman, N. L. (2004). *Kaufman Assessment Battery for Children, Second Edition*. San Antonio, TX: Pearson/PsychCorp.

Kolar, G. M. (2001). *A literature review and critical analysis of the concurrent validity of the Differential Ability Scales and the Cognitive Assessment System*. Unpublished master's thesis, University of Wisconsin-Stout, Menomonie, WI.

Layzer, D. (1995). Science or superstition? In R. Jacoby & N. Glauberman (Eds.), *The bell curve debate: History, documents, opinions* (pp. 653–681). New York, NY: Times Books/Random House.

Lewontin, R. C. (1982). *Human diversity*. New York, NY: Freeman.

Lia-Hoagberg, B., Rode, P., Skovholt, C., Oberg, C., Berg, C. Mullett, S., & Choi, T. (1990). Barriers and motivators to prenatal care among low-income women. *Social Science and Medicine*, 30, 487–495.

Liaw, F. R., & Brooks-Gunn, J. (1994). Cumulative familial risks and low birthweight children's cognitive and behavioral development. *Journal of Clinical Child Psychology*, 23, 360–372.

Lind, M. (1995). Brave new right. In S. Fraser (Ed.), *The bell curve wars: Race, intelligence, and the future of America* (pp. 172–178). New York, NY: BasicBooks.

Littlefield, A., Lieberman, L., & Reynolds, L. T. (1982). Redefining race: The potential demise of a concept in anthropology. *Current Anthropology*, 23, 641–647.

Massey, J. T. (1980). A comparison of interviewer observed race and respondent reported race in the National Health Interview Survey. In *Proceedings of the American Statistical Association Proceedings, Social Statistics Section* (pp. 425–428). Washington, DC: American Statistical Association.

Matthews, K. A., Kelsey, S. F., Meilahn, E. N., Kuller, L. H., & Wing, R. R. (1989). Educational attainment and behavioral and biologic risk factors for coronary heart disease in middle-aged women. *American Journal of Epidemiology, 129*, 1132–1144.

McCardle, J. J. (1998). Contemporary statistical models for examining test bias. In J. J. McCardle & R. W. Woodcock (Eds.), *Human cognitive abilities: Theory and practice* (pp. 157–196). Mahwah, NJ: Erlbaum.

McLoyd, V. C. (1998). Socioeconomic disadvantage and child development. *American Psychologist, 53*, 185–204.

Messick, S. (1989). Validity. In R. L. Linn (Ed.), *Educational measurement* (3rd ed., pp. 13–103). Old Tappan, NJ: Macmillan.

Messick, S. (1995). Validity of psychological assessment: Validation of inferences from persons' responses and performances as scientific inquiry into score meaning. *American Psychologist, 50*, 741–749.

Naglieri, J. A., & Das, J. P. (1997). *Das-Naglieri Cognitive Assessment System*. Rolling Meadows, IL: Riverside.

National Research Council. (1999). *Equity and adequacy in education finance: Issues and perspectives*. Washington, DC: National Research Council Committee on Education Finance.

Neisser, U. (1998). Rising test scores. In U. Neisser (Ed.), *The rising curve* (pp. 3–22). Washington, DC: American Psychological Association.

Nisbett, R. (1995). Race, IQ, and scientism. In S. Fraser (Ed.), *The bell curve wars: Race, intelligence, and the future of America* (pp. 36–57). New York, NY: BasicBooks.

Noble, K., Norman, M., & Farah, M. (2005). Neurocognitive correlates of socioeconomic status in kindergarten children. *Developmental Science*, 8(1), 74–87.

O'Campo, P., Xue, X., Wang, M. C., & Caughy, M. (1997). Neighborhood risk factors for low birthweight in Baltimore: A multilevel analysis. *American Journal of Public Health*, 87, 1113–1118.

O'Grady, K. (1989). Factor structure of the WISC-R. *Multivariate Behavioral Research, 24*, 177–193.

O'Grady, K. (1990). A confirmatory maximum factor analysis of the WPPSI. *Personality and Individual Differences, 11*, 135–190.

Onwuegbuzie, A. J. (2003). Expanding the framework of internal and external validity in quantitative research. *Research in the Schools*, 10(1), 71–90.

Onwuegbuzie, A. J., & Daley, C. E. (1996, May). *Myths surrounding racial differences in intelligence: A statistical, sociological, social psychological, and historical critique of The Bell Curve*. Paper presented to students and faculty at the University of Cape Town, South Africa.

Onwuegbuzie, A. J., & Daley, C. E. (2001). Racial differences in IQ revisited: A synthesis of nearly a century of research. *Journal of Black Psychology, 27*, 209–220.

Onwuegbuzie, A. J., Daniel, L. G., & Collins, K. M. T. (2009). A meta-validation model for assessing the score-validity of student teacher evaluations. *Quality & Quantity: International Journal of Methodology, 43*, 197–209.

Pamuk, E., Makuc, D., Heck, K., Reuben, C., & Lochner. K. (1998). *Socioeconomic status and health chartbook. Health, United States, 1998*. Hyattsville, MD: National Center for Health Statistics.

Pearson, H. (1995). Developing the rage to win. In S. Fraser (Ed.), *The bell curve wars: Race, intelligence, and the future of America* (pp. 164–171). New York: BasicBooks.

Plomin, R., & Kosslyn, S. M. (2001). Genes, brain and cognition. *Nature Neuroscience, 4*, 1153–1154.

Raven, J., Raven, J. C., & Court, J. H. (1995). *Manual for Raven's Progressive Matrices and Vocabulary Scales* (Section J, General Overview). Oxford, UK: Oxford Psychologists Press.

Ridley, M. (2003). *Nature via nurture: Genes, experience, and what makes us human*. New York, NY: Harper Collins.

Robbins, J. M., Vaccarino, V., Zhang, H., & Kasl, S. V. (2001). Socioeconomic status and type 2 diabetes in African American and non-Hispanic white women and men: Evidence from the Third National Health and Nutrition Examination Survey. *American Journal of Public Health, 91*, 76–83.

Roid, G. H. (2003). *Stanford-Binet Intelligence Scales, Fifth Edition*. Rolling Meadows, IL: Riverside.

Rosenberg, N. A., Pritchard, J. K., Weber, J. L., Cann, H. M., Field, K. K., Zhivotovsky, L. A., & Feldman, M. A. (2002). Genetic structure of human populations. *Science, 298*, 2381–2385.

Rushton, J. P. (2000). *Race, evolution, and behavior: A life-history perspective* (3rd ed.). Port Huron, MI: Charles Darwin Research Institute.

Rushton, J. P., Skuy, M., & Fridjohn, P. (2003). Performance on Raven's Advanced Progressive Matrices by African, East Indian, and

White engineering students in South Africa. *Intelligence*, 31, 123–137.

Schaefer, R. T. (1988). *Racial and ethnic groups* (3rd ed.). Glenview, IL: Scott, Foresman.

Skuy, M., Gewer, A., Osrin, Y., Khunou, D., Fridjohn, P., & Rushton, J. P. (2002). Effects of mediated learning experiences on Raven's matrices scores of African and non-African university students in South Africa. *Intelligence*, 30, 221–232.

Smedley, A., & Smedley, B. (2005). Race as biology is fiction, racism as a social problem is real. *American Psychologist*, 60, 16–26.

Smith, J., Brooks-Gunn, J., & Klebanov, P. (1997). Consequences of living in poverty for young children's cognitive and verbal ability and early school achievement. In G. Duncan & J. Brooks-Gunn (Eds.), *Consequences of growing up poor* (pp. 132–189). New York, NY: Russell Sage.

Steele, C. M., & Aronson, J. (1995). Stereotype threat and the intellectual performance of African Americans. *Journal of Personality and Social Psychology*, 69, 797–811.

Sternberg, R. J. (1997a). *Successful intelligence*. New York, NY: Plume.

Sternberg, R. J. (1997b). The triarchic theory of intelligence. In D. P. Flanagan, J. L. Genshaft, & P. L. Harrison (Eds.), *Contemporary intellectual assessment: Theories, tests, and issues* (pp. 92–104). New York, NY: Guilford Press.

Sternberg, R.J. (2000). Implicit theories of intelligence as exemplar stories of success: Why intelligence test validity is in the eye of the beholder. *Psychology, Public Policy, and Law*, 6, 159–167.

Sternberg, R. J., Grigorenko, E. L., & Kidd, K. K. (2005). Intelligence, race, and genetics. *American Psychologist*, 60(1), 46–59.

Sternberg, R. J., Grigorenko, E. L., Ngorosho, D., Tantufuye, E., Mbise, A., Nokes, C., et al. (2002). Assessing intellectual potential in rural Tanzanian school children. *Intelligence*, 30, 141–162.

Stoddard, G. D. (1943). *The meaning of intelligence*. New York, NY: Macmillan.

Telzrow, C. F. (1990). Does *PASS* pass the test? A critique of the Das-Naglieri Cognitive Assessment System. *Journal of Psychoeducational Assessment*, 6, 344–355.

Tishkoff, S. A., & Kidd, K. K. (2004). Implications of biogeography of human populations for "race" and medicine. *Nature Genetics*, 36(11, Suppl.), S21–S27.

Toga, A. W., & Thompson, P. M. (2005). Genetics of brain structure and intelligence. *Annual Review of Neuroscience*, 28, 1–23.

Turkheimer, E., Haley, A., Waldron, M., D'Onofrio, B., & Gottesman, I. (2003). Socioeconomic status modifies heritability of IQ in young children. *Psychological Science*, 14, 623–628.

Watkins, T. J. (1997). Teacher communications, child achievement, and parent traits in parent involvement models. *Journal of Educational Research*, 91, 3–14.

Wechsler, D. (1958). *The measurement and appraisal of adult intelligence* (4th ed.). Baltimore, MD: Williams & Wilkins.

Wechsler, D. (2002). *Wechsler Preschool and Primary Scale of Intelligence, Third Edition*. San Antonio, TX: Pearson/PsychCorp.

Wechsler, D. (2003). *Wechsler Intelligence Scale for Children, Fourth Edition*. San Antonio, TX: Pearson/PsychCorp.

Wechsler, D. (2008). *Wechsler Adult Intelligence Scale, Fourth Edition*. San Antonio, TX: Pearson/PsychCorp.

Wenglinsky, H. (1998). Finance equalization and within-school equity: The relationship between education spending and the social distribution of achievement. *Educational Evaluation and Policy Analysis*, 20, 269–283.

Wilson, D. K., Kirtland, K. A., Ainsworth, B. E., & Addy, C. L. (2004). Socioeconomic status and perceptions of access and safety for physical activity. *Annals of Behavioral Medicine*, 28, 20–28.

Wilson, W. J. (1987). The hidden agenda. In W. J. Wilson (Ed.), *The truly disadvantaged: The inner city, the underclass and public policy* (pp. 140–164). Chicago. IL: University of Chicago Press.

Wilson, L. C., & Williams, D. R. (1998). Issues in the quality of data on minority groups. In V. C. McLoyd & L. Steinberg (Eds.), *Studying minority adolescents: Conceptual, methodological, and theoretical issues* (pp. 237–250). Mahwah, NJ: Erlbaum.

Woodcock, R. W., McGrew, K. S., & Mather, N. (2007). *Woodcock-Johnson III NU Tests of Cognitive Abilities*. Rolling Meadows, IL: Riverside.

Part IV

BIOLOGY OF INTELLIGENCE

CHAPTER 16

Animal Intelligence

Thomas R. Zentall

The notion of an evolutionary scale with humans at the top is popularly held but also self-serving. We tend to undervalue the exceptional sensory skills of tracking and drug-detecting dogs as well as the navigational abilities of homing pigeons, whales, and monarch butterflies. Conversely, we tend to overvalue our problem-solving ability, capacity to modify our environment, and ability to communicate with each other. This bias notwithstanding, taken as a whole, clearly the sum of our intellectual capacity, measured in almost any way, exceeds that of other animals. The role of our intelligence in the domination of our species over others seems obvious, but in the broader perspective of evolutionary success, as measured by the number of surviving members of a species, intelligence, as a general characteristic, correlates only superficially (and perhaps even negatively) with most measures of evolutionary success. Consider the relatively small numbers of our closest relatives, the great apes, compared with the large numbers of considerably more "primitive" insects, bacteria, and viruses. And it is estimated that if a massive disaster were to occur (e.g., if Earth were hit by a large asteroid or suffered a self-inflicted nuclear disaster), many simpler organisms would likely survive much better than large intelligent animals like us.

From a purely biological perspective, the ideal survival machine is a simple, perhaps even one-celled, organism (e.g., the amoeba) that has survived in one of two ways. Either it has needed to undergo little change in morphology or behavior for millions of years because it exists in a remarkably stable (predictable) environment, in which case there has been little need for change, or if its environment does change, it relies on natural selection by means of very rapid reproduction and mutation (e.g., bacteria and viruses). This ability to reproduce quickly and often, ensures the survival of many of these organisms (albeit not necessarily in the same form) even in the event of a major catastrophe. Many other organisms whose rate of reproduction has not been able to keep up with relatively rapid changes in the environment have relied on the ability to modify their behavior during their lifetime. Intelligence, in its simplest form, can be thought of as the genetic flexibility that allows organisms to adjust their behavior to relatively rapidly changing environments. For some animals, a stable supply of a highly specific food may be predictable (e.g., eucalyptus leaves for the koala or bamboo leaves for the giant panda) – at least until recently. For most animals, however, environments are much less predictable and their predisposed eating preferences have had to be much more flexible. For still other animals, the environment is sufficiently unpredictable that it is impossible to specify (by genetic means) what food will be available to an individual (consider the varied diet of the city-dwelling rat). For these animals to survive, more general (abstract) rules must be available. Rules about what to eat may not be based on the sight or taste of what is ingested but on its consequences. Instead of instructing the animal to eat eucalyptus leaves or to eat a certain class of seeds, these genes tell the animal that if it feels sick after eating a new food, it should avoid eating more of that food. Such general rules allow for the behavioral flexibility that we call learning.

But there is a price to pay for this added flexibility. The animal must sometimes suffer the consequences of eating something bad. If the novel food is poisonous, the animal may not survive to use its newfound knowledge. The creation and maintenance of a nervous system capable of such learning represents a cost as well. For many animals, the benefits of the capacity for simple associative learning outweigh the cost, and for some animals, the negative consequences are sufficiently costly that simple learning rules are not enough.

Some animals have found ways to reduce this cost. Rats, which live in highly unpredictable environments, have evolved the ability to learn the consequences of eating a small amount of a novel food in a single experience, even when those consequences are experienced hours after the food was ingested (Garcia & Koelling, 1966). Rats have also developed the ability to transmit food preferences socially. If a rat experiences the smell of a novel food on the breath of another rat, it will prefer food with that smell over another, equally novel food (Galef, 1988x) and it may also be able to assess the consequences to the other rat of having eaten a novel food (Kuan & Colwill, 1997).

But what if this degree of flexibility in learning is still not enough to allow for survival? In the case of humans, for example, our poorly developed sense of smell, our relatively poorly developed gross motor response (e.g., slow running speed), and our relative physical weakness may not have allowed us to hunt competitively with other predators (e.g., large cats). The competition with other animals for food must have come about slowly enough for us to develop weapons and tools, complex forms of communication (language), and complex social structure (allowing for cooperation, teamwork, and reciprocation). According to this view, although our intellect appears to have given us a clear advantage over other animals, its evolution is likely to have emerged because of our relative weakness in other areas. Other animals have compensated for their weaknesses by developing strengths in nonintellectual areas (e.g., the snail compensates for its lack of rapid mobility by building a protective shell around itself). Discussions of animal intelligence often assume, inappropriately, that intelligence is inherently good. In our case, it has turned out to be generally true (at least to the present). For us, intelligence has had a runaway effect on our ability to adapt to change (an effect that Dawkins, 1976, calls *hypergamy*), which has allowed us to produce radical changes in our environment. However, from a biological perspective, in general, intelligence can be viewed as making the best out of a bad situation, or producing a complex solution to problems that other species have often solved in simpler ways. As we evaluate the various intellectual capacities of nonhuman animals, let us try to keep in mind that they have survived quite well (until recently) without the need for our complex intellectual skills.

The Comparative Approach: Two Warnings

First, most people have a vague idea of the relative intelligence of animals. As a general rule, those species that are more like us physically are judged to be more intelligent. But we must be careful in making such judgments because we humans are the ones deciding what intelligent behavior is. We make up the rules and the testing procedures and those tests may be biased in favor of our particular capacities. Isn't it interesting that animals that are more similar to us, that have similar sensory, motor, and motivational systems, just happen to be judged as more intelligent?

Bitterman (1975) has suggested that a relational view of animal learning should be used to correct for peripheral differences in sensory capacity and motor coordination. He suggests that rather than looking for differences in the rate at which different species can learn, we might look at differences, for example, in an animal's ability to learn *from the experience of learning.* In other words, to what extent can learning facilitate new learning (*learning to learn*)? Then, using the rate of original learning as a baseline, one can determine the degree to which later learning, presumably involving the same processes, is facilitated. However, this approach is not always possible and we must be aware that our assessment may be biased by the use of testing procedures not well suited for the species we are studying. Second, we must guard against the opposite bias – the tendency to interpret behavior as intelligent because of its similarity to intelligent human behavior. In evaluating research addressing the cognitive capacity of animals I will adopt C. Lloyd Morgan's (1894) position that it is not necessary to interpret behavior as complex (more cognitive) if a simpler (less cognitive) account will suffice. Thus, higher level cognitive interpretations will always be contrasted with simpler, contiguity- and contingency-based, associative-learning accounts. I will start with several classical issues concerned with the nature of learning and intelligence in animals, move to more complex behavior thought to be uniquely human, and end with examples of presumably complex behavior that are likely to be based on simpler predisposed processes.

1. Absolute Versus Relational Learning

One of the most basic cognitive functions is not being bound to the absolute properties of a stimulus. Although Hull (1943) claimed that learning involves solely the absolute properties of a stimulus, he proposed that animals will appear to respond relationally because they will respond similarly to similar stimuli, a process known as stimulus generalization. Spence (1937) elaborated on this theory by proposing that discrimination learning establishes predictable gradients of excitation and inhibition that summate algebraically. And this theory of generalization gradient summation can account for a number of phenomena that were formerly explained as relational learning (see Riley, 1968). The fact that one sees little discussion of this issue in the modern literature suggests that animals are capable of using either the absolute or relative properties of a stimulus in making discriminations.

2. Learning to Learn

Can an animal use prior learning to facilitate new learning? That is, can animals learn to learn? If an animal learns a simple discrimination between two stimuli (an S+, to which responses are reinforced and an S- to which responses are extinguished) and then, following acquisition, the discrimination is reversed (the S+ becomes S- and the S- becomes S+), and then reversed again, repeatedly, are successive reversals learned faster than earlier reversals? Animals trained on such a serial-reversal task often show improvement within a few reversals and the rate of improvement can be used as a measure of learning to learn. For example, rats show more improvement than pigeons, and pigeons show more improvement than gold fish (Bitterman & Mackintosh, 1969). Mackintosh (1969) attributes these differences in serial-reversal learning to the differential ability of these species to maintain attention to the relevant dimension.

A different approach to learning to learn is to look for improvement in the rate at which discriminations involving *new* stimuli are learned. This phenomenon, known as learning set (Harlow, 1949), has been studied primarily using visual discriminations with monkeys but good evidence for such effects has also been found with olfactory discriminations with rats (Slotnick & Katz, 1974). In the limit, learning of a new discrimination, or of a reversal, can occur in a single trial. When it does, it is referred to as a win-stay-lose-shift strategy because stimulus choice is completely controlled by the consequences of choice on the preceding trial. One means of developing such a strategy is to *learn to forget* the consequences of trials prior to the immediately preceding trial. In fact, research has shown that memory for the specific characteristics of the stimuli from prior discriminations does decline as the number of discriminations learned increases (Meyer, 1971). Thus, animals approach optimal learning by learning to ignore the effects of all but the most recent experience.

3. Stimulus Class Formation

A. *Perceptual Classes*

Pigeons are remarkably adept at responding selectively to photographs of natural scenes, depending on whether the scene involves a human form (Herrnstein & Loveland, 1964) or trees or water (Herrnstein, Loveland, & Cable, 1976) and those objects need not be anything that they might have actually encountered in their past (e.g., underwater pictures of fish; Herrnstein & deVilliers, 1980). To demonstrate that the pigeons do not simply memorize a list of pictures and their appropriate responses, Herrnstein et al. showed that the pigeons would respond appropriately to new examples of the positive and negative stimulus sets.

What is interesting about perceptual classes is that it is difficult to specify what features humans or pigeons use to discriminate members from nonmembers of the perceptual class. However, examination of the kinds of errors made can tell us about the attributes that were used to categorize the exemplars and the similarities in the underlying processes. For example, pigeons make errors similar to those of young children (e.g., they often erroneously assign a picture of a bunch of celery to the category "tree").

B. *Equivalence Relations*

The emergent relations that may arise when arbitrary, initially unrelated stimuli are associated with the same response are often referred to as functional equivalence (see Zentall & Smeets, 1996) because the two stimuli can be thought of as "having the same meaning. The most common procedure for demonstrating functional equivalence involves training on two conditional discriminations. In the first, for example, a red hue (sample) signals that a response to a circle will be reinforced (but not a response to a dot) and a green hue signals that a response to a dot will be reinforced (but not a response to a circle; see Figure 16.1). In the second conditional discrimination, a vertical line signals that a response to the circle will be reinforced (but not a response to the dot) and a horizontal line signals that a response to the dot will be reinforced (but not a response to the circle). Thus, red and vertical line mean choose the circle and green and horizontal line mean choose the dot. This procedure has been referred to as many-to-one matching because training involves the association of two samples with the same comparison stimulus. To show that an emergent relation has developed between the red hue and the vertical line and between green hue and the horizontal line, one can train new associations between one pair of the original sample (e.g., the red and green hues) and a new pair of comparison stimuli (e.g., blue and white hues, respectively). Then on test trials one can show that emergent relations have developed when, without

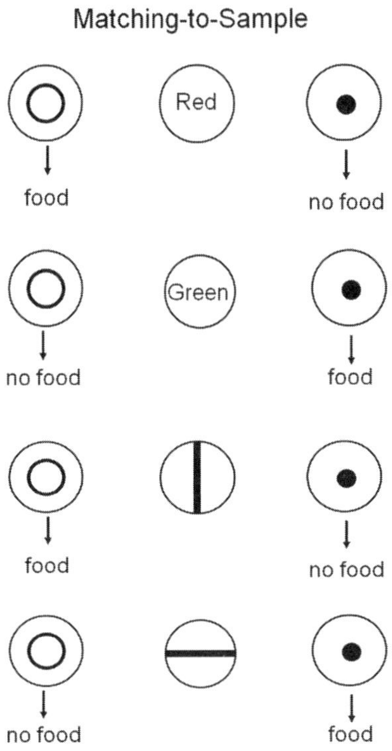

Figure 16.1. Many-to-one matching training used to show that pigeons will learn that red and vertical (as well as green and horizontal) "mean the same thing." If red and green samples are now associated with new comparison stimuli, blue and white, respectively, there is evidence that the vertical- and horizontal-line are also associated with the blue and white stimuli, respectively.

further training, an animal chooses blue when the sample is a vertical line and chooses white when the sample is a horizontal line (Urcuioli, Zentall, Jackson-Smith, & Steirn, 1989; Wasserman, DeVolder, & Coppage, 1992; Zentall, 1998).

The ability of animals to develop emergent stimulus classes involving arbitrary stimuli has important implications for human language learning because stimulus class formation plays an integral role in the acquisition of that aspect of human language known as *semantics* – the use of symbols (words) to stand for objects, actions, and attributes. The ability of small-brained organisms like pigeons to develop *arbitrary* stimulus classes suggests that this capacity is much more pervasive than once thought.

4. Memory Strategies

The task most often used to study memory in animals is delayed matching-to-sample, in which following acquisition of matching-to-sample, a delay is inserted between the offset of the sample and the onset of the comparison stimuli (Roberts & Grant, 1976). However, the retention functions typically found with this procedure generally greatly underestimate the animal's memory capacity for two reasons. First, in many studies, the novel delay interval is quite similar to the intertrial interval, the end of the trial event. When the delay interval and the intertrial interval are made distinctive, the retention functions obtained may provide a very different picture of the animal's memory (Sherburne, Zentall, & Kaiser, 1998). Second, the novelty of the delays may result in a generalization decrement that is confounded with memory loss. When pigeons are trained with delays, considerably flatter retention functions have been found (Dorrance, Kaiser, & Zentall, 2000). Of more interest in the assessment of animal intelligence are strategies that animals may use to enhance memory.

A. *Prospective Processes*

Traditionally animal memory has been viewed as a rather passive process. According to this view, sensory events can leave a trace that may control responding even when the event is no longer present (Roberts & Grant, 1976). However, it has been suggested that animals can also actively translate or code the representation of a presented stimulus into an expectation of a yet-to-be-presented event (Honig & Thompson, 1982). The use of expectations, or prospective coding processes, has important implications for the cognitive capacities of animals. If the expectation of a stimulus, response, or outcome can serve as an effective cue for responding, it suggests that animals may be capable of exerting active control over memory, and in particular, it may suggest they have the capacity for active planning.

The notion of expectancy as an active purposive process can be attributed to Tolman (1932). Although one can say that a dog salivates when it hears a bell because it *expects* food to be placed in its mouth, the demonstration that an expectation can serve as a discriminative stimulus (i.e., as the basis for making a choice) suggests that the expectancy has additional cognitive properties.

The differential outcomes effect. If a conditional discrimination is designed such that a correct response following one sample results in one kind of outcome (e.g., food) and following the other sample results in a different kind of outcome (e.g., water), one can show that acquisition of the conditional discrimination is faster (Trapold, 1970) and retention is better when a delay is inserted between the conditional and choice stimuli (Peterson, Wheeler, & Trapold, 1980). Furthermore, there is evidence from transfer-of-training experiments that in the absence of other cues, outcome anticipations can serve as sufficient cues for comparison choice. That is, if the original samples are replaced by other stimuli associated with the same differential outcomes, positive transfer has been found (Edwards, Jagielo, Zentall, & Hogan, 1982; Peterson, 1984). This line of research indicates that presentation of a sample creates an expectation of a particular kind of outcome, and that expectation can then serve as the basis for comparison choice. In most cases, the differential outcomes have differential hedonic value (e.g., a high probability of food versus a low probability of food) and it is possible that outcome anticipation can elicit differential emotional states in the animal. But there is also evidence that nondifferentially hedonic events such as the anticipation of a particular stimulus can affect response accuracy (Kelly & Grant, 2001; Miller, Friedrich, Narkavic, & Zentall, 2009; Williams, Butler, & Overmier, 1990).

Planning ahead. One of the hallmarks of human cognitive behavior is our ability to consciously plan for the future. Although animals sometimes appear to plan for the future (birds build nests, rats hoard food), these behaviors are likely to be under genetic control. To distinguish between planning for the future and learning with a long delay of reinforcement, Suddendorf and Corballis (1997) have suggested that the behavior must occur in the absence of the relevant motivation. Thus, Roberts (2002) reported the absence of planning by monkeys which, when given their daily portion of food, after eating, threw out of their cage whatever food remained but requested more food later in the day. Further laboratory research suggested, however, that monkeys could learn to plan for the future and would choose a smaller amount of food over a larger amount (1) if more food would be provided later after they selected the smaller amount but not the larger amount or (2) if choosing the larger amount resulted in the removal of much of what was selected (Naqshbandi & Roberts, 2006).

More convincing evidence for planning was reported by Raby, Alexis, Dickinson, and Clayton (2007). Western scrub jays, which cache food for future use, learned that they would spend the night in a compartment in which they would find one kind of food (peanuts) in the morning or in a compartment in which they would find a different kind of food (kibble) in the morning. On test trials, they were allowed to eat and cache food in either compartment the night before. When they were given peanuts they tended to cache them in the kibble compartment and when they were given kibble they tended to cache them in the peanut compartment (i.e., the compartment in which they would not find the particular cached food in the morning).

B. *Directed (Intentional) Forgetting*

The notion of directed or intentional forgetting is borrowed from human memory research. It implies that memory is an active rather than an automatic process. Presumably, following presentation, items that participants are instructed to forget may not be well stored or maintained in memory and thus should not be well retained. In a directed forgetting task with animals, for example, pigeons are trained on a matching task and then a delay of a fixed duration is introduced between the sample and the comparisons. On "forget" trials, during the delay, the pigeons are cued that there will be no test of sample memory. On probe trials, the forget cue is presented but there is also a test of sample memory. Matching accuracy on these probe trials is generally below that of "remember" trials on which there was an expected test of sample memory (Grant, 1981). But this design confounds differential motivation on remember and forget trials with sample memory effects. In a more complex design that controls for motivational effects and that better approximates the human directed forgetting procedure by allowing the animal to *reallocate* its memory from the sample to an alternative memory on forget trials in training, better evidence for directed forgetting in pigeons has been demonstrated (Roper, Kaiser, & Zentall, 1995). Thus, under certain conditions it appears that animals do have active control over memory processes.

C. *Episodic Memory*

Human memory can be identified by the kinds of processes presumed to be involved. Procedural memory involves memory for actions (e.g., riding a bicycle) and it has been assumed that most learned behavior by animals involves this kind of memory. Human declarative memory is assumed to be more cognitive because it involves memory for facts (semantic memory) and memory of personal experiences (episodic memory). Although animals cannot typically describe factual information, their conditional rule-based learning can be thought of as a kind of semantic memory (e.g., if the sample is red choose the vertical line, if the sample is green choose the horizontal line). But do animals have episodic memory?

Tulving (1972) proposed that an episodic memory should include the *what, where,* and *when* of an experience. Clayton and Dickinson (1999) showed that western scrub jays that cached peanuts and wax worms (what) on one side or the other of an ice cube tray (where) learned that their preferred wax worms would be edible after one day but after four days only the peanut would be edible (when; see also Babb & Crystal, 2006, for a similar finding with rats). But it can be argued that it is insufficient to retrieve the *what, where,* and *when* of an episode because those have been explicitly trained (i.e., they are semantic or rule-based memories). Instead, better evidence for episodic memory would come from the finding that animals can retrieve information about a past episode when there is no expectation that they will be requested to do so in the future (Zentall, Clement, Bhatt, & Allen, 2001). That is, imagine that pigeons are first trained to report the location where they recently pecked and then are trained on an unrelated conditional discrimination in which choice of a vertical line was correct when the sample was blue and choice of the horizontal line was correct when the sample was yellow. Singer and Zentall (2007) found that on probe trials on which following a vertical- or horizontal-line comparison response the pigeons were asked unexpectedly to report the location that they had pecked, they reliably did so. Thus, by either criterion (what-where-when or responding to an unexpected question), pigeons show some evidence of episodic-like memory.

5. Navigation

Compared to many animals, humans have relatively poor navigational skills. Consider how dependent we are on external supports such as compasses, maps, and more recently global positioning devices. Many animals (e.g., migrating whales, birds, monarch butterflies) can navigate over many hundreds of miles using magnetic fields, chemical gradients, and star patterns. And homing pigeons use a number of these navigational systems including landmarks consisting of natural and man-made geographic features (Lipp et al., 2004).

However, many humans have the ability to imagine a route that they will take and even to imagine how to get to a familiar destination by a novel path. This ability, known as cognitive mapping, consists of knitting together landmarks one has experienced, such that the relation among them can be used to determine a novel path to arrive at a goal. Landmarks are needed to *form* a cognitive map but they should not be necessary to *use* it. Can animals form a cognitive map?

Some animals have the remarkable ability to navigate in the absence of landmarks or other external cues. This ability, known as path integration (or dead reckoning), involves the representation of direction and distance one has traveled from a starting point. Desert ants are particularly adept at path integration as can be shown not only by the direct path that they take to return to their nest after a foraging trip but also by the systematic error incurred if they are displaced just before they attempt to return home (Collette & Graham, 2004). The distinction between path integration and cognitive mapping has been a point of controversy. However, under conditions that cannot be accounted for with either landmark use or path integration, there is evidence for the development of a simple cognitive map in rats (Singer, Abroms, & Zentall, 2007) and dogs (Chapuis & Varlet, 1987).

6. Counting

The term "numerical competence" is often used in animal research because the more common term, "counting," carries with it the surplus meaning that accompanies the human verbal labels given to numbers. That this distinction is an arbitrary one, based on limitations of response (output) capacity rather than conceptual ability, is suggested by Pepperberg's (1987) work with generalized number use (in verbal English) in an African gray parrot.

An excellent review of the animal counting literature is provided by Davis and Memmott (1982), who conclude that counting does not come easily to animals. "Although counting is obtainable in infra humans, its occurrence requires considerable environmental support" (Davis & Memmott, p. 566). In contrast, Capaldi (1993) concludes that under the right conditions, animals count routinely. In simple but elegant experiments, Capaldi and Miller (1988) demonstrated that following training, rats can anticipate whether they will get fed or not for running down an alley depending solely on the number of successive times they have run down that alley and found food on successive earlier trials.

The difference in the conclusions reached by Davis and Memmott (1982) and by Capaldi and Miller (1988) has general implications for the study of intelligence in animals (including humans). The context in which one looks for a particular capacity may determine whether one will find evidence for it. Because we, as human experimenters, devise the tasks that serve as the basis for the assessment of intelligence, we must be sensitive to the possibility that these tasks may not be optimal for eliciting the behavior we are assessing. As noted earlier, much of our view of the evolutionary scale of intelligence may be biased in this way by species differences in sensory, response, and motivational factors. Perhaps the most impressive demonstration of numerical competence in an animal was reported by Boysen and Berntson (1993). A chimpanzee, Sheba, was first trained on the correspondence between Arabic numerals and number of objects. When she was then shown a number of objects seen at two different locations (e.g., three objects at one site and one object at another), she pointed to the numeral "4," the sum of the objects. Finally, she was shown Arabic numerals at two different sites and she spontaneously pointed to the numeral that represented the sum of the two numerals she had seen.

7. Reasoning

Reasoning can be thought of as a class of cognitive behavior for which correct responding on test trials requires an inference based on incomplete experience. Although, for obvious reasons, most research on reasoning in animals has been done with higher primates (e.g., chimpanzees), there is evidence that some reasoning-like behavior can be demonstrated in a variety of species.

A. *Transitive Inference*

In its simplest form, the transitive inference task can be described as follows: if A is greater than B (A>B), and B is greater than C (B>C), then it can be inferred that A>C (where the letters A, B, and C represent arbitrary stimuli). A correct response on this relational learning task requires that an inference be made about the relation between A and C that can only be derived from the two original propositions. To avoid potential problems with "end-point effects" that could produce a spurious nonrelational solution (i.e., C is never greater and A is always greater), experimental research typically uses a task that involves four propositions: A > B, B > C, C > D, and D > E and the test involves the choice between B and D, each of which is sometimes greater and sometimes lesser.

When humans are tested for transitive inference, the use of language allows for the propositions to be completely relational. Relative size may be assigned to individuals identified only by name (e.g., given that Anne is taller than Betty, and Betty is taller than Carol, who is taller, Anne or Carol?). With animals, however, there is no way to present such relational propositions without also presenting the actual stimuli. And if the stimuli differ in observable value (e.g., size), then a correct response can be made without the need to make an inference.

McGonigle and Chalmers (1977) suggested that a nonverbal relational form of the task could be represented by simple simultaneous discriminations in which one stimulus is associated with reinforcement (+) and the other is not (–). A > B can be represented as A + B-, B > C as B + C-, and so on. With four propositions an animal would be exposed to A + B-, B + C-, C + D-, and D + E-. A is always positive and E is always negative but B and D, stimuli that were never paired during training, would share similar reinforcement histories. If animals order the stimuli from A is best to E is worst, then B should be preferred over D.

Findings consistent with transitive inference have been reported in research with species as diverse as chimpanzees (Gillan, 1981), rats (Davis, 1992), and pigeons (Fersen, Wynne, Delius, & Staddon, 1991). Although some have argued that these results can be accounted for without postulating that an inference has been made (Couvillon & Bitterman, 1992; Fersen et al., 1991; Steirn, Weaver, & Zentall, 1995), transitive inference effects have been found when these presumably simpler mechanisms have been controlled (Lazareva & Wasserman, 2006; Weaver, Steirn, & Zentall, 1997). Thus, although it is not clear what mechanism produces it, pigeons clearly show transitive choice that is not produced by differential reinforcement history or differential value transfer from the positive to the negation stimulus in a simultaneous discrimination.

B. *Conservation*

The conservation of liquid volume task, made popular as a test of cognitive development by Piaget (1952), was developed to test for the inference that if two liquid volumes are initially the same and one of the volumes is transformed by pouring it into a container of a different shape (following transformation, the heights of the liquids in the two containers are quite different), the volumes are still the same. Woodruff, Premack, and Kennel (1978) developed a nonverbal version of this task that they used to test for conservation in Sarah, a chimpanzee. Not only did Sarah indicate (by means of previously acquired use of tokens representing "same" and "different") that transformation of shape did not cause two like volumes to be different, but she also indicated that two dissimilar volumes continued to be different following a transformation that resulted in liquid levels of similar height. Furthermore,

Sarah was unable to correctly judge the relative volume of the liquids if the transformation was made out of sight. Thus, correct responding required observation of the original state of the containers and the transformation. This series of experiments is particularly noteworthy for its careful control of possible extraneous variables.

C. *Analogical Reasoning*

Another example of reasoning by a chimpanzee, analogical reasoning, has been reported by Gillan, Premack, and Woodruff (1981). Sarah, the chimpanzee, was shown pictures of objects she had previously encountered in the relation A is to B as A' is to X, with a choice of B' and C' as a replacement for X. Sarah's reliance on the analogical relationship was tested by varying only the initial stimulus pair. Thus, on one trial she was presented with, for example, "lock" is to "key" as "paint can" is to "?" with a choice of "can opener" and "paint brush," and on another trial with "paper" is to "pencil" as "paint can" is to "?" with a choice of the same "can opener" and "paint brush." In the first case Sarah selected the "can opener" (indicating something with which to open the paint can), in the second, the "paint brush" (indicating something with which to paint). Thus, at least one chimpanzee appears to understand and can use analogical reasoning.

8. Language

We are the only species to develop, on our own, the flexible form of communication based on arbitrary symbols that we call language. With training, however, other species may be able to acquire a rudimentary form of symbolic communication. One of the most widely reported and least understood lines of research in animal intelligence involves projects concerned with the acquisition of language by chimpanzees. The three best known of these projects are Gardner and Gardner's (1965) sign learning project (see also Patterson's [1978] work with a gorilla and Herman, Pack, and Morrel-Samuels's [1993] work with dolphins), Premack's (1976) token learning project, and the Rumbaughs' (Rumbaugh, 1977) keyboard learning project.

Although these projects are identified by the nature of the responses required of their animals, they are better distinguished by differences in their conceptual approaches. The Gardners chose sign language because it is an accepted form of human language, and acquisition and mastery skills by a chimpanzee could be compared directly with those of humans by objective sign-trained observers unfamiliar with the animals. The use of tokens in Premack's research allowed for more careful control over the set of possible responses. Premack's research focused more on the *conceptual* nature of language, including such characteristics as same/different learning, negation, property of, and causality. The Rumbaughs' work with Austin and Sherman focused on the functional use of language in communication (Savage-Rumbaugh, 1984). For example, they established conditions in which solution of a problem by one chimpanzee required the production and reception by another chimpanzee of a list of symbols representing a request for a tool.

Whether the communication skills acquired by these chimpanzees qualify as language depends in part on how language is defined. Unfortunately, there is little agreement on the necessary and sufficient characteristics of language. Such a definition must be sufficiently liberal to include not only hearing impaired humans who use sign language but also young children and many developmentally delayed adults who have restricted but functionally adequate language skills.

9. Taking the Perspective of Others

An organism can take the perspective of another when it demonstrates an understanding of what the other may know. For example, when Susan sees a hidden object moved to a second hidden location after

Billy has left the room and Susan understands that Billy will probably look for the object in the first location rather than second, we would say that Susan can take the perspective of Billy or has a theory of mind because she understands that Billy doesn't know that the object has been moved (see Frye, 1993). To demonstrate perspective taking in an animal is a bit more complex because, in the absence of language, theory of mind must be inferred from other behavior.

A. *Self-Recognition*

Recognition of the similarity between ourselves and other humans would seem to be a prerequisite for perspective taking. If we can recognize ourselves in a mirror, we can see that we are similar to others of our species. Gallup (1970) has shown that not only will chimpanzees exposed to a mirror use it for grooming, but if their face is marked while they are anesthetized, they will use the mirror to explore the mark visually and tactually (i.e., they pass the mark test). Furthermore, both prior experience with the mirror and the presence of the mirror following marking appear to be necessary for mark exploration to occur. Although mirror-directed mark exploration appears to occur in other higher apes (orangutans and perhaps also in gorillas), no evidence of self-recognition has been found in monkeys, even with extensive mirror experience (Gallup & Suarez, 1991). On the other hand, there is some evidence of self-recognition in both dolphins (Reiss & Marino, 2001) and elephants (Plotnik, de Waal, & Reiss, 2006). Thus, self-recognition appears to occur in several species thought to have other cognitive skills.

B. *Imitation*

A more direct form of perspective taking involves the capacity to imitate another (Piaget, 1951), especially opaque imitation for which the observer cannot see itself perform the response (e.g., clasping one's hands behind one's back). But evidence for true imitative learning requires that one rule out (or control for) other sources of facilitated learning following observation (see Whiten & Ham, 1992; Zentall, 1996). A design that appears to control for artifactual sources of facilitated learning following observation is the two-action procedure based on a method developed by Dawson and Foss (1965). For example, imitation is said to occur if observers, exposed to a demonstrator performing a response in one of two topographically different ways, perform the response with the same topography as their demonstrator (Heyes & Dawson, 1990). Akins and Zentall (1996) trained Japanese quail demonstrators to either step on a treadle or peck the treadle for food reinforcement. When observer quail were exposed to one or the other demonstrator, they matched the behavior of their demonstrator with a high probability (see also Zentall, Sutton, & Sherburne, 1996, for similar evidence with pigeons). Furthermore, there is some evidence that pigeons can imitate a sequence of two responses, operating a treadle (by stepping or pecking) and pushing a screen (to the left or to the right; Nguyen, Klein, & Zentall, 2005).

Perhaps the most impressive example of animal imitation comes from a test of generalized imitative learning reported by Hayes and Hayes (1952) with a home-raised chimpanzee named Viki. Using a set of 70 gestures, Viki was trained to replicate each gesture when the experimenter said, "Do this." More important, Viki also accurately performed 10 novel arbitrary gestures when directed to with the "Do this" command (see also Custance, Whiten, & Bard, 1995).

If Piaget is correct, the ability to imitate requires the ability to take the perspective of another. But children do not develop the ability to take the perspective of another until they are 5–7 years old, yet they are able to imitate others at a much earlier age. Furthermore, if pigeons and Japanese quail can imitate, it is unlikely that they do so by taking the perspective of the demonstrator, in the sense that Piaget implied. Thus, although cognitively interesting, imitation may not provide evidence for the kind of cognitive behavior implied by perspective taking.

C. *Animal Culture*

When a particular behavior is imitated by all members of a group, some researchers have taken it as evidence that the species has a form of culture (see Laland & Galef, 2009) but this question depends in part on how one defines culture. If one defines culture as an anthropologist might, characterized by a group having socially learned laws, ethics, rituals, religion, and morality, then no group of nonhuman animals has culture. If, however, one defines culture as the transmission of innovations among members of a group (some have argued that tradition may be a less controversial term; Laland & Galef, 2009), then animals may have such a capacity. Much of the evidence for culture in animals comes from animals living in natural settings in which the members of one group exhibit a particular behavior whereas those of other nearby groups do not (e.g., grooming posture in chimpanzees; McGrew & Tutin, 1978). The problem is, if group differences in behavior are to be attributed to culture, it must be clearly shown that they do not result either from genetic difference between the groups or from environmental differences that could have encouraged one group to develop the novel behavior by individual learning.

Better controlled studies can be carried out in the laboratory, where one can control for the environmental conditions and for genetic differences as well by randomly assigning animals to groups (see, e.g., the serial transmission of food preference among rats;Galef & Whiskin, 1998).

D. *Theory of Mind*

A version of the child's game with a hidden object described earlier (Frye, 1993) was attempted by Povinelli, Nelson, and Boysen (1990). Chimpanzees were trained to select a box toward which a trainer was pointing to receive a reward. When they were tested with two trainers (who were pointing at different boxes) – one who had been present when the box was baited (the "knower") and the other who had been absent (the "guesser") – the chimpanzees chose the box indicated by the "knower" over that indicated by the "guesser." But as Heyes (1998) has noted, in this and other similar procedures (involving, for example, a "guesser" with a bag over his head), the preference for the "knower" did not show up on early trials and the number of test trials was sufficient that the chimpanzees could have *learned* to use the "knower's" behavior as a cue.

A different approach to theory of mind focused on the natural competitiveness and dominance hierarchy of chimpanzees (e.g., Hare, Call, & Tomasello, 2001). They found that when a subordinate chimpanzee could observe that a dominant chimpanzee could see where food was hidden, it avoided that location. But the subordinate did not avoid a location when the dominant had not seen where food was hidden. Although these and related experiments provide the best evidence to date for theory of mind in animals, it may be that cues provided by the dominant chimpanzee played a role in the results. That is, if the dominant chimpanzee was staring at the location where it saw food hidden, it may have inhibited the subordinate from approaching that location.

E. *Deception*

If an animal can purposefully deceive another, one could argue that it must be able to take the perspective of the other. Certainly, functional deception can be trained. Woodruff and Premack (1979) trained chimpanzees to point to the container that held food in order to receive the food. The chimpanzees then learned that one trainer would give them the food for pointing to the correct container whereas the other would allow them to have the food only if they pointed to an incorrect container. Although the chimpanzees learned to respond appropriately, there was no indication that they *intended* to deceive the trainer (Dennett, 1983). One can find anecdotes in the literature suggestive of intentional deception (e.g., Heyes, 1998) but the problem with the attribution of deception is that intentionality must be inferred from behavior, and intentionality is particularly difficult to assess in a nonverbal organism.

F. *Cooperation and Altruism*

Cooperation and altruism are special cases of intelligent behavior because they represent a form of social behavior for which the actions of the organism have implications for the well-being of another. Although true cooperation and altruism are closely related to theory of mind, many forms of these behaviors (e.g., the cooperation among dogs hunting in a pack, and maternal behavior) are strongly biologically predisposed and so cognitive accounts are unnecessary. Other cases of cooperation can more parsimoniously be interpreted as the use of another animal as a discriminative stimulus. Skinner (1962) for example trained pigeons to "hunt," on each trial, for the response location to which a response would be reinforced. He then placed two pigeons side by side and added the contingency that the two correct response locations (which were always at the same vertical level) should be pecked nearly simultaneously. The pigeons readily adjusted to the new contingency and often got fed, but their functional cooperation can be explained as the use of the movement of one pigeon toward a response location as a discriminative stimulus for the other pigeon to peck the location at the same level at the same time.

Examples of altruistic behavior based on variants of parental behavior (e.g., adoption of an unrelated offspring) can be explained more parsimoniously in terms of "errors" in biologically predisposed behavior. Even altruistic acts such as those that occur between unrelated humans in wartime may be based on biological predispositions that evolved in hunter-gatherer times as a form of kin selection (the tendency that genes predispose the bodies that they are in to look out for themselves and copies of themselves in others – i.e., kin). In the case of wartime bravery, the closeness of the military unit may mimic the relatedness of the hunting party. Furthermore, one could argue that although a certain level of intelligence may be required to produce true, cognitively based cooperation and altruism in humans, considering the range of individual differences among humans, intelligence is certainly not predictive of either. Theory of mind in animals is a relatively new area of research that is fraught with problems of interpretation; however, clever techniques for assessing what animals know (e.g., Gallup, 1970; Hare et al., 2001) promise to get us closer to the goal of understanding the relation between the cognitive abilities of humans and those of other animals.

What Animals Can Tell Us About Human Reasoning

Cognitive Dissonance

I have saved for last the discussion of two lines of research directed to similarities between the behavior of humans and that of other animals because they both have important implications for how we interpret human behavior. The first has to do with a phenomenon extensively studied in humans called cognitive dissonance. Cognitive dissonance is the discomfort that comes when there is a discrepancy between one's beliefs and one's behavior. For example, if one believes that one should tell the truth, one is likely to feel dissonance on occasions when one fails to do so. That dissonance may be resolved by deciding that there are some conditions under which lying is appropriate or the person lied to may have deserved it. Cognitive dissonance presumably comes about because of a need to be consistent or to avoid being labeled a hypocrite. Does this represent a kind of social intelligence? And if so, would nonhuman animals show a similar effect? But how would one go about asking this question of animals?

One approach involves a version of cognitive dissonance called justification of effort (Aronson & Mills, 1959). In their study, undergraduates who underwent an unpleasant initiation to become part of a group reported that they wanted to join the group more than those who underwent a less unpleasant initiation. It is assumed that those individuals gave more value to membership in the group to justify undergoing the unpleasant initiation.

The justification of effort design allows for a direct test of cognitive dissonance in animals. For example, if on some trials a pigeon has to work hard to receive Signal A that says food is coming and on other trials the pigeon does not have to work hard to receive Signal B that says the same food is coming, will the pigeon show a preference for Signal A over Signal B? Several studies have shown that they will (e.g., Clement, Feltus, Kaiser, & Zentall, 2000; Kacelnik, & Marsh 2002). But is this cognitive dissonance? Do animals need to justify to themselves why they worked harder for one signal than the other?

Alternatively, we have suggested that this choice behavior results from the contrast between the relatively negative emotional state of the organism at the end of the effort and upon presentation of the signal (Zentall & Singer, 2007). That difference would be greater when more effort is involved. Thus, the subjective value of the signal for reinforcement might be judged to be greater. Contrast provides a more parsimonious account of the pigeons' choice behavior. Could contrast also be involved in the similar behavior shown by humans? This possibility should be examined by social psychologists.

Maladaptive Gambling Behavior

Humans often gamble (e.g., play the lottery) even though the odds against winning are very high. This behavior may be attributable to an inaccurate assessment of the probability of winning, perhaps resulting in part from public announcements of the winners but not the losers (an availability heuristic). Would animals show a similar kind of maladaptive gambling behavior? According to optimal foraging theory, they should not because such inappropriate behavior should have been selected against by evolution. Furthermore, if the choice is to have any meaning for the animal, it would have to have experienced the probability associated with winning (reinforcement) and that should reduce the likelihood that the animal would not be able to assess the probability of winning and losing. However, we have recently found conditions under which pigeons will prefer 50% reinforcement over 75% reinforcement. The procedure is as follows: If the pigeon chooses the left alternative, half of the time a red stimulus appears and is followed by food 10 seconds later. The remainder of the time it chooses the left alternative; a green stimulus appears and is never followed by food. Thus, food appears 50% of the time for the choice of left. If the pigeon chooses the right alternative, half of the time a yellow stimulus appears and the remainder of the time a blue stimulus appears and both colors are followed by food 75% of the time. Thus, food appears 75% of the time for the choice of right. Curiously, the pigeons prefer the left alternative 2 to 1 over the right alternative and they do so in spite of the fact that they would get 50% more food for choosing the right alternative.

This result suggests that gambling behavior is likely to have a simple biological basis and although social and cognitive factors may contribute to human gambling behavior, the underlying mechanism is likely to present in other animals. A more nearly complete analysis of the mechanisms responsible for this maladaptive behavior and its relation to human gambling will have to wait for further research, but at this point it is clear that pigeons are no more appropriate in their choice behavior than are humans.

Conclusions

The broad range of positive research findings that have come from investigating the cognitive abilities of animals suggests that many of the "special capacities" attributed to humans may be more quantitative than qualitative. In the case of many cognitive learning tasks, once we learn how to ask the question appropriately (i.e., in a way that is accommodating to the animal), we may often be surprised with the capacity of animals to use complex relations.

In evaluating the animal (and human) intelligence literature, we should be sensitive to both overestimation of capacity (what appears to be higher level functioning in animals that can be accounted for more parsimoniously at a lower level; see Zentall, 1993) and underestimation of capacity (our bias to present animals with tasks convenient to our human sensory, response, and motivational systems). Underestimation can also come from the difficulty in providing animals with task instructions as one can quite easily do with humans (see Zentall, 1997). The accurate assessment of animal intelligence will require vigilance, on the one hand, to evaluate cognitive functioning against simpler accounts and, on the other hand, to determine the conditions that will maximally elicit the animal's cognitive capacity.

Acknowledgments

Preparation of this chapter was made possible by Grant MH 63726 from the National Institute of Mental Health and Grant HD60996 from the National Institute of Child Heath and Human Development.

References

Akins, C., & Zentall, T. R. (1996). Evidence for true imitative learning in Japanese quail. *Journal of Comparative Psychology*, 110, 316–320.

Aronson, E., & Mills, J. (1959). The effect of severity of initiation on liking for a group. *Journal of Abnormal and Social Psychology*, 59, 177–181.

Bitterman, M. E. (1975). The comparative analysis of learning. *Science*, 188, 699–709.

Bitterman, M. E., & Mackintosh, N. J. (1969). Habit reversal and probability learning: Rats, birds, and fish. In R. M. Gilbert & N. S. Sutherland (Eds.), *Animal discrimination learning* (pp. 163–185). New York, NY: Academic Press.

Boysen, S. T., & Berntson, G. G. (1989). Numerical competence in a chimpanzee (Pan troglodytes). *Journal of Comparative Psychology*, 103, 23–31.

Capaldi, E. J. (1993). Animal number abilities: Implications for a hierarchical approach to instrumental learning. In S. T. Boysen & E. J. Capaldi (Eds.), *The development of numerical competence* (pp. 191–209). Hillsdale, NJ: Erlbaum.

Capaldi, E. J., & Miller, D. J. (1988). Counting in rats: Its functional significance and the independent cognitive processes that constitute it. *Journal of Experimental Psychology: Animal Behavior Processes*, 14, 3–17.

Chapuis, N., & Varlet, C. (1987). Short cuts by dogs in natural surroundings. *Quarterly Journal of Experimental Psychology*, 39, 49–64.

Clayton, N. S., & Dickinson, A. (1999). Scrub jays (Aphelocoma coerulescens) remember the relative time of caching as well as the location and content of their caches. *Journal of Comparative Psychology*, 113, 403–416.

Clement, T. S., Feltus, J., Kaiser, D. H., & Zentall, T. R. (2000). "Work ethic" in pigeons: Reward value is directly related to the effort or time required to obtain the reward. *Psychonomic Bulletin & Review*, 7, 100–106.

Collette, T. S., & Graham, P. (2004). Animal navigation: Path integration, visual landmarks and cognitive maps. *Current Biology*, 14, 475–477.

Cook, R. G., Brown, M. F., & Riley, D. A. (1985). Flexible memory processing by rats: Use of prospective and retrospective information in the radial maze. *Journal of Experimental Psychology: Animal Behavior Processes*, 11, 453–469.

Couvillon, P. A., & Bitterman, M. E. (1992). A conventional conditioning analysis of "transitive inference" in pigeons. *Journal of Experimental Psychology: Animal Behavior Processes*, 18, 308–310.

Custance, D. M., Whiten, A., & Bard, K. A. (1995). Can young chimpanzees imitate arbitrary actions? Hayes and Hayes (1952) revisited. *Behaviour*, 132, 837–859.

Davis, H. (1992). Transitive inference in rats (Rattus norvegicus). *Journal of Comparative Psychology*, 106, 342–349.

Davis, H., & Memmott, J. (1982). Counting behavior in animals: A critical evaluation. *Psychological Bulletin*, 92, 547–571.

Dawkins, R. (1976). *The selfish gene*. New York, NY: Oxford University Press.

Dawson, B. V., & Foss, B. M. (1965). Observational learning in budgerigars. *Animal Behaviour*, **13**, 470–474.

Dennett, D. C. (1983). Intentional systems in cognitive ecology: The "panglossian paradigm" defended. *Behavioral and Brain Sciences*, 6, 343–355.

Dorrance, B. R., Kaiser, D. H., & Zentall, T. R. (2000). Event duration discrimination by pigeons: The choose-short effect may result from retention-test novelty. *Animal Learning & Behavior*, **28**, 344–353.

Edwards, C. A., Jagielo, J. A., Zentall, T. R., & Hogan, D. E. (1982). Acquired equivalence and distinctiveness in matching-to-sample by pigeons: Mediation by reinforcer-specific expectancies. *Journal of Experimental Psychology: Animal Behavior Processes*, 8, 244–259.

Edwards, C. A., & Honig, W. K. (1987). Memorization and "feature selection" in the acquisition of natural concepts in pigeons. *Learning and Motivation*, 18, 235–260.

Farthing, G. W., Wagner, J. W. Gilmour, S., & Waxman, H. M. (1977). Short-term memory and information processing in pigeons. *Learning and Motivation*, 8, 520–532.

Fersen, L. V., Wynne, C. D. L., Delius, J. D., & Staddon, J. E. R. (1991). Transitive inference formation in pigeons. *Journal of Experimental Psychology: Animal Behavior Processes*, 17, 334–341.

Frye, D. (1993). Causes and precursors of children's theory of mind. In D. F. Hay & A. Angold (Eds.), *Precursors and causes of development and psychopathology*. Chichester, UK: Wiley.

Galef, B. G., Jr. (1988). Imitation in animals: History, definition, and interpretation of data from the psychological laboratory. In T. R. Zentall & B. G. Galef, Jr. (Eds.), *Social learning: Psychological and biological perspectives* (pp. 3–28). Hillsdale, NJ: Erlbaum.

Galef, B. G., Jr., & Whiskin, E. E. (1998). Determinants of the longevity of socially learned food preferences of Norway rats. *Animal Behaviour*, **55**, 967–975.

Gallup, G. G. (1970). Chimpanzees self-recognition, *Science*, **167**, 86–87.

Gallup, G. G., & Suarez, S. D. (1991). Social responding to mirrors in rhesus monkeys: Effects of temporary mirror removal. *Journal of Comparative Psychology*, **105**, 376–379.

Garcia, J., & Koelling, R. A. (1966). Relation of cue to consequence in avoidance learning. *Psychonomic Science*, **4**, 123–124.

Gardner, R. A., & Gardner, B. T. (1964). Teaching sign language to a chimpanzee. *Science*, **165**, 664–672.

Gillan, D. J. (1981). Reasoning in the chimpanzee: II. Transitive inference. *Journal of Experimental Psychology: Animal Behavior Processes*, 7, 150–164.

Gillan, D. J., Premack, D., & Woodruff, G. (1981). Reasoning in the chimpanzee: I. Analogical reasoning. *Journal of Experimental Psychology: Animal Behavior Processes*, 7, 1–17.

Hall, G. (1996). Learning about associatively activated stimulus representations: Implications for acquired equivalence and perceptual learning. *Animal Learning & Behavior*, **24**, 233–255.

Hare, B., Call, J., & Tomasello, M. (2001). Do chimpanzees know what conspecifics know? *Animal Behaviour*, **61**, 139–151.

Harlow, H. F. (1949). The formation of learning sets, *Psychological Review*, **56**, 51–65.

Hayes, K. J., & Hayes, C. (1952). Imitation in a home-raised chimpanzee. *Journal of Comparative and Physiological Psychology*, **45**, 450–459.

Herman, L. M., Pack, A. A., & Morrel-Samuels, P. (1993). Representational and conceptual skills of dolphins. In H. L. Roitblat, L. M. Herman, & P. E. Nachtigall (Eds.), *Language and communication: Comparative perspectives* (pp. 403–442). Hillsdale, NJ: Erlbaum.

Herrnstein, R. J., & deVilliers, P. A. (1980). Fish as a natural category for people and pigeons. *Psychology of Learning and Motivation*, **14**, 59–95.

Herrnstein, R. J., & Loveland, D. H. (1964). Complex visual concept in the pigeon. *Science*, **146**, 549–551.

Herrnstein, R. J., Loveland, D. H., & Cable, C. (1976). Natural concepts in pigeons. *Journal of Experimental Psychology: Animal Behavior Processes*, **2**, 285–301.

Heyes, C. M. (1998). Theory of mind in nonhuman primates. *Behavioral and Brain Sciences*, **21**, 101–134.

Heyes, C. M., & Dawson, G. R. (1990). A demonstration of observational learning in rats using a bidirectional control. *Quarterly Journal of Experimental Psychology*, **42B**, 59–71.

Honey, R. C., & Hall, G. (1989). The acquired equivalence and distinctiveness of cues. *Journal of Experimental Psychology: Animal Behavior Processes*, **15**, 338–346.

Honig, W. K., & Thompson, R. K. R. (1982). Retrospective and prospective processing in animal working memory. In G. Bower (Ed.), *The psychology of learning and motivation* (Vol. 16, pp. 239–283). Orlando, FL: Academic Press.

Hull, C. L. (1943). *Principles of behavior.* New York, NY: Appleton-Century-Crofts.

Kacelnik, A., & Marsh, B. (2002). Cost can increase preference in starlings. *Animal Behaviour*, **63**, 245–250.

Kaiser, D. H., Sherburne, L. M., & Zentall, T. R. (1997). Directed forgetting in pigeons produced by the reallocation of memory-maintaining processes on forget-cue trials. *Psychonomic Bulletin & Review*, 4 559–565

Kelly, R., & Grant, D. S. (2001). A differential outcomes effect using biologically neutral outcomes in delayed matching-to-sample with pigeons. *Quarterly Journal of Experimental Psychology*, **54B**, 69–79.

Kendler, T. S. (1950). An experimental investigation of transposition as a function of the difference between training and test stimuli. *Journal of Experimental Psychology*, 40, 552–562.

Kuan, L.-A., & Colwill, R. (1997). Demonstration of a socially transmitted taste aversion in the rat. *Psychonomic Bulletin & Review*, 4, 374–377.

Lawrence, D. H. (1952). The transfer of a discrimination along a continuum. *Journal of Comparative and Physiological Psychology*, **45**, 511–516.

Lawrence, D. H. (1955). The applicability of generalization gradients to the transfer of a discrimination. *Journal of Genetic Psychology*, **52**, 37–48.

Lazareva, O. F., & Wasserman, E. A. (2006). Effect of stimulus orderability and reinforcement history on transitive responding in pigeons. *Behavioural Processes*, **72**, 161–172.

Lea, S. E. G. (1984). In what sense do pigeons learn concepts? In H. L. Roitblat, T. G. Bever, & H. S. Terrace (Eds.), *Animal cognition* (pp. 263–276). Hillsdale, NJ: Erlbaum.

Lipp, H.-P., Vyssotski, A. L., Wolfer, D. P., Renaudineau, S., Savini, M., Tröster, G., & Dell'Omo, G. (2004). Pigeon homing along highways and exits. *Current Biology*, **14**, 1239–1249.

Logan, F. A. (1966). Transfer of discrimination. *Journal of Experimental Psychology*, **71**, 616–618.

Mackintosh, N. J. (1965). Selective attention in animal discrimination learning. *Psychological Bulletin*, 64, 124–150.

Mackintosh, N. J. (1969). Comparative studies of reversal and probability learning: Rats, birds, and fish. In R. M. Gilbert, & N. S. Sutherland (Eds.), *Animal discrimination learning* (pp. 137–162). New York, NY: Academic Press.

McGonigle, B. O., & Chalmers, M. (1977). Are monkeys logical? *Nature*, **267**, 694–696.

Meyer, D. R. (1971). Habits and concepts of monkeys. In L. E. Jarrard (Ed.), *Cognitive processes of nonhuman primates* (pp. 83–102). New York, NY: Academic Press.

Miller, H. C., Friedrich, A. M., Narkavic, R. J., & Zentall, T. R. (2009). A differential outcomes effect using hedonically-nondifferential outcomes with delayed matching-to-sample by pigeons. *Learning & Behavior*, **37**, 161–166.

Morgan, C. L. (1894). *An introduction to comparative psychology*. London: Scott.

Naqshbandi, M., & Roberts, W. A. (2006). Anticipation of future events in squirrel monkeys (Saimiri sciureus) and rats (Rattus norvegicus): Tests of the Bischof-Kohler hypothesis. *Journal of Comparative Psychology*, **120**, 345–357.

Nguyen, N. H., Klein, E. D., & Zentall, T. R. (2005). Imitation of two-action sequences by pigeons. *Psychonomic Bulletin & Review*, **12**, 514–518.

Patterson, F. G. (1978). The gestures of a gorilla: Language acquisition in another pongid. *Brain and Language*, **5**, 72–97.

Pepperberg, I. M. (1987). Interspecies communication: A tool for assessing conceptual abilities in an African Grey parrot. In G. Greenberg & E. Tobach (Eds.), *Language, cognition, and consciousness: Integrative levels* (pp. 31–56). Hillsdale, NJ: Erlbaum.

Peterson, G. B. (1984). How expectancies guide behavior. In H. L. Roitblat, T. G. Bever, & H. S. Terrace (Eds.), *Animal cognition* (pp. 135–148). Hillsdale, NJ: Erlbaum.

Peterson, G. B., Wheeler, R. L., & Trapold, M. A. (1980). Enhancement of pigeons' conditional discrimination performance by expectancies of reinforcement and nonreinforcement. *Animal Learning & Behavior*, 8, 22–30.

Plotnik, J. M., de Waal, F. B. M., & Reiss, D. (2006). Self-recognition in an Asian elephant. *Proceedings of the National Academy of Sciences*, **103**, 17053–17057.

Piaget, J. (1951). *Play, dreams, and imitation in childhood*. New York, NY: W.W. Norton.

Piaget, J. (1952). *The child's concept of number.* New York, NY: W. W. Norton.

Povinelli, D. J., Nelson, K. E., & Boysen, S. T. (1990). Inferences about guessing and knowing by chimpanzees. *Journal of Comparative Psychology*, **104**, 203–210.

Premack, D. (1976). *Intelligence in ape and man.* Hillsdale, NJ: Erlbaum.

Raby, C. R., Alexis, D. M., Dickinson, A., & Clayton, N. S. (2007). Empirical evaluation of mental time travel. *Behavioral Brain Sciences*, 30, 330–331.

Reid, L. S. (1953). Development of noncontinuity behavior through continuity learning. *Journal of Experimental Psychology*, 46, 107–112.

Reiss, D., & Marino, L. (2001). Self-recognition in the bottlenose dolphin: A case of cognitive convergence. *Proceedings of the National Academy of Sciences*, 98, 5937– 5942.

Riley, D. A. (1968). *Discrimination learning.* Boston, MA: Allyn & Bacon.

Roberts, W. A. (2002) Are animals stuck in time? *Psychological Bulletin*, **128**, 473–489.

Roberts, W. A., & Grant, D. S. (1976). Studies of short-term memory in the pigeon using the delayed matching-to-sample procedure. In D. L. Medin, W. A. Roberts, & R. T. Davis (Eds.), *Processes of animal memory* (pp. 79–112). Hillsdale, NJ: Erlbaum.

Roper, K. L., Kaiser, D. H., & Zentall, T. R. (1995). Directed forgetting in pigeons: The role of alternative memories in the effectiveness of forget cues. *Animal Learning & Behavior*, **23**, 280–285.

Roper, K. L., & Zentall, T. R. (1993). Directed forgetting in animals. *Psychological Bulletin*, **113**, 513–532.

Rumbaugh, D. M. (Ed.). (1977). Language learning by a chimpanzee: *The Lana project*. New York: Academic Press.

Savage-Rumbaugh, E. S. (1984). Acquisition of functional symbol use in apes and children. In H. L. Roitblat, T. G. Bever, & H. S. Terrace (Eds.), *Animal cognition* (pp. 291–310). Hillsdale, NJ: Erlbaum.

Sherburne, L. M., Zentall, T. R., & Kaiser, D. H. (1998). Timing in pigeons: The choose-short effect may result from "confusion" between delay and intertrial intervals. *Psychonomic Bulletin & Review*, **5**, 516–522.

Singer, R. A., Abroms, B. D., & Zentall, T. R. (2007). Formation of a simple cognitive map by rats. *International Journal of Comparative Psychology*, **19**, 417–425.

Skinner, B. F. (1962). Two "synthetic social relations." *Journal of the Experimental Analysis of Behavior*, **5**, 531–533.

Slotnick, B. M., & Katz, H. M. (1974). Olfactory learning-set formation in rats. *Science*, **185**, 796–798.

Spence, K. W. (1937). The differential response in animals to stimuli varying within a single dimension. *Psychological Review*, **44**, 430–444.

Steirn, J. N., Weaver, J. E., & Zentall, T. R. (1995). Transitive inference in pigeons: Simplified procedures and a test of value transfer theory. *Animal Learning & Behavior*, **23**, 76–82.

Steirn, J. N., Zentall, T. R., & Sherburne, L. M. (1992). Pigeons' performances of a radial–arm–maze analog task: Effect of spatial distinctiveness. *Psychological Record*, **42**, 255–272.

Suddendorf, T., & Corballis, M. C. (1997). Mental time travel and the evolution of the human mind. *Genetic, Social, and General Psychology Monographs* **123**, 133–167.

Tolman, E. C. (1932). *Purposive behavior in animals and men*. New York, NY: Century.

Trapold, M. A. (1970). Are expectancies based on different reinforcing events discriminably different? *Learning and Motivation*, **1**, 129–140.

Tulving, E. (1972). Episodic and semantic memory. In E. Tulving & W. Donaldson (Eds.), *Organization of memory* (pp. 382–403). New York, NY: Academic Press.

Urcuioli, P. J., & Zentall, T. R. (1986). Retrospective memory in pigeons' delayed matching–to–sample. *Journal of Experimental Psychology: Animal Behavior Processes*, **12**, 69–77.

Urcuioli, P. J., Zentall, T. R., Jackson–Smith, P., & Steirn, J. N. (1989). Evidence for common coding in many–to–one matching: Retention, intertrial interference, and transfer. *Journal of Experimental Psychology: Animal Behavior Processes*, **15**, 264–273.

Vaughan, W., Jr. (1988). Formation of equivalence sets in pigeons. *Journal of Experimental Psychology: Animal Behavior Processes*, **14**, 36–42.

Wasserman, E. A., DeVolder, C. L., & Coppage, D. J. (1992). Non-similarity based conceptualization in pigeons via secondary or mediated generalization. *Psychological Science*, 6, 374–379.

Weaver, J. E., Steirn J. N., & Zentall, T. R. (1997). Transitive inference in pigeons: Control for differential value transfer. *Psychonomic Bulletin and Review*, 4, 113–117.

Whiten, A., & Ham, R. (1992). On the nature and evolution of imitation in the animal kingdom: Reappraisal of a century of research. *Advances in the Study of Behavior*, **21**, 239–283.

Williams, D. A., Butler, M. M., & Overmier, J. B. (1990). Expectancies of reinforcer location and quality as cues for a conditional discrimination in pigeons. *Journal of Experimental Psychology: Animal Behavior Processes*, **16**, 3–13.

Woodruff, G., & Premack, D. (1979). Intentional communication in the chimpanzee: The development of deception. *Cognition*, 7, 333–362.

Woodruff, G., Premack D., & Kennel, K. (1978). Conservation of liquid and solid quantity by the chimpanzee. *Science*, 202, 991–994.

Zentall, T. R. (1993). Animal cognition: An approach to the study of animal Behavior. In T. R. Zentall (Ed.), *Animal cognition: A tribute to Donald A. Riley* (pp. 3–15). Hillsdale, NJ: Erlbaum.

Zentall, T. R. (1996). An analysis of imitative learning in animals. In C. M. Heyes & B. G. Galef, Jr. (Eds.), *Social learning and tradition in animals* (pp. 221–243). New York, NY: Academic Press.

Zentall, T. R. (1997). Animal memory: The role of instructions. *Learning and Motivation*, 28, 248–267.

Zentall, T. R. (1998). Symbolic representation in pigeons: Emergent stimulus relations in conditional discrimination learning. *Animal Learning & Behavior*, 26, 363–377.

Zentall, T. R., Clement, T. S., Bhatt, R. S., & Allen, J. (2001). Episodic-like memory in pigeons. *Psychonomic Bulletin & Review*, 8, 685–690.

Zentall, T. R., & Singer, R. A. (2007). Within-trial contrast: Pigeons prefer conditioned reinforcers that follow a relatively more rather than less aversive event. *Journal of the Experimental Analysis of Behavior*, 88, 131–149.

Zentall, T. R., & Smeets, P. M. (Eds.). (1996). *Stimulus class formation in humans and animals.* Amsterdam, the Netherlands: North Holland.

Zentall, T. R., Steirn, J. N., & Jackson–Smith, P. (1990). Memory strategies in pigeons' performance of a radial–arm–maze analog task. *Journal of Experimental Psychology: Animal Behavior Processes*, 16, 358–371.

Zentall, T. R., Steirn, J. N., Sherburne, L. M., & Urcuioli, P. J. (1991). Common coding in pigeons assessed through partial versus total reversals of many-to-one conditional discriminations. *Journal of Experimental Psychology: Animal Behavior Processes*, 17, 194–201.

Zentall, T. R., Sutton, J. E., & Sherburne, L. M. (1996). True imitative learning in pigeons. *Psychological Science*, 7, 343–346.

Zentall, T. R., Urcuioli, P. J., Jagielo, J. A., & Jackson-Smith, P. (1989). Interaction of sample dimension and sample-comparison mapping on pigeons' performance of delayed conditional discriminations. *Animal Learning & Behavior*, 17, 172–178.

CHAPTER 17

The Evolution of Intelligence

Liane Gabora and Anne Russon

How did the human species evolve the capacity not just to communicate complex ideas to one another but to hold such conversations from across the globe, using remote devices constructed from substances that do not exist in the natural world, the raw materials for which may have been hauled up from the bowels of the earth? How did we come to be so intelligent? Research at the interface of psychology, biology, anthropology, archaeology, and cognitive science is culminating in an increasingly sophisticated understanding of how human intelligence evolved. Studies of the brains of living humans and great apes and the intellectual abilities they support are enabling us to assess what is unique about human intelligence and what we share with our primate relatives. Examining the habitats and skeletons of our ancestors gives cues as to environmental, social, and anatomical factors that both constrain and enable the evolution of human intelligence. Relics of the past also have much to tell us about the thoughts, beliefs, and abilities of the individuals who invented and used them.

The chapter starts with an introduction to some key issues in the evolution of intelligence. We then consider what is unique about human intelligence compared to our closest living biological relatives, the great apes – chimpanzees, bonobos, gorillas, and orangutans. The process by which the human intelligence came about is the next topic. Finally, we address the question of *why* human intelligence evolved – did it evolve purely due to biological forces, that is, does intelligence merely help us solve survival problems and attract mates, or are nonbiological factors such as culture involved?

Key Issues

We begin by laying out some of the fundamental issues that arise in considerations of the evolution of human intelligence. First, we address some issues of definition. Second, we comment on challenges to the accurate assessment of intelligence, particularly when comparing intelligence across different species. A third, related issue is the question of the extent to which there are special qualities of intelligence that only humans attain.

Assessing Intelligence and Its Evolution

Many methods are used to assess intelligence and its evolution. These include (1) *behavioral measures*, which may involve naturalistic observation or analyzing responses in laboratory experiments; (2) *artifactual measures*, which involve analysis of tools, art, and so forth; and (3) *anatomical/neurological measures*, which involve studies of the brain and cranium. Ideally, all three would converge upon a unified picture of how intelligence evolved. However, this is not always the case, and indeed, the assessment of intelligence is fraught with challenges.

An obvious one is that we cannot perform behavioral or neurological studies of our ancestors, so we are forced to rely on bones and artifacts. Moreover, the further back in time one looks, the more fragmentary the archaeological record becomes. To explore the ancestral roots of our intelligence, we therefore also partly rely on studying the intelligence and brains of the great apes, our closest biological relatives. We share a common ancestor with great apes as recently as 4–6 million years ago (mya): No living species are more closely related. Other species such as dolphins and crows share some complex intellectual abilities with great apes and humans, but their abilities probably evolved independently and operate differently. Dolphins' and crows' brains differ strikingly from ours, for instance, whereas great ape brains are exceptionally similar to ours (Emery & Clayton, 2004; Hof, Chanis, & Marino, 2005; MacLeod, 2004).

What the great apes offer to the study of the evolution of human intelligence is the best living model of the intelligence that existed in our common great ape ancestors before our unique evolutionary lineage, the hominins, diverged. Modern human intelligence evolved from earlier forms of intelligence in response to selective pressures generated by ancestral living conditions. Understanding its evolution therefore entails looking into the past for the changes that occurred within the hominins – but also for earlier intellectual traits upon which the hominins built and the changes that led to the their divergence from ancestral great apes. If we can identify complex behaviors that great apes share with humans but not with other nonhuman primates, then these behaviors and the intellectual qualities they imply may have been shared by our common ancestors.

To use great apes to contribute to understanding the evolution of human intelligence, especially inferring what intellectual capacities evolved uniquely in the hominins, we need to assess their intellectual ceiling, that is, their top adult-level capabilities near the human boundary. The intelligence of great apes is highly malleable and dependent on the developmental and learning history of the individual (Matsuzawa, Tomonaga, & Tanaka, 2006; Parker & McKinney 1999; de Waal, 2001), as it is in humans. Conclusions about great ape cognition and comparisons with human cognition must therefore be made with care. In part because this care has not always been taken, the literature on how human intelligence evolved does not present as straightforward a picture as one might hope. Nevertheless, an integrated account is starting to emerge.

What Distinguishes Human From Nonhuman Intelligence?

Many have attempted to specify what marks the intellectual divide between humans and other species. Some follow Aristotle's proposal that it is reason (French, 1994), or symbolic thinking. Symbols are arbitrary signs with conventional meanings that are used to represent (stand for) other things or relationships between them, and that generally have conventionally accepted meanings. Another suggestion is that human intelligence is distinguished by the ability to develop complex, abstract, internally coherent systems of symbol use (Deacon, 1997). Others propose that it is creativity, such as is required to invent tools, or abilities associated with creativity, such as cognitive fluidity (combining concepts or ideas, or adapting them to new contexts), or the ability to generate and understand analogies (Fauconnier & Turner, 2002; Mithen, 1996). Still other proposals single out key abilities for dealing with the social world, such as demonstration teaching, imitative learning, cooperative problem solving, or communicating about the past and future. A related proposal is that the divide owes to the onset of what Premack and Woodruff (1978) refer to as *theory of mind* – the capacity to reason about mental states of others (Mithen, 1998).

The more we learn about nonhuman intelligence, however, the more we find that abilities previously thought to be uniquely human are not. Many of the abilities listed earlier have been found to varying degrees in the great apes. For example, it was thought until the 1960s that humans alone make tools. But then Jane Goodall (1963) found wild chimpanzees making them. Later, several other species were found making tools too (Beck, 1980). Thus, ideas about what marks the boundary between human and nonhuman intelligence have undergone repeated revision.

Although a large gulf separates human abilities from those of other species, it is not as easy as we hoped to pinpoint in a word or two what distinguishes humans. That does not mean that a more complex explanation is not forthcoming. For example, it may be that it is not creativity per se that distinguishes human intelligence, but the proclivity to take existing ideas and adapt them to new contexts or to one's own unique circumstances – that is, to put one's own spin on them, such that they become increasingly complex. The question of what separates human intelligence from that of other species is a recurring theme that will be fleshed out in the pages that follow.

Intelligence in Our Closest Relatives: The Great Apes

This section summarizes the current picture of great ape intelligence, focusing on qualities once thought to be uniquely human. While some monkeys have shown similar achievements, great apes consistently achieve higher levels (Parker & McKinney, 1999).

We now possess a rich body of data on great ape intelligence (Byrne, 1995; Gómez, 2004; Matsuzawa et al., 2006; Parker & Gibson, 1990; Povinelli, 2000; Rumbaugh & Washburn, 2003; Russon, Bard, & Parker, 1996; Tomasello & Call, 1997; de Waal, 2001). Great apes have shown many social cognitive abilities thought uniquely human. They show imitative learning and demonstration teaching powerful enough to sustain simple cultures (Boesch, 1991; Byrne & Russon, 1998; Parker 1996; van Schaik et al., 2003; Whiten et al., 1999). Some have solved problems cooperatively (Boesch & Boesch-Achermann, 2000; Hirata & Fuwa, 2007) and show some understanding of others' mental states (e.g., knowledge, competence; Parker & McKinney, 1999). Captives have acquired basic sign language, including learning and inventing arbitrary conventional signs and simple grammar (Blake, 2004). Some great ape gestures qualify as symbolic by standards used in early language studies, including tree-drumming and covering both eyes with fingertips in a V-shape to mean view-master (Blake, 2004).

Great apes can understand simple analogies and engage in analogical reasoning (Thompson & Oden, 2000). They are considered to achieve basic symbolic abilities in several problem domains; they can do simple arithmetic and master simple language, for example (Parker & McKinney, 1999; Thompson & Oden, 2000).

A certain degree of creativity may be normal in great apes (and other nonhuman species; Reader & Laland 2003). Their creativity includes smearing leaf pulp foam on their body (perhaps as an analgesic), inventing new tools (e.g., branch hook tools, termite fishing brush tools), primitive swimming, and fishing (Russon et al., 2009; Sanz & Morgan, 2004). They have invented gestures and signs such as hand shaking and tree drumming (Boesch, 1996; Goodall, 1986). Some have mimed inventively; examples are making hitting actions toward nuts they want cracked, blowing between thumb and forefinger to represent a balloon, and making twisting motions at containers they want opened (Miles et al., 1996; Russon, 2002; Savage-Rumbaugh et al., 1986).

One approach to assessing the intelligence of great apes is measuring their performances against children's on the same cognitive task. Chimpanzees can use scale models, for instance, which children first master in their third year (Kuhlmeier, Boysen, & Mukobi, 1999). Chimpanzees and orangutans have solved *reverse contingency* tasks, which allow a subject to choose one of two sets of items (e.g., different amounts of candies) but then give the subject the set *not* chosen (Boysen et al., 1996; Shumaker et al., 2001). Chimpanzees who understood number symbols solved this task (chose the smaller amount to receive the larger) when amounts were shown by symbols, but failed with real foods. Children first solve this task between 3 and 3.5 years of age, and 3-year-olds show limitations like the chimpanzees' (Carlson, Davis, & Leach, 2005). Thus some great apes show certain symbolic logical abilities comparable to those of 3.5-year-old children. To date, great apes have not shown evidence of the symbol systems that Deacon (1997) proposes to distinguish human intelligence.

Summary and Implications of Great Ape Research for Human Intelligence

There is now fairly strong agreement that great apes share a grade of intelligence of intermediate complexity that goes beyond that of other nonhuman primates and includes abilities previously thought uniquely human (Byrne, 1995; Gómez, 2004; Langer, 1996; Matsuzawa, 2001b; Parker & McKinney, 1999, Russon, 2004). A minority of primatologists view great ape intelligence as not significantly different from that of other nonhuman primates, on the one hand, or as more powerful but not reaching the currently defined human boundary, on the other (e.g., Povinelli, 2000; Suddendorf &Whiten, 2002; Tomasello & Call, 1997). Disagreement is due partly to emphasizing weak performances, interpreting monkey evidence too generously, neglecting great apes' most complex achievements, or incorrectly discounting them as artificially boosted by human enculturation. All-in-all, however, the evidence remains consistent with Premack's (1988) rule of thumb: Under normal circumstances great apes can reach levels of intelligence of 3.5-year-old children, but not beyond.

In short, within the primates, many of the intellectual enhancements once considered uniquely hominin adaptations probably originated in the older and broader great ape lineage. Paleological evidence is consistent with a great ape grade of intelligence evolving with mid-Miocene hominids, as part and parcel of a biological package that includes larger brains, larger bodies, longer lives, and the mix of socioecological pressures the hominids faced and created (Russon & Begun, 2004). If so, these intellectual enhancements evolved as hominid adaptations to increasingly difficult life in moist tropical forests – not hominin adaptations to savanna life.

The Intelligence of Early Humans

This section examines the archaeological evidence for the earliest indications of human intelligence and anthropological evidence for concurrent changes in the size and shape of the cranial cavity. It discusses the implications for the evolution of human intelligence.

Homo habilis

Ancestral humans started diverging from ancestral great apes approximately six million years ago. The first Homo lineage, *Homo habilis*, appeared approximately 2.4 million years ago in the Lower Paleolithic and persisted until 1.5 mya. The earliest known human inventions, referred to as *Oldowan* artifacts (after Olduvai Gorge, Tanzania, where they were first found), are widely attributed to *Homo habilis* (Semaw et al., 1997), although it is possible that they were also used by late australopithecenes (de Baune, 2004). They were simple, mostly single-faced stone tools, pointed at one end (Leakey, 1971). These tools were most likely used to split fruits and nuts (de Baune, 2004), although some of the more recently constructed ones have sharp edges and are found with cut-marked bones, suggesting that they were used to sharpen wood implements and butcher small game (Bunn & Kroll, 1986; Leakey, 1971).

Although these carefully planed and deliberately fashioned early tools are seen as marking a momentous breakthrough for our lineage, they were nevertheless simple and unspecialized; by our standards they were not indicative of a very flexible or creative kind of intelligence. The same tools were put to many uses instead of being adapted to precisely meet the task at hand. Mithen (1996) refers to minds at this time as possessing *generalized intelligence*, reflecting his belief that associative-level domain-general learning mechanisms, such as operant and Pavlovian conditioning, predominated. The minds of these early hominins have been referred to as *pre-representational*, because available artifacts show no indication that the hominins were capable of forming representations that deviated from their concrete sensory perceptions; their experience is considered to have been *episodic*, or tied to the present moment (Donald, 1993). Donald characterized their intelligence as governed by procedural memory. They could store perceptions of events and recall them in the presence of a reminder or cue, but they had little voluntary access to episodic memories without environmental cues. They were therefore unable to voluntarily shape, modify, or practice skills and actions, and they were unable to invent or refine complex gestures or means of communicating.

The Massive Modularity Hypothesis

Evolutionary psychologists claim that the intelligence of *Homo* arose due to *massive modularity* (Buss, 1999, 2004; Barkow, Cosmides, & Tooby, 1992; Rozin, 1976; for an extensive critique see Buller, 2005, and Byrne, 2000). Cosmides and Tooby (1992) proposed that human intelligence evolved in the form of hundreds or thousands of functionally encapsulated (that is, not accessible to each other) cognitive modules. Each module was specialized to accomplish a specific task or solve a specific problem encountered by ancestral humans in their *environment of evolutionary adaptedness*, taken to be hunter-gatherer life in the Pleistocene. Modules for language, theory of mind, spatial relations, and tool use are among the modules proposed. These modules are supposedly content rich, pre-fitted with knowledge relevant to hunter-gatherer problems. It is also claimed that these modules exist today in more or less the same form as they existed in the Pleistocene, because too little time has passed for them to have undergone significant modification.

What is the current status of these ideas? Although the mind exhibits an intermediate degree of functional and anatomical modularity, neuroscience has not revealed vast numbers of hardwired, encapsulated, task-specific modules; indeed, the brain has been shown to be more highly subject to environmental influence than we thought (Wexler, 2006). Nevertheless, evolutionary psychology has made a valuable contribution by heightening awareness that the human mind is not an optimally designed machine; its structure and function reflect the pressures it was subjected to in over its long evolutionary history.

Homo erectus

Approximately 1.9 million years ago, *Homo ergaster* and *Homo erectus* appeared, followed by archaic *Homo sapiens* and *Homo neanderthalensis*. The size of the *Homo erectus* brain was approximately 1,000 cc, about 25% larger than that of *Homo habilis*, at least twice as large as the brains of living great apes, and 75% the cranial capacity of modern humans (Aiello, 1996; Ruff et al.,

1997). *Homo erectus* exhibited many indications of enhanced ability to adapt to the environment to meet the demands of survival, including having sophisticated, task-specific stone handaxes, complex stable seasonal home bases, and long-distance hunting strategies involving large game. By 1.6 mya, *Homo erectus* had dispersed as far as Southeast Asia, indicating the ability to adjust its lifestyle to different climates and habitats (Anton & Swisher, 2004; Cachel & Harris, 1995; Swisher, Curtis, Jacob, Getty, & Widiasmoro, 1994; Walker & Leakey, 1993). By 1.4 mya in Africa, West Asia, and Europe, *Homo erectus* had produced the Aschulean handaxe (Asfaw et al., 1992), a do-it-all tool that may have functioned as a social status symbol (Kohn & Mithen, 1999). The most notable characteristic of these tools is their biface (two-sided) symmetry. They probably required several stages of production, bifacial knapping, and considerable skill and spatial ability to achieve their final form.

Though anatomical evidence indicates the presence of Broca's area in the brain, suggesting that the capacity for language was present by this time (Wynn, 1998), verbal communication is thought to have been limited to (at best) pre-syntactical proto-language involving primarily short, non-grammatical utterances of one or two words (Dunbar, 1996). Mental processes during this time period probably strayed little from concrete sensory experience. The capacity for abstract thought and for thinking about what one is thinking about (that is, metacognition) had not yet appeared.

Social Explanations

There are multiple versions of the hypothesis that the origins of human intellect and onset of the archaeological record reflect a transition in cognitive or social abilities. *Homo erectus* were indeed probably the earliest humans to live in hunter-gatherer societies. One suggestion has been that they owe their achievements to onset of theory of mind (Mithen, 1998). However, as we have seen, there is evidence that other species possess theory of mind (Heyes, 1998), yet do not compare to modern humans in intelligence.

Self-Triggered Recall and Rehearsal Loop

Donald (1991) proposed that with the enlarged cranial capacity of *Homo erectus*, the human mind underwent the first of three transitions by which it – and the cultural matrix in which it is profoundly embedded – evolved from the ancestral, pre-hominin condition. Each transition entailed a new way of encoding representations in memory and storing them in collective memory so that they can later be drawn upon and shared with others.

This first transition is characterized by a shift from an *episodic* to a *mimetic mode* of cognitive functioning, made possible by onset of the capacity for voluntary retrieval of stored memories, independent of environmental cues. Donald refers to this as a "self-triggered recall and rehearsal loop." Self-triggered recall enabled hominins to access memories voluntarily and thereby act out[1] events that occurred in the past or that might occur in the future. Thus not only could the mimetic mind temporarily escape the here and now, but by miming or gesture, it could communicate similar escapes in other minds. The capacity to mime thus ushered forth what is referred to as a *mimetic* form of cognition and brought about a transition to the mimetic stage of human culture. The self-triggered recall and rehearsal loop also enabled hominins to engage in a stream of thought. One thought or idea evokes another, revised version of it, which evokes yet another, and so forth recursively. In this way, attention is directed away from the external world toward one's internal model of it. Finally, self-triggered recall allowed actors to take control over their own output, including voluntary rehearsal and refinement, and mimetic skills such as pantomime, reenactive play, self-reminding, imitative learning, and proto-teaching. In effect, it allows systematic evaluation and

1 The term *mimetic* is derived from "mime," which means "to act out."

improvement of motor acts and adapting them to new situations, resulting in more refined skills and artifacts, and the capacity to use one's body as a communication device to act out events.

Donald's scenario becomes even more plausible in light of the structure and dynamics of associative memory (Gabora, 1998, 2003, 2007, 2010; Gabora & Aerts, 2009). Neurons are sensitive to *microfeatures* – primitive stimulus attributes such as a sound of a particular pitch, or a line of a particular orientation. Episodes etched in memory are *distributed* across a bundle or cell assembly of these neurons, and likewise, each neuron participates in the encoding of many episodes. Finally, memory is *content-addressable*, such that similar stimuli activate and get encoded in overlapping distributions of neurons. With larger brains, episodes are encoded in more detail, allowing for a transition from more coarse-grained to more fine-grained memory. Fine-grained memory means more microfeatures of episodes tend to be encoded, so there are more ways for distributions to overlap. Greater overlap meant more routes by which one memory can evoke another, making possible the onset of self-triggered recall and rehearsal, and paving the way for a more integrated internal model of the world, or worldview.

Over a Million Years of Stasis

The handaxe persisted as the almost exclusive tool preserved in the archaeological record for over a million years, spreading by 500,000 years ago into Europe, where was it used until about 200,000 years ago. During this period, there was almost no change in tool design and little other evidence of new forms of intelligent behavior, with the exception of the first solid evidence for controlled use of fire, approximately 800,000 years ago (Goren-Inbar et al., 2004). There is, however, some evidence (such as charred animal bones at *Homo ergaster* sites) that fire may have been used substantially earlier.

A Second Increase in Brain Size

Between 600,000 and 150,000 years ago there was a second spurt in brain enlargement (Aiello, 1996; Ruff et al., 1997), which marks the appearance of anatomically modern humans. It would make our story simple if the increase in brain size coincided with the burst of creativity in the Middle/Upper Paleolithic (Bickerton, 1990; Mithen, 1998), to be discussed shortly. But although *anatomically* modern humans had arrived, *behavioral* modernity had not. Leakey (1984) writes of anatomically modern human populations in the Middle East with little in the way of evidence for the kind of intelligence of modern humans and concludes, "The link between anatomy and behavior therefore seems to break" (p. 95). An exception to the overall lack of evidence for intellectual progress at this time is the advancement of the Levallois flake, which came into prominence approximately 250,000 years ago in the Neanderthal line. This suggests that cognitive processes were primarily first order (tied to concrete sensory experience) rather than second order (derivative, or abstract).

Perhaps this second spurt in encephalization exerted an impact on expressions of intelligence that left little trace in the archaeological record, such as ways of coping with increasing social complexity or manipulating competitors (Baron-Cohen, 1995; Byrne & Whiten, 1988; Dunbar, 1996; Humphrey, 1976; Whiten, 1991; Whiten & Byrne, 1997; Wilson et al., 1996). Another possible reason for the apparent rift between anatomical and behavioral modernity is that while genetic changes necessary for cognitive modernity arose at this time, the fine-tuning of the nervous system to fully capitalize on these genetic changes took longer, or the necessary environmental conditions were not yet in place (Gabora, 2003). It is worth noting that other periods of revolutionary innovation, such as the Holocene transition to agriculture and the modern Industrial Revolution, occurred long after the biological changes that made them cognitively possible.

The Spectacular Intelligence of Modern Humans

The European archaeological record indicates that an unparalleled transition occurred between 60,000 and 30,000 years ago at the onset of the Upper Paleolithic (Bar-Yosef, 1994; Klein, 1989; Mellars, 1973, 1989a, 1989b; Soffer, 1994; Stringer & Gamble, 1993). Considering it "evidence of the modern human mind at work," Richard Leakey (1984, pp. 93–94) writes: "[It was] unlike previous eras, when stasis dominated, . . . [with] change being measured in millennia rather than hundreds of millennia." Similarly, Mithen (1996) refers to the Upper Paleolithic as the "big bang" of human culture, exhibiting more innovation than had occurred in the previous six million years of human evolution.

At this time we see the more or less simultaneous appearance of traits considered diagnostic of behavioral modernity. They include the beginning of a more organized, strategic, season-specific style of hunting involving specific animals at specific sites; elaborate burial sites indicative of ritual and religion; evidence of dance, magic, and totemism; the colonization of Australia; and replacement of Levallois tool technology by blade cores in the Near East. In Europe, complex hearths and many forms of art appeared, including naturalistic cave paintings of animals, decorated tools and pottery, bone and antler tools with engraved designs, ivory statues of animals and sea shells, and personal decoration such as beads, pendants, and perforated animal teeth, many of which may have indicated social status (White, 1989a, 1989b). White (1982, p. 176) also wrote of a "total restructuring of social relations." What is perhaps most impressive about this period is not the novelty of any particular artifact but that the overall pattern of change is cumulative; more recent artifacts resemble older ones but have modifications that enhance their appearance or functionality. This cumulative change is referred to as the *ratchet effect* (Tomasello, Kruger, & Ratner, 1993), and it has been suggested that it is uniquely human (Donald, 1998).

Whether this period was a genuine revolution culminating in behavioral modernity is hotly debated because claims to this effect are based on the European Paleolithic record and largely exclude the African record (Henshilwood & Marean, 2003; McBrearty & Brooks, 2000). Indeed, most of the artifacts associated with a rapid transition to behavioral modernity at 40,000–50,000 years ago in Europe are found in the African Middle Stone Age tens of thousands of years earlier. These artifacts include blades and microliths, bone tools, specialized hunting, long-distance trade, art and decoration (McBrearty & Brooks, 2000), the Berekhat Ram figurine from Israel (d'Errico & Nowell, 2000), and an anthropomorphic figurine of quartzite from the Middle Ascheulian site of Tan-tan in Morocco (Bednarik, 2003). Moreover, gradualist models of the evolution of cognitive modernity well before the Upper Paleolithic find some support in archaeological data (Bahn, 1991; Harrold, 1992; Henshilwood & Marean, 2003; White, 1993; White et al., 2003). If modern human behaviors were indeed gradually assembled as early as 250,000–300,000 years ago, as McBrearty and Brooks (2000) argue, the transition falls more closely into alignment with the most recent spurt in human brain enlargement. However, the traditional and currently dominant view is that modern behavior appeared in anatomically modern humans in Africa between 50,000 and 40,000 years ago due to biologically evolved cognitive advantages, and that anatomically modern humans spread replacing existing species, including the Neanderthals in Europe (e.g., Ambrose, 1998; Gamble, 1994; Klein, 2003; Stringer & Gamble, 1993). Thus, from this point onward, there was only one hominin species: the modern *Homo sapiens*.

Despite lack of overall increase in cranial capacity, the prefrontal cortex and particularly the orbitofrontal region increased disproportionately in size (Deacon, 1997; Dunbar, 1993; Jerison, 1973; Krasnegor, Lyon, & Goldman-Rakic, 1997; Rumbaugh, 1997) and it was likely a time of major neural reorganization (Henshilwood, d'Errico, Vanhaeren, van Niekerk, & Jacobs, 2004; Klein, 1999). These brain changes may have given rise to metacognition, or what Feist (2006) refers to as "meta-representational thought," that is, the ability to reflect on representations and think about thinking.

Whether or not it is considered a "revolution," it is accepted that the Middle/Upper Paleolithic was a period of unprecedented intellectual activity. How and why did it occur? Let us now review the most popular hypotheses for how and why behavioral modernity and its underlying intellectual capacities arose.

Syntactic Language and Symbolic Reasoning

It has been suggested that at this time humans underwent a transition from a predominantly gestural to a vocal form of communication (Corballis, 2002). Although the ambiguity of the archaeological evidence means we may never know exactly when language began (Bednarik, 1992, p. 30; Davidson & Noble, 1989), most scholars agree that earlier *Homo* and even Neanderthals may have been capable of primitive proto-language, and that the grammatical and syntactic aspects emerged at the start of the Upper Paleolithic (Aiello & Dunbar, 1993; Bickerton, 1990, 1996; Dunbar, 1993, 1996; Tomasello, 1999).

Carstairs-McCarthy (1999) presented a modified version of this proposal, suggesting that although some form of syntax was present in the earliest languages, most of the later elaboration, including recursive embedding of syntactic structure, emerged in the Upper Paleolithic. Syntax enabled the capacity to state more precisely how elements are related, and to embed them in other elements. Thus it enabled language to become general-purpose and applied in a variety of situations.

Deacon (1997) stresses that the onset of complex language reflects onset of the capacity to internally represent complex, abstract, internally coherent systems of meaning using symbols – items, such as words, that arbitrarily stand for other items, such as things in the world. The advent of language made possible what Donald (1991) refers to as the *mythic* or storytelling stage of human culture. It enhanced not just the ability to communicate with others, spread ideas from one individual to the next, and collaborate (thereby speeding up cultural innovation), but also the ability to think things through for oneself and manipulate ideas in a controlled, deliberate fashion (Reboul, 2007).

Cognitive Fluidity, Connected Modules, and Cross-Domain Thinking

Another proposal is that the exceptional abilities exhibited by *Homo* in the Middle/Upper Paleolithic were due to the onset of *cognitive fluidity* (Fauconnier & Turner, 2002). Cognitive fluidity involves the capacity to draw analogies, to combine concepts and adapt ideas to new contexts, and to map across different knowledge systems, potentially employing multiple "intelligences" simultaneously (Gardner, 1983; Langer, 1996; Mithen, 1996). Cognitive fluidity would have facilitated the weaving of experiences into stories, parables, and broader conceptual frameworks, and thereby the integration of knowledge and experience (Gabora & Aerts, 2009).

A related proposal has been put forward by Mithen (1996). Drawing on the evolutionary psychologist's notion of massive modularity, he suggests that the abilities of the modern human mind arose through the interconnecting of preexisting intellectual modules (that is, encapsulated or functionally isolated *specialized intelligences*, or cognitive domains) devoted to natural history, technology, social processes, and language. This interconnecting, he claims, is what enabled the onset of cognitive fluidity and allowed humans to map, explore, and transform conceptual spaces. Sperber (1994) proposed that the connecting of modules involved a special module, the "module of meta-representation," which contains "concepts of concepts" and enabled cross-domain thinking, and particularly analogies and metaphors.

Contextual Focus: Shifting Between Explicit and Implicit Modes of Thought

These proposals for what kinds of cognitive change could have led to the Upper Paleolithic transition stress different aspects of cognitive modernity. Acknowledging a possible seed of truth in each, we begin to converge toward a common (if more complex) view. Concept combination is characteristic of *divergent thought*, which tends to be intuitive, diffuse, and associative. Divergent thought is on the opposite end of the spectrum from the *convergent thought* stressed by Deacon, which tends to be logical, controlled, effortful, and reflective and symbolic. Converging evidence suggests that the modern mind engages in both (Arieti, 1976; Ashby & Ell, 2002; Freud, 1949; Guilford, 1950; James, 1890/1950; Johnson-Laird, 1983; Kris, 1952; Neisser, 1963; Piaget, 1926; Rips, 2001; Sloman, 1996; Stanovich & West, 2000; Werner, 1948; Wundt, 1896). This is sometimes referred to as dual-process theory (Chaiken & Trope, 1999; Evans & Frankish, 2009) and it is consistent with some current theories of creativity (Finke, Ward, & Smith, 1992; Gabora, 2000, 2003, 2010; S. B. Kaufman, Chapter 22, Intelligence and the Cognitive Unconscious, this volume. Divergent processes are hypothesized to facilitate insight and idea generation, while convergent processes predominate during the refinement, implementation, and testing of an idea.

It has been proposed that the Paleolithic transition reflects genetic changes involved in the fine-tuning of the biochemical mechanisms underlying the capacity to shift between these modes of thought, depending on the situation, by varying the specificity of the activated cognitive receptive field (Gabora, 2003, 2007; for related proposals see Howard-Jones & Murray, 2003; Martindale, 1995). This capacity is referred to as *contextual focus*[2] because it requires the ability to focus or defocus attention in response to the context or situation one is in. Defocused attention, by diffusely activating a broad region of memory, is conducive to divergent thought; it enables obscure (but potentially relevant) aspects of the situation to come into play. Focused attention is conducive to convergent thought; memory activation is constrained enough to home in and perform logical mental operations on the most clearly relevant aspects. Note that contextual focus enables dynamic "resizing" of the activated brain region in response to the situation (as opposed to rigid compartmentalization).

Once the capacity to shrink or expand the field of attention came about, thereby improving the capacity to tailor one's mode of thought to the demands of the current situation, tasks requiring convergent thought (e.g., mathematical derivation), divergent thought (e.g., poetry), or both (e.g., technological invention) could be carried out more effectively. When the individual is fixated or stuck, and progress is not forthcoming, defocusing attention enables the individual to enter a more divergent mode of thought, and peripherally related elements of the situation begin to enter working memory until a potential solution is glimpsed. At this point attention becomes more focused, and thought becomes more convergent, as befits the fine-tuning of the idea and manifestation of it in the world.

Thus, the onset of contextual focus would have enabled hominins to adapt ideas to new contexts or combine them in new ways through divergent thought and fine-tune these unusual new combinations through convergent thought. In this way, the fruits of one mode of thought provide the ingredients for the other, culminating in a more fine-grained internal model of the world.

2 For those who think in neural net terms, contextual focus amounts to the capacity to spontaneously and subconsciously vary the shape of the activation function, flat for divergent thought and spiky for analytical.

A related proposal is that this period marks the onset of the capacity to move between explicit and implicit modes of thought (Feist, 2007). Explicit thought involves the executive functions concerned with control of cognitive processes such as planning and decision making, while implicit thought encompasses the ability to automatically and nonconsciously detect complex regularities, contingencies, and covariances in our environment (Kaufman, DeYoung, Gray, Jiménez, Brown, & Mackintosh, N., under revision). A contributing factor to the emergence of the ability to shift between them may have been the expansion of the prefrontal cortex. This expansion probably enhanced the executive functions as well as the capacity to maintain and manipulate information in an active state in working memory. Indeed, individual differences in working memory capacity are strongly related to fluid intelligence in modern humans (Conway, Jarrold, Kane, & Miyake, 2007; Engle, Tuholski, Laughlin, & Conway, 1999; Kane, Hambrick, & Conway, 2005; Kaufman, DeYoung, Gray, Brown, & Mackintosh, 2009).

Synthesizing the Various Accounts

The notion of mental modules amounts to an explicit compartmentalization of the brain for different tasks. However, this kind of division of labor – and the ensuing intelligence – would emerge unavoidably as the brain got larger *without* explicit high-level compartmentalization, due to the sparse, distributed, content-addressable manner in which neurons encode information (Gabora, 2003). Because neurons are tuned to respond to different microfeatures and a systematic relationship exists between the content of a stimulus and the distributed set of neurons that respond to it, neurons that respond to similar microfeatures are near one another (Churchland & Sejnowski, 1992; Smolensky, 1988). Thus, as the brain got larger and the number of neurons increased, and the brain accordingly responded to a greater variety of microfeatures, neighboring neurons tended to respond to microfeatures that were more similar, and distant neurons tended to respond to microfeatures that were more different. There were more ways in which distributed representations could overlap and new associations be made. Thus a weak modularity of sorts can emerge at the neuron level without any explicit compartmentalization going on, and it need not necessarily correspond to how humans carve up the world, that is, to categories such as natural history, technology, and so forth. Moreover, explicit connecting of modules is not necessary for new associations to be made; all that is necessary is that the relevant domains or modules be simultaneously accessible (Gabora, 2003).

Let us return briefly to the question of why the burst of innovation in the Upper Paleolithic became apparent well after the second rapid increase in brain size approximately 500,000 years ago. A larger brain provided more room for episodes to be encoded, and particularly more association cortex for connections between episodes to be made, but it doesn't follow that this increased brain mass could straightaway be optimally navigated. It is reasonable that it took time for the anatomically modern brain to fine-tune how its components "talk" to each other such that different items could be merged or recursively revised and recoded in a coordinated manner (Gabora, 2003). Only then could the full potential of the large brain be realized. Thus the bottleneck may not have been sufficient brain size but sufficient sophistication in the *use of* the capacities that became available – for example, by way of contextual focus, or shifting between implicit and explicit thought.

"Recent" Breakthroughs in the Evolution of Intelligence

Of course, the story of how human intelligence evolved does not end with the arrival of anatomical and behavioral modernity. The end of the ice age around 10,000–12,000 years ago witnessed the beginnings of agriculture and the invention of the wheel. Written languages developed around 5,000–6,000 years ago, and approximately 4,000 years ago astronomy and mathematics appear on the scene. We see the expression of philosophical ideas around 2,500 years ago, invention of the printing press 1,000 years ago, and the modern scientific method about 500 years ago. The past 100 years have yielded a technological explosion that has completely altered the daily routines of humans (as well as other species), the consequences of which remain to be seen. Donald (1991) claims that in recent time the abundance of new means of altering our environment and thereby creating an external, communally accessible form of memory brought about what he refers to as the *theoretic* stage of human cognition.

Why Did Intelligence Evolve?

We have examined how the *capacity* for human intelligence evolved over millions of years. We now address a fundamental question: *Why* did human intelligence evolve?

Biological Explanations

We begin with biological explanations for the evolution of human intelligence. Biological explanations generally invoke natural selection as underlying the mechanism; that is, those who displayed a certain characteristic or behavior leave behind more offspring, or are "selected for." Thus, biological explanations have to do with competitive exclusion or "survival of the fittest." Because modifications that are acquired over the course of a lifetime – for example, through learning – do not get incorporated into the organism's genome or DNA, they are not inherited. Because they are not passed on to the next generation, they are not selected for. However, in some cases they may play an indirect role. We now look at a few of the factors that can influence what gets selected for, and thereby influence, the evolution of intelligence.

Intelligence as Evolutionary Spandrel

Some products of intelligence enhance survival and thus reproductive fitness. For example, the invention of weapons most likely evolved as an intelligent response to a need for protection from enemies and predators. For other expressions of intelligence, however, such as art, music, humor, fiction, religion, and philosophy, the link to survival and reproduction is not clear-cut. Why do we bother? One possibility is that art and so forth are not real adaptations but evolutionary spandrels: side-effects of abilities that evolved for other purposes (Dennett, 1995; Pinker, 1997). Dennett argued that even language originally arose as an evolutionary spandrel.

Group Selection

Even if intelligence is at least in part driven by individual-level biological selection forces, other forces may also be at work. Natural selection is believed to operate at multiple levels, including gene-level selection, individual-level election, sexual selection, kin selection, and group selection. Although there is evidence from archaeology, anthropology, and ethnography that individual-level selection plays a key role in human intelligence, other levels may have an impact as well.

Sexual Selection

Some (e.g., Miller, 2000 a, b) argue for a possible role of sexual selection in shaping intelligent behavior. According to the sexual-selection account, there is competition to mate with individuals who exhibit intelligence because it is (in theory) a reliable indicator of fitness. Intelligence may be the result of complex psychological adaptations whose primary functions were to attract mates, yielding reproductive rather than survival benefits. According to the "sexy-handaxe hypothesis" hypothesis, sexual selection pressures may have caused men to produce symmetric handaxes as a reliable indicator of cognitive, behavioral, and physiological fitness (Kohn, 1999; Kohn & Mithen, 1999). As Mithen (1996) noted, the symmetry of handaxes is attractive to the eye, but these tools require a huge investment in time and energy to make – a burden that makes their evolution difficult to account for in terms of strictly practical, survival purposes.

The Baldwin Effect

Not all believe that the spandrel idea can account for the evolution of language. Pinker (1997) invoked the *Baldwin effect*. To understand how this works, note first that genetic diversity within a population is costly because if a superior trait exists, ideally all members of the population should converge on it. However, the advantage of genetic diversity comes to light in uncertain or changing environments; if one variant does not excel under the new conditions, another variant may. Baldwin's insight was that learning may increase the likelihood of evolutionary change by increasing behavioral flexibility, thereby reducing the evolutionary cost of genetic diversity. The idea is that if environmental uncertainty is being effectively dealt with at the *behavioral level*, it need no longer be looked after at the *genetic level*. Thus, although selective pressures cannot preserve the *results* of learning, they can act on any possible genetic factors underlying the *propensity* to learn.

The greater the proportion of individuals in a population who express themselves with language or use other kinds of symbols, the greater the value of language or symbol use to *other* individuals in this population. Therefore, natural selection can start to act on the genetic variation underlying the ability to learn. Individuals whose genetic makeup does *not* predispose them to use language or symbols are not selected for. In this way, the Baldwin effect provides a theoretically justifiable Darwinian explanation for evolution of the propensity to acquire language, use symbols, or indeed any trait whose complexity makes it difficult to see how it can be accounted for by orthodox natural selection.

According to Pinker, this is how the ability to learn language evolved. The Baldwin effect led to the evolution of a set of innate brain functions that (following Chomsky) he refers to as the *Language Acquisition Device*, or LAD. It is because the LAD is innate that there are developmental windows for language learning. This, he claims, is also the reason humans tend to learn language-typical sounds, words, and grammatical rules according to a stereotyped series of steps. Deacon (1997) also saw the Baldwin effect as playing an essential role in the evolution of human language, but in his account, acquisition of symbol use is emphasized much more than grammar.

Empirical proof that any particular facet of human intelligence can be accounted for by the Baldwin effect is difficult to obtain, but it does have computational support. Hinton and Nowlan (1987) ran a computer simulation using a "sexually reproducing" population of neural networks, which showed over generations a progressive increase in genes that enabled learning, accompanied by reduced genetic diversity (increased fixation). In other words, they provided computational evidence for the feasibility of the Baldwin effect.

Cultural Explanations of Intelligence

The Baldwin effect predisposes us to face challenges and uncertainties through behavioral flexibility and learning (rather than exhibit hardwired diversity in the hopes that at least one of us will possess the right genes to meet whatever challenge comes along). It thus sets the stage for brain tissue that is relatively undifferentiated and adaptable, and subject to substantial modification through *other, nonbiological* influences such as culture. The drive to create is often compared with the drive to procreate, and evolutionary forces may be at the genesis of both. In other words, we may be tinkered with by two evolutionary forces: one that prompts us to act in ways that foster the proliferation of our biological lineage, and one that prompts us to act in ways that foster the proliferation of our cultural lineage. For example, it has been suggested that we exhibit a cultural form of altruism, such that we are kinder to those with whom we share ideas and values than to those with whom we share genes for eye color or blood type (Gabora, 1997). By contributing to the well-being of those who share our cultural makeup, we aid the proliferation of our "cultural selves." Similarly, when we are on the verge of an intellectual breakthrough, it may be that forces originating as part of cultural evolution are compelling us to give all we have to our ideas and thereby impact our cultural lineage, much as biological forces compel us to provide for our children.

It has been proposed that the evolution of ideas through culture works in a manner akin to the evolution of the earliest life forms (Gabora & Aerts, 2009; Gabora, 1998, 2000, 2004, 2008). Recent work indicates that early life emerged and replicated through a self-organized process referred to as *autocatalysis*, in which a set of molecules catalyzes (speeds up) the reactions that generate other molecules in the set, until as a whole they self-replicate (Kauffman, 1993). Such a structure is *self-regenerating* because the whole is reconstituted through the interactions of the parts (Maturana & Varela, 1980). These earliest precursors of life evolved not through natural selection and competitive exclusion or "survival of the fittest," like present-day life, but rather by transformation and communal exchange (Gabora, 2006; Vetsigian et al. 2006). Because replication of these pre-DNA life forms occurred through regeneration of catalytic molecules rather than (as with present-day life) by using a genetic self-assembly code, acquired traits were inherited. In other words, their evolution was, like that of culture, Lamarckian.

This suggests that it is worldviews that evolve through culture, through the same non-Darwinian process as the earliest forms of life evolved, and products of our intelligence such as tools and architectural plans are external manifestations of this process; they reflect the states of the particular worldviews that generate them (Gabora, 1998, 2000, 2004, 2008). The idea is that like these early life forms, worldviews evolve not through natural selection but through self-organization and communal exchange of innovations. One does not accumulate elements of culture transmitted from others like items on a grocery list but hones them into a unique tapestry of understanding, a worldview, which like these early life forms is autopoietic in that the whole emerges through interactions among the parts. It is *self-mending* in the sense that, just as injury to the body spontaneously evokes physiological changes that bring about healing, events that are problematic or surprising or evoke cognitive dissonance spontaneously evokes streams of thought that attempt to generate an intelligent solution to the problem or reconcile the dissonance (Gabora, 1999). Thus it is proposed that what fuels intelligent thought is the self-organizing, self-mending nature of a worldview.

Conclusions

This chapter began with an overview of the primate context out of which human intelligence emerged, concentrating on the modern great apes. Modern great apes offer the best and indeed the only living models of the cognitive platform from which human intelligence evolved. The cognitive abilities that great apes demonstrate suggest that a more sophisticated intelligence predated the human lineage than we have traditionally believed. Many of the intellectual qualities believed to have evolved in early *Homo* are now recognized in the great apes – including basic symbolic cognition, creativity, and cultural transmission – so they most likely evolved in ancestral great apes of the mid-Miocene era, well before the hominins diverged. The evolutionary changes proposed to have culminated in modern human intelligence may remain correct, but when and where they occurred and what the archaeological record implies about hominin intelligences may need to be reconsidered.

We continued to a brief tour of the history of *Homo sapiens*, starting six million years ago when we began diverging from ancestral large apes. The earliest signs of creativity in *Homo* are simple stone tools, thought to be made by *Homo habilis*, just over two million years ago. Though primitive, they marked a momentous breakthrough: the arrival of a species within our own lineage that would eventually refashion to its liking an entire planet. With the arrival of *Homo erectus* roughly 1.8 million years ago, there was a dramatic enlargement in cranial capacity coinciding with solid evidence of enhanced intelligence: task-specific stone handaxes, complex stable seasonal habitats, and signs of coordinated, long-distance hunting. The larger brain may have allowed items encoded in memory to be more fine-grained, which facilitated the forging of richer associations between them, and paved the way for self-triggered thought and rehearsal and refinement of skills, and thus the ability mentally go beyond "what is" to "what could be."

Another rapid increase in cranial capacity occurred between 600,000 and 150,000 years ago. It preceded by some hundreds of thousands of years the sudden flourishing of human-made artifacts between 60,000 and 30,000 years ago in the Middle/Upper Paleolithic, which is associated with the beginnings of art, science, politics, religion, and probably syntactical language. The time lag suggests that behavioral modernity arose due not to new brain parts or increased memory but to a more sophisticated way of *using* memory, which may have involved the enhancement of symbolic thinking, cognitive fluidity, and the capacity to shift between convergent and divergent or explicit and implicit modes of thought. Also, the emergence of meta-cognition enabled our ancestors to reflect on and even override their own nature.

The breadth of material that must be weighed to reconstruct models of how and why human intelligence evolved is vast, ranging from characterizations of modern human intelligence and brains to inferring ancestral intelligences from the fragmentary evidence available, identifying and weighing how ecological and social pressures may have guided evolutionary change, and reconstructing when and where these changes occurred. As we continue to study, our understanding of these factors continues to change. An important task facing us now is adjusting views that were built on evidence from within the *Homo* lineage in light of evidence on the hominid lineage from which *Homo* evolved – especially, evidence of greater similarities between humans and great apes in intelligence than traditionally believed.

The striking pattern that emerges from juxtaposing these two perspectives is a disjunction: Based on comparing great apes' tool use with *Homo* tool artifacts, for instance, living great apes show evidence of intellectual capabilities that resemble those inferred in early *Homo* (Byrne, 2004). Great apes' ancestors from the mid-late Miocene had brains of comparable size, so these intellectual capabilities may have been potentiated as early as 12–14 mya (Begun & Kordos, 2004). One implication is that a grade of intelligence that generates basic symbolism and creativity evolved as an adaptation to forested environments of Eurasia during the Miocene, not much more recent savanna habitats in East Africa. If hominids could evolve larger brains and enhanced intelligence, why did they stop at moderate enhancements? A good guess is that they never really got away from fruit diets and this may have limited their capacity to take in enough energy to enlarge their brains more. If so, what ancestral hominins' mix of social and ecological pressures (e.g., savanna life, eating more meat) enabled was evolutionary enlargement of hominid brains, which enabled elaborations to hominid intelligence. The intellectual advances that evolved with *Homo* may have been higher level, not basic, symbolism – possibly, symbol systems. These hominin elaborations beyond great ape intelligence are what need evolutionary explanation, and they make better sense in light of great apes' grade of intelligence and its evolutionary history.

This chapter also addressed the question, at some level, of *why* human intelligence evolved, and whether it is still evolving. Several biological explanations for the evolution of intelligence have been proposed. One is that certain of its expressions emerged as evolutionary spandrels. Sexual selection, group selection, and the Baldwin effect have also been implicated as playing a role in shaping intelligence. Another possibility derives from the theory that culture constitutes a second form of evolution, and that our thought and behavior are shaped by *two* distinct evolutionary forces. Just as the drive to procreate ensures that at least some of us make a dent in our biological lineage, the drive to create may enable us to make a dent in our cultural lineage. It was noted that the self-organized, self-regenerating autocatalytic structures widely believed to be the earliest forms of life did not evolve through natural selection either, but through a Lamarckian process involving communal exchange of innovations. It has been proposed that what evolves through culture is individuals' internal models of the world, or worldviews, and that like early life they are self-organized and self-regenerating. They evolve not through survival of the fittest but through transformation. By understanding the evolutionary origins of human intelligence, we gain perspective on pressing issues of today and are in a better position to use our intelligence to direct the future course of our species and our planet.

Acknowledgments

This work was funded in part by grants to the first author from the Social Sciences and Humanities Research Council of Canada (SSHRC) and the GOA Project of the Free University of Brussels, and grants to the second author from the Natural Sciences and Engineering Research Council of Canada, the LSB Leakey Foundation, and York University.

References

Aiello, L. C. (1996). Hominine preadaptations for language and cognition. In P. Mellars & K. Gibson (Eds.), *Modeling the early human mind* (pp. 89–99). Cambridge, UK: McDonald Institute Monographs.

Aiello, L. C., & Dunbar, R. (1993). Neocortex size, group size, and the evolution of language. *Current Anthropology*, 34, 184–193.

Ambrose, S. H. (1998). Chronology of the later stone age and food production in East Africa. *Journal of Archaeological Science*, 25, 377–392.

Antón, S. C., & Swisher, C. C. (2004). Early dispersals of homo from Africa. *Annual Review of Anthropology*, 33, 271–296.

Arieti, S. (1976). *Creativity: The magic synthesis*. New York, NY: Basic Books.

Asfaw, B., Yonas, B., Gen, S., Walterm R. C., White, T. D., et al. (1992). The earliest acheulean from konso-gardula. *Nature*, 360, 732–735.

Ashby, F. G., & Ell, S. W. (2002). Single versus multiple systems of learning and memory. In J. Wixted & H. Pashler (Eds.), *Stevens' handbook of experimental psychology: Vol. 4. Methodology in experimental psychology*. New York, NY: Wiley.

Aunger, R. (2000). *Darwinizing culture*. Oxford, UK: Oxford University Press.

Bahn, P. G. (1991). Pleistocene images outside Europe. *Proceedings of the Prehistoric Society*, 57, 99–102.

J. H. Barkow, L. Cosmides, & J. Tooby, Eds. (1992). *The adapted mind: Evolutionary psychology and the generation of culture*. New York, NY: Oxford University Press.

Bar-Yosef, O. 1994. The contribution of southwest Asia to the study of the origin of modern humans. In M. Nitecki & D. Nitecki (Eds.), *Origins of anatomically modern humans*. New York, NY: Plenum Press.

Bar-Yosef, O., Vandermeersch, B., Arensburg, B., Goldberg, P., & Laville, H. (1986). New data on the origin of modern man in the Levant. *Current Anthropology*, 27, 63–64.

Beck, B. B. (1980). *Animal tool behavior: The use and manufacture of tools by animals*. New York, NY: Garland STPM Press.

Bednarik, R. G. (1992). Paleoart and archaeological myths. *Cambridge Archaeological Journal*, 2, 27–57.

Bednarik, R. G. (2003). A figurine from the African Acheulian. *Current Anthropology, 44*, 405–413.

Begun, D. R., & Kordos, L. (2004). Cranial evidence and the evolution of intelligence in fossil apes. In A. E. Russon & D. R. Begun (Eds.), *The evolution of thought: Evolutionary origins of great ape intelligence* (pp. 260–279). Cambridge, UK: Cambridge University Press.

Bentley, R. A., Hahn, M. W., & Shennan, S. J. (2004). Random drift and culture change. *Proceedings of the Royal Society: Biology, 271*, 1443–1450.

Bickerton, D. (1990). *Language and species*. Chicago: Chicago University Press.

Bickerton, D. (1996). *Language and human behavior*. London: UCL Press.

Blackmore, S. J. (1999). *The meme machine*. Oxford: Oxford University Press.

Blake, J. (2004). Gestural communication in the great apes. In A. E. Russon & D. R. Begun (Eds.), *The evolution of thought: Evolutionary origins of great ape intelligence* (pp. 61–75). Cambridge, UK: Cambridge University Press.

Boden, M. (1990). *The creative mind: Myths and mechanisms*. Grand Bay, NB: Cardinal.

Boesch, C. (1991). Teaching in wild chimpanzees. *Animal Behaviour, 41*, 530–532.

Boesch, C. (1996). Three approaches for assessing chimpanzee culture. In A. E. Russon, K. A. Bard, & S. T. Parker (Eds.), *Reaching into thought: The minds of the great apes* (pp. 404–429). Cambridge, UK: Cambridge University Press.

Boesch, C., & Boesch-Achermann, H. (2000). *The chimpanzees of the Taï Forest: Behavioural ecology and evolution*. Oxford, UK: Oxford University Press.

Boyd, R., & Richerson, P. (1985). *Culture and the evolutionary process*. Chicago, IL: University of Chicago Press.

Boysen, S. T., Berntson, G. G., Hannan, M. B., & Cacioppo, J. T. (1996). Quantity-based inference and symbolic representations in chimpanzees (*Pan troglodytes*). *Journal of Experimental Psychology: Animal Behavior Processes, 22*, 76–86.

Buller, D. J. (2005). *Adapting minds*. Cambridge, MA: MIT Press.

Bunn, H. T., & Kroll, E. M. (1986). Systematic butchery by plio/pleistocene hominids at Olduvai Gorge, Tanzania. *Current Anthropology, 27*, 431–452.

Buss, D. M. (1994). *The evolution of desire: Strategies of human mating*. New York, NY: Basic Books.

Buss, D. M. (1999/2004). *Evolutionary psychology: The new science of the mind*. Boston, MA: Pearson.

Byrne, R. W. (1995). *The thinking ape*. Oxford, UK: Oxford University Press.

Byrne, R. W. (2000). Evolution of primate cognition. *Cognitive Science, 24*(3), 543–570.

Byrne, R. W. (2004). The manual skills and cognition that lie behind hominid tool use. In A. E. Russon & D. R. Begun (Eds.), *The evolution of thought: Evolutionary origins of great ape intelligence* (pp. 31–44). Cambridge, UK: Cambridge University Press.

Byrne, R. W., & Russon, A. E. (1998). Learning by imitation: A hierarchical approach. *Behavioural and Brain Sciences, 21*, 667–721.

Byrne, R. W., & Whiten, A. (1990). Tactical deception in primates: The 1990 database. *Primate Report, 27*, 1–101.

Byrne, R. W., & Whiten, A. (Eds.). (1988). *Machiavellian intelligence: Social expertise and the evolution of intellect in monkeys, apes, and humans*. Oxford, UK: Clarendon Press.

Cachel, S., & Harris, J. W. K. (1995). Ranging patterns, land-use and subsistence in homo erectus from the perspective of evolutionary ecology. In J. R. F. Bower & S. Sartono (Eds.), *Evolution and ecology of homo erectus* (pp. 51–66). Leiden, the Netherlands: Pithecanthropus Centennial Foundation.

Carlson, S. M., Davis, A. C., & Leach, J. G. (2005). Less is more: Executive function and symbolic representation in preschool children. *Psychological Science, 16*, 609–616.

Carstairs-McCarthy, A. (1999). *The origins of complex language*. Oxford, UK: Oxford University Press.

Cavalli-Sforza, L. L., & Feldman, M. W. (1981). *Cultural transmission and evolution: A quantitative approach*. Princeton, NJ: Princeton University Press.

Chaiken, S., & Trope, Y. (1999). *Dual-process theories in social psychology*. New York, NY: Guilford Press.

Churchland, P. S., & Sejnowski, T. (1992). *The computational brain*. Cambridge, MA: MIT Press.

Conway, A. R. A., Jarrold, C., Kane, M. J., Miyake, A., & Towse, J. N. (2007). *Variation in working memory*. New York, NY: Oxford University Press.

Corballis, M. (2002). *From hand to mouth: The origins of language*. Princeton, NJ: Princeton University Press.

Cosmides, L., & Tooby, J. (1992). Cognitive adaptations for social exchange. In J. Barkow, L. Cosmides, & J. Tooby (Eds.), *The adapted mind* (pp. 163–228). New York, NY: Oxford University Press.

Darwin, C. (1871). *The descent of man, and selection in relation to sex* (2 vols.). London, UK: John Murray.

Davidson, I., & Noble, W. (1989) The archaeology of perception: Traces of depiction and language. *Current Anthropology*, 30(2), 125–155.

Dawkins, R. (1975). *The selfish gene*. Oxford, UK: Oxford University Press.

Deacon, T. W. (1997). *The symbolic species: The coevolution of language and the brain*. New York, NY: W.W. Norton.

de Beaune, S. A. (2004). The invention of technology: Prehistory and cognition. *Current Anthropology*, *45*, 139–162.

Dennett, D. (1976). Conditions of personhood. In A. Rorty (Ed.), *The identities of persons* (pp. 175–197). Berkeley: University of California Press.

Dennett, D. (1995). *Darwin's dangerous idea: Evolution and the meaning of life*. New York, NY: Simon & Schuster.

D'Errico, F., & Nowell, A. (2000). A new look at the berekhat ram figurine: Implications for the origins of symbolism. *Cambridge Archaeological Journal*, *10*, 123–167.

Donald, M. (1991). *Origins of the modern mind: Three stages in the evolution of culture and cognition*. Cambridge, MA: Harvard University Press.

Donald, M. (1993). "Précis of *Origins of the Modern Mind*" with multiple reviews and author's response. *Behavioral and Brain Sciences*, *16*(4), 737–791.

Donald, M. (1998). Hominid enculturation and cognitive evolution. In Colin Renfrew & C. Scarre (Eds.), *Cognition and material culture: The archaeology of symbolic storage* (pp. 7–17). McDonald Institute Monographs.

Dugatkin, L. A. (2001). *Imitation factor: Imitation in animals and the origin of human culture*. New York, NY: Free Press.

Dunbar, R. (1993). Coevolution of neocortical size, group size, and language in humans. *Behavioral and Brain Sciences*, *16*(4), 681–735.

Dunbar, R. (1996). *Grooming, gossip, and the evolution of language*. London, UK: Faber & Faber.

Durham, W. (1991). *Coevolution: Genes, culture, and human diversity*. Stanford, CA: Stanford University Press.

Emery, N. J., & Clayton, N. S. (2004). The mentality of crows: Convergent evolution of intelligence in corvids and apes. *Science*, *306*, 1903–1907.

Engle, R. W., Tuholski, S. W., Laughlin, J. E., & Conway, A. R. A. (1999). Working memory, short-term memory and general fluid intelligence: A latent variable approach. *Journal of Experimental Psychology: General*, *128*, 309–331.

Evans, J., & Frankish, K. (2009). *In two minds: Dual processes and beyond*. New York, NY: Oxford University Press.

Fauconnier, G., & Turner, M. (2002). *The way we think: Conceptual blending and the mind's hidden complexities*. New York, NY: Basic Books.

Feist, G. (2006). *The psychology of science and the origins of the scientific mind*. New Haven, CT: Yale University Press.

Finke, R. A., Ward, T. B., & Smith, S. M. (1992). *Creative cognition: Theory, research, and applications*. Cambridge, MA: MIT Press.

French, R. (1994). *Ancient natural history*. London, UK: Routledge.

Freud, S. (1949). *An outline of psychoanalysis*. New York, NY: W.W. Norton.

Gabora, L. (1995). Meme and variations: A computer model of cultural evolution. In L. Nadel & D. Stein (Eds.), *Lectures in complex systems* (pp. 471–486). Reading, MA: Addison-Wesley.

Gabora, L. (1997). The origin and evolution of culture and creativity. *Journal of Memetics: Evolutionary Models of Information Transmission*, *1*(1).

Gabora, L. (1998). Autocatalytic closure in a cognitive system: A tentative scenario for the origin of culture. *Psycoloquy*, 9(67).

Gabora, L. (1999). Weaving, bending, patching, mending the fabric of reality: A cognitive science perspective on worldview inconsistency. *Foundations of Science*, 3(2), 395–428.

Gabora, L. (2000). Conceptual closure: Weaving memories into an interconnected worldview. In G. Van de Vijver & J. Chandler (Eds.), *Closure: Emergent organizations and their dynamics*. New York, NY: Annals of the New York Academy of Sciences.

Gabora, L. (2003). Contextual focus: A tentative cognitive explanation for the cultural transition of the middle/upper Paleolithic. In R. Alterman & D. Hirsch (Eds.), *Proceedings of the 25th annual meeting of the Cognitive Science Society*. Boston. MA: Erlbaum.

Gabora, L. (2004). Ideas are not replicators but minds are. *Biology & Philosophy*, 19(1), 127–143.

Gabora, L. (2006). Self-other organization: Why early life did not evolve through natural selection. *Journal of Theoretical Biology*, 241(3), 443–450.

Gabora, L. (2008). The cultural evolution of socially situated cognition. *Cognitive Systems Research*, 9(1–2), 104–113.

Gabora L., & Aerts, D. (2009). A model of the emergence and evolution of integrated worldviews. *Journal of Mathematical Psychology*, 53, 434–451.

Gabora, L. (2010). Revenge of the "neurds": Characterizing creative thought in terms of the structure and dynamics of human memory. *Creativity Research Journal*, 22(1), 1–13.

Gamble, C. (1994). *Timewalkers: The prehistory of global colonization*. Cambridge, MA: Harvard University Press.

Gardner, H. (1983). *Frames of mind: The theory of multiple intelligences*. New York, NY: Basic Books.

Gardner, H. (1993). *Creating minds: An anatomy of creativity seen through the lives of Freud, Einstein, Picasso, Stravinsky, Eliot, Graham and Gandhi*. New York, NY: Basic Books.

Gómez, J.-C. (2004). *Apes, monkeys, children, and the growth of mind*. Cambridge, MA: Harvard University Press.

Goodall, J. (1963). My life among wild chimpanzees. *National Geographic*, 124, 272–308.

Goodall, J. (1986). *The chimpanzees of Gombe: Patterns of behavior*. Cambridge, MA: Harvard University Press.

Goren-Inbar, N., Alperson, N., Kislev, M. E., Simchoni, O., & Melamed., Y. (2004). Evidence of Hominin control of fire at Gesher Benot Ya'aqov, Israel. *Science*, 304, 725–727.

Guilford, P. J. (1950). Creativity. *American Psychologist*, 5, 444–454.

Harrold, F. (1992.) Paleolithic archaeology, ancient behavior, and the transition to modern Homo. In G. Bräuer & F. Smith (Eds.), *Continuity or replacement: Controversies in Homo sapiens evolution* (pp. 219–30). Rotterdam: Balkema.

Henshilwood, C., d'Errico, F., Vanhaeren, M., van Niekerk, K., & Jacobs, Z. (2004). Middle stone age shell beads from South Africa, *Science*, 304, 404.

Henshilwood, C. S., & Marean, C. W. (2003). The origin of modern human behavior. *Current Anthropology*, 44, 627–651.

Heyes, C. M. (1998). Theory of mind in nonhuman primates. *Behavioral and Brain Sciences*, 211, 104–134.

Hinton, G. E., & Nowlan, S. J. (1987). How learning can guide evolution. *Complex Systems*, 1, 495–502.

Hirata, S., & Fuwa, K. (2007). Chimpanzees (*Pan troglodytes*) learn to act with other individuals in a cooperative task. *Primates*, 48, 13–21.

Hof, P. R., Chanis, R., & Marino, L. (2005). Cortical complexity in cetacean brains. *Anatomical Record Part A*, 287a, 1142–1152.

Howard-Jones, P.A., & Murray, S. (2003). Ideational productivity, focus of attention, and context. *Creativity Research Journal*, 15(2&3), 153–166.

Howes, J. M. A. (1999). Prodigies and creativity. In R. J. Sternberg (Ed.), *Handbook of creativity*. Cambridge, UK: Cambridge University Press.

Humphrey, N. (1976). The social function of intellect. In P. P. G. Bateson & R. A. Hinde (Eds.), *Growing points in ethology* (pp. 303–317). Cambridge, UK: Cambridge University Press.

Jablonka, E., & Lamb, M. (2005). *Evolution in four dimensions: Genetic, epigenetic, behavioural and symbolic variation in the history of life*. Cambridge MA: MIT Press.

James, W. (1890/1950). *The principles of psychology*. New York, NY: Dover.

Jerison, H. J. (1973). *Evolution of the brain and intelligence*. New York, NY: Academic Press.

Johnson-Laird, P. N. (1983). *Mental models*. Cambridge, MA: Harvard University Press.

Kane, M. J., Hambrick, D. Z., & Conway, A. R. A. (2005). Working memory capacity and fluid intelligence are strongly related constructs: Comment on Ackerman, Beier, and Boyle. *Psychological Bulletin*, 131, 66–71.

Kauffman, S. (1993). *Origins of order*. New York, NY: Oxford University Press.

Kaufman, S. B., DeYoung, C. G., Gray, J. R., Brown, J., & Mackintosh, N. (2009). Associative learning predicts intelligence above and beyond working memory and processing speed. *Intelligence*, 37, 374–382.

Kaufman, S. B., DeYoung, C. G., Gray, J. R., Jiménez, L., Brown, J., & Mackintosh, N. (under revision). *Implicit learning as an ability*.

Klein, R. G. (1989). Biological and behavioral perspectives on modern human origins in South

Africa. In P. Mellars & C. Stringe (Eds.), *The human revolution*. Edinburgh, UK: Edinburgh University Press.

Klein, R. G. (1999). *The human career: Human biological and cultural origins*. Chicago, IL: University of Chicago Press.

Klein, R. G. (2003). Whither the Neanderthals? *Science*, 299, 1525–1527.

Kohn, M. (1999). A race apart. *Index on Censorship*, 28(3), 79.

Kohn, M., & Mithen, S. (1999). Handaxes: Products of sexual selection? *Antiquity*, 73, 281.

Krasnegor, N., Lyon, G. R., & Goldman-Rakic, P. S. (1997). *Prefrontal cortex: Evolution, development, and behavioral neuroscience*. Baltimore, MD: Brooke.

Kris, E. (1952). *Psychoanalytic explorations in art*. New York, NY: International Universities Press.

Kuhlmeier, V. A., Boysen, S. T., & Mukobi, K. L. (1999). Scale-model comprehension by chimpanzees (*Pan troglodytes*). *Journal of Comparative Psychology*, 113, 396–402.

Langer, J. (1996). Heterochrony and the evolution of primate cognitive development. In A. E. Russon, K. A. Bard, & S. T. Parker (Eds.), *Reaching into thought: The minds of the great apes* (pp. 257–277). Cambridge, UK: Cambridge University Press.

Leakey, M. D. (1971). *Olduvai gorge: Excavations in beds I and II*, 1960–1963. Cambridge, UK: Cambridge University Press.

Leakey, R. (1984). *The origins of humankind*. New York, NY: Science Masters Basic Books.

Leijnen, S., Gabora, L., & von Ghyczy, T. (in press). Is it better to invent or imitate? A computer simulation. *International Journal of Software and Informatics*.

MacLeod, C. (2004). What's in a brain? The question of a distinct brain anatomy in great apes. In A. E. Russon & D. R. Begun (Eds.), *The evolution of thought: Evolutionary origins of great ape intelligence* (pp. 105–121). Cambridge, UK: Cambridge University Press.

Martindale, C. (1995). Creativity and connectionism. In S. M. Smith, T. B. Ward, & R. A. Finke (Eds.), *The creative cognition approach* (pp. 249–268). Cambridge MA: MIT Press.

Matsuzawa, T. (1991). Nesting cups and metatools in chimpanzees. *Behavioral and Brain Sciences*, 14(4), 570–571.

Matsuzawa, T. (2001). Primate foundations of human intelligence: A view of tool use in nonhuman primates and fossil hominids. In T. Matsuzawa (Ed.), *Primate origins of human cognition and behavior* (pp. 3–25). Tokyo: Springer-Verlag.

Matsuzawa, T., Tomonaga, M., & Tanaka, M. (Eds.). (2006). *Cognitive development in chimpanzees*. Tokyo: Springer.

Maturana, R. H., & Varela, F. J. (1980). *Autopoiesis and cognition: The realization of the living*. New York, NY: Springer.

McBrearty, S., & Brooks, A. S. (2000). The revolution that wasn't: A new interpretation of the origin of modern human behavior. *Journal of Human Evolution*, 39, 453–563.

Mellars, P. (1973). The character of the middle-upper transition in South-West France. In C. Renfrew (Eds.), *The explanation of culture change*. London, UK: Duckworth.

Mellars, P. (1989a). Technological changes in the middle-upper Paleolithic transition: Economic, social, and cognitive perspectives. In P. Mellars & C. Stringer (Eds.), *The human revolution*. Edinburgh, UK: Edinburgh University Press.

Mellars, P. (1989b). Major issues in the emergence of modern humans. *Current Anthropology*, 30, 349–385.

Miles, H. L., Mitchell, R. W., & Harper, S. (1996). Simon says: The development of imitation in an enculturated orangutan. In A. E. Russon, K. A. Bard, & S. T. Parker (Eds.), *Reaching into thought: The minds of the great apes* (pp. 278–299). Cambridge, UK: Cambridge University Press.

Miller, G. F. (2000a). *The mating mind: How sexual choice shaped the evolution of human nature*. London, UK: Vintage.

Miller, G. F. (2000b). Sexual selection for indicators of intelligence. *Novartis Foundation Symposium*, 233, 260–270; discussion 270–280.

Mithen, S. (1996). *The prehistory of the mind: The cognitive origins of art and science*. London, UK: Thames and Hudson.

Mithen, S. (Ed.). (1998). *Creativity in human evolution and prehistory*. London, UK: Routledge.

Neisser, U. (1963). The multiplicity of thought. *British Journal of Psychology*, 54, 1–14.

Newman, S. A. & Müller, G. B. (1999). Morphological evolution: Epigenetic mechanisms. In *Embryonic encyclopedia of life sciences*. London, UK: Nature Publishing Group.

Parker, S. T. (1996). Apprenticeship in tool-mediated extractive foraging: The origins of imitation, teaching, and self-awareness in great apes. In A. E. Russon, K. A. Bard, & S. T. Parker (Eds.), *Reaching into thought: The minds of the great apes* (pp. 348–370). Cambridge, UK: Cambridge University Press.

Parker, S. T., & Gibson, K. R. (Eds.). (1990). *"Language" and intelligence in monkeys and apes: Comparative developmental perspectives*. Cambridge, UK: Cambridge University Press.

Parker, S. T., & McKinney, M. (1999). *Origins of intelligence: The evolution of cognitive development in monkeys, apes, and humans*. Baltimore, MD: Johns Hopkins University Press.

Piaget, J. (1926). *The language and thought of the child*. Kent, UK: Harcourt Brace.

Pinker, S. (1997). *How the mind works*. New York, NY: W. W. Norton.

Potts, R. (2004). Paleoenvironments and the evolution of adaptability in great apes. In A. E. Russon & D. R. Begun (Eds.), *The evolution of thought: Evolutionary origins of great ape intelligence* (pp. 237–259). Cambridge, UK: Cambridge University Press.

Povinelli, D. (2000). *Folk physics for apes: The chimpanzee's theory of how the world works*. New York, NY: Oxford University Press.

Premack, D. (1988). "Does the chimpanzee have a theory of mind?" revisited. In R. W. Byrne & A. Whiten (Eds.), *Machiavellian intelligence: Social expertise and the evolution of intellect in monkeys, apes and humans* (pp. 160–179). Oxford, UK: Oxford University Press.

Premack, D., & Woodruff, G. (1978). Does the chimpanzee have a theory of mind? *Behavioral and Brain Sciences*, **1**, 515–526.

Reader, S. M., & Laland, K. N. (Eds.). (2003). *Animal innovation*. Oxford, UK: Oxford University Press.

Reboul, A. (2007). Does the Gricean distinction between natural and non-natural meaning exhaustively account for all instances of communication? *Pragmatics & Cognition*, **15**(2), 253–276.

Rips, L. (2001). Necessity and natural categories. *Psychological Bulletin*, **127**(6), 827–852.

Rosch, R. H. (1975). Cognitive reference points. *Cognitive Psychology*, 7, 532–47.

Rozin, P. (1976). The evolution of intelligence and access to the cognitive unconscious. In J. M. Sprague & A. N. Epstein (Eds.), *Progress in psychobiology and physiological psychology*. New York, NY: Academic Press.

Ruff, C., Trinkaus, E., & Holliday, T. (1997). Body mass and encephalization in Pleistocene Homo. *Nature*, 387, 173–176.

Rumbaugh, D. M. (1997). Competence, cortex, and primate models: A comparative primate perspective. In N. A. Krasnegor, G. R. Lyon, & P. S. Goldman-Rakic (Eds.), *Development of the prefrontal cortex: Evolution, neurobiology, and behavior* (pp. 117–139). Baltimore, MD: Paul H. Brookes.

Rumbaugh, D. M., & Washburn, D. A. (2003). *Intelligence of apes and other rational beings*. New Haven, CT: Yale University Press.

Russon A. E. (1998). The nature and evolution of intelligence in orangutans (Pongo pygmaeus). *Primates*, **39**, 485–503.

Russon, A. E. (1999). Naturalistic approaches to orangutan intelligence and the question of enculturation. *International Journal of Comparative Psychology*, **12**, 181–202.

Russon, A. E. (2002). Pretending in free-ranging rehabilitant orangutans. In R. W. Mitchell (Ed.), *Pretending and imagination in animals and children* (pp. 229–240). Cambridge, UK: Cambridge University Press.

Russon, A. E. (2003). Innovation and creativity in forest-living rehabilitant orangutans. In S. M. Reader & K. N. Laland (Eds.), *Animal innovation* (pp. 279–306). Oxford, UK: Oxford University Press.

Russon, A. E. (2004). Great ape cognitive systems. In A. E. Russon & D. R. Begun (Eds.), *The evolution of thought: Evolutionary origins of great ape intelligence* (pp. 76–100). Cambridge, UK: Cambridge University Press.

Russon, A. E., Bard, K. A., & Parker, S. T. (Eds.). (1996). *Reaching into thought: The minds of the great apes*. Cambridge, UK: Cambridge University Press.

Russon, A. E., & Begun, D. R. (2004). Evolutionary origins of great ape intelligence. In A. E. Russon & D. R. Begun (Eds.), *The evolution of thought: Evolutionary origins of great ape intelligence* (pp. 353–368). Cambridge, UK: Cambridge University Press.

Russon, A.E., van Schaik, C. P., Kuncoro, P., Ferisa, A., Handayani, P., & van Noordwijk, M. A. (2009). Innovation and intelligence in orangutans. In S. A. Wich, S. S. Utami Atmoko, T. Mitra Setia, & C. P. van Schaik (Eds.), *Orangutans: Geographic variation in behavioral ecology and conservation* (pp. 279–298). Oxford, UK: Oxford University Press.

Sanz, C. M., & Morgan, D. B. (2007). Chimpanzee tool technology in the Goualougo Triangle, Republic of Congo. *Journal of Human Evolution*, **52**, 420–433.

Savage-Rumbaugh, S., McDonald, K., Sevcik, R. A., Hopkins, W. D., & Rubert, E. (1986). Spontaneous symbol acquisition and communicative use by pygmy chimpanzees (*Pan*

paniscus). *Journal of Experimental Psychology: General, 115*, 211–235.
Schwartz, J. H. (1999). *Sudden origins*. New York, NY: Wiley.
Semaw, S., Renne, P., Harris, J. W. K., Feibel, C. S., Bernor, R. L., et al. (1997). 2.5-million-year-old stone tools from Gona, Ethiopia. *Nature, 385*, 333–336.
Shumaker, R. W., Palkovich, A. M., Beck, B. B., Guagnano, G. A., & Morowitz, H. (2001). Spontaneous use of magnitude discrimination and ordination by the orangutan (*Pongo pygmaeus*). *Journal of Comparative Psychology, 115*, 385–391.
Sloman, S. (1996). The empirical case for two systems of reasoning. *Psychological Bulletin*, 9(1), 3–22.
Smith, W. M., Ward, T. B., & Finke, R. A. (1995). *The creative cognition approach*. Cambridge, MA: MIT Press.
Smolensky, P. (1988). On the proper treatment of connectionism. *Behavioral and Brain Sciences*, 11(1), 1–23.
Soffer, O. (1994). Ancestral lifeways in Eurasia – The middle and upper Paleolithic records. In M. Nitecki & D. Nitecki (Eds.), *Origins of anatomically modern humans*. New York, NY: Plenum Press.
Sperber, D. (1994). The modularity of thought and the epidemiology of representations. In L. A. Hirshfield & S. A. Gelman (Eds.), *Mapping the mind: Domain specificity in cognition and culture*. Cambridge, UK: Cambridge University Press.
Stanovich, K. E. (2005). *The robot's rebellion: Finding meaning in the age of Darwin*. Chicago, IL: University of Chicago Press.
Stanovich, K. E., & West, R. F. (2000). Individual differences in reasoning: Implications for the rationality debate? *Behavioral and Brain Sciences, 23*, 645–726.
Sternberg, R. J. (2001). Why schools should teach for wisdom: The balance theory of wisdom in educational settings. *Educational Psychologist, 36*, 227–245.
Stringer, C., & Gamble, C. (1993). *In search of the Neanderthals*. London, UK: Thames and Hudson.
Suddendorf, T., & Whiten, A. (2002). Mental evolution and development: Evidence for secondary representation in children, great apes, and other animals. *Psychological Bulletin, 127*, 629–650.
Swisher, C. C., Curtis, G. H., Jacob, T., Getty, A. G., Suprijo, A., et al. (1994). Age of the earliest known hominids in java, Indonesia. *Science, 263*, 118–121.
Thompson, R. K. R., & Oden, D. L. (2000). Categorical perception and conceptual judgments by nonhuman primates: The paleological monkey and the analogical ape. *Cognitive Science, 24*, 363–396.
Tomasello, M., Kruger, A. C., & Ratner, H. H. (1993). Cultural learning. *Behavioral and Brain Sciences, 16*, 495–552.
Tomasello, M. (1999). *The cultural origins of human cognition*. Cambridge, MA: Harvard University Press.
Tomasello, M., & Call, J. (1997). *Primate cognition*. New York, NY: Oxford University Press.
van Schaik, C. P., Ancrenaz, M., Borgen, G., Galdikas, B., Knott, C. D., Singleton, I., Suzuki, A., Utami, S. S., Merrill, M. (2003). Orangutan cultures and the evolution of material culture. *Science, 299*, 102–105.
Vetsigian, K., Woese, C., & Goldenfeld, N. (2006). Collective evolution and the genetic code. *Proceedings of the New York Academy of Science USA, 103*, 10696–10701.
de Waal, F. B. M. (2001). *The ape and the sushi master: Cultural reflections by a primatologist*. New York, NY: Basic Books.
Walker, A. C. & Leakey, R. E. (1993). *The Nariokotome Homo erectus skeleton*. Cambridge, MA: Harvard University Press.
Werner, H. (1948). *Comparative psychology of mental development*. New York, NY: International Universities Press.
White, R. (1982). Rethinking the middle/upper Paleolithic transition. *Current Anthropology, 23*, 169–189.
White, R. (1989a). Production complexity and standardization in early Aurignacian bead and pendant manufacture: Evolutionary implications. In P. Mellars & C. Stringer (Eds.), *The human revolution: Behavioral and biological perspectives on the origins of modern humans* (pp. 366–90). Cambridge, UK: Cambridge University Press.
White, R. (1989b). Toward a contextual understanding of the earliest body ornaments. In E. Trinkhaus (Eds.), *The emergence of modern humans: Biocultural adaptations in the later Pleistocene*. Cambridge, UK: Cambridge University Press.
White, R. (1993). Technological and social dimensions of "Aurignacian-age" body ornaments across Europe. In H. Knecht, A. Pike-Tay, & R. White (Eds.), *Before Lascaux: The complex*

record of the early upper Paleolithc. New York, NY: CRC Press.

White, T., Asfaw, B., Degusta, D., Gilbert, H., Richards, G. D., et al. (2003). Pleistocene Homo sapiens from middle awash, Ethiopia. *Nature*, 423, 742–747.

Whiten, A. (Ed.). (1991). *Natural theories of mind*. Oxford, UK: Basil Blackwell.

Whiten, A., & Byrne, R. (Eds.). (1997). *Machiavellian intelligence II: Extensions and evaluations*. Cambridge, UK: Cambridge University Press.

Whiten, A., Goodall, J., McGrew, W. C., Nishida, T., Reynolds, V., Sugiyama, Y., Tutin C. E. G., Wrangham, R. W., & Boesch, C. (1999). Culture in chimpanzees. *Nature*, 399, 682–685.

Whiten, A., Schick, K., & Toth, N. (2009). The evolution and cultural transmission of percussive technology: Integrating evidence from palaeoanthropology and primatology. *Journal of Human Evolution*, 57, 420–435.

Wilson, D. S., Near, D., & Miller, R. R. (1996). Machiavellianism: A synthesis of the evolutionary and psychological literatures. *Psychological Bulletin*, 119, 285–299.

Wundt, W. (1896). *Lectures on human and animal psychology*. New York, NY: Macmillan.

Wynn, T. (1998). Did Homo erectus speak? *Cambridge Archaeological Journal*, 8, 78–81.

CHAPTER 18

Biological Basis of Intelligence

Richard J. Haier

There is no longer any controversy about whether there is a genetic component to intelligence (Bouchard, 2009; Deary, Johnson, & Houlihan, 2009). Since genes work through biology, there must be a biological basis to intelligence. A major neuroscience challenge is to identify specific properties of the brain that are responsible for intelligence. Modern neuroimaging research techniques are providing important data and insights. Before describing these new findings, we will review some earlier pre-imaging attempts to study the relationship between brain properties and intelligence. These early studies are important historically because they introduce concepts of current interest like whether intelligence is localized in the brain and whether efficient communication among brain areas helps explain intelligence. Then we will review the first phase of neuroimaging/intelligence studies beginning in 1988 and ending with a comprehensive review in 2007 that proposed a specific model of the neuro-anatomy of intelligence. Finally, we will review some of the newest imaging data published since 2007 that are defining the emerging field of "neuro-intelligence."

Two brief introductory comments are necessary. First, the definition of intelligence and how it is measured develop hand in hand. Consensus agreement is not necessary for progress. After all, there is still controversy about the definition of a "gene" (Silverman, 2004). Neuroimaging offers the possibility for new, objective assessment of intelligence using brain parameters (Haier, 2009 a, b). Already, psychometric measures of intelligence, once alleged to be "meaningless" by some critics, have received powerful new validity based on their relationship to brain structure and function. Understanding these relationships is now the focus of many research groups around the world.

Second, once any brain property is found to be associated with intelligence, a separate issue is how that property develops and how it may be influenced by other biological and nonbiological factors to create individual differences. How genes are expressed biologically can depend on interaction with environmental factors. Although the mechanisms are largely unknown, they are biological and the subject of the emerging field of epigenetic research. The importance of identifying these factors and interactions is that there may be ways to influence them to maximize intelligence, especially during brain development in early life. In some cases, treatments might be possible for the low IQ that defines mental retardation. It may even be possible to develop drugs, diets, or lifestyle changes to increase IQ across the normal range so that everyone is smarter, just as genetic medicine hopes to influence genetic effects on health. As we learn more and more about brain properties and neural mechanisms associated with intelligence, the possibilities for increasing intelligence become less and less far-fetched.

Pre-Imaging Studies

Brain Waves

The brain is constantly active as billions of neurons react to chemical and electrical interactions. The main measure of the electrical activity produced as neurons fire on and off is the electroencephalogram (EEG). Since the 1960s, many studies have correlated EEG parameters, assessed under a wide variety of experimental conditions and stimulus types, to measures of intelligence. In general, modest correlations have been reported. One explanation for these correlations is that higher IQ subjects process information more efficiently than lower IQ subjects. In early studies using average EEG following repeated stimuli (i.e., the average evoked potential, or AEP), Schafer reported smaller amplitudes to unexpected stimuli were found in higher IQ subjects (Schafer, 1982). He suggested, "A brain that uses fewer neurons (smaller AEP amplitudes) to process a foreknown sensory input saves its limited neural energy and functions in an inherently efficient manner" (p. 184). Schafer also developed an index of "neural adaptability" based on AEP parameters and this index correlated to IQ ($r = .66$). Others reported shorter AEP latencies in higher IQ subjects (Chalke & Ertl, 1965; Ertl & Schafer, 1969). They argued that this result was a consequence of having a fast mind. Another study reported that the complexity of AEP waveforms was greater in higher IQ subjects than in lower IQ subjects, suggesting less neural transmission error and more efficiency in the high-IQ subjects. Other researchers have pursued using EEG and evoked potential measures to assess IQ or learning potential, but findings continue to be inconsistent (Barrett & Eysenck, 1994).

A more recent series of AEP studies focused on how high- and low-IQ individuals differ with respect to the temporal sequence of activation of different brain areas as various cognitive stimuli are processed (Neubauer, Fink, & Schrausser, 2002; Neubauer, Freudenthaler, & Pfurtscheller, 1997; Van Rooy, Stough, Pipingas, Hocking, & Silberstein, 2001). Using multiple electrodes across the entire scalp, researchers can create maps of brain activity as information flows among cortical areas millisecond by millisecond. These studies suggest that high- and low-IQ subjects show differences in a complex temporal sequence of brain activity (measured as various amplitudes and latencies) across multiple areas during performance on cognitive tasks related to intelligence. The differences have been interpreted as consistent with the view that higher IQ is associated with more efficient brain processing.

The biological basis for EEG/AEP correlations to intelligence measures, however, is not yet clear. Neural transmission speed (often measured as nerve conduction velocity) and the degree of myelination surrounding neurons have been proposed as potentially important variables for individual differences in intelligence (Miller, 1994; Reed & Jensen, 1992, 1993; Vernon, 1993). However, the research relating these variables to intelligence measures is inconsistent.

Lesion Studies

Where in the brain is intelligence? It has long been observed that significant brain damage often does not result in a dramatic lowering of IQ. Even "psychosurgery" to sever the connections between the frontal lobes and the rest of the brain, practiced in earlier decades (but rarely used today) to treat schizophrenia and other mental conditions, produced little apparent impairment in tests of general intelligence (O'Callaghan & Carroll, 1982). Similarly, early animal lesion experiments found that the severity of impaired performance during learning experiments was more related to the size rather than to the location of a brain injury (Lashey, 1964). This indicated that general intelligence may be diffusely represented throughout the brain rather than reside in specific "centers." Retrospective clinical studies of humans after brain injury do not provide definitive maps of "intelligence areas" and the brain injury data related to intelligence are inconsistent (Duncan, Emslie, Williams, Johnson, & Freer, 1996). As discussed later, however, new neuroimaging data of lesion patients shows considerable progress (Glascher et al., 2009).

Experimental animal lesion studies suggest one set of brain areas may be related to performance on specific problem-solving tasks and another set of areas may be related to a general problem-solving ability (Thompson, Crinella, & Yu, 1990). In these studies, researchers created lesions in more than 1,000 rats to determine "the functional organization of the brain in relation to problem solving ability and intelligence" (p. 7). They systematically created surgical lesions in 50 brain areas; each rat received a lesion to only one area (and there were at least seven rats with each lesion). Following recovery from the surgery, each rat was trained to perform a battery of problem-solving tasks. A control group of rats with sham surgery was also trained on the same battery of tasks. The tasks included a variety of climbing detour problems, puzzle box problems, and maze learning problems.

The results identified eight brain areas where lesions caused significant impairment in the performance of all tasks in the battery. These areas were thought to represent a nonspecific mechanism that influenced general problem-solving ability, termed "biological g." Lesions in any of these eight areas resulted in poor performance on all tasks. These areas were ventrolateral thalamus, pontine reticular formation, dorsal caudatoputamen, globus pallidus, substantia nigra, ventral tegmental areas, median raphe, and superior colliculus.

In the next step, the statistical technique of factor analysis was used to determine how performance on each problem-solving task in the sham group was related to performance on the other tasks. One factor accounted for most task variance, just as one factor accounts for most variance among humans on psychometric measures of intelligence. This main factor is usually referred to as "g," following Spearman (Spearman, 1904). In the rat data, the *g* factor was most related to the complex tasks. Each of the 50 lesion locations was ranked for its statistical relationship to this *g* factor. Six regions were most related: superior colliculus, posterior cingulate, dorsal hippocampus, posterolateral hypothalamus, parietal cortex, and occipitotemporal cortex. These may represent those brain areas required for good performance on complex tasks, similar to "psychometric *g*" in humans.

The importance of this elaborate rat lesion study is that it indicates specific brain areas that underlie individual differences in performance of general problem-solving ability. To the extent that the tasks used in the rats are similar to measures of human intelligence, and this seems also to be the case in mice (Matzel et al., 2003), the search for analogous areas in humans could be successful, although the rat and human brains are quite different and, of course, lesion studies cannot be done in humans. However, if human "intelligence areas" exist, modern noninvasive brain imaging techniques should be able to identify them.

The First Phase of Neuroimaging Studies (1988–2007)

Positron Emission Tomography

Positron Emission Tomography (PET) scanning provides unique information about brain function and it was the first modern imaging technique applied to the study of intelligence. The technique is based on injecting a low-level radioactive tracer into a subject. The tracer is chemically designed to carry a positron-emitting isotope like F^{18} into neurons by attaching the F^{18} to a special glucose. The result is flurodeoxyglucose (FDG). Glucose is sugar, and every time a neuron fires, glucose is consumed. The harder a brain area is working, the more glucose it uses and the more FDG is deposited in that area. PET scanning reveals the amount of radiation coming from the FDG in all parts of the brain and computes an image showing where the most activity occurred. This is a measure of glucose metabolic rate (GMR). The pattern of GMR in the brain changes depending on what the brain is doing following the injection of the FDG. For example, the pattern will differ if the person is awake or asleep, dreaming or not dreaming, doing mental arithmetic or silent reading. This is a powerful technique for psychology, especially since radiolabels for neurotransmitters can be used in addition to FDG.

Our group used PET in a series of studies to determine whether there are "intelligence centers" in the brain. In the first study (Haier et al., 1988), eight males were injected with FDG and then solved problems on the Raven's Advanced Progressive Matrices (RAPM). The RAPM is a standard test of nonverbal abstract reasoning problems with a high loading on the *g* factor. Each test item is a matrix of symbols arranged according to a pattern or rule, but one symbol is missing from the matrix. Once the pattern or rule is discerned, the missing symbol can be identified from eight choices. The test has 36 items that get progressively more difficult. The harder any brain area worked while solving these problems, the more FDG would accumulate. Controls performed a simple test of attention that required no problem solving. Results revealed that several cortical regions distributed throughout the brain were uniquely activated during the RAPM (i.e., higher GMR) compared to the control conditions. We correlated each person's RAPM score with his MR in each cortical region that was significantly different from the comparison tasks. Our expectation was that the higher the score, the higher the GMR would be in these brain areas. Several correlations were statistically significant but, surprisingly, they were all negative (−.72 to −.84). That is, high RAPM scores were correlated to *low* GMR. We interpreted this as evidence consistent with a brain efficiency hypothesis for complex problem solving and intelligence.

Soon thereafter, another PET study with a larger sample size (N = 16) also reported widespread inverse correlations between performance on a measure of verbal fluency (a measure correlated to general intelligence) and brain function (Parks et al., 1988). We reanalyzed our data with a more accurate method for defining anatomical localization of cortical areas. Although still primitive by today's standard, we found even stronger inverse correlations in some areas, especially in the temporal lobes bilaterally (Haier, 1993).

At the time, inverse correlations between brain activation and test performance were novel and we wondered what might make a brain efficient. In a second study, we tested whether there were activity decreases after learning, using the computer game Tetris (Haier, Siegel, MacLachlan, et al., 1992). Eight subjects completed PET before and after 50 days of practice. At the time, Tetris had just been introduced in the United States and none of the subjects had ever seen or played it. As predicted by an efficiency hypothesis, activity decreased in some brain areas after practice even though game performance was better and required faster processing and decision making for more stimuli than at the baseline. Some of the areas implicated were areas identified in rat/lesion studies of problem solving (R. Thompson et al., 1990), but given small sample sizes and the difficulties in matching rat and human brain areas, these comparisons are illustrative only (Haier, Siegel, Crinella, & Buchsbaum, 1993). Moreover, each subject in the Tetris experiment completed the RAPM on a separate occasion. Those subjects with the highest scores on the RAPM showed the largest GMR decreases with practice, especially in frontal cortical and in cingulate areas (Haier, Siegel, Tang, Abel, & Buchsbaum, 1992). Thus, the most intelligent subjects showed the greatest brain efficiency with learning.

One hypothesis to explain increased brain efficiency is that decreased activity results from an increase in gray matter. More gray matter might mean that having more brain resources would result in less work required for solving a problem. To examine this hypothesis, we recently conducted a new MRI study (Haier, Karama, Leyba, & Jung, 2009), again using Tetris to assess structural and functional brain changes after learning. The subjects were adolescent girls; 15 played Tetris for three months and 11 controls did not. The functional (fMRI) results showed activity decreases after three months of practice, especially in frontal areas (the 1992 study in young men found decreases mostly in parietal areas). The structural MRI results showed thicker cortex, relative to controls, in the girls who practiced Tetris; these changes were most significant in the frontal Brodmann Area (BA) 6 and in temporal BA 22. Contrary to our prediction, there was no overlap between the structural and functional changes, suggesting that efficiency is not a function of increased gray matter. Moreover, this study, unlike the 1992 study, found no relationship between brain changes and intelligence scores.

After the original Tetris study, we also tested whether people with mild mental retardation (IQ between 50 and 75; n = 10) of unknown etiology had *higher* cerebral GMR than 10 normal controls (Haier, Chueh, Touchette, Lott, et al., 1995). A group with Down syndrome (n = 7) was included for comparison. At the time, no other PET studies of low-IQ individuals had been done, and the expectation of most researchers was that we would find lower GMR reflecting brain damage. That low IQ people would show high GMR because they had too many circuits (i.e., the inefficiency hypothesis) was counterintuitive, but this is what we found. Outcomes for the normal controls were lower than for either of the low-IQ groups. These results were consistent with the brain inefficiency prediction, although in Down syndrome, the explanation for increased GMR may be related to a compensatory brain reaction in response to a very early stage of dementia (Haier, Alkire, et al., 2003; Haier, Head, Head, & Lott, 2008; Head, Lott, Patterson, Doran, & Haier, 2007).

Each subject in this study also completed structural MRI determinations of brain volume. For the combined group of all subjects (N = 26), the correlation between brain volume and GMR was –.69, suggesting that bigger brains use less glucose. A similar inverse correlation between brain size and GMR had been reported earlier (Hatazawa, Brooks, Di Chiro, & Bacharach, 1987). This suggested that neural density or packing of neurons may be an important factor for individual differences in intelligence.

In addition to general intelligence, we also used PET to investigate a specific cognitive ability, and we designed the study as one of the first to examine sex differences with neuroimaging (Haier & Benbow, 1995). Male and female college students were selected for high or average mathematical reasoning ability using the SAT. Each person then solved mathematical reasoning problems during FDG uptake. Based on the brain efficiency hypothesis, we expected students selected for high math ability would have lower cerebral GMR than the subjects selected for average ability.

A total of 44 right-handed students participated. Eleven males had SAT-Math scores (for college entrance) of 700 or higher (95th percentile of college-bound high school seniors) as did 11 females. Another 11 males and 11 females had SAT-Math scores between 410 and 540 (30th to 68th percentile). Contrary to the prediction of brain efficiency, the subjects selected for high math ability did not show lower cerebral GMR. In the 22 males, there were, however, positive correlations between GMR in temporal lobe areas (bilaterally) and math score attained on the test given during the FDG uptake period. These correlations ranged between .42 and .55 for the areas of middle, inferior, and posterior temporal cortex in left and in right hemispheres. In the women, there were no significant correlations between GMR and math score. Thus, although failing to substantiate brain efficiency in the high-ability group, this study showed a clear sex difference. Recent imaging research has clarified sex differences in math performance (Keller & Menon, 2009), and new structural imaging studies of intelligence described later in the chapter also reveal sex differences.

One inherent problem with functional imaging is that results depend on the problem-solving task used, so any correlations between brain activity and intelligence test scores can be confounded with task demands. We used PET in students while they watched videos with no problem-solving task. Based on 44 scans, we correlated activation during this "passive" task with RAPM scores. Activation in posterior areas, especially Brodmann areas 37 and 19, was correlated with scores on the RAPM (Haier, White, & Alkire, 2003). Since watching videos had no problem-solving component, it appears that more intelligent people activate sensory processing and integration brain areas more than less intelligent ones. The results of this study are consistent with the view that brain areas related to intelligence are distributed throughout the brain and that intelligence depends on the integration of activity among these areas.

It should be noted that one PET study of 13 subjects reported that only frontal lobe areas were activated when tasks related to different levels of "*g*" were performed (Duncan et al., 2000). However, the subjects did not complete any IQ testing so we don't know their level of intelligence (high-IQ subjects might need to expend less effort), the tasks used did not represent a sufficient range of *g*-loadings, only a single trial of each task was used (reducing reliability), and the small sample size of this study limited the statistical power to determine whether other areas might also be activated. In fact, the idea that intelligence is related to activation of only frontal lobe areas is not consistent with either previous or subsequent imaging studies and is considered unlikely by most researchers.

Magnetic Resonance Imaging

Magnetic resonance imaging (MRI) is based on strong magnetic fields that create a north/south alignment of protons in hydrogen atoms found in water throughout the body. This alignment by itself does not produce an image. However, when radio frequencies are rapidly pulsed into the magnetic field, each pulse briefly throws the protons out of the north/south alignment. Since the body is still in the magnetic field, the protons snap back into alignment between pulses. As this sequence is repeated rapidly, different radio frequencies are produced from the changing energy emanating from the spinning protons. These frequencies are detected by antenna-like coils inside the scanner. By using a gradient magnetic field, the radio frequencies produced also contain spatial information that is mathematically converted to an image. Since the brain has high water content, it shows considerable structural detail with this technique. MRI also can be used to produce functional images (fMRI) by rapidly scanning changes in oxygen content in blood. Prabhakaran and colleagues first used fMRI to study intelligence using the RAPM (Prabhakaran, Smith, Desmond, Glover, & Gabrieli, 1997). A number of fMRI studies of intelligence subsequently appeared; most findings supported earlier PET results (Jung & Haier, 2007). Functional MRI is easier to use than PET because no isotopes are required, and the shorter time resolution allows for better experimental control. Nonetheless, interpretation of results, like those in PET studies, is dependent on the cognitive tasks used during the scanning. Structural MRI results are the same no matter what the cognitive or mental state of the subject, so interpretation of structural imaging results can be more straightforward.

Structural MRI studies confirmed earlier research using head measurements that showed higher intelligence was associated with bigger brains. It is now generally accepted that the correlation between brain size, as measured by MRI scans, and most intelligence measures is about r = .40 (Gignac, Vernon, & Wickett, 2003; McDaniel, 2005). However, is whole brain size the most important variable or is the size of specific areas more important? This was difficult to determine with methods based on defining a region-of-interest (ROI) and then outlining this region on individual brain images where there often is no clear visual boundary between one area and another, especially in cortex. Newer techniques to assess gray and white matter concentrations in the brain addressed this problem. Voxel-Based Morphometry (VBM) uses algorithms to differentiate and quantify gray and white matter for each voxel of the image throughout the entire brain. No predefined ROIs are required for this technique. Even newer, the assessment of cortical thickness has advantages over VBM and may be more accurate. Diffusion Tensor Imaging (DTI) shows white matter tracts in great detail. These methods have been applied to intelligence studies.

Using data collected from two research centers, we correlated gray and white matter assessed with VBM to Full Scale IQ (FSIQ) scores in 47 normal volunteers (Haier, Jung, Yeo, Head, & M.T., 2004). The amount of gray matter was strongly correlated with FSIQ in six areas of the frontal lobes as well as in five areas of the temporal lobes. The frontal areas included BA 10 (bilaterally), BA 46 (left hemisphere; an area related to language), BA 9 (right inferior and pre-central), and BA 8 (left). The temporal areas included BA 21 (left; 2 separate areas), BA 37 (right), BA 22 (left), and BA 42 (left). White matter showed the strongest relationship near BA 39, one area where Albert Einstein's brain differed from controls (Diamond, Scheibel, Murphy, & Harvey, 1985).

However, when we subsequently analyzed these data separately for males and females (Haier, Jung, Yeo, Head, & Alkire, 2005), we saw completely different results. The areas where brain tissue was correlated to IQ in the males were different from those in the females. Frontal areas were more prominent in the females; posterior areas were more prominent in the males. Since the men and women were matched on IQ scores, this was a surprising result. Could it be that evolution has created at least two different brain architectures equally related to intelligence? This possibility implies that not all brains work the same way and that there may be alternative combinations of brain parameters that lead to equal cognitive abilities. This view reinforces the importance of individual differences for interpreting imaging results and the need to analyze data separately for males and females. Schmithorst and Holland demonstrated this convincingly using fMRI during a verb generation task. They studied over 300 children and adolescents aged 5–18 years old, and showed brain development pattern differences between males and females for the areas related to intelligence scores (Schmithorst & Holland, 2006); they also showed sex differences in the connectivity among the areas related to intelligence (Schmithorst & Holland, 2007).

One major issue not addressed in most of the early imaging studies concerned the intelligence measures used. Most used only one measure either as a summary of all intelligence factors (like IQ scores), or as an estimate of the *g* factor (the general factor underlying all mental tests, as first identified by Spearman (1904). Colom and colleagues addressed this issue in two complementary studies using voxel-based morphometry (VBM) to assess gray matter. First, they correlated gray matter with three subtest scores of the Wechsler Adult Intelligence Scale (WAIS) IQ test. Each subtest has a different *g*-loading – low, medium, and high. The higher the *g*-loading, the more gray matter clusters were correlated to the subtest score (Colom, Jung, & Haier, 2006a). They also computed correlations with gray matter for the subtests with the two highest *g*-loadings (Vocabulary and Block Design) to estimate correlates of the *g* factor. In the second study, they used Jensen's Method of Correlated Vectors (Jensen, 1998) and showed a near-perfect correlation between

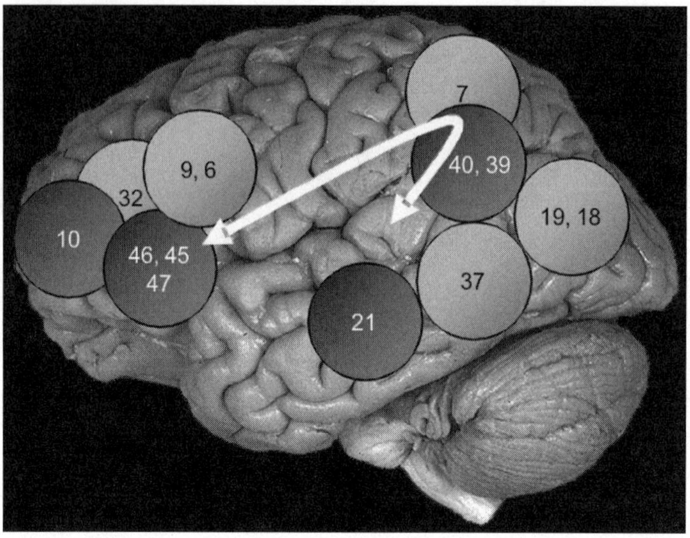

Figure 18.1. The P-FIT model brain regions by Brodmann area (BA) associated with better performance on measures of intelligence. Numbers refer to BAs; dark circles denote predominant left hemisphere associations; light circles denote predominant bilateral associations; white arrow denotes arcuate fasciculus.

the *g*-loading of the subtest and the number of brain areas where gray matter correlated with the subtest score (Colom, Jung, & Haier, 2006b). Lee and colleagues did a similar study (Lee et al., 2006). These studies focused more attention on the brain correlates of the *g* factor common to all tests rather than on composite measures like IQ that estimate intelligence in general. Research on this distinction continues.

The P-FIT Model

In December of 2003, the International Society of Intelligence Researchers (ISIR) hosted a symposium on brain-imaging studies of intelligence at their annual meeting, the first symposium of its kind. One outcome of that symposium was an appreciation of an emerging field of "neuro-intelligence" research. In our presentations, Rex Jung and I independently concluded that the brain areas most likely involved with intelligence were distributed throughout the brain rather than only in the frontal lobes. Subsequently, we reviewed 37 neuroimaging studies of intelligence that existed at the time. These included functional imaging (PET, fMRI, MRI spectroscopy) and structural MRI imaging; a wide variety of intelligence measures were represented. We identified brain areas related to intelligence with some consistency across these methodologically disparate studies (Jung & Haier, 2007). These areas were distributed throughout the brain but were most prominent in parietal and frontal areas. We proposed a model called the parieto-frontal integration theory (P-FIT) of intelligence to emphasize the importance of information flow among these areas.

The P-FIT areas are shown in Figure 18.1 and can be characterized as stages of information processing. In the first stage, temporal and occipital areas process sensory information: the extrastriate cortex (BAs 18 and 19) and the fusiform gyrus (BA 37), involved with recognition, imagery, and elaboration of visual inputs, as well as the Wernicke's area (BA 22) for analysis and elaboration of syntax of auditory information. The second stage implicates integration and abstraction of this information by parietal BAs 39 (angular gyrus), 40 (supramarginal gyrus), and 7 (superior parietal lobule). In the third stage, these parietal areas interact with the frontal lobes, which serve to problem solve, evaluate, and hypothesis test. Frontal BAs 6, 9, 10, 45, 46, and 47 are prominent. In the final stage, the anterior cingulate (BA 32) is implicated for response selection and inhibition of alternative responses, once the best solution is determined in the previous stage. White matter, especially the arcuate fasciculus, plays a critical role for reliable communication of information among these processing units.

The P-FIT recognizes that there may be different combinations of areas that lead to the same cognitive performance. Individual differences in the pattern of P-FIT areas, and the white matter tracts that connect them, may account for individual differences in cognitive strengths and weakness assessed by scores on factors of intelligence denoting specific abilities as well as on the *g* factor. The 2007 P-FIT review included commentaries by 19 other researchers and responses (Haier & Jung, 2007). The comments mostly supported the fundamental idea of a distributed network and enumerated many testable hypotheses and issues for future research including the need for larger samples and multiple measures of intelligence.

Recent Imaging Studies (POST 2007)

The first 37 neuroimaging studies of intelligence appeared over a 20-year period. As this chapter is being finalized in the early fall of 2009, there is an astonishing number of at least 40 new studies published after the 2007 P-FIT review, attesting to the exponential growth of this field. Eleven of these new studies appeared in a special issue of *Intelligence* devoted to imaging research; see the overview by Haier (2009a). A comprehensive review of all 40 new studies is beyond the scope of this summary, but we will note some of the most interesting findings and issues.

Developmental Studies

Structural neuroimaging studies with large samples continue to relate intelligence to brain development. Karama and colleagues studied 216 children and adolescents aged 6 to 18 years old from an NIH-sponsored multicenter sample (Karama et al., 2009). They correlated *g*-scores derived from WAIS subtests with cortical thickness. Results confirmed a distributed network including P-FIT areas, especially multimodal association areas. These areas were the same for the full range of ages studied and largely replicated the findings of Shaw and colleagues (2006). Schmithorst and colleagues continue their impressive series of developmental studies with new findings in more than 100 children and adolescents aged 5–18 years old studied with Diffusion Tensor Imaging (DTI), an MRI technique that images the integrity of white matter tracts. The focus was specifically on sex differences (Schmithorst, 2009; Schmithorst et al., 2008). The findings showed significant sex-by-IQ interactions, especially in left frontal lobe, in fronto-parietal areas bilaterally, and in the arcuate fasciculus bilaterally, consistent with the P-FIT. Girls showed positive correlations of white matter integrity with IQ, and boys showed a negative correlation. That is, *less* white matter in a specific tract may be related to higher IQs in older males. These findings demonstrate the necessity of analyzing imaging data separately for males and females, and they are consistent with new studies of connectivity and efficiency described below.

Network Efficiency Studies

Studies of intelligence and brain efficiency continue to reveal complexities, especially interactions with age, sex, and task type and difficulty – see the review by Neubauer and Fink (2009a). There is increasing attention to methods of assessing functional connectivity among brain areas and relating efficiency of connectivity to intelligence. Given previous findings of sex differences, Neubauer and Fink (2009b) used EEG techniques to assess synchrony among brain areas during different tasks in 30 males and 31 females. In general, brighter subjects showed an increase in functional coupling (especially frontal and parietal areas) during a spatial task, although males showed less activation in frontal areas whereas females showed greater activation. These authors hypothesize that efficiency in females may be a function of neural connectivity but in males, efficiency may be a function of activation/deactivation patterns.

In groundbreaking work, Li and colleagues (Y. H. Li, et al., 2009) assessed connectivity using Diffusion Tensor Tractography (DTT) in 79 young adults and found higher intelligence scores corresponded to a shorter characteristic path length and a higher global efficiency of the networks, indicating a more efficient parallel information transfer in the brain. They conclude that their findings supported the P-FIT anatomy and added direct evidence that, as predicted by the P-FIT, efficient information flow in this network was related to IQ scores. In a smaller study (N = 18), Van den Heuvel and colleagues (2009) also assessed pathway distances among areas to provide estimates of efficiency of connections. They similarly found that IQ scores were related to the global efficiency of connections, but especially in frontal and parietal areas. Song and colleagues (2008) used resting fMRI and examined functional connectivity based on correlations of BOLD signal among all voxels. Even though no task was involved during the imaging, they also found correlations between IQ scores and connectivity measures, especially frontal/posterior areas. Unfortunately, these studies did not examine sex differences, but they clearly illustrate new approaches for testing specific hypotheses about communication among brain areas with advanced image analyses.

Functional Studies

A number of new functional imaging studies use sophisticated experimental designs to examine cognitive and psychometric components of intelligence, although sample sizes still tend to be relatively small and sex differences are not routinely examined. Rypma and Prabhakaran (2009) studied young adults with fMRI in two separate experiments (n = 12 each) focused on separating effects of processing capacity and processing speed as determinants of brain efficiency. Their results "support a model of neural efficiency in which individuals differ in the extent of direct processing links between neural nodes. One benefit of direct processing links may be a surplus of resources that maximize available capacity permitting fast and accurate performance." With respect to the P-FIT, they note, "Our results extend [the P-FIT model] by suggesting that optimal performance occurs when posterior brain regions (parietal cortex and ventrolateral pre-frontal cortex . . .) can operate with minimal executive dorsolateral pre-frontal cortex control. Slower performance occurs when greater dorsolateral pre-frontal cortex involvement is required to provide top-down control of task-relevant brain regions." Waiter and colleagues (2009) also used fMRI and experimental cognitive psychology approaches in older adults (aged 68 years) during two tasks – n-back test of working memory (n = 37) and inspection time task of processing speed (n = 47) – and related activation patterns to task performance and scores on the Raven's test. They found several interaction effects and there was partial replication of results reported by a similar earlier study in young adults (Gray, Chabris, & Braver, 2003). Separate analyses for males and females may provide additional clarification and insights of interactions among these cognitive components and intelligence measures.

Analogical reasoning is a key component of fluid intelligence (Geake & Hansen, 2005). Geake and Hanson (2010) used fMRI and tests of analogical reasoning in 16 subjects (13 female). Activations during an analogy test that required fluid reasoning were compared to activations during an analogy test that required crystallized knowledge. Differences where activations differed between tasks included "bilateral frontal and parietal areas associated with WM load and fronto-parietal models of general intelligence." Wartenburger and colleagues (2009) studied 15 males with fMRI during a geometric analogy task with easy and hard conditions before and after training. They found both increased activity in a fronto-parietal network as the task got harder and increased brain efficiency in this network after training. Similarly, Perfetti and colleagues (2009) compared fMRI activity during easy and hard fluid reasoning tasks in small samples of high- and low-IQ young adults (n = 8 and 10, respectively). They found two opposite patterns of neural activity. When complexity increased, high-IQ subjects showed more activation in some frontal and parietal regions, whereas low-IQ subjects showed deceases in the same areas. Masunaga and colleagues (2008) used another nonverbal measure of fluid intelligence, the Topology Test; it assesses the ability to locate objects in space. They found activations in parietal and frontal areas during fMRI (N = 18 graduate students).

Finally, Jung and colleagues (2009) used an MRI method called proton magnetic resonance spectroscopy to investigate correlates of IQ scores in 63 young adults. This technique assays specific brain neurochemistry in vivo – in this case, N-acetylaspartate (NAA), a marker of neuronal density. They found that lower NAA within right anterior gray matter predicted better scores on verbal IQ, possibly consistent with efficient function; higher NAA within the right posterior gray matter region predicted better performance as assessed by IQ scores. The findings tended to be stronger in the males. MRI spectroscopy has considerable potential for identifying details of the neurochemistry underlying other functional and structural correlates of intelligence test scores.

Structural Studies

Structural imaging shows anatomical detail, especially when strong magnets are used in MRI, but has no functional information (e.g., a structural scan can show the location of a tumor, but a functional scan can show how active the tumor is). These studies also continue to be used in studies of intelligence with more sophisticated designs, image analyses, and larger samples. Luders and colleagues (2009) have reviewed neuro-anatomical correlates of intelligence, including studies of regional and global volume, gray and white matter assessments, cortical thickness (Narr et al., 2007), cortical convolution (Luders et al., 2008), and assessment of the corpus callosum (Luders et al., 2007); see also Hutchinson and colleagues (2009). Their review supports the distributed nature of intelligence-related areas throughout the brain and reinforces the P-FIT.

An interesting paper, appearing too late for inclusion in the Luders et al. review, correlated IQ scores with the size of the hippocampus and amygdala, as determined by region-of-interest analysis of high resolution MRIs, in 34 adults (Amat et al., 2008). There were no findings for the amygdala, but hippocampus volumes correlated significantly and inversely with FSIQ. Left and right hippocampus volumes correlated respectively with verbal and performance IQ subscales. Higher IQs were associated with large inward deformations of the surface of the anterior hippocampus bilaterally. The findings suggested to the authors that a smaller anterior hippocampus "contributes to an increased efficiency of neural processing that subserves overall intelligence." Unfortunately, sex differences were not examined.

One of the most compelling structural studies used MRI and voxel-based lesion-symptom mapping in 241 patients with focal brain damage (Glascher et al., 2009). Four cognitive indices of intelligence (perceptual organization, working memory, verbal comprehension, and processing speed) were determined from the WAIS subtests and correlated to lesion location. Each index showed correlates distributed throughout the brain, with considerable anatomical overlap for verbal comprehension and working memory; perceptual organization and processing speed had more distinct anatomical correlates with the pattern for processing speed most similar to the P-FIT. Interestingly, separate analyses by age and sex revealed no interactions, suggesting that any influence of these variables was overwhelmed by lesion location. There was no analysis of a *g* factor in this report but there will be in a future one, so comparisons will be possible between lesion location effects on a general factor of intelligence and on more specific factors. Following seminal experimental lesion studies in rats (Lashey, 1964; R. Thompson et al., 1990), this study clearly illustrates that neuroimaging techniques in humans with lesions can provide important new insights about intelligence and cognition – see also Nachev and colleagues (Nachev, Mah, & Husain, 2009).

Multiple Measurement Studies

Based on 100 years of psychometric research, most researchers assume that mental abilities are organized in a hierarchy with a general factor (*g*) underlying all tests and that a small number of primary factors account for specific abilities (Jensen, 1998). The first phase of imaging studies mostly focused on single measures of the general factor. Some newer studies use a battery of tests from which a general factor can be extracted along with specific factors. Colom and colleagues (2009) used this approach in 100 college students and correlated intelligence factors with gray matter using VBM. The results showed some overlap for certain factors and some unique neuro-anatomy for others. Many P-FIT areas were found where more gray matter was associated with higher factor scores. Haier and colleagues (Haier, Colom, et al., 2009) used a different battery of tests in 40 young adults and extracted a general factor and specific factors. Correlations with amount of gray matter determined by VBM for the general factor did not match the areas found in the Colom analysis very well, although there was a good match for the spatial factor. The inconsistencies for the general factor may be due to the small sample size studied by Haier et al, although *g* factors extracted from different test batteries should be nearly equivalent. At this time, it is not yet determined whether there is an anatomic network specific for the *g* factor ("neuro-g") that is unique from networks associated with specific factors (derived with *g* variance removed). Colom and colleagues (2007), for example, found considerable overlap in the brain areas where gray matter correlated with scores on general intelligence and working memory. Johnson and colleagues (Johnson et al., 2008; van der Maas et al., 2006) investigated gray and white matter correlates of other cognitive factors that were derived independent of IQ. Two dimensions, rotation–verbal and focus–diffusion, were studied in adults (N = 45). There were correlations in brain areas that did not correspond to those reported for IQ. These data demonstrate that there is more to learn about the neural basis of cognitive abilities after removing variance contributed by general intelligence.

Such neuroimaging results contribute to the recent reexamination of some psychometric assumptions about *g* and the hierarchical structure of mental abilities (van der Maas et al., 2006). It should be noted that there is also growing interest in using the metric of reaction time in milliseconds to assess intelligence as a substitute for psychometric approaches (Jensen, 2006), although this topic is beyond the scope of this chapter.

Genetic/Imaging Studies

The combination of neuroimaging and genetic research is one of the most powerful new approaches to understanding the neural basis of intelligence. Studies show that regional gray matter and white matter are largely under genetic control and share common genes with intelligence (Hulshoff Pol et al., 2006; Peper, Peper et al., 2007; Posthuma et al., 2002; P. M. Thompson et al., 2001; Toga & Thompson, 2005). Particularly noteworthy, for example, Chiang and colleagues (Chiang et al., 2009) studied identical (n = 22 pairs) and fraternal twins (n = 23 pairs) who had completed MRI-based DTI and IQ testing in young adulthood. White matter integrity was highly heritable (75%–90% variance accounted for by genetics; contributions from shared environmental factors were not detectable) and most significant in parietal, frontal, and occipital tracts. White matter integrity in several regions was also correlated to IQ scores. The authors concluded that "common genetic factors mediated the correlation between IQ and white matter integrity, suggesting a common physiological mechanism for both, and common genetic determination." There is tentative evidence that variation in the COMT (catechol-O-methyltransferase) 158MET gene may underlie the relationship between white matter integrity in frontal and hippocampal areas and IQ (J. Li et al., 2009). COMT 158MET may also be related to fMRI activations in frontal and parietal areas during tasks of fluid intelligence (Bishop, Fossella, Croucher, & Duncan, 2008). Because white matter underlies communication among brain areas, these genetic studies complement and extend the studies of efficiency described earlier.

There are also noteworthy genetic findings related to intelligence in children. Van Leeuwen and colleagues (2009) studied 112 twin pairs (48 identical pairs and 64 fraternal pairs) at age 9 years. Phenotypic correlations between whole brain volumes and different intelligence tests were modest, but the correlation between brain volume and intelligence was entirely explained by a common set of genes influencing both sets of phenotypes. These studies illustrate the powerful potential for future developmental studies in large twin sets, genetically characterized in detail, and assessed with longitudinal data from imaging and intelligence testing.

What Is the Goal?

One consequence of understanding details about the biological basis of intelligence is that neural mechanisms can be adjusted. This is the goal of research into the biology of all health-related issues, especially those that are brain-based like Alzheimer's disease or schizophrenia. Certainly, a laudable goal of intelligence research is to find a way to increase intelligence in those with mental retardation. What about increasing intelligence in everyone else?

Consider if there were a safe drug that influenced gray matter volume development, white matter integrity, or relevant neurotransmitter activity that regulated communication among neurons and across brain areas and, consequently increased IQ by 15 points (one standard deviation). This is a substantial increase that would likely result in much improved school and work performance and new possibilities for personal and professional development. Would you take the drug? Should the drug be mandated for everyone, like fluoride in the municipal water supply, based on the moral prescription that more intelligence is always better than less? Imagine that this drug was expensive so that only wealthy people could afford it. Should insurance companies pay for the drug just for low-IQ people or for anyone who wished to be smarter? Suppose it only worked in children as the brain developed; should parents be allowed to give a child the drug? Would it be regarded as cheating if college students took the drug? Learning and memory are key components of intelligence and they are the mental abilities that deteriorate in Alzheimer's disease (AD). Given the intense worldwide efforts to find drugs to slow, stop, or reverse these declines in AD, drugs to increase intelligence are on the way. It is only a matter of time before difficult and complex questions about their use in nonpatients will need answers.

Conclusion

As the 21st century begins, neuroimaging research into the biological basis of intelligence is increasing rapidly: 37 studies were published between 1988 and 2007 and there are 40 new studies since 2007. So far, the data show that brain areas related to intelligence are distributed throughout the brain. Brain efficiency continues to develop as a concept that shows promise as a measurable feature of connectivity and information flow around brain networks that may help define intelligence. The relevant networks may depend on whether intelligence is assessed as *g* or as specific factors. Apparently, not all brains work the same way, as evidenced by the imaging data that show different brain areas related to intelligence according to age and sex. Therefore, influences of age, sex, and intelligence need to be addressed systematically in future studies of cognition. The evolution of imaging studies of intelligence already includes greatly increased sample sizes, more sophisticated image analyses, and more complex, hypothesis-driven research designs. We have data on brain development trajectories related to intelligence and we have genetic analyses that indicate common genes for brain structures and intelligence. We may be on the verge of using neuroimaging data to assess individual differences in intelligence using measures of gray matter volume, white matter integrity and connectivity, degree of regional activation or deactivation, and the efficiency of information flow through specific networks. Certainly, such advances will have implications for education, aging, and the treatment of brain deficits, damage, and disorders. Intelligence research is no longer bound by psychometric controversies. Neuroimaging tools continue to advance our understanding of what intelligence is and how the brain makes it so.

Acknowledgment

A partial version of this chapter dealing with early studies was published previously: Haier, R. (2006).Teoria da biologia da inteligencia. In *Introducao a psicologia das diferencas individuais*, chap. 6, pp. 136–142. Porto Alegre, Brazil: Artmed Editora.

References

Amat, J. A., Bansal, R., Whiteman, R., Haggerty, R., Royal, J., & Peterson, B. S. (2008). Correlates of intellectual ability with morphology of the hippocampus and amygdala in healthy adults. *Brain and Cognition*, *66*(2), 105–114.

Barrett, P. T., & Eysenck, H. J. (1994). The relationship between evoked-potential component amplitude, latency, contour length, variability, zero-crossings, and psychometric intelligence. *Personality and Individual Differences*, *16*(1), 3–32.

Bishop, S. J., Fossella, J., Croucher, C. J., & Duncan, J. (2008). COMT val(158)met genotype affects recruitment of neural mechanisms supporting fluid intelligence. *Cerebral Cortex*, *18*(9), 2132–2140.

Bouchard, T. J., Jr. (2009). Genetic influence on human intelligence (Spearman's g): how much? *Ann Hum Biol*, *36*(5), 527–544.

Chalke, F. C., & Ertl, J. (1965). Evoked potentials and intelligence. *Life Sci*, *4*(13), 1319–1322.

Chiang, M. C., Barysheva, M., Shattuck, D. W., Lee, A. D., Madsen, S. K., Avedissian, C., et al. (2009). Genetics of brain fiber architecture and intellectual performance. *J Neurosci*, *29*(7), 2212–2224.

Colom, R., Haier, R. J., Head, K., Alvarez-Linera, J., Quiroga, M. A., Shih, P. C., et al. (2009). Gray matter correlates of fluid, crystallized, and spatial intelligence: Testing the P-FIT model. *Intelligence*, *37*(2), 124–135.

Colom, R., Jung, R. E., & Haier, R. J. (2006a). Distributed brain sites for the g-factor of intelligence. *NeuroImage*, *31*(3), 1359–1365.

Colom, R., Jung, R. E., & Haier, R. J. (2006b). Finding the g-factor in brain structure using the method of correlated vectors. *Intelligence*, *34*(6), 561.

Colom, R., Jung, R. E., & Haier, R. J. (2007). General intelligence and memory span: Evidence for a common neuroanatomic framework. *Cognitive Neuropsychology*, *24*(8), 867–878.

Deary, I. J., Johnson, W., & Houlihan, L. M. (2009). Genetic foundations of human intelligence. *Hum Genet*, *126*(1), 215–232.

Diamond, M. C., Scheibel, A. B., Murphy, G. M., Jr., & Harvey, T. (1985). On the brain of a scientist: Albert Einstein. *Exp Neurol*, 88(1), 198–204.

Duncan, J., Emslie, H., Williams, P., Johnson, R., & Freer, C. (1996). Intelligence and the frontal lobe: The organization of goal-directed behavior. *Cognit Psychol*, *30*(3), 257–303.

Duncan, J., Seitz, R. J., Kolodny, J., Bor, D., Herzog, H., Ahmed, A., et al. (2000). A neural basis for general intelligence. *Science*, *289*(5478), 457–460.

Ertl, J. P., & Schafer, E. W. (1969). Brain response correlates of psychometric intelligence. *Nature*, *223*(204), 421–422.

Geake, J. G., & Hansen, P. C. (2005). Neural correlates of intelligence as revealed by fMRI of fluid analogies. *NeuroImage*, *26*(2), 555–564.

Geake, J. G., & Hansen, P. C. (2010). Functional neural correlates of fluid and crystallized analogizing. *NeuroImage, 49*, 3489–3497.
Gignac, G., Vernon, P. A., & Wickett, J. C. (2003). Factors influencing the relationship between brain size and intelligence. In H. Nyborg (Ed.), *The scientific study of general intelligence* (pp. 93–106). Amsterdam: Pergamon.
Glascher, J., Tranel, D., Paul, L. K., Rudrauf, D., Rorden, C., Hornaday, A., et al. (2009). Lesion mapping of cognitive abilities linked to intelligence. *Neuron, 61*(5), 681–691.
Gray, J. R., Chabris, C. F., & Braver, T. S. (2003). Neural mechanisms of general fluid intelligence. *Nat Neurosci, 6*(3), 316–322.
Haier, R. J. (1993). Cerebral glucose metabolism and intelliegnce. In P. Vernon (Ed.), *Biological approaches to the study of human intelligence* (pp. 317–332). Norwood, NJ: Ablex.
Haier, R. J. (2009). Neuro-intelligence, neurometrics and the next phase of brain imaging studies. *Intelligence, 37*(2), 121–123.
Haier, R. J. (2009, November–December). What does a smart brain look like? *Scientific American Mind*, 26–33.
Haier, R. J., Alkire, M. T., White, N. S., Uncapher, M. R., Head, E., Lott, I. T., et al. (2003). Temporal cortex hypermetabolism in Down syndrome prior to the onset of dementia. *Neurology, 61*(12), 1673–1679.
Haier, R. J., & Benbow, C. P. (1995). Sex differences and lateralization in temporal lobe glucose metabolism during mathematical reasoning. *Developmental Neuropsychology, 11*(4), 405–414.
Haier, R. J., Chueh, D., Touchette, P., Lott, I. T., et al. (1995). Brain size and cerebral glucose metabolic rate in nonspecific mental retardation and Down syndrome. *Intelligence, 20*(2), 191–210.
Haier, R. J., Colom, R., Schroeder, D. H., Condon, C. A., Tang, C., Eaves, E., et al. (2009). Gray matter and intelligence factors: Is there a neuro-g? *Intelligence, 37*(2), 136–144.
Haier, R. J., Head, K., Head, E., & Lott, I. T. (2008). Neuroimaging of individuals with Down's syndrome at-risk for dementia: Evidence for possible compensatory events. *NeuroImage, 39*(3), 1324–1332.
Haier, R. J., & Jung, R. E. (2007). Beautiful minds (i.e., brains) and the neural basis of intelligence. *Behavioral and Brain Sciences, 30*(02), 174–178.
Haier, R. J., Jung, R. E., Yeo, R. A., Head, K., & Alkire, M. T. (2004). Structural brain variation and general intelligence. *NeuroImage, 23*(1), 425–433.
Haier, R. J., Jung, R. E., Yeo, R. A., Head, K., & Alkire, M. T. (2005). The neuroanatomy of general intelligence: Sex matters. *NeuroImage, 25*(1), 320–327.
Haier, R. J., Karama, S., Leyba, L., & Jung, R. E. (2009). MRI assessment of cortical thickness and functional activity changes in adolescent girls following three months of practice on a visual-spatial task. *BMC Res Notes, 2*, 174.
Haier, R. J., Siegel, B., Tang, C., Abel, L., & Buchsbaum, M. S. (1992). Intelligence and changes in regional cerebral glucose metabolic-rate following learning. *Intelligence, 16*(3–4), 415–426.
Haier, R. J., Siegel, B. V., Jr., Crinella, F. M., & Buchsbaum, M. S. (1993). Biological and psychometric intelligence: Testing an animal model in humans with positron emission tomography. In E. Douglas & K. Detterman (Eds.), *Individual differences and cognition* (pp. 317–331): New York, NY: Ablex.
Haier, R. J., Siegel, B. V., Jr., MacLachlan, A., Soderling, E., Lottenberg, S., & Buchsbaum, M. S. (1992). Regional glucose metabolic changes after learning a complex visuospatial/motor task: A positron emission tomographic study. *Brain Res, 570*(1–2), 134–143.
Haier, R. J., Siegel, B. V., Nuechterlein, K. H., Hazlett, E., Wu, J. C., Paek, J., et al. (1988). Cortical glucose metabolic-rate correlates of abstract reasoning and attention studied with positron emission tomography. *Intelligence, 12*(2), 199–217.
Haier, R. J., White, N. S., & Alkire, M. T. (2003). Individual differences in general intelligence correlate with brain function during nonreasoning tasks. *Intelligence, 31*(5), 429–441.
Hatazawa, J., Brooks, R. A., Di Chiro, G., & Bacharach, S. L. (1987). Glucose utilization rate versus brain size in humans. *Neurology, 37*(4), 583–588.
Head, E., Lott, I. T., Patterson, D., Doran, E., & Haier, R. J. (2007). Possible compensatory events in adult Down syndrome brain prior to the development of Alzheimer disease neuropathology: Targets for non-pharmacological intervention. *Journal of Alzheimer's Disease, 11*(1), 61–76.
Hulshoff Pol, H. E., Schnack, H. G., Posthuma, D., Mandl, R. C. W., Baare, W. F., van Oel,

C., et al. (2006). Genetic contributions to human brain morphology and intelligence. *J. Neurosci.*, 26(40), 10235–10242.

Hutchinson, A. D., Mathias, J. L., Jacobson, B. L., Ruzic, L., Bond, A. N., & Banich, M. T. (2009). Relationship between intelligence and the size and composition of the corpus callosum. *Experimental Brain Research*, 192(3), 455–464.

Jensen, A. R. (1998). *The g factor: The science of mental ability*. Westport, CT: Praeger.

Jensen, A. R. (2006). *Clocking the mind: Mental chronometry and individual differences*. New York, NY: Elsevier.

Johnson, W., Jung, R. E., Colom, R., & Haier, R. J. (2008). Cognitive abilities independent of IQ correlate with regional brain structure. *Intelligence*, 36(1), 18–28.

Jung, R., & Haier, R. (2007). The parieto-frontal integration theory (P-FIT) of intelligence: Converging neuroimaging evidence. *Behavioral and Brain Sciences*, 30(02), 135–154.

Jung, R. E., Gasparovic, C., Chavez, R. S., Caprihan, A., Barrow, R., & Yeo, R. A. (2009). Imaging intelligence with proton magnetic resonance spectroscopy. *Intelligence*, 37(2), 192–198.

Karama, S., Ad-Dab'bagh, Y., Haier, R. J., Deary, I. J., Lyttelton, O. C., Lepage, C., et al. (2009). Positive association between cognitive ability and cortical thickness in a representative US sample of healthy 6- to 18-year-olds. *Intelligence*, 37(4), 431–442.

Keller, K., & Menon, V. (2009). Gender differences in the functional and structural neuroanatomy of mathematical cognition. *NeuroImage*, 47(1), 342–352.

Lashey, K. S. (1964). *Brain mechanisms and intelligence*. New York, NY: Hafner.

Lee, K. H., Choi, Y. Y., Gray, J. R., Cho, S. H., Chae, J. H., Lee, S., et al. (2006). Neural correlates of superior intelligence: Stronger recruitment of posterior parietal cortex. *NeuroImage*, 29(2), 578–586.

Li, J., Yu, C., Li, Y. H., Liu, B., Liu, Y., Shu, N., et al. (2009). COMT Val158Met modulates association between brain white matter architecture and IQ. *American Journal of Medical Genetics Part B-Neuropsychiatric Genetics*, ***150B***(3), 375–380.

Li, Y. H., Liu, Y., Li, J., Qin, W., Li, K. C., Yu, C. S., et al. (2009). Brain anatomical network and intelligence. *Plos Computational Biology*, 5(5), 1–17.

Luders, E., Narr, K. L., Bilder, R. M., Szeszko, P. R., Gurbani, M. N., Hamilton, L., et al. (2008). Mapping the relationship between cortical convolution and intelligence: Effects of gender. *Cereb Cortex*, 18(9), 2019–2026.

Luders, E., Narr, K. L., Bilder, R. M., Thompson, P. M., Szeszko, P. R., Hamilton, L., et al. (2007). Positive correlations between corpus callosum thickness and intelligence. *NeuroImage*, 37(4), 1457–1464.

Luders, E., Narr, K. L., Thompson, P. M., & Toga, A. W. (2009). Neuroanatomical correlates of intelligence. *Intelligence*, 37(2), 156–163.

Masunaga, H., Kawashima, R., Horn, J. L., Sassa, Y., & Sekiguchi, A. (2008). Neural substrates of the Topology Test to measure fluid reasoning: An fMRI study. *Intelligence*, 36(6), 607–615.

Matzel, L. D., Han, Y. R., Grossman, H., Karnik, M. S., Patel, D., Scott, N., et al. (2003). Individual differences in the expression of a "general" learning ability in mice. *Journal of Neuroscience*, 23(16), 6423–6433.

McDaniel, M. A. (2005). Big-brained people are smarter: A meta-analysis of the relationship between in vivo brain volume and intelligence. *Intelligence*, 33(4), 337–346.

Miller, E. (1994). Intelligence and brain myelination. *Personality and individual differences*, 17, 803–832.

Nachev, P., Mah, Y. H., & Husain, M. (2009). Functional neuroanatomy: The locus of human intelligence. *Curr Biol*, 19(10), R418–420.

Narr, K. L., Woods, R. P., Thompson, P. M., Szeszko, P., Robinson, D., Dimtcheva, T., et al. (2007). Relationships between IQ and regional cortical gray matter thickness in healthy adults. *Cereb Cortex*, 17(9), 2163–2171.

Neubauer, A. C., & Fink, A. (2009a). Intelligence and neural efficiency. *Neuroscience and Biobehavioral Reviews*, 33(7), 1004–1023.

Neubauer, A. C., & Fink, A. (2009b). Intelligence and neural efficiency: Measures of brain activation versus measures of functional connectivity in the brain. *Intelligence*, 37(2), 223–229.

Neubauer, A. C., Fink, A., & Schrausser, D. G. (2002). Intelligence and neural efficiency: The influence of task content and sex on the brain-IQ relationship. *Intelligence*, 30(6), 515–536.

Neubauer, A. C., Freudenthaler, H. H., & Pfurtscheller, G. (1997). Intelligence and spatio-temporal patterns of event-related cortical desynchronization. *Journal of Psychophysiology*, 11(4), 375–375.

O'Callaghan, M. A., & Carroll, D. (1982). *Psychosurgery: A scientific analysis*. Ridgewood, NJ: George A. Bogden.

Parks, R. W., Loewenstein, D. A., Dodrill, K. L., Barker, W. W., Yoshii, F., Chang, J. Y., et al. (1988). Cerebral metabolic effects of a verbal fluency test – a PET scan study. *Journal of Clinical and Experimental Neuropsychology*, *10*(5), 565–575.

Peper, J. S., Brouwer, R. M., Boomsma, D. I., Kahn, R. S., & Poll, H. E. H. (2007). Genetic influences on human brain structure: A review of brain imaging studies in twins. *Human Brain Mapping*, *28*(6), 464–473.

Perfetti, B., Saggino, A., Ferretti, A., Caulo, M., Romani, G. L., & Onofrj, M. (2009). Differential patterns of cortical activation as a function of fluid reasoning complexity. *Human Brain Mapping*, *30*(2), 497–510.

Posthuma, D., De Geus, E. J., Baare, W. F., Hulshoff Pol, H. E., Kahn, R. S., & Boomsma, D. I. (2002). The association between brain volume and intelligence is of genetic origin. *Nat Neurosci*, *5*(2), 83–84.

Prabhakaran, V., Smith, J. A., Desmond, J. E., Glover, G. H., & Gabrieli, J. D. (1997). Neural substrates of fluid reasoning: An fMRI study of neocortical activation during performance of the Raven's Progressive Matrices Test. *Cognit Psychol*, *33*(1), 43–63.

Reed, T. E., & Jensen, A. R. (1992). Conduction-velocity in a brain nerve pathway of normal adults correlates with intelligence level. *Intelligence*, *16*(3–4), 259–272.

Reed, T. E., & Jensen, A. R. (1993). Choice-reaction time and visual pathway nerve-conduction velocity both correlate with intelligence but appear not to correlate with each other – Implications for information-processing. *Intelligence*, *17*(2), 191–203.

Rypma, B., & Prabhakaran, V. (2009). When less is more and when more is more: The mediating roles of capacity and speed in brain-behavior efficiency. *Intelligence*, *37*(2), 207–222.

Schafer, E. W. (1982). Neural adaptability: A biological determinant of behavioral intelligence. *Int J Neurosci*, *17*(3), 183–191.

Schmithorst, V. J. (2009). Developmental sex differences in the relation of neuroanatomical connectivity to intelligence. *Intelligence*, *37*(2), 164–173.

Schmithorst, V. J., & Holland, S. K. (2006). Functional MRI evidence for disparate developmental processes underlying intelligence in boys and girls. *NeuroImage*, *31*(3), 1366–1379.

Schmithorst, V. J., & Holland, S. K. (2007). Sex differences in the development of neuroanatomical functional connectivity underlying intelligence found using Bayesian connectivity analysis. *NeuroImage*, *35*(1), 406.

Schmithorst, V. J., Holland, S. K., & Dardzinski, B. J. (2008). Developmental differences in white matter architecture between boys and girls. *Human Brain Mapping*, *29*(6), 696–710.

Shaw, P., Greenstein, D., Lerch, J., Clasen, L., Lenroot, R., Gogtay, N., et al. (2006). Intellectual ability and cortical development in children and adolescents. *Nature*, *440*(7084), 676–679.

Silverman, P. H. (2004). Rethinking genetic determinism. *The Scientist*, *18*(10), 32–33.

Song, M., Zhou, Y., Li, J., Liu, Y., Tian, L., Yu, C., et al. (2008). Brain spontaneous functional connectivity and intelligence. *NeuroImage*, *41*(3), 1168–1176.

Spearman, C. (1904). General intelligence objectively determined and measured. *American Journal of Psychology*, *15*, 201–293.

Thompson, P. M., Cannon, T. D., Narr, K. L., van Erp, T., Poutanen, V. P., Huttunen, M., et al. (2001). Genetic influences on brain structure. *Nat Neurosci*, *4*(12), 1253–1258.

Thompson, R., Crinella, F. M., & Yu, J. (1990). *Brain mechanisms in problem solving and intelligence: A survey of the rat brain*. New York, NY: Plenum Press.

Toga, A. W., & Thompson, P. M. (2005). Genetics of brain structure and intelligence. *Annu Rev Neurosci*, *28*, 1–23.

Van Den Heuvel, M. P., Stam, C. J., Kahn, R. S., & Hulshoff Pol, H. E. (2009). Efficiency of functional brain networks and intellectual performance. *J Neurosci*, *29*(23), 7619–7624.

Van Der Maas, H. L. J., Dolan, C. V., Grasman, R., Wicherts, J. M., Huizenga, H. A., & Raijmakers, M. E. J. (2006). A dynamical model of general intelligence: The positive manifold of intelligence by mutualism. *Psychological Review*, *113*(4), 842–861.

van Leeuwen, M., Peper, J. S., van den Berg, S. M., Brouwer, R. M., Pol, H. E. H., Kahn, R. S., et al. (2009). A genetic analysis of brain volumes and IQ in children. *Intelligence*, *37*(2), 181–191.

Van Rooy, C., Stough, C., Pipingas, A., Hocking, C., & Silberstein, R. B. (2001). Spatial working memory and intelligence – Biological correlates. *Intelligence*, *29*(4), 275–292.

Vernon, P. A. (1993). Intelligence and neural efficiency. In D. K. Detterman (Ed.), *Current topics in human intelligence: Individual differences and cognition* (Vol. 3, pp. 171–188). Norwood, NJ: Ablex.

Waiter, G. D., Deary, I. J., Staff, R. T., Murray, A. D., Fox, H. C., Starr, J. M., et al. (2009). Exploring possible neural mechanisms of intelligence differences using processing speed and working memory tasks: An fMRI study. *Intelligence*, 37(2), 199–206.

Wartenburger, I., Heekeren, H. R., Preusse, F., Kramer, J., & Van Der Meer, E. (2009). Cerebral correlates of analogical processing and their modulation by training. *NeuroImage*, 48(1), 291–302.

Part V

INTELLIGENCE AND INFORMATION PROCESSING

CHAPTER 19

Basic Processes of Intelligence

Ted Nettelbeck

The search for basic processes that support intelligence has a long history. This endeavor rests on the assumption that there are individual differences in structures of the central nervous system (CNS) whereby information critical to decision making is conducted more or less rapidly. Reductionist theory has linked intelligent behaviors with low-level perceptual sensitivity since Galton's (1883) explorations of individual differences in sensory discriminations and reaction times. This approach was adjudged nonproductive around the beginning of the 20th century because studies measuring reaction time (RT) had, to that time, failed to support the theory (Jensen, 1982). At around the same time, Binet developed a practical measure of intelligence and behaviorism, and psychoanalysis successfully captured mainstream interest within psychology (Deary, 2000). Together, these circumstances established an orthodoxy that eschewed attempts to address theory about putative biological bases to intelligence for more than half a century.

Instead, the main focus for differential psychology became the further development and validation of tests of higher order mental abilities. This approach to defining intelligence struggled initially to avoid the circularity of using description as explanation; but, arguably, modern tests do have good construct validity for culturally valued behaviors held by consensus to require intelligence (Jensen, 1998). This is important because the vast majority of researchers following a reductionist paradigm have relied on IQ-type tests to provide an (imperfect) proxy for intelligence.

Recent Interest in Speeded Tasks

From about the 1960s there has been renewed interest in mental speed as somehow fundamental to intelligence (Eysenck, 1987). Broadly, speeded tasks have been of two kinds.

In the first, generally drawn from mainstream cognitive psychology and neuropsychology, tasks have been conceived as measuring individual differences in cognitive subsystems that traditionally have been incorporated within psychometric accounts of intelligence, such as attention (e.g., orientation, focused, divided, sustained) or short-term, working, and long-term memory. The reductionist account assumes that individual differences in response latencies reflect underlying stages or mechanisms essential to the specified construct. Examples are S. Sternberg's (1975) four-stage short-term memory scanning model, Posner's (1978) long-term encoding function task, and R. J. Sternberg's (1977) componential analysis of analogical reasoning, which led him to invoke metacognition to direct processing resources where most required. Such tasks have successfully discriminated between people with brain damage or an intellectual disability and those without; but results have not generally located these differences within set processing stages or convincingly demonstrated that bottom-up processing, as opposed to top-down processing, was involved (Nettelbeck & Wilson, 1997). Within the normal population, correlations between such measures and IQ have typically been modest (Jensen 2006) but stronger for more cognitively demanding tasks (Schweizer et al., 2000). However, Deary (2000) expressed strong reservations about the utility of these more demanding tasks to reductionist theory because of uncertainty about what they measure.

The second category of speeded performance has included tasks assumed to reflect more general basic functions, like *perceptual speed* and *information-processing speed*. As will be clear from what follows, there is uncertainty about the precise meaning of these terms. However, perceptual speed has commonly been defined as speediness on very simple tasks (Nettelbeck, 1994), whereas speed of information processing is a generic term, referring to the rate at which hypothetical basic mechanisms within the brain and CNS operate.

Theoretical accounts for why such tasks might correlate with intelligence have postulated that the brain has limited capacity to process incoming information simultaneously, so that short-term storage is lost without rehearsal. Faster processing therefore confers advantage, particularly for complex decision making. Jensen (1982) proposed a model of this kind that derived from "neural oscillation" whereby variability in performance, rather than central tendency, is the key to understanding timed performance. Consistent individual biological differences are held to exist in the rate at which cells in a neural network oscillate between excitatory and refractory phases. A fast rate means that, irrespective of when a response is required, excitatory potential is closer to threshold, resulting in faster and less variable reactions than are generated from a slower rate of oscillation. Capacity to encode information more quickly therefore equates with a more efficient processing system at a given point in time because more information, critical to the integration of different essential elements of a problem, is acquired from the environment and/or existing long-term storage and is retained in working memory (WM). This account implies that processing speed is central to WM, the capacity to retrieve, manipulate. and rehearse information within a very short time frame. If information quality is degraded because of limited capacity before processing has been completed, the accumulation of task-relevant knowledge will be less effective. Extending this theory to an account of intelligence, Jensen's argument becomes that the more efficient system conveys cumulative advantage for the acquisition of knowledge over time. This theory has influenced current research directions, as described later.

Reliable correlations between speeded measures and cognitive tests are now established for children. Whether faster RTs with age are confounded by higher order responding strategies that reflect maturing problem-solving skills (Anderson, Nettelbeck, & Barlow, 1997) or reflect more functional basic cognitive development as a child grows older (Jensen, 1982) is still not known, although recent results from Edmonds et al. (2008) appear to favor the latter interpretation. This distinction notwithstanding, however, the evidence is overwhelming that speed on tasks with low knowledge requirements, like RT and inspection time (IT; see later in the chapter for definition), improves markedly from preschool years to adolescence, in parallel with increasing problem-solving capacities (Edmonds et al., 2008; Fry & Hale, 2000; Kail, 1991; Nettelbeck & Wilson, 1985).

Jensen (2006) has observed that the course of cognitive decline during old age that accompanies slowing processing speed appears to be "a mirror image" (p. 97) of how improving cognitive maturity and increasing processing speed develop during childhood. Whether this is literally so remains to be tested, but large bodies of cross-sectional and longitudinal research, conducted over several decades, have confirmed that slowing processing speed accounts substantially, if not entirely, for age-related changes in fluid cognitive abilities (Gf; coping with novel situations), as opposed to crystallized abilities (Gc; using acquired knowledge to solve problems) (Finkel, Reynolds, McArdle, & Pedersen, 2007; Salthouse, 1996; Schaie, 2005). Thus, whereas tests for vocabulary and cultural knowledge show little decline throughout adult life, tests for inductive reasoning, WM, and spatial orientation on average show very marked effects, and individual differences in these abilities become more substantial with age. Moreover, when speeded performances of elderly persons on diverse tasks, supposedly requiring different processes, are plotted against the performances of young adults on the same tasks (so-called Brinley plots), the outcome is a single function (Cerella, 1985; Madden, 2001), consistent with theory that a general speed factor is responsible for age-related cognitive differences. Nonetheless, there are grounds for challenging whether a general speed factor provides a sufficient account for such differences. Following Danthiir, Wilhelm, Schulze, and Roberts' (2005) finding that both a general mental speed factor and independent, specific speed factors were incrementally related to differences in higher reasoning among university students, Danthiir, Burns, Nettelbeck, Wilson, and Wittert (2009) have confirmed a similar multifaceted speed structure with elderly participants. Age effects on speed were general, with a strong general mental speed factor accounting substantially for age-related variance in reasoning and WM. However, there were also direct effects of age, unrelated to speed, on reasoning and WM. Moreover, the best-fitting structural model for these data included additional, specific speed factors that reflected performance on tests of RT and perceptual speed. Identifying age effects unrelated to speed and better defining the nature of specific speed influences are therefore prospects for future research.

Sheppard and Vernon (2008) compiled results from 172 studies of processing speed and intelligence, conducted between 1955 and 2005 and involving more than 53,500 participants. Correlations between diverse measures of processing speed (choice RT, IT, perceptual speed, more complex short-term memory processing, or long-term retrieval) and various tests of intelligence remind us that although understanding differences in mental speed may be essential to an improved understanding of intelligence, these differences do not on current evidence provide a full account of differences in intelligence. Measures of mental speed, whether tapping more or less complex decisions, correlated reliably with intelligence, whether categorized as general, fluid or crystallized but the n-weighted mean coefficient overall from single speed measures was only –.24. This is typical of RT studies and reflects the fact from Sheppard and Vernon's review that RT measures under conditions requiring low prior knowledge have vastly outnumbered other forms of speed measurement. Moreover, as will be explored further in what follows, more substantial correlations have been found with other forms of measurement.

Current widespread interest in whether a reductionist approach utilizing speeded performance can deliver a better understanding of intelligence is a major change of direction within differential psychology. Strong skepticism three decades ago as to whether more than trivial correlation between mental speed and intelligence could be established, captured the Zeitgeist at that time (see Jensen, 2006, pp. 155–158). However, the volume of ongoing research currently addressing whether and, if so, to what extent basic speed processes contribute to intelligence suggests that these questions are now recognized by researchers as future priorities.

Several reviews of the field have been published in the past decade (Deary, 2000; Deluca & Kalmar, 2007; Jensen, 2006; Roberts & Stankov, 1999). It is clear from these reviews, however, that although mental speed is widely recognized as a facet of intelligence, there is divergent opinion about the nature of this association. Brand (1996) held speed and intelligence to be isomorphic. Eysenck (1987) gave mental speed primacy as a fundamental cognitive variable that, together with aspects of personality, was responsible for individual differences in intelligence. He also speculated that accuracy of neuronal transmission might provide the biological basis to mental speed. Jensen's position has been similar but with a focus on speed as central to his definition for Spearman's *g*, that is, the first unrotated principal component extracted from performance on a battery of ability tests. Deary (2000) considered restricting intelligence to a general factor to be too narrow a description of human abilities and allowed that mental speed could prove to be more closely aligned with some specific cognitive abilities than with a general ability.

Others have pointed out that speed-IQ correlation could reflect individual differences in attentional and memory processes applied in all tasks, rather than a basic rate of processing at a biological level (Carlson, Jensen, & Widaman, 1983; Detterman, 1987; Hunt, 1980; Mackintosh, 1998; Marr & Sternberg, 1987). Alternatively, as demonstrated by substantial practice effects on elementary cognitive tasks (ECTs, that is, tasks with low knowledge requirements; see later in the chapter), it is possible that higher IQ determines capacity to render response organization more automatic (Rockstroh & Schweizer, 2004).

Studies of cognitive development have pointed to a close association between improving processing speed and WM. Thus, Fry and Hale (2000) described this relationship as part of a "cognitive developmental cascade" whereby cognitive maturation depends on improving processing speed, which results in improved WM, which in turn influences fluid reasoning. Salthouse (1996) has expressed the same idea, but in reverse, to account for cognitive aging. There are grounds, however, to question whether the simple cascade model provides a sufficient account for cognitive performance, either in older or younger adults. Thus, Gregory, Nettelbeck, Howard, and Wilson (2009) reported a direct path between age and WM for elderly participants that excluded speed differences; and Conway, Cowan, Bunting, Therriault, and Minkoff (2002) found strong support for a model wherein WM in young adults strongly predicted fluid reasoning whereas processing speed did not. Following Engle, Tuholski, Laughlin, and Conway (1999), they suggested that strong correlation between WM and general ability may reflect executive attentional processes.

Recent research, particularly within Germany, has explored relationships between attention, WM, speed, and intelligence. Buehner, Krumm, Ziegler, and Pluecken (2006) provide a good example of this approach, set within debate about whether WM and intelligence are essentially isomorphic (Kyllonen & Christal, 1990) or substantially independent (Ackerman, Beier, & Boyle, 2005). Buehner et al. used an extensive test battery, requiring up to nine hours of testing for timing and accuracy on tests of WM, sustained attention, intelligence, and two-choice RT to diverse verbal, numerical, and spatial stimuli. They found that aspects of WM responsible for brief retention of new information and for coordination/integration of operations, rather than a general speed factor, were central to reasoning, but that WM and reasoning were nonetheless distinguishable. Sustained attention was equivalent to coordination. Speed of WM operations, particularly for selective attention, conferred performance advantage, but this was independent from the influence of a general factor derived from all tests of WM, Gf, and Gc. By this account, therefore, speed is essential, but does not provide a sufficient explanation for, intelligence. This conclusion has received strong support from a recent study by Kaufman, DeYoung, Gray, Brown, and Mackintosh (2009). They found that general associative learning, WM, and a composite speed variable (derived from verbal, numerical, and figural speed tests) all had incremental validity for a general intelligence factor defined by verbal, perceptual reasoning and mental rotation abilities.

We have already raised earlier the possibility that mental speed is multifaceted. In fact, within psychometric theory, Horn consistently raised doubts about speed as a unitary process, distinguishing between broad group factors for speediness (Gs; quick responding on very simple tasks) and correct decision speed (CDS; responding speed on cognitively demanding tasks) while acknowledging that CDS has been less reliably identified (Horn & Noll, 1997). Further, Danthiir, Wilhelm, and Schacht (2005) found distinguishable but correlated CDS factors that related to Gf and Gc, respectively, but that resulted from confounding between speed, ability levels, and item difficulty. Similar to Sternberg (1977), Danthiir et al. found that although more intelligent participants were generally quicker overall, they took longer than less intelligent participants on the most difficult items. As Danthiir et al. pointed out, irrespective of whether these differences reflected task characteristics like higher complexity of difficult items, or person characteristics like more persistence among smarter participants, they did not support a simple explanation for higher reasoning in terms of faster basic processing.

Carroll's (1993) taxonomy for intelligence included Gs as a second-stratum factor, which he distinguished from processing speed (Gt) and psychomotor speed (Gp) components from ECTs. It has not always been clear, however, that such theoretical distinctions have been justified by empirical evidence. Confusion about what constructs different tests represent has sometimes been the consequence of different assessment traditions, for example, neuropsychological versus psychometric. For example, Krumm, Schmidt-Atzert, Michalczyk, and Danthiir (2008) found that a latent variable sustained attention (a neuropsychological construct) was virtually indistinguishable from psychometric Gs, which, however, closely resembled Carroll's psychometric Gt.

Roberts and Stankov (1999) provided detailed consideration of methodological issues that research should confront and reported a large-scale investigation of speed in relation to a hierarchical, multivariate model of intelligence. Their battery included multiple ECTs and psychometric tests representing seven of the nine broad group factors that define Horn's Gf-Gc theory. Roberts and Stankov concluded that mental speed is complex and described by a hierarchical model with a broad cognitive speed factor extracted from five separable, less broad speed factors and located on the same level as their seven broad cognitive abilities.

Jensen's (2006) comprehensive overview of the history of "mental chronometry" is the most recent substantial account of research in this field and it is clear that he remains convinced that an emerging "science of chronometry" can further understanding of intelligence. Both Roberts and Stankov (1999) and Jensen (2006) emphasized that before attempting to answer how mental speed relates to intelligence, there are two fundamental theoretical issues to be addressed by future research. The first is how best to describe intelligence; and the second is to determine whether speed is better represented as unitary or multifaceted.

Defining Intelligence

Many researchers correlating individual differences in ECTs with differences in intelligence have assumed that a single test like Raven's Progressive Matrices provided a sufficient account of intelligence, a practice criticized by Juhel (1991) as inadequate. However, although we have witnessed growing acceptance during the past two decades that relying on a single test as a marker for intelligence is not adequate, the definition of intelligence accepted for much of the research with ECTs still lacks consensual definition. Jensen (1998) has argued that "intelligence" is so vague as to be scientifically useless, proposing instead that the core aspect of mental ability be represented by Spearman's *g*. Others have disagreed, arguing that although a general factor represents commonality among whichever tests comprise the test battery, this will reflect different content across batteries, so that other aspects of intelligence, defined by hierarchical psychometric models, should be taken into account (Horn & Noll, 1997; Roberts & Stankov, 1999).

This debate also reflects uncertainty about the causal function of a general factor. Although evidence for psychometric *g* is strong (Jensen, 1998), it does not necessarily follow that there is a single property that is invested in all mental activities. For example, as Detterman (1982) pointed out, individual differences in *g* could be the consequence of relative efficiencies within a system composed of independent functions, like executive control of attention, a perceptual register, WM, long-term memory, and a response mechanism. Although he defined them as separate components, Detterman conceptualized these functions as interrelated within the system because all would be necessary for the system to operate; and in this view all would be involved to varying degrees in all mental activities.

There is now at least considerable agreement among researchers in the field that the psychometric intelligence for which reductionist accounts are sought is multifaceted. Therefore, explanations for individual differences in intelligence require taking account of some 9–10 broad, relatively independent factors that nonetheless share variance that defines a substantial general factor. These broad factors are derived from a larger number of more narrowly defined ability factors, with these in turn defined by performance on a potentially limitless number of tests. Because most hierarchical models require a strong general factor to provide a comprehensive psychometric description of test variance, they accommodate both sides of the long debate about whether intelligence is better described as a single entity or as multiple abilities.

Several different versions of a hierarchical structure have been proposed, but the taxonomy currently attracting widest acceptance derives from the three-stratum account of cognitive abilities advanced by Carroll (1993). Following adoption of Carroll's taxonomy as compatible with Horn's and appropriate to underpin the development of the Woodcock Johnson III Tests of Cognitive Abilities (McGrew, 2005), it has become widely referred to as C-H-C theory (i.e., Cattell-Horn-Carroll). This account of intelligence has explanatory value insofar as test scores can be shown to predict important life outcomes. However, this conception, although multifaceted, does not extend to include suggestions about the importance of practical intelligence or creativity (R. J. Sternberg, 2003), or musical or bodily-kinesthetic abilities (Gardner, 1983), or emotional intelligence (Matthews, Zeidner, & Roberts, 2007).

Speed of Information Processing and Elementary Cognitive Tasks

Different terms have described quick responding – processing speed, cognitive speed, psychometric speed, perceptual speed, and so on. As clarified, speed of information processing is a generic term referring to putative basic processes whereby external events are registered and manipulated, so as to give rise to observable behaviors. Methodology derived from speeded tasks assumes that cognitive processes intervening between stimulus and response can at least be relatively isolated by appropriate manipulation of experimental conditions.

The term *elementary cognitive task* was first coined by John Carroll around 1980 to describe tests of timed performance, assumed to require few cognitive processes, that could be completed satisfactorily by anyone in the absence of time constraints (see Carroll, 1993, pp. 11–13). Current acceptance that speed of information processing, after all, may be an important aspect of intelligence dates from the last four decades of the 20th century. This research has focused on correlations between ECTs and scores on a diverse range of IQ tests, foremost among these being the Wechsler scales and matrices tests like Raven's and Cattell's.

Deary (2000) criticized use of the term ECT – and others, like speed of information processing, perceptual speed, and mental speed – as lacking explanatory value because they have remained poorly defined. Various speed terms have been used interchangeably, implying that all mean the same thing, although this has not been established. Arguably, however, although such terms reflect limited current understanding, they do capture aspects of mental activities that are intrinsic to human nature. Moreover, they are what we currently have to work with and theoretical formulation of some kind is a necessary first step to scientific progress. Thus, it does not follow that because a construct is poorly understood, future improvement in understanding is impossible.

It is also apparent that the complexity of content of different speeded tasks varies. Thus, Jensen (1998) has maintained that information-processing speed is different from Gs, typically measured from pencil–and-paper psychometric tests. Most recently, Jensen (2006) has raised the possibility that speed from more simple RT tasks might be distinguishable from speed on tasks developed to tap more complex cognitive processes. Detterman (1987) earlier outlined a possible way forward on issues of this kind: to use factor analysis to clarify the definition of commonalities among and specificities within multiple speeded tasks and then to test these structures against multifaceted models for intelligence. Although some researchers have followed this path (Burns & Nettelbeck, 2003; Danthiir, Wilhelm, Schulze et al., 2005; Neubauer & Bucik, 1996; Roberts & Stankov, 1999), the matter is certainly not yet resolved (Jensen, 2006). As foreshadowed earlier, debate continues about whether there are individual differences in different kinds of processing speed that are specific to different capacities or in a single, basic speed construct (Anderson, 1992), although most recent evidence suggests that speed is multifaceted (Danthiir et al., 2009).

Widespread use of the term *ECT* today is principally the consequence of its adoption by Jensen (e.g., 1998), the most prolific researcher during the past 30 years of a relationship between speeded performance and intelligence. Attempts to better understand the nature of intelligence by the study of ECTs rest on the reductionist assumption that such tasks, although not strictly biological, predominantly isolate low-level processes that operate to generate and manipulate knowledge within storage and retrieval structures. This theory holds that individual differences in measures of intelligence, and therefore in real-life achievements, are to some extent the consequence of differences in ECT performance. Broadly, two different approaches to measuring processing speed have been used: reaction time (RT), whereby the time of making a detection or discrimination is measured by the duration between a presented stimulus and the registration of a reaction; and inspection time (IT), whereby the time to make a decision is inferred from accuracy of judgments under time constraints but without requiring quick reactions.

Jensen's Studies of Reaction Times

The most comprehensive body of data assembled to test the theory that processes responsible for speed on ECTs are the same as those responsible for complex intelligent actions comes from Jensen's studies of simple and choice RTs, made principally from the late 1970s through the 1980s. Jensen (1982, 1987, 1998, 2006) has provided extensive accounts of this research involving more than 2,000 participants, which has been reviewed by several authors (Carroll, 1987; Deary, 2000, 2003; Longstreth, 1984; Mackintosh, 1998; Nettelbeck, 1998; Neubauer,

1997). Although reviewers have not reached consensus about how Jensen's results should be interpreted, there is now general agreement that stronger correlations can be found between RT and intelligence tests than was previously thought.

Jensen adopted an apparatus designed to decouple a decision time (DT) from movement time (MT) in a two-stage responding process (see Figure 19.1 and Jensen, 2006, pp. 27–29, for detailed description). Jensen's main objective was to test the hypothesis that individual differences in the slope of the linear regression of latency on the number of target alternatives (expressed as binary logarithmic transformations) are the principal source of correlations between RT and intelligence (Hick, 1952). Specifically, if DT taps processing speed, then flatter slopes should reflect higher intelligence, whereas MT should be constant across degrees of choice and therefore not correlate with intelligence. This hypothesis has been tested, predominantly using scores on Raven's Matrices as an index for general intelligence, by comparing groups with different average abilities and by within-group correlation between various parameters of distributions of DT and MT with intelligence scores. In some instances, substantial correlations have been demonstrated between latency and intelligence measures; but results have generally not supported the hypothesis.

Although group data have generally conformed closely to Hick's theory, individual data have fitted less well. Moreover, following Longstreth (1984), several critics have challenged Jensen's interpretation, which attributes a causal function to processing speed. Subsequent consideration has probably successfully discounted alternative explanations for the observed correlations in terms of cognitive strategies reflecting sundry methodological variables (configuration of potential targets, order of presentation for choice alternatives, putative visual attentional biases linked to set size, different set sizes requiring different physical responses, opportunities for speed-accuracy trade-off). Nor were these correlations the consequence of speed constraints on intelligence items (Vernon, 1987). It is possible, nonetheless, that Jensen's procedure provided insufficient practice to discount a possibility that higher IQ participants adapted to task requirements more efficiently (Nettelbeck, 1985).

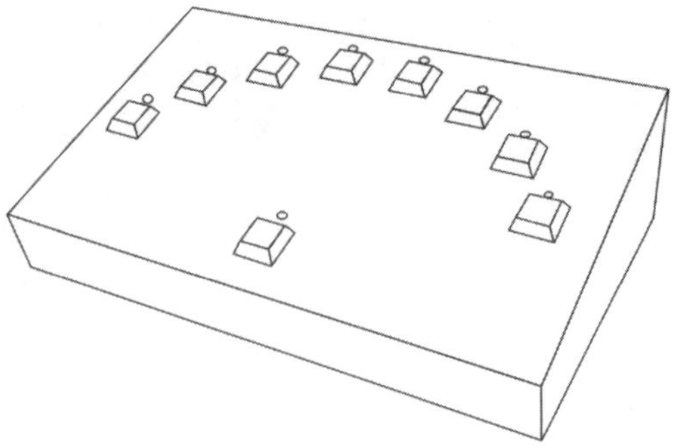

Figure 19.1. Reaction time apparatus, following Jensen (1987). The eight alternative stimulus lights are equidistant from the home button. When a stimulus light is illuminated, two timers register (i) time to lift-off from the home button (decision time); and (ii) time from lift-off to turning off the target (movement time).

Most critically, however, correlations involving individual regression slopes (proposed by Hick, 1952, to capture information-processing speed) were not reliably stronger than those involving other parameters of RT, like regression intercept for DT, mean or median DT, or even MT. Using multiple regression, Jensen demonstrated that different combinations of latency variables can account for as much as about 50% of variance in intelligence scores. However, such analyses did not identify an optimal set of parameters that might advance explanation for the correlation. Particularly troublesome have been significant correlations involving MT because the theory provides no basis for these. A likely explanation is that these have reflected confounding between DT and MT as a consequence of occasional early detection responses (i.e., an as-yet unlocated illuminated target is detected but before the discrimination judgment has formed; Smith & Carew, 1987).

Nonetheless, although Deary (2000, p. 181) concluded that attempts to decompose RT into underlying cognitive constructs were not convincing, the accumulated evidence led him to believe that correlations between RTs and psychometric ability were sufficiently substantial to warrant continuing interest. In his subsequent comments on this matter (Deary, 2003), he noted that the more complex response actions required with Jensen's apparatus may have introduced unexpected top-down strategic processes and that future work should therefore rely on the traditional apparatus (individual fingers for alternative responses). However, whether adopting the earlier techniques will improve prospects for advancing knowledge is, at this time, unclear. Deary's point was well made. Arguably, however, all ECTs are to some extent confounded by idiosyncratic cognitive strategies that cannot be excluded (Nettelbeck, 1998), and although this need not be a critical obstacle to progress if acceptably robust construct validity for such tasks can be established, it may be that different kinds of apparatuses will prove to be better suited to different circumstances. For example, removing or reducing motor influences from responding requirements could be more of an issue for elderly than for younger respondents.

Deary (2003) made two further points for future consideration. First, relying on untransformed data from simple and choice RT conditions, rather than continuing with parameters extracted from the Hick function, should be more tractable for theory buiding. Second, despite a very large body of research published in this area, the effect size of the RT-intelligence correlation had not yet been determined. Deary, Der, and Ford (2001) addressed the second question for a large representative sample of Scottish men and women in their 50s who were participants in a large, ongoing population-based study, begun in 1988. Scores on a widely used British test of general mental ability (Alice Heim Part 1; AH4) correlated with simple and four-choice RT. Corrected for test unreliability, "true" effect size was about −.5, independent from sex, social class, and education, confirming Deary's conviction that there is a substantial relationship to be explained.

In a follow-up after 13 years, Deary, Allehand, and Der (2009) applied cross-lagged correlational analyses to test the hypothesis that faster processing speed is responsible for more successful cognitive aging. The rationale for this design rests on the assumption that correlation between antecedent and subsequent variables establishes consequence, from former to latter. Structural equation modeling defined latent factors for processing speed from simple and four-choice RT at both baseline and time 2; and latent factors for intelligence from the AH4 tests. Correlations between latent speed and ability factors were as expected from the 2001 study, (−.49 and −.41 for times 1 and 2, respectively). However, contrary to prediction, only the path from the first latent ability factor to the later processing speed factor was statistically significant (−.21), leading the authors to suggest that "higher general intelligence might be associated with lifestyle and other factors that preserve processing speed" (p. 40). This may be so; but, as outlined later in the section titled Inspection Time, it does not exclude the possibility that antecedent measures of processing speed can predict subsequent cognitive integrity. It is possible too that Deary et al.'s (2009) result owed something to the relatively low test-retest reliability of their speed construct (.49 compared to .89 for the ability factor). Indeed, insofar as their RT apparatus confounded cognitive and motor responding (a problem that Jensen's apparatus tends to reduce), this outcome may have reflected deteriorating motor dexterity in 69-year-olds.

Variability of Individual Reaction Times

Recent theoretical interest about how RT relates to intelligence has tended to shift from measures of central tendency in RT to variability in trial-to-trial performance. This has followed observations (Baumeister & Kellas, 1968; Brewer & Smith, 1984; Jensen, 1987) that even between groups with widely disparate abilities, fastest RTs differ little, and differences are captured by the extent to which individual distributions are positively skewed. When a respondent's RTs within a set condition are ranked from fastest to slowest, within-rank correlation with intelligence increases from the fastest to the slowest RTs. This finding has resulted in a focus on *worst performance* (WP; Larson & Alderton, 1990). Variability of responding also increases systematically as RTs slow, implying that it is increasing unreliability of responding that is responsible for higher correlation between intelligence and worst-performance RTs. The relationship appears to apply for cognitive abilities that have higher *g*-loading but not for tasks that do not. Moreover, mean levels of WP reliably differentiate between groups with different mean IQs when RTs in these groups are measured by the same procedures, principally because more marked skewing of RT distributions is related to lower intelligence.

Coyle (2003) reviewed relevant research, including consideration of possible causes for these relationships. He acknowledged that WP could reflect psychological variables like lapses in attention or WM but argued that these can represent functioning at a fundamental biological level rather than top-down cognitive influences influenced by conceptual knowledge. He favored Jensen's theory of individual differences in rate of neural oscillations and outlined an agenda for future WP research.

More recently, Schmiedek, Oberauer, Schmiedek et al. (2007) have drawn from three previously largely separate strands of research to test whether efficiency of RT performance relates to intelligence. First, they pointed out that reliability of WP analyses derived from separate RT bands is limited by small numbers of trials within bands. However, the ex-Gaussian distribution (a normal-like distribution obtained by convolving a Gaussian with an exponential distribution) provides an appropriate description for RT distributions. Specifically, in addition to mean and standard deviation, the distribution parameter tau (τ) integrates information from all trials but predominantly reflects skewness, particularly at the extreme tail. Tau is therefore sensitive to the slowest RTs; and Schmiedek et al. noted evidence that linked τ with fluctuation in attention. Second, Schmiedek et al. considered evidence that WM and reasoning (core abilities to *g*) reflect attentional control, both over distraction and for maintaining focus. This theory therefore predicts that slower RT is the consequence of poorer executive attention, which impacts WM, which in turn impacts reasoning ability. Third, however, Schmiedek et al. sought an alternative to attention as a causal explanation, drawing on the diffusion model of choice RT (Ratcliff & Smith, 2004). This is a *random walk* model for two-choice decision making that assumes that information on which a decision is reached is accumulated sequentially over time. The two most critical parameters of this model for current discussion are the *response criterion* (i.e., level of information required before responding) and *drift rate* (mean rate of decision making). Because drift rate is essentially an index for the quality of information processed, it should be the most sensitive to slower RTs and therefore most related to τ.

Latent trait analyses of multiple tasks for WM, reasoning, and RTs for verbal classification, quantitative decision, and spatial orientation tasks confirmed commonalities within parameters across different tasks. Reaction time (mean, SD, τ) accounted for more than 50% of variance in working memory and reasoning factors; but τ showed stronger correlations with the cognitive traits (around −.7). Similarly, compared with parameters for response criterion and nondecision components of RT, drift rate extracted from a scaled-down diffusion model was by far the strongest predictor of WM (.68) and reasoning (.79).

These results were consistent with theory that lower intelligence reflects poorer executive control but, as Schmiedek et al. argued, they could also mean that differences in τ, representing efficiency of information processing, can provide a more parsimonious account. They tested this idea by simulating model and distribution parameters, demonstrating that the strong correlation between τ and the WM factor was wholly accounted for by drift rate. A second simulation introduced trial-to-trial variability into drift rate, to represent occasional lapses of attention that could interrupt information accumulation. This simulation produced lower τ-WM correlation than was determined empirically, so that it was improbable that the observed correlation was due to attentional fluctuations, although not excluding this possibility.

Schmiedek et al.'s account therefore avoided introducing an attentional construct in addition to drift rate. To account for what is responsible for the efficiency construct, these authors proposed their theory that the function of WM is to make and maintain temporary "bindings" between stimulus and response representations. (Binding is the mechanism whereby separate elements of knowledge are accessed within memory and coordinated and synthesized as required, to produce new knowledge.) This theory therefore holds that efficiency of the binding mechanism located in WM, which relies on consistency in speeded performance, is central to intelligence. This work represents an advance and sets a promising future research agenda that focuses on the relevance of individual differences in response variability to improved understanding of differences in intelligence.

Inspection Time

Inspection time (IT) was conceived by Douglas Vickers around 1970 as a fundamental limitation on the rate at which external information critical to making a decision can be accumulated in temporary sensory stores. Vickers' theory was heavily influenced by earlier ideas about a "perceptual moment" (Stroud, 1956) and limitations to processing efficiency dictated by "single channel operation" (Welford, 1968). (See also Lehrl and Fischer, 1990, for their account of the history of such ideas within the German information-processing tradition).

Vickers proposed an optional-stopping, random walk model of decision making whereby information is initially briefly stored at an early stage of visual processing by a series of discrete sequential samples ("inspections") from proximal stimulation, made against a background of "noise" both internal and external, in accordance with an internally held standard for what constitutes sufficient evidence to permit a decision. The duration of an inspection, which determined the rate at which information is accumulated, was held to be independent from the criterion for sufficient evidence. The measurement of IT was operationalized as the minimum time to accumulate sufficient information to make a decision with high reliability about which of two highly discriminable lines of different lengths was longer (or shorter).

Several challenges to the construct validity for this account of IT have been acknowledged (Deary, 2000; Nettelbeck, 2001). Here, IT is used to refer to the measure, not a putative sampling mechanism. Figure 19.2 illustrates a current version of this task. Alternative targets are briefly displayed, with duration varying in accordance with the viewer's accuracy. Consistent accuracy results in shortened target duration but an error results in lengthened duration. Exposure duration is set by presentation of a second figure, termed a backward pattern mask, which disrupts perception of the target. Phenomenologically the target disappears, becoming integrated with the contours of the masking figure. Based on theory advanced by Turvey (1973), Nettelbeck and Wilson (1985) demonstrated by experiment that this masking effect was located centrally, beyond the peripheral visual system.

The viewer indicates whether the shorter (or longer) line was located to left or right but speed of this response is not relevant to the determination of IT. Instead, processing speed is inferred from accuracy of performance under conditions that limit exposure of the target to the duration between the target onset and the onset of the mask that follows (stimulus-onset-asynchrony SOA). IT has been measured by different methods, with different criteria for accuracy, and

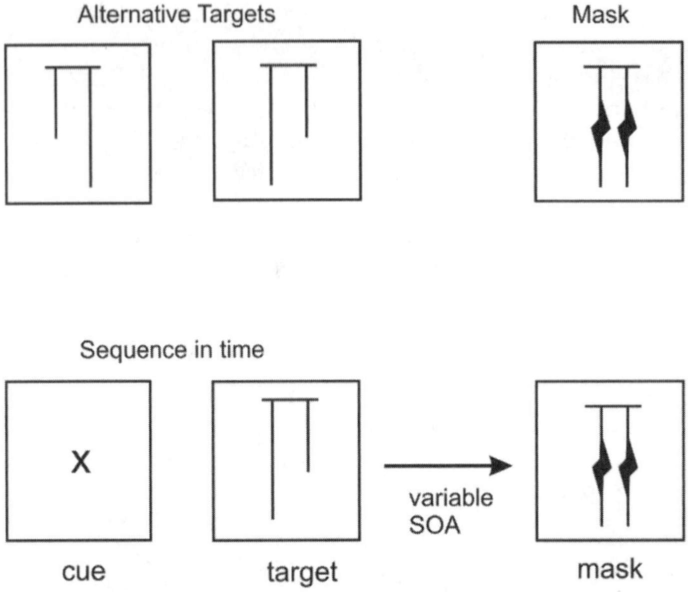

Figure 19.2. A procedure for measuring visual inspection time.

using different targets and a variety of masking procedures.

There have been attempts to measure IT in other sensory modalities, on grounds that similar results across modalities would strengthen the conclusion that IT tapped central, not peripheral, processes. The first such task, developed by Brand and Deary (1982), required auditory discrimination between two tones presented for varying lengths of time as either high-low or low-high sequences. Just as in the visual IT paradigm, the critical variable was the shortest tone duration at which a listener achieved specified high accuracy. Subsequently, other researchers devised different versions of this task that manipulated the pitch difference between the tones or used different forms of auditory masking. However, problems in achieving effective masking, together with the realization that 35% to 50% of participants encountered difficulty in completing the task, led Olsson, Björkman, Haag, and Juslin (1998) to develop a task in which loud-soft or soft-loud alternatives replaced pitch discrimination (see Deary, 2000, chapter 7, for a detailed account of this work). Parker, Crawford, and Stephen (1999) developed an auditory discrimination task that requires locating a target tone in space, with tone duration at which high accuracy is achieved as the critical variable. Zajac and Burns (2007) have recently compared performance of children aged 10–12 years on both visual IT and auditory IT requiring spatial location. They concluded that both versions, together with a coding task (Gs), shared sufficient variance to implicate common central processes. However, correlations between the three tasks were markedly stronger for children with slower ITs, implying that children with faster and slower ITs may be using different strategies. Only one study (Nettelbeck & Kirby, 1983) has sought to measure IT in the touch modality, and this encountered a problem with diminishing tactile sensitivity as a consequence of direct stimulation. To summarize, only limited attempts have been made to measure IT in different sensory modalities, with most research limited to visual IT.

Correlation Between IT and IQ

The first actualization of the now widely applied visual version of IT (Vickers, Nettelbeck, & Willson, 1972) was observed by Nettelbeck and Lally (1976) to correlate with

IQ. The considerable body of research generated by this initial finding has been previously reviewed on a number of occasions and the interested reader is referred to Brand and Deary (1982), Deary (2000, chapter 7), Deary and Stough (1996), and Nettelbeck (1987, 2001, 2003).

Nettelbeck and Lally's assumption that IT represented early perceptual efficiency, and might therefore reveal some basic aspect of intelligence, was soon challenged by suggestions that those with higher IQ performed more effectively than those with lower IQ on simple and complex tasks alike because they were capable of generating better learning strategies, including being prepared to try harder (Mackintosh, 1986). Deary (2000, chapter 7) has provided a detailed review of research that has attempted to resolve this matter, concluding that there was no evidence to suppose that the relationship was principally the consequence of better learning strategies or motivation or the effects of personality. This conclusion is challenged, however, by evidence that extended practice tends to reduce range of individual differences in IT (Nettelbeck & Vita, 1992) and that even limited task experience can produce larger improvement in children's ITs than maturation (Anderson, Reid, & Nelson, 2001). Currently, it remains plausible that IT taps some low-level aspect of perceptual learning (Burns, Nettelbeck, McPherson, & Stankov, 2007).

Nonetheless, 25 years of research into the relationship between IT and IQ (Grudnik & Kranzler, 2001) has established that a moderately strong correlation exists. Grudnick and Kransler's meta-analyses were based on more than 4,000 participants in 92 studies – 62 involving adults and 30 with children. Ten studies involved auditory IT; but the mean correlations with IQ from auditory and visual tasks were virtually identical. Across all studies, the uncorrected mean correlation was –.3. Corrected for sampling error, attenuation and range variation, this correlation was –.51. The mean corrected correlation among children was slightly lower (–.44) but still substantial. Corrected correlation for self-identified strategy users (those who acknowledge associating apparent movement cues with the shorter line when the backward mask appears) was statistically significantly lower that that for nonusers (–.60 and –.77 respectively), although still substantial. Clearly, this result was consistent with Egan's (1994) conclusion that IT-IQ correlation is not explained simply by assuming that smarter people have access to smarter strategies for both easy and more challenging tasks. Reliability of IT, estimated for both test-retest and internal consistency, was good, averaging .8.

Inspection Time as a Lead Marker for Unfavorable Aging

Although noticeable decline in WM and fluid abilities accompanies normal aging, particularly beyond the sixth decade, chronological age (CA) is a poor predictor for individual functioning because different functions change at different rates, highly practiced skills may be relatively protected, and, despite average trends, there are marked individual differences in onset and progress of age-related changes accepted as normal. Moreover, some individuals experience more severe decline, which may reflect the impact of age-related dementia-type diseases, the prevalence of which increases with old age. A major challenge is therefore to develop quantitative lead markers that can detect early preclinical signs of deterioration before this becomes established. It is assumed that if this could be successfully done, further decline might be prevented by appropriate intervention. Although there is currently debate about the effectiveness of available interventions (Salthouse, 2006), a considerable body of recent research has provided grounds for optimism (Hertzog, Kramer, Wilson, & Lindenberger, 2008). Related to this prospect, recent research has suggested that slower and/or slowing IT may provide a *biomarker* for less favorable aging (Gregory, Callaghan, Nettelbeck, & Wilson, 2009; Gregory, Nettelbeck, Howard, & Wilson, 2008; Gregory, Nettelbeck, & Wilson, 2009).

Birren and Fisher (1992) have set out requirements for a quantitative biomarker; and IT meets several of these. It is noninvasive, convenient, and reliable, with low knowledge requirements; it isolates cognitive performance from motor competence; and it monitors a process that reflects normal age-related cognitive decline, slowing steadily and appreciably across adulthood (Nettelbeck et al., 2008). It is also sensitive to abnormal cognitive decline in people with mild cognitive impairment (Bonney et al., 2006) and Alzheimer's disease (Deary, Hunter, Langan, & Goodwin, 1991).

Most important, Gregory et al. (2008) have shown that ITs from elderly persons aged 70–91 predict performances 18 months later on fluid reasoning, WM and decline in WM over this time. Moreover, slowing IT from baseline across both 6 and 18 months correlated with fluid reasoning 18 months later. These results were not found with concurrent physiological measures for grip strength, systolic blood pressure, and visual acuity. Follow-up 42 months from baseline (Gregory, Nettelbeck, & Wilson, 2009) showed that IT trajectories across this time were markedly different depending on whether participants at 42 months showed incipient cognitive decline not apparent at baseline. For those with only marginally poorer recall and recognition memory, ITs had slowed appreciably at a constant rate, whereas ITs were unchanged for those without signs of memory decline. Gregory et al. (2009) examined the potential relevance of slower IT for future practical, everyday functioning by comparing two samples of elderly persons matched at baseline for age, gender, education, and visual acuity, but with initial nonoverlapping distributions for faster and slower ITs. At baseline the two samples did not differ for self-reported functioning on activities of daily living such as housekeeping, gardening, shopping, and moving around their communities. However, direct observations of performances 42 months later on everyday tasks (understanding medication instructions, telephone use, managing finances, understanding instructions for food preparation) clearly confirmed that those persons with initially slower ITs now made more errors and were slower on the tasks of everyday functioning. To summarize, slowing IT in old age predicted subsequent decline in cognitive and everyday functioning well before these changes were detectable. This result strongly suggests that IT is sensitive to changes in basic processes. What those processes are has not been determined; but the tasks of everyday functioning all relied substantially on WM. Taken together with Gregory et al.'s (2008) finding that IT predicted WM functioning at 18 months and decline over this time, these results raise the possibility that the IT task measures speed of some basic aspect of WM.

The Nature of Inspection Time

Crawford, Deary, Allan, and Gustafsson (1998) were first to attempt to locate IT within a psychometric model for intelligence. They found that IT loaded only weakly on an orthogonal general factor defined by all WAIS-R subtests but moderately on a broad perceptual-organization factor defined by the Performance subtests. There was no relationship between IT and the group factor attention-concentration although some research has implicated attention as responsible for IT differences (Bors, Stokes, Forrin, & Hodder, 1999; Fox, Roring, & Mitchum, 2009; Nettelbeck & Young, 1989). Results similar to Crawford et al.'s were reported for children by Petrill (Petrill et al., 2001), using the Wechsler Intelligence Scale for Children–Revised (WISC-R) to define orthogonal broad factors for verbal, performance, and freedom-from-distractibility, together with a strong psychometric general factor (*g*). Confirmatory factor analysis found that several ECTs combined to define a latent speed trait that shared substantial variance with *g*. IT shared variance with the speed factor but predominantly contributed to performance and *g* via substantial residual paths. Thus, IT predicted *g* by two pathways; one shared variance with other ECTs but the other reflected different sources of variance unique to IT.

These results are consistent with speculation that IT is psychologically complex (Nettelbeck, 2001); and also with a suggestion by Gregory et al. (2008) that IT is linked with WM, at least in elderly persons.

Mackintosh and Bennett (2002) tested relationships between IT and markers for Gc, Gf, and Gs, concluding that IT correlated with Gs. Similarly, Burns and Nettelbeck (2003) used a test battery selected to return broad factors from Gf-Gc theory of Gf, Gc, Gs, Gv (visual processing) and Gsm (short-term memory), and included two different methods for estimating IT, as well as a backward masking task involving alphanumeric stimuli and up to four degrees of choice. All of these tasks loaded strongly on Gs, which in turn loaded strongly on a general factor, although the strength of this association doubtless reflected speed constraints on many of the tests in this battery. Subsequent unpublished analyses have established strong commonality among these three tasks, thereby defining a latent IT variable with high loading on the general factor.

Burns and Nettelbeck (2003) also included "odd-man-out" RT (Frearson & Eysenck, 1986). For each trial, three stimulus lights on the panel of the apparatus in Figure 19.1 are illuminated so that two are adjacent and one is farther away. The required response is a fast reaction to the latter. Unlike IT, performance on this task loaded strongly on Gf, suggesting that the two tasks measure different processes. However, O'Connor and Burns (2003) obtained results that questioned this conclusion.

O'Connor and Burns used exploratory and confirmatory factor analysis to locate IT within a hierarchical model for different speed factors derived from traditional perceptual speed tasks, choice and odd-man-out RT (decoupled into DT and MT), and cognitively more demanding tasks involving evaluation and manipulation of digit and letter displays. IT correlated with group factors visualization speed and perceptual speed, which together with decision time and movement time defined a general factor Gs. However, the IT-perceptual speed correlation was entirely accounted for by correlation between visualization speed and perceptual speed. In short, this study found four different kinds of speed, with IT relating to only one. The correlation between IT and IQ depended on Gs via visualization speed, defined in terms of an ability to visualize complex rules, principally about how triplets of ordinal digits were presented. However, odd-man-out DT also had its strongest loading on visualization speed, contrary to Burns and Nettelbeck's result. Thus, whether IT taps processes different from those measured by the odd-man-out task remains unresolved.

Basic Processes

Belief is now widespread that measures of IT and RT tap individual differences in a fundamental, biological property of the CNS that limits speed of information processing (Madden, 2001). Nonetheless, evidence for this theory is suggestive rather than conclusive. As Mackintosh (1998, p. 246) has pointed out, as correlation between IQ and RT principally reflects a capacity of those with higher IQ to avoid the slower responding that characterizes the performance of those with lower IQs, this must mean that RT involves more than the speed of nerve conduction.

Event-related potential (ERP) recordings – made at the scalp of changes in cortical activity following presentation of target stimuli – have found correlations between IQ and the latency, rise time, amplitude, and complexity of waveforms, particularly the positive peaks found approximately 100–300ms after stimulus onset (Deary, 2000). However, Deary has cautioned against accepting such results as establishing direct links between intelligence and basic biological speed differences. Limits to current knowledge mean that there is uncertainty about the nature of ongoing brain activities that are captured by the ERP (Burns, Nettelbeck, & Cooper, 2000). For example, these may reflect "neural adaptability" (Schafer, 1985) – that is, the effectiveness of processing strategies, not differences in speed of neuronal transmission.

A recent procedure developed by Sculthorpe, Stelmack, and Campbell (2009) as a variant on the widely used "oddball" ERP task may have potential for addressing this theoretically important distinction. Sculthorpe et al.'s task differed from the parent version in a number of respects not important here, but, in common, required detection of occasional deviant auditory stimuli located within a common pattern of tone sequences. Critically, their version included both an active detection condition and a passive condition (concurrent reading task with the sequence of tone stimuli presented but ignored). Electrophysiological responses to the unattended deviant stimuli were measured by "mismatch negativity" (MMN) – amplitude departures from the standard level of activity (regular tone patterns) in the time frame 110–350 ms following a deviant stimulus. As predicted by earlier research, higher IQ participants were more effective (shorter latencies; higher amplitudes in the ERP P300 component; shorter, less variable RTs) at detecting pattern "violations." Most important, similar results held for MMN in the passive condition. The authors argued that because attention was focused on the reading task in the passive condition, these results excluded involvement of higher level conscious processes. This argument relies on the difficult to confirm assumption that participants complied with instructions; but comparison of average ERP waveforms across the active and passive conditions was consistent with this interpretation, and this paradigm therefore offers promise for future research of this kind.

There have been attempts to relate intelligence to more direct measures of speed of information transmission in the CNS. Thus, Vernon and Mori (1992) reported low-moderate correlations between peripheral nerve conduction velocity (NCV) in the arms, general RT extracted from several RT tasks and general psychometric intelligence, but they also found that the RT-IQ correlation did not depend on NVC. Reed and Jensen (1992; Reed, Vernon, & Johnson, 2004) tried to estimate individual differences in brain NVC and correlate these with measures of intelligence and with RT (Reed & Jensen, 1993). However, although Reed and Jensen (1993) found low but statistically significant correlations between NCV and nonverbal IQ and between nonverbal IQ and choice RT, the expected correlation between NCV and choice RT was not found. Reviews of these and similar studies have concluded that results have not been convincing (Deary, 2000; Vernon, Wickett, Bazana, & Stelmack, 2000).

Strachan et al. (2001) attempted to clarify relations between NCV, psychometric speeded tasks, and ECTs by experiment. They manipulated the blood glucose levels of healthy participants while measuring performance on RT and IT. As predicted by knowledge about the effects of hypoglycemia, lowered blood glucose resulted in significant slowing on all tasks; but this did not affect the velocity of motor nerve conduction in the arms or legs of participants. This result suggests that speed measured by these tasks is not at the level of nerve conduction. Although differences in neural transmission time may account for some small part of variance in cognitive functioning, RT and IT differences do not appear to reflect these.

Recent twin studies have reported that IT has moderate heritability (Edmonds et al., 2008; Luciano et al., 2001; Luciano et al., 2004; Posthuma, de Geus, & Boomsma, 2001). Correlation between IT and IQ has been accounted for by common genetic influences. Patterns of results have been similar for children, adolescents, young adults, and middle-aged adults and for males and females. Consistent results have been found for two-choice RT (Luciano et al., 2004).

Demonstrating that a trait is in part heritable implicates biological processes but does not of itself establish that these are low-level, as opposed to top-down, strategic processes. A demonstration by Deary et al. (2001) using functional resonance imaging technology during IT performance is similarly difficult to interpret. Deary et al. found that areas of brain activation during a difficult discrimination condition (short SOA) and deactivation during an easy condition (long SOA) overlapped with areas in the lateral frontal cortex that Duncan et al. (2000) proposed are the basis for *g*. These results are consistent with the theory that IT and abstract problem solving share common processes but do not reveal the direction of causality. Luciano et al. (2004) acknowledged that their results would be equally well explained by a top-down explanation involving attention. Similarly, Edmonds et al. (2008) noted substantial correlations between IT and neuropsychological functions, including attention/executive, language, and memory, all of which were substantially correlated with IQ. However, Posthuma et al. (2001) have considered a bottom-up account more likely. Drawing on research into conduction velocity in early visual pathways in the monkey brain, they concluded that "genes related to CNS axonal conduction velocity constitute good candidate genes for intelligence" (p. 601). Similarly, both Luciano et al. (2004) and Edmonds et al. (2008) have speculated that processing speed may be related to basic brain characteristics, like the quality of axonal myelination.

A promising line of enquiry, supporting theory that IT does measure basic processes underpinning intelligence, has been pointed by Stough and colleagues (reviewed by Stough, Thompson, Bates, & Nathan, 2001). Their research derived from initial observation that acute nicotine dosage improves speed of processing, vigilance, attention, and memory. Pharmacological theory has implicated nicotine in enhanced synaptic transfer of acetylcholine. By systematically testing changes in IT coincident with neurochemical interventions, Stough and others have demonstrated that administering nicotine enhances IT whereas blocking nicotinic receptors impairs IT. Other neurotransmitters – serotonin, noradrenaline, and dopamine – which also contribute to effective cognitive performance, were found not to influence IT. Stough et al. have therefore proposed that IT is specifically a marker for the integrity of the cholinergic system, which uses acetylcholine to transmit nerve impulses, and is involved in regulation of memory and learning. These ideas align with the suggestion that processing speed provides a necessary but insufficient condition for intelligence (Nettelbeck & Wilson, 1985) and with Detterman's (1982) model for intelligence as a system of different cognitive functions.

Conclusions

After more than a century beyond Galton's speculations about the bases of intelligence, a growing body of evidence provides support for his ideas. An improved understanding of processing speed will prove fundamental to an understanding of intelligence, but current evidence suggests that speed constructs will not provide a sufficient explanation and, moreover, the influence of speed may be manifest by different pathways. Although the extent to which IT and RT measure the same or different processes is still an open question, there is compelling evidence that correlation between IQ and processing speed estimated by IT or choice RT reflects shared genetic influences. Although these influences might implicate higher order strategic-based processing, the current balance of opinion appears to favor a role for basic perceptual processes. These may rely on the quality of brain white matter communication systems, perhaps even at the level of chemical neurotransmitters responsible for specific functions, although this has not been established and currently there is uncertainty about the influence of white matter abnormalities, which increase with normal aging, on cognitive functioning among healthy elderly persons. There is considerable evidence that white matter lesions are associated with slower processing speed and poorer performance on tests of attention and memory (Gunning-Dixon & Raz, 2000). However, whereas some researchers have found no evidence to link the extent of lesions to intelligence (Gunning-Dixon & Raz, 2000; Rabbitt et al., 2007), others have (Deary et al., 2006; Deary, Leaper, Murray,

Staff, & Whalley, 2003). Deary's studies are persuasive because they have controlled for prior IQ. They found that both IQ measured at age 11 and contemporaneous white matter integrity independently accounted for variance in general cognitive ability in elderly participants, with the latter mediated by standard deviation for simple RT. Moreover, IQ at age 11 predicted both general cognitive ability and white matter integrity some 70 years later. By this account, cognitive integrity throughout life reflects white matter integrity, which determines efficiency of information processing. This is an intriguing scenario; but, clearly, further research is required that better defines more comprehensive models for processing speed, psychometric intelligence, and white-matter structures.

Future Directions

The foregoing account has identified the major questions that future research should attempt to address. An important next step is to determine whether different kinds of speed are required to account for differences in intelligence. It is possible that different ECTs tap different processes underlying different components, all of which contribute to individual differences in intelligence. However, identifying different kinds of speed would not rule out the possibility that there are also individual differences in a general speed factor that reflects some fundamental biological constraint and that has some important explanatory value for understanding differences in higher level abilities. Thus, a clearer definition of basic processes requires that commonalities and specificities within batteries of speeded tasks, that encompass a range of cognitive demand from simple to more complex, are first identified. On current evidence, there should be a focus on response variability rather than relying on measures of central tendency. These endeavors should be theory driven and based on more comprehensive, multivariate models for intelligence than have typically been applied in the past and should attempt, moreover, to encourage closer collaboration between the cognitive, neurological, and psychometric traditions.

Promising directions have been suggested by attempts to establish links between speeded performance and biochemical and neurophysiological features of the brain. Attempts to test the adequacy of statistical models that include the independent contribution of both higher order cognitive constructs and speed variables to intelligence also have potential to improve understanding in reductionist terms. And if it can be established that prior levels of speed and/or changes in speed precede subsequent cognitive changes, this finding would provide powerful evidence for a causal relationship. Research that addresses developmental cascade theory across a longitudinal timeframe, both with children and with elderly adults, would contribute to knowledge here. Of course, it is possible that changing processing speed during childhood and old age has a different role in relation to intelligence than is the case for middle life. Moreover, although improving processing speed during normal childhood development may be the consequence of increasingly complex brain structures, which later deteriorate during normal adult aging, it is also possible that declining processing speed reflects, at least in part, different biological states from those associated with improving speed.

Finally, the major challenge is to ascertain whether the speed of bottom-up processes is primarily responsible for developmental trends and individual differences in higher reasoning abilities, as opposed to whether speed differences are the consequence of top-down strategic functions, or whether both mechanisms interact. These are open questions that so far have proved difficult to resolve, but it is already clear that the potential utility of bottom-up explanation does not exclude the possibility that higher order functions influenced by responding strategies can have a nontrivial explanatory role. In fact, future confirmation that the brain's neural structures have potential to change in response to idiosyncratic behaviors and experience (Doidge, 2007) would point toward theory that bottom-up and top-down processes are inextricably linked.

Acknowledgments

Preparation of this chapter was supported by grant DP0772346 from the Australian Research Council. I am grateful to Nick Burns, Tess Gregory, and Carlene Wilson for their comments on a draft.

References

Ackerman, P. L., Beier, M. E., & Boyle, M. O. (2005). Working memory and intelligence. *Psychological Bulletin*, *131*, 30–60.

Anderson, M., Nettelbeck, T., & Barlow, J. (1997). Reaction time measures of speed of processing: Speed of response selection increases with age but speed of stimulus categorization does not. *British Journal of Developmental Psychology*, *15*, 145–157.

Anderson, M., Reid, C., & Nelson, J. (2001). Developmental changes in inspection time; What a difference a year makes. *Intelligence*, *29*, 475–486.

Baumeister, A. A., & Kellas, G. (1968). Reaction time and mental retardation. In N. R. Ellis (Ed.), *International review of research in mental retardation* (Vol. 3, pp. 163–193). New York, NY: Academic Press.

Birren, J. E., & Fisher, L. M. (1992). Aging and slowing of behavior: Consequences for cognition and survival. In T. B. Sonderegger (Ed.), *Nebraska symposium on motivation 1991* (pp. 1–37). Lincoln: University of Nebraska Press.

Bonney, K. R., Almeida, O. P., Flicker, L., Davies, S., Clarnette, R., Anderson, M., et al. (2006). Inspection time in non-demented older adults with mild cognitive impairment. *Neuropsychologia*, *44*, 1452–1456.

Bors, D. A., Stokes, T. L., Forrin, B., & Hodder, S. L. (1999). Inspection time and intelligence: Practice, strategies and attention. *Intelligence*, *27*, 111–129.

Brand, C. R. (1996). *The g factor: General intelligence and its implications*. Chichester, UK: Wiley.

Brand, C. R., & Deary, I. J. (1982). Intelligence and "inspection time." In H. J. Eysenck (Ed.), *A model for intelligence* (pp. 133–148). New York, NY: Springer-Verlag.

Brewer, N., & Smith, G. A. (1984). How normal and retarded individuals monitor and regulate speed and accuracy of responding in serial choice tasks. *Journal of Experimental Psychology: General*, *113*, 71–93.

Buehner, M., Krumm, S., Ziegler, M., & Pluecken, T. (2006). Cognitive abilities and their interplay: Reasoning, crystallized intelligence, working memory components, and sustained attention. *Journal of Individual Differences*, *27*, 57–72.

Burns, N. R., & Nettelbeck, T. (2003). Inspection time in the structure of cognitive abilities: Where does IT fit? *Intelligence*, *31*, 237–255.

Burns, N. R., Nettelbeck, T., & Cooper, C. J. (2000). Event-related potential correlates of some human cognitive ability constructs. *Personality and Individual Differences*, *29*, 157–168.

Burns, N. R., Nettelbeck, T., McPherson, J., & Stankov, L. (2007). Perceptual learning on inspection time and motion perception. *Journal of General Psychology*, *134*, 83–100.

Carlson, J. S., Jensen, C. M., & Widaman, K. (1983). Reaction time, intelligence and attention. *Intelligence*, *7*, 329–344.

Carroll, J. B. (1987). Jensen's mental chronometry: Some comments and questions. In S. Modgil & C. Modgil (Eds.), *Arthur Jensen: Consensus and controversy* (pp. 297–301 and 310–311). New York, NY: Falmer.

Carroll, J. B. (1993). *Human cognitive abilities: A survey of factor analytic studies*. Cambridge, UK: Cambridge University Press.

Cerella, J. (1985). Information processing rates in the elderly. *Psychological Bulletin*, *98*, 67–83.

Conway, A. R. A., Cowan, N., Bunting, M. F., Therriault, D. J., & Minkoff, S. R. B. (2002). A latent variable analysis of working memory capacity, short-term memory capcity, processing speed, and general fluid intelligence. *Intelligence*, *30*, 163–183.

Coyle, T. R. (2003). A review of the worst performance rule: Evidence, theory, and alternative hypotheses. *Intelligence*, *31*, 567–587.

Crawford, J. R., Deary, I. J., Allan, K. M., & Gustafsson, J. E. (1998). Evaluating competing models of the relationship between inspection time and psychometric intelligence. *Intelligence*, *26*, 27–42.

Danthiir, V., Burns, N. R., Nettelbeck, T., Wilson, C., & Wittert, G. (2009, July 18–22). *Relationships between age, processing speed, working memory, inhibition and fluid intelligence in older adults*. Paper presented at the International Society for the Study of Individual Differences, Chicago, IL.

Danthiir, V., Wilhelm, O., & Schacht, A. (2005). Decision speed in intelligence tasks: Correctly an ability? *Psychology Science*, 47, 200–229.

Danthiir, V., Wilhelm, O., Schulze, R., & Roberts, R. D. (2005). Factor structure and validity of paper-and-pencil measures of mental speed: Evidence for a higher-order model? *Intelligence*, 33, 491–514.

Deary, I. J. (2000). *Looking down on human intelligence: From psychophysics to the brain.* Oxford, UK: Oxford University Press.

Deary, I. J. (2003). Reaction time and psychometric intelligence: Jensen's contributions. In H. Nyborg (Ed.), *The scientific study of general intelligence: Tribute to Arthur R. Jensen* (pp. 53–75). Amsterdam, the Netherlands: Pergamon.

Deary, I. J., Allerhand, M., & Der, G. (2009). Smarter in middle age, faster in old age: A cross-lagged panel analysis of reaction time and cognitive ability over 13 years in the West of Scotland Twenty-07 study. *Psychology and Aging*, **24**, 40–47.

Deary, I. J., Bastin, M. E., Pattie, A., Clayden, J. D., Whalley, L. J., Starr, J. M., et al. (2006). White matter integrity and cognition in childhood and old age. *Neurology*, 66, 505–512.

Deary, I. J., Der, G., & Ford, G. (2001). Reaction times and intelligence differences: A population-based cohort study. *Intelligence*, **29**, 389–399.

Deary, I. J., Hunter, R., Langan, S. J., & Goodwin, G. M. (1991). Inspection time, psychometric intelligence and clinical estimates of cognitive ability in pre-senile Alzheimer's disease and Korsakoff's psychosis. *Brain*, **114**, 2543–2554.

Deary, I. J., Leaper, S. A., Murray, A. D., Staff, R. T., & Whalley, L. J. (2003). Cerebral white matter abnormalities and lifetime cognitive change: A 67-year follow-up of the Scottish Mental Survey of 1932. *Psychology and Aging*, **18**, 140–148.

Deary, I. J., Simonotto, E., Marshall, A., Marshall, I., Goddard, N., & Wardlaw, J. M. (2001). The functional anatomy of inspection time: A pilot fMRI study. *Intelligence*, **29**, 497–510.

Deary, I. J., & Stough, C. (1996). Intelligence and inspection time: Achievements, prospects and problems. *American Psychologist*, **51**, 599–608.

Deluca, J., & Kalmar, J. H. (2007). *Information processing speed in clinical populations.* New York, NY: Psychology Press.

Detterman, D. K. (1982). Does g exist? *Intelligence*, 6, 99–108.

Detterman, D. K. (1987). What does reaction time tell us about intelligence? In P. A. Vernon (Ed.), *Speed of information processing and intelligence* (pp. 177–200). Norwood, NJ: Ablex.

Doidge, N. (2007). *The brain that changes itself.* New York, NY: Viking Press.

Duncan, J., Seitz, R. J., Koldny, J., Bor, D., Herzog, H., Ahmed, A., Newell, F. N., & Emslie, H. (2000). A neural basis for general intelligence. *Science*, 289, 457–460.

Edmonds, C. J., Isaacs, E. B., Visscher, P. M., Rogers, M., Lanigan, J., Singhal, A., et al. (2008). Inspection time and cognitive abilities in twins aged 7 to 17 years: Age-related changes, heritability and genetic covariance. *Intelligence*, 36, 210–255.

Egan, V. (1994). Intelligence, inspection time and cognitive strategies. *British Journal of Psychology*, 85, 305–316.

Engle, R. W., Tuholski, S. W., Laughlin, J. E., & Conway, A. R. A. (1999). Working memory, short-term memory and general fluid intelligence: A latent variable approach. *Journal of Experimental Psychology: General*, **128**, 309–331.

Eysenck, H. J. (1987). Speed of information processing, reaction time, and the theory of intelligence. In P. A. Vernon (Ed.), *Speed of information processing and intelligence* (pp. 21–67). Norwood, NJ: Ablex.

Finkel, D., Reynolds, C. A., McArdle, J. J., & Pedersen, N. L. (2007). Age changes in processing speed as a leading indicator of cognitive aging. *Psychology and Aging*, **22**, 558–568.

Fox, M. C., Roring, R. W., & Mitchum, A. L. (2009). Reversing the speed-IQ correlation: Intra-individual variability and attentional control in the inspection time paradigm. *Intelligence*, 37, 76–80.

Frearson, W., & Eysenck, H. J. (1986). Intelligence, reaction time (RT) and a new 'odd-man-out' RT paradigm. *Personality and Individual Differences*, 7, 807–817.

Fry, A. F., & Hale, S. (2000). Relationships among processing speed, working memory, and fluid intelligence in children. *Biological Psychology*, **54**, 1–34.

Galton, F. (1883). *Inquiries into human faculty and its development.* London, UK: Macmillan.

Gardner, H. (1983). *Frames of mind: The theory of multiple intelligences.* New York, NY: Harper and Row.

Gregory, T., Callaghan, A., Nettelbeck, T., & Wilson, C. (2009). Inspection time predicts individual differences in everyday functioning among elderly adults: Testing discriminant validity. *Australasian Journal on Ageing, 28,* 87–92.

Gregory, T., Nettelbeck, T., Howard, S., & Wilson, C. (2008). Inspection time: A biomarker for cognitive decline. *Intelligence, 36,* 664–671.

Gregory, T., Nettelbeck, T., Howard, S., & Wilson, C. (2009). A test of the Cascade model in the elderly. *Personality and Individual Differences, 46,* 71–73.

Gregory, T., Nettelbeck, T., & Wilson, C. (2009). Within-person changes in inspection time predict memory. *Personality and Individual Differences, 46,* 741–743.

Grudnik, J. L., & Kranzler, J. H. (2001). Meta-analysis of the relationship between intelligence and inspection time. *Intelligence, 29,* 523–535.

Gunning-Dixon, F. M., & Raz, N. (2000). The cognitive correlates of white matter abnormalities in normal aging: A quantitative review. *Neuropsychology, 14,* 224–232.

Hertzog, C., Kramer, A. F., Wilson, R. S., & Lindenberger, U. (2008). Enrichment effects on adult cognitive development: Can the functional capacity of older adults be preserved and enhanced? *Psychological Science in the Public Interest, 9,* 1–65.

Hick, W. (1952). On the rate of gain of information. *Quarterly Journal of Experimental Psychology, 4,* 11–26.

Horn, J. L., & Noll, J. (1997). Human cognitive capabilities: Gf-Gc theory. In D. P. Flanagan, J. L. Genshaft, & P. L. Harrison (Eds.), *Contemporary intellectual assessment: Theories, tests, and issues* (pp. 53–91). New York, NY: Guilford Press.

Hunt, E. (1980). Intelligence as an information processing concept. *British Journal of Psychology, 71,* 449–474.

Jensen, A. R. (1982). Reaction time and psychometric g. In H. J. Eysenck (Ed.), *A model for intelligence* (pp. 93–132). New York, NY: Springer-Verlag.

Jensen, A. R. (1987). Individual differences in the Hick paradigm. In P. A. Vernon (Ed.), *Speed of information-processing and intelligence* (pp. 101–175). Norwood, NJ: Ablex.

Jensen, A. R. (1998). *The g factor: The science of mental ability.* New York: Praeger.

Jensen, A. R. (2006). *Clocking the mind: Mental chronometry and individual differences.* Amsterdam, the Netherlands: Elsevier.

Juhel, J. (1991). Relationships between psychometric intelligence and information-processing speed indexes. *European Bulletin of Cognitive Psychology, 11,* 73–105.

Kail, R. (1991). Developmental change in speed of processing during childhood and adolescence. *Psychological Bulletin, 109,* 490–501.

Kaufman, S. B., DeYoung, C. G., Gray, J. R., Brown, J., & Mackintosh, N. (2009). Associative learning predicts intelligence above and beyond working memory and processing speed. *Intelligence,* doi: 10.1016/j.intell.2009.03.004.

Krumm, S., Schmidt-Azert, L., Michalczyk, K., & Danthiir, V. (2008). Speeded paper-pencil sustained attention and mental speed tests. *Journal of Individual Differences, 29,* 205–216.

Kyllonen, P. C., & Christal, R. E. (1990). Reasoning ability is (little more than) working memory capacity? *Intelligence, 14,* 389–433.

Larson, G. E., & Alderton, D. L. (1990). Reaction time variability and intelligence: A "worst performance" analysis of individual differences. *Intelligence, 14,* 309–325.

Lehrl, S., & Fischer, B. (1990). A basic information psychological parameter (BIP) for the reconstruction of concepts of intelligence. *European Journal of Personality, 4,* 259–286.

Longstreth, L. E. (1984). Jensen's reaction time investigations of intelligence: A critique. *Intelligence, 8,* 139–160.

Luciano, M., Smith, G. A., Wright, M. J., Geffen, G. M., Geffen, L. B., & Martin, N. G. (2001). On the heritability of inspection time and its covariance with IQ: A twin study. *Intelligence, 29,* 443–457.

Luciano, M., Wright, M. J., Geffen, G. M., Geffen, L. B., Smith, G. A., & Martin, N. G. (2004). A genetic investigation of the covariation among inspection time, choice reaction time, and IQ subtest scores. *Behavior Genetics, 34,* 41–50.

Mackintosh, N. J. (1986). The biology of intelligence? *British Journal of Psychology, 77,* 1–18.

Mackintosh, N. J. (1998). *IQ and human intelligence.* Oxford, UK: Oxford University Press.

Madden, D. J. (2001). Speed and timing in behavioral processes. In J. E. Birren & K. W. Schaie (Eds.), *Handbook of the psychology of aging* (5th ed., pp. 288–312). San Diego, CA: Academic Press.

Marr, D. B., & Sternberg, R. J. (1987). The role of mental speed in intelligence: A triarchic perspective. In P. A. Vernon (Ed.), *Speed of information-processing and intelligence* (pp. 271–294). Norwood, NJ: Ablex.

Matthews, G., Zeidner, M., & Roberts, R. D. (2007). *The science of emotional intelligence: Knowns and unknowns.* Oxford, UK: Oxford University Press.

McGrew, K. S. (2005). The Cattell-Horn-Carroll theory of cognitive abilities: Past, present and future. In D. P. Flanagan & P. L. Harrison (Eds.), *Contemporary intellectual assessment* (2nd ed., pp. 156–182). New York, NY: Guilford.

Nettelbeck, T. (1985). What reaction times time. *Behavioral and Brain Sciences, 8*, 235.

Nettelbeck, T. (1987). Inspection time and intelligence. In P. A. Vernon (Ed.), *Speed of information-processing and intelligence* (pp. 295–346). Norwood, NJ: Ablex.

Nettelbeck, T. (1994). Speediness. In R. J. Sternberg (Ed.), *Encyclopedia of human intelligence* (pp. 1014–1019). New York, NY: Macmillan.

Nettelbeck, T. (1998). Jensen's chronometric research: Neither simple nor sufficient but a good place to start. *Intelligence, 29*, 233–241.

Nettelbeck, T. (2001). Correlation between inspection time and psychometric abilities: A personal interpretation. *Intelligence, 29*, 459–474.

Nettelbeck, T. (2003). Inspection time and g. In H. Nyborg (Ed.), *The scientific study of general intelligence: Tribute to Arthur R. Jensen* (pp. 77–91). Amsterdam, the Netherlands: Pergamon.

Nettelbeck, T., Gregory, T., Wilson, C., Burns, N., Danthiir, V., & Wittert, G. (2008, December 11–13). *Inspection time: A marker for less successful ageing.* Paper presented at the Ninth Annual Conference of the International Society for Intelligence Research (ISIR), Decatur, GA.

Nettelbeck, T., & Kirby, N. H. (1983). Measures of timed performance and intelligence. *Intelligence, 7*, 39–52.

Nettelbeck, T., & Lally, M. (1976). Inspection time and measured intelligence. *British Journal of Psychology, 67*, 17–22.

Nettelbeck, T., & Vita, P. (1992). Inspection time in two childhood age cohorts: A constant of a developmental function? *British Journal of Developmental Psychology, 10*, 189–198.

Nettelbeck, T., & Wilson, C. (1985). A cross-sequential analysis of developmental differences in speed of visual information processing. *Journal of Experimental Child Psychology, 40*, 1–22.

Nettelbeck, T., & Wilson, C. (1997). Speed of information processing and cognition. In W. E. J. Maclean (Ed.), *Ellis' handbook of mental deficiency, psychological theory and research* (3rd ed., pp. 245–274). Mahwah, NJ: Erlbaum.

Nettelbeck, T., & Young, R. (1989). Inspection time and intelligence in 6 year old children. *Personality and Individual Differences, 10*, 605–614.

Neubauer, A. C. (1997). The mental speed account to the assessment of intelligence In J. S. Carlson, J. Kingma, & W. Tomic (Eds.), *Advances in cognition and educational practice: Reflections on the concept of intelligence* (Vol. 4, pp. 149–173). Greenwich, CT: JAI Press.

Neubauer, A. C., & Bucik, V. (1996). The mental speed-IQ relationship: Unitary or modular? *Intelligence, 22*, 23–48.

O'Connor, T. A., & Burns, N. R. (2003). Inspection time and general speed of processing. *Personality and Individual Differences, 35*, 713–724.

Olsson, H., Björkman, C., Haag, K., & Juslin, P. (1998). Auditory inspection time: On the importance of selecting the appropriate sensory continuum. *Personality and Individual Differences, 25*, 627–634.

Parker, D. M., Crawford, J. R., & Stephen, E. (1999). Auditory inspection time and intelligence: A new spatial localization task. *Intelligence, 27*, 131–139.

Petrill, S. A., Luo, D., Thompson, L. A., & Detterman, D. K. (2001). Inspection time and the relationship among elementary cognitive tasks, general intelligence, and specific cognitive abilities. *Intelligence, 29*, 487–496.

Posner, M. I. (1978). *Chronometric explorations of mind.* Hillsdale, NJ: Erlbaum.

Posthuma, D., de Geus, E. J. C., & Boomsma, D. I. (2001). Perceptual speed and IQ are associated through common genetic factors. *Behavior Genetics, 31*, 593–602.

Rabbitt, P., Scott, M., Lunn, M., Thacker, N., Lowe, C., Pedleton, N., et al. (2007). White matter lesions account for all age-related declines in speed but not in intelligence. *Neuropsychology, 21*, 363–370.

Ratcliff, R., & Smith, P. L. (2004). A comparison of sequential sampling models for two-choice reaction time. *Psychological Review, 111*, 333–367.

Reed, T. E., & Jensen, A. R. (1992). Conduction velocity in a brain nerve pathway of normal adults correlates with intelligence level. *Intelligence, 16*, 259–272.

Reed, T. E., & Jensen, A. R. (1993). Choice reaction time and visual pathway nerve conduction velocity both correlate with intelligence but appear not to correlate with each other: Implications for information processing. *Intelligence, 17*, 191–203.

Reed, T. E., Vernon, P. A., & Johnson, A. M. (2004). Confirmation of correlation between brain nerve conduction velocity and intelligence level in normal adults. *Intelligence, 32*, 563–572.

Roberts, R. D., & Stankov, L. (1999). Individual differences in speed of mental processing and human cognitive abilities: Toward a taxonomic model. *Learning and Individual Differences, 11*, 1–120.

Rockstroh, S., & Schweizer, K. (2004). The effect of retest practice on the speed-ability relationship. *European Psychologist, 9*, 24–31.

Salthouse, T. A. (1996). The processing-speed theory of adult age differences in cognition. *Psychological Review, 103*, 403–428.

Salthouse, T. A. (2006). Mental exercise and mental aging. *Perspectives on Psychological Science, 1*, 68–87.

Schafer, E. P. W. (1985). Neural adaptability: A biological determinant of *g* factor intelligence. *Behavioral and Brain Sciences, 8*, 240–241.

Schaie, K. W. (2005). *Developmental influences on adult intelligence*. Oxford, UK: Oxford University Press.

Schmiedek, F., Oberauer, K., Wilhelm, O., Süß, H.-M., & Wittmann, W. W. (2007). Individual differences in components of reaction time distributions and their relations to working memory and intelligence. *Journal of Experimental Psychology: General, 136*, 414–429.

Schweizer, K., Zimmermann, P., & Koch, W. (2000). Sustained attention, intelligence, and the crucial role of perceptual processes. *Learning and Individual Differences, 12*, 271–287.

Sculthorpe, L. D., Stelmack, R. M., & Campbell, K. B. (2009). Mental ability and the effect of pattern violation discrimination on P300 and mismatch negativity. *Intelligence, 37*, 405–411.

Sheppard, L. D., & Vernon, P. A. (2008). Intelligence and speed of information-processing: A review of 50 years of research. *Personality and Individual Differences, 44*, 535–551.

Smith, G. A., & Carew, M. (1987). Decision time unmasked: Individuals adopt different strategies. *Australian Journal of Psychology, 39*, 339–351.

Sternberg, R. J. (1977). *Intelligence, information processing, and analogical reasoning: The componential analysis of human abilities*. Hillsdale, NJ: Erlbaum.

Sternberg, R. J. (2003). *Wisdom, intelligence and creativity synthesized*. Cambridge, UK: Cambridge University Press.

Sternberg, S. (1975). Memory scanning: New findings and current controversies. *Quarterly Journal of Experimental Psychology, 27*, 1–32.

Stough, C., Thompson, J. C., Bates, T. C., & Nathan, P. J. (2001). Examining neurochemical determinants of inspection time: Development of a biological model. *Intelligence, 29*, 511–522.

Strachan, M. W. J., Deary, I. J., Ewing, F. M. E., Ferguson, S. S. C., Young, M. J., & Frier, B. M. (2001). Acute hypoglycemia impairs the functioning of the central but not peripheral nervous system. *Physiology & Behavior, 72*, 83–92.

Stroud, J. M. (1956). The fine structure of psychological time. In H. Quastler (Ed.), *Information theory in psychology*. Glencoe, Scotland: Free Press.

Turvey, M. T. (1973). On peripheral and central processes in vision: Inferences from an information-processing analysis of masking with patterned stimuli. *Psychological Review*, 80, 1–52.

Vernon, P. A. (1987). New developments in reaction time research. In P. A. Vernon (Ed.), *Speed of information-processing and intelligence* (pp. 1–20). Norwood, NJ: Ablex.

Vernon, P. A., & Mori, M. (1992). Intelligence, reaction times, and peripheral nerve conduction velocity. *Intelligence, 16*, 273–288.

Vernon, P. A., Wickett, J. C., Bazana, P. C., & Stelmack, R. M. (2000). The neuropsychology and psychophysiology of human intelligence. In R. J. Sternberg (Ed.), *Handbook of intelligence*. Cambridge, UK: Cambridge University Press.

Vickers, D., Nettelbeck, T., & Willson, R. J. (1972). Perceptual indices of performance: The measurement of "inspection time" and "noise" in the visual system. *Perception, 1*, 263–295.

Welford, A. T. (1968). *Fundamentals of skill*. London, UK: Methuen.

Zajac, I. T., & Burns, N. R. (2007). Measuring auditory inspection time in primary school children. *Journal of Individual Differences, 28*, 45–52.

CHAPTER 20

Working Memory and Intelligence

Andrew R. A. Conway, Sarah J. Getz, Brooke Macnamara, and Pascale M. J. Engel de Abreu

We want to understand intelligence, not only map its network of correlations with other constructs. This means to reveal the functional – and ultimately, the neural – mechanisms underlying intelligent information processing. Among the theoretical constructs within current theories of information processing, [working memory capacity] WMC is the one parameter that correlates best with measures of reasoning ability, and even with g_f and g. Therefore, investigating WMC, and its relationship with intelligence, is psychology's best hope to date to understand intelligence.

Oberauer, Schulze, Wilhelm, & Süß (2005)

Working memory (WM) is a construct developed by cognitive psychologists to characterize and help further investigate how human beings maintain access to goal-relevant information in the face of concurrent processing and/or distraction. For example, suppose you are fixing a cocktail for your spouse, who has just arrived home from work. You need to remember that for the perfect Manhattan, you need two ounces of bourbon, one ounce of sweet vermouth, a dash of bitters, and a splash of maraschino cherry juice, and at the same time you need to listen to your spouse tell you about his or her day. WM is required to remember the ingredients without repeatedly consulting the recipe and to process the incoming information to understand the conversation. Many important cognitive behaviors, beyond cocktail mixing – such as reading, reasoning, and problem solving – require WM because for each of these activities, some information must be maintained in an accessible state while new information is processed and potentially distracting information is ignored. If you have experience preparing this particular drink, then you could rely on procedural memory to perform the task. If not, however, WM is required to simultaneously remember the ingredients and comprehend the conversation.

Working memory is a limited-capacity system. That is, there is only so much information that can be maintained in an accessible state at one time. There is also substantial variation in WM capacity (WMC) across individuals: Older children have greater capacity than younger children, the elderly tend to have lesser capacity than younger adults, and patients with certain types of neural damage or disease have lesser capacity than healthy adults. There is even a large degree of variation in WMC within healthy adult samples of subjects, such as within college student samples.

It is important to clarify at the outset the distinction between working memory and working memory capacity. Working memory refers to the cognitive system required to maintain access to information in the face of concurrent processing and/or distraction (including mechanisms involved in stimulus representation, maintenance, manipulation, and retrieval), while working memory capacity refers to the maximum amount of information an individual can maintain in a particular task that is designed to measure some aspect(s) of WM. This has caused some confusion in the literature because different researchers operationally define WM in different ways, and this has implications for the relationship between WM and intelligence. For example, two researchers may share the same exact definition of WM but they may operationalize WM differently, which could result in a different perspective on WMC and its correlates.

The focus of this chapter is on the relationship between WMC and fluid intelligence (g_f) in healthy young adults. Recent meta-analyses, conducted by two different groups of researchers, estimate the correlation between WMC and g_f to be somewhere between $r = .72$ (Kane, Hambrick, & Conway, 2005) and $r = .85$ (Oberauer et al., 2005). Thus, according to these analyses, WMC accounts for at least half the variance in g_f. This is impressive, yet for this line of work to truly inform theoretical accounts of intelligence, we need to better understand the construct of WM and discuss the various ways in which it is measured.

The emphasis here is on fluid intelligence rather than crystallized intelligence, general intelligence (g), or intelligence more broadly defined because most of the research linking WM to the concept of intelligence has focused on fluid abilities and reasoning rather than on acquired knowledge or skill (however, see Hambrick, 2003; Hambrick & Engle, 2002; Hambrick & Oswald, 2005). This is a natural place to focus our microscope because WM is most important in situations that do not allow for the use of prior knowledge and less important in situations in which skills and strategies guide behavior (Ackerman, 1988; Engle, Tuholski, Laughlin, & Conway, 1999). That said, we acknowledge that fluid intelligence is a fuzzy concept. The goal of this chapter and much of the research reviewed in it is to move away from such nebulous constructs and toward more precisely defined cognitive mechanisms that underlie complex cognition.

The chapter begins with a brief review of the history of working memory, followed by our own contemporary view of WM, which is largely shaped by Cowan's model (1988, 1995, 2001, 2005) but also incorporates ideas from individual differences research (for a review, see Unsworth and Engle, 2007), neuroimaging experiments (for a review, see Jonides et al., 2008), and computational models of WM (Ashby, Ell, Valentin, & Casale, 2005; O'Reilly & Frank, 2006). We then discuss the measurement of WMC. These initial sections allow for a more informed discussion of the empirical work that has linked WMC and g_f. We then consider various theories on the relationship between WMC and g_f, and propose a novel perspective, which we call the *multi-mechanism view*. We conclude with a discussion of a recent trend in research on WM and intelligence: WM training and its effect on g_f.

Historical Perspective on Working Memory

The *concept* of WM was first introduced by Miller, Galanter, and Pribram (1960) in their influential book, *Plans and the Structure of Behavior*. Recognized as one of the milestones of the cognitive revolution, the book is also known for introducing the iterative problem-solving strategy known as TOTE, or Test – Operate – Test – Exit. The TOTE strategy is often implemented as people carry out plans and pursue goal-directed behavior. For example, when mixing the drink for your spouse, you could perform a *Test* (is the drink done?), and if not, then perform an *Operation* (add bourbon, which would require remembering that bourbon is one of the ingredients), and test again, and so on until the goal is achieved, at which point you *Exit* the plan. Miller et al. realized that a dynamic and flexible short-term memory system is necessary to engage the TOTE strategy and to structure and execute a plan. They referred to this short-term memory system as a type of "working memory" and speculated that it may be dependent upon the prefrontal cortex.

The *construct* WM was introduced in the seminal chapter by Baddeley and Hitch (1974). Prior to their work, the dominant theoretical construct used to explain short-term memory performance was the short-term store (STS), epitomized by the so-called modal model of memory popular in the late 1960s (e.g., Atkinson & Shiffrin, 1968). According to these models, the STS plays a central role in cognitive behavior, essentially serving as a gateway to further information processing. It was therefore assumed that the STS would be crucial for a range of complex cognitive behaviors, such as planning, reasoning, and problem solving. The problem with this approach, as reviewed by Baddeley and Hitch, was that disrupting the STS with a small memory load had very little impact on the performance of a range of complex cognitive tasks, particularly reasoning and planning. Moreover, patients with severe STS deficits – for example, a digit span of only two items – functioned rather normally on a wide range of complex cognitive tasks (Shallice & Warrington, 1970; Warrington & Shallice, 1969). This would not be possible if the STS were essential for information processing, as proposed by the modal model.

Baddeley and Hitch therefore proposed a more complex construct, *working memory*, that could maintain information in a readily accessible state, consistent with the STS, but could also engage in concurrent processing, as well as maintain access to more information than the limited capacity STS could purportedly maintain. According to this perspective, a small amount of information can be maintained via "slave" storage systems, akin to the STS, but more information can be processed and accessed via a central executive, which was poorly described in the initial WM model but has since been refined and will be discussed in more detail later in the chapter.

Baddeley and Hitch argued that WM but not the STS plays an essential role in a range of complex cognitive tasks. According to this perspective, WMC should be more predictive of cognitive performance than the capacity of the STS. This prediction was first supported by an influential study by Daneman and Carpenter (1980), which explored the relationship between the capacity of the STS, WMC, and reading comprehension, as assessed by the Verbal Scholastic Aptitude Test (VSAT). STS capacity was assessed using a word span task, in which a series of words was presented, one word per second, and at the end of a series the subject was prompted to recall all the words in correct serial order. Daneman and Carpenter developed a novel task to measure WMC. The task was designed to require short-term storage, akin to word span, but also to require the simultaneous processing of new information. Their *reading span* task required subjects to read a series of sentences aloud and remember the last word of each sentence for later recall. Thus, the storage and recall demands of reading span are the same as for the word span task, but the reading span task has the additional requirement of reading sentences aloud while trying to remember words for later recall. This type of task is thought to be an ecologically valid measure of the WM construct proposed by Baddeley and Hitch.

Consistent with the predictions of WM theory, the reading span task correlated more strongly with VSAT ($r = .59$) than the word span task ($r = .35$). This may not seem at all surprising, given that both the VSAT and reading span involve *reading*. However, subsequent work by Turner and Engle (1989) and others showed that the processing component of the WM span task does not have to involve reading for the task to be predictive of VSAT. They had subjects solve simple mathematical operations while remembering words for later recall and showed, consistent with Daneman and Carpenter (1980), that the operation span task predicted VSAT more strongly than did the word span task. More recent research has shown that a variety of WM span tasks, similar in structure to reading span and operation span but with various processing and storage demands, are strongly predictive of a wide range of complex cognitive tasks, suggesting that the relationship between WM span performance and complex cognition is largely domain-general (e.g., Kane, Hambrick, Wilhelm, Payne, Tuholski, & Engle, 2004).

In sum, WM is a relatively young construct in the field of psychology. It was proposed as an alternative conception of short-term memory performance in an attempt to account for empirical evidence that was inconsistent with the modal model of memory that included an STS to explain short-term memory. Original measures of WMC, such as reading span and operation span (also known as complex span tasks; see the section titled Measurement of WMC), were shown to be more strongly correlated with measures of complex cognition, including intelligence tests, than are simple span tasks, such as digit span and word span. Recent work has called into question this simple distinction between complex and simple span tasks, which we discuss later in the chapter, but here at the outset it is important to highlight that Baddeley and Hitch (1974) proposed WM as an alternative to the concept of an STS. Indeed, referring to WM as a "system" and using the digit span task as a marker of the STS, Baddeley and Hitch concluded:

> *This system [WM] appears to have something in common with the mechanism responsible for the digit span, being susceptible to disruption by a concurrent digit span task, and like the digit span showing signs of being based at least in part upon phonemic coding. It should be noted, however, that the degree of disruption observed, even with a near-span concurrent memory load, was far from massive. This suggests that although the digit span and working memory overlap, there appears to be a considerable component of working memory which is not taken up by the digit span task (p. 76).*

Contemporary View of Working Memory

Delineating the exact characteristics of WM and accounting for variation in WMC continues to be an extremely active area of research. There are, therefore, several current theoretical models of WM and several explanations of WMC variation. In this section we introduce just one view of WM, simply to provide the proper language necessary to explain WM measurement and the empirical data linking WMC to intelligence. Later in the chapter we will consider alternative theoretical accounts. Our view is largely shaped by Cowan's model (1988, 1995, 2001, 2005) rather than the recent incarnation of Baddeley's model (2007) because we argue that Cowan's model is more amenable to recent findings from neuroimaging studies of WM (Jonides et al., 2008; Postle, 2006). We also prefer Cowan's model to computational modeling approaches to WM (e.g., Ashby et al., 2005; O'Reilly & Frank, 2006) because Cowan's model, while less specified mechanistically, addresses a broader range of phenomena, including the correlation between WMC and g_f.

Cowan's model (see Figure 20.1) assumes that WM consists of activated long-term memory representations (see also Anderson, 1983; Atkinson & Shiffrin, 1971; Hebb, 1949) and a central executive responsible for cognitive control (for work that

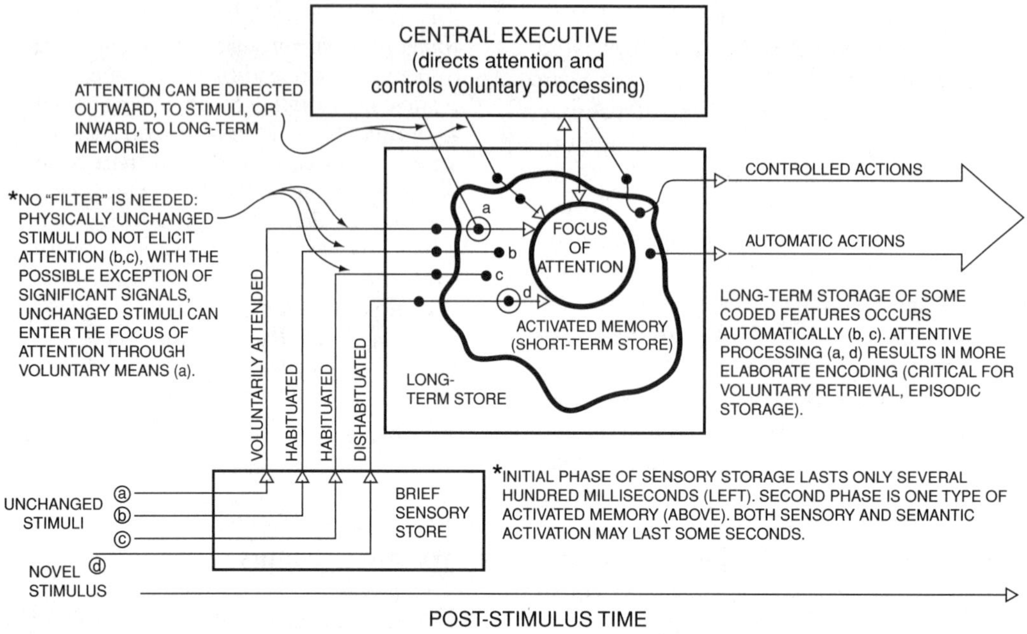
CENTRAL EXECUTIVE
(directs attention and controls voluntary processing)
ATTENTION CAN BE DIRECTED OUTWARD, TO STIMULI, OR INWARD, TO LONG-TERM MEMORIES
*NO "FILTER" IS NEEDED: PHYSICALLY UNCHANGED STIMULI DO NOT ELICIT ATTENTION (b,c), WITH THE POSSIBLE EXCEPTION OF SIGNIFICANT SIGNALS, UNCHANGED STIMULI CAN ENTER THE FOCUS OF ATTENTION THROUGH VOLUNTARY MEANS (a).
CONTROLLED ACTIONS
AUTOMATIC ACTIONS
FOCUS OF ATTENTION
ACTIVATED MEMORY (SHORT-TERM STORE)
LONG-TERM STORE
LONG-TERM STORAGE OF SOME CODED FEATURES OCCURS AUTOMATICALLY (b, c). ATTENTIVE PROCESSING (a, d) RESULTS IN MORE ELABORATE ENCODING (CRITICAL FOR VOLUNTARY RETRIEVAL, EPISODIC STORAGE).
VOLUNTARILY ATTENDED
HABITUATED
HABITUATED
DISHABITUATED
BRIEF SENSORY STORE
*INITIAL PHASE OF SENSORY STORAGE LASTS ONLY SEVERAL HUNDRED MILLISECONDS (LEFT). SECOND PHASE IS ONE TYPE OF ACTIVATED MEMORY (ABOVE). BOTH SENSORY AND SEMANTIC ACTIVATION MAY LAST SOME SECONDS.
UNCHANGED STIMULI
NOVEL STIMULUS
POST-STIMULUS TIME

Figure 20.1. Cowan, N. (1988). Evolving conceptions of memory storage, selective attention, and their mutual constraints within the human information processing system. *Psychological Bulletin*, 104, 163–191. Published by the American Psychological Association. Reprinted with permission.

explains cognitive control without reference to a homuncular executive, see O'Reilly and Frank, 2006). Within this activated set of representations, or "short-term store," there is a focus of attention that can maintain approximately four items in a readily accessible state (Cowan, 2001). In other words, we can "think of" approximately four mental representations at one time.

Our own view is quite similar to the model in Figure 20.1. However, we make three modifications. First, we prefer "unitary store" models of memory rather than multiple store models and therefore do not think of the activated portion of long-term memory (LTM) as a "store." The reason for this distinction is that there is very little neuroscience evidence to support the notion that there is a neurologically separate "buffer" responsible for the short-term storage of information (see Postle, 2006). We acknowledge that there are memory phenomena that differ as a function of retention interval (for a review, see Davelaar, Goshen-Gottstein, Ashkenazi, Haarmann, and Usher, 2005) but we argue that these effects do not necessitate the assumption of a short-term store (for a review see Sederberg, Howard, and Kahana, 2008). Second, recent work has shown that the focus of attention may be limited to just one item, depending on task demands (Garavan, 1998; McElree, 2001; Nee & Jonides, 2008; Oberauer, 2002). We therefore adopt Oberauer's view that there are actually three layers of representation in WM: (1) the focus of attention, limited to one item; (2) the region of direct access, limited to approximately four items; and (3) representations active above baseline but no longer in the region of direct access. To avoid confusion over Cowan and Oberauer's terminology, we will use the phrase "scope of attention" to refer to the limited number of items that are readily accessible, recognizing that one item may have privileged access. Third, and most important for the current chapter, we argue that Cowan's view of WMC is too limited to account for complex cognitive activity, such as reasoning. Complex cognitive behavior, such as reasoning, reading, and problem solving, requires rapid access to more than four items at one time. WM therefore must also consist of a retrieval mechanism that allows for the rapid retrieval of information from LTM. This notion has been referred to as long-term WM (Ericcson & Kintsch, 1995).

Thus, we view WM as consisting of at least three main components: (1) cognitive control mechanisms (or the central executive), which are most likely governed by the prefrontal cortex (PFC), anterior-cingulate cortex (ACC), and subcortical structures including the basal ganglia and thalamus (Ashby et al. 2005; Botvinick, 2007; Miller & Cohen, 2001; O'Reilly & Frank, 2006); (2) one to four representations in the scope of attention, which are most likely maintained via activity in a frontal-parietal network (Todd & Marois, 2004; Vogel & Machizawa, 2004); and (3) a retrieval mechanism responsible for the rapid retrieval of information from LTM. This process is most likely achieved via cortical connections from the PFC to the medial temporal lobe (MTL), including the hippocampus (Chein, Moore, & Conway, 2010; Nee & Jonides, 2008; Ranganath, 2006; O'Reilly & Norman, 2002; Unsworth & Engle, 2007).

Assuming this general architecture, consider Figure 20.2, from Jonides et al. (2008), which depicts the processing and neural representation of a single stimulus over the course of a few seconds in a hypothetical WM task, consisting of the presentation of three stimuli followed by a probe. Note that three brain regions, PFC, parietal cortex, and MTL, are integral to processing. This framework is consistent with our view and with recent individual differences research on WM proposing that variation in WMC is partly due to active maintenance of information, achieved via PFC-parietal connections, and controlled retrieval of information achieved via PFC-MTL connections (Unsworth & Engle, 2007). We further propose that WMC is partly determined by cognitive control mechanisms, such as interference control (Burgess, Braver, Conway, & Gray, 2010). We elaborate upon this multi-mechanism view later in the chapter.

Measurement of Working Memory Capacity

Several different WM tasks are used in contemporary research. These tasks vary in extremely important ways, which we discuss. As well, the extent to which WMC predicts g_f is largely dependent upon which set of tasks one uses to measure WMC. Thus, a detailed discussion of various WM tasks is essential here. We mainly consider WM tasks that have shown strong correlations with measures of g_f in a domain-general fashion, for example, a verbal WM task predicting a spatial reasoning task and vice versa.

Complex Span Tasks

As discussed, complex span tasks, such as reading span (Daneman & Carpenter, 1980) and operation span (Turner & Engle, 1989), were designed from the perspective of the original WM model. Other complex span tasks include the counting span task (Case, Kurland, & Goldberg, 1982), as well as various spatial versions (see Kane et al., 2004; Shah & Miyake, 1996). Complex span tasks require participants to engage in some sort of simple processing task (e.g., reading unrelated sentences aloud or completing a math problem, as in reading span and operation span, respectively) between the presentations of to-be-remembered items (e.g., letters, words, digits, spatial locations). After several items have been presented, typically between two and seven, the subject is prompted to recall all the to-be-remembered items in correct serial order.

For example, in the counting span task, subjects are presented with an array of items, such as blue and red circles and squares, and instructed to count a particular class of items, such as blue squares. After counting aloud, subjects are required to remember the total and are then presented with another array. They again count the number of blue squares aloud and remember the total. After a series of arrays they are required to recall all the totals in correct serial order. Thus, the storage and recall

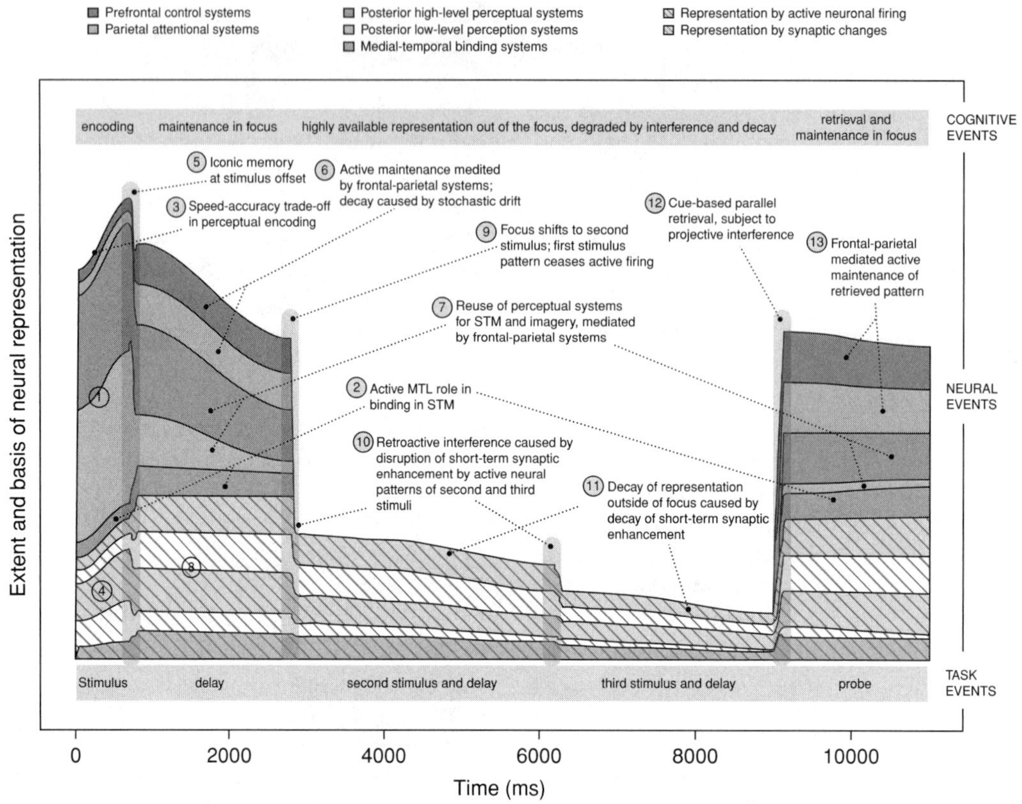

Figure 20.2. Jonides, J., Lewis, R. L., Nee, D. E., Lustig, C. A., Berman, M. G., and Moore K. S. (2008). The mind and brain of short-term memory. *Annual Review of Psychology*, 59, 193–224. Copyright 2008 by Annual Reviews, Inc. Reproduced with permission of Annual Reviews, Inc. The processing and neural representation of one item in memory over the course of a few seconds in a hypothetical short-term memory task, assuming a simple single-item focus architecture. The cognitive events are demarcated at the top; the task events, at the bottom. The colored layers depict the extent to which different brain areas contribute to the representation of the item over time, at distinct functional stages of short-term memory processing. The colored layers also distinguish two basic types of neural representation: Solid layers depict memory supported by a coherent pattern of active neural firing, and hashed layers depict memory supported by changes in synaptic patterns. The example task requires processing and remembering three visual items; the figure traces the representation of the first item only. In this task, the three items are sequentially presented, and each is followed by a delay period. After the delay following the third item, a probe appears that requires retrieval of the first item.

demands are the same as a simple digit span task, but there is the additional requirement of counting the arrays, which demands controlled attention (Treisman & Gelade, 1980) and therefore disrupts active maintenance of the digits. Again, this is thought to be an ecologically valid measure of WM as proposed by Baddeley and Hitch (1974) because it requires access to information (the digits) in the face of concurrent processing (counting) (for more details, see Conway, Kane, Bunting, Hambrick, Wilhelm, and Engle, 2005).

As mentioned earlier, complex span tasks reveal strong correlations with the VSAT (*r*s approximately .5; see Daneman and Carpenter, 1980, 1983; Turner and Engle, 1989) and other measures of reading comprehension (*r*s ranging from .50 to .90 depending on the comprehension task). Complex span tasks also correlate highly with each other regardless of the processing and storage task

(Turner & Engle, 1989). For example, Kane et al. (2004) administered several verbal and several spatial complex span tasks and the range of correlations among all the tasks was $r = .39$ to $r = .51$. Moreover, the correlation between latent variables representing spatial complex span and verbal complex span was $r = .84$ and the correlation between a latent variable representing all complex span tasks and g_f was $r = .76$. These results suggest that complex span tasks tap largely domain-general mechanisms, which makes them good candidates for exploring the relationship between WMC and g_f.

Simple Span Tasks

Simple span tasks (e.g., digit span, word span, letter span), in contrast to complex span, do not include an interleaved processing task between the presentation of to-be-remembered items. For example, in digit span, one digit is presented at a time, typically one per second, and after a series of digits the subject is asked to recall the digits in correct serial order. Simple span tasks are among the oldest tasks used in memory research – for example, digit span was included in the first intelligence test (Binet, 1903) – and continue to be popular in standardized intelligence batteries (e.g., WAIS, WISC).

As discussed earlier, simple span tasks like digit span correlate less well with measures of complex cognition than complex span tasks (Conway, Cowan, Bunting, Therriault, & Minkoff, 2002; Daneman & Carpenter, 1980; Daneman & Merikle, 1996; Engle et al., 1999; Kane et al., 2004). As well, simple span tasks are thought to be more domain-specific than complex span tasks, such that within-domain correlations among simple span tasks are higher than cross-domain correlations among simple span tasks (Kane et al., 2004). Moreover, this domain-specific dominance is greater in simple span tasks than in complex span tasks (Kane et al., 2004). These results would suggest that simple span tasks are not ideal candidates for exploring the relationship between WMC and g_f. However, recent research has shown that in some situations simple span tasks correlate as well with measures of g_f as complex span tasks, and in some cases they tap domain-general WM processes. We discuss three of these situations here: (1) simple span with very rapid presentation of items, known as running span; (2) simple span with spatial stimuli, known as spatial simple span; and (3) simple span with long lists of items, known as long-list simple span.

In a running memory span task (Pollack, Johnson, & Knaff, 1959), subjects are rapidly presented with a very long list of to-be-remembered items, the length of which is unpredictable. At the end of the list the subject is prompted to recall as many of the last few items as possible. Cowan et al. (2005) found that running span correlates well with various measures of cognitive ability in children and adults (see also Mukunda & Hall, 1992). Cowan et al. argued that the rapid presentation (e.g., four items per second as compared to one item per second in digit span) prevents verbal rehearsal and that any WM memory task that prevents well-learned maintenance strategies, such as rehearsal and chunking, will serve as a good predictor of complex cognition, including g_f.

This same explanation may demonstrate why simple span tasks with spatial stimuli tend to show strong correlations with measures of g_f (Kane et al., 2004; Miyake et al., 2001). For example, in a computerized version of the corsi blocks task, subjects are presented with a 4×4 matrix and a series of cells in the matrix flash, one location at a time, typically at a rate of one location per second. At the end of a series, the subject is required to recall the flashed locations in correct serial order. Kane et al. found that a latent variable derived from three spatial simple span tasks correlates as well with g_f as a latent variable derived from three spatial complex span tasks. Note, however, that the g_f variance accounted for by complex span and spatial simple span does not completely overlap, a point we will return to later in the chapter.

Simple span tasks are also strong predictors of g_f when only trials with long lists are considered. Reanalyzing data from

Kane et al. (2004), Unsworth and Engle (2006) showed that the correlation between simple span and g_f increased as the number of to-be-remembered items in the span task increased. In contrast, the correlation between complex span and g_f remained stable as the number of items in the complex span task increased. Also, the correlation between simple span and g_f was equivalent to the correlation between complex span and g_f for lists of four or more items. Unsworth and Engle therefore argued that controlled retrieval of items is needed when the number of items exceeds the scope of attention, that is, approximately four items. According to this perspective, simple span tasks with long lists require the same retrieval mechanism as complex span tasks because in each type of task, some information is lost from the scope of attention and must be recovered at the recall prompt. In the case of long-list simple span, some items are lost because the scope of attention is full and in the case of complex span items are lost because attention is shifted to the processing component of the task.

Scope of Attention Tasks

Running memory span and spatial simple span tasks with short lists, discussed earlier, might also be considered "scope of attention" tasks. Cowan (2001) reviewed evidence from a variety of tasks that prevents simple maintenance strategies such as rehearsal and chunking and found that for most of these tasks the number of items that could be maintained was about four. As mentioned above, other researchers have shown that in some tasks, one item in the focus of attention has privileged access (Garavan, 1998; McElree, 2001; Nee & Jonides, 2008; Oberauer, 2002) but according to Cowan's (2001) review, the *scope* of attention is approximately four items. While running span and spatial simple span may be considered part of this class, they are not ideal measures of the scope (and control) of attention because the to-be-remembered items must each be recalled and therefore performance is susceptible to output interference. In other words, it's possible that more than four items are actively maintained but some representations are lost during recall.

For this reason, the visual array comparison task (Luck & Vogel, 1997) is considered a better measure of the scope of attention. There are several variants of the visual array comparison task, but in a typical version subjects are briefly presented (e.g., 100 ms) with an array of several items that vary in shape and color. After a short retention interval (e.g., 1 s), they are then presented with another array and asked to judge whether the two arrays are the same or different. On half the trials the two arrays are the same and on the other half one item in the second array is different. Thus, if all items in the initial array are maintained, then subjects will be able to detect the change. Most subjects achieve 100% accuracy on this task when the number of items is fewer than four but performance begins to drop as the number of items in the array increases beyond four.

Tasks that are designed to measure the scope of attention, like visual array comparison tasks, have not been used in studies of WM and g_f as often as in complex and simple span tasks, but recent research shows that scope of attention tasks account for nearly as much variance in cognitive ability as complex span tasks (Awh, Fukuda, Vogel, & Mayr, 2009; Cowan et al., 2005; Cowan et al., 2006). This work will be discussed in more detail later in the chapter.

Coordination and Transformation Tasks

All of the above mentioned tasks require subjects to recall or recognize information that was explicitly presented. In some WM tasks, which we label "coordination and transformation" tasks, subjects are presented with information and required to manipulate and/or transform that information to arrive at a correct response. We include in this class backward span, letter-number sequencing, and alphabet recoding, as well as more complex tasks used by Kyllonen and Christal (1990) and Oberauer and colleagues (Oberauer et al., 2003; Oberauer, 2004; Süß et al., 2002).

Backward span tasks are similar to simple span tasks except that the subject is required to recall the items in reverse order. Thus, the internal representation of the list must be transformed for successful performance. In letter-number sequencing, the subject is presented with a sequence of letters and numbers and required to recall first the letters in alphabetical order and then the numbers in chronological order. In alphabet recoding the subject is required to perform addition and subtraction using the alphabet, for example, C – 2 = A. The subject is presented with a problem and required to generate the answer. Difficulty is manipulated by varying the number of letters presented, as CD – 2 = AB.

Kyllonen and Christal (1990) found very strong correlations between WMC and reasoning ability, using a variety of WM tasks that can all be considered in this "coordination and transformation" class (*r*s between .79 and .91). Also, Oberauer and colleagues showed that the correlation between WMC and g_f does not depend upon whether WM is measured using complex span tasks or these types of transformation tasks, suggesting that coordination and transformation tasks tap the same mechanisms as complex span tasks. Importantly, this suggests that the dual-task nature of complex span tasks (i.e., processing and storage) is not necessary for a WM task to be predictive of g_f, a point we return to later.

N-Back Tasks

In an n-back task the subject is presented with a series of stimuli, one at a time, typically one every two to three seconds, and must determine if the current stimulus matches the one presented n-back. The stimuli may be verbal, such as letters or words, or visual objects, or spatial locations. N-back tasks have been used extensively in functional magnetic resonance imaging (fMRI) experiments, and more recently in WM training experiments. Gray, Chabris, and Braver (2003) showed that a verbal n-back task was a strong predictor of a spatial reasoning task (Raven's Advanced Progressive Matrices), making n-back a class of WM tasks to consider as we discuss the relationship between WMC and g_f.

Empirical Evidence Linking WMC and g_f

Now that we have considered various measures of WMC, we turn to a review of the empirical evidence linking WMC and g_f. As mentioned, two recent meta-analyses, conducted by two different groups of researchers, estimated the correlation between WMC and g_f to be somewhere between r = .72 (Kane et al., 2005) and r = .85 (Oberauer et al., 2005). Kane et al. summarized the studies included in their meta-analysis in a table, which is reproduced here (see Table 20.1). Each of the studies included in the meta-analysis administered several tests of WMC and several tests of g_f , and latent variable analysis was used to determine the strength of the relationship between the two constructs. A variety of WM tasks was used in these studies, including complex span, simple span, and coordination and transformation tasks. None of the studies referenced in Table 20.1 used tests designed to measure the scope of attention, like visual array comparison, or n-back tasks.

One finding that has emerged from these studies is that complex span tasks are a stronger predictor of g_f than is a simple span (Conway et al., 2002; Daneman & Carpenter, 1980; Daneman & Merikle, 1996; Engle et al., 1999; Kane et al., 2004). However, as mentioned above, more recent research has demonstrated that this is only true for verbal simple span tasks (Kane et al., 2004; Miyake et al., 2001), and then, it is only true for verbal simple span tasks that do not include long lists (Unsworth & Engle, 2006, 2007). Unsworth and Engle have now repeatedly shown that simple span tasks with long lists correlate as strongly with measures of g_f as complex span tasks. Also, Kane et al. found that simple span tasks with spatial stimuli revealed correlations with measures of g_f as high as complex span tasks did.

Table 20.1. Correlations Between WMC and Gf/Reasoning Factors Derived From Confirmatory Factor Analyses of Data From Latent-Variable Studies With Young Adults

Study	*WMC tasks*	*Gf/reasoning tasks*	*r*(95% *CI*)
Kyllonen & Christal (1990) Study 2: $n = 399$	ABC numerical assignment, mental arithmetic, alphabet recoding	Arithmetic reasoning. AB grammatical reasoning, verbal analogies, arrow grammatical reasoning, number sets	.91 (.89, .93)
Study 3: $n = 393$	Alphabet recoding, ABC21	Arithmetic reasoning, AB grammatical reasoning, ABCD arrow, diagramming relations, following instructions, letter sets, necessary arithmetic operations, nonsense syllogisms	.79 (.75, .82)
Study 4: $n = 562$	Alphabet recoding, mental math	Arithmetic reasoning, verbal analogies, number sets, 123 symbol reduction, three term series, calendar test	.83 (.80, 85)
Engle, Tuholski, et al. (1999; $N =$ 133)	Operation span, reading span, counting span, ABCD, keeping track, secondary memory/ immediate free recall	Raven, Cattell culture fair	.60 (.48, .70)
Miyake et al. (2001; $N = 167$)	Letter rotation, dot matrix	Tower of Hanoi, random generation, paper folding, space relations, cards, flags	.64 (.54, .72)
Ackerman et al. (2002; $N = 135$)	ABCD order, alpha span, backward digit span, computation span, figural-spatial span, spatial span, word-sentence span	Raven, number series, problem solving, necessary facts, paper folding, spatial analogy, cube comparison	.66 (.55, . 75)
Conway et al. (2002; $N = 120$)	Operation span, reading span, counting span	Raven, Cattell culture fair	.54 (.40, .66)
SUB et al. (2002; $N = 121^a$)	Reading span, computation span, alpha span, backward digit span, math span, verbal span, spatial working memory, spatial short-term memory, updating numerical, updating spatial, spatial coordination, verbal coordination	Number sequences, letter sequences, computational reasoning, verbal analogies, fact/opinion, senseless inferences, syllogisms, figural analogies, Charkow, Bongard, figure assembly, surface development	.86 (.81, .90)
Hambrick (2003; $N = 171$)	Computation span, reading span	Raven, Cattell culture fair, abstraction, letter sets	.71 (.63, .78)
Mackintosh & Bennett (2003; $N = 138b$)	Mental counters, reading span, spatial span	Raven, mental rotations	1.00
Colom et al. (2004) Study 1: $n = 198$	Mental counters, sentence verification, line formation	Raven, surface development	.86 (.82, .89)

Study	*WMC tasks*	*Gf/reasoning tasks*	*r(95% CI)*
Study 2: $n = 203$	Mental counters, sentence verification, line formation	Surface development, cards, figure classification	.73 (.82, .89)
Study 3; $n = 193$	Mental counters, sentence verification, line formation	Surface development, cards, figure classification	.41 (.29, .52)
Kane et al. (2004; $N = 236$)	Operation span, reading span, counting span, rotation span, symmetry span, navigation span	Raven, WASI matrix, BETA III matrix, reading comprehension, verbal analogies, inferences, nonsense syllogisms, remote associates, paper folding, surface development, form board, space relations, rotated blocks	.67 (.59, .73)

Note. WMC = working memory capacity; Gf = general fluid intelligence; 95% CI = the 95% confidence interval around the correlations; WASI = Wechsler Abbreviated Scale of Intelligence.
[a] *N* with the complete data set available (personal communication, K. Oberauer, July 7, 2004).
[b] *N* for each pairwise correlation ranged from 117 to 127.

These recent findings have important implications for theories of the relationship between WMC and g_f. However, it is important to note that in each of these cases, simple span with spatial stimuli, and simple span with long lists, the variance explained in g_f is not entirely the same as the variance explained by complex span. To illustrate this, we reanalyzed data from Kane et al. (2004). We conducted a series of hierarchical regression analyses to determine the variance in g_f that is either uniquely or commonly explained by complex span and simple span (cf. Chuah & Mayberry, 1999). The results of this analysis are presented in Figure 20.3, panel A. As the figure illustrates, simple span with spatial stimuli accounts for a substantial portion of variance in g_f, and some of that variance is shared with complex span but some of it is unique to simple span with spatial stimuli. At first glance, this finding indicates that spatial simple span is tapping a mechanism that is important to g_f but is not common to complex span. However, the battery of reasoning tasks used by Kane et al. to derive the g_f factor had a slight bias toward spatial reasoning tests. When we model g_f from only the verbal reasoning tests, we observe a different result (see Figure 20.3, panel B). This suggests that spatial simple span does *not* account for any domain-general variance in g_f above and beyond complex span.

Unsworth and Engle (2006) conducted a similar analysis with respect to the relationship between complex span, simple span with short and long lists, and g_f. The results of their analysis are reproduced here in Figure 20.4. As with simple span with spatial stimuli, simple span with long lists (5–7 items) accounts for a substantial percentage of variance in g_f (22.5%). However, most of that variance is shared with complex span (79%). This suggests that simple span with long lists and complex span tap similar mechanisms.

As mentioned above, none of the studies in the meta-analyses conducted by Kane et al. (2005) included tasks specifically designed to measure the scope of attention. However, Cowan and his colleagues have conducted several recent studies to explore the relationship among scope of attention tasks, complex span, and cognitive ability in both children and adults. The results from just one of these studies are reproduced in Figure 20.5. Here we see that the variance in g_f accounted for by scope of attention

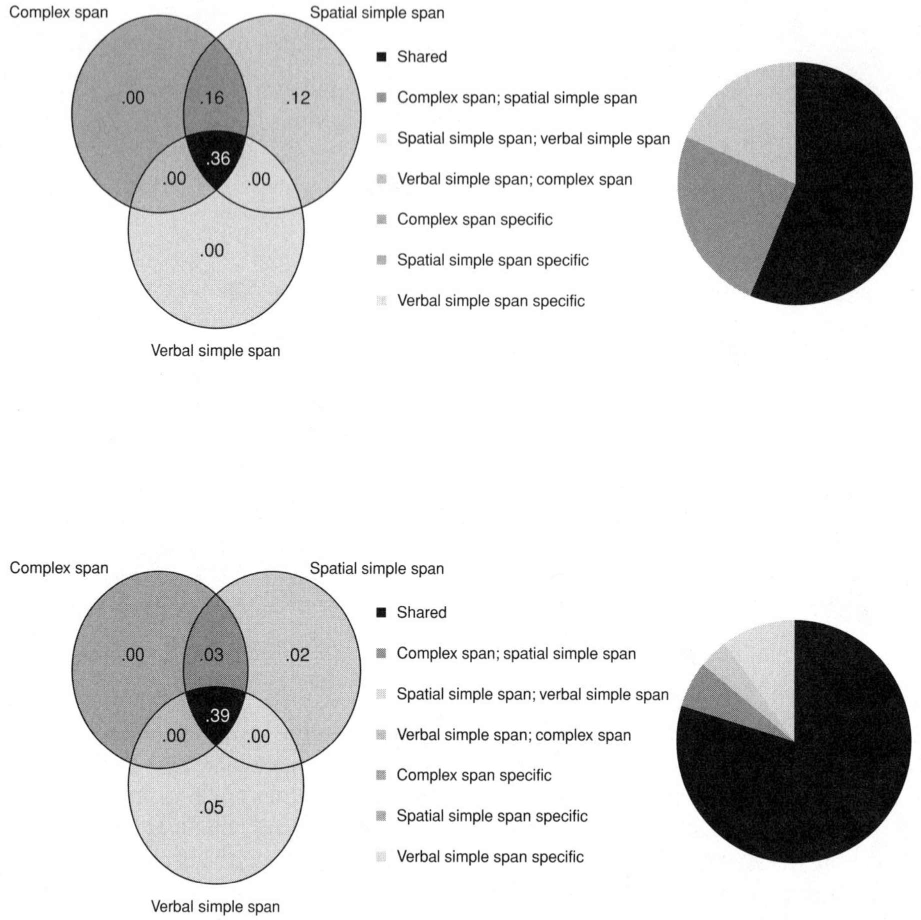

Figure 20.3. Reanalysis of Kane, M. J., Hambrick, D. Z., Tuholski, S. W., Wilhelm, O., Payne, T. W., & Engle, R. W. (2004). The generality of working memory capacity: A latent-variable approach to verbal and visuospatial memory span and reasoning. *Journal of Experimental Psychology: General, 133*, 189–217. Published by the American Psychological Association. Reprinted with permission. Panel A: Complex span, spatial simple span, and verbal simple span predicting Gf indexed by verbal reasoning, spatial reasoning, and figural matrix tasks. Panel B: Complex span, spatial simple span and verbal simple span predicting verbal reasoning.

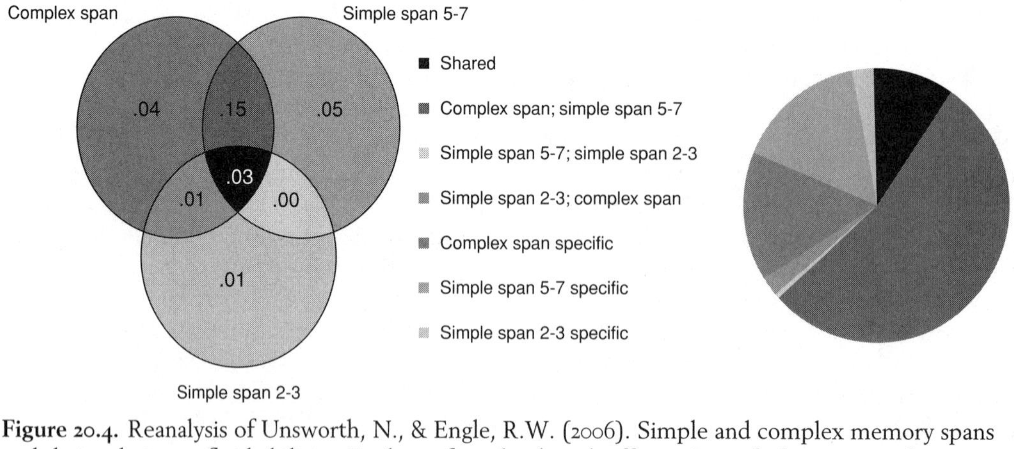

Figure 20.4. Reanalysis of Unsworth, N., & Engle, R.W. (2006). Simple and complex memory spans and their relation to fluid abilities: Evidence from list-length effects. *Journal of Memory and Language, 54*, 68–80. Reprinted with permission from Elsevier.

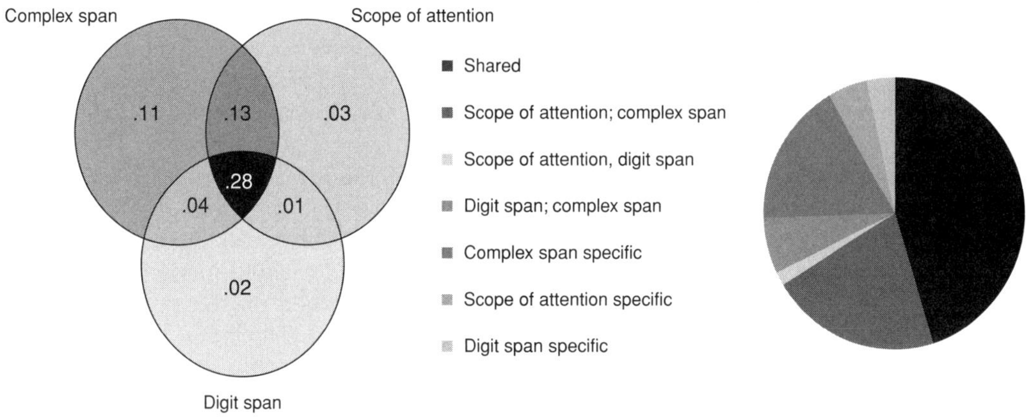

Figure 20.5. Reanalysis of Cowan, N., Elliott, E. M., Saults, J. S., Morey, C. C., Mattox, S., Hismjatullina, A., & Conway, A. R. A. (2005). On the capacity of attention: Its estimation and its role in working memory and cognitive aptitudes. *Cognitive Psychology*, 51, 42–100. Reprinted with permission from Elsevier.

tasks is largely shared by complex span tasks but that complex span tasks account for variance in g_f above and beyond scope of attention tasks. This result suggests that complex span and scope of attention tasks tap some overlapping mechanisms but complex span taps something that is important to g_f that is not required by scope of attention tasks.

Finally, recent studies by Jeremy Gray and colleagues have considered the relationship among complex span, g_f, and n-back. An important feature of Gray's n-back task is the inclusion of lure trials, which are trials in which the current stimulus matches a recently presented stimulus, but not the one n-back (e.g., n-1 or n+1 back). Accuracy to lure trials is lower than accuracy to non-lure foils, and accuracy to lure trials correlates more strongly with complex span tasks and with tests of g_f than accuracy to non-lure trials (Burgess et al., 2010; Gray et al., 2003; Kane et al., 2007). Burgess et al. examined the relationship between lure accuracy, complex span, and g_f. The results of their analyses are reproduced in Figure 20.6. Here again, n-back and complex span account for much of the same variance in g_f but complex span accounts for a substantial portion of variance in g_f that is not explained by n-back (see also Kane et al., 2007). As with the scope of attention tasks, this suggests that complex span and n-back tap some mechanisms that are common and important to g_f but that they also tap some mechanisms that are unique and important to g_f.

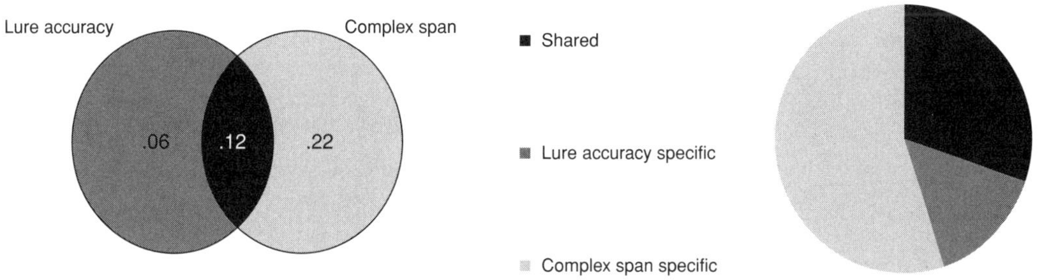

Figure 20.6. Reanalysis of Burgess, G. C., Braver, T. S., Conway, A. R. A., & Gray, J. R. (2010). Neural mechanisms of interference control underlie the relationship between fluid intelligence and working memory span. Manuscript under review.

Theoretical Accounts of the Link between WM and g_f

Several theoretical accounts have been offered to account for the strong relationship between WMC and g_f. It should be stated at the outset that these different accounts vary more in terms of emphasis and approach than they do in terms of the data they explain or the predictions they make. Furthermore, we believe that these various accounts can be encompassed by one theory, our multi-mechanism view, which we discuss at the end of this section.

Executive Attention

The first comprehensive theoretical account of the relationship between WMC and g_f was offered by Engle and colleagues, and particularly in the work of Engle and Kane (Engle & Kane, 2004; Kane & Engle, 2002). This view has been referred to as the "controlled attention" or "executive attention" theory. According to this perspective, individuals with greater cognitive control mechanisms, such as goal maintenance, selective attention, and interference resolution (inhibition), will perform better on a variety of tasks, including measures of WMC and tests of g_f. There is a great deal of support for this theory, and an exhaustive review is not possible here. Instead, we will highlight a few important findings. First, performance on various WM tasks has been linked to mechanisms of cognitive control, such as inhibition. For example, individuals who perform better on complex span tasks do so in part because they are better at resolving proactive interference from previous trials (Bunting, 2006; Unsworth & Engle, 2007). Similarly, individuals who perform better on complex span tasks are also more accurate on lure trials in the n-back task and lure trials predict g_f better than non-lure trials (Burgess et al., 2010; Gray et al., 2003; Kane et al., 2007). As well, tasks that place heavy demands on cognitive control but little demand on memory predict g_f (Dempster & Corkill, 1999).

Perhaps most striking, the correlation between complex span and g_f increases as a function of the amount of proactive interference (PI) in the task (Bunting, 2006). Bunting had subjects perform a complex span task and manipulated the category from which the to-be-remembered items were drawn (words or digits). The category was repeated for three items (to build PI) and then switched on the fourth item (to release PI). The correlation between complex span and Raven's Progressive Matrices, a marker of g_f, increased linearly as PI increased and dropped significantly when PI was released.

While executive attention theory has enjoyed considerable support, a fair criticism is that the empirical evidence is overly reliant on studies using complex span tasks. This is problematic because complex span tasks are, as the name suggests, complex. Thus, while Engle and colleagues have argued that "executive attention" is the primary source of variation in these tasks, other researchers have emphasized the fact that other sources of variance are at play as well, such as domain-specific abilities required to perform the processing component of the task (e.g., mathematical ability, in the case of operation span; or verbal ability, in the case of reading span; Bayliss, Jarrold, Gunn, & Baddeley, 2003; Daneman & Carpenter, 1983; Shah & Miyake, 1996). As well, performance of complex span tasks can be influenced by strategy deployment, such that a person may perform above average on a complex span task because he or she implements an effective strategy, not because the person actually has superior WMC (Dunlosky & Kane, 2007; McNamara & Scott, 2001; Turley-Ames & Whitfield, 2003).

Scope and Control of Attention

According to Cowan's approach, the scope of attention is limited to about four items, and individual differences in the scope and control of attention are what drive the correlation between measures of WMC and g_f (for a similar perspective on capacity limitations, see Drew and Vogel, 2009). The difference between Cowan's approach and that of Engle and colleagues, however, may be just one of emphasis. Cowan's recent work has emphasized the scope of attention while Engle's recent work, particularly that of Unsworth and Engle, has emphasized retrieval of information that has been lost from the focus of attention. Thus, we do not see these views as necessarily incompatible and we incorporate both into our multi-mechanism view, articulated later. One issue of debate, however, is whether scope of attention tests of WMC, like visual array comparison, account for the same variance in g_f as complex span tasks. The results of Cowan et al. (2005), reproduced here in Figure 20.5, suggest that complex span tasks have something in common with g_f that scope of attention tasks do not. However, Cowan et al. reported confirmatory factor analyses indicating that a two-factor model of the WM tasks, dissociating scope of attention and complex span, did *not* fit the data better than a single-factor model. Also, more recent work has demonstrated correlations between scope of attention tasks and g_f that are as strong as correlations typically observed between complex span tasks and g_f (Awh et al., 2009; Cowan et al., 2006). More research is needed to further investigate the relationship among scope of attention tasks, complex span tasks, and g_f.

Binding Limits

Oberauer and colleagues characterize the relationship between WMC and g_f as one of "binding limits" rather than one of attention. Oberauer argues that memory requires the binding of features into objects and the binding of objects into episodes. There is a limit to the number of bindings that can be actively maintained at once and this causes WMC. Importantly, more complex tasks require more bindings, and Oberauer has shown that more complex WM tasks tend to show stronger correlations with tests of g_f, which themselves are complex tasks. Of particular importance is the finding, mentioned earlier, that WM tasks that require multiple bindings, such as coordination and transformation tasks, predict g_f just as well as do complex span tasks, and account for largely the same variance in g_f as complex span tasks (Oberauer et al., 2003; Süß et al., 2002). This suggests that the dual-task nature of complex span tasks is not necessary to predict g_f and calls into question a basic tenet of executive attention theory, that is, that cognitive control mechanisms are responsible for the relationship between WMC and g_f. That said, an unresolved issue is the relationship between attention and binding. Hence, it isn't clear if Oberauer's view is incompatible with Engle and/or Cowan's view.

Active Maintenance and Controlled Retrieval

Unsworth and Engle (2007) argue that there are two dissociable domain-general mechanisms that influence WMC: (1) a dynamic attention component that is responsible for maintaining information in an accessible state; and (2) a probabilistic cue-dependent search component, which is responsible for searching for information that has been lost from the focus of attention. For example, as a subject performs a complex span task, the dynamic attention component is necessary to coordinate the processing and storage demands of the task and to maintain the to-be-remembered items in an accessible state. The search component is necessary at the recall prompt to recover to-be-remembered items that may have been lost from the focus of attention because of the demands of the processing component of the task.

Empirical support for this theory comes from simple span tasks with long lists and from serial free recall tasks designed to assess primacy and recency effects. As mentioned, Unsworth and Engle (2006, 2007) have shown that simple span tasks with long lists correlate as well with g_f as measures of complex span tasks and much of the variance explained by simple span with long lists is shared with complex span (see Figure 20.4). They argue that simple span with long lists taps the same controlled retrieval mechanism as complex span because the focus of attention is overloaded and items displaced from the focus of attention must be recovered during recall. More recent work demonstrates that individual differences in the primacy portion of free recall account for different variance in g_f than individual differences in the recency portion (Unsworth, Spillers, & Brewer, 2010). Unsworth et al. argue that variance in the primacy effect is driven by individual differences in controlled retrieval, and variance in the recency effect is driven by individual differences in active maintenance via attention.

While Unsworth and Engle (2007) do not provide a neural model of their theory, the dynamic attentional processes implicated in their account are consistent with recent computational models of WM that implicate PFC, ACC, and parietal cortex as regions involved in the active maintenance, updating, and monitoring of information in WM (Botvinick et al., 2001; Frank et al., 2001; Miller & Cohen, 2001; O'Reilly & Frank, 2006). Indeed, neuroimaging studies of complex span tasks show that PFC, ACC, and parietal areas are more strongly recruited in complex span tasks than during simple span tasks (Bunge et al., 2000; Chein et al., 2010; Kondo et al., 2004; Osaka et al., 2003; Osaka et al., 2004; Smith et al., 2001).

Unsworth and Engle further speculate that the medial temporal lobes (MTL) are also important for WM performance, which is a relatively novel prediction (but see Ranganath, 2006). In particular, they argue that the cue-dependent search process implicated during recall relies on coordinated activity between PFC and MTL. This view is also consistent with computational models that examine the interaction between PFC and MTL in a variety of memory tasks (O'Reilly & Norman, 2002). Indeed, a recent fMRI study indicates greater PFC and hippocampal activity during recall in complex span tasks than during recall in simple span tasks (Chein et al., 2010).

A Multi-Mechanism View

We argue that there are multiple domain-general cognitive mechanisms underlying the relationship between WMC and g_f. Our view is largely shaped by Unsworth and Engle's account discussed earlier, but also by computational models and neuroimaging data that similarly fractionate WM into dissociable mechanisms. Most important among these are the scope and control of attention, updating and conflict monitoring, interference resolution, and controlled retrieval. These mechanisms have been linked to neural activity in specific brain regions: PFC-parietal connections for the scope and control of attention (Todd & Marois, 2004; Vogel & Machizawa, 2004); a PFC-ACC-basal ganglia-thalamus network for updating and conflict monitoring (Ashby et al. 2005; Botvinick, 2007; O'Reilly & Frank, 2006); inferior frontal cortex for interference resolution (Aron, Robbins, & Poldrack, 2004); and PFC-hippocampal connections for controlled retrieval (Chein, et al., 2010; Nee & Jonides, 2008; Ranganath, 2006).

This multi-mechanism view of the relationship between WMC and g_f is consistent with the parieto-frontal integration theory (P-FIT) of intelligence (Jung & Haier, 2007), according to which, intelligence and reasoning are particularly dependent upon connections between parietal and prefrontal cortices. The current view is consistent with P-FIT but suggests that subcortical structures, such as the basal ganglia and thalamus, and medial temporal regions, such as the hippocampus, are also important. In fact, at the end of their review, Jung and Haier (2007) speculated: "there are likely other brain regions critical to intelligence and the implementation of intelligent behavior, including regions identified in studies of discrete cognitive processes, such as the basal ganglia, thalamus, hippocampus, and cerebellum."

Multi-mechanism, or multiple component theories of intelligence are not new. In fact, they date back to the beginning of the debate about the basis of Spearman's *g* (Thompson, 1916). Spearman described the underlying source of variance in *g* as a unitary construct, reflecting some sort of cognitive resource, or "mental energy." However, early critics of Spearman's work illustrated that *g* could be caused by multiple factors as long as the battery of tasks from which *g* is derived tap all of these various factors in an overlapping fashion. That is, any one individual task does not have to tap all the common factors across a battery of tasks but each task must have at least one factor in common with another task. These theories have been referred to as "sampling theories" of *g* and are best represented by the work of Thomson (1916) and Thorndike (1927). According to sampling theories, *g* will emerge from a battery of tasks that "sample" an array of "elements" that, in combination, constitute the cognitive abilities measured by the tests (Jensen, 1998). Thomson (1916) provided a mathematical proof of this by randomly sampling various sized groups of digits. In his terms, the groups represented mental tests and the digits represented elements. In our view, the "elements" are the various domain-general mechanisms tapped by the mental tests. Thomson showed that the groups of digits will be correlated with each other in terms of the number of digits any two random samples have in common. Thus, *g* may not reflect a unitary construct. Instead, *g* will emerge from a battery of tasks that tap various important domain-general mechanisms in an overlapping fashion.

Recent Trend: Training Working Memory to Boost Intelligence

One interpretation of the relationship between WMC and g_f is that WMC *constrains* intelligent behavior. According to this perspective, if people were able to increase their WMC, then they would be able to effectively increase their intelligence. Jaeggi, Buschkuehl, Jonides, and Perrig (2008) attempted to do just this and made what has been described as a "landmark" finding: training on a continuously adaptive dual n-back task transfers to performance on tests of g_f, such that subjects who underwent WM training performed better on tests of fluid intelligence than a control group that did not get WM training.

Subjects in the study underwent 8, 12, 17, or 19 days of training on a continuously adaptive dual n-back task. The dual n-back consisted of two strings of stimuli, letters and spatial locations (see Figure 20.7). Subjects were instructed to indicate whether the current stimulus was the same as the stimulus *n* back in the series. The value of *n* increased or decreased from block to block as performance improved or worsened. Thus, the task was titrated to individual performance and was consistently demanding. Participants were pre- and posttested on different forms of a measure of g_f. A control group did not undergo any training and completed only the pre- and posttest measures. As previously mentioned, the training groups underwent 8, 12, 17, or 19 days of n-back training, though not all groups received the same format of the test of g_f. This aspect of the design has received some criticism, as described later.

Jaeggi et al. (2008) found that all the training groups showed improvements in g_f, and the magnitude of the improvement increased with more training (see Figure 20.8). The control group also showed a significant increase in g_f, most likely due to practice effects. After taking pretest g_f scores into account (as a covariate), a trend toward significant group differences emerged after 12 training days. After 17 training days, the difference in g_f between the training and control group was significant. Thus, transfer of training to g_f was dosage dependent – gains in fluid intelligence were a function of the amount of training. If reliable, this effect clearly has tremendous implications. However, several critiques of this work have been presented recently. We consider these, as well as our own, in the later discussion.

One curious aspect of the Jaeggi et al. results, which is particularly relevant to this chapter, is that subjects showed training-related transfer to digit span but *not* to the reading span task. As mentioned earlier, reading span is considered a complex span task, dependent on active maintenance and controlled retrieval, whereas n-back is considered an updating task, dependent on active maintenance and cognitive control but not necessarily retrieval (indeed, fMRI studies of n-back typically show prefrontal

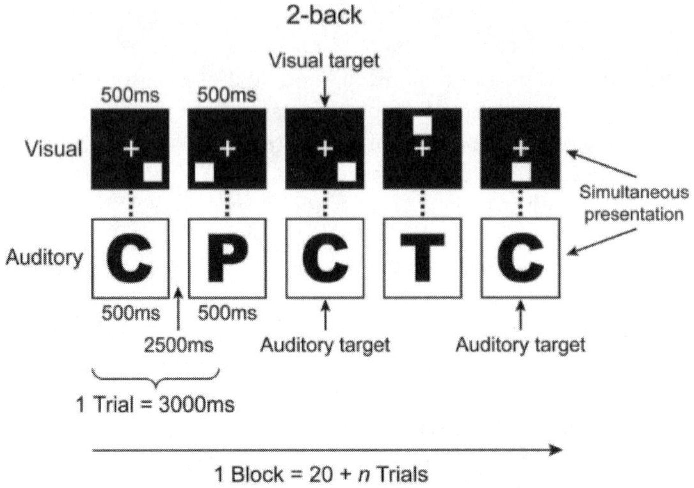

Figure 20.7. The *n*-back task that was used as the training task, illustrated for a two-back condition. The letters were presented auditorily at the same rate as the spatial material was presented visually.

and parietal activation but not hippocampal activation). Thus, an intriguing possibility is that their WM training regimen tapped the PFC-parietal aspect of WM but not the PFC-MTL component and that a more comprehensive training regimen would show even stronger gains in g_f.

The choice of tasks used by Jaeggi et al. (2008) to assess g_f has also come under criticism. Moody (2009) made the important point that while the group that received eight days of training was tested on Raven's Advanced Progressive Matrices (RAPM) and showed little improvement between pre- and posttests, the other groups, that did show improvement, were tested using the Bochumer Matrices Test (BOMAT) (Hossiep, Turck & Hasella, 1999). Jaeggi et al. provide no rationale for switching from one test to another. RAPM and BOMAT are similar in that they both use visual analogies in matrix format and both tests are progressive, such that the items become successively more difficult. Typical administration

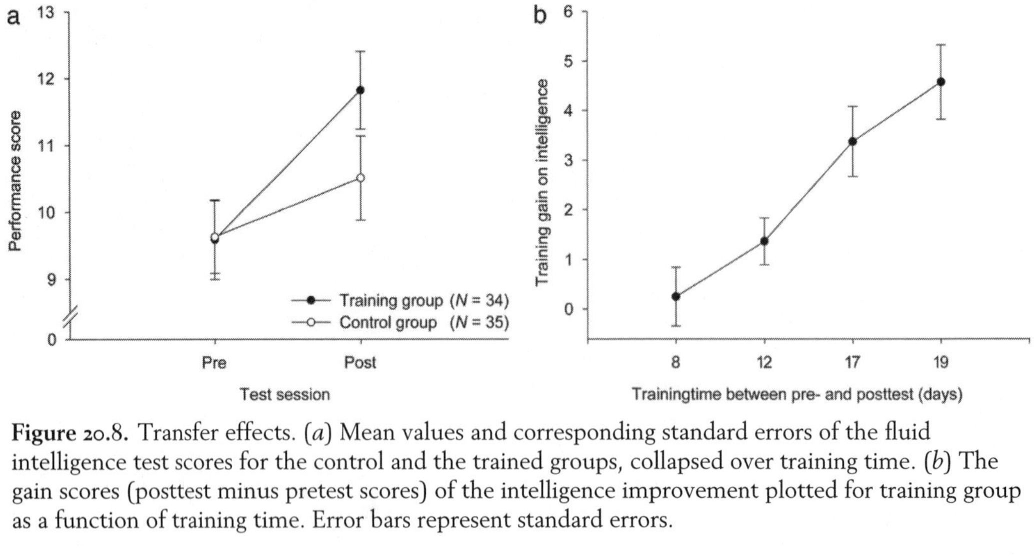

Figure 20.8. Transfer effects. (*a*) Mean values and corresponding standard errors of the fluid intelligence test scores for the control and the trained groups, collapsed over training time. (*b*) The gain scores (posttest minus pretest scores) of the intelligence improvement plotted for training group as a function of training time. Error bars represent standard errors.

of the BOMAT takes 45 minutes; however, Jaeggi et al. allowed only 10 minutes. Moody argues that the speeded nature of the administration did not allow subjects to advance to more difficult problems and thus "transformed it from a test of fluid intelligence into a speed test of ability to solve the easier visual analogies" (Moody, 2009, pp. 327).

Jaeggi et al. (2008) are not the first to target improvements in cognition via WM training, nor or they the first to document transfer of WM training to a nontrained task. Klingberg, Forssberg, and Westerberg (2002) administered intensive and adaptive WM training to young adults with and without attention deficit hyperactivity disorder (ADHD). These authors observed significant improvements post-training on RAPM as well as on a nontrained visuospatial WM task in both groups. A relative strength of this investigation was the use of an active control group that played computer games over the duration of training so as to control for the amount of time spent in front of the computer. A weakness of this study, however, was the small sample size of only four participants. Olesen, Westerberg, and Klingberg (2003) were able to pinpoint a biological mechanism for increased WMC after WM training for five weeks in three subjects. The authors propose that after training, the increased activity in the middle frontal gyrus and superior and inferior parietal cortices might be indicators of training-induced plasticity. While this finding is very suggestive, the claim must be supported by future studies with a larger sample size.

Future investigations of WM training and transfer to intelligence should aim to find transfer to complex span tasks for the reasons discussed. Moreover, it is crucial that pre- and post-measures of g_f be consistent and administered in a valid manner. Further, an active control group would address the issue of training gains based on repeated exposure to a testing environment alone. Last, and perhaps most important, the durability of training must be assessed. Jaeggi et al. fail to address the durability of the transfer of training to g_f. Their claims about increases in fluid intelligence would be further substantiated if they were able to demonstrate that these changes are not transient. A longitudinal follow up on participants' g_f would address this issue.

Conclusion

Working memory has emerged as a very useful construct in the field of psychology. Various measures of WMC have been shown to correlate quite strongly with measures of intelligence, accounting for at least half the variance in g_f. We argue that these correlations exist because tests of WMC and tests of g_f tap multiple domain-general cognitive mechanisms required for the active maintenance and rapid controlled retrieval of information. Also, recent research indicates that training WM, or specific aspects of WM, increases g_f, although more research is necessary to establish the reliability and durability of these results.

More research is also needed to better specify the various mechanisms underlying performance of WM and reasoning tests. Neuroimaging studies on healthy adults and neuropsychological tests of patients with various neurological damage or disease will be especially fruitful. For example, recent fMRI studies have illustrated that individual differences in activity in PFC during a WM task partly accounts for the relationship between WMC and g_f (Burgess et al., 2010; Gray et al., 2003). One intriguing possibility is that individual differences in activity in different brain regions (or network of regions) account for *different* variance in g_f. For example, based on the work of Unsworth and Engle (2007), it may be possible to demonstrate that individual differences in activity in the PFC, ACC, and parietal cortex, reflecting active maintenance during a WM task, account for different variance in g_f rather than individual differences in activity in PFC and hippocampus, reflecting controlled retrieval during a WM task.

The multi-mechanism view also has implications for research on WM training and for cognitive therapy for the elderly and patients with neural damage or disease. That is, rather than treat WM as a global construct, training and remediation could be tailored more specifically. Instead of "WM training" we envisage mechanism-specific training. That is, training a specific domain-general cognitive mechanism should result in improved performance across a variety of tasks. There is now some research supporting this idea (Dahlin, Neely, Larsson, Bäckman, & Nyberg, 2009; Karbach & Kray, in press) but again, more work is needed to confirm the reliability and durability of these results.

In sum, WMC is strongly correlated with g_f. We argue that the relationship between these constructs is driven by the operation of multiple domain-general cognitive mechanisms that are required for the performance of tasks designed to measure WMC and for the performance of test batteries designed to assess fluid intelligence. Future research in cognitive psychology and neuroscience will hopefully refine our understanding of these underlying mechanisms, which will in turn sharpen the multi-mechanism view.

References

Ackerman, P. L. (1988). Determinants of individual differences during skill acquisition: Cognitive abilities and information processing. *Journal of Experimental Psychology: General, 117*, 288–318.

Ackerman, P. L., Beier, M. E., & Boyle, M. O. (2002). Individual differences in working memory within a nomological network of cognitive and perceptual speed abilities. *Journal of Experimental Psychology: General, 131*, 567–589.

Anderson, J. R. (1983). *The architecture of cognition*. Cambridge, MA: Harvard University Press.

Aron, A. R., Robbins, T. W., & Poldrack, R. A. (2004). Inhibition and the right inferior frontal cortex. *Trends in Cognitive Sciences, 8*, 170–177.

Ashby, F. G., Ell, S. W., Valentin, V. V., & Casale, M. B. (2005). FROST: A distributed neurocomputational model of working memory maintenance. *Journal of Cognitive Neuroscience, 17*, 1728–1743.

Atkinson, R. C., & Shiffrin, R. M. (1968). Human memory: A proposed system and its control processes. In K. W. Spence & J. T. Spence (Eds), *The psychology of learning and motivation* (Vol. 2). New York, NY: Academic Press.

Atkinson, R. C., & Shiffrin, R. M. (1971). The control of short-term memory. *Scientific American, 225*, 82–90.

Awh, E., Fukuda, K., Vogel, E. K., & Mayr, U. (2009). *Quantity not quality: The relationship between fluid intelligence and working memory capacity*. Paper presented at the 50th annual meeting of the Psychonomic Society, Boston, MA.

Baddeley, A. D., & Hitch, G. (1974). Working memory. In G. A. Bower (Ed.), *The psychology of learning and motivation* (Vol. 8, pp. 47–89). New York, NY: Academic Press.

Bayliss, D. M., Jarrold, C., Gunn, D. M., & Baddeley, A. D. (2003). The complexities of complex span: Explaining individual differences in working memory in children and adults. *Journal of Experimental Psychology: General, 132*, 71–92.

Bors, D. A., & Bigneau, G. (2003). The effect of practice on Raven's Advanced Progressive Matrices. *Learning and Individual Differences, 13*, 291–312.

Botvinick, M. (2007). Conflict monitoring and decision making: Reconciling two perspectives on anterior cingulate function. *Cognitive, Affective and Behavioral Neuroscience, 7*, 356–366.

Botvinick, M. M., Braver, T. S., Barch, D. M., Carter, C. S., & Cohen, J. D. (2001). Conflict monitoring and cognitive control. *Psychological Review, 108*, 624–652.

Bunge, S. A., Klingberg, T., Jacobsen, R. B., & Gabrieli, J. D. E. (2000). A resource model of the neural basis of executive working memory. *Proceedings of the National Academy of Sciences, 97*, 3573–3578.

Bunting, M. F. (2006). Proactive interference and item similarity in working memory. *Journal of Experimental Psychology: Learning, Memory, and Cognition, 32*, 183–196.

Burgess, G. C., Braver, T. S., Conway, A. R. A., & Gray, J. R. (2010). Neural mechanisms of interference control underlie the relationship between fluid intelligence and working memory span. Manuscript under review.

Carpenter, P. A., Just, M. A., & Shell, P. (1990). A theoretical account of the processing in the Raven Progressive Matrices Test. *Psychological Review, 97*, 404–431.

Case, R., Kurland, M. D., & Goldberg, J. (1982). Operational efficiency and the growth of

short-term memory span. *Journal of Experimental Child Psychology*, 33, 386–404.
Chein, J. M., Moore, A. B., & Conway, A. R. A. (2010). Domain-general mechanisms of active maintenance and serial recall in complex working memory span. Manuscript under review.
Chuah, Y. M. L., & Maybery, M. T. (1999). Verbal and spatial short-term memory: Common sources of developmental change? *Journal of Experimental Child Psychology*, 73, 7–44.
Colom, R., Rebollo, I., Palacios, A., Juan-Espinosa, M., & Kyllonen, P. C. (2004). Working memory is (almost) perfectly predicted by g. *Intelligence*, 32, 277–296.
Conway, A. R. A., Cowan, N., Bunting, M. F., Therriault, D., & Minkoff, S. (2002). A latent variable analysis of working memory capacity, short term memory capacity, processing speed, and general fluid intelligence. *Intelligence*, 30, 163–183.
Conway, A. R. A., & Engle, R. W. (1994). Working memory and retrieval: A resource-dependent inhibition model. *Journal of Experimental Psychology: General*, 123, 354–373.
Conway, A. R. A., & Engle, R. W. (1996). Individual differences in working memory capacity: More evidence for a general capacity theory. *Memory*, 4, 577–590.
Conway, A. R. A., Jarrold, C., Kane, M. J., Miyake, A., & Towse, J. (2007). *Variation in working memory*. Oxford, UK: Oxford University Press.
Conway, A. R. A., Kane, M., J., Bunting, M. F., Hambrick, D. Z., Wilhelm, O., & Engle, R. W. (2005). Working memory span tasks: A methodological review and user's guide. *Psychonomic Bulletin & Review*, 12(5), 769–786.
Conway, A. R. A., Kane, M. J., & Engle, R. W. (2003). Working memory capacity and its relation to general intelligence. *Trends in Cognitive Sciences*, 7, 547–552.
Cowan, N. (1988). Evolving conceptions of memory storage, selective attention, and their mutual constraints within the human information processing system. *Psychological Bulletin*, 104, 163–191.
Cowan, N. (1995). *Attention and memory: An integrated framework*. Oxford, UK: Oxford University Press.
Cowan, N. (2001). The magical number 4 in short-term memory: A reconsideration of mental storage capacity. *Behavioral and Brain Sciences*, 24, 87–185.
Cowan, N. (2005). *Working memory capacity*. Hove, East Sussex, UK: Psychology Press.
Cowan, N., Elliott, E. M., Saults, J. S., Morey, C. C., Mattox, S., Hismjatullina, A., & Conway, A. R. A. (2005). On the capacity of attention: Its estimation and its role in working memory and cognitive aptitudes. *Cognitive Psychology*, 51(1), 42–100.
Cowan, N., Fristoe, N. M., Elliott, E. M., Brunner, R. P., & Saults, J. S. (2006). Scope of attention, control of attention, and intelligence in children and adults. *Memory & Cognition*, 34, 1754–1768.
Dahlin, E., Bäckman, L., Neely, A. S., & Nyberg, L. (2009). Training of the executive component of working memory: Subcortical areas mediate transfer effects. *Restorative Neurology and Neuroscience*, 27(5), 405–419.
Dahlin, E., Neely, A. S., Larsson, A., Bäckman, L., & Nyberg, L. (2008). Transfer of learning after updating training mediated by the striatum. *Science*, 320, 1510–1512.
Daneman, M., & Carpenter, P. A. (1980). Individual differences in working memory and reading. *Journal of Verbal Behavior and Verbal Learning*, 19, 450–466.
Daneman, M., & Carpenter, P. A. (1983). Individual differences in integrating information between and within sentences. *Journal of Experimental Psychology: Learning, Memory, and Cognition*, 9, 561–584.
Daneman, M., & Merikle, P. M. (1996). Working memory and language comprehension: A meta-analysis. *Psychonomic Bulletin & Review*, 3, 422–433.
Davelaar, E. J., Goshen-Gottstein, Y., Ashkenazi, A., Haarmann, H. J., & Usher, M. (2005). The demise of short-term memory revisited: Empirical and computational investigations of recency effects. *Psychological Review*, 112, 3–42.
Dempster, F. N., & Corkill, A. J. (1999). Interference and inhibition in cognition and behavior: Unifying themes for educational psychology. *Educational Psychology Review*, 11, 1–88.
Dunlosky, J., & Kane, M. J. (2007). The contributions of strategy use to working memory span: A comparison of strategy-assessment methods. *Quarterly Journal of Experimental Psychology*, 60, 1227–1245.
Engle, R. W., & Kane, M. J. (2004). Executive attention, working memory capacity, and a two-factor theory of cognitive control. In B. Ross (Ed.), *The psychology of learning and motivation* (pp. 145–199). New York, NY: Academic Press.

Engle, R. W., Tuholski, S. W., Laughlin, J. E., & Conway, A. R. A. (1999). Working memory, short-term memory and general fluid intelligence: A latent variable approach. *Journal of Experimental Psychology: General*, **128**, 309–331.

Ericsson, K. A., & Kintsch, W. (1995). Long-term working memory. *Psychological Review*, **102**(2), 211–245.

Frank, M. J., Loughry, B., & O'Reilly, R. C. (2001). Interactions between the frontal cortex and basal ganglia in working memory: A computational model. *Cognitive, Affective, & Behavioral Neuroscience*, **1**, 137–160.

Garavan, H. (1998). Serial attention within working memory. *Memory & Cognition*, **26**, 263–276.

Gray, J. R., Chabris, C. F., & Braver, T. S. (2003). Neural mechanisms of general fluid intelligence. *Nature Neuroscience*, **6**, 316–322.

Hambrick, D. Z. (2003). Why are some people more knowledgeable than others? A longitudinal study of real-world knowledge acquisition. *Memory & Cognition*, **31**, 902–917.

Hambrick, D. Z., & Engle, R. W. (2002). Effects of domain knowledge, working memory capacity, and age on cognitive performance: An investigation of the knowledge-is-power hypothesis. *Cognitive Psychology*, **44**, 339–387.

Hambrick, D. Z., & Oswald, F. L. (2005). Does domain knowledge moderate involvement of working memory capacity in higher-level cognition? A test of three models. *Journal of Memory and Language*, **52**, 377–397.

Hebb, D. O. (1949). *Organization of behavior*. New York, NY: Wiley.

Hossiep, R., Turck, D., & Hasella, M. (1999). *Bochumer Matrizentest: BOMAT Advanced-Short Version*. Göttingen: Hogrefe.

Jaeggi, S. M., Buschkuehl, M., Jonides, J., & Perrig, W. J. (2008). Improving fluid intelligence with training on working memory. *Proceedings of the National Academy of Sciences*, **105**, 6829–6833.

Jensen, A. R. (1998). *The g factor: The science of mental ability*. Westport, CT: Praeger.

Jonides, J., Lewis, R. L., Nee, D. E., Lustig, C. A., Berman, M. G., & Moore K. S. (2008). The mind and brain of short-term memory. *Annual Review of Psychology*, **59**, 193–224.

Jung, R. E., & Haier, R. J. (2007). The parieto-frontal integration theory (P-FIT) of intelligence: Converging neuroimaging evidence. *Behavioral and Brain Sciences*, **30**, 135–187.

Kane, M. J., Conway, A. R. A., Miura, T. K., & Colflesh, G. J. H. (2007). Working memory, attention control, and the *n*-back task: A question of construct validity. *Journal of Experimental Psychology: Learning, Memory, and Cognition*, **33**, 615–622.

Kane, M. J., & Engle, R. W. (2000). Working memory capacity, proactive interference, and divided attention: Limits on long-term memory retrieval. *Journal of Experimental Psychology: Learning, Memory, and Cognition*, **26**, 333–358.

Kane, M. J., & Engle, R. W. (2002). The role of prefrontal cortex in working-memory capacity, executive attention, and general fluid intelligence: An individual-differences perspective. *Psychonomic Bulletin & Review*, **9**, 637–671.

Kane, M. J., & Engle, R. W. (2003). Working-memory capacity and the control of attention: The contributions of goal neglect, response competition, and task set to Stroop interference. *Journal of Experimental Psychology: General*, **132**, 47–70.

Kane, M. J., Hambrick, D. Z., & Conway, A. R. A. (2005). Working memory capacity and fluid intelligence are strongly related constructs: Comment on Ackerman, Beier, and Boyle (2005). *Psychological Bulletin*, **131**, 66–71.

Kane, M. J., Hambrick, D. Z., Tuholski, S. W., Wilhelm, O., Payne, T. W., & Engle, R. W. (2004). The generality of working memory capacity: A latent-variable approach to verbal and visuospatial memory span and reasoning. *Journal of Experimental Psychology: General*, **133**, 189–217.

Karbach, J., & Kray, J. (in press). How useful is executive control training? Age differences in near and far transfer of task-switching training. *Developmental Science*.

Klingberg, T., Forssberg, H., & Westerberg, H. (2002). Training of working memory in children with ADHD. *Journal of Clinical and Experimental Psychology*, **24**, 781–791.

Kondo, H., Morishita, M., Osaka, N., Osaka, M., Fukuyama, H., & Shibasaki, H. (2004). Functional roles of the cingulo-frontal network in performance on working memory. *Neuroimage*, **21**, 2–14.

Kyllonen, P. C., & Christal, R. E. (1990). Reasoning ability is (little more than) working-memory capacity?! *Intelligence*, **14**, 389–433.

Luck, S. J., & Vogel, E. K. (1997). The capacity of visual working memory for features and conjunctions. *Nature*, **390**, 279–281.

Mackintosh, N. J., & Bennett, E. S. (2003). The fractionation of working memory maps onto different components of intelligence. *Intelligence, 31*, 519–531.

McNamara, D. S., & Scott, J. L. (2001). Working memory capacity and strategy use. *Memory & Cognition, 29*, 10–17.

McElree, B. (2001). Working memory and focal attention. *Journal of Experimental Psychology: Learning, Memory & Cognition, 27*, 817–835.

Miller E. K., & Cohen J. D. (2001). An integrative theory of prefrontal cortex function. *Annual Review of Neuroscience, 24*, 167–202.

Miller, G. A., Galanter, E., & Pribram, K. H. (1960). *Plans and the structure of behavior*. New York: Holt.

Miyake, A., Friedman, N. P., Emerson, M. J., Witzki, A. H., & Howerter, A. (2000). The unity and diversity of executive functions and their contributions to complex "frontal lobe" tasks: A latent variable analysis. *Cognitive Psychology 41*, 49–100.

Miyake, A., Friedman, N. P., Rettinger, D. A., Shah, P., & Hegarty, M. (2001). How are visuospatial working memory, executive functioning, and spatial abilities related? A latent variable analysis. *Journal of Experimental Psychology: General, 130*, 621–640.

Miyake, A., & Shah, P. (1999). *Models of working memory: Mechanisms of active maintenance and executive control*. New York: Cambridge University Press.

Moody, D. E. (2009). Can intelligence be increased by training on a task of working memory? *Intelligence, 37*, 327–328.

Mukunda K. V., & Hall V. C. (1992). Does performance on memory for order correlate with performance on standardized measures of ability? A meta-analysis. *Intelligence, 16*, 81–97.

Nee, D. E., & Jonides, J. (2008). Neural correlates of access to short-term memory. *Proceedings of the National Academy of Sciences, 105*, 14228–14233.

Norman, K. A., & O'Reilly, R. C. (2003). Modeling hippocampal and neocortical contributions to recognition memory: A complementary learning systems approach. *Psychological Review, 110*, 611–646.

Oberauer, K. (2002). Access to information in working memory: Exploring the focus of attention. *Journal of Experimental Psychology: Learning, Memory, and Cognition* 2002, *28*, 411–421.

Oberauer, K. (2004). The measurement of working memory capacity. In O. Wilhelm & R. W. Engle (Eds.), *Handbook of understanding and measuring intelligence*. London: Sage.

Oberauer, K. (2005). Binding and inhibition in working memory – individual and age differences in short-term recognition. *Journal of Experimental Psychology: General, 134*, 368–387.

Oberauer, K., Schulze, R., Wilhelm, O., & Süß, H. M. (2005). Working memory and intelligence – their correlation and their relation: A comment on Ackerman, Beier, and Boyle (2005). *Psychological Bulletin, 131*, 61–65.

Oberauer, K., Süß, H. M., Wilhelm, O., & Wittman, W. W. (2003). The multiple faces of working memory: Storage, processing, supervision, and coordination. *Intelligence, 31*, 167–193.

Oleson, P. J., Westerberg, H., & Klingberg, T. (2003). Increased prefrontal and parietal activity after training of working memory. *Nature Neuroscience, 7*, 75–79.

O'Reilly, R. C., Braver, T. S., & Cohen, J. D. (1999). A biologically-based computational model of working memory. In A. Miyake and P. Shah (Eds.), *Models of working memory: Mechanisms of active maintenance and executive control* (pp. 102–134). Cambridge, UK: Cambridge University Press.

O'Reilly, R. C., & Frank, M. J. (2006). Making working memory work: A computational model of learning in the prefrontal cortex and basal ganglia. *Neural Computation. 18*, 283–328.

O'Reilly, R. C., & Norman, K. A. (2002). Hippocampal and neocortical contributions to memory: Advances in the complementary learning systems framework. *Trends in Cognitive Sciences, 6*(12), 505–510.

Osaka, M., Osaka, N., Kondo, H., Morishita, M., Fukuyama, H., Aso, T., & Shibasaki, H. (2003). The neural basis of individual differences in working memory capacity: an fMRI study. *Neuroimage, 18*, 789–797.

Osaka, N., Osaka, M., Kondo, H., Morishita, M., Fukuyama, H., & Shibasaki, H. (2004). The neural basis of executive function in working memory: An fMRI study based on individual differences. *Neuroimage, 21*, 623–631.

Pollack, I., Johnson, I. B., & Knaff, P. R. (1959). Running memory span. *Journal of Experimental Psychology, 57*, 137–146.

Ranganath, C. (2006). Working memory for visual objects: Complementary roles of inferior temporal, medial temporal, and prefrontal cortex. *Neuroscience, 139*(1), 277–289.

Shah, P., & Miyake, A. (1996). The separability of working memory resources for spatial thinking and language processing: An individual differences approach. *Journal of Experimental Psychology: General*, 125, 4–27.

Shallice, T., & Warrington, E. K. (1970). Independent functioning of verbal memory stores: A neuropsychological study. *Quarterly Journal of Experimental Psychology*, 22, 261–273.

Sederberg P. B., Howard M. W., & Kahana M. J. (2008). A context-based theory of recency and contiguity in free recall. *Psychological Review*, 115, 893–912.

Smith, E. E., Geva, A., Jonides, J., Miller, A., Reuter-Lorenz, P., & Koeppe, R. A. (2001). The neural basis of task-switching in working memory: Effects of performance and aging. *Proceedings of the National Academy of Sciences*, 98, 2095–2100.

Suß, H. M., Oberauer, K., Wittman, W. W., Wilhelm, O., & Schulze, R. (2002). Working memory capacity explains reasoning ability – and a little bit more. *Intelligence*, 30, 261–288.

Thompson, G. (1916). A hierarchy without a general factor. *British Journal of Psychology*, 8, 271–281.

Todd, J. J., & Marois, R. (2004). Capacity limit of visual short-term memory in human posterior parietal cortex. *Nature*, 428, 751–754.

Turley-Ames, K. J., & Whitfield, M. M. (2003). Strategy training and working memory task performance. *Journal of Memory and Language*, 49, 446–468.

Turner, M. L., & Engle, R. W. (1989). Is working memory capacity task dependent? *Journal of Memory and Language*, 28, 127–154.

Treisman, A., & Gelade, G. (1980). A feature integration theory of attention. *Cognitive Psychology*, 12, 97–136.

Unsworth, N., & Engle, R. W. (2006). Simple and complex memory spans and their relation to fluid abilities: Evidence from list-length effects. *Journal of Memory and Language*, 54, 68–80.

Unsworth, N., & Engle, R.W. (2006). A temporal-contextual retrieval account of complex span: An analysis of errors. *Journal of Memory and Language*, 54, 346–362.

Unsworth, N., & Engle, R. W. (2007). The nature of individual differences in working memory capacity: Active maintenance in primary memory and controlled search from secondary memory. *Psychological Review*, 114, 104–132.

Unsworth, N., Spillers, G. J., & Brewer, A. (2010). The contributions of primary and secondary memory to working memory capacity: An individual differences analysis of immediate free recall. *Journal of Experimental Psychology: Learning, Memory, and Cognition*, 36, 240–247.

Vogel, E. K., & Machizawa, M. G. (2004). Neural activity predicts individual differences in visual working memory capacity. *Nature*, 428, 784–775.

Warrington, E. K., & Shallice, T. (1969). The selective impairment of auditory verbal short-term memory. *Brain*, 92, 885–96.

CHAPTER 21

Intelligence and Reasoning

David F. Lohman and Joni M. Lakin

The topic of reasoning has always been central to Western philosophy. Early psychological speculations about the nature of reasoning (e.g., James, 1890/1950, chap. 22) grew out of these traditions, especially from the work of philosophers such as David Hume and John Locke. Normative standards for good reasoning are fundamental to philosophy. Building on this legacy, some psychologists have studied reasoning on formal-logic tasks and the consistent violations of these normative standards that characterize much of human reasoning (see Chapter 39, Intelligence and Rationality, this volume). Researchers in this tradition study logical problem solving using the methods of inquiry developed in cognitive psychology (Leighton & Sternberg, 2004). A related tradition has focused on probabilistic reasoning in knowledge-rich domains such as law or medicine (Ellsworth, 2005; Patel, Arocha, & Zhang, 2005). Other researchers focus instead on individual differences in reasoning and the place of reasoning abilities within the larger domain of human abilities (Carroll, 1993). Typically, these researchers in the psychometric tradition administer batteries of psychological tests to large samples of people and study the patterns of covariation among test scores using latent variable models. Finally, other researchers have attempted to understand individual differences in reasoning by modeling the processes individuals use when solving items on tests that define reasoning abilities in these latent-variable models (e.g., Pellegrino, 1985; Sternberg, 1986).

Reasoning is closely allied with other domains of inquiry in psychology. Reasoning, problem solving, and decision-making represent different but overlapping aspects of human intelligence. Although interrelated, research on each of these three aspects of thinking is enormous (e.g., Holyoak & Morrison, 2005). In this chapter, we will survey only a small part of the field. Our emphasis will be on individual differences in reasoning as it is reflected in solving problems taken from or modeled after those used on psychometric tests of reasoning.

Defining Reasoning

Reasoning refers to the process of drawing conclusions or inferences from information. In logic, an inference is called *deductive* if the truth of the initial information (or premises) guarantees the truth of the conclusion. The inference is called *inductive* if the truth of the premises makes the conclusion probable but not certain. Distinctions between deductive and inductive reasoning can be important in understanding logic; but in practice, these distinctions may exist more in the mind of the researcher developing a task than in the performance of examinees on that task. Many researchers have found that performance on deductive and inductive tests is strongly related (Wilhelm, 2005).

These caveats aside, it is helpful at the outset to consider a more nuanced definition of these two aspects of reasoning. When people reason, they must, in Bruner's (1957) helpful phrase, go "beyond the information given." They do this in one or both of the following ways:

- They attempt to *infer* (either automatically or deliberately) concepts, patterns, or rules that best (i.e., most uniquely) characterize the relationships or patterns they perceive among all the elements (e.g., words, symbols, figures, sounds, movements) in a stimulus set. Better reasoning is characterized by the use of concepts or rules that simultaneously satisfy the opposing needs for abstraction (or generalization) and specificity. Such concepts or rules tend to be at least moderately abstract yet precisely tuned. Put differently, a poor inference is often vague and captures only a subset of the relationships among the elements in the set.
- They attempt to *deduce* the consequences or implications of a rule, set of premises, or statements using warrants that are rendered plausible by logic or by information that is either given in the problem or assumed to be true within the community of discourse. They often seem to do this by creating and manipulating mental models of the situation. Such models tend to represent explicitly only what is assumed to be true about the situation. Better reasoning involves providing warrants that are more plausible or consistent with the rules of logic or the conditions embodied in a comprehensive mental model. More advanced deductive reasoning involves providing either multiple (possibly divergent) warrants for a single claim or an increasingly sophisticated chain of logically connected and separately warranted assertions.

Cognitive-Psychological Studies of Reasoning

Those researchers following the *cognitive-psychological approach* to the study of reasoning typically study the responses of a small number of participants to logical tasks such as syllogisms or formal logic tasks. Researchers analyze how features of the problem influence the types of errors that participants make and often base their generalizations on the proportion of participants making certain errors (e.g., Stanovich, 1999). One source of debate in the cognitive approach is whether humans are fundamentally rational, as Aristotle assumed, or whether consistent demonstrations of irrational behaviors in the laboratory mean that humans function with pervasive biases that impede or prevent rational decision making. Researchers who conclude that humans operate with biases cite instances showing that people are swayed by personal testimony that is contrary to data and readily accept believable conclusions that are based on unlikely premises. However, critics of this research argue that the abstract structure of the problems can influence how they are solved and participants' misunderstandings of the format may explain some of these apparent failures in logical reasoning (Leighton, 2004). In some cases, illogical behavior on artificial tasks can disappear when the task is framed in a more meaningful way (Evans & Feeney, 2004; Stenning & Monaghan, 2004).

Followers of the cognitive-psychological approach have debated how best to explain variation in performance across tasks: Although some have argued that failures of logical reasoning are caused by random errors, others have shown that these errors are correlated across tasks. The observation that some people make more errors than others suggests computational limitations that vary systematically across individuals (Stanovich, 1999). That such a finding could be controversial would astonish most researchers coming from the psychometric approach.

Mental Rules or Mental Models?

Two theories have dominated psychological theorizing about reasoning: mental rules and mental models. Both theories were first applied to the study of deductive reasoning tasks such as syllogisms and then later applied to a broader range of reasoning tasks. The mental rules theory of deductive reasoning (Rips, 1994) posits mental processes common to all normally developed adults that operate directly on the representations of the premises. Humans are assumed to be natural logicians who are sometimes fallible because of errors in processing or because of limitations of the human cognitive system. According to mental rules theory, the basic processes involved in solving deductive reasoning problems are (1) encoding the premises into representations stored in working memory, (2) applying abstract, rule-based schemas to these representations to derive a conclusion, and (3) applying other rules to check the contents of working memory for incompatibilities. Although the model posits several sources of error, the number of steps to be executed in applying rules is the major source of difficulty. Errors in performance are thus primarily attributable to working memory overload (Gilhooly, 2004).

The mental models theory (Johnson-Laird, 2004) of deductive reasoning posits that the individual first transforms the premises of an argument into another representation (i.e., a mental model) that is consistent with the premises. Importantly, multiple mental models that are consistent with the premises must often be constructed and then compared in order for a valid conclusion to be reached. Each mental model represents a possible state of affairs that must be evaluated. Bara, Bucciarelli, and Johnson-Laird (1995) identified the following factors that affect syllogistic inference in the mental models approach: (1) assembling a propositional representation of premises; (2) constructing models that integrate information from premises; (3) formulating a conclusion that integrates relationships not expressed in the premises; (4) searching for alternative models to refute conclusions; and (5) recognizing similarities between models. All these processes require working memory resources. Limitations of working memory are considered especially important in this theory in understanding individual differences in reasoning, because working memory limits the number of mental models that can be held in mind at once. Individuals with limited working memory capacity can fail to generate enough models to evaluate the validity of a conclusion (Stanovich, Sá, & West, 2004).

The mental rules and mental models theories of reasoning propose universal but somewhat contradictory mechanisms for deductive reasoning (Roberts, 1993). Furthermore, advocates of both theories have been able to marshal considerable evidence in support of their position. Research that explicitly attempts to account for individual differences in reasoning offers a possible explanation for this paradox: On some problems, the behavior of some reasoners is more consistent with the mental models theory, whereas the behavior of other reasoners is more consistent with the predictions of a mental rules theory (Stanovich et al., 2004). In addition to stable individual differences in propensity to solve reasoning problems in one way or another, how the problem is presented can encourage individuals to change their strategies across items (Galotti, Baron, & Sabini, 1986). Therefore, what a task measures cannot be determined by simple inspection. Rather, what is measured depends on a complex interaction between the characteristics of the examinee, the task, and the situation. This does not mean, however, that one cannot know what tasks typically measure when they are attempted by individuals of known characteristics, but what tasks measure and for whom and under what circumstances are inferences that must be supported by other data – not merely presumed to be the case.

Tacit and Explicit Processes

Human reasoning occurs at different levels of awareness. Most cognitive scientists distinguish between tacit and intentional (or explicit) reasoning processes (Evans & Over, 1996; Stanovich, 1999). *Tacit* processes that facilitate reasoning occur without conscious intervention and outside awareness; they typically do not require attention. Such thinking is sometimes described as *associative* because it depends on the network of ideas and associations in memory (James, 1890/1950). Tacit processes are used when we make a decision in a quick or intuitive way, often because it feels right rather than because we have a clearly articulated set of reasons. We are aware of the outcome of these tacit processes but not of the processes themselves.

Tacit processes are particularly important in focusing attention and in building an initial mental model of a problem. Effective problem solvers typically attend to different features of the problem than those attended to by less effective problem solvers. Effective problem solvers know what to seek and know what to ignore (Horn & Masunaga, 2006). In part, this is due to greater experience, and in part, to better use of past experiences. Other researchers describe this automatic attention as the extent to which the person is attuned to certain aspects of a situation and not others (Gobet & Waters, 2003). By temperament or training, some people are more attuned to the distress of others, the beauty in a painting, the mathematical properties of objects, or the alliteration in a poem. Tacit processes are also importantly linked to feelings, which seem essential for solving ill-structured problems of all sorts. This runs counter to the belief that emotion interferes with reasoning. Yet without ready access to the affective associates of memories, problem solvers seem to drown in a sea of equally plausible but equally bland alternatives (Damasio, 1994).

Intentional reasoning processes, on the other hand, occur within the sphere of our conscious awareness. We are aware not only of the outcome of our thinking (as with tacit processes) but also with the processes themselves. This is the type of reasoning that is most distinctly human. Such thinking is often described as *strategic* or rule based. It typically requires effort, and it allows us to bypass the relatively slow accumulation of experiences that underlie tacit learning. We can thereby transfer principles (e.g., *always capitalize proper nouns*) rather than an accumulation of varied experiences (e.g., *I always capitalize this word*). Put differently, tacit processes are generally fast but limited to the range of contexts repeatedly experienced. Intentional reasoning processes, on the other hand, are comparatively slow and effortful, but flexible.

Thus, reasoning involves both conscious (or explicit) and unconscious (or tacit) processes. Although some refer to both explicit and tacit reasoning processes, other psychologists argue that tasks elicit reasoning only to the extent that they require conscious application of particular mental processes (Elshout, 1985; Sternberg, 1986).

The Role of Knowledge in Reasoning

Reasoning well in domains of nontrivial complexity depends importantly on knowledge. Expertise is rooted in knowledge, and experts reason differently about problems than do novices (Feltovich, Prietula, & Ericsson, 2006). Because of this, some have erroneously assumed that good reasoning is nothing more than good knowledge. This does not take into account the importance of good reasoning in the acquisition of a well-ordered knowledge base. Everyday reasoning depends heavily on the efficacy of past reasoning processes (stored as knowledge) as well as the efficacy of present reasoning processes. An increasingly sophisticated knowledge base supports increasingly sophisticated forms of reasoning. A more sophisticated knowledge base has richer, more abstract associative connections between concepts and more metacognitive knowledge that links strategies to goals. This frees working memory resources for problem solving (Gobet & Waters, 2003; Feltovich et al., 2006; Horn & Masunaga, 2006; Proctor & Vu, 2006).

Experienced problem solvers form problem representations that are not only more abstract than those of novices but are also more finely tuned to the problem at hand. Markman and Gentner (2001) argue that the formation of moderately abstract conceptual relations may be a precursor to the detection of coherent patterns that help successful problem solvers make connections to similar problems with known solutions. Further, moderately abstract, principle-based concepts are easier to retain and manipulate in working memory, thereby freeing attentional resources for higher level processes. There is thus an important synergy between good knowledge and good reasoning.

Studies of tasks modeled after item types on intelligence tests often ignore these contributions of knowledge – particularly domain-specific knowledge – to reasoning. The loss is probably most obvious in the domain of verbal reasoning. The verbal reasoning skills of lawyers or scientists go well beyond the sorts of decontextualized reasoning abilities assessed on most mental tests. A rich understanding of a domain and of the conventions of argumentation in that domain are needed to identify relevant rather than irrelevant information when understanding the problem, to decide which alternatives are most plausible and need to be considered, and then to decide how best to marshal evidence in support of a position. Strong warrants for an argument are considered highly plausible by those evaluating it. Plausibility judgments reflect both the beliefs of listeners and their assessment of the logical consistency of the argument. Standards for evaluating arguments are thus necessarily somewhat subjective. Nevertheless, some types of arguments are widely recognized as logically unsound. Toulmin, Rieke, and Janik (1984) classify these as (1) missing grounds (e.g., begging the question); (2) irrelevant grounds (e.g., red herring); (3) defective grounds (e.g., hasty generalization); (4) unwarranted assumptions; and (5) ambiguities.

Careful studies of reasoning in knowledge-rich contexts also show processes that generalize across domains. Newell and Simon's (1972) distinction between strong and weak methods of reasoning is especially helpful here. *Strong methods* of reasoning rely heavily on knowledge within a particular domain, whereas *weak methods* depend less on content and context. That is, strong (or domain-specific) methods describe what people do when they *do know* what to do; weak (or domain-general) methods describe what people do when they *do not know* what to do. Therefore, children and novices are more likely to use domain-general methods. Strong methods are closer to the construct of fluid reasoning ability whereas weak methods are closer to the construct of crystallized ability, at least as Cattell (1963) originally defined these constructs. Note, however, that evidence showing transfer of strong problem-solving methods concurs with the finding that fluid reasoning abilities are developed, not fixed.

A Classification Scheme for Reasoning Processes

Sternberg (1986) offered a helpful way to categorize the kinds of mental processes used on commonly investigated reasoning tasks: He calls them *selective encoding, selective comparison,* and *selective combination.* We will alter these labels somewhat in the discussion that follows. Recall from the discussion of mental models that although a test item or experimental task may elicit these processes for some or even most people, it may elicit other (nonreasoning) processes for any particular person or item. As Sternberg puts it, "the extent to which a task elicits reasoning is a function of the interaction between person and task, rather than merely a function of the task" (p. 287).

Selective encoding refers to the process of distinguishing relevant from irrelevant information. Such encoding can be effortful and deliberate, in which case it is clearly a reasoning process, or automatic, in which case it is at best a process that facilitates reasoning. For example, expert problem solvers generally attend to the deep structure of a problem and notice features and task similarities invisible to the untrained eye, whereas novices attend to the problem's surface features. For the expert, then, encoding processes facilitate problem solution but are automatized and not truly part of reasoning on the task; for the novice, however, attempting to encode the most important features is an effortful and multistep process that can impede problem solution. Learning what to notice and what to ignore is the essential first step in reasoning about any problem.

Whereas selective encoding means attending only to a subset of the information in a situation, *selective comparison* means retrieving and then comparing only a subset of the potentially relevant information about these concepts from long-term memory. We know a lot about many things that we think we do not know very well, and vastly more about things we know intimately; choosing what knowledge to apply to a new problem is a nontrivial source of reasoning complexity. Developmental psychologists have long known that children reveal much about the sophistication of their reasoning by how they classify or sort objects: on the basis of an arbitrary association, by using perceptual characteristics, or, at the highest level, by using several different abstract concepts (e.g., Piaget, 1963). Therefore, deciding how best to describe the relationships among two or more concepts is the critical second step in reasoning. For example, consider the analogy:

teacher : student :: coach : (a) athlete (b) child

There are many things a particular examinee knows about teachers: that teachers are people, that her English teacher is Mrs. Smith, that teachers are adults, that teachers have college degrees, and so on. Solving the analogy requires that the student focus on that small subset of features of the concept *teacher* that overlaps with the concept *student*. Comparison refers to the inference process – that is, the process of finding relationships between the two concepts and then selecting one that best characterizes the type of association between them given other contextual clues. For example, a vague relationship would be that teachers and students are both people, but this will not lead to a unique answer in this problem. One of the critical differences between good and poor reasoners is that poor reasoners often settle for a vague relationship or rule rather than a more exact one (Sternberg, 1985). This could be because they terminate the search for a rule or relationship too quickly, or because they do not critically examine how well candidate rules or relationships describe the data, or because they simply do not see or know the rule. Thus, what is called the comparison phase of reasoning actually has two parts: (1) the generation of plausible rules or relationships and (2) the evaluation of these rules or relationships. Oftentimes the problem itself provides the context for at least a partial evaluation of the rule. In an analogy, the relationship between the first two terms (A and B) must also be applicable to the third term (C) and one of the options (D_1, D_2, . . .). If the A-B relationship cannot be mapped on to one of the C-D pairs, then one must try to generate other possible relationships. Similarly, when inferring the meaning of a word or phrase in a text, the surrounding text provides the context for evaluation.

Finally, the third category of reasoning processes may be called an orderly, strategic, or planful combination of information in working memory. *Strategic combination* is often required on tasks that require deductive reasoning, such as formulating a logical argument or a mathematical proof. Syllogisms capture key aspects of this type of reasoning, albeit in an artificial format. Consider the following syllogism:

All A are B.
Some B are C.
Some C are A. (True or False?)

The difficulty in such problems lies not in discovering relationships or in understanding the meaning of concepts such as *all* or *some*. Rather, the difficulty lies in keeping track of all the ways in which the three terms (A, B, and C) can be combined. This quickly taxes working memory and can lead to a failure to consider combinations that disprove the rule (Stanovich et al., 2004). Memory burdens (and thus errors) are reduced if one has or can assemble a systematic method for solving the problem. For example, abstract syllogisms can be made more understandable by replacing abstractions (A, B, and C) with concrete nouns:

All dogs are animals.
Some animals are cats.
Some cats are dogs. (True or False?)

Sternberg claims that the major difference between inductive and deductive reasoning is that the difficulty of the former derives mainly from the selective encoding and comparison processes, whereas the difficulty of the latter derives mainly from the selective combination process. Because of the importance of strategy use in deductive reasoning, many investigators have noted that such tasks are particularly susceptible to training. This also means that deductive reasoning tests can measure different abilities in examinees who have learned strategies for solving problems like those used on the test than for examinees who must invent a strategy on the spot.

There are several other processes that, while not reasoning processes, are often essential. All are routinely used to regulate processing in working memory. Particularly important are the executive functions of self-monitoring and coordination. In order to be strategic or planful in working out the ways in which concepts can be combined or rules can be applied, one must monitor the success of one's efforts. Thoughtful adaptation of old strategies, the invention of new strategies, or the ability to learn from each problem attempted all depend on the ability to monitor the success of one's efforts. Thus, self-monitoring is a critical skill. Similarly, when solving reasoning problems, one must frequently coordinate different types of mental models. Understanding a text, for example, requires that one coordinate what Kintsch and Greeno (1985) call a text-based model (i.e., the network of ideas) with a situation model (often an envisioning of the situation being described).

Evidence of the nature and importance of these sorts of metacognitive skills for the development of intelligence is well documented in developmental psychology (e.g., Siegler & Alibali, 2005). For adults, some of the most striking evidence comes from studies of patients with damage to the prefrontal cortex. Such patients often retain the component skills that problems demand but cannot coordinate them. For example, a cook might remember recipes, measurements, and cooking techniques, but be unable to prepare a simple meal because he is unable to assemble a plan (see Damasio, 1994). We shall return to this issue later in the chapter. For now, the important point is that the development and use of intelligence requires more than efficient component processes for encoding, comparison, and combination. Unpacking the modifier "selective" (as in "selective encoding") shows that much more is required.

Working Memory

One of the more important controversies about reasoning abilities is the extent to which individual differences in reasoning abilities overlap with individual differences in working memory capacity. Kyllonen and Christal (1990) sparked the controversy with their finding that latent variables for working memory and reasoning factors correlated $r =$ .80 to .88 in four large studies with U.S. Air Force recruits. Other researchers also found large path coefficients between measures of working memory and measures of fluid reasoning abilities (Conway, Cowan, Bunting, Therriault, & Minkoff, 2002; Süß, Oberauer, Wittman, Wilhelm, & Schulze, 2002). However, critics complained that some tasks used to estimate working memory in these studies were indistinguishable from tasks used to estimate reasoning. Other critics (e.g., Fry & Hale, 1996) have argued that processing speed accounts for most of the relationship between the reasoning and working memory constructs in these studies. Ackerman, Beier, and Boyle (2002) note that processing speed is itself a multidimensional construct. They conclude that although there is little doubt that measures of working memory are significantly associated with measures of general intelligence, the two are not synonymous. Indeed, a meta-analysis of the existing data yielded a true-score correlation of $r = .48$ between working memory and *g*, far below the unity some claim (Ackerman, Beier, & Boyle, 2005).

In part, this is a problem of words. The term *working memory* connotes too small a construct; *reasoning* connotes too large a construct – especially given the way each is typically measured. Consider first the reasoning construct. In the best of these studies, reasoning is estimated by performance on a series of short, puzzle-like tasks. More commonly, it is estimated by a single test such as Raven's Progressive Matrices (Raven, Court, & Raven, 1977) which uses a single item format. As Ackerman et al. (2002) note, "if the Raven is not an exemplary measure of general intelligence (or even Gf), any corroborations between experimental measures (such as [working memory]) and Raven . . . are apt to miss important variance . . . and result in distortion of construct validity" (p. 586). Indeed, figural reasoning tests such as the Raven are typically much poorer predictors of both real-world learning and academic achievement than measures of verbal and quantitative reasoning. For example, Lohman, Korb, and Lakin (2008) administered the Standard Progressive Matrices (Raven et al., 1977), the Naglieri Nonverbal Ability test (Naglieri, 1996), and Form 6 of the Cognitive Abilities test (Lohman & Hagen, 2001) to approximately 1,200 children in grades K–6. Correlations with multiple measures of reading and mathematics achievement varied from $r = .3$ to $.7$ for all three nonverbal reasoning tests. The corresponding correlations for the CogAT Verbal and Quantitative batteries ranged from $r = .7$ to $.8$. Technical manuals for ability tests that are co-normed with achievement tests provide similar information, but on large nationally representative samples of students in grades K–12 (e.g., Lohman & Hagen, 2002). Raven was well aware of the restricted construct representation of the Progressive Matrices test. Because of this, he advised never to administer the test alone when making decisions about students but always to administer a verbal reasoning test as well (Raven, Court, & Raven, 1977). Therefore, whether measured by one task or several short tasks, the reasoning construct is underrepresented in virtually all research studies.

On the other hand, the construct measured by the series of working memory tests is much more complex than its label suggests. These tasks generally require participants to understand and follow a sometimes complex set of directions; to assemble and then revise a strategy for performing a difficult, attention-demanding task; to maintain a high level of effort across a substantial number of trials; and then to repeat the process for a new task with a new set of directions. In addition, many working memory tasks require individuals to process simultaneously one set of ideas while remembering another set. Although the individual tasks are generally thought to be easy, they are certainly not trivial, especially when performed under memory load. These tasks elicit executive functions such as the monitoring of processes, controlling their rate and sequence of operation, inhibiting inappropriate response processes, coordinating information from different domains, and integrating ideas into a coherent mental model. Such executive functions clearly overlap with many researchers' conceptions of reasoning or even of general intelligence. This heated debate may boil down to a difference in branding caused by the parallel development of closely related constructs in both psychometric and cognitive traditions.

Measuring Reasoning Abilities

Performance on one item provides little information about individual differences that would generalize to a test composed of similar items, and even less information about the broader ability construct defined by performance on several tests. Research on reasoning requires a method for measuring reasoning abilities. Although a single test-task is often used in experimental research, the term "ability" implies consistency in performance across some defined class of tasks. Indeed, some of the confusions and controversies in the field stem from equating performance on a particular task with the broader psychological construct. Psychological tests are simply organized collections of such tasks. However, typically less than half of the variation on well-constructed, reliable tests is shared with other tests that measure the same construct using somewhat different kinds of test tasks. An early but still reasonable rule in psychological measurement is that when measuring any ability, one should combine performance across at least three different measures that use different formats to reduce the specific effects of individual tasks (Süß & Beauducel, 2005).

Although many different tasks have been used to measure reasoning, a few are used much more commonly than others: analogies, matrix problems, series completions, and classification tasks. Some test batteries also measure verbal reasoning through sentence completion tests, sentence comprehension tests, and even vocabulary. Others include more specific spatial tasks, such as form boards or paper-folding tests. And others use quantitative tests that require examinees to make relational judgments (such as *greater than* or *less than*) between quantitative concepts or to determine how numbers and mathematical operators can be combined to generate a product.

Examples of the nine reasoning tasks used in the most recent revision of Thorndike and Hagen's Cognitive Abilities Test (CogAT, Lohman, in press) are presented in Figure 21.1. Although unfamiliar to most researchers, the CogAT is the most widely used group ability test in the United States and the United Kingdom. The three reasoning abilities measured by the test correspond with the three aspects of fluid reasoning ability identified in Carroll's (1993) compendium. Carroll's analyses of the fluid reasoning factor show that it is defined by three reasoning abilities: (1) sequential reasoning – verbal, logical, or deductive reasoning; (2) quantitative reasoning – inductive or deductive reasoning with quantitative concepts; and (3) inductive reasoning – the core component of most figural reasoning tasks. These correspond with the three CogAT batteries: verbal reasoning, quantitative reasoning, and figural/nonverbal reasoning. As shown in Figure 21.1, each reasoning ability is estimated by three subtests that require somewhat different processing.

Uses of Reasoning Tests

Traditionally, tests such as the CogAT or the SAT have been used (1) to predict achievement, (2) to provide a measure of cognitive development that supplements or can be contrasted with other measures of a student's cognitive development, and (3) to guide efforts to adapt instruction to the abilities of students. One need not have much of a theory of reasoning abilities to use a test such as the SAT Reasoning Test to predict college grade-point average (GPA). Indeed, the primary contribution of a theory of reasoning in such cases would be to avoid misinterpretation of predictions. Naive interpreters will see causal arrows running only from reasoning ability to achievement (or GPA), rather than seeing both as outcomes of education and experience (Snow, 1996). Understanding of the nature of reasoning abilities is also required when scores on an ability test are used as a measure of a student's level of cognitive development. For example, SAT scores can provide new information on a student's cognitive development only if the interpreter has some

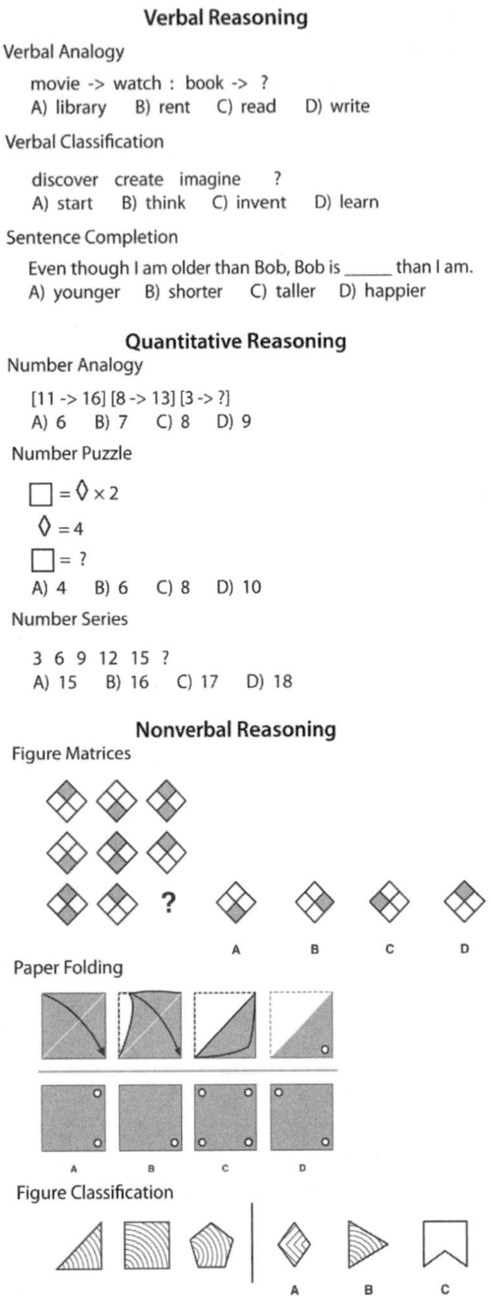

Verbal Reasoning
Verbal Analogy
movie -> watch : book -> ?
A) library B) rent C) read D) write
Verbal Classification
discover create imagine ?
A) start B) think C) invent D) learn
Sentence Completion
Even though I am older than Bob, Bob is ______ than I am.
A) younger B) shorter C) taller D) happier
Quantitative Reasoning
Number Analogy
[11 -> 16] [8 -> 13] [3 -> ?]
A) 6 B) 7 C) 8 D) 9
Number Puzzle
□ = ◊ × 2
◊ = 4
□ = ?
A) 4 B) 6 C) 8 D) 10
Number Series
3 6 9 12 15 ?
A) 15 B) 16 C) 17 D) 18
Nonverbal Reasoning
Figure Matrices
?
A B C D
Paper Folding
A B C D
Figure Classification
A B C

Figure 21.1. Reasoning subtests on Form 7 of the Cognitive Abilities Test (Lohman, in press): (1) Verbal Analogies (ans. = C); (2) Verbal Classification (ans. = C), (3) Sentence Completion (ans. = C); (4) Number Analogies (ans. = C), (5) Number Puzzles (ans. = C), (6) Number Series (ans. = *D*); (7) Figure Matrices (ans. = *A*); (8) Paper Folding (ans. = *D*), (9) Figure Classification (ans. = *B*).

understanding of what reasoning abilities are and how they develop. Diagnostic interpretations of test scores attempt to provide this information at a more skill-based level (see Mislevy, 2006).

The third use of reasoning tests – to guide instructional adaptations – often requires the most sophisticated understanding of reasoning abilities. Every effort to make instructional adaptations on the basis of student performance on an ability test makes some implicit or explicit assumption about what those measured abilities are. For example, if ability is primarily a matter of speed of processing, then slowing the pace of instruction may be the most effective adaptation for students with relatively poorly developed reasoning abilities. If, on the other hand, reasoning has more to do with the type of thinking one uses to solve problems than the speed of processing, then slowing the pace of instruction may not be the most effective adaptation. Knowing what elements of a task elicit or circumvent reasoning helps us better understand what those abilities are and how instruction might be modified to require or circumvent the need for those abilities.

One really does not know what abilities are unless one knows how they develop. Reasoning abilities are not only critical aptitudes for learning but they are also among its most important outcomes. Instructional interventions that explicitly require and succeed in developing students' reasoning abilities comprise one of the best sources of evidence on the construct validity of reasoning tests (Snow & Lohman, 1989).

The Construct Validity of Reasoning Tests

Inferences about the psychological constructs that a test measures in any particular application require multiple sources of evidence. The two major aspects of construct validation are nicely captured in Embretson's (1983) distinction between *construct representation* and *nomothetic span*. *Construct representation* refers to the identification of psychological constructs (e.g., component processes, strategies, structures) that individuals typically use in responding to items on a test. The cognitive psychological research on families of reasoning tests or tasks summarized in previous sections of this chapter provides the foundation for this aspect of construct validation.

However, inferences about processes do not depend on or explain individual differences on a task. Of the many processes that are involved in performance on a particular task, only some will be shared with other tasks. And of these common processes, an even smaller subset will be responsible for major sources of individual differences across several tasks. And only a part of these common individual differences will be attributed to the latent variable that best represents the reasoning construct. In other words, even processes and structures that are common to all tests in a family of reasoning tasks may contribute little or not at all to individual differences in reasoning ability.

Nomothetic span, on the other hand, concerns evidence on the nature of a construct that derives from its relationships with other constructs. For constructs that are grounded in individual differences, these inferences are based on the complex web of relationships among scores on tests that are designed to measure different constructs. Since the patterns of individual differences on a test depend on the characteristics of both the sample of test takers and of the number and nature of other tests included in the study, inferences about the nomothetic span of a test gain credence only after the test has been used in many different studies. The aspect of construct validation captured by nomothetic span affirms the importance of understanding individual differences on families of reasoning tasks, not simply on one or two tasks that have sparked interest among researchers. It follows that using a test in which all items follow the same format to define *reasoning* (or even worse, to define *intelligence*) reflects a fundamental misunderstanding of psychological measurement.

Nomothetic Span of Reasoning Tests

Psychologists have been investigating the number and organization of cognitive abilities for over a century now. Carroll (1993) reanalyzed and then summarized much of this work. His conclusions generally conform with those of other researchers in the field (McGrew, 2005). The first important finding is that human abilities are organized hierarchically. This means that some cognitive competencies are more broadly useful than others. It also means that theories that postulate an independent set of abilities (Gardner, 1983; Thurstone, 1938) or only one ability of any consequence (Jensen, 1998) are fundamentally flawed. The hierarchy that Carroll proposes starts with *g* (general mental ability) at the topmost level: Although the broadest factor in the model, *g* is also the least psychologically transparent. Eight broad group factors that are somewhat more psychologically transparent define the second level. These factors vary in their closeness or association with *g*. The closest is an ability factor that Cattell (1963) called *Gf* (general fluid ability). Other broad factors closely related to *g* at this level include *Gc* (General verbal crystallized ability), *Gv* (general spatial visualization ability), and *Gm* (general memory ability). Finally, a longer list of primary factors that are even more psychologically transparent defines the third level. These factors include such abilities as verbal comprehension, verbal fluency, inductive reasoning, spatial visualization, perceptual speed, and number facility. Most of these specific abilities have quite narrow predictive ranges.

The second critical finding in the literature on human abilities is that the general reasoning factor (*Gf*) may be decomposed into subfactors: (a) sequential reasoning (verbal logical or deductive reasoning), (b) quantitative reasoning (inductive or deductive reasoning with quantitative concepts), and (3) inductive reasoning (often measured with figural tasks). A good reasoning test, then, should probably measure all three of these reasoning factors – or at least not be strongly biased toward one (Wilhelm,

2005). This fact is commonly overlooked in studies that represent fluid reasoning abilities with a single figural reasoning test such as the Progressive Matrices test (Raven et al., 1977).

The third critical finding is that the topmost factor in the hierarchy (*g*) is virtually synonymous with the factor called *Gf* (general fluid ability) at the second level. And *Gf* is in turn virtually synonymous with the primary factor called inductive reasoning (IR). Gustafsson (1988; Kvist & Gustafsson, 2008) claims that the three factors are in fact identical (i.e., $g = Gf = \text{IR}$). Others would describe the relationship between *g* and *Gf* as more of an approximation than an identity (Carroll, 1993; Horn & Blankson, 2005). In either case, however, we are left with the important insight that reasoning abilities are at the core of human cognitive competence. In other words, the least psychologically transparent dimension (*g*) is in large measure isomorphic with one of the most psychologically transparent dimensions (IR).

Evidence from School Learning

Information on the nomothetic span of a test also comes from the sorts of criterion behaviors that the test predicts. Measures of general reasoning ability (or *Gf*) are good predictors of success in learning a broad range of tasks. Correlations are generally highest for the early phases of learning new, especially open-ended skills (Ackerman, 1988) and for learning the sorts of organized systems of meaningful concepts that are commonly required in formal schooling. Population correlations with measures of school success range from $r = .4$ to .8, depending on the criterion measure (e.g., grades, achievement tests) and of content of reasoning test (e.g. verbal, quantitative, or figural reasoning). Predictive and concurrent correlations based on representative samples of U.S. schoolchildren are commonly reported in technical manuals for group ability and achievement tests, most of which are updated and renormed every 6 to 10 years (e.g., Lohman & Hagen, 2002).

Reasoning tests correlate with academic success because school learning requires reasoning abilities. Understanding a story, inferring the meaning of an unfamiliar word, detecting patterns and regularities in information, abstracting the information given to form more general rules or principles, applying mathematical concepts to solve a problem . . . in these ways and in a hundred other ways, successful learning requires reasoning strategies. Indeed, the best way to develop reasoning abilities is through challenging instruction that requires students to exercise old reasoning strategies and to invent or learn new ones (Martinez, 2000; Nickerson, 2004).

These important reasoning skills are captured even by what some would consider narrow measures of achievement like vocabulary tests. Individual differences on vocabulary tests may arise from variance in how well learners use certain metacognitive or performance processes when learning – such as systematically testing alternative interpretations of a word when it is used in unfamiliar contexts – that then lead to a richer and more usefully organized knowledge base to guide new learning (e.g., Robinson & Hayes, 1978). Marshalek (1981) concludes that the ability to infer word meanings from the contexts in which they occur is the cause of the high correlations typically observed between vocabulary and reasoning tests. But there is also a synergism in that vocabulary knowledge allows comprehension and expression of a broader array of ideas, which in turn facilitate the task of learning new words and concepts. Thus, language functions as a vehicle for the expression, refinement, and acquisition of thought, and the humble vocabulary test masks an enormous amount of reasoning and remembering.

Aptitude-Treatment Interaction Research

One of the best sorts of evidence for construct validity via nomothetic span comes from experiments in which the treatment conditions are designed to vary in their demands for the construct presumably measured by a test (Messick, 1989). Those who understand that abilities are multiple, not unitary, have always believed that students' profiles on the sort of primary abilities that Thurstone (1938) identified would be the key to effective instructional adaptation. In the 1950s, research on the problem began in earnest (see Cronbach, 1957). The idea is straightforward. First, measure students' abilities. Then, randomly assign them to different instructional treatments, each of which is designed to appeal to students with different patterns of abilities. Finally, measure outcomes to see whether students with a particular ability profile performed better in one instructional treatment than another treatment. Statistically, the goal is to look for interactions between aptitude variables (such as verbal ability or spatial ability) and treatments (such as the use of demonstrations and films versus written texts) or aptitude by treatment interactions (ATI).

Hundreds of ATI studies have been conducted. Cronbach and Snow (1977) provided an initial summary; more recently, Corno et al. (2002) have updated the record. The most astonishing finding in this vast research effort is this: Contrary to the expectations of virtually all, the profile of specific abilities or learning styles generally does not account for much of the variation in outcomes. Indeed, interactions between learning styles (such as verbalizer versus visualizer) and instructional methods (such as an emphasis on visual versus verbal media) are usually small and frequently in opposite directions in different studies. Instead, the ability dimensions that routinely interact with instructional methods are *Gc* (general verbal-crystallized achievement), *Gf* (general fluid reasoning abilities), or *Gv* (general spatial visualization abilities). This means that what matters most when deciding how best to help students learn is their knowledge and skills in a domain, and their abilities to reason in the symbol system of that domain. For example, it is not the ability to generate visual images that matters, but rather the ability to reason with and about those images. Similarly, it is not the ability to remember words or to speak with fluency but rather to reason about what concepts the words signify.

The nature of the statistical interaction between instructional treatments and reasoning abilities is straightforward. Instructional methods that place the burden of making inferences and deductions on the student increase the relationship between reasoning abilities and achievement. Instructional methods that scaffold, remove, or otherwise reduce this burden reduce the relationship between reasoning abilities and achievement. The relationship is moderated by other variables, particularly anxiety, but reasoning abilities and prior knowledge in the domain are clearly the most important aptitudes for learning from instruction. Put differently, those who hope to enhance the probability of successful completion of school by offering different instructional opportunities are most likely to succeed if the adaptations are based on the developed broad reasoning abilities of students rather than narrow cognitive styles.

In summary, studies that address the nomothetic span of reasoning tests show that they (1) are at the core of human cognitive abilities, (2) are among the best predictors of meaningful learning, and (3) routinely interact with instructional methods that vary in the demands placed on students to think for themselves. Such evidence confirms the important role that reasoning tests play in human abilities. But other information is needed to understand exactly what these tests measure.

Hypotheses About the Construct Representation of Reasoning Tests

Hundreds of studies have estimated relationships between reasoning tests and other kinds of ability tests and show that reasoning tests are good measures of the general ability (*g*). But evidence of construct representation is needed to explain *why* reasoning tests are such good measures and what essential processes they tap into that could explain this relationship. Two-dimensional scalings of the correlations among large batteries of tests reveal something that can serve

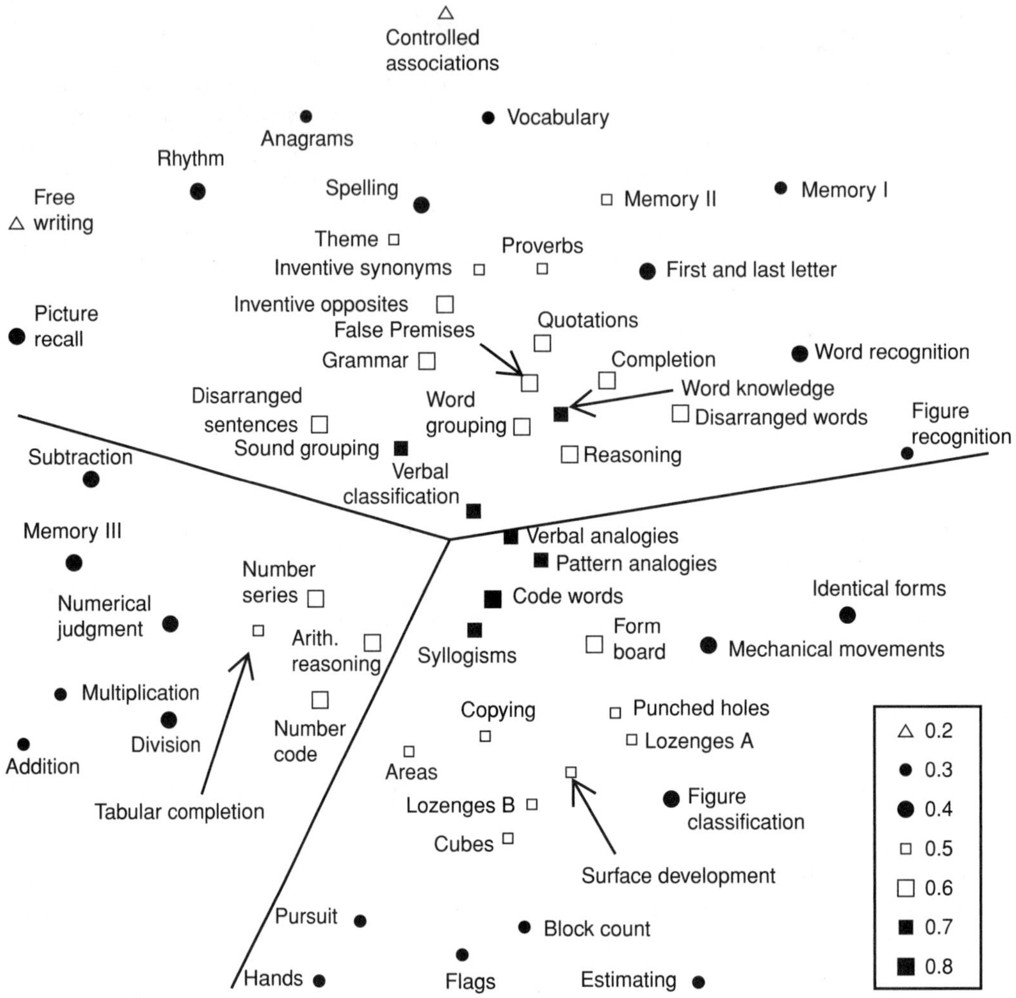

Figure 21.2. Nonmetric scaling of ability test intercorrelations. The symbols indicate the correlation of the test with the general factor. Data from L. L. Thurstone (1938). Plot coordinates from Snow, Kyllonen, and Marshalek (1984). Copyright 1984 by Lawrence Erlbaum Associates. Adapted by permission.

as a useful bridge between the cognitive-psychological studies that investigate the construct representation of reasoning tests and the correlational studies that address the nomothetic span of reasoning tests. In these scalings, complex tests that load heavily on *g* (or *Gf*) fall near the center of the plot, whereas simpler tasks are distributed around the periphery. (See Figure 21.2.) Complex reasoning tasks occupy the spots closest to the center.

Several hypotheses have been advanced to explain how processing complexity increases along the various spokes that run from the periphery to *g*: (1) an increase in the number of component processes; (2) an accumulation of differences in speed of component processing; (3) an increase in the involvement of one or more critically important performance components, such as the inference process; (4) an increase in demands on limited working memory or attention; and (5) an increase in demands on adaptive functions, including assembly, control, and monitoring functions. Clearly these explanations are not independent. For example, it is impossible to get an accumulation of speed differences over components (Hypothesis 2) without also increasing the number of component processes required

(Hypothesis 1). Despite this overlap, these hypotheses provide a useful way to organize the discussion.

More Component Processes

Even the most superficial examination of tasks that fall along one of the spokes of the plot shown in Figure 21.2 reveals that more central or *g*-loaded tasks require subjects to do more than the more peripheral tests. Many years ago, Zimmerman (1954) demonstrated that a form-board test could be made to load more on perceptual speed, spatial relations, visualization, and reasoning factors, in that order, by increasing the complexity of the items. Snow, Kyllonen, and Marshalek's (1984) reanalysis of old learning-task and ability-test correlation matrices showed similar continua. Spilsbury (1992) argued that the crucial manipulation was an increase in the factorial complexity of a task (that is, the number of different abilities required). However, increases in the number or difficulty of task steps beyond a certain point can decrease the correlation with *g* (Crawford, 1988; Raaheim, 1988; Swiney, 1985). Thus, one does not automatically increase the relationship with *g* simply by making problems harder, or even by increasing the factorial complexity of a task. Indeed, there are many hard problems (e.g., memorizing lists of randomly chosen numbers or words) that are not particularly good measures of *g*. Furthermore, even for problems that do require the type of processing that causes the test to measure *g*, problems must be of the appropriate level of difficulty for subjects.

Speed or Efficiency of Elementary Processing

This hypothesis has taken several forms. In its strongest form, the assertion has been that individuals differ in the general speed or efficiency with which they process information, possibly as a result of more efficient brain structures (Jensen, 1998). Although disattenuated correlations between reaction time (RT) and *g* can be substantial when samples vary widely in ability (even, for example, including mentally retarded participants), samples more typical of those used in other research on abilities yield correlations between RT and *g* in the $r = -.1$ to $-.4$ range (Deary & Stough, 1996; Jensen, 1982; Roberts & Stankov, 1999; Sternberg, 1985). In principle, processing speed could be estimated on any elementary cognitive task that minimizes the import of learning, motivation, strategy, and other confounding variables. In fact, response latencies on many tasks show a pattern of increasing correlation with an external estimate of *g* as task complexity decreases. In other words, response latencies for simpler tasks typically show higher correlations with *g* than do response latencies for more complex tasks. But this is unsurprising. The more complex the task, the more room there is for subjects to use different strategies or even to be inconsistent in the execution of different components across items.

In its weak form, the hypothesis has been that although speed of processing on any one task may be only weakly correlated with more complex performances, such small differences cumulate over time and tasks. Thus, Hunt, Frost, and Lunneborg (1973) noted that although latency differences in the retrieval of overlearned name codes correlated only $r = .3$ with verbal ability, such small differences on individual words cumulate to substantial differences in the course of a more extended activity such as reading comprehension. Detterman (1986) emphasized the cumulation across different component processes rather than across time. He showed that although individual component processes were only weakly correlated with *g*, their combined effect on a complex task was more substantial.

Although individual differences in speed of processing are an important aspect of *g*, *g* is more than rapid or efficient information processing. Furthermore, the strength of the relationship between speed of processing and *g* varies considerably across domains, being strongest ($r \approx -.4$) in the verbal domain and weakest ($r \approx -.2$) in the spatial domain. Indeed, for complex spatial tasks, the speed with which individuals perform different spatial operations is usually much less predictive of overall performance than the richness or quality of the mental representations they create (Lohman, 1988; Salthouse, Babcock, Mitchell, Palmon, & Skovronek, 1990).

More Involvement of Critical Performance Components

If the *g*-loading of a test is not simply a reflection of more or faster processing, might it be the case that *g* really reflects the action of particular mental processes? Spearman (1927) was one of the first to argue for this alternative. For him, the essential processes were the "eduction of relations," which Sternberg (1977) calls *inference*, and the "eduction of correlates," which Sternberg calls *mapping* and *application*. Evidence favoring this hypothesis is substantial. A common characteristic of tests that require eduction of relations such as the matrices, letter/number series, analogies, classification, and various quantitative reasoning tests is that they are all measures of reasoning, particularly inductive reasoning. Many school learning tasks, particularly in science and mathematics, bear formal similarity to these reasoning tests. Greeno (1978) refers to such tasks, collectively, as problems of inducing structure. Indeed, the need for learners to induce structure in instruction is probably why reasoning tests correlate with achievement tests (Snow, 1980). But to describe the overlap in this way is not to explain it.

Evidence unequivocally supporting the hypothesis that individual differences in particular component processes correlate strongly with *g* has been surprisingly difficult to obtain. Sternberg's (1977) investigations of analogical reasoning found little generalizability across tasks or scores for the inference component (Spearman's eduction of relations), and at best inconsistent correlations of these scores with reference reasoning tests. Rather, it was the intercept (or "wastebasket" parameter) that showed more consistent correlations with reference abilities. We now know that this was in large measure an inevitable consequence of the way component scores are estimated (Lohman, 1994): Individual differences that are consistent across items intended to require different amounts of particular component processes will appear in the intercept (the mean score of the individual across items) rather than in the component scores (reflecting factors that vary within the individual). Therefore, low or inconsistent correlations between scores for particular component processes and other variables do not provide much evidence against the hypothesis that these processes are important because estimates of component processes omit important variance due to differences in reasoning – both between and within individuals.

A second line of evidence on the centrality of particular component processes comes from demonstrations that certain types of task manipulations are more likely than others to increase the *Gf*-loading of a task (Pellegrino, 1985; Sternberg, 1986). Sternberg (1986) focused on manipulations that affected the demands placed on his three component processes: selective encoding, selective comparison, and selective combination, described previously. Demands on selective encoding skills are amplified by increasing distractions caused by salient but irrelevant information, or, when solving items on mental tests, by preventing examinees from looking ahead to the alternatives before studying the stem (Bethell-Fox, Lohman, & Snow, 1984). Demands on selective comparison are increased by manipulating the familiarity of concepts. Presenting somewhat unfamiliar concepts or using familiar concepts in unfamiliar ways places heavy demands on the ability to retrieve and compare information. Selective combination can be manipulated by providing algorithms or strategies that reduce working memory burdens. Practice on items that are similar to those used on a test can undermine the *Gf*-loading of a test because the processes and strategies used become increasingly automatized; this is especially apparent on deductive reasoning tasks and their demands on selective combination (Sternberg, 1986).

Attention and Working Memory Capacity

All information-processing models of memory and cognition posit the existence of a limited capacity working memory that functions not only as a central processor but also as a bottleneck in the system. Some see this in terms of structure or capacity limitations, others in terms of attentional resources, and yet others in terms of differences in knowledge or experience (see Miyake & Shah, 1999). Hunt and Lansman (1982) and Ackerman (1988) argue that tasks that show higher correlations with *g* require more attentional resources. Attempts to manipulate the attentional demands of tasks often use a dual-task paradigm. Here, participants are required to do two things simultaneously, such as searching for a particular stimulus in a visual display while simultaneously listening for a specified auditory stimulus. Differences between more and less able subjects are typically greater in the dual task than in the single task condition. However, interpretation of this finding is problematic. For example, in one study, Stankov (1988) found that correlations with both *Gc* and *Gf*, but especially *Gf*, were higher for dual tasks than for single tasks. However, high levels of performance in the dual task situation were due to a strategy of momentarily ignoring one task while attending to the other. Thus, what on the surface seemed to implicate greater attentional resources on closer inspection implicated self-monitoring and the shifting of attentional resources.

Attentional requirements of tasks vary according to an individual's familiarity with the task and to the susceptibility of the task to automatization. Tasks – or task components – in which there is a consistent mapping between stimulus and response can be automatized in this way (Ackerman & Woltz, 1994). Attributing individual differences in reasoning to individual differences in working memory capacity parallels the attentional explanation. Many researchers have claimed that a major source of individual differences on reasoning tasks lies in how much information one must maintain in working memory, especially while effecting some transformation of that information (Engle, Tuholski, Laughlin, & Conway, 1999; Holzman, Pellegrino, & Glaser, 1982). Controlling attention in this way is a critical aspect of both selective encoding and goal management within the constraints of working memory (Primi, 2001). Furthermore, as Kyllonen and Christal (1990) noted, most of the performance processes (such as encoding and inference) and executive processes (such as goal setting, goal management, and monitoring) are presumed to occur in working memory. Thus, even though a chosen strategy may be effective, it must be performed within the limits of the working memory system while sharing resources with retrieval, executive, and other processes. Therefore, although many different processes may be executed in the solution of a task, individual differences in them may primarily reflect individual differences in working memory resources to maintain these competing processes.

Adaptive Processing

While acknowledging that individual differences in *g* reflected differences in all of these levels – in the speed and efficacy of elementary processes, in attentional or working memory resources, in the action of processes responsible for inference and abstraction (which includes knowledge, skill, and attunement to affordances in the task situation) – several theorists have argued that more is needed. Sternberg (1985) argued that intelligent action requires the application of control processes that decide what the problem is, select lower-order components and organize them into a strategy, select a mode for representing or organizing information, allocate attentional resources, monitor the solution process, and attend to external feedback.

Marshalek, Lohman, and Snow (1983), on the other hand, focused more narrowly on assembly and control processes: They hypothesized that

> *more complex tasks may require more involvement of executive assembly and control processes that structure and analyze the problem, assemble a strategy of attack on it, monitor the performance process, and adapt these strategies as performance proceeds, within as well as between items in a task, and between tasks. (Marshalek et al., 1983, p. 124)*

The Carpenter, Just, and Shell (1990) analysis of the Raven test supports this hypothesis. In their simulation, the crucial executive functions were (1) the ability to decompose a complex problem into simpler problems and (2) the ability to manage the hierarchy of goals and subgoals generated by this decomposition.

In general, assembly processes are reflected in activities in which an individual must organize a series of overt acts or covert cognitive processes into a sequence. They are thus essential for all high-level thinking and complex problem solving. These processes are greatly facilitated by the ability to envision future states (i.e., goals) that differ from present states (i.e., what is currently in mind or in view). This is an especially important activity when attempting novel or ill-structured tasks. Control processes are more diverse, although all involve the ability to monitor the effects of one's cognitions and actions and adjust them according to feedback from the environment or one's body. Both types of processing depend heavily on the ability to maintain ideas or images in an active state in working memory, especially when several ideas must be considered simultaneously or when goal images differ from images activated by perceptions.

Several investigators have attempted to manipulate the extent to which items require assembly and control processes and thereby alter their relationship with *g*. For example, Swiney (1985) sought to test the hypothesis that correlations between performance on geometric analogies and *g* would increase as more flexible adaptation was required, at least for easy and moderately difficult problems. Correlations with *g* were expected to decline if task difficulty was too great. Adaptation was manipulated by grouping items in different ways. In the blocked condition, inter-item variation was minimized by grouping items with similar processing requirements (estimated by the number of elements, and the number and type of transformations). In the mixed condition, items were grouped to be as dissimilar as possible requiring maximally flexible adaptation.

Results showed that low-ability students were more adversely affected by mixing items than were high-ability students, regardless of treatment order. Relationships between task accuracy and *g* varied systematically as a function of item difficulty and task requirements. Strongest relationships were observed for items that required students to identify or apply difficult rules. Retrospective reports supported the conclusion that high-*g* subjects were better able to adapt their strategies flexibly to meet changing task demands. Swiney (1985) also found that low-*g* subjects overestimated their performance on highly difficult items; they also consistently underestimated the difficulty of problems. This suggests differences in monitoring and evaluation processes.

Chastain (1992) reported three similar studies contrasting blocked versus mixed item presentations and found small relationships consistent with Swiney's (1985) hypotheses that mixed items would show greater *g*-loading. An opposite finding, however, was reported in a study by Carlstedt, Gustafsson, and Ullstadius (2000). Three kinds of inductive reasoning problems were administered to groups of Swedish military recruits. Carlstedt et al. unexpectedly found that *g*-loadings were higher in the blocked condition than in the mixed condition; they argued that the homogeneous arrangement affords better possibilities for learning and transfer across items. However, items were extremely difficult, and so generalization is limited.

To summarize: On plots of two-dimensional scalings of test correlations, tests increase in apparent complexity as one moves from the periphery to the center of the plot. Tasks near the center typically require more steps or component processes and emphasize accuracy rather than speed of response. But this does not mean that speed of processing is unimportant or that the addition of any type of process will increase the correlation with *g*. Increasing the demand on certain types of processing, which Sternberg describes as selective encoding, comparison, and combination, also increases the correlation with *g*. Importantly, though, such processes require controlled, effortful thinking and place heavy demands on working memory resources. They also require subjects to be more strategic or flexible or adaptive in their problem solving, or to learn from easy items rules that will be needed in combination to solve hard items. All of these elements may be necessary to explain the relationships among batteries of diverse collections of ability tests.

Conclusions

Reasoning abilities are not static. They are developed through experience and rendered easier to perform through exercise. Recall that individual differences in reasoning are substantially correlated with the amount of information individuals can hold in working memory while performing some transformation on it. The ability to do this depends in large measure on the attentional resources individuals bring to a task, their familiarity with the to-be-remembered information, and their skill in performing the required transformations. Thus, prior knowledge and skill are critical determiners of the level of reasoning that one can exhibit both on reasoning tests and in everyday tasks. The dependence on prior knowledge is most pronounced on tasks that require deductive reasoning with authentic stimulus materials, and it is least pronounced on tasks that require inferential reasoning with simple geometric or alphanumeric stimuli. The processes that support sophisticated reasoning by experts in a knowledge-rich domain, however, appear to be largely the same as those which enable the novice to infer consistencies or deduce likely consequents in novel problem solving.

There are many sources of evidence that bear on the construct validity and practical importance of reasoning tests. First, reasoning is the central or most general cognitive ability in any diverse battery of tests. Second, reasoning tests predict success in academic learning because – as Snow, Greeno, Resnick, Bruner, and others have pointed out – academic learning is at its core one grand game of inference and deduction making. All instruction is incomplete in some respects. Effective learning requires that the student continually go beyond the information given to find similarities and differences between new patterns and concepts already in memory. Third, reasoning abilities are the critical moderator of instructional adaptations. By tracking what increases or decreases the relationship between reasoning ability and learning outcomes, we understand better both what reasoning abilities are and how instruction can be made more effective for more learners. Fourth, there is now a substantial research base in cognitive psychology on the nature of human reasoning (e.g., Evans & Over, 1996; Holyoak & Morrison, 2005; Johnson-Laird, 1999; Leighton & Sternberg, 2004; Rips, 1994; Stanovich, 1999). Especially helpful are studies of individual differences in reasoning measured on test-like tasks modeled after those used on ability tests. Indeed, one would be hard-pressed to think of any construct in psychology that is better understood, and whose practical relevance for education at all levels is better demonstrated than reasoning abilities.

References

Ackerman, P. L. (1988). Determinants of individual differences during skill acquisition: Cognitive abilities and information processing. *Journal of Experimental Psychology: General, 117*, 288–318.

Ackerman, P. L., Beier, M., & Boyle, M. O. (2002). Individual differences in working memory within a nomological network of cognitive and perceptual speed abilities. *Journal of Experimental Psychology: General*, **131**, 567–589.

Ackerman, P. L., Beier, M. E., & Boyle, M. O. (2005). Working memory and intelligence: The same or different constructs? *Psychological Bulletin*, **131**, 30–60.

Ackerman, P. L., & Woltz, D. J. (1994). Determinants of learning and performance in an associative memory/substitution task: Task constraints, individual differences, volition, and motivation. *Journal of Educational Psychology*, *86*, 487–515.

Bara, B. G., Bucciarelli, M., & Johnson-Laird, P. N. (1995). Development of syllogistic reasoning. *American Journal of Psychology*, **108**, 157–193.

Bethell-Fox, C. E., Lohman, D. F., & Snow, R. E. (1984). Adaptive reasoning: Componential and eye movement analysis of geometric analogy performance. *Intelligence*, *8*, 205–238.

Bruner, J. S. (Ed.). (1957). Going beyond the information given. In *Contemporary approaches to cognition: A symposium held at the University of Colorado* (pp. 41–69). Cambridge, MA: Harvard University Press.

Carlstedt, B., Gustafsson, J.-E., & Ullstadius, E. (2000). Item sequencing effects on the measurement of fluid intelligence. *Intelligence*, *28*, 145–160.

Carpenter, P. A., Just, M. A., & Shell, P. (1990). What one intelligence test measures: A theoretical account of the processing in the Raven Progressive Matrices test. *Psychological Review*, *97*, 404–431.

Carroll, J. B. (1993). *Human cognitive abilities. A survey of factor-analytic studies*. Cambridge, UK: Cambridge University Press.

Cattell, R. B. (1963). Theory of fluid and crystallized intelligence: A critical experiment. *Journal of Educational Psychology*, *54*, 1–22.

Chastain, R. L. (1992). *Adaptive processing in complex learning and cognitive performance*. Unpublished doctoral dissertation, Stanford University, Stanford, CA.

Conway, A. R. A., Cowan, N., Bunting, M. F., Therriault, D. J., & Minkoff, S. R. B. (2002). A latent variable analysis of working memory capacity, short-term memory capacity, processing speed, and general fluid intelligence. *Intelligence*, **30**, 163–183.

Corno, L., Cronbach, L. J., Kupermintz, H., Lohman, D. F., Mandinach, E. B., Porteus, A. W., & Talbert, J. (2002). *Remaking the concept of aptitude: Extending the legacy of Richard E. Snow*. Hillsdale, NJ: Erlbaum. (Educational psychology series; work completed by the Stanford Aptitude Seminar after the death of R. E. Snow; L. J. Cronbach, Ed.).

Crawford, J. (1988). *Intelligence, task complexity and tests of sustained attention*. Unpublished doctoral dissertation, University of New South Wales, Sydney, Australia.

Cronbach, L. J. (1957). The two disciplines of scientific psychology. *American Psychologist*, **12**, 671–684.

Cronbach, L. J., & Snow, R. E. (1977). Aptitudes and instructional methods: *A handbook for research on interactions*. New York, NY: Irvington.

Damasio, A. (1994). *Descartes' error: Emotion, reason, and the human brain*. New York, NY: Putnam.

Deary, I. J., & Stough, C. (1996). Intelligence and inspection time: Achievements, prospects, and problems. *American Psychologist*, **51**, 599–608.

Detterman, D. K. (1986). Human intelligence is a complex system of separate processes. In R. J. Sternberg & D. K. Detterman (Eds.), *What is intelligence? Contemporary viewpoints on its nature and definition* (pp. 57–61). Norwood, NJ: Ablex.

Ellsworth, P. C. (2005). Legal reasoning. In K. J. Holyoak & R. G. Morrison (Eds.), *The Cambridge handbook of thinking and reasoning* (pp. 685–704). New York, NY: Cambridge University Press.

Elshout, J. J. (1985, June). *Problem solving and education*. Paper presented at the annual meeting of the American Educational Research Association, San Francisco, CA.

Embretson, S. E. (1983). Construct validity: Construct representation versus nomothetic span. *Psychological Bulletin*, *93*, 179–197.

Engle, R. W., Tuholski, S. W., Laughlin, J. E., & Conway, A. R. A. (1999). Working memory, short-term memory, and general fluid intelligence: A latent-variable approach. *Journal of Experimental Psychology: General*, **128**, 309–331.

Evans, J. St. B. T., & Feeney, A. (2004). The role of prior belief in reasoning. In J. P. Leighton & R. J. Sternberg (Eds.), *The nature of reasoning* (pp. 78–102). New York, NY: Cambridge University Press.

Evans, J. S. B. T., & Over, D. E. (1996). *Rationality and reasoning*. Hove, UK: Psychology Press.

Feltovich, P. J., Prietula, M. J., & Ericsson, K. A. (2006). Studies of expertise from psychological perspectives. In K. A. Ericsson, N. Charness, P. J. Feltovich, & R. R. Hoffman (Eds.), *The Cambridge handbook of expertise and expert performance* (pp. 41–68). New York, NY: Cambridge University Press.

Fry, A. F., & Hale, S. (1996). Processing speed, working memory, and fluid intelligence: Evidence for a developmental cascade. *Psychological Science, 7,* 237–241.

Galotti, K. M., Baron, J., & Sabini, J. P. (1986). Individual differences in syllogistic reasoning: Deduction rules or mental models? *Journal of Experimental Psychology: General, 115,* 16–25.

Gardner, H. (1983). *Frames of mind: The theory of multiple intelligences.* New York, NY: Basic Books.

Gilhooly, K. J. (2004). Working memory and reasoning. In J. P. Leighton & R. J. Sternberg (Eds.), *The nature of reasoning* (pp. 49–77). New York, NY: Cambridge University Press.

Gobet, F., & Waters, A. J. (2003). The role of constraints in expert memory. *Journal of Experimental Psychology: Learning, Memory and Cognition, 29,* 1082–1094.

Greeno, J. G. (1978). A study of problem solving. In R. Glaser (Ed.), *Advances in instructional psychology* (Vol. 1, pp. 13–75). Hillsdale, NJ: Erlbaum.

Gustafsson, J.- E. (1988). Hierarchical models of individual differences in cognitive abilities. In R. J. Sternberg (Ed.), *Advances in the psychology of human intelligence* (Vol. 4, pp. 35–71). Hillsdale, NJ: Erlbaum.

Holyoak, K. J., & Morrison, R. G. (Eds.). (2005). *The Cambridge handbook of thinking and reasoning.* New York, NY: Cambridge University Press.

Holzman, T. G., Pellegrino, J. W., & Glaser, R. (1982). Cognitive dimensions of numerical rule induction. *Journal of Educational Psychology, 74,* 360–373.

Horn, J. L., & Blankson, N. (2005). Foundations for better understanding of cognitive abilities. In D. P. Flanagan & P. L. Harrison (Eds.), *Contemporary intellectual assessment: Theories, test, and issues* (2nd ed., pp. 41–68). New York, NY: Guilford Press.

Horn, J., & Masunaga, H. (2006). A merging theory of expertise and intelligence. In K. A. Ericsson, N. Charness, P. J. Feltovich, & R. R. Hoffman (Eds.), *The Cambridge handbook of expertise and expert performance* (pp. 587–612). New York, NY: Cambridge University Press.

Hunt, E. B., Frost, N., & Lunneborg, C. (1973). Individual differences in cognition: A new approach to intelligence. In G. Bower (Ed.), *The psychology of learning and motivation* (Vol. 7, pp. 87–122). New York, NY: Academic Press.

Hunt, E., & Lansman, M. (1982). Individual differences in attention. In R. J. Sternberg (Ed.), *Advances in the psychology of human abilities* (Vol. 1, pp. 207–254). Hillsdale, NJ: Erlbaum.

James, W. (1950). *Principles of psychology* (Vol. 2). New York, NY: Dover. (Original work published in 1890)

Jensen, A. R. (1982). The chronometry of intelligence. In R. J. Sternberg (Ed.), *Advances in the psychology of human intelligence* (Vol. 1, pp. 255–310). Hillsdale, NJ: Erlbaum.

Jensen, A. R. (1998). *The g factor: The science of mental ability.* Westport, CT: Praeger.

Johnson-Laird, P. N. (1999). Deductive reasoning. *Annual Review of Psychology, 50,* 109–135.

Johnson-Laird, P. N. (2004). Mental models and reasoning. In J. P. Leighton, & R. J. Sternberg (Eds.), *The nature of reasoning* (pp. 169–204). New York, NY: Cambridge University Press.

Kintsch, W., & Greeno, J. G.,(1985). Understanding and solving word arithmetic problems. *Psychological Review, 92,* 109–129.

Kvist, A.V., & Gustafsson, J.- E. (2008). The relation between fluid intelligence and the general factor as a function of cultural background: A test of Cattell's investment theory. *Intelligence, 36,* 422–436.

Kyllonen, P. C., & Christal, R. E. (1990). Reasoning ability is (little more than) working-memory capacity?! *Intelligence, 14,* 389–433.

Leighton, J. P. (2004). The assessment of logical reasoning. In J. P. Leighton & R. J. Sternberg (Eds.), *The nature of reasoning* (pp. 291–312). New York, NY: Cambridge University Press.

Leighton, J. P., & Sternberg, R. J. (Eds.). (2004). *The nature of reasoning.* New York, NY: Cambridge University Press.

Lohman, D. F. (1988). Spatial abilities as traits, processes, and knowledge. In R. J. Sternberg (Ed.), *Advances in the psychology of human intelligence* (Vol. 4, pp. 181–248). Hillsdale, NJ: Erlbaum.

Lohman, D. F. (1994). Component scores as residual variation (or why the intercept correlates best). *Intelligence, 19,* 1–11.

Lohman, D. F. (in press). *Cognitive Abilities Test (Form 7).* Rolling Meadows, IL: Riverside.

Lohman, D. F., & Hagen, E. (2001). *Cognitive Abilities Test (Form 6).* Itasca, IL: Riverside.

Lohman, D. F., & Hagen, E. (2002). *Cognitive Abilities Test (Form 6): Research handbook*. Itasca, IL: Riverside.

Lohman, D. F., Korb, K., & Lakin, J. (2008). Identifying academically gifted English language learners using nonverbal tests: A comparison of the Raven, NNAT, and CogAT. *Gifted Child Quarterly*, *52*, 275–296.

Markman, A. B., & Gentner, D. (2001). Thinking. *Annual Review of Psychology*, *52*, 223–247.

Marshalek, B. (1981). *Trait and process aspects of vocabulary knowledge and verbal ability* (Tech. Rep. No. 15). Stanford, CA: Stanford University, Aptitude Research Project, School of Education. (NTIS No. AD-A102 757).

Marshalek, B., Lohman, D. F., & Snow, R. E. (1983). The complexity continuum in the radex and hierarchical models of intelligence. *Intelligence*, *7*, 107–128.

Martinez, M. E. (2000). *Education as the cultivation of intelligence*. Mahwah, NJ: Erlbaum.

McGrew, K. S. (2005). The Cattell-Horn-Carroll Theory of cognitive abilities: Past, present, and future. In D. P. Flanagan & P. L. Harrison (Eds.), *Contemporary intellectual assessment: Theories, test, and issues* (2nd ed., pp. 136–181). New York, NY: Guilford Press.

Mislevy, R. J. (2006). Cognitive psychology and educational assessment. In R. L. Brennan (Ed.), *Educational measurement* (4th ed., pp. 257–353). Westport, CT: American Council on Educational/Praeger.

Miyake, A., & Shah, P. (1999). *Models of working memory: Mechanisms of active maintenance and executive control*. Cambridge, UK: Cambridge University Press.

Naglieri, J. A. (1996). *Naglieri Nonverbal Ability Test*. San Antonio, TX: Harcourt Brace Educational Measurement.

Newell, A., & Simon, H. A. (1972). *Human problem solving*. Englewood Cliffs, NJ: Prentice-Hall.

Nickerson, R. S. (2004). Teaching reasoning. In J. P. Leighton & R. J. Sternberg (Eds.), *The nature of reasoning* (pp. 410–442). New York, NY: Cambridge University Press.

Patel, V. L., Arocha, J. F., & Zhang, J. (2005). Thinking and reasoning in medicine. In K. J. Holyoak & R. G. Morrison (Eds.), *The Cambridge handbook of thinking and reasoning* (pp. 727–750). New York, NY: Cambridge University Press.

Pellegrino, J. W. (1985). Inductive reasoning ability. In R. J. Sternberg (Ed.), *Human abilities: An information-processing approach* (pp. 195–225). New York, NY: Freeman.

Piaget, J. (1963). *The psychology of intelligence*. New York, NY: International Universities Press.

Primi, R. (2001). Complexity of geometric inductive reasoning tasks contribution to the understanding of fluid intelligence. *Intelligence*, *30*, 41–70.

Proctor, R. W., & Vu, K. L. (2006). Laboratory studies of training, skill acquisition, and retention of performance. In K. A. Ericsson, N. Charness, P. J. Feltovich, & R. R. Hoffman (Eds.), *The Cambridge handbook of expertise and expert performance* (pp. 265–286). New York, NY: Cambridge University Press.

Raaheim, K. (1988). Intelligence and task novelty. In R. J. Sternberg (Ed.), *Advances in the psychology of human intelligence* (Vol. 4, pp. 73–97). Hillsdale, NJ: Erlbaum.

Raven, J. C., Court, J. H., & Raven, J. (1977). *Raven's Progressive Matrices and Vocabulary Scales*. New York, NY: Psychological Corporation.

Rips, L. J. (1994). *The psychology of proof*. Cambridge, MA: MIT Press.

Roberts, M. J. (1993). Human reasoning: Deductive rules or mental models, or both? *Quarterly Journal of Experimental Psychology*, *46A*, 569–589.

Roberts, R. D., & Stankov, L. (1999). Individual differences in speed of mental processing and human cognitive abilities: Toward a taxonomic model. *Learning and Individual Differences*, *11*, 1–120.

Salthouse, T. A., Babcock, R. L., Mitchell, D. R. D., Palmon, R., & Skovronek, E. (1990). Sources of individual differences in spatial visualization ability. *Intelligence*, *14*, 187–230.

Siegler, R. S., & Alibali, M. W. (2005). *Children's thinking* (4th ed.). Upper Saddle River, NJ: Pearson Prentice Hall.

Snow, R. E. (1980). Aptitude and achievement. *New Directions for Testing and Measurement*, *5*, 39–59.

Snow, R. E. (1994). Abilities in academic tasks. In R. J. Sternberg & R. K. Wagner (Eds.), *Mind in context: Interactionist perspectives on human intelligence* (pp. 3–37). Cambridge, UK: Cambridge University Press.

Snow, R. E. (1996). Aptitude development and education. *Psychology, Public Policy, and Law*, *2*, 536–560.

Snow, R. E., Kyllonen, P. C., & Marshalek, B. (1984). The topography of ability and learning correlations. In R. J. Sternberg (Ed.), *Advances in the psychology of human intelligence* (Vol. 2, pp. 47–104). Hillsdale, NJ: Erlbaum.

Snow, R. E., & Lohman, D. F. (1989). Implications of cognitive psychology for educational measurement. In R. Linn (Ed.), *Educational measurement* (3rd ed., pp. 263–331). New York, NY: Macmillan.
Spearman, C. E. (1927). *The abilities of man*. London, UK: Macmillan.
Spilsbury, G. (1992). Complexity as a reflection of the dimensionality of a task. *Intelligence, 16*, 31–45.
Stankov, L. (1988). Single tests, competing tasks and their relationship to broad factors of intelligence. *Personality and Individual Differences, 9*, 25–33.
Stanovich, K. E. (1999). *Who is rational? Studies of individual differences in reasoning*. Mahwah, NJ: Erlbaum.
Stanovich, K. E., Sá, W. C., & West, R. F. (2004). Individual differences in thinking, reasoning, and decision making. In J. P. Leighton & R. J. Sternberg (Eds.), *The nature of reasoning* (pp. 375–409). New York, NY: Cambridge University Press.
Stenning, K., & Monaghan, P. (2004). Strategies and knowledge representation. In J. P. Leighton & R. J. Sternberg (Eds.), *The nature of reasoning* (pp. 129–168). New York, NY: Cambridge University Press.
Sternberg, R. J. (1977). *Intelligence, information processing, and analogical reasoning: The componential analysis of human abilities*. Hillsdale, NJ: Erlbaum.
Sternberg, R. J. (1985). *Beyond IQ: A triarchic theory of human intelligence*. Cambridge, England: Cambridge University Press.
Sternberg, R. J. (1986). Toward a unified theory of human reasoning. *Intelligence, 10*, 281–314.
Süß, H.- M. & Beauducel, A. (2005). Faceted models of intelligence. In O. Wilhelm & R. W. Engle (Eds.), *Handbook of measuring and understanding intelligence* (pp. 313–332). Thousand Oaks, CA: Sage.
Süß, H.- M., Oberauer, K., Wittmann, W. W., Wilhelm, O., & Schulze, R. (2002). Working memory capacity explains reasoning ability – and a little bit more. *Intelligence, 30*, 261–288.
Swiney, J. F. (1985). *A study of executive processes in intelligence*. Unpublished doctoral dissertation, Stanford University, Stanford, CA.
Thurstone, L. L. (1938). Primary mental abilities. *Psychometric Monographs, 1*.
Toulmin, S., Rieke, R., & Janik, A. (1984). *An introduction to reasoning* (2nd ed.). New York, NY: Macmillan.
Wilhelm, O. (2005). Measuring reasoning ability. In O. Wilhelm & R. W. Engle (Eds.), *Handbook of measuring and understanding intelligence* (pp. 373–392). Thousand Oaks, CA: Sage.
Zimmerman, W. S. (1954). The influence of item complexity upon the factor composition of a spatial visualization test. *Educational and Psychological Measurement, 14*, 106–119.

CHAPTER 22

Intelligence and the Cognitive Unconscious

Scott Barry Kaufman

The definition of genius is that it acts unconsciously; and those who have produced immortal works, have done so without knowing how or why. The greatest power operates unseen, and executes its appointed task with as little ostentation as difficulty.

– *William Hazlitt*[1]

Intelligence tests were originally created with the practical goal of identifying students in need of alternative education (Binet & Simon, 1916). Because intelligence tests were originally devised to predict school grades, the items were intentionally designed to measure a general ability to profit from explicit instruction, concentrate on a task, and engage in intellectual material. Indeed, research shows that such a general ability does seem to exist. Over a century ago, Spearman (1904) discovered that when a wide range of cognitive tests that have explicit instructions and require effortful concentration is administered to a diverse group of people, all of the tests tend to be positively correlated with one another, a finding often referred to as a "positive manifold." Spearman labeled the factor on which all individual tests loaded *g*, for general intelligence.

Over the past 100 years, the existence of *g* as a statistical phenomenon is one of the most replicable findings in all of psychology (Carroll, 1993; Chabris, 2007; Jensen, 1998). Nonetheless, there is still work to be done to determine what explains the positive manifold (see Maas et al., 2006), the cognitive mechanisms that support *g* (see Chapter 20, Working Memory and Intelligence, this volume; Kaufman, DeYoung, Gray, Brown, & Mackintosh, 2009; Sternberg & Pretz, 2005), and whether there are other forms of cognition that display meaningful individual differences and predict intelligent behavior above and beyond *g* and the cognitive mechanisms that support *g*.

This chapter presents evidence that mechanisms relating to the *cognitive unconscious* – "mental structures, processes, and

[1] William Hazlitt (1846), "Essay IV. Whether Genius Is Conscious of Its Powers?" in *Table Talk: Opinions on Books, Men, and Things*, Second Series, Part I (pp. 37–49). New York, NY: Wiley & Putnam.

states[2] that can influence experience, thought, and actions outside phenomenal awareness and voluntary control" (Dorfman, Shames, & Kihlstrom, 1996, p. 259) also make an important contribution to intelligent behavior. Although intelligence testers have done a remarkable job developing tests that measure individual differences in explicit, controlled cognitive processes, the investigation of individual differences in implicit, nonconscious processes has not received nearly as much attention (Kaufman, 2009a, b).

Furthermore, researchers have created clever experiments to probe the nature of the cognitive unconscious by looking at implicit memory, implicit perception, and other forms of implicit cognition and thought[3] (for reviews, see Kihlstrom, 1987, and Litman & Reber, 2005), but they have focused primarily on group-level data, ignoring individual differences (see Cronbach, 1957). Additionally, some researchers have downplayed the existence of continuous individual differences in the cognitive unconscious that are meaningfully related to important life outcomes (Reber, 1993; Stanovich, 2009).

There have been some recent studies, however, that look at *individual differences* in the cognitive unconscious. This chapter focuses on individual differences and reviews recent empirical work on relations among the cognitive processes underlying psychometric intelligence and the cognitive processes underlying the cognitive unconscious, attempting to bridge two major research programs that, until recently, have traveled on separate but parallel paths.

[2] I include "implicit thought" in this definition as well, although Kihlstrom tends to refer to "implicit cognition" differently from the "cognitive unconscious" (Dorfman, Shames, & Kihlstrom, 1996).

[3] I assume in this chapter that intelligent "thought" can operate either with or without awareness of that thought. As Dorfman, Shames, and Kihlstrom (1996) astutely note, the idea of "implicit thought" is a difficult concept because the notion of thinking has traditionally been equated with notions of consciousness. For instance, William James (1890) thought the notion of "unconscious thought" was a contradiction in terms!

Integrating Two Research Traditions

The 20th century witnessed at least two major paradigm shifts within psychological science. One major shift was from behaviorism to the "cognitive revolution," which brought along with it a shift in focus from learning and conditioning toward investigating the mental processes involved in conscious thought, including memory, thinking, and problem solving (Miller, 2003). This shift has had an enduring effect on conceptualizations of human intelligence as well as research methodology. Indeed, one of the earliest investigators of the development of intelligence in children was Jean Piaget (1952), whose focus was on conscious higher order reasoning and how children at different ages think. This emphasis on age differences in thought as well as the notion that intelligence involves conscious, deliberate reasoning also underlies the logic behind the first widely administered intelligence test, the Binet-Simon Scale (Binet & Simon, 1916). Furthermore, the discovery that performances on diverse tests of explicit cognitive ability tend to correlate with one another – Spearman's (1904) so-called positive manifold – further supported the idea that intelligence tests are tapping into a "general cognitive ability."

Around the same time the shift from behaviorism to the cognitive revolution was taking place, another dramatic shift in psychology was occurring. The conceptualization of the unconscious that was predominant with psychodynamic theories of personality was slowly being transformed into an unconscious recognized to serve many adaptive functions among both modern-day humans and our evolutionary ancestry (Epstein, 1991; Hassin, Uleman, & Bargh, 2005; Wilson, 2004). Over 30 years of research in cognitive science reveals that a considerable amount of information processing takes place on a daily basis automatically – without our intent, awareness, and deliberate encoding – and plays an important role in structuring our skills, perceptions, and behavior (Epstein, 1991; Hassin et al., 2005; Kihlstrom, 1987; Lewicki & Hill,

1987; Reber, 1993; Stadler & Frensch, 1997) as well as facilitating problem solving and creativity (Dijksterhuis & Nordgren, 2006; Dorfman, Shames, & Kihlstrom, 1996; Litman & Reber, 2005).

Kihlstrom (1987) distinguishes between three types of nonconscious mental structures that together constitute the domain of the "cognitive unconscious." *Unconscious* representations fit within the domain of procedural knowledge and are inaccessible to introspection under any circumstances. "By virtue of routinization (or perhaps because they are innate), such procedures operate on declarative knowledge without either conscious intent or conscious awareness, in order to construct the person's ongoing experience, thought, and action" (p. 1450; also see Anderson, 1982). Subliminal perception, implicit memory, and implicit learning fit the category of *preconscious* declarative knowledge structures. In contrast to unconscious representations, preconscious structures can be available to phenomenal awareness and can be introspected upon, but they can also influence ongoing experience, thought, and action without ever entering into working memory. Finally, Kihlstrom describes *subconscious* declarative knowledge mental representations such as those activated during hypnosis, which can be quite available to introspection but inaccessible to phenomenal awareness.[4]

Note that even though some nonconscious representations have such high levels of activation that they enter working memory, they still might not meet the criteria of conscious awareness. As noted by Kihlstrom, William James (1890) suggested over a century ago in his *Principles of Psychology* that the key to consciousness is *self-reference*:

> *In order for ongoing experience, thought, and action to become conscious, a link must be made between its mental representation and some mental representation of the self as agent or experiencer – as well, perhaps, as some representation of the environment in which these events take place. These episodic representations of the self and context reside in working memory, but apparently the links in question are neither automatic nor permanent, and must be actively forged . . . without such linkages certain aspects of mental life are dissociated from awareness, and are not accompanied by the experience of consciousness. (Kihlstrom, 1987, p. 1451)*

A great deal of research has demonstrated the sophisticated and intelligent nature of the cognitive unconscious (Epstein, 2001; Lewicki, Hill, & Czyzewska, 1992; Loftus & Klinger, 1992). For instance, after reviewing the literature on the nonconscious acquisition of information, Lewicki, Hill, and Czyzewska (1992) asked, "Is the nonconscious information-processing system 'intelligent'?" – to which they concluded:

> *The answer to the question about intelligence would be affirmative if intelligence is understood as "equipped to efficiently process complex information." In this sense, our nonconscious information-processing system appears to be incomparably more able to process formally complex knowledge structures, faster and "smarter" overall than our ability to think and identify meanings of stimuli in a consciously controlled manner. (p. 801)*

The idea that the unconscious can be smart is also illustrated by the title of a recent popular summary of the fast-and-frugal heuristics literature: *Gut Feelings: The Intelligence of the Unconscious* (Gigerenzer, 2007).[5] Today there is a strong consensus

[4] Note that only Kihlstrom's (1987) notion of "unconscious" mental structures meets all four of Bargh's (2004) horsemen of automaticity: lack of awareness, lack of intention, high efficiency, and inability to control. Kihlstrom's notion of the preconscious lacks intention, but only under some circumstances is efficient, lacks awareness, and can't be controlled. Kihlstrom's notion of the subconscious can be intentional and efficient, and even can be controlled, but the key to defining the subconscious according to Kihlstrom is the lack of phenomenal awareness.

[5] But note that Gigerenzer (2007; Gigerenzer & Brighton, 2009), in contrast to those who view the cognitive unconscious as able to process complex information, views the cognitive unconscious as operating by the principle "less is more," selecting the right rule of thumb for the right situation.

among contemporary researchers in cognitive science, philosophy, cognitive psychology, social psychology, reasoning, and morality that humans possess two quite distinct modes of thought – one controlled and the other more automatic (Epstein, 2003; Evans & Frankish, 2009; Stanovich & West, 2002). Indeed, dual-process theories of cognition are becoming increasingly necessary for explaining a wide variety of cognitive, personality, social developmental, and cross-cultural phenomena (Evans & Frankish, 2009). For instance, Klaczynski (2009) makes a case for adopting and developing a comprehensive dual-process theory of development, reviewing studies from such diverse research topics as memory, judgments and decisions, reasoning, motivated reasoning, stereotypes, and magical reasoning to support his argument.

Dual-Process Theories of Cognition

Type 1 processes[6] are thought to comprise a set of autonomous subsystems (Stanovich, 2004) that include both innate input modules (Fodor, 1983) and domain-specific knowledge acquired by domain-general learning mechanisms that operate automatically and efficiently (Reber, 1993). Type 1 processes process information fast (relative to type 2 processes); are heavily influenced by context, biology, and past experience; and aid humans in mapping and assimilating newly acquired stimuli into preexisting knowledge structures.

An advantage of type 1 processes over type 2 processes is that the former require little conscious cognitive effort and free attentional resources for computationally complex reasoning. According to Lewicki, Hill, and Czyzewska (1992),

> *Data indicate that as compared with consciously controlled cognition, the nonconscious information-acquisition processes are not only much faster but are also structurally more sophisticated, in that they are capable of efficient processing of multidimensional and interactive relations between variables. Those mechanisms of non-conscious acquisition of information provide a major channel for the development of procedural knowledge that is indispensable for such important aspects of cognitive functioning as encoding and interpretation of stimuli and the triggering of emotional reactions. (p. 796)*

The advantages of type 1 processes can also become disadvantages under certain circumstances. When thinking is dominated by type 1 processes, task representations are highly contextualized. This contextualization can lead to the thoughtless application of judgment and decision heuristics. According to Stanovich and West (2000), this mode of thought is in fact the "default" mode in humans. They refer to this tendency toward automatic contextualization of problems as the "fundamental computational bias" in human cognition (Stanovich & West, 2000). A similar idea can be found in Chaiken's (1987) heuristic systematic model of persuasion, according to which people are guided in part by a "principle of least effort." Because people have limited cognitive resources, and because heuristic processing is easy and adequate for most tasks, heuristic processing from type 1 is generally used unless there is a special need to engage in systematic processing (see also Simon, 1979). In line with this idea, Klaczynski and Cottrell (2004) have argued that "metacognitive intercession" often occurs, whereby responses derived from intuition are available in working memory, where reflection is possible. However, according to Klaczynski, most people do not take advantage of the opportunity to reflect on the contents of working memory, taking the contents from the experiential system as self-evidently valid. Finally, the view of type 1 processes as the default mode of human cognition is also present in Haidt's (2001)

[6] Many dual-process theorists refer to two "systems" (see Kahneman & Frederick, 2002). In recent years, however, critics of dual-system theorists have called for the use of a different name, arguing that "system" carries with it a lot of conceptual baggage (see Evans, 2008; Keren & Schul, 2009). In line with Evans's (2008) suggestion, I refer here to "types" of thought processes instead of "systems."

social intuitionist model of moral reasoning, in which it is posited that intuitive processing is the default process, with deliberate reasoning called upon only when intuitions conflict with reason (see also Stanovich & West, 2000).

In contrast, *type 2 processes* are typically characterized by deliberately controlled, effortful, and intentional cognition. Individual differences in this system have been linked in the past to psychometric intelligence (see Stanovich, 2009). According to Stanovich and West (1997), a hallmark of this type of thought is the ability to decontextualize task representations.[7] Type 2 processes can deal with abstract content under conditions of awareness[8] and are not dominated by the goal of attributing intentionality nor by the search for conversational relevance (Margolis, 1987). It has been posited that type 2 processes are evolutionarily more recent and uniquely developed in humans than type 1 processes (Epstein, 2003; Evans, 2008; Gabora & Kaufman, 2009).

Note that while some aspects are common across most dual-process theories, there are also distinct differences (Evans, 2008). Most dual-process theorists agree on the automatic/controlled distinction between the two modes of thought, as well as the idea that type 2 processes are constrained by a central working memory system whereas type 1 processes are unconstrained by a central pool of resources. Dual-process theorists differ, however, in terms of other features they attribute to the two modes of thought. For instance, some dual-process theorists emphasize the affective nature of type 1 processes (Epstein, 1994; Metcalfe & Mischel, 1999; Zajonc, 1980), whereas emotions are not a key component of other models of implicit cognition (e.g., Reber, 1993).

Also, as Evans (2008) rightly points out, some of the distinctions between the two modes of thought (e.g., abstract vs. contextualized, associative vs. rule-based, shared with other animals vs. unique to humans) are not as neat and clear-cut when one considers that type 1 isn't a unitary system, but includes a set of autonomous systems, some of which are innately specified and some of which come about through learning and practice (Stanovich, 2004; but see Epstein, 2010). Evans (2008) also points out that "type 2" is most likely not a unitary system, suggesting that not all type 2 processes are consciously controlled. Additionally, Cokely and Kelley (2009) and Cokely, Parpart, and Schooler (2009) have noted that even controlled processes may rely on automatic processes for processing, even at the stage of early attentional selection. Other criticisms (see Aczel, 2009; Gigerenzer & Regier, 1996; Keren & Schul, 2009) have been leveled against dual-system models, a sign that the study of the dual-process nature of the mind is an active area of research and debate. In line with these criticisms, the remainder of this chapter will refer to "dual-process" theories instead of "dual-system" theories and will assume that the various processes are not completely independent but can interact with each other and facilitate (or inhibit) each other in important ways.

Indeed, in his review of dual-process accounts of reasoning, judgment, and social cognition, Evans (2008) notes two distinct kinds of dual-process theories. One kind, which he refers to as "parallel-competitive" forms of dual-process theory, states that there are two forms of learning that lead to two forms of knowledge (explicit and implicit) and each form competes for the control of behavior. Evans refers to another category of dual-process researchers as the "default-interventionists," who assume that rapid preconscious processes supply content for conscious processing and that the explicit system can intervene with the application of controlled processes. It should be noted that not all dual-process theories fall neatly into one category or the other. For instance, Epstein (2003) assumes that the two systems operate in parallel and are bi-directionally

7 Although note that this system can also deal with contextualized content (see Cokely & Kelley, 2009; Cokely, Parpart, & Schooler, 2009).

8 Although note that some researchers have argued that aspects of System 1 (e.g., implicit learning) can also deal with abstract material (see Reber, 1989).

interactive. As the implicit system has a faster reaction time it is more likely to initiate an action sequence. Nonetheless, Evans (2008) does offer a useful classification of different dual-process theories.

There is evidence for both categories; fMRI evidence suggests that the type of processes are independent – under processing conditions that favor automatic processing, automatic cognitive processes and the brain regions supporting those processes are more active than the brain regions supporting controlled cognition. Conversely, under conditions that favor controlled processing, controlled cognitive processes and the brain regions supporting those processes (such as the dorsolateral prefrontal cortex) are more active than the brain regions supporting automatic cognitive processes (Lieberman, 2007).

There is also support for the default-interventionists' view in that humans on average have a tendency to contextualize information (i.e., automatic cognition is the default mode in most humans) and that in some instances it is important for controlled cognition to reflect on that contextualization and potentially override the outputs of automatic cognition (Kahneman & Frederick, 2002; Chapter 39, Intelligence and Rationality, this volume). Nonetheless, in some situations the output of the automatic system is beneficial for intelligent behavior, and controlled cognition is not necessary, or can even get in the way.

Interestingly, a number of neuroimaging studies in humans and lesion studies on rodents have found that the basal ganglia and medial temporal lobe (mTL) function competitively (Packard, Hirsh, & White, 1989; Poldrack & Packard, 2003). In an interesting study, Packard, Hirsh, and White (1989) found that rats with basal ganglia lesions performed better than normal rats on an mTL-specific task, and rats with mTL lesions performed better than normal on the basal ganglia–specific task. These results suggest that the presence of a normally functioning medial temporal lobe may interfere with performance on tasks that strongly recruit basal ganglia functions, and performance is thus improved on these tasks when the medial temporal lobe is removed (Lieberman, 2007).

Therefore, intelligence and the cognitive unconscious mostly work in concert with each other during our daily lives, but in some situations they may be competitive – and depending on the situation, either controlled or spontaneous cognitions will be the more important contributor to intelligent behavior.

Interestingly, while various dual-process theories of *cognition* have been proposed over the years, only two are explicitly theories of *human intelligence*. Below I will review both: Anderson's (M. Anderson, 2005) *theory of the minimal cognitive architecture underlying intelligence and development* and the recent *dual-process (DP) theory of human intelligence* (Kaufman, 2009a).

The Theory of the Minimal Cognitive Architecture underlying Intelligence and Development

Based on Fodor's (1983) distinction between central processes of thought and dedicated processing input modules, Anderson's (2005) theory synthesizes the idea of general and specific abilities and incorporates the notion of development. Anderson argues that knowledge is acquired through two different "processing routes," with central processes (route 1) being tied to individual differences and input modules being tied to cognitive development (route 2). According to Anderson, route 1 involves "thoughtful problem solving" and is constrained by the speed of a basic processing mechanism. Anderson argues that "it is this constraint that is the basis of general intelligence and the reason why manifest specific abilities are correlated" (p. 280). Anderson's basic processing mechanism comprises both a verbal and a spatial processor that are normally distributed, uncorrelated with each other, and each having their own predictive powers.

In contrast, the second route for acquiring knowledge in Anderson's model is tied to dedicated information-processing modules, such as perception of three-dimensional space, syntactic parsing, phonological encoding, and theory of mind. According to Anderson, this route is tied to cognitive development as these modules undergo developmental changes in cognitive competence across the life span. Anderson acknowledges that modular processes can be acquired through extensive practice, but both are similar in that they operate automatically and independently of the first route and are therefore unconstrained by the speed of the basic processing mechanism.

Anderson makes the case that the modular component of his cognitive theory allows for an integration of Gardner's "multiple intelligences" and "general intelligence," as the theory includes domain-specific modular functions as well as a basic processing mechanism. Anderson also argues that his theory explains how low-IQ individuals can be capable of remarkable cognitive feats (e.g., "savant" abilities), including various practical skills, such as the ability to acquire language or see in three dimensions that are considerably more computationally complex than the abilities that are tapped by IQ tests. Anderson argues that his theory also can explain how developmental disabilities such as dyslexia and autism can exist in the presence of typical or even above-average IQ (Anderson, 2008).

Note that in Anderson's model there is little room for individual differences in route 2. Furthermore, Anderson does not propose any domain general learning mechanisms that are part of route 2, focusing instead on the Fodorian definition of modules. By limiting the cognitive mechanisms associated with each "route," the total amount of other research that could be brought to bear on the cognitive processes underlying the two information-processing routes becomes unnecessarily restricted. Nonetheless, Anderson's model makes an important contribution to the investigation of intelligence by expanding modes of thought and incorporating development.

Dual-Process (DP) Theory of Human Intelligence

The dual-process theory of human intelligence aims to integrate modern dual-process theories of cognition (e.g., Evans & Frankish, 2009) with research on intelligence (Kaufman, 2009a). The theory is an organizing framework for various constructs relating to human cognition that are at least partially separable and display individual differences that are meaningfully related to a wide range of socially valued intelligent behaviors. A main goal of the theory is to expand both the range of methodologies and the dependent measures traditionally studied by intelligence researchers in order to more clearly define the cognitive mechanisms underlying each construct and to develop interventions to increase these abilities in everyone.

According to the theory, performance across a wide range of intelligent behaviors can be predicted through a hierarchical structure of controlled and spontaneous cognitive processes. Controlled cognitions are goal directed and consume limited central executive resources, whereas spontaneous cognitions aren't constrained by the same limited pool of attentional resources. An assumption of the theory is that both controlled and spontaneous cognitive processes to some degree jointly determine all intelligent behaviors, although in varying degrees. For instance, prediction of performance on an IQ test will maximize the measurement of controlled cognitive processes whereas performance on a test that requires the incidental learning of a complex pattern or performance in a domain in which someone has acquired a large body of expertise will maximize the measurement of spontaneous cognitive processes.

Echoes of this idea can be found in Hammond, Hamm, Grassia, and Pearson (1987) when they argue that different decision-making situations will draw on different strategies in a continuum between pure intuition and pure rational analysis. According to the dual-process theory, neither component is more important than the other, but what is important is the ability to flexibly switch between modes of cognition depending on the task requirements (for applications of this idea to creativity, see Chapter 17, The Evolution of Intelligence, this volume; Gabora & Kaufman, 2009; Howard-Jones & Murray, 2003; Martindale, 1995; Vartanian, 2009). According to the theory, what has traditionally been labeled general intelligence (*g*) is primarily tapping into explicit cognitive ability, and the theory predicts that individual differences in *spontaneous cognition* will predict variance in a wide variety of intelligent behaviors above and beyond the variability in *g*, which itself is thought to be only a part of *controlled cognition*.

Both forms of cognition involve the *ability* and the *tendency* to *engage* in each mode of thought. The two are related because people tend to engage in things they are good at and avoid engaging in things they aren't good at. A key assumption of the dual-process theory is that abilities are not static entities but are constantly changing through the life span as the person continually engages with the world. The more a person engages in a mode of thought, the more that individual will develop skills in that modality, which in turn increases the desire for engaging with that skill. Indeed, research on expertise skill acquisition shows that engagement in a domain through many hours of deliberate practice contributes to the generation of mental structures that can surpass information-processing limitations when performing within that domain (Ericsson & Charness, 1994; Ericsson & Kintsch, 1995; Ericsson & Lehmann, 1996, but see Kaufman, 2007).

Controlled cognition is at the top of the hierarchy (alongside *spontaneous cognition*) because the capacity for goal-directed action is an important component of human intelligence. Controlled cognition consists of a class of cognitive processes that involve the ability and tendency across situations to think about thinking (i.e., "metacognition" – see Dennett, 1992; Hertzog & Robinson, 2005), reflect on prior behavior, and use that information to modify behavior and plan for the future.[9] Constructs that are part of the controlled cognition hierarchy include central executive functions (updating, cognitive inhibition, and mental flexibility), reflective engagement, explicit cognitive ability (the skill sets that lie at the heart of highly *g*-loaded tasks), intellectual engagement, and elementary cognitive tasks that support explicit cognitive ability.[10] What links all of the processes together is that they all draw on a limited capacity pool of attentional resources.

The second main component (alongside *controlled cognition*) of the dual-process theory, and the component that contains processes relating to the cognitive unconscious, is *spontaneous cognition*. At the broadest level, individual differences in spontaneous cognition reflect the *ability* to acquire information automatically and the *tendency* to engage in spontaneous forms of cognition. For instance, whereas most people have the *ability* to spontaneously experience emotions and daydream, there may be individual differences in the extent to which people are willing to *engage* in their emotions and to daydream (see Pacini & Epstein, 1999; Zhiyan & Singer, 1997).[11] Constructs that are part of the spontaneous cognition hierarchy include spontaneous information acquisition abilities (implicit learning, reduced latent inhibition, etc.), spontaneous forms of engagement (affective engagement,

9 Note that other definitions of "controlled cognition" have been put forward (see Schneider & Shiffrin, 1977).

10 It should be noted, however, that elementary cognitive tasks (ECTs) are not process pure, and motivation, strategy use, and the allocation of attentional resources play an important role in performance (see Chapter 37, Intelligence and Motivation, this volume; Cokely, Kelley, & Gilchrist 2006; Fox, Roring, & Mitchum, 2009).

11 Note that the distinction between controlled and spontaneous cognition is not always the same as the distinction between conscious and unconscious modes of thought. Spontaneous cognitions can be either conscious, such as when individuals are consciously aware of their daydreaming, fantasy, or mind wandering, or nonconscious such as when individuals are dreaming, daydreaming without conscious awareness, or implicitly learning the underlying rule structure of the environment without awareness of how that tacit knowledge is affecting their behavior.

aesthetic engagement, and fantasy engagement), and various implicit domains of mind that are universal human domains pertaining to knowledge of people, language, numbers, animals, music, visual images, aesthetics, or the inanimate physical world (see Carey & Spelke, 1994; Feist, 2001; Hirschfeld & Gelman, 1994).[12]

Other technical details about the theory, including the hierarchical nature of the model can be found in Kaufman (2009a). Thus far, there is support for the theory from different branches of psychology and neuropsychology. The theory has not received many criticisms, but it is still new; thus, the extent to which the dual-process theory of human intelligence advances the field by making new, testable predictions and the extent to which the theory more clearly defines various constructs relating to intelligence is still to be determined.

The rest of this chapter reviews recent empirical work on linkages between the cognitive processes underlying psychometric intelligence and various aspects of the cognitive unconscious. First, relations between individual differences in controlled cognitive processing and individual differences in two forms of preconscious processing, implicit learning, and latent inhibition will be discussed. Because intuitions and insights generally follow preconscious processing, the next section of this chapter reviews evidence on the relation between intelligence and individual differences in both intuition and insights. The following section will then look at the implications of intelligence and the cognitive unconscious for two major domains of human cognitive functioning: social cognition and creative cognition. The chapter will then conclude with a call for more research. The review of studies in this chapter is by no means exhaustive but is meant to highlight some of the latest thinking and research on the relation between individual differences in psychometric intelligence and individual differences in the cognitive unconscious.

[12] Implicit domains of mind are similar to group factors in hierarchical models of intelligence. Indeed, research shows that group factors, such as mathematical, spatial, and verbal reasoning abilities provide incremental validity for predicting associated vocations above and beyond general intelligence (Achter, Lubinski, Benbow, & Eftekhari-Sanjani, 1999; Humphreys, Lubinski, & Yao, 1993). These domains of mind are also related to Howard Gardner's "multiple intelligences" (Gardner, 1993, 1999), although the dual-process theory acknowledges that there are also more general forms of cognition that contribute to intelligent behavior, a criticism that is often leveled against theories of multiple intelligences (see Lohman, 2001).

Intelligence and Preconscious Processing

Intelligence and Implicit Learning

According to Reber (1993), implicit learning is "a fundamental root process... that lies at the very heart of the adaptive behavioral repertoire of every complex organism" and can be characterized as "the acquisition of knowledge that takes place largely independent of conscious attempts to learn and largely in the absence of explicit knowledge about what was acquired" (p. 5; for a similar view see Epstein & Meier, 1989). We frequently encounter many complex contingencies and patterns, and the ability to preconsciously learn patterns and then use that knowledge to recognize and detect patterns in the future is an important component of intelligence (see Hawkins, 2005).

What is the link between psychometric intelligence and implicit learning? According to Reber (1993) and Epstein and Meier (1989), individual differences in implicit learning should be unrelated to individual differences in measures of explicit cognition. Applying principles of evolutionary biology, they argue that the capacity for explicit cognition arrived later on the evolutionary scene than did implicit cognition. Nonetheless, the older implicit learning mechanisms were unaffected by the emergence of explicit thought and continue to function autonomously.

Thus far, the majority of the evidence supports the notion that implicit learning ability is independent of IQ. Some implicit learning tasks have never demonstrated a relation with explicit cognitive ability (e.g., *artificial grammar learning*; Gebauer & Mackintosh, 2007; McGeorge, Crawford, & Kelly, 1997; Reber, Walkenfeld, & Hernstadt, 1991), whereas other tasks have not shown a significant association in the majority of the studies (e.g., *serial reaction time learning*; Feldman, Kerr, & Streissguth, 1995; Kaufman, DeYoung, Gray, Jiménez, Brown, & Mackintosh, 2010; Pretz, Totz, & Kaufman, 2010; Unsworth & Engle, 2005 – but see Salthouse, McGuthry, & Hambrick, 1999). One other implicit learning task, which involves unintentional exposure to pictures, did show an association once with explicit cognitive ability (Fletcher, Maybery, & Bennett, 2000). These results may be mixed as different implicit learning tasks are only weakly correlated with each other (Gebauer & Mackintosh, 2007, 2009; Salthouse et al., 1999). Further, some implicit learning paradigms may better capture implicit cognition than others, which may draw more on explicit cognition (e.g., Seger, 1994). An important future line of research to better understand the relation of implicit learning to psychometric intelligence will be to construct reliable measures that more accurately assess implicit learning. Then, the factorial structure of implicit learning tasks can be assessed and the convergent-discriminant validity can be compared to other measures of psychometric intelligence.

Another methodology with which to investigate the link between implicit and explicit cognition is to compare implicit and explicit versions of the same task. In one condition, experimenters instructed participants to find the pattern, whereas in another condition participants received no such instruction, thereby making learning unintentional. When this methodology is employed, psychometric intelligence is more highly correlated with the task under explicit instructions compared with the condition in which participants are not instructed to intentionally search for the pattern (Gebauer & Mackintosh, 2007; Unsworth & Engle, 2005). Using a similar methodology, Feldman, Kerr, and Streissguth (1995) separated an intentional declarative component of an implicit learning task from the procedural component using a sample of 455 adolescents; they found that while the declarative learning component significantly correlated with explicit cognition, the procedural component did not. In another line of research, using a population of individuals with autistic spectrum condition (ASC), Brown et al. (2010) found that matching for IQ, there was statistical equivalence between participants with ASC and typically developing individuals on four implicit learning tasks. Further, this finding was not a consequence of compensation by explicit learning ability or IQ. Taken together, the research supports the separation of explicit and implicit cognition and the notion that individual differences in psychometric intelligence are only weakly if at all associated with individual differences in implicit learning (e.g., McGeorge et al., 1997; Reber et al., 1991).

Recent research has found that individual differences in implicit learning make an independent contribution to complex cognition above and beyond psychometric intelligence. Gebauer and Mackintosh (2009) administered a large battery of implicit learning and intelligence tests to 195 German students. A factor analysis of all the tasks revealed two second-order principal components: the first consisting primarily of the intelligence measures and the second consisting of the measures of implicit learning. Both factors were only weakly related to each other. Additionally, the implicit learning second-order factor was significantly related to math and English grades, subjects that were foreign languages for the German students in the sample. Controlling for the intelligence second-order factor, the association between the implicit learning factor and English remained whereas the association with math was no longer significant.

Consistent with this finding, Pretz, Totz, and Kaufman (2010) found a relation between a probabilistic sequence learning task and both the American College Testing (ACT) math and English scores, and these effects were in the middle third of effect sizes reported in psychology ($r = .2$ to $.3$; Hemphill, 2003). In another recent study, Kaufman et al. (2010) investigated the association of individual differences in implicit learning with a variety of cognitive and personality variables in a sample of English 16- to 17-year-olds. Probabilistic sequence learning was related to intentional associative learning more strongly than psychometric intelligence, and it was not associated with working memory. Furthermore, structural equation modeling revealed that individual differences in implicit learning were independently related to verbal analogical reasoning and processing speed, and implicit learning was significantly correlated with academic performance on two foreign language exams (French and German). Implicit learning also was positively related to self-report measures of personality, including intuition, Openness to Experience, and impulsivity. Also, a double dissociation was found between a latent Intellect factor and a latent Openness to Experience factor – with Intellect relating to working memory (.29) but not implicit learning (.00) and Openness to Experience relating to implicit learning (.31) but not working memory (.13).

This lack of association between implicit learning and working memory is consistent with other research on attention and executive functioning. Research shows that those high in working memory are better able to control their attention and stay on task when there is interference (Kane, Bleckley, Conway, & Engle, 2001) and this ability is associated with psychometric intelligence (see Chapter 20, Working Memory and Intelligence, this volume). There is an emerging consensus that implicit learning requires selective attention to the relevant stimuli but then learning about the selected stimuli operates automatically, independent of an intention to learn and without drawing on further central executive processing (e.g., Baker, Olson, & Behrmann, 2004; Frensch & Miner, 1995; Jiang & Chun, 2001; Jiménez & Mendez, 1999; Turke-Browne, Junge, & Scholl, 2005).

Indeed, researchers have proposed that central executive functions should be engaged only under intentional learning conditions to aid in focusing attention, whereas only selective attention processes are necessary for learning stimuli incidentally (Cowan, 1988; Frensch & Miner, 1995, Johnson & Hirst, 1993). In support of this view, Unsworth and Engle (2005) found that variations in working memory were associated with an implicit learning task only when participants were instructed to explicitly detect the covariation, but no association with working memory was found when participants were not given that instruction. Feldman, Kerr, and Streissguth (1995) also found no relation between implicit learning and measures of working memory.

In sum, while the literature is not large, the evidence that does exist suggests that implicit learning is often unrelated to psychometric intelligence or working memory but is independently associated with specific forms of complex cognition, academic achievement, and particular aspects of personality related to Openness to Experience and impulsivity. Future research on the topic is needed to clarify and extend these findings.

Intelligence and Latent Inhibition

It can be important in our everyday lives to be able to automatically distinguish relevant from irrelevant stimuli and to filter out information irrelevant to the task at hand. For instance, when trying to concentrate on writing poetry, it's important to filter out the rattle of the radiator. Such a mechanism has been investigated and is called latent inhibition (Lubow, 1989). Latent inhibition is often characterized as a preconscious gating mechanism that screens from current focus those stimuli that have previously been regarded as irrelevant (Lubow, 1989). Those with *increased* latent inhibition show higher levels of this form of inhibition (Peterson, Smith, & Carson, 2002). Variation in latent inhibition has been documented across a variety of mammalian species and, at least in other animals, has known biological substrates (Lubow & Gewirtz, 1995). Prior research has shown a relation between *decreased* latent inhibition and acute-phase schizophrenia (Baruch, Hemsley, & Gray, 1988a, 1988b; Lubow, Ingberg-Sachs, Zalstein-Orda, & Gewirtz, 1992). People with schizophrenia also tend to have reduced ability for central executive functioning (Barch, 2005).

Recent research suggests that reduced latent inhibition can also have its advantages. In students with a high IQ (and presumably a high level of central executive functioning), *decreased* latent inhibition is associated with higher scores on a self-report measure of creative achievement (Carson, Peterson, & Higgins, 2003). Interestingly, the researchers did not find a correlation between fluid intelligence and latent inhibition. Kaufman (2009a) also did not find an association between variations in *g* and variations in latent inhibition. Additionally, Kaufman (2009a, b) examined the relationship between latent inhibition and individual differences in the tendency to rely on intuition to make decisions. Indeed, latent inhibition is conceptually related to intuition: Jung's original conception of intuition is "perception via the unconscious" (Jung, 1921/1971, p. 538). Kaufman hypothesized that an intuitive cognitive style would be related to reduced latent inhibition. Results showed that those with higher scores on a faith in intuition factor (consisting of intuition items related to affect) tended to have reduced latent inhibition. Further, latent inhibition was not associated with an intuition factor consisting of items having to do with holistic processing of information or a rational cognitive style. There was also a tendency for those scoring high (as compared to medium or low) on the faith in intuition factor to benefit more from a preexposure condition where participants received the relevant stimuli in the first part of the task. Therefore, current research suggests that decreased latent inhibition is unrelated to general intelligence or a rational cognitive style. Since decreased latent inhibition may make an individual more likely to perceive and make connections that others do not see, this ability in combination with high psychometric intelligence can lead to the highest levels of creative achievement.

Intelligence, Intuition, and Insight

Various researchers have come to the conclusion that in many naturalistic situations, such as decision making in groups, very little controlled cognition is required (Klein, 1999; also see Gladwell, 2007, for a summary of relevant research). Instead, they note that expertise seems to be related to recognition of a situation that had been encountered previously and the retrieval of schemas that match the situation.[13] They argue that while controlled cognition is sometimes important, the key to intelligent behavior is the automatic retrieval process.

Similarly, Reyna (2004) argued that experts acquire knowledge that allows them to make fast, intuitive, and effective decisions whereas novices need to rely on deliberate, effortful reasoning. Reyna noted, however, that automatic processes can lead to bias and error when experts are presented with novel problems (also see Chabris & Simons, 2010, for a summary of research showing the potential perils of relying on intuition when making expert as well as novel decisions). Wilson and Schooler (1991) also showed the importance of automatic processing in decision making – they demonstrated that when making a decision that is complex and multi-attributed, people do better when conscious deliberation is intentionally prevented. This idea is also a major tenet of the unconscious thought theory (UTT), in which it is argued that decisions about simple issues can be better tackled by conscious thought, whereas decisions about complex matter can be better approached with unconscious thought (Dijksterhuis & Nordgren, 2006, but see Aczel, 2009; Newell, Wong, & Cheung, 2009; Payne, Samper, Bettman, & Luce, 2008; Thorsteinson & Withrow, 2009).

[13] For more on the relations between intelligence and the acquisition of expertise more generally, see Ackerman (Chapter 41, Intelligence and Expertise, this volume). In this section I focus instead on the relation between intelligence and intuition, particularly from an individual differences perspective.

Along similar lines, Hogarth (2005) distinguished between deliberate and tacit cognitive processes. According to Hogarth, complex decisions will benefit from tacit processing whereas less complex decisions will benefit from deliberate processing. An additional component in Hogarth's model is the degree of bias in the original learning environment. If the feedback presented in the original learning environment regarding decision accuracy is clear and immediate, the environment is considered "kind," and accurate causal relationships can be learned. Environments in which feedback is unclear and not available in a timely manner are considered "wicked" and are considered highly biased. In wicked learning environments, the intuitive system is prone to errors. According to Hogarth, intentional, deliberate thought is best suited to biased learning environments where the complexity of the task is low, whereas intuitive processing is best suited to learning environments in which bias is low and complexity of the task is high (see Epstein, 2003, and Kahneman, 2009, for related ideas, including the notion that the quality of an intuitive judgment is dependent upon the predictability of the environment in which the judgment is made and the individual's opportunity to learn the regularities in that environment).

Recently, researchers have investigated the role of individual differences in the use of intuition. With the aim of integrating the psychodynamic focus on unconscious processing with the cognitive focus on rational conscious thinking, Seymour Epstein put forth the cognitive-experiential self-theory (CEST; Epstein, 1994), which was an outgrowth of ideas presented in Epstein (1973). The theory posits that humans have two parallel but interacting modes of information processing. The *rational system* is analytic, logical, abstract, experienced actively and consciously, is slower to process information, and requires justification via logic and evidence. In contrast, the *experiential system* is holistic, affective, concrete, experienced passively, processes information automatically, and is self-evidently valid (experience alone is enough for belief).

Epstein's experiential system is related to intuition in the sense of "gut-feelings" that guide behavior. Based on his theory, Epstein developed the Rational-Experiential Inventory (REI; Pacini & Epstein, 1999), which measures individual differences in the tendency to rely on each mode of thought. His research program has discovered that the intelligence of each system is independent of, or very weakly correlated with, the intelligence of the other (Epstein & Meier, 1989), and each subscale (analytical and experiential) has unique predictive validity for a wide range of intelligent behaviors (see Epstein, 2003, for a review). In general, the rational scale is more strongly *positively* related to measures of intellectual performance such as scores on the Scholastic Aptitude Test (SAT) and grade point averages (GPA) than is the experiential scale, whereas the experiential scale is more strongly positively related to Extroversion, agreeableness, favorable interpersonal relationships, empathy, creativity, emotionality, sense of humor, and art appreciation than is the rational scale. The rational scale is more strongly *negatively* associated with Neuroticism, depression, anxiety, stress in college life, subtle racism, extreme conservatism, alcohol abuse, and naïve optimism than is the experiential scale, whereas the experiential scale is more strongly negatively associated with distrust and intolerance than is the rational scale. Many of these relations held even after controlling for the NEO Five Factor Inventory (NEO-FFI; Costa & McCrae, 1989), which measures the Big Five factors of personality. Other researchers have used the REI to investigate human cognition. For instance, Klaczynski (2009) reviews a number of studies he and his collaborators conducted using the REI to investigate the development of dual processes across the life span.

Pretz (2008) has extended both the experimental work on intuition and the cognitive styles approach by looking at the effects of individual differences in an analytical versus intuitive strategy and level of experience on practical problem solving. Pretz reasoned that the more experienced an individual is with a task, the less complex the task and the more decomposable the problem will appear to that individual. Pretz noted that the relevant knowledge associated with an everyday problem-solving task is likely to be acquired through informal experience, and individuals with more experience will therefore have more tacit knowledge but will also be able to better articulate that knowledge. As a result, the expert can use metacognitive skills to explicitly identify the main problem, identify the most relevant information, and identify the consequences of various courses of action (Antonakis et al., 2002).

In Pretz's study, college students were instructed to use either holistic intuition (bringing to mind all relevant information and trusting hunches) or analysis (defining the problem, distinguishing the relevant from irrelevant information, and monitoring the problem carefully) when solving various practical problems dealing with college life. Pretz found that the effectiveness of the strategy on task performance interacted with the participant's level of experience: analysis worked better for more experienced individuals whereas novices were slightly more successful when they employed a holistic, intuitive strategy. A similar pattern was found looking at existing individual differences in strategy preference.

Pretz's study suggests that among individuals with an intermediate level of expertise, analytical problem solving can be helpful in perceiving the logic and structure of the problem, and intuition can distract the expert from this critical information. In contrast, intuitive, holistic thought may be best suited for novices in a domain who see the task as ill-defined and need to bring to mind the relevant information. An implication of Pretz's study is that intermediate experts should rely on an analytical strategy when solving complex, practical problems. Full-blown experts who have fully automatized their task may benefit from an intuitive mode of thought.

This distinction between holistic intuition (of the sort studied in Pretz's study) and inferential intuition (full automatization) was made by Hill (1987–1988); the ideas are consistent with Baylor's (Baylor, 2001) U-shaped model of expertise and intuition and research showing the facilitation of intuition for complex, high-stakes decision making (Klein, 1999). Indeed, Pretz and Totz (2007) have developed a scale to measure individual differences in the tendency to rely on three different forms of intuition: affective, heuristic, and holistic. Another implication of Pretz's study is that many social problems may be better suited to the cognitive unconscious, as they may be more complex than nonsocial problems. Whereas individual differences in the cognitive unconscious can be adaptive for some social problems, there may be instances of social cognition in which the cognitive unconscious can lead to undesirable outcomes (see Implicit Social Cognition section).

Another line of research has investigated the intimate connection between intuition and insight. Anecdotally, insight has played a crucial role in the generation of creative ideas. The great French mathematician Henri Poincaré (1921) described incidents in which an answer came to him only after his conscious attention was directed away from the problem and he wasn't consciously deliberating on the problem. Poincaré argued that these moments of sudden inspiration are the result of unconscious thinking. Based on reflections of his creative thought process, he argued that the creative process starts with conscious work on a problem, followed by unconscious work, and then, if insight is successful, another stage of conscious work to verify that the ideas makes sense and to work out the implications of the idea. Indeed, insight is considered an important component of the creative process (Wallas, 1926).

Empirical work supports these anecdotes. In reviewing a number of experiments relating to implicit thought, intuition, and insights, Kihlstrom, Shames, and Dorfman (1996) have this to say about the nature of intuition:

> *From the experiments described in this chapter, it appears that the processes underlying intuitions closely resemble those*

which underlie implicit memory. In recognition, people's intuitions about the past – the feeling of familiarity, in the absence of full recollection – seems to be based on the perceptual fluency that comes with priming.... We actually think of these mental states as implicit thoughts: instances in which an idea or image influences experience, thought, or action in the absence of conscious awareness of what that idea or image is.

As for the link between intuitions and insight, they then go on to say:

... it is clear that problem solutions, like memories, are not discontinuous, all-or-none affairs, remaining entirely unconscious until they emerge full-blown into the full light of consciousness. There is a point, as they approach and cross what Wallas (1926), following William James (1890), called the "fringe" of consciousness, when we know they are coming, even when we do not know what they are. This is the point, between preparation and insight, where intuitions occur. (p. 19)

Other researchers have investigated the controlled and spontaneous cognitive mechanisms that underlie insight (see Sternberg & Davidson, 1995, for a review of research on insight). A methodology that is often employed is the Accumulated Clues Task (ACT), in which participants must discover a word, but are given clues (e.g., words that are associated with the answer) along the way. After each clue is presented, participants are required to provide an answer. The clues get increasingly helpful (are more related to the answer) and the answers given by the participants get objectively closer to the answer in an incremental fashion that occurs before their subjective ratings of feeling close to an answer, which they often report occurring to them in a sudden flash of insight (Bowers, Farvolden, & Mermigis, 1995; Dorfman, Shames, & Kihlstrom, 1996). Research has shown that individual differences in how long it takes participants to arrive at the correct answer correlate with verbal intelligence.

Recent research, however, suggests that different components of the task may differentially relate to controlled cognition. Reber, Ruch-Monachon, and Perrig (2007) first replicated earlier research on the ACT by finding that participants often underestimated their degree of closeness to the answer; these subjective reports of closeness exhibited a positive slope, suggesting that participants possessed implicit knowledge about the task and indeed felt hunches about their progress that weren't necessarily aligned with objective incremental progress. The researchers then distinguished between performance level, processing style, implicit knowledge, and subjective feeling of closeness to the solution on the ACT. While performance level correlated with verbal intelligence, processing style and implicit knowledge were not correlated with verbal intelligence. Further, a faith in intuition cognitive style and the Big Five personality traits Openness to Experience and Conscientiousness were all correlated with processing style, but not with implicit knowledge on the task. These results suggest that a promising research direction is to decompose problem-solving tasks into their processing style and intuitive components and investigate relations between individual differences in these components and individual differences in various processes and thinking styles relating to intelligence and the cognitive unconscious.

Domains

Implicit Social Cognition

There is an emerging consensus in the social cognition literature that many of our social behaviors and judgments are made automatically, without intention, effort, or awareness (Bargh & Chartrand, 1999; Bargh & Morsella, 2008). Research on automatic evaluation, impression formation, and automatic characterization all demonstrate the prevalence of automaticity in social life. It is generally thought now that mere perception of a stimulus can lead instantly and automatically to a judgment without any conscious reflection or reasoning. Indeed, until the 1980s, attitudes were mostly assumed to rely on consciously available information (Nosek, Greenwald, & Banaji, 2007).

Recently, researchers have investigated individual differences in implicit social cognition, using a variety of measures "that avoid requiring introspective access, decrease the mental control available to produce the response, reduce the role of conscious intention, and reduce the role of self-reflective, deliberative processes" (Nosek et al., 2007, p. 267). Greenwald and Banaji (1995) have been among the most active researchers investigating the role of implicit cognition in various social psychology constructs such as attitudes, stereotypes, and self-esteem. In their research, they attempt to "reveal traces of past experience that people might explicitly reject because it conflicts with values or beliefs, or might avoid revealing because the expression could have negative social consequences. Even more likely, implicit cognition can reveal information that is not available to introspective access even if people were motivated to retrieve and express it" (Nosek et al., 2007, p. 266; see Wilson, Lindsey, & Schooler, 2000, for related ideas about attitudes).

One of the best-validated measures of implicit social cognition is the Implicit Association Test (IAT; Greenwald, McGhee, & Schwartz, 1998). The IAT requires the participant to categorize various stimulus exemplars representing four concepts (e.g., men, women, good, bad) using two response options. When concepts that share a response are strongly associated, it is expected that the sorting task will be easier for the participant (as indexed by faster responses and fewer errors) than when the concepts are weakly associated. Thus, the IAT affords insight into automatic associative processes that are introspectively inaccessible. Over the last decade, the IAT has been adapted for use in various disciplines (see Nosek et al., 2007, for a review) and to assess implicit attitudes related to categories such as race, gender, and even insects. In studies that involve some measure of discrimination toward a social group, both explicit and IAT measures predict behavior, with the IAT offering superior prediction (Greenwald, Poehlman, Uhlmann, & Banaji, 2009). Furthermore, it has been demonstrated that people with the strongest automatic racial biases are most likely to engage in a wide variety of discriminatory behavior, including overt behavior (Rudman & Ashmore, 2007, but see van Ravenzwaaij, van der Maas, & Wagenmakers for an alternative account).

Therefore, research on how individual differences in intelligence and the cognitive unconscious interact to produce stereotyping and attitude formation is of both theoretical and practical interest. Recent research utilizing fMRI techniques provides some clues. Chee, Sriam, Soon, and Less (2000) used fMRI to examine participants while these individuals were taking the IAT. The researchers found that the left dorsolateral prefrontal cortex and to a lesser degree the anterior cingulate were most active during conditions in which items from incongruent categories (e.g., insect + pleasant) shared a response key than when items from congruent categories (e.g., flower + pleasant) shared a key. According to the researchers, this suggests that greater controlled cognition was required in conditions in which it was necessary to overcome the prepotent tendency to map emotionally congruent items to the same response key. In another study, Phelps et al. (2000) had White participants view faces of unfamiliar Black and White males. Participants who showed greater activation of the amygdala (a region of the brain associated with fear and negative emotions) while viewing Black faces relative to White faces tended to score higher on two measures of unconscious race evaluation: the IAT and the eyeblink response. In a second experiment, the researchers did not find the same pattern of brain activation when the faces were familiar and the participants regarded the Black and White individuals positively. In a related study, Cunningham et al. (2004) had participants view Black and White faces either subliminally or supraliminally during fMRI. When presented subliminally, the amygdala was more active for Black faces relative to White faces. This effect was reduced when the faces were presented supraliminally. Further, control regions in the prefrontal cortex (which are also activated during working memory and psychometric intelligence tests) showed greater activation for Black faces than White faces when presented supraliminally. Race bias as assessed by the IAT was related to a greater difference in amygdala activation for Black faces relative to White faces, and activity in the prefrontal cortex predicted a reduction in amygdala activation from the subliminal to the supraliminal condition. According to the researchers, this provides evidence for neural distinctions between automatic and controlled processing of social groups, suggesting that controlled processes (which support performance on measure of psychometric intelligence) may modulate automatic evaluation.

These results suggest that individual differences in measures of controlled cognition may predict the extent to which automatic evaluations influence behavior. To expand the range of individual differences in implicit social cognition investigated, it may be useful to construct new implicit learning tasks that consist of stimuli relating to the learning of real-world contingencies in the social domain. Tasks that already exist that could be adapted include the task used by Lewicki, Hill, and Sasaki (1989), in which participants implicitly learn to judge the intelligence of individuals from brain scans or the adaptation of that task employed by Woolhouse and Bayne (2000), in which participants implicitly learn to judge the job suitability of job candidates based on their personality profile. Such research can help distinguish between situations in which individual differences in the cognitive unconscious contribute to intelligent behavior (for example, when a person is engaging in an area of expertise or generating novel ideas), and situations in which controlled cognition may be the better predictor of intelligent behavior (since it helps override generalizations that can lead to explicit prejudice and stereotyping). Such research would further illustrate the need for measuring individual differences in both controlled and automatic cognitive processes in order to predict various forms of intelligent behavior.

Creative Cognition

Creativity requires both novelty and usefulness (Kaufman, 2007). The Creative Cognition Approach endeavors to identify and investigate the role of mental processes in creative cognition at various stages in the creative process (Finke, Ward, & Smith, 1992, 1995; Ward, Smith, & Finke, 1999). Creative cognition researchers have identified two main phases of creative invention that occur in a cyclical fashion in ordinary individuals. During the *generative* phase, the individual generates numerous candidate ideas or solutions and forms a mental representation (referred to as a preinventive structure). Then during the *exploratory* stage, the individual examines the candidate mental representations and ideas and consciously and sometimes painstakingly works out their implications. Cognitive unconscious processes activated through defocused attention most likely play more of a role during the generative stage, whereas controlled cognitive processes activated through focused attention most likely play more of a role during the exploratory stage. The highest levels of creativity, however, most likely require the ability for both modes of thought and the flexibility to switch modes of thought throughout the creative process.

On the one hand, behavioral and brain studies suggest that creative people are characterized by a lack of inhibition (Eysenck, 1995; Martindale, 1999), and case studies repeatedly show that creative people do describe the creative process as effortless and lacking in deliberation (Csikzentmihalyi, 1996). However, studies also show that creative individuals defocus their attention when approaching a creative task but they are capable of focusing their attention when it comes time to make the ideas practical (Martindale, 1999). In recent years, Oshin Vartian and colleagues have extended this research by showing in a series of clever experiments that creative people are able to adjust their focus of attention, depending on the demands of the task.

In one study, Vartanian, Martindale, and Kwiatkowski (2007) found a *negative* correlation between creative potential (measured by fluency scores) and speed of information processing on two tasks that did not involve interference or ambiguity, and a *positive* correlation between creative potential and speed of information processing on two tasks that did require the inhibition of interfering information. Therefore, subjects with greater creative potential were better able to slow down or speed up their information processing, depending on the task demands. A follow-up study found similar results and extended the earlier results in a sample of high school students in Russia (2008). The same pattern was found between creative potential (as measured by fluency, flexibility, and originality) and response latency as in the earlier study, and the findings held, correcting for IQ. In a third study, participants were instructed to judge whether two concepts were related or unrelated (Vartanian, Martindale, & Matthews, 2009). The rationale was that creativity is frequently defined as the novel and useful association of concepts that are not traditionally related. Therefore, this important cognitive process relies at least in part on a person's ability to quickly assess the degree of relationship between concepts. The researchers manipulated the degree of association between word pairs. Participants with greater creative potential (assessed by a measure of divergent thinking) exhibited a faster reaction time when judging the relatedness of the concepts. Psychometric intelligence didn't account for additional variance above and beyond divergent thinking scores in predicting the variability in reaction time performance. The researchers conclude that the ability of individuals with higher creative potential to more quickly judge the degree of association between words can lead to an advantage over time in the total number of potentially relevant conceptual associations that can be considered. The researchers argued that the task they used involved unambiguous task instructions and associations and that it is just these conditions in which those with better divergent thinking skills focus their attention, which can result in a faster reaction time.

An interesting question raised by Vartanian, Martindale, and Matthews (2009) is whether the mechanism that regulates the focus of attention is itself automatic or requires self-control. They have argued that the unambiguous nature of their task led to automatic regulation of attention. They point to evidence that in other circumstances, top-down processing can also play an important role in creative cognition. Vartanian, Martindale, and Kwiatkowski (2003) investigated the role of strategic flexibility in creative problem solving. They administered a rule discovery task and found that participants with higher creative potential (as measured by fluency scores) were better at discovering the rules. Further, the strategy of generating disconfirmatory hypotheses played an important role for successful participants in the later stages of hypothesis testing after the first feedback was given. Having already formed a representation of the problem space after feedback, successful participants were flexibly able to switch to a more successful strategy following initial feedback. Similar results have been found by Gilhooly, Fiortou, Anthony, and Wynn (2007), who found using think-aloud protocols that alternative uses for a task generated earlier in the course of the task drew primarily on memory-based strategies, whereas uses generated later drew on a more limited range of strategies requiring executive processes, such as imagining the disassembly of the object and using the parts or recombining the parts into other objects that could be applied in other ways. Similar to the results of the Vartanian, Martindale, and Kwiatkowki (2003) study, novelty of responses was affected by the ability to use a specific strategy later in the course of problem solving, supporting the view that creative people switch strategies during the course of a task but also suggesting that top-down processing can play an important role in creative problem solving. Vartanian, Martindale, and Kwiatkowski (2003) suggested a bi-directional model of creativity in which the focus of attention is modulated according to top-down as well as bottom-up processes, with the use of bottom-up processing determined by the stage of the problem (bottom-up processing primarily during the earlier stages, and top-down processing primarily during the later stages). Both Vartanian, Martindale, and Kwiatkowski (2003) and Vartanian (2009) mentioned that an important future line of research will be to investigate the underlying mechanism(s) that enable the modulation of information-processing strategies during the course of creative problem solving.

Drawing more on the memory and brain literature, Bristol and Viskontas (2006) came to similar conclusions. They proposed that creative individuals are good at modulating inhibitory processes, so that they have both the capability for cognitive control and the capacity for disinhibition and can switch fluidly from one mode to another. In particular, they argue that creative individuals can defocus their attention at the early stages of creative cognition so that they grasp the whole set of potential covariations; then, during the retrieval and elaboration stage, they can control attention so that they can inhibit prepotent responses and thereby allow remote associations to enter into consciousness without intrusions. Therefore, the researchers argue that creative individuals are both able to overcome cognitive inhibition and are capable of suppressing undesired responses. They claim that this skill requires the ability to *activate* the dorsolateral prefrontal cortex and inhibit retrieval-related processes that may interfere with accessing remote associations, as well as to *deactivate* the dorsolateral prefrontal cortex, depending on the context of the task and the goals of the individual. They also left as an interesting open question determining the precise brain mechanisms that can modulate between the different brain activations and deactivations depending on the demands of the task.

Conclusion

In his 1957 presidential address to the American Psychological Association, Lee Cronbach pleaded his case for uniting the burgeoning field of cognitive psychology, with its focus on the experimental psychology of higher order information processing, with the study of individual differences in Spearman's *g*. Cronbach's call set off a great deal of research that would demonstrate that the newer theories regarding the nature of intelligence and the burgeoning field of information-processing psychology were indeed quite compatible. The work by Hunt (Hunt, Frost, & Lunneborg, 1973) and Sternberg (1977) helped lay the foundation for the experimental study of intelligent reasoning processes that are deliberate and effortful. Subsequent research has tended to focus on both lower level as well as higher level correlates of general intelligence.

One particular set of cognitive processes that has not been investigated as thoroughly as the others from an individual differences perspective is the set related to the cognitive unconscious. This situation of mutual neglect has had the unfortunate consequence of limiting our picture of the nature of both human intelligence and the cognitive unconscious, thus potentially limiting our understanding of the role of individual differences in information processing in complex cognition more generally. The study of individual differences in the cognitive unconscious can increase our understanding of the nature of intelligence by helping us find boundary conditions for so-called general intelligence (*g*) and by doing so, discovering where *g* breaks down. Similarly, the study of individual differences in general intelligence and its associated cognitive mechanisms can elucidate the nature of the cognitive unconscious by helping to clarify and delineate automatic, spontaneous, and rapid information-processing mechanisms.

By charting new terrains, researchers can increase understanding of the determinants of intelligent behavior. A potentially fruitful line of research is to adapt already existing experimental paradigms and construct new tests that tap the cognitive unconscious. Individual differences in such tasks may not be strongly related to psychometric intelligence but may still explain intelligent behavior independent of psychometric intelligence. Researchers can then investigate the precise cognitive and neural mechanisms that underlie measures of the cognitive unconscious and develop interventions to raise these skills in everyone. By fostering collaborations across the various areas of psychology and related disciplines, and incorporating dual-process theory into our thinking, we should be able to come to a fuller, more complete understanding of human intelligence.

Acknowledgments

I would like to thank Edward Cokely, Seymour Epstein, Jean Pretz, and Robert Sternberg for their insightful suggestions on an earlier draft.

References

Achter, J. A., Lubinski, D., Benbow, C. P., & Eftekhari-Sanjani, H. (1999). Assessing vocational preferences among gifted adolescents adds incremental validity to abilities: A discriminant analysis of educational outcomes over a 10-year interval. *Journal of Educational Psychology, 91*, 777–786.

Aczel, B. (2009). *Attention and awareness in human learning and decision making* (Unpublished doctoral dissertation). University of Cambridge, Cambridge, UK.

Anderson, J. R. (1982). Acquisition of cognitive skill. *Psychological Review, 89*, 369–406.

Anderson, M. (2005). Marrying intelligence and cognition: A developmental review. In R. J. Sternberg & J. E. Pretz (Eds.), *Cognition & intelligence: Identifying the mechanisms of the mind* (pp. 268–288). Cambridge, UK: Cambridge University Press.

Anderson, M. (2008). What can autism and dyslexia tell us about intelligence? *Quarterly Journal of Experimental Psychology, 61*, 116–128.

Antonakis, J., Hedlund, J., Pretz, J., & Sternberg, R. J. (2002). *Exploring the nature and acquisition of tacit knowledge for military leadership* (Research Note 2002–04). Alexandria, VA: Army Research Institute for the Behavioral and Social Sciences.

Baker, C. I., Olson, C. R., & Behrmann, M. (2004). Role of attention and perceptual grouping in visual statistical learning. *Psychological Science, 15*, 460–466.

Barch, D. M. (2005). The cognitive neuroscience of schizophrenia. *Annual Review of Clinical Psychology, 1*, 321–353.

Bargh, J. A. (2004). The four horsemen of automaticity: Awareness, intention, efficiency, and control in social cognition. In R. S. Wyer & T. K. Srull (Eds.), *Handbook of social cognition* (pp. 1–41). Hillsdale, NJ: Erlbaum.

Bargh, J. A., & Chartrand, T. L. (1999). The unbearable automaticity of being. *American Psychologist, 54*, 462–479.

Bargh, J. A., & Morsella, E. (2008). The unconscious mind. *Perspectives on Psychological Science, 3*, 73–79.

Baruch, I., Hemsley, D. R., & Gray, J. A. (1988a). Latent inhibition and "psychotic proneness" in normal subjects. *Personality and Individual Differences, 9*, 777–783.

Baruch, I., Hemsley, D. R., & Gray, J. A. (1988b). Differential performance of acute and chronic schizophrenics in a latent inhibition task. *Journal of Nervous and Mental Disease, 176*, 598–606.

Baylor, A. L. (2001). A U-shaped model for the development of intuition by level of expertise. *New Ideas in Psychology, 19*, 237–244.

Binet, A., & Simon, T. (1916). *The development of intelligence in children* (E. S. Kite, Trans.). Baltimore, MD: Williams & Wilkens.

Bowers, K. S., Farvolden, P., & Mermigis, L. (1995). Intuitive antecedents of insight. In S. M. Smith, T. B. Ward & R. A. Finke (Eds.), *The creative cognition approach* (pp. 27–51). Cambridge, MA: MIT Press.

Bristol, A. S., & Viskontas, I. V. (2006). Dynamic processes within associative memory stores: Piecing together the neural basis of creative cognition. In J. C. Kaufman & J. Baer (Eds.), *Creativity and reason in cognitive development* (pp. 60–80). New York, NY: Cambridge University Press.

Brown, J. B., Aczel, B., Jimenez, L., Kaufman, S. B., Mackintosh, N., & Plaisted, K. (2010). Intact implicit learning in autism spectrum conditions. *Quarterly Journal of Experimental Psychology*, **1**, 1–24.

Carey, S., & Spelke, E. (1994). Domain-specific knowledge and conceptual change. In L. A. Hirschfeld & S. A. Gelman (Eds.), *Mapping the mind: Domain specificity in cognition and culture* (pp. 169–200). New York, NY: Cambridge University Press.

Carroll, J. B. (1993). *Human cognitive abilities: A survey of factor-analytic studies*. Cambridge, UK: Cambridge University Press.

Carson, S. H., Peterson, J. B., & Higgins, D. M. (2003). Decreased latent inhibition is associated with increased creative achievement in high-functioning individuals. *Journal of Personality and Social Psychology*, **85**, 499–506.

Chabris, C. F. (2007). Cognitive and neurobiological mechanisms of the Law of General Intelligence. In M. J. Roberts (Ed.), *Integrating the mind: Domain general vs. domain specific processes in higher cognition* (pp. 449–491). New York, NY: Psychology Press.

Chabris, C.F., & Simons, D. (2010). *The invisible gorilla: And other ways our intuitions deceive us*. New York, NY: Crown Archetype.

Chaiken, S. (1987). The heuristic model of persuasion. In M. P. Zanna, J. M. Olson, & C. P. Herman (Eds.), *Social influence: The Ontario symposium* (vol. 5, pp. 3–39). Hillsdale, NJ: Erlbaum.

Chee, M. W. L., Sriram, N., Soon, C. S., & Lee, K. M. (2000). Dorsolateral prefrontal cortex and the implicit association of concepts and attributes. *Neuroreport: For Rapid Communication of Neuroscience Research*, **11**, 135–140.

Cokely, E. T., & Kelley, C. M. (2009). Cognitive abilities and superior decision making under risk: A protocol analysis and process model evaluation. *Judgment and Decision Making*, **4**, 20–33.

Cokely, E. T., Parpart, P., & Schooler, L.J. (2009). On the link between cognitive control and heuristic processes. In N. A. Taatgen & H. v. Rijn (Eds.), *Proceedings of the 31st Annual Conference of the Cognitive Science Society* (pp. 2926–2931). Austin, TX: Cognitive Science Society.

Cokely, K., Kelley, C. M., & Gilchrist, A. L. (2006). Sources of individual differences in working memory: Contributions of strategy to capacity. *Psychonomic Bulletin & Review*, **13**, 991–997.

Costa, P. T., & McCrae, R. R. (1989). *The NEO-PI/NEO-FFI manual supplement*. Odessa, FL: Psychological Assessment Resources.

Cowan, N. (1988). Evolving conceptions of memory storage, selective attention, and their mutual constraints within the human information-processing system. *Psychological Bulletin*, **104**, 163–191.

Cronbach, L. J. (1957). The two disciplines of scientific psychology. *American Psychologist*, **12**, 671–684.

Csikzentmihalyi, M. (1996). *Creativity: Flow and the psychology of discovery and invention*. New York, NY: Harper Collins.

Cunningham, W. A., Johnson, M. K., Raye, C. L., Gatenby, J. C., Gore, J. C., & Banaji, M. R. (2004). Separable neural components in the processing of black and white faces. *Psychological Science*, **15**, 806–813.

Dennett, D. C. (1992). *Consciousness explained*. New York, NY: Back Bay Books.

Dijksterhuis, A., & Nordgren, L. F. (2006). A theory of unconscious thought. *Perspectives on Psychological Science*, **1**, 95–109.

Dorfman, J., Shames, V. A., & Kihlstrom, J. F. (1996). Intuition, incubation, and insight: Implicit cognition in problem solving. In G. D. M. Underwood (Ed.), *Implicit cognition* (pp. 257–296). New York, NY: Oxford University Press.

Dorfman, L., Martindale, C., Gassimova, V., & Vartanian, O. (2008). Creativity and speed of information processing: A double dissociation involving elementary versus inhibitory cognitive tasks. *Personality and Individual Differences*, **44**, 1382–1390.

Epstein, S. (1973). The self-concept revisited or a theory of a theory. *American Psychologist*, **28**, 404–416.

Epstein, S. (1991). Cognitive-experiential self-theory: An integrative theory of personality. In R. Curtis (Ed.), *The relational self: Convergences in psychoanalysis and social psychology* (pp. 111–137). New York, NY: Guilford Press.

Epstein, S. (1994). Integration of the cognitive and the psychodynamic unconscious. *American Psychologist*, **49**, 709–724.

Epstein, S. (2001). *Manual for the Constructive Thinking Inventory*. Odessa, FL: Psychological Assessment Resources.

Epstein, S. (2003). Cognitive-experiential self-theory of personality. In T. Millon & M. J. Lerner (Eds.), *Comprehensive handbook of psychology* (Vol. 5, pp. 159–184). Personality and social psychology. Hoboken, NJ: Wiley.

Epstein, S. (2010). Demystifying intuition: What it is, what it does, and how it does it. *Psychological Inquiry*, **21**, 295–312.
Epstein, S., & Meier, P. (1989). Constructive thinking: A broad coping variable with specific components. *Journal of Personality and Social Psychology*, 57, 332–349.
Ericsson, K. A., & Charness, N. (1994). Expert performance: Its structure and acquisition. *American Psychologist*, 49, 725–747.
Ericsson, K. A., & Kintsch, W. (1995). Long-term working memory. *Psychological Review*, **102**, 211–245.
Ericsson, K. A., & Lehmann, A. C. (1996). Expert and exceptional performance: Evidence of maximal adaptation to task constraints. *Annual Review of Psychology*, 47, 273–305.
Evans, J. S. B. T. (2008). Dual-processing accounts of reasoning, judgment, and social cognition. *Annual Review of Psychology*, 59, 255–278.
Evans, J. S. B. T., & Frankish, K. (2009). *In two minds: Dual processes and beyond*. New York, NY: Oxford University Press.
Eysenck, H. J. (1995). Creativity as a product of intelligence and personality. In D. Saklofske & M. Zeidner (Eds.), *International handbook of personality and intelligence: Perspectives on individual differences* (pp. 231–247). New York, NY: Plenum Press.
Feist, G. J. (2001). Natural and sexual selection in the evolution of creativity. *Bulletin of Psychology and the Arts*, **2**, 11–16.
Feldman, J., Kerr, B., & Streissguth, A. P. (1995). Correlational analyses of procedural and declarative learning performance. *Intelligence*, **20**, 87–114.
Finke, R. A., Ward, T. B., & Smith, S. M. (1992). *Creative cognition: Theory, research, and applications*. Cambridge, MA: MIT Press.
Fletcher, J., Maybery, M. T., & Bennett, S. (2000). Implicit learning differences: A question of developmental level? *Journal of Experimental Psychology: Learning, Memory, and Cognition*, **26**, 246–252.
Fodor, J. (1983). *The modularity of mind*. Boston, MA: MIT Press.
Fox, M. C., Roring, R. W., & Mitchum, A. L. (2009). Reversing the speed-IQ correlation: Intra-individual variability and attentional control in the inspection time paradigm. *Intelligence*, 37(76–80).
Frensch, P. A., & Miner, C. S. (1995). Zur Rolle des Arbeitsgedächtnisses beim impliziten Sequenzlernen [The role of working memory in implicit sequence learning]. *Zeitschrift für Experimentelle Psychologie*, 42, 545–575.
Gabora, L., & Kaufman, S. B. (2009). Evolutionary approaches to creativity. In J. C. Kaufman & R. J. Sternberg (Eds.), *Cambridge handbook of creativity*. Cambridge, UK: Cambridge University Press. Manuscript in preparation.
Gardner, H. (1993). *Frames of mind: The theory of multiple intelligences* (2nd ed.). New York, NY: Basic Books.
Gardner, H. (1999). *Intelligence reframed: Multiple intelligences for the 21st century*. New York, NY: Basic Books.
Gebauer, G. F., & Mackintosh, N. J. (2007). Psychometric intelligence dissociates implicit and explicit learning. *Journal of Experimental Psychology: Learning, Memory, and Cognition*, 33, 34–54.
Gebauer, G. F., & Mackintosh, N. J. (2009). Implicit learning and intelligence: A principal component analysis. Manuscript submitted for publication.
Gigerenzer, G. (2007). *Gut feelings: The intelligence of the unconscious*. New York, NY: Viking.
Gigerenzer, G., & Brighton, H. (2009). Homo heuristicus: Why biased minds make better inferences. *Topics in Cognitive Science*, **1**, 107–143.
Gigerenzer, G., & Regier, T. (1996). How do we tell an association from a rule? Comment on Sloman (1996). *Psychological Bulletin*, **119**, 23–26.
Gilhooly, K. J., Fiortou, E., Anthony, S. H., & Wynn, V. (2007). Divergent thinking: Strategies and executive involvement in generating novel uses for familiar objects. *British Journal of Psychology*, 98, 611–625.
Gladwell, M. (2007). *Blink: The power of thinking without thinking*. New York, NY: Back Bay Books.
Greenwald, A. G., & Banaji, M. R. (1995). Implicit social cognition: Attitudes, self-esteem, and stereotypes. *Psychological Review*, **102**, 4–27.
Greenwald, A. G., McGhee, D. E., & Schwartz, J. L. K. (1998). Measuring individual differences in implicit cognition: The Implicit Association Test. *Journal of Personality and Social Psychology*, 74, 1464–1480.
Greenwald, A. G., Poehlman, T. A., Uhlmann, E., & Banaji, M. R. (2009). Understanding and

using the Implicit Association Test: III. Meta-analysis of predictive validity. *Journal of Personality and Social Psychology*, 97, 17–41.

Haidt, J. (2001). The emotional dog and its rational tail: A social intuitionist approach to moral judgment. *Psychological Review*, 108, 814–834.

Hammond, K. R., & Hamm, R. M., Grassia, J., & Pearson, T. (1987). Direct comparison of the efficacy of intuitive and analytical cognition in expert judgment. *IEEE Transactions on Systems, Man, and Cybernetics, SMC*, 17, 753–770.

Hassin, R. R., Uleman, J. S., & Bargh, J. A. (2005). *The new unconscious*. New York, NY: Oxford University Press.

Hawkins, J. (2005). *On intelligence*. New York, NY: Holt.

Hemphill, J. F. (2003). Interpreting the magnitudes of correlation coefficients. *American Psychologist*, 58, 78–79.

Hertzog, C., & Robinson, A. E. (2005). Metacognition and intelligence. In O. Wilhelm & R. W. Engle (Eds.), *Handbook of understanding and measuring intelligence* (pp. 101–123). Thousand Oaks, CA: Sage.

Hill, O. W. (1987–1988). Intuition: Inferential heuristic or epistemic mode? *Imagination, Cognition and Personality*, 7, 137–154.

Hirschfeld, L. A., & Gelman, S. A. (1994). *Mapping the mind: Domain specificity in cognition and culture*. New York, NY: Cambridge University Press.

Hogarth, R. M. (2005). Deciding analytically or trusting your intuition? The advantages and disadvantages of analytic and intuitive thought. In T. Betsch & S. Haberstroh (Eds.), *Routines of decision making* (pp. 67–82). Mahwah, NJ: Erlbaum.

Howard-Jones, P. A., & Murray, S. (2003). Ideational productivity, focus of attention, and context. *Creativity Research Journal*, 15, 153–166.

Humphreys, L. G., Lubinski, D., & Yao, G. (1993). Utility of predicting group membership and the role of spatial visualization in becoming an engineer, physical scientist, or artist. *Journal of Applied Psychology*, 78, 250–261.

Hunt, E., Frost, N., & Lunneborg, C. (1973). Individual differences in cognition: A new approach to intelligence. In G. H. Bower (Ed.), *The psychology of learning and motivation: Advances in research and theory*. Oxford, UK: Academic Press.

James, W. (1890). *The principles of psychology*. New, York, NY: Dover.

Jensen, A. R. (1998). *The g factor: The science of mental ability*. Westport, CT: Praeger.

Jiang, Y., & Chun, M. M. (2001). Selective attention modulates implicit learning. *Quarterly Journal of Experimental Psychology*, **54A**, 1105–1124.

Jiménez, L., & Mendez, C. (1999). Which attention is needed for implicit sequence learning? *Journal of Experimental Psychology: Learning, Memory, and Cognition*, 25, 236–259.

Johnson, M. K., & Hirst, W. (1993). MEM: Memory subsystems as processes. In A. F. Collins, S. E. Gathercole, M. A. Conway, & P. E. Morris (Eds.), *Theories of memory* (pp. 241–286). Hillsdale, NJ: Erlbaum.

Jung, C. G. (1921/1971). *Psychological types* (H. G. Baynes, Trans.). Princeton, NJ: Princeton University Press. (revised by R.F.C. Hull).

Kahneman, D., & Klein, G. (2009). Conditions for intuitive expertise. *American Psychologist*, 64, 515–526.

Kahneman, D., & Frederick, S. (2002). Representativeness revisited: Attribute substitution in intuitive judgment. In T. Gilovich, D. Griffin, & D. Kahneman (Eds.), *Heuristics and biases: The psychology of intuitive judgment* (pp. 49–81). New York, NY: Cambridge University Press.

Kane, M. J., Bleckley, M. K., Conway, A. R. A., & Engle, R. W. (2001). A controlled-attention view of working-memory capacity. *Journal of Experimental Psychology: General*, 130, 169–183.

Kaufman, S. B. (2007). Creativity. In C. R. Reynolds & E. Fletcher-Janzen (Eds.), *Encyclopedia of special education* (3rd ed.). New York, NY: Wiley.

Kaufman, S. B. (2007). Investigating the role of domain general mechanisms in the acquisition of domain specific expertise. *High Ability Studies*, 18, 71–73.

Kaufman, S. B. (2009a). *Beyond general intelligence: The dual-process theory of human intelligence* (Doctoral dissertation). Yale University, New Haven, CT.

Kaufman, S. B. (2009b). Faith in intuition is associated with decreased latent inhibition in a sample of high-achieving adolescents. *Psychology of Aesthetics, Creativity, and the Arts*, 3, 28–34.

Kaufman, S. B., DeYoung, C. G., Gray, J. R., Brown, J., & Mackintosh, N. (2009). Associative learning predicts intelligence above and beyond working memory and processing speed. *Intelligence*, 37, 374–382.

Kaufman, S. B., DeYoung, C. G., Gray, J. R., Jiménez, L., Brown, J. B., & Mackintosh, N. (2009). Implicit learning as an ability. *Cognition, 116*, 321–340.

Keren, G., & Schul, Y. (2009). Two is not always better than one: A critical evaluation of two-system theories. *Perspectives on Psychological Science, 4*, 533–550.

Kihlstrom, J. F. (1987). The cognitive unconscious. *Science, 237*(4821), 1445–1452.

Kihlstrom, J. F., Shames, V. A., & Dorfman, J. (1996). Intimations of memory and thought. In L. M. Reder (Ed.), *Implicit memory and metacognition*. Hillsdale, N.J.: Erlbaum.

Klaczynski, P. A. (2009). Cognitive and social cognitive development: Dual-process research and theory. In S. B. T. Evans & K. Frankish (Eds.), *In two minds: Dual processes and beyond*. New York, NY: Oxford University Press.

Klaczynski, P. A., & Cottrell, J. M. (2004). A dual-process approach to cognitive development: The case of children's understanding of sunk cost decisions. *Thinking & Reasoning, 10*, 147–174.

Klein, G. (1999). *Sources of power: How people make decisions*. Cambridge, UK: Cambridge University Press.

Lewicki, P., & Hill, T. (1987). Unconscious processes as explanations of behavior in cognitive, personality, and social psychology. *Personality and Social Psychology Bulletin, 13*, 355–362.

Lewicki, P., Hill, T., & Czyzewska, M. (1992). Nonconscious acquisition of information. *American Psychologist, 47*, 796–801.

Lewicki, P., Hill, T., & Sasaki, I. (1989). Self-perpetuating development of encoding biases. [Empirical Study]. *Journal of Experimental Psychology: General, 118*, 323–337.

Lieberman, M. D. (2007). The X- and C-systems: The neural basis of automatic and controlled social cognition. *Social neuroscience: Integrating biological and psychological explanations of social behavior*, 290–315.

Litman, L., & Reber, A. S. (2005). Implicit cognition and thought. In K. J. Holyoak & R. G. Morrison (Eds.), *The Cambridge handbook of thinking and reasoning* (pp. 431–453). New York, NY: Cambridge University Press.

Loftus, E. F., & Klinger, M. R. (1992). Is the unconscious smart or dumb? *American Psychologist, 47*, 761–765.

Lohman, D. F. (2001). Fluid intelligence, inductive reasoning, and working memory: Where the theory of multiple intelligences falls short. In N. Colangelo & S. G. Assouline (Eds.), *Talent development IV: Proceedings from the 1998 Henry B. and Jocelyn Wallace National Research Symposium on Talent Development* (pp. 219–227). Scottsdale, AZ: Gifted Psychology Press.

Lubow, R. E. (1989). *Latent inhibition and conditioned attention theory*. Cambridge, UK: Cambridge University Press.

Lubow, R. E., & Gewirtz, J. C. (1995). Latent inhibition in humans: Data, theory, and implications for schizophrenia. *Psychological Bulletin, 117*, 87–103.

Lubow, R. E., Ingberg-Sachs, Y., Zalstein-Orda, N., & Gewirtz, J. C. (1992). Latent inhibition in low and high "psychotic-prone" normal subjects. *Personality and Individual Differences, 13*, 563–572.

Maas, H. L. J., Dolan, C. V., Grasman, P. P. P., Wicherts, J. M., Huizenga, H. M., & Raijmakers, M. E. J. (2006). A dynamical model of general intelligence: The positive manifold of intelligence by mutualism. *Psychological Review, 113*, 842–861.

Margolis, H. (1987). *Patterns, thinking, and cognition: A theory of judgment*. Chicago, IL: University of Chicago Press.

Martindale, C. (1995). Creativity and connectionism. In S. M. Smith, T. B. Ward, & R. A. Finke (Eds.), *The creative cognition approach* (pp. 249–268). Cambridge, MA: MIT Press.

Martindale, C. (1999). Biological bases of creativity. In R. J. Sternberg (Ed.), *Handbook of creativity* (pp. 137–152). Cambridge, UK: Cambridge University Press.

McGeorge, P., Crawford, J. R., & Kelly, S. W. (1997). The relationships between psychometric intelligence and learning in an explicit and an implicit task. *Journal of Experimental Psychology: Learning, Memory, and Cognition, 23*, 239–245.

Metcalfe, J., & Mischel, W. (1999). A hot/cool-system analysis of delay of gratification: Dynamics of willpower. *Psychological Review, 106*, 3–19.

Miller, G. A. (2003). The cognitive revolution: A historical perspective. *Trends in Cognitive Sciences, 7*, 141–144.

Newell, B. R., Wong, K.Y., & Cheung, J. C. H. (2009). Think, blink or sleep on it? The impact of modes of thought on complex decision making. *Quarterly Journal of Experimental Psychology, 62*, 707–732.

Nosek, B. A., Greenwald, A. G., & Banaji, M. R. (2007). The Implicit Association Test at age

7: A methodological and conceptual review. In J. A. Bargh (Ed.), *Social psychology and the unconscious: The automaticity of higher mental processes* (pp. 265–292). New York, NY: Psychology Press.

Pacini, R., & Epstein, S. (1999). The relation of rational and experiential information processing styles to personality, basic beliefs, and the ratio-bias phenomenon. *Journal of Personality and Social Psychology, 76*, 972–987.

Packard, M. G., Hirsh, R., & White, N. M. (1989). Differential effects of fornix and caudate nucleus lesions on two radial maze tasks: Evidence for multiple memory systems. *Journal of Neuroscience, 9*, 1465–1472.

Payne, J. W., Samper, A., Bettman, J. R., & Luce, M. F. (2008). Boundary conditions on unconscious thought in complex decision making. *Psychological Science, 19*, 1118–1123.

Peterson, J. B., Smith, K. W., & Carson, S. (2002). Openness and extraversion are associated with reduced latent inhibition: Replication and commentary. *Personality and Individual Differences, 33*, 1137–1147.

Phelps, E. A., O'Connor, K. J., Cunningham, W. A., Funayama, E. S., Gatenby, J. C., Gore, J. C., et al. (2000). Performance on indirect measures of race evaluation predicts amygdala activation. *Journal of Cognitive Neuroscience, 12*, 729–738.

Piaget, J. (1952). *The origins of intelligence in children*. Madison, CT: International Universities Press.

Poincaré, H. (1921). *The foundations of science* (G. B. Halstead, Trans.). New York, NY: Science Press.

Poldrack, R. A., & Packard, M. G. (2003). Competition among multiple memory systems: Converging evidence from animal and human brain studies. *Neuropsychologia, 41*, 245–251.

Pretz, J. E. (2008). Intuition versus analysis: Strategy and experience in complex everyday problem solving. *Memory & Cognition, 36*, 554–566.

Pretz, J. E., & Totz, K. S. (2007). Measuring individual differences in affective, heuristic, and holistic intuition. *Personality and Individual Differences, 43*, 1247–1257.

Pretz, J. E., Totz, K. S., & Kaufman, S. B. (2010). The effects of mood, cognitive style, and cognitive ability on implicit learning. *Learning and Individual Differences, 20*, 215–219.

Reber, A. S. (1989). Implicit learning and tacit knowledge. *Journal of Experimental Psychology: General, 118*, 219–235.

Reber, A. S. (1993). *Implicit learning and tacit knowledge: An essay on the cognitive unconscious*. New York, NY: Oxford University Press.

Reber, A. S., Walkenfeld, F. F., & Hernstadt, R. (1991). Implicit and explicit learning: Individual differences and IQ. *Journal of Experimental Psychology: Learning, Memory, and Cognition, 17*, 888–896.

Reber, R., Ruch-Monachon, M.-A., & Perrig, W. J. (2007). Decomposing intuitive components in a conceptual problem solving task. *Consciousness and Cognition: An International Journal, 16*, 294–309.

Reyna, V. F. (2004). How people make decisions that involve risk: A dual-processes approach. *Current Directions in Psychological Science, 13*, 60–66.

Rudman, L. A., & Ashmore, R. D. (2007). Discrimination and the Implicit Association Test. *Group Processes & Intergroup Relations, 10*, 359–372.

Salthouse, T. A., McGuthry, K. E., & Hambrick, D. Z. (1999). A framework for analyzing and interpreting differential aging patterns: Application to three measures of implicit learning. *Aging, Neuropsychology, and Cognition, 6*, 1–18.

Schneider, W., & Shiffrin, R. M. (1977). Controlled and automatic human information processing: I. Detection, search, and attention. *Psychological Review, 84*, 1–66.

Seger, C. A. (1994). Implicit learning. *Psychological Bulletin, 115*, 163–196.

Simon, H. A. (1979). *Models of thought*. New Haven, CT: Yale University Press.

Smith, S. M., Ward, T. B., & Finke, R. A. (1995). *The creative cognition approach*. Cambridge, MA: MIT Press.

Spearman, C. (1904). "General intelligence," objectively determined and measured. *American Journal of Psychology, 15*, 201–293.

Stadler, M. A., & Frensch, P. A. (1997). *Handbook of implicit learning*. Thousand Oaks, CA: Sage.

Stanovich, K. (1999). *Who is rational? Studies of individual differences in reasoning*. Mahwah, NJ: Erlbaum

Stanovich, K. E. (2004). *The robot's rebellion: Finding meaning in the age of Darwin*. Chicago, IL: University of Chicago Press.

Stanovich, K. E. (2009). Distinguishing the reflective, algorithmic, and autonomous minds: Is it time for a tri-process theory. In J. S. B. T. Evans & K. Frankish (Eds.), *In two minds: Dual processes and beyond*. Oxford, UK: Oxford University Press.

Stanovich, K. E., & West, R. F. (1997). Reasoning independently of prior belief and individual differences in actively open-minded thinking. *Journal of Educational Psychology*, 89, 342–357.

Stanovich, K. E., & West, R. F. (2000). Individual differences in reasoning: Implications for the rationality debate? *Behavioral and Brain Sciences*, 23, 645–726.

Stanovich, K. E., & West, R. F. (2002). Individual differences in reasoning: Implications for the rationality debate? In T. Gilovich, D. Griffin, & D. Kahneman (Eds.), *Heuristics and biases: The psychology of intuitive judgment* (pp. 421–440). New York, NY: Cambridge University Press.

Sternberg, R. J. (1977). Component processes in analogical reasoning. *Psychological Review*, 84, 353–378.

Sternberg, R. J., & Davidson, J. E. (1995). *The nature of insight*. Cambridge, MA: MIT Press.

Sternberg, R. J., & Pretz, J. E. (2005). *Cognition & intelligence: Identifying the mechanisms of the mind*. New York, NY: Cambridge University Press.

Thorsteinson, T. J., & Withrow, S. (2009). Does unconscious thought outperform conscious thought on complex decisions? A further examination. *Judgment and Decision Making*, 4, 235–247.

Turke-Browne, N. B., Junge, J. A., & Scholl, B. J. (2005). The automaticity of visual statistical learning. *Journal of Experimental Psychology: General*, **134**, 552–564.

Unsworth, N., & Engle, R. W. (2005). Individual differences in working memory capacity and learning: Evidence from the serial reaction time task. *Memory & Cognition*, 33, 213–220.

van Ravenzwaaij, D., van der Maas, H.L., & Wagenmakers, E.J. (in press). Does the name-race implicit association test measure racial prejudice? *Experimental Psychology*, doi: 10.1027/1618-3169/a000093.

Vartanian, O. (2009). Variable attention facilitates creative problem *Psychology of Aesthetics, Creativity, and the Arts*, 3, 57–59.

Vartanian, O., Martindale, C., & Kwiatkowski, J. (2003). Creativity and inductive reasoning: The relationship between divergent thinking and performance on Wason's 2–4–6 task. *Quarterly Journal of Experimental Psychology*, 34, 1370–1380.

Vartanian, O., Martindale, C., & Kwiatkowski, J. (2007). Creative potential, attention, and speed of information processing. *Personality and Individual Differences*, 43, 1470–1480.

Vartanian, O., Martindale, C., & Matthews, J. (2009). Divergent thinking ability is related to faster relatedness judgments. *Psychology of Aesthetics, Creativity, and the Arts*, 3, 99–103.

Wallas (1926). *The art of thought*. New York, NY: Harcourt Brace.

Ward, T. B., Smith, S. M., & Finke, R. A. (1999). Creative cognition. In R. J. Sternberg (Ed.), *Handbook of creativity* (pp. 189–212). New York, NY: Cambridge University Press.

Wilson, T. (2004). *Strangers to ourselves: Discovering the adaptive unconscious*. Boston, MA: Harvard University Press.

Wilson, T. D., Lindsey, S., & Schooler, T. Y. (2000). A model of dual attitudes. *Psychological Review*, **107**, 101–126.

Wilson, T. D., & Schooler, J. W. (1991). Thinking too much: Introspection can reduce the quality of preferences and decisions. *Journal of Personality and Social Psychology*, 60, 181–192.

Woolhouse, L. S., & Bayne, R. (2000). Personality and the use of intuition: Individual differences in strategy and performance on an implicit learning task. *European Journal of Personality*, **14**, 157–169.

Zajonc, R. B. (1980). Feeling and thinking: Preferences need no inferences. *American Psychologist*, 35, 151–175.

Zhiyan, T., & Singer, J. L. (1997). Daydreaming styles, emotionality and the Big Five personality dimensions. *Imagination, Cognition and Personality*, 16, 399–414.

CHAPTER 23

Artificial Intelligence

Ashok K. Goel and Jim Davies

Artificial intelligence (AI) is the field of research that strives to understand, design, and build cognitive systems. From computer programs that can beat top international grand masters at chess to robots that can help detect improvised explosive devices in war, AI has had many successes. As a science, it differs from cognitive psychology in two ways. First, its main methodology is the exploration of cognitive theory by building intelligent artifacts. Though the design of any intelligent artifact would be classified as an AI, AI as a discipline is united in the core belief that intelligence is a kind of computation. Thus, in practice, AI artifacts are almost always computers or computer programs. This also explains why AI laboratories typically are found in computer science departments.

Second, psychology is mostly interested in the understanding of intelligence found naturally in humans and other animals, whereas, in addition, AI concerns itself with the understanding of intelligence in agents it designs. From the AI perspective, the concept of intelligence is not one that should be limited to the abilities of humans or even animals in general, but it should cover potentially any kind of intelligent system, be it human, computer, animal, or alien. Albus (1991, p. 474) puts it eloquently: "A useful definition of intelligence ... should include both biological and machine embodiments, and these should span an intellectual range from that of an insect to that of an Einstein, from that of a thermostat to that of the most sophisticated computer system that could ever be built."

To demonstrate this latter difference, it is helpful to distinguish AI research into two kinds. *Engineering AI* is concerned with how to design the smartest intelligent artifacts possible, regardless of whether the processes implemented reflect those found in natural intelligences. The vast majority of AI research falls into this category. *Cognitive AI*, in contrast, endeavors to design artifacts that think the way people (or sometimes other animals) do. A subcategory of cognitive AI is *cognitive modeling*, which tries to quantitatively model empirical human participant data. Many cognitive modeling groups are working in psychology departments. AI cognitive models differ from other models in psychology in that AI always implements *information-processing* theories. That is, the theory describes intelligence in terms of content, representation, access, use, and acquisition of information, as opposed to, for example, a statistical model of the influences on IQ (e.g., age) in a population.

This article focuses on cognitive AI for several reasons: The original dream of AI was to develop human-level intelligence, this handbook is intended for an audience of cognitive scientists, and the authors themselves work in this paradigm.

Be it a leftover from Cartesian dualism or a desperate hold onto the uniqueness of humanity, many people have an almost mystical view of intelligence. One result is that when an AI program manages to accomplish some cognitive task, a common reaction is to claim that it's not an example of intelligence. Indeed, at one point, arithmetic calculation was thought to be one of best displays of intelligence, but now almost no one wants to say a calculator is intelligent. Because of this moving of the goalposts, AI has been jokingly referred to as standing for "Almost Implemented." For the most part, this is only a semantic issue. In fact, AI discoveries have revolutionized our world; although not always labeled AI, the findings of the field have been used so widely in the software the runs our businesses and financial transactions that our economy as we know it would grind to a halt without the work of AI-inspired programs (Kurzweil, 2005). Among many, many other applications, AIs help land our airplanes, understand our voices on the phone in automated systems, and detect credit card fraud.

1. What AI Brings to Cognitive Sciences

Critics of AI from psychology sometimes view AI programs as being psychologically implausible. Indeed, cognitive claims of AI theories typically are underconstrained by empirical human data, and thus, for the most part, criticisms of AI from psychology are not inaccurate. Most AI is engineering AI, and even cognitive AI must go out on limbs simply because there are just not enough data to constrain all the choices AI scientists need to make. However, AI contributes to the understanding of intelligence in several ways.

First, although they can be underconstrained, *AI programs demonstrate what kinds of data need to be collected*. Because AI works at a very precise level of detail, it brings to light theoretical ambiguities that psychology might not immediately or explicitly realize it needs to acknowledge. For example, it is one thing to say that a person can only comprehend one speaking voice heard at a time. It is quite another to create a computer implementation of this attentional effect – to do so requires making decisions about the interaction and influences of volume, which one voice you are listening to first, what factors affect attentional switching, among many other issues. The level of detail that makes AI programs underconstrained is the very quality that brings to light previously unconceived factors.

Humans obviously have only limited information and information-processing resources, and, thus, their rationality is intrinsically bounded (Simon, 1969). However, it is also true that many cognitive problems people routinely solve are computationally intractable. For example, deciding how to design a poster for a concert offers more possibilities than can possibly be considered in a reasonable time. *AI approaches to solving intractable problems shed light on what ways will not work*. If AI shows that a means for solving a problem will take too long to be practical, then AI has shown that people cannot be doing it that way, at least not routinely.

On the other hand, *AI can show that certain methods are possible*. Though showing that something is possible is far from proving that it *is*, many current theories in psychology do not have such proof. AI serves a valuable function as creating proofs-of-concept.

Another thing AI is particularly good at is *exploring the benefits and limitations of various ways to represent and organize knowledge in memory*. Many of these benefits are clear only when dealing with a strict information-processing level of detail. Are beliefs represented as words, pictures, or something else? Given all of the cognitive tasks memories are supposed to contribute to, AI is in a good position to shed light on such issues. As we will describe in more detail later, this subfield of AI is known as "knowledge representation."

Finally, once there is an AI program that resembles some part of human thinking to a researcher's satisfaction, *it is possible to run experiments on the program that are either unethical or too expensive (in terms of time or money) to run on living beings*. In simulation you can run thousands of experiments in a day, with exquisite control over all variables.

2. Navigational Planning: An Illustrative Example

We want to illustrate a simple example of AI in some detail so that this chapter is more than just so many big words. Let us suppose that Sunny, a cheerful AI agent, is about to start a new job in a new city. Sunny starts its car at its apartment and needs to navigate to an office building downtown. How might Sunny think and what might Sunny do, given that this is its first day in the city and it has never been to the office building? Our goals in this section are to explain some dimensions in designing AI agents as well as describe some issues in putting multiple capabilities into an AI agent.[1]

2.1 *Action, Perception, and Cognition*

To reach its office from its apartment, Sunny might use one (or more) of several possible strategies. For example, it might drive its car a short distance in some direction and then see if it has reached the office building. If it has, then it has accomplished its goal. If it has not, then it might again drive a short distance in some direction, and then again see if has reached the building. Sunny could repeat this process until it reaches its goal. Blindly moving about like this would likely take a very long time, but in terms of internal processing, this method is very efficient. This *perceive-act* internal computational processing, called *situated action* (or *reactive control;* Arkin, 1999), works by perceiving the immediate environment, acting based on those perceptions, and then repeating. The computational processing in reactive control is very efficient and requires no memory. However, depending on the environment and the goal, it may produce needlessly complicated external behavior since Sunny could be driving short distances in arbitrary directions for a very long time before it reaches its goal. In fact, this strategy does not guarantee that the goal will ever be reached.

Alternatively, when Sunny started at its apartment, it might simply ask Honey, a sweet AI agent who happens to be passing by, how to reach the office building. Honey, a longtime resident of the city, might give Sunny detailed directions, which Sunny could simply follow. In contrast to the previous strategy, this strategy produces very efficient output behavior: Assuming that Honey's directions are good, Sunny should reach its goal quite efficiently. However, this strategy of *asking* requires a society of intelligent agents (human or AI), each with different knowledge. It also requires a culture in which Sunny may in fact approach Honey for directions; Honey might in fact stop to help Sunny, and the two can communicate in a shared language; Sunny might trust Honey, a total stranger, enough to follow its directions in a new city; and so on. AI research on robot societies and human-robot interaction is in its early stages, and so here we will briefly mention only a small set of selected issues.

How can Sunny and Honey talk with each other? How can Sunny talk with a

1 Much of our discussion of this problem is based on the work of the first author and his students in the early 1990s when they developed a computer program called Router for addressing this class of problems (Goel, Ali, Donnellan, Gomez, & Callantine, 1994) and instantiated Router on a mobile reactive robot called Stimpy (Ali & Goel 1996). They also developed a knowledge-based shell called Autognostic for learning by reflection on the Router program embodied in Stimpy (Stroulia & Goel 1999) as well as reflection on Stimpy's reactive controller (Goel, Stroulia, Chen, & Rowland, 1997).

human? Understanding and generating natural language is the goal of the AI subdiscipline of *natural language processing* (NLP). Researchers in the area of natural language understanding take written text or spoken language and create accurate knowledge representations reflecting the meaning of the input. Natural language generation works roughly in the reverse – taking in knowledge and generating appropriate words and speech to communicate that meaning; this has received much less attention in AI. Two robots might be able to share knowledge very efficiently if that knowledge is represented in the same way. However, there is little agreement in AI over how knowledge should be represented in general. Different knowledge representation strategies appear to be better for different tasks.

When Honey gives advice, how is Sunny to know whether that advice is plausible? Except for limited environments, this problem seems to require general *commonsense reasoning*, a field closely related to knowledge representation. It is a widely held belief that most computer programs' lack of common knowledge and inability to reason with it effectively are major problems for much of AI. The subfield of commonsense reasoning endeavors to overcome this challenge. The most famous is the Cyc project (Lenat & Guha, 1990), a major project to manually encode all human commonsense knowledge. More recent strategies include Web-based knowledge collection methods, such as OpenMind Commonsense (Singh, Lin, Meuller, Lim, Perkins, & Zhu, 2002) and Peekaboom (von Ahn, Liu, & Blum, 2006).

Here is another strategy by which Sunny may reach its office building: Let us suppose that when Sunny was originally built in an AI laboratory, it was bootstrapped with some knowledge. Some of this knowledge may have been *heuristic* in its content and encoded in the form of a *production rule*. A heuristic is like a "rule of thumb," and a production is an "If x then do y" kind of rule. So, for example, Sunny might be bootstrapped with the knowledge that "if the goal is to reach downtown in a city, then move in the direction of the tallest buildings." This knowledge directly uses the goal (reaching downtown) to suggest a high-level action (move in the direction of the tallest buildings) and is heuristic in its nature since it may not correctly apply in all cities. If Sunny had this knowledge, then it might begin by perceiving the environment around it, locating the tallest buildings in the horizon, deciding to head in their direction, and moving toward them. When it reaches the next intersection, Sunny might again locate the tallest buildings relative to its current location, change its direction if needed, and so on. This strategy of *perceive-think-act* not only requires some knowledge but also must use more complex internal processing than the simpler perceive-act strategy of situated action. On the other hand, depending on the environment, perceive-think-act may result in a far simpler external behavior because now the behavior is more explicitly directed by the goal.

This kind of strategy can be implemented as a *production system* (Newell & Simon, 1972), which represents "what to do," or procedural knowledge, with if-then rules. In Sunny's case, the rules dictate physical action in the environment. Production systems are often used for making changes in memory as well. Rules can add, change, and remove goals and elements in memory. Surprisingly complex behavior can result with this method. This particular approach has been very successful in cognitive modeling. Well-known cognitive architectures such as Soar (Laird, Newell, & Rosenbloom) and ACT-R (Anderson & Lebiere, 1998) are production systems at heart. Production systems have representations of declarative and procedural knowledge. Declarative knowledge is relatively static and is used by the productions (the procedural knowledge), and it is often represented as *frames* (Minsky, 1975). Frames are similar to classes in object-oriented programming: They define a class of entities and what attributes they have. Instances of these frames take particular values for these attributes. For example, the frame for PERSON might contain the attributes NAME and AGE, and an instance of person might have a NAME of "Julie" and an AGE of "45." Like frames, *semantic networks* (Sowa, 1987) are a widely used representation scheme in AI. One can imagine a semantic network as a map of concepts, with nodes representing concepts (such as MAN and DOG) and labeled links between them (labeled, for example, with OWNS). Frames and semantic networks are thought to be informationally equivalent, which means that there is no loss of information when translating from one to another. Semantic networks are one kind of belief representation, called in the AI literature *knowledge representation*.

Another long-standing and still very strong area of AI is representation and processing based on *logic*. Logic is used for inference but has also been adapted for use in many other specific tasks, such as theorem proving (McCarthy, 1988).

Let us consider one other strategy for Sunny's task before we move on to the next topic: Sunny might consult a map of the new city. The important characteristics of a city map in this context are that it is an external representation of the world (i.e., it is not stored internally in Sunny) and that it is a visuospatial model of the world (i.e., there is a one-to-one structural correspondence between selected spatial objects and relations in the world and the objects and relations on the map; see Glasgow, Narayanan, & Chandrasekaran, 1995). Sunny can use this map to plan a navigation route to the office building and then execute the plan. This too is a perceive-think-act strategy. However, as compared to the heuristic method, the "thinking" in this strategy uses very different content and representation of knowledge. The internal processing in this strategy in general might be more costly than the processing in a heuristic search; however, depending on the environment, this strategy might lead to a solution that has a better chance of success – for example, the solution generated by this model-based method is less likely to get stuck in some cul-de-sac than the solution generated by the heuristic method.

Once Sunny has studied the map, it has some version of it stored in its memory. When Sunny needs to navigate to a location on the map, it can refer to the map. Finding a route on a map is not trivial, however. At each intersection, a choice must be made. One of the first insights of the field was that a great many cognitive problems can be solved by systematically evaluating available options. This method of searching through a space of choices is applicable in many domains and is still widely used. Researchers focusing on *search* compare the various search methods that have been invented and describe the classes of problems to which each is most applicable. Because most interesting search spaces are enormous (e.g., there are more possible chess game configurations than there are atoms in the universe), researchers invent heuristics to guide the AI to explore the more promising areas of the search space. One problem for which search has been particularly useful is in *planning*, which is the generation of an ordered sequence of actions prior to actually executing those actions.

Of course we can easily think of several other strategies for addressing Sunny's task, especially in today's world of the Internet and the global positioning system. But more important for our present discussion, we also can see some of the dimensions of designing an AI agent. First, an AI agent lives in some environment, and what and how an agent can think depends in large part on the environment in which the agent lives. Some environments might contain other agents, who may be cooperative, competitive, or combative. Some environments are dynamic. Some environments are only partially observable. Some environments are nondeterministic, and so on. One of the many contributions of AI is a more precise characterization and analysis of different kinds of environments, though much of the AI analysis so far has focused mostly on physical, not social, environments. Second, an agent might have access to different kinds of knowledge contents and representations. The knowledge may be engineered or acquired. The representations can be internal or external. The knowledge contents range from nil to heuristic rules to detailed, high-fidelity models of the environment. Another major AI contribution is a more precise and detailed account of knowledge contents and representations. Third, different strategies lead to very different trade-offs among knowledge requirements, the computational efficiency of internal processing, and the quality of generated solutions and behaviors. Yet another contribution of AI is more precise enumeration and analysis of these trade-offs.

2.2 *Reasoning, Learning, and Memory*

So far we have talked only about what our hypothetical AI agent, Sunny, might think and do when trying to reach its office for the first time. However, because Sunny is an AI agent, it shall also learn from its interactions with the environment. What and how might Sunny learn from its experiences? Sunny acquires a new experience each time it interacts with the environment, including navigating from its apartment to its office, talking with Honey, and so on, irrespective of what internal strategy it uses. Further, to the degree to which Sunny's internal processing is accessible to it, it may also acquire an internal experience each time it does internal processing. In addition, when Sunny executes a plan or an action on the environment, the environment might provide it with feedback. This feedback might come immediately after the execution of an action (e.g., taking a turn at an intersection and getting caught in a cul-de-sac), or after a series of actions (e.g., taking a sequence of turns and reaching the goal). The feedback might simply be the outcome – success or failure – of a plan, or it might contain more information, for example, a specific action in the plan failed because it led to a cul-de-sac. Thus, an experience might contain not only an interaction with the environment but also some feedback on the interaction, and perhaps also a trace of the internal processing in that interaction.

Sunny might potentially learn many different things from its experiences in the environment. For example, Sunny might simply encapsulate experiences as *cases* and store them in memory for reuse in the future. On the first day, for example, Sunny might use a map to plan a navigation route and then execute the plan in the environment, as indicated in the previous subsection. The next day, when Sunny again faces the task of navigating to its office from its apartment, it might find a solution simply by retrieving the navigation plan in the case acquired from the previous day rather than relying on general-purpose knowledge and rules. This is called *case-based reasoning* (Kolodner, 1993). This approach views reasoning largely as a memory task, that is, as a task of retrieving and modifying almost correct solutions from memory to address the current problem.

As Sunny learns from its experiences, its internal processing as well as its external behaviors can change. Initially, for example, Sunny might use a map of the environment for navigating through the new city. However, as it navigates through the world and stores its experiences as cases in its memory, it can increasingly generate new navigation plans by case-based reasoning. However, as the number of cases in memory increases, the cost of retrieving the case appropriate for a new problem also increases. Thus, again, each reasoning strategy offers computational trade-offs among knowledge requirements, processing efficiency, and solution quality.

More generally, AI typically thinks of each strategy for action selection discussed in the previous subsection as setting up an associated learning goal, which in turn requires a corresponding strategy for learning from experiences. Let us suppose, for example, that Sunny uses the strategy of situated action for action selection. It might, for example, use a table (called a *policy*) that specifies mappings from percepts of the world into actions on it. Then, from the feedback, or the reward, on a series of actions, Sunny can learn updates to the policy so that over time its action selection is closer to optimal. This is called *reinforcement learning* (Sutton & Barto,1998). Note that if the series of actions results in success, then the reward will be positive; otherwise it is negative. Reinforcement learning is an especially useful learning strategy when the reward is delayed, that is, it comes after a series of actions rather than immediately after an action. Alternatively, suppose that Sunny employs the strategy of using production rules such as "If x then do y" to select actions. In this case, Sunny can use the learning strategy of *chunking* (Laird, Newell, & Rosenbloom, 1987) to learn new rules from its experiences over time. Thus, just as AI has developed many reasoning strategies for action selection, it has developed many learning strategies for acquiring the knowledge needed by the reasoning strategies. Further, just like the reasoning strategies, the learning strategies too offer trade-offs among knowledge requirements, computational efficiency, and solution quality.

Most of the methods described thus far fall roughly into a category that can be described as "symbolic" approaches, characterized by the manipulation of qualitative, recognizable, discrete symbols. Another broad approach is quantitative or subsymbolic. Though the border between these two approaches is fuzzy, we can think of a symbolic representation having a symbol for the letter "R" and a subsymbolic system representing the letter with the dots that make it up on a screen. Since the dots, or pixels, are not meaningful in themselves, they are thought to be at a level of description below the symbol. The rest of the methods described in this subsection tend to use subsymbolic representations.

So far we have assumed that Sunny has perfect knowledge of the environment, even if that knowledge is limited. However, many real-world domains involve uncertainty, and AI methods based on *probability* have been very successful at working in these environments. Probability theory has been used in algorithms that use *Hidden Markov Models* to predict events based on what has happened in the past. Hidden Markov Models are mathematical representations that predict the values of some variables given a history of how the values of these and other variables have changed over time (Raibiner & Juang, 1986). Probabilities are also used to determine beliefs, such as how likely it is that a street Sunny wants to use has been closed, given that the rain in that part of the city was 80% likely to have been freezing. Bayes' Rule is useful for determining such conditional probabilities of some events (e.g., a road being closed) given the probability of others (e.g., freezing rain). *Bayesian belief networks* are mathematical representations that predict the probability of certain beliefs being true, given the conditional probabilities of other beliefs being true (Pearl, 2000). These networks are useful for updating probabilities of beliefs as information about events in the world arrives.

Statistics is the foundation of much of *machine learning*, a subdiscipline of AI that aims to create programs that use data and limited previous beliefs to create new beliefs. There are a great many kinds of learning algorithms, including artificial *neural networks*, which are the basis of connectionism in cognitive science (Rumelhart, McClleland, & the PDP Research Group, 1986; McCelland, Rumelhart, and the PDP Research Group, 1986). Whereas most of the systems we've discussed process recognizable symbols, neural networks represent information at a subsymbolic level (such as in pixels or bits of sound) as activations of nodes in a network. The processing of a neural network depends on how the nodes change each other's activations. The output of a neural network is an interpretation of the activations of certain nodes (for example, indicating whether or not a room is dark). *Genetic algorithms* are another means of computation that is (often) based on processing subsymbolic representations. Inspired by the theory of biological evolution, genetic algorithms create solutions to problems by applying some fitness function to a population of potential solutions (Mitchell, 1998). Solutions with a high fitness are used to generate members of the next generation (often with some mutation or crossover of features), after which the process repeats.

2.3 *Deliberation and Situated Action*

Although above we briefly discussed situated action (reactive control) and situated learning (reinforcement learning), much of our discussion about Sunny, our friendly robot, pertained to deliberation. While AI theories of deliberative action selection typically are explicitly goal directed, goals in situated action often are only implicit in the design of an AI agent. Deliberation and situated action in AI agents occur at different time scales, with deliberation typically unfolding at longer time scales than situated action. In general, designs of AI agents include both deliberative and situated components. For example, the design of Sunny, our friendly robot, might contain a deliberative planner that generates plans to navigate from one location in a city to another. Note that because there are many people and other robots working or walking on the roads, Sunny's environment is dynamic in that the state of the world can change during the time Sunny takes to generate a plan. How can Sunny navigate from its apartment to its office building in this dynamic environment?

Sunny of course can use the deliberative planner to plan a path between offices. However, while the planner can produce navigation plans, it might not represent the movements of all the people and other robots on the roads. So deliberation by itself is not good enough for the dynamic urban environment. Alternatively, Sunny can use situated action (i.e., *perceive-act*) that we described in the previous section. While this can help Sunny avoid collisions with moving people – as soon as Sunny senses the nearby presence of a person, it can move away – its progress toward the goal of reaching a specific office is likely to be slow, perhaps painfully slow.

Yet another alternative is to endow Sunny with the capability of both deliberative planning and situated action. In fact, this is exactly what many practical robots do. As a result, Sunny becomes capable of both long-range planning and short-range reaction. It can use its deliberative planner to come up with a plan for reaching the office building. Then, as it is executing the navigation plan, it constantly monitors the world around it and acts to avoid collisions with moving people. Next, as soon as it has moved away from a collision, it reverts to execution of its navigation plan. In this way, Sunny combines both deliberation and situated action. While this integration of deliberation and situated action has obvious benefits, it also has additional knowledge requirements as well as additional computational costs of shifting between strategies.

So far we have talked of perceiving the environment as though it were a minor task. For human beings, perception often appears to be effortless, but automating perception in AI agents has proven to be one of the many difficult problems in AI. The field of *computer vision* creates programs that take photos and video as input and generates beliefs about objects, textures, and movements, as well as higher level features such as emotions, movement styles, and gender. *Speech recognition* is another major field in perception. The ability of computers to understand your credit card number when you speak it into the phone is the result of over 50 years of AI work. Many of the algorithms used to understand speech and sound are shared with those of machine learning.

Likewise, achieving physical motion in the real world is difficult. *Robotics* is the field of AI that controls machines that interact directly with the physical world (as opposed to a program that, say, buys stocks electronically). Robotics uses computational perception, machine learning, and sometimes natural language processing. Some of the major problems specific to robotics are navigation and the handling of objects. Robots can work in collaboration with each other; the field of *intelligent agents* or *agent-based AI* builds intelligent programs that operate through the interaction of many individual agents whereas in *swarm intelligence* the individual agents do not have much intelligence individually. For example, two intelligent robots cooperating to assemble a desk would be an example of agent-based AI, and a large number of simple agents, reacting to their environment only locally to find the fastest route, much as ants do, would be an example of swarm intelligence.

2.4 *Deliberation and Reflection*

We have briefly discussed the need for both longer range planning and shorter range situated action in autonomous AI agents because the environment in which they reside is dynamic. However, changes in the environments themselves can unfold over different time scales. In the short term, for example, people and robots might be moving around on the roads of a Sunny's city. In the long term, roads themselves change, new apartments and office buildings are be constructed, and other changes occur. Then the navigation plan that Sunny's deliberative planner produces will start failing upon execution. How might Sunny adapt its knowledge of the environment as the environment changes? Alternatively, if Sunny had been designed incorrectly to begin with, how might it adapt its reasoning process?

Recent AI research on meta-reasoning is starting to design AI agents capable of self-adaptation. Such an AI agent might contain a specification of its own design. For example, the meta-reasoner in Sunny may have a specification of Sunny's design, including its functions (e.g., its goals) and its mechanisms for achieving the functions (e.g., the method of map-based navigation planning). When Sunny generates a plan that fails upon execution, Sunny's meta-reasoner uses the specification of its design to diagnose and repair its reasoning process. If the feedback from the world on the failed plan pertains to an element of knowledge (e.g., at intersection A, I expected a road going directly toward downtown but when I reached there, I found no such road), then Sunny enters this new knowledge in its map of the city. Thus, while the deliberative planner in Sunny reasons about actions in the external world, Sunny's reflective meta-reasoner reasons about its external world as well as its internal knowledge and reasoning.

2.5 *Putting It All Together*

In this section, we took navigational planning as an example to illustrate how AI is putting together multiple capabilities ranging from perception, cognition, and action, to reasoning, learning, and memory, and on to reflection, deliberation, and situated action. Of course, the design choices we have outlined are exactly that: choices. For example, instead of using deliberation to mediate between reflection and situated action as described above, an AI agent can reflect directly on situated action. In a way, the enterprise of AI is to explore such design choices and examine the computational trade-offs that each choice offers.

What has emerged out of this line of work is an understanding that the design of an AI agent depends on the environment it lives in, and that no one design is necessarily the best for all environments. Further, the design of an AI agent in any nontrivial environment requires multiple capabilities and multiple methods for achieving any capability such as reasoning and learning.

3. A Very Brief History of Artificial Intelligence

In the middle of the 20th century, the scientific world experienced a shift in focus from descriptions of matter and energy to descriptions of information. One manifestation of information theory applied to real-world problems was the field of *cybernetics* (Weiner, 1948, 1961), the study of communication and control in self-regulating analog systems. Cybernetics' focus on analog signal contributed to its losing ground against symbolic-based approaches, such as AI. Not only did AI approaches come to dominate the research into the same problems, but the symbol-processing approach came to dominate cognitive psychology as well.

Search was the first major paradigm of AI. The first artificial intelligence program ever written is the Logic Theorist (Newell, Shaw, & Simon, 1958). Many of the problems early AI researchers focused on were, in retrospect, simple. The early exuberance of AI was tempered with the first "AI Winter" that dominated the late 1960s and the 1970s, characterized by a decrease of optimism and funding, and caused by unfulfilled expectations. Early interest in associative processing was diminished by an influential book *Perceptrons* (Minsky & Papert, 1969) around the same time. This rigorous book showed that the state of the art associative systems of the time could not implement any task that was not linearly separable, including the simple logical operator "exclusive or."

The AI Winter of the 1970s, however, also witnessed the emergence of new theories and paradigms. For example, ANALOGY (Evans 1968) solved simple geometric analogy problems that appear on some intelligence tests. SHRDLU (Winograd, 1972) performed natural language processing to understand commands to a robot to pick up and manipulate blocks. Marr (1982) developed a three-stage computational theory of vision. Schank (1975) first developed a theory of conceptual structures for natural language understanding (Schank 1975) and then a theory of memory, reasoning, and learning (Schank 1982).

Working in a different paradigm, Feigenbaum, Buchanan, and their colleagues first developed an expert system called Dendral that could generate hypotheses about molecular structures from spectroscopic data (Lindsay et al., 1980), and then an expert system called Mycin that could generate hypotheses about E. coli bacterial diseases from heterogeneous patient data (Buchanan & Shortliffe, 1984). AI's revival in the 1980s was due in part to the success of these *expert systems* that were designed to replicate the expertise of individuals with a great deal of domain knowledge. Knowledge engineers would interview and observe experts, and then attempt to encode their knowledge into some form that an AI program could use. This was done with a variety of methods, including *decision trees* (which can be thought of as using the answers to a series of questions to classify some input, as in the game Twenty Questions). Since expert systems were of use to business, there was a renewed interest in AI and its applications. Funding for AI research increased.

One of the ideological debates of the 1980s was between the "neats" and the "scruffies": the neats used a formal, often logic-based approach and the scruffies focused on modeling human intelligence and getting AIs to use semantic information processing. Geographically, the neats were based at Stanford University and the West Coast, and in Japan, and the scruffies were at MIT and the East Coast. Neats thought that knowledge representation and processing should be mathematically rigorous and elegant, and evaluations should involve proofs. Scruffies believed that intelligence is so complex that it is unwise to put such constraints on at this early stage of development of AI theory and methodology. Today, most of the engineering AI research would be classified as neat. A good deal of, but not all, contemporary cognitive AI is scruffy.

In the 1980s, interest in artificial neural networks and associative AI was revived through cognitive modeling by *connectionists* (Rumelhart, McClelland, & the PDP Research Group, 1986; McClelland, Rumelhart, & the PDP Research Group, 1986). Connectionism continues to have influence in modern cognitive science; in engineering AI, artificial neural networks are regarded as just one of many statistical learning mechanisms (such as Markov models and other methods mentioned in the previous section.) Interestingly, some of the approaches and ideas of the cyberneticists have had a revival in these subsymbolic approaches to AI.

Over time, the limits of expert systems became clear. As they grew in size, they became difficult to maintain and could not learn. As a knowledge base grows, inconsistencies between different chunks of knowledge tend to arise. In part again because of unfulfilled expectations, in the 1990s, AI entered a second "winter," with diminished optimism, interest, and funding. However, during the second winter, again, new frameworks appeared, including *embodied cognition, situated cognition,* and *distributed cognition.* These frameworks emphasize how the body and environment both constrain and afford cognition, how cognition always is in the context of the physical and social worlds where these worlds themselves afford information to the cognitive agent. Similarly, *agent-based AI* on one hand seeks to unify cognition with perception and action, and on the other, studies AI agents as members of a team of other agents (artificial or human).

At present, AI appears to have entered a new phase of revival. This is in part due to the new frameworks that appeared in the 1990s, especially agent-based AI. By now, AI is ubiquitous in industrialized societies, though it often does not go by that name. Many researchers avoid the term, feeling that it has been tarnished by the boom-and-bust cycle of interest and funding it has experienced in its 50-year history. However, techniques from AI are used in many practical applications: allowing your voice to be understood when you talk to an automated phone system, using your past purchases to make recommendations for books when you shop online, efficiently matching flights to gates at airports, directing the path-finding of characters in computer games, generating Web search engine results, enabling face detection in cameras and online photo archives, and doing automatic translation.

4. Measuring the Intelligence of AIs

When measuring the intelligence of human beings, the test need not have questions representing every kind of intelligent thing a person could do. Rather, the test result is intended to measure the general intelligence of the test taker (Wechsler, 1939; Raven, 1962). When one form of intelligence (e.g., mathematical) does not predict another (e.g., verbal), two tests are required.

In artificial intelligence, the problem is much bigger. Since AIs are designed by people, they have enormous variety, depending on the goals of the researcher creating them. As such, an AI that scores well on the SAT verbal section, like Latent Semantic Analysis (Landauer, 1998), will likely not only score poorly when tested on other cognitive tasks but will probably not be able to take those tests at all. In short, performance on any given human IQ test will predict general intelligence in an AI even more poorly than it does in human beings. Depending on how the AI is built, it can have unique combinations of sensors, actuators, and ways to think. Not only are these often completely different from those of other AI programs, but they are also often very alien to our own experiences as human beings.

A further problem is that AIs tend to be computer programs that run on computers, which vary in speed. A program running on a faster computer will be much more effective, and in any timed test this will make an enormous difference. It is a philosophical question whether the computer's speed should affect how we regard the intelligence of the AI. The chess playing programs of the early days of AI did not fail because of their bad algorithms; the computers they ran on were too slow to make those algorithms effective. Current chess champion AIs, such as Hydra (Donninger & Lorentz, 2004), are run on normal commercial PCs rather than the special-purpose hardware required with the Deep Blue project that defeated Kasparov (Hsu, Campbell, & Hoane, 1995). The effectiveness of an algorithm can be dependent, in part, on the speed of the computer running it.

In the past, certain tasks, such as memory use and speed of calculation, were thought to be excellent examples of intelligence, and even modern tests often measure these things. These tasks are very easy for computer programs, but, for whatever reason, we are reluctant to attribute high intelligence to computer programs for being able to do them. Even chess can largely be played well using "brute-force" search methods (Hsu et al., 1995). Algorithms that don't work well today might work just fine on faster computers of the future. Note also, however, that if we were to find a human who could evaluate moves like a computer could, we would regard her as very intelligent indeed, at least in her own way.

AI researchers usually evaluate their programs with idiosyncratic methodology appropriate to the task. Though these evaluations are not thought of as intelligence tests, they could be thought of as specialized intelligence tests, just as there are sometimes special tests for certain subpopulations of human beings, such as children (Legg & Hutter, 2007). In contrast, PERI (Bringsjord, Selmer, Schimanski, & Bettina, 2003) is an AI project with the explicit goal of passing intelligence tests. As of 2003, it performed well on block design problems in the Wechsler Adult Intelligence Scale (WAIS; Wechsler 1939). Even if we could think of a single test for all AIs, the variance in their scores would be enormous in comparison to people, for whom the IQ of an individual can usefully be scored relative to a large group (Legg & Hutter, 2007).

The most famous proposed test for AI is the "imitation game," or, as it is more popularly called, the Turing test (Turing, 1950). In this test, computers and human beings are put in typed chat sessions with human judges. If computers can reliably fool the judges into thinking they are human, they pass the test. Turing formulated this test in response to the question "Can machines think?" Rather than answering that question, he reformulated it into a more concrete question of whether a machine could fool a human interrogator. Though Turing played it a bit safe, most interpretations of him do not, interpreting the purpose of the test as to distinguish programs that have human-level intelligence from those that do not (e.g., Harnad, 1992). In this interpretation, the test is not a measurement of intelligence in the sense of giving a score that accurately reflects cognitive abilities, but is a pass-or-fail litmus test of general intelligence.

It has proven to be a very difficult test to pass, although some surprisingly simple programs, such as ELIZA (Weizenbaum, 1966) and PARRY (Raphael, 1976), sometimes fool some people for short times. Because of this difficulty, competitions usually restrict judges to specific topics, as the general topic version is impossible for state-of-the-art AIs to pass. Some programs can pass the restricted test (according to Turing's suggested numbers), but they appear to do so at least in part because of aspects that are not relevant to intelligence, such as demonstrating typing errors (Johnson, 1992). Recently there even have been Turing test competitions and prizes (e.g., http://www.loebner.net/Prizef/loebner-prize.html).

4. Conclusion

In this chapter we have reviewed the history of AI and its major subfields, illustrated AI as a science and as a technology, and discussed the problems of the measurement of intelligence in AIs. The field has made so much progress that now every year the Association for Advancement of Artificial Intelligence (http://www.aaai.org/home.html) organizes a conference for deployed AI applications (called Innovative Applications of Artificial Intelligence, http://www.aaai.org/Conferences/IAAI/iaai10.php).

Of course, we have not tried to cover every topic in AI. For example, over the last decade, there has been much AI research on designing the *semantic web* (Berners-Lee, Hendler, & Lassial 2001), a new version of the World Wide Web that would be capable of understanding information (e.g., Web pages) stored on it. As another example, just over the last few years, *interactive games* have emerged as an important arena for AI research, especially agent-based AI. Nor, in this article, have we attended to AI ethics, which is becoming an increasingly important issue.

A somewhat surprising lesson from the history of AI is that cognitive tasks that seem difficult for humans to solve (e.g., mathematical, logical, and chess problems) are relatively easy to make programs solve, and those cognitive tasks that are apparently easy for humans to address (e.g., walking, talking, and perceiving) are extraordinarily difficult to make computers solve. This apparent paradox has meant that repeated predictions about bold AI successes have gone unfulfilled.

We suggest two reasons for this paradox. First, our difficult problems require deliberate thought and strategies that are explicitly learned. As a result, we can often gain insight into how they are solved through introspection. Indeed, many of these strategies are actually written down, to be learned through reading. In contrast, nobody needs to tell human beings how to see, walk, or speak. As a result, our intuitions about how these processes work are, to put it mildly, unhelpful.

The second, perhaps more important, reason is that deliberate processing is likely a serial process running as a virtual machine on a network of neurons, whereas the automatic processes, the easy tasks, are running directly on the neural network. These easy tasks (called System 1 in Stanovich & West, 2003) are evolutionarily older, and the parts of our brains that accomplish them (generally near the back of the head; Anderson, 2007) evolved to do just those things. In contrast, the more deliberate processing is evolutionarily younger and makes use of the kind of hardware designed for System 1 tasks. System 2 struggles to do rational, serial processing on an essentially parallel pattern-matching machine (Stanovich, 2004). In Chapter 22, Intelligence and the Cognitive Unconscious, of this volume, S. B. Kaufman provides a review of such dual-process theories.

Computers, and the languages we program them with, are naturally serial processors. When we implement artificial neural networks, we are doing it backward from nature: Whereas System 2 is a serial virtual machine running on parallel hardware, our artificial neural networks are parallel virtual machines running on serial hardware. Given this and the fact that we have no conscious access to System 1 processes, it is no wonder that the AI community has had to work very hard to make progress in these areas. As a result, we have chess programs that can beat world grand masters, but no robots that can walk down a street even as well as a 5-year-old child. We expect that neuroscience findings may illuminate the nature of these processes, and the AI community will be able to build on them.

Given the track record of predictions about the future of AI, we will refrain from making our own (see Kurzweil, 2005, for one possible future). What we can and will claim is that AI already has had a profound impact not only on computer science and information technology but also more generally on our culture and our philosophy. If the last 50-year history of AI is any guide, then the next 50 years will not only be full of exciting discoveries and bold inventions, but they will also raise new questions about who we are as humans and what we want to be.

Acknowledgments

We thank the editors of this volume and members of the Design and Intelligence Laboratory at Georgia Tech for their comments on earlier drafts of this article. During the writing of this article, Goel's writing has been partially supported by NSF grants (#0632519, Learning About Complex Systems in Middle School by Constructing Structure-Behavior-Function Models; #0613744, Teleological Reasoning in Adaptive Software Design; and #0855916, Computational Tools for Enhancing Creativity in Biologically Inspired Engineering Design).

References

Ali, K., & Goel, A. (1996). Combining navigational planning and reactive control. *Proceedings of the AAAI-96 Workshop on Reasoning About Actions, Planning and Control: Bridging the Gap* (pp. 1–7), Portland.

Albus, J. S. (1991). Outline for a theory of intelligence. *IEEE Transactions on Systems, Man, and Cybernetics*, **21**(3), 473–509.

Anderson, J. R., & Lebiere, C. (1998). *The atomic components of thought*. Mahwah, NJ: Erlbaum.

Anderson, M. L. (2007). Massive redeployment, exaptation, and the functional integration of cognitive operations. *Synthese*, **159**(3), 329–345.

Arkin, R. (1999). *Behavior-based robotics*. Cambridge, MA: MIT Press.

Berners-Lee, T., Hendler, J., & Lassila, O. (2001, May). Semantic web. *Scientific American*, pp. 35–43.

Bringsjord, S. (1998). Chess is too easy. *Technology Review*, 101(2), 23–28.

Bringsjord, S., & Schimanski, B. (2003). What is artificial intelligence? Psychometric AI as an answer. *Proceedings of the 18th International Joint Conference on Artificial Intelligence (IJCAI–03)* (pp. 887–893). San Francisco, CA: Morgan Kaufmann.

Buchanan, B., & Shortliffe, E. (1984). *Rule based expert systems: The Mycin experiments of the Stanford Heuristic Programming Project*. Boston, MA: Addison-Wesley.

Donninger, C., & Lorenz, U. (2004). The chess monster hydra. *Proceedings of the 14th International Conference on Field-Programmable Logic and Applications (FPL)* (pp. 927–932). Antwerp, Belgium: LNCS 3203.

Evans, T. G. (1968). A program for the solution of a class of geometric-analogy intelligence-test questions. In M. Minsky (Ed.), *Semantic information processing* (pp. 271–353). Cambridge, MA: MIT Press.

Glasgow, J., Narayanan, N. H., & Chandrasekaran, B. (Eds.). (1995). *Diagrammatic reasoning: Cognitive and computational perspectives*. Cambridge, MA: MIT Press.

Goel, A., Ali, K., Donnellan, M., Gomez, A., & Callantine, T. (1994). Multistrategy adaptive navigational path planning. *IEEE Expert*, 9(6), 57–65.

Goel, A., Stroulia, E., Chen, Z., & Rowland, P. (1997). Model-based reconfiguration of schema-based reactive control architectures. *Proceedings of the AAAI Fall Symposium on Model-Directed Autonomous Systems*, Cambridge, MA, AAAI.

Harnad, S. (1992). The Turing Test is not a trick: Turing indistinguishability is a scientific criterion. *SIGART Bulletin*, 3(4), 9–10.

Hsu, F. H., Campbell, M. S., & Hoane, A. J. (1995). Deep Blue system overview. *Proceedings of the 1995 International Conference on Supercomputing* (pp. 240–244).

Johnson, W. L. (1992). Needed: A new test of intelligence. *SIGART Newsletter*, 3(4), 7–9.

Kolodner, J. (1993). *Case-based reasoning*. San Francisco, CA: Morgan Kaufmann.

Kurzweil, R. (2005). *The singularity is near: When humans transcend biology*. New York, NY: Viking Adult.

Laird, J., Newell, A., & Rosenbloom, P. (1987). Soar: An architecture for general intelligence. *Artificial Intelligence*, 33, 1–64.

Landauer, T. K. (1998). Learning and representing verbal meaning: The latent semantic analysis theory. *Current Directions in Psychological Science*, 7(5), 161–164.

Legg, S., & Hutter, M. (2007). Universal intelligence: A definition of machine intelligence. *Minds & Machines*, 17(4), 391–444.

Lindsay, R., Buchanan, B., Feigenbaum, E., & Lederberg, J. (1980). *Applications of artificial intelligence for chemical inference: The Dendral project*. New York, NY: McGraw-Hill.

Lenat, D., & Guha, R. (1990). *Building large knowledge based systems: Representation and inference in the Cyc project*. Boston, MA: Addison-Wesley Longman.

Marr, D. (1982). *Vision*. New York, NY: Henry Holt.

McCarthy, J. (1988). Mathematical logic in AI. *Daedalus*, 117(1), 297–311.

McClelland, J. L., Rumelhart, D. E., & PDP Research Group. (1986). *Parallel distributed processing: Explorations in the microstructure of cognition: Volume 2, Psychological and biological models*. Cambridge, MA: MIT Press.

Minsky, M. L., & Papert S. A. (1969). *Perceptrons*. Cambridge, MA: MIT Press.

Minsky, M. L. (1975). *A framework for representing knowledge*. In Patrick Henry Winston (Ed.), *The psychology of computer vision*. New York, NY: McGraw-Hill.

Mitchell, M. (1998). *An introduction to genetic algorithms*. Cambridge, MA: MIT Press.

Newell, A., Shaw, J. C., & Simon, H. A. (1958). Elements of a theory of problem solving. *Psychological Review*, 63(3), 151–166.

Newell, A., & Simon, H. A. (1972). *Human problem solving*. Englewood Cliffs, NJ: Prentice-Hall.

Pearl, J. (2000). *Causality: Models, reasoning and inference*. New York, NY: Cambridge University Press.

Rabiner, L., & Juang, B. H. (1986, January). An introduction to hidden Markov models. *IEEE AASP Magazine*, pp. 4–16.

Raphael, B. (1976). *The thinking computer*. New York, NY: W. H. Freeman.

Raven, J.C. (1962). *Advanced Progressive Matrices Set II*. London, UK: H. K. Lewis.

Rumelhart, D.E., McClelland, J. L., & PDP Research Group. (1986). *Parallel distributed processing: Explorations in the microstructure of cognition: Volume 1, Foundations*. Cambridge, MA: MIT Press.

Schank, R.C. (1975). *Conceptual information processing*. New York, NY: Elsevier.

Schank, R.C. (1982). *Dynamic memory* (2nd ed.). New York, NY: Cambridge University Press.

Simon, H. A. (1969). *Sciences of the artificial*. Cambridge, MA: MIT Press.

Singh, P., Lin T., Mueller, E.T., Lim, G., Perkins, T., & Zhu, W. L. (2002). Open mind common sense: Knowledge acquisition from the general public. *Proceedings of the First International Conference on Ontologies, Databases, and Applications of Semantics for Large Scale Information Systems* (pp. 1223–1237).

Sowa, J. (1987). Semantic networks. In S. Shapiro (Ed.), *Encylopedia of AI* (pp. 1011–1024). New York, NY: Wiley.

Stanovich, K. E. (2004). *The robot's rebellion*. Chicago, IL: University of Chicago Press.

Stanovich, K.E., & West, R.F (2003). The rationality debate as a progressive research program. *Behavioral and Brain Sciences*, 26(4), 531–533.

Stroulia, E., & Goel, A. K. (1999). Evaluating problem-solving methods in evolutionary design: The autognostic experiments. *International Journal of Human-Computer Studies*, 51, 825–847.

Sutton, R. S., & Barto, A. (1998). *Reinforcement learning: An introduction*. Cambridge, MA: MIT Press.

Turing, A. M. (1950). Computing machinery and intelligence. *Mind*, 59, 433–460.

Von Anh, L., Liu, R., & Blum, M. (2006). Peekaboom: A game for locating objects in images. *Proceedings of the SIGCHI Conference on Human Factors in Computing Systems* (pp. 55–64). (Montreal, April 22–27). New York, NY: ACM Press.

Wechsler, David. (1939). *The measurement of adult intelligence*. Baltimore, MD: Williams & Wilkins.

Weiner, N. (1948). *Cybernetics*. Cambridge, MA: MIT Press.

Weiner, N. (1961). *Cybernetics* (2nd ed.). Cambridge, MA: MIT Press.

Weizenbaum, J. (1966). ELIZA – a computer program for the study of natural language communication between man and machine. *Communications of the ACM*, 9(1), 36–45.

Winograd, T. (1972). *Understanding natural language*. San Diego, CA: Academic Press.

Part VI

KINDS OF INTELLIGENCE

CHAPTER 24

The Theory of Multiple Intelligences

Katie Davis, Joanna Christodoulou, Scott Seider, and Howard Gardner

Part 1: Background

The theory of multiple intelligences, developed by psychologist Howard Gardner in the late 1970s and early 1980s, posits that individuals possess eight or more relatively autonomous intelligences. Individuals draw on these intelligences, individually and corporately, to create products and solve problems that are relevant to the societies in which they live (Gardner, 1983, 1993, 1999, 2006b, 2006c). The eight identified intelligences include linguistic intelligence, logical-mathematical intelligence, spatial intelligence, musical intelligence, bodily-kinesthetic intelligence, naturalistic intelligence, interpersonal intelligence, and intrapersonal intelligence (Gardner, 1999). According to Gardner's analysis, only two intelligences – linguistic and logical mathematical – have been valued and tested for in modern secular schools; it is useful to think of that language-logic combination as "academic" or "scholarly intelligence." In conceiving of intelligence as multiple rather than unitary in nature, the theory of multiple intelligences – hereafter MI theory – represents a departure from traditional conceptions of intelligence first formulated in the early 20th century, measured today by IQ tests, and studied in great detail by Piaget (1950, 1952) and other cognitively oriented psychologists.

As described elsewhere in this volume, French psychologist Alfred Binet (Binet & Simon, 1911; Binet & Simon, 1916) designed the precursor to the modern-day intelligence test in the early 1900s to identify French schoolchildren in need of special educational interventions. Binet's scale, along with the contemporaneous work of English psychologist Charles Spearman (1904, 1927) on general intelligence or *g*, served as the principal catalysts for conceiving of all forms of intellectual activity as stemming from a unitary or general ability for problem solving (Perkins & Tishman, 2001). Within academic psychology, Spearman's theory of general intelligence (or *g*) remains the predominant conception of intelligence (Brody, 2004; Deary et al., 2007; Jensen, 2008) and the basis for more than 70 IQ tests in circulation (e.g., Stanford-Binet Intelligence Scales Fifth Edition, 2003;

Wechsler Adult Intelligence Scales Third Edition, 2008). MI theory, in contrast, asserts that individuals who demonstrate a particular aptitude in one intelligence will not necessarily demonstrate a comparable aptitude in another intelligence (Gardner, 2006b). For example, an individual may possess a profile of intelligences that is high in spatial intelligence but moderate or low in interpersonal intelligence or vice versa. This conception of intelligence as multiple rather than singular forms the primary distinction between MI theory and the conception of intelligence that dominates Western psychological theory and much of common discourse.

A second key distinction concerns the origins of intelligence. While some contemporary scholars have asserted that intelligence is influenced by environmental factors (Diamond & Hopson, 1998; Lucas, Morley, & Cole, 1998; Neisser et al., 1996; Nisbett, 2009), many proponents of the concept of general intelligence conceive of intelligence as an innate trait with which one is born and which one can therefore do little to change (Eysenck, 1994; Herrnstein & Murray, 1994; Jensen, 1980, 1998). In contrast, MI theory conceives of intelligence as a combination of heritable potentials and skills that can be developed in diverse ways through relevant experiences (Gardner, 1983). For example, one individual might be born with a high intellectual potential in the bodily-kinesthetic sphere that allows him or her to master the intricate steps of a ballet performance with relative ease. For another individual, achieving similar expertise in the domain of ballet requires many additional hours of study and practice. Both individuals are capable of becoming strong performers – experts – in a domain that draws on their bodily-kinesthetic intelligence; however, the pathways along which they travel to become strong performers may well differ quantitatively (in terms of speed) and perhaps qualitatively (in terms of process).

MI theory is neither the sole challenger to Spearman's (1904, 1927) conception of general intelligence nor the only theory to conceive of intelligence as pluralistic. Among others, Thorndike (1920; Thorndike, Bregman, Cobb, & Woodyard, 1927) conceived of intelligence as the sum of three parts: abstract intelligence, mechanical intelligence, and social intelligence. Thurstone (1938, Thurstone & Thurstone, 1941) argued that intelligence could better be understood as consisting of seven primary abilities. Guilford (1967; Guilford & Hoepfner, 1971) conceptualized intelligence as consisting of four content categories, five operational categories, and six product categories; he ultimately proposed 150 different intellectual faculties. Sternberg (1985, 1990) offered a triarchic theory of intelligence that identified analytic, creative, and practical intelligences. Finally, Ceci (1990, 1996) has described multiple cognitive potentials that allow for knowledge to be acquired and relationships between concepts and ideas to be considered.

Gardner's theory of multiple intelligences, however, is perhaps the best known of these pluralistic theories. This notoriety is due, in part, to the sources of evidence on which Gardner drew, and, in part, to its enthusiastic embrace by the educational community (Armstrong, 1994; Kornhaber, 1999; Shearer, 2004). Many hundreds of schools across the globe have incorporated MI principles into their mission, curriculum, and pedagogy; and hundreds of books have been written (in numerous languages) on the relevance of MI theory to educators and educational institutions (Chen, Moran, & Gardner, 2009). In 2005, a 10-acre "science experience park" opened in Sonderberg, Denmark, with more than 50 different exhibits through which participants can explore their own profile of intelligences (Danfoss Universe, 2007). In what follows, we outline the major claims of this far-reaching theory as well as some of the adjustments to the theory made over the past 25 years.

It should be pointed out that Gardner's conceptualization of multiple intelligence does not belong exclusively to Gardner; other scholars and practitioners have made numerous applications of the principal tenets, sometimes with little regard for Gardner's own claims. In this chapter, however, we focus principally on MI theory and practices as put forth by Gardner.

Gardner's (1983, 1999) conception of intelligence as pluralistic grew out of his observation that individuals who demonstrated substantial talent in domains as diverse as chess, music, athletics, politics, and entrepreneurship possessed capacities in these domains that should be accounted for in conceptualizing intelligence. Accordingly, in developing MI theory and its broader characterization of intelligence, Gardner did not focus on the creation and interpretation of psychometric instruments. Rather, he drew upon research findings from evolutionary biology, neuroscience, anthropology, psychometrics, and psychological studies of prodigies and savants. Through synthesis of relevant research across these fields, Gardner established several criteria for identification of a unique intelligence (see Table 24.1).

Drawing on these criteria, Gardner initially identified seven intelligences. However, in the mid-1990s, he concluded that an eighth intelligence, naturalistic intelligence, met the criteria for identification as an intelligence as well (see Table 24.2). Naturalistic intelligence allows individuals to identify and distinguish among products of the natural world such as animals, plants, types of rocks, and weather patterns (Gardner, 1999). Meteorology, botany, and zoology are all professions in which one would likely find individuals who demonstrate high levels of naturalistic intelligence. In a world where this particular skill is less important for survival than it was in earlier times, naturalistic capacities are brought to bear in making consequential distinctions with respect to man-made objects displayed in a consumer society.

These descriptions of the eight intelligences that comprise MI theory relied upon the *domains or disciplines* in which one typically finds individuals who demonstrate high levels of each intelligence. This is because we do not yet have psychometric or neuroimaging techniques that directly assess an individual's capacity for a particular intelligence. For example, no test has been devised to assess directly whether an individual possesses a profile of intelligences high in spatial intelligence; however, one might reasonably infer that an individual who demonstrates excellent performance in the domain of architecture or sculpture or geometry possesses high spatial intelligence. Likewise, excellence in the domains of ballet or orthopedic surgery suggests the possession of high bodily-kinesthetic intelligence. It is possible that in the future more direct methods of measuring intelligences may be devised – for example, through evidence about neural structures or even through genetic markers.

Table 24.1. Criteria for Identification of an Intelligence

- It should be seen in relative isolation in prodigies, autistic savants, stroke victims, or other exceptional populations. In other words, certain individuals should demonstrate particularly high or low levels of a particular capacity in contrast to other capacities.
- It should have a distinct neural representation – that is, its neural structure and functioning should be distinguishable from that of other major human faculties.
- It should have a distinct developmental trajectory. That is, different intelligences should develop at different rates and along paths which are distinctive.
- It should have some basis in evolutionary biology. In other words, an intelligence ought to have a previous instantiation in primate or other species and putative survival value.
- It should be susceptible to capture in symbol systems, of the sort used in formal or informal education.
- It should be supported by evidence from psychometric tests of intelligence.
- It should be distinguishable from other intelligences through experimental psychological tasks.
- It should demonstrate a core, information-processing system. That is, there should be identifiable mental processes that handle information related to each intelligence.

(Gardner 1983; Kornhaber, Fierros, & Veneema, 2004)

Table 24.2. Gardner's Eight Intelligences

Intelligence	*Description*
Linguistic	An ability to analyze information and create products involving oral and written language such as speeches, books, and memos.
Logical-Mathematical	An ability to develop equations and proofs, make calculations, and solve abstract problems.
Spatial	An ability to recognize and manipulate large-scale and fine-grained spatial images.
Musical	An ability to produce, remember, and make meaning of different patterns of sound.
Naturalist	An ability to identify and distinguish among different types of plants, animals, and weather formations that are found in the natural world.
Bodily-Kinesthetic	An ability to use one's own body to create products or solve problems.
Interpersonal	An ability to recognize and understand other people's moods, desires, motivations, and intentions.
Intrapersonal	An ability to recognize and understand one's own moods, desires, motivations, and intentions.

In the 25-year history of the theory, numerous researchers have proposed additional intelligences that range from moral intelligence to humor intelligence to cooking intelligence (Boss, 2005; Goleman, 1995). Gardner (2006b) himself has speculated about an existential intelligence that reflects an individual's capacity for considering "big questions" about life, death, love, and being. Individuals with high levels of this hypothesized intelligence might likely be found in philosophy departments, religious seminaries, or the ateliers of artists. To date, however, naturalistic intelligence has been the only definitive addition to the original set of seven intelligences. In Gardner's judgment, neither existential intelligence nor any of the other proposed intelligences sufficiently meet the criteria for identification as a unique intelligence (a discussion of the reliability of these criteria in identifying candidate intelligences is offered in Part 2 of this chapter). In future years, new proposed intelligences might be found to meet the criteria for identification as a unique intelligence (Battro & Denham, 2007; Chen & Gardner, 2005). Conversely, future research may reveal that existing intelligences such as linguistic intelligence are more accurately conceived of as several subintelligences. These inevitable adjustments and adaptations of MI theory, however, are less important than the theory's overarching principle: namely, that intelligence is better conceived of as multiple and content-specific rather than unitary and general.

In describing intelligence(s) as pluralistic, MI theory conceives of individuals as possessing a profile of intelligences in which they demonstrate varying levels of strengths and weakness for each of the eight intelligences. It is a misstatement within the MI framework, then, to characterize an individual as possessing "no" capacity for a particular intelligence (Gardner, 1999). Individuals may certainly demonstrate low levels of a particular intelligence, but, except in cases involving severe congenital or acquired brain damage, all individuals possess the full range of intelligences. It would be equally inaccurate within the MI framework, however, to assert that everyone demonstrates superiority or giftedness in at least one of the intelligences (Gardner, 1999). As a pluralistic theory, the fundamental assertion of MI theory is that individuals *do* demonstrate variation in their levels of strength and weakness across the intelligences. Unfortunately, this variation does not mean that every individual will necessarily demonstrate superior aptitude in one or more of the intelligences.

After 25 years of reflection on the theory, Gardner accentuates two primary claims: (1) All individuals possess the full range of intelligences – the intelligences are what define human beings, cognitively speaking; (2) no two individuals, not even identical twins, exhibit precisely the same profile of intellectual strengths and weaknesses. These constitute the principal scientific claims of the theory; educational or other practical implications go beyond the scope of the theory, in a strict sense.

Part 2: Review of Issues and Pseudo-Issues Spawned by the Theory

During the years since its inception, MI theory has drawn considerable attention, primarily from psychologists and educators. The attention has come in many forms, from scholarly critiques regarding the development, scope, and empirical basis of the theory, to educational curricula that claim to develop children's intelligences in an optimal way. This attention has led to new developments in the theory and promising practical applications in the classroom. Yet, several reviews and critiques of MI theory reveal misunderstandings regarding its empirical foundation and theoretical conception of human cognition. In this section, we use these misunderstandings as a springboard for exploring the theory in greater depth, with the purpose of illuminating its major claims and conceptual contours.

The Foundation and Province of MI Theory

Some critics of MI theory argue that it is not grounded in empirical research and cannot, therefore, be proved or disproved on the basis of new empirical findings (Waterhouse, 2006; White, 2006). In fact, MI theory is based entirely on empirical findings. The intelligences were identified on the basis of hundreds of empirical studies spanning multiple disciplines (Gardner, 1983, 1993; Gardner & Moran, 2006). Noted, too, is the relative lack of empirical studies specifically designed to test the theory as a whole (Visser, Ashton, & Vernon, 2006). Like other broad theories, such as evolution or plate tectonics, which synthesize experimental, observational, and theoretical work, MI theory cannot be proved or disproved on the basis of a single test or experiment. Rather, it gains or loses credibility as findings accumulate over time. Indeed, subsequent findings have prompted ongoing review and revisions of MI theory, such as the addition of new intelligences and the conceptualization of intelligence profiles. Much of the empirical work conducted since 1983 lends support to various aspects of the theory. For instance, studies on children's theory of mind and the identification of pathologies that involve losing a sense of social judgment provide strong evidence for a distinct interpersonal intelligence (Gardner, 1993; Gardner, Feldman & Krechevsky, 1998a, 1998b, 1998c; Malkus, Feldman, & Gardner, 1988; Ramos-Ford, Feldman, & Gardner, 1988).

Relatively few critiques of MI theory have addressed the criteria used to identify and evaluate a candidate intelligence. This state of affairs is somewhat unexpected, since the criteria serve as the theory's foundation. Moreover, by drawing on cross-disciplinary sources of evidence, the criteria represent a pioneering effort to broaden the way in which human intellectual capacities are identified and evaluated. White (2006) is one of the few scholars to question this effort. He suggests that the selection and application of the criteria is a subjective – and therefore flawed – process. A psychologist with a different intellectual biography, he argues, would have arrived at a different set of criteria and, consequently, a different set of intelligences.

The professional training that preceded MI theory no doubt played an important role in its formulation. We do not argue the fact of this influence, simply its effect. MI theory is the product of several years spent examining human cognition through several disciplinary lenses, including psychology, sociology, neurology, biology, and anthropology, as well as the arts and humanities. The criteria that emerged from this examination formed the basis of a systematic investigation of candidate faculties. Thus, in contrast to White's depiction of an idiosyncratic process marked by one researcher's intellectual preoccupations, the identification and application of the criteria represent a systematic and comprehensive approach to the study of human intelligence. Moreover, any attempt to pluralize intelligence inevitably involves either an agreed-upon stopping point (an acceptance of the criterion as stated) or an infinite regress (what stimulated this criterion rather than another criterion?). Nonetheless, White is correct that ultimately the ascertainment of what is, or is not, a separate intelligence involves a synthesizing frame of mind (Gardner, 2006a), if not a certain degree of subjectivity.

Many critiques of MI theory pay scant attention to the criteria and focus instead on the level of analysis used to classify human intellectual faculties. Some scholars argue that the eight intelligences are not specific enough. Indeed, findings from neuroscience lend support to the call for increased specificity in the classification of intellectual capacities. As Gardner pointed out in the original publications (Gardner, 1983, 1993), it is likely that musical intelligence comprises several subintelligences relating to various dimensions of music, such as rhythm, harmony, melody, and timbre. An analogous comment can be stated for each of the other intelligences. In fact, one test of MI theory would be whether the subintelligences within each intelligence correlate more highly with each other than they correlate with subintelligences within other intelligences. Were the classification of intelligences expanded to include such specific faculties, however, the number would quickly become unwieldy and virtually untranslatable to educators. At the other extreme are those scholars who claim that MI theory expands the definition of intelligence to such a degree that it is no longer a useful construct. Gardner has argued elsewhere that a concept of intelligence that is yoked to linguistic and logical-mathematical capacities is too narrow and fails to capture the wide range of human intellectual functioning (Gardner, 1993; Gardner & Moran, 2006). MI theory seeks a middle ground between an innumerable set of highly specific intelligences, on the one hand, and a single, all-purpose intelligence, on the other.

The description of individuals in terms of several relatively independent computational capacities would seem to put MI theory at odds with *g* (psychometricians' term for general intelligence). Willingham (2004) argues that a theory of intelligence that does not include *g* is inconsistent with existing psychometric data. These data, consisting typically of correlations between scores on a series of oral questions or paper-and-pencil instruments, do provide considerable evidence for the existence of *g*. They do not, however, provide insight into the scope of *g*, or its usefulness as a construct. Neither Willingham nor other "geocentric" theorists have yet provided a satisfactory definition for *g*. One might argue that *g* is merely the common factor that underlies the set of tasks devised by psychologists in their attempt to predict scholastic success. Perhaps *g* measures speed or flexibility of response; capacity to follow instructions; or motivation to succeed at an artificial, decontextualized task. None of these possibilities necessarily places *g* at odds with MI theory – and indeed Gardner has never denied the existence or utility of *g* for certain analytic purposes. The current perseveration on *g* does, however, suggest a narrowness that fails to capture adequately the broad range of human cognition. Just how much of excellence across the range of intelligences reflects a current or future version of *g* is at present not known.

Delineating the Boundaries of an Intelligence

It is sometimes challenging to draw clear distinctions between intelligences and other human capacities (Gardner, 2006c). Indeed, even when we have mapped out completely the neurological underpinnings of the human mind, the drawing of these boundaries will probably continue to involve considerable judgment. At the same time, the undergirding criteria and level of analysis of MI theory can be usefully employed to draw a number of key distinctions. For instance, since intelligences operate on specific content (e.g., language, music, the apprehension of other persons), they can be separated from so-called across the board or "horizontal" capacities like attention, motivation, and cognitive style. Whereas these general capacities are thought to apply across a range of situations, the "vertical" intelligences are used by individuals to make sense of specific content, information, or objects in the world. Thus, while attention is required to engage in any type of intellectual work and motivation is needed to sustain and enhance it, attention and motivation remain separate from the operation of an intelligence. Moreover, it is possible that an individual may be quite attentive and/or motivated with respect to one kind of content and much less so with respect to other contents.

Similarly, an individual's cognitive style (sometimes referred to as a learning or working style) is not tied to specific content in the same way as is an intelligence (Gardner, 1995). A cognitive style putatively denotes the general manner in which an individual approaches cognitive tasks. For instance, where one person may approach a range of situations with careful deliberation, another person may respond more intuitively. In contrast, the operation of an intelligence entails the computation of specific content in the world (such as phonemes, numerical patterns, or musical sounds). A closer look at individuals' cognitive styles may reveal content-specificity. For instance, a student who approaches a chemistry experiment in a methodical and deliberative manner may be less reflective when practicing the piano or writing an essay. By the same token, individuals bring to bear different styles depending on the intelligence or group of intelligences they are using. The key distinction is that one can bring either a deliberative or intuitive style to the interpretation of a poem, but there is no question that some degree of linguistic intelligence will be needed.

Indeed, in an illuminating discussion of the relation between style and intelligence, Silver and Strong (1997) suggest that an introvert strong in linguistic intelligence might become a poet, while an extrovert with comparable linguistic competence is more likely to become a debater. This observation also highlights the fact that there is not a one-to-one correspondence between specific types of content and the intelligences. Writing a poem and engaging in a debate are two distinct activities that each draw on linguistic intelligence. Moreover, it is not the case that a skilled debater will necessarily be a successful poet. In addition to using linguistic intelligence, a debater may employ logical-mathematical intelligence to structure a coherent argument, whereas a poet may draw on musical intelligence to compose a sonnet. Other factors besides intelligence, such as motivation, personality, and will power, will likely prove influential, as well.

Other putative general capacities, like memory and critical thinking, may not be so general, either. For instance, we know that individuals draw on different types of memory for different purposes. Episodic memory enables us to remember particular events like a high school graduation or wedding, whereas procedural memory allows us to recall how to drive a car or knit a scarf. These different types of memory draw on different neural systems of the brain. Neuropsychological evidence documents that memory for one type of content, such as language, can be separated from memory for other types of content, such as music, shapes, movement, and so on (Gardner, 2006b). Similarly, the kind of critical thinking required to edit a book is certainly different from the kind of critical thinking required to balance a budget, plan a dinner party, transpose a piece of music, or resolve a domestic conflict.

The understanding that intelligences operate on specific content can also help to distinguish them from sensory systems. Whereas sensory systems are the means through which the brain receives information from the outside world, the intelligences have been conceptualized as computational systems that make sense of that information *once it has been received and irrespective of the means of reception*. Thus, the senses and the intelligences are independent systems. The type and quality of the information received by a sensory system determines the intelligence, or set of intelligences, employed, not the sensory system itself. Thus, linguistic intelligence can operate equivalently on language that is perceived through eye, ear, or touch. Even musical intelligence, which is most closely linked to a specific sensory system (audition), may be fractionated into information that can be obtained via diverse transducers (e.g., rhythm, timbre).

The distinction between an intelligence and a skill is another common source of confusion. Unlike sensory systems, which precede intellectual work, skills manifest as a product of such work. More specifically, they are the cognitive performances that result from the operation of one or more intelligences (Gardner & Moran, 2006). Within and across cultures, the types of skills displayed by individuals vary widely, from cartoon drawing to swimming, from writing computer code to navigating ships. Skills act on the external world. As a result, they are shaped by the supports and constraints of the environment. Thus, whether an individual's bodily-kinesthetic and spatial intelligences are put to use in swimming or marine navigation depends on an individual's access to a body of water, a willing instructor, and time for practice. Living in a culture that values the ability to swim or sail (or scuba dive or catch fish) is another influential factor.

Skills can be grouped according to the domain in which they operate. A domain (a neutral term designed to encompass a profession, discipline, or craft) is any type of organized activity in a society in which individuals demonstrate varying levels of expertise. A list of domains can readily be generated by considering the broad range of occupations in a society, such as lawyer, journalist, dancer, or electrician. (In modern society, the yellow pages serve as a convenient index of significant domains.) As such, a domain is a social construct that exists outside the individual, in society; skills in that domain can be acquired through various routes. An intelligence, on the other hand, is a biopsychological potential that all individuals possess by virtue of being human.

Because some domains have the same name as certain intelligences, they are often conflated. However, an individual can, and often does, draw on several intelligences when performing in a given domain. A successful musical performance, for example, does not simply depend on musical intelligence; bodily-kinesthetic, spatial, and even interpersonal and intrapersonal intelligences are likely at work, as well. By the same token, fluent computation of an intelligence does not dictate choice of profession; a person with high interpersonal intelligence might choose to enter teaching, acting, public relations, sales, therapy, or the ministry.

Domains are continually being reshaped by the work of creative individuals (Feldman, 1980). Newton changed the domain of physics with his universal law of gravitation and laws of motion, and Einstein reconceptualized it again with his theory of relativity. Like intelligences, creativity involves solving problems or fashioning products; however, creativity requires doing so in *a novel way*. Yet, novelty in itself does not constitute creativity. An individual who fashions a novel product may not necessarily alter a domain. Sufficient mastery of a domain is required to detect certain anomalies and formulate new techniques or ideas that resolve these anomalies. Since it generally takes 10 years, or several thousand hours, to master a domain, and several more years to alter it (Hayes, 1989; Simon & Chase, 1973), creativity requires concerted focus and dedication to one domain. For this reason, a person rarely achieves high levels of creativity in more than one domain. Moreover, individuals do not have the final word on their creativity. According to Csikszentmihalyi (1996), creativity is a communal judgment that is ultimately rendered by the gatekeepers and practitioners of the domain; there is no statute of limitations as to when these judgments are made.

In contrast, the intelligences are used daily across a variety of domains. In one day, a person may use linguistic intelligence to write a letter to a friend, read the assembly instructions for a piece of furniture, and question the fairness of a government policy in a class debate. In developing one or more intelligences to a high degree, individuals become experts in a domain and are readily recognized as such. It may well be that individuals who become experts exhibit a personality configuration and motivational structure quite different from that displayed by creators (Gardner, 1993). For example, creators are likely to take on risks and deal easily with setbacks, while experts may be risk-averse and aim toward perfection in well-developed spheres.

In delineating the boundaries of an intelligence, Gardner hesitated to posit an executive function (a "central intelligences agency") that coordinates the relationships among the intelligences, or between the intelligences and other human capacities (Gardner, 1983, 2006b). The first problem one encounters when considering an executive function is the prospect of infinite regression: who is in charge of the executive? Further, it is worth noting that many human groups, whether artistic, athletic, or corporate, follow a decentralized model of organization and perform effectively without an executive whose role it is to coordinate and direct behavior. At the same time, neuropsychological evidence suggests that particular executive functions, such as self-regulation and planning, are controlled by mechanisms in the frontal lobe. Instead of viewing such functions as constituting a separate entity that oversees the intelligences and other human capacities, Gardner and Moran (2007) argue that executive functions are likely one, clearly vital, emerging component of intrapersonal intelligence. Defined as the capacity to discern and use information about oneself, intrapersonal intelligence engenders a sense of personal coherence in two ways: by providing understanding of oneself, or self-awareness; and by regulating goal-directed behavior, or executive function. Thus, executive function is that part of intrapersonal intelligence responsible for planning and organizing actions in a deliberative and strategic way. Viewed in this way, executive function does not form the apex of a hierarchical structure but rather constitutes one vital component of an essentially decentralized process.

Assessing Candidate Intelligences

Over the years, there have been many calls for new intelligences to be added to the original list of seven. Yet, as noted, in more than 25 years, the list has grown by only one (and a possible second). This relatively small expansion is partly due to Gardner's intellectual conservatism; mostly, however, it can be attributed to the failure of candidate intelligences to meet sufficiently the criteria for inclusion. For instance, some of the proposed intelligences are really general capacities that do not operate on specific content. Posner's (2004) "attention intelligence" and Luhrmann's (2006) "absorption intelligence" fall into this category. Absorption is arguably one component of attention and both are prerequisites for intellectual work. It is not evident how either one is tied to specific content, information, or objects in the world. For this reason, attention and absorption are perhaps more properly viewed as components of the sensory systems that precede and facilitate the operation of any one of the intelligences.

Artistic intelligence is another candidate intelligence that is not tied to any specific content. Since each intelligence can be used in an artistic or a nonartistic way, it does not make sense to speak of a separate artistic intelligence. Linguistic intelligence is used by both playwrights and lawyers, and spatial intelligence is used by sculptors and building contractors. Musical intelligence may be used to compose a symphony, to announce the arrival of horses onto a race track, or to soothe pain in the dental chair. The decision to deploy an intelligence more or less artistically is left to the individual. The culture in which he or she lives can also prove consequential, as cultures vary in the degree to which they encourage and support artistic expression.

Candidate intelligences raise additional considerations. Scholars (including Gardner himself) have explored the possibility of a moral intelligence (Boos, 2005; Gardner, 1997, 2006b). Morality is clearly an important component of human society, but it is not clear that it is felicitously described as an intelligence. MI theory is descriptive, not normative. As computational capacities based in human biology and human psychology, intelligences can be put to either moral or immoral uses in society. Martin Luther King, Jr., used his linguistic intelligence to craft and deliver inspiring speeches about the quest for civil rights through peaceful means. In stark contrast, Slobodan Milosevic used his linguistic intelligence to call for the subjugation and eventual extermination of entire groups of people. The two men also deployed their interpersonal intelligences in distinct ways. MI theory merely delineates the boundaries of biopsychological capacities; the way in which one decides to use these capacities is a separate matter.

A closer look at another oft-proposed candidate – humor intelligence – underscores a second ploy. There is no need to add a new intelligence when it can be explained through a combination of existing intelligences. Thus, humor can be seen as a playful manipulation of our logical capacity. Comedians draw on their logical-mathematical intelligence to turn the logic of everyday experience on its head. They also employ their interpersonal intelligence to "read" an audience and make decisions about the timing of individual jokes and the overall direction of their act. In this way, it is more appropriate to speak of comedians as exercising a particular blend of logical-mathematical and interpersonal intelligences rather than as displaying separate humor intelligence. In a similar manner, Battro and Denham (2007) make an intriguing case for a digital intelligence, but it is not clear whether or how digital intelligence can be untangled from logical-mathematical intelligence (with a smidgeon of bodily-kinesthetic intelligence tacked on).

Cooking is another candidate intelligence that is more properly viewed as an amalgam of existing intelligences. In preparing a meal, for instance, one might draw on interpersonal intelligence to decide on a menu that will please the guests; linguistic intelligence to read the recipe; logical-mathematical intelligence to adjust the ingredient measurements for the size of the party; and bodily-kinesthetic intelligence to dice the vegetables, tenderize the meat, and whip the cream. The preparation of a fine meal may also draw on the only full-fledged addition to the original list of intelligences: naturalist intelligence. Cooks will draw on their naturalist intelligence to distinguish among ingredients and perhaps tweak a recipe by combining ingredients in an unexpectedly flavorful way. Of course, sensory systems are important in cooking, but it is the operations performed upon the sensory information that yields intelligent (or nonintelligent!) outcomes.

Part 3: Scholarly Work in the Wake of MI Theory

Since its inception, the theory of multiple intelligences has been a subject of scholarly inquiry and educational experimentation. We here examine three major fronts: research, assessment, and educational interventions.

Research

A notable point of departure is the problem of how to decide which research is relevant to testing MI theory as it has been described in these pages. Some research that is described in MI terms may be irrelevant (e.g., informal and unvalidated questionnaires, assessments using paper and pencil or multiple-choice tests alone), whereas research that does not mention MI explicitly could be important (e.g., transfer and correlations between competencies, aptitude-treatment interactions, parsimonious models of cognitive neuroscience brain activation patterns, etc.). Other conceptions of intellect have faced a similar challenge in psychology (Mayer & Caruso, 2008).

Cognitive Neuroscience and MI

Evidence for the several intelligences came originally from the study of how mental faculties were associated or dissociated as a consequence of damage to the brain, and especially to cortical structures. With the surge in the types of neuroimaging tools in the recent decades, far more specified inquiries relevant to MI are possible. Nowadays a consensus obtains that there is not a one-to-one correspondence between types of intelligence and areas of the cortex. Nonetheless it is still germane to detail how the constructs outlined by MI can relate to brain structure and function.

Until this point, most neuroimaging studies of intellect have examined the brain correlates of general intelligence (IQ). These studies have revealed that general intelligence is correlated with activations in frontal regions (Duncan et al., 2000) as well as several other brain regions (e.g., Jung & Haier, 2007), with speed of neural conduction (Gogtay et al., 2004). An analogous kind of study can be carried out with respect to specific intelligences (cf. emotional intelligence as reviewed by Mayer, Roberts, & Barsade, 2008). Ultimately it would be desirable to secure an atlas of the neural correlates of each of the intelligences, along with indices of how they do or do not operate in concert. Researchers should remain open to the possibility that intelligences may have different neural representations, in different cultures – the examples of linguistic intelligence (speaking, reading, writing) comes to mind.

From a neuropsychological point of view, the critical test for MI theory will be the ways in which intellectual strengths map onto neural structures and connections. It could be, as proponents of general intelligence claim, that individuals with certain neural structures and connections will be outstanding in all or at least, predictably, in some intelligences. Were this to be the case, the neuropsychological underpinnings of MI theory would be challenged. It could also be the case that individuals with intellectual strengths in a particular area show similar brain profiles, and that those who exhibit contrasting intellectual strengths show a contrasting set of neural profiles. It might also be the case that certain neural structures (e.g., precociously developing frontal lobes) or functions (speed of conduction) place one "at promise" for intellectual precocity more generally, but that certain kinds of experiences then cause specialization to emerge – in which case, a profile of neurally discrete intelligences will ultimately consolidate.

Similar lines of argument can unfold with respect to the genetic basis of intelligence. To this point, those with very high or very low IQs display distinct combinations of genes, though it is already clear that there will not be a single gene, or even a small set of genes, that codes for intellect. What remains to be determined is whether those with quite distinctive behavioral profiles (e.g., individuals who are highly musical, highly linguistic, and/or highly skilled in physical activities) exhibit distinctive genetic clusters as well. Put vividly, can the Bach family or the Curie family or the Polgar family be distinguished genetically from the general population and from one another? Or, as with the neural argument just propounded, certain genetic profiles may aid one to achieve expertise more quickly, but the particular area of expertise will necessarily yield quite distinctive cognitive profiles in the adult.

It is germane to inquire whether, should neural evidence and genetic evidence favor the notion of a single general intelligence and provide little evidence for biological markers of the specific intelligences, MI theory will be disproved scientifically. A question will still remain about how individuals end up possessing quite distinct profiles of abilities and disabilities. Whether the answer to that question will lie in studies drawn from genetics, neurology, psychology, sociology, anthropology, or some combination thereof, remains to be determined.

MI Assessments

From the start, a distinctive hallmark of MI theory has been its spurning of simple paper-and-pencil or "one shot" behavioral measures. Instead, with respect to assessment, Gardner has called for multiple measures of performance and ecologically valid testing environments and tasks. This approach to MI has been actualized by a large initiative for children, Project Spectrum.

Project Spectrum is an assessment system for young children that features a classroom rich in opportunities to work with different materials – in the manner of a well-stocked children's museum (Gardner et al., 1998a, 1998b, 1998c; Malkus et al., 1988; Ramos-Ford, Feldman, & Gardner, 1988; see also http://www.pz.harvard.edu/research/Spectrum.htm). The Spectrum approach yields information based on meaningful activities that allow for a demonstration of the strengths of the several intelligences. While validity is not something that can be examined with preschoolers, Spectrum tasks have been shown to demonstrate reliability (Gardner et al., 1998a, 1998b, 1998c).

Spectrum transcends traditional assessments such as the IQ tests in several ways. First, it highlights components of thought (e.g., musical competence, knowledge of other persons) that are not typically considered indices of smartness (Gardner, 1993). Second, the assessment is based on "hands on" activities that have proved to be engaging and meaningful for preschool children drawn from a range of social backgrounds (Chen & Gardner, 1997). Third, the initiative seeks to document approaches to learning (working styles) as well as the distribution of strengths and weaknesses across the several intelligences – the so-called Spectrum Profile. (For a comprehensive description of components and guidelines by domain for *activities*, see Adams & Feldman, 1993; Krechevsky, 1998; Krechevsky & Gardner, 1990; for *observational guidelines* see Chen & Gardner, 1997).

Empirical studies using the Project Spectrum materials have been instructive and useful. In one study, researchers worked with at-risk students in a local elementary school's first grade (Chen & Gardner, 1997). The majority of students (13/15) demonstrated identifiable strengths based on assessments spanning many areas of performance including visual arts, mechanical science, movement, music, social understanding, mathematics, science, and language (Chen & Gardner, 1997). Gardner (1993) has described this approach as efforts to identify *how* a student is smart as opposed to *whether* the student is smart. Identifying such strengths has the potential to detach an at-risk or struggling student from unidimensional labels and offer a more holistic formulation with respect to student strengths and potentials.

Other empirical investigations have sought to document the validity of MI claims. Visser et al. (2006) operationalized the eight intelligences and selected two assessments for each. Further, the researchers categorized the intelligences into purely cognitive (linguistic, spatial, logical-mathematical, naturalistic, and interpersonal), motor (bodily-kinesthetic), a combination of cognitive and personality (intrapersonal and possibly interpersonal), and a combination of cognitive and sensory (musical). Study results showed a strong loading on *g*, or general intelligence, for intelligences categorized as cognitive as well as intercorrelations among intelligences, suggesting that strong MI claims are not held up empirically.

The study findings stand in contrast to those reported from Project Spectrum studies, as well as those put forth by other investigators (e.g., Maker, Nielson, & Rogers, 1994). These contrasting results may be attributed to the use of standard psychometric measures, as opposed to the employment of broader (but less specific) tasks that aim for ecological validity and that can be used routinely in the course of daily school activities.

As a visit to any search engine will document, many researchers and practitioners of an educational bent have developed rough-and-ready measures of the several intelligences. The best known such effort is

Branton Shearer's Multiple Intelligences Developmental Assessment Scale (MIDAS, 1999), which has been used as a tool for measuring MI in many research projects, has been translated into several languages and has been administered to thousands of subjects all over the world (Shearer, 2007). The MIDAS, and other less widely used instruments, provide a useful snapshot of how individuals view their own intellectual profiles. Such self-descriptions do not, however, allow one to distinguish one's own preferences from one's own computational abilities, nor is it clear that individuals are necessarily competent to assess their areas of strength. (How many persons consider themselves in the bottom half of the population with respect to driving skill, or sense of humor?) Optimally, descriptions of a person should come from several knowledgeable individuals, not just the person him self or herself. And optimally, the measures should tap actual intellectual strengths. Of the methods with which we are familiar, Project Spectrum comes closest to meeting these desiderata.

With respect to assessment generally, Gardner and colleagues (Chen & Gardner, 1997) have advocated several key points. As reviewed earlier, an important starting point is the assumption that intelligence may be pluralistic rather than a unitary entity. Another key point is that the intelligences are shaped by cultural and educational influences; it follows that measuring them in natural contexts is preferable, if the results are to be ecologically valid. Recognizing the limitations of static assessment is also important – while such assessment sessions may serve other purposes, they do not fulfill the tenets of MI which calls for dynamic assessment to accompany the use of intelligences in culturally meaningful contexts.

Perhaps most important, intelligences can never be observed in isolation; they can only be manifest in the performance and tasks of skills that are available, and optimally, valued in a cultural context. Hence the notion of a single measure of an intelligence makes little sense. Rather, any intelligence – say, linguistic – ought to be observed in several contexts: speaking, reading, telling a story, making an argument, learning a foreign language, and so on. Taken together, such diverse measures would converge on linguistic intelligence; one assumes that what each task shares in common with the remaining tasks is reliance on some facet of linguistic intelligence. In sum, MI assessment calls for multiple measures for each intelligence and "intelligence-fair" materials that do not rely on verbal or logical-mathematical skills. Gold standard MI assessments should avoid several pitfalls and aim for several goals, summarized in Table 24.3.

Research on MI as an Educational Intervention

We turn finally to studies of educational settings that have developed methods based on the core ideas of MI theory. In the most ambitious study to date, Kornhaber, Fierros, and Veenema (2004) compiled data on the impact of these methods across many educational settings using interview and questionnaire data to collect educators' perceptions of the impact of MI-based methods. Featured were interview data from 41 schools, which had been implementing MI-inspired curricular practices for at least three years. Staff at four-fifths of the schools associated improvements in standardized test scores with the implementation of MI-based practices. Additionally, use of these methods was also associated with improvements in student discipline (54% of schools), parent participation (60% of schools), and performances of students diagnosed with learning disabilities (78% of schools). The researchers attributed the success of MI-based practices to six *compass point practices*: attention to the school culture, readiness to subscribe to the ideas from the theory of Multiple Intelligences and building classroom and school capacity to use the theory, use of the theory as a framework for improving work quality, collaborations, opportunities for choice, and a role for the arts.

Investigations of MI in educational settings have taken several forms, including

Table 24.3. Assessment Characteristics for the Multiple Intelligences and Traditional Counterparts

Traditional Assessment	*MI Assessment*
Over-reliant on linguistic and logical mathematical abilities and measures	Samples the gamut of intelligences and domains
Deficit-focused	Identifies relative and absolute strengths
Limited connection between assessment and curricular activity/tasks	Gives immediate feedback to students; is meaningful for students; uses materials with which children are familiar
Captures performance in a single score	Produces scores on a range of tasks, across several domains for each intelligence
Is detached from context	Has ecological validity; presents problems in the context of problem solving; is instructive for teachers

(Adapted from Chen & Gardner, 1997).

descriptions of how the theory contributes to education (e.g., Barrington, 2004), how MI can be applied in the curriculum (e.g., Dias Ward & Dias, 2004; Nolen, 2003; Özdemir, Güneysu, & Tekkaya, 2006; Wallach & Callahan, 1994), and how MI operates within or across schools (e.g., Campbell & Campbell, 1999; Greenhawk, 1997; Hickey, 2004; Hoerr, 1992, 1994, 2004; Wagmeister & Shifrin, 2000). MI approaches have been credited with better performance and retention of knowledge as compared to a traditional approach (for science instruction for fourth-graders) (Ozdemir et al., 2006) and with understanding content in more complex ways (Emig, 1997). Similarly, MI approaches in the curriculum have been credited with giving teachers a framework for making instructional decisions (Ozdemir et al., 2006). Teele, who has devised one of the principal MI self-administered instruments, suggests that "intrinsic motivation, positive self-image, and a sense of responsibility develop when students become stakeholders in the educational process and accept responsibility for their own actions" (1996, p. 72).

Part 4: Conclusion: Looking Ahead

In a number of ways, MI theory differs from other psychological approaches to intelligence. Rather than proceeding from or creating psychometric instruments, the theory emerged from an interdisciplinary consideration of the range of human capacities and faculties. The theory has garnered considerable attention, far more in educational circles than in the corridors of standard psychological testing and experimentation. Consistent with that emphasis, numerous educational experiments build on MI theory, and many of them claim success. However, because MI theory does not dictate specific educational practices, and because any educational intervention is multifaceted, it is not possible to attribute school success or failure strictly to MI interventions. Direct experimental tests of the theory are difficult to implement and so the status of the theory within academic psychology remains indeterminate. The biological basis of the theory – its neural and genetic correlates – should be clarified in the coming years. But in the absence of consensually agreed upon measures of the intelligences, either individually or in conjunction with one another, the psychological validity of the theory will continue to be elusive.

What does the future hold for MI theory? It seems reasonable to expect that these ideas will continue to be of interest to educators and other practitioners. Having initially catalyzed an interest in elementary schools, particularly with respect to students with learning problems, the theory has been picked up by schools of all sorts, as well as museums and other institutions of informal learning. MI ideas are also invading other occupational spheres, such as business, and have proved of special interest to those charged with hiring, assembling teams, or placing personnel (Moran & Gardner, 2006).

Uses of MI ideas within and outside formal educational settings hold great promise. In particular, new digital media and virtual realities offer numerous ways in which learners can master required knowledge and skills. At one time, it may have seemed advisable or even necessary to search for the "one best way" to teach a topic. Now, at a time when computers can deliver contents and processes in numerous ways, and when learners can take increasing control of their own educational destinies, a plurality of curricula, pedagogy, and assessments figures to become the norm. Individualized education does not depend on the existence of MI theory; and yet MI-inspired practices provide promising approaches for effective teaching and learning (Birchfield et al., 2008). Moreover, as lifelong learning becomes more important around the world, the prospects of developing, maintaining, and enhancing the several intelligences gain urgency.

Initially, MI ideas were introduced in the United States and the first MI-inspired experiments took place there. But over the last two decades, MI ideas and practices have spread to numerous countries and regions. There are both striking similarities and instructive differences in the ways in which these regions implement MI ideas, formally and informally. An initial survey appears in *Multiple Intelligences Around the World* (Chen, Moran, & Gardner, 2009). In addition to chronicling numerous implementations of MI theory in more than a dozen countries, this work also provides a fascinating and original portrait of how "memes" about intelligence take and spread in different educational soils.

Gardner has long maintained that MI cannot be an educational goal in itself. Educational goals, value judgments, must emerge from discussions and debates among responsible leaders and citizens. Once goals have been laid out, the question then arises: How and in what ways, can MI ideas aid in the achievement of these goals? To be sure, a tight answer to that question can rarely be given. Nonetheless, over time it should certainly become clearer which MI ideas, in combination with which goals, have pedagogical effectiveness and which do not. Within Project Zero, the research group with which Gardner has been associated since its inception in 1967, MI ideas have proved particularly congenial with the goal of "education for deep understanding" (Gardner 1999, 2006b).

Whether or not explicitly recognized as such, MI ideas are likely to endure within the worlds of education, business, and daily practice – like the terms *emotional intelligence* and *social intelligence* (Goleman 1995, 2006), they are already becoming part of the conventional wisdom. The status of MI theory within psychology, biology, and other social and natural sciences remains to be determined. Attempts will be made to define and redefine the set of intelligences, to evaluate the criteria by which they are identified and measured, to consider their relationships to one another, and their status vis-à-vis "general intelligence." In all probability, like other attempts at intellectual synthesis, some facets will become accepted in scholarship, while other parts will fade away or remain topics for debate. What is most likely to last in MI theory is the set of criteria for what counts as an intelligence and the idea of intelligence as pluralistic, with links to specific contents in the human and primate environments. The particular list of intelligences and subintelligences will doubtless be reformulated as a result of continuing studies in psychology, neuroscience, and genetics.

References

Adams, M., & Feldman, D. H. (1993). Project Spectrum: A theory-based approach to early education. In R. Pasnak & M. L. Howe (Eds.), *Emerging themes in cognitive development*. New York, NY: Springer-Verlag.

Armstrong, T. (1994). *Multiple intelligences in the classroom*. Alexandria, VA: Association for Supervision and Curriculum Development.

Barrington, E. (2004). Teaching to student diversity in higher education: How multiple intelligence theory can help. *Teaching in Higher Education*, 9, 421–434.

Battro, A. M., & Denham, P. J. (2007). *Hacia una inteligencia*. Buenos Aires, Argentina: Academia Nacional de Educación.

Binet, A., & Simon, T. (1911). *A method of measuring the development of the intelligence of young children*. Lincoln, IL: Courier.

Binet, A., & Simon, T. (1916). *The development of intelligence in children*. Baltimore, MD: Williams & Wilkins.

Birchfield, D., Thornburg, H., Megowan-Romanowicz, C., Hatton, S., Mechtley, B., Dolgov, I., & Burleson, W. (2008). Embodiment, multimodality, and composition: Convergent themes across HCI and education for mixed-reality learning environments. *Journal of Advances in Human-Computer Interaction*, 2008, Article ID 874563.

Boss, J. (2005). The autonomy of moral intelligence. *Educational Theory*, 44(4), 399–416.

Brody, N. (2004). What cognitive intelligence is and what emotional intelligence is not. *Psychological Inquiry*, 15(3), 234–238.

Campbell, L., & Campbell, B. (1999). *Multiple intelligences and student achievement*. Alexandria, VA: ASCD.

Ceci, S. J. (1990). *On intelligence, more or less: A bioecological treatise on intellectual development*. Englewood Cliffs, NJ: Prentice-Hall.

Ceci, S. J. (1996). *On intelligence* (rev. ed.). Cambridge, MA: Harvard University Press.

Chen, J.-Q., & Gardner, H. (1997). Assessment based on multiple-intelligences theory. In D. P. Flanagan & P. L. Harrison (Eds.), *Contemporary intellectual assessment: Theories, tests, and issues* (Vol. 2, pp. 77–102). New York, NY: Guilford Press.

Chen, Jie-Qi, & Gardner, H. (2005). Multiple intelligences: Assessment based on multiple-intelligence theory. In D. Flanagan & P. Harrison (Eds.), *Contemporary intellectual assessment: Theories, tests and issues*. New York: Guilford Press.

Chen, J., Moran, S., & Gardner, H. (2009). *Multiple intelligences around the world*. New York, NY: Jossey-Bass.

Csikszentmihalyi, M. (1996). *Creativity: Flow and the psychology of discovery and invention*. New York: HarperCollins.

Danfoss Universe. (2007). Retrieved July 1, 2007, from http://www.danfossuniverse.com.

Deary, I., Strand, S., Smith, P., & Fernandes, C. (2007). Intelligence and educational achievement. *Intelligence*, 35, 13–21.

Diamond, M., & Hopson, J. (1998). *Magic trees of the mind: How to nurture your child's intelligence, creativity, and healthy emotions from birth through adolescence*. New York, NY: Dutton.

Dias Ward, C., & Dias, M. J. (2004). Ladybugs across the curriculum. *Science and Children*, 41(7), 40–44.

Duncan, J., Seitz, R.J., Kolodny, J., Bor, D., Herzog, H., Ahmed, A., Newell, F.N., & Emslie, H. (2000). A neural basis for general intelligence. *Science*, 289(5478), 457–460.

Emig, V. B. (1997). A multiple intelligences inventory. *Educational Leadership*, 55(1), 47.

Eysenck, H. (1994). *Manual for the Eysenck personality questionnaire* (EPQ-R Adult). San Diego, CA: Educational Industrial Testing Service.

Feldman, D. H. (1980). *Beyond universals in cognitive development*. Norwood, NJ: Ablex.

Gardner, H. (1983). *Frames of mind: The theory of multiple intelligences*. New York, NY: Basic Books.

Gardner, H. (1993). *Frames of mind: The theory of multiple intelligences* (10th anniversary ed.). New York, NY: Basic Books.

Gardner, H. (1997). Is there a moral intelligence? In M. Runco (Ed.), *The creativity research handbook*. Cresskill, NJ: Hampton Press.

Gardner, H. (1999). *The disciplined mind: What all students should understand*. New York, NY: Simon & Schuster.

Gardner, H. (2006a). *Five minds for the future*. Boston, MA: Harvard Business School Press.

Gardner, H. (2006b). *Multiple intelligences: New horizons*. New York, NY: Basic Books.

Gardner, H. (2006c). Replies to my critics. In J. A. Schaler (Ed.), *Howard Gardner under fire: The rebel psychologist faces his critics* (pp. 277–344). Chicago, IL: Open Court.

Gardner, H., Feldman, D. H., & Krechevsky, M. (Gen. Eds.). (1998a). *Project Zero frameworks for early childhood education: Volume 1, Building on children's strengths: The experience of Project Spectrum* (Volume authors J.-Q. Chen, M. Krechevsky, & J. Viens, with

E. Isberg). New York, NY: Teachers College Press. Translated into Chinese, Italian, Spanish, and Portuguese.

Gardner, H., Feldman, D. H., & Krechevsky, M. (Gen. Eds.). (1998b). *Project Zero frameworks for early childhood education: Volume 2, Project Spectrum early learning activities* (Volume author J-Q. Chen, with E. Isberg and M. Krechevsky). New York, NY: Teachers College Press. Translated into Chinese, Italian, Spanish, and Portuguese.

Gardner, H., Feldman, D. H., & Krechevsky, M. (Gen. Eds.). (1998c). *Project Zero frameworks for early childhood education: Volume 3, Project Spectrum preschool assessment handbook* (Volume author M. Krechevsky). New York, NY: Teachers College Press. Translated into Chinese, Italian, Spanish, and Portuguese.

Gardner, H., & Laskin, E. (1995). *Leading minds: An anatomy of leadership*. New York, NY: BasicBooks.

Gardner, H., & Moran, S. (2006). The science of multiple intelligences theory: A response to Lynn Waterhouse. *Educational Psychologist*, 41(4), 227–232.

Gogtay, N., Giedd, J. N., Lusk, L., Hayashi, K. M., Greenstein, D., Vaituzis, A. C., et al. (2004). Dynamic mapping of human cortical development during childhood through early adulthood. *PNAS*, 101(21), 8174–8179.

Goleman D. 1995. *Emotional intelligence*. New York, NY: Bantam Books.

Goleman, D. (2006). *Social intelligence: The new science of human relationships*. New York, NY: Bantam Books.

Greenhawk, J. (1997). Multiple intelligences meet standards. *Educational Leadership*, 55(1), 62–64.

Guilford, J. P. (1967). *The nature of human intelligence*. New York, NY: McGraw-Hill.

Guilford, J. P., & Hoepfner, R. (1971). *The analysis of intelligence*. New York, NY: McGraw-Hill.

Haier, R. J., & Jung, R. E. (2007). Beautiful minds (i.e., brains) and the neural basis of intelligence. *Behavioral and Brain Sciences*, 30(2), 174–178.

Hayes, J. R. (1989). Cognitive processes in creativity. In J. A. Glover, R. R. Ronning, & C. R. Reynolds (Eds.), *Handbook of creativity* (pp. 135–145). New York, NY: Plenum Press.

Hickey, G. (2004). "Can I pick more than one project? Case studies of five teachers who used MI-based instructional planning". *Teachers College Record*, 106(1), 77–86.

Herrnstein, R.J., & Murray, C. (1994). *The bell curve: Intelligence and class structure in American life*. New York, NY: Free Press.

Hoerr, T. (2004). How MI informs teaching at New City School. *Teachers College Record*, 106(1), 40–48.

Hoerr, T. R. (1992). How our school applied multiple intelligences theory. *Educational Leadership*, 50(2), 67–68.

Hoerr, T. R. (1994). How the New City School applies the multiple intelligences. *Educational Leadership*, 52(3), 29–33.

Jensen, A. R. (1980). *Bias in mental testing*. New York, NY: Free Press.

Jensen, A. R. (1998). *The g factor: The science of mental ability*. Westport, CT: Praeger/Greenwoood.

Jensen, A. (2008). Why is reaction time correlated with psychometric 'g'? *Current Directions in Psychological Science*, 2(2), 53–56.

Jung, R. E. & Haier, R. J. (2007). The parieto-frontal integration theory (P-FIT) of intelligence: Converging neuroimaging evidence. *Behavioral and Brain Sciences*, 30(2), 135–154.

Kornhaber, M. (1999). Multiple intelligences theory in practice. In J. H. Block, S. T. Everson, & T. R. Guskey (Eds.), *Comprehensive school reform: A program perspective*. Dubuque, IA: Kendall/Hunt.

Kornhaber, M., Fierros, E., & Veenema, S. (2004). *Multiple intelligences: Best ideas from research and practice*. Boston, MA: Pearson Education.

Krechevsky, M. (1998). *Project Spectrum preschool assessment handbook*. New York, NY: Teachers College Press.

Krechevsky, M., & Gardner, H. (1990). The emergence and nurturance of multiple intelligences: The Project Spectrum approach. In M. J. Howe (Ed.), *Encouraging the development of exceptional skills and talents*. Leicester, UK: British Psychological Society.

Lucas, A., Morley, R., & Cole, T. (1998). Randomised trial of early diet in preterm babies and later intelligence quotient. *British Medical Journal*, 317, 1481–1487.

Luhrmann, T. M. (2006). On spirituality. In J. A. Schaler (Ed.), *Howard Gardner under fire: The rebel psychologist faces his critics* (pp. 115–142). Chicago, IL: Open Court.

Maker, C. J., Nielson, A. B., & Rogers, J. A. (1994). Giftedness, diversity, and problem-solving. *Teaching Exceptional Children, 27*(1), 4–19.

Malkus, U. C., Feldman, D. H., & Gardner, H. (1988). Dimensions of mind in early childhood. In A. D. Pellegrini (Ed.), *Psychological bases for early education* (pp. 25–38). Oxford, UK: John Wiley.

Mayer, J. D., Roberts, R. D., & Barsade, S. G. (2008). Human abilities: Emotional intelligence. *Annual Review of Psychology, 59*(1), 507–536.

Moran, S., & Gardner, H. (2006). Multiple intelligences in the workplace. In H. Gardner, *Multiple intelligences: New horizons* (pp. 213–232). New York, NY: BasicBooks.

Moran, S., & Gardner, H. (2007). "Hill, skill, and will": Executive function from a multiple-intelligences perspective. In L. Meltzer (Ed.), *Executive function in education: From theory to practice* (pp. 19–38). New York, NY: Guilford Press.

Neisser, U., Boodoo, G., Bouchard, T., Boykin, A. W., Brody, N., Ceci, S. J., Halpern, D., Loehlin, J., Perloff, R., Sternberg, R., & Urbina, S. (1996) Intelligence: Knowns and unknowns. *American Psychologist* **51**, 77–101.

Nisbett, R. E. (2009). *Intelligence and how to get it: Why schools and cultures count*. New York, NY: W. W. Norton.

Nolen, J. L. (2003). Multiple intelligences in the classroom. *Educational Leadership,* **124**(1), 115–119.

Özdemir, P., Güneysu, S., & Tekkaya, C. (2006). Enhancing learning through multiple intelligences. *Journal of Biological Education,* **40**(2), 74–78.

Perkins, D., & Tishman, S. (2001). Dispositional aspects of intelligence. In J. Collis, S. Messick, & U. Scheifele (Eds.), *Intelligence and personality: Bridging the gap in theory and measurement*. Mahwah, NJ: Erlbaum.

Piaget, J. (1950). *The psychology of intelligence*. London: Routledge & Kegan Paul.

Piaget, J. (1952). *The origins of intelligence in children*. New York, NY: International Universities Press.

Posner, M. I. (2004). Neural systems and individual differences. *Teachers College Record,* **106**(1), 24–30.

Ramos-Ford, V., Feldman, D. H., & Gardner, H. (1988). A new look at intelligence through project spectrum. *New Horizons for Learning,* 8(3), 6–15.

Shearer, B. (1999). *Multiple intelligences developmental assessment scale*. Kent, OH: Multiple Intelligences Research and Consulting.

Shearer, C. B. (2004). Using a multiple intelligences assessment to promote teacher development and student achievement. *Teachers College Record,* **106**(1), 147–162.

Shearer, C. B. (2007). *The MIDAS: Professional manual* (rev. ed.). Kent, OH: MI Research and Consulting.

Silver, H., & Strong, R. (1997). Integrating learning styles and multiple intelligences. *Educational Leadership,* **55**(1), 22.

Simon, H. A., & Chase, W. (1973). Skill in chess. *American Scientist,* **61**, 394–403.

Spearman, Charles. (1904). General intelligence, objectively determined and measured. *American Journal of Psychology.* **15**, 201–293.

Spearman, C. (1927). *The abilities of man*. London, UK: Macmillan.

Stanford-Binet Intelligences Scales (SB5), Fifth Edition. (2003). Rolling Meadows, IL: Riverside Publishing. http://www.riverpub.com/products/sb5/scoring.html.

Sternberg, R. J. (1985). *Beyond IQ: A triarchic theory of human intelligence*. New York, NY: Cambridge University Press.

Sternberg, R. J. (1990). *Metaphors of mind*. New York, NY: Cambridge University Press.

Teele, S. (1996). Redesigning the educational system to enable all students to succeed. *NASSP Bulletin,* 80(583), 65–75.

Thorndike, E. (1920). A constant error in psychological ratings. *Journal of Applied Psychology,* **4**, 25–29.

Thorndike, E., Bregman, E., Cobb, M., & Woodyard, E. (1927). *The measurement of intelligence*. New York, NY: Teachers College Bureau of Publications.

Thurstone, L. (1938). *Primary mental abilities*. Chicago, IL: University of Chicago Press.

Thurstone, L. L., & Thurstone, T. G. (1941). *Factorial studies of intelligence*. Chicago, IL: University of Chicago Press.

Visser, B. A., Ashton, M. C., & Vernon, P. A. (2006). Beyond *g*: Putting multiple intelligences theory to the test. *Intelligence,* **34**(5), 487–502.

Wagmeister, J., & Shifrin, B. (2000). Thinking differently, Learning differently. *Educational Leadership,* 58(3), 45.

Wallach, C., & Callahan, S. (1994). The 1st grade plant museum. *Educational Leadership,* **52**(3), 32–34.

Waterhouse, L. (2006). Multiple intelligences, the Mozart effect, and emotional intelligence: A critical review. *Educational Psychologist*, 41(4), 207–225.

Wechsler Adult Intelligence Scales, Fourth Edition. (2008). Pearson. http://www.pearsonassess.com

White, J. (2006). Multiple invalidities. In J. A. Schaler (Ed.), *Howard Gardner under fire: The rebel psychologist faces his critics* (pp. 45–72). Chicago, IL: Open Court.

Willingham, D. T. (2004). Reframing the mind. *Education Next*, 4(3), 19–24.

CHAPTER 25

The Theory of Successful Intelligence

Robert J. Sternberg

My mother once told me I was smart in school but lacked common sense. Although her judgment of me was woefully mistaken – I hope – she, in effect, adumbrated and perhaps prompted what I have come to call the "theory of successful intelligence." In this chapter, I describe the theory of successful intelligence (Sternberg, 1997, 2003e, 2005, 2009, 2010). The history of the theory presented here has been documented, to some extent, in two earlier theoretical articles in the *Behavioral and Brain Sciences* (Sternberg, 1980b, 1984) and one in the *Review of General Psychology* (Sternberg, 1999c). In the first article (Sternberg, 1980b) a theory of components of intelligence ("componential subtheory of intelligence") was presented, with the argument that intelligence could be understood in terms of a set of elementary information-processing components that contributed to people's intelligence and individual differences in it. In the second article (Sternberg, 1984) the theory was expanded ("triarchic theory of intelligence") to include not just the analytical aspect of intelligence, which had been the emphasis of the earlier article, but the creative and practical aspects of intelligence as well. By the third article (Sternberg, 1999c), the "theory of successful intelligence" was emphasizing not only levels of abilities but also how one capitalizes on one's strengths in abilities and compensates for or corrects one's weaknesses. It also emphasized the importance of the adaptive nature of intelligence rather than the importance of psychometric tests.

The Nature of Intelligence

There are many definitions of intelligence, although intelligence is typically defined in terms of a person's ability to adapt to the environment and to learn from experience (Sternberg & Detterman, 1986). The definition of intelligence here is somewhat more elaborate and is based on my (Sternberg, 1997, 1998a, 1999c, 2003e) theory of successful intelligence. According to this definition, (successful) intelligence is (1) the ability to achieve one's goals in life, given one's sociocultural context, (2) by capitalizing on strengths and correcting or compensating for weaknesses (3) in order to adapt to, shape, and select environments (4) through a combination of analytical, creative, and practical abilities. In recent years, I have emphasized that intelligence best serves individuals and societies when it is augmented by wisdom (Sternberg, 1998a, 2003b, 2008), the utilization of our abilities and knowledge, through the infusion of positive ethical values, toward a common good.

Consider first Item 1. Intelligence involves formulating a meaningful and coherent set of goals, and having the skills and dispositions to reach those goals. The important question typically is not so much what career or personal goals individuals have chosen, but rather, whether those goals make sense for the person and what he or she has done to be able to realize those goals in a meaningful way. Thus, this item actually includes three subitems: (a) identifying meaningful goals; (b) coordinating those goals in a meaningful way so that they form a coherent story of what one is seeking in life; and (c) moving a substantial distance along the path toward realizing those goals.

This first item recognizes that "intelligence" means a somewhat different thing to each individual. The individual who wishes to become a Supreme Court judge will be taking a different path from the individual who wishes to become a distinguished novelist – but both will have formulated a set of coherent goals toward which to work. A full evaluation of intelligence should focus not on what goals are chosen but rather on (1) whether the individual has chosen a worthwhile set of goals compatible with the skills and dispositions he or she has that are needed to achieve those goals; and (2) whether the individual is on the way toward achieving those goals.

Item 2 recognizes that although psychologists sometimes talk of a "general" factor of intelligence (Jensen, 1998; Spearman, 1927; see essays in Sternberg, 2000; Sternberg & Grigorenko, 2002b), really, virtually no one is good at everything or bad at everything. People who are the positive intellectual forces in society have identified their strengths and weaknesses, and have found ways to work effectively within that pattern of strengths and weaknesses.

There is no uniform way to succeed in any career. Consider, for example, teaching. Educators often try to distinguish characteristics of expert teachers (see Sternberg & Williams, 2010), and indeed, they have distinguished some such characteristics. But the truth is that teachers can excel in many different ways. Some teachers are better in giving large lectures; others in small seminars; others in one-on-one mentoring. There is no one formula that works for every teacher. Good teachers figure out their strengths and try to arrange their teaching so that they can capitalize on their strengths and at the same time either compensate for or correct their weaknesses. Team teaching is one way of doing so, as one teacher can compensate for what the other does not do well. The same would be true of people in any career.

Item 3 recognizes that intelligence broadly defined refers to more than just "adapting to the environment," which is the mainstay of conventional definitions of intelligence. The theory of successful intelligence distinguishes among adapting, shaping, and selecting.

In adaptation to the environment, one modifies oneself to fit an environment. The ability to adapt to the environment is important in life and is especially important to individuals entering a new program. Most of them will be entering a new environment that is quite different from the one in which they previously have spent time. If they are not adaptable, they may not be able to transfer the skills they showed in the previous environment to the new one. Over the course of a lifetime, environmental conditions change greatly. For example, financial investments that succeed greatly at one time may fail miserably at another time. Clearly, adaptability is a key skill in any definition of intelligence.

In life, adaptation is not enough, however. Adaptation needs to be balanced with shaping. In shaping, one modifies the environment to fit what one seeks of it, rather than modifying oneself to fit the environment. Truly great people in any field are not just adaptors; they are also shapers. They recognize that they cannot change everything, but that if they want to have an impact on the world, they have to change some things. Part of successful intelligence is deciding what to change, and then how to change it (Sternberg, 2003a).

Sometimes, one attempts unsuccessfully to adapt to an environment and then also fails in shaping that environment. No matter what one does to try to make the environment work out, nothing in fact seems to work. In such cases, the appropriate action may be to select another environment.

Many of the greatest people in any one field are people who started off in another field and found that the first field was not really the one in which they had the most to contribute. Rather than spend their lives doing something that turned out not to match their pattern of strengths and weaknesses, they had the sense to find something else to do where they really had a contribution to make. They selected a new environment.

Item 4 points out that successful intelligence involves a broader range of abilities than is typically measured by tests of intellectual and academic skills. Most of these tests measure primarily or exclusively memory and analytical abilities. With regard to memory, they assess the abilities to recall and recognize information. With regard to analytical abilities, they measure the skills involved when one analyzes, compares and contrasts, evaluates, critiques, and judges. These are important skills during the school years and in later life. But they are not the only skills that matter for school and life success. One needs not only to remember and analyze concepts, but one also needs to be able to generate and apply them. Memory pervades analytic, creative, and practical thinking, and is necessary for their execution; but it is far from sufficient.

According to the proposed theory of human intelligence and its development (Sternberg, 1980a, 1984, 1985a, 1990a, 1997, 1999a, 2003e, 2004, 2009), a common set of processes underlies all aspects of intelligence. These processes are hypothesized to be universal. For example, although the solutions to problems that are considered intelligent in one culture may be different from the solutions considered to be intelligent in another culture, the need to define problems and translate strategies to solve these problems exists in any culture. Even within cultures, there may be differences in what different groups mean by intelligence (Okagaki & Sternberg, 1993; Sternberg, 1985b).

Metacomponents, or executive processes, plan what to do, monitor things as they are being done, and evaluate things after they are done. Examples of metacomponents are recognizing the existence of a problem, defining the nature of the problem, deciding on a strategy for solving the problem, monitoring the solution of the problem, and evaluating the solution after the problem is solved.

Performance components execute the instructions of the metacomponents. For example, inference is used to decide how two stimuli are related and application is used to apply what one has inferred (Sternberg, 1977). Other examples of performance components are comparison of stimuli, justification of a given response as adequate although not ideal, and actually making the response.

Knowledge-acquisition components are used to learn how to solve problems or simply to acquire declarative knowledge in the first place (Sternberg, 1985a). Selective encoding is used to decide what information is relevant in the context of one's learning. Selective comparison is used to bring old information to bear on new problems. And selective combination is used to put together the selectively encoded and compared information into a single and sometimes insightful solution to a problem.

Although the same processes are used for all three aspects of intelligence universally, these processes are applied to different kinds of tasks and situations depending on whether a given problem requires analytical thinking, creative thinking, practical thinking, or a combination of these kinds of thinking. In particular, analytical thinking is invoked when components are applied to fairly familiar kinds of problems abstracted from everyday life. Creative thinking is invoked when the components are applied to relatively novel kinds of tasks or situations. Practical thinking is invoked when the components are applied to experience to adapt to, shape, and select environments. One needs creative skills and dispositions to generate ideas, analytical skills and dispositions to decide if they are good ideas, and practical skills and dispositions to implement one's ideas and to convince others of their worth. Because the theory of successful intelligence comprises three subtheories – a componential subtheory dealing with the components of intelligence, an experiential subtheory dealing with the importance of coping with relative novelty and of automatization of information processing, and a contextual subtheory dealing with processes of adaptation, shaping, and selection, the theory has been referred to from time to time as *triarchic*.

Intelligence is not, as Edwin Boring (1923) once suggested, merely what intelligence tests test. Intelligence tests and other tests of cognitive and academic skills measure part of the range of intellectual skills. They do not measure the whole range. One should not conclude that a person who does not test well is not smart. Rather, one should merely look at test scores as one indicator among many of a person's intellectual skills. Moreover, the kinds of skills posited by hierarchical theories (e.g., Carroll, 1993; Cattell, 1971; Vernon, 1971) are viewed only as a subset of the skills important in a broader conception of intelligence.

The Assessment of Successful Intelligence

Our assessments of intelligence have been organized around the analytical, creative, and practical aspects of it. We discuss those assessments here, singly and collectively.

Analytical Intelligence

Analytical intelligence is involved when the information-processing components of intelligence are applied to analyze, evaluate, judge, or compare and contrast. It typically is involved when components are applied to relatively familiar kinds of problems where the judgments to be made are of a fairly abstract nature.

Some early work showed how analytical kinds of problems, such as analogies or syllogisms, can be analyzed componentially (Guyote & Sternberg, 1981; Sternberg, 1977, 1980b, 1983; Sternberg & Gardner, 1983; Sternberg & Turner, 1981), with response times or error rates decomposed to yield their underlying information-processing components. The goal of this research was to understand the information-processing origins of individual differences in (the analytical aspect of) human intelligence. With componential analysis, one could specify sources of individual differences underlying a factor score such as that for "inductive reasoning." For example, response times on analogies (Sternberg, 1977) and linear syllogisms (Sternberg, 1980a) were decomposed into their elementary performance components. The general strategy of such research is to (1) specify an information-processing model of task performance; (2) propose a parameterization of this model, so that each information-processing component is assigned a mathematical parameter corresponding to its latency (and another corresponding to its error rate); and (3) construct cognitive tasks administered in such a way that it is possible through mathematical modeling to isolate the parameters of the mathematical model. In this way, it is possible to specify, in the solving of various kinds of problems, several sources of important individual or developmental differences: (1) What performance components are used? (2) How long does it takes to execute each component? (3) How susceptible is each component to error? (4) How are the components combined into strategies? (5) What are the mental representations upon which the components act?

As an example, through componential analysis, it was possible to decompose inductive-reasoning performance into a set of underlying information-processing components (Sternberg, 1977). The analogy *A : B : C : D1, D2, D3, D4* will be used as an example to illustrate the components. These components are (1) *encoding*, the amount of time needed to register each stimulus (*A, B, C, D1, D2, D3, D4*); (2) *inference*, the amount of time needed to discern the basic relation between given stimuli (*A to B*); (3) *mapping*, the amount of time needed to transfer the relation from one set of stimuli to another (needed in analogical reasoning) (*A to C*); (4) *application*, the amount of time needed to apply the relation as inferred (and sometimes as mapped) to a new set of stimuli (*A to B to C to?*); (5) *comparison*, the amount of time needed to compare the validity of the response options (*D1, D2, D3, D4*); (6) *justification*, the amount of time needed to justify one answer as the best of the bunch (e.g., *D1*); and (7) *preparation-response*, the amount of time needed to prepare for problem solution and to respond.

Studies of reasoning need not use artificial formats. In one study, a colleague and I looked at predictions for everyday kinds of situations, such as when milk will spoil (Sternberg & Kalmar, 1997). In this study, the investigators looked at both predictions and postdictions (hypotheses about the past where information about the past is unknown) and found that postdictions took longer to make than did predictions.

Research on the components of human intelligence yielded some interesting results. Consider some examples. First, execution of early components (e.g., inference and mapping) tends exhaustively to consider the attributes of the stimuli, whereas execution of later components (e.g., application) tends to consider the attributes of the stimuli in self-terminating fashion, with only those attributes processed that are essential for reaching a solution (Sternberg, 1977). Second, in a study of the development of figural analogical reasoning, it was found that although children generally became quicker in information processing with age, not all components were executed more rapidly with age (Sternberg & Rifkin, 1979). The encoding component first showed a decrease in component time with age and then an increase. Apparently, older children realized that their best strategy was to spend more time in encoding the terms of a problem so that they later would be able to spend less time in operating on these encodings. A related, third finding was that better reasoners tend to spend relatively more time than do poorer reasoners in global, up-front metacomponential planning, when they solve difficult reasoning problems. Poorer reasoners, on the other hand, tend to spend relatively more time in local planning (Sternberg, 1981). Presumably, the better reasoners recognize that it is better to invest more time up front so as to be able to process a problem more efficiently later on. Fourth, it also was found in verbal analogical reasoning that, as children grew older, their strategies shifted so that they relied on word association less and abstract relations more (Sternberg & Nigro, 1980).

Some of the componential studies concentrated on knowledge-acquisition components rather than performance components or metacomponents. For example, in one set of studies, the investigators were interested in sources of individual differences in vocabulary (Sternberg & Powell, 1983; Sternberg, Powell, & Kaye, 1983; see also Sternberg, 1987a, 1987b). We were not content just to view these as individual differences in declarative knowledge because we wanted to understand why some people acquired this declarative knowledge and others did not. What we found is that there are multiple sources of individual and developmental differences. The three main sources were in knowledge-acquisition components, use of context clues, and use of mediating variables. For example, in the sentence, "The blen rises in the east and sets in the west," the knowledge-acquisition component of selective comparison is used to relate prior knowledge about a known concept, the sun, to the unknown word (neologism) in the sentence, "blen." Several context cues appear in the sentence, such as the fact that a blen rises, the fact that it sets, and the information about where it rises and sets. A mediating variable is that the information can occur after the presentation of the unknown word.

My colleagues and I did research such as that described above because we believed that conventional psychometric research sometimes incorrectly attributed individual and developmental differences. For example, a verbal analogies test that might appear on its surface to measure verbal reasoning might in fact measure primarily vocabulary and general information (Sternberg, 1977; Sternberg & Gardner, 1983). In fact, in some populations, reasoning might hardly be a source of individual or developmental differences at all. And if researchers then look at the sources of the individual differences in vocabulary, they would need to understand that the differences in knowledge did not come from nowhere: Some children had much more frequent and better opportunities to learn word meanings than did others.

In the componential-analysis work described above, correlations were computed between component scores of individuals and scores on tests of different kinds of psychometric abilities. First, in the studies of inductive reasoning (Sternberg, 1977; Sternberg & Gardner, 1982, 1983), it was found that although inference, mapping, application, comparison, and justification tended to correlate with such tests, the highest correlation typically was with the preparation-response component. This result was puzzling at first, because this component was estimated as the regression constant in the predictive regression equation. This result ended up giving birth to the concept of the metacomponents: higher order processes used to plan, monitor, and evaluate task performance. It was also found, second, that the correlations obtained for all the components showed convergent-discriminant validation: They tended to be significant with psychometric tests of reasoning but not with psychometric tests of perceptual speed (Sternberg, 1977; Sternberg & Gardner, 1983). Moreover, third, significant correlations with vocabulary tended to be obtained only for encoding of verbal stimuli (Sternberg, 1977, Sternberg & Gardner, 1983). Fourth, it was found in studies of linear-syllogistic reasoning (e.g., *John is taller than Mary; Mary is taller than Susan; who is tallest?*) that components of the proposed (mixed linguistic-spatial) model that were supposed to correlate with verbal ability did so and did not correlate with spatial ability; components that were supposed to correlate with spatial ability did so and did not correlate with verbal ability. In other words, it was possible successfully to validate the proposed model of linear-syllogistic reasoning not only in terms of the fit of response-time or error data to the predictions of the alternative models, but also in terms of the correlations of component scores with psychometric tests of verbal and spatial abilities (Sternberg, 1980a). Fifth and finally, it was found that there were individual differences in strategies in solving linear syllogisms, whereby some people used a largely linguistic model, others a largely spatial model, and most the proposed linguistic-spatial mixed model. Thus, sometimes less than perfect fit of a proposed model to group data may reflect individual differences in strategies among participants.

In more recent work, discussed in more detail later (Sternberg, 2009, 2010; Sternberg & Coffin, 2010; Sternberg & the Rainbow Project Collaborators, 2006), we have used analytical essays as well as multiple-choice items, for example, asking examinees to analyze a book or an idea. We have found, as have others, that almost all analytical tests tend to correlate highly with each other, although essays introduce some variation beyond what is found in multiple-choice assessments.

Creative Intelligence

Intelligence tests contain a range of problems, some of them more novel than others. In some of the componential work we have shown that when one goes beyond the range of unconventionality of the conventional tests of intelligence, one starts to tap sources of individual differences that are measured little or not at all by the tests. According to the theory of successful intelligence, creative intelligence is particularly well measured by problems assessing how well an individual can cope with relative novelty.

We presented 80 individuals with novel kinds of reasoning problems that had a single best answer. For example, they might be told that some objects are green and others blue; but still other objects might be grue, meaning green until the year 2000 and blue thereafter, or bleen, meaning blue until the year 2000 and green thereafter. Or they might be told of four kinds of people on the planet Kyron, blens, who are born young and die young; kwefs, who are born old and die old; balts, who are born young and die old; and prosses, who are born old and die young (Sternberg, 1982; Tetewsky & Sternberg, 1986). Their task was to predict future states from past states, given incomplete information. In another set of studies, 60 people were given more conventional kinds of inductive reasoning problems, such as analogies, series completions, and classifications, but they were told to solve them. However, the problems had premises preceding them that were either conventional (dancers wear shoes) or novel (dancers eat shoes). The participants had to solve the problems as though the counterfactuals were true (Sternberg & Gastel, 1989a, 1989b).

In these studies, we found that correlations with conventional kinds of tests depended on how novel or nonentrenched the conventional tests were. The more novel are the items, the higher are the correlations of our tests with scores on successively more novel conventional tests. Thus, the components isolated for relatively novel items would tend to correlate more highly with more unusual tests of fluid abilities (e.g., that of Cattell & Cattell, 1973) than with tests of crystallized abilities. We also found that when response times on the relatively novel problems were componentially analyzed, some components better measured the creative aspect of intelligence than did others. For example, in the "grue-bleen" task mentioned earlier, the information-processing component requiring people to switch from conventional green-blue thinking to grue-bleen thinking and then back to green-blue thinking again was a particularly good measure of the ability to cope with novelty.

In our original work with divergent reasoning problems having no one best answer, we asked 63 people to create various kinds of products (Lubart & Sternberg, 1995; Sternberg & Lubart, 1991, 1995, 1996) where an infinite variety of responses was possible. Individuals were asked to create products in the realms of writing, art, advertising, and science. In writing, they were asked to write very short stories for which we would give them a choice of titles, such as "Beyond the Edge" or "The Octopus's Sneakers." In art, the participants were asked to produce art compositions with titles such as "The Beginning of Time" or "Earth from an Insect's Point of View." In advertising, they were asked to produce advertisements for products such as a brand of bow tie or a brand of doorknob. In science, they were asked to solve problems such as one asking them how people might detect extraterrestrial aliens among us who are seeking to escape detection. Participants created two products in each domain.

We found, first, that creativity comprises the components proposed by Sternberg and Lubart's (1995) investment model of creativity: intelligence, knowledge, thinking styles, personality, and motivation. Second, we found that creativity is relatively although not wholly domain-specific. Correlations of ratings of the creative quality of the products across domains were lower than correlations of ratings within domains and generally were at about the .4 level. Thus, there was some degree of relation across domains, at the same time that there was plenty of room for someone to be strong in one or more domains but not in others. Third, we found a range of correlations of measures of creative performance with conventional tests of abilities. As was the case for the correlations obtained with convergent problems, correlations were higher to the extent that problems on the conventional tests were nonentrenched. For example, correlations were higher with fluid than with crystallized ability tests, and correlations were higher the more novel the fluid test was. These results suggest that tests of creative intelligence have some overlap with conventional tests (e.g., in requiring verbal skills or the ability to analyze one's own ideas – Sternberg & Lubart, 1995) but they also tap skills beyond those measured even by relatively novel kinds of items on the conventional tests of intelligence.

Practical Intelligence

Practical intelligence involves individuals applying their abilities to the kinds of problems that confront them in daily life, such as on the job or in the home. Practical intelligence involves applying the components of intelligence to experience so as to (1) adapt to, (2) shape, and (c) select environments. People differ in their balance of adaptation, shaping, and selection, and in the competence with which they balance among the three possible courses of action.

Much of our work on practical intelligence has centered on the concept of tacit knowledge. We have defined this construct as what one needs to know in order to work effectively in an environment that one is not explicitly taught and that often is not even verbalized (Sternberg et al., 2000; Sternberg & Hedlund, 2002; Sternberg & Wagner, 1993; Sternberg, Wagner, & Okagaki, 1993; Sternberg, Wagner, Williams, & Horvath, 1995; Wagner, 1987; Wagner & Sternberg, 1986; Williams et al., 2002). We represent tacit knowledge in the form of production systems, or sequences of "if-then" statements that describe procedures one follows in various kinds of everyday situations.

We typically have measured tacit knowledge using work-related situations that present problems one might encounter on the job. We have measured tacit knowledge for both children and adults, and among adults, for people in over two dozen occupations, such as management, sales, academia, teaching, school administration, secretarial work, and the military. In a typical tacit-knowledge problem, people are asked to read a story about a problem someone faces and to rate, for each statement in a set of statements, how adequate a solution the statement represents. For example, in a paper-and-pencil measure of tacit knowledge for sales, one of the problems deals with sales of photocopy machines. A relatively inexpensive machine is not moving out of the showroom and has become overstocked. The examinee is asked to rate the quality of various solutions for moving the particular model out of the showroom. In a performance-based measure for sales people, the test taker makes a phone call to a supposed customer, who is actually the examiner. The test taker tries to sell advertising space over the phone. The examiner raises various objections to buying the advertising space. The test taker is evaluated for the quality, rapidity, and fluency of the responses on the telephone.

In the tacit-knowledge studies, we have found, first, that practical intelligence as embodied in tacit knowledge increases with experience, but it is *profiting* from experience, rather than experience per se, that results in increases in scores. Some people can have been in a job for years and still have acquired relatively little tacit knowledge. Second, we also have found that subscores on tests of tacit knowledge – such as for managing oneself, managing others, and managing tasks – correlate significantly with each other. Third, scores on various tests of tacit knowledge, such as for academics and managers, are also correlated fairly substantially (at about the .5 level) with each other. Thus, fourth, tests of tacit knowledge may yield a general factor across these tests. However, fifth, scores on tacit-knowledge tests do not correlate with scores on conventional tests of intelligence, whether the measures used are single-score measures or multiple-ability batteries. Thus, any general factor from the tacit-knowledge tests is not the same as any general factor from tests of academic abilities (suggesting that neither kind of *g* factor is truly general, but rather, general only across a limited range of measuring instruments). Sixth, despite the lack of correlation of practical-intellectual with conventional measures, the scores on tacit-knowledge tests predict performance on the job as well as or better than do conventional psychometric intelligence tests. In one study done at the Center for Creative Leadership, we further found, seventh, that scores on our tests of tacit knowledge for management were the best single predictor of performance on a managerial simulation. In a hierarchical regression, scores on conventional tests of intelligence, personality, styles, and interpersonal orientation were entered first and scores on the test of tacit knowledge were entered last. Scores on the test of tacit knowledge were the single best predictor of managerial simulation score. Moreover, these scores also contributed significantly to the prediction even after everything else was entered first into the equation. In recent work on military leadership (Hedlund et al., 2003; Sternberg & Hedlund, 2002; Sternberg et al., 2000), it was found, eighth, that scores of 562 participants on tests of tacit knowledge for military leadership predicted ratings of leadership effectiveness, whereas scores on a conventional test of intelligence and on a tacit-knowledge test for managers did not significantly predict the ratings of effectiveness. In work with Eskimos (Grigorenko et al., 2004), it was found that low achievers in school can have exceptionally high practical adaptive skills at home.

We also have done studies of social intelligence, which is viewed in the theory of successful intelligence as a part of practical intelligence. In these studies, 40 individuals were presented with photos and were asked to make judgments about the photos. In one kind of photo, they were asked to evaluate whether a male-female couple was a genuine couple (i.e., really involved in a romantic relationship) or a phony couple posed by the experimenters. In another kind of photo, they were asked to indicate which of two individuals was the other's supervisor (Barnes & Sternberg, 1989; Sternberg & Smith, 1985). We found females to be superior to males on these tasks. Scores on the two tasks did not correlate with scores on conventional ability tests, nor did they correlate with each other, suggesting a substantial degree of domain specificity in the task.

Even stronger results have been obtained overseas. In a study in Usenge, Kenya, near the town of Kisumu, we were interested in school-age children's ability to adapt to their indigenous environment. We devised a test of practical intelligence for adaptation to the environment (see Sternberg & Grigorenko, 1997; Sternberg, Nokes, Geissler, Prince, Okatcha, Bundy, et al., 2001; see Sternberg, 2004, 2007 for more examples of cultural work relevant to the theory). The test of practical intelligence measured children's informal tacit knowledge for natural herbal medicines that the villagers believe can be used to fight various types of infections. Most villagers certainly believe in their efficacy, as shown by the fact that children in the villages use their knowledge of these medicines an average of once a week in medicating themselves and others. Thus, tests of how to use these medicines constitute effective measures of one aspect of practical intelligence as defined by the villagers as well as their life circumstances in their environmental contexts. Middle-class Westerners might find it quite a challenge to thrive or even survive in these contexts, or, for that matter, in the contexts of urban ghettos often not distant from their comfortable homes.

We measured the Kenyan children's ability to identify the medicines, where they come from, what they are used for, and what appropriate doses are. Based on work we had done elsewhere, we expected that scores on this test would not correlate with scores on conventional tests of intelligence. To test this hypothesis, we also administered to the 85 children the Raven Coloured Progressive Matrices Test, which is a measure of fluid or abstract-reasoning-based abilities, as well as the Mill Hill Vocabulary Scale, which is a measure of crystallized or formal-knowledge-based abilities. In addition, we gave the children a comparable test of vocabulary in their own Dholuo language. The Dholuo language is spoken in the home, English in the schools.

We did indeed find no correlation between the test of indigenous tacit knowledge and scores on the fluid-ability tests. But to our surprise, we found statistically significant correlations of the tacit-knowledge tests with the tests of crystallized abilities. The correlations, however, were *negative*. In other words, the higher the children scored on the test of tacit knowledge, the lower they scored, on average, on the tests of crystallized abilities. This surprising result can be interpreted in various ways, but based on the ethnographic observations of the anthropologists on the team, Geissler and Prince, the researchers concluded that a plausible scenario takes into account the expectations of families for their children.

Many children drop out of school before graduation, for financial or other reasons, and many families in the village do not particularly value formal Western schooling. There is no reason they should, as the children of many families will for the most part spend their lives farming or engaged in other occupations that make little or no use of Western schooling. These families emphasize teaching their children the indigenous informal knowledge that will lead to successful adaptation in the environments in which they will really live. Children who spend their time learning the indigenous practical knowledge of the community generally do not invest themselves heavily in doing well in school, whereas children who do well in school generally do not invest themselves as heavily in learning the indigenous knowledge – hence the negative correlations.

The Kenya study suggests that if we identify a general factor of human intelligence, this factor may tell us more about how abilities interact with patterns of schooling and especially Western patterns of schooling than it does about the structure of human abilities. In Western schooling, children typically study a variety of subject matters from an early age and thus develop skills in a variety of skill areas. This kind of schooling prepares the children to take a test of intelligence, which typically measures skills in a variety of areas. Often intelligence tests measure skills that children were expected to acquire a few years before taking the intelligence test. But as Rogoff (1990) and others have noted, this pattern of schooling is not universal and has not even been common for much of the history of humankind. Throughout history and in many places still, schooling, especially for boys, takes the form of apprenticeships in which children learn a craft from an early age. They learn what they will need to know to succeed in a trade, but not a lot more. They are not simultaneously engaged in tasks that require the development of the particular blend of skills measured by conventional intelligence tests. Hence it is less likely that one would observe a general factor in their scores, much as the investigators discovered in Kenya.

We have considered each of the aspects of intelligence separately. How do they fare when they are assessed together?

All Three Aspects of Intelligence Together

Internal-validity studies. Several separate factor-analytic studies support the internal validity of the theory of successful intelligence.

In one study (Sternberg, Grigorenko, Ferrari, & Clinkenbeard, 1999), we used the so-called Sternberg Triarchic Abilities Test (STAT – Sternberg, 1993) to investigate the internal validity of the theory. Three hundred twenty-six high school students, primarily from diverse parts of the United States, took the test, which comprised 12 subtests in all. There were four subtests each measuring analytical, creative, and practical abilities. For each type of ability, there were three multiple-choice tests and one essay test. The multiple-choice tests, in turn, involved, respectively, verbal, quantitative, and figural content. Consider the content of each test:

1. Analytical-Verbal: Figuring out meanings of neologisms (artificial words) from natural contexts. Students see a novel word embedded in a paragraph and have to infer its meaning from the context.

2. Analytical-Quantitative: Number series. Students have to say what number should come next in a series of numbers.
3. Analytical-Figural: Matrices. Students see a figural matrix with the lower right entry missing. They have to say which of the options fits into the missing space.
4. Practical-Verbal: Everyday reasoning. Students are presented with a set of everyday problems in the life of an adolescent and have to select the option that best solves each problem.
5. Practical-Quantitative: Everyday math. Students are presented with scenarios requiring the use of math in everyday life (e.g., buying tickets for a ballgame), and have to solve math problems based on the scenarios.
6. Practical-Figural: Route planning. Students are presented with a map of an area (e.g., an entertainment park) and have to answer questions about navigating effectively through the area depicted by the map.
7. Creative-Verbal: Novel analogies. Students are presented with verbal analogies preceded by counterfactual premises (e.g., money falls off trees). They have to solve the analogies as though the counterfactual premises were true.
8. Creative-Quantitative: Novel number operations. Students are presented with rules for novel number operations, for example, "flix," which involves numerical manipulations that differ as a function of whether the first of two operands is greater than, equal to, or less than the second. Participants have to use the novel number operations to solve presented math problems.
9. Creative-Figural: In each item, participants are first presented with a figural series that involves one or more transformations; they then have to apply the rule of the series to a new figure with a different appearance, and complete the new series.
10. Analytical-Essay: This essay requires students to analyze the use of security guards in high schools: What are the advantages and disadvantages and how can these be weighed to make a recommendation?
11. Practical-Essay: Give three practical solutions to a problem you are currently having in your life.
12. Creative-Essay: Describe the ideal school.

Confirmatory factor analysis on the data was supportive of the triarchic theory of human intelligence, yielding separate and uncorrelated analytical, creative, and practical factors. The lack of correlation was due to the inclusion of essay as well as multiple-choice subtests. Although multiple-choice tests tended to correlate substantially with multiple-choice tests, their correlations with essay tests were much weaker. The multiple-choice analytical subtest loaded most highly on the analytical factor, but the essay creative and practical subtests loaded most highly on their respective factors. Thus, measurement of creative and practical abilities probably ideally should be accomplished with other kinds of testing instruments that complement multiple-choice instruments.

In another study, conducted with 3,252 students in the United States, Finland, and Spain, we used the multiple-choice section of that STAT to compare five alternative models of intelligence, again via confirmatory factor analysis. A model featuring a general factor of intelligence fit the data relatively poorly. The triarchic model, allowing for intercorrelation among the analytic, creative, and practical factors, provided the best fit to the data (Sternberg, Castejón, Prieto, Hautakami, & Grigorenko, 2001).

In a further study, we (Grigorenko & Sternberg, 2001) tested 511 Russian schoolchildren (ranging in age from 8 to 17 years) as well as 490 mothers and 328 fathers of these children. We used entirely distinct measures of analytical, creative, and practical intelligence. Consider, for example, the tests used for adults. Similar tests were used for children.

Fluid analytical intelligence was measured by two subtests of a test of nonverbal intelligence. The *Test of g: Culture Fair, Level II* (Cattell & Cattell, 1973) is a test of fluid intelligence designed to reduce, as much as possible, the influence of verbal comprehension, culture, and educational level, although no test eliminates such influences totally. In the first subtest, *Series*, individuals were presented with an incomplete, progressive series of figures. The participants' task was to select, from among the choices provided, the answer that best continued the series. In the *Matrices* subtest, the task was to complete the matrix presented at the left of each row.

The test of crystallized intelligence was adapted from existing traditional tests of analogies and synonyms/antonyms used in Russia. We used adaptations of Russian rather than American tests because the vocabulary used in Russia differs from that used in the United States. The first part of the test included 20 verbal analogies (KR20 = 0.83). An example is *circle – ball = square–? (a) quadrangular, (b) figure, (c) rectangular, (d) solid, (e) cube*. The second part included 30 pairs of words, and the participants' task was to specify whether the words in the pair were synonyms or antonyms (KR20 = 0.74). Examples are *latent–hidden*, and *systematic–chaotic*.

The measure of creative intelligence also comprised two parts. The first part asked the participants to describe the world through the eyes of insects. The second part asked participants to describe who might live and what might happen on a planet called "Primliava." No additional information on the nature of the planet was specified. Each part of the test was scored in three different ways to yield three different scores. The first score was for originality (novelty); the second was for the amount of development in the plot (quality); and the third was for creative use of prior knowledge in these relatively novel kinds of tasks (sophistication). The measure of practical intelligence was self-report and also comprised two parts. The first part was designed as a 20-item, self-report instrument, assessing practical skills in the social domain (e.g., effective and successful communication with other people), in the family domain (e.g., how to fix household items, how to run the family budget), and in the domain of effective resolution of sudden problems (e.g., organizing something that has become chaotic). The second part had four vignettes, based on themes that appeared in popular Russian magazines in the context of discussion of adaptive skills in the current society. The four themes were, respectively, how to maintain the value of one's savings, what to do when one makes a purchase and discovers that the item one has purchased is broken, how to locate medical assistance in a time of need, and how to manage a salary bonus one has received for outstanding work. Each vignette was accompanied by five choices and participants had to select the best one. Obviously, there is no one "right" answer in this type of situation. Hence Grigorenko and Sternberg used the most frequently chosen response as the keyed answer. To the extent that this response was suboptimal, this suboptimality would work against the researchers in subsequent analyses relating scores on this test to other predictor and criterion measures.

In this study, exploratory principal-component analysis for responses of both children and adults yielded very similar factor structures. Both varimax and oblimin rotations yielded clear-cut analytical, creative, and practical factors for the tests. Thus, a sample of a different nationality (Russian), a different set of tests, and a different method of analysis (exploratory rather than confirmatory analysis) again supported the theory of successful intelligence.

The analytical, creative, and practical tests the investigators employed were used to predict mental and physical health among the Russian adults. Mental health was measured by widely used paper-and-pencil tests of depression and anxiety, and physical health was measured by self-report. The best predictor of mental and physical health was the practical-intelligence measure. Analytical intelligence came second, and creative intelligence came third. All three contributed to prediction, however. Thus, the researchers again concluded that a theory of intelligence encompassing all three elements provides better prediction of success in life than does a theory comprising just the analytical element.

External validity studies. We have also looked at the external validity of tests assessing successful intelligence.

The Rainbow Project. In a study supported by the College Board (Sternberg & the Rainbow Project Collaborators, 2006), we used an expanded set of tests on 1,015 students at 15 different institutions (13 colleges and 2 high schools). Our goal was not to replace the SAT but to devise tests that would supplement the SAT, measuring skills that this test does not measure. In addition to the multiple-choice STAT tests described earlier, we used three additional measures of creative skills and three of practical skills:

Creative skills. The three additional tests were as follows:

1. *Cartoons*. Participants were given five cartoons purchased from the archives of the *New Yorker*, but with the caption removed. The participant's task was to choose three cartoons and to provide a caption for each cartoon. Two trained judges rated all the cartoons for cleverness, humor, and originality. A combined creativity score was formed by summing the individual ratings on each dimension.
2. *Written Stories*. Participants were asked to write two stories, spending about 15 minutes on each, choosing from the following titles: "A Fifth Chance," "2983," "Beyond the Edge," "The Octopus's Sneakers," "It's Moving Backwards," and "Not Enough Time." A team of four judges was trained to rate the stories for originality, complexity, emotional evocativeness, and descriptiveness. These stories were based on work originally done to measure creativity (Sternberg & Lubart, 1995), described in more detail later.
3. *Oral Stories*. Participants were presented with five sheets of paper, each containing a set of pictures linked by a common theme. For example, participants might receive a sheet of paper with images of a musical theme, a money theme, or a travel theme. The participant then chose one of the pages and was given 15 minutes to formulate a short story and dictate it into a cassette recorder. The dictation period was not to be more than five minutes long. The process was then repeated with another sheet of images so that each participant dictated a total of two oral stories. Six judges were trained to rate the stories for originality, complexity, emotional evocativeness, and descriptiveness.

Practical skills. The three additional tests were as follows:

1. *Everyday Situational Judgment Inventory (Movies)*. This video-based inventory presents participants with seven brief vignettes that capture problems encountered in general, everyday life, such as determining what to do when one is asked to write a letter of recommendation for someone one does not know particularly well.
2. *Common Sense Questionnaire*. This written inventory presents participants with 15 vignettes that capture problems encountered in general business-related situations, such as managing tedious tasks or handling a competitive work situation.
3. *College Life Questionnaire*. This written inventory presents participants with 15 vignettes that capture problems encountered in general college-related situations, such as handling trips to the bursar's office or dealing with a difficult roommate.

We found that our tests significantly and substantially improved upon the validity of the SAT for predicting first-year college grades (Sternberg & the Rainbow Project Collaborators, 2006). The test also improved equity: Using the test to admit a class would result in greater ethnic diversity than would using just the SAT or just the SAT and grade-point average.

The Kaleidoscope Project. The Kaleidoscope Project (2009, 2010; Sternberg & Coffin, 2010) has been used over the past four years to admit undergraduate students to Tufts University. Each year, all 15,000+ applicants are given a selection of essays assessing analytical, creative, practical, and also wisdom-based skills. The applicants have the option of completing one of the essays, and then the analytical, creative, practical, and wisdom-based skills demonstrated through these essays and other aspects of the application are rated.

The exact Kaleidoscope prompts vary from year to year. Here are sample exercises used for the 2009 admissions cycle:

1. Since the silent movies of the 1920s first flickered on the screen, the medium of film has inspired, provoked, entertained, and educated. Select a film whose message or imagery resonated with you long after the credits rolled. How did it capture your imagination or affect your consciousness? [primarily analytical]
2. Engineers and scientists like astronomer Edwin Powell Hubble discover new solutions to contemporary issues. "Equipped with his five senses," Hubble said, "man explores the universe around him and calls the adventure Science." Using your knowledge of scientific principles, identify "an adventure" in science you would like to pursue and tell us how you would investigate it. [primarily creative]
3. The human narrative is replete with memorable characters like America's Johnny Appleseed, ancient Greece's Perseus or the Fox Spirits of East Asia. Imagine one of humanity's storied figures is alive and working in the world today. Why does Joan of Arc have a desk job? Would Shiva be a general or a diplomat? Is Quetzalcoatl trapped in a zoo? In short, connect your chosen figure to the contemporary world and imagine the life he/she/it might lead. [primarily creative]
4. Use an 8.5 × 11 inch sheet of paper to create something. You can blueprint your future home, create a new product, draw a cartoon strip, design a costume or a theatrical set, compose a score or do something entirely different. Let your imagination wander. [primarily creative]
5. Use one of the following topics to create a short story:
   a. The Spam Filter
   b. Seventeen Minutes Ago . . .
   c. Two by Two
   d. Facebook
   e. Now There's the Rub . . .
   f. No Whip Half-Caf Latte
   g. The Eleventh Commandment [primarily creative]
6. The 44th president of the United States will be inaugurated on January 20, 2009. If the 2008 presidential primaries were an indicator, young voters will have had a substantial voice in the selection of the next American president. Offer an open letter to the new president: what issue would you like to see addressed in the first 100 days of the new administration. Why does this matter to you? [primarily practical and wisdom]

Note that the questions differ in the skills they emphasize. No question is a "pure" measure of any single component of successful intelligence. Scoring of the exercises is holistic and is completed by admissions officers using rubrics with which they are provided by the Center for the Psychology of Abilities, Competencies, and Expertise at Tufts (PACE Center). We have found that, with training, admissions officers can achieve good interrater reliability (consistency) in their evaluations.

The early results at Tufts illustrate that a highly selective college can introduce an "unconventional" exercise into its undergraduate admissions process without disrupting the quality of the entering class. It is important to underscore the point that academic achievement has always been and remains the most important dimension of Tufts' undergraduate admissions process. Since we introduced the Kaleidoscope pilot in 2006, applications have remained roughly steady or increased slightly, and the mean SAT scores of accepted and enrolling students increased to new highs. In addition, we have not detected statistically meaningful ethnic group differences on the Kaleidoscope measures. Controlling for the academic rating given to applicants by admissions officers (which combines information from the transcript and standardized tests), students rated for Kaleidoscope achieved significantly higher academic averages in their undergraduate work than students who were not so rated by the admissions staff. In addition, research found that students with higher Kaleidoscope ratings were more involved in, and reported getting more out of, extracurricular, active-citizenship and leadership activities in their first year at Tufts.

The positive effects of Kaleidoscope on the university's undergraduate applicant pool and enrolled class should not be disentangled from the effects of other initiatives, especially increased undergraduate financial aid – which at Tufts is always need-based. Initiatives like Kaleidoscope can help identify an able, diverse group of students but, without adequate financial aid and university commitment, the effects of the program will not be fully shown in actual matriculation figures.

In sum, as Tufts seeks to identify and develop new leaders for a changing world, Kaleidoscope provides a vehicle to help identify the potential leaders who may be best positioned to make a positive and meaningful difference to the world in the future. In the fast-paced, data-driven atmosphere of highly competitive college admissions, Kaleidoscope validates the role of qualitative measures of student ability and excellence.

Instruction for Successful Intelligence

Instructional studies are a further means of testing the theory (Sternberg, Grigorenko, & Zhang, 2008; Sternberg, Jarvin, & Grigorenko, 2009). We have used instruction both in cognitive skills, in general, and in academic skills, in particular.

Cognitive Skills

The kinds of analytical, creative, and practical abilities discussed in this chapter are not fixed, but rather, modifiable. They are essentially cognitive skills (Sternberg & Pretz, 2005).

Analytical skills can be taught. For example, in one study, I (Sternberg, 1987a) tested whether it is possible to teach people to improve their skills in decontextualizing the meanings of unknown words presented in context. In one study, I gave 81 participants in five conditions a pretest on their ability to decontextualize word meanings. Then the participants were divided into five conditions, two of which were control conditions that lacked formal instruction. In one condition, participants were not given any instructional treatment. They were merely asked later to take a posttest. In a second condition, they were given practice as an instructional condition, but there was no formal instruction, per se. In a third condition, they were taught knowledge-acquisition component processes that could be used to decontextualize word meanings. In a fourth condition, they were taught to use context cues. In a fifth condition, they were taught to use mediating variables. Participants in all three of the theory-based formal-instructional conditions outperformed participants in the two control conditions, whose performance did not differ. In other words, theory-based instruction was better than no instruction at all or just practice without formal instruction.

Creative-thinking skills also can be taught, and a program has been devised for teaching them (Sternberg & Williams, 1996; see also Sternberg & Grigorenko, 2007; Sternberg, Jarvin, & Grigorenko, 2009). In some relevant work, the investigators divided 86 gifted and nongifted fourth-grade children into experimental and control groups. All children took pretests on insightful thinking. Then some of the children received their regular school instruction whereas others received instruction on insight skills. After the instruction of whichever kind, all children took a posttest on insight skills. We found that children taught how to solve the insight problems using knowledge-acquisition components gained more from pretest to posttest than did students who were not so taught (Davidson & Sternberg, 1984).

Practical-intelligence skills also can be taught. We have developed a program for teaching practical intellectual skills, aimed at middle-school students, that explicitly teaches students "practical intelligence for school" in the contexts of doing homework, taking tests, reading, and writing (Gardner, Krechevsky, Sternberg, & Okagaki, 1994; Williams et al., 1996; Williams et al., 2002). We have evaluated the program in a variety of settings (Gardner et al., 1994; Sternberg, Okagaki, & Jackson, 1990) and found that students taught via the program outperform students in control groups that did not receive the instruction.

Individuals' use of practical intelligence can be to their own gain in addition to or instead of the gain of others. People can be practically intelligent for themselves at the expense of others. It is for this reason that wisdom needs to be studied in its own right in addition to practical or even successful intelligence (Baltes & Staudinger, 2000; Sternberg, 1998b).

In sum, practical intelligence, like analytical intelligence, is an important antecedent of life success. Because measures of practical intelligence predict everyday behavior at about the same level as do measures of analytical intelligence (and sometimes even better), the sophisticated use of such tests roughly could double the explained variance in various kinds of criteria of success. Using measures of creative intelligence as well might increase prediction still more. Thus, tests based on the construct of successful intelligence might take us to new and higher levels of prediction. At the same time, expansions of conventional tests that stay within the conventional framework of analytical tests based on standard psychometric models do not seem likely greatly to expand our predictive capabilities (Schmidt & Hunter, 1998).

We view intelligence as a form of developing expertise (Sternberg, 1998a, 1999a, 2003a). Indeed, some of our tests may seem more like tests of achievement or of developing expertise (see Ericsson, 1996; Howe, Davidson, & Sloboda, 1998) than of intelligence. But it can be argued that intelligence is itself a form of developing expertise – that there is no clear-cut distinction between the two constructs (Sternberg, 1998a, 1999a). Indeed, all measures of intelligence, one might argue, measure a form of developing expertise. And expertise can actually undermine creative thinking in some cases (Frensch & Sternberg, 1989).

An example of how tests of intelligence measure developing expertise emanates from work we have done in Tanzania. A study done in Tanzania (see Sternberg & Grigorenko, 1997; Sternberg, Grigorenko, et al., 2002) points out the risks of giving tests, scoring them, and interpreting the results as measures of some latent intellectual ability or abilities. We administered to 358 school children between the ages of 11 and 13 years near Bagamoyo, Tanzania, tests including a form-board classification test, a linear syllogisms test, and a Twenty Questions Test, which measure the kinds of skills required on conventional tests of intelligence. Of course, we obtained scores that could be analyzed and evaluated, ranking the children in terms of their supposed general or other abilities. However, we administered the tests dynamically rather than statically (Brown & Ferrara, 1985; Budoff, 1968; Day, Engelhardt, Maxwell, & Bolig, 1997; Feuerstein, 1979; Grigorenko & Sternberg, 1998; Guthke, 1993; Haywood & Tzuriel, 1992; Lidz, 1987, 1991; Sternberg & Grigorenko, 2002a; Tzuriel, 1995; Vygotsky, 1978). Dynamic testing is like conventional static testing in that individuals are tested and inferences about their abilities are made. But dynamic tests differ in that children are given some kind of feedback to help them improve their scores. Vygotsky

(1978) suggested that the children's ability to profit from the guided instruction they received during the testing session could serve as a measure of children's zone of proximal development (ZPD), or the difference between their developed abilities and their latent capacities. In other words, testing and instruction are treated as being of one piece rather than as being distinct processes.

This integration makes sense in terms of traditional definitions of intelligence as the ability to learn ("Intelligence and Its Measurement," 1921; Sternberg & Detterman, 1986). What a dynamic test does is directly measure processes of learning in the context of testing rather than measuring these processes indirectly as the product of past learning. Such measurement is especially important when not all children have had equal opportunities to learn in the past.

In our assessments, children were first given the ability tests. In an experimental group, they then were given a brief period of instruction in which they were able to learn skills that would potentially enable them to improve their scores. In a control group, they were not given this intervention. Then they were tested again. Because the instruction for each test lasted only about 5–10 minutes, one would not expect dramatic gains. Yet, on average, the gains were statistically significant in the experimental group, and statistically greater than in the control group. In the control group, pretest and posttest scores correlated at the .8 level. In the experimental group, however, scores on the pretest showed only weak although significant correlations with scores on the posttest. These correlations, at about the .3 level, suggested that when tests are administered statically to children in developing countries, they may be rather unstable and easily subject to influences of training. The reason could be that the children are not accustomed to taking Western-style tests, and so profit quickly even from small amounts of instruction as to what is expected from them. Of course, the more important question is not whether the scores changed or even correlated with each other, but rather how they correlated with other cognitive measures. In other words, which test was a better predictor of transfer to other cognitive performance, the pretest score or the posttest score? We found the posttest score to be the better predictor.

Academic Skills

Several sets of studies investigated instruction for academic skills. Four sets are briefly described here.

In a first set of studies, researchers explored the question of whether conventional education in school systematically discriminates against children with creative and practical strengths (Sternberg & Clinkenbeard, 1995; Sternberg, Ferrari, Clinkenbeard, & Grigorenko, 1996; Sternberg, Grigorenko, Ferrari, & Clinkenbeard, 1999). Motivating this work was the belief that the systems in most schools strongly tend to favor children with strengths in memory and analytical abilities. However, schools can be unbalanced in other directions as well. One school Elena Grigorenko and I visited in Russia in 2000 placed a heavy emphasis upon the development of creative abilities – much more so than on the development of analytical and practical abilities. While on this trip, we were told of yet another school – catering to the children of Russian businessmen – that strongly emphasized practical abilities, and in which children who were not practically oriented were told that, eventually, they would be working for their classmates who were practically oriented.

The investigators used the Sternberg Triarchic Abilities Test, as described earlier, in some of our instructional work. The test was administered to 326 children around the United States and in some other countries who were identified by their schools as gifted by any standard whatsoever. Children were selected for a summer program in (college-level) psychology if they fell into one of five ability groupings: high analytical, high creative, high practical, high balanced (high in all three abilities), or low balanced (low in all three abilities). Students who came to Yale were then divided into four instructional groups. Students in all four instructional groups used the same introductory-psychology textbook (a preliminary version of Sternberg [1995]) and listened to the same psychology lectures. What differed among them was the type of afternoon discussion section to which they were assigned. They were assigned to an instructional condition that emphasized memory, analytical, creative, or practical instruction. For example, in the memory condition, they might be asked to describe the main tenets of a major theory of depression. In the analytical condition, they might be asked to compare and contrast two theories of depression. In the creative condition, they might be asked to formulate their own theory of depression. In the practical condition, they might be asked how they could use what they had learned about depression to help a friend who was depressed.

Students in all four instructional conditions were evaluated in terms of their performance on homework, a midterm exam, a final exam, and an independent project. Each type of work was evaluated for memory, analytical, creative, and practical quality. Thus, all students were evaluated in exactly the same way.

Our results suggested the utility of the theory of successful intelligence. This utility showed itself in several ways.

First, we observed when the students arrived at Yale that the students in the high-creative and high-practical groups were much more diverse in terms of racial, ethnic, socioeconomic, and educational backgrounds than were the students in the high-analytical group, suggesting that correlations of measured intelligence with status variables such as these may be reduced by using a broader conception of intelligence. Thus, the kinds of students identified as strong differed in terms of populations from which they were drawn in comparison with students identified as strong solely by analytical measures. More important, just by expanding the range of abilities measured, the investigators discovered intellectual strengths that might not have been apparent through a conventional test.

Second, we found that all three ability tests – analytical, creative, and practical – significantly predicted course performance. When multiple-regression analysis was used, at least two of these ability measures contributed significantly to the prediction of each of the measures of achievement. Perhaps as a reflection of the difficulty of deemphasizing the analytical way of teaching, one of the significant predictors was always the analytical score. (However, in a replication of our study with low-income African American students from New York, Deborah Coates of the City University of New York found a different pattern of results. Her data indicated that the practical tests were better predictors of course performance than were the analytical measures, suggesting that which ability test predicts which criterion depends on population as well as mode of teaching.)

Third and most important, there was an aptitude-treatment interaction whereby students who were placed in instructional conditions that better matched their pattern of abilities outperformed students who were mismatched. In other words, when students are taught in a way that fits how they think, they do better in school. Children with creative and practical abilities, who are almost never taught or assessed in a way that matches their pattern of abilities, may be at a disadvantage in course after course, year after year.

A follow-up study (Sternberg, Torff, & Grigorenko, 1998a, 1998b) examined learning of social studies and science by third-graders and eighth-graders. The 225 third-graders were students in a very low income neighborhood in Raleigh, North Carolina. The 142 eighth-graders were students who were largely middle to upper middle class studying in Baltimore, Maryland, and Fresno, California. In this study, students were assigned to one of three instructional conditions. In the first condition, they were taught the course that basically they would have learned had there been no intervention. The emphasis in the course was on memory. In a second condition, students were taught in a way that emphasized critical (analytical) thinking. In the third condition, they were taught in a way that emphasized analytical, creative, and practical thinking. All students' performance was assessed for memory learning (through multiple-choice assessments) as well as for analytical, creative, and practical learning (through performance assessments).

As expected, students in the successful-intelligence (analytical, creative, practical) condition outperformed the other students in terms of the performance assessments. One could argue that this result merely reflected the way they were taught. Nevertheless, the result suggested that teaching for these kinds of thinking succeeded. More important, however, was the result that children in the successful-intelligence condition outperformed the other children even on the multiple-choice memory tests. In other words, to the extent that one's goal is just to maximize children's memory for information, teaching for successful intelligence is still superior. It enables children to capitalize on their strengths and to correct or to compensate for their weaknesses, and it allows children to encode material in a variety of interesting ways.

We extended these results to reading curricula at the middle school and the high school level. In a study of 871 middle school students and 432 high school students, we taught reading either triarchically or through the regular curriculum. At the middle school level, reading was taught explicitly. At the high school level, reading was infused into instruction in mathematics, physical sciences, social sciences, English, history, foreign languages, and the arts. In all settings, students who were taught triarchially substantially outperformed students who were taught in standard ways (Grigorenko, Jarvin, & Sternberg, 2002).

The largest scale study, described in Sternberg, Grigorenko, and Zhang (2007), was conducted with 196 teachers and 7,702 students. The study spanned 4 years, 9 states, 14 school districts, and 110 schools. It showed that, with many thousands of fourth-graders, it was possible to obtain gains in fourth-grade reading and mathematics that were greater for triarchic instruction for critical thinking or memory. This study suggested that triarchic instruction can be "scaled up" to reach children across a wide variety of geographic areas as well as subject matter areas.

Thus the results of these sets of studies suggest that the theory of successful intelligence is valid as a whole. Moreover, the results suggest that the theory can make a difference not only in laboratory tests but in school classrooms and even the everyday life of adults as well.

Conclusions

This chapter has presented the theory of successful intelligence. Some psychologists believe the theory departs too much from the conventional theory of general intelligence proposed by Spearman (1904): Some disagree with parts of the theory (e.g., Brody, 2003a, 2003b) and some disagree with the whole thing, vehemently (Gottfredson, 2003a, 2003b). Others believe the theory does not depart from conventional *g* theory enough (Gardner, 1983, 2006). Still others have theories that are more compatible, in spirit, with that proposed here, at least for intelligence (Ceci, 1996). The theory is rather newer than that of, say, Spearman (1904), and has much less work to support is, as well as a lesser range of empirical support. I doubt the theory is wholly correct – scientific theories so far have not been – but I hope at the same time it serves as a broader basis for future theories than, perhaps, Spearman's theory of general intelligence. No doubt, there will be those who wish to preserve this and related older theories, and those who will continue to do research that replicates hundreds and thousands of time that so-called general intelligence does indeed matter for success in many aspects of life. I agree. At the same time, I suspect it is not sufficient, and also, that those who keep replicating endlessly the findings of the past are unlikely to serve as the positive intellectual leaders of the future. But only time will tell.

The educational system in the United States, as in many other countries, places great emphasis on instruction and assessments that tap into two important skills: memory and analysis. Students who are adept at these two skills tend to profit from the educational system because the ability tests, instruction, and achievement tests we use all largely measure products and processes emanating from these two kinds of skills. There is a problem, however – namely, that children whose strengths are in other kinds of skills may be shortchanged by this system. These children might learn and test well if only they were given an opportunity to play to their strengths rather than their weaknesses.

As a society, we can create a closed system that advantages only certain types of children and that disadvantages other types. Children who excel in memory and analytical abilities may end up doing well on ability tests and achievement tests, and hence find the doors of opportunity open to them. Children who excel in other abilities may end up doing poorly on the tests and find the doors shut. By treating children with alternative patterns of abilities as losers, we may end up creating harmful self-fulfilling prophecies.

Institutions should consider pooling their resources and developing a common model and common methods of assessment. By working separately, they fail to leverage their strengths and to share information regarding the best ways to make decisions. In essence, each institution "reinvents the wheel." A consortium would be far more powerful than each institution working on its own. Successful intelligence is one model such a consortium might use. Doubtless there are many others. The important thing is to work together toward a common good – toward devising the best ways to select students so as to maximize their positive future impact. We all wish our intellectual leaders to show wisdom. We ourselves need to do the same.

By the way, regarding my mother's comment that I lack common sense, which I told you about at the beginning of this article: Please don't tell her I told you!

References

Baltes, P. B., & Staudinger, U. M (2000). Wisdom: A metaheuristic (pragmatic) to orchestrate mind and virtue toward excellence. *American Psychologist*, 55, 122–135.

Barnes, M. L., & Sternberg, R. J. (1989). Social intelligence and decoding of nonverbal cues. *Intelligence*, 13, 263–287.

Boring, E. G. (1923, June 6). Intelligence as the tests test it. *New Republic*, 35–37.

Brody, N. (2003a). What Sternberg should have concluded. *Intelligence*, 31(4) 339–342.

Brody, N. (2003b). Construct validation of the Sternberg Triarchic abilities test: Comment and reanalysis. *Intelligence*, 31(4), 319–329.

Brown, A. L., & Ferrara, R. A. (1985). Diagnosing zones of proximal development. In J. V. Wertsch (Ed.), *Culture, communication, and cognition: Vygotskian perspectives*, (pp. 273–305). New York, NY: Cambridge University Press.

Budoff, M. (1968). Learning potential as a supplementary assessment procedure. In J. Hellmuth (Ed.), *Learning disorders* (Vol. 3, pp. 295–343). Seattle, WA: Special Child.

Carroll, J. B. (1993). *Human cognitive abilities: A survey of factor-analytic studies*. New York, NY: Cambridge University Press.

Cattell, R. B. (1971). *Abilities: Their structure, growth and action*. Boston, MA: Houghton Mifflin.

Cattell, R. B., & Cattell, H. E. P. (1973). *Measuring intelligence with the Culture Fair Tests*. Champaign, IL: Institute for Personality and Ability Testing.

Ceci, S. J. (1996). *On intelligence* (rev. and exp. ed.). Cambridge, MA: Harvard University Press.

Davidson, J. E., & Sternberg, R. J. (1984). The role of insight in intellectual giftedness. *Gifted Child Quarterly*, 28, 58–64.

Day, J. D., Engelhardt, J. L., Maxwell, S. E., & Bolig, E. E. (1997). Comparison of static and dynamic assessment procedures and their relation to independent performance. *Journal of Educational Psychology*, 89(2), 358–368.

Dewey, J. (1933). *How we think*. Boston, MA: Heath.

Ericsson, K. A. (Ed.). (1996). *The road to excellence*. Mahwah, NJ: Erlbaum.

Feuerstein, R. (1979). *The dynamic assessment of retarded performers: The learning potential assessment device theory, instruments, and techniques* Baltimore, MD: University Park Press.

Frensch, P. A., & Sternberg, R. J. (1989). Expertise and intelligent thinking: When is it worse to know better? In R. J. Sternberg (Ed.), *Advances in the psychology of human intelligence* (Vol. 5, pp. 157–188). Hillsdale, NJ: Erlbaum.

Gardner, H. (1983). *Frames of mind: The theory of multiple intelligences*. New York, NY: Basic.

Gardner, H. (2006). *Multiple intelligences: New horizons in theory and practice*. New York, NY: Basic.

Gardner, H., Krechevsky, M., Sternberg, R. J., & Okagaki, L. (1994). Intelligence in context: Enhancing students' practical intelligence for school. In K. McGilly (Ed.), *Classroom lessons: Integrating cognitive theory and classroom practice* (pp. 105–127). Cambridge, MA: MIT Press.

Gottfredson, L. S. (2003a). Discussion: On Sternberg's "Reply to Gottfredson." *Intelligence*, **31**(4), 415–424.

Gottfredson, L. S. (2003b). Dissecting practical intelligence theory: Its claims and evidence. *Intelligence*, **31**(4), 343–397.

Grigorenko, E. L., Jarvin, L., & Sternberg, R. J. (2002). School-based tests of the triarchic theory of intelligence: Three settings, three samples, three syllabi. *Contemporary Educational Psychology*, **27**, 167–208.

Grigorenko, E. L., Meier, E., Lipka, J., Mohatt, G., Yanez, E., & Sternberg, R. J. (2004). Academic and practical intelligence: A case study of the Yup'ik in Alaska. *Learning and Individual Differences*, **14**, 183–207.

Grigorenko, E. L., & Sternberg, R. J. (1998). Dynamic testing. *Psychological Bulletin*, **124**, 75–111.

Grigorenko, E. L., & Sternberg, R. J. (2001). Analytical, creative, and practical intelligence as predictors of self-reported adaptive functioning: A case study in Russia. *Intelligence*, **29**, 57–73.

Guthke, J. (1993). Current trends in theories and assessment of intelligence. In J. H. M. Hamers, K. Sijtsma, & A. J. J. M. Ruijssenaars (Eds.), *Learning potential assessment* (pp. 13–20). Amsterdam, the Netherlands: Swets & Zeitlinger.

Guyote, M. J., & Sternberg, R. J. (1981). A transitive-chain theory of syllogistic reasoning. *Cognitive Psychology*, **13**, 461–525.

Haywood, H. C., & Tzuriel, D. (1992). Epilogue: The status and future of interactive assessment. In H. C. Haywood & D. Tzuriel (Eds.), *Interactive assessment* (pp. 38–63). New York, NY: Springer-Verlag.

Hedlund, J., Forsythe, G. B., Horvath, J. A., Williams, W. M., Snook, S., & Sternberg, R. J. (2003). Identifying and assessing tacit knowledge: Understanding the practical intelligence of military leaders. *Leadership Quarterly*, **14**, 117–140.

Howe, M. J., Davidson, J. W., & Sloboda, J. A (1998). Innate talents: Reality or myth? *Behavioral & Brain Sciences*, **21**, 399–442.

"Intelligence and its measurement": A symposium (1921). *Journal of Educational Psychology*, **12**, 123–147, 195–216, 271–275.

Jensen, A. R. (1998). *The g factor: The science of mental ability*. Westport, CT: Praeger/Greenwoood.

Lidz, C. S. (Ed.). (1987). *Dynamic assessment*. New York, NY: Guilford Press.

Lidz, C. S. (1991). *Practitioner's guide to dynamic assessment*. New York, NY: Guilford Press.

Lubart, T. I., & Sternberg, R. J. (1995). An investment approach to creativity: Theory and data. In S. M. Smith, T. B. Ward, & R. A. Finke (Eds.), *The creative cognition approach*. Cambridge, MA: MIT Press.

Okagaki, L., & Sternberg, R. J. (1993). Parental beliefs and children's school performance. *Child Development*, **64**(1), 36–56.

Rogoff, B. (1990). *Apprenticeship in thinking. Cognitive development in social context*. New York, NY: Oxford University Press.

Schmidt, F. L., & Hunter, J. E. (1998). The validity and utility of selection methods in personnel psychology: Practical and theoretical implications of 85 years of research findings. *Psychological Bulletin*, **124**, 262–274.

Spearman, C. (1904). "General intelligence," objectively determined and measured. *American Journal of Psychology*, **15**(2), 201–293.

Spearman, C. (1927). *The abilities of man*. London, UK: Macmillan.

Sternberg, R. J. (1977). *Intelligence, information processing, and analogical reasoning: The componential analysis of human abilities*. Hillsdale, NJ: Erlbaum.

Sternberg, R. J. (1980a). Representation and process in linear syllogistic reasoning. *Journal of Experimental Psychology: General*, **109**, 119–159.

Sternberg, R. J. (1980b). Sketch of a componential subtheory of human intelligence. *Behavioral and Brain Sciences*, **3**, 573–584.

Sternberg, R. J. (1981). Intelligence and nonentrenchment. *Journal of Educational Psychology*, **73**, 1–16.

Sternberg, R. J. (1982). Natural, unnatural, and supernatural concepts. *Cognitive Psychology, 14*, 451–488.
Sternberg, R. J. (1983). Components of human intelligence. *Cognition, 15*, 1–48.
Sternberg, R. J. (1984). Toward a triarchic theory of human intelligence. *Behavioral and Brain Sciences, 7*, 269–287.
Sternberg, R. J. (1985a). *Beyond IQ: A triarchic theory of human intelligence*. New York, NY: Cambridge University Press.
Sternberg, R. J. (1985b). Implicit theories of intelligence, creativity, and wisdom. *Journal of Personality and Social Psychology, 49*(3), 607–627.
Sternberg, R. J. (1987a). Most vocabulary is learned from context. In M. G. McKeown & M. E. Curtis (Eds.), *The nature of vocabulary acquisition* (pp. 89–105). Hillsdale, NJ: Erlbaum.
Sternberg, R. J. (1987b). The psychology of verbal comprehension. In R. Glaser (Ed.), *Advances in instructional psychology* (Vol. 3, pp. 97–151). Hillsdale, NJ: Erlbaum.
Sternberg, R. J. (1990a). *Metaphors of mind*. New York, NY: Cambridge University Press.
Sternberg, R. J. (1990b). Understanding wisdom. In R. J. Sternberg (Ed.), *Wisdom: Its nature, origins, and development* (pp. 3–9). New York, NY: Cambridge University Press.
Sternberg, R. J. (1993). *Sternberg Triarchic Abilities Test*. Unpublished test.
Sternberg, R. J. (1995). *In search of the human mind*. Orlando, FL: Harcourt Brace College.
Sternberg, R. J. (1997). *Successful intelligence*. New York, NY: Plume.
Sternberg, R. J. (1998a). Abilities are forms of developing expertise. *Educational Researcher, 27*, 11–20.
Sternberg, R. J. (1998b). A balance theory of wisdom. *Review of General Psychology, 2*, 347–365.
Sternberg, R. J. (1998c). Metacognition, abilities, and developing expertise: What makes an expert student? *Instructional Science, 26*, 127–140.
Sternberg, R. J. (1999a). Intelligence as developing expertise. *Contemporary Educational Psychology, 24*, 359–375.
Sternberg, R. J. (1999b). A propulsion model of types of creative contributions. *Review of General Psychology, 3*, 83–100.
Sternberg, R. J. (1999c). The theory of successful intelligence. *Review of General Psychology, 3*, 292–316.
Sternberg, R. J. (Ed.). (2000). *Handbook of intelligence*. New York, NY: Cambridge University Press.
Sternberg, R. J. (2001). Why schools should teach for wisdom: The balance theory of wisdom in educational settings. *Educational Psychologist, 36*(4), 227–245.
Sternberg, R. J. (Ed.). (2003a). *The anatomy of impact: What has made the great works of psychology great?* (pp. 223–228). Washington, DC: American Psychological Association.
Sternberg, R. J. (Ed.). (2003b). *Psychologists defying the crowd: Stories of those who battled the establishment and won*. Washington, DC: American Psychological Association.
Sternberg, R. J. (2003c). What is an expert student? *Educational Researcher, 32*(8), 5–9.
Sternberg, R. J. (2003d). WICS: A model for leadership in organizations. *Academy of Management Learning & Education, 2*, 386–401.
Sternberg, R. J. (2003e). *WICS: A theory of wisdom, intelligence, and creativity, synthesized*. New York, NY: Cambridge University Press.
Sternberg, R. J. (2003f). WICS as a model of giftedness. *High Ability Studies, 14*, 109–137.
Sternberg, R. J. (2004). Culture and intelligence. *American Psychologist, 59*(5), 325–338.
Sternberg, R. J. (2005). The theory of successful intelligence. *Interamerican Journal of Psychology, 39*(2), 189–202.
Sternberg, R. J. (2007). Culture, instruction, and assessment. *Comparative Education, 43* (1), 5–22.
Sternberg, R. J. (2008). Schools should nurture wisdom. In B. Z. Presseisen (Ed.), *Teaching for intelligence* (2nd ed., pp. 61–88). Thousand Oaks, CA: Corwin.
Sternberg, R. J. (2009). Wisdom, intelligence, and creativity synthesized. *School Administrator, 66*(2), 10–14.
Sternberg, R. J. (2010). WICS: A new model for cognitive education. *Journal of Cognitive Education and Psychology, 9*, 34–46.
Sternberg, R. J. (2009). The Rainbow and Kaleidoscope projects: A new psychological approach to undergraduate admissions. *European Psychologist, 14*, 279–287.
Sternberg, R. J. (2010). *Seeking the best: A new approach to college admissions*. Cambridge, MA: Harvard University Press.
Sternberg, R. J., Castejón, J. L., Prieto, M. D., Hautamäki, J., & Grigorenko, E. L. (2001). Confirmatory factor analysis of the Sternberg triarchic abilities test in three international samples: An empirical test of the triarchic

theory of intelligence. *European Journal of Psychological Assessment*, 17(1) 1–16.

Sternberg, R. J., & Clinkenbeard, P. R. (1995). The triarchic model applied to identifying, teaching, and assessing gifted children. *Roeper Review*, 17(4), 255–260.

Sternberg, R. J., & Coffin L. A. (2010). Admitting and developing "new leaders for a changing world." *New England Journal of Higher Education*, Winter, 24, 12–13.

Sternberg, R. J., & Detterman, D. K. (Eds.). (1986). *What is intelligence?* Norwood, NJ: Ablex.

Sternberg, R. J., Ferrari, M., Clinkenbeard, P. R., & Grigorenko, E. L. (1996). Identification, instruction, and assessment of gifted children: A construct validation of a triarchic model. *Gifted Child Quarterly*, 40(3), 129–137.

Sternberg, R. J., Forsythe, G. B., Hedlund, J., Horvath, J., Snook, S., Williams, W. M., Wagner, R. K., & Grigorenko, E. L. (2000). *Practical intelligence in everyday life*. New York, NY: Cambridge University Press.

Sternberg, R. J., & Gardner, M. K. (1982). A componential interpretation of the general factor in human intelligence. In H. J. Eysenck (Ed.), *A model for intelligence* (pp. 231–254). Berlin, Germany: Springer–Verlag.

Sternberg, R. J., & Gardner, M. K. (1983). Unities in inductive reasoning. *Journal of Experimental Psychology: General*, 112, 80–116.

Sternberg, R. J., & Gastel, J. (1989a). Coping with novelty in human intelligence: An empirical investigation. *Intelligence*, 13, 187–197.

Sternberg, R. J., & Gastel, J. (1989b). If dancers ate their shoes: Inductive reasoning with factual and counterfactual premises. *Memory and Cognition*, 17, 1–10.

Sternberg, R. J., & Grigorenko, E. L. (1997, Fall). The cognitive costs of physical and mental ill health: Applying the psychology of the developed world to the problems of the developing world. *Eye on Psi Chi*, 2(1), 20–27.

Sternberg, R. J., & Grigorenko, E. L. (2007). *Teaching for successful intelligence* (2nd ed.). Thousand Oaks, CA: Corwin.

Sternberg, R. J., & Grigorenko, E. L. (2002a). *Dynamic testing*. New York, NY: Cambridge University Press.

Sternberg, R. J., & Grigorenko E. L. (Eds.). (2002b). *The general factor of intelligence: How general is it?* Mahwah, NJ: Erlbaum.

Sternberg, R. J., Grigorenko, E. L., Ferrari, M., & Clinkenbeard, P. (1999). A triarchic analysis of an aptitude-treatment interaction. *European Journal of Psychological Assessment*, 15(1), 1–11.

Sternberg, R. J., Grigorenko, E. L., & Jarvin, L. (2001). Improving reading instruction: The triarchic model. *Educational Leadership*, 58(6), 48–52.

Sternberg, R. J., Grigorenko, E. L., & Zhang, L.-F. (2008). Styles of learning and thinking matter in instruction and assessment. *Perspectives on Psychological Science*, 3(6), 486–506.

Sternberg, R. J., Grigorenko, E. L., Ngrosho, D., Tantufuye, E., Mbise, A., Nokes, C., Jukes, M., & Bundy, D. A. (2002). Assessing intellectual potential in rural Tanzanian school children. *Intelligence*, 30, 141–162.

Sternberg, R. J., & Hedlund, J. (2002). Practical intelligence, *g*, and work psychology. *Human Performance* 15(1/2), 143–160.

Sternberg, R. J., Jarvin, L., & Grigorenko, E. L. (2009). *Teaching for wisdom, intelligence, creativity, and success*. Thousand Oaks, CA: Corwin.

Sternberg, R. J., & Kalmar D.A. (1997). When will the milk spoil? Everyday induction in human intelligence. *Intelligence*, 25(3), 185–203.

Sternberg, R. J., Kaufman, J. C., & Pretz, J. E. (2002). *The creativity conundrum: A propulsion model of kinds of creative contributions*. New York, NY: Psychology Press.

Sternberg, R. J., Kaufman, J. C., & Pretz, J. E. (2003). A propulsion model of creative leadership. *Leadership Quarterly*, 14, 455–473.

Sternberg, R. J., & Lubart, T. I. (1991). An investment theory of creativity and its development. *Human Development*, 34(1), 1–31.

Sternberg, R. J., & Lubart, T. I. (1995). *Defying the crowd: Cultivating creativity in a culture of conformity*. New York: Free Press.

Sternberg, R. J., & Lubart, T. I. (1996). Investing in creativity. *American Psychologist*, 51(7), 677–688.

Sternberg, R. J., & Nigro, G. (1980). Developmental patterns in the solution of verbal analogies. *Child Development*, 51, 27–38.

Sternberg, R. J., Nokes, K., Geissler, P. W., Prince, R., Okatcha, F., Bundy, D. A., & Grigorenko, E. L. (2001). The relationship between academic and practical intelligence: A case study in Kenya. *Intelligence*, 29, 401–418.

Sternberg, R. J., & O'Hara, L. (1999). Creativity and intelligence. In R. J. Sternberg (Ed.), *Handbook of creativity* (pp. 251–272). New York, NY: Cambridge University Press.

Sternberg, R. J., Okagaki, L., & Jackson, A. (1990). Practical intelligence for success in school. *Educational Leadership, 48*, 35–39.
Sternberg, R. J., & Powell, J. S. (1983). Comprehending verbal comprehension. *American Psychologist, 38*, 878–893.
Sternberg, R. J., Powell, J. S., & Kaye, D. B. (1983). Teaching vocabulary-building skills: A contextual approach. In A. C. Wilkinson (Ed.), *Classroom computers and cognitive science* (pp. 121–143). New York, NY: Academic Press.
Sternberg, R. J., & Pretz, J. E. (Eds.). (2005). *Cognition and intelligence: Identifying the mechanisms of the mind*. New York, NY: Cambridge University Press.
Sternberg, R. J., & The Rainbow Project Collaborators. (2006). The Rainbow Project: Enhancing the SAT through assessments of analytical, practical and creative skills. *Intelligence*, 34(4), 321–350.
Sternberg, R. J., & Rifkin, B. (1979). The development of analogical reasoning processes. *Journal of Experimental Child Psychology, 27*, 195–232.
Sternberg, R. J., & Smith, C. (1985). Social intelligence and decoding skills in nonverbal communication. *Social Cognition, 2*, 168–192.
Sternberg, R. J., Torff, B., & Grigorenko, E. L. (1998a). Teaching for successful intelligence raises school achievement. *Phi Delta Kappan, 79*, 667–669.
Sternberg, R. J., Torff, B., & Grigorenko, E. L. (1998b). Teaching triarchically improves school achievement. *Journal of Educational Psychology, 90*, 374–384.
Sternberg, R. J., & Turner, M. E. (1981). Components of syllogistic reasoning. *Acta psychologica, 47*, 245–265.
Sternberg, R. J., & Vroom, V. H. (2002). The person versus the situation in leadership. *Leadership Quarterly, 13*, 301–323.
Sternberg, R. J., & Wagner, R. K. (1993). The *g*-ocentric view of intelligence and job performance is wrong. *Current Directions in Psychological Science*, 2(1), 1–4.
Sternberg, R. J., Wagner, R. K., & Okagaki, L. (1993). Practical intelligence: The nature and role of tacit knowledge in work and at school. In H. Reese & J. Puckett (Eds.), *Advances in lifespan development* (pp. 205–227). Hillsdale, NJ: Erlbaum.
Sternberg, R. J., Wagner, R. K., Williams, W. M., & Horvath, J. A. (1995). Testing common sense. *American Psychologist*, 50(11), 912–927.
Sternberg, R. J., & Williams, W. M. (1996). *How to develop student creativity*. Alexandria, VA: Association for Supervision and Curriculum Development.
Sternberg, R. J., & Williams, W. M. (2010). *Educational psychology* (2nd ed.). Boston, MA: Allyn & Bacon.
Tetewsky, S. J., & Sternberg, R. J. (1986). Conceptual and lexical determinants of nonentrenched thinking. *Journal of Memory and Language*, 25, 202–225.
Tzuriel, D. (1995). *Dynamic-interactive assessment: The legacy of L. S. Vygotsky and current developments*. Unpublished manuscript.
Vernon, P. E. (1971). *The structure of human abilities*. London, UK: Methuen.
Vygotsky, L. S. (1978). *Mind in society: The development of higher psychological processes*. Cambridge, MA: Harvard University Press.
Wagner, R. K. (1987).Tacit knowledge in everyday intelligent behavior. *Journal of Personality & Social Psychology*, 52(6), 1236–1247.
Wagner, R. K., & Sternberg, R. J. (1986). Tacit knowledge and intelligence in the everyday world. In R. J. Sternberg & R. K. Wagner (Eds.), *Practical intelligence: Nature and origins of competence in the everyday world* (pp. 51–83). New York, NY: Cambridge University Press.
Williams, W. M., Blythe, T., White, N., Li, J., Sternberg, R. J., & Gardner, H. I. (1996). *Practical intelligence for school: A handbook for teachers of grades* 5–8. New York, NY: HarperCollins.
Williams, W. M., Blythe, T., White, N., Li, J., Gardner, H., & Sternberg, R. J. (2002). Practical intelligence for school: Developing metacognitive sources of achievement in adolescence. *Developmental Review*, 22(2), 162–210.

CHAPTER 26

Emotional Intelligence

John D. Mayer, Peter Salovey, David R. Caruso, and Lillia Cherkasskiy

Emotional Intelligence at 20 Years

A comprehensive initial theory of emotional intelligence (EI) and a preliminary demonstration that it could be measured appeared 20 years ago in the scientific literature (Mayer, Salovey, & DiPaolo, 1990; Salovey & Mayer, 1990). In the 2000 edition of the *Handbook of Intelligence* we defined emotional intelligence as

> *the ability to perceive and express emotion, assimilate emotion in thought, understand and reason with emotion, and regulate emotion in the self and others. (Mayer, Salovey, & Caruso, 2000, p. 396; see also Mayer & Salovey, 1997)*

Today, EI is conceived of in much the same way by many investigators, and there is a much better sense of what EI is, how it can be measured, and what it predicts than there was two or even one decade ago. Although alternative uses of the term EI exist, they are more likely to refer to a group of diverse positive traits and competencies, not all having to do with emotions, intelligence, or their intersection. There is increasing recognition that this latter use of the term *emotional intelligence* is confusing (e.g., Daus & Ashkanasy, 2003).

Emotional Intelligence Over 20 Years

Before the 1990 articles on emotional intelligence, the term was used on a mostly occasional and inconsistent basis. A literary critic commented that some of Jane Austen's characters exhibited an "emotional intelligence" (Van Ghent, 1953). In a prefeminist German article on motherhood, the author speculated that women might reject their roles as housewives and mothers due to a lack of emotional intelligence (Leuner, 1966). (We note that Leuner proposed LSD as a treatment for such women!) A more focused approach appeared in a dissertation by Payne (1986), who argued that "the mass suppression of emotion throughout the civilized world has stifled our growth emotionally."

In addition to these uses of the term, a number of related concepts also emerged by the late 20th century. Influenced by the Hindu yogic traditions, Carl Jung (1921) suggested that some people used a *feeling function* to understand the world: thinking with their hearts. Much later, Steiner (1984) proposed the existence of *emotional literacy* and argued that greater emotional awareness could improve a person's well-being (see also Steiner, 1986, 2003; Steiner & Perry, 1997). Saarni (1990, 1997) argued for a general emotional competence and proposed a model for tracking its development in children (Saarni, 1990, 1997, in press). In the intelligence tradition, Gardner (1993) proposed an *intrapersonal intelligence* that was especially focused on the awareness of feelings.

Relevant empirical work emerged as well. Investigators studying nonverbal perception had begun to examine people's accuracy at recognizing emotions in facial expressions and bodily postures (e.g., Buck, 1984; Rosenthal et al., 1979). And a number of researchers became interested in how emotions influence thought and vice versa (see reviews by Matthews et al., 2002; Mayer, 2000; Oatley, 2004). Our own model of emotional intelligence emerged in the context of these related lines of work.

Within a few years after publication of our initial articles in 1990, a book about EI written for a general audience appeared, selling millions of copies worldwide (Goleman, 1995). The book covered much of the literature reviewed in the aforementioned articles as well as considerable additional research on emotions and brain function, emotions and social behavior, and school-based programs designed to help children develop emotional and social skills.

Goleman's book emphasized earlier comments we had made concerning how people with emotional intelligence might be more socially effective than others in certain respects (Salovey & Mayer, 1990). Particularly strong claims were made as to emotional intelligence's contribution to the individual and society (Goleman, 1995, p. xii). This combination of science and human potential attracted extensive media coverage, culminating, perhaps, when *Time* magazine asked the question "What's your EQ?" on its cover, and stated:

> *It's not your IQ. It's not even a number. But emotional intelligence may be the best predictor of success in life, redefining what it means to be smart.* (Time, 1995)

In short order, the phrase "emotional intelligence" became widely known, appearing in many magazine and newspaper articles (e.g., Bennetts, 1996; Henig, 1996; Peterson, 1997), books (e.g., Cooper & Sawaf, 1997; Gottman, 1997; Salerno, 1996; Segal, 1997; Shapiro, 1997; Simmons & Simmons, 1997; Steiner & Perry, 1997; Weisinger, 1997), and even in popular comic strips, Dilbert (Adams, 1997) and Zippy the Pinhead (Griffith, 1996). Although the phrase was widely disseminated, its exact meaning often became distorted, and discussions in the popular media were rarely rooted in the scientific literature on the topic.

The first portion of this chapter reviews the concept of emotional intelligence. Some attention is paid to what is meant by the terms *emotion*, *intelligence*, and *emotional intelligence*. A distinction is drawn between models of emotional intelligence that focus on mental abilities and alternative models that, increasingly, are recognized as speaking more generally of personality. Measures of emotional intelligence are examined in the chapter's second section. Findings concerning what emotional intelligence predicts are the topic of the chapter's third section. And finally, we take a look forward in the general discussion.

Theoretical Considerations

The Terms Emotion *and* Intelligence

Theories should be internally consistent, make meaningful use of technical language, and provide the basis for useful predictions. One issue in studying emotional intelligence is that some theories pertain to emotions and intelligence, whereas others seem far broader. Therefore, it is worth examining the constituent terms, *emotion*, *intelligence*, and their combination at the outset.

CONCEPTIONS OF EMOTION

Emotions are recognized as one of three or four fundamental classes of mental operations. These classes include motivation, emotion, cognition, and (less frequently) consciousness (Bain, 1855/1977; Izard, 1993; MacLean, 1973; Mayer, 1995a, 1995b; Plutchik, 1984; Tomkins, 1962; see Hilgard, 1980; Mayer, Chabot, & Carlsmith, 1997, for reviews). Among the triad of motivation, emotion, and cognition, basic motivations arise in response to internal bodily states and include drives such as hunger, thirst, need for social contact, and sexual desires. Motivations are responsible for directing the organism to carry out simple acts so as to satisfy survival and reproductive needs. In their basic form, motivations follow a relatively determined time course (e.g., thirst rises until quenched) and are typically satisfied in a specific fashion (e.g., thirst is satisfied by drinking fluids).

Emotions form the second class of this triad. Emotions appear to have evolved across mammalian species so as to signal and respond to changes in relationships between the individual and the environment (including one's imagined place within it). For example, anger arises in response to perceived threat or injustice; fear arises in response to perceived danger. Emotions respond to perceived changes in relationships. Moreover, each emotion organizes several basic behavioral responses to the relationship; for example, fear organizes freezing or fleeing. Emotions are therefore more flexible than motivations, though not quite so flexible as cognition.

Cognition, the third member of the triad, allows the organism to learn from the environment and to solve problems in novel situations. This is often in the service of satisfying motives or keeping emotions positive. Cognition includes learning, memory, and problem solving. It is ongoing, and involves flexible, intentional information processing based on learning and memory (see Mayer et al., 1997, for a review of these concepts).

The term *emotional intelligence*, then, implies something having to do with the intersection of emotion and cognition. From our perspective, evaluating theories of emotional intelligence requires an assessment of the degree to which the theory actually pertains to this intersection.

CONCEPTIONS OF INTELLIGENCE

An intelligence researcher was invited mistakenly to a conference on military intelligence by someone who noticed he was an expert on intelligence – but did not notice the kinds of intelligence he studied.[1] Howard Gardner (1997) uses this true story about himself to make the point that *intelligence* is used differently by different people. Although we acknowledge different meanings of the term, we also believe intelligence possesses a core meaning in the sciences. Artificial intelligence, human intelligence, even Offices of Military Intelligence all imply gathering information, learning about that information, and using it to guide reasoning and solve problems. Human and artificial intelligence both imply a mental ability associated with cognitive operations. The mental ability model was represented in pure form by Terman (1921, p. 128), who stated, "An individual is intelligent in proportion as he is able to carry on abstract thinking." In fact, symposia on intelligence over the years repeatedly conclude that the first hallmark of intelligence is the capacity to carry out valid abstract reasoning (Sternberg, 1997).

Intelligence, conceptualized as abstract thinking, has often been demonstrated to predict one or another type of success, particularly academic success. But although it is a potent predictor, it is far from a perfect one, leaving the vast amount of variance

1 The problem of the meaning of intelligence is an old one in the field and should not discourage us. Spearman (1927, p. 24) noted:

> The most enthusiastic advocates of intelligence become doubtful of it themselves. From having naively assumed that its nature is straightway conveyed by its name, they now set out to discover what this nature really is. In the last act, the truth stands revealed, that the name really has no definite meaning at all; it shows itself to be nothing more than a hypostatized word, applied indiscriminately to all sorts of things.

in successful behavior unexplained. As Wechsler (1940, p. 444) put it, "individuals with identical IQs may differ very markedly in regard to their effective ability to cope with the environment." One way to regard this limitation is to view human life as naturally complex and as subject both to chance events and to complicated interactions. A second approach is to search for better ways to assess intelligence (e.g., Sternberg, 1997). A third approach is to attribute the difference to a combination of nonintellective factors, such as personality traits. These approaches are all complementary and have all been used with different degrees of effectiveness in enhancing psychological predictions of positive outcomes.

Note, however, that there is a fourth alternative to dealing with limitations of IQ's predictive ability. That is to redefine intelligence itself as a combination of mental ability and personality traits. This approach seems very unsatisfactory because it overrides a century of conceptual usage of the term *intelligence*. Labeling nonintellectual characteristics intelligence potentially obscures their meaning (cf. Salovey & Mayer, 1994; Sternberg, 1997). Scarr (1989) notes that goodness in human relationships, athletic ability (i.e., kinesthetic ability), and certain talents in music, dance, and painting have all been labeled intelligence at one time or another. She cautions, however, that "to call them intelligence does not do justice either to theories of intelligence or to the personality traits and special talents that lie beyond the consensual definition of intelligence" (p. 78). Nonetheless, some investigators in the emotional intelligence field have proposed this approach – and we cover them briefly in the section on what we term *mixed models*.

Emotional Intelligence

Both in Western history and in psychology, emotions and reasoning sometimes have been viewed in opposition to one another (e.g., Schaffer, Gilmer, & Schoen, 1940; Publilius Syrus, 100 BCE/1961; Woodworth, 1940; Young, 1936). The contemporary view that emotions convey information about relationships, however, suggests that emotions and intelligence can work hand in hand. Emotions reflect relationships between a person and a friend, a family, the situation, a society, or more internally, between a person and a reflection or memory. For example, joy might indicate one's identification with a friend's success; sadness might indicate disappointment with one's self. Emotional intelligence refers in part to an ability to recognize the meanings of such emotional patterns and to reason and problem solve on the basis of them (Mayer & Salovey, 1997; Salovey & Mayer, 1990).

ABILITY MODELS: SPECIFIC AND INTEGRATIVE

Intelligences are mental abilities, and in the emotional intelligence area, some research focuses on specific abilities related to emotional intelligence, and other research examines many abilities together. Specific-ability models examine a particular realm of emotional intelligence in depth – for example, perceiving emotion in faces. Global ability models look at the general overall pattern of EI. Parallel to such approaches, the emotional intelligence area has given rise to tools for assessment that focus on specific areas and global areas. Specific measures examine just the recognition of emotions in faces, or solely the capacity to be aware of subtle emotional meanings; as such, the specific approaches have the advantage of assessing EI in depth in a particular area and understanding how a person reasons about a given subject matter. Integrative models better allow for an overview of how the parts of EI fit together to form an overall intelligence.

AN EXAMPLE OF AN INTEGRATIVE APPROACH

In this section, we examine an integrative approach to emotional intelligence, the Four-Branch Model of Emotional Intelligence (Mayer & Salovey, 1997). An integrative approach can provide a reasonable first overview of an area because it draws together examples of the specific areas that make up reasoning about emotions and emotional information. For reviews of specific-ability areas, the reader is referred to Matsumoto et al. (2000) and Roseman & Evdokas (2004) for examples involving facial emotion recognition and emotional appraisal, respectively.

To return to the integrative approach, as we now view it, emotional intelligence draws together emotional abilities from four classes or branches, as shown in Table 26.1. (The specific skills listed in Column 1 are meant to be representative; there are other skills that could be included on each branch as well as the ones shown.) The most basic skills involve the perception and appraisal of emotion. For example, early on, an infant learns to perceive emotions in facial expressions. The infant cries in distress, or smiles in joy, and watches her reaction mirrored in the parent's face, as the parent empathically reflects those feelings. As the child grows, he or she discriminates more finely among genuine versus merely polite smiles and other gradations of expression. People also read emotional information in the objects they encounter, interpreting emotionally the expansiveness of a dining hall, or the stoicism of a simple and spare Shaker chair (cf. Arnheim, 1974).

The second set of emotional intelligence skills involves using emotional experiences to promote thinking, including weighing emotions against one another and against other sensations and thoughts, and allowing emotions to direct attention. For example, a manager may use a low-energy emotion to help her focus on the detailed editing of a budget spreadsheet.

The third branch involves understanding and reasoning about emotions and using language to describe them. The experience of specific emotions – happiness, anger, fear, and the like – is rule-governed. Anger generally rises when justice is denied; fear often changes to relief; dejection may separate us from others. Sadness and anger "move" according to their own characteristic rules, just as the knight and bishop on a chessboard move in different ways. Consider a woman who is extremely angry and an hour later ashamed. It is likely that certain events in particular may have intervened: she might have expressed her anger more forcefully than she intended, or discovered she falsely believed that a friend had betrayed her. Emotional understanding involves the ability to recognize the emotions, to know

Table 26.1 Overview of an Integrative-Model Approach to Emotional Intelligence Overall Definition

	Examples of Specific Areas
Perception and Expression of Emotion	Identifying and expressing emotions in one's physical states, feelings, and thoughts.
	Identifying and expressing emotions in other people, artwork, language, etc.
Assimilating Emotion in Thought	Using emotions to prioritize thinking in productive ways
	Generating emotions as aids to judgment and memory
Understanding and Analyzing Emotion	Labeling emotions, including complex emotions, and recognizing simultaneous feelings
	Understanding relationships associated with shifts of emotion
Reflective Regulation of Emotion	Staying open to feelings
	Being able to reflectively monitor and regulate emotions to promote emotional and intellectual growth (after Mayer & Salovey, 1997, p. 11)

"Emotional intelligence is the set of abilities that account for how people's emotional perception and understanding vary in their accuracy. More formally, we define emotional intelligence as the ability to perceive and express emotion, assimilate emotion in thought, understand and reason with emotion, and regulate emotion in the self and others" (after Mayer & Salovey, 1997).

how they unfold, and to reason about them accordingly.

The fourth branch of emotional intelligence involves the management and regulation of emotion in oneself and others, such as knowing how to calm down after feeling angry or being able to alleviate the anxiety of another person. Tasks defining these four branches are described in greater detail in the section concerning scale development below.

This mental ability model of emotional intelligence makes predictions about the internal structure of the intelligence, and also its implications for a person's life. The theory predicts that emotional intelligence is, in fact, an intelligence like other intelligences in that it meets three empirical criteria. First, mental problems have right or wrong answers, as assessed by the convergence of methods for scoring the correctness of an answer. Second, the measured skills correlate with other measures of mental ability (because mental abilities tend to intercorrelate), and correlate moderately with socioemotional traits hypothesized to promote or covary with higher emotional intelligence, including Agreeableness, empathy, and Openness (the latter trait correlates generally with intelligences; Mayer, DiPaolo, & Salovey, 1990; Mayer, Roberts, & Barsade, 2008). Third, the absolute ability level at emotional problem solving rises with age into middle adulthood.

The model further predicts that emotionally intelligent individuals are more likely to (1) have been raised by socioemotionally sensitive parents, (2) be able to communicate and discuss feelings, (3) be nondefensive more generally, (4) be able to cope with emotions effectively and, if desirable, (5) develop expert knowledge in a particular emotional area such as aesthetics, moral or ethical responsiveness, social problem solving, leadership, or spiritual feeling (Mayer & Salovey, 1995).

For us, the limits of EI correspond to basic problem solving that centers on emotional reasoning itself. There are likely other, important abilities that blend into emotional intelligence. For example, recognizing cultural differences in emotional expression is related to EI but might better be considered an aspect of cultural intelligence because the information is as relevant to sociocultural as to emotional understanding (e.g., Earley & Ang, 2003). Although these related abilities are not part of our model, they likely overlap with EI.

Models Labeled "Emotional Intelligence"

BACKGROUND TO MIXING INTELLIGENCE(S) WITH PERSONALITY TRAITS

In addition to models of emotional intelligence, there are models labeled "emotional intelligence" but that include many nonintelligence qualities and traits that, to our minds, more clearly belong to other areas of personality. The idea of mixing intelligence with other factors surely is not new. No less an eminent figure than David Wechsler (1943, p. 103) wondered "whether nonintellective, that is, affective and conative [motivational] abilities are admissible as factors in general intelligence." He suggests that such traits might be. A few sentences thereafter, however, he qualifies the notion: they predict intelligent *behavior* (as opposed to being a part of intelligence per se). Wechsler straddled the fence, as it were. On the one hand, he at times defined intelligence as involving "the aggregate or global capacity of the individual to act purposefully, to think rationally and to *deal effectively with his environment*" (italics added; Wechsler, 1958, p. 7). On the other hand, the intelligence tests that carry his name focus on measuring mental abilities.

MIXED MODELS: SETS OF PERSONALITY CHARACTERISTICS INCLUDING SOME RELATED TO EMOTIONAL INTELLIGENCE

After Wechsler's work, the matter seems to have been settled to most people's satisfaction: Intelligence is a mental ability. However, some people doing work on emotional intelligence have generated mixed models: that is, personality characteristics mixed in with the abilities of emotional intelligence. We acknowledge that our first articles on emotional intelligence could have been construed in such a manner (e.g., Mayer, DiPaolo, & Salovey, 1990; Salovey & Mayer, 1990). Although (to us) these articles set out a clear mental ability conception of emotional intelligence, they also freely described personality characteristics that might accompany such an intelligence. Emotional intelligence was said to distinguish those who are "genuine and warm . . . [from those who] appear oblivious and boorish." Emotionally intelligent individuals were also said to exhibit "persistence at challenging tasks' and have "positive attitudes toward life . . . that lead to better outcomes and greater rewards for themselves and others" (Salovey & Mayer, 1990, pp. 199–200). We ourselves may have seemed to mix clear mental abilities with their outcomes and consequences in these initial articles.

Almost immediately after these initial articles on emotional intelligence appeared, we recognized that it was crucial to distinguish more clearly the mental ability concept from its outcomes. Although traits such as warmth and persistence are important, we believe they are better addressed directly, and as distinct from emotional intelligence (Mayer & Salovey, 1993, 1997).

Whether or not our own early writings contributed to the confusion, Goleman's (1995) account of emotional intelligence included a number of personality qualities clearly outside the realm of the intelligences. The five areas Goleman lists are depicted in the first column of Table 26.2, including (1) knowing one's emotions, (2) managing emotions, (3) motivating oneself, (4) recognizing emotions in others, and (5) handling relationships. Each area is further divided. Goleman's specific attributes under motivation, for example, include marshaling emotions, delaying gratification, and entering flow states (Goleman, 1995, p. 43). Even though this was a journalistic account rather than a scientific work, Goleman recognized that he was moving from emotional intelligence to something far broader. He states that "'ego resilience,' . . . is quite similar to [this model of] emotional intelligence" in that it includes social (and emotional) competencies (Goleman, 1995, p. 44). He noted, "There is an old-fashioned word for the body of skills that emotional intelligence represents: *character*" (Goleman, 1995, p. 285).

Goleman (1995) also appeared to make extraordinary claims for the predictive validity of his mixed model. Emotional intelligence, he argued, would confer:

> *an advantage in any domain in life, whether in romance and intimate relationships or picking up the unspoken rules that govern success in organizational politics. (Goleman, 1995, p. 36)*

Arguing that "at best, IQ contributes about 20% to the factors that determine life success," he seemed to us and to others to imply that emotional intelligence would account for much of the "80% [left] to other factors" (Goleman, 1995, p. 34). " What data exist," Goleman wrote of emotional intelligence, "suggest it can be as powerful, and at times more powerful, than IQ." The misimpressions created by these arguments have been addressed by Goleman in an excellent introductory chapter to the 10th anniversary edition of his book (Goleman, 2005).

In the earlier edition of this chapter (Mayer, Salovey, & Caruso, 2000), and in several other articles, we described in considerable detail why his claims were not only unsupported by the evidence, but deeply implausible (Mayer, 1998; Mayer & Cobb, 2000; Mayer & Salovey, 1997). In the 10th anniversary edition of his book, Goleman (2005) said he had been misunderstood and acknowledged that such ideas were unrealistic. It is understandable that a book on EI written for the general public would stretch the boundaries of available empirical findings to make a point. It is also understandable that the popular media might embrace such claims. As we see it, however, other scientists should have employed a more critical eye regarding such a loose rendering of a scientific construct.

A number of ensuing mixed models using the name *emotional intelligence* appeared. For

Table 26.2 Evolution of the Journalistic Account of "Emotional Intelligence"

Goleman (1995) *Overall Definition(s)*	*Bar-On (1997)* *Overall Definition*	*Petrides and Furnham (2003)* *Overall Definition*
"the abilities called here *emotional intelligence*, which include self-control, zeal and persistence, and the ability to motivate oneself" (Goleman, 1995, p. xii). [. . . and . . .] "There is an old-fashioned word for the body of skills that emotional intelligence represents: *character*" (Goleman, 1995, p. 28). Major Areas of Skills and Specific Examples *Knowing One's Emotions* *recognizing a feeling *as it happens* *monitoring feelings from moment to moment *Managing Emotions* *handling feelings so they are appropriate *being able to soothe oneself *being able to shake off rampant anxiety, gloom, or irritability *Motivating Oneself* *marshaling emotions in the service of a goal *delaying gratification and stifling impulsiveness *being able to get into the "flow" state *Recognizing Emotions in Others* *having empathic awareness *being attuned to what others need or want *Handling Relationships* *having skill in managing emotions in others *interacting smoothly with others	"Emotional intelligence is . . . an array of noncognitive capabilities, competencies, and skills that influence one's ability to succeed in coping with environmental demands and pressures" (Bar-On, 1997, p. 14). Major Areas of Skills and Specific Skills *Intrapersonal Skills* *Emotional self-awareness *Assertiveness *Self-Regard *Self-Actualization *Independence *Interpersonal Skills* *Interpersonal relationships *Social responsibility *Empathy *Adaptability Scales* *Problem solving *Reality testing *Flexibility *Stress-Management Scales* *Stress tolerance *Impulse control *General Mood* *Happiness *Optimism	"a constellation of emotion-related self-perceptions and dispositions, assessed through self-report. The precise composition of these self-perceptions and dispositions varies across different conceptualizations, with some . . . being broader than others" (Petrides & Furnham, 2003, p. 40). Major Areas of Skills and Specific Skills *Adaptability *Assertiveness *Emotional appraisal (self and *others) *Emotion expression *Emotion management (others) *Emotion regulation *Impulsiveness *Relationship skills *Self-esteem *Self-motivation *Social competence *Stress management *Trait empathy *Trait happiness *Trait optimism (Petrides & Furnham, 2001, p. 428)

example, Bar-On's (1997) model of emotional intelligence was intended to answer the question "Why are some individuals more able to succeed in life than others?" A more recent model by Petrides and Furnham (2001, 2003) seems to cover much the same ground. Other, similar approaches have been proposed (e.g., Tett, Fox, & Wang, 2005). Two of these models are summarized in Table 26.2. For example, in his self-report assessment, Bar-On included such characteristics as emotional self-awareness, assertiveness, self-regard, self-actualization, and independence.

ARE MIXED MODELS OF EMOTIONAL INTELLIGENCE REALLY EMOTIONAL INTELLIGENCE?

Mixed models have come in for a good deal of criticism in the psychological literature. Referring specifically to Goleman's (1998) model of emotional intelligence, Locke (2005) referred to it as "preposterous." In fairness, however, Goleman writes as a journalist, not as a scientist. The 2008 *Annual Review of Psychology* coverage of the field concluded the concept of mixed models was questionable (Mayer, Roberts, & Barsade, 2008). Perhaps more important, recent reviews increasingly reflect the idea that the measurement project emanating from such models has failed (Daus & Ashkanasy, 2003; Grubb & McDaniel, 2007; Mayer, Roberts, & Barsade, 2008; Mayer, Salovey, & Caruso, 2008; Zeidner, Roberts, & Matthews, 2008). We will discuss these problems briefly later in this chapter.

The problem is that the concept of mixed-model emotional intelligence is unmoored from the twin concepts of emotion and of intelligence. Recall that Goleman (1995) acknowledges that his model is little different from Block and Block's (1980) model of ego-strength. Petrides and Furnham (2003) acknowledge the content overlap between what they are discussing and the Big Five personality traits. The Big Five are often-measured traits including Extraversion-Introversion, Stability-Neuroticism, Openness-Closedness, Conscientiousness-Carelessness, and Agreeableness-Disagreeableness (e.g., Goldberg, 1990); they seem to have little to do with emotional intelligence. These mixed models, unmoored from the concepts of "emotion" and "intelligence," also have included concepts of constructive thinking (Epstein & Meier, 1989), ego strength (Block & Block, 1980), social desirability (Paulhus, 1991), social insight (Chapin, 1967), and many other constructs.

The Measurement of Emotional Intelligence

Mental ability models of emotional intelligence, as well as mixed models, have prompted the construction of instruments to measure emotional intelligence. Mental ability models of emotional intelligence are most directly assessed by ability measures. Ability measures have the advantage of representing an individual's performance level on a task. We deal with those here, reserving a brief section later for mixed-model measures.

Measures of Emotional Intelligence

EARLY WORK

Emotional Intelligence Measurement before Emotional Intelligence Theory We refer readers to our chapter in the original *Handbook* for an examination of the early measures that led up to contemporary work in emotional intelligence research (Mayer, Salovey, & Caruso, 2000). That earlier chapter examines precursor specific-ability measures related to perceiving emotion. Included were a number of scales of the nonverbal assessment of emotion, for example, of faces (Buck, 1976; Campbell, Kagan, & Krathwohl, 1971; Kagan, 1978; Rosenthal et al., 1979), as well as some additional background on our own work in developing measures of emotional intelligence.

In the past 20 years, a great number of improved, revised ability scales of EI have been introduced and we briefly outline them here. As with models of emotional intelligence more generally, ability scales of EI can be divided into "specific-ability" measures and "integrative-model" measures. Specific-ability tests focus on a single area or subarea of emotional intelligence and the integrative-model approach involves tests that span several different ability areas of emotional intelligence. Here, we describe several examples of such scales.

EXAMPLES OF SPECIFIC-ABILITY MEASURES

Perhaps the most highly developed area of specific-ability measurement in emotional intelligence concerns assessments of people's abilities to discern emotional facial expressions. Among these measures, perhaps the most widely used group is the Diagnostic Analysis of Nonverbal Accuracy (DANVA) tests developed by Nowicki and colleagues (e.g., Nowicki & Carton, 1993; Pitterman & Nowicki, 2004). The different versions of these tests measure people's abilities to assess emotions in faces, posture, and auditory perception. For example, in the adult faces version of the test, participants are exposed to a series of 24 faces divided among basic emotions and equated for gender. Then, they must indicate the emotion present in the given face. Another relatively recent scale of note in this area is the Japanese and Caucasian Brief Affect Recognition Test (JACBART; Matsumoto et al., 2000).

Beyond the emotion-in-faces area, recent additions to ability scales have appeared in the areas of understanding emotions and emotion management. These include the Situational Test of Emotional Understanding (STEU) and the Situational Test of Emotion Management (STEM; MacCann & Roberts, 2008). The STEU asks questions about a person's ability to appraise and react to complicated emotional situations. Some questions are phrased to be low in context while others are higher in context. An example of a low-context item is this:

> *An unwanted situation becomes less likely or stops altogether. The person involved is most likely to feel: (a) regret, (b) hope, (c) joy, (d) sadness, (e) relief. (MacCann & Roberts, 2008, p. 542)*

High context items are similar but add in specifics, for example,

> *A supervisor who is unpleasant to work for leaves Alfonso's work. Alfonso is most likely to feel . . . ? (McCann & Roberts, 2008, p. 542)*

Answers to the STEU are keyed to an emotional appraisal theory developed by Roseman (2001); the correct answer for the question above in Roseman's system is "(e) relief."

The STEM focuses on emotion management, as opposed to the STEU's focus on understanding. The STEM, a situational judgment task type of assessment, presents brief vignettes to people; then, correct answers as to management are keyed to responses indicated by two expert groups who answered the scale.

EXAMPLES OF INTEGRATIVE-MODEL MEASURES

Integrative-model measures are similar to specific-ability measures described earlier, but rather than measure just one area of emotional intelligence, they measure multiple areas. As such, they generally are longer and more comprehensive than specific-ability measures. Schultz and Izard's Assessment of Children's Emotion Skills, or ACES (e.g., Schultz et al., 2001), measures children's abilities to assess emotions in pictures of faces, understand the emotions generated by social situations, and appreciate the emotions stemming from social behavior. It has been successfully used in a number of research studies (one to be described in the section, "Examples of EI Research").

In our own laboratory, we have developed the Mayer-Salovey-Caruso Emotional Intelligence Test or MSCEIT. The MSCEIT is a 141-item scale that measures (1) perceiving emotions, (2) using emotions to facilitate thought, (3) understanding emotions, and (4) managing emotions: four areas corresponding to the four branches of our model. Each branch contains two tasks. The perceiving-emotions area, for example, is divided into "faces" and "pictures" tasks. In the "faces" task, test takers view a series of faces and respond as to how much a specific emotion (e.g., sadness, fear, happiness, etc.) might be present, using a 5-point scale for each emotion. "Pictures" is similar except that abstract images and landscape photos are employed in place of faces.

The facilitation area is measured with "sensations" and "facilitation" tasks. For the sensations task, for example, test takers are asked to generate a moderate level of an emotion (e.g., joy) and then to match sensations such as a sweet taste or a cool temperature to those feelings. The facilitation task asks participants to match a mood to the kind of thinking it might enhance.

The understanding emotions area is measured by "blends" and "changes." In the blends task, participants match combinations of basic emotions to more complex blends: for example, "anger" and "disgust" might match reasonably closely to "contempt." In the changes task, one kind of item asks what emotion might result if another emotion were intensified (e.g., intensified frustration might lead to rage).

The management area is assessed by emotion management and emotional relationship tasks. Each presents brief vignettes about an emotion-eliciting event and asks the best way to manage emotions in relation to it. Emotion management focuses on regulating one's own emotions; emotional relationships focuses on regulating the feelings of others.

Scoring the MSCEIT Scoring of the MSCEIT and its precursors has generated several potential criteria for correct answers. These include identifying correct answers according to a general population group consensus (i.e., of the standardization sample), or the consensus of emotion experts. A third possibility, having targets describe their emotions, is possible for some tasks such as faces, where the photographed person can describe his or her feelings at the time of the picture. Work with the earlier Multifactor Emotional Intelligence Scale indicated that consensus, expert, and target scoring methods for the same tasks converged on the same answers (Mayer & Geher, 1996). Work with the MSCEIT employed more rigorous procedures. Twenty-one emotions experts provided answers to the test. These expert-identified answers converged dramatically with consensus-identified correct answers in the general sample. Such convergence adds confidence to the expert scoring approach, perhaps, as the optimal method. The nature of emotional information differs from information that is often included in standard intelligence tests, and thus, necessitates the use of different scoring methods. However, the existence of two, independent scoring keys has proven confusing to some, and the lack of a true, veridical scoring key is problematic to others (Matthews, Zeidner, & Roberts, 2002).

The Cohesiveness of the MSCEIT Tasks Integrative-model approaches to emotional intelligence tell us about how the different areas of emotional intelligence may relate to each other – if at all. The MSCEIT and its precursors make clear that emotional intelligence is a unitary ability. That is, the tasks are generally positively intercorrelated with one another. Beyond that general factor of EI, a number of subsidiary factors can be identified. One solution for the MSCEIT's factorial structure divides emotional intelligence into three areas: (1) emotional perception, (2) emotional understanding, and (3) emotional management. Others solutions are consistent with the four-factor model. However, some studies have recommended alternative factor models for the MSCEIT (Palmer et al., 2005).

EMOTIONAL INTELLIGENCE AS A MIXED MODEL MEASURED BY SELF-REPORT SCALES

Just as the ability model of emotional intelligence has generated measures of emotional intelligence, so have mixed models. These models are almost entirely based on self-report. As such, they are filtered through a person's self-concept and impression management motives.

Ability measurement possesses *process* validity evidence. For example, intelligence tests include a scoring process that verifies that participants can solve problems correctly, independently of the test taker's claims. Self-report lacks such validity evidence; consider the validity of a hypothetical self-report intelligence measure that asks, simply, "How smart do you think you are?" In fact, self-reported intelligence has a relatively low correlation with actual, measured intelligence via ability scales (e.g., Paulhus, Lysy, & Yik, 1998). This also is the case for emotional intelligence, where correlations between the MSCEIT and a self-report scale based on our four-branch model ranged between $r = .07$ and .19 in two samples (Brackett et al., 2006).

Most mixed-model scales, in addition to using self-report, simply measure traits drawn from personality research that are unrelated to emotional intelligence. Bar-On's Emotional Quotient Inventory (EQ_i) includes factors more or less consistent with the individual attributes listed in Table 26.2 of this chapter, ranging from self-actualization to happiness.

Such tests represent, in substantial part, a positive-negative halo effect in how people describe themselves. The Bar-On EQi, for example, correlates negatively and highly (in the $r = -.50$ to $-.75$ range) with measures of negative affect such as the Beck Depression Inventory and the Zung Self-Rating Depression Scale. It also correlates positively with traits related to positive affect. A cross-national administration of the Bar-On and the 16PF (e.g., Cattell, Cattell, & Cattell, 1993) indicated that the Bar-On was consistently positively correlated (mostly between $r = .40$ and .60) with emotional stability, and with components of extraversion including social boldness and social warmth (Bar-On, 1997, pp. 110–111). Tests such as the Bar-On, the Tett (Tett, Fox, & Wang, 2005), and the scales by Petrides and Furnham (2001, 2003) overlap with personality scales such as the NEO-PI measure of the Big Five as highly as do measures expressly developed as alternative measures of the Big Five itself (Mayer, Salovey, & Caruso, 2008, Table 1).

What Does Emotional Intelligence Predict?

We next turn to the predictive validity of emotional intelligence (excluding mixed-model measures). Emotional intelligence predicts specific outcomes in limited but important domains of social interaction. Although emotional intelligence identifies unique variance, it also overlaps, at least at low levels, with other commonly assessed variables. For that reason, researchers interested in emotional intelligence should examine incremental validity of EI in their work, comparing EI assessments with measures of cognitive ability and of other commonly measured personality traits such as the Big Five. Finally, given that some studies have shown differential gender effects, we suggest that researchers examine their data to determine whether EI's effects are similar for men and women. We begin with just two examples of some of the intriguing research in the area and then talk more globally of what EI predicts.

Examples of EI Research

Rosete (2005, 2009) conducted a workplace study that illustrates why it is critical to examine multiple aspects of managerial performance. He studied 117 managers from an Australian public service organization, administering the MSCEIT as well as a personality scale (16 PF) and an EI self-report scale. He also collected performance management ratings based on an extensive data collection and discussion process between the manager and his or her supervisor. These performance behaviors had two dimensions: "what they accomplish" and "how they accomplish it." The "what they accomplish" scale indicated the extent to which the manager hit certain targets such as reaching tax revenue goals or decreasing health insurance costs. The "how they accomplish it" ratings examined leadership behaviors such as "facilitates cooperation and partnerships," "communicates clearly," and "inspires a sense of purpose and direction." The MSCEIT significantly predicted performance "what's," accounting for 5% of the variance after controlling for cognitive ability and personality. More interesting, however, was that EI accounted for 22% of the variance for performance "how's," even after accounting for cognitive ability and personality. These results suggest that EI may play a more important role in how managers do their work rather than in what they accomplish.

In a series of studies, Trentacosta and Izard (2007) examined children's emotional knowledge and its relation to academic performance. For example, these authors tested 193 children attending kindergarten in an urban school system chiefly serving low-income and minority children. Of these kindergarteners, 142 were followed up in first grade (Trentacosta & Izard, 2007). The researchers collected various measures of attention, verbal ability, student-teacher closeness, and academic competence. They also employed a measure of "emotional regulation" – a measure of emotional negativity and instability similar to Neuroticism on the Big Five, and the Assessment of Children's Emotion Skills (ACES), which measures knowledge of emotional facial expressions, the emotions involved in social situations, and emotions in social behaviors.

In this particular study, high ACES scorers exhibited better attention to the teacher and to in-class test materials, higher verbal ability, and better overall academic performance in the $r = .20$ to $.40$ range. (These findings are similar to those found by these authors and their colleagues in other studies.) In a path-analytic model generated using structural equation modeling, the authors concluded that emotion knowledge has a direct, independent influence on academic achievement of $r = .17$ ($p < .05$) after controlling for the many other variables of the study, including intelligence, emotionality, and attention.

Reviewing Recent Reviews

The aforementioned research studies represent just two examples of the burgeoning empirical work in the EI area. The field of emotional intelligence has recently seen three highly visible reviews and critiques that focus especially on ability-based measures. We will summarize the major points and conclusions of those reviews briefly here in regard to what EI predicts.

An article by Zeidner, Roberts, and Matthews (2008), "The Science of Emotional Intelligence," appeared in the *European Psychologist*. The writers divide EI research into four conceptual approaches, but then reduce these, when it comes to measurement, to two: the ability and mixed-model approaches we describe here, writing that "reviews of the various measures of EI . . . have generally been structured around this distinction" (Zeidner et al., 2008, p. 68). In their test-criterion section, they report some selected findings in favor of both types of instruments. Later, however, they conclude that a moratorium on the development of new self-report instruments is needed, while further objective (i.e., ability) measures should be developed. The basis for this recommendation appears to be their conclusion that mixed-model scales are difficult to distinguish from well-known personality dimensions.

To find out more about what EI predicts, it is necessary to move to one of the other two reviews discussed here: Mayer, Salovey, and Caruso's (2008) article, "Emotional Intelligence: New Ability or Eclectic Traits?" appearing in the *American Psychologist*. This review was organized around the schism in the field between ability and mixed models and argued (much as we have here) that the emotional intelligence term was best applied only to the ability approach. The empirical review of measures was summarized, in large part, in a table concerning representative EI results. This table addressed concerns about the incremental validity of EI in predicting various measures of social behavior, with such traits as the Big Five and verbal intelligence partialed out. Five studies illustrated such incremental prediction.

Relative to the other two reviews, *Annual Review* coverage was most focused on outcomes of EI. This review can be regarded more as a consensus document, as it drew authors from both of the other reviews mentioned earlier, and a third independent emotions expert. The authors provided a qualitative review of results from all known ability measures of EI, with results from 1990 forward. Their conclusions for emotional intelligence were presented in their Table 2 and related discussion (Mayer, Roberts, & Barsade, 2008, p. 525).

They concluded the following: Children, adolescents, and adults higher in emotional intelligence exhibited better social relations than others. In most studies reviewed, EI correlated positively with indices of good social relations and social competencies, and negatively with the use of destructive interpersonal strategies and indices of social deviance. Moreover, individuals with high EI were perceived as more pleasant, empathic, and socially adroit than others. As might be expected, these results generalized to better intimate and family relations (for which, however, there were fewer relevant studies and results). The findings also generalized to work environments, where employees exhibited more positive performance, engaged in better negotiations with others, and left others feeling better in stressful work encounters. Of specific interest to intelligence researchers and educators, although EI was correlated with better academic achievement, this often washed out when IQ was partialed out. Finally, those with higher emotional intelligence also experienced higher levels of subjective well-being than did their lower-EI counterparts.

Most of the relationships reviewed between EI and the criteria mentioned earlier were in the $r = .20$ to $.30$ range, and many relationships remained significant after partialing out a number of control variables. However, such results can disappoint readers who are expecting that a single psychological construct accounts for 80% of the variance in important life outcomes! To put these EI results in context, Meyer and colleagues (2001) noted that psychologists ought to be pleased to find relationships at this level – which are comparable to those between, for example, college grades and job performance ($r = .16$), criminal history and recidivism ($r = .18$), and gender and weight ($r = .26$), among others.

The Future of Emotional Intelligence

Capturing the Energy of Mixed-Model Approaches

Earlier in this chapter, it probably seemed as if we dismissed mixed-model approaches to emotional intelligence. Although we are skeptical that this approach will lead to advances in our understanding of emotional intelligence per se, we do acknowledge that many of the traits studied in mixed models are of considerable importance. That is why we recommend calling those traits what they are: aspects of personality, rather than emotional intelligence.

Some psychologists have raised the idea that such traits should be called emotional intelligence simply because they do not fit comfortably into, say, the Big Five approach to personality. The Big Five (described earlier) are five traits often used to represent some of the basic aspects of personal functioning. There is nothing in the discipline of personality psychology, however, that ought to pressure researchers into an either-or choice between emotional intelligence and the Big Five.

In fact, there are several recent contemporary models of personality that can harness the power of studying traits such as optimism and the achievement motive, and competencies such as diversity-sensitivity, and the like. Some models allow for broad organizations of traits, such as the Big Five approach, and contemporary variations of it such as the HEXACO and 10-Aspects models (e.g., DeYoung, Quilty, & Peterson, 2007; Goldberg, 1990). Other models divide personality into functional areas such as a person's mental energy (e.g., motives and emotions), or self-regulation (e.g., self-monitoring, self-control and planning). These latter models include Mischel and Shoda's Cognitive-Affective Personality System (CAPS) model (e.g., Mischel, 2004) and the Systems Set division (e.g., Mayer, 2003, 2005). McAdams and Pal's (2006) "New Big Five" is a hybrid model that divides personality into traits, characteristic adaptations, and other qualities.

The aforementioned Systems Set divides personality into four areas and may be especially suitable for the organization of mixed-model personality characteristics (Mayer, 2003). The first is *Energy Development*, which concerns how the person's motives and emotions combine to enhance an individual's psychological energy. Second is *Knowledge Guidance*, which concerns how intelligences and knowledge combine together to guide mental energy. Third is *Action Implementation*, which includes a person's plans and procedures for operating in the situations she or he faces. Finally, there is *Executive Consciousness*, which involves self-monitoring and self-guidance. The four parts of the Systems Set are illustrated in Figure 26.1.

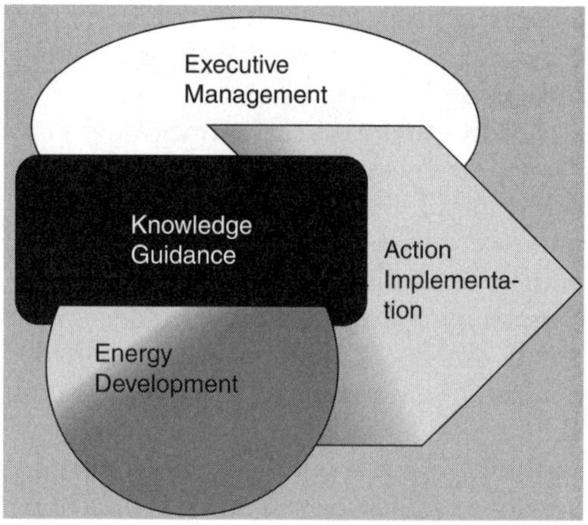

Figure 26.1. The four areas of the systems set. This four-part division of personality has advantages for classifying traits and other qualities of personality. *Energy Development* involves the interactions of motivations and emotions. *Knowledge Guidance* helps direct mental energy toward goals. *Action Implementation* contains plans and skills for operating in the outside environment, and *Executive Management* helps monitor and control the rest. For a further discussion, please refer to the text. Detail from Mayer, J. D. (2009). Psychotherapist's Wall Chart. Lulu.com. Reproduced with permission.

The Systems Set serves as a reasonable organizer for personality traits. In one study, for example, participants using the four-fold division were able to sort 70 commonly studied personality traits into its four categories far better than they could sort the traits using alternative divisions of personality. Using the Systems Set in that study, 97% of the traits could be assigned an area, and judges agreed to such assignments at levels well above chance (Mayer, 2003).

An example of how EI related characteristics might be organized is illustrated in Table 26.3. At the top are the four areas of personal function, as divided according to the Systems Set model. Immediately below are four brief descriptions of the areas. Below that are some prototypical traits that describe each area. For example, Energy Development is described by such traits as the *need for achievement* and *positive affect*. Or, to take another example, *Executive Consciousness* is described by such traits as self-awareness and self-monitoring.

In the last row of Table 26.3, the method is applied to the Trait Emotional Intelligence Questionnaire (TEIQue; Petrides & Furnham, 2003). This self-report, mixed-model measure assesses 15 qualities including Adaptability, Assertiveness, Emotion Perception, Emotion Expression, and so on. These traits are difficult to make congruent with emotional intelligence as reasonably defined. They are, however, very easy to organize within the Systems Set, as shown in the last row of Table 26.3.

When, in the *American Psychologist* article, we recommended that personality traits be labeled as personality traits, part of the reason was to ensure that the field of emotional intelligence survives and thrives as a reputable scientific area. The other reason, however, is that much of the energy behind mixed models, we believe, can contribute more generally to the contemporary field of

Table 26.3 The Systems Set and Its Integration of Personality Parts

	The Systems Set's Four Areas			
Names of the Systems Set	*Energy Development*	*Knowledge Guidance*	*Executive Management*	*Action Implementation*
Brief Description	Motives and emotions join together to enhance an individual's psychic energy	Intelligences operate on knowledge to enhance problem solving	Self-monitoring, self-regulation, defense and coping	Customary styles of carrying out behavior along with plans for action
Generally relevant traits	Specific motivations of achievement, power, affiliation; positive and negative emotionality as well as specific tendencies toward emotions (e.g., happiness, sadness, etc.)	Intelligence, emotional intelligence, competencies, optimism-pessimism, actual self, ideal self, self-esteem, etc.; mental models of other people and the world	Self-awareness, self-monitoring, defensiveness, repression-sensitization, problem-focused coping, emotion-focused coping	Secure attachment, sociability, shyness, social skills, group competencies
Traits of the TEIQue organized accordingly	Self-motivation; Trait happiness	Emotional perception; Self-esteem; Social awareness; Trait empathy; Trait optimism	Adaptability; Emotional regulation; Impulsiveness (low); Stress management	Assertiveness; Emotional expression; Emotional management of others; Relationships

personality psychology if researchers in the area see how to integrate their work in that now-burgeoning area. We hope our earlier description can serve as one illustration of how this might be done.

THE MENTAL ABILITY OF EMOTIONAL REASONING: REALLY AN INTELLIGENCE?

To return to the mental ability conception of emotional intelligence, there are two further questions often asked about EI. The first is, Is emotional intelligence (as an ability) an intelligence, or a talent, or an acquired skill? Whether EI is an intelligence is, to some extent, a matter of one's definition of "intelligence," "talent," and "skill." To us, an intelligence is a mental ability that involves abstract reasoning with information in an area of some breadth and consequence. Consequently, verbal-comprehension, perceptual-organizational abilities, and emotional intelligence all represent intelligences. By contrast, "talents" begin to mix in highly practiced, physical operations with mental operations, for example, in certain forms of musical performance and athletic prowess. Mental skills, such as those displayed in the game of chess, involve highly focused abilities at limited domains. Because the exact demarcation among intelligences, talents, and skills is difficult to fix at present, this will be a matter of some opinion.

Another issue that speaks to whether EI is a true intelligence is its universality versus cross-cultural nature. We believe emotional intelligence is universal or nearly so, and that such universality bolsters its status as an intelligence. The MSCEIT has been translated into such different languages as French, Spanish, Japanese, and Norwegian, and appears to perform comparably in different cultures. Another specific-ability test of EI, the Japanese and Caucasian Brief Affect Recognition Test (JACBART), relies on faces from two different cultures for participants to examine, and the test has been used and is valid with people from many parts of the world. That said, translators of the MSCEIT, for example, have often needed to change items to suit a particular culture so that its content fits with national cultural expectations. Although EI may be universal, in other words, the interpretation of specific items may vary somewhat from culture to culture. There exist, it appears, both universal aspects of emotional understanding and aspects of such understandings that are culturally specific. This seems, once again, consistent with the intelligence concept as presently understood.

Further Research Needed

We have noted that emotional intelligence is part of a larger group of hot intelligences (Mayer, Salovey, & Caruso, 2004). These intelligences are called "hot" because they concern personally relevant information to which people often have personal reactions: of pain, pleasure, defensiveness, emotionality, or moral judgment. Of the partly overlapping intelligences, social intelligence is being newly reoperationalized as a mental ability and has recently seen a revival of interest (e.g., Legree, 1995; Sternberg & Smith, 1985; Weis & Süß, 2007; Wong, Day, Maxwell, & Meara, 1995). A growing body of research supports a practical or successful intelligence (Sternberg, 2003). There also are recent mentions of cultural, personal, and spiritual intelligences (Earley & Ang, 2003; Emmons, 2000; Mayer, 2009). Research on the degree these intelligences overlap and interpenetrate is needed – and remarkably little exists. Moreover, once more is understood about the hot intelligences as a group, their relation and integration with the "cool" intelligences will require further understanding.

Justifiable Excitement Over Emotional Intelligence

To return to emotional intelligence itself, we believe emotional intelligence is worth the excitement. The rigorous search for new intelligences can result in important, incremental predictive power over current measures of intelligence. We believe that emotional intelligence identifies a previously overlooked area of ability critical to certain important areas of human functioning. Before the theory, emotionally intelligent skills lay hidden in the boundary area between mental ability and noncognitive dispositions. Many intelligence researchers were relieved when Scarr (1989) came to the defense of traditional intelligence with the statement that "human virtues . . . such as goodness in human relationships, and talents in music, dance, and painting, should not be called intelligent." Yet there is a borderland between the two. Musical ability, after all, is related to intelligence (e.g., Schellenberg, 2006). Our own intuition was that there was something more than simple emotionality among those people sometimes labeled as touchy-feely, bleeding hearts, sensitive, or empathic souls. Emotional intelligence is the mental ability that lurks amidst the emotions.

There is a social implication of this finding. Scarr (1989) believes that labeling an attribute as an intelligence adjusts social behavior so as to value the entity more than before. She suspects this is one reason some have labeled nonintelligences, such as warmth, as intelligence. Identifying an actual intelligence, therefore, might possibly readjust values. For example, people who have different kinds of skills often can communicate more convincingly about their abilities and limitations. We have often noticed that people in cars readily say, "Oh, I can't navigate well" (low spatial intelligence) and pass the map over to someone else, or turn on the global positioning system (GPS).

We look forward to the day when, rather than dismiss someone else as a "bleeding heart," or a "touchy feely type," or "oversensitive," a person will feel comfortable saying, "Oh, I can't read emotions; you help me understand how to make my friend feel better." Passing the job of emotional reading over to the individual who can perform it (or, indeed, passing it to some future emotion-sensing device) would be readjusting social values in a way that might make good sense for all parties.

Conclusion

There is growing consensus that emotional intelligence involves the capacity to reason accurately with emotion and emotional information, and of emotion to enhance thought. There is an increasing call to "weed out" those conceptualizations that do not make sense to be called *emotional intelligence*. Alternatively, they can be transplanted in the soil of personality psychology, where they better belong. Current research suggests that mental ability models of emotional intelligence can be described as a standard intelligence, and they empirically meet the criteria for a standard intelligence. Emotional intelligence therefore provides a recognition of an exciting new area of human ability.

Acknowledgment

The first three authors disclose that they receive royalty payments from the sale of an assessment tool, the Mayer-Salovey-Caruso Emotional Intelligence Test (MSCEIT) published by MHS, Inc., and discussed in this chapter.

References

Adams, S. (1997, April 7). Dilbert. In *Boston Globe* (comics section), Boston, MA.

Arnheim, R. (1974). *Art and visual perception (The new version)*. Berkeley: University of California Press.

Bain, A. (1855/1977). *The senses and the intellect*. London: John W. Parker & Son. [Reprinted in D. N. Robinson (Ed.), *Significant contributions to the history of psychology: 1750–1920 [Series A: Orientations; Vol. 4]*. Washington, DC: University Publications of America.

Bar-On, R. (1997). *The Emotional Quotient Inventory (EQ-i): Technical manual*. Toronto, Canada: Multi-Health Systems.

Bennetts, L. (March, 1996). Emotional savvy. *Parents*, 56–61.

Block, J., & Block, J. H. (1980). The role of ego-control and ego resiliency in the organization of behavior. In W. A. Collins (Ed.), *The Minnesota symposium on child psychology* (Vol. 13, pp. 33–101). Hillsdale, NJ: Erlbaum.

Brackett, M., & Mayer, J. D. (2003). Convergent, discriminant, and incremental validity of competing measures of emotional intelligence. *Personality and Social Psychology Bulletin, 64*, 1147–1158.

Brackett, M. A., Rivers, S. E., Shiffman, S., Lerner, N., & Salovey, P. (2006). Relating emotional abilities to social functioning: A comparison of self-report and performance measures of emotional intelligence. *Journal of Personality and Social Psychology, 91*, 780–795.

Buck, R. (1976). A test of nonverbal receiving ability: Preliminary studies. *Human Communication Research, 2*, 162–171.

Buck, R. (1984). *The communication of emotion*. New York, NY: Guilford Press.

Buck, R., Miller, R. E., & Caul, D. F. (1974). Sex, personality, and physiological variables in the communication of emotion via facial expression. *Journal of Personality and Social Psychology, 30*, 587–596.

Campbell, R. J., Kagan, N. I., & Krathwohl, D. R. (1971). The development and validation of a scale to measure affective sensitivity (empathy). *Journal of Counseling Psychology, 18*, 407–412.

Cattell, R. B., Cattell, A. K., & Cattell, H. E. P. (1993). *Sixteen Personality Factor Questionnaire* (5th ed.). Champaign, IL: Institute for Personality and Ability Testing.

Chapin, F. S. (1967). *The social insight test*. Palo Alto, CA: Consulting Psychologists Press.

Cooper, R. K., & Sawaf, A. (1997). *Executive EQ: Emotional intelligence in leadership and organizations*. New York, NY: Grosset/Putnam.

Daus, C. S., & Ashkanasy, N. M. (2003). Will the real emotional intelligence please stand up? On deconstructing the emotional intelligence "debate." *Industrial–Organizational Psychologist, 41*, 69–72.

DeYoung, C. G., Quilty, L. C., & Peterson, J. B. (2007). Between facets and domains: 10 aspects of the Big Five. *Journal of Personality and Social Psychology, 93*, 880–896.

Earley, P. C., & Ang, S. (2003). Cultural intelligence: *Individual interactions across cultures*. Palo Alto, CA: Stanford University Press.

Ekman, P. (1973). *Darwin and facial expression: A century of research in review*. New York, NY: Academic Press.

Emmons, R. A. (2000). Is spirituality an intelligence? Motivation, cognition, and the psychology of ultimate concern. *International Journal for the Psychology of Religion, 10*, 3–26.

Epstein, S., & Meier, P. (1989). Constructive thinking: A broad coping variable with specific components. *Journal of Personality and Social Psychology, 54*, 332–350.

Gardner, H. (1993). *Frames of mind* (10th anniversary ed.). New York, NY: Basic Books.

Gardner, H. (March, 1997). "Who owns 'intelligence?'" Invited talk, in G. Sinatra (Chair) and C. Bereiter (Discussant), *Expanding our concept of intelligence: What's missing and what could we gain?* Symposium at the Annual Meeting of the American Educational Research Association, Chicago, IL.

Goldberg, L. R. (1990). An alternative "description of personality": The *Big-Five* factor solution. *Journal of Personality and Social Psychology, 59*, 1216–1229.

Goleman, D. (1995). *Emotional intelligence*. New York, NY: Bantam Books.

Goleman, D. (1998). *Working with emotional intelligence*. New York, NY: Bantam.

Goleman, D. (2005). *Emotional intelligence* (10th anniversary ed.). New York, NY: Bantam.

Gottman, J. (1997). *The heart of parenting: How to raise an emotionally intelligent child*. New York, NY: Simon & Schuster.

Griffith, B. (1996, November 17). Zippy the Pinhead. *Boston Globe (comics section)*, Boston, MA.

Grubb, W. L., & McDaniel, M. A. (2007). The fakability of Bar-On's Emotional Quotient Inventory Short Form: Catch me if you can. *Human Performance, 20*, 43–59.

Henig, R. M. (1996, June). Are you smarter than you think? *McCall's*, 84–91.

Hilgard, E. R. (1980). The trilogy of mind: Cognition, affection, and conation. *Journal of the History of the Behavioral Sciences, 16*, 107–117.

Izard, C. E. (1993). Four systems for emotion activation: Cognitive and noncognitive processes. *Psychological Review, 100*, 68–90.

Jung, C. (1921/1971). *Psychological types* (H. G. Baynes, Trans.; R. F. C. Hull, Rev. Trans.). Princeton, NJ: Princeton University Press. [Original work published 1921]

Kagan, N. (1978). *Affective sensitivity test: Validity and reliability*. Paper presented at the 86th meeting of the American Psychological Association, San Francisco, CA.

Legree, P. J. (1995). Evidence for an oblique social intelligence factor established with a Likert-based testing procedure. *Intelligence, 21*, 247–266.

Leuner, B. (1966). Emotional intelligence and emancipation. *Praxis der Kinderpsychologie und Kinderpsychiatie, 15*, 193–203.

Leuner B. (1966). Emotional intelligence and emancipation. *Praxis Kinderpsychol. Kinderpsychiatrie, 15*, 193–203.

MacCann, C., & Roberts, R. (2008). New paradigms for assessing emotional intelligence: Theory and data. *Emotion, 8*, 540–551.

MacLean, P. D. (1973). *A triune concept of the brain and behavior*. Toronto, Canada: University of Toronto Press.

Matsumoto, D., LeRoux, J., & Wilson-Cohn, C., Raroque, J., Kooken, K., Ekman, P., Yrizarry, N., Loewinger, S., Uchida, H., Yee, A., Amo, L., & Goh, A. (2000). A new test to measure emotion recognition ability: Matsumoto and Ekman's Japanese and Caucasian Brief Affect Recognition Test (JACBART). *Journal of Nonverbal Behavior, 24*, 179–209.

Matthews, G., Zeidner, M., & Roberts, R. D. (2002). *Emotional intelligence: Science and myth*. Cambridge, MA: MIT Press.

Mayer, J. D. (1995a). The System-Topics Framework and the structural arrangement of systems within and around personality. *Journal of Personality, 63*, 459–493.

Mayer, J. D. (1995b). A framework for the classification of personality components. *Journal of Personality, 63*, 819–877.

Mayer, J. D. (1999). Emotional intelligence: Popular or scientific psychology? *APA Monitor, 30*, 50.

Mayer J. D. (2000). Emotion, intelligence, emotional intelligence. In J. P. Forgas (Ed.), *The Handbook of Affect and Social Cognition* (pp. 410–31). Mahwah, NJ: Erlbaum.

Mayer, J. D. (2003). Structural divisions of personality and the classification of traits. *Review of General Psychology, 7*, 381–401.

Mayer, J. D. (2005). A tale of two visions: Can a new view of personality help integrate psychology? *American Psychologist, 60*, 294–307.

Mayer, J. D. (2009). Personal intelligence expressed: A theoretical analysis. *Review of General Psychology, 13*, 46–58.

Mayer, J. D., Chabot, H. F., & Carlsmith, K. M. (1997). Conation, affect, and cognition in personality. In G. Matthews (Ed.), *Cognitive science perspectives on personality and emotion* (pp. 31–63). New York, NY: Elsevier.

Mayer, J. D., & Cobb, C. D. (2000). Educational policy on emotional intelligence: Does it make sense? *Educational Psychology Review, 12*, 163–183.

Mayer, J. D., DiPaolo, M. T., & Salovey, P. (1990). Perceiving affective content in ambiguous visual stimuli: A component of emotional intelligence. *Journal of Personality Assessment, 54*, 772–781.

Mayer, J. D., & Geher, G. (1996). Emotional intelligence and the identification of emotion. *Intelligence, 22*, 89–113.

Mayer, J. D., Roberts, R. D., & Barsade, S. G. (2008). Human abilities: Emotional intelligence. *Annual Review of Psychology, 59*, 507–536.

Mayer, J. D., & Salovey, P. (1993). The intelligence of emotional intelligence. *Intelligence, 17*, 433–442.

Mayer, J. D., & Salovey, P. (1995). Emotional intelligence and the construction and regulation of feelings. *Applied and Preventive Psychology, 4*, 197–208.

Mayer, J. D., & Salovey, P. (1997). What is emotional intelligence? In P. Salovey & D. Sluyter (Eds.). *Emotional development and emotional intelligence: Implications for educators* (pp. 3–31). New York, NY: Basic Books.

Mayer, J. D., Salovey, P., & Caruso, D. (1997). *Emotional IQ test* (CD ROM). Needham, MA: Virtual Knowledge.

Mayer, J. D., Salovey, P., & Caruso, D. R. (2000). Models of emotional intelligence. In R. J. Sternberg (Ed.), *Handbook of intelligence* (pp. 396–420). New York, NY: Cambridge University Press.

Mayer, J. D., Salovey, P., & Caruso, D. R. (2004). Emotional intelligence: Theory, findings, and implications. *Psychological Inquiry, 60*, 197–215.

Mayer, J. D., Salovey, P., & Caruso, D. R. (2008). Emotional intelligence: New ability or eclectic traits? *American Psychologist, 63*, 503–517.

Mayer, J.D., & Stevens, A. (1994). An emerging understanding of the reflective (meta-) experience of mood. *Journal of Research in Personality, 28*, 351–373.

McAdams, D. P., & Pals, J. L. (2006). A new Big Five: Fundamental principles for an integrative science of personality. *American Psychologist, 61*, 204–217.

Meyer, G. J., Finn, S. E., Eyde, L. D., Kay, G. G., Moreland, K. L., Dies, R. R., Eisman, E. J., Kubiszyn, T. W., & Read, G. M. (2001). Psychological testing and psychological assessment: A review of evidence and issues. *American Psychologist, 52*, 128–165.

Mischel, W. (2004). Toward an integrative science of the person. *Annual Review of Psychology, 55*, 1–22.

Nowicki S. J., & Carton J. (1993). The measurement of emotional intensity from facial expressions. *Journal of Social Psychology, 133*, 749–750.

Oatley, K. (2004). Emotional intelligence and the intelligence of emotions. *Psychological Inquiry, 15*, 216–221.

Palmer, B. R., Gignac, G., Manocha, R., & Stough, C. (2005). A psychometric evaluation of the Mayer-Salovey-Caruso Emotional Intelligence Test Version 2.0. *Intelligence, 33*, 285–305.

Paulhus, D. L. (1991). Measurement and control of response bias. In J. P. Robinson, P. R. Shaver, & L. S. Wrightsman (Eds.), *Measures of personality and social psychological attitudes* (pp. 17–60). New York, NY: Academic Press/Harcourt Brace Jovanovich.

Paulhus D. L., Lysy D. C., & Yik M. S. M. (1998). Self-report measures of intelligence: Are they useful as proxy IQ tests? *Journal of Personality, 66*, 525–554.

Payne, W. L. (1986). A study of emotion: Developing emotional intelligence; Self-integration; relating to fear, pain and desire. *Dissertation Abstracts International, 47*, (01), p. 203A. (University Microfilms No. AAC 8605928).

Peterson, K. S. (1997, February 18). Signs of intelligence: Do new definitions of smart dilute meaning? *USA Today*, Section D, p. 1.

Petrides, K. V., & Furnham, A. (2001). Trait emotional intelligence: Psychometric investigation with reference to established trait taxonomies. *European Journal of Personality, 15*, 425–448.

Petrides, K. V., & Furnham, A. (2003). Trait emotional intelligence: Behavioural validation in two studies of emotion recognition and reactivity to mood induction. *European Journal of Personality*, 17, 39–57.

Pitterman H., & Nowicki S. J. 2004. A test of the ability to identify emotion in human standing and sitting postures: The diagnostic analysis of nonverbal accuracy-2 posture test (DANVA2-POS). *Genetic Social and General Psychological Monographs*, 130, 146–162.

Plutchik, R. (1984). Emotions: A general psychoevolutionary theory. In K. R. Scherer & P. Ekman (Eds.), *Approaches to emotion* (pp. 197–219). Hillsdale, NJ: Erlbaum.

Publilius Syrus. (1961). "Sententiae." In J. W. Duff & A. M. Duff (Eds.), *Minor Latin poets*. Cambridge, MA: Harvard University Press. [Original work published c. 100 BCE]

Rosenthal, R., Hall, J. A., DiMatteo, M. R., Rogers, P. L., & Archer, D (1979). *Sensitivity to nonverbal communication: The PONS Test*. Baltimore, MD: Johns Hopkins University Press.

Roseman, I. J., & Evdokas, A. (2004). Appraisals cause experienced emotions: Experimental evidence. *Cognition and Emotion*, 18, 1–28.

Rosete, D. (2005, June 12–14). *A leaders edge – what attributes make an effective leader?* Paper presented at the Fifth Annual Emotional Intelligence Conference, the Netherlands.

Rosete, D. (2009). *A leaders edge – what attributes make an effective leader?* Manuscript in preparation.

Saarni, C. (1990). Emotional competence: How emotions and relationships become integrated. In R. A. Thompson (Ed.), *Socioemotional development: Nebraska symposium on motivation* (Vol. 36, pp. 115–182). Lincoln: University of Nebraska Press.

Saarni, C. (1997). Emotional competence and self-regulation in childhood. In P. Salovey & D. J. Sluyter, *Emotional development and emotional intelligence* (pp. 35–66). New York, NY: Basic Books.

Saarni, C. (in press). *Developing emotional competence*. New York, NY: Guilford Press.

Salerno, J. G.,(1996). *The whole intelligence: Emotional quotient (EQ)*. Oakbank, South Australia: Noble House of Australia.

Salovey, P., & Mayer, J. D. (1990). Emotional intelligence. *Imagination, Cognition, and Personality*, 9, 185–211.

Salovey, P., & Mayer, J. D. (1994). Some final thoughts about personality and intelligence. In R. J. Sternberg, & P. Ruzgis (Eds.), *Personality and intelligence* (pp. 303–318). Cambridge, UK: Cambridge University Press.

Salovey, P., Mayer, J. D., Goldman, S., Turvey, C., & Palfai, T. (1995). Emotional attention, clarity, and repair: Exploring emotional intelligence using the Trait Meta-Mood Scale. In J. W. Pennebaker (Ed.), *Emotion, disclosure, and health* (pp. 125–154). Washington, DC: American Psychological Association.

Scarr, S. (1989). Protecting general intelligence: Constructs and consequences for interventions. In R. L. Linn (Ed.), *Intelligence: Measurement, theory, and public policy*. Urbana: University of Illinois Press.

Schaffer, L. F., Gilmer, B., & Schoen, M. (1940). *Psychology* (p. xii). New York: Harper & Brothers.

Schellenberg, E. G. (2006). Long-term positive associations between music lessons and IQ. *Journal of Educational Psychology*, 98, 457–468.

Schultz, D., Izard, C. E., Ackerman, B. P., & Youngstrom, E. A. (2001). Emotion knowledge in economically disadvantaged children: Self-regulatory antecedents and relations for to social difficulties and withdrawal. *Development and Psychopathology*, 13, 53–67.

Segal, J. (1997). *Raising your emotional intelligence*. New York, NY: Holt.

Shapiro, L. E. (1997). *How to raise a child with a high E.Q: A parents' guide to emotional intelligence*. New York, NY: HarperCollins.

Simmons, S., & Simmons, J. C. (1997). *Measuring emotional intelligence with techniques for self-improvement*. Arlington, TX: Summit Publishing Group.

Spearman, C. (1927). *The abilities of man*. New York, NY: Macmillan.

Steiner, C. M. (1986). *When a man loves a woman*. New York, NY: Grove Press.

Steiner, C. M. (2003). *Emotional literacy: Intelligence with a heart*. Fawnskin, CA: Personhood Press.

Steiner, C., & Perry, P. (1997). *Achieving emotional literacy: A program to increase your emotional intelligence*. New York, NY: Avon.

Sternberg, R. J. (1988). *The triarchic mind: A new theory of human intelligence*. New York, NY: Penguin Books.

Sternberg, R. J. (1996). *Successful intelligence: How practical and creative intelligence determine success in life*. New York, NY: Simon & Schuster.

Sternberg, R. J. (2003). A broad view of intelligence: The theory of successful intelligence. *Consulting Psychology Journal: Practice and Research*, 55, 139–154.

Sternberg, R. J., & Smith, C. (1985). Social intelligence and decoding skills in nonverbal communication. *Social Cognition*, 3, 168–192.

Taylor, G. J., Ryan, D., & Bagby, R. M. (1985). Toward the development of a new self-report alexithymia scale. *Psychotherapy and psychosomatics*, 44, 191–199.

Terman, L. M. (1921). II [Second contribution to "Intelligence and its measurement: A symposium"]. *Journal of Educational Psychology*, 12, 127–133.

Tett, R. P., Fox, K. E., & Wang, A. (2005). Development and validation of a self-report measure of emotional intelligence as a multidimensional trait domain. *Personality and Social Psychology Bulletin*, 31, 859–888.

Thorndike, R. L., & Stein, S. (1937). An evaluation of the attempts to measure social intelligence. *Psychological Bulletin*, 34, 275–284.

Time. (1995, October 2). [Cover]. New York: Time Warner.

Tomkins, S. S. (1962). *Affect, imagery, consciousness: Vol. 1, The positive affects*. New York, NY: Springer.

Trentacosta, C. J., & Izard, C. E. (2007). Kindergarten children's emotion competence as a predictor of their academic competence in first grade. *Emotion*, 7, 77–88.

Van Ghent D. (1953). *The English novel: Form and function*. New York, NY: Harper & Row.

Wechsler, D. (1940). Nonintellective factors in general intelligence. *Psychological Bulletin*, 37, 444–445.

Wechsler, D. (1943). Non-intellective factors in general intelligence. *Journal of Abnormal Social Psychology*, 38, 100–104.

Wechsler, D. (1958). *The measurement and appraisal of adult intelligence* (4th ed.). Baltimore, MD: Williams & Wilkins.

Weis, S., & Süß, H. M. (2007). Reviving the search for social intelligence – A multitrait-multimethod study of its structure and construct validity. *Personality and Individual Differences*, 42, 3–14.

Weisinger, H. (1997). *Emotional intelligence at work*. New York: Jossey-Bass.

Wong, C. T., Day, J. D., Maxwell, S. E., & Meara, N. M. (1995). A multitrait-multimethod study of academic and social intelligence in college students. *Journal of Educational Psychology*, 87, 117–133.

Woodworth, R. S. (1940). *Psychology* (4th ed.). New York, NY: Henry Holt.

Young, P. T. (1936). *Motivation of behavior*. New York, NY: Wiley.

Zeidner, M., Roberts, R. D., & Matthews, G. (2008). The science of emotional intelligence: Current consensus and controversies. *European Psychologist*, 13, 64–78.

CHAPTER 27

Practical Intelligence

Richard K. Wagner

What is practical intelligence? How is practical intelligence related to other forms of intelligence? Can the development of practical intelligence be facilitated? This chapter attempts to answer these questions. The field of practical intelligence is well characterized by the yin and yang of two complementary enterprises. The first has been to determine whether practical intelligence exists as a separate form of intelligence. The second has been to determine how practical intelligence fits in the larger context of intelligence broadly defined. More recently, a third area of interest has emerged, namely, whether and how the development of practical intelligence might be enhanced. This chapter is divided into four parts. The first part reviews research that addresses whether practical intelligence exists as a separate form of intelligence. The second part reviews research that seeks to incorporate practical intelligence into larger frameworks. The third part reviews research on facilitating the development of practical intelligence. The final part addresses some the future of the field of practical intelligence.

What Is Practical Intelligence?

Defining any kind of intelligence has not been an easy task. When the *Journal of Educational Psychology* asked 17 leading researchers to define intelligence in 1921, the results were 14 different definitions and 3 nonreplies. Sixty-five years later, leading researchers were asked to respond to the identical question. Again the results were characterized by more diversity than consistency (Sternberg & Detterman, 1986). An analysis of this second group of definitions identified an unwieldy set of 27 different attributes of intelligence (Sternberg & Berg, 1986). Although definitions of practical intelligence vary to a similar extent, it is useful to spend a little time considering them as a first pass at describing what is meant by the term *practical intelligence*.

Exclusionary Definitions

An exclusionary definition is a definition of something based on describing what it is not. A classic example is provided by Frederiksen

(1986), who described practical intelligence as being reflected in our cognitive responses to most things that happen outside the school setting. Frederiksen's research interests centered on practical intelligence as manifested by managers in various industries. He measured their practical intelligence by simulating what they might do in their daily work using an "in-basket" technique. The in-basket technique requires managers to sit at a desk and work their way through an in-basket that contains simulated memos, phone messages, and other items.

Observers classified what the managers did as they worked their way through the in-basket using phrases such as "delegates task to subordinate," "seeks additional information," and "asks for advice." The in-basket technique has been used to study managerial performance in a variety of managerial domains including business, government, the military, and school administration. Performance has been found to depend on two key attributes: domain knowledge and ideational fluency. Domain knowledge refers to knowledge acquired from doing similar tasks in one's job. Ideational fluency refers to the number of relevant ideas and information produced in the in-basket simulation.

Defining practical intelligence in terms of cognitive responses to problems that occur outside the school setting implies important differences between the kinds of problems found inside and outside of school settings. Problems found in school settings and also on IQ tests typically (1) are well defined, (2) are formulated by others, (3) come with all necessary information, (4) have a single correct solution, (5) have only one or at most a couple of ways of obtaining the correct solution, and (6) are unrelated to everyday experience (Neisser, 1976; Wagner & Sternberg, 1985). Problems found outside the classroom setting differ in that they typically (1) are ill-defined; (2) require formulation by the problem solver; (3) have missing information that must be acquired; (4) have multiple solutions, each with liabilities as well as assets; (5) have multiple methods for achieving solutions; and (6) are related to everyday experience.

Empirical support for the distinction between in-school and out-of-school problems comes from predictive validity studies of IQ tests and of measures of practical problem solving. The average predictive validity coefficient between IQ scores and job performance is about .2 (Hartigan & Wigdor, 1989; Sternberg, Wagner, Williams, & Horvath, 1995; Wigdor & Garner, 1982). An average predictive validity coefficient of .2 means that IQ accounts for only 4% of the variance in job performance. In contrast, the average predictive validity coefficient between IQ scores and performance in job training is .4, which means that 16% of variance in training performance is accounted for by IQ. IQ then accounts for four times as much variance in the more school-like criterion of performance in job training programs than in the less school-like criterion of actual job performance.

Observed validity coefficients can be inaccurate indices of the theoretical relations between IQ and performance. They are affected by range restriction and measurement error. Range restriction refers to the fact that samples available to be used in predictive validity studies of job performance are limited in range of scores because they can include only individuals actually hired by a company. Low scorers are less likely to be hired, leaving a restricted range of both test and job performance for hired individuals compared to an unselected sample. Measurement error refers to the fact that unreliability in the test or the criterion measure reduces the size of the observed validity coefficient. Correcting for both measurement error and range restriction increases the average validity coefficient between IQ and job performance to .5. However, this value inflates the actual unique importance of using IQ tests to predict job performance for an important reason beyond the fact that measurement error exists in practice. Validity coefficients are simple correlations between test scores and criterion measures, and simple correlations overestimate the unique predictive power of a variable when multiple sources of information are used to select individuals (Wagner, 1997). Most individuals are selected using a variety of sources of information such as grade-point average, letters of recommendations, personal statements, previous experience, educational attainment, and interviews. Validity coefficients overestimate the value of any single source of information when multiple, correlated sources of information are related to the criterion.

A problem with defining practical intelligence as intellectual performance in out-of-school settings is a lack of specificity that makes it difficult to study or measure practical intelligence. For these reasons, others have attempted to define practical intelligence more specifically.

Practical Know-How

Cross-cultural studies from a large number of societies provide examples of practical intelligence manifested as practical know-how. Berry and Irvine (1986) provided the example of individuals who repair machines and appliances without the benefit of sophisticated diagnostic equipment or even replacement parts. If you live in a modern society and have a problem with your automobile, repairing it often is a fairly straightforward matter. Test equipment and a computer on your automobile that records malfunctions are used to identify the problem part or component. Most repairs are done by replacing defective parts as opposed to repairing them. In contrast, automobiles in poorer countries are kept in running condition without test equipment or even replacement parts. Problems are identified by a diagnostic process that relies heavily on previous experience as opposed to technical manuals. Solving the problem often involves actually repairing defective parts or modifying parts from another model to fit the model of automobile being repaired. Berry and Irvine (1986) used the concept of the *bricoleur* to describe individuals who do this kind of repair. The term comes from Levi-Strauss (1966), who used the term *bricolage* to describe odd-job type work. As used by Beery and Irvine, a bricoleur will size up the situation and the available resources and devise an improvisational solution.

Another example of practical know-how is provided by the ocean navigation skills of the Puluwat people of Micronesia (Gladwin, 1970). They travel the islands of Micronesia in large oceangoing canoes. The Puluwat navigate using a system in which the islands are considered to be moving as opposed to the canoe they are traveling in. Although this seems counterintuitive, if you actually are on board a canoe, the islands appear to be moving. They either show up on or disappear from the horizon, and move closer, farther away, or along a parallel course as the journey takes place.

The Puluwat's system of navigation divides a journey into three phases: selecting the destination island; maintaining a course toward the destination island; and locating the destination island. Selecting the destination island involves consideration of the purpose of the trip and the wind, weather, and season. The second phase begins by identifying the correct course to the destination island. This is accomplished by going out to a departure point in the harbor and drawing an imaginary line from a point on the departure island that is known to indicate the approximate direction to the destination island. Extending this line through the canoe and out to the horizon marks the desired course. Various sources of information are used to maintain the desired course once the departure island is out of sight. Dead reckoning in the form of keeping track of the estimated course, speed, and time is used for estimating present position, as is marking the passage of known islands and reefs. Stars are used for navigation at night. They also are used at dusk and at dawn in conjunction with known islands in a type of navigation aid called *etak*. This involves dividing the ocean into sectors on the basis of imaginary lines drawn with reference to the island and selected visible stars. The final phase of navigation – locating the destination island – is nontrivial. Navigation accuracy falls short of what is possible using modern technology. Missing an island is easy to do and can be life threatening. Determining that the destination island has actually been overshot can be difficult, and because journeys are planned to take advantage of prevailing winds and waves, little headway may be possible after reversing course in the belief that the destination island was missed. To detect the destination island, the navigator attempts to detect odors, sounds, and changes in wind direction and velocity that can signal presence of a land mass. Observing birds at dusk that are known to roost on land at night also signals the presence of land.

Grigorenko et al. (2004) reported a case study of practical as well as academic intelligence in Yup'ik Alaskan communities. They found that performance on a measure of practical intelligence was related to rated possession of desired Yup-ik traits. Performance on practical intelligence was distinct from the measures of fluid and crystallized intelligence.

Everyday mathematics provides another example of practical know-how. Nuñes, Schliemann, and Carraher (1993) studied the children of street vendors in Brazil. Children help out their parents by completing transactions with customers while their parents are busy with other customers or running errands. For the children to complete transactions, they needed to be able to solve practical mathematics problems without the aid of paper and pencil or calculators. Children are adept at solving these problems despite having little formal schooling. In an interesting study, Carraher, Carraher, and Schliemann (1985) gave identical problems to the children of street vendors in three contexts: an informal context, a formal word-problem context, and a formal arithmetic operations context. For purposes of illustrating the three contexts, it helps to have an example problem: How much change must be given back if a customer buys three apples at a cost of 50 cruzeiros each and pays for them with a 500 cruzeiros bill? An informal context involved treating the problems as real transactions at the parents' street vendor location. A formal word-problem context required having children solve the same problems using paper and pencil, with the problems presented as word problems. For this example, the word problem would be represented as it was described above. A formal arithmetic operations context consisted of simply presenting the problems as math problems (e.g., $500 - 3 \times 50$). The key result was that the average accuracy for solving the identical problems varied across the three contexts. For the informal context that consisted of actually doing problems at work, average accuracy was 98%. For the formal word-problem context, average accuracy dropped to 74%. For the formal arithmetic operations context, average accuracy fell to only 37%. For these children, performance was dramatically better in the practical context compared to the more academic contexts.

Studies of everyday mathematics also have been carried out using educated grocery shoppers. Lave, Murtaugh, and de la Rocha (1984) observed California grocery shoppers who were trying to determine the most economical size of a product to buy. The study was carried out before labels included the price per ounce as is common today. For the majority of products, the largest size was the most economical but this was not true universally. The shoppers solved these mathematical problems by using mental shortcuts that were not perfectly accurate but were good enough for the task at hand. For example, the shopper had to decide between a 10 ounce box of oatmeal that cost 98 cents and a 24 ounce box for $2.29. Shoppers solved the problem by considering 10 ounces at 98 cents is about 10 cents per ounce. At 10 cents per ounce, 24 ounces would be $2.40. Because $2.29 was noticeably less than $2.40, the larger size was judged to be more economical than the smaller size. As a follow-up, the shoppers were given a test of mental arithmetic. Accuracy at picking the best buys was unrelated to mental arithmetic test performance.

Another example of everyday mathematics is provided by a study of workers at a milk processing plant (Scribner, 1984). The workers studied were assemblers whose job it was to assemble orders of cases that varied in terms of both products (e.g., whole milk, low-fat milk) and quantities (e.g., pints, quarts, and gallons). Experienced workers filled orders by combining existing partially filled cases using a strategy that minimized the number of moves required. Implementing the strategy required the workers to carry out calculations in their heads that involved using different base number systems. Performance at assembling orders was unrelated to IQ, arithmetic test scores, or school grades. The assemblers were able to use the complex strategy efficiently despite being the least educated workers in the plant. In fact, when more highly educated white-collar workers had to fill in on a temporary basis, they were not as efficient at assembling orders as the less educated assemblers.

A final example of everyday mathematics comes from a study of expert racetrack handicappers (Ceci & Liker, 1988). Of particular interest were the strategies used to estimate post-time odds. Expert handicappers were found to use a complicated strategy that involved adjusting a horse's previous quarter-mile times for various conditions that affect them. Race times are divided into quarter-mile times, and time over each quarter mile of a previous race is published. Examples of conditions that affect quarter-mile times include condition of the track, speed of the other horses in the race, and where the horse was running relative to the rail if the quarter mile was part of a curve rather than a straightaway. The accuracy with which handicappers estimated post-time odds was unrelated to their IQs.

For other examples of cross-cultural studies of practical know-how, see Berry and Irvine (1986); Burton Jones and Kronner (1976); Cole, Gay, Glick, and Sharp (1971); Laboratory of Comparative Human Cognition (1982); Levy-Strauss (1966); and Scribner and Cole (1981).

Tacit Knowledge

A particular form of practical know-how that figures prominently in research on practical intelligence is tacit knowledge. Tacit knowledge has been defined as practical knowledge that usually is not openly expressed or taught directly (Wagner & Sternberg, 1985). Three key features of tacit knowledge have been proposed by Sternberg et al. (2000). First, tacit knowledge typically is acquired with little or no environmental support. As such, it is typically acquired on one's own without formal means for its transmission. Perhaps the closest tacit knowledge comes to being "taught" is when a mentor makes an effort to "show the ropes" to a mentee. Second, tacit knowledge is procedural rather than declarative, using Anderson's (1983) terminology; it is a form of knowing how as opposed to knowing that. It is knowledge that guides action or behavior without typically being subject to conscious introspection. Third, tacit knowledge is practically useful. It serves an instrumental role in attainment of desired goals.

The concept of tacit knowledge was popularized by Polanyi (1958, 1966), who argued that such knowledge routinely underlies task performance. According to Polanyi, tacit knowledge even is involved when a hammer is used to strike an object (Cianciolo et al., 2006). When you use a hammer, you are unaware how the sensation the tool is producing in your palm corresponds to the velocity and direction with which the hammer is moving to its target. Others have pursued understanding of the nature of tacit knowledge in a variety of domains, including cognitive psychology (Reber, 1989; Reber & Lewis, 1977), differential psychology (Sternberg et al., 2000), linguistics (Dahl, 2000), and management (Nonaka & Takeuchi, 1995).

Performance on measures of tacit knowledge has been shown to predict a variety of outcomes. Wagner (1987) administered a measure of tacit knowledge about academic psychology to college professors, graduate students, and undergraduates. For college professors, the correlation between tacit knowledge scores and number of citations reported in the *Social Sciences Citation Index* was .44. There also was a significant linear trend of increasing tacit knowledge from undergraduates to graduate students to professors. Similar results were reported for a measure of tacit knowledge about business management that was given to undergraduates, business graduate students, and managers.

Wagner and Sternberg (1985) reported significant correlations between tacit knowledge about management and salary (r = .46) and size of company (r = .34) for a sample of managers. In a second study of bank managers, tacit knowledge predicted success in generating new business (r = .56) and percentage of merit salary increase (r = .48). Similarly, Wagner and Sternberg (1990) reported a correlation of .61 between tacit knowledge and performance ratings on management simulations given in a leadership-development program. Turning to the domain of auditing, Tan and Libby (1997) reported significantly higher tacit knowledge about auditing for top performers compared to bottom performers in a sample of audit managers. Tacit knowledge has also predicted criterion performance in several military settings (Hedlund et al., 2003; Legree et al., 2003).

Grigorenko, Sternberg, and Strauss (2006) developed a measure of tacit knowledge about teaching (see also Stemier et al., 2006). Teachers who scored higher on the measure were rated as more effective by their principals. The researchers administered the measure in both the United States and Israel and found the measure to perform comparably across the two cultures.

Measures of practical intelligence based on the tacit knowledge framework and Sternberg's theory of successful intelligence have been evaluated in the context of admissions testing (Sternberg, 2004). Hedlund et al. (2006) developed a practical intelligence supplement to the Graduate Management Admission Test (GMAT) in the form of two measures that assessed business practical knowledge. Evaluation of the measures showed that they provided a small but statistically significant increment to prediction beyond the GMAT. Performance on the practical tests also showed less disparity across gender and racial/ethnic groups than did the GMAT. Sternberg (2006) developed supplementary tasks including measures of practical know-how to be used in conjunction with the SAT in his Rainbow Project. The supplementary tasks enhanced the predictive validity of high school grade-point average and also showed less disparity associated with ethnic group differences.

How Is Practical Intelligence Related to Other Forms of Intelligence?

Although practical intelligence is related to performance in a variety of domains, studies in which both practical intelligence – primarily various measures of tacit knowledge – and IQ have been measured demonstrate that practical intelligence is distinct from fluid and crystallized intelligence (Cianciolo, Antonakis, & Sternberg, 2004; Collonia-Willner, 1998, Legree et al., 2003; Sternberg et al., 2001; Tan & Libby, 1997; Wagner, 1997; Wagner & Sternberg, 1985, 1990). For example, Cianciolo et al. (2006) created three tacit-knowledge inventories to assess relatively general aspects of everyday life as opposed to job or domain-specific knowledge. They reported three studies that used factor analysis to examine relations among tacit knowledge, fluid intelligence, and crystallized intelligence. The results supported a coherent practical intelligence factor that was distinct from both fluid and practical intelligence. Although these studies support the idea that assessments of practical intelligence measure something different from what traditional IQ tests measure, where does practical intelligence fit in the context of intelligence broadly defined?

One answer to this question has been to challenge the idea that practical intelligence exists as a form of intelligence (Gottfredson, 2003). For example, Schmidt and Hunter (1993) consider measures of practical intelligence to be tests of job knowledge. A conventional view of job performance is that performance depends upon general intelligence and job knowledge. Job knowledge typically is conveyed through job training. Job knowledge is considered to be explicit rather than implicit in nature (Schmidt &

Hunter, 1998). Sternberg (2003; Sternberg & Wagner, 1993) countered that this conceptualization of job knowledge does not do justice to the features of tacit knowledge described previously. He and his colleagues also have questioned the interpretation that IQ tests are direct measures of intelligence or cognitive ability. They have argued that IQ tests do not measure intelligence directly, but also assess formal knowledge, among other things. If everyone has an equal opportunity to acquire the formal knowledge and equal motivation for doing so, the inference is made that a person who has acquired more knowledge has more intelligence compared to a person who has acquired less knowledge. This same logic can be applied to practical intelligence as being reflected in individual differences in the acquisition of tacit as opposed to formal knowledge.

Another answer to the question of how practical intelligence is related to other forms of intelligence is provided by theories of intelligence that posit multiple forms of intelligence or competence. For example, Greenspan and colleagues (Greenspan, 1981; Greenspan & Driscoll, 1997; Greenspan & Granfield, 1992) identified four broad domains of competence: physical, affective, everyday, and academic. The broad domains are further subdivided into subdomains. For everyday competence, the subdomains are practical intelligence and social intelligence.

Ford and colleagues (Ford, 1982, 1986, 1994; Ford & Ford, 1987; Ford & Maher, 1998) developed a theory of social competence that culminated in the Living Systems Framework (LSF). In this system, intelligence is viewed as the effective pursuit of goals in a given setting or domain of activity. Everyday life consists of a continuous series of context-specific, goal-directed behavior.

Gardner (1983) proposed multiple intelligences that include linguistic intelligence (i.e., sensitivity to spoken and written languages), musical intelligence (i.e., sensitivity to rhythm, pitch, and timbre), logical-mathematical intelligence (i.e., facility with numbers and hypothetical statements), spatial intelligence (i.e., sensitivity to visual-spatial elements and the ability to transform them), bodily-kinesthetic intelligence (sensitivity to and control over one's body), intrapersonal intelligence (i.e., understanding of one's personal strengths, weaknesses, and feelings), and interpersonal intelligence (i.e., sensitivity to the intentions and desires of others). Gardner's theory incorporates both practical and academic aspects of intelligence. In its most recent version, it also incorporates naturalist intelligence (Gardner, 1999).

Sternberg's triarchic theory of human intelligence (Sternberg, 1985) and his follow-up theory of successful intelligence (Sternberg, 1997) both incorporate practical intelligence within a larger framework of intelligence. The triarchic theory depicts three kinds of intelligence: analytical, practical, and creative. The theory of successful intelligence represents a broader and more integrated conceptualization of intelligence. The goal of the theory is to explain relations between intelligence and three critical aspects of intellectual competence. The first of these aspects is the internal world of the individual, which refers to the mental mechanisms that underlie intelligent behavior. The second aspect is the external world of the individual, which refers to the use of cognitive mechanisms in everyday life to obtain and maintain a functional fit to the environment. The third and final aspect is experience, which refers to the passage through life between the internal and external worlds. These three aspects are referred to as the componential subtheory, the contextual subtheory, and the experiential subtheory, respectively. The contextual subtheory is where practical intelligence is incorporated into the broader theory.

Can the Development of Practical Intelligence Be Facilitated?

If being able to respond in a practically intelligent manner depends in part on one's store of tacit knowledge, then it may be worthwhile to attempt to facilitate the acquisition of tacit knowledge. Two potential ways of doing so are by making tacit knowledge explicit and sharing it, and by improving people's ability to acquire tacit knowledge from their environment (Wagner & Sternberg, 1990). Examples of attempts to enhance the acquisition of tacit knowledge using either or both of these methods are summarized in Cianciolo et al. (2006).

One potential mechanism for sharing tacit knowledge is through communities of practice. Communities of practice refer to self-selected groups of individuals who come together informally to exchange knowledge and experience in a given domain (Gheradi, Nicolini, & Odella, 1998; Lesser & Storck, 2001; Nonaka & Takeuchi, 1995; Wenger, 2000). For example, product-delivery consultants employed by Hewlett-Packard have organized monthly teleconferences to solve problems with software products (Wenger & Snyder, 2000). For a second example, a community of practice has developed in an educational technology doctoral program at Pepperdine University for the purpose of capturing and sharing the knowledge of its members (Adams & Freeman, 2000). A military community of practice around the topic of leading soldiers has arisen in the form of a professional forum called CompanyCommand.mil (Dixon et al., 2005). Although communities of practice are widespread, their effectiveness as vehicles for facilitating the development of tacit knowledge has yet to be examined rigorously.

Sternberg, Wagner, and Okagaki (1993) attempted to facilitate the acquisition of tacit knowledge by providing training in three components that have been proposed as mechanisms by which it is acquired: selective encoding, selective combination, and selective comparison (Sternberg, 1985). Training facilitated performance in a knowledge acquisition task that required participants to play the role of a personnel manager evaluating potential job candidates.

A larger scale attempt to improve practical intelligence is represented by the Practical Intelligence for School project (Williams et al., 1996, 2002). The training program was based on Sternberg's (1997) theory of practical intelligence and Gardner's (1983, 1999) theory of multiple intelligences. The program targeted practical thinking skills of middle school students in two states. After two years, program participants showed significant gains on practical assessments of reading, writing, homework, and test taking compared to controls. For a related approach to improving practical thinking in the classroom, see Sternberg and Grigorenko (2004).

Future Directions

Among the most interesting pages of any handbook are the few that make up the table of contents. The contents provides an editor's view of what constitutes a field at a point in history. The original *Handbook of Human Intelligence* (Sternberg, 1982) did not include a chapter on practical intelligence. Indeed, the term *practical intelligence* could not even be found in the index. The follow-up edition (Sternberg, 2000) included a separate chapter on practical intelligence and the length of the entry in the index was among the longer entries, comparable to those of memory, mental abilities, and information processing. The present edition follows from the previous edition in having a separate chapter devoted to practical intelligence. Will a subsequent volume do likewise?

One reason a separate chapter may not be needed is a growing convergence of theoretical perspectives. Consider three examples. First, proponents of practical intelligence have begun to embrace concepts and constructs from other areas of psychology, such as life span development and expertise. Second, proponents of traditional views of intelligence have also begun to embrace the same constructs of life span development and expertise. Third, the field of cognitive psychology – the area of psychology that studies key components of human intellect including language, reasoning, problem solving, and thought – is undergoing a revolution. The traditional view that human intellect deals primarily in abstract symbols is being challenged by the view that cognition is grounded in perception and action. According to this view, cognition has evolved in response to the need to adapt to a challenging environment: Abstract cognition is giving way to a more practical form of cognition.

Proponents of Practical Intelligence Embracing Other Areas of Psychology

Sternberg has been the most forceful proponent of the concept of practical intelligence as one of three, distinct form of intelligence (Sternberg, 1985, 1997; Sternberg & Wagner, 1986; Wagner & Sternberg, 1985). However, his theory of intelligence evolved in a major way when he began viewing intelligence in the context of developing expertise (Sternberg, 1997, 1998). Developing expertise is defined by Sternberg as the "ongoing process of the acquisition and consolidation of a set of skills needed for a high level of mastery in one or more domains of life performance" (Sternberg, 1999, p. 359). According to the developing-expertise model, individuals are constantly engaged in the process of developing expertise in one or more domains. Although individual differences in rates of development and ultimate level of accomplishment are acknowledged, the main constraint on developing competence is amount of purposeful engagement rather than fixed levels of capacity.

The developing-expertise theory integrates traditional views of intelligence and IQ tests into the theory by viewing them as measuring aspects of developing expertise, but limited aspects relative to the full range of skill levels and domains. One important difference between the developing-expertise view of intelligence and traditional views is the importance given to instruction and other means provided by societies for developing expertise. Galton (1869/1979) provided an account of individual differences in attainment in terms of experience and innate capacities that remains influential today. Everyone initially improves with experience, but eventually the amount of improvement is limited by basic abilities, capacities, and talents that are not affected by training (Ericsson, 2006). More recent accounts often rely on the distinction between fluid and crystallized intelligence (Catell, 1971; Horn, 1994). Fluid intelligence represents the ability to acquire and reason with new information; crystallized intelligence represents the ability to use the information that has been acquired over the years via fluid intelligence. According to the traditional view, fluid intelligence peaks in late adolescence and is relatively unaffected by instruction whereas crystallized intelligence can be influenced by instruction. In contrast, the developing-expertise view considers all forms of intelligence, including fluid intelligence, to be responsive to instruction and other developmental experiences (Sternberg, 1997). Consequently, considerable effort has been devoted to developing intelligence.

Proponents of Traditional Intelligence Embracing Other Areas of Psychology

Horn and Masunaga (2006) provide an account of the merging of a theory of intelligence with a theory of expertise. The particular theory of intelligence used is the extended theory of fluid (Gf) and crystallized (Gc) intelligence. According to the theory, fluid and crystallized intelligence are manifested to varying degrees in eight second-order factors.

1. *Acculturation knowledge*. The extent to which the knowledge and language of the dominant culture has been acquired.
2. *Fluid reasoning*. Reasoning as evidenced by performance on tasks that require reasoning over relatively brief periods of time about problems that are relatively novel.
3. *Short-term apprehension and retrieval*. The ability to remember information over brief periods of time as assessed by performance on short-term memory and working memory tasks.
4. *Fluency of retrieval from long-term storage*. The ability to retrieve information learned over a longer period of time from long-term memory.

5. *Visual processing.* The ability to do visual processing tasks such as completing incomplete figures and figure rotation.
6. *Auditory processing.* The ability to recognize sound patterns, including awareness of order and rhythm.
7. *Processing speed.* Basic processing speed as measured by tasks such as rapid scanning and comparison of simple figures.
8. *Quantitative knowledge.* The ability to think quantitatively and solve mathematical problems.

Fluid intelligence is a primary determinant of performance on the factors that reflect processing speed (visual processing, auditory processing, and processing speed), storage over short periods of time (short-term apprehension and retrieval), and reasoning when presented with novel problems (fluid reasoning). Crystallized intelligence is a primary determinant of performance on the factors that reflect knowledge accumulation (acculturation knowledge, quantitative knowledge) and long-term storage of information (fluency of retrieval from long-term storage).

Fluid and crystallized intelligence can be distinguished reliably from age 3 onward. Developmental studies document decline associated with aging in fluid intelligence factors but not in acculturative knowledge or fluency of retrieval from long-term storage. The primary limitation in extended Gf-Gc theory that motivated Horn and Masunaga (2006) to incorporate ideas from the study of expertise comes from developmental studies. The substantial declines found for abilities described by the theory do not characterize adult intellectual functioning. The individuals given the most responsibility by society are given such responsibility at a time during which significant decline has occurred in most of the abilities measured by the theory. It is true that acculturative knowledge and fluency of retrieval from long-term storage do not show age-related decline, but Horn and Masunaga consider these two factors to represent only an impoverished view of the broad and diverse range of knowledge and intellectual skill that adults demonstrate. Consequently, they have begun to turn to theories of expertise to flesh out what remains unaffected by aging.

Three theoretical accounts have been proposed to account for the fact that expert levels of performance are observed even in older age (Krampe & Charness, 2006). The first is that older experts had extraordinarily high levels of underlying skills and abilities required for the area of expertise even prior to acquiring their expertise. They thus are able to withstand some decrement in abilities because of their high starting values. The second account is that the process of acquiring expertise results in gradual improvement in abilities such as working memory that are required for expert performance, while other abilities may show typical age-related decline. The third account is that expert performance is based upon domain-specific mechanisms that arise through training and that can be maintained through adulthood with continued training. The third account appears to enjoy considerably more empirical support than the first two.

Practical Cognition

Standard theories of cognition and processing analyses of tasks found on IQ tests make fundamental assumptions about information processing that are facing increasing challenge (Barsalou, 2008). These standard theories assume that cognition results from a processing system based on symbols that are independent of perception, action, and introspection or simulation. Information obtained from the physical senses is transduced into amodal (i.e., a form different from its origin in the perceptual or motor system that generated it) symbols that represent knowledge in semantic memory.

The increasingly influential alternative is *embodied* or *grounded cognition.* According to this alternative, cognition is directly related to perception, action, and mental simulation. The part of embodied cognition of particular relevance for practical intelligence is found in theories of situated action (Clark, 1997; Gibson, 1979; Spivey, 2007; Thelen &

Smith, 1994; Van Orden, Holden, & Turvey, 2005). The key idea is that cognition involves a close coupling of perception and action during meaningful goal achievement. Relevant to practical intelligence, theories of situated action propose that embodied cognitive mechanisms arise as a consequence of adapting to the environment.

According to this view, cognition has evolved from the need to act successfully in a dynamic and potentially dangerous world. Taken seriously, adequate measures of practical cognition would seem to require simulation of real-world tasks as opposed to measuring facility at manipulation abstract symbols (Sternberg, Wagner, Williams, & Horvath, 1995).

Whether the next *Handbook of Intelligence* will include a separate chapter on the topic of practical intelligence is uncertain. If it does not include a separate chapter on practical intelligence, it won't be because its key ideas turned out to be wrong. Rather, it will be because the key ideas have become adopted so pervasively that a separate chapter no longer makes sense.

References

Adams, E. C., & Freeman, C. (2000). Communities of practice: Bridging technology and knowledge assessment. *Journal of Knowledge Management*, 4, 38–42.

Barsalou, L. W. (2008). Grounded cognition. *Annual Review of Psychology*, 59, 617–645.

Berry, J. W., & Irvine, S. H. (1986). Bricolage: Savages to it daily. In R. J. Sternberg & R. K. Wagner (Eds.), *Practical intelligence: Nature and origins of competence in the everyday world* (pp. 271–306). New York, NY: Cambridge University Press.

Burton Jones, N., & Kronner, M. (1976). Kung knowledge of animal behavior. In R. B. Lee & I. DeVore (Eds.), *Kalahari hunter-gatherers* (pp. 326–348). Cambridge, MA: Harvard University Press.

Carraher, T. N., Carraher, D. W., & Schliemann, A. D. (1985). Mathematics in the streets and in schools. *British Journal of Developmental Psychology*, 3, 21–29.

Cattell, R. B. (1971). *Abilities: Their structure, growth, and action.* Boston, MA: Houghton Mifflin.

Ceci, S. J., & Liker, J. (1988). Stalking the IQ-expertise relationship: When the critics go fishing. *Journal of Experimental Psychology: General*, 117, 96–100.

Cianciolo, A. T., Matthew, C., Sternberg, R. J., & Wagner, R. K. (2006). Tacit knowledge, practical intelligence, and expertise. In K. A. Ericsson, N. Charness, P. J. Feltovich, & R. R. Hoffman (Eds.), *The Cambridge handbook of expertise and expert performance* (pp. 613–632). New York, NY: Cambridge University Press.

Cianciolo, A. T., Antonakis, J., & Sternberg, R. J. (2004). Practical intelligence and leadership: Using experience as a "mentor." In D. Day, S. Zaccaro, & S. Halpin (Eds.), *Leader development for transforming organizations – growing leaders for tomorrow* (pp. 211–236). Mahwah, NJ: Erlbaum.

Cianciolo, A. T., Grigorenko, E. L., Jarvin, L., Gil, G., Drebot, M. E., & Sternberg, R. J. (2006). Practical intelligence and tacit knowledge: Advancements in the measurement of developing expertise. *Learning & Individual Differences*, 16, 235–253.

Clark, A. (1997). *Being there: Putting brain, body, and world together again.* Cambridge, MA: MIT Press.

Cole, M., Gay, J., Glick, J., & Sharp, D. (1971). *The cultural context of learning and thinking.* New York, NY: Basic.

Collonia-Willner, R. (1998). Practical intelligence at work: Relationship between aging and cognitive efficiency among managers in a bank environment. *Psychology & Aging*, 13, 45–57.

Dahl, T. (2000). Text summarization: From human activity to computer program. The problem of tacit knowledge. *Journal of Linguistics*, 25, 113–131.

Dixon, N. M., Allen, N., Burgess, T., Kilner, P., & Schweitzer, S. (2005). *CompanyCommand: Unleashing the power of the Army profession.* West Point, NY: Center for the Advancement of Leader Development and Organization Learning.

Ericsson, K. A. (2006). The influence of experience and deliberate practice on the development of superior expert performance. In K. A. Ericsson, N. Charness, P. J. Feltovich, & R. R. Hoffman (Eds.), *The Cambridge handbook of expertise and expert performance* (pp. 683–703). New York, NY: Cambridge University Press.

Frederiksen, N. (1986). Toward a broader conception of human intelligence. In R. J. Sternberg & R. K. Wagner (Eds.), *Practical intelligence: Nature and origins of competence in the everyday world* (pp. 84–116). New York, NY: Cambridge University Press.

Ford, M. E. (1982). Social cognition and social competence in adolescence. *Developmental Psychology*, *18*, 323–340.

Ford, M. E. (1986). For all practical purposes: Criteria for defining and evaluating practical intelligence. In R. J. Sternberg & R. K. Wagner (Eds.), *Practical intelligence: Nature and origins of competence in the everyday world* (pp. 183–200). New York, NY: Cambridge University Press.

Ford, M. E.(1994). *Humans as self-constructing living systems: A developmental perspective on behavior and personality* (2nd ed.). State College, PA: Ideals.

Ford, M. E., & Ford, D. H. (1987). *Humans as self-constructing living systems: Putting the framework to work*. Mahwah, NJ: Erlbaum.

Ford, M. E., & Maher, M. A. (1998). Self-awareness and social intelligence. In M. Ferrari & R. Sternberg (Eds.), *Self awareness: Its nature and development* (pp. 191–218). New York, NY: Guilford Press.

Galton, F. (1869/1979). *Hereditary genius: An inquiry into its laws and consequences*. London: Julian Friedman. (Originally published in 1869)

Gardner, H. (1983). *Frames of mind. The theory of multiple intelligences*. New York, NY: Basic.

Gardner, H. (1999). *Intelligence re-framed: Multiple intelligences for the 21st century*. New York, NY: Basic.

Gheradi, S., Nicolini, D., & Odella, F. (1998). Toward a social understanding of how people learn in organizations. *Management Learning*, *29*, 273–297.

Gibson, J. J. (1979). *The ecological approach to visual perception*. New York, NY: Houghton Mifflin.

Gladwin, T. (1970). *East is a big bird: Navigation and loci on the Puluwat atoll*. Cambridge, MA: Harvard University Press.

Gottfredson, L. S. (2003). Dissecting practical intelligence theory: Its claims and evidence. *Intelligence*, *31*, 343–397.

Greenspan, S. (1981). Defining childhood social competence: A proposed working model. In B. K. Keogh (Ed.), *Advances in special education* (Vol. 3, pp. 1–39). Greenwich, CT: JAI Press.

Greenspan, S., & Driscoll, J. (1997). The role of intelligence in a broad model of personal competence. In D. P. Flanagan & J. L. Genshaft (Eds.), *Contemporary intellectual assessment: Theories, tests, and issues* (pp. 131–150). New York, NY: Guilford Press.

Greenspan, S., & Garfield, J. M. (1992). Reconsidering the construct of mental retardation: Implications of a model of social competence. *American Journal on Mental Retardation*, *96*, 442–453.

Grigorenko, E. L., Meier, E., Lipka, J., Mohatt, G., Yanez, E., & Sternberg, R. J. (2004). Academic and practical intelligence: A case study of the Yup'ik in Alaska. *Learning & Individual Differences*, *14*, 183–207.

Grigorenko, E. L., Sternberg, R. J., & Strauss, S. (2006). Practical intelligence and elementary-school teacher effectiveness in the United States and Israel: Measuring the predictive power of tacit knowledge. *Thinking Skills and Creativity*, *1*, 14–33.

Hartigan, J. A., & Wigdor, A. K. (1989). *Fairness in employment testing*. Washington, DC: National Academy Press.

Hedlund, J., Forsythe, G. B., Horvath, J. A., Williams, W. M., Snook, S., & Sternberg, R. J. (2003). Identifying and assessing tacit knowledge: Understanding the practical intelligence of military leaders. *Leadership Quarterly*, *14*, 117–140.

Hedlund, J., Wilt, J. M., Nebel, K. L., Ashford, S. J., & Sternberg, R. J. (2006). Assessing practical intelligence in business school admissions: A supplement to the Graduate Management Admissions Test. *Learning & Individual Differences*, *16*, 101–127.

Horn, J. L. (1994). Fluid and crystallized intelligence. In R. J. Sternberg (Ed.), *Encyclopedia of human intelligence* (Vol. 1, pp. 443–451). New York, NY: Macmillan.

Horn, J. L., & Masunaga, H. (2006). A merging theory of expertise and intelligence. In K. A. Ericsson, N. Charness, P. J. Feltovich, & R. R. Hoffman (Eds.), *The Cambridge handbook of expertise and expert performance* (pp. 587–611). New York, NY: Cambridge University Press.

Krampe, R. T., & Charness, N. (2006). Aging and expertise. In K. A. Ericsson, N. Charness, P. J. Feltovich, & R. R. Hoffman (Eds.), *The Cambridge handbook of expertise and expert performance* (pp. 723–742). New York, NY: Cambridge University Press.

Laboratory of Comparative Human Cognition. (1982). Culture and intelligence. In R. J. Sternberg (Ed.), *Handbook of human intelligence* (pp. 642–719). New York, NY: Cambridge University Press.

Lave, J., Murtaugh, M., & de la Rocha, O. (1984). The dialectic of arithmetic in grocery shopping. In B. Rogoff & J. Lace (Eds.), *Everyday cognition* (pp. 67–94). Cambridge, MA: Harvard University Press.

Legree, P. J., Heffner, T. S., Psotka, J., Martin, D. E., & Medsker, G. J. (2003). Traffic crash involvement: Experiential driving knowledge and stressful contextual antecedents. *Journal of Applied Psychology*, 88, 15–26.

Lesser, E. L., & Storck, J. (2001). Communities of practice and organizational performance. *IBM Systems Journal*, *40*, 831–841.

Levi-Strauss, C. (1966). *The savage mind*. London, UK: Weidenfield & Nicholson.

Neisser, U. (1976). General, academic, and artificial intelligence. In L. Resnick (Ed.), *Human intelligence: Perspectives on its theory and measurement* (pp. 179–189). Norwood, NJ: Ablex.

Nonaka, I., & Takeuchi, H. (1995). *The knowledge creating company: How Japanese companies create the dynamics of innovation*. New York, NY: Oxford University Press.

Nunes, T., Schliemann, A. D., & Carraher, D. W. (1993). *Street mathematics and school mathematics*. New York, NY: Cambridge University Press.

Polanyi, M. (1958). *Personal knowledge: Towards a post-critical philosophy*. Chicago, IL: University of Chicago Press.

Polanyi, M. (1966). *The tacit dimension*. New York, NY: Doubleday.

Reber, A. S. (1989). Implicit learning and tacit knowledge. *Journal of Experimental Psychology: General*, *118*, 219–235.

Reber, A. S., & Lewis, S. (1977). Implicit learning: An analysis of the form and structure of a body of tacit knowledge. *Cognition*, *5*, 333–361.

Schmidt, F. L., & Hunter, J. E. (1993). Tacit knowledge, practical intelligence, general mental ability, and job knowledge. *Current Directions in Psychological Science*, *1*, 8–9.

Schmidt, F. L., & Hunter, J. E. (1998). The validity and utility of selection methods in personnel psychology: Practical and theoretical implications of 85 years of research findings. *Psychological Bulletin*, *124*, 262–274.

Scribner, S. (1984). Studying workplace intelligence. In S. Scribner (Ed.), *Everyday cognition: Its development in social context* (pp. 9–40). Cambridge, MA: Harvard University Press.

Scribner, S., & Cole, M. (1981). *The psychology of literacy*. Cambridge, MA: Harvard University Press.

Spivey, M. (2007). *The continuity of mind*. New York, NY: Oxford University Press.

Stemier, S. E., Elliott, J. G., Grigorenko, E. L., & Sternberg, R. J. (2006). There's more to teaching than instruction: Seven strategies for dealing with the practical side of teaching. *Educational Studies*, *32*, 101–118.

Sternberg, R. J. (1985). *Beyond IQ: A triarchic theory of human intelligence*. New York, NY: Cambridge University Press.

Sternberg, R. J. (1997). *Successful intelligence*. New York, NY: Plume.

Sternberg, R. J. (1998). Abilities are forms of developing expertise. *Educational Researcher*, *27*, 11–20.

Sternberg, R. J. (1999). Intelligence as developing expertise. *Contemporary Educational Psychology*, *24*, 359–375.

Sternberg, R. J. (2003). Our research program validating the triarchic theory of successful intelligence: Reply to Gottfredson. *Intelligence*, *31*, 399–413.

Sternberg, R. J. (2004). Theory-based university admissions testing for a new millennium. *Educational Psychologist*, *39*, 185–198.

Sternberg, R. J. (2006). The rainbow project: Enhancing the SAT through assessments of analytical, practical, and creative skills. *Intelligence*, *34*, 321–350.

Sternberg, R. J., & Berg, C. A. (1986). Quantitative integration: Definitions of intelligence: A comparison of the 1921 and 1986 symposia. In R. J. Sternberg & D. K. Detterman (Eds.), *What is intelligence?* (pp. 155–162). Norwood, NJ: Ablex.

Sternberg, R. J., & Detterman, D. K. (Eds.). (1986). *What is intelligence?* Norwood, NJ: Ablex.

Sternberg, R. J., & Grigorenko, E. L. (2004). Successful intelligence in the classroom. *Theory into Practice*, *43*, 274–280.

Sternberg, R. J., Nokes, K., Geissler, P. W., Prince, R., Okatcha, F., Bundy, D. A., & Grigorenko, E. L. (2001). The relationship between academic and practical intelligence: A case study in Kenya. *Intelligence*, *29*, 401–418.

Sternberg, R. J., & Wagner, R. K. (Eds.). (1986). *Practical intelligence: Nature and origins of competence in the everyday world*. New York, NY: Cambridge University Press.

Sternberg, R. J., & Wagner, R. K. (1993). The geocentric view of intelligence and job performance is wrong. *Current Directions in Psychological Science*, 2, 1–5.

Sternberg, R. J., Wagner, R. K., & Okagaki, L. (1993). Practical intelligence: The nature and role of tacit knowledge in work and at school. In J. Puckett & H. Reese (Eds.), *Mechanisms of everyday cognition* (pp. 205–223). Mahwah, NJ: Erlbaum.

Sternberg, R. J., Wagner, R. K., Williams, W. M., & Horvath, J. A. (1995). Testing common sense. *American Psychologist*, 50, 912–927.

Tan, H., & Libby, R. (1997). Tacit managerial versus technical knowledge as determinants of adit expertise in the field. *Journal of Accounting Research*, 35, 97–113.

Thelen, E., & Smith, L. B. (1994). *A dynamic systems approach to the development of cognition and action*. Cambridge, MA: MIT Press.

Van Orden, G. C., Holden, J. G., & Turvey, M. T. (2005). Human cognition and 1/f scaling. *Journal of Experimental Psychology: General*, 134, 117–123.

Wagner, R. K. (1997). Intelligence, training, and employment. *American Psychologist*, 52, 1059–1069.

Wagner, R. K., & Sternberg, R. J. (1985). Practical intelligence in real-world pursuits: The role of tacit knowledge. *Journal of Personality and Social Psychology*, 49, 436–458.

Wagner, R. K., & Sternberg, R. J. (1990). Street smarts. In K. E. Clark & M. B. Clark (Eds.), *Measures of leadership* (pp. 493–504). West Orange, NJ: Leadership Library of America.

Wenger, E. C. (2000). Communities of practice and social learning systems. *Organization*, 7, 225–246.

Wenger, E. C., & Snyder, W. M. (2000, January–February). Communities of practice: The organizational frontier. *Harvard Business Review*, 139–145.

Wigdor, A. K., & Garner, W. R. (Eds.). (1982). *Ability testing: Uses, consequences, and controversies*. Washington, DC: National Academy Press.

Williams, W., Blythe, T., White, N., Li, J., Gardner, H., & Sternberg, R. J. (2002). Practical intelligence for school: Developing metacognitive sources of achievement in adolescence. *Developmental Review*, 22, 162–210.

Williams, W., Blythe, T., White, N., Li, J., Sternberg, R. J., & Gardner, H. (1996). *Practical intelligence for school handbook*. New York, NY: Harper Collins.

CHAPTER 28

Social Intelligence

John F. Kihlstrom and Nancy Cantor

The term *social intelligence* was first used by Dewey (1909) and Lull (1911), but the modern concept has its origins in E. L. Thorndike's (1920) division of intelligence into three facets pertaining to the ability to understand and manage ideas (abstract intelligence), concrete objects (mechanical intelligence), and people (social intelligence). In Thorndike's classic formulation: "By social intelligence is meant the ability to understand and manage men and women, boys and girls – to act wisely in human relations" (p. 228). Similarly, Moss and Hunt (1927) defined social intelligence as the "ability to get along with others" (p. 108). Vernon (1933) provided the most wide-ranging definition of social intelligence as the "ability to get along with people in general, social technique or ease in society, knowledge of social matters, susceptibility to stimuli from other members of a group, as well as insight into the temporary moods or underlying personality traits of strangers" (p. 44).

By contrast, Wechsler (1939, 1958) gave scant attention to social intelligence in the development of the Wechsler Adult Intelligence Scale (WAIS) and similar instruments. He did acknowledge that the Picture Arrangement subtest of the WAIS might serve as a measure of social intelligence because it assesses the individual's ability to comprehend social situations (see also Rapaport, Gill, & Shafer, 1968; Campbell & McCord, 1996). In his view, however, "social intelligence is just general intelligence applied to social situations" (1958, p. 75). This dismissal was repeated in Matarazzo's (1972, p. 209) fifth and final edition of Wechsler's monograph, in which *social intelligence* dropped out as an index term.

Measuring Social Intelligence

Defining social intelligence seems easy enough, especially by analogy to abstract intelligence. When it came to *measuring* social intelligence, however, Thorndike (1920) noted somewhat ruefully that "convenient tests of social intelligence are hard to devise.... Social intelligence shows itself abundantly in the nursery, on the playground, in barracks and factories and salesroom [*sic*], but it eludes the formal standardized conditions of the testing laboratory. It requires human beings to respond to, time to adapt its responses, and face, voice, gesture, and mien as tools" (p. 231). Nevertheless, true to the goals of the psychometric tradition, researchers quickly translated the abstract definitions of social intelligence into standardized laboratory instruments for measuring individual differences in social intelligence (for thorough reviews of research published before 2000, see Kihlstrom & Cantor, 2000; Landy, 2006; Taylor, 1990; Walker & Foley, 1973).

The George Washington Social Intelligence Test

The first of these was the George Washington Social Intelligence Test (GWSIT; Hunt, 1928; Moss, 1931; Moss, Hunt, Omwake, & Ronning, 1927; for later editions, see Moss, Hunt, & Omwake, 1949; Moss, Hunt, Omwake, & Woodward, 1955). Like the Stanford-Binet Intelligence Test or WAIS, the GWSIT was composed of a number of subtests, which can be combined to yield an aggregate score. Four subtests – Judgment in Social Situations, Memory for Names and Faces, Observation of Human Behavior, and Recognition of the Mental States Behind Words – were employed in all editions of the GWSIT. Subtests of Facial Expression and Social Information subtests were included in early editions but dropped from in later editions, and a Humor subtest was added.

Hunt (1928) originally validated the GWSIT through its correlations with adult occupational status, the number of extracurricular activities pursued by college students, and supervisor ratings of employees' ability to get along with people. However, some controversy ensued about whether social intelligence should be correlated with personality measures of sociability or extraversion. Most important, however, the GWSIT came under immediate criticism for its relatively high correlation with abstract intelligence. Thorndike and Stein (1937) concluded that the GWSIT "is so heavily loaded with ability to work with words and ideas, that differences in social intelligence tend to be swamped by differences in abstract intelligence" (p. 282).

The inability to discriminate between social intelligence and IQ, coupled with difficulties in selecting external criteria against which the scale could be validated, led to declining interest in the GWSIT, and indeed in the whole concept of social intelligence as a distinct intellectual entity. Spearman's *g* afforded no special place for social intelligence, of course; nor was social intelligence included, or even implied, in Thurstone's list of primary mental abilities.

Social Intelligence in Guilford's Structure of Intellect

After an initial burst of interest in the GWSIT, work on the assessment and correlates of social intelligence fell off sharply until the 1960s (Walker & Foley, 1973), when this line of research was revived within the context of Guilford's Structure of Intellect model of intelligence. Guilford postulated a system of at least 120 separate intellectual abilities, based on all possible combinations of five categories of operations (cognition, memory, divergent production, convergent production, and evaluation), with four categories of content (figural, symbolic, semantic, and behavioral) and six categories of products (units, classes, relations, systems, transformations, and implications). Within this more differentiated system, social intelligence is represented by the domain of behavioral operations. In contrast to its extensive work on semantic and figural content, Guilford's group addressed issues of behavioral content only very late in their program of research. Of the 30 facets of social intelligence predicted by the structure-of-intellect model (5 operations × 6 products), actual tests were devised for only six cognitive abilities (O'Sullivan et al., 1965; Hoepfner & O'Sullivan, 1969) and six divergent production abilities (Hendricks, Guilford, & Hoepfner, 1969).

O'Sullivan et al. (1965) defined the category of behavioral cognition as representing the "ability to judge people" (p. 5) with respect to "feelings, motives, thoughts, intentions, attitudes, or other psychological dispositions which might affect an individual's social behavior" (O'Sullivan et al., p. 4). They made it clear that someone's ability to judge individual people was not the same as his or her comprehension of people in general, or "stereotypic understanding" (p. 5), and bore no *a priori* relation to one's ability to understand oneself. Apparently, these two aspects of social cognition lie outside the standard structure-of-intellect model.

In constructing their tests of behavioral cognition, O'Sullivan et al. (1965) assumed that "expressive behavior, more particularly facial expressions, vocal inflections, postures, and gestures, are the cues from which intentional states are inferred" (p. 6). While recognizing the value of assessing the ability to decode these cues in real-life contexts with real people serving as targets, economic constraints forced the investigators to rely on photographs, cartoons, drawings, and tape recordings (the cost of film was prohibitive); verbal materials were avoided wherever possible, presumably to avoid contamination of social intelligence by verbal abilities. Their study yielded six factors clearly interpretable as cognition of behavior, which were not contaminated by nonsocial semantic and spatial abilities. However, echoing earlier findings with the GWSIT, later studies found substantial correlations between IQ and scores on the individual Guilford subtests as well as various composite social intelligence scores (Riggio, Messamer, & Throckmorton, 1991; Shanley, Walker, & Foley, 1971). Still, Shanley et al. (1971) conceded that the correlations obtained were not strong enough to warrant Wechsler's assertion that social intelligence is nothing more than general intelligence applied in the social domain.

In one of the last test-construction efforts by Guilford's group, Hendricks et al. (1969) attempted to develop tests for coping with other people, not just understanding them through their behavior – what they referred to as "basic solution-finding skills in interpersonal relations" (p. 3). Because successful coping involves the creative generation of many and diverse behavioral ideas, these investigators labeled these divergent-thinking abilities *creative social intelligence*. As with the behavioral cognition abilities studied by O'Sullivan et al. (1965), the very nature of the behavioral domain raised serious technical problems for test development in the behavioral domain, especially with respect to contamination by verbal (semantic) abilities. As might be expected, scoring divergent productions proved considerably harder than scoring cognitions, as in the former case there is no one best answer, and subjects' responses must be evaluated by independent judges for quality as well as quantity. Nevertheless, a factor-analytic study yielded six factors clearly interpretable as divergent production in the behavioral domain, which were essentially independent of both divergent semantic production and (convergent) cognition in the behavioral domain.

A later study by Chen and Michael (1993), employing more modern factor-analytic techniques, essentially confirmed these findings – although Snyder and Michael (1983) had earlier found significant correlations between some of these tests of social intelligence and tests of verbal and mathematical ability. A similar reanalysis of the O'Sullivan et al. (1965) data by Romney and Pyryt (1999) found that all the tests loaded on a single factor rather than the six independent factors predicted by Guilford's Structure of Intellect theory. In neither domain is there much evidence for the ability of any of these tests to predict external criteria of social intelligence.

Tests of the remaining three structure-of-intellect domains (memory, convergent production, and evaluation) had not been developed by the time the Guilford program came to a close. Hendricks et al. (1969) noted that "these constitute by far the greatest number of unknowns in the [Structure of Intellect] model" (p. 6). However, O'Sullivan et al. (1965) did sketch out how these abilities were defined. *Convergent production* in the behavioral domain was defined as "doing the right thing at the right time" (p. 5), and presumably might be tested by a knowledge of etiquette. *Behavioral memory* was defined as the ability to remember the social characteristics of people (e.g., names, faces, and personality traits), while *behavioral evaluation* was defined as the ability to judge the appropriateness of behavior.

Convergent and Discriminant Validity in Social Intelligence

Following the Guilford studies, a number of investigators continued the attempt to define social intelligence and determine its relation to general abstract intelligence. Most of these studies explicitly employed the logic of the multitrait-multimethod matrix (MTMM; Campbell & Fiske, 1959), employing multiple measures of social and nonsocial intelligence, and examining the convergent validity of alternative measures within each domain and their discriminant validity across domains (e.g., Sechrest & Jackson, 1961). For example, Day and his group showed that multiple measures of social insight and social intelligence were poorly correlated with academic intelligence (Jones and Day,1997; Lee, Wong, Day, Maxwell, & Thorpe, 2000; Lee, Day, Meara, & Maxwell, 2002; Wong, Day, Maxwell, & Meara, 1995). Weis and Suss (2007) obtained similar results for measures of social understanding and social knowledge, but not for social memory.

Marlowe (1986) and his colleagues assembled a large battery of personality measures ostensibly tapping various aspects of social intelligence. Factor analysis of these instruments yielded five dimensions of social intelligence: interest and concern for other people, social performance skills, empathic ability, emotional expressiveness and sensitivity to others' emotional expressions, and social anxiety and lack of social self-efficacy and self-esteem. Factor scores on these dimensions of social intelligence were essentially unrelated to measures of verbal and abstract intelligence. In evaluating studies like this, however, note that the apparent independence of social and general intelligence may be at least partially an artifact of method variance. Unlike the GWSIT and the batteries of cognitive and divergent-production measures devised by the Guilford group, Marlowe's ostensible measures of social intelligence are all self-report scales, whereas his measures of verbal and abstract intelligence were the usual sorts of objective performance tests. The measurement of individual differences in social intelligence by means of self-report scales is a major departure from the tradition of intelligence testing, and it seems important to confirm Marlowe's findings using objective performance measures of the various facets of social intelligence.

The Prototype of Social Intelligence

Although social intelligence has proved difficult for psychometricians to operationalize, it does appear to play a major role in people's näive, intuitive concepts of intelligence. Sternberg and his colleagues asked subjects to list the behaviors which they considered characteristic of intelligence, academic intelligence, everyday intelligence, and unintelligence; two additional groups of subjects rated each of 250 behaviors from the first list in terms of how "characteristic" each was of the ideal person possessing each of the three forms of intelligence (Sternberg, Conway, Ketron, & Bernstein, 1981). Factor analysis of ratings provided by laypeople yielded a factor of "social competence" in each context. Prototypical behaviors reflecting social competence were these:

> *Accepts others for what they are; admits mistakes; displays interest in the world at large; is on time for appointments; has social conscience; thinks before speaking and doing; displays curiosity; does not make snap judgments; makes fair judgments; assesses well the relevance of information to a problem at hand; is sensitive to other people's needs and desires; is frank and honest with self and others; and displays interest in the immediate environment.*

Interestingly, a separate dimension of social competence did not consistently emerge in ratings made by a group of experts on intelligence. Rather, the experts' dimensions focused on verbal intelligence and problem-solving ability, with social competence expressly emerging only in the ratings of the ideal "practically intelligent" person. Perhaps these experts shared Wechsler's dismissive view of social intelligence.

Similar studies were conducted by Kosmitzki and John (1993), and by Schneider, Ackerman, and Kanfer (1996), and obtained similar results. In the Schneider et al. study, factor analysis revealed seven dimensions of social competence that were essentially uncorrelated with measures of quantitative and verbal/reasoning ability. On the basis of these findings, Schneider et al. concluded that "it is time to lay to rest any residual notions that social competence is a monolithic entity, or that it is just general intelligence applied to social situations" (p. 479). As with Marlowe's (1986) study, however, the reliance on self-report measures of social intelligence compromises this conclusion, which remains to be confirmed using objective performance measures of the various dimensions in the social domain.

Social intelligence played little role in Sternberg's early componential view of human intelligence (e.g., Sternberg, 1977), which was intended to focus on reasoning and problem-solving skills as represented by traditional intelligence tests. However, social intelligence is explicitly represented in Sternberg's more recent *triarchic* view of intelligence (e.g., Sternberg, 1988), according to which intelligence is composed of analytical, creative, and practical abilities. Practical intelligence is defined in terms of problem-solving in everyday contexts and explicitly includes social intelligence (Sternberg & Wagner, 1986). According to Sternberg, each type of intelligence reflects the operation of three different kinds of component processes: performance components, which solve problems in various domains; executive metacomponents, which plan and evaluate problem solving; and knowledge-acquisition components, by which the first two components are learned. For Sternberg, these abilities, and thus their underlying components, may well be somewhat independent of each other; but the actual relation among various intellectual abilities is an open, empirical question.

Answering this question, of course, requires that we have psychometrically adequate instruments for assessing social intelligence. This brings us back to our starting point – the question of how social intelligence is to be measured. Future investigators who wish to make the attempt might be well advised to begin with the intuitive concept of social intelligence held in the mind of the layperson. When Alfred Binet was given the task of devising an intelligence test for French schoolchildren, he began by examining the kinds of things that they were asked to do in school. If a new generation of psychometricians undertakes the task of assessing social intelligence, they might well begin by looking at how that construct is represented in the mind of real people engaged in the ordinary course of everyday living. After all, social intelligence is a social construct, not just an academic one.

The Development of Social Intelligence

While the psychometric research just reviewed has focused – though not quite exclusively – on normal adults, there is also a long-standing interest in social intelligence among developmental psychologists (for a review, see Greenspan & Love, 1997) – particularly among those psychologists concerned with the assessment, treatment, and rehabilitation of children (and adults) with developmental disorders such as mental retardation and autism.

Mental Retardation

Of course, social intelligence has always played a role in the assessment of mental retardation. This psychiatric diagnosis requires not only evidence of subnormal intellectual functioning (i.e., IQ < 70) but also demonstrated evidence of impairments in "communication, self-care, home living, social and interpersonal skills, use of community resources, self-direction, functional academic skills, work, leisure, health, and safety" (American Psychiatric Association, 1994, p. 46). In other words, the diagnosis of mental retardation involves deficits in social as well as academic intelligence. Furthermore, the wording of the diagnostic criteria implies that social and academic intelligence are not highly correlated – it requires positive evidence of *both* forms of impairment, meaning that the presence of one cannot be inferred from the presence of the other.

While the conventional diagnostic criterion for mental retardation places primary emphasis on IQ and intellectual functioning, Greenspan and Love (1997) argued that it should emphasize social and practical intelligence instead. To this end, they proposed a hierarchical model of social intelligence. In this model, social intelligence consists of three components: *social sensitivity*, reflected in role-taking and social inference; *social insight*, including social comprehension, psychological insight, and moral judgment; and *social communication*, subsuming referential communication and social problem solving. Social intelligence, in turn, is only one component of *adaptive intelligence* (the others being *conceptual intelligence* and *practical intelligence*), which in turn joins *physical competence* and *socioemotional adaptation* (temperament and character) as the major dimensions of personal competence broadly construed. Greenspan and Love did not propose specific tests for any of these components of social intelligence but implied that they could be derived from experimental procedures used to study social cognition in general.

All this is well and good, but while the criterion for impaired intellectual functioning is clearly operationalized by an IQ threshold, there is as yet no standard by which impaired social functioning – impaired *social intelligence* – can be determined. The Vineland Social Maturity Scale (Doll, 1947) was an important step in this direction: This instrument yields aggregate scores of *social age* (analogous to mental age) and *social quotient* (by analogy to the intelligence quotient, calculated as social age divided by chronological age). The Vineland has been recently revised (Sparrow, Balla, & Cicchetti, 1984), but its adequacy as a measure of social intelligence is compromised by the fact that linguistic functions, motor skills, occupational skills, and self-care and self-direction are assessed as well as social relations. As an alternative, Taylor (1990) has proposed a semistructured Social Intelligence Interview covering such domains as social memory, moral development, recognition of and response to social cues, and social judgment. However, Taylor concedes that such an interview, being idiographically constructed to take account of the individual's particular social environment, cannot easily yield numerical scores by which individuals can be compared and ranked. More important than ranking individuals, from Taylor's point of view, is identifying areas of high and low functioning within various environments experienced by the individual, and determining the goodness of fit between the individual and the environments in which he or she lives.

Autism

Another group of developmental disabilities, autistic spectrum disorders, also invokes the concept of social intelligence. Kanner's (1943) classic description of autism portrays children who do not seem to be capable of engaging in normal social behavior or of maintaining normal social relationships, and the diagnostic criteria specified in the *Diagnostic and Statistical Manual of Mental Disorders (DSM-IV;* American Psychiatric Association, 1994) emphasize deficits in social relations: impairments in nonverbal behavior, failures to develop peer relationships, lack of spontaneous sharing and other aspects of social reciprocity; impairments in communication, including an inability to initiate or sustain conversations or social imitative play; and stereotyped patterns of behavior, including inflexibility in various behavioral routines. All of these features suggest that autism is characterized not just by social withdrawal and language impairment but by a specific impairment in the abilities that underlie effective social interaction.

Specifically, it has been proposed that autistic children and adults lack a "theory of mind" (Wellman, 1990) by which they can attribute mental states to other people and reflect on their own mental lives (Baron-Cohen, 1995; Baron-Cohen et al., 1993; see also Tager-Flusberg, 2007). This hypothesis brought the problem of assessing social intelligence in disabled populations (including mental retardation as well as autism) directly in contact with a literature on the development of social cognition in normal children. Still, Bruner and Feldman (1993) have argued that deficits in social cognition, such as those seen in autism, are actually secondary to deficits in general cognitive functioning. The fundamental question endures: Is social cognition a separate faculty from nonsocial cognition? Is social intelligence anything different from general intelligence applied to the social domain?

Moral Reasoning

Another trend contributing to revived interest in social intelligence was the upsurge of interest in moral reasoning following the publication of Kohlberg's Piagetian theory of moral reasoning (e.g., Kohlberg, 1963). As Turiel (2006) notes, Piaget himself had viewed moral reasoning within the wider context of the child's knowledge and judgment of social relationships. So, just as Thorndike raised the question of how social intelligence related to academic intelligence, the Piaget-Kohlberg trend raised the question of how age differences in moral reasoning were related to social reasoning in general. One answer is that they do not relate much at all, because moral judgments are based on unconscious, intuitive processes that are based more on emotion than reason; in this view, the reasons we give for our judgments are little more than after-the-fact rationalizations (e.g., Greene, Sommerville, Nystrom, Darley, & Cohen, 2001; Haidt, 2001). Another approach is that moral reasoning, while obviously related to social reasoning and to reasoning in general, constitutes a separate domain of reasoning that might follow its own unique principles, developmental trajectory, and the like. This does not rule out a role for emotional processes, but it keeps social cognition at the center of the study of moral reasoning

According to *social-cognitive domain theory* (Turiel, Killen, & Helwig, 1987; Smetana, 2006), morality is only one of several aspects of the social world about which children and adults acquire knowledge, and about which they engage in reasoning, judgment, and decision making. The "conventional" domain of social knowledge has to do with norms of social behavior that vary from one context to another. The "personal" domain has to do with our understanding of individual persons as psychological entities, including the attributions that we make for our own and others' behaviors, and our ability to infer meaning in social situations. The "moral" domain concerns universally applicable and obligatory concepts of harm, welfare, fairness, and rights. Most of the focus in social-cognitive domain theory has been on the moral domain and on children's developing the ability to understand moral concepts and render judgments of right and wrong. As a developmental theory, social-cognitive domain theory assumes that social-cognitive abilities are heterogeneous – that children's (and adults') abilities to reason about the social world and the trajectory of their development may well differ from one domain to another. But for present purposes, social-cognitive domain theory offers an alternative description of the domains in which children and adults apply distinctively social intelligence.

The Fall and Rise of Social Intelligence

Reviewing the literature published up to 1983, Landy (2006) characterized the search for social intelligence as "long, frustrating, and fruitless." Certainly it has been long and frustrating. Decade by decade, Landy traces a record of "disappointing empirical results and substantial theoretical criticism" (p. 82). This record did not, however, diminish the enthusiasm of both basic and applied social psychologists for the concept of social intelligence. Landy's review essentially stopped at 1983, and for good reason – for very soon events were to give social intelligence a new lease on life.

The Theory of Multiple Intelligences

The milestone event here was the theory of *multiple intelligences* proposed by Gardner (1983, 1993, 1999; Walters & Gardner, 1984). Unlike Spearman and other advocates of general intelligence, Gardner proposed that intelligence is not a unitary cognitive ability but that there are seven (and perhaps more) quite different kinds of intelligence, each hypothetically dissociable from the others, and each hypothetically associated with a different brain system. While most of these proposed intelligences (linguistic, logical-mathematical, spatial, musical, and bodily-kinesthetic) are "cognitive" abilities somewhat reminiscent of Thurstone's primary mental abilities, two are explicitly personal and social in nature. *Intrapersonal intelligence* is the ability to gain access to one's own internal emotional life, and *interpersonal intelligence* is the ability to notice and make distinctions among other individuals.

Although Gardner's (1983) multiple intelligences are individual-differences constructs, in which some people or some diagnostic groups are assumed to have more of these abilities than others, Gardner does not rely on the traditional psychometric procedures – scale construction, factor analysis, multitrait-multimethod matrices, external validity coefficients, and so on – for documenting individual differences. Rather, his preferred method is a somewhat impressionistic analysis based on a convergence of signs provided by eight different lines of evidence – chief among which are *isolation by brain damage*, such that one form of intelligence can be selectively impaired, leaving other forms relatively unimpaired; and *exceptional cases*, individuals who possess extraordinary levels of ability in one domain against a background of normal or even impaired abilities in other domains (alternatively, a person may show extraordinarily *low* levels of ability in one domain against a background of normal or exceptionally high levels of ability in others). In addition, Gardner postulated several other signs suggesting different types of intelligence. Among these are *identifiable core operations*, coupled with *experimental tasks* that permit analysis of these core operations and *psychometric tests* that reveal individual differences in the ability to perform them. In addition to experimental and psychometric evidence, Gardner (1983) also assumes that qualitatively different forms of intelligence will show *distinctive developmental histories*, in terms of different developmental trajectories, from infancy through adolescence and adulthood to old age – and, perhaps, different evolutionary pathways as well. Finally, Gardner argues that each form of intelligence is encoded in a *unique symbol system* by which the ability in question can be manipulated and transmitted by a culture. For social intelligence, this is, at least in part, the language of traits – the thousands of terms that we use to describe each other's mental states, but which do not apply to nonsentient objects (e.g., Allport & Odbert, 1937).

Gardner did not offer any new tests of social intelligence, nor did he provide compelling evidence that his multiple intelligences were really qualitatively different from each other. But in the context of a growing interest in cognitive neuroscience, and a growing inclination among psychologists to take neurobiological data as the gold standard of what is psychologically "real," claims for a neuropsychological dissociation between interpersonal intelligence and other forms of intelligence (e.g., that damage to the prefrontal cortex can selectively impair intrapersonal and interpersonal intelligence while leaving other abilities intact) gave new life to the notion that social intelligence can be distinguished from linguistic, logical-mathematical, and spatial intelligence.

Emotional Intelligence

The idea of social intelligence also got a boost from arguments in favor of individual differences in *emotional* intelligence, defined as "the ability to monitor one's own and others' feelings, to discriminate among them, and to use this information to guide one's thinking and action" (Salovey & Mayer, 1990, p. 189; see also Mayer, Roberts, & Barsade, 2008; Mayer, Salovey, & Caruso, 2008; Salovey & Grewal, 2005). Emotional intelligence subsumes four component abilities: the ability to perceive emotions in oneself and others; to use emotions in the service of thinking and problem solving; to understand emotions and the relations among them; and to manage emotions in oneself and others. Emotional intelligence and social intelligence are not the same thing: There is nothing particularly social about snake phobia, and there are many aspects of social cognition where emotion plays little or no role. But, as the listing of the component abilities indicates, emotion is frequently evoked in a social context, so emotional intelligence and social intelligence do share a sort of family resemblance.

The idea of emotional intelligence was popularized by Daniel Goleman in a series of books (e.g., Goleman, 1995) and quickly caught on in both academic and applied psychology. A search of the PsycInfo database reveals that before 1990, only three items had the phrase "emotional intelligence" in their title or abstract, compared to 253 for "social intelligence." For the decade 1990–1999, emotional intelligence had 77 such items, compared to 97 for social intelligence. But for the decade 2000–2009, emotional intelligence garnered 1,838 items (this is not a misprint), compared to 289 for social intelligence. Whereas Thorndike (1920) postulated social intelligence as the third member of a triad of intelligences, along with mechanical and abstract intelligence, it seems possible that, as suggested by Mayer, "Emotional intelligence could be . . . the replacement member of the triumvirate where social intelligence failed" (quoted in Goleman, 2006, p. 330).

This explosion of interest in emotional intelligence probably has much to do with what might be called the "affective counter-revolution" in psychology – the feeling that, since the cognitive revolution of the 1950s and 1960s, psychology had gone overboard in emphasizing epistemology and needed to pay more attention to feelings and desires. Certainly there is little reason to think that emotional intelligence is a clearer concept than social intelligence, or any easier to measure (Murphy, 2006). Whatever the reason, the upsurge of interest in emotional intelligence seems to have carried social intelligence along with it, so that we can look forward to a revival of research interest in this topic.

Social Neuroscience

All the more so, perhaps, now that Goleman (2006) has done for social intelligence what he did earlier for emotional intelligence. The premise of Goleman's book is that rewarding social relationships are the key to happiness and health (roughly half of the book reviews research on the social psychology of health) and that the key to rewarding social relationships is social intelligence. Therefore, we need new tools for the assessment of individual differences in social intelligence, but – more to the point – we need educational programs that will enable people to learn how to increase their emotional intelligence and therefore to be happier and healthier, as well as wiser. Whereas Gardner had postulated a single social intelligence, or perhaps two (*intra*personal and *inter*personal intelligence), Goleman argues for a highly differentiated set of social intelligences, grouped under two major headings. *Social awareness* (corresponding to the "self-awareness" domain of emotional intelligence) includes the ability to perceive other people's internal mental states, to understand their feelings and thoughts, and to comprehend the demands of complex social situations. It includes modules dedicated to primal empathy, empathic accuracy, attunement, and social cognition. *Social facility*, or relationship management (corresponding to the "self-management" domain), "builds on social awareness to allow smooth, effective interactions" (p. 84) and includes interaction synchrony, self-presentation, influence, and concern for others.

Goleman provocatively characterizes previous work on social intelligence as a "scientific backwater" (p. 330) in need of total rethinking. Taking a key from Gardner (1999; Walters & Gardner, 1984), who relied more on neuropsychology than on psychometrics, as well as the doctrine of modularity as it has developed in contemporary cognitive and social neuroscience (Fodor, 1983; Kihlstrom, in press), Goleman hypothesizes that social intelligence is mediated by an extensive network of neural modules, each dedicated to a particular aspect of social interaction. But more than that, Goleman asserts that "new neuroscientific findings have the potential to reinvigorate the social and behavioral sciences," just as "the basic assumptions of economics ... have been challenged by the emerging 'neuroeconomics,' which studies the brain during decision-making" (p. 324). Perhaps this prediction will come true. At the same time, however, it is a matter of historical fact that the real revolution in economics – the advances that garnered the Nobel Prizes – flowed from observational field studies (e.g., Simon, 1947, 1955) and paper-and-pencil questionnaires (Kahneman, 2003; Tversky & Kahneman, 1974). But even if cognitive and social neuroscience do not prove to be the saviors of social intelligence (or of cognitive and social psychology in general), Goleman's list of social-intelligence abilities is as good a place as any to start developing a new generation of instruments for assessing social intelligence.

The Knowledge View of Social Intelligence

Intelligence, as defined in standard dictionaries, has two rather different meanings. In its most familiar meaning, intelligence has to do with the individual's ability to learn and reason. It is this meaning that underlies common psychometric notions such as *intelligence testing*, the *intelligence quotient*, and the like. As originally coined by E. L. Thorndike (1920) and pursued in the studies reviewed so far, *social intelligence* referred to the person's ability to understand and manage other people, and to engage in adaptive social interactions. In its less common meaning, intelligence has to do with a body of information and knowledge. This second meaning is implicated in the titles of certain government organizations, such as the Central Intelligence Agency in the United States, and its British counterparts MI-5 and MI-6. Both meanings are invoked by the concept of social intelligence. But from Thorndike and Guilford to Gardner and Goleman, and beyond, social intelligence research and theory has been predicated almost exclusively on what might be called the "ability view."

On the other hand, Cantor and Kihlstrom have offered an alternative "knowledge view" of social intelligence that refers simply to the individual's fund of knowledge about the social world (Cantor & Kihlstrom, 1987, 1989; Kihlstrom & Cantor, 1989, 2000). In contrast to the ability view of social intelligence, the knowledge view does not conceptualize social intelligence as a trait, or group of traits, on which individuals can be compared and ranked on a dimension from low to high. Rather, the knowledge view of personality begins with the assumption that social behavior is *intelligent* – that it is mediated by what the person knows and believes to be the case, and by cognitive processes of perception, memory, reasoning, and problem solving, rather than being mediated by innate reflexes, conditioned responses, evolved genetic programs, and the like. Accordingly, the social intelligence view construes individual differences in social behavior – the public manifestations of personality – to be the product of individual differences in the knowledge that individuals bring to bear on their social interactions. Differences in social knowledge cause differences in social behavior, but it does not make sense to construct measures of social IQ. The important variable is not *how much* social intelligence the person has but rather *what* social intelligence he or she possesses – what the individual knows about himself or herself, other people, the situations in which people encounter each other, and the behaviors they exchange when they are in them.

The Evolution of Cognitive Views of Personality

The social intelligence view of personality has its origins in the social-cognitive tradition of personality theory, in which construal and reasoning processes are central to issues of social adaptation. Thus, Kelly (1955) characterized people as näive scientists generating hypotheses about future interpersonal events based on a set of personal constructs concerning self, others, and the world at large. These constructs were idiographic with respect to both content and organization. Individuals might be ranked in terms of the complexity of their personal construct systems, but the important issue for Kelly was knowing *what* the individual's personal constructs were. Beyond complexity, the idiosyncratic nature of personal construct systems precluded much nomothetic comparison.

While Kelly's theory was somewhat iconoclastic, similar developments occurred in the evolution of social learning theories of personality. The initial formulation of social learning theory (Miller & Dollard, 1941), a combination of Freudian psychoanalysis and Hullian learning theory, held that personality was largely learned behavior and that understanding personality required understanding the social conditions under which it was acquired. However, the slow rise of cognitive theories of learning soon lent a cognitive flavor to social learning theory itself (Bandura & Walters, 1963; Rotter, 1954). Bandura (1973) argued for the acquisition of social knowledge through precept and example rather than the direct experience of rewards and punishment, and later (1986) he distinguished between the outcome expectancies emphasized by Rotter and expectancies of self-efficacy – the individual's judgment or belief concerning his or her ability to carry out the actions required to achieve control over the events in a situation. Although Rotter (1966) proposed an individual-differences measure of internal versus external locus of control, it would never occur to Bandura to propose a nomothetic instrument for measuring individual differences in generalized self-efficacy expectations. The important consideration is not whether an individual is relatively high or low in self-perceptions of competence, or even actual competence, but rather whether the person *believes* that he or she is competent to perform a particular behavior in some particular situation.

The immediate predecessor to the social-intelligence view of personality is Mischel's (1968, 1973) cognitive social-learning reconceptualization of personality. Although sometimes couched in behaviorist language, an emphasis on the *subjective meaning* of the situation marked even Mischel's 1968 theory as cognitive in nature. Since that time, Mischel has broadened his conceptualization of personality to include a wide variety of different constructs, some derived from the earlier work of Kelly, Rotter, Bandura, and others reflecting the importation into personality theory of concepts originating in the laboratory study of human cognitive processes. From Mischel's (1973) point of view, the most important product of cognitive development and social learning is the individual's repertoire of *cognitive and behavioral construction competencies* – the ability to engage in a wide variety of skilled, adaptive behaviors, including both overt action and covert mental activities. These construction competencies are as close as Mischel gets to the ability view of social (or, for that matter, *non*social) intelligence.

On the other hand, the importance of perception and interpretation of events in Mischel's system calls for a second set of person variables, having to do with *encoding strategies* governing selective attention and *personal constructs* – Kelly-like categories that filter people's perceptions, memories, and expectations. Then, of course, following Rotter and Bandura, Mischel also stresses the role of stimulus-outcome, behavior-outcome, and self-efficacy *expectancies*. Also in line with Rotter's theory, Mischel notes that behavior will be governed by the *subjective values* associated with various outcomes. A final set of relevant variables consists of *self-regulatory systems and plans*, self-imposed goals and consequences that govern behavior in the absence (or in spite) of social monitors and external constraints. These variables are more in line with the knowledge view of social intelligence.

Social Intelligence as Social Knowledge

Following Winograd (1975) and Anderson (1976), Cantor and Kihlstrom (1987) classified social intelligence into two broad categories: *declarative social knowledge*, consisting of abstract concepts and specific memories, and *procedural social knowledge*, consisting of the rules, skills, and strategies by which the person manipulates and transforms declarative knowledge and translates knowledge into action. Following Tulving (1983), the individual's fund of declarative social knowledge, in turn, can be broken down further into context-free *semantic* social knowledge about the social world in general and *episodic* social memory for the particular events and experiences that make up the person's autobiographical record. Similarly, procedural knowledge can be subclassified in terms of cognitive and motoric social skills. These concepts, personal memories, interpretive rules, and action plans are the cognitive structures of personality. Together, they constitute the expertise that guides an individual's approach to solving the problems of social life.

The cognitive architecture of social intelligence will be familiar from the literature on social cognition (for an overviews, see Fiske & Taylor, 2007) – a literature that, interestingly, had its beginnings in early psychometric efforts to measure individual differences in social intelligence. For example, Vernon (1933) argued that one of the characteristics of a socially intelligent person was that he or she was a good judge of personality – a proposition that naturally led to inquiries into how people form impressions of personality. Research on person perception, in turn, led to an inquiry into the implicit theories of personality that provide the cognitive basis for impression formation. Specifically, Cronbach argued that one's implicit theory of personality consisted of his or her knowledge of "the generalized Other" (1955, p. 179) – a mental list of the important dimensions of personality and estimates of the mean and variance of each dimension within the population, as well as estimates of the covariances among the several dimensions. Cronbach argued that this intuitive knowledge might be widely shared and could be acquired as a consequence of socialization and acculturation processes; but he also assumed that there would be individual and cultural differences in this knowledge, leading to individual and group differences in social behavior. Studies of impression formation, implicit personality theory, and later, causal attributions, social categories, scripts, and person memories provided the foundation for the social-intelligence analysis of personality structures and processes.

Following Kelly (1955) and Mischel (1973), Cantor and Kihlstrom (1987) accorded *social concepts* a central status as cognitive structures of personality. If the purpose of perception is action, and if every act of perception is an act of categorization (Bruner, 1957), the particular categories that organize people's perception of the social world assume paramount importance in a cognitive analysis of personality. Some of these concepts concern the world of other people and the places we encounter them: knowledge of personality types, social groups, and social situations. Other concepts concern the *intra*personal world: the kinds of people we are, both in general and in particular classes of situations, and our theories of how we got that way. Some of these conceptual relations may be universal, and others may be highly consensual within the individual's culture; but, as Kelly (1955) argued, some may be quite idiosyncratic. Regardless of whether they are shared with others, the individual's conceptual knowledge about the social world forms a major portion of his or her declarative social knowledge.

Another important set of declarative social knowledge structures represents the individual's autobiographical memory (Kihlstrom, 2009). In the context of social intelligence, autobiographical memory includes a narrative of the person's own actions and experiences, but it also includes what he or she has learned through direct and vicarious experience about the actions and experiences of specific other people, and the events that have transpired in particular situations. In addition, every piece of conscious autobiographical memory is linked to a mental representation of the self as the agent or patient of some action, or the stimulus or experiencer of some state (Kihlstrom, Beer, & Klein, 2002).

On the procedural side, a substantial portion of the social intelligence repertoire consists of interpretive rules for making sense of social experience: for inducing social categories and deducing category membership, making attributions of causality, inferring other people's behavioral dispositions and emotional states, forming judgments of likability and responsibility, resolving cognitive dissonance, encoding and retrieving memories of our own and other people's behavior, predicting future events, and testing hypotheses about our social judgments. Some of these procedures are algorithmic in nature, while others may entail heuristic shortcuts (Nisbett & Ross, 1980). Some are enacted deliberately, while others may be evoked automatically, without much attention and cognitive effort on our part (Bargh, 1997; but see also Kihlstrom, 2008). They are all part of our repertoire of procedural social knowledge.

Social Intelligence in Life Tasks

It should be clear that from the knowledge view of social intelligence, the assessment of social intelligence has quite a different character than it does from the ability view. From a psychometric point of view, the questions posed have answers that are right or wrong: Are smart people also friendly? How do you know when a person is happy or sad? Is it proper to laugh at a funeral? In this way, it is possible, at least in principle, to evaluate the accuracy of the person's social knowledge and the effectiveness of his or her social behaviors. However, as noted at the outset, the social intelligence approach to personality abjures such rankings of people (Cantor, 2003). Rather than asking how socially intelligent a person *is*, compared to some norm, the social intelligence view of personality asks what social intelligence a person *has*, which he or she can use to guide his or her interpersonal behavior. In fact, the social intelligence approach to personality is less interested in assessing the individual's repertoire of social intelligence than in seeking to understand the general cognitive structures and processes out of which individuality is constructed, how these develop over the life course of the individual, and how they play a role in ongoing social interactions. For this reason, Cantor and Kihlstrom (1987, 1989; Kihlstrom & Cantor, 1989) have not proposed any individual-differences measures by which the person's social intelligence can be assessed.

Although the social intelligence view of personality diverges from the psychometric approach to social intelligence on the matter of assessment, it agrees with some contemporary psychometric views that intelligence is context-specific. Thus, in Sternberg's (1988) triarchic theory, social intelligence is part of a larger repertoire of knowledge by which the person attempts to solve the practical problems encountered in the physical and social world. According to Cantor and Kihlstrom (1987), social intelligence is specifically geared to solving the problems of social life, and in particular managing the *life tasks, current concerns* (Klinger 1977), or *personal projects* (Little, 2005) that people select for themselves, or that other people impose on them from outside. Put another way, one's social intelligence cannot be evaluated in the abstract but only with respect to the domains and contexts in which it is exhibited and the life tasks it is designed to serve. And even in this case, "adequacy" cannot be judged from the viewpoint of the external observer but must come from the point of view of the particular person whose life tasks are in play.

Life tasks provide an integrative unit of analysis for studying the interaction between the person and the situation (Cantor & Fleeson, 1994; Cantor & Harlow, 1994; Cantor, Kemmelmeier, Basten, & Prentice, 2002; Cantor & Langston, 1989; Cantor & Malley, 1991). They may be explicit or implicit, abstract or circumscribed, universal or unique, enduring or stage-specific, rare or commonplace, poorly defined or well defined. Whatever their features, they give meaning to the individual's life and serve to organize his or her daily activities. They are defined from the subjective point of view of the individual: They are the tasks that the person perceives himself or herself as "working on and devoting energy to solving during a specified period in life" (Cantor & Kihlstrom, 1987, p. 168). First, life tasks are articulated by the individual as self-relevant, time-consuming, and meaningful. They provide a kind of organizing scheme for the individual's activities, and they are embedded in the individual's ongoing daily life. And they are responsive to the demands, structure, and constraints of the social environment in which the person lives. Life tasks are often willingly undertaken, but they can also be imposed on people from outside, and the ways in which they are approached may be constrained by sociocultural factors. Unlike the stage-structured views of Erikson and his popularizers, however, the social-intelligence view of personality does not propose that everyone at a particular age is engaged in the same sorts of life tasks. Instead, periods of transition, when the person is entering into new institutions, are precisely those times when individual differences in life tasks become most apparent.

The intelligent nature of life-task pursuit is clearly illustrated by the strategies deployed in its service. People often begin to comprehend the problem at hand by simulating a set of plausible outcomes, relating them to previous experiences stored in autobiographical memory. They also formulate specific plans for action and monitor their progress toward their goals, taking special note of environmental factors that stand in the way and determining whether the actual outcome meets their original expectations. Much of the cognitive activity in life-task problem solving involves forming causal attributions about outcomes and in surveying autobiographical memory for hints about how things might have gone differently. Particularly compelling evidence of the intelligent nature of life-task pursuit comes when, inevitably, plans go awry or some unforeseen event frustrates progress. Then, the person will map out a new path toward the goal or even choose a new goal compatible with a superordinate life task. Intelligence frees us from reflex, tropism, and instinct in social life as in nonsocial domains.

QUO VADIS?

It is possible that the concept of social intelligence has outlived its usefulness and will be supplanted by emotional intelligence. Alternatively, it is possible that neuroscientific analyses will give new life to the study of social intelligence, as they promise to do in other areas of psychology. On the other hand, perhaps we should abandon the "ability" model of social intelligence completely, along with its psychometric emphasis on developing instruments for the measuring of individual differences in social competencies of various sorts – tests intended to rank people, and on which some people must score high and others must score low. Instead of focusing on *how people compare*, perhaps we should focus on *what people know*, and how they bring their social intelligence to bear on their interactions with other people, on the tasks life has set for them, and on the tasks they have set for themselves. In this way, we would honor the primary idea of the cognitive view of social interaction, which is that interpersonal behavior is intelligent, based on what the individual knows and believes – no matter how smart or stupid it may appear to other people.

References

Allport, G. W., & Odbert, H. S. (1937). Trait-names: A psycho-lexical study. *Psychological Monographs*, 47 (Whole No. 211).

American Psychiatric Association. (1994). *Diagnostic and statistical manual of mental disorders* (4th ed.). Washington, DC: American Psychiatric Association.

Anderson, J. R. (1976). *Language, memory, and thought*. Hillsdale, NJ: Erlbaum.

Bandura, A. (1973). *Aggression: A social learning analysis*. Englewood Cliffs, NJ: Prentice-Hall.

Bandura, A. (1986). *Social foundations of thought and action: A social cognitive theory*. Englewood Cliffs, NJ: Prentice-Hall.

Bandura, A., & Walters, R. H. (1963). *Social learning and personality development*. New York: Holt, Rinehart and Winston.

Bargh, J. A. (1997). The automaticity of everyday life. In R. S. Wyer (Ed.), *Advances in social cognition* (Vol. 10, pp. 1–61). Mahwah, NJ: Erlbaum.

Baron-Cohen, S. (1995). *Mindblindness: An essay on autism and theory of mind*. Cambridge, MA: MIT Press.

Baron-Cohen, S., Tager-Flusberg, H., & Cohen, D. J. (1993). Does the autistic child have a "theory of mind"? *Cognition*, *21*, 37–46.

Bruner, J. S. (1957). On perceptual readiness. *Psychological Review*, *64*, 123–152.

Bruner, J. S., & Feldman, C. (1993). Theories of mind and the problem of autism. In S. Baron-Cohen, H. Tager-Flusberg, & D. J. Cohen (Eds.), *Understanding other minds: Perspectives from autism* (pp. 267–291). Oxford, UK: Oxford University Press.

Campbell, D. T., & Fiske, D. W. (1959). Convergent and discriminant validation by the multitrait-multimethod matrix. *Psychological Bulletin*, *56*, 81–105.

Campbell, J. M., & McCord, D. M. (1996). The WAIS-R Comprehension and Picture Arrangement subtests as measures of social intelligence: Testing traditional interpretations. *Journal of Psychoeducational Assessment*, *14*, 240–249.

Cantor, N. (2003). Constructive cognition, personal goals, and the social embedding of personality. In L. G. Aspinwall & U. M. Staudinger (Eds.), *A psychology of human strengths: Fundamental directions and future directions for a positive psychology* (pp. 49–60). Washington, DC: American Psychological Association.

Cantor, N., & Fleeson, W. (1994). Social intelligence and intelligent goal pursuit: A cognitive slice of motivation. In W. D. Spaulding (Ed.), *Integrative views of motivation, cognition, and emotion. Nebraska Symposium on Motivation*, *41*, 125–180.

Cantor, N., & Harlow, R. (1994). Social intelligence and personality: Flexible life-task pursuit. In R. J. Sternberg & P. Ruzgis (Eds.), *Personality and intelligence* (pp. 137–168). Cambridge, UK: Cambridge University Press.

Cantor, N., Kemmelmeier, M., Basten, J., & Prentice, D. A. (2002). Life-task pursuit in social groups: Balancing self-exploration and social integration. *Self & Identity*, *1*, 177–184.

Cantor, N., & Kihlstrom, J. F. (1987). *Personality and social intelligence*. Englewood Cliffs, NJ: Prentice-Hall.

Cantor, N., & Kihlstrom, J. F. (1989). Social intelligence and cognitive assessments of personality. In R. S. Wyer & T. K. Srull (Eds.), *Advances in social cognition* (Vol. 2, pp. 1–59). Hillsdale, NJ: Erlbaum.

Cantor, N., & Langston, C. A. (1989). "Ups and downs" of life tasks in a life transition. In L. A. Pervin (Ed.), *Goal concept in personality and social psychology* (pp. 127–168). Hillsdale, NJ: Erlbaum.

Cantor, N., & Malley, J. (1991). Life tasks, personal needs, and close relationships. In G. J. O. Fletcher & F. D. Fincham (Eds.), *Cognition in close relationships* (pp. 101–125). Hillsdale, NJ: Erlbaum.

Chen, S. A., & Michael, W. B. (1993). First-order and higher-order factors of creative social intelligence within Guilford's structure-of-intellect model: A reanalysis of a Guilford data base. *Educational & Psychological Measurement*, *53*, 619–641.

Cronbach, L. J. (1955). Processes affecting scores on "understanding of others" and "assumed similarity." *Psychological Bulletin*, *52*, 177–193.

Dewey, J. (1909). *Moral principles in education*. New York: Houghton Mifflin.

Doll, E. A. (1947). *Social maturity scale*. Circle Pines, MN: American Guidance Service.

Fiske, S. T., & Taylor, S. E. (2007). *Social cognition: From brains to culture*. New York, NY: McGraw-Hill.

Fodor, J. A. (1983). *The modularity of the mind*. Cambridge, MA: MIT Press.

Gardner, H. (1983). *Frames of mind: The theory of multiple intelligences*. New York, NY: BasicBooks.

Gardner, H. (1993). *Multiple intelligences: The theory in practice*. New York, NY: BasicBooks.

Gardner, H. (1999). *Intelligence reframed : Multiple intelligences for the 21st century*. New York, NY: BasicBooks.

Goleman, D. (1995). *Emotional intelligence*. New York, NY: Bantam.

Goleman, D. (2006). *Social intelligence: The new science of human relationships*. New York, NY: Bantam Books.

Greene, J. D., Sommerville, R. B., Nystrom, L. E., Darley, J. M., & Cohen, J. D. (2001). An fMRI investigation of emotional engagement in moral judgment. *Science*, **293**, 2105–2108.

Greenspan, S., & Love, P. F. (1997). Social intelligence and developmental disorder: mental retardation, learning disabilities, and autism. In W. E. MacLean (Ed.), *Ellis' handbook of mental deficiency: Psychological theory and research* (3rd ed., pp. 311–342). Mahwah, NJ: Erlbaum.

Haidt, J. (2001). The emotional dog and its rational tail: A social intuitionist approach to moral judgment. *Psychological Review*, **108**(4), 814–834.

Hendricks, M., Guilford, J. P., & Hoepfner, R. (1969). Measuring creative social intelligence. *Reports from the Psychological Laboratory, University of Southern California*, No. 42.

Hoepfner, R., & O'Sullivan, M. (1969). Social intelligence and IQ. *Educational & Psychological Measurement*, **28**, 339–344.

Hunt, T. (1928). The measurement of social intelligence. *Journal of Applied Psychology*, **12**, 317–334.

Jones, K., & Day, J. D. (1997). Discrimination of two aspects of cognitive-social intelligence from academic intelligence. *Journal of Educational Psychology*, **89**, 486–497.

Kahneman, D. (2003). A perspective on judgment and choice: Mapping bounded rationality. *American Psychologist*, **58**(9), 697–720.

Kanner, L. (1943). Autistic disturbances of affective contact. *Nervous Child*, **2**, 217–250.

Kelly, G. (1955). *The psychology of personal constructs*. New York, NY: W. W. Norton.

Kihlstrom, J. F. (2008). The automaticity juggernaut. In J. Baer, J. C. Kaufman, & R. F. Baumeister (Eds.), *Are we free? Psychology and free will* (pp. 155–180). New York, NY: Oxford University Press.

Kihlstrom, J. F. (2009). "So that we might have roses in December": The functions of autobiographical memory. *Applied Cognitive Psychology*, **23**, 1179–1192.

Kihlstrom, J. F. (2010). Social neuroscience: The footprints of Phineas Gage. *Social Cognition*, 28(6), pp. 757–783.

Kihlstrom, J. F., Beer, J. S., & Klein, S. B. (2002). Self and identity as memory. In M. R. Leary & J. Tangney (Eds.), *Handbook of self and identity* (pp. 68–90). New York, NY: Guilford Press.

Kihlstrom, J. F., & Cantor, N. (2000). Social intelligence. In R. J. Sternberg (Ed.), *Handbook of intelligence* (pp. 359–379). New York, NY: Cambridge University Press.

Kihlstrom, J. F., & Cantor, N. (1989). Social intelligence and personality: There's room for growth. In R. S. Wyer & T. K. Srull (Eds.), *Advances in social cognition* (Vol. 2, pp. 197–214). Hillsdale, NJ: Erlbaum.

Klinger, E. (1977). *Meaning and void: Inner experience and the incentives in people's lives*. Minneapolis: University of Minnesota Press.

Kohlberg, L. (1963). The development of children's orientations toward a moral order: I. Sequence in the development of moral thought. *Vita Humana*, 6, 11–33.

Kosmitzki, C., & John, O. P. (1993). The implicit use of explicit conceptions of social intelligence. *Personality & Individual Differences*, **15**, 11–23.

Landy, F. J. (2006). The long, frustrating and fruitless search for social intelligence: A cautionary tale. In K. R. Murphy (Ed.), *A critique of emotional intelligence: What are the problems and how can they be fixed?* (pp. 81–123). Mahwah, NJ: Erlbaum.

Lee, J.-E., Wong, C. T., Day, J. D., Maxwell, S., & Thorpe, S. (2000). Social and academic intelligences: A multitrait-multimethod study of their crystallized and fluid characteristics. *Personality & Individual Differences*, **29**, 539–553.

Lee, N.-E., Day, J. D., Meara, N. M., & Maxwell, S. (2002). Discrimination of social knowledge and its flexible application from creativity: A multitrait-multimethod approach. *Personality & Individual Differences*, **32**, 913–928.

Little, B. R. (2005). Personality science and personal projects: Six impossible things before breakfast. *Journal of Research in Personality*, **39**, 4–21.

Lull, H. G. (1911). Moral instruction through social intelligence. *American Journal of Sociology*, **17**, 47–60.

Marlowe, H. A. (1986). Social intelligence: Evidence for multidimensionality and construct independence. *Journal of Educational Psychology*, **78**, 52–58.

Matarazzo, J. D. (1972). *Wechsler's measurement and appraisal of adult intelligence* (5th ed.). Baltimore, MD: Williams & Wilkins.

Mayer, J. D., Roberts, R. D., & Barsade, S. G. (2008). Human abilities: Emotional intelligence. *Annual Review of Psychology*, 59, 507–536.

Mayer, J. D., Salovey, P., & Caruso, D. R. (2008). Emotional intelligence: New ability or eclectic traits? *American Psychologist*, 63, 503–517.

Miller, N. E., & Dollard, J. H. (1941). *Social learning and imitation*. New Haven, CT: Yale University Press.

Mischel, W. (1968). *Personality and assessment*. New York, NY: Wiley.

Mischel, W. (1973). Toward a cognitive social learning reconceptualization of personality. *Psychological Review*, 80, 252–283.

Moss, F. A. (1931). Preliminary report of a study of social intelligence and executive ability. *Public Personnel Studies*, 9, 2–9.

Moss, F. A., & Hunt, T. (1927). Are you socially intelligent? *Scientific American*, 137, 108–110.

Moss, F. A., Hunt, T., & Omwake, K. T. (1949). *Manual for the Social Intelligence Test, Revised Form*. Washington, DC: Center for Psychological Service.

Moss, F. A., Hunt, T., Omwake, K. T., & Ronning, M. M. (1927). *Social Intelligence Test*. Washington, DC: Center for Psychological Service.

Moss, F. A., Hunt, T., Omwake, K. T., & Woodward, L. G. (1955). *Manual for the George Washington University Series Social Intelligence Test*. Washington, DC: Center for Psychological Service.

Murphy, K. R. (Ed.). (2006). *A critique of emotional intelligence: What are the problems and how can they be fixed?* Mahwah, NJ: Erlbaum.

Nisbett, R. E., & Ross, L. (1980). *Human inference: Strategies and shortcomings in social judgment*. Englewood Cliffs, NJ: Prentice-Hall.

O'Sullivan, M., Guilford, J. P., & deMille, R. (1965). The measurement of social intelligence. *Reports from the Psychological Laboratory, University of Southern California*, No. 34.

Rapaport, D., Gill, M. M., & Schafer, R. (1968). *Diagnostic psychological testing* (Rev. ed.). New York, NY: International Universities Press.

Riggio, R. E., Messamer, J., & Throckmorton, B. (1991). Social and academic intelligence: Conceptually distinct but overlapping constructs. *Personality & Individual Differences*, 12, 695–702.

Romney, D. M., & Pyryt, M. C. (1999). Guilford's concept of social intelligence revisited. *High Ability Studies*, 10, 137–199.

Rotter, J. B. (1954). *Social learning and clinical psychology*. Englewood Cliffs, NJ: Prentice-Hall.

Rotter, J. B. (1966). Generalized expectancies for internal versus external control of reinforcement. *Psychological Monographs*, 80(1, Whole No. 609).

Salovey, P., & Grewal, D. (2005). The science of emotional intelligence. *Current Directions in Psychological Science*, 14(6), 281–285.

Salovey, P., & Mayer, J. D. (1990). Emotional intelligence. *Imagination, Cognition, and Personality*, 9, 185–211.

Schneider, R. J., Ackerman, P. L., & Kanfer, R. (1996). To "act wisely in human relations": Exploring the dimensions of social competence. *Personality & Individual Differences*, 21, 469–482.

Sechrest, L., & Jackson, D. N. (1961). Social intelligence and the accuracy of interpersonal predictions. *Journal of Personality*, 29, 167–182.

Shanley, L. A., Walker, R. E., & Foley, J. M. (1971). Social intelligence: A concept in search of data. *Psychological Reports*, 29, 1123–1132.

Simon, H. A. (1947). *Administrative behavior*. New York, NY: Macmillan.

Simon, H. A. (1955). A behavioral model of rational choice. *Quarterly Journal of Economics*, 69, 99–118.

Smetana, J. G. (2006). Social-cognitive domain theory: Consistencies and variations in children's moral and social judgments. In M. Killen & J. G. Smetana (Eds.), *Handbook of moral development* (pp. 119–153). Mahwah, NJ: Erlbaum.

Snyder, M., & Cantor, N. (1998). Understanding personality and social behavior: A functionalist strategy. In D. T. Gilbert & S. T. Fiske (Eds.), *Handbook of social psychology* (4th ed., Vol. 2, pp. 635–679). Boston, MA: McGraw-Hill.

Snyder, S. D., & Michael, W. B. (1983). The relationship between performance on standardized tests in mathematics and reading to two measures of social intelligence and one of academic self-esteem of primary school children. *Educational and Psychological Measurement*, 43, 1141–1148.

Sparrow, S. S., Balla, D. A., & Cicchetti, D. V. (1984). *Vineland Adaptive Behavior Scale*. Circle Pines, MN: American Guidance Service.

Spearman, C. (1927). *The abilities of man*. New York, NY: Macmillan.

Sternberg, R. J. (1977). *Intelligence, information processing, and analogical reasoning: The componential analysis of human abilities*. Hillsdale, NJ: Erlbaum.

Sternberg, R. J. (1988). *The triarchic mind: A new theory of intelligence*. New York, NY: Viking.

Sternberg, R. J. Conway, B. E., Ketron, J. L., & Bernstein, M. (1981). People's conceptions of intelligence. *Journal of Personality & Social Psychology, 41*, 37–55.

Sternberg, R. J., & Wagner, R. (Eds.). (1986). *Practical intelligence: Nature and origins of competence in the everyday world*. Cambridge, UK: Cambridge University Press.

Tager-Flusberg, H. (2007). Evaluating the theory-of-mind theory of autism. *Current Directions in Psychological Science, 16*, 311–315.

Taylor, E. H. (1990). The assessment of social intelligence. *Psychotherapy, 27*, 445–457.

Thorndike, E. L. (1920). Intelligence and its use. *Harper's Magazine, 140*, 227–235.

Thorndike, R. L., & Stein, S. (1937). An evaluation of the attempts to measure social intelligence. *Psychological Bulletin, 34*, 275–285.

Tulving, E. (1983). *Elements of episodic memory*. New York, NY: Oxford University Press.

Turiel, E. (2006). The development of morality. In N. Eisenberg, W. Damon, & R. M. Lerner (Eds.), *Handbook of child psychology: Social emotional, and personality development* (6th ed., Vol. 3, pp. 789–857). Hoboken, NJ: Wiley.

Turiel, E., Killen, M., & Helwig, C. (1987). Morality: Its structure, functions, and vagaries. In J. Kagan & M. Lamb (Eds.), *The emergence of morality in young children*. Chicago, IL: University of Chicago Press.

Tversky, A., & Kahneman, D. (1974). Judgment under uncertainty: Heuristics and biases. *Science, 185*, 1124–1131.

Vernon, P. E. (1933). Some characteristics of the good judge of personality. *Journal of Social Psychology, 4*, 42–57.

Walker, R. E., & Foley, J. M. (1973). Social intelligence: Its history and measurement. *Psychological Reports, 33*, 839–864.

Walters, J. M., & Gardner, H. (1986). The theory of multiple intelligences: Some issues and answers. In R. J. Sternberg & R. Wagner (Eds.), *Practical intelligence: Origins of competence in the everyday world* (pp. 163–182). Cambridge, UK: Cambridge University Press.

Wechsler, D. (1939). *The measurement and appraisal of adult intelligence*. Baltimore, MD: Williams & Wilkins.

Wechsler, D. (1958). *The measurement and appraisal of adult intelligence* (4th ed.). Baltimore: Williams & Wilkins.

Weis, S., & Suss, H.-M. (2007). Reviving the search for social intelligence – A multitrait-multimethod study of its structure and construct validity. *Personality and Individual Differences, 42*(1), 3–14.

Wellman, H. M. (1990). *The child's theory of mind*. Cambridge, MA: MIT Press.

Winograd, T. (1975). Frame representations and the procedural-declarative controversy. In D. Bobrow & A. Collins (Eds.), *Representation and understanding: Studies in cognitive science* (pp. 185–210). New York, NY: Academic Press.

Wong, C.-M. T., Day, J. D., Maxwell, S. E., & Meara, N. M. (1995). A multitrait-multimethod study of academic and social intelligence in college students. *Journal of Educational Psychology, 87*, 117–133.

CHAPTER 29

Cultural Intelligence

Soon Ang, Linn Van Dyne, and Mei Ling Tan

1.0 Introduction and Historical Background

Earley and Ang introduced the concept of cultural intelligence in their Stanford University Press book published in 2003. Cultural intelligence refers to an individual's capability to function effectively in situations characterized by cultural diversity (Ang & Van Dyne, 2008; Earley & Ang, 2003).

Cultural intelligence was conceived at the turn of the 21st century, when the world was experiencing unprecedented globalization and interconnectedness. Advanced communication and transportation technologies have made traveling to and sojourning in foreign soils more affordable and accessible. Cultural intelligence (CQ) was also conceived at a time in which ideological clashes and cultural conflict culminated in the tragic events of September 11, 2001. Nobel Prize laureate Elie Wiesel identified "cultural hatred" – hatred directed toward culturally different individuals – as *the* major source of problems between people, across all times. The *Los Angeles Times* estimates that there are over 50 hot spots in the world where cultural conflicts occur every day. Cultural wars in Serbia, Croatia, Bosnia, Rwanda, Burundi, Angola, and Afghanistan have plagued the globe. Thus, although globalization may lead some to regard the world as "flat," cultural hatred is a major destabilizing factor in the contemporary world. Although technology is often a force for convergence, deep-seated cultural differences and cultural diversity present critical challenges to people all over the world. In sum, globalization increases intercultural interactions and also increases the probability of cultural misunderstandings, tensions, and conflicts.

The driving question behind the idea of cultural intelligence is, *Why do some but not other individuals easily and effectively adapt their views and behaviors cross-culturally?* (Van Dyne, Ang, & Livermore, 2010). This question has long interested researchers across diverse disciplines in psychology, sociology, management, health care, military, education, and other fields. Thus, it is not surprising that a wide array of frameworks and intercultural instruments (see

Paige, 2004, for a comprehensive review) purport to assess cultural competencies.

Nevertheless, Gelfand, Imai, and Fehr (2008) described the existing cultural-competency literature as lacking a coherent theoretical foundation and confusing because it often mixes ability and nonability characteristics. In their words, the literature on cultural competency can best be characterized as suffering from the "jingle and jangle fallacy – where constructs with the same meaning are labeled differently while constructs with different meanings are labeled similarly" (p. 375). Because there is no overarching theoretical framework to tie the numerous cultural competency constructs together and there is little consensus on operationalizations, questions of construct validity arise and compromise the practical utility of the concept.

It is within this context that the concept of cultural intelligence (CQ) was formulated. Drawing on the theory of multiple loci of intelligence (Sternberg & Detterman 1986), Earley and Ang (2003) conceptualized cultural intelligence as a set of four capabilities – based specifically on the theory of multiple loci of intelligence. Accordingly, CQ is a "cleaner" construct that assesses multiple aspects of intercultural competence based on a theoretically grounded, comprehensive, and coherent framework.

Since 2003, the concept of cultural intelligence has attracted significant attention worldwide and across diverse disciplines. Despite being relatively new, the concept has been cited in over 60 journals in disciplines as diverse as applied, cognitive, and social psychology; mental health; international business; management; organizational behavior; human resources; human relations; industrial relations; intercultural relations; sociology; education; communications; knowledge management; decision sciences; information science; the military; architecture; economics; and engineering.

This chapter provides an overview of research on cultural intelligence, the nomological network of cultural intelligence, and future directions for research on cultural intelligence. We aim to help readers think more deeply about their own cultural intelligence capabilities. We also aim to stimulate additional theorizing, empirical research, and practical application in diverse countries and cultures across the globe.

2.0 The Four-Factor Model of Cultural Intelligence

2.1 *Conceptualization of* CQ

Although early research tended to view intelligence narrowly as the ability to grasp concepts and solve problems in academic settings, there is now a consensus that intelligence applies beyond the classroom. The growing interest in "real-world" intelligence has identified new types of nonacademic intelligences (Sternberg, 1997) that focus on specific content domains such as social intelligence (Thorndike & Stein, 1937), emotional intelligence (Mayer & Salovey, 1993), and practical intelligence (Sternberg & Wagner, 2000).

Cultural intelligence builds upon some of these same ideas but instead focuses on a specific domain – intercultural settings – and is motivated by the practical reality of globalization (Earley & Ang, 2003). Just as EQ (emotional intelligence) complements IQ (cognitive intelligence) as important for work effectiveness and high-quality interpersonal relationships in this increasingly interdependent world (Earley & Gibson, 2002), cultural intelligence is another complementary form of intelligence that can explain variability in coping with diversity and functioning in new cultural settings. Since the norms for social interaction vary from culture to culture, it is unlikely that cognitive intelligence, emotional intelligence, or social intelligence will translate automatically into effective cross-cultural adjustment, interaction, and effectiveness.

CULTURAL INTELLIGENCE AS A MULTIDIMENSIONAL CONSTRUCT

Earley and Ang (2003) built on the increasing consensus that intelligence should go beyond mere cognitive abilities. They drew on Sternberg and Detterman's (1986) integration of the myriad views of intelligence as comprising four complementary ways of conceptualizing individual-level intelligence: metacognitive, cognitive, motivational, and behavioral.

Sternberg and Detterman's framework is noteworthy because it proposes intelligence as having different "loci" within the person – metacognition, cognition, and motivation are mental capabilities that reside within the "head" of the person, while overt actions are behavioral capabilities. Metacognitive intelligence refers to the control of cognition – the processes individuals use to acquire and understand knowledge. Cognitive intelligence refers to a person's knowledge structures and is consistent with Ackerman's (1996) intelligence-as-knowledge concept, which similarly argues for the importance of knowledge as part of a person's intellect. Motivational intelligence refers to the mental capacity to direct and sustain energy on a particular task or situation. The concept of motivational intelligence is based on contemporary views that motivational capabilities are critical to "real-world" problem solving. Without motivation, cognition such as problem solving, reasoning, or decision making may not even be activated. Therefore, it is useless to focus simply on cognition and ignore the motivation aspect of intelligence (e.g., Ceci, 1996). Behavioral intelligence refers to outward manifestations or overt actions – what the person does rather than what he or she thinks (Sternberg, 1986). Hence, metacognitive, cognitive, and motivational intelligence involve mental functioning, and behavioral intelligence is the capability to display actual behaviors. In parallel fashion, Earley and Ang (2003) described cultural intelligence as a complex, multifactor individual attribute that is composed of metacognitive, cognitive, motivational, and behavioral factors.

Metacognitive CQ. This aspect of CQ refers to an individual's level of conscious cultural awareness during cross-cultural interactions. Metacognitive cultural intelligence involves higher level cognitive strategies – strategies that allow individuals to develop new heuristics and rules for social interaction in novel cultural environments by promoting information processing at a deeper level.

People with high metacognitive CQ consciously question their own cultural assumptions, reflect during interactions, and adjust their cultural knowledge when they interact with those from other cultures. For example, a Western business executive with high metacognitive CQ would be aware, vigilant, and mindful about the appropriate time to speak up during meetings with Asians. Those with high metacognitive CQ would typically observe interactions and the communication style of their Asian counterparts (such as turn-taking) and think about what is appropriate before speaking up.

The metacognitive factor of CQ is a critical component of cultural intelligence because it promotes active thinking about people and situations in different cultural settings, triggers active challenges to rigid reliance on culturally bounded thinking and assumptions, and drives individuals to adapt and revise their strategies so that they are more culturally appropriate and more likely to achieve desired outcomes in cross-cultural encounters.

Cognitive CQ. While metacognitive CQ focuses on higher order cognitive processes, cognitive CQ reflects knowledge of norms, practices, and conventions in different cultures acquired from education and personal experiences. Cognitive CQ includes knowledge of cultural universals as well as knowledge of cultural differences. It is an individual's level of cultural knowledge, knowledge of the cultural environment, and knowledge of self as embedded in the cultural context of the environment. Traditional approaches to intercultural competency typically emphasize cognitive CQ. While valuable, the knowledge that comes from cognitive CQ must be combined with the other three factors of CQ or its relevance to the real demands of leadership is questionable and potentially detrimental.

Cultural norms and values are the varying ways cultures approach things like time, authority, and relationships. Thus, understanding how a family system works becomes critically relevant when developing human-resource policies for employees from cultures in which employees are expected to care for senior members of their extended family. Likewise, the value a culture places upon time and relationships becomes highly germane when an American is trying to get a contract signed with a potential affiliate in China or Brazil or Saudi Arabia or Spain, where norms for time differ from those in Western settings.

The cognitive factor of CQ is a critical component of cultural intelligence because knowledge of culture influences people's thoughts and behaviors. By understanding a society's culture and the components of culture, individuals gain a better understanding of the systems that shape and cause patterns of social interaction within a culture. Consequently, those with high cognitive CQ are less disoriented when interacting with people from different societies.

Motivational CQ. Motivational CQ reflects the capability to direct attention and energy toward learning about and functioning in culturally diverse situations. Kanfer and Heggestad (1997, p. 39) argued that such motivational capacities "provide agentic control of affect, cognition and behavior that facilitate goal accomplishment." According to the expectancy-value theory of motivation (Eccles & Wigfield, 2002), the direction and magnitude of energy channeled toward a particular task involve two elements – the expectation of successfully accomplishing the task and the value associated with accomplishing the task. Those with high motivational CQ direct attention and energy toward cross-cultural situations based on intrinsic interest (Deci & Ryan, 1985) and confidence in cross-cultural effectiveness (Bandura, 2002).

Motivational CQ is a critical component of cultural intelligence because it is a source of drive. It triggers effort and energy directed toward functioning in novel cultural settings. For example, a Chinese executive who has a good command of Japanese and likes interacting with those from other cultures would not hesitate to initiate a conversation with a fellow colleague from Japan. In contrast, another Chinese executive who is just learning Japanese or dislikes cross-cultural encounters would be more reticent to engage in such a cross-cultural interaction.

Behavioral CQ. Finally, behavioral CQ reflects an individual's capability to exhibit appropriate verbal and nonverbal actions when interacting with people from different cultures. Behavioral CQ is a critical component of CQ because actions are the most salient features of social interactions. As Hall (1959) emphasized, mental capabilities for cultural understanding and motivation must be complemented with the ability to exhibit appropriate verbal and nonverbal actions, based on cultural values of a specific setting. When individuals initiate and maintain face-to-face interactions, they do not have access to each other's latent thoughts, feelings, or motivation. Yet, they can rely on what they see and hear in the other person's verbal, vocal, facial, and other bodily expressions.

The behavioral factor of CQ includes the capability to be flexible in verbal and nonverbal actions. It also includes appropriate flexibility in speech acts – the exact words and phrases used when communicating specific messages. While the demands of intercultural settings make it impossible for anyone to master all the etiquettes and the dos and don'ts of various cultures, individuals should modify certain behaviors when interacting with different cultures. For example, Westerners need to learn the importance of carefully studying business cards presented by those from most Asian contexts. In sum, almost every approach to cross-cultural work has insisted on the importance of flexibility. Behavioral CQ provides a way of exploring how to enhance this flexibility.

2.2 *Conceptual Distinctiveness of Cultural Intelligence*

To further clarify the nature of CQ, we need to describe what CQ is not. Specifically, we discuss the differences and similarities of CQ compared to personality, cognitive ability, and emotional intelligence.

CQ AND PERSONALITY

CQ is a set of abilities or individual capabilities. Abilities are those personal characteristics that relate to the capability to perform the behavior of interest. As such, CQ is clearly different from personality traits, which are nonability individual differences. CQ focuses on culturally relevant capabilities. Thus, it is more specific than personality or general cognitive ability. Note, however, that CQ is not specific to a particular culture. Instead, CQ is specific to particular types of situations (culturally diverse), and it is not culture-specific.

It is also critical to note that CQ is malleable and can be enhanced through experience, education, and training. While personality is a relatively stable, trait-like individual difference, CQ is more of a state-like individual difference that can evolve over time.

CQ IN RELATION TO OTHER INTELLIGENCE CONSTRUCTS

CQ is similar to general cognitive ability (e.g., Schmidt & Hunter, 1998) and emotional intelligence (Mayer & Salovey, 1993) because it deals with a set of abilities. CQ differs, however, from the two other intelligences in the nature of the ability examined. General cognitive ability, the ability to learn, predicts performance across many jobs and settings, but it is not specific to certain contexts – such as culturally diverse situations. In addition, it does not include behavioral or motivational aspects of intelligence. Emotional intelligence (EQ) is the ability to deal with personal emotions. Thus, it is similar to CQ because it goes beyond academic and mental intelligence, but it differs from CQ because it focuses on the general ability to perceive and manage emotions without consideration of cultural context. Given that emotional cues are symbolically constructed within a culture, emotional intelligence in the home culture does not automatically transfer to unfamiliar cultures (Earley & Ang, 2003). Thus, EQ is culture-bound and a person who has high EQ in one cultural context may not be emotionally intelligent in another culture. In contrast, CQ is not culture-specific and refers to a general set of capabilities with relevance to situations characterized by cultural diversity.

2.3 *Measurement of Cultural Intelligence – the Cultural Intelligence Scale (CQS)*

Ang and associates (2007) and Van Dyne, Ang, and Koh (2008) initiated a series of studies to develop, validate, and cross-validate (N > 1500) the first Cultural Intelligence Scale – the 20-item CQS. Below, we describe development, validation, and cross-validation of the CQS. First, 53 items (13–14 items per CQ dimension) were generated for the initial item pool. These items were assessed for clarity, readability, and definitional fidelity, and the 10 best items for each dimension were retained (40 items). In Study 1, business school undergraduates in Singapore (N = 576) completed the 40 items. Based on a comprehensive series of specification searches, we deleted items with high residuals, low factor loadings, small standard deviations or extreme means, and low item-to-total correlations. We retained the 20 items with the strongest psychometric properties as the CQS: four metacognitive CQ, six cognitive CQ, five motivational CQ, and five behavioral CQ. Figure 29.1 lists the 20 items in the CQS. Confirmatory factor analysis (CFA) (LISREL 8: maximum likelihood estimation and correlated factors) demonstrated good fit of the hypothesized four-factor model to the data.

We next cross-validated the CQS across samples, time, countries, and methods (Studies 2, 3, 4, and 5, respectively). In Study 2, a second, nonoverlapping sample of undergraduate students in Singapore (N = 447) completed the CQS. CFA confirmed the four-factor structure in this cross-validation sample. In Study 3, a subset of respondents in Study 2 completed the CQS again four months later. We used these data to assess temporal stability of the CQS; results provided evidence of test-retest reliability. In Study 4, a sample of undergraduates (N = 337) at a large school in the Midwestern United States completed the CQS. Multiple group tests of invariance using structural equation modeling demonstrated

Figure 29.1 Cultural Intelligence Scale (CQS) – Self-Report.[a] Read each statement and select the response that best describes your capabilities. Select the answer that BEST describes you AS YOU REALLY ARE (1 = strongly disagree; 7 = strongly agree).

CQ *Factor*	*Questionnaire Items*
Metacognitive CQ	
MC1	I am conscious of the cultural knowledge I use when interacting with people with different cultural backgrounds.
MC2	I adjust my cultural knowledge as I interact with people from a culture that is unfamiliar to me.
MC3	I am conscious of the cultural knowledge I apply to cross-cultural interactions.
MC4	I check the accuracy of my cultural knowledge as I interact with people from different cultures.
Cognitive CQ	
COG1	I know the legal and economic systems of other cultures.
COG2	I know the rules (e.g., vocabulary, grammar) of other languages.
COG3	I know the cultural values and religious beliefs of other cultures.
COG4	I know the marriage systems of other cultures.
COG5	I know the arts and crafts of other cultures.
COG6	I know the rules for expressing nonverbal behaviors in other cultures.
Motivational CQ	
MOT1	I enjoy interacting with people from different cultures.
MOT2	I am confident that I can socialize with locals in a culture that is unfamiliar to me.
MOT3	I am sure I can deal with the stresses of adjusting to a culture that is new to me.
MOT4	I enjoy living in cultures that are unfamiliar to me.
MOT5	I am confident that I can get accustomed to the shopping conditions in a different culture.
Behavioral CQ	
BEH1	I change my verbal behavior (e.g., accent, tone) when a cross-cultural interaction requires it.
BEH2	I use pause and silence differently to suit different cross-cultural situations.
BEH3	I vary the rate of my speaking when a cross-cultural situation requires it.
BEH4	I change my nonverbal behavior when a cross-cultural situation requires it.
BEH5	I alter my facial expressions when a cross-cultural interaction requires it.

Note. Use of this scale is granted to academic researchers for research purposes only. For information on using the scale for purposes other than academic research (e.g., consultants and nonacademic organizations), please send an email to cquery@commat;culturalq.com.

The citation for this scale is

Ang, S., Van Dyne, L., Koh, C., Ng, K. Y., Templer, K., Tay, C., & Chandrasekar, N. A. (2007). Cultural intelligence: Its measurement and effects on cultural judgment and decision making, cultural adaptation and task performance. *Management and Organization Review*, 3, 335–371.

A short version Mini-CQS can be found in

Ang, S., & Van Dyne, L. (Eds.). (2008). *Handbook of cultural intelligence: Theory, measurement, and applications* (p. 391). New York, NY: M. E. Sharpe.

that the four-factor structure held across the two countries – Singapore and the United States – thereby establishing generalizability across countries.

Last, we cross-validated the CQS across methods. We developed an observer version of the scale, such that the items reflected observer ratings rather than self-ratings. Managers participating in an executive MBA program at a large university in the United States (N = 142, 47% female, average age 35) completed Web questionnaires that included self-report of CQ and interactional adjustment. In addition, participants also completed an observer questionnaire with peer-report of CQ and interaction adjustment on one randomly assigned peer from their MBA team. Multitrait multimethod (MTMM) analysis provided evidence of convergent, discriminant, and criterion validity of the CQS across self- and peer ratings.

Collectively, the five studies provide evidence of the psychometric stability of the 20-item CQS across samples, time, countries, and methods (self- versus peer report). Analyses of additional questionnaires in Study 2 and Study 4 showed that CQ differed from general mental ability (*g*), emotional intelligence, cultural judgment and decision making, interactional adjustment, and mental well-being.

2.4 *Predictive Validity of the CQS – Initial Evidence*

We next conducted three substantive studies on the predictive validity of the CQS (N = 794) in field and educational settings across two national contexts – the United States and Singapore.

In Study 1, two samples of undergraduates (N = 235: Midwestern USA; N = 358: Singapore) completed the CQS, cultural judgment and decision making (CJDM) scenarios, rated their cultural adaptation, and provided information on demographics, general mental ability, cross-cultural adaptability, and cross-cultural experiences. In Study 2, international managers (N = 98) participating in a three-day executive development program at a public university in Singapore completed the CQS and CJDM scenarios, and were rated for performance in an extended case analysis. In Study 3, working adults at an information technology consulting firm in Singapore completed Web questionnaires on cultural adjustment and well-being. Supervisors completed Web questionnaires on task performance and employee adjustment (interactional adjustment and work adjustment).

Across these instructional and work settings, results demonstrated a consistent pattern of relationships between CQ and three forms of intercultural effectiveness. The mental capabilities of metacognitive CQ and cognitive CQ predicted CJDM. Motivational CQ and behavioral CQ predicted sociocultural and psychological adjustment (see Section 3.4 for description of adjustment variables). Metacognitive CQ and behavioral CQ predicted task performance.

These results suggest that cognitive capabilities such as questioning assumptions, adjusting mental models, and having rich cultural knowledge schemas are especially important for making accurate judgments and decisions when situations involve cultural diversity. Results also show that the motivational capability to channel energy productively, even when intercultural situations are stressful, and the behavioral capability to exhibit flexible, culturally appropriate actions are especially important for coping with experiences in culturally diverse situations. The finding that metacognitive CQ and behavioral CQ predicted task performance in intercultural settings is consistent with existing conceptual and empirical research on organizational diversity. For instance, Caldwell and O'Reilly (1982) demonstrated that those who monitored the situation (metacognition) and adapted to the environment (behavioral flexibility) were more effective in boundary-spanning jobs that required interactions across groups with different norms. In sum, results highlight the value of carefully aligning specific

CQ capabilities with specific aspects of intercultural effectiveness.

2.5 *Nomological Network of Cultural Intelligence*

To facilitate future research, Ang and Van Dyne (2008) proposed an initial nomological network with antecedents, consequences, mediators, and moderators with relevance to CQ. The nomological network contains four basic relationships.

First, distal individual differences such as personality as well as demographic and biographical characteristics such as intercultural education and experiences (Stokes, Mumford, & Owens 1994) should predict the more state-like four factors of cultural intelligence. Second, the four factors of cultural intelligence should influence subjective perceptions of cultural encounters, subjective perceptions of uncertainty and anxiety in cross-cultural communication (Gudykunst, 2004), and participation and involvement in cross-cultural activities.

Third, the nomological network also incorporates other intelligences, including cognitive ability, social intelligence (Thorndike & Stein, 1937), emotional intelligence (Mayer & Salovey, 1993), and practical intelligence (Sternberg & Wagner, 2000), as correlates of CQ. Finally, the nomological network recognizes the importance of context. Specifically, when situations are weak, people have to rely on CQ as a guide for action (Earley & Ang, 2003). Restated, the four factors of cultural intelligence should have stronger effects on perceptions of the intercultural environment and participation in intercultural activities when norms are more ambiguous (weak situations). In other words, situational strength is an important moderator that qualifies the effects of cultural intelligence. Weak situations are vague, generating mixed expectations of the desired behavior. In strong situations, where the task environment is well structured and there are clear cues for task performance, cultural intelligence will have weaker effects.

3.0 Recent Empirical Evidence

Empirical research on CQ has proliferated ever since construct and predictive validity of the CQS scale were established by Ang and colleagues (2007). To date, scholars from different cultures around the world have used the CQS instrument to increase our understanding of correlates, predictors, consequences, and moderators in the nomological network of CQ.

3.1 CQ *in Relation to Other Intelligences*

Given that cultural intelligence is a form of nonacademic intelligence that goes beyond the traditional mental and academic intelligences, a number of studies have tried to examine whether CQ is empirically distinct from EQ and social intelligence. Moon (2010), through confirmatory factor analyses, found that CQ and EQ are distinct. In Moon's study, correlations between CQ dimensions and EQ dimensions ranged between .20 and .41. Kim, Kirkman, and Chen (2008), using multitrait-multimethod (MTMM) analyses, showed self-rated CQ correlated with friend-rated CQ (.43) more strongly than with friend-rated EQ (.26). Kim et al.'s (2008) confirmatory factor analyses also showed discriminant validity between CQ and EQ. Crowne (2009) found CQ to be discriminant from EQ and social intelligence and CQ to be related to EQ at .31 and to social intelligence at .42. Rockstuhl, Ng, Seiler, Ang, and Annen (2009b) showed that CQ correlated more strongly with EQ (.62) than with general intelligence (.15). Thus far, studies have consistently shown that CQ is related to but distinct from other forms of nonacademic intelligences.

3.2 *Personality and* CQ

Stable personality traits describe *typical behavior* across situations and times. In contrast, CQ describes a person's ability to be effective in culturally diverse settings. Since personality influences choice of behaviors and experiences, some personality traits should be related to CQ. Empirically, Ang, Van Dyne, and Koh (2006) showed discriminant validity of the four dimensions of CQ compared to the Big Five personality traits and demonstrated that openness to experience, the tendency to be imaginative, creative, and adventurous (Costa & McCrae, 1992), was related to all four dimensions of CQ. This makes sense because CQ is a set of capabilities targeted at novel cultural situations. Moody (2007) also found that openness to experience predicted CQ, and Oolders, Chernyshenko, and Stark (2008) demonstrated that the six subfacets of openness to experience – intellectual efficiency, ingenuity, curiosity, aesthetics, tolerance, and depth – were significantly related to the four facets of CQ.

Evidence of the openness to experience-CQ relationship has also led to studies on CQ as a mediator of the relationship between personality and adaptation-related outcomes. CQ partially mediates the relationship between openness to experience and adaptive performance (Oolders et al., 2008). CQ also mediates the relationship between flexibility, one of the subscales of the Multicultural Personality Questionnaire (MPQ; van der Zee & van Oudenhoven, 2000) and general cross-cultural adjustment (Ward & Fischer, 2008).

These studies provide fresh impetus for personality research on openness to experience. The typical view of openness has been that it is a relatively useless trait because it previously did not demonstrate consistent relationships with job-related outcomes, unlike the other dimensions of the Big Five (Barrick, Mitchell, & Stewart, 2003). However, the research cited here suggests that openness to experience might be a critical personality factor in intercultural situations. These research results should trigger additional research on openness to experience, particularly in dynamic work situations where curiosity, broad-mindedness, and imagination are valued.

3.3 *International Experience and* CQ

CQ is a malleable individual difference. Accordingly, experience can increase an individual's CQ. To date, the relationship between international experience and CQ has attracted a large amount of research attention worldwide.

Some studies examine specific features of international experience. Wilson and Stewart (2009) studied voluntary international service programs and found that CQ increased the most for those experiencing their first international service assignment, suggesting diminishing marginal increments in CQ as the number of international experiences increased. Crawford-Mathis (2009) showed the importance of depth of cross-cultural experience because volunteers in Belize who spent more time interacting with local citizens had higher increases in CQ at the end of their service project. Likewise, staying in a hostel in a different country and eating with local residents increased CQ, while staying in an expatriate compound or residence reduced opportunities for contact with local citizenry (Crowne, 2007). Finally, Shokef and Erez (2008) found that multicultural team experience increased CQ over time.

Other studies used operationalizations of international experience that fall within Takeuchi, Tesluk, Yun, and Lepak's (2005) framework of international experience, which differentiates work and nonwork international experience as well as nonwork travel and study experience. Shannon and Begley (2008) found that the number of countries worked in predicted metacognitive CQ and motivational CQ. Crowne (2008) showed that number of countries visited for employment predicted metacognitive CQ, cognitive CQ, and behavioral CQ, but not motivational CQ. Tay, Westman, and Chia (2008) found that length of international work experiences predicted cognitive CQ. For nonwork experience, Crowne (2008) showed that number of countries visited for educational purposes predicted cognitive CQ and behavioral CQ and that number of countries visited for vacation predicted motivational CQ. In contrast, Tarique and Takeuchi (2008) demonstrated that number of countries visited predicted all four facets of CQ, and also they showed that length of travel predicted metacognitive CQ and cognitive CQ.

The differences across these studies indicate that the international experience hypothesis needs theoretical refinement to unravel inconsistent results. One possibility would be to consider dynamic interactions. For example, Tay et al. (2008) found that the positive relationship between international work experience and CQ was stronger for business travelers when their need for control was lower. They reasoned that those with low need for control might have been better able to capitalize on international work experiences because they did less pre-trip preparation and might have had fewer preconceived notions than those with high need for control. A second possibility proposed by Ng, Van Dyne, and Ang (2009) is the value of thinking about CQ as an essential learning capability that is required to transform international experiences into effective experiential learning in culturally diverse contexts, rather than conceptualizing international experience as a predictor of CQ.

3.4 *CQ and Cultural Adaptation*

Research demonstrates that CQ predicts cultural adaptation – a key outcome in psychological research on sojourners (Church, 1982). Cultural adaptation comprises two dimensions: sociocultural and psychological adjustment. Sociocultural adjustment includes general adjustment to foreign living conditions; work adjustment to foreign work culture; and interactional adjustment – the extent of socializing and getting along with those from another culture. Psychological adjustment refers to a person's general mental well-being when immersed in another culture.

Ang et al.'s (2007) series of CQ studies shows that undergraduates and IT professionals with higher motivational and behavioral CQ have better general, work, and interactional adjustment, as well as enhanced mental well-being in multicultural settings. Templer, Tay, and Chandrasekar (2006) showed that motivational CQ predicted work and general adjustment of global professionals over and above realistic job preview information – the extent to which the employer accurately portrayed relevant job-related aspects at the time global professionals accepted their job and realistic living conditions preview – the extent to which the global professionals had gathered accurate information on general living conditions in the host country prior to relocation. Williams's (2008) study of American expatriates living and working in China showed that cognitive CQ predicted sociocultural adjustment, while motivational CQ predicted sociocultural adjustment and psychological adjustment. Chen, Kirkman, Kim, Farh, and Tangirala (2010) incorporated contextual moderators and showed that motivational CQ influenced work adjustment of expatriates more when cultural distance and subsidiary support were low.

Using a different operationalization, Gong and colleagues (Gong & Chang, 2007; Gong & Fan, 2006) decomposed motivational CQ into self-efficacy (social self-efficacy) and valence (social interaction goals) components. Their results showed that motivational CQ predicted sojourner social adjustment. Collectively, these studies point to the importance of motivational CQ in predicting cultural adaptation.

3.5 *CQ and Performance*

Work performance is a multidimensional construct (Campbell, 1990), and empirical evidence is increasingly showing that CQ predicts various aspects of performance. Ang et al. (2007) showed that individuals with higher metacognitive CQ and cognitive CQ performed better at cultural decision making, and those with higher metacognitive CQ and behavioral CQ demonstrated higher task performance. Refining these results, Chen et al. (2010) showed that CQ influenced performance by enhancing cultural adaptation.

Research also shows that CQ predicts effectiveness in intercultural negotiation. Specifically, Imai and Gelfand's (2010) negotiation simulation demonstrated that motivational CQ predicted negotiation effectiveness in dyads. Moreover, the minimum CQ score was enough to predict integrative behaviors, which in turn predicted joint profits. Another important outcome is strategic decision-making effectiveness. For example, Prado (2006) showed that cognitive CQ increased perceived cross-border environmental uncertainty among managers who evaluated cross-border opportunities. This finding has implications for strategic decision-making effectiveness and cross-border business performance because firms can mitigate uncertainties with risk management tools only if the uncertainties are perceived.

To date, most studies have focused on the positive outcomes of CQ capabilities. Beyene (2007), however, uncovered a dark side of CQ. In a global organization that mandated employees to use English as their common language, or lingua franca, she found that CQ appeared to motivate nonnative English speakers to engage in frequent interactions with native English-speaking colleagues. However, this can create problems because lingua franca communication creates a socially stigmatizing context for less fluent communicators, engenders feelings of incompetence and inferiority, and can cause stigmatized employees to withdraw from communication situations. This research highlights the importance of language fluency and suggests that future research should assess boundary conditions of CQ-performance relationships.

3.6 CQ *and Global Leadership*

Leaders in global organizations face the stark reality that employees and customers are increasingly culturally diverse. More than ever, global leaders require cultural competencies to operate effectively in cross-border, multi-ethnic environments (Livermore, 2009). To date, research has examined both qualitative and quantitative aspects of CQ and global leadership.

Among the qualitative studies, Dean (2007) found that global leaders endorse and adopt metacognitive CQ principles in leadership processes. Deng and Gibson's (2008) in-depth interviews with Western expatriates and Chinese managers showed that motivational CQ is a sine qua non for cross-cultural leadership effectiveness.

Among the quantitative studies, Elenkov and Manev (2009) studied senior corporate leaders and their subordinates in 27 countries of the European Union and showed that senior expatriate managers' CQ magnified the effects of visionary-transformational leadership on organizational innovation. CQ enabled these leaders to set culturally suitable goals, achieve clarity in leadership, and implement more organizational innovations. Rockstuhl et al. (2009b) examined general intelligence, EQ, and CQ of Swiss military leaders. After accounting for controls – experience and Big Five personality traits – general intelligence predicted leadership effectiveness in both domestic and cross-border contexts. Interestingly, above and beyond general intelligence, EQ was a stronger predictor of leadership effectiveness in domestic contexts while CQ was a stronger predictor of leadership effectiveness in cross-border contexts. This shows that effective domestic leaders are not necessarily effective global leaders, with CQ a key differentiating factor (Alon & Higgins, 2005).

3.7 CQ *and Multicultural Teams*

With globalization and persistent challenges facing groups composed of individuals from different parts of the world, research on CQ has galvanized around multicultural teams. Studies show that multicultural teams can draw on the CQ of their members to overcome potential negative processes associated with team diversity and instead tap diversity of member knowledge as a strength (Moynihan, Peterson, & Earley, 2006).

Rockstuhl and Ng (2008) found that higher metacognitive and cognitive CQ enhanced affect-based trust in culturally diverse dyad partners. They also showed that higher behavioral CQ displayed by a dyad partner led to higher affect-based trust in the dyad partner.

Chua and Morris's (2009) study of executives from diverse backgrounds (European, Asian, African American, Middle Eastern) showed that overall CQ increased affect-based trust (but not cognitive-based trust) among culturally different members of multicultural professional networks, which in turn led to sharing new ideas, exchanging ideas, and cross-pollination of ideas. High CQ in team members also expedites team integration (Flaherty, 2008), promotes team cohesion (Moynihan et al., 2006), and fosters global identity (Shokef & Erez, 2008). Collectively, these studies show that CQ mitigates emotional conflict typically associated with demographic diversity in teams.

3.8 *CQ and Social Networks*

Research has begun to consider the extent to which CQ, as an individual capability, can facilitate development of network ties that span geographical, cultural, and ethnic boundaries. For example, Ang and Ng (2005) theorized that an agile and adaptive military force requires leaders with the ability to manage complex relationships arising from diverse cultural contexts and the capacity to network both internally and externally. Thus, CQ could facilitate military operations through network relationships that sustain coalition teams in multinational military and peacekeeping efforts.

Fehr and Kuo (2008) studied individuals in a multicultural university living community (Americans, Asian, Europeans, South Americans, and Australians). Students lived in close quarters and participated in structured communal activities, including visits to museums and field trips. Results showed that CQ predicted denser relationship networks. In another study, they found that CQ predicted development of relationship networks during studying abroad – controlling for international experience, host country language fluency, and cultural distance. In both of these studies, greater relationship networks predicted greater belongingness as well as fewer withdrawal cognitions and behaviors. Torp and Gjertsen (2009) surveyed engineers from 12 nationalities drawn from Northern Europe and Asia and showed that those with high CQ had higher centrality in friendship networks for social support at work but had lower centrality in advice networks at work. Instead, those with longer tenure and more position power occupied central positions in advice networks. They commented that CQ may have less of an effect on advice networks in highly technical industries where technical jargon leaves less room for cross-cultural misinterpretation in task resolution.

In sum, theory and research suggest that CQ facilitates formation of expressive ties. In contrast, the role of CQ relative to formation of instrumental ties requires further investigation.

4.0 Future Directions

4.1 *Deepening the Conceptualization of CQ*

This integrative review of CQ research summarizes initial empirical evidence of the nomological network of CQ. This research complements the construct validity of Ang and colleagues (2007) and suggests the benefits of future research that deepens understanding of each of the four factors of CQ – with special attention to research on the subfacets of each of the four factors as well as research on interrelationships among the four factors.

Gelfand and colleagues (2008) called for theory and research on interrelationships among the four factors of CQ. Van Dyne et al. (2010) developed a conceptual model of interrelationships among the four factors, such that motivational CQ – defined as the capability to direct attention and energy toward cultural differences – drives the development of the mental metacognitive and cognitive CQ. Then, motivational and mental capabilities influence enactment of behavioral CQ. Alternatively, it seems plausible that the two mental capability factors (metacognitive and cognitive CQ) drive behavioral CQ, but this relationship is moderated by motivational CQ. Another promising direction for future research would be examining the compensatory effects of the CQ factors in combination with each other. For example, it is possible that negative effects of a low score on one CQ factor can be mitigated by high scores on other CQ factors. Alternatively, it is possible that maximum intercultural effectiveness requires moderate to high scores on all four factors. To address this question, we recommend configurational studies (Meyer, Tsui, & Hinings, 1993) that assess the extent to which CQ factors complement or substitute for each other. These are exciting ideas for future research.

Future research is also needed on subfactors of each of the four factors because each of the factors is multidimensional in nature and needs to be understood more deeply at the subfacet level. Van Dyne et al. (2010) theorized that metacognitive CQ includes the cognitive processes of (1) awareness, (2) planning, and (3) checking mental models; that cognitive CQ includes knowledge of cultural systems as well as cultural norms and values; that motivational CQ includes intrinsic motivation, extrinsic motivation, and self-efficacy; and that behavioral CQ includes flexibility in verbal and nonverbal actions as well as flexibility in speech acts. Thomas (2006) proposed that cultural mindfulness could be a useful theoretical frame for deeper consideration of the awareness dimension of metacognitive CQ. Klafehn, Banerjee, and Chiu (2008) proposed that flexibility in cultural frame switching is a cognitive mechanism for enhancing metacognitive capabilities.

Linguistics research has important relevance to subfactors of behavioral CQ. For example, Spencer-Oatey and Xing (2000) analyzed interactions between culturally diverse persons and identified discourse domain, stylistic domain, nonverbal domain, participation domain, and illocutionary domain as important to effectiveness. Some of these domains, such as stylistic (e.g., stylistic aspects of interchange, such as choice of tone) and nonverbal (e.g., gestures, body movements, eye contact, and proxemics) have already been discussed by Earley and Ang (2003) and are included in the CQS. Incorporating additional domains (discourse, participation, and illocutionary) could further refine the conceptualization and assessment of behavioral CQ. Molinsky's (2007) work on cross-cultural code-switching also has important relevance to behavioral CQ. Specifically, Molinsky proposed that behavioral CQ has a performance dimension and an identity dimension. Thus intercultural effectiveness requires the performance challenge of successfully enacting a novel set of behaviors and the identity challenge of behaving in a manner that is potentially in conflict with personal core values. For example, deviating from accustomed behavior and displaying a different set of appropriate behaviors in a cross-cultural interaction can exact a psychological toll and elicit feelings of guilt, distress, and anxiety that deplete psychological resources for subsequent interactions. In sum, we emphasize the value of future research on subfacets of the four CQ factors.

4.2 *Expanding the Nomological Network of CQ*

Although our summary of research indicates exciting and growing knowledge of the CQ nomological network, many relationships within the CQ nomological network remain untested. For example, much research has considered EQ and CQ, but less research focuses on CQ and other nonacademic intelligences such as practical intelligence (Sternberg, 2008).

To date, research theorizes and demonstrates that because CQ is a state-like individual difference (Ang & Van Dyne, 2008; Earley & Ang, 2003; Van Dyne et al., 2008), it is predicted by some personality traits. Specifically, research consistently shows that openness to experience is a key predictor of overall CQ and the facets of CQ. Results on other Big Five personality characteristics, however, are equivocal – with significant relationships in some studies but not others (see Ang et al., 2006; Moody, 2007). Thus, future research is needed on personality and subfacets of personality as they relate to CQ. In addition, this research would benefit from consideration of demographics and biographical characteristics as moderators that influence other relationships involving CQ.

Research that considers other aspects of personality that go beyond the Big Five personality characteristics is growing. For example, need for control – defined as an individual's desire and intent to exert influence over situations – is positively related to all four facets of CQ (Tay et al. 2008). Crawford-Mathis (2009) demonstrated that the self-presentation facet of self monitoring personality predicted increases in CQ based on participation in voluntary philanthropic service projects. Research also shows that global identity – defined as self-transcendence toward universalism and benevolence and a person's sense of belongingness to the human species – predicts CQ and leader emergence in multicultural teams (Lee, Masuda, & Cardona, 2009; Shokef & Erez, 2008). In addition, other personal attributes and traits have been postulated as antecedents of CQ but remain untested. These include biculturalism, ethnocentrism, core self-evaluation, need for closure, and social axioms.

Further, some relationships have been demonstrated empirically but remain theoretically underdeveloped. For example, Alon and Higgins (2005) demonstrated a positive relationship between language skills and CQ. At the same time, they called for additional research on linguistic competence (see also Beyene, 2007, Section 3.5).

Another important emerging topic focuses on contextual conditions that influence CQ. Ng, Tan, and Ang (in press) proposed that multinational corporations with firm-level global cultural capital – which refers to global mind-set values and organizational routines that support such values – could impact employees' cultural intelligence via the process of situated learning. Specifically, firms that emphasize global mind-sets and actively promote organizational routines that facilitate employees' acquisition and integration of local knowledge create more opportunities for employees to experience intercultural interactions across geographical locations and this should enhance cultural intelligence capabilities.

To date, research on the consequences side of the nomological network of CQ has focused primarily on the direct effects of CQ on cultural adaptation and performance. Gelfand et al. (2008) called for research that goes beyond "quasi-tautological" reasoning (where CQ affects outcomes in cross-cultural context because people know more about culture) and instead recommended research that focuses on intermediate outcomes and mediators so that we refine our understanding of how CQ leads to distal outcomes such as adaptation and performance. Obviously the link between CQ and performance requires more refined conceptual thought and empirical investigation. For example, more complex models that include mediating processes as well as situational moderators would add value to the field.

As an example, Shaffer and Miller (2008) proposed a complex moderated-mediated model that distinguishes CQ from performance outcomes in the context of expatriation. This model suggests interaction effects between CQ and Big Five personality, role clarity, role discretion, role novelty, and role conflict in predicting expatriate adjustment, performance, retention, and career success. As another example of making explicit the link between CQ and performance, Mannor (2008) postulated relationships between CQ and top executives' information processing, decision making, and performance. Mannor's theoretical arguments suggest that top executives who are more culturally intelligent are better able to scan their environments for relevant and accurate information and use this higher quality information to make better decisions and take better calculated risks, with positive implications for stakeholder evaluations of firm and top executive performance.

4.3 *Developing Complementary Measures of Cultural Intelligence*

To date, most of the empirical research on cultural intelligence has used the Cultural Intelligence Scale (CQS) (Ang et al., 2007). The scale can be used for self- or observer report of CQ. Reported measures of intelligence have advantages because they provide important perspectives and they reliably predict performance and other outcomes. Nevertheless, future research should assess alternative ways of measuring cultural intelligence because reported measures can be upward biased (based on individual self-enhancement or on a self-enhancing culture) or downward biased (based on modesty or a self-effacing culture). To that end, Harris and Lievens (2005) proposed an assessment center approach that uses a range of behavioral and cognitive tests. Gelfand et al. (2008) suggested a plethora of other ways of assessing cultural intelligence, including implicit measures of cultural knowledge using priming techniques, objective tests of cultural knowledge, cognitive mapping that assesses the complexity of cultural knowledge, and physiological probes of cultural intelligence.

More recently, Rockstuhl, Ang, Ng, Van Dyne, and Lievens (2009a) developed a performance-based assessment of mental CQ (metacognitive and cognitive CQ) using a multimedia situational judgment test methodology with the objective of complementing the existing CQS Likert-type scale. Subjects watch a series of enacted intercultural dilemmas and indicate what they would do in each dilemma. Responses are coded for effectiveness of subjects' resolutions to the dilemmas. Results demonstrated the benefits of both Likert-type and performance-based measures. The self-report measure of CQ predicted cross-cultural leader emergence – as measured by peers over and above IQ, EQ, openness to experience, and international experience. In addition, the performance-based measure of CQ increased explained variance in cross-cultural leader emergence above and beyond self-report of CQ. Thus, we recommend future research that builds on Rockstuhl et al.'s (2009a) research and considers other complementary approaches to assessing CQ.

4.4 *Going Beyond the Individual Level of Analysis*

Cultural intelligence was originally conceptualized as an individual capability. As such, much of the empirical research has focused on the construct at the individual level of analysis. A growing body of research, however, is beginning to consider cultural intelligence in teams and social networks (see Sections 3.7 and 3.8). Given that cultural intelligence focuses on the capability to function effectively in culturally diverse situations, CQ capabilities are inherently embedded in the individual's web of intercultural interactions.

Accordingly, we recommend the value of future research that considers cultural intelligence as a characteristic of intercultural dyads and multicultural teams. This will require consideration of alternative compositional models that specify the functional relationships of cultural intelligence at the dyadic, team, and higher levels. It will also require additional research on the validity of CQ at higher levels of analysis. For example, it would be possible to assess dyadic or team-level CQ using direct consensus or referent shift models. Alternatively, research could consider dispersion models of how CQ is distributed within teams or comparison of an individual's CQ relative to the mean level of CQ. All of these approaches, however, will require explicit theorizing.

Cultural intelligence could also be conceptualized at the organizational level – as a property of the firm. For example, van Driel (2008) explored two competing approaches for assessing CQ at the organizational level of analysis: aggregated individual responses using the direct consensus approach versus a 25-item self-report measure of organizational-level cultural intelligence based on synthesis of CQ and the organizational intelligence literature. Results in a military context showed that the self-report scale of the organization's capability to deal with intraorganizational diversity was a better predictor of equal opportunity behaviors and organizational performance than the direct consensus composition measure. Drawing on the resource-based view of the firm, Ang and Inkpen (2008) developed an alternative model of organizational-level cultural intelligence with three components: managerial CQ, competitive CQ, and structural CQ. Specifically, they argue that firm-level cultural intelligence is an important competitive resource in the context of international business ventures and they predict that firms must be culturally intelligent to leverage off shoring and other ventures.

These concepts of dyadic-, team-, and organizational-level CQ are still nascent. Thus, future research could theorize about the extent to which CQ models have homology where parallel relationships are theorized and tested across different levels of analysis. Future research could also delineate and test more comprehensive, dynamic, and complex nomological networks that include multilevel and cross-level relationships that link higher level CQ with individual, dyadic, team, and organizational outcomes.

5.0 Conclusion

Cultural intelligence is an exciting new construct that has important theoretical and practical implications as evidenced by the expanding interest exhibited by scholars, managers, employees, educators, and consultants. Clearly, CQ resonates with researchers and practitioners who are concerned with adaptation to and effectiveness in multicultural settings.

Although the concept of CQ was originally developed in the context of global business environments, it has been applied to numerous other disciplines and contexts, including cross-cultural applied linguistics (Rogers, 2008), military operations (Ang & Ng, 2005; Ng, Ramaya, Teo, & Wong, 2005; Selmeski, 2007), United Nations peacekeeping operations (Seiler, 2007), transnational families (Janhonen-Abruquah, 2006), immigrants (Leung & Li, 2008), international missionary work (Livermore, 2006, 2008, 2009), spiritual leadership (Tavanti, 2005), mental health counseling (Goh, Koch, & Sanger, 2008; Jennings, D'Rozario, Goh, Sovereign, Brogger, & Skovholt, 2008), and library management (Wang & Su, 2006). Educators have also realized the importance of preparing students for demands in diverse workplaces and in the global workforce. Education researchers are calling for increased awareness of cultural differences in learning styles (Joy & Kolb, 2009) and for development of CQ in teachers and students (Gokulsing, 2006; Griffer & Perlis, 2007; Tomalin, 2007). In addition, CQ can also be meaningfully applied in the contexts of international relations, marketing, and marketing education.

As summarized in this integrative literature review, we have learned a lot about CQ. More important, we have described important topics and areas that require future research and practical application.

References

Ackerman, P. L. (1996). A theory of adult intellectual development: Process, personality, interests, and knowledge. *Intelligence, 22,* 227–257.

Alon, I., & Higgins, J. M. (2005). Global leadership success through emotional and cultural intelligences. *Business Horizons, 48,* 501–512.

Ang, S., & Inkpen, A. C. (2008). Cultural intelligence and offshore outsourcing success: A framework of firm-level intercultural capability. *Decision Sciences, 39,* 337–358.

Ang, S., & Ng, K. Y. (2005). Cultural and network intelligences: The twin pillars in leadership development for the 21st century era of global business and institutional networks. In K. Y. Chan, et al. (Eds.), *Systems and spirit* (pp. 46–48). Singapore Armed Forces Military Institute Monograph, Singapore.

Ang, S., & Van Dyne, L. (2008). Conceptualization of cultural intelligence: Definition, distinctiveness, and nomological network. In S. Ang & L. Van Dyne (Eds.), *Handbook of cultural intelligence: Theory, measurement, and applications* (pp. 3–15). New York, NY: M. E. Sharpe.

Ang, S., Van Dyne, L., & Koh, C. (2006). Personality correlates of the four-factor model of cultural intelligence. *Group and Organization Management*, *31*, 100–123.

Ang, S., Van Dyne, L., Koh, C., Ng, K. Y., Templer, K. J., Tay, C., & Chandrasekar, N. A. (2007). Cultural intelligence: Its measurement and effects on cultural judgment and decision making, cultural adaptation and task performance. *Management and Organization Review*, *3*, 335–371.

Bandura, A. (2002). Social cognitive theory in cultural context. *Applied psychology: An international review*, *51*, 269–290.

Barrick, M. R., Mitchell, T. R., & Stewart, G. L. (2003). Situational and motivational influences on trait-behavior relationships. In M. R. Barrick & A. M. Ryan (Eds.), *Personality and work* (pp. 60–82). San Francisco, CA: Jossey-Bass.

Beyene, T. (2007). *Fluency as a stigma: Implications of a language mandate in global work*. Unpublished doctoral dissertation, Stanford University.

Caldwell, D. F., & O'Reilly, C. A., III. (1982). Boundary spanning and individual performance: The impact of self-monitoring. *Journal of Applied Psychology*, *67*, 124–127.

Campbell, J. P. (1990). Modeling the performance prediction problem in industrial and organizational psychology. In M. Dunnette & L. M. Hough (Eds.), *Handbook of industrial and organizational psychology* (Vol. 1, 2nd ed., pp. 687–731). Palo Alto, CA: Consulting Psychologists Press.

Ceci, S. J. (1996). *On intelligence: A bioecological treatise on intellectual development*. Cambridge, MA: Harvard University Press.

Chen, G., Kirkman, B. L., Kim, K., Farh, C. I. C., & Tangirala, S. (2010). When does cross-cultural motivation enhance expatriate effectiveness? A multilevel investigation of the moderating roles of subsidiary support and cultural distance. *Academy of Management Journal*, *53*, 1110–1130.

Chua, R. Y., & Morris, M. W. (2009). *Innovation communication in multicultural networks: Deficits in inter-cultural capability and affect-based trust as barriers to new idea sharing in inter-cultural relationships*. Working paper, Harvard Business School.

Church, A. (1982). Sojourner adjustment. *Psychological Bulletin*, *91*, 540–572.

Costa, P. T., & McCrae, R. R. (1992). *Revised NEO-Personality Inventory (NEO-PI-R) and NEO Five Factor Inventory (NEO-FFI) professional manual*. Odessa, FL: Psychological Assessment Resources.

Crawford-Mathis, K. (2009). *A longitudinal study of cultural intelligence and self-monitoring personality*. Paper presented at the Academy of Management Meeting, Chicago, IL.

Crowne, K. (2007). *The relationships among social intelligence, emotional intelligence, cultural intelligence, and cultural exposure*. Unpublished doctoral dissertation, Temple University.

Crowne, K. A. (2008). What leads to cultural intelligence? *Business Horizons*, *51*, 391–399.

Crowne, K. (2009). *Social intelligence, emotional intelligence, cultural intelligence and leadership: Testing a new model*. Paper presented at the Academy of Management Meeting, Chicago, IL.

Dean, B. P. (2007). *Cultural intelligence in global leadership: A model for developing culturally and nationally diverse teams*. Unpublished doctoral dissertation, Regent University.

Deci, E. L., & Ryan, R. M. (1985). *Intrinsic motivation and self-determination in human behavior*. New York, NY: Plenum.

Deng, L., & Gibson, P. (2008). A qualitative evaluation on the role of cultural intelligence in cross-cultural leadership effectiveness. *International Journal of Leadership Studies*, *3*, 181–197.

Earley, P. C., & Ang, S. (2003). *Cultural intelligence: Individual interactions across cultures*. Palo Alto, CA: Stanford University Press.

Earley, P. C., & Gibson, C. B. (2002). *Multinational work teams: A new perspective*. Hillsdale, NJ: Erlbaum.

Eccles, J. S., & Wigfield, A. (2002). Motivational beliefs, values, and goals, In S. T. Fiske, D. L. Schacter, & C. Zahn-Waxler (Eds.), *Annual review of psychology* (Vol. 53, pp. 109–132). Palo Alto, CA: Annual Reviews.

Elenkov, D. S., & Manev, I. M. (2009). Senior expatriate leadership's effects on innovation and the role of cultural intelligence. *Journal of World Business*, *44*, 357–369.

Fehr, R., & Kuo, E. (2008). *The impact of cultural intelligence in multicultural social networks*. Paper presented at the 23rd Annual Conference of the Society for Industrial and Organizational Psychology (SIOP), San Francisco, CA.

Flaherty, J. E. (2008). The effects of cultural intelligence on team member acceptance and integration in multinational teams. In S. Ang & L. Van Dyne (Eds.), *Handbook of cultural intelligence: Theory, measurement, and applications* (pp. 192–205). New York, NY: M. E. Sharpe.

Gelfand, M. J., Imai, L., & Fehr, R. (2008). Thinking intelligently about cultural intelligence: The road ahead. In S. Ang & L. Van Dyne (Eds.), *Handbook of cultural intelligence: Theory, measurement, and applications* (pp. 375–387). New York, NY: M. E. Sharpe.

Goh, M., Koch, J. M., & Sanger, S. (2008). Cultural intelligence in counseling psychology: Applications for multicultural counseling competence. In S. Ang & L. Van Dyne (Eds.), *Handbook of cultural intelligence: Theory, measurement, and applications* (pp. 257–270). New York, NY: M. E. Sharpe.

Gokulsing, K. M. (2006). Without prejudice: An exploration of religious diversity, secularism and citizenship in England (with particular reference to the state funding of Muslim faith schools and multiculturalism). *Journal of Education Policy*, **21**, 459–470.

Gong, Y., & Chang, S. (2007). The relationships of cross-cultural adjustment with dispositional learning orientation and goal setting: A longitudinal analysis. *Journal of Cross-Cultural Psychology*, 38, 19–25.

Gong, Y., & Fan, J. (2006). Longitudinal examination of the role of goal orientation in cross-cultural adjustment. *Journal of Applied Psychology*, **91**, 176–184.

Griffer, M. R., & Perlis, S. M. (2007). Developing cultural intelligence in preservice speech-language pathologists and educators. *Communication Disorders Quarterly*, **29**, 28–35.

Gudykunst, W. B. (2004). *Bridging differences* (4th ed.). Thousand Oaks, CA: Sage.

Hall, E. T. (1959). *The silent language*. New York, NY: Doubleday.

Harris, M., & Lievens, F. (2005). Selecting employees for global assignments: Can assessment centers measure cultural intelligence? In A. M. Rahim (Ed.), *Current topics in management* (Vol. 10, pp. 221–239). Greenwich, CN: JAI Press.

Imai, L., & Gelfand, M. J. (2010). The culturally intelligent negotiator: The impact of cultural intelligence (CQ) on negotiation sequences and outcomes. *Organizational Behavior and Human Decision Processes*, **112**, 83–98.

Janhonen-Abruquah, H. (2006). *Eco-cultural theory in the research of trans-national families and their daily life*. Paper presented at the Second EURODIV conference "Qualitative Diversity Research: Looking Ahead," Leuven, Belgium.

Jennings, L., D'Rozario, V., Goh, M., Sovereign, A., Brogger, M., & Skovholt, T. (2008). Psychotherapy expertise in Singapore: A qualitative investigation. *Psychotherapy Research*, **18**, 508–522.

Joy, S., & Kolb, D. A. (2009). Are there cultural differences in learning style? *International Journal of Intercultural Relations*, 33, 69–85.

Kanfer, R., & Heggestad, E. D. (1997). Motivational traits and skills: A person-centered approach to work motivation. *Research in Organizational Behavior*, **19**, 1–56.

Kim, K., Kirkman, B. L., & Chen, G. (2008). Cultural intelligence and international assignment effectiveness. In S. Ang & L. Van Dyne (Eds.), *Handbook of cultural intelligence: Theory, measurement, and applications* (pp. 71–90). New York, NY: M. E. Sharpe.

Klafehn, J., Banerjee, P. M., & Chiu, C.-Y. (2008). Navigating cultures: The role of metacognitive cultural intelligence. In S. Ang & L. Van Dyne (Eds.), *Handbook of cultural intelligence: Theory, measurement, and applications* (pp. 318–331). New York, NY: M. E. Sharpe.

Lee, Y-T., Masuda, A. D., & Cardona, P. (2009). *Leadership perception and individual performance in multicultural teams: The role of cultural intelligence and cultural identities*. Symposium presented at the Academy of Management Meetings, Chicago, IL.

Leung, K., & Li, F. (2008). Social axioms and cultural intelligence: Working across cultural boundaries. In S. Ang & L. Van Dyne (Eds.), *Handbook of cultural intelligence: Theory, measurement, and applications* (pp. 332–341). New York, NY: M. E. Sharpe.

Livermore, D. (2006). *Serving with eyes wide open: Doing short-term missions with cultural intelligence*. Grand Rapids, MI: Baker Books.

Livermore, D. A. (2008). Cultural intelligence and short-term missions: The phenomenon of the fifteen-year-old missionary. In S. Ang & L. Van Dyne (Eds.), *Handbook of cultural intelligence: Theory, measurement, and applications* (pp. 271–285). New York, NY: M.E. Sharpe.

Livermore, D. A. (2009). *Cultural intelligence: Improving your CQ to engage our multicultural world*. Grand Rapids, MI: Baker Academic.

Mannor, M. J. (2008). Top executives and global leadership: At the intersection of cultural intelligence and strategic leadership theory. In S. Ang & L. Van Dyne (Eds.), *Handbook of cultural intelligence: Theory, measurement, and applications* (pp. 91–106). New York, NY: M. E. Sharpe.

Mayer, J. D., & Salovey, P. (1993). The intelligence of emotional intelligence. *Intelligence, 17*, 433–442.

Meyer, A. D., Tsui, A. S., & Hinings, C. R. (1993). Configurational approaches to organizational analysis. *Academy of Management Journal, 36*, 1175–1195.

Molinsky, A. (2007). Cross-cultural code-switching: The psychological challenges of adapting behavior in foreign cultural interactions. *Academy of Management Review, 32*, 622–640.

Moody, M. C. (2007). *Adaptive behavior in intercultural environments: The relationship between cultural intelligence factors and Big Five personality traits*. Unpublished doctoral dissertation, George Washington University.

Moon, T. (2010). Emotional intelligence correlates of the four-factor model of cultural intelligence. *Journal of Managerial Psychology, 25*, 876–898.

Moynihan, L. M., Peterson, R. S., & Earley, P. C. (2006). Cultural intelligence and the multinational team experience: Does the experience of working in a multinational team improve cultural intelligence? In Y-R. Chen (Ed.), *Research on managing groups and teams* (Vol. 9, pp. 299–323). Bingley, UK: Emerald Group.

Ng, K.Y., Tan, M. L., & Ang, S. (in press). Culture capital and cosmopolitan human capital: The impact of global mindset and organizational routines on developing cultural intelligence & international experiences in organizations. In A. Burton & J. C. Spender (Eds.), *The Oxford handbook of human capital*.

Ng, K.Y., Van Dyne, L., & Ang, S. (2009). From experience to experiential learning: Cultural intelligence as a learning capability for global leader development. *Academy of Management Learning and Education*, 8, 511–526.

Ng, K.Y., Ramaya, R., Teo, T. M. S., & Wong, S. K. (2005). *Cultural intelligence: Its potential for military leadership development*. Paper presented at the 47th International Military Testing Association, Singapore.

Oolders, T., Chernyshenko, O. S., & Stark, S. (2008). Cultural intelligence as a mediator of relationships between openness to experience and adaptive performance. In S. **Ang** & L. Van Dyne (Eds.), *Handbook of cultural intelligence: Theory, measurement, and applications* (pp. 145–158). New York, NY: M. E. Sharpe.

Paige, R. M. (2004). Instrumentation in intercultural training. In D. Landis, J. M. Bennett, & M. J. Bennett (Eds.), *Handbook of intercultural training* (3rd ed., pp. 85–128). Thousand Oaks, CA: Sage.

Prado, W. H. (2006). *The relationship between cultural intelligence and perceived environmental uncertainty*. Unpublished doctoral dissertation, University of Phoenix.

Rockstuhl, T., Ang, S., Ng, K.Y., **Van** Dyne, L., & Lievens, F. (2009a). *Cultural intelligence and leadership emergence in multicultural teams*. Symposium presented at the Academy of Management meeting, Chicago, IL.

Rockstuhl, T., Ng, K.Y., Seiler, S., Ang, S., & Annen, H. (2009b). *Emotional intelligence and cultural intelligence in global leadership effectiveness*. Paper presented at the 24th Annual Conference of the Society for Industrial and Organizational Psychology meeting (SIOP), New Orleans, LA.

Rockstuhl, T., & Ng, K-Y. (2008). The effects of cultural intelligence on interpersonal trust in multicultural teams. In S. **Ang** & L. Van Dyne (Eds.), *Handbook of cultural intelligence: Theory, measurement, and applications* (pp. 206–220). New York, NY: M. E. Sharpe.

Rogers, P. S. (2008). The challenge of behavioral cultural intelligence: What might dialogue tell us? In S. Ang & L. Van Dyne (Eds.), *Handbook of cultural intelligence: Theory, measurement, and applications* (pp. 243–256). New York, NY: M. E. Sharpe.

Schmidt, F. L., & Hunter, J. E. (1998). The validity and utility of selection methods in personnel psychology: Practical and theoretical implications of 85 years of research findings. *Psychological Bulletin*, **124**, 262–274.

Seiler, S. (2007). Determining factors of intercultural leadership – A theoretical framework. In C. M. Coops & T. S. Tresch (Eds.), *Cultural challenges in military operations*. Rome, Italy: NATO Defence College.

Selmeski, B. R. (2007). *Military cross-cultural competence: Core concepts and individual development*. (Occasional Paper Series – Number 1). Ontario, Canada: Royal Military College of Canada, Centre for Security, Armed Forces, and Society.

Shaffer, M., & Miller, G. (2008). Cultural intelligence: A key success factor for expatriates. In S. Ang & L. Van Dyne (Eds.), *Handbook of cultural intelligence: Theory, measurement, and applications* (pp. 107–125). New York, NY: M. E. Sharpe.

Shannon, L. M., & Begley, T. M. (2008). Antecedents of the four-factor model of cultural intelligence. In S. Ang & L. Van Dyne (Eds.), *Handbook of cultural intelligence: Theory, measurement, and applications* (pp. 41–55). New York, NY: M. E. Sharpe.

Shokef, E., & Erez, M. (2008). Cultural intelligence and global identity in multicultural teams. In S. Ang & L. Van Dyne (Eds.), *Handbook of cultural intelligence: Theory, measurement, and applications* (pp. 177–191). New York, NY: M. E. Sharpe.

Spencer-Oatey, H., & Xing, J. (2000). A problematic Chinese business visit to Britain: Issues of face. In H. Spencer-Oatey (Ed.), *Culturally speaking: Managing rapport in talk across cultures* (pp. 272–288). London, UK: Continuum.

Sternberg, R. J. (1986). A framework for understanding conceptions of intelligence. In R. J. Sternberg & D. K. Detterman (Eds.), *What is intelligence?* (pp. 3–18). Norwood, NJ: Ablex.

Sternberg, R. J. (1997). *Successful intelligence: How practical and creative intelligence determine success in life*. New York, NY: Plume.

Sternberg, R. J. (2008). Successful intelligence as a framework for understanding cultural adaptation. In S. Ang & L. Van Dyne (Eds.), *Handbook of cultural intelligence: Theory, measurement, and applications* (pp. 306–317). New York, NY: M. E. Sharpe.

Sternberg, R. J., & Detterman, D. K. (1986). *What is intelligence?* Norwood, NJ: Ablex.

Sternberg, R. J., & Wagner, R. J. (2000). Practical intelligence. In R. J. Sternberg (Ed.), *Handbook of intelligence* (pp. 380–395). New York, NY: Cambridge University Press.

Stokes, G. S., Mumford, M. D., & Owens, W. A. (1994). Biodata handbook: *Theory, research, and use of biographical information in selection and performance prediction*. Palo Alto, CA: CPP Books.

Takeuchi, R., Tesluk, P. E., Yun, S., & Lepak, D. P. (2005). An integrative view of international experience. *Academy of Management Journal*, *48*, 85–100.

Tarique, I., & Takeuchi, R. (2008). Developing cultural intelligence: The roles of international nonwork experiences. In S. Ang & L. Van Dyne (Eds.), *Handbook of cultural intelligence: Theory, measurement, and applications* (pp. 56–70). New York, NY: M. E. Sharpe.

Tavanti, M. (2005). Cross-cultural Vincentian leadership: The challenge of developing culturally intelligent leaders. *Vincentian Heritage Journal*, *26*, 201–225.

Tay, C., Westman, M., & Chia, A. (2008). Antecedents and consequences of cultural intelligence among short-term business travelers. In S. Ang & L. Van Dyne (Eds.), *Handbook of cultural Intelligence: Theory, measurement, and applications* (pp. 126–144). New York, NY: M. E. Sharpe.

Templer, K. J., Tay, C., & Chandrasekar, N. A. (2006). Motivational cultural intelligence, realistic job preview, realistic living conditions preview, and cross-cultural adjustment. *Group and Organization Management*, *31*, 154–173.

Thomas, D. C. (2006). Domain and development of cultural intelligence: The importance of mindfulness. *Group and Organization Management*, *31*, 78–99.

Thorndike, R., & Stein, S. (1937). An evaluation of the attempts to measure social intelligence. *Psychological Bulletin*, *34*, 275–285.

Tomalin, E. (2007). Supporting cultural and religious diversity in higher education: Pedagogy and beyond. *Teaching in Higher Education*, *12*, 621–634.

Torp, A. N., & Gjertsen, T. (2009). *Social network centrality and brokerage: The effect of cultural intelligence*. Master of Science Thesis, BI Norwegian School of Management.

van Driel, M. (2008). *Cultural intelligence as an emergent organizational level construct*. Unpublished doctoral dissertation, Florida Institute of Technology.

Van Dyne, L., Ang, S., & Koh, C. (2008). Development and validation of the CQS: The cultural intelligence scale. In S. Ang & L. Van Dyne (Eds.), *Handbook of cultural intelligence: Theory, measurement, and applications* (pp. 16–38). New York, NY: M. E. Sharpe.

Van Dyne, L., Ang, S., & Livermore, D. (2010). Cultural intelligence: A pathway for leading in a rapidly globalizing world. In K. M. Hannum. B. McFeeters, & L. Booysen (Eds.), *Leading across differences: Cases and perspectives*. San Francisco, CA: Pfeiffer.

Van Der Zee, K. I., & van Oudenhoven, J. P. (2000). The Multicultural Personality Questionnaire: A multidimensional instrument of multicultural effectiveness. *European Journal of Personality*, *14*, 291–309.

Wang, X., & Su, C. (2006). Develop future library leaders with global literacy in the context of cultural intelligence. *Chinese*

Librarianship: An International Electronic Journal, 22. Retrieved July 1, 2009, from http://www.iclc.us/cliej/cl22WangSu.htm.

Ward, C., & Fischer, R. (2008). Personality, cultural intelligence and cross-cultural adaptation: A test of mediation hypothesis. In S. Ang & L. Van Dyne (Eds.), *Handbook of cultural intelligence: Theory, measurement, and applications* (pp. 159–173). New York, NY: M. E. Sharpe.

Williams, M. E. (2008). *Individual differences and cross-cultural adaptation: A study of cultural intelligence, psychological adjustment, and socio-cultural adjustment*. Unpublished doctoral dissertation, TUI University.

Wilson, C. E., & Stewart, A. C. (2009). *Developing ethically & culturally-intelligent leaders through international service experiences*. Paper presented at the Academy of Management Meeting, Chicago, IL.

CHAPTER 30

Mating Intelligence

Glenn Geher and Scott Barry Kaufman

Mating Intelligence Defined

In the broadest terms, we see *mating intelligence* (MI) as the cognitive abilities that bear on mating-relevant outcomes – in short: the mind's reproductive system (Geher, Miller, & Murphy, 2008). Mating intelligence differs from the broader field of mating psychology per se, as mating intelligence focuses on relatively high-level cognitive processes – intelligence that underlies the domain of human mating – while mating psychology writ large has focused on relatively basic, unconscious, low-level psychological processes – such as the effects of ovulation on attraction (Miller, Tybur, & Jordan, 2007) or the nature of the human voice as a courtship device (e.g., Pipitone & Gallup, 2008). A mountain of research on human mating makes it abundantly clear that many basic psychological processes comprise evolved mating adaptations in our species.

Mating intelligence is different in that it focuses on the richer, more abstract, and more intellectual nature of human psychology in the domain of mating. Clearly, there are low-level, physiological, and emotional aspects of human mating that seem like important products of our evolutionary heritage. Mating intelligence suggests that there are also high-level, cognitive aspects of human psychology that also primarily reflect mating-relevant adaptations resulting from our evolutionary heritage.

Summary of Geher, Camargo, and O'Rourke's (2008) Model

In summarizing the first 15 chapters of the book *Mating Intelligence*, Geher, Camargo, and O'Rourke (2008) provide a framework for conceptualizing this new construct. First, these authors draw important distinctions between the *fitness indicator* component of mating intelligence and the *cognitive mating mechanisms* component.

Rooted in Miller's (2000a) conception of high-order human intelligence as having evolved for courtship purposes, the fitness-indicator component of mating intelligence corresponds to areas of intelligence that are uniquely human (including, for instance, artistic and linguistic elements), that vary dramatically from person to person, that are partly heritable, and that are attractive in the mating domain. Such forms of intelligence may include, for instance, art (Nettle & Clegg, 2006), creative writing (Nettle, 2009), humor (see Kaufman et al., 2010; Kaufman, Kozbelt, Bromley & Miller, 2008), and vocabulary (see Rosenberg & Tunney, 2008). Importantly, while these hypothesized mental fitness indicators have been shown to act as courtship signals, they do not necessarily directly bear on mating issues. Thus, the fitness-indicator component of mating intelligence is thought to comprise higher order intellectual processes (e.g., the ability to write and recite a high-quality poem), but the links between these processes and mating outcomes are conceptualized as indirect. So while poetic ability, for instance, may have evolved partly because success in this area was related to success in attracting high-quality mates, the thoughts that underlie poetry need not be directly mating-relevant or, indeed, publicly advertised as part of courtship (Nettle, 2009; although they may be – see Gottschall & Wilson, 2005).

On the other hand, *cognitive mating mechanisms* are proposed to be relatively high-level cognitive abilities that bear directly on mating-relevant issues. In successful mating, one must effectively engage in a host of such processes – such as accurate cross-sex mind reading (to know whether a potential mate is interested, to know what a current mate wants, etc.), strategic flexibility in mating strategies (knowing when it is optimal to pursue long-term versus short-term strategies), being able to read cues that reliably indicate that a mate has cheated in a relationship, being able to outcompete intrasexual rivals while keeping an eye toward presenting oneself as kind and other-oriented, and so on. In short, there are many cognitive processes that are directly relevant to the domain of mating. We conceptualize these processes as the cognitive mating mechanisms of mating intelligence.

Two important superordinate variables underlie the nature of mating intelligence in the model proposed by Geher, Camargo, and O'Rourke (2008). The first is biological sex. In many regards, human mating processes have been shown to be sex-differentiated. While dramatic intrasex variability tends to exist for mating-relevant variables, consistent sex differences on such variables are reliably found – often across disparate cultures – suggesting that males are more likely than females to pursue short-term mating strategies across the gamut of mating-relevant behavioral traits (see Buss, 2003). As such, male mating intelligence is predicted to be more honed toward optimizing short-term mating opportunities while female mating intelligence is predicted to be more honed toward optimizing long-term opportunities. This prediction follows from asymmetries in parental investment across the sexes that benefit males, the lower investing sex, in short-term strategies and that benefit females, the higher investing sex, in long-term strategies (cf. Buss, 2003).

Life-history strategy is a similarly important superordinate variable (see Figueredo et al., 2008). This idea, adapted from evolutionary ecology, suggests that organisms unconsciously strategize to find an optimal balance between somatic effort (facilitating their own survival) and reproductive effort (facilitating the replication of their genes into future generations via reproduction). This concept was initially designed by biologists to characterize different kinds of species – those that are *k-selected* – defined as "expecting" a long life within a stable environment (e.g., elephants) versus those that are *r-selected* – defined as "expecting" an unpredictable life, within an unstable environment (e.g., rabbits; see MacArthur & Wilson, 1967). While humans are k-selected as a species, there are clearly differences among human environments in terms of predictability of resources and long-term stability. With this idea in mind, Figuredo et al. (2008) and others (see Giosan, 2006) propose that people differ in terms of the degree to which they follow a prototypical k-selected strategy. As such, these scholars conceptualize a k-differential continuum as typifying humans, with some people being relatively *high k* (these would be individuals who are raised in relatively resource-rich and stable backgrounds) and others being relatively *low k* (individuals raised in harsh and relatively resource-poor and unstable backgrounds and/or high in mortality). A great deal of recent research has shown that the differential-k continuum is strongly predictive of general behavioral strategies – with *high-k* individuals being more likely to delay gratification and take long-term approaches to solving problems (mating and otherwise) and *low-k* individuals being more likely to seek instant gratification and to take short-term approaches to solving problems (see Kruger, Reischl, & Zimmerman, 2008). Such a strategies approach allows for plasticity and malleability of human adaptations and are in concordance with evolutionary principles in behavioral ecology, in which adaptations vary by specific environmental demands, as these constraints influence the expression of adaptations (Wilson, 2007). Consequently, this plasticity of adaptations also allows for considerable individual differences, the focus of the mating intelligence construct.

Geher, Camargo, and O'Rourke (2008) propose that the differential-k continuum is a major variable that underlies mating intelligence. To the extent that the elements of mating intelligence are adaptations, designed to facilitate long-term reproductive success, it makes sense that the nature of mating intelligence would change as a function of an individual's placement on the differential-k continuum. High-k individuals are expected to be most likely to pursue long-term mating strategies and to ultimately engage in high levels of parental effort while low-k individuals are expected to be most likely to pursue short-term mating opportunities. As such, high-k individuals are predicted to have cognitive sets that facilitate long-term mating, often at a cost to success in the area of short-term mating, while low-k individuals are predicted to be characterized by cognitive sets that, on the other hand, facilitate success in short-term mating. Thus, the nature of mating intelligence likely takes on different forms in light of the k-differential continuum. Someone high in general intelligence who comes from an unstable childhood background and develops a low-k life-history strategy may well make mating decisions in adulthood that seem highly unintelligent (consider Bill Clinton's scandal with Monica Lewinsky, as an example).

Finally, Geher, Camargo, and O'Rourke (2008) propose that the different elements of mating intelligence – including the fitness indicators and cognitive mating mechanisms – ultimately should predict Darwin's bottom line of reproductive success. In fact, from an evolutionary perspective, all adaptations are adaptations because they gave our ancestors reproductive advantages. Biologists who study nonhumans are able to see whether certain traits are more likely to lead to higher numbers of viable offspring compared with other traits. However, the study of humans from an evolutionary perspective runs into an idiosyncratic quagmire regarding this issue: birth control. The presence of birth control in most Westernized societies makes it nearly impossible to study contemporary human behavior optimally from an evolutionary perspective, as hypothesized human evolutionary adaptations cannot typically be examined vis-à-vis reproductive success. A researcher who, for instance, hypothesizes that relatively deep voices in males evolved because women are attracted to such voices and ultimately are more willing to become pregnant and bear children of men with deep voices runs into a problem – such women may well be taking oral contraceptives – so this researcher will have a difficult time counting viable offspring as a way of testing his or her adaptationist hypothesis.

This problem, which ends up as a major concern for all evolutionary approaches to humans, needs to be addressed. Geher, Camargo, and O'Rourke (2008) and others (e.g., Pérusse, 1993) propose that we need to measure indicators of mating success as a proxy for reproductive success to be better able to test evolutionary hypotheses. If mating intelligence does comprise an important set of adaptations, then measures of mating intelligence should predict reproductive success. Since we cannot typically measure reproductive success effectively in large samples of modern humans, predictions regarding mating intelligence should seek to predict mating success that may be addressed in terms of behavioral outcomes as well as potential reproductive fitness outcomes such as sperm quality (cf. Arden, Gottfredson, Miller, & Pierce, 2009). Mating success is defined largely as including outcomes that would have likely led to reproductive success under precontraceptive conditions. For males, such outcomes would include, for a straightforward example, having had sexual intercourse with multiple women and, in particular, attracting women who are physically attractive. Of course, males also are often motivated to pursue long-term strategies (see Simpson & Gangestad, 2000), and, as such, a measure of mating success for males should also include such outcomes as being courted by kind, intelligent, and socially connected females for long-term relationships. For females, outcomes associated with mating success would include, for instance, having a history of dating relatively successful men and having had multiple men spend high amounts of money on gifts for them (see Camargo, Geher, Fisher, & Arrabacca, under review, for a thorough treatment of operationalizing mating success in modern humans). Importantly, mating success, in this context refers to outcomes that would have led to increased fitness relative to same-sex competitors under ancestral conditions – we are not referring to more intuitive conceptions such as relationship happiness in long-term mateships.

In sum, this model of MI suggests that it (1) is broken into fitness indicators and cognitive mating mechanisms, (2) is moderated importantly by the superordinate variables of biological sex and the differential-k continuum, and (3) ultimately predicts mating success.

What's New Here?

What's new here? Any time someone proposes a novel psychological construct, educated psychological researchers automatically raise a skeptical eye – rightfully so. The modern behavioral sciences are rooted in methods for objectively collecting and analyzing observable data. Psychology is an empirical science – and psychologists demand evidence for any and all claims. While this skeptical approach may make psychological research difficult to conduct and to publish, it is, without question, a good thing. The scientifically rigorous approach that underlies modern research psychology makes it so that the material taught to students in psychology classes in modern universities is based on data rather than opinion.

When Geher and Miller launched the construct of mating intelligence in their book by the same name (2008), they knew full well that this construct would be under a good bit of scrutiny. In fact, several of the chapters in that edited volume on mating intelligence included comments that were critical of the concept writ large. Never one to mince words, Satoshi Kanazawa (2008) wrote, "Intelligence, in its original definition, referred to purely cognitive abilities. . . . I personally would have preferred to keep it that way" (p. 283). Similar concerns are expressed in chapters by Figueredo, Brumbach, Jones, Sefcek, Vasquez, and Jacobs (2008) as well as in David Buss's (2008) foreword to the book.

While the basic idea of mating intelligence has generally been well received in both academic (see Springer, 2009) and popular circles (see Perina, 2007), we think it is important to address criticisms of this construct up front. As is true of any newly introduced psychological construct, the main criticism launched at mating intelligence has been essentially this: What's new here?

The Heuristic Value of Mating Intelligence (What's New Here)

Sometimes, progressive scientific ideas form from stepping back and looking at things from a new angle (see Dawkins, 2005). We believe that the unification of the fields of mating and intelligence, implied in the mating intelligence construct, provides such a new angle on many areas of the behavioral sciences. In a thorough consideration of the areas potentially illuminated by this construct, Miller (2008) argues that mating intelligence has potential to improve our understanding of such disparate facets of human functioning as medicine, psychiatry, economics, marketing, political science, sociology, education, and law. Here, we discuss specific areas of psychological research that may benefit – or that have already benefited – from the MI construct.

The study of individual differences from an evolutionary perspective has been, to this point, largely incomplete. With a major focus on human universals, evolutionary psychology has often either dismissed or ignored individual differences in important behavioral traits. While there are some important exceptions to this generalization, such as Nettle and Clegg's (2008) work on understanding superordinate trait dimensions in terms of balancing selection forces and Simpson and Gangestad's (1991) groundbreaking work on individual differences in sociosexuality (see also Penke, Denissen, & Miller, 2007), by and large, mating research conducted from an evolutionary perspective focuses on human universals such as sex-specific tactics to derogate mates (e.g., Buss & Schmitt, 1996), universals in the nature of human jealousy (Buss, Larsen, Weston, & Semmelroth, 1992), universals in features of attractive faces and bodies (Hughes & Gallup, 2003), and universals in qualities desired in long-term versus short-term mates (Gangestad & Simpson, 2000).

While the universalist approach that characterizes most evolutionary-psychology research clearly has shed light on many important aspects of the human condition, it fails to do justice to the myriad traits in our species that demonstrate reliable individual differences. Our conception of mating intelligence as including both mental fitness indicators and cognitive mating mechanisms opens the door for two important areas of individual-differences research. The study of mental fitness indicators addresses many cognitively laden traits that seem to act as courtship mechanisms. Such traits include verbal fluency (Rosenberg & Tunney, 2008), humor (Greengross & Miller, 2008; Kaufman et al., 2008), conspicuous altruism (see Miller, 2007), and creative writing (Kaufman & Kaufman, 2009).

The study of cognitive mating mechanisms has potential to provide insights into many areas of mating psychology that have been primarily studied from a universalist perspective. For instance, while mating psychologists have previously documented sex-specific features of deception in the mating domain (e.g., Haselton, Buss, Oubaid, & Angleitner, 2005), a mating intelligence approach to this issue may address individual differences in mate-deception efficacy (e.g., O'Brien, Geher, Gallup, Garcia, & Kaufman, 2010). Similarly, while prior researchers have addressed universals in responses to infidelity, it may be that there are individual differences in such processes as (1) the ability to accurately detect infidelity, (2) the ability to engage in infidelity with a high-quality mate, (3) the ability to deceive a partner about one's history of infidelity, and so forth. The study of individual differences in mating-relevant trait dimensions should be a major product of the mating intelligence construct.

In formulating our model of mating intelligence (Geher, Camargo, & O'Rourke, 2008), the importance of mating success became clear. Intelligence research of all kinds focuses on predicting success in some area. Research on cognitive, or general intelligence, has focused on predicting success in various academic arenas (see Sternberg, 1996); research on social intelligence has sought to pinpoint the predictors of success in such areas as marriage and career (Cantor & Kihlstrom, 1987); research on emotional intelligence has examined the predictors of success in such areas as intimate relationships (Casey, Garrett, Brackett, & Rivers, 2008), health (Matthews, Zeidner, & Roberts, 2002), and education (Brackett, Alster, Wolfe, Katulak, & Fale, 2007). Given the evolutionary roots that underlie mating intelligence, it quickly becomes clear that the main kind of success that should result from mating intelligence would be *reproductive success* (RS), which is essentially Darwin's bottom line – ultimately bearing on the number of viable descendants that reach future generations (taking quality of descendants into account, as well, to the extent that quality facilitates gene proliferation overall across generations). Whether a trait is adaptive in the Darwinian sense corresponds, ultimately, to whether certain levels of that trait led to increases in RS in our ancestors. As such, the main outcome that should be predicted by any adaptation is RS – often framed in terms of the number of viable offspring produced.

An important hurdle to the study of mating intelligence, then, becomes apparent. Given the widespread use of birth control in so many modern societies, RS, operationalized in terms of number of offspring, has little construct validity. A tall, muscular, symmetrical, dominant, and intelligent male in a modern society may well attract many high-quality (attractive, healthy, and free from debilitating mental illness) sexual partners, but his consistent use of birth control may reduce his RS to zero. As such, the widespread use of birth control renders RS nearly impossible to operationalize in modern human populations. For this reason, we propose that RS needs to be approximated with measures of mating success – defined as including outcomes that would have corresponded to RS under pre-contraceptive conditions (see Geher, Camargo, & O'Rourke, 2008). While previous scholars have considered the importance of operationalizing mating success (e.g., Pérusse, 1993), the mating intelligence framework makes the need for valid measures of mating success extremely clear. One of the important outcomes of the mating intelligence construct should pertain to thorough psychometric work on mating success.

Intelligence and Mental Fitness Indicators

Human courtship has a distinct flavor compared to the courtship behavior of other species. We sing tunes designed to coordinate with lyrics, write poems, and paint wonderfully complex and aesthetic pictures to attract mates. We go on dates, exchange witty banter, and engage in long conversations about preferences and values. Why do we bother?

When we seek a mate, we surely look for someone whom we can connect with on a personal level, who shares our hopes, desires, goals, and fears. As such, mate selection in humans consistently focuses on qualities that are optimal for short-term as well as long-term partners. But at another level, our genes pull us toward individuals high in fitness (heritable genetic quality). Most animals in the animal kingdom advertise fitness by displaying elaborate structures that don't appear to serve a survival function. The peacock's tail, the elk's antlers, and the nightingale's voice are all examples of adaptations that signal fitness.

Humans are unique, however, in the amount of fitness information that is contained in the brain. And because the brain is the source of human intelligence, intelligence is fair game for sexual selection. According to the principle of sexual selection, reproduction is just as much a struggle as survival. Thus, while adaptations for survival surely come to typify organisms via evolutionary processes, adaptations that are primarily about successful reproduction share the front seat. Sexually selected traits (as opposed to traits operating under the forces of natural selection) display high variance because there is competition for individuals to mate with those who exhibit traits that are metabolically expensive, hard to maintain, not easily counterfeited, and highly sensitive to genetic mutations. Such traits that display these properties are the most reliable indicators of genetic fitness. According to Zahavi's (1997) handicap principle, even though fitness indicators may impair the odds of survival (creating a handicap), they can offer reproductive benefits that outweigh the survival costs. The peacock's tail may make it difficult for the peacock to walk, and may make the peacock more visible to predators, but the peacock's tail attracts mates. Likewise with the human brain – while there may be metabolic costs associated with having such a heavy brain, the costs may be outweighed by reproductive benefits. Those animals who can display such structures that go beyond survival are advertising that they have the resources not only to survive; they also have resources left over to invest in excess. An analogy can be found in Veblen's (1899) idea of conspicuous consumption. According to Veblen, wasteful display of wealth is a reliable indicator of wealth since the poor cannot afford such waste. From Zahavi's perspective, such characteristics represent *costly signals*, which evolve as hard-to-fake, honest advertisements of heritable qualities.

In recent years, Geoffrey Miller has applied Zahavi's handicap principle to the evolution of human intelligence, arguing that sexual selection played a much greater role than natural selection in shaping the most distinctively human aspects of our minds, including storytelling, art, music, sports, dance, humor, kindness, and leadership (Miller, 1998, 2000a, 2000b, 2000c, 2001; Kaufman et al., 2008). Miller argues that these behaviors are the result of complex psychological adaptations whose primary functions were to attract mates, yielding reproductive rather than survival benefits. Germs of this idea can be traced back to Darwin: "It appears probable that the progenitors of man, either the males or females or both sexes, before acquiring the power of expressing mutual love in articulate language, endeavored to charm each other with musical notes and rhythm" (Darwin, 1871, p. 880).

Taking as the assumption that the general factor of human intelligence (i.e., *g*) is synonymous with human intelligence, Miller argues that behaviors that show a strong influence of general intelligence (i.e., are highly *g*-loaded) should be sexually attractive since they are indicators of a superordinate *fitness factor* (*f* factor). Indeed, evidence has been accumulating that suggests the existence of an *f* factor. Various threads of research show a correlation between *g* and many biological traits such as height, health, longevity, bodily symmetry, and even sperm quality (Arden et al., 2009; Banks, Batchelor, & McDaniel, 2010; Bates, 2007; Calvin et al., 2010; Furlow et al., 1997; Jensen, 1998; Prokosch, Yeo, & Miller, 2005; Silventoinen, Posthuma, van Beijsterveldt, Bartels, & Boomsma, 2006; Sundet, Tambs, Harris, Magnus, & Torjussen, 2005; also see Intelligence as a Predictor of Health, Illness, and Death, Chapter 34 of this volume); *g* may therefore be an indicator of deleterious mutation load, which would affect many interacting genes and thereby have an effect on the entire biological system.

There is also accumulating evidence that intelligence and creativity (which Miller argues is an indicator of intelligence) are sexually attractive traits. Buss (1989) investigated mate preferences across 37 cultures and found that intelligence was the second-most-desired trait in a sexual partner, right below kindness. Experimental research shows that intelligent and creative individuals are considered more attractive, and have a higher number of sexual partners (Buss, 1989; Griskevicius, Cialdini, & Kenrick, 2006; Haselton & Miller, 2006; Nettle & Clegg, 2006; Prokosch, Coss, Scheib, & Blozis, 2009).

Various scholars have elaborated and clarified Miller's theory. Feist (2001) notes that Miller focuses on sexual selection and artistic creativity at the exclusion of the evolution of scientific creativity and technology, which Feist argues is more likely to have been shaped by natural selection pressures. Further, Feist (2001) argues that natural selection has driven mainly the more applied or technological aspects of creativity that have clear survival benefits, such as advances in science and engineering, whereas sexual selection may have driven more ornamental or aesthetic aspects of creativity, including art, music, dance, and humor; forms of creativity that have come along more recently on the evolutionary scene.

Therefore, not all creative displays may be considered equally as sexually attractive. More "nerdy" displays of creativity, such as in math, engineering, and the sciences, may be considered less attractive, on average, than more "artistic" displays of creativity such as in poetry, music, and art. Recent research does suggest that collapsing over individual differences, more artistic forms of creativity are considered more sexually attractive than more scientific forms of creativity (Kaufman et al., 2009). However, individual differences were found in that those who reported higher levels of creative achievement in scientific forms of creativity did tend to find scientific forms of creativity sexually attractive (as well as some artistic forms of creativity) whereas those who reported higher levels of creative achievement in artistic forms of creativity did tend to find artistic forms of creativity sexually attractive, but did not report finding scientific forms of creativity sexually attractive. Future research should clarify these issues, testing Feist's hypothesis at both the group and individual level of analysis.

In a related line of thought, Feist argues that Miller's account of sexual selection does not fully connect with the creativity literature. In this body of literature, creativity is defined as both novel and adaptive behavior (Sternberg, 1998), not as novel creative displays that attract the attention of potential mates. Feist also notes that there is evidence that creative people tend to be less likely to marry and when they do, they have relatively *few* children (Harrison, Moore, & Rucker, 1985), a factor that surely also impacts on reproductive success. Also, it should be noted that time spent on creative projects may be time taken away from mating and child rearing (Gabora & Kaufman, 2010). And it is also possible that creative individuals may have trouble in relationships, on average, as well, due to their unique constellation of personality traits, including being less conventional and conscientious, and more driven, ambitious, dominant, hostile, and impulsive than less creative individuals (see Feist, 1998).

In a related line of research, Mithen (2006) presents evidence that the musicality of our ancestors and relatives may in fact have had considerable *survival value* as a means of communicating emotions, intentions, and information, and facilitating cooperation. Thus, sexual selection may not be the primary selective pressure for musicality. He also notes that while it may appear at first blush that creative men have more short-term sexual partners because of their creativity, their attractiveness may be more the combination of good looks, style, and an antiestablishment persona. Mithen also points out that the finding (Miller, 1999) that males produce at least 10 times more music than females and are the most productive around the age of 30 (in which men are in their peak mating effort and activity) could more parsimoniously be explained by the particular structure and attitudes of 20th-century Western society. Perhaps the most reasonable conclusion is that sexual selection helped ramp up the evolution of intelligence and creativity, exaggerating certain forms, or making them not only functional but also ornamental. In this way they went beyond the realm of practicality to the realm of aesthetic functionality.

From a different angle, Kanazawa (2008) argues that individuals with greater general intelligence do not have greater mating intelligence, except in areas where the mechanisms underlying mating intelligence operate on evolutionarily novel stimuli. Kanazawa (2004, 2010) proposed that general intelligence evolved as a domain-specific psychological mechanism to solve evolutionarily novel problems (for a different perspective on the evolution of general intelligence, see Borsboom & Dolan, 2006; Chiappe & MacDonald, 2005; Geary, 2004, 2009; Girotto & Tentori, 2008; Kaufman, DeYoung, Reis, & Gray, in press; Penke, 2010; Woodley, 2010). With this theory as a foundation, Kanazawa (2008) argues that general intelligence is independent of other adaptations, including mating intelligence. Kanazawa presents evidence that those higher in verbal intelligence are relatively ineffective at evolutionarily familiar tasks such as finding mates, having children, and getting and staying married (see Taylor et al., 2005 for further evidence on the negative association between IQ and marriage). Kanazawa presents evidence that those with higher verbal intelligence are better, however, at voluntarily controlling fertility, a finding Kanazawa interprets as reflecting the better ability of those with higher verbal intelligence in dealing with evolutionarily novel means of contraception in the current environment. Accordingly, Kanazawa and others see this tendency for individuals high in general intelligence to take steps to inhibit reproduction as consistent with the dysgenic hypothesis, that low intelligence drives out high intelligence.

Perhaps it is important to distinguish between the sexual attractiveness of intelligence and the use of human intelligence to navigate the mating domain. An interesting irony may be that while intelligence might be a sexually attractive trait, those with high intelligence may have no advantage in actually navigating the mating domain (unless the domain consists of evolutionary novelty). It is to the cognitive mechanisms underlying mating intelligence that we now turn.

Mating-Relevant Cognitive Mechanisms

As stated in prior work, we believe that the cognitive mating mechanisms of MI include both species-typical and individual-differences features (Miller, 2008). Species-typical (i.e., universalist) mating mechanisms include the many mating qualities that have been studied by prior researchers that may be thought of as characterizing a human universal mating intelligence. Such qualities include, as examples, the tendencies to (1) advertise qualities that are attractive to potential mates (Buss & Schmitt, 1996), (2) engage in adaptive mating-relevant self-deception (O'Sullivan, 2008), (3) demonstrate meta-strategic flexibility, by changing one's mating strategy as a function of current ecological conditions (such as the prevailing sex ratios; see Schmitt 2005), and (4) hold biased mating-relevant beliefs that may be evolutionarily adaptive (Haselton & Buss, 2000). To a large extent, the edifice of mating psychology comprises the species-typical portion of MI's cognitive mating mechanisms.

As a recent example of a mating-relevant psychological process framed as a cognitive mating mechanism, consider Geher's (2009) work on cross-sex mind reading. Rooted in methods borrowed from the field of emotional intelligence research (Geher, 2004), this work explored the ability to accurately guess the mating desires of the opposite sex in a large sample of heterosexual adults. Being able to read the thoughts of the opposite sex (literally, not in an extrasensory manner!) comprises an important set of cognitive skills that are crucial for mating success. Thus, this ability is a crucial cognitive mating mechanism that underlies mating intelligence. In this research, participants were presented with real personal ads written by members of their own sex – and they were asked to judge which ad (in clusters of three) was rated as most attractive for either a long-term or short-term mating partner by members of the opposite sex. In a separate part of the study, members of the opposite sex rated these same ads, so the actual answers could be determined. Ads were all content coded for the presence of sexual content in a blind process by two independent judges.

Across both short- and long-term items, women showed a strong tendency to overestimate the degree to which males were attracted to ads of women who included sexual content. These findings are consistent with an *adaptive bias* account of cross-sex mind reading, suggesting that women may be particularly prone to think that men are only interested in sex; such a judgment may encourage women to be especially skeptical of men's intentions. Such commitment skepticism may be part of a broad long-term female mating strategy designed to reduce the likelihood of a female's being impregnated by a nonfaithful male and, thus, bearing the evolutionary tax of raising an offspring alone.

In terms of accuracy in cross-sex mind reading, the findings were revealing. Each sex turned out to be relatively expert at guessing the mating-relevant thoughts of the opposite sex when the judgments corresponded to the dominant strategy of the opposite sex. Thus, females outperformed males in guessing short-term desires, while males outperformed females in guessing long-term desires. Accordingly, it seems that cross-sex mind reading seems particularly honed when it comes to knowing what the opposite sex wants in the areas that are prioritized by the opposite sex.

While Geher (2009) explicates the utility of the mating intelligence construct to generate new research and new findings, this study was limited when it came to understanding cross-sex mind reading in terms of individual differences. An attempt to measure cross-sex mind reading in terms of individual differences did not yield internally reliable scales. While this fact was somewhat disappointing, it is worth noting that this same issue typified the earliest attempts to create ability-based measures of emotional intelligence (Mayer & Geher, 1996). Attempts to operationalize emotional intelligence in terms of individual differences have increased markedly in their success across time (Geher, 2004). We expect that attempts to measure the mating mechanisms of mating intelligence as individual-differences variables will also succeed in time.

In fact, another thread of recent work has demonstrated that mating intelligence may prove to be a valid individual-differences construct. Geher and Kaufman (2007) created a self-report measure of MI to appear alongside a popular article on this topic published in *Psychology Today* (Perina, 2007). While this scale was not initially designed with scholarly goals in mind, several recent studies that have included this measure have demonstrated its internal reliability as well as its predictive utility (O'Brien, Geher, Gallup, Garcia & Kaufman, 2010). Male and female versions of this scale, created primarily for use with heterosexual populations, tap several major dimensions that underlie mating intelligence, including (1) accuracy in cross-sex mind reading, (2) effective deception in the mating domain (a characteristic that likely pertains to both short-term and long-term mating strategies), (3) adaptive self-deception in the mating domain, (4) adaptive mating-relevant bias (with the male subscale corresponding to overestimating the degree to which women find males sexually attractive and the female subscale corresponding to being hyper skeptical of males' intentions), and (5) effective behavioral courtship display. Thus, this scale is designed to tap both mental fitness indicators as well as mating mechanisms in terms of individual differences.

It is important to note that this measure uses self-report methods and that, without question, work on this scale represents the nascent stage of psychometric efforts on this construct that are needed. Previous research on aspects of human intelligence using self-report methods has generally cast a critical eye on such approaches (Geher & Renstrom, 2004). Ultimately, ability-based measures would likely have more face validity as well as, perhaps, more predictive validity. Still, both the male and female versions of this measure (based on total scale scores) demonstrated high internal-consistency reliability. Further, in two studies on young heterosexual adults, this scale demonstrated a strong ability to predict important variables related to reproductive success. In the first study, males' scores were positively predictive of having had more sexual partners in the past year as well as more lifetime partners, whereas females' scores showed a more nuanced pattern, with high mating intelligence for females corresponding to having had sexual relations relatively early in life, but not having a relatively high number of sexual partners in the last year. Thus, for males, high mating intelligence seems to correspond to more sexual partners overall whereas for females, high mating intelligence corresponds to having more sexual experience but *not* a more promiscuous current strategy (O'Brien et al., under review).

A second study explored mating intelligence in the context of hookups, generally defined as short-term sexual relationships with no explicit long-term relationship attached (Garcia & Reiber, 2008). In addition to measuring mating intelligence, this study asked participants if they had ever engaged in Type-I hookups (with strangers), Type-II hookups (with acquaintances), and Type-III hookups (with individuals they defined as *friends*). Again, the MI scale demonstrated sensitivity to important sex-differentiated features of relationships. For males, higher mating intelligence corresponded to having engaged in each kind of hookup, whereas for females, high mating intelligence corresponded to having engaged in hookups with acquaintances (Type-II), but not either of the other kinds. These findings make sense from an evolutionary perspective, as it may be particularly costly for a female to engage in sex with a stranger, about whom she has little information. Such relationships, started with minimal baseline information, could put a female at high risk for such adverse outcomes as violence, desertion, or disease. On the other hand, prior research has demonstrated that it is not adaptive for females to have sexual relations with close opposite-sex friends; and, in fact, females typically do not report having opposite-sex friends for sexual reasons (Bleske-Recheck & Buss, 2001). Relations with individuals defined as acquaintances may well strike a balance.

The findings from the aforementioned studies (Geher, 2009; O'Brien et al., 2010) are presented to give a face to the field of mating intelligence. Some of these findings bear primarily on species-typical mating mechanisms whereas others focus on individual differences in the different elements of mating intelligence. While this work provides an important first step in carving out the nature of mating intelligence and its contribution to the field of psychology, more research is surely needed to help the mating intelligence construct realize its potential.

The Future of Mating Intelligence

By proposing the mating intelligence construct, we hope to stimulate research on the connection between human sexuality and human intelligence. A large part of the relatively nascent field of evolutionary psychology includes the study of human mating (see Buss, 2005). However, evolutionary psychology has traditionally focused on human universals instead of individual differences, and has traditionally focused on lower level cognitive processes instead of higher level cognitive functions. We hope the mating intelligence construct will provide a missing piece of the human cognitive puzzle for the fields of both human intelligence and evolutionary psychology and will stimulate cross-talk between the two fields of inquiry.

The integrative model of mating intelligence outlined here and first proposed by Geher, Camargo, and O'Rourke (2008) includes two main components. The first class of cognitive processes relate to mating-relevant cognitive domains that are thought to primarily serve courtship-display functions. While evolutionary psychology has tended to focus mainly on behavioral displays of physical qualities such as strength, virility, and athleticism, the MI construct focuses on psychological qualities (*mental fitness indicators*) such as confidence, kindness, creativity, intelligence, resourcefulness, status, humor, and mental health.

According to the fitness-indicator model, humans are particularly attuned to behavioral qualities of potential mates that reveal *good genes* in the evolutionary sense in that they reveal a relatively low mutation load (in other words, a relatively low number of genetic mutations) as well as genes that are generally associated with health, survival, and successful reproductive abilities (see Keller & Miller, 2006). Therefore, much of human mate choice can be explained as an adaptive (unconscious) fear of heritable mutations – as *mutation phobia*. According to this idea of mutation phobia, people are repulsed by features of potential mates that have a strong latent correlation with high mutation load. In the biological literature, body asymmetry or dullness of plumage are often given as examples (see Hasson, 2006).

It is not clear, however, whether such mate choice operates in a continuous or categorical manner. It is entirely possible that our mate preferences have been shaped more to avoid mating with high-mutation-load individuals who have obvious physical or psychological problems than to make very fine discriminations among individuals who seem more or less average in terms of mutation load. Zebrowitz and Rhodes (2004) offer evidence that, at least in some cases, mate choice operates in a categorical manner. They found that people could accurately predict overall health and intelligence for targets with relatively unattractive faces, but not for targets with relatively attractive faces. Facial attractiveness was predictive of health and intelligence for targets and intelligence only at the low-fitness extremes.

Such a curvilinear relationship between indicator quality and sexual attractiveness (concave-downward, with rapidly diminishing returns above the mean of indicator quality) may be seen in the domain of mating intelligence. For example, someone with an IQ of 90 may be much more attractive than someone with an IQ of 70, but a potential mate with an IQ of 150 may only be a little more attractive than one whose IQ is 130. Research should attempt to investigate the (probably nonlinear) functions that relate mutation load to mental fitness indicators and that relate indicator quality to attractiveness in mating. Such research should sample populations from all strata of society. Indeed, if it turns out that fitness indicators correlate differently at low-quality and high-quality extremes, and assortative mating on IQ is a predominant occurrence, then bright, healthy, college sophomores may not be the best and/or only population we should be studying for mating intelligence research on the display, judgment, and sexual attractiveness of fitness indicators!

Another issue in the understanding of mental fitness indicators has to do with the relation of each fitness indicator to general intelligence. In conceiving of *g*-loaded mental traits as having arisen from sexual selection processes, Miller (2000a) posits that *g* is essentially an index of neurodevelopmental stability and brain efficiency that taps any overall fitness factor (roughly, the first principal component of genetic quality across all fitness-related traits). Further, Miller proposes that the existence of this superordinate fitness factor should be manifest as a positive manifold (all-positive correlations) among fitness indicators in general. Future research should attempt to tests Miller's (2000c) predictions and shed light on the nature of the courtship-display components of MI. One such method would be to simply assess the *g*-loadings of a variety of mental fitness indicators and compare the relationship of the *g*-loadings to ratings of sexual attractiveness of each fitness indicator. According to Miller, there should be a positive relationship.

Future research should also try to elucidate the particular characteristics of various mental displays that are sexually attractive. Various forms of creativity (e.g., artistic) may be considered more attractive than other forms of creativity (e.g., scientific) not only due to indications of *g* (indeed, scientific forms of creativity are probably more *g*-loaded than artistic forms of creativity) but also due to fitness indications of kindness, emotional expressivity, and so on. Future research should also assess the importance of individual differences in preferences for various mental fitness indicators. Preliminary research in this regard is under way (Kaufman et al., 2009) and suggests that at the group level, artistic forms of creativity are considered more sexually attractive than scientific forms of creativity, with substantial individual differences in preferences for forms of creative display that can at least partly be predicted by an individual's personality, intelligence, and creativity.

The second class of cognitive processes act as mating mechanisms. Such potentially fruitful domains of MI that can be classified under the mating mechanisms component of MI include *mate-choice mechanisms* for evaluation and choosing among potential sexual partners (e.g., Penke et al., 2008); *self-evaluation mechanisms* for assessing one's own mate value (O'Brien et al., under review); *mechanisms for making context-sensitive decisions about mating strategies* (Schmitt, 2005) such as whether to pursue short-term or long-term relationships;

cross-sex mind reading mechanisms (Geher, 2009) for understanding and influencing the behavior of potential mates, and of their friends, families, and children; and *same-sex mind reading mechanisms* for understanding and influencing the behavior of potential sexual rivals, and of their friends, families, and allies (Fisher, 2004). Future research should also attempt to investigate relations between mental fitness indicators and mating mechanisms. For instance, are those with higher IQ better able to detect interest in a potential mate? Are those who are higher in fitness displays such as humor production better able at assessing their own mate value? Such an investigation of how various fitness indicators relate to one another and with other mating mechanisms will help clarify the structure of mating intelligence.

One step toward this clarification would be to develop a performance measure of mating intelligence. The mating mechanisms in our model may be interrelated much like the abilities that underlie emotional intelligence (see Emotional Intelligence, Chapter 26 of this volume). The ability-based model of emotional intelligence presented by the authors of that chapter suggests that there are four basic facets of emotional intelligence, which are somewhat interrelated and mildly *g*-loaded. These facets include the ability to identify emotions, assimilate emotion into thought, understand emotions, and manage emotions (in one's self and others). This framework might be useful for producing a test of mating intelligence as well as understanding the structure of mating intelligence. Just as emotional intelligence may have basic interrelated components that underlie it, mating intelligence may also have basic elements (such as the ability to accurately assess one's own mate value) which may be interrelated and found to comprise a distinct set of mating-relevant cognitive abilities. The important distinction between emotional intelligence and mating intelligence here pertains to content – with emotional intelligence dealing with emotion-relevant stimuli and processes and mating intelligence focusing on content tied to the mating domain.

In addition to such basic psychometric qualities as internal reliability of measuring instruments, this work will need to assess whether (1) different elements of mating intelligence are mildly interrelated, (2) they are somewhat related to *g*, (3) they are not redundant with well-established personality traits such as the Big Five, and (4) the abilities that comprise mating intelligence are, indeed, predictive of mating success (such as the abilities to attract, choose, court, and retain high-quality sexual partners, and to deter sexual rivals and infidelities). Such psychometric work will be crucial in determining whether mating intelligence is a useful individual-differences construct within psychology writ large. Further, given that emotional intelligence is predictive of success in intimate relationships, research on the interface between emotional intelligence and mating intelligence could be both theoretically and practically valuable. Finally, future research needs to focus on measuring mating intelligence in an ability-based manner. Work on the parallel construct of emotional intelligence has clearly demonstrated that indices of this construct as an ability are not fully correlated with indices of this construct measured via self-report measures (see Geher, 2004). Ability-based measures of mating intelligence might use work in emotional intelligence as a guide, examining such abilities as, for instance, the ability to know what is attractive to a large group of potential mates, the ability to effectively deceive others regarding mating-relevant stimuli, and so on. Future research along these lines should be very fruitful in carving out the nature of this construct.

In terms of the practical value of mating intelligence, there are important potential applications of the MI framework to society. Awareness of mating intelligence in the larger society should increase our appreciation of psychological and mental qualities in a potential mate in addition to purely physical qualities. Further, sex education in the schools can be improved by being informed by the MI framework. In particular, by embracing the fact that much of the human mind is really about mating, sex education classes could teach students the importance of mental indicators and the various skills necessary to successfully navigate the mating domain. Informed by the complexities of human mating research, such education could address the fact that there are multiple routes to success in mating – with males and females both armed with a variety of long- and short-term strategies that are highly context-sensitive. The mating intelligence idea underscores this complexity, but also places these ideas within a coherent framework informed by evolutionary theory.

It is our hope that the mating intelligence construct, by providing an evolutionarily informed understanding of human intelligence that takes into account the important domain of human mating, can allow us to come toward a more complete understanding of human intelligence.

Acknowledgments

We greatly appreciate the diligent work of senior editor Robert Sternberg during the editorial process and we thank Justin Garcia for offering his thoughtful guidance and insights regarding biological aspects of this work. We also thank Megan Geher for her excellent editorial help.

References

Arden, R., Gottfredson, L. S., Miller, G., & Pierce, A. (2009). Intelligence and semen quality are positively correlated. *Intelligence*, *37*, 277–282.

Banks, G. C., Batchelor, J. H., & McDaniel, M. A. (2010). Smarter people are (a bit) more symmetrical: A meta-analysis of the relationship between intelligence and fluctuating asymmetry. *Intelligence*, *4*, 393–401.

Bates, T. C. (2007). Fluctuating asymmetry and intelligence. *Intelligence*, *35*, 41–46.

Bleske-Recheck, A. L., & Buss, D. M. (2001). Opposite-sex friendship: Sex differences and similarities in initiation, selection, and dissolution. *Personality and Social Psychology Bulletin*, *27*, 1310–1327.

Brackett, M. A., Alster, B., Wolfe, C. J., Katulak, N. A., & Fale, E. (2007). Creating an emotionally intelligent school district: A skill based approach In R. Bar-On, J. G. Maree, & M. J. Elias (Eds.), *Educating people to be emotionally intelligent* (pp. 123–137). Westport, CT: Praeger.

Buss, D. M. (1989). Sex differences in human mate selection: Evolutionary hypothesis tested in 37 cultures. *Behavioral and Brain Sciences*, **12**, 1–49.

Buss, D. M. (2003). *The evolution of desire: Strategies of human mating*. New York, NY: Basic Books.

Buss, D. M. (2005). *The handbook of evolutionary psychology*. New York, NY: Wiley.

Buss, D. M. (2009). *Evolutionary psychology: The new science of the mind*. Boston, MA: Pearson.

Buss, D. M. (2008). The future of mating intelligence. *Mating intelligence: Sex, relationships, and the mind's reproductive system*. Mahwah, NJ: Erlbaum.

Borsboom, D., & Dolan, C. V. (2006). Why *g* is not an adaptation: A comment on Kanazawa (2004). *Psychological Review*, **113**, 433–437.

Buss, D. M., Larsen, R. J., Weston, D., & Semmelroth, J. (1992). Sex differences in jealousy: Evolution, physiology, and psychology. *Psychological Science*, *3*, 251–255.

Buss, D. M., & Schmitt, D. P. (1996). Strategic self-promotion and competition derogation: Sex and conflict effects on perceived effectiveness of mate attraction tactics. *Journal of Personality and Social Psychology*, *70*, 1185–1204.

Calvin, C. M., Deary, I. J., Fenton, C., Roberts, B. A., Der, G., Leckenby, N., & Batty, G. D. (2010). Intelligence in youth and all-cause-mortality: Systematic review with meta-analysis. *International Journal of Epidemiology*. doi:10.1093/ije/dyq190.

Camargo, M. A., Geher, G., Fisher, M., & Arrabacca, A. (under review). The relationship between hypothesized psychological genetic fitness indicators and indices of mating success.

Cantor, N., & Kihlstrom, J. F. (1987). *Personality and social intelligence*. Englewood Cliffs, NJ: Prentice-Hall.

Casey, J. J., Garrett, J., Brackett, M. A., & Rivers, S. (2008). Emotional intelligence, relationship quality, and partner selection. In G. Geher & G. F. Miller (Eds.), *Mating intelligence: Sex, relationships, and the mind's reproductive system*. Mahwah, NJ: Erlbaum.

Chiappe, D., & MacDonald, K. (2005). The evolution of domain-general mechanisms in intelligence and learning. *Journal of General Psychology*, 132, 5–40.

Darwin, C. (1871). *The descent of man, and selection in relation to sex* (2 vols.). London, UK: John Murray.

Dawkins, R. (2005). Afterword. In D. M. Buss (Ed.), *The handbook of evolutionary psychology*. New York, NY: Wiley.

Feist, G. (1998). A meta-analysis of personality in scientific and artistic creativity. *Personality and Social Psychology Review*, 2, 290–309.

Feist, G. (2001). Natural and sexual selection in the evolutionary of creativity. *Bulletin of Psychology and the Arts*, 2, 11–16.

Fisher, M. L. (2004). Female intrasexual competition decreases female facial attractiveness. *Proceedings of the Royal Society*, 271, 283–285.

Furlow, B., Armijo-Prewitt, T., Gangestad, S. W., & Thornhill, R. (1997). Fluctuating asymmetry and psychometric intelligence. *Proceedings of the Royal Society of London. Series B, Biological Sciences*, 264, 823–829.

Figueredo, A. J., Brumbach, B. H., Jones, D. N., Sefcek, J. A., Vasquez, G., & Jacobs, W. J. Ecological constraints on mating tactics. In G. Geher & G. F. Miller (Eds.), *Mating Intelligence: Sex, relationships, and the mind's reproductive system*. Mahwah, NJ: Erlbaum.

Gabora, L., & Kaufman, S. B. (2010). Evolutionary approaches to creativity. R. J. Sternberg & J. C. Kaufman (Eds.), *The Cambridge Handbook of Creativity* (pp. 279–301). New York, NY: Cambridge University Press.

Gangestad, S.W., & Simpson, J. A. (2000). The evolution of human mating: Trade-offs and strategic pluralism. *Behavioral and Brain Sciences*, 23, 573–644.

Garcia, J. R., & Reiber, C. (2008). Hook-up behavior: A biopsychosocial perspective. *Journal of Social, Evolutionary, and Cultural Psychology*, 2, 192–208.

Geary, D. C. (2004). *Origin of mind: Evolution of brain, cognition, and general intelligence*. Washington, DC: American Psychological Association.

Geary, D. C. (2009). Evolution of general fluid intelligence. In S. M. Platek & T. K. Shackelford (Eds.), *Foundations in evolutionary cognitive neuroscience* (pp. 25–26). Cambridge, MA: MIT Press.

Geher, G. (2009). Accuracy and oversexualization in cross-sex mind-reading: An adaptationist approach. *Evolutionary Psychology*, 7, 331–347.

Geher, G. (Ed.). (2004). *Measuring emotional intelligence: Common ground and controversy*. New York, NY: Nova Science.

Geher, G., & Kaufman, S. B. (2007). The mating intelligence scale. *Psychology Today*, 40, 78–79.

Geher, G., Camargo, M. A., & O'Rourke, S. (2008). Future directions in research on mating intelligence. In G. Geher & G. F. Miller (Eds.), *Mating intelligence: Sex, relationships, and the mind's reproductive system* (pp. 395–425). Mahwah, NJ: Erlbaum.

Geher, G., Miller, G., & Murphy, J. (2008). Mating intelligence: Toward an evolutionarily informed construct. In G. Geher & G. Miller (Eds.), *Mating intelligence: Sex, relationships, and the mind's reproductive system* (pp. 3–34). Mahwah, NJ: Erlbaum.

Geher, G., & Miller, G. F. (Eds.). (2008). *Mating intelligence: Sex, relationships, and the mind's reproductive system*. Mahwah, NJ: Erlbaum.

Geher, G., & Renstrom, K. L. (2004). Measurement issues in emotional intelligence research. In G. Geher (Ed.), *Measuring emotional intelligence: Common ground and controversy*. New York, NY: Nova Science.

Giosan, C. (2006). High-k strategy scale: A measure of the high-k independent criterion of fitness. *Evolutionary Psychology*, 4, 394–405.

Girotto, V., & Tentori, K. (2008). Is domain-general thinking a domain-specific adaptation? *Mind & Society*, 7, 167–175.

Greengross, G., & Miller, G. F. (2008). Dissing oneself versus one's rivals. *Evolutionary Psychology*, 6, 393–408.

Griskevicius, V., Cialdini, R. B., & Kenrick, D. T. (2006). Peacocks, Picasso, and parental investment: The effects of romantic motives on creativity. *Journal of Personality and Social Psychology*, 91, 63–76.

Gottschall, J., & Wilson, D. S. (2005). *The literary animal: Evolution and the nature of narrative*. Evanston, IL: Northwestern University Press.

Harrison, A., Moore, M., & Rucker, M. (1985). Further evidence on career and family compatibility among eminent women and men. *Archivio di Psicologia, Neurologia e Psichiatria*, 46, 140–155.

Haselton, M. G., & Miller, G. F. (2006). Women's fertility across the cycle increases the short-term attractiveness of creative intelligence compared to wealth. *Human Nature*, 17, 50–73.

Haselton, M. G. (2007). Error management theory. In R. F. Baumeister & K. D. Vohs (Eds.), *Encyclopedia of social psychology* (Vol. 1, pp. 311–312). Thousand Oaks, CA: Sage.

Haselton, M. G., & Buss, D. M. (2000). Error management theory: A new perspective on biases in cross-sex mind reading. *Journal of Personality and Social Psychology*, 78, 81–91.

Haselton, M. G., Buss, D. M., Oubaid, V., & Angleitner, A. (2005). Sex, lies, and strategic interference: The psychology of deception between the sexes. *Personality and Social Psychology Bulletin*, **31**, 3–23.

Hasson, O. (2006). The role of amplifiers in sexual selection: An integration of the amplifying and the Fisherian mechanisms. *Evolutionary Ecology*, **4**, 277–289.

Hughes, S., & Gallup, G. G. Jr. (2003). Sex differences in morphological predictors of sexual behavior: Shoulder to hip and waist to hip ratios. *Evolution and Human Behavior*, **24**, 173–178.

Jensen A. (1998). *The g factor: The science of mental ability*. London, UK: Praeger.

Kanazawa, S. (2004). General intelligence as a domain-specific adaptation. *Psychological Review*, **111**, 512–523.

Kanazawa, S. (2010). Evolutionary psychology and intelligence research. *American Psychologist*, **65**, 279–289.

Kanazawa, S. (2008). The independence of mating intelligence and general intelligence. In G. Geher & G. F. Miller (Eds.), *Mating intelligence: Sex, relationships, and the mind's reproductive system*. Mahwah, NJ: Erlbaum.

Kaufman, S. B., DeYoung, C. G., Reis, D. L., & Gray, J. R. (in press). *The role of general intelligence in contextualized deductive reasoning. Intelligence*.

Kaufman, S. B., Erickson, J. E., Huang, J. Y., Ramesh, S., Thompson, S., Kozbelt, A., Paul, E., & Kaufman, J. C. (2009). *Art as an aphrodisiac*. Paper presented at the Northeastern Evolutionary Psychology Society Conference, Oswego, NY.

Kaufman, S. B., Erickson, J. E., Ramesh, S., Kozbelt, A., Magee, M., & Kaufman, J. C. (2010). *What are funny people like?* Paper presented at the Human Behavior and Evolution Society Conference, Eugene, OR.

Kaufman, S. B., & Kaufman, J. C. (Eds.). (2009). *The psychology of creative writing*. Cambridge, UK: Cambridge University Press

Kaufman, S. B., Kozbelt, A., Bromley, M. L., & Miller, G. F. (2008). The role of creativity and humor in human mate selection. In G. Geher & G. F. Miller (Eds.), *Mating intelligence: Sex, relationships, and the mind's reproductive system* (pp. 227–263). Mahwah, NJ: Erlbaum.

Keller, M., & Miller, G. F. (2006). An evolutionary framework for mental disorders: Integrating adaptationist and evolutionary genetics models. *Behavioral and Brain Sciences*, **29**, 429–452.

Kruger, D. J., Reischl, T. M., & Zimmerman, M. A. (2008). Time perspective as a mechanism for functional developmental adaptation. *Journal of Social, Evolutionary, and Cultural Psychology*, **2**, 1–22.

MacArthur, R. H., & Wilson, E. O. (1967). *Theory of island biogeography*. Princeton, NJ: Princeton University Press.

Matthews, G., Zeidner, M., & Roberts, R. D. (2002). *Emotional intelligence: Science and myth*. Cambridge, MA: MIT Press.

Mayer, J. D., & Geher, G. (1996). Emotional intelligence and the identification of emotion. *Intelligence*, **22**, 89–113.

Mayer, J. D., Salovey, P., & Caruso, D. (2000). Models of emotional intelligence. In R. J. Sternberg (Ed.), *The handbook of intelligence* (pp. 396–420). New York, NY: Cambridge University Press.

Miller, G. F. (1998). How mate choice shaped human nature: A review of sexual selection and human evolution. In C. B. Crawford & D. L. Krebs (Eds.), *Handbook of evolutionary psychology: Ideas, issues, and applications* (pp. 87–129). Mahwah, NJ: Erlbaum.

Miller G. F. (1999). Sexual selection for cultural displays. In R. Dunbar, C. Knight, & C. Power (Eds.), *The evolution of culture* (pp. 71–91). Edinburgh, UK: Edinburgh University Press.

Miller, G. F. (2000a). *The mating mind: How sexual choice shaped the evolution of human nature*. New York, NY: Doubleday.

Miller, G. F. (2000b). Mental traits as fitness indicators: Expanding evolutionary psychology's adaptationism. In D. LeCroy & P. Moller (Eds.), *Evolutionary perspectives on human reproductive behavior* (pp. 62–74). New York: New York Academy of Sciences.

Miller, G. F. (2000c). Sexual selection for indicators of intelligence. *Novartis Foundation Symposium*, **233**, 260–270; discussion 270–280.

Miller, G. F. (2001). Aesthetic fitness: How sexual selection shaped artistic virtuosity as a fitness indicator and aesthetic preferences as mate choice criteria. *Bulletin of Psychology and the Arts*, **2**, 20–25.

Miller, G. F. (2007). Sexual selection for moral virtues. *Quarterly Review of Biology*, 82(2), 97–125.

Miller, G. F. (2008). Mating intelligence: Frequently asked questions. In G. Geher & Miller, G. F. (Eds.), *Mating intelligence: Sex, relationships, and the mind's reproductive system* (pp. 367–393). Mahwah, NJ: Erlbaum.

Miller, G. F., Tybur, J., & Jordan, B. (2007). Ovulatory cycle effects on tip earnings by lap-dancers: Economic evidence for human estrus? *Evolution and Human Behavior, 28*, 375–381.

Mithen, S. (2006). *The singing Neanderthals: The origins of music, language, mind, and body.* London: Weidenfeld and Nicolson.

Nettle, D. (2009). The evolution of creative writing. In S. B. Kaufman & J. C. Kaufman (Eds.), *The psychology of creative writing* (pp. 101–117). Cambridge, UK: Cambridge University Press.

Nettle, D. (2006). Schizotypy and mental health amongst poets, artists, and mathematicians. *Journal of Research in Personality, 40*, 876–890.

Nettle, D., & Clegg, H. (2006). Schizotypy, creativity and mating success in humans. *Proceedings of the Royal Society: B, 273*, 611–615.

Nettle, D., & Clegg, H. (2008). Personality, mating strategies, and mating intelligence. In G. Geher & G. F. Miller (Eds.), *Mating intelligence: Sex, relationships, and the mind's reproductive system.* Mahwah, NJ: Erlbaum.

O'Brien, D., Geher, G., Gallup, A., Garcia, J., & Kaufman, S. B. (2010). Self-perceived mating intelligence predicts sexual behavior in college students: Empirical validation of a theoretical construct. *Imagination, Cognition and Personality, 29*, 341–362.

O'Sullivan, M. (2008). Deception and self-deception as strategies in short- and long-term mating. In G. Geher & G. F. Miller (Eds.), *Mating intelligence: Sex, relationships, and the mind's reproductive system.* Mahwah, NJ: Erlbaum.

Penke, L., Denissen, J. J., & Miller, G. F. (2007). The evolutionary genetics of personality [target article]. *European Journal of Personality, 21*, 549–587.

Penke, L., Todd, P., Lenton, A. P., & Fasolo, B. (2008). How self-related cognitions can guide human mating decisions. In G. Geher & G. F. Miller (Eds.), *Mating Intelligence: Sex, relationships, and the mind's reproductive system.* Mahwah, NJ: Erlbaum.

Perina, K. (2007). Love's loopy logic. *Psychology Today, 40*, 68–77.

Pérusse, D. (1993). Cultural and reproductive success in industrial societies: Testing the relationship at the proximate and ultimate levels. *Behavioral and Brain Sciences, 16*, 267–322.

Pipitone, R. N., & Gallup, G. G. (2008). Women's voice attractiveness varies across the menstrual cycle. *Evolution and Human Behavior, 29*, 268–274.

Prokosch, M. D., Coss, R. G., Scheib, J. E., & Blozis, S. A. (2009). Intelligence and mate choice: Intelligent men are always appealing. *Evolution and Human Behavior, 30*, 11–20.

Prokosch, M. D., Yeo, R. A., & Miller, G. F. (2005). Intelligence tests with higher g-loadings show higher correlations with body symmetry: Evidence for a general fitness factor mediated by developmental stability. *Intelligence, 33*, 203–213.

Rosenberg, J., & Tunney, R. J. (2008). Human vocabulary use as display. *Evolutionary Psychology, 6*, 538–549.

Schmitt, D. P. (2005). Fundamentals of human mating strategies. In D. M. Buss (Ed.), *The Handbook of Evolutionary Psychology.* New York, NY: Wiley.

Silventoinen, K., Posthuma, D., van Beijsterveldt, T., Bartels, M., & Boomsma, D. I. (2006). Genetic contributions to the association between height and intelligence: Evidence from Dutch twin data from childhood to middle age. *Genes, Brain and Behavior, 5*, 585–595.

Simpson, J. A., & Gangstead, S.W. (1991). Individual differences in sociosexuality: Evidence for convergent and discriminant validity. *Journal of Personality and Social Psychology, 60*, 870–883.

Springer, J. (2009). Evolution's Match.com. PsychCRITIQUES, 53.

Sternberg, R. J. (1996). *Successful intelligence.* New York, NY: Simon & Schuster.

Sternberg, R. J. (1998). *Handbook of creativity.* Cambridge, UK: Cambridge University Press.

Sundet, J. M., Tambs, K., Harris, J. R., Magnus, P., & Torjussen, T. M. (2005). Resolving the genetic and environmental sources of the correlation between height and intelligence: A study of nearly 2600 Norwegian male twin pairs. *Twin Research and Human Genetics, 8*, 307–311.

Taylor, M. D., Hart, C. L., Smith, G. D., Whalley, L. J., Hole, D. J., Wilson, V., & Deary, I. J. (2005). Childhood IQ and marriage by mid-life: The Scottish Mental Survey 1932 and the Midspan studies. *Personality and Individual Differences*, 38, 1621–1630.

Trivers, R. (1985). *Social evolution*. San Francisco, CA: Benjamin Cummings.

Veblen, T. (1899). *The theory of the leisure class*. New York, NY: Macmillan.

Wilson, D. S. (2007). *Evolution for everyone*. New York, NY: Bantam.

Zahavi, A. (1997). *The handicap principle: A missing piece of Darwin's puzzle*. New York, NY: Oxford University Press.

Zebrowitz, L.A., & Rhodes, G. (2004). Sensitivity to "bad genes" and the anomalous face overgeneralization effect: Cue validity, cue utilization, and accuracy in judging intelligence and health. *Journal of Nonverbal Behavior*, 28, 167–185.

Part VII

INTELLIGENCE AND SOCIETY

CHAPTER 31

Intelligence in Worldwide Perspective

Weihua Niu and Jillian Brass

For thousands of years of human history, understanding the nature of "intelligence" has been a quest of the utmost importance, attracting many sages and intellects around the world. In ancient Greek culture, Plato (428/427–348/347 B.C.E.) expressed his belief that human beings are born with different levels of intelligence, strength, and courage. In his opinion, those who were not overly bright, strong, or brave were suited to various trades such as farming, blacksmithing, and building, whereas those who were somewhat bright, strong, and especially courageous were suited to defensive and policing professions. Those who were extraordinarily intelligent, virtuous, and brave were suited to run the state itself as part of the aristocracy, a Greek word for "rule by the best" (Hooker & Hines, 1996; Plato, 1992).

In ancient Chinese culture, Confucius (551–479 B.C.E.) presented a different view of intelligence from that of Plato. Using the words "intelligence (智)" and "knowledge (知)" almost interchangeably, Confucius believed that people varied in their levels of intelligence by how knowledge was acquired and utilized. In the *Doctrine of the Mean*, Confucius (2010) said, "Some are born with the knowledge of those duties; some know them by study; and some acquire the knowledge after a painful feeling of their ignorance. But the knowledge being possessed, it comes to the same thing. Some practice it with a natural ease; some from a desire for its advantages; and some by strenuous effort. But the achievement being made, it comes to the same thing" (p. 9). "或生而知之,或学而知之,或困而知之,及其知之一也。或安而行之,或利而行之,或勉强而行之,及其成功一也。"

Although acknowledging that some people are born with knowledge or intelligence, Confucius believed that these people are extremely rare and truly exceptional. Confucius would not consider even himself to be one of them. Therefore, Confucius emphasized the importance of learning and self-cultivation in acquiring knowledge or intelligence.

This discrepancy in philosophical views is one of the first pieces of evidence that people from different cultures view intelligence differently. To Plato, intelligence is something that one is born with whereas to Confucius, intelligence is something that one can earn and accumulate throughout one's life. Both Plato and Confucius have had a profound impact on the development of great civilizations in the world, and their views on intelligence also deeply affect how people across the world currently perceive and attempt to measure intelligence.

Many scholarly works examine the role of culture in understanding and measuring intelligence, including several comprehensive reviews (e.g., Serpell, 2000; Sternberg 2004, Sternberg & Grigorenko, 2006). This chapter first summarizes some of the main points and findings from studies on implicit theories of intelligence, adding new evidence from recent studies, particularly originating in East Asia. It then reviews some new developments in measures of intelligence in different countries from different continents. Finally, it concludes with a presentation of our views on the ways in which culture affects people's perception of intelligence and the practice of measuring intelligence.

Implicit Theories of Intelligence Across Different Cultures

What is intelligence? Many psychologists around the world have proposed theories to answer this question. There are probably as many definitions of intelligence as there are experts who study it. As noted by Determan (1986), there is no definitive definition of intelligence; the concept has evolved and will continue to evolve over time. Many researchers also recognize that intelligence cannot be understood outside a cultural context (Greenfield, 1997; Sternberg 2004). People from different cultures may perceive intelligence differently, depending on what is considered to be important in that culture.

One important approach to studying people's conceptions of intelligence is through investigating the cultural prototype of an intelligent person. This approach is relatively straightforward: Lay people are asked to list characteristics associated with the term "intelligence" or "an intelligent person." Many researchers credit Neisser (1979) for his acknowledgment of the importance of this approach. Sternberg coined the term "implicit theories of intelligence" to describe this approach, in comparison to the other type of approach, based on experts' explicit theories of intelligence. Sternberg and his colleagues conducted a series of empirical studies in the 1980s (Sternberg, 1985; Sternberg, Conway, Ketron, & Bernstein, 1981), studying laypeople's implicit theories of intelligence. These studies generated wide interest around the world in investigating definitions of intelligence within each specific culture.

In a seminal work studying people's implicit theories of intelligence, Sternberg, Conway, Ketron, and Bernstein (1981) asked members of the general public to list behaviors that characterize intelligence, academic intelligence, everyday intelligence, and unintelligence. They then recorded the frequency with which each behavior for each type of intelligence was listed by participants in each setting, looking at both self-evaluation and evaluation of others. They later asked another group of people from varying backgrounds to indicate the importance and characteristics of each behavior associated with their ideal concepts of intelligence, academic intelligence, and everyday intelligence. Findings from this study suggested that people have well-developed implicit theories of intelligence that they use both in self-evaluation and in the evaluation of others. These theories identify intelligence as consisting of at least three common components: problem-solving abilities, verbal abilities, and social competence. Importantly, such core components of intelligence have been found to be shared by both laypeople and experts who study intelligence. The difference between their evaluations of intelligence is that laypeople did not consider motivation to be an important ingredient of "academic" intelligence, whereas the experts did. Additionally, laypeople placed somewhat greater emphasis on practical intelligence than did the experts.

Emphasizing the importance of cognitive abilities in intelligence was also evident in some earlier work on people's perceptions of intelligence. For example, Neisser (1979) asked college students to list characteristics of intelligent people and found that characteristics such as "the ability to think logically" "verbal fluency," "wide general knowledge and common sense," "openness to experiences," and "sensitivity to one's own limitations" were important in the conception of intelligence. Bruner, Shapiro, and Tagiuri (1958) conducted a similar study and found that intelligent people were characterized as clever, deliberate, efficient, and energetic. People tended not to associate social aspects such as "dishonest," "apathetic," and "unreliable" with intelligence. This view is consistent with many popular intelligence measurements based on earlier explicit theories of intelligence.

However, this conception of intelligence is not consistently shared by people from other parts of world, especially Asia and Africa where social and emotional competence and even moral character are important in people's implicit theories of intelligence.

Asia

In Asia, many studies have been conducted to investigate people's implicit theories of intelligence using samples from Mainland China, Taiwan, Hong Kong, Japan, Korea, India, and Malaysia.

The literate translation of the Chinese phrase for "intelligence" (聪明) is "to have sharp hearing and clear vision," or "to have a clear understanding (of a situation)." The phrase itself reflects the Chinese view of intelligence, which has historically emphasized the correctness of one's perception and comprehension. The implied meaning is that with a clear perception and understanding of a situation, one can act properly. This notion of intelligence is supported by empirical studies on implicit theories of intelligence in China.

For example, in Mainland China, Fang and Keats (1987) did a study in the early 1980s comparing Australian and Chinese conceptions of intelligence. They found that both Chinese people and Australians shared some common views regarding intelligence, yet there were substantial discrepancies in prioritizing attributes of intelligences. More specifically, the Chinese participants valued analytical ability, memory skills, correctness, and carefulness more in their conceptions of intelligence than did their Australian counterparts. Additionally, although both Chinese people and Australians included personality traits in interpreting intelligence, Chinese participants placed more emphasis on characteristics such as modesty, remaining calm in the face of difficulties, and perseverance. They also found that there was significantly more consistency across all age groups in Chinese participants than in the Australian participants.

In the 1990s in Beijing, Zhang and Wu (1994) studied laypeople's implicit theories of intelligence. They found that, similar to findings from the West, curiosity, logic, and reasoning, adapting to new environments, creativity, and self-confidence were listed as the most important components of being an intelligent person; moreover, having a good memory was believed to be extremely important.

In a more recent study, Bai, Liu, and Hu (2007) surveyed both teachers and adolescents (aged between 12 and 18 years old) from four different schools in Tianjing, asking them to prioritize 15 attributes (obtained from a previous study) that characterize an intelligent adolescent. The results showed substantial differences between teachers and students in defining an intelligent student. To Chinese teachers, an intelligent student needed to have "strong comprehension skills," "communication skills," and "balanced psychological characteristics," along with other characteristics such as "being hardworking" and "being knowledgeable." To Chinese adolescents, the most important characteristics of intelligence were "open-mindedness," "thirst for knowledge," "creativity," "being hardworking," "leadership," and "balanced psychological characters." Overall, from this study, one can see that having balanced psychological characters, being hardworking, and having a thirst for knowledge are important attributes of Chinese conceptions of intelligence.

Using a similar approach, some studies also examined ethnic differences within China. For example, in a study investigating adolescents' conceptions of intelligence among five different ethnic groups in southwest China, Cai and Jiang (1995) found that participants across all five ethnic groups agreed about some core components of intelligence such as confidence, diligence, creativity, imagination, enjoyment of thinking, being knowledgeable, and being able to grasp the points of a problem. Ethnic differences existed primarily in terms of prioritizing these attributes (no detailed information was provided in the paper), and those differences were found to be more evident in the younger age group of participants (12-year-olds) than in the older participants (18-year-olds), showing the effects of schooling and cultural integration on conceptions of intelligence.

In another study, Wan, Li, and Jing (1997) surveyed adolescents of three different ethnicities (12 to 18 years old) in northwest China. The three ethnic groups were Han Chinese (constituting 92% of the Chinese population in the People's Republic of China or the PRC), Tibetan (constituting 0.5% of the Chinese population in the PRC, within which most observe Tibetan Buddhism), and Dongxiang (constituting 0.05% of the Chinese population in the PRC, within which most observe Sunni Islam). Although there were some shared attributions among the three groups, the ethnic differences were prominent in terms of prioritizing these attributes. For example, whereas Han Chinese adolescents prioritized logical thinking ability and analytical ability in understanding intelligence, both Tibetan and Dongxiang adolescents prioritized "having aspirations to go to college" and "having religious belief" in their conceptions of intelligence. Similar to the findings of Cai and Jiang (1995), this study also demonstrated that the ethnic differences shrank with schooling such that the views of intelligence among all three groups of students were more consistent when they were about to graduate from high school.

Implicit theories of intelligence among Chinese people were also investigated in Taiwan and Hong Kong. In Taiwan, for example, by asking 434 Taiwanese adults to rate the relative frequency and importance of 120 attributes (generated from a previous study) in an intelligent person, Yang and Sternberg (1997b) found five major factors in characterizing Taiwanese conceptions of intelligence: (1) general cognitive ability, (2) interpersonal intelligence, (3) intrapersonal intelligence, (4) intellectual self-promotion, and (5) intellectual self-effacement (including attributes such as "is lonesome," "likes to think quietly," or "likes to be lost in thinking"). Such a view is discrepant with implicit theories of intelligence in the United States, based on other studies (Berg & Sternberg, 1992, Sternberg, 1985; Sternberg, Conway, Ketron, & Bernstein, 1981). It seems that Taiwanese Chinese people place more emphasis on the importance of intellectual balance and integration in their conception of intelligence than do Westerners.

In explaining their results, Yang and Sternberg (1997b) attribute their findings to the influence of two major philosophical schools in the Chinese culture on Chinese people's implicit theories of intelligence. They wrote,

> *As noted earlier, full self-knowledge and being perceptive and responsive to changes in immediate circumstances are key aspects of intelligence in the Taoist tradition; cultivation of character and lifelong learning in the context of everyday life are key aspects of intelligence in the Confucian tradition. To a certain extent, conceptions of intelligence are cultural inventions that reflect the values of a given culture.*

The cultural influences on the Taiwanese Chinese conception of intelligence were also observed in an earlier study. Using a slightly different approach, Chen et al. (1982) studied cultural differences in people's conception of intelligence by asking Australian and Taiwanese college students to list the importance of 27 items selected from two well-known Western intelligence tests (the Stanford-Binet and the Wechsler Adult Intelligence Scale). A noticeable finding from this study is that although both Australian and Chinese conceptions of intelligence include three main factors – nonverbal reasoning, verbal reasoning, and rote memory – when judging the task difficulty of items for each of these three aspects, Taiwanese Chinese judged rote memory to be easier than did their Australian counterparts. Similar results were also found in another study using Hong Kong Chinese (Chen & Chen, 1988). Based on the consistent findings from these two studies, Chen (1994) concluded that compared with the Australian culture, Chinese culture values people's memory skills more in explaining intelligence, a possible result of different instructional practices and values in Chinese and Australian schools. Chen noted that whereas Australian culture is predominantly modern industrial, Chinese culture has only recently evolved from a traditional agricultural background that put great demands on memory skills.

From the abovementioned studies, one may see that some distinct attributes in people's implicit theories of intelligence are shared by all Chinese people, including diligence, thirst for knowledge, and being knowledgeable. Some studies also found that balanced psychological characters, knowing how to express one's self appropriately in a social context, a high level of self-knowledge, being perceptive and responsive to changes in immediate circumstances, and having good memory skills were also consistently noted as important attributes. These characteristics represent the deep influence of cultural heritage in China, namely, the influence of Confucianism and Taoism. Whereas the former emphasizes benevolence, appropriate behavior and conversation in a social context, and self-cultivation, the latter emphasizes seeking harmony between humanity and nature, health and longevity, and action through inaction (not to act immediately but to go with the natural flow of the situation; Yang & Sternberg, 2007a). Both views dominated mainstream Chinese culture for over 2,000 years and still have a significant impact on the way people think, not only in China but also in other East Asian countries such as Japan and Korea.

How Do Other Asian People View Intelligence?

In a study examining Japanese implicit theories of intelligence, Azuma and Kashiwagi (1987) asked Japanese college students and middle-aged female adults to rate each of 67 descriptors with regard to an intelligent person. One important finding of this study was that characteristics related to receptive social competence, such as being sympathetic, modest, and tender-hearted, tended to be associated with high intelligence, especially when the person described was a woman. Overall, the study demonstrated that the implicit theory of Japanese intelligence placed more emphasis on social competence than did the American implicit theories of intelligence reported by Sternberg et al. (1981).

In another study, Ueda (1989) gave 701 Japanese school-aged children (from third grade to senior year of high school) a list of 43 characteristics and asked them to rate the extent to which each characteristic was typical of an intelligent child. The Japanese children put more emphasis on classroom behavior and seemingly innate abilities such as "can remember well what has been learned before," "having his or her own way of thinking," and "good in mathematics," but the older Japanese students focused more on organization, management, planning, and social factors such as responsibility and sociability in their conception of intelligence. Interestingly, all age groups of Japanese students disassociated arrogance and selfishness from intelligence. They also consistently rated memory and good concentration skills as being important to the concept of intelligence. This study suggests that Japanese students and Chinese students show some similarities in their conceptions of intelligence.

When asked, "How can people become more intelligent?" Japanese students across all age groups placed great emphasis on effort-related descriptions, such as "engaging in everything seriously," "making an effort (try harder)," and "trying everything without giving up." In other words, Japanese students believe working hard makes people more intelligent.

Emphasizing the importance of effort in conceptions of intelligence and related concepts in Japanese culture was also found in many cross-cultural studies examining attribution theories. Overall, Japanese students placed greater emphasis on effort whereas American students placed greater emphasis on one's innate ability (for a review, see Holloway, 1988).

The importance of modesty in Japanese conceptions of intelligence is also evident from another set of studies examining how people estimate and compare their own intelligence with that of other people. In a study in which 198 Japanese laypeople estimated their own intelligence and the intelligence of their children, Furnham and Fukumoto (2008) found that the Japanese tend to underestimate their own intelligence compared with people from other countries, including Zulu-speaking South Africans (in comparisons made with earlier studies; see Furnham & Mkhize, 2004, and Furnham, Mkhize, & Mndaweni, 2004). Such a finding is consistent with earlier cross-cultural studies looking at American, British, and Japanese self-estimation of intelligence (Furnham, Hosoe, & Tang, 2002), which demonstrated that among the three groups, Americans gave themselves the highest rating overall (108.73), followed by the British (106.78), and last, the Japanese (101.73).

In summary, three main attributes appear to characterize Japanese conceptions of intelligence: social competence, diligence, and modesty.

Cultural influence on people's implicit theories of intelligence was not found to be salient in studies from Korea. Lim, Plucker, and Im (2002) replicated an earlier study (Sternberg et al., 1981) using a sample of both Korean college students and members of the general public, who were approached at a railway station. They found that Korean participants' theories of intelligence were only slightly different from those of Americans. Similar to findings from studies of the Chinese and Japanese, Korean participants emphasized social competence in their conception of intelligence. However, when Korean participants were asked to evaluate other people's intelligence, they emphasized problem-solving ability over all other factors, an evaluation that shows much similarity with the views of their American counterparts.

Although also geographically in Asia, Indian societies represent a different culture from that of the East Asians. India also has a long history of cultural tradition that still deeply affects the lives of modern Indian people and their ways of thinking. In studying Indians' understanding of intelligence, Srivastava and Misra (2001) surveyed 1,885 participants from five representative geographic regions, careful to mirror the population of India in terms of ecological context (rural vs. urban), and age composition. Participants were asked to list attributes that characterize an intelligent person, which yielded a total of 7,931 attributes. After factor analysis, four meaningful factors were revealed: (1) cognitive competence (such as sensitivity to context, reflection, communication, and decision making), (2) social competence (such as helping the needy, obedience, service to elders, and following norms), (3) emotional competence (such as control of emotions and patience), and (4) competence in actions (such as commitment and efficiency). More important, among the 7931 attributes generated by Indians, only one-third of the attributes referred to the cognitive domain. Even within the category of cognitive competence, sensitivity to context refers to understanding the significance of the relationship between person, time, and ecology, a much more comprehensive concept than cognitive ability. In other words, an intelligent person knows how to speak and behave in a context-sensitive manner and is able to value options and make wise generalizations and discriminations. In India, someone who communicates effectively speaks only when necessary, can make his or her intent clear using minimum words, is able to master a polite and subtle language that often has hidden meanings in the words, and remains focused on the problem under discussion. Srivastava and Misra concluded:

> *This study shows that instead of valuing mere possession of cognitive competence, the application of these abilities in real-life situations is glorified in the Indian context.... According to this study, the Indian conception of intelligence is situated more in the practices and performances distributed across several domains. For example, respect for and service to elders, parents, and guests; being obedient; and following social norms were shared by all the groups. This is in line with the earlier findings showing social concern as an important aspect of achievement concerns among Indians.*

Malaysia represents another type of Asian culture, in which Islam is the official and most widespread religion. Gill and Keats (1980) studied Malay University students' views of intellectual competence, in comparison with those of Australians. They found that whereas Australian students rated academic skills more highly and stressed the ability to adapt to new events, Malays placed great emphasis on social and practical skills along with speed and creativity.

In a recent study, Swami et al. (2008) asked 235 college students in Malaysia, along with 347 college students from Britain and 137 college students from the United States, to indicate their agreement with 30 statements about what intelligence is, the source and stability of between group differences in intelligence, and the practical relevance as well as social implications of intelligence. Most of the statements were derived from a summary of a psychological study asking 50 Western experts in intelligence and applied fields about their views of intelligence. Similar to the findings of Gill and Keats (1980), this study also demonstrated that Malaysians place more emphasis than do their Western counterparts on social competence and the practical aspects of intelligence.

Africa

Not only people from Asia (typically viewed as the East) view intelligence differently from people in the West; people from Africa also have different conceptions from those of Westerners. According to Sternberg (2004), African conceptions are more consistent with Eastern than with Western views. In a review examining the relationship between personality and intelligence in a cultural context, Ruzgis and Grigorenko (1994) argued that the implicit theories of Africans revolve largely around skills that help to facilitate harmonious and stable intergroup relationships. Such a view is supported by many empirical studies from Africa.

Using semantic-differential scales, Wober (1974) studied conceptions of intelligence among members of different tribes in Uganda as well as within various subgroups of the tribes. In results surprising to many Westerners, traditional Ugandans associated intelligence with slowness, gradualness, and taking one's time, whereas Western-educated Ugandans and Indians in Uganda associated it with speed. There is also a difference in conceptions of intelligence both within and between tribes. People of the Beganda tribe associated intelligence with words such as persistent and hardworking, whereas the Batoro thought of it as soft, obedient, and yielding.

Serpell (1974) asked Chewa adults in rural eastern Zambia to rate village children on how well they could perform tasks requiring adaptation in the everyday world (practical and social intelligence). He found that the ratings did not relate to children's cognitive IQ test scores, which had been assessed by the investigators. The results suggested that Chewa criteria for judgments of intelligence were not the same as Western notions of intelligence. In many places in Africa, the games people play, such as "kala," encourage the development of numerical ability (Gardner, 1983). In a series of experimental studies, Cole, Gay, and Glick (1967) found that Kpelle adults in Liberia succeeded far better than American adults in estimating the quantity of a group of objects.

More recently, Grigorenko et al. (2001) investigated the implicit theories of intelligence in a Kenyan village. They found that in rural Kenya, intelligence consists of four different concepts: knowledge and skills, respect, comprehension of how to handle real-life problems, and taking initiative. Of these four skills, only the first relates to cognitive skills while the other three fall into the social domain.

South America and East Europe

Implicit theories in South America and Eastern Europe fall somewhere in between the views of the East and the West. In Chile, for example, Garcia-Cepero and McCoach (2009) surveyed 372 schoolteachers and college professors with regard to their implicit theories of intelligence. Using both Sternberg's theory of successful intelligence and Gardner's theory of multiple intelligence as their framework to design questionnaires, the researchers asked participants whether they agreed with views relating to these two theories. They found that Chilean educators acknowledge the importance of practical, analytical, and creative attributes in their prototypes of an intelligence person. However, participants were fairly neutral about whether interpersonal and intrapersonal attributes characterized intelligent people.

In Eastern Europe, Kopic, Vranic, and Zarevski (2009) asked 330 eighth-graders from Croatia to list attributes associated with an intelligent person; five meaningful factors emerged as associated with intelligence: (1) cognitive abilities, (2) practical intelligence, (3) interpersonal characteristics, (4) motivation, and (5) "academic" intelligence and verbal abilities. All five characteristics had been included in previous studies using Western samples (such as studies of Sternberg and colleagues); however, the importance of interpersonal characteristics and practical intelligence seem to be recognized more in the Croatian culture than in Western culture.

In summary, studies of implicit theories of intelligence in different parts of the world suggest that intelligence may not mean the same thing in different cultures. In Western Europe and North America, where many modern intelligence theories and measurements have been generated, intelligence is largely related to one's cognitive abilities, whereas the rest of the world seems to view other aspects of intelligence such as social acuity, emotional intelligence, and morality to be more important than did their Western counterparts. Even within the domain of cognitive functioning, some areas are emphasized more in some cultures (such as memory skills in China), or may mean different things (such as the meaning of sensitivity to information having much more comprehensive implications in Indian culture). However, this does not mean that social, emotional, and moral components of intelligence are entirely excluded from the Western notion of intelligence, nor does it mean that cognitive functioning is not valued in other parts of the world. In fact, despite the differences in components of intelligence, people around the world share some core views in their conceptions of intelligence, including cognitive competence (both verbal and nonverbal) and social-emotional competence. Most attempts at measurement of intelligence have been focused on the former (cognitive competence), even though there has been an increasing amount of effort in recent years to develop scales to measure the latter. The next section primarily focuses on examining measures of intelligence in the former area (cognitive competence).

Measurements of Intelligence Around the World

As noted in the first section of the chapter, ideas about intelligence vary across cultures and sometimes even within cultures. Just as definitions of intelligence exist throughout the world, instruments used to try to measure and quantify intelligence are used worldwide. Many countries generate their own tests through psychometric research using their own conceptualizations of intelligence, and those tests are then translated and exported to other countries. Therefore, while some tests may measure constructs that are particularly important to the culture they were created for, the fact that the same or similar tests are used in so many different countries means that many different cultures are actually measuring the same constructs despite differences in ideology regarding intelligence.

The process of translating tests is not straightforward or simple. Van De Vijver (2003) argues that when test constructors translate tests into other languages, they can take several different routes . An *application* refers to a close translation of the original test, while an adaptation makes changes to the instrument (for instance, substituting words for more appropriate ones or task materials for ones more familiar to the target audience) to emphasize measuring the same underlying constructs. Oftentimes, a literal translation will be inappropriate in a different language or culture. *Assembly* refers to the construction of an entirely new instrument. Test constructors must decide how an instrument would best fit the population of their country and work accordingly, trying as much as possible to reduce cultural bias that occurs because a test was originally developed for use in a different culture.

One major question hotly debated by psychologists is whether intelligence tests should be measuring the same processes cross-culturally. Are the abilities and skills measured by intelligence tests equally relevant in all parts of the world? Are underlying cognitive processes valued in the same way in a small town in Africa and in Akron, Ohio? For that matter, do people think in the same ways in these different areas? One school of thought is that tests designed by a certain culture primarily measure skills and abilities most valued by that culture that are not as applicable elsewhere. On the other hand, the globalization of tests such as the Wechsler Intelligence Scale for Children (WISC) comes with a certain implication that it is appropriate and even useful to measure the same processes valued in the United States in a multitude of other geographic areas with different values and cultures. Although there is no apparent resolution to bridge these viewpoints, it is evident that, just as with definitions of intelligence worldwide, there will be some discrepancies as well as some similarities in what different cultures want to measure in quantifying or even qualifying intelligence.

As illustrated in the previous section of this chapter, most cultural differences in people's implicit theories of intelligence reflect their cultural value systems. One example lies in Asian cultures seeing effort as being a part of intelligence. However, most intelligence tests developed in the United States and Europe do not measure this factor, as these cultures tend to see intelligence as inherent or based on ability than rather than as a result of hard work.

The philosophical questions of the degree to which intelligence tests should be specific to the culture in which they are used continue to be studied; even so, it is clear that certain tests such as the Wechsler tests, the Stanford-Binet, and the Kaufman Assessment Battery for Children (K-ABC) have been exported and are now used in many countries around the world (Lautrey & de Ribaupierre, 2004; Sato, Namiki, Ando, & Hatano, 2004). Using the same test cross-culturally often tempts researchers to make comparisons between intelligence test scores in different geographic regions. How intelligent we are relative to other cultures and to people from different geographical locations has become a question of great interest and, at times, of national importance. Years ago, worries about the United States falling behind relative to other countries sparked renewed interest in programs such as gifted education. In modern times, we have the instruments necessary to screen and document intelligence test scores of populations. However, there are major problems with making cross-cultural comparisons of intelligence, the largest and most important of which is inaccuracy.

The validity of making comparisons across different tests, or even the same test adapted and normed for a different population, is questionable. Cross-cultural comparisons that look specifically at numbers are inherently based on the idea that when we are measuring intelligence, we are all measuring the same thing. The problem is that more often than not, what we are measuring is quite different.

Even when the same test is used, major differences can exist in the equivalence of the test across cultures. The Wechsler Intelligence Scale for Children (WISC), in its fourth edition in the United States, where it originated, has been adapted and renormed all over the world (Georgas et al., 2003). In a survey of European countries, Muñiz and colleagues (2001) asked what the most frequently used psychological tests were in each country; only the WISC and Wechsler Adult Intelligence Scale (WAIS) were in the top 10 of each country surveyed. Muñiz et al. (1999) also found that the Wechsler scales rank in the top 10 tests used in Spanish- and Portuguese-speaking countries, including Spain, Portugal, and 14 countries in Latin America. These studies provide evidence of the popularity of the Wechsler Intelligence instruments across countries, languages, and continents. Many different countries now have their own versions of the WISC, though not all of them have been readapted based on the most recent U.S. edition.

Although many countries are using the same tests, significant issues in translation and adaptation, as well as appropriateness to a new population, affect whether cross-cultural comparisons of scores on this instrument reflect true cross-cultural differences. How relevant and accurate cross-cultural comparisons are seems to depend on the factor being examined.

Psychologists involved in cross-cultural analysis of the WISC have noted that the performance subtests in particular are easily adaptable to other cultures, as the skills they measure – analysis of visual material, pattern completion, and visual-motor integration, for example – are practical across cultures and have a universal feel to them; there are probably very few cultures in which abilities such as visual-motor integration or visual analysis, which are generally adaptive skills from an evolutionary standpoint, are irrelevant. (Georgas, Van de Vijver, Weiss, & Saklofske, 2003).

However, looking at the verbal subtests opens a host of larger problems. Evidence suggests that verbal thinking is not necessarily the same cross-culturally, and therefore a test measuring verbal abilities in the United States may not be as relevant elsewhere. For instance, a study by Peng and Nisbett (1999) suggested that people in China think differently from those in the United States. When Chinese people were presented with a seemingly contradictory statement, they tended to try to resolve the two sides and find a compromise between them, which the authors termed "dialectical thinking." When presented with the same contradiction, people in the United States tended to polarize their views by picking the half of the apparent contradiction they felt was more accurate and rejecting the other half, a process termed "differentiation of thinking" by the authors. These results seemed to suggest that cognitive processes are different between Chinese individuals and those from the United States.

Problems with subtest translation are not limited to underlying conceptual issues – they also involve the more practical elements of test adaptation. One such problem is the vocabulary subtest of the WISC, which asks children to define words. In adapting this subtest, many countries have found that not all the vocabulary words are directly translatable and that, if they are, the same word in a different language might not have an equivalent "difficulty" level – the word might be more or less common than its English counterpart, which in turn changes the difficulty of the entire subtest. Substituting a more appropriate word for equivalent difficulty would change the content of the subtest; both solutions compromise the integrity of cross-cultural comparisons of ability on this task (Georgas et al., 2003).

As an example, Beller and Gafni note that when a test originally written in Hebrew was translated into Russian, Russians did more poorly on a specific analogy when the answer involved understanding the relationship between a dictionary and a definition. The authors noted that in the Russian language, dictionaries are used to translate, not to define, which led to Russians not being able to recognize this relationship as the correct response for "Telephone book: telephone number." However, Russians performed better on a different analogy, "plough: furrows," as "furrows" in its appropriate translation is a more common word in Russian than it is in Hebrew (Beller & Gafni, 1995).

Another task on the WISC, designed to measure working memory, requires children to repeat a series of numbers first forward and then, later, backward. This task was designed in the United States, where the numbers used in the task have fairly distinct, one-syllable names. Countries that do not have similar ways of naming their numbers might have difficulty constructing an equivalent of this subtest that would measure precisely the same process (Georgas et al., 2003; Kwak, 2003).

Another important issue in cross-cultural comparisons is the familiarity that the test audience has with both the modality of an intelligence test – the methods of administration and materials used – and with the information or experiential bases necessary to succeed. While doing research with children from Tanzania, Sternberg and colleagues noted that a short intervention could raise test scores. This result suggested that familiarity and training play key roles in scores, and that giving an unfamiliar test to a group of children is likely not to be an accurate measure of cognitive ability alone (Sternberg et al., 2002).

Serpell and Jere-Folotiya (2008) noted that in Zambia, pencils and paper are rare playthings for children before entering school. They found in studies that children from England performed superiorly to children from Zambia in a pencil-and-paper task. However, when the same task was presented in the media of small twisted wires, something with which Zambian children are familiar and English children less so, the performance of the Zambian children was superior. This study suggested that the way in which a task is presented affects performance on the task, depending on the test takers' familiarity with and training in the presented media.

Another issue to consider is whether children who have access to schooling will do better on cognitive tests, which would suggest that pure, untrained cognitive ability is not the underlying construct being measured. Even if children have a history of schooling, Sternberg et al. (2002) point out that children in some parts of Africa do not have equal opportunity to take advantage of their schooling, as the environment in which they are schooled, in terms of stressors and opportunities, is not comparable to school environments in the United States or Western Europe.

Europe

Europe has a rich history of intelligence testing. Even before the Binet-Simon intelligence scale was published in 1905, beginning a new age of formal intelligence testing, other researchers and psychologists had invented ways to measure aspects of intelligence. Some subtests that are now established parts of the Wechsler intelligence instruments, such as digit span and coding, appear to have their origins in tests developed in Europe in the late 19th and early 20th centuries. In 1909, the Binet-Simon was grouped into age levels so that the administration of the instrument would begin at a predetermined level deemed appropriate for a child's chronological age and proceed to more difficult questions or fall back to questions at a lower level depending on the child's performance. This structure is now commonly used across intelligence tests. Several years after its development, the Binet-Simon came into widespread use across Europe and North America, bringing with it an era of intelligence testing that would continue in spirit to the present day (Boake, 2002).

In contemporary Europe, many countries use versions of tests such as the Wechsler Scales, the Kaufman-ABC, and the Stanford-Binet. However, many European countries have also created their own instruments to suit their own specific needs. This section will focus on instruments indigenous to European countries.

One important test developed in the United Kingdom is the British Ability Scales (Deary & Smith, 2004). As early as the 1960s, British psychologists, who heavily relied on American tests such as the WISC or Stanford-Binet without norms applicable to the United Kingdom or adaptation of content, recognized that the instruments they had were often inadequate for their purposes. In 1965 the British Psychological Society commissioned a contemporary British test to measure intelligence, leading to the development of the British Ability Scales (BAS), which were produced in 1979. The current version, the BAS II, consists of two separate batteries; the Early Years for children age 2.6 to 5.11, and the School Age Scales, for children 6.0 to 17.11. The scales contain seven core scales, seven diagnostic scales, and three achievement scales (number skills, spelling, and word reading), and measure the underlying processes of verbal intelligence, visual/spatial intelligence, and nonverbal intelligence, all of which then contribute to general intelligence. One feature of the BAS II is that subtest scores are robust and easily interpretable, meaning that psychologists can choose to give individual subtests targeting a student's specific issues rather than administering the entire test (Hill, 2005).

While France is not focused on developing new intelligence tests, emphasis is placed on the process used to problem-solve on tests, looking at individual differences in established tests. Approach and strategy on tasks are observed and analyzed (Lautrey & de Ribaupierre, 2004). This approach places a clear priority on the process rather than the magnitude of skills and abilities.

In the Netherlands, the Revised Amsterdam Child Intelligence Test (RAKIT) was developed by Bleichrodt, Drenth, Zaal, and Resing in the 1980s (te Nijenhuis et al., 2004). Although the test was created in the Netherlands, it has been exported to other cultures as well. The test, which is intended for children of ages 4 through 12, is partially based on Thurstone's primary-factor theory (Bleichrodt, Hoksbergen, & Khire, 1999). Since this theory is important in the Dutch understanding of intelligence, it follows that a test measuring intelligence to be used in the Netherlands would be structured around Thurstone's conceptualization. Specific tasks include recognition of incomplete pictures, recalling pictures in a certain order, mazes, deciding which object does not belong to a category, quantitative tasks, receptive vocabulary, remembering names, finding hidden figures, naming items belonging to a given category, a motor task involving placing discs over pins, and storytelling. Some of these subtests measure processes not directly or singularly emphasized by the Wechsler scales, such as ideational fluency and verbal inductive reasoning. Performance subtests also differ somewhat from the WISC, with an emphasis on closure in some subtests. Since Thurstone theorized seven primary mental abilities, the RAKIT by nature must measure a wide range of processes (Bleichrodt, Hoksbergen, & Khire, 1999; te Nijenhuis et al., 2004).

Another test developed in the Netherlands is the Snijders-Oomen Nonverbal Intelligence Scale for Children (SON), which was originally designed for the assessment of deaf children; it does not require a testee to be verbal to understand or respond to the test. However, the test is also normed for and can be administered to hearing children. The SON is made up of five untimed subtests, which test nonverbal skills such as sorting, copying patterns, assembling completed pictures from parts, visual-spatial memory, and visual-motor integration (Harris, 1982; Tellegen & Laros, 1993).

Sweden has a history of indigenous test construction. One widely used cognitive test, the Swedish Scholastic Aptitude Test, or SweSAT, is somewhat comparable in terms of purpose to the American SAT (Carlstedt, Gustafsson, & Hautamäki, 2004). Since 1977, the test has been used as part of the admissions process for higher education in Sweden and is designed to assess the abilities necessary to be successful in this area. The SweSAT consists of five sections, which measure vocabulary, numerical problem solving and reasoning, reading comprehension in both Swedish and English, and the ability to utilize information from different sources such as maps, tables, and graphs (Cliffordson, 2004; Carlstedt & Gustafsson, 2005).

Another important cognitive test developed and used in Sweden is the enlistment battery, known as the CAT-SEB, which is a general intelligence test used to screen men who want to enlist in the military. Unlike the SweSAT, the CAT-SEB is based on a specific intelligence model and seeks to measure the constructs of general intelligence, crystallized intelligence, and broad visual perception. The test is computer administered and consists of 10 subtests, which include verbal and nonverbal tasks and require knowledge of vocabulary, spatial reasoning ability, logic, and problem-solving (Carlstedt & Gustafsson, 2005).

Also from the Nordic region are the KTK Performance Scales from Finland. One of the goals in developing this test was to make it as nearly "culture free" as possible, so that exposure to different objects or ideas would not heavily influence scores. This instrument originated as a performance-based test for children ages 2.5 to 11, with subtests such as figures drawn from memory, a block design using multicolored blocks to replicate a pattern, dot patterns in which children have to locate and trace shapes, block analogies in which children must select a block to complete a pattern, and sorting based on Vygotsky blocks (blocks of different sizes, shapes, colors, textures, and thicknesses; Elonen, Takala, & Ruopilla, 1963).

Often, an indigenous intelligence test focuses on aspects of intelligence that are deemed important by the particular country in which it was created, either as part of that country's model of intelligence or as a contribution to the type of intelligence research being conducted. For instance, in Germany, a large amount of research has been done on information processing and how the speed of processing correlates with other intellectual functions (Li & Kunzmann, 2004). A group of psychologists, including Frank and Lehrl, would come to be known as the Erlangen school. Their major research contribution was the idea that information processing, which consists of both speed of information processing and short-term memory, is a major facet of intelligence, which can account for individual differences in intelligence as measured psychometrically. As would be expected, several tests created in Germany have a focus on information processing. One of these tests is the Zahlen-Verbindungs Test (ZVT), a trail-making test developed in 1978 by Oswald and Roth. This test measures processing speed by timing participants while they draw lines to connect, in order, circles containing the numbers 1–90, which are distributed randomly on the page. The completion time is usually one minute or less (Vernon, 1993). This measure was reported in the manual by Oswald and Roth (as cited by Vernon, 1993) to be highly correlated with other measures of intelligence, such as the Raven's Progressive Matrices and other general IQ tests, including the Hamburg-Wechsler-Intelligenztest fur Erwachsene (Oswald & Roth, 1987). The ZVT also exists in several alternate forms, which use the same basic concept but change the rules and patterns of the search or whether the circles contain numbers, letters, or both (Vernon, 1993).

Another test developed in Germany is the Kurztest fur Allgemeine Intelligenze (KAI), developed by Lehrl. Also based on an information-processing theory of intelligence, the KAI is a very brief intelligence test that consists of two subtests. The first involves reading letters aloud quickly and is scored based on completion time, and the second involves repeating remembered sequences of numbers and letters and is scored based on the longest sequence that has been correctly recalled (Wolters, 2005).

Africa

Africa is one of the sites where the indigenous versus adapted test debate is hotly contested. The processes measured by imported tests often do not fully encompass the idea of intelligence held by societies in Africa, which as noted previously can have less to do with cognitive skills and more to do with practical abilities and social competences. Serpell and Pitts Haynes (2004) describe some current problems with intelligence testing in Africa, noting that while the tests are used to "fit" people to professions that would best suit them, how well they ultimately perform in the selected profession is not well predicted by the tests. Most countries in Africa were found to use achievement tests rather than aptitude tests, and those that used aptitude tests were faced with problems of boys and people from urban as opposed to rural settings seemingly being favored by the test. This bias was justified by some as the proper selection of people who are likely to do well in a system based on the same intellectual values measured by the test, but Serpell and Pitts Haynes (2004) rejected this explanation, noting that it amounts to little beyond the circular reasoning that what is measured by an intelligence test must be intelligence.

Another issue that creates bias in tests is that instruments are sometimes not restandardized on local populations before being administered, a phenomenon noted particularly in Zimbabwe by Mpofu and Nyanungo (1998). The purpose of standardization is to create a large, representative sample of the population to which the test will be administered, which can then be used to locate where any given test taker's score falls relative to his or her population. When tests are not restandardized on local populations, test takers are being compared to populations in the location where the test was originally standardized, with corresponding demographics, rather than to people in their own communities, which often have dramatically different demographics. Naturally, the people who will rise to the top on this test are those who are most similar in background to the ones on whom the test was originally standardized, and scores of all test takers will have little contextual relevance. Others, such as Kathuria and Serpell (1998), noted that even when tests are restandardized, those with similarity to populations for whom the tests were originally intended will still be favored, as the test was written with the original population in mind.

Mpofu and Nyanungo (1998) noted that intelligence testing in schools in Zimbabwe largely used imported tests from the United States and Europe, with the Goodenough Draw-a-Person Test and the WISC-R as the most popular instruments. Only the WISC-R and Goodenough tests had local norms established. Zimbabwean children tended to score lower on the WISC-R and British Ability Scales (BAS) than their European and American counterparts, a difference attributed to test items that were more appropriate for children from locations for which the test was originally intended. The authors specifically cited as an example a question regarding the distance between two cities in England. This question was more appropriate for English children than for children in Zimbabwe. Scores on the Goodenough, however, were similar cross-culturally, suggesting less cultural bias. The authors noted that the test is one that can be group administered. Because it is nonverbal, it is convenient to use with a variety of populations in Zimbabwe.

Intelligence tests in Zimbabwean schools are mainly used for classification but are also used by educational psychologists to explore how children think. For the latter purpose, test procedures such as discontinuing time limits are usually not followed, and the "right" answers are not as important as how children arrived at their answers. This fact suggests that the way intelligence is viewed in Zimbabwe emphasizes the process of thinking rather than simple results that do not convey how a child obtained a certain answer – a notion similar to the one used in France (Mpofu & Nyanungo, 1998). This difference in emphasis could certainly signify a difference in conceptualizations of intelligence.

Since cultural bias plays a role in many imported tests used in Africa, some researchers have tried to find ways to overcome these contextual issues. Kathuria and Serpell (1998) standardized the Panga Munthu test, intended to measure the intellectual abilities of children in Zambia in a culturally fair way. In this assessment, children are asked to represent a person using clay, a material found to be familiar to children of this target population, in a task somewhat similar to the Draw-a-Person test. The representations are then judged against predetermined criteria, and children receive points for every criterion met by their representation. The emphasis of this test is on knowledge of basic human anatomy, something most individuals have access to and are exposed to continuously, rather than on knowledge obtained through education or perceptual skills.

Although many countries in Africa, like many countries worldwide, import intelligence measures, several tests have been constructed there as well, particularly in South Africa. The Junior South African Intelligence Scale (JSAIS), intended for the cognitive assessment of children, was published in 1981 for use with both English and Afrikaans-speaking children. The test consists of 22 subtests, 12 of which produce a general intelligence quotient, as well as scores on verbal, performance, and memory scales. Tasks included noting missing parts, judging what was incorrect in absurdities, measuring forms meaningfully as well as tests of verbal general knowledge, picture riddles, word association, and story memory. While some tasks, such as block design, general knowledge, and absurdities seem familiar in concept to modern versions of the Wechsler or Stanford-Binet scales, others such as story memory are less frequently employed by American intelligence tests (Luiz & Heimes, 1988).

Asia

China has a long history of educational testing and is believed to be the first nation to employ intelligence tests in personnel selection (Niu, 2007; Grigorenko, Jarvin, Niu, & Preiss, 2007; Shi, 2004; Zhang, 1988). Interest in Western intelligence tests began in 1916, when the Stanford-Binet was introduced into China and was eventually turned into the Chinese-Binet Intelligence Test by Lu Zhiwei (Song & Zhang, 1987). Many other Western tests were imported, translated, adapted, and standardized during the first half of the 20th century. By the early 1930s, a total of 20 intelligence and personality tests, as well as 50 educational achievement tests, had been introduced into China, initiating the rise in popularity of Western test instruments (Shi, 2004). Such developments led to the establishment of the Society of Psychological Testing in 1931 and the creation of a professional journal named *Testing* in 1932 (Zhang, 1988). The trend of introducing and revising Western psychological testing experienced a downturn between 1949 and 1978 as a result of various political movements in China. China reopened its doors to the West in early 1980s, and began modernizing its agriculture, industry, and technology, a process that necessitated having talented and intelligent people in various fields. Identification of these people became important, and one test created in China was the Cognitive Ability Test for Identifying Supernormal Children (CATISC), developed by Zha and colleagues. This test was built around the belief that the most important components of intelligence include memory, analogy, observation, and creative thinking as well as certain personality traits, indicating a tendency toward a more Eastern than Western conception, as personality is often left entirely out of the Western definitions of intelligence (Niu, 2007; Shi, 2004).

One recently designed measure in China is the Chinese Intelligence Scale for Young Children (CISYC). The test is suitable for children ages 3 through 7, and consists of 10 subtests, which are grouped on verbal comprehension and spatial perception factors. Subtests include familiar ones from the Wechsler scales such as cancellation, block design, digit span, picture vocabulary, picture concepts, arithmetic, and information, as well as "tangram," which involves forming figures with tangram pieces; "spatial imagination," in which children view the same object from different angles to identify it; and "window," in which a child must memorize and repeat the sequence in which a toy cat sticks it head out of different windows. Guo, Aveyard, and Dai (2009) recently looked at the CISYC to learn whether the four-factor structure employed by the WISC would make more sense as a factor structure for this test as well, adding processing speed and working memory as factors. The main issue they hoped to address was the bias in intelligence testing caused by the discrepant situations of urban versus rural children in China; vast differences between these groups had led to separate norms for each group due to an invariant factor structure between them. They indeed found no evidence of cultural bias when interpreting the test using the four-factor model, despite the differences in educational level and socioeconomic status of these two groups – the factor structure was equivalent for both. Although this test was developed in China, the test was not developed to be significantly more reflective of the Chinese view of intelligence than a more Westernized view. Though some tasks are different, emphasizing things like visual memory and three-dimensional spatial understanding, which are not specifically focused on in the regular version of the WISC, the test can be interpreted using the factor structure used in the WISC and contains many similar subtests. Because the test ultimately measures the same concepts, it cannot stray very far from the Wechsler operationalization of intelligence.

Although Japan is not geographically close to Europe, the epicenter of intelligence testing, the trend caught on quickly (Osaka, 1961). Educators in Japan found themselves interested in understanding the intelligence level of their students in the interest of providing the best education for each and were therefore ready and willing to accept the idea of intelligence testing (Sato et al., 2004). By 1908, the 1905 version of the Binet-Simon Intelligence Test had been brought to Japan by K. Miyake and Ikeda of Tokyo Imperial University. Ueno, a psychologist, brought later versions of the scale to educational leaders (Osaka, 1961). Intelligence testing became an important, at times even overused, method for evaluating students' suitability for higher education and constructing educational plans that addressed students' individuality (Sato et al., 2004).

Following World War I, competition for admission to secondary schools became so fierce that the problem of admission decisions and the basis on which they were made needed to be addressed, leading to the creation of an entrance exam for the Attached Secondary School of Tokyo Higher Normal School, which measured skills in language and mathematics. Although the test fell out of use soon after its development due to the amount of work that specialists needed to put into it every year, this test caught the attention of many and triggered a period of intelligence test construction in Japan. The first large-scale test intended to measure group intelligence in Japan was the Group National Intelligence Test, created by Watanabe and colleagues in 1921 for the purpose of measuring intelligence in elementary school students (Osaka, 1961). Verbal and nonverbal tests adapted from the U.S. Army test also saw widespread use. Intelligence testing spread to areas outside education, for example, to people entering military or industry fields (Sato et al., 2004).

From 1931 to the end of World War II, the intelligence measurement movement died down and the Japanese people became increasingly discontent with relying on methods of intelligence measurement developed by the Western world. During this time, tests were developed for infant assessment, and K. Tanaka tested people cross-culturally to compare Japanese children with children in China and the United States, concluding that the Japanese children had intelligence superior to children from other nations, on the basis more of qualitative observations than of quantitative data (Osaka, 1961).

After World War II, a period of educational assessment and reform led to renewed interest in ways to measure achievement and intelligence, and many individual and group intelligence instruments were developed. On the recommendation of an educational advisor from the United States, Japan adopted the SAT college entrance exam, to be administered to all candidates for national and prefectural colleges. In 1947, about 115,000 students were tested using this instrument; by 1954, the number had risen to more than 338,500 students, and the SAT had become a factor of great influence in college-admissions decisions. Controversy soon began to develop, as people wondered how valid the test was – if it served its purpose well, it should correspond highly with regular examinations given to the students in school. However, too high a correspondence would suggest that the SAT was redundant and not necessary as a separate entity from regular school testing, while too low a correspondence would suggest low validity (Osaka, 1961). In addition, the SAT was incompatible with one of the major tenets of the Japanese view of intelligence, the idea that effort is important in intelligence; the SAT catered more to the American view that ability is what matters most in intelligence (Sato et al., 2004). In the wake of this disagreement, the National Association of High School Principals passed a resolution to abolish the SAT, and it fell out of use after 1955. Meanwhile, adapted versions of Western tests, such as a Japanese adaptation of the Wechsler Bellevue Intelligence Test for Children by Kodama and Shinagawa in 1953, began to be recognized as some of the most reliable tests available for use. In the period following, test development began to level off, with differentiation of tests – for instance, tests for different age levels or different points in the school year – taking a more prominent role than development of new tests. Tests for groups such as the deaf and gifted were also created. By the 1960s, Osaka (1961) reported that at least 50 intelligence tests were in circulation.

One significant instance of indigenous test development was the Kyoto University NX Intelligence Test, developed in 1953 by R. Osaka and A. Umemoto, which is still currently in use in Japan. The test is intended for group administration, and different versions target different age levels. An SX version is also available for testing gifted individuals above the age of 15, as one goal of test development was to have a test to measure extremes of intelligence (Sato et al., 2004). Processes tapped by this test include spatial reasoning, quantitative reasoning, verbal fluency, verbal reasoning, and memory, and the test developers hoped to measure both inherent and acquired intelligence (Osaka, 1961).

Interest in Western intelligence tests has also been evident in other parts of Asia. In Israel, for example, the Psychometric Entrance Test (PET) is used for the higher admissions process. It is similar to the American SAT (Zeidner, Matthews, & Roberts, 2004). Although the PET originally contained subtests measuring general intelligence and figural reasoning, it was changed in the early 1990s to more closely mimic the SAT. It now consists of verbal reasoning, which generally contains synonyms, antonyms, analogies, sentence completions, logic, and reading comprehension; quantitative reasoning, which involves numerical and algebraic problem solving as well as numerical data analysis; and a section evaluating the ability to understand English as a foreign language, which tests the ability to comprehend academic level texts in English through sentence completions, reading comprehension, and restatements (Beller, 2001; Beller & Gafni, 1995).

Alnabhan and Harwell (2001) discussed the work being done to establish an aptitude test to be used as part of the admissions process for higher education in Jordan. Anticipation of a need for a well-educated workforce led the Jordanian Council of Higher Education to look for a way to make decisions about who would be successful in college. The team constructing the test consisted of experts in the domains of statistics, English, Arabic, mathematics, and science. Questions for a pilot test were of a multiple choice format in domains such as verbal skills.

Although tests around the world contain tasks different from those in some of the Western tests we are familiar with in this country, very few seem to be based on entirely different models of intelligence. Even countries that incorporate different ideas such as effort or social responsibility into their conceptualizations of intelligence do not frequently incorporate these ideas into tests used to measure intelligence in their citizens. Generally, countries that have constructed their own tests also rely on translations or adaptations of instruments such as the Wechsler scales or Stanford-Binet. While these instruments have proven to be reliable and valid, they do not always match the values of the cultures in which they are being used. Although intelligence is defined differently throughout the world, the testing of intelligence suggests that what we are content to measure as intelligence may remain far more consistent than our definitions across cultures.

Conclusion

The major quest of this chapter has been to investigate how people from different cultures perceive and measure intelligence. To answer the first part of the question, we reviewed studies on implicit theories of intelligence from some selected cultures around the world. The overall picture is that intelligence is defined and perceived differently by people from different parts of the world, and that these difference are largely reflective of long-standing cultural traditions. Just as Greenfield observed (1998), "cultures define intelligence by what is adaptive in their particular niche," reflecting the multifaceted nature of intelligence. Many contemporary experts on theories of intelligences have addressed this multidimensionality of intelligence (Gardner, 1993, 1995; Mayer, Salovey, & Caruso, 2000; Sternberg, 1997), discussing multiple intelligences (Gardner, 1993), successful intelligences, (Sternberg, 1997), or simply an inclusion of emotional intelligence (Mayer, Salovey, & Caruso, 2000; Sternberg, 1997). In other words, most people would agree that there are many aspects of intelligence, but what is emphasized depends on culture. For example, many studies have documented that the Western notion of intelligence places more emphasis on cognitive competencies such as attention, speed of learning, logical reasoning, and language comprehension than is considered important in other cultures (Sternberg et al., 1981). This distinction may reflect the cultural tradition of the West, where behaviors leading to control over the physical environment are highly valued (White, 1959). The Western notion of intelligence also strongly emphasizes one's innate ability, a value that can be traced back to ancient Western philosophers such as Plato. Different from the notion of the West, people from the rest of world have their own distinctive focuses. In many Chinese societies, despite the differences in political ideology, economic development, and even ethnic background, most people believe that knowledge and intelligence are closely related to each other. In their conception, one should also have good comprehension skills and good judgment about the immediate surroundings. Therefore, an intelligent person should have good cognitive competence, a curious mind, a thirst for knowledge, a wide range of knowledge, and a good memory (that is ready to take in yet more knowledge). These qualities are closely related to the Chinese cultural tradition of Confucianism, the ideas of which regarding intelligence were quoted in the beginning of the chapter. Although the Japanese view of intelligence was also influenced by Confucianism, the concept of effort, which is very important in the Japanese implicit theory of intelligence, is also largely a result of past and present societal values. In India, following from a cultural tradition in which individuals are evaluated by how sensitive they are to the social context, as well as by possession of qualities such as chivalry, rectitude, and righteousness, cognitive competence accounts for only one-third of what lay Indians see as intelligence. A full two-thirds of their implicit theory refers to domains such as social competence, emotional competence, and competence in action. Recognizing the importance of maintaining harmonious and stable intergroup relationships, the African conception of intelligence strongly emphasizes practical and social components.

The answer to the second part of the question presents a totally different picture from that of the first part; that is, although intelligence is perceived differently, similar measures of intelligence are widely adopted by people across different cultures. Many countries have constructed their own measures of intelligence to suit both their own purposes, such as admissions to schools or professions, and their own values, such as information-processing tests in Germany. However, these measures often seem to be used in conjunction with measures imported from Western countries such as the Wechsler scales, Stanford-Binet, and K-ABC, and many countries rely solely on these imported instruments. Therefore, while understandings of intelligence throughout the world are multifaceted, nuanced, and varied in terms of underlying intellectual qualities, what is measured as intelligence across many countries is largely consistent. A benefit of using an instrument such as the WISC is its proven reliability and validity in measuring its underlying construct of intelligence, which is solely cognitively based. The mismatch comes when imported tests based only on cognitive ability are used in countries that value social, emotional, or practical everyday aspects in construing one's general intelligence level, as imported tests largely do not meet these purposes.

What causes this discrepancy between the conception of intelligence and the measurement of intelligence? We believe there are at least four factors accounting for this departure. First, although there might be different foci in terms of what constitutes intelligence, people from different cultures all recognize the importance of cognitive components in their conceptions of intelligence. This part of intelligence can be viewed as more nearly universal and hence can be measured by similar tests. Second, measures of intelligence are primarily used for academic placement, such as for school entrance and tracking. Although many people criticize such a practice, it is still regarded as an effective way of allocating resources and of helping route students into specific areas of the labor market. This is especially the case in many developing societies, where resources are limited and a need for a quick and relatively objective way to place people is dire. Despite their many limitations, compared to other types of measurements, IQ tests still demonstrate the highest predictive validity of one's academic achievement. Third, studies have consistently shown a moderate to strong correlation between a person's academic achievement and the analytical component of intelligence, measured by traditional IQ tests such as the Cognitive Abilities Tests (CAT) and the WISC-III (Brody, 1992; Frey & Detterman, 2004; Jensen, 1998; Neisser et al., 1996; Sternberg, Grigorenko, & Bundy, 2001; Watkins, Glutting, & Lei, 2007). It is not surprising that both researchers and educators still use traditional types of IQ tests in assessing individuals. Last, creation of a new measurement based on contemporary theories of intelligences with a broader coverage to measure one's true intelligence is extremely difficult. Although there have been several such attempts (Brackett & Mayer, 2003; Gardner, 1993; 1995; Mayer, Salovey, & Caruso, 2000, 2002, 2004; Stemler & Sternberg, 2006; Sternberg, 2003; Tirri & Nokelainen, 2008), the road to perfecting these measurements while also meeting people's practical needs is still long and rough. It took many decades for the traditional IQ tests to mature and to be accepted by people in just one culture; it may require more intensive work to make new measurements capturing the important features of intelligence that will suit each particular society's need.

We also observe an interesting phenomenon from reviewing recent studies on implicit views of intelligence in the West: Just like the expert explicit theories of intelligence, Western laypeople's implicit theories of intelligence have gradually evolved from primarily focusing on cognitive abilities to emphasizing a comprehensive list of attributes including social competence and even moral components of intelligence.

Paulhus, Whr, Harms, and Strasser (2002) asked American and Canadian college students to list names of well-known people in history or current affairs who are ideal examples of intelligent individuals. The results showed that the individuals named can be clustered into five distinctive categories, representing five different types of intelligences, such as scientific intelligence (e.g., Einstein and Hawking), artistic intelligence (e.g., Mozart and Shakespeare), entrepreneurial intelligence (e.g., Turner, Trump, and Gates), communicative intelligence (e.g., President Clinton, Prime Minister Jean Chrétien, Oprah Winfrey), and moral intelligence (e.g., Gandhi and Martin Luther King, Jr.).

In other words, it seems that not only did Western notions of intelligence influence people's perception and practice in measuring intelligence across the rest of the world but also that other cultures and their views of intelligence have helped shape what contemporary Westerners view as intelligence. Conceptions of intelligence are more inclusive than they used to be. Although there will always be multiple views regarding intelligence, we believe knowing how people from different parts of the world define intelligence will only enhance our ability to capture the concept better, and to measure it more accurately.

References

Alnabhan, M., & Harwell, M. (2001). Psychometric challenges in developing a college admission test for Jordan. *Social Behavior and Personality*, 29(5), 445–458.

Azuma, H., & Kashiwagi, K. (1987). Descriptions for an intelligent person: A Japanese study. *Japanese Psychological Research*, 29, 17–26.

Bai, X. Liu, H., & Hu, X. (2007). Development of high school teachers and students' view on implicit theories of intelligence. [Chinese]. *Studies of Psychology and Behavior*, 5(2), 81–85.

Beller, M. (2001). Admission to higher education in Israel and the role of the psychometric entrance test: Educational and political dilemmas. *Assessment in Education*, 8(3), 2001.

Beller, M., & Gafni, N. (1995). Equating and validating translated scholastic aptitude tests: The Israeli case. In G. Ben-Shakhar & A. Lieblich (Eds.), *Studies in psychology in honor of Solomon Kugelmass* (pp. 202–219). Jerusalem, Israel: Magnes Press.

Berg, L. A., & Sternberg, R. J. (1992). Adults' conceptions of intelligence across the adult life span. *Psychology and Aging*, 7, 221–231.

Bleichrodt, N., Hoksbergen, R. A. C., & Khire, Usha. (1999). Cross-cultural testing of intelligence. *Cross-Cultural Research: The Journal of Comparative Social Science*, 33(1), 3–25.

Boake, C. (2002) From the Binet-Simon to the Wechsler-Bellevue: Tracing the history of intelligence testing. *Journal of Clinical and Experimental Neuropsychology*, 24(3), 383–405.

Brackett, M. A., & Mayer, J. D. (2003). Convergent, discriminate, and incremental validity of competing measures of EI. *Personality and Social Psychology Bulletin*, 29(9), 1147–1158.

Brody, N. (1992). *Intelligence* (2nd ed.). San Diego, CA: Academic Press.

Bruner, J. S., Shapiro, D., & Tagiuri, R. (1958). The meaning of traits in isolation and in combination. In R. Tagiuri & L. Petrullo (Eds.), *Person perception and interpersonal behavior* (pp. 278–288). Stanford, CA: Stanford University Press.

Cai, X., & Jiang, L. (1995). A cross-cultural study of the intellectual concepts of junior and senior middle school students from five nationalities in Southwest China. [Chinese] *Science of Psychology*, 18, 346–350.

Carlstedt, B., & Gustafsson, J. (2005). Construct validation of the Swedish Scholastic Aptitude Test by means of the Swedish Enlistment Battery. *Scandinavian Journal of Psychology*, 46(1), 31–42.

Carlstedt, B., Gustafsson, J., & Hautamäki, J. (2004). Intelligence – theory, research, and testing in the Nordic countries. In R. J. Sternberg (Ed.), *International handbook of intelligence* (pp. 49–78). New York, NY: Cambridge University Press.

Chen, M. J. (1994). Chinese and Australian concepts of intelligence. *Psychology and Developing Societies*, *6*, 101–117.

Chen, M. J., Braithwaite, V., & Huang, J. T. (1982). Attributes of intelligent behaviour: Perceived relevance and difficulty by Australian and Chinese students. *Journal of Cross-Cultural Psychology*, **13**, 139–156.

Chen, M. J., & Chen, H. C. (1988). Conceptions of intelligence: A comparison of Chinese graduates from Chinese and English schools in Hong Kong. *International Journal of Psychology*, **23**, 471–487.

Cliffordson, C. (2004). Effects of practice and intellectual growth on performance on the Swedish Scholastic Aptitude Test (SweSAT). *European Journal of Psychological Assessment*, **20**(3), 192–204.

Cole, M., Gay, J., & Glick, J. (1967). A cross-cultural study of clustering in free recall. *Psychonomic Bulletin*, **1**(2), 18.

Comaroff, J. (1975). Talking politics: Oratory and authority in a Tswana Chiefdom. In M. Bolch (Ed.), *Political language and oratory in traditional society*. London, UK: Academic Press.

Comaroff, J., & Roberts, S. A. (1981). *Rules and process: The cultural logic of dispute in an African context*. Chicago, IL: University of Chicago Press.

Confucius. (2010). The doctrine of the mean (J. Leggs, Trans.) .Whitefish, MT: Kessinger. (Original translation published 1893)

Deary, I. J., & Smith, P. (2004). Intelligence research and assessment in the United Kingdom. In R. J. Sternberg (Ed.), *International handbook of intelligence* (pp. 1–48). New York, NY: Cambridge University Press.

Detterman, D. K. (1986). Qualitative integration: The last word? In R. J. Sternberg & D. K. Detterman (Eds.), *What is intelligence: Contemporary viewpoints on its nature and definition* (pp. 163–166). Norwood, NJ: Ablex.

Elonen, A. S., Takala, M., & Ruoppila, I. (1963). *A study of intellectual functions in children by means of the KTK performance scales*. Oxford, UK: Kystantajat.

Fang, F., & Keat, D. (1987). A cross-cultural study on the conception of intelligence. [Chinese] *Acta Psychologica Sinica*, **19**(3), 255–262.

Frey, M.C., & Detterman, D. K. (2004). Scholastic assessment or g? The relationship between the scholastic assessment test and general cognitive ability. *Psychological Science*, **15**(6), 373–378.

Furnham, A., & Fukumoto, S. (2008). Japanese parents' estimates of their own and their children's multiple intelligences: Cultural modesty and moderate differentiation. *Japanese Psychological Research*, **50**(2), 63–76.

Furnham, A., Hosoe, T., & Tang, T. (2002). Male hubris and female humility? A cross-cultural study of ratings of self, parental and sibling multiple intelligences in America, Britain and Japan. *Intelligence*, **30**, 101–105.

Furnham, A., & Mkhize, N. (2004). Indian and Isi-Zulu-speaking South African parents' estimates of their own and their children's intelligence. *South African Journal of Psychology*, **34**, 363–385.

Garcia-Cepero, M. C., & McCoach, D. B. (2009). Educators' implicit theories of intelligence and beliefs about the identification of gifted students. *Universitas Psychologica*, 8(2), 295–310.

Gardner, H. (1995). Reflections on multiple intelligences: Myths and messages. *Phi Delta Kappan*, 77, 200–203, 206–209.

Gardner, H. (1993). *Multiple intelligences: The theory in practice*. New York, NY: Basic Books.

Georgas, J., Van de Vijver, F. J. R., Weiss, L. G., & Saklofske, D. H. (2003). In J. Georgas, L. G. Weiss, F. J. Van de Vijver, & D. H. Saflofske (Eds.), *Culture and children's intelligence: Cross-cultural analysis of the WISC-III* (pp. 227–240). San Diego, CA: Academic Press.

Gill, R., & Keats, D. (1980). Elements of intellectual competence: Judgments by Australian and Malay university students. *Journal of Cross-Cultural Psychology*, **11**, 233–243.

Greenfield, P. M. (1997). You can't take it with you: Why ability assessments don't cross cultures. *American Psychologist*, **52**, 1115–1124.

Greenfield, P. M. (1998). The cultural evolution of IQ. In U. Neisser (Ed.), *The rising curve: Long term gains in IQ and related measures* (pp. 81–123). Washington, DC: American Psychological Association.

Grigorenko, E. L., Geissler, P. W., Prince, R., Okatcha, F., Nokes, C., et al. (2001). The organisation of Luo conceptions of intelligence: A study of implicit theories of Kenya village. *International Journal of Behavioral Development*, **25**(4), 367–378.

Grigorenko, E. L., Jarvin, L., Niu, W., & Preiss, D. (2007). Is there a standard for standardized testing? In P.C. Kyllonen, R. D. Roberts, & L. Stankov (Eds.), *Extending intelligence: Enhancement and new constructs* (pp. 157–182). Mahwah, NJ: Erlbaum.

Guo, B., Aveyard, P., & Dai, X. (2009). The Chinese Intelligence Scale for Young Children: Testing factor structure and invariance using the framework of the Wechsler Intelligence Tests. *Educational and Psychological Measurement*, 69(3), 459–474.

Harris, S. H. (1982). An evaluation of the Snijders-Oomen Nonverbal Intelligence Scale for Children. *Journal of Pediatric Psychology*, 7(3), 239–251.

Hill, V. (2005). Through the past darkly: A review of the British Ability Scales, second edition. *Child and Adolescent Mental Health*, 10(2), 87–98.

Holloway, S. D. (1988). Concepts of ability and effort in Japan and the United States. *Review of Educational Research*, 58(3), 327–345.

Hooker, R., & Hines, R. K. (1996). *World civilizations: A world classroom and anthology – Plato.* Retrieved January 21, 2010, from http://wsu.edu/~dee/GREECE/PLATO.HTM.

Jensen, A. (1998). The suppressed relationship between IQ and the reaction time slope parameter of the Hick function. *Intelligence*, 26(1), 43–52.

Kathuria, R., & Serpell, R. (1998). Standardization of the Panga Munthu test: A nonverbal cognitive test developed in Zambia. *Journal of Negro Education*, 67(3), 228–241.

Kopic, K., Vranic, A., & Zarevski, P. (2009). Implicit theories of intelligence in elementary school eighth-grade pupils. *Drustvena Istrazivanja*, 18(3), 503–521.

Kwak, K. (2003). South Korea. In J. Georgas, L. G. Weiss, F. J. Van de Vijver, & D. H. Saflofske (Eds.), *Culture and children's intelligence: Cross-cultural analysis of the WISC-III* (227–240). San Diego, CA: Academic Press.

Lautrey, J., & Ribaupierre, A. (2004). Psychology of human intelligence in France and French-speaking Switzerland. In R. J. Sternberg (Ed.), *International handbook of intelligence* (pp. 104–134). New York, NY: Cambridge University Press.

Li, S., & Kunzmann, U. (2004). Research on intelligence in German-speaking countries. In R. J. Sternberg (Ed.), *International handbook of intelligence* (pp. 135–169). New York, NY: Cambridge University Press.

Lim, W., Plucker, J. A., & Im, K. (2002). We are more alike than we think we are: Implicit theories of intelligence with a Korean sample. *Intelligence*, 30(2),185–208.

Luiz, D. M., & Heimes, L. (1988). The Junior South African Intelligence Scales and the Griffiths Scale of Mental Development: A correlative study. In D. M. Luiz (Ed.), *Griffith Scales of Mental Development* (pp. 1–15). Port Elizabeth, South Africa: University of Port Elizabeth.

Mayer, J. D., Salovey, P., & Caruso, D. (2004). Emotional intelligence: Theory, findings, and implications. *Psychological Inquiry*,15(3), 197–215.

Mayer, J. D., Salovey, P., & Caruso, D. (2002). *Mayer-Salovey-Caruso Emotional Intelligence Test (MSCEIT)*, Version 2.0. Toronto, Canada: Multi-Health Systems.

Mayer, J. D., Salovey, P., & Caruso, D. (2000). Models of emotional intelligence. In R. J. Sternberg (Ed.), *Handbook of intelligence* (pp. 396–420). New York, NY: Cambridge University Press.

Mpofu, E., & Nyanungo, K. R. (1998). Educational and psychological testing in Zimbabwean schools: Past, present and future. *European Journal of Psychological Assessment*, 4(1), 71–90.

Muñiz, J., Bartram, D., Evers, A., Boben, D., Matesic, K., Glabeke, K., et al. (2001). Testing practices in European countries. *European Journal of Psychological Assessment*, 17(3), 201–211.

Muñiz, J., Prieto, G., Almeida, L., & Bartram, D. (1999). Test use in Spain, Portugal and Latin American countries. *European Journal of Psychological Assessment*, 15(2), 151–157.

Neisser, U. (1979). The concept of intelligence. In R. J. Sternberg & D. T. Detterman (Eds.), *Human intelligence: Perspectives on its theory and measurement* (pp.179–189). Norwood, NJ: Ablex.

Neisser, U., Boodoo, G., Bouchard, T. J., Boykin, A.W., Brody, N., Ceci, S. J., et al. (1996). Intelligence: Knowns and unknowns. *American Psychologist*, 51(2), 77–101.

Niu, W. (2007). Western influence on Chinese educational testing system. *Comparative Education*, 43(1), 71–91.

Osaka, R. (1961). Intelligence tests in Japan. *Psychologia, Kyoto*, 4(4), 218–234.

Oswald, W. D., & Roth, E. (1987). *Der Zahlen-Verbindungs-Test (ZVT) Handanweisung (Manual)*. Gottingen, Germany: Hogrefe.

Paulhus, D. L. Wehr, P., Harms, P. D., & Strasser, D. I. (2002). Use of exemplar surveys to reveal implicit types of intelligence. *Personality and Social Psychology Bulletin*, 28, 1051–1062.

Peng, K., & Nisbett, R. E. (1999). Culture, dialectics, and reasoning about contradiction. *American Psychologist*, 54(9), 741–754.

Plato. (1992). *The Republic* (G. M. A. Grube, Trans., 2nd ed.). Indianapolis, IN: Hackett.

Rosas, R. (2004). Intelligence research in Latin America. In R. J. Sternberg (Ed.), *International handbook of intelligence* (pp. 391–410). New York, NY: Cambridge University Press.

Ruzgis, P. M., & Grigorenko, E. L. (1994). Cultural meaning systems, intelligence and personality. In R. J. Sternberg & P. Ruzgis (Eds.), *Personality and intelligence* (pp. 248–270). New York, NY: Cambridge University Press.

Sato, T., Namiki, H., Ando, J., & Hatano, G. (2004). Japanese conception of and research on human intelligence. In R. J. Sternberg (Ed.), *International handbook of intelligence* (pp. 302–324). New York, NY: Cambridge University Press.

Serpell, R. (1974). Aspects of intelligence in a developing country. *African Social Research*, 17, 576–596.

Serpell, R. (2000). Intelligence and culture. In R. J. Sternberg (Ed.), *Handbook of intelligence* (pp. 549–580). New York, NY: Cambridge University Press.

Serpell, R., & Jere-Folotiya, J. (2008). Developmental assessment, cultural context, gender, and schooling in Zambia. *International Journal of Psychology*, 43(2), 88–96.

Serpell, R., & Pitts Haynes, B. (2004). The cultural practice of intelligence testing: Problems of international export. In R. J. Sternberg & E. L. Grigorenko (Eds.), *Culture and competence: Contexts of life success* (pp. 163–185). Washington, DC: American Psychological Association.

Shi, J. (2004). Diligence makes people smart: Chinese perspectives of intelligence. In R. J. Sternberg (Ed.), *International handbook of intelligence* (pp. 325–343). New York, NY: Cambridge University Press.

Song, W., & Zhang, Y. (1987) *Psychology measurement*. Beijing, China: Science Press.

Srivastava, A. K., & Misra, G. (2001). Lay people's understanding and use of intelligence: An Indian perspective. *Psychology Developing Societies*, 13, 25–49.

Stemler, S. E., & Sternberg, R. J. (2006). Using situational judgment tests to measure practical intelligence. In J. A.Weekley & R. E. Ployhart (Eds.), *Situational judgment tests: Theory, measurement, and application* (pp. 107–131). Mahwah, NJ: Erlbaum.

Sternberg, R. J. (1985). Implicit theories of intelligence, creativity, and wisdom. *Journal of Personality and Social Psychology*, 49, 607–627.

Sternberg, R. J. (1997). *Successful intelligence*. New York, NY: Plume.

Sternberg, R. J. (2003). Construct validity of the theory of successful intelligence. In R. J. Sternbger, J. Lautrey, & Lubart, T. I. (Eds.), *Models of intelligence: International perspectives* (pp. 55–77). Washington, DC: American Psychological Association.

Sternberg, R. J. (2004). Culture and intelligence. *American Psychologist*, 59, 325–338.

Sternberg, R. J., Conway, B. E., Ketron, J. L., & Bernstein, M. (1981). People's conceptions of intelligence. *Journal of Personality and Social Psychology*, 41(1), 37–55.

Sternberg, R. J., & Grigorenko, E. L. (2004). Why we need to explore development in its cultural context. *Merrill-Palmer Quarterly*, 50(3), 369–386.

Sternberg, R. J., & Grigorenko, E. L. (2006). Cultural intelligence and successful intelligence. *Group & Organization Management*, 31(1), 27–39.

Sternberg, R. J., & Grigorenko, E. L. (2007). Ability testing across cultures. In L. Suzuki (Ed.), *Handbook of multicultural assessment* (3rd ed., pp. 449–470). San Francisco, CA: Jossey-Bass.

Sternberg, R. J., Grigorenko, E. L., Ngorosho, D., Tantufuye, E., Mbise, A., Nokes, Catherine, et al. (2002). Assessing intellectual potential in rural Tanzanian school children. *Intelligence*, 30(2), 141–162.

Sternberg, R. J., Grigorenko, E. L., & Brundy, D. A. (2001). The predictive value of IQ. *Merrill-Palmer Quarterly*, 47(1), 1–41.

Sternberg, R. J., Nokes, C., Geissler, P. W., Prince, R., Okatcha, F., Bundy, D. A., et al. (2001). The relationship between academic and practical intelligence: A case study in Kenya. *Intelligence*, 29(5), 401–418.

Swami, V., Furnham, A., Maakip, I., Ahmad, M. S., Naw, N. H. M., Voo P. S. K., et al. (2008). Beliefs about the meaning and measurement of intelligence: A cross-cultural comparison of American, British, and Malaysian undergraduates. *Applied Cognitive Psychology*, 22(2), 235–246.

te Nijenhuis, J., Tolboom, E., Resing, W., & Bleichrodt, N. (2004). Does cultural background influence the intellectual performance of children from immigrant groups? The RAKIT intelligence test for immigrant children. *European Journal of Psychological Assessment*, 20(1), 10–26.

Tellegen, P., & Laros, J. (1993). The construction and validation of a nonverbal test of intelligence: The revision of the Snijders-Oomen Tests. *European Journal of Psychological Assessment*, 9(2), 147–157.

Tirri, K., & Nokelainen, P. (2008). Identification of multiple intelligences with the Multiple Intelligence Profiling Questionnaire III. *Psychology Science*, 50(2), Special issue: High Ability Assessment, 206–221.

Van de Vijver, F. J. R. (2003). Principles of adaptation of intelligence tests to other cultures. In J. Georgas, L. G. Weiss, F. J. Van de Vijver, & D. H. Saflofske (Eds.), *Culture and children's intelligence: Cross-cultural analysis of the WISC-III* (pp. 255–263). San Diego, CA: Academic Press.

Ueda, N. (1989). *Japanese children's personal theories of intelligence: A developmental study*. Doctoral dissertation, Harvard University. ProQuest Digital Dissertation, AAT 9000889.

Vernon, P. (1993). Der Zahlen-Verbindungs-Test and other trail-making correlates of general intelligence. *Personality and Individual Differences*, 14(1), 35–40.

Wan, M., Li, N., & Jing, Q. (1997). A cross-cultural study on middle school and high school students' implicit theories of intelligence: Comparison among Han, Tabitan, and Dongxiang Chinese students. [Chinese] *Psychological Development and Education*, 2, 1–6.

Watkins, M. W., Glutting, J. J., & Lei, P-W. (2007). Validity of the full-scale IQ when there is significant variability among WISC-III and WISC-IV factor scores. *Applied Neuropsychology*, 14(1),13–20.

White, R. W. (1959). Motivation reconsidered: The concept of competence. *Psychological Review*, 66, 297–333.

Wober, M. (1974). Towards an understanding of the Kigranda concept of intelligence. In J. W. Berry & P. R. Dasen (Eds.), *Culture and cognition* (pp. 261–280). London, UK: Methuen.

Wolters, M., Hickstein, M., Flintermann, A., Tewes, U., & Hahn, A. (2005). Cognitive performance in relation to vitamin status in healthy elderly German women – the effect of a 6- month multivitamin supplementation. *Preventative Medicine*, 41, 253–259.

Yang, S. -Y., & Sternberg, R. J. (1997a). Conceptions of intelligence in ancient Chinese philosophy. *Journal of Theoretical and Philosophical Psychology*, 17,101–119.

Yang, S. -Y., & Sternberg, R. J. (1997b). Taiwanese Chinese people's conceptions of intelligence. *Intelligence*, 25, 21–36.

Zeidner, M., Matthews, G., & Roberts, R. D. (2004). Intelligence theory, assessment, and research: The Israeli experience. In R. J. Sternberg (Ed.), *International handbook of intelligence* (pp. 212–247). New York, NY: Cambridge University Press.

Zhang, H. (1988) Psychological measurement in China. *International Journal of Psychology*, 23,101–117.

Zhang, H., & Wu, Z. (1994). People's conceptions of intelligence: A study of Beijing residents' conceptions of intelligence. (Chinese) *Science of Psychology*, 17(2), 65–69, 81.

CHAPTER 32

Secular Changes in Intelligence

James R. Flynn

Whether the 20th century has seen intelligence gains is controversial. Whether there have been massive IQ gains over time is not. This difference orders my task. I will (1) describe the range and pattern of IQ gains; (2) discuss their cognitive significance; (3) describe their significance for today's world; (4) argue that they suggest a new theory of intelligence; (5) speculate about what may happen during the 21st century.

The Evidence and Its Peculiarities

Reed Tuddenham (1948) was the first to present convincing evidence of massive gains on mental tests using a nationwide sample. He showed that U.S. soldiers had made about a 14-point gain on Armed Forces tests between World War I and World War II or almost a full standard deviation (SD = 15 throughout). The tests in question had a high loading on the kind of material taught in the classroom and he thought the gains were primarily a measure of improved schooling. Therefore, they seemed to have no theoretical implications, and because the tests were not among those used by clinical psychologists, the practical implications were ignored. It was when Flynn (1984, 1987) showed that massive gains had occurred in the United States on Wechsler and Stanford-Binet IQ tests, and that they had occurred throughout the industrialized world, even on tests thought to be pure measures of intelligence, that IQ gains took center stage. Within a decade, Herrnstein and Murray (1994), the authors of *The Bell Curve*, called the phenomenon "the Flynn effect."

Nations with data about IQ trends stand at 30. Scandinavian nations show that IQ gains may not last much beyond the end of the 20th century, at least in the developed world. Their scores peaked about 1990 and since then, may have gone into mild decline. Several other nations still show robust gains. Americans are still gaining at their historic rate of 0.30 points per year (WAIS 1995–2006; WISC 1989–2002). British children were a bit below that on Raven's from 1980 to 2008, but their current rate of gain is higher than in the earlier period from 1943 to 1980. Other gains cover long periods, so whether the rate varied approaching the present is unknown. Urban Argentines (ages 13 to 24) made a 22-point gain on Raven's between 1964 and 1998. Children in urban Brazil (1930–2002), Estonia (1935–1998), and Spain (1970–1999) made gains akin to the U.S. rate (Colom, Lluis Font, & Andres-Pueyo, 2005; Colom, Flores-Mendoza, & Abad, 2007; Emanuelsson, Reuterberg, & Svensson, 1993; Flynn, 2009a,b,c; Flynn & Rossi-Casé, under review; Must, Must, & Raudik, 2003; Schneider, 2006; Sundet, Barlaug, & Torjussen, 2004; Teasdale & Owen, 1989, 2000).

The developing world shows explosive gains in rural Kenya and the Caribbean. In Sudan, large fluid gains (WAIS Performance Scale) were accompanied by a small loss for crystallized intelligence (Daley et al., 2003; Khaleefa, Sulman, & Lynn, 2009; Meisenberg et al., 2005). If third-world nations continue to gain over the 21st century, and the developed nations do not, the present IQ gap between the two will disappear.

Dutch data illustrate why IQ gains were so disturbing. Between 1952 and 1982, young Dutch males gained 20 IQ points on a test of 40 items selected from Raven's Progressive Matrices (Flynn, 1987). The sample was exhaustive. Raven's was supposed to be the exemplar of a culturally reduced test, one that should have shown no gains over time as culture evolved. These 18-year-olds had reached the age at which performance on Raven's peaks. Therefore, their gains could not be dismissed as early maturation, that is, it was not just a matter that children today matured about two years earlier than the children of yesterday. Current people would have a much higher IQ than the last generation even after both had reached maturity.

These gains created a crisis of confidence: How could such huge gains be intelligence gains? The gains amounted to 1.33 SDs. This would put the average Dutchman of 1982 at the 90th percentile of Dutch in 1952. Psychologists faced a paradox: Either the people of today were far brighter than their parents or, at least in some circumstances, IQ tests were not good measures of intelligence.

Table 32.1 reveals some of the peculiarities of IQ gains. First, it shows how large American gains have been on the most frequently used tests, namely, the Wechsler tests. Both the WISC (Wechsler Intelligence Scale for Children) and the WAIS (Wechsler Adult Intelligence Scale) show full-scale IQ gains proceeding at 0.30 points per year over the last half of the 20th century, a rate often found in other nations, for a total gain of over 15 points. If we link this to earlier data, like that of Tuddenham, the gain over the whole 20th century has been at least 30 points. Second, for children, there is a marked contrast between small gains on subtests close to school-taught subjects (Information, Arithmetic, Vocabulary) and large gains on subtests that require solving a problem on the spot (Picture Completion, Block Design, Coding). The former are often classified as *crystallized* subtests, those that measure what an intelligent person is likely to learn over a lifetime, and the latter as *fluid* subtests, those that measure intelligence by forcing you to solve problems in the test room for which you have no previously learned method.

This WISC pattern of larger gains on fluid than crystallized subtests is international. For example, Raven's gains are huge everywhere and it is the epitome of a fluid test: You study a matrix pattern with a piece missing and must recognize that piece from alternatives, only one of which is correct. For later reference, look at the bottom of the table and note the huge gains on the Similarities subtest, which is a measure of the ability to classify and defies to some degree the crystallized/fluid dichotomy. Also note a new peculiarity that has just come to light. Adults differ from children: The fluid gains of the latter are five times their crystallized gains, while the fluid gains of the former are only slightly greater. This is largely because since 1950, U.S. children have made only a minimal vocabulary gain of 4.40 points, while U.S. adults have made a huge gain of 17.80 points. It is not yet known whether this is an international phenomenon. Other U.S. data suggest that the growing discrepancy between U.S. adults and their children is largely active vocabulary, the words you use, rather than passive vocabulary, the words

Table 32.1. American WISC (Schoolchildren) and WAIS (Adults) Gains

	Rising Full-Scale IQ			
	1947.5	1972	1989	2001.75
WISC	100.00	107.63	113.00	117.63
	1953.5	1978	1995	2006
WAIS	100.00	107.50	111.70	115.07

Contrast between gains on crystallized and fluid subtests (over a shared period of 54 years)

	WISC	*WAIS*
Information (C)	2.15	8.40
Arithmetic (C)	2.30	3.50
Vocabulary (C)	4.40	17.80
Average crystallized	**2.95**	**9.90**
Picture Completion (F)	11.70	11.20
Block Design (F)	15.90	10.25
Coding (F)	18.00	16.15
Average fluid	**15.20**	**12.53**

Subtests ranked by the difference between adult and child gains (over a shared period of 54 years)

	Difference IQ points		*Difference percentages*	
	WAIS – WISC	*Points*	*WAIS/WISC*	*Percentages*
Vocabulary	17.80 – 4.40 =	13.40	17.80 / 4.40 =	405
Information	8.40 – 2.15 =	6.25	8.40 / 2.15 =	391
Comprehension	13.80 – 11.00 =	2.80	13.80 /11.00 =	125
Arithmetic	3.50 – 2.30 =	1.20	3.50 / 2.30 =	152
Picture Completion	11.20 – 11.70 =	–0.50	11.20/ 11.70 =	96
Coding	16.15 – 18.00 =	–1.85	16.15/ 18.00 =	92
Similarities	19.55 – 23.85 =	–4.30	19.55/23.85 =	82
Block Design	10.25 – 15.90 =	–5.65	10.25/ 15.90 =	64

Sources: Flynn, 2009b; 2009c; under review-b.

you understand when you hear them used (Flynn, under review-b).

The only thing that can be said at present is that the discrepancy does not seem to be because adults have their university education behind them, while their children are still in school. Perhaps it is symptomatic of a trend over the last 50 years for U.S. teenagers to retreat into the subculture of their peers with its own peculiar dialect; and then join the adult speech community as they age and participate in the world of work.

The pattern of IQ gains over time has a final peculiarity, namely, it is not consistently factor-invariant (Wicherts et al., 2004). Factor analysis is a technique that measures the extent to which those who excel on some IQ subtests also excel on others. The tendency toward general excellence is not peculiar to cognitive tests. Just as those who have larger vocabularies also tend to be better at arithmetical reasoning and solving matrices problems, so people who are good at one musical instrument are often good at another, and people good at one sport are often good at almost all sports. The measure of the tendency for a variety of skills to intercorrelate is call *g* (the general intelligence factor). If the top person on one subtest of the WISC topped all the others, and so on down the line, *g* would "explain" 100 percent of the pattern of test performance and have a value of 1.00. If a person's score on each subtest were no more of an indication of their performance on any other subtest than a score chosen at random, *g* would be zero.

One subtest may have a higher *g*-loading than another. This means that it is a better guide as to who will do well on the other subtests. For example, if you added an 11th WISC subtest on shoe tying, it would have a *g*-loading of close to zero: How fast you tie your shoes would have little relation to the size of your vocabulary. On the other hand, your score on the Vocabulary subtest might be a pretty good predictor of your scores on the other subtests (except shoe tying) and get a *g*-loading of 0.75. You could then rank the subtests into a hierarchy according to the size of their *g*-loadings. When this is done, it is evident that the skills with the greatest cognitive complexity top the *g*-loading hierarchy, which is to say that the more complex the task, the greater will be the gap between high-IQ people and the average person. This seems to give *g* a good case to be identified with intelligence and suggests that there might be a latent trait, general intelligence; and that to the extent to which a person possesses that trait, the better he or she will do on a whole range of cognitive tasks.

We can now understand why it is thought significant that IQ gains are not consistently factor invariant. As far as *g* is concerned, this means that when we rank subtests by their *g*-loadings, we find that the magnitude of IQ gains on the various subtest does not tally: The largest IQ gain over time may be on a subtest with an average *g*-loading and the smallest gain may be on a subtest with an above-average *g*-loading. This convinced Jensen (1998) that the bulk of IQ gains were not *g* gains and therefore, were not intelligence gains. He suggests that IQ gains may be largely "hollow," that is, they are a bundle of subtest-specific skills that have little real-world significance.

Two Kinds of Significance

Before we accept the interpretation of IQ gains as hollow, it is useful to supplement factor analysis with functional analysis. Factor analysis may disclose latent traits but no one can do latent traits. What we do in the real world is perform, better or worse, functional activities, such as speaking, solving arithmetic problems, and reasoning about scientific and moral questions. To contrast the two kinds of analysis, I will use a sports analogy.

If we factor analyzed performances on the 10 events of the decathlon, a general factor or *g* would emerge and very likely subordinate factors representing speed (the sprints), spring (jumping events), and strength (throwing events). We would get a *g* because at a given time and place, performance on the 10 events would be intercorrelated, that is, someone who tended to be superior on any one would tend to be above average on all. We would also get various *g*-loadings for the 10 events, that is, superior performers would tend to rise further above average on some of them than on the others. The 100 meters would have a much higher *g* loading than the 1,500 meters, which involves an endurance factor not clearly necessary in the other events.

Decathlon *g* might well have much utility in predicting performance differences between athletes of the same age cohort. However, if we used it to predict progress over time and forecast that trends on the 10 events would move in tandem, we would go astray. That is because decathlon *g* cannot discriminate between pairs of events in terms of the extent to which they are functionally related.

Let us assume that the 100 meters, the hurdles, and the high jump all had large and similar *g* loadings, as they almost certainly would. A sprinter needs upper body strength as well as speed, a hurdler needs speed and spring, a high jumper needs spring and timing. I have no doubt that a good athlete would best the average athlete handily on all three at a given place and time. However, over time, social priorities change. People become obsessed with the 100 meters as the most spectacular spectator event (the world's fastest human). Young people find success in this event a secondary sex characteristic of great allure. Over 30 years, performance escalates by a full SD in the 100 meters, by half a standard deviation in the hurdles, and not at all in the high jump.

In sum, the trends do not mimic the relative *g* loadings of the "subtests." One pair of events highly correlated (sprint and hurdles) shows a modest trend for both to move in the same direction and another pair equally highly correlated (sprint and high jump) shows trends greatly at variance. Factor loadings have proved deceptive about whether various athletic skills are functionally independent. We can react to this in two ways: Either confront the surprising autonomy of various skills and seek a solution by depth analysis of how they function in the real world; or deny that anything real has happened and classify the trends over time as artifacts. The second option is sterile. It is equivalent to saying that if trends are not factor invariant, they are artifacts by definition.

It is better to talk to some athletics coaches. They tell us that over the years, everyone has become focused on the 100 meters and it is hard to get people to take other events as seriously as in the past. They point out that sprint speed may be highly correlated with high jump performance but past a certain point, it is actually counterproductive. If you hurl yourself at the bar at maximum speed, your forward momentum cannot be converted into upward lift and you are likely to time your jump badly. They are not surprised that increased sprint speed has made some contribution to the hurdles because speed between the hurdles is important. But it is only half the story: You have to control your speed so that you take the same number of steps between hurdles and always jump off the same foot. If you told these coaches that you found it surprising that real-world shifts in priorities, and the real-world functional relationships between events, ignored the factor loadings of the events, they would find your mind-set surprising.

Back to the WISC subtests: Arithmetic, Information, Vocabulary, and Similarities all load heavily on *g* and on a shared verbal factor. Despite this, as Table 32.1 shows, between 1947 and 2002, American children gained 24 points on Similarities, 4 points on Vocabulary, and only 2 points on Arithmetic and Information. This is to say that the pattern of gains bears little relation to factor loadings and cannot qualify as factor invariant. However, as usual, factor analysis was done in a static setting with social change held constant. It has no necessary applicability to the dynamic scenario of social priorities altering over time. Thus, *g*-loadings turn out to be bad guides as to which real-world cognitive skills are merely correlated and which are functionally related. To anticipate, a social change over time like people putting on scientific spectacles might greatly enhance the ability to classify (Similarities) without affecting everyday vocabulary or fund of general information. Nonetheless all of these trends would be of great significance, and to dismiss them as "hollow" would be a barrier to understanding the cognitive history of our time.

Interpretation and Causes

Ideally, everyone would approach the cause of massive IQ gains evidentially. But inevitably, a scholar's interpretation of their significance affects his or her list of what causes seem most likely.

If you think that IQ trends are significant as barometers of a shift in cognitive priorities over time, you are likely to focus on cultural factors. But if you believe that they are mainly hollow with a residue that is true intelligence or *g* gains, and that *g* is a latent trait that has its home in brain physiology, you will turn to causes that might affect brain physiology, such as improved nutrition or hybrid vigor (Lynn, 1989, 1990, 1993, 1998; Migronni, 2007). The latter refers to the fact that too much inbreeding is a negative influence on a whole range of human traits including intelligence, as inbreeding between first and second cousins eventually produces IQ deficits. If a nation's population was divided at the beginning of the 20th century into small and inbred communities and then, over time, became more mobile, it would reap the benefits of out-breeding (hybrid vigor) and the nation's mean IQ would rise.

The evidence calls enhanced out-breeding into question as an important cause, at least in developed nations in the 20th century. America was never a collection of isolated communities that discovered geographical mobility only in the 20th century. Right from the start, there was a huge influx of migrants who settled in both urban and rural areas. There were major population shifts during settlement of the West, after the Civil War, and during the World Wars. The growth of mobility has been modest: In 1870, 23% of Americans were living in a state other than the one of their birth; in 1970, the figure was 32% (Mosler & Catley, 1998). Recent data from Norway compare the scores of males as they reach 18 with the scores of their older siblings who reached 18 a few years earlier. If the younger sibling outscores the older, this signals an IQ gain over time (the reverse would signal a loss over time). The IQ trends yielded by these comparisons exactly match the magnitude of the nation's IQ trends (Sundet et al., in press). Because siblings cannot differ in their degree of out-breeding, this shows that hybrid vigor has not been a factor in modern Scandinavia. If it had, the within-sibling estimate would fall short of the actual trend.

In the developed world, better nutrition was probably a factor before 1950, but not since. The nutrition hypothesis posits greater IQ gains in the lower half of the IQ curve than the upper half. The assumption is that even in the past, the upper classes were well fed, while the nutritional deficiencies of the lower classes have gradually diminished. IQ gains have been concentrated in the lower half of the curve in Denmark, Spain, and Norway, but not in Argentina, France, the Netherlands, and the United States. Norway is actually a counterexample: Height gains were larger in the upper half of the distribution while IQ gains were higher in the lower half (Sundet, Barlaug, & Torjussen, 2004). It is unlikely that enhanced nutrition both raises height more than IQ and IQ more than height. British trends are fatal. They do not show the IQ gap between the top and bottom halves reducing over time. The difference was large on the eve of the Great Depression, contracted 1940 to 1942, expanded 1964 to 1971, contacted 1972 to 1977, and has expanded ever since. No coherent dietary history of England can offer the alteration of feast and famine needed to explain these trends (Flynn, 2009a, 2009c).

As noted, those who think IQ trends are barometers that register a shift in cognitive priorities over time will look toward cultural evolution for causes. Flynn (2009a) tried to simplify the explanatory task by focusing on the observation that the largest IQ gains were on Raven's Progressive Matrices and the Similarities subtest of the Wechsler battery.

He asked what "habits of mind" people needed to get the right answers as given in the scoring manuals. Take Similarities: When asked, "What do dogs and rabbits have in common?" the correct answer is that "they are both mammals" rather than "we use dogs to hunt rabbits." The right answer assumes that you are conditioned to look at the world through scientific spectacles – as something to be understood by classification rather than through utilitarian spectacles – as something to be manipulated to advantage. Raven's is all about using logic to deal with sequences of abstract shapes that have no counterpart in concrete reality. If a mind is habituated to taking hypothetical problems seriously and to using logic to deal with the hypothetical, this seems perfectly natural. If you are unaccustomed to using logic for anything but to deal with the concrete world, and indeed distrust reasoning that is not grounded in the concrete, you are unaccustomed to the change of gears that Raven's requires. Like classification, the reasoning rewarded is of the sort that science, which is all about taking explanatory hypotheses seriously, entails.

The next step is rather like an archaeological excavation: Dig into the past hoping to find evidence that appears relevant and assemble it bit by bit. Fortunately, Luria recorded interviews with isolated rural people (Russians in the 1920s) who still lived in prescientific cognitive environments. Here is one about classification:

Fish and Crows (Luria, 1976, p. 82)

Q: What do a fish and a crow have in common?
A: A fish – it lives in water. A crow flies. If the fish just lies on top of the water, the crow could peck at it. A crow can eat a fish but a fish can't eat a crow.
Q: Could you use one word for them both?
A: If you call them "animals," that wouldn't be right. A fish isn't an animal and a crow isn't either. A crow can eat a fish but a fish can't eat a bird. A person can eat a fish but not a crow.

Note that even after an abstract term is suggested, the "correct" answer is still alien. Today we are so familiar with the categories of science that it seems obvious that the most important attribute things have in common is that they are both animate, or mammals, or chemical compounds. However, people attached to the concrete will not find those categories natural at all. First, they will be far more reluctant to classify. Second, when they do classify, they will have a strong preference for concrete similarities (two things look alike, two animals are functionally related, for example, one eats the other) over a similarity in terms of abstract categories. The Similarities subtest assumes exactly the opposite, that is, it damns the concrete in favor of the abstract.

Here is an interview about using logic to analyze the hypothetical:

Camels and Germany (Luria, 1976, p. 112)

Q: There are no camels in Germany; the city of B is in Germany; are there camels there or not?
A: I don't know, I have never seen German villages. If B is a large city, there should be camels there.
Q: But what if there aren't any in all of Germany?
A: If B is a village, there is probably no room for camels.

Today, we are accustomed to detaching logic from the concrete, and say, "of course there would be no camels in this hypothetical German city." The person whose life is grounded in concrete reality rather than in a world of symbols is baffled. Who has ever seen a city of any size without camels? The inhibition is not primarily due to limited experience but rather to a refusal to treat the problem as anything other than concrete. Imagine that the syllogism said there were no dogs in a large German city. The concrete response is that there *must* be dogs in German cities – who would want or be able to exterminate them all? And if one is not practiced in dealing with using logic on hypothetical problems that at least use concrete imagery, what of the hypothetical problems of Raven's that are stated in terms of abstractions with no concrete referent?

Unlike today, when we are bombarded with symbols, the Americans of 1900 had a poverty of experience with such. The only artificial images they saw were drawings or photographs, both of which tended to be representational. Aside from basic Arithmetic, nonverbal symbols were restricted to musical notation (for an elite) and playing cards (except for the religious). They saw the world through utilitarian spectacles:

Their minds were focused on ownership, the useful, the beneficial, and the harmful; and not on the hypothetical and abstract classification.

Genovese (2002) has done his own dig into America's past. He compared the exams the state of Ohio gave to 14-year-old schoolchildren between 1902 and 1913 and between 1997 and 1999. The former tested for in-depth knowledge of culturally valued information; the latter expected only superficial knowledge of such information and tested for understanding complex relationships between concepts. The former were likely to ask you to name the capitals of the (then) 48 states. The latter tended to ask you why the largest city of a state was rarely the state capital (rural members dominated state legislatures, hated the big city, and bestowed the capital on a rural town). Genovese (2002, p. 101) concludes: "These findings suggest that there have been substantial changes in the cognitive skills valued by Ohio educators over the course of the 20th century." We now have a clue as to why there have been virtually no score gains on the WISC general information subtest.

Thus far, the proffered causes of the huge gains on Similarities and Raven's have to do with the minds that took the tests. A full analysis would be multilayered. The ultimate cause of IQ gains is the Industrial Revolution. The intermediate causes are probably its social consequences, such as a better ratio of adults to children, richer interaction between parent and child, better schooling, more cognitively demanding jobs, and cognitively challenging leisure (Neisser, 1998). Donning scientific spectacles with the attendant emphasis on classification and logical analysis is only the proximate cause.

In fairness, biological causes like hybrid vigor and nutrition are usually precise enough to be at risk of falsification. Cultural history, like all history, suggests causes that may be plausible but difficult to quantify and test. More digging is needed if the scenario offered herein is to inspire confidence.

Interpretation and Effects

There is another avenue toward enhanced plausibility. Make "predictions" about what we ought to find in the real world – *if* trends on the WISC subtests are clues to the evolution of functional skills rather than "hollow." Here are a half a dozen: (1) Tutoring children on Raven's should do little to improve their mathematical problem-solving skills. (2) Enhanced performance on school reading and English courses should decline after the age of 14. (3) Enhanced performance in school mathematics should show the same pattern. (4) Popular entertainment should be more cognitively complex and less "literal" in its plot lines. (5) Cognitively demanding games like chess should show large performance gains over time. (6) The quality of moral and political debate should have risen over time.

It is tempting to identify mathematical thinking with the cognitive problems posed by Raven's. Raven's demands that you think out problems on the spot without a previously learned method for doing so, and Mathematics requires mastering new proofs dealing with nonverbal material. They are highly correlated in terms of factor loadings, which seems to signal that they require similar cognitive skills. Therefore, it seems sensible to teach young children Raven's-type problems in the hope that they will become better mathematics problem solvers. U.S. schools have been doing that since 1991 (Blair, Gamson, Thorne, & Baker, 2005, pp. 100–101).

Here IQ gains validate their credentials as a diagnostician of functional relationships between cognitive skills. The large gains on Raven's since 1950 and the virtually nil gains on Arithmetic (see Table 32.1) show that the relationship between the two is no more functional than the relationship between sprinting and the high jump. Sadly, our understanding of the functional process for learning Arithmetic is far behind our understanding of the high jump. Some speculation: Except for mathematicians who link the formulas with proofs, mathematics is less a logical enterprise than a separate reality with its own laws that are at variance with those of the natural world. Therefore, just as infants explore the natural world, children must explore the world of mathematics themselves and become familiar with its "objects" by self-discovery.

Subtests that show minimal gains have as much explanatory potential as those that show huge gains. Since 1950, there have been very minimal gains on the WISC subtests that measure whether children have an adequate fund of general information and a decent vocabulary and whether they can reason arithmetically (Table 32.1). These are very close to school-taught skills. Let us see what they tell us about U.S. trends on the National Association of Educational Progress (NAEP) tests, often called the nation's report card.

The NAEP tests are administered to large representative samples of 4th-, 8th-, and 12th-graders. From 1971 to 2002, 4th- and 8th-graders (average age 11 years old) made a reading gain equivalent to almost four IQ points. However, by the 12th grade, the reading gain drops off to almost nothing (U.S. Department of Education, 2000, pp. 104, 110; 2003, p. 21). The IQ data suggest an interesting possibility. For the sake of comparability, we will focus on WISC trends from 1972 to 2002, rather than on the full period beginning in 1947. Between 1972 and 2002, U.S. schoolchildren made no gain in their store of general information and only minimal vocabulary gains (Flynn, 2009c). Therefore, while today's children may learn to master preadult literature at a younger age, they are no better prepared for reading more demanding adult literature.

You cannot enjoy *War and Peace* if you have to run to the dictionary or encyclopedia every other paragraph. Take Browning's poem:

> Over the Kremlin's pavement bright
> With serpentine and syenite,
> Steps, with other five generals
> That simultaneously take snuff,
> For each to have pretext enough
> And kerchiefwise unfold his sash
> Which, softness self, is yet the stuff
> To hold fast where a steel chain snaps,
> And leave the grand white neck no gash

If you do not know what the Kremlin is, or what "serpentine" means, or that taking snuff involves using a snuff rag, you will hardly realize that these generals caught the czar unaware and strangled him.

In other words, today's schoolchildren opened up an early lead on their parents (who were schoolchildren circa 1972) by learning the mechanics of reading at an earlier age. But by age 17, their parents had caught up. And because current students are no better than their parents in terms of vocabulary and general information, the two generations at 17 are dead equal in their ability to read the adult literature expected of a senior in high school.

From 1973 to 2000, the Nation's Report Card shows 4th- and 8th-graders making mathematics gains equivalent to almost seven IQ points. These put the young children of 2000 at the 68th percentile of their parents' generation. But once again, the gain falls off at the 12th grade, this time to literally nothing (U.S. Department of Education, 2000, pp. 54, 60–61; 2001, p. 24). And once again, the relevant WISC subtest suggests why.

The Arithmetic subtest and the NAEP mathematics tests present a composite picture. An increasing percentage of young children have been mastering the computational skills the Nation's Report Card emphasizes at those ages. However, WISC Arithmetic measures both computational skills and something extra. The questions are put verbally and often in a context that requires more than a times-table-type answer. For example, take an item like this: "If 4 toys cost $6, how much do 7 cost?" Many subjects who can do straight paper calculations cannot diagnose the two operations required: that you must first divide and then multiply. Others cannot do mental arithmetic involving fractions. In other words, WISC Arithmetic also tests for the kind of mind that is likely to be able to reason mathematically.

My hypothesis is that during the period in which children mastered calculating skills at an earlier age, they made no progress in acquiring mathematical reasoning skills. Reasoning skills are essential for higher mathematics. Therefore, by the 12th grade, the failure to develop enhanced mathematical problem-solving strategies begins to bite. American schoolchildren cannot do Algebra and Geometry any better than the previous generation. Once again, although the previous generation was slower to master computational skills, they were no worse off at graduation.

We turn to the worlds of leisure and popular entertainment. Greenfield (1998) argues that videogames, popular electronic games, and computer applications cause enhanced problem solving in visual and symbolic contexts; if that is so, that kind of enhanced problem solving is necessary if we are to fully enjoy our leisure. Johnson (2005) points to the cognitive demands of videogames, for example, the spatial geometry of Tetris, the engineering riddles of Myst, and the mapping of Grand Theft Auto.

However, Johnson's most important contribution is his analysis of television. TV aims at a mass audience and therefore, its level of cognitive complexity is based on an estimate of what the average person can assimilate. Johnson shows convincingly that today's popular TV programs make unprecedented cognitive demands. The popular shows of a generation ago, such as *I Love Lucy* and *Dragnet* and *Starsky and Hutch*, were simplistic, requiring virtually no concentration to follow. Beginning in 1981 with *Hill Street Blues*, single-episode drama began to be replaced with dramas that wove together as many as 10 threads into the plot line. A recent episode of the hit drama *24* connected the lives of 21 characters, each with a distinct story.

Howard (1999) uses traditional games as an informal measure of cognitive gains. He speaks of "cascading feed-back loops": More people want to play chess, the average skill rises, chess clubs form, coaching and chess books improve with rising demand, so you have even better average performance, and so on. He evidences the trend toward enhanced skills by documenting the decline in the age of chess grandmasters. There is no doubt that the standard of play in chess tournaments has risen (Nunn, 1999). Howard makes the same case, although the evidence is less compelling, for feedback loops in other leisure activities that are cognitively demanding such as bridge and go.

Has the quality of political debate risen over the 20th century? Rosenau and Fagan (1997) compare the 1918 debate on women's suffrage with recent debates on women's rights and make an excellent case that the latter shows less contempt for logic and relevance. Note the setting, namely, debate that goes into the *Congressional Record*. That members of Congress have become unwilling to give their colleagues a mindless harangue to read does not mean that all forms of political debate have improved.

We need more research with a proper focus. I suspect that improvement has been limited to written material of some length, that is, material designed to persuade the solitary reader who can take as long as he or she likes to mull over what is said. I anticipate no improvement in two categories. First, speeches to live audiences meant to reduce them to an unthinking mob. William Jennings Bryan's dreadful "Cross of Gold" speech sets the standard for stump oratory today as much as it did over a century ago. Second, there are media events in which the speaker has a few minutes to pack in the most effective sound bites. This is the natural arena of the spin doctor and its standard was set in New Zealand by a candidate who catapulted his party up the polls by using the words "family," "moderate," and "reasonable" more often in five minutes than one would think possible. What we need is a survey covering 50 years of news stories and opinion essays in semiserious publications like *Newsweek* and the *New York Times*.

I know of no study that measures whether the quality of moral debate has risen over the 20th century. However, I will show why it should have. The key is that more people take the hypothetical seriously, and taking the hypothetical seriously is a prerequisite to getting serious moral debate off the ground. When my brother and I would argue with our father about race, and when he endorsed discrimination, we would say, "But what if your skin turned black?" A man born in 1885, and firmly grounded in the concrete, he would reply, "That is the dumbest thing you have ever said – whom do you know whose skin has ever turned black?" I have never encountered contemporary racists who responded in that way. They feel that they must take the hypothetical seriously, and see that they are being challenged to use reason detached from the concrete to show that their racial judgments are logically consistent. The possibility of better moral debate is so important that it too must be subject to systematic investigation.

We can now offer a summary of the real-world implications of IQ gains. Not IQ gains as such, of course, because they have no real-world implications. Rather, it is a summary of the real-world effects of the cognitive trends that IQ scores have registered. Let's take Raven's and the various Wechsler subtests (Table 32.1) one by one:

Raven's: Massive gains show that people have freed logic from analyzing concrete situations to deal with problems put abstractly. This has been a prerequisite for the vast expansion of tertiary education and professional jobs requiring university skills and creative solution of problems on the spot (Schooler, 1998). Taking hypothetical situations seriously may have rendered moral and political debate more reflective. The full potential of this has not been realized because even the best universities do not give their graduates the tools they need to analyze the modern world except perhaps in their area of specialization (Flynn, under review-a).

Similarities: The huge gains mark a transition from regarding the world as something to be manipulated for use to classifying it using the vocabulary of science. This habit of mind is also a prerequisite for higher education.

Performance subtests: Large gains on these are more difficult to interpret. Certainly, the gains on Block Design signal enhanced ability to solve on the spot problems that require more than the mere application of learned rules.

Comprehension: Since 1947, adults have gained the equivalent of almost 14 IQ points and children 11. This subtest measures the ability to comprehend how the concrete world is organized (why streets are numbered in sequence). The greater complexity of life today seems to pose a challenge the average person has risen to meet.

Information: Over 8 points for adults but only 2 points for children. Presumably this reflects the influence on adults of the expansion of tertiary education.

Arithmetic: The small gains here reveal the failure of education on any level to significantly improve arithmetical reasoning.

Vocabulary: A wider gulf exists between parent and child as noted earlier. Serious writers have a larger adult audience able to read their works, although the visual culture of our time may limit the number of those willing to do so.

Another real-world implication of IQ gains: Past standardization samples performed worse than recent ones, and set lower norms. Therefore, obsolete IQ tests give higher scores than up-to-date ones. Therefore, someone who took an obsolete test may get 74 when his or her IQ on current norms would be 69. Since a score of 70 is the cutting line for immunity from the death penalty in America, obsolete tests have literally cost lives (Flynn, 2009b).

Measurement Versus History

The phenomenon of IQ gains has created unnecessary controversy because of conceptual confusion. Imagine an archaeologist from the distant future who excavates our civilization and finds a record of performances over time on measures of marksmanship. The test is always the same, that is, how many bullets you can put in a target 100 meters away in a minute. Records from 1865 (the U.S. Civil War) show the best scoring as 5, records from 1898 (Spanish-American War) show 10, while records from 1918 (World War I) show 50.

A group of "marksmanship-metricians" looks at these data. They find it worthless for measuring marksmanship. They make two points. First, they distinguish between the measure and the trait being measured. The mere fact that performance on the test has risen in terms of "items" correct does not mean that marksmanship ability has increased. All we know is that the test has gotten easier. Many things might account for that. Second, they stress that we have only relative and no absolute scales of measurement. We can rank soldiers against one another at each of the three times. But we have no measure that would bridge the transition from one shooting instrument to another. How could you rank the best shot with a rifle against the best shot with a bow and arrow? At this point, the marksmanship-metrician either gives up or looks for something that would allow him to do his job, perhaps some new data that would afford an absolute measure of marksmanship over time.

However, a group of military historians are also present and it is at this point they get excited. They want to know why the test got easier, irrespective of whether the answer aids or undermines the measurement of marksmanship over time. They ask the archaeologists to look further. If they are lucky, battlefields specific to each time will be discovered. The 1865 battlefields disclose the presence of primitive rifles, the 1898 ones, repeating rifles, and the 1918 ones, machine guns. Now we know why it was easier to get more bullets into the target over time and we can confirm that this was no measure of enhanced marksmanship. But it was of enormous historical and social significance: Battle casualties, the industries needed to arm the troops, and so forth altered dramatically.

Any confusion about the two roles has been dispelled. If the battlefields had been the artifacts first discovered, there would have been no confusion because no one uses battlefields as instruments for measuring marksmanship. It was the fact that the first artifacts were also instruments of measurement that put historians and metricians at cross-purposes. Now they see that different concepts dominate their two spheres: social evolution in weaponry – whose significance is that we have become much better at solving the problem of how to kill people quickly; marksmanship – whose significance is determining which people have the ability to kill more skillfully than other people can. The metrician would not deny that the historian's account is important. The historian has done nothing to undermine what the metrician does. Results on his tests have great external validity. They tell us who is likely to be promoted in each of the three wars (insofar as marksmanship is a criterion) and which of two armies equal in other respects is likely to win a battle (the one with the best marksmen).

I hope this analogy will convince psychometricans (whose job it is to measure cognitive skill differences between people) that my interpretation of the significance of IQ gains over time is not adversarial. Let me make its import explicit.

Some years ago, acting as an archaeologist, I amassed a large body of data showing that IQ tests had gotten much easier over the 20th century in America and elsewhere. Over the century, the average person was getting many more items correct on tests like Raven's and Similarities. The response of intelligence- or *g*-metricians was dual: first, to distinguish IQ tests as measuring instruments from the trait being measured, that is, from intelligence or *g* (if you will); second, to note that in the absence of an absolute scale of measurement, the mere fact that the tests had gotten easier told us nothing about whether the trait was being enhanced. The difficulty was inherent. IQ tests were only relative scales of measurement ranking the members of a group in terms of items they found easy to items they found difficult. A radical shift in the ease/difficulty of items meant all bets were off. At this point, the *g*-metrician decides that he cannot do his job of measurement and begins to look for an absolute measure that would allow him to do so.

However, as a cognitive historian, this was where I began to get excited: Why had the items gotten so much easier over time? Where was the alteration in our mental weaponry that was analogous to the transition from the rifle to the machine gun? This meant returning to the role of archaeologist and finding battlefields of the mind that distinguished 1900 from the year 2000. I found evidence of a profound shift from an exclusively utilitarian attitude to concrete reality toward a much more abstract attitude – to assuming that it was important to classify concrete reality in abstract terms (the more abstract the better); and that taking hypothetical situations seriously had freed logic to deal with not only hypothetical questions but also with symbols that had no concrete referents.

It was the initial artifacts that caused all the trouble. Because they were performances on IQ tests, and IQ tests are instruments of measurement, the roles of the cognitive historian and the *g*-metrician were confused. Finding the causes and developing the implications of a shift in habits of mind over time is simply not equivalent to a task of measurement, even the measurement of intelligence. Now all should see that different concepts dominate two spheres: society's demands – whose evolution from one generation to the next dominates the realm of cognitive history; and *g* – which measures individual differences in cognitive ability. And just as the *g*-metrician should not undervalue the nonmeasurement task of the historian, so the historian does nothing to devalue the measurement of which individuals are most likely to learn fastest and best when in competition with one another.

The direct challenge to those who use conventional IQ tests or the *g* derived from them to measure individual differences comes not from cognitive history but from those who believe they have discovered better measures. No one denies that *g*-loaded IQ tests are useful predictors of things like academic achievement and life outcomes like employment or obedience to the law, and whether children are born in or out of wedlock. However, Sternberg has developed tests that measure creativity and practical intelligence as well the analytic skills emphasized in school, and these may give even better predictions of university marks and job performance (Sternberg, 1988, 2006; Sternberg et al., 2000). Heckman has developed research designs that indicate that noncognitive traits are at least as influential as cognitive traits (Heckman & Rubenstein, 2001; Heckman, Stixrud, & Urzua, 2006).

I have used an analogy to break the steel chain of ideas that circumscribed our ability to see the light IQ gains shed on cognitive history. But an analogy that clarifies one thing can introduce a new confusion. The reciprocal causation between developing new weapons and the physique of marksmen is a shadow of the interaction between developing new habits of mind and the brain.

The new weapons were a technological development of something *outside* ourselves that had minimal impact on biology: Perhaps our trigger fingers got slightly different exercise when we fired a machinegun rather than a musket. But the evolution from preoccupation with the concrete and the literal to the abstract and hypothetical was a profound change *within* our minds that involved new problem-solving activities. Reciprocal causation between mind and brain entails that our brains may well be different from those of our ancestors. It is a matter of use and structure.

If people switch from swimming to weight lifting, the new exercise develops different muscles and the enhanced muscles make them better at the new activity. Everything we know about the brain suggests that it is similar to our muscles. Maguire et al. (2000) found that the brains of the best and most experienced London taxidrivers were peculiar. They had an enlarged hippocampus, which is the brain area used for navigating three-dimensional space. Here we see one area of the brain being developed without comparable development of other areas in response to a specialized cognitive activity. It may well be that when we do "Raven's-type" problems, certain centers of our brain are active that used to get little exercise; or it may be that we increase the efficiency of synaptic connections throughout the brain. If we could scan the brains of people in 1900, who knows what differences we would see?

So if we can say that the marksman today shoots a *superior gun* to that of his predecessors, can we not say we have a *superior brain* to that of our ancestors? Not superior in every way, of course. The machine gun's gain in firepower is bought at the price of less maneuverability: If someone approaches you from the rear, you would do better to have a rifle that you can turn around in an instant. Our brain may have lost something our ancestors had – something like the wonderful mapping system that Australian Aborigines use in the outback. But, even granting that each generation has a brain adapted to the society of its day, do not our brains deal with an environment of greater cognitive complexity than in 1900? And is that not sufficient reason to say that we are more intelligent?

We can now resolve the question asked at the beginning: Do the huge IQ gains of the 20th century mean we are more intelligent than our ancestors? If the question is, Do we have better brain potential at conception or were our ancestors too stupid to deal with the concrete world of everyday life, the answer is no. If the question is, Do we live in a time that poses a wider range of cognitive problems than those our ancestors encountered, and have we developed new cognitive skills and the kind of brain that can deal with them, the answer is yes. Once we understand what has happened, we can communicate with one another, even if some prefer the label "more intelligent" and others prefer "different." To care passionately about which label we use is to surrender to the tyranny of words.

The Theory of Intelligence

The thesis about psychometics and cognitive history – that they actually complement one another – and the remarks made about the brain imply a new approach to the theory of intelligence. I believe we need a BIDS approach: one that treats the brain (B), individual differences (ID), and social trends (S) as three distinct levels, each having equal integrity. The three are interrelated and each has the right to propose hypotheses about what ought to happen on another level. It is our job to investigate them independently and then integrate what they tell us into a coherent whole.

The core of a BIDS approach is that each of those levels has its own organizing concept and it is a mistake to impose the architectonic concept of one level on another. The best analogy I can find from the history of science is the controversy between Huygens, who championed the wave theory of light, and Newton, who held that light was a stream of corpuscles (particles). Much time was wasted before someone realized that light could act like a wave in certain of its manifestations and like a stream of particles in other manifestations. We have to realize that intelligence can act like a highly correlated set of abilities on one level (individual differences), like a set of functionally independent abilities on another level (cognitive trends over time), and like a mix on a third level (the brain), whose structure and operations underlie what people do on both of the other two levels. Let us look at the levels and their organizing concepts.

Individual differences. Performance differences between individuals on a wide variety of cognitive tasks are correlated primarily in terms of the cognitive complexity of the task (fluid *g*) – or the posited cognitive complexity of the path toward mastery (crystallized *g*). Information may not seem to differentiate individuals for intelligence, but if two people have the same opportunity, the better mind is likely to accumulate a wider range of information. I will call the appropriate organizing concept "General Intelligence" or *g*, without intending to foreclose improved measures that go beyond the limitations of "academic" intelligence.

Society. Various real-world cognitive skills show different trends over time as a result of shifting social priorities. I will call this concept "Social Adaptation." As I have argued, the major confusion thus far has been *either* to insist on using the organizing concept of the individual differences level to assess cognitive evolution, and call IQ gains "hollow" if they are not *g* gains; *or* to insist on using the organizing concept of the societal level to characterize the measurement of individual differences in intelligence, and to deny that some individuals really do have better minds and brains to deal with the dominant cognitive demands of their time.

The brain. Localized neural clusters are developed differently as a result of specialized cognitive exercise. There are also important factors that affect all neural clusters such as blood supply, dopamine as a substance that render synapses receptive to registering experience, and the input of the stress-response system. Let us call its organizing concept "Neural Federalism." The brain is a system in which a certain degree of autonomy is limited by a "higher" organizational structure.

Here I will linger a bit because researchers on this level have the difficult task of explaining what occurs on both of the other two levels. The task of the brain physiologist is reductionist. To illustrate, assume that physiologists have almost perfect knowledge of the brain: When supplied with data on how cognition varies from person to person and from time to time, they can map exactly what brain "locations" underlie the social and life histories supplied. To flesh this out, make the simplifying assumption that the mind performs only four operations when cognizing: classification or CL (of the Similarities sort); liberated logic or LL (of the Raven's sort); practical intelligence or PI (needed to manipulate the concrete world); and vocabulary and information acquisition or VI.

We will posit that the brain is neatly divided into four sectors active respectively when the mind performs the four mental operations, that is, it is divided into matching CL, LL, PI, and VI sectors. Through magnetic resonance imaging scans (MRI) of the brain, we have "pictures" of these sectors. For example, somehow we have MRIs from 1900 that we can compare to MRIs of 2000. When we measure the connections between neurons within the CL and LL sectors, we find that the later brains have thicker connections, and that the extra thickness exactly predicts the century's enhanced performance on Similarities and Raven's.

As for individual differences, we have equally informative pictures of what is going on in the brains of two people in the VI sector as they enjoy the same exposure to new vocabulary. We note that the neurons (and connections between neurons) of one person are better nourished than those of the other due to optimal blood supply (we know just what the optimum is). We note that when the neurons are used to learn new vocabulary, the connections between the neurons of one person are sprayed with the optimum amount of dopamine and the connections of the other are less adequately sprayed. And we can measure the exact amount of extra thickening of the connections the first person enjoys compared to the second. All of this allows us to actually predict their different performances on the WISC Vocabulary subtest.

Given all of the above, brain physiology would have performed its reductionist task: It would have reduced problem-solving differences between individuals and between generations to brain functions; and it would have accommodated both the tendency of various cognitive skills to be correlated on the individual differences level, and their tendency to show functional autonomy on the societal level.

Our Ancestors and Ourselves

IQ trends over time have opened our eyes to a great romance: the cognitive history of the 20th century. Science altered our lives and then liberated our minds from the concrete.

This history has not been written because, as children of our time, we do not perceive the gulf that separates us from our distant ancestors: the difference between their world and the world seen through scientific spectacles. Moreover, because the ability to cope with the concrete demands of everyday life has not been much enhanced, our distant ancestors appear fully human. People use their minds to adapt to the demands of their social environment. Long before the beginning of the 20th century, people felt a strong need to be cognitively self-sufficient in everyday life and long before 1900, virtually everyone who could meet the demands of everyday life had done so. The small percentage that cannot (those who are genuinely mentally retarded) has not varied much over the last 100 years.

Before 1900, most Americans had a few years of school and then worked long hours in factories, shops, or agriculture. Kinship and church provided identity. Slowly society began to demand that the mass of people come to terms with the cognitive demands of secondary education, and contrary to the confident predictions of the privileged, they met that challenge to a large degree. Mass graduation from secondary school had profound real-world effects. The search for identity became a more individual quest. Education created a mass clientele for books, plays, and the arts, and culture was enriched by contributions from those whose talents had hitherto gone undeveloped.

After 1950, the emergence of a new visual culture and perhaps a resistance to the ever increased demands of classroom subjects brought progress to an end in areas like school mathematics and the appreciation of serious literature. Nonetheless, post-1950 IQ cognitive gains have been significant. More and more people continued to put on scientific spectacles. As use of logic and the hypothetical moved beyond the concrete, people developed new habits of mind. The scientific ethos provided the prerequisites for this advance. However, once minds were prepared to attack these new problems, certain social triggers enhanced performance greatly. Post-1950 affluence meant that people sought cognitive stimulation from leisure. It meant that parents had to rear fewer children and they became preoccupied with affording their children a cognitively stimulating environment. Schools became filled with children and teachers less friendly to rote learning, and the world of work offered more and more professional and managerial jobs. These jobs both required and stimulated the new habits of mind. As this last implies, there was causal interaction: New problems developed new skills and better skills allowed us to cope with an even wider range of problems.

The expanded population of secondary school graduates was a prerequisite for the educational advance of the post-1950 era, that is, the huge increase in the number of university graduates. These graduates have gone the farthest toward viewing the world through scientific spectacles. They are more likely to be innovative and independent and therefore, can meet professional and managerial demands. A greater pool of those suited by temperament to be mathematicians or theoretical scientists or even philosophers, more contact with people who enjoy playing with ideas for its own sake, the improvement of managerial efficiency, the enhancement of leisure, the enhancement of moral and political debate – these things are not to be despised.

Quo Vadis

Lynn and Vanhanen (2002) have engendered pessimism by showing that the mean IQs of many nations in the developing world are well below those in the developed world. However, there are signs that IQ gains may cease in developed nations in the 21st century and evidence that they are just taking off in the developing world. These trends would close the developed/developing IQ gap and falsify the hypothesis that some nations lack the intelligence to industrialize. In 1917, Americans had a mean IQ of 70 (against today's norms), which matches the lowest IQs found in the developing world. IQ does not leap from 70 to 100 as a prerequisite for industrial development. The first step toward modernity raises IQ a bit, which paves the way for the next step, which raises IQ a bit more, and so on. The converging IQ trends may be fragile: An environmental crisis might merely inconvenience rich nations while sending poor nations into a downward spiral toward starvation and anarchy.

Despite static IQ, the developed world may enjoy a century of cognitive progress just as exciting as the last 100 years. Science has not only freed logic from the concrete but has also bestowed a second gift, one on which we have not yet capitalized. I refer to a set of wonderful concepts that allow us to critically analyze the modern world: market analysis, basic social science methodology, analytic concepts that make sense of international relations, philosophical progress toward identifying bad argument particularly in ethics, and so forth. But there is no reason for optimism. Universities seem determined to give each graduate one or two of these tools at best. In the larger society, uncritical minds use logic and the vocabulary of science to argue for nonsense (creation science) and fill the schools with confusion. Even universities have become a home to academics that kill critical acumen: those who deny science and reason any special role in the search for truth.

IQ gains over time signal the evolution of minds that can be better educated. They provide no guarantee that the educating will be done.

References

Blair, C., Gamson, D., Thorne, S., & Baker, D. (2005). Rising mean IQ: Cognitive demand of mathematics education for young children, population exposure to formal schooling, and the neurology of the prefrontal cortex. *Intelligence*, 33, 93–106.

Colom, R., Flores-Mendoza, C. E., & Abad, F. J. (2007). Generational changes on the Draw-a-Man Test: A comparison of Brazilian urban and rural children tested in 1930, 2002, and 2004. *Journal of Biosocial Science*, 39, 79–89.

Colom, R., Lluis Font, J. M., & Andres-Pueyo, A. (2005). The generational intelligence gains are caused by decreasing variance in the lower half of the distribution: Supporting evidence for the nutrition hypothesis. *Intelligence*, 2005, 33, 83–92.

Daley, T. C., Whaley, S. E., Sigman, M. D., Espinosa, M. P., & Neumann, C. (2003). IQ on the rise: The Flynn effect in rural Kenyan children. *Psychological Science*, 14, 215–219.

Emanuelsson, I., Reuterberg, S.-E., & Svensson, A. (1993). Changing differences in intelligence? Comparisons between groups of thirteen-year-olds tested from 1960 to 1990. *Scandinavian Journal of Educational Research*, 37, 259–277.

Flynn, J. R. (1984). The mean IQ of Americans: Massive gains 1932 to 1978. *Psychological Bulletin*, 95, 29–51.

Flynn, J. R. (1987). Massive IQ gains in 14 nations: What IQ tests really measure. *Psychological Bulletin*, 101, 171–191.

Flynn, J. R. (2009a). Requiem for nutrition as the cause of IQ gains: Raven's gains in Britain 1938 to 2008. *Economics and Human Biology*, 7, 18–27.

Flynn, J. R. (2009b). The WAIS-III and WAIS-IV: Daubert motions favor the certainly false over the approximately true. *Applied Neuropsychology*, 16, 1–7.

Flynn, J. R. (2009c). *What is intelligence? Beyond the Flynn Effect*. Expanded paperback edition. New York, NY: Cambridge University Press.

Flynn, J. R. (under review-a). *How to improve your mind*.

Flynn, J. R. (under review-b). *The vocabularies of adults and school children drift apart: WAIS and WISC subtest gains*.

Flynn, J. R., & Rossi-Casé (under review). *IQ gains in Argentina between 1964 and 1998*.

Genovese, J. E. (2002). Cognitive skills valued by educators: Historic content analysis of testing in Ohio. *Journal of Educational Research*, 96, 101–114.

Greenfield, P. (1998). The cultural evolution of IQ. In U. Neisser, (Ed.), *The rising curve: Long-term gains in IQ and related measures* (pp. 67–79). Washington, DC: American Psychological Association.

Heckman, J. J., & Rubenstein, Y. (2001). The importance of non-cognitive skills: Lessons from the GED testing program. *American Economic Review*, 91, 145–149.

Heckman, J. J., Stixrud, J., & Urzua, S. (2006). The effects of cognitive and non-cognitive

abilities on labor market outcomes and social behavior. *Journal of Labor Economics*, 24, 411–482.
Herrnstein, R. J., & Murray, C. (1994). *The bell curve: Intelligence and class in American life*. New York, NY: Free Press.
Howard, R. W. (1999). Preliminary real-world evidence that average intelligence really is rising. *Intelligence*, 27, 235–250.
Khaleefa, O., Sulman, A., & Lynn, R. (2009). An increase of intelligence in Sudan, 1987–2007. *Journal of Biosocial Science*, 41, 279–83.
Jensen, A. R. (1998). *The g factor: The science of mental ability*. Westport, CT: Praeger.
Johnson, S. (2005). *Everything bad is good for you: How today's popular culture is actually making us smarter*. New York, NY: Rimerhead Books.
Luria, A. R. (1976). *Cognitive development: Its cultural and social foundations*. Cambridge MA: Harvard University Press.
Lynn, R. (1989). Positive correlation between height, head size and IQ: A nutrition theory of the secular increases in intelligence. *British Journal of Educational Psychology*, 59, 372–377.
Lynn, R. (1990). The role of nutrition in secular increases in intelligence. *Personality and Individual Differences*, 11, 273–275.
Lynn, R. (1993). Nutrition and intelligence. In P. A. Vernon (Ed.), *Biological approaches to the study of intelligence* (pp. 105–121). Norwood, NJ: Ablex.
Lynn, R. (1998). In support of nutrition theory. In U. Neisser (Ed.), *The rising curve: Long-term gains in IQ and related measures* (pp. 67–79). Washington, DC: American Psychological Association.
Lynn, R., & Vanhanen, T. (2002). *IQ and the wealth of nations*. Westport, CT: Praeger.
Maguire, E. A., Gadian, D. G., Johnsrude, I. S., Good, C. D., Ashburner, J., Frackowiak, R. S. J., & Frith, C. D. (2000). Navigation-related structural change in the hippocampi of taxi drivers. *Proceedings of the National Academy of Sciences*, 97, 4398–4403.
Meisenberg, G., Lawless, E., Lambert, E., & Newton, A. (2005). The Flynn effect in the Caribbean: Generational change in test performance in Dominica. *Mankind Quarterly*, 46, 29–70.
Mingroni, M. A. (2007). Resolving the IQ paradox: Heterosis as a cause of the Flynn effect and other trends. *Psychological Review*, 114, 806–829.
Mosler, D., & Catley, B. (1998). *America and Americans in Australia*. Westport, CT: Praeger.
Must, O., Must, A., & Raudik, V. (2003). The secular rise in IQs: In Estonia, the Flynn effect is not a Jensen effect. *Intelligence*, 31, 461–471.
Neisser, U. (Ed.). (1998). *The rising curve: Long term gains in IQ and related measures*. Washington, DC: American Psychological Association.
Nunn, J. (1999). *John Nunn's chess puzzle book*. London: Gambit.
Rosenau, J. N., & Fagan, W. M. (1997). A new dynamism in world politics: Increasingly skilled individuals? *International Studies Quarterly*, 41, 655–686.
Schneider, D. (2006). Smart as we can get? *American Scientist*, 94, 311–312.
Schooler, C. (1998). Environmental complexity and the Flynn effect. In U. Neisser (Ed.), *The rising curve: Long-term gains in IQ and related measures* (pp. 67–79). Washington, DC: American Psychological Association.
Sternberg, R. J. (1988). *The triarchic mind: A new theory of human intelligence*. New York, NY: Penguin.
Sternberg, R. J. (2006). The Rainbow Project: Enhancing the SAT through assessments of analytic, practical, and creative skills. *Intelligence*, 34, 321–350.
Sternberg, R. J., Forsythe, G. B., Hedlund, J., Horvath, J. A., Wagner, R. K., Williams, W. M., Snook, S. A., & Grigorenko, E. L. (2000). *Practical intelligence in everyday life*. New York, NY: Cambridge University Press.
Sundet, J. M., Barlaug, D. G., & Torjussen, T. M. (2004). The end of the Flynn effect? A study of secular trends in mean intelligence test scores of Norwegian conscripts during half a century. *Intelligence*, 32, 349–362.
Sundet, J. M., et al. (in press). The Flynn effect in sibships: Investigating the role of age differences between siblings. *Intelligence*.
Teasdale, T. W., & Owen, D. R. (1989). Continued secular increases in intelligence and a stable prevalence of high intelligence levels. *Intelligence*, 13, 255–262.
Teasdale, T. W., & Owen, D. R.. (2000). Forty-year secular trends in cognitive abilities. *Intelligence*, 28, 115–120.
Tuddenham, R. D. (1948). Soldier intelligence in World Wars I and II. *American Psychologist*, 3, 54–56.

U.S. Department of Education, Institute of Education Sciences, National Center for Educational Statistics. (2003). *The nation's report card: Reading* 2002, NCES 2003–521, by W. S. Grigg, M. C. Daane, Y. Jin, & J. R. Campbell. Washington, DC: Author.

U.S. Department of Education, Office of Educational Research and Improvement, National Center for Educational Statistics. (2000). *NAEP 1996 Trends in Academic Progress,* NCES 97–985r, by J. R. Campbell, K. E. Voelkl, & P. L. Donahue. Washington, DC: Author.

U.S. Department of Education, Office of Educational Research and Improvement, National Center for Educational Statistics. (2001). *The Nation's Report Card: Mathematics* 2000, NCES 2001–517, by J. S. Braswell, A. D. Lutkus, W. S. Grigg, S. L. Santapau, B. Tay-Lim, & M. Johnson. Washington, DC: Author.

Wicherts, J. M., Dolan, C. V., Hessen, D. J., Oosterveld, P., van Baal, G. C. M., Boomsma, D. I., & Span, M. M. (2004). Are intelligence tests measurement invariant over time? Investigating the Flynn effect. *Intelligence,* **32**, 509–538.

CHAPTER 33

Society and Intelligence

Susan M. Barnett, Heiner Rindermann, Wendy M. Williams, and Stephen J. Ceci

There are large between-country differences in measures of economic well-being and noneconomic well-being (democracy, rule of law, human rights, health) – but why? Many researchers from diverse disciplines view increasing the stock of human capital as the key to raising economic development, promoting democratization, and improving health, and hence improving overall societal well-being. The single most studied aspect of human capital concerns *cognitive competence* – the capacity to assess and solve problems by the use of thinking (intelligence), to acquire, to possess and use knowledge. Some have suggested that differences in population cognitive competence might explain these societal differences (e.g., Hanushek & Woessmann, 2008; Hart, 2007; Kanazawa, 2006; McDaniel, 2006). At the individual level, cognitive competence is broadly believed to increase productivity and quality in many realms (employment, child rearing, health and political decisions, to name a few). Substantial correlations between schooling attainment (i.e., highest completed school grade or level) and these societal and individual outcomes have been interpreted to support the proposition that cognitive competence, the best-known measures of which are psychometric intelligence tests, is influenced by schooling, and in turn drives international differences in health, wealth, and modernity. Understanding the processes by which cognitive dimensions of human capital are fostered represents a key issue of our time. Unsurprisingly, many researchers have toiled on this issue in recent years, focusing on the relationship between transnational gaps in cognitive competence and international differences in wealth, longevity, democratization, and so on.

For example, there are hundreds of empirical studies that are interpreted as showing the impact of cognitive and other skills obtained through education on wages or incomes; the vast majority of them use schooling attainment to represent these skills (see Psacharopolous & Patrinos, 2004). A small number instead use direct measures of adult cognitive skills (e.g., Alderman et al., 1996; Boissiere, Knight, & Sabot, 1985;

Glewwe, 1996; Murnane, Willet, & Levy, 1995). The many empirical studies of the effects of cognitive and other skills on outcomes such as health, nutrition, and fertility almost all use schooling attainment to represent these skills (see Strauss & Thomas, 1998).

What if genetic differences in intelligence of the populations of each country contributed to international gaps in economic growth and health? This hypothesis was advanced in *IQ and the Wealth of Nations*, by the British intelligence researcher Richard Lynn and the Finnish political scientist Tatu Vanhanen (2002). In it, these authors discussed the relationship between national IQ and national income for a sample of 81 countries, concluding that the results imply that since largely genetically driven IQ differences are the cause of differences in national income, it will be impossible to eradicate the gap between rich and poor nations and there is little hope for most poor nations ever to catch up with the rich nations (p. 184).

Using a similarly broad swath of nations, Rindermann (2008a) and Rindermann and Ceci (2009) also reported strong relationships between cognitive competence scores that are highly correlated with IQ, which they derived from a variety of international achievement tests (e.g., TIMSS, PISA, and PIRLS), and a host of outcomes that include gross domestic product (GDP), health, human rights, rule of law, and measures of modernity. However, these authors, while not ruling out genetic contributions to cognitive competence within individual countries, concluded that the biggest contributor of transnational gaps was within-country differences in educational attainment. They suggest that changes in national educational policies can be expected to close these international gaps in GDP, health, rule of law, and so on.

However, a correlation between cognitive competence and these measures of societal well-being does not imply causality. Indeed, both could be consequences of some other, third factor, or causality could be the other way round – that is, societal differences could cause differences in cognitive competence. For example, rich countries can afford better schools and better schools could lead to higher scores on measures of cognitive competence (whether directly school-related, such as achievement test scores, or indirectly school-related, such as measures of abstract reasoning embodied in IQ tests, e.g., Raven's matrices), without that higher cognitive competence necessarily leading back to greater national wealth. The direction of causality is important if the goal is to change the level of economic and noneconomic well-being of a country. If cognitive competence causes societal differences, then changing cognitive competence might be one solution to alleviating some of the problems some societies are facing. If, on the other hand, causality is the other way around, and cognitive differences are merely a consequence of societal differences, modifying cognitive competence cannot be the solution. If cognitive competence is deemed to be a cause of societal differences, the next question is, Can cognitive competence be changed? If cognitive competence is defined as intelligence, as measured by an IQ test, then the issue becomes, Can intelligence be altered? Some have argued that it cannot, pointing to the substantial heritability of IQ within societies as evidence. Others have pointed to the malleability of IQ and other measures of cognitive competence as a result of, for example, schooling, to suggest that providing more/better access to education could change cognitive competence and hence broad societal outcomes (Ceci & Williams, 1997). This chapter will discuss each of these issues in turn.

International Differences in Cognitive Competence

There are large international differences on measures of cognitive competence, whether measured by IQ tests or by tests designed to assess school-related achievement. We will discuss each of these types of measure in turn. Lynn and Vanhanen (2002) compiled results from myriad studies of intelligence throughout the world. They found wide variability in measures of national IQ. For example, even within Europe, national average IQ estimates range from 90 in Croatia to 102 in Austria, Germany, Italy, and the Netherlands. Outside Europe they found a much larger range. For example, the Hong Kong estimate is 107, while the estimate for India is 81 and for South Africa it is 72. The lowest IQ estimate in their 81-nation sample is Ethiopia, at 63.[1] These authors note, in particular, the low scores shown by black, sub-Saharan African samples, which they calculate to have a median score of 69. As we will see, results of different tests, including culture-reduced figural relations as well as achievement tests, depend on school quantity and quality.

However, as we discuss later, some authors have questioned the validity (both internal and external) of Lynn and Vanhanen's results, particularly pointing to the unrepresentativeness of some of their samples and the meaningfulness of applying generally U.S./UK-oriented paper-and-pencil tests to people growing up in very different cultures (Barnett & Williams, 2004, 2005; Hunt & Carlson, 2007). Wicherts and colleagues (Wicherts, Dolan, & van der Maas, 2010; Wicherts, Dolan, Carlson & van der Maas, in press) also reviewed evidence of differences in national IQ. Disagreeing with Lynn and Vanhanen's claim that the IQ of black sub-Saharan African nations averaged below 70, their systematic review suggested a figure of approximately 80 IQ points, the discrepancy between the two due mainly to different choices regarding sample inclusion. Wicherts and colleagues also share some of Barnett and Williams's concerns regarding the meaning of these tests for individuals in undeveloped countries.

[1] The mean of IQ tests is set at 100 for the UK, with the standard deviation at 15 ("Greenwich IQ"). We do not mention Equatorial Guinea with IQ 59 (was a mistake in Lynn and Vanhanen's book).

What Do International Differences in IQ/Assessment Test Performance Mean?

To make international comparisons meaningful as indicators of some underlying, culture-independent ability, tests must be measuring the same thing – with equal difficulty – in all countries. But intelligence tests were developed in Western countries, and because of this they are sometimes suspected to measure only an adaptation to a particular culture ("How well can they do our tricks?" Wober, 1969, p. 488). Intelligence should be defined as thinking ability independent of culture, but numerous examples can be cited of cultural variability on cognitive tasks, even very basic perceptual processes involved in spatial cognition (Henrich, Heine, & Norenzayan, 2010). This issue of cross-cultural validity is not a simple matter, due to differences in language, culture, and knowledge, and it seems fair to say that no test, no matter how "culture-free" it is claimed to be, is impervious to the effects of culture and schooling. Having stated this, it also seems evident that some tests are far more influenced by culture than others.

Tests include items of many different types, including explicit tests of vocabulary and figural problems. For example, the Draw-a-Man test (DAM; Goodenough, 1926; Harris, 1963) is a nonverbal intelligence test in which children are required to draw a man. It is often used in African samples, even though it is not generally considered as good an indicator of general intelligence as regular IQ tests (Wicherts, Dolan, & van der Maas, 2010). Lynn and Vanhanen (2002, 2006) included some samples using the Draw-a-Man test. Wicherts et al. suggest that the use of such samples is fraught with difficulties (e.g., in some cases the children completing the test had never used a pencil, had no schooling, and were unfamiliar with two-dimensional pictures). The tests were also being scored according to culturally loaded criteria including whether or not the children correctly drew Western clothes on their figures, despite being naked themselves. Other culture-dependent tests include the Kaufmann Assessment Battery for Children, which includes items that are likely to be unfamiliar to many test takers in less developed countries, such as telephones (Wicherts et al., 2010). Other well-known tests are also culture dependent, for example, the WISC-III: "Questions referring to, for example, 'advantages of getting news from a newspaper rather than from a television news program' (Wechsler, 1991, WISC-III Manual Comprehension subtest, p. 138), 'why it is important for cars to have license plates' (Wechsler, 1991, WISC-III Manual Comprehension subtest, p. 137), 'why you should turn off lights when no one is using them' (Wechsler, 1991, WISC-III, Manual Comprehension subtest, p. 134), 'what is an umbrella?' (Wechsler, 1991, WISC-III Manual Vocabulary subtest, p. 108), and 'in what way are a telephone and a radio alike?' (Wechsler, 1991, WISC III Manual Similarities subtest, p. 78), would not be equally difficult, even when translated, for individuals from more and less developed countries" (Barnett & Williams, 2004, p. 390). Wicherts and colleagues noted that small alterations to the WISC-R, to reduce language and other difficulties, made a large difference in scores of Zimbabwean children, which again raises the question of what these tests are measuring.

Even tests that appear to be less culturally loaded, such as the Raven's matrices tests, are considered to have questionable psychometric meaning (Wicherts, Dolan, Carlson, & van der Maas, in press) due to test takers' lack of familiarity with stimulus materials (colored geometric shapes, multiple choice format, etc.). Wicherts and his colleagues stated, "Factor analyses show that the *g* loading of the Raven's tests is considerably smaller in African than in western samples" (p. 145) and "it is unclear whether Raven's tests afford an adequate comparison of western and African samples in terms of the construct of *g*" (p. 145).

Some have gone so far as to claim that "intelligence cannot be fully or even meaningfully understood outside its cultural context" (Sternberg, 2004, p. 325). Sternberg uses the term "successful intelligence" to refer to the practical utility of understanding behaviors within the individual's own particular environment and suggests that if tests are used cross-culturally, " the psychological meanings to be assigned to the scores will differ from one culture to another" (p. 327). The successful intelligence approach is based on the idea that "components of intelligence and the mental representations on which they act are universal" (p. 327) but "the mental contents (i.e., types and items of knowledge) to which processes such as these are applied and the judgments as to what are considered 'intelligent' applications of the processes to these contents" (p. 327) vary across cultures. Aspects of a test that are familiar in one situation or culture might be less familiar, and therefore potentially more difficult, in another situation or culture, both for individuals from different cultures in the same test situation and for the same individual in different situations (at home in a village while tracking livestock versus sitting at a desk in a school building surrounded by strangers).

The latter is an example of the context or domain specificity of expertise, knowledge, and understanding. An extensive body of research over the last century has shown that learning does not always readily transfer to novel contexts (see Barnett & Ceci, 2002, for an overview). An individual may behave intelligently in a familiar context but not successfully apply that intelligence to an unfamiliar context.

Thus, even if an intelligence test is capable of making meaningful distinctions between individuals who have similar life experiences (whether that distinction is phrased in terms of a latent construct such as "*g*," or in terms of motivational or other causes of differential learning from the same experiences, or in terms of attentional or other constraints on demonstrated performance) it may not have the same meaning when comparing individuals with different life experiences. For example, if individuals in one group have spent several hours a day for several years sitting at a desk in a school listening to a teacher and working with paper and pencil on writing and mathematics, and another group has never set foot in such a place and never worked with a paper and pencil, any difference in performance is a confound of what that difference would have been had they had the same experience, and the differences caused by the differential experience.

So, in light of this, what do international differences in IQ test performance mean?[2] Researchers do not want to unjustifiably disparage the abilities of people from other cultures (Ceci & Williams, 2009). Culture has a strong impact on forms of education, on the esteem a given culture assigns to abstract thinking and knowledge, on diligence and effort (Flynn, 2007), on thinking styles and worldviews. However, this acknowledgment does not obviate the possibility of making cross-cultural comparisons. Cross-cultural research provides a means of identifying both large background factors and the many small ideological, institutional, and behavioral mechanisms through which the worldviews of cultures work to shape cognitive competencies.

Although some (e.g., Lynn & Vanhanen, 2002) would argue that differences are indicative of underlying general intelligence, the latent construct "*g*," the foregoing suggests they are, at best, a not error-free measure. The relative magnitude of the signal (*g*) and noise (experientially driven differences) is open to debate. Resolving this debate rests, in part, on the issue of malleability (sensitivity to education and other experiential differences) of IQ, which we discuss later in this chapter. However, even if they do not measure pure "*g*," IQ tests measure something, and if that "something" can be used to make useful predictions, it may be worth understanding. For example, if national IQ measurements (from appropriately representative samples, etc.) are an indicator of national absorption of formal education, and if the effect of widespread formal education is beneficial for society, then the factors that boost national IQ may be worth investment.

An alternative way to measure the effects of formal education is to do so directly, with tests of academic achievement. Using more knowledge-based student achievement tests, which had been applied in a few sub-Saharan countries (where IQ scores are also low), Rindermann, Sailer, and Thompson (2009) and Lynn and Meisenberg (2009) have demonstrated, with measures transformed into IQ equivalent scores, averages of around 66 for these countries (e.g., South Africa, Botswana, and Ghana). Measures of cognitive competence other than IQ show large ranges similar to less knowledge-based figural tests such as mazes (e.g., CPM, SPM, and APM).[3] For example, the Trends in International Mathematics and Science Study (TIMSS), a series of international assessments carried out in 59 participating countries and 8 benchmarking locations around the world to assess mathematics and science learning in the fourth and eighth grades, found large differences in mathematical performance at both age levels (Mullis, Martin, et al., 2009). In the eighth-grade sample, Taiwan and South Korea recorded the highest average scaled scores, at 598 and 597, respectively, while Qatar and Ghana scored the lowest, at 307 and 309, respectively. (The mean is 500, the standard deviation, 100.) In the younger age group, the top scorers were Hong Kong and Singapore, at 607 and 599, while the lowest were Yemen and Qatar, at 224 and 296 – a difference of nearly three standard deviations! Findings were similar in the 2003 version of the study (Mullis, Martin, et al., 2005). In the

[2] There is considerable debate about the meaning of intelligence and whether IQ tests really measure it (Ceci, 1996). However, we will not discuss this wider debate here, except to address issues particular to the interpretation of international comparisons of IQ.

[3] CPM, SPM and APM – psychometric paper-and-pencil tests using only abstract figures (similar nonverbal-figural scales of CogAT) – are less overtly related to explicitly, school-taught knowledge than intelligence tests using verbal and math tasks or student assessment tests (using verbal and math tasks and knowledge questions). But performance on these tests and intelligence underlying the performance on them are not independent of school attendance and instructional quality (Becker, Lüdtke, Trautwein, Köller, & Baumert, 2007; Cahan & Cohen, 1989; Ceci, 1991; Stelzl, Merz, Remer, & Ehlers, 1995).

eighth-grade sample, Singapore and South Korea recorded the highest average scaled scores, at 605 and 589, respectively, while South Africa and Ghana scored the lowest, at 264 and 276, respectively. In the younger age group, the top scorers were Singapore and Hong Kong, at 594 and 575, and the lowest were Tunisia and Morocco, at 339 and 347. In summary, the well-known large-scale student assessment studies also demonstrate very large transnational differences in cognitive competence.

The relationship between these two measures of cognitive competence – intelligence and achievement – is a contentious topic. Some psychometricians argue that intelligence tests, particularly those assessing fluid intelligence (Cattell, 1987), are tapping an innate ability driven by brain differences related to neuronal processing time and working memory capacity, and as such are measuring something completely different from more knowledge-based performance on school-related assessment tests (for a review, see Neisser et al., 1996). However, high correlations between aptitude and achievement test scores in intranational samples (Ceci, 1991), coupled with similar cognitive demands and very high correlations at the between-country level (Rindermann, 2007), lead to the conclusion that the various measures of cognitive competence are largely tapping the same characteristic. Translating international score differences into an easy to understand metric, "years-behind-at-school," suggests that the larger transnational gaps are equivalent to about 5–10 years of schooling among children, adolescents, and young adults between 10 and 30 (Rindermann & Ceci, 2009).

Cognitive Competence and Societal Measures

Many have noted that cognitive competence appears to be related to societal measures of economic and noneconomic well-being. Lynn and Vanhanen (2002) assessed the correlation between national IQ estimates and national per capita income (GDP per capita), and found a correlation of $r = .62$, for 199/8, with higher IQ countries showing higher per capita income. Whetzel and McDaniel (2006) reached a similar conclusion using updated data. They avoided some of the methodological issues raised concerning Lynn and Vanhanen's study by truncating all IQ scores below 90 to equal 90; the relationship between IQ and GDP remained strong. Other researchers using student achievement studies or further control variables and different statistical methods found supporting positive relationships (Hanushek & Woessmann, 2008; Jones & Schneider, 2006; Weede & Kämpf, 2002).[4]

Additionally, there are positive correlations between measures of cognitive abilities and noneconomic aspects of national well-being such as democracy, the rule of law, and political liberty. For example, Glaeser, Ponzetto, and Shleifer (2007) have argued that the causal path runs from increased education to increased democracy. Positive effects remain significant when income is controlled (Rindermann, 2008b): Cognitive ability correlates with democracy ($N = 183$) at $r = .56$ (partial correlation with GDP controlled = .23); cognitive ability correlates with the rule of law ($N = 131$) at $r = .64$ ($r_p = .27$). The level of democracy was measured by two indices: one combining variables such as the fragmentation of the vote between political parties and the level of voter turnout, the second aggregating essential political indicators such as guarantees of civil liberties (Rindermann, 2008b). The rule of law was measured by indices focusing on protection of property rights and judicial independence (Rindermann, 2008b). The correlations are not extremely high, thus leaving space for exceptions like high levels of intelligence and knowledge in Singapore or China and only low or zero levels of democracy. At the individual data

[4] Describing the positive impact of one variable on the other does not imply that other variables have no influence. Intelligence is not the only determinant for wealth, for example. There are additional factors behind intelligence (e.g., culture) and between intelligence and positive outcomes (like the quality and functionality of institutions).

level (Cunha, Heckman, Lochner, & Masterov, 2006; Ellis & Walsh, 2003; Thomson, 1937) cognitive ability is negatively correlated with violent crime. Rushton and Templer (Rushton &Templer, 2009) also report noneconomic national well-being correlates, using Lynn and Vanhanen's national IQ data: "Cross-national differences in rate of violent crime (murder, rape, and serious assault) were significantly correlated with a country's IQ scores (mean r = −.25, such that the higher the IQ, the lower the rate of crime)" (p. 345). The relationship remains robust excluding sub-Saharan African countries for which IQ estimates may be less valid ($r = -.35$). These same authors also investigated the relationship between national IQ and health measures, reporting correlations between IQ and the rate of HIV/AIDS ($r = -.52$), infant mortality ($r = -.67$), and life expectancy ($r = .74$). Thus, measures of cognitive competence and indicators of economic and noneconomic national well-being have been shown to be significantly correlated. Even if these cognitive measures are not assessing potential but merely some form of realized potential in academic-style tasks, their relationship with measures of national well-being merit further investigation.

Direction of Causality

Given a correlation between higher national cognitive competence and positive societal outcomes, the question remains: Does higher cognitive competence (howsoever derived) cause the positive outcomes (i.e., smarter people make better decisions and end up richer and healthier), do the positive "outcomes" cause higher cognitive competence scores (i.e., rich, healthy people have time and energy to devote to learning and so end up smarter), or could the relationship go in both directions? It may be easier to study, learn, and score high on cognitive tests if you are healthy and live in a law-abiding democracy that allows all children to attend, and afford, good schools, and studying and learning may lead to better lifestyle decisions. It is also possible that some of the correlations mentioned above are not causal in either direction but are both the consequence of some other factor, such as culture.

Although random assignment, experimental studies are impractical, individual, within country, quasi-experimental data do provide some evidence for a causal link between education and earnings. For example, Angrist and Krueger (1991) investigated the way that compulsory schooling age rules affect the amount of education children receive – depending on whether they are born earlier or later compared to the age cutoff – and the subsequent effect this exerts on earnings. Those students "who are compelled to attend school longer by compulsory schooling laws earn higher wages as a result of their extra schooling" (p. 1010). Unfortunately, investigation of the relationship between education and earnings *between* countries is even more difficult, due to the many potential confounded variables.

One way to examine such relationships is to look at the correlation between potentially causal factors at some point in history with potential dependent variables at a later time, controlling for the level of likely confounds. Rindermann (2008a, 2008b) adopted this approach. A longitudinal cross-lagged analysis on a sample of 17 (largely developed) nations was used to assess the possible direction of causality between cognitive ability (measured by student assessments) and national income (Rindermann, 2008a). Longitudinally, the standardized path coefficient for the impact of cognitive abilities on gross domestic product was .29 while the coefficient for the impact of gross domestic product on cognitive abilities was .21. So there may be effects of cognitive ability on wealth (e.g., through increased efficiency at the job and increased efficiency of institutions) and vice versa (e.g., by higher quality of nutrition and health services). Overall model fit was good. The impact of cognitive ability on GDP was similar when a larger sample of 88 nations' educational measures (average years of school attendance) were used as proxies or causal factors of cognitive competence ($\beta_{Edu1 \rightarrow GDP2} = .40$).

However, the reverse effect was not found ($\beta_{GDP1 \rightarrow Edu2} = -.06$). The finding of an effect of cognitive ability and education on GDP, in both samples, provides support for claims of generalizability. There is also a suggestion of the effects of the "classical" factor economic freedom on GDP (cognitive ability model, $\beta_{EF1 \rightarrow GDP2} = .10$; education model, $\beta_{EF1 \rightarrow GDP2} = .23$). In turn, cognitive competence and education also seem to have positive impacts on economic freedom ($\beta_{CA1 \rightarrow EFP2} = .25$; $\beta_{ED1 \rightarrow EF2} = .54$): Cognitive competence and education enable individuals and societies to act successfully to establish a liberal economy. The coefficients for the effect of economic freedom on cognitive competence and education are smaller (cognitive ability model, $\beta_{EF1 \rightarrow CA2} = .17$; education model, $\beta_{EF1 \rightarrow Edu2} = .09$).

Unconfounded data to further elucidate the relationship between wealth and cognition are difficult to find, but Rindermann and Ceci (2009, p. 554) described one natural experiment by comparing cognitive assessments for Arab countries with varying levels of mineral wealth. Results suggest no effects of such independently generated affluence on cognitive ability, at least for the way that influx of wealth was spent. In an update of these results using only student assessment results (Rindermann, Sailer, & Thompson, 2009), a similar outcome appears: Oil-rich countries (Bahrain, Kuwait, Qatar, Saudi Arabia, Emirates) reach a mean of 80 (result of Program of International Student Assessment – PISA, Third International Mathematics and Science Study – TIMSS and Progress in International Reading Literacy Study – PIRLS averaged and renormed on an IQ-scale with UK = 100) with a GDP per capita of U.S.$18,203 in purchasing power parity. But 10 poorer Arab countries without such large per capita oil resources (Algeria, Egypt, Iran, Jordan, Lebanon, Morocco, Oman, Syria, Tunisia, and Yemen) had similar average IQ (79) but a GDP of only U.S.$5,566. A similar pattern is seen within Scandinavia if oil-rich Norway (IQ 96, GDP U.S.$37,670) is compared with Finland, Denmark, Sweden, and Iceland (mean IQ 99, GDP U.S.$29,269). In sum, in these cases, money appears to neither foster intelligence nor increase knowledge – maybe because the additional affluence was not spent for the improvement of environmental conditions furthering cognitive development.

The impact of pure economic factors has also been found to be weak at the individual data level, if the socioeconomic status variable (SES) is divided into two of its components: educational attainment and wealth (Rindermann & Thompson, 2009). Using datasets from Austria, Germany, the United States (the latter from Hart & Risley, 1995), Costa Rica, and Ecuador (indigenous people), the educational level of parents was always more important for explaining (at least statistically) the cognitive ability level of children than the parental level of financial affluence. (Similar findings have been reported by Melhuish et al., 2008.) Rindermann and Ceci (2009) suggested that income at the national level could be more important indirectly, depending on the distribution and use of wealth within a country. Economic resources spent for sufficient and high-quality nutrition (proteins, vitamins, minerals; Eysenck & Schoenthaler, 1997; Lynn, 2009) and health care (from pregnancy on to anti-worm treatment and to vaccinations such as against measles; Glewwe & Kremer, 2006) reaching the whole population (including the poor, orphans, and children of poorly educated parents) provide a basis for a healthy cognitive (and physical) development.

There is some evidence that measures of noneconomic well-being can also be affected by cognitive competence. Within-country evidence shows a statistical relationship between individual differences in childhood cognitive ability and adult health, even after controlling for SES (Gottfredson & Deary, 2004). Although these researchers' methodology was not experimental, the longitudinal nature of their study suggests that cognitive ability differences may be causal. However, in the absence of intervention studies, evaluating causality from between-country cognitive competence differences to between-country health differences is more difficult due to the necessity of more extensive controls for other variables, such as access to health care. Nevertheless, different authors using different data sources (educational or competence measures) have come to the conclusion that human capital is more important than wealth even for health factors such as a reduction in the spread of HIV (Lakhanpal & Ram, 2008; Rindermann & Meisenberg, 2009).

As mentioned earlier, correlational analyses also found statistical relationships between measures of cognitive competence and democracy. Within-country longitudinal evidence, which supports a causal interpretation, also exists for a relationship between childhood cognitive ability and adult voter turnout, after controlling for various personality and social variables (Denny & Doyle, 2008). Voting – engagement in the political process – could be viewed as an indicator of democratization in general. The same is true for attitudes of tolerance and liberty (Deary, Batty, & Gale, 2008).

Thus, cognitive competence and education may help improve societal well-being, including wealth, and evidence suggests a link between education and wealth, not purely a consequence of wealth buying education. However, generalizability of quasi-experimental data is limited. Perhaps, if oil-rich countries had spent their windfall differently, the consequences for cognitive development could also have been different.

Malleability of Ability

Even if there is a causal relationship between cognitive competence and desirable societal outcomes, there may be nothing that can be done to promote these desirable outcomes unless cognitive competence is malleable. Some have claimed that cognitive competence, as measured by IQ, is largely determined by genetics, and thus is not very malleable in response to policy interventions (see, e.g., Lynn & Vanhanen's comments regarding the impossibility of eradicating the difference between poor and rich countries, mentioned earlier). High heritability within a population does not, however, necessarily imply (or preclude) equivalent heritability for differences between populations. Given the obvious difficulty of conducting behavioral genetic twin and adoption studies between populations and countries (take two U.S. identical twins separated at birth, send one to live in a village in sub-Saharan Africa and one to live in Pittsburgh, then take two African identical twins separated at birth and . . .), Rushton, Bons, Vernon, and Cvorovic (2007) attempted to address these questions by comparing the patterns of item difficulty and heritability for IQ test items across populations. They used the Raven's Progressive Matrices test, which is often considered one of the least culture-bound tests, and compared groups from Canada, the United States, Serbia, and South Africa. Within the South African sample, they also compared different ethnic/racial groups. They found that population differences on item scores correlated with item heritability within the Canadian and U.S. twin samples, leading them to suggest that IQ differences *between* populations, as well as individual differences *within* populations, are highly genetically driven and hence nonmalleable. These data are also open to alternative explanations. For example, if heritability was driven by attention differences, with more heritable items being those requiring the most careful concentration, international differences due to lack of experience with schooling and sit down, paper-and-pencil tests might also correlate with this, but for environmental rather than genetic reasons. That is, test takers in a less developed country, where they did not have so much experience with concentrating for long periods of time on written materials, might do poorly on items requiring such careful concentration, compared to test takers in a more developed country where they have much more experience with such tasks. Admittedly, this is speculative and perhaps even far-fetched, but it illustrates the difficulty of making transnational inferences based on within-country heritability estimates obtained in developed nations.

Moreover, there is also considerable evidence that IQ, and other measures of cognitive competence, can be changed by education (see, e.g., Ceci, 1991; Hansen, Heckman, & Mullen, 2004; Nisbett, 2009), despite strong genetic effects (Neisser et al., 1996). It has been suggested that schooling and school-related activities foster the development of cognitive competencies that promote performance on most intelligence tests (Cahan & Cohen, 1989). Perfectly controlled experiments are impossible to conduct – children cannot be randomly assigned to be deprived of an education in the name of research – but researchers have provided several sources of evidence to support this claim. Some analyses are correlational, such as analyses of the relationship between IQ and number of years in school. However, many come from natural experiments. Ceci (1991) reviewed studies in which IQ has been shown to decline during summer vacations and among those who have been unable to reliably attend school due to their parents' occupation or the unavailability of schools. For example, children living in remote "hollows" in mountains west of Washington, D.C., early in the 20th century, had reduced exposure to school compared to those in less remote areas, presumably independent from genetic background. IQ scores were found to vary with availability of schooling. Further studies found that delayed onset of schooling depresses IQ scores, whether the delay was due to war, unavailability of teachers, closure due to racial desegregation, or school entry cutoff dates (Cahan & Cohen, 1989; Ceci, 1991; Stelzl, Merz, Remer, & Ehlers, 1995). School age cutoffs were used by Cahan and Cohen in their quasi-experimental study of the effect of amount of schooling on fifth- and sixth-graders' scores on various verbal and nonverbal intelligence tests, including the Cognitive Abilities Test and Raven's Matrices. They concluded, "The results unambiguously point to schooling as the major factor underlying the increase in intelligence test scores as a function of age" (p. 1239). Similar results were found by Stelzl et al. (1995). They also used a quasi-experimental design to separate schooling from age effects on intelligence test scores of 10-year-old children. Their results showed considerable schooling effects on all tests, including the tests of fluid intelligence.

And academic activities such as training on a task that exercises working memory have been shown to enhance so-called culture-reduced tests of fluid intelligence similar to Raven's Matrices. For example, Klauer and Phye (2008) have shown in a meta-analysis of 73 studies with 79 comparisons a mean effect of cognitive training on intelligence (mainly measures of fluid intelligence, using Cattell's Culture Fair Test) of $d = 0.52$.

Thus, at least within countries, there is considerable evidence that IQ is malleable and that education can lead to changes in cognitive competence, as assessed by measures such as IQ tests. Between-country evidence also shows a correlation between schooling and IQ.

In assessing the benefits of education, it is important to distinguish between the benefits in terms of increases in cognitive competence and the benefits in terms of gaining credentials the world might interpret as a signal of increased cognitive competence (or other related skills), whether actual or not. The latter has been termed the *signal theory* of educational effects (Spence, 1973). Signal theory argues that educational attainments *only* serve to signal the competence level of individuals. For example, college education does not further cognitive competence, but merely signals competence; persons intelligent enough to get through college and to receive a degree are assumed to possess a minimum level of intelligence and beneficial personality traits (e.g., conscientiousness), but college attendance or school education themselves do not increase abilities (e.g., Charlton, 2009; Murray, 2008). Signal theory is of course controversial and is not compatible with the results of much empirical research: Too many quasi-experimental studies have shown that the quantity of education alters cognitive competence (academic achievement and IQ; e.g., Cahan & Cohen, 1989; Stelzl et al. 1995). Thus, whether or not there may also be a signaling effect of educational credentials, signal theory cannot explain all of the benefits of education.

And at the cross-country level, signal theory is irrelevant – why should the overall economy develop better if people are absent from the labor market to spend their time on "learning" if it brings no real benefit? It seems unlikely that international investors or importers would invest in or buy from a country purely because of the educational credentials of its population.

Policy Implications

If schooling can change cognitive competence, and cognitive competence affects national economic and noneconomic well-being, then investment in raising the national level of schooling might be a good way to alleviate some of society's ills. Reviewing evidence of the interrelationship between schooling, intelligence, and income, several authors concluded, for different countries (including the United States, the UK, South Africa, Sweden, and Germany), that schooling increases individual income, both directly and via enhancement of intelligence (Bond & Saunders, 1999; Ceci & Williams, 1997). However, variations in individual IQ only explain a small amount of variance in individual income in the intranational samples.

Psacharopoulos and Patrinos (2004) reviewed studies of the return on investment in education in the tradition of the pioneering work of Angrist and Krueger (1991), based on human capital theory. Return on investment is measured by the increase in per capita income for each additional year of schooling. Their review encompasses studies from many countries, each evaluating intranational returns on investment, focusing only on individual income differences but considering both individual and social costs. (Note that the income benefit may include both increases due to increased competences, cognitive and other, and increases due to signaling effects.) Rates of return vary by geographic region and are higher for less well developed nations. Returns are also higher for primary education than for secondary or higher education, a finding consistent with Heckman and Masterov (2007). Private returns for primary education in sub-Saharan Africa are shown to be very high (37.6%), while social returns (including shared, "social" costs) are still high (25.4%).

An investigation by Rindermann and Ceci (2009) of the relationships between aspects of national educational systems and cognitive competencies aimed to determine the optimal educational policy choices to efficiently promote cognitive competence. The most important factor seems to be a general high educational level of society (high adult literacy rate, adults who have attended many years of school, adults who completed secondary or at least primary school). Cognitive competence is defined by Rindermann and Ceci as the mean cognitive competence level of students at school (measured using large-scale international student assessments such as TIMSS, PIRLS, and PISA), and the mean intelligence level in society, adapted from Lynn and Vanhanen (2006; see also Barber, 2005). Strong, positive relationships were found between kindergarten attendance and subsequent cognitive competence, even after controlling for other factors such as GDP, suggesting that early education provides a basis for subsequent successful ability development. Similar beneficial results of preschool education were found within different countries (e.g., W. S. Barnett & Boocock, 1998; Cunha et al., 2006). Number of instructional hours is also correlated with competence, leading to the conclusion that the more formal education students receive – and the younger they are when they begin to receive it – the higher their achieved cognitive competence levels are (at the individual data level, see also Ceci, 1991). However, just spending more money seems to be ineffective: Although educational expenditures are highly correlated with cognitive outcomes, the relationship disappears when GDP is partialed out.

Large class sizes were found to have a negative effect on cognitive competence, though this can be alleviated by cram school attendance, where available, and good discipline helps promote success, as do the use of achievement tests and central exit exams. Discipline and behavioral education seem to be especially important for pupils from families with low educational background (Woodworth, David, Guha, Wang, & Lopez-Torkos, 2008).[5] More time spent on homework has a negative effect on cognitive performance in poor school systems (but only at the cross-country level!). Overall, the results of Rindermann and Ceci's study suggest that increased gross and net learning *time* (from kindergarten and early school enrollment to adults' level of education) is important for the development of cognitive competence. However, as Hanushek and Woessmass (2008) note, quality of education is also important: "Knowledge rather than just time in school is what counts. . . . School attainment has a positive impact only if it raises the cognitive skills of students – something that does not happen with sufficient regularity in many developing countries" (p. 658). Discipline of students (e.g., attending school regularly, not coming late, not disturbing lessons), effective classroom management by teachers, and the use of high-stakes tests also lead to more net learning time.

Caveats

Education is not an isolated factor. Several studies have shown strong relationships between educational level and attributes of educational systems on the one hand and cognitive competence on the other. The obvious consequence would be to recommend the extension of education and the improvement of educational systems as described above. But the realization as well as outcomes of such reforms could be faced with several problems:

1. Educational attributes of societies do *not* exist *accidentally*. For instance, the existence of a large private school population in the United States and the absence of this sector in Scandinavia have their roots in cultural, historical, and social features of societies that cannot be neglected.
2. The same attributes of educational systems could have *differential impacts* depending on other educational and cultural features of societies. For example, late school enrollment in Finland is not detrimental because traditionally literacy education (at least the beginning of literacy education) occurs in families. Large class sizes in East-Asian countries do not impede achievement because the entire culture emphasizes personal effort and discipline and because regular instruction in school is accompanied by instruction in cram schools. So in these countries, reforms leading to earlier school onset or smaller classes would likely have rather small effects.
3. Educational attributes like kindergarten attendance, discipline, central exams, the use of tests, age at which students are first segregated into more versus less academic tracks, and instructional techniques cannot be easily manipulated. Educational traditions react sluggishly to attempts to change their direction. Additionally, pressure groups could oppose reforms, and there could be conflicts of interests between parties, trade unions, parental organizations, and media.
4. Educational reforms have *side effects*. For instance, if in less developed countries the educational level is raised, traditional aspects of societies from familial cohesion up to the influence of an old religious elite (e.g., mullahs and sangomas – healers in sub-Saharan Africa) may be weakened. A culture

[5] We use the term "low educational background" instead of the usually used term "minority" because the decisive variable seems to be not the status as a (quantitative) minority as opposed to a majority (e.g., Chinese or Jewish students in the United States versus Whites or Gentiles) but the educational background of the parents and their values and abilities.

might change when educational levels increase. Single modifications like earlier tracking could increase within-country differences or, like delaying tracking, the "bright flight" to private schools where a more tailored academic experience can be offered for those who can afford it.

Reciprocal causation. Neither at the level of individuals nor at the level of nations is education the single determinant of cognitive ability differences or of development processes. Numerous other factors (e.g., culture and genetics) have been empirically verified (for a list, see Rindermann & Ceci, 2009). And of course there are reciprocal effects: Education nurtures ability and ability promotes insight into the benefits of education and more generally into the advantages of a stimulating environment and lifestyle. Intelligence and knowledge enhance the ability to understand causal relationships, to anticipate future events, to act in a rational manner, and to modify environments – from their physical aspects to their social and cultural dimensions. So intelligent people may start with a higher probability of modifying their physical, social, and cultural world, and be able to construct this world in a more beneficial and more complex way. And such an environment will have an impact on ability.

Recommendation for Future Research

Psychological research and the economic sciences have done many statistical studies to research possible benefits of cognitive competences and education and why countries differed in economic and (relatively new) in cognitive development. In future research, this approach should be complemented by case studies of single countries and their educational policies and the possible effects of other social, economic and cultural conditions supporting or impeding ability development. Such studies should start with countries at the top of international competence studies, like the culturally very different Finland and Singapore. Possibly their experiences could not only increase our knowledge of determinants for cognitive enhancement but also assist other countries in their educational reforms.

Conclusion

Research on this topic is difficult due to the inappropriateness of experimental methods for many questions. Inferences must be derived from nonexperimental, correlational data whether cross-sectional, cross-lagged longitudinal, or quasi-experimental. Conclusions cannot be based on a single, watertight experiment but must be generated by converging weaker evidence from multiple sources. That being said, for some questions, enough such data exist to allow tentative conclusions. Evidence suggests that education does build cognitive competence, and education and cognitive competence promote better social outcomes, in terms of both economic and noneconomic factors. Cognitive competence here is used to refer to ability demonstrated in academic style, paper-and-pencil tasks of the sorts of skills schools seem to build. These studies do not assess practical abilities, creativity, and so on. Such skills are certainly useful and may or may not correlate (positively or negatively) with education, GDP, and other societal outcomes. However, within the limited sphere of the cognitive tests discussed here, cognitive competence appears malleable, education fruitful, and beneficial to society.

References

Alderman, H., Behrman, J. R., Ross, D., & Sabot, R. (1996). The returns to endogenous human capital in Pakistan's rural wage labor market. *Oxford Bulletin of Economics and Statistics*, 58, 29–55.

Angrist, J., & Krueger, A. B. (1991). Does compulsory schooling affect schooling and earnings? *Quarterly Journal of Economics*, 106, 979–1014.

Barber, N. (2005). Educational and ecological correlates of IQ: A cross-national investigation. *Intelligence, 33*, 273–284.

Barnett, S. M., & Ceci, S. J. (2002). When and where do we apply what we learn? A taxonomy for far transfer. *Psychological Bulletin, 128*(4), 612–637

Barnett, S. M., & Williams, W. M. (2004). National intelligence and the emperor's new clothes. *Contemporary Psychology, 49*, 389–396.

Barnett, S. M., & Williams, W. M. (2005). IQ-income data do not prove poor countries must remain poor. *PsycCRITIQUES, 50*(13), no pagination specified.

Barnett, W. S., & Boocock, S. S. (Eds.). (1998). *Early care and education for children in poverty. Promises, programs, and long-term results.* Albany: State University of New York Press.

Becker, M., Lüdtke, O., Trautwein, U., Köller, O., & Baumert, J. (2007). *The effect of schooling on psychometric intelligence: Does school quality make a difference?* Unpublished paper. Berlin: Max-Planck-Institute for Human Development.

Bond, R., & Saunders, P. (1999). Routes of success: Influences on the occupational attainment of young British males. *British Journal of Sociology, 50*, 217–249.

Boissiere, M., Knight, J. B., & Sabot, R. (1985). Earnings, schooling, ability and reading-comprehension cognitive skills. *American Economic Review, 75*, 1016–1030.

Botticini, M., & Eckstein, Z. (2007). From farmers to merchants, conversions and diaspora: Human capital and Jewish history. *Journal of the European Economic Association, 5*, 885–926.

Bruner, J. S., Olver, R. R., & Greenfield, P. M. (1966). *Studies in cognitive growth.* New York, NY: Wiley.

Cahan, S., & Cohen, N. (1989). Age versus schooling effects on intelligence development. *Child Development, 60*, 1239–1249.

Cattell, R. B. (1987). *Intelligence: Its structure, growth and action.* Amsterdam, the Netherlands: Elsevier.

Ceci, S. J. (1991). How much does schooling influence general intelligence and its cognitive components? A reassessment of the evidence. *Developmental Psychology, 27*, 703–722.

Ceci, S. J. (1996). *On intelligence: A bioecological treatise on intellectual development.* Cambridge, MA: Harvard University Press.

Ceci, S. J., & Williams, W. M. (1997). Schooling, intelligence, and income. *American Psychologist, 52*, 1051–1058.

Ceci, S. J., & Williams, W. M. (2009). Should scientists study race and IQ? Yes: The scientific truth must be pursued. *Nature, 457*, 788–789.

Charlton, B. G. (2009). Replacing education with psychometrics. *Medical Hypotheses, 73*, 273–277.

Clark, G. (2007). *A farewell to alms. A brief economic history of the world.* Princeton, NJ: Princeton University Press.

Cunha, F., Heckman, J. J., Lochner, L., & Masterov, D. V. (2006). Interpreting the evidence on life cycle skill formation. In E. A. Hanushek & F. Welch (Eds.), *Handbook of the economics of education* (Vol. 1, pp. 697–812). Amsterdam, the Netherlands: North-Holland.

Dar, Y., & Resh, N. (1986). Classroom intellectual composition and academic achievement. *American Educational Research Journal, 23*, 357–374.

Deary, I. J., Batty, G. D., & Gale, C. R. (2008). Bright children become enlightened adults. *Psychological Science, 19*, 1–6.

Denny, K., & Doyle, O. (2008). Political interest, cognitive ability and personality: Determinants of voter turnout in Britain. *British Journal of Political Science, 38*, 291–310.

Ellis, L., & Walsh, A. (2003). Crime, delinquency and intelligence: A review of the worldwide literature. In H. Nyborg (Ed.), *The scientific study of general intelligence. Tribute to Arthur R. Jensen* (pp. 343–365). Oxford, UK: Pergamon.

Eysenck, H. J., & Schoenthaler, S. J. (1997). Raising IQ level by vitamin and mineral supplementation. In R. J. Sternberg & E. L. Grigorenko (Eds.), *Intelligence, heredity and environment* (pp. 363–392). Cambridge, UK: Cambridge University Press.

Flynn, J. R. (2007). *What is intelligence? Beyond the Flynn effect.* Cambridge, UK: Cambridge University Press.

Glaeser, E., Ponzetto, G., & Shleifer, A. (2007). Why does democracy need education? *Journal of Economic Growth, 12*, 77–99.

Glewwe, P. (1996). The relevance of standard estimates of rates of return to schooling for education policy: A critical assessment. *Journal of Development Economics 51*, 267–290.

Glewwe, P., & Kremer, M. (2006). Schools, teachers, and education outcomes in developing countries. In E. A. Hanushek & F. Welch

(Eds.), *Handbook of the economics of education* (Vol. 2, pp. 945–1017). Amsterdam, the Netherlands: North-Holland.

Goodenough, F. L. (1926). *Measurement of intelligence by drawings*. Chicago, IL: World Book.

Gottfredson, L. S. (2005). Suppressing intelligence research: Hurting those we intend to help. In R. H. Wright & N. A. Cummings (Eds.), *Destructive trends in mental health: The well-intentioned path to harm* (pp. 155–186). New York, NY: Taylor and Francis.

Gottfredson, L., & Deary, I. J. (2004). Intelligence predicts health and longevity, but why? *Current Directions in Psychological Science, 13*, 1–4.

Hansen, K. T., Heckman, J. J., & Mullen, K. J. (2004). The effect of schooling and ability on achievement test scores. *Journal of Econometrics, 121*, 39–98.

Hanushek, E. A., & Woessmann, L. (2008). The role of cognitive skills in economic development. *Journal of Economic Literature, 46*, 607–668.

Harris, D. B. (1963). *Children's drawings as measures of intellectual maturity*. New York, NY: Harcourt, Brace & World.

Harris, L. (2007). *The suicide of reason: Radical Islam's threat to the West and enlightenment*. New York, NY: Basic Books.

Hart, B., & Risley, T. R. (1995). *Meaningful differences in the everyday experience of young American children*. Baltimore, MD: Paul Brookes.

Hart, M. (2007). *Understanding human history. An analysis including the effects of geography and differential evolution*. Augusta, GA: Washington Summit.

Heckman, J. J., & Masterov, D. V. (2007, April). *The productivity argument for investing in young children*. NBER Working Paper 13016. Cambridge, MA: National Bureau of Educational Research.

Henrich, J., Heine, S., & Norenzayan, A. (2010). The WEIRDEST people in the world? *Behavioral and Brain Sciences*, 33(2–3), 61–83.

Hunt, E., & Carlson, J. (2007). Considerations relating to the study of group differences in intelligence. *Perspectives on Psychological Science, 2*, 194–213.

Klauer, K. J., & Phye, G. D. (2008). Inductive reasoning: A training approach. *Review of Educational Research*, 78, 85–123.

Johnson, W., Bouchard, Th. J., Mcgue, M., Segal, N. L., Tellegen, A., Keyes, M., & Gottesman, I. I. (2007). Genetic and environmental influences on the Verbal-Perceptual-Image Rotation (VPR) model of the structure of mental abilities in the Minnesota study of twins reared apart. *Intelligence, 35*, 542–562.

Jones, G., & Schneider, W. J. (2006). Intelligence, human capital, and economic growth: A Bayesian Averaging of Classical Estimates (BACE) approach. *Journal of Economic Growth, 11*, 71–93.

Kanazawa, S. (2006). IQ and the wealth of states. *Intelligence, 34*, 593–600.

Komlos, J., & Kriwy, P. (2003). The biological standard of living in the two Germanies. *German Economic Review, 4*, 493–507.

Lakhanpal, M., & Ram, R. (2008). Educational attainment and HIV/AIDS prevalence: A cross-country study. *Economics of Education Review, 27*, 14–21.

Levels, M., Dronkers, J., & Kraaykamp, G. (2008). Immigrant children's educational achievement in Western countries: Origin, destination, and community effects on mathematical performance. *American Sociological Review*, 73, 835–853.

Lynn, R. (2009). What has caused the Flynn effect? Secular increases in the development quotients of infants. *Intelligence, 37*, 16–24.

Lynn, R., & Meisenberg, G. (2009). The average IQ of sub-Saharan Africans: Comments on Wicherts, Dolan, and van der Maas. *Intelligence* 38(1), 21–29.

Lynn, R., & Vanhanen, T. (2002). *IQ and the wealth of nations*. Westport, CN: Praeger.

Lynn, R., & Vanhanen, T. (2006). *IQ and global inequality*. Augusta, GA: Washington Summit.

McDaniel, M. A. (2006). Estimating state IQ: Measurement challenges and preliminary correlates. *Intelligence, 34*, 607–619.

Meisenberg, G. (2004). Talent, character, and the dimensions of national culture. *Mankind Quarterly, 45*, 123–168.

Melhuish, E. C., Phan, M. B., Sylva, K., Sammons, P., Siraj-Blatchford, I., & Taggart, B. (2008). Effects of the home learning environment and preschool center experience upon literacy and numeracy development in early primary school. *Journal of Social Issues, 64*, 95–114.

Meyer, J. W., Ramirez, F. O., & Soysal, Y. N. (1992). World expansion of mass education, 1870–1980. *Sociology of Education, 65*, 128–149.

Mullis, I. V. S., Martin, M. O., & Foy, P. (2005). *IEA's TIMSS 2003 international report on achievement in the mathematics cognitive domains: Findings from a developmental project.*

Chestnut Hill: International Association for the Evaluation of Educational Achievement.

Mullis, I. V. S., Martin, M. O., & Foy, P. (2009). *TIMSS 2007 international mathematics report: Findings from IEA's trends in international mathematics and science study at the fourth and eighth grades*. Chestnut Hill: International Association for the Evaluation of Educational Achievement.

Murnane, R. J., Willet, J. B., & Levy, F. (1995). The growing importance of reading comprehension cognitive skills in wage determination. *Review of Economics and Statistics, 77,* 251–266.

Murray, Ch. (2003). *Human accomplishment: The pursuit of excellence in the arts and sciences, 800 B.C. to 1950*. New York, NY: Harper-Collins.

Murray, Ch. (2008). *Real education: Four simple truths for bringing America's schools back to reality*. New York, NY: Crown Forum.

Neisser, U., Boodoo, G., Bouchard, Th. J., Boykin, A. W., Brody, N., Ceci, St. J., Halpern, D. F., Loehlin, J. C., Perloff, R., Sternberg, R. J., & Urbina, S. (1996). Intelligence: Knowns and unknowns. *American Psychologist*, **51**, 77–101.

Nisbett, R. E. (2009). *Intelligence and how to get it. Why schools and cultures count*. New York, NY: W. W. Norton.

Nyborg, H. (2009). The intelligence-religiosity nexus: A representative study of white adolescent Americans. *Intelligence, 37,* 81–93.

Oesterdiekhoff, G. W. (2008). Magic and animism in old religions: The relevance of sun cults in the world-view of traditional societies. *Croatian Journal of Ethnology and Folklore Research*, **45**, 43–66.

Priester, E. (1949). *Kurze Geschichte Österreichs. Band II*. [Short history of Austria. Volume II.] Wien, Austria: Globus.

Psacharopoulos, G., & Patrinos, H. A. (2004). Returns to investment in education: A further update. *Education Economics*, **12**, 111–134.

Rindermann, H. (2007). The *g*-factor of international cognitive ability comparisons: The homogeneity of results in PISA, TIMSS, PIRLS and IQ-tests across nations. *European Journal of Personality*, **21**, 667–706.

Rindermann, H. (2008a). Relevance of education and intelligence at the national level for the economic welfare of people. *Intelligence, 36,* 127–142.

Rindermann, H. (2008b). Relevance of education and intelligence for the political development of nations: Democracy, rule of law and political liberty. *Intelligence, 36,* 306–322.

Rindermann, H., & Ceci, S. J. (2009). Educational policy and country outcomes in international cognitive competence studies. *Perspectives on Psychological Science*, **4**(6), 551–577.

Rindermann, H., & Meisenberg, G. (2009). Relevance of education and intelligence at the national level for health: The case of HIV and AIDS. *Intelligence, 37,* 383–395.

Rindermann, H., Sailer, M., & Thompson, J. (2009). The impact of smart fractions, cognitive ability of politicians and average competence of peoples on social development. *Talent Development and Excellence*, **1**, 3–25.

Rindermann, H., & Thompson, J. (2009). *Parents' education, and not their money, nurtures the intelligence of their children*. Graz, Institute for Psychology. Manuscript in preparation.

Rushton, J. Ph., Bons, T. A., Vernon, Ph. A., & Cvorovic, J. (2007). Genetic and environmental contributions to population group differences on the Raven's Progressive Matrices estimated from twins reared together and apart. *Proceedings of the Royal Society*, **274**, 1773–1777.

Rushton, J. Ph., & Templer, D. I. (2009). National differences in intelligence, crime, income, and skin color. *Intelligence, 37,* 341–346.

Sackett, P. R., Kuncel, N. R., Arneson, J. J., Cooper, S. R., & Waters, Sh. D. (2009). Does socioeconomic status explain the relationship between admissions tests and post-secondary academic performance? *Psychological Bulletin*, **135**, 1–22.

Schmidt, F. L., & Hunter, J. E. (2004). General mental ability in the world of work: Occupational attainment and job performance. *Journal of Personality and Social Psychology, 86,* 162–173.

Schwekendiek, D., & Pak, S. (2009). Recent growth of children in the two Koreas: A meta-analysis. *Economics and Human Biology, 7,* 109–112.

Shayer, M., & Ginsburg, D. (2009). Thirty years on – a large anti-Flynn effect (II)? 13- & 14-year-olds. Piagetian tests of formal operations norms 1976–2006/7. *British Journal of Educational Psychology, 79,* 409–418.

Spence, M. (1973). Job market signaling. *Quarterly Journal of Economics, 87,* 355–374.

Stelzl, I., Merz, F., Remer, H., & Ehlers, Th. (1995). The effect of schooling on the development of fluid and chrystallized intelligence: A quasi-experimental study. *Intelligence*, *21*, 279–296.

Strauss, J., & Thomas, D. (1998). Health, nutrition, and economic development. *Journal of Economic Literature* 36, 766–817.

te Nijenhuis, J., de Jong, M.-J., Evers, A., & van der Flier, H. (2004). Are cognitive differences between immigrant and majority groups diminishing? *European Journal of Personality*, *18*, 405–434.

Thomson, G. H. (1937/1936). Intelligence and civilisation: A Ludwig Mond lecture delivered at the University of Manchester on October 23, 1936. *Journal of the University of Manchester*, *1*, 18–38.

Weber, M. (2001/1905). *The Protestant ethic and the spirit of capitalism*. London, UK: Routledge.

Weede, E., & Kämpf, S. (2002). The impact of intelligence and institutional improvements on economic growth. *Kyklos*, *55*, 361–380.

Whetzel, D. L., & McDaniel, M. A. (2006). Prediction of national wealth. *Intelligence*, *34*, 449–458.

Wicherts, J. M., Dolan, C. V., Carlson, J. S., & van der Maas, H. L. J. (2010). Raven's Test performance of sub-Saharan Africans: Average performance, psychometric properties, and the Flynn effect. *Learning and Individual Differences*, *20(3)*, 135–151.

Wicherts, J. M., Dolan, C. V., & van der Maas, H. L. J. (2010). A systematic literature review of the average IQ of sub-Saharan Africans. *Intelligence*, 38(1), 1–20.

Wober, M. (1969). Distinguishing centri-cultural from cross-cultural tests and research. *Perceptual and Motor Skills*, *28*, 488.

Woodworth, K. R., David, J. L., Guha, R., Wang, H., & Lopez-Torkos, A. (2008). *San Francisco Bay Area KIPP schools: A study of early implementation and achievement. Final report.* Menlo Park, CA: SRI International.

CHAPTER 34

Intelligence as a Predictor of Health, Illness, and Death

Ian J. Deary and G. David Batty

Introduction

In the last 10 years, psychometric intelligence has become established as a significant correlate of death, illness, and health outcomes. This adds considerably to the already known predictive power that intelligence test scores have for educational and occupational outcomes. In this chapter we show that lower intelligence test scores from early life – childhood and early adulthood – are associated with earlier death, an increased risk of specific diseases, and less advantageous health-related behaviors. The causal direction is thought to be from intelligence to these later outcomes, because intelligence is typically assessed decades before them. The field of study that examines the associations between intelligence and health, illness, and death is called cognitive epidemiology. Already, there are some brief overviews of the field (e.g., Deary, 2008), and a glossary of terms used in the field (Deary & Batty, 2007). There is a systematic review of the first nine studies – conducted between 1984 and 2006 – that established the association between lower intelligence and earlier death from all causes (Batty, Deary, & Gottfredson, 2007). "All-cause" mortality is a phrase used within epidemiology to mean mortality per se, no matter what the cause of death. This review also provided a theoretical framework for exploring possible reasons for the association, which expanded upon an original series of suggestions by Whalley and Deary (2001). This framework is shown in Figure 34.1, and we encourage the reader to use this as a reference when the individual studies are described below. There is also a special issue of the journal *Intelligence* devoted to the topic of cognitive epidemiology (see Deary, 2009).

Since the association between intelligence and death was established, research on cognitive epidemiology has explored a number of specific issues. These issues include the ages across which the intelligence-death association applies; the causes of death with which intelligence is associated; the types of physical and mental illness with which intelligence is associated; the health behaviors with which intelligence is associated; and possible causes of, and mediators through

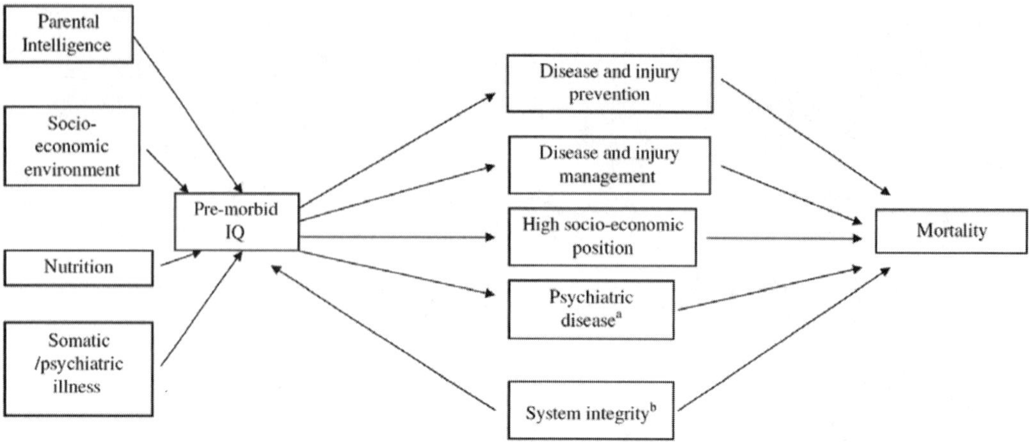

Figure 34.1 Simplified model of influences on premorbid IQ and potential pathways linking premorbid IQ with later mortality. [a]Although psychiatric disease is shown as a possible mediating variable between IQ and mortality, it might also be an antecedent variable if, for example, suboptimal neurodevelopment were the prior cause of both psychiatric disease and early mortality. [b]Note that system integrity is shown as antecedent to both IQ and mortality. In this pathway, lower IQ is not a cause of mortality, but both IQ and mortality are influenced by this more fundamental physiological integrity. From Batty, G. D., Deary, I. J., & Gottfredson, L. S. (2007). Premorbid (early life) IQ and later mortality risk: Systematic review. Annals of Epidemiology, 17, 278–288. Reproduced with permission.

which, intelligence and health and death are associated. These will be recounted in the present chapter.

The first peer-reviewed study in the field to find that higher individually tested intelligence was associated with lower mortality (in men between the ages of 22 and 40) was O'Toole and Stankov's (1992) report based on Australian Vietnam veterans who had taken the Australian Army General Classification Test. The result was found for all-cause mortality, and for mortality from motor vehicle accidents and suicides. The authors emphasized the importance of education and the difficulty of separating it, as a cause, from intelligence. Prior to that, Maller (1933) had noted a strong, linear association between mean childhood intelligence test scores and mortality rates in areas of New York. Furu, Lingarde, and Ljung (1984) found – in the Malmo (Sweden) cohort followed from 1938 to 1979 – an association between intelligence tests taken at age 10 and 20 and the 61 deaths that occurred among the 831 men. The results were published in a non-peer-reviewed report.

Note on the Organization of the Chapter

To conduct studies in cognitive epidemiology requires study samples that are unusual in intelligence research. The samples must be large (ranging from hundreds to over one million), they must have mental test data, and they must then be followed up for health-related information. This makes the studies rather special. They are, typically, cohort studies: that is, longitudinal studies of people born in the same time period and with other similar characteristics. This is a far stronger design than the more usual cross-sectional studies, often performed on convenience samples. These samples also tend to be idiosyncratic with respect to the background population (in terms of age, sex, and geography) they represent, the data they have available (risk factors, potential confounders and mediators, and outcomes), and the period(s) of time over which they have been studied. Therefore, in this chapter, we have adopted an approach that takes the reader through many of the most impressive and informative cohorts that have contributed to cognitive epidemiology. We describe the characteristics of each cohort in outline. We then summarize the cohort's principal published contributions to cognitive epidemiology, with the following order: associations between intelligence and all-cause mortality, then specific causes of mortality, then specific disease states, and then other health outcomes and health behaviors. We end each section with any other interesting findings between intelligence and health-relevant factors. There are several reasons for presenting the results by cohort: The field is new, and readers need to be convinced of the strengths of the cohorts that provide the results; it has publications scattered over many medical and psychological journals; to recall which cohorts have which types of participants and data can be confusing; and we think that the strength of this new field is most clearly signaled by a clear presentation of the strength of its evidence base in this way. To assist with integration of results between cohorts, we often compare and contrast individual results. Our opinion is that the style of presentation makes the origins and strengths of the data and results from each cohort explicit and accessible. We appreciate that to integrate across outcomes – for example, all-cause mortality – some cross-cohort inspection is required. However, we consider this to be at least as easy as having to recall all of the characteristics of each cohort with respect to any given health outcome.

Note on the Presentation of Statistical Results in the Chapter

A few notes are needed for readers unfamiliar with the largely epidemiological statistical analyses that are presented below. Analyses in epidemiology typically use Cox proportional hazards regression or logistic regression, which produce hazard ratios and odds ratios, respectively (Cox, 1972). These have similar meanings, except that the Cox method is sensitive to the time at which the outcome event occurs. A hazard ratio of exactly 1.0 means there is no association between the predictor (typically intelligence test scores) and the outcome (typically a dichotomous health variable, such as mortality or a specific illness). If the hazard ratio is greater than 1.0, then the predictor is associated with an increased risk of the outcome. If the hazard ratio is less than 1.0, then the risk is lower. For example, a hazard ratio of 1.29 means that there is a 29% increase in the hazard per unit of measurement of the predictor; often, we use a standard deviation of intelligence as the predictor to make the ratios comparable between studies. A hazard ratio of 0.86 means there is a 14% decrease in the hazard. Typically, for ease of reading, we refer to the percentage change to the hazard ratio instead of the actual hazard ratio. Therefore, a decrease of 26% refers to a hazard ratio of 0.74, an increase of 37% refers to a hazard ratio of 1.37, and an increase of, say, 217% refers to a hazard ratio of 3.17. Hazard ratios are often presented with 95% confidence intervals. If this interval includes 1.0, then the ratio is not statistically significant at the $p < .05$ level. The research papers to which we refer often contain many such regression models. These tend to start with age and – if appropriate – sex-adjusted models, and then further models that adjust for potentially confounding and mediating variables. Here, in our necessarily brief summaries of each study, we tend to present the age- (and sex-) adjusted model results. This is in part to let the reader view the basic associations, and in part because many of the statistical adjustments are contentious, because they include variables – such as education and socioeconomic status – with which intelligence is strongly correlated and on which intelligence might have a causal influence. However, in many instances we discuss the degree of attenuation caused by such adjustments and also the possible conclusions that may be drawn from them.

The Scottish Mental Surveys of 1932 and 1947

The Scottish Mental Survey of 1932 took place on June 1, 1932. It tested the intelligence of almost everyone born in 1921 and attending school in Scotland, at a mean age of 11 years. The test used was a version of the Moray House Test No. 12. This is a group-administered, general ability-type test with many of the items requiring verbal reasoning, though there are also some nonverbal reasoning items. There were 87,498 subjects in the study, about 95% of the 1921-born population. The Scottish Mental Survey of 1947 – implemented to test for any change in the mean of the Scottish population's mental ability, since 1932 – took place on June 4, 1947. It used the same mental test as the 1932 Survey. There were 70,805 subjects in the study, again about 95% of the whole population born in 1936. Both studies were conducted by the Scottish Council for Research in Education, which retained the data and later made them available for linkage to social and health records. A description of both Scottish Mental Surveys is available in Deary, Whalley, and Starr (2009). Studies in cognitive epidemiology have tended to use various subsamples of these surveys.

A number of reports from the Scottish Mental Surveys have examined the association between intelligence at age 11 and all-cause mortality and specific causes of death. The children who took the Mental Survey 1932 test in Aberdeen (N = 2,792) were sought in public and health records for vital status as of January 1, 1997; 2,230 were found (Whalley & Deary, 2001). A 15-point disadvantage in intelligence at age 11 was associated with a 21% increased risk of dying by age 76 (Figure 34.2). The exception was that men who died in active service in World War II tended to have higher than average intelligence. This study suggested a research agenda for the field, by hypothesizing that there were at least four nonexclusive possible explanations for the association between intelligence and mortality: that intelligence was a record of perinatal and childhood insults; that intelligence was a marker for good general system integrity; that intelligence was a predictor of safer occupational and other environments; and that intelligence was a predictor of health behaviors and management. As studies are described later in the chapter, we shall see tests of all of these ideas. An expanded version of these possibilities is shown in Figure 34.1.

Confirmation of the childhood intelligence-mortality association came from analyses based in the west of Scotland when the data from the Scottish Mental Survey 1932 were linked with the Midspan studies of cardiovascular health (Hart, MacKinnon et al., 2005). Combining the studies meant that there was a new "life course" dataset with intelligence at age 11, many physical health variables in middle age (taken in the 1970s), and follow-up for mortality across 25 years from the 1970s to 2002 (Hart et al., 2003). In this sample of over 900 people, a standard deviation disadvantage in intelligence at age 11 was associated with a 17% higher risk of dying in the 25-year follow-up period. Adjustment for adult occupational social class and a measure of the deprivation of the area of residence reduced this to 12%, though it was still significant. There were significant associations between childhood intelligence and dying from cardiovascular disease and lung cancer. Further analyses of the association between childhood intelligence and death up to age 81 in this sample showed that there was a significant association with deaths before age 65 (a standard deviation disadvantage in intelligence at age 11 was associated with a 36% increased risk) but not after 65 years (Hart, Taylor, et al., 2005). Deaths before 65 years are often characterized as being more preventable, which would accord with the view that intelligence relates to healthier lifestyle choices and better health management.

A wholly representative subsample (N = 1,181) of the Scottish Mental Survey 1936 was rated at age 14 by teachers on the personality trait of dependability (closely associated with conscientiousness in the Five-Factor Model of personality traits), in addition to having taken the 1947 Survey intelligence test at age 11 (Deary et al., 2008). These data were also linked to death records between 1968 and 2003. With both childhood factors included in the analysis, a standard deviation

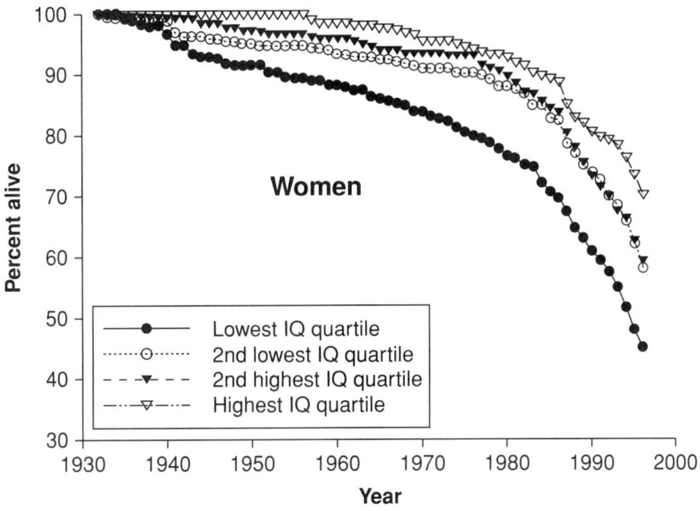

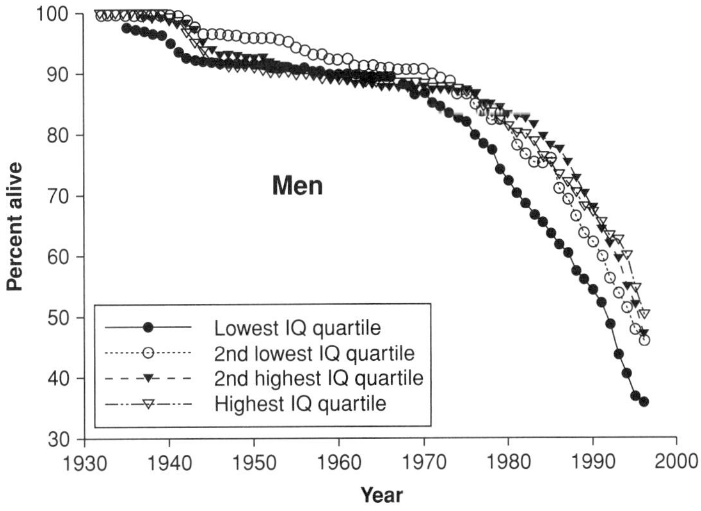

Figure 34.2 Relationship between IQ at age 11 in the Scottish Mental Survey 1932 and survival to age 76 on January 1, 1997, for women and for men. From "IQ at Age 11 and Longevity: Results From a Follow Up of the Scottish Mental Survey 1932" (Figure 1, p. 157), in *Brain and Longevity: Perspectives in Longevity*, by C. Finch, J.-M. Robine, & Y. Christen (Eds.), 2003, Berlin: Springer. Copyright 2003 by Springer. Adapted with permission.

decrease in intelligence and dependability from childhood was associated with a 20% and 23% reduction in survival, respectively. Children in the lower half of the distribution for intelligence and dependability in childhood were more than 2.5 times as likely to be dead by their mid-60s when compared with those in the top half for both traits.

A number of reports from the Scottish Mental Surveys have examined the association between intelligence at age 11 and the risk of developing specific illnesses later in life. The combined Scottish Mental Survey 1932-Midspan dataset showed that a standard deviation disadvantage in intelligence at age 11 was associated with a 16% increased risk of hospital admission for, or death from, coronary heart disease (Hart et al., 2004). The effect was found for events occurring before but not after age 65. Linkage of the Scottish Mental Survey 1932 data to dementia records in Scotland revealed that higher childhood intelligence was associated with lower risk of late onset dementia, but that there was no association with early-onset dementia (Whalley et al., 2000). Later and more detailed exploration of late onset dementia cases within the Edinburgh area suggested that higher intelligence in childhood was associated with lower risk of vascular dementia, but that there was no association with Alzheimer's-type dementia (McGurn, Deary, & Starr, 2008). Analyses of psychiatric case records in the northeast of Scotland found that a standard deviation disadvantage in IQ was associated with a 12% increased risk of contact with psychiatric services up to age 77 (Walker et al., 2002).

A number of reports from the Scottish Mental Surveys have examined the association between intelligence at age 11 and risk factors for ill health later in life, particularly coronary heart disease. The combined Scottish Mental Survey 1932-Midspan dataset showed that a standard deviation disadvantage in intelligence at age 11 was significantly associated with a 3.15 mmHg increase in systolic, and 1.5 mmHg increase in diastolic blood pressure in mid-life (Starr et al., 2004). These are relatively small effects for individuals, but this magnitude of difference could have a large effect on hypertension-related pathology (such as stroke) in a population. The same study and the Lothian Birth Cohort 1921 – a follow-up of 550 of the Edinburgh-based Scottish Mental Survey 1932 participants in old age (Deary et al., 2004) – both found that higher childhood intelligence was associated with better lung function – as assessed by the forced expiratory volume in one second – in middle and old age, respectively (Hart et al., 2004; Deary et al., 2006). Smaller subsamples from the Lothian Birth Cohort 1921 found that childhood intelligence was correlated ($r \approx 0.4$) significantly with lower integrity of the brain's white matter in the region of the centrum semiovale (Shenkin et al., 2003, Deary et al., 2006). More evidence in this field has come from the Lothian Birth Cohort 1936 – a follow-up study of 1,091 of the Edinburgh-based Scottish Mental Survey 1932 participants in old age (Deary et al., 2007). While investigating the cross-sectional association between cognitive ability at age 70 years and levels of C-reactive protein – a marker for systemic bodily inflammation in old age – it was found that lower intelligence at age 11 was associated with greater levels of C-reactive protein (more inflammation; Luciano et al., 2009). Also, adjusting for intelligence at age 11 reduced the correlation between intelligence at 70 and C-reactive protein (the variance accounted for was about 1%, which is typical for this association in other studies) to nonsignificant levels, an example of possible reverse causation, or an indication that both inflammation and intelligence in old age are associated with some more fundamental processes, which bring about a spurious correlation between them.

With regard to health behaviors, the combined Scottish Mental Survey 1932-Midspan dataset revealed that a standard deviation advantage in intelligence at age 11 was associated with a 33% increase in giving up smoking by mid-life (in the 1970s) (Taylor et al., 2003). However, there was no significant association between childhood intelligence and having started smoking. It should be noted that at the time when most of this cohort began smoking, there was little knowledge of, or publicity for, the health risks of smoking.

The Swedish Conscripts Study

The Swedish Conscripts Study makes use of the near-universal military conscription in Sweden. The study cohort includes non-adopted men born between 1950 and 1976 who were conscripted. This has resulted in a sample of over 1.3 million men. This is almost the whole male population born in the relevant years. The only men excused from the conscription examination are those with foreign citizenship or a severe medical condition or disability. The conscription examination includes four mental tests covering the mental domains of logical reasoning, verbal ability, spatial ability, and

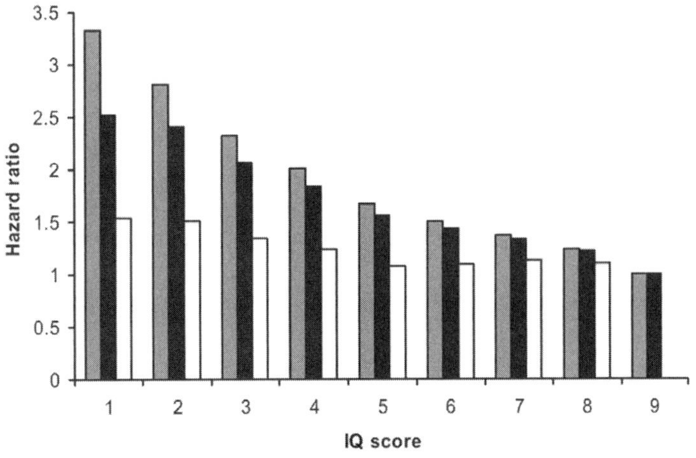

Figure 34.3 Hazard ratios for the relation of IQ score with total mortality (N = 994,262). Basic adjustment (gray bars); full adjustment without education (black); full adjustments with education (white). The referent is the highest scoring IQ group (category 9). From, Batty, G. D., Wennerstad, K. M., Davey Smith, G., Gunnell, D., Deary, I. J., Tylenius, P., & Rasmussen, F. (2009). IQ in early adulthood and mortality by middle age: Cohort study of one million Swedish men. *Epidemiology*, 20, 100–109. Reproduced with permission.

technical (physics and chemistry) ability. The four tests together make up a general ability score: all four tests correlated highly, and principal components analysis revealed only one component, on which all tests loaded strongly. Also included in the conscription examination were height, weight, blood pressure, smoking, and a short interview by a physician to record physical and psychiatric illnesses. Sweden's Multi-Generation Register was used to link a personal identifier to the following Swedish registers: the Military Service Conscription Register, the Cause of Death Register, Population and Housing Censuses records, and the register of Education. From these, there is information on parental and conscripts' occupational social class, and on conscript's education and vital status. Studies in cognitive epidemiology from this study have sometimes used a narrow range of birth years, and sometimes the whole range available within this study. An example of a paper that describes this study is by Batty, Wennerstad, et al. (2007). This study is the largest and one of the most productive in cognitive epidemiology. However, because of the range of birth years included, the study necessarily is relevant only to male deaths and illness at relatively young ages.

A number of reports from the Swedish Conscripts Study have examined the association between intelligence at conscription and all-cause mortality and specific causes of death. There were 14,498 deaths among the million or so men in the follow-up period. A one standard deviation disadvantage in intelligence at conscription was associated with a 32% increased risk of death from all causes (Batty, Wennerstad, et al., 2009). There was little attenuation after adjusting for childhood social circumstances, or concurrently measured (with intelligence) blood pressure, body mass index, or smoking. Therefore, intelligence influences survival to middle as well as old age. A notable finding was that when the risk of death was examined in each of the nine intelligence groups – from highest to lowest – it increased monotonically and appeared mostly linear (Figure 34.3). Therefore, the intelligence-mortality association does not appear, at least in men in this age range and culture, to be caused merely by an excess of deaths among the lowest IQ groups. There were also significant associations between intelligence and conscription and death from (percentage of increased risk per one standard deviation disadvantage in intelligence at conscription) coronary heart disease (31%) (previously shown in a slightly smaller sample, of almost 700,000 of the cohort; Silventoinen et al., 2007), accidents (22%), suicide (22%; previously shown by Gunnell, Magnusson, & Rasmussen, 2005); and other deaths (41%), but not from all cancers (3%). A further study examined death by type of unintentional injury (accident) and divided intelligence scores into four groups (Batty, Gale, et al., 2009). Compared with the highest scoring intelligence group, the hazard ratios increased (%) as follows for the lowest scoring group: poisonings = 482%; fire = 339%; falls = 217%; drowning = 216%; road injury = 117%. Homicide was the cause of death for 191 out of the approximately 1,000,000 men in the follow-up period. A one standard deviation advantage in intelligence at conscription was associated with a 51% reduction in the risk of being murdered (Batty, Deary, et al., 2008b). Those in the lowest tertile of intelligence had about five times the risk of those in the highest tertile. This finding posed especially tricky considerations concerning possible mechanisms, and four were suggested: that higher verbal skills might be associated with successful conflict resolution; that individuals with lower intelligence might tend to live in more dangerous localities; that lower intelligence might be associated with poorer risk perception; and that it might in fact be the perpetrators that have lower intelligence, and that the apparent risk is because of social selection of intelligence that tends to result in people with similar intelligence levels being in proximity.

Reports from the Swedish Conscripts Study have examined the association between intelligence at conscription and the risk of developing specific illnesses in the follow-up period other than those described above. There were over 10,000 incident cancers (fatal and nonfatal) among the million men after 19.5 years of follow-up. People with higher intelligence at conscription had a significantly decreased risk (% per standard deviation disadvantage in intelligence) of cancer of the stomach (18%), and a significantly increased risk of skin cancer (18%). The latter could be due to a lifestyle that afforded more time exposed to the sun. There were nonsignificant associations with many other cancers tested. Over the same period, using the same metric, lower intelligence was associated with increased risk of being hospitalized for the following psychiatric disorders (Gale, Batty, et al., 2010): schizophrenia (60%), other nonaffective psychosis (49%), mood disorders (50%), neurotic and somatoform disorders (51%), adjustment disorders (60%), personality disorders (75%), alcohol-related disorders (75%), other substance-use disorders (85%), and any other psychiatric diagnosis (55%).

A report from a smaller sample (over 49,000) of the Swedish Conscripts Study found an inverse association between intelligence at conscription (65% increased odds per category change, out of nine, in intelligence test score) and taking up smoking in adolescence, but not with quitting in the follow-up period (Hemmingsson et al., 2008). Though these results in a different country appear to disagree with those found in the Scottish Mental Survey of 1932 (Taylor et al., 2003), they could be explained by the increased knowledge and dissemination of the health effects of smoking in the period between the birth years of the two cohorts' subjects.

The Vietnam Experience Study

The Vietnam Experience Study draws its subjects from men who started military service between the start of 1965 and the end of 1971. From a random sample of over 48,500 men, excluding those who died, who could not be traced, or who did not meet inclusion criteria, 18,313 were selected to form the cohort. Of these, around 20 years later,

15,288 took part in a telephone interview in 1985, and 4,462 took part in a medical examination in 1986. Mental ability was tested using the Army General Technical Test at the time of enlistment. During the telephone interview, the data gathered included study participant-reported information on occupation, income and health, and smoking. During the medical examination, the types of data collected included blood being assessed for a number of disease biomarkers; blood pressure and heart rate; lung function; body mass index; subtests from the Wechsler Intelligence Scale; a readministration of the Army General Technical Test; and, very unusually given the sample size – but perhaps owing to lay and health practitioner concerns over mental health in Vietnam war veterans – a standardized psychiatric interview. The cohort was followed up for deaths to the end of 2000. A description of this study is available in the Centres for Disease Control Vietnam Experience Study (2004), and in Batty, Shipley, et al. (2008a).

Reports from the Vietnam Experience Study have examined the association between intelligence at conscription and all-cause mortality and specific causes of death. In a study of 4,316 men, one standard deviation advantage in intelligence at enlistment was associated with a 29% reduction of the risk of all-cause mortality in men (Batty Shipley, et al., 2008a). A particular strength of this study is the large number of possible mediating factors that were assessed. Each of the following factors was tested one at a time and had very little attenuating effect on the association: depression, body mass index, pulse rate, post-traumatic stress disorder, somatic disease, marital status, alcohol consumption, systolic blood pressure, diastolic blood pressure, blood glucose, generalized anxiety disorder, smoking, lung function, occupational prestige, and educational grade. Only family income had a substantial mediating effect, reducing the influence of intelligence by about half. Therefore, income might mediate the influence of intelligence on mortality, but it could merely be acting as a surrogate for mental ability. More specifically, one standard deviation disadvantage in intelligence at enlistment was associated with a 34% increase in the risk of coronary heart disease mortality (Batty, Shipley, et al., 2008b). This effect was reduced by just under half after adjusting for possible mediating factors of blood pressure, blood lipids, blood glucose, lung function, and body mass index, all being known risk factors for coronary heart disease. There was almost complete attenuation of the effect after adjustment for education, income, and occupational prestige, but again, it is not clear how to interpret this, because these variables are likely to be substantially influenced by earlier intelligence. One standard deviation disadvantage in intelligence at enlistment was also associated with a 27% increase in the risk of death from all cancers, and a 37% increase in the risk of death from smoking-related cancers (Batty, Mortensen, et al., 2009). These are dissimilar to the more nearly null results in cancer deaths from the Swedish Conscripts Study; the number of cancer deaths was small in the Vietnam Experience Study, and the Swedish Conscripts Study had a far larger number of cancer cases. There were 21 deaths by homicide in the Vietnam Experience Study over the follow-up period. The hazard ratio for risk of death by homicide, expressed as the risk per standard deviation of intelligence at enlistment, was 15.20 (Batty, Mortensen, et al., 2008). However, because of the small number of cases, the 95% confidence interval is very large (2.62 to 88.10), and the Swedish Conscripts Study of the same outcome – albeit it in a different country – provides a more robust estimate.

One study used cognitive ability at enlistment, and later cognitive ability and the personality trait of neuroticism from the clinical examination, as predictors of mortality in the follow-up period (Weiss et al., 2009). The modeling used was novel. It used a structural equation modeling framework, including latent traits for intelligence and poor health; an interaction term between intelligence and neuroticism; Cox proportional hazards modeling for the associations with mortality; and mediating effects,

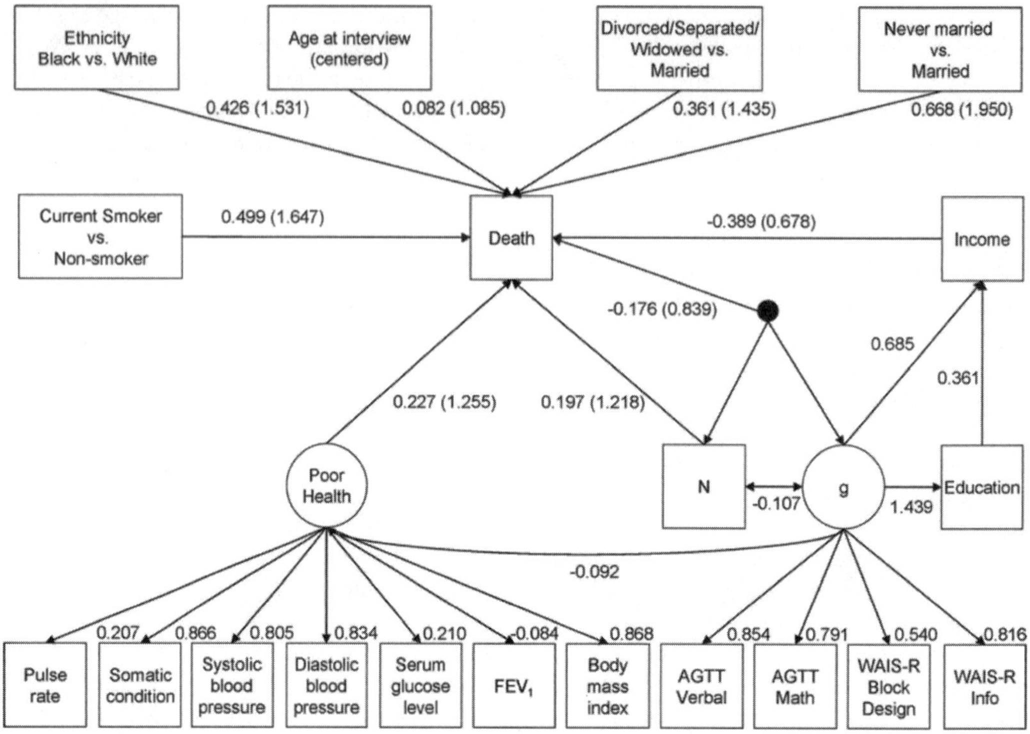

Figure 34.4 Structural equation model for predicting mortality in the Vietnam Experience Study. Numbers in parentheses are exponentiated path coefficients (hazard ratios). N = neuroticism; g = cognitive ability; AGTT = Army General Technical Test; WAIS-R = Wechsler Adult Intelligence Scale-Revised; FEV1 = forced expiratory volume in 1 second. Measured (manifest) variables are indicated by rectangles and latent traits by circles. The small black circle indicates an interaction between general intelligence and neuroticism on mortality. Note that the influence of intelligence on mortality is wholly mediated and that the influence of neuroticism is direct. From Weiss, A., Gale, C. R., Batty, G. D., & Deary, I. J. (2009). Emotionally stable, intelligent men live longer: The Vietnam Experience Study. *Psychosomatic Medicine*, 71, 385–394. Reproduced with permission.

especially education and income as potential mediators of intelligence (Figure 34.4). For a standard deviation increase in neuroticism there was a 33% increase in the risk of mortality, and a 27% decreased risk for each standard deviation advantage in intelligence. They were mutually independent predictors of mortality. In addition to this, the two psychological factors interacted: There was more effect of neuroticism at low levels of intelligence, and a greater effect of intelligence at high levels of neuroticism. The effects of intelligence were mediated via education, income, and poor health, with no direct effects after adjusting for these factors. There were no variables studied that mediated the effects of neuroticism; it had a direct effect on mortality.

The Vietnam Experience Study was also used to test whether intelligence could predict total and cardiovascular disease mortality as strongly as established risk factors (Batty, Shipley, et al., 2008c). The relative index of inequality was used to derive hazard ratios that were comparable between predictors; this method effectively compares the extremes of any predictor with regard to its influence on the outcome. For sex-adjusted models, the hazard ratios for total and cardiovascular disease mortality, respectively, were family income = 7.46, 6.58; intelligence in middle age = 4.41, 4.70; smoking = 4.02, 3.96; educational attainment = 3.81, 3.29; pulse rate = 3.40, 2.88; intelligence at enlistment = 3.26, 2.88; occupational prestige = 3.02, 3.97; fasting blood glucose = 1.69,

4.29; systolic blood pressure = 1.66, 2.75; HDL cholesterol = 1.66, 4.08; diastolic blood pressure = 1.59, 2.31; total cholesterol = 1.07, 5.55; body mass index = 0.91, 5.12. These data were used for a different purpose by inquiring whether intelligence was more effective in accounting for the well-documented influence of indicators of socioeconomic position (army income, occupational prestige, mid-life income, and education) on cardiovascular disease mortality than the combined influence of a basket of traditional risk factors (systolic and diastolic blood pressure, total cholesterol, HDL cholesterol, body mass index, smoking, blood glucose, resting heart rate, FEV1; Batty, Shipley, et al., 2009). The mean attenuation of the socioeconomic association with cardiovascular disease mortality was 55.3% using the intelligence test at the clinical examination, and 40.4% for the basket of traditional risk factors. Therefore, intelligence ranks highly as a mortality risk factor, and intelligence on its own can account for more of the socioeconomic influence on cardiovascular disease mortality than a whole range of physiological and biochemical risk factors.

Reports from the Vietnam Experience Study have examined the association between intelligence at conscription and the risk of developing specific illnesses in the follow-up period. In a study of 4,157 of the veterans studied between enlistment (mean age 20.4 years) and the clinical examination (mean age 38.3 years), a standard deviation advantage in intelligence at enlistment was associated with a 13% reduction in the risk of developing the metabolic syndrome (Batty, Gale, et al., 2008). This is a group of factors, including being overweight or obese, and having high cholesterol, poor glucose metabolism, and hypertension. Developing the metabolic syndrome is associated with increased risk of mortality, especially from cardiovascular disease. Therefore, the Vietnam Experience Study sample was used to ask whether developing the metabolic syndrome might be a mediating factor in the association between intelligence and death from cardiovascular disease. This was true to an extent; statistical adjustment for metabolic syndrome attenuated the association between intelligence and death from cardiovascular disease by about a third. In addition to somatic outcomes, mental health status was also recorded in this study. Over the 20.4 years of follow-up in 3,285 of the veterans, a one standard deviation disadvantage in intelligence at enlistment was associated with an increased risk (%) of the men currently suffering from the following mental disorders at the medical examination: depression = 32%; generalized anxiety disorder = 43% (replicated in around 700 people in a study of the National Collaborative Perinatal Project, in which one standard deviation advantage in intelligence at age 7 years was associated with 50% lower risk in adulthood; Martin et al., 2007); alcohol abuse or dependence = 20%; post-traumatic stress disorder = 39%; post-traumatic stress disorder and generalized anxiety disorder = 150%; post-traumatic stress disorder and generalized anxiety disorder and depression = 117%; all four disorders = 177% (Gale, Deary, et al., 2008).

The West of Scotland Twenty-07 Study

The West of Scotland Twenty-07 study started in 1988, drawing subjects from the large urban area surrounding Glasgow City in Scotland. It is a population-based longitudinal study of men and women. The study originally recruited three narrow-age cohorts, aged around 15, 35, and 55 years when first tested, and has now followed each of these for twenty years. The cohort that has been used in cognitive epidemiology studies is the 55-year-old group, with 1,042 subjects. At the first wave of study, the subjects were visited twice at home, where they were administered a series of social and health questionnaires and health measurements. They also took Part I of the Alice Heim 4 Test of General Intelligence and simple and 4-choice reaction time. The subjects were flagged at the United Kingdom National Health Service Central Registry, which sent a copy of the death certificate to the study office when subjects died. A description of this cohort may be found in Ford et al. (1994). It should be noted that this sample does not have intelligence tested from early life, and so the results are not necessarily comparable with those studies that have such data.

The West of Scotland Twenty-07 study was used to test whether intelligence from age 55 could predict total and cardiovascular disease mortality over the next two decades as strongly as established risk factors (Batty et al., 2010). Again, the relative index of inequality was used to derive hazard ratios that were comparable between predictors. For sex-adjusted models, the hazard ratios for total and cardiovascular disease mortality, respectively, were smoking = 4.60, 5.58; intelligence = 3.48, 3.76, income = 2.90, 3.20; physical activity = 2.27, 2.06; education = 2.07, 1.81; occupational social class = 1.84, 1.56; systolic blood pressure = 1.42, 2.61; diastolic blood pressure = 1.06, 1.67; body mass index = 0.94, 1.24. Therefore, intelligence again ranks highly – here, just below smoking – as a predictor of death. It should be made clear that, here as elsewhere, less smoking and higher intelligence are associated with death; the numbers here are given as absolute coefficients, without signs, because the direction of risk is assumed to be obvious for each variable.

One of the hypotheses mooted to explain the association between intelligence and death is the notion of system integrity (Figure 34.1): that intelligence is a marker for a body that is well assembled, and can return to equilibrium after challenges with allostatic load. This idea would suggest that other complex systems that deal with the environment – for example, those that contribute to general fitness (Arden, Gottfredson, & Miller, 2009) – should be markers of system integrity too, and related to intelligence. The problem was to find another marker for this construct, and to test whether it could account for the influence of intelligence on death. In the West of Scotland Twenty-07 study, in the 55-year-old sample, a standard deviation disadvantage in intelligence and mean 4-choice reaction time were associated with a 42% and 41%, respectively, increased risk of mortality to age 70. Intelligence and 4-choice reaction time correlated .49 in this sample. Adjusting for smoking, social class (the sample was tested against the background population and found to be representative on social class), and years of education had little influence on the effects. The effect of intelligence on mortality was no longer significant after adjustment for reaction time. This implied that speed of information processing – perhaps a marker of system integrity – could account for much of the intelligence-death association.

The West of Scotland Twenty-07 study was also used to test Gottfredson's (2004) hypothesis that IQ is a fundamental cause of socioeconomic inequalities in health (Batty, Der, Macintyre, & Deary, 2006). The study provided a good test: It had six health outcomes – total and coronary heart disease mortality over 15 years, long-term illness, self-perceived health, psychological distress, and respiratory function – and five indices of socioeconomic position – father's occupation, own occupation, income, deprivation index, and education. This question was posed: How much attenuation of the socioeconomic-health association, if any, occurs after adjusting for intelligence? For the two mortality outcomes and their association with the two key socioeconomic indicators – the person's own occupational social class and education – the answer was about 100%, providing statistical confirmation for Gottfredson's hypothesis. Other attenuations – especially for the more subjective health indicators of self-perceived health and psychological distress – were modest to large.

The United Kingdom Health and Lifestyle Survey

The United Kingdom Health and Lifestyle Study began in 1984. From the UK electoral register, 12,254 addresses were taken at random. One individual aged 18 years or over was chosen from each household. There were 9,003 subjects interviewed, ranging in age from 18 to 99 years. The survey provides a reasonably representative sample of the adult population. Over 7,400 of the subjects also took part in a session of physical measurements. Data are available on social class, education, smoking status, alcohol, physical activity, lung function, blood pressure, and body mass index. The physical measurements included simple and 4-choice reaction time tests, and short tests of verbal declarative memory and visuospatial reasoning. The same procedures were repeated seven years later in over 5,300 of the subjects. Subjects in the study have been flagged with the UK's National Health Service Central Registry that gives dates and causes of deaths. A description of the two waves of this study may be found in Shipley et al. (2006, 2007), and in greater detail in Cox (1987) and Cox, Huppert and Whichelow (1993). The principal interest here is in the results of 4-choice reaction time: first, because these offer an assessment of brain information processing that is less likely to be affected by education and other cultural effects; and, second, because the other cognitive assessments were made on so few items that they are relatively low in reliability. Also, in the results presented below we concentrate on 4-choice reaction time mean. Generally, the results are just as strong for 4-choice reaction time variability, and less strong, but still typically highly statistically significant, for simple reaction time mean and variability.

Over a follow-up period of 19 years, a standard deviation disadvantage in 4-choice reaction time was associated with an 18% increased risk of death in the whole sample (Shipley et al., 2006). This reduced only slightly – to 15% – after adjusting for occupational social class and education. An especially informative aspect of this study was the estimate of the 4-choice reaction time-mortality association in different adult age bands. A standard deviation disadvantage in 4-choice reaction time was associated with a 62% increased risk of death in the 20–39-year-olds, 20% in the 40–59-year-olds, and 17% in those aged 60 and over. Further analyses were performed with respect to specific causes of death. In the analyses with all ages included, there were significant associations between 4-choice reaction time mean and deaths from all cardiovascular disease, coronary heart disease, stroke, respiratory disease, and lung cancers but not for non-lung cancers. Effect sizes were typically around 20% increased risk for a standard deviation disadvantage in 4-choice reaction time mean. Most of the effect was found in the group aged 60 years and over. Effects for 4-choice reaction time variability and simple reaction time mean and variability were weaker, though often significant.

A further study examined the association between reaction time change (independently of baseline reaction time) over seven years and mortality (Shipley et al., 2007). A standard deviation relative disadvantage in 4-choice reaction time slowing over the seven years after baseline testing was associated with a 20% increased risk of death in the whole sample, with similar effects in the 40–59-year-olds and in those aged 60 and over (there were too few deaths to analyze in the younger age band). The results were similarly strong and significant for deaths from all cardiovascular disease, coronary heart disease, stroke, respiratory disease, but not significant for lung cancers or nonlung cancers. The failure to find an association with lung cancer could reflect the fact that it is associated with the level but not the change in reaction time.

The United Kingdom Health and Lifestyle study was also used to test whether 4-choice reaction time mean could predict total and cardiovascular disease mortality as strongly as established risk factors (Roberts et al., 2009). As described earlier, the relative index of inequality was used to derive hazard ratios that were comparable between predictors. For sex-adjusted models, the hazard ratios for total and cardiovascular disease mortality, respectively, were smoking = 3.03, 1.85; 4-choice reaction time mean = 2.57, 2.31, physical activity = 2.27, 1.74; education = 2.07, 1.81; occupational social class = 1.84, 1.56; systolic blood pressure = 1.63, 4.37; resting heart rate = 1.59, 1.32; psychological distress (General Health Questionnaire-30) = 1.53, 1.46; waist-hip ratio = 1.22, 1.26; alcohol = 1.05, 0.88; body mass index = 0.95, 1.43. As above, these have been given as absolute numbers, and it is assumed that the directions of risk are obvious, for example, more smoking, lower intelligence, less education, more manual social class, and so on. Therefore, 4-choice reaction time ranks highly – just below smoking, as was found in the similar analysis described for intelligence in the West of Scotland Twenty-07 study – as a predictor of death.

The British Birth Cohorts of 1946, 1958, and 1970

All three of these British birth cohorts each has a very useful "cohort profile," a journal report describing exactly whom they involve and what was tested and when (Wadsworth, 2006; Power & Elliot, 2006; Elliot & Shepherd, 2006). They each involve several thousands of people born in the UK in the years 1946, 1958, or 1970.

1946 *British Birth Cohort*

The 1946-born cohort is called the National Survey of Health and Development. Its target sample was all births in England, Scotland, and Wales in one week in March 1946. There are data from five detailed waves of collection from birth to age 53. These data include, for example, cognitive data from age 8 years, and health, illness, and mortality data up to age 53. The health and illness data include cardiovascular and lung function, mental health, and smoking, exercise, and diet. The cohort profile was written by Wadsworth et al. (2006).

Data from the 1948 British birth cohort have examined the association between childhood intelligence and mortality. Based on intelligence measured at age 8 and deaths between ages 9 and 54 years, the risk of dying for men in the bottom quarter of IQ scores was about twice when compared with the other groups combined (Kuh et al., 2004). There was no significant effect in women, probably because there had been, as yet, few deaths in this relatively small and young cohort. When the study was extended to age 60 – based on 4,461 male and female participants and 332 deaths – there was a significant association between mortality and intelligence measured at age 8 years, 11 years, and 15 years (Kuh et al., 2009). Those in the lowest quarter were about twice as likely to have died as those in the top quarter. The largest attenuating factor on the effect was home ownership. The same study reported – but did not show statistical results for – a similar association between childhood intelligence and deaths from cancer and cardiovascular disease. This study also showed that adjusting for childhood intelligence had a small attenuating effect on the association between childhood circumstances and later mortality.

Data from the 1946 British birth cohort have examined the association between childhood intelligence and later health outcomes. Intelligence at age 8 years was significantly associated with developing the metabolic syndrome, with a 14% increase in the risk per standard deviation disadvantage in childhood intelligence (Richards et al., 2009). This is similar in effect size to the finding by Batty, Gale, et al. (2008) in the Vietnam Experience Study. However, there was more statistical mediation of the effect by education in the 1946 British birth cohort. Data from this cohort showed a significant linear association between cognitive ability at age 15 years and lung function – measured using the forced expiratory volume from the lungs in one second – at age 43 years (Richards et al., 2005), as was found in the Lothian Birth Cohort 1921 sample (Deary et al., 2006). The effect was still significant after adjustment for childhood and adult socioeconomic status and education. It was speculated that there might be influences of endocrine, autonomic, and motor control systems that acted in parallel on mental and respiratory functions.

1958 *British Birth Cohort*

The 1958 birth cohort is also known as the National Child Development Study and was based upon all births in England, Scotland, and Wales in one week in 1958. There were seven data sweeps up to 2004. These include a wide range of social, psychological, medical, and most recently, biomedical data. There are cognitive test data from age 11 (verbal and nonverbal tests from the National Foundation for Educational Research). The cohort profile was written by Power and Elliot (2006).

Data on over 14,000 participants in the 1958 British birth cohort were used to examine the association between intelligence at age 11 and all-cause mortality up to age 46. By age 46 there were 124 deaths: with intelligence from age 11 divided into tertiles, 3.4% of the lowest intelligence group were dead, but only 1.7% of the highest intelligence group. One standard deviation disadvantage in intelligence at age 11 was associated with a 24% reduction in the risk of death during that period, with very similar results for men and women (Jokela et al., 2009).

Reports from the 1958 birth cohort have examined the association between intelligence at age 11 and health behaviors in adulthood. One standard deviation disadvantage in intelligence at age 11 was associated with a 38% increased risk of obesity at age 42 years in women, and 26% in men (Chandola et al., 2006). Moreover, structural equation growth curve models showed that lower childhood intelligence was associated with greater weight gain between age 16 and 42 years. The effects appeared to be statistically mediated via education and eating a healthy diet in adulthood.

Data from the 1958 British Cohort Study were used to test the system integrity hypothesis in cognitive epidemiology (Gale, Batty, et al., 2009). It was hypothesized that in addition to intelligence – and, perhaps, reaction time – physical coordination might be another indicator of system integrity. The following health outcomes were assessed at age 33 years: psychological distress, poor self-rated health, and obesity. Physical coordination was quantified using principal components analysis of a number of upper and lower limb tests from age 11 years. Three outcomes were predicted if the system integrity hypothesis was correct. First, intelligence and coordination should be significantly correlated: This was found, with $r = .18$ ($p < .001$). Second, intelligence and coordination from age 11 should be significantly associated with the health outcomes at age 33; they were. Third, adjusting the influence of intelligence for coordination (and vice versa) on the health outcomes should lead to substantial attenuation (since they are both markers for the same underlying trait of system integrity). This failed to occur: There was very little attenuation of intelligence's effects on the health outcomes after adjusting for coordination, and vice versa. Intelligence and coordination from childhood were independent predictors of the health outcomes. Another possible aspect of system integrity is cortisol function. There is evidence that lower cognitive ability is associated with an intact diurnal rhythm for cortisol (Power, Li, & Hertzman, 2008). One marker of disruption to this diurnal rhythm is having a low level of cortisol after morning waking. This was supported in the finding that intelligence at age 11 was associated with a greater likelihood of not showing the morning cortisol peak and diurnal rhythm (Power, Li, & Hertzman, 2008). For example, for males and females at age 45 years, there was a 29% and 18% reduction in odds ratio, respectively, of being in the lowest 5% for morning cortisol per standard deviation advantage of nonverbal intelligence at age 11 years. One interpretation offered was that people with higher intelligence have had less accumulated biological aging over the life course on the hypothalamic-pituitary-adrenal axis.

Results from 3,325 women in the 1958 British birth cohort at age 33 suggest that intelligence from childhood might be associated with the health of the next generation. Intelligence at age 11 was associated with a greater likelihood of smoking during pregnancy (data collected at age 33 years; Gale et al., 2009). Women who smoked during pregnancy were a mean of 5.3 IQ points lower than those who did not. There was statistical mediation of the effects via education and age at first pregnancy.

1970 *British Birth Cohort*

The 1970 British Cohort Study was based upon all births in England, Scotland, and Wales in one week in 1970. Up to 2004, there were six data sweeps. These include a wide range of social, psychological, and medical data. There are, for example, intelligence test data (four subtests from the British Ability Scales) from age 10, and many health behaviors at age 30. The cohort profile was written by Elliot and Shepherd (2006). Studies described below typically involve more than 8000 individuals.

Reports from the 1970 birth cohort have examined the association between intelligence at age 11 and health and health behaviors in adulthood. One study – based on 8,282 cohort members with complete data – examined diet preferences and exercise at age 30. A standard deviation advantage in intelligence at age 10 years was significantly associated with the following at age 30 years (percentage difference in odds ratios): greater likelihood of eating fresh fruit (30%), cooked vegetables (26%), salads and raw vegetables (27%), wholemeal bread (23%), fish (27%), food fried in vegetable oil (19%), and taking regular exercise (20%); and lower likelihood of eating nonwholemeal breads (14%), red meat (7%), cakes and biscuits (5%), and french-fried potatoes (26%; Batty, Deary, et al., 2007a). A standard deviation advantage in intelligence at age 10 years was associated with the following at age 30 years: a 16% decreased risk of smoking; a 12% decreased risk of being overweight; a 16% decreased risk of obesity; and a 25% greater likelihood of giving up smoking (Batty, Deary, et al., 2007b). Similar results were obtained when intelligence scores from age 5 years were used. Therefore, intelligence from a very young age is associated with adult health factors that are associated with later life chronic illness and death. It is possible that these choices are made via intelligent people gaining and reasoning with more health-relevant information. A standard deviation advantage in intelligence at age 10 years was associated with a 38% increase in the likelihood of being vegetarian at age 30 years (Gale et al., 2007). Vegetarians also had higher mean social class and more education, but not greater incomes than nonvegetarians. It was not clear whether this was associated with better objective health, or whether choosing to be a vegetarian was one of a number of arbitrary lifestyle decisions that tend to be made by people with higher intelligence. In a study with 6,074 cohorts members, a standard deviation advantage in intelligence at age 10 years was significantly associated with a 23% reduced odds ratio for psychological distress – anxiety and depression measured with the Rutter Malaise Inventory – at age 30 years (Gale, Hatch, et al., 2009). An apparent reversal of all of these trends occurred with the finding that childhood intelligence was associated with (percentage increase in odds ratio per standard deviation of intelligence at age 10) more alcohol problems (men = 13%, women = 44%); drinking alcohol more frequently (men = 36%; women = 54%); and higher weekly alcohol intake (men = 11%; women = 26%; Batty, Deary, et al., 2008a).

Data from the 1970 British Cohort Study were used to test the system integrity hypothesis in cognitive epidemiology, alongside data from the 1958 British birth cohort (Gale, Batty, et al., 2009). Results were very similar to those described above for the 1958 cohort.

The Whitehall II Study

The Whitehall II study includes London-based civil servants. It began in 1985 when employees were invited to take part by letter: 73% (6,895 men, 3,413 women) agreed. The first study wave occurred during 1985–1988. It collected data by questionnaire and in-person examination. Data were collected on demographics, health, lifestyle, social factors, blood pressure, body measurements, disease biomarkers, and cardiovascular function. Five further study waves occurred up to 2001, and they are, at the time of writing, up to Wave 9. There are detailed data on education, income, and occupational status (father's and proband's). Mental ability was first assessed on the full sample between 1997 and 1995 (Wave 5) using Part I of the Alice Heim 4 Test of general intelligence. This includes 65 items of verbal and numerical reasoning. Subjects in the study have been flagged with the UK's National Health Service Central Registry that gives dates and causes of deaths. Health was assessed using history, validated questionnaires (for physical and mental health), and investigations such as electrocardiogram. A description of this study up to Phase 7 may be found in Marmot and Brunner (2005).

Data from the Whitehall II study have been used to examine the association between intelligence and mortality in midlife up to 2006. The follow-up period was short for this type of study, only eight years (Sabia et al., 2010). For a standard deviation disadvantage in the Alice Heim 4 test of general intelligence, there was a 16% increase in the risk of death over the period. Memory was also significantly associated, but not vocabulary or fluency measures.

Data from the Whitehall II study have been used to examine the association between intelligence and incident (new cases of) coronary heart disease in over 5,000 people who did not have such disease at baseline. For a standard deviation disadvantage in the Alice Heim 4 test of general intelligence there was a 24% increase in the risk of coronary heart disease over the follow-up period (Singh-Manoux et al., 2009). There were similarly sized, slightly lower, significant effects for Mill Hill Vocabulary and a general intelligence factor, and nonsignificant effects for fluency and memory. The effects were not reduced after adjusting for socioeconomic status, education, cardiovascular disease risk factors (diabetes, blood pressure, cholesterol, cardiovascular disease medication), or for health behaviors (smoking, alcohol, diet, physical activity). As was noted in the West of Scotland Twenty-07 Study, this sample does not have intelligence tested from early life, and so the results are not necessarily comparable with those studies that have such data.

Data from the Whitehall II study were used to test Gottfredson's (2004) hypothesis that intelligence might account for the association between socioeconomic factors and health. They found that intelligence was associated with coronary heart disease, physical functioning, mental functioning (men only), and self-rated health (Singh-Manoux et al., 2005). However, for these four variables, intelligence accounted for only 17%, 33%, 12%, and 39%, respectively, of the association between socioeconomic position and health outcome. A later test of this hypothesis was described earlier (Batty, Der, Macintyre, & Deary, 2006); it had better outcome variables, and a longitudinal design, and appeared more strongly to support Gottfredson's hypothesis.

U.S. National Longitudinal Survey of Youth 1979

The total sample of more than 12,000 individuals comprises people originally aged from 15 to 22. They were drawn from three sources: a representative population sample, excluding those in institutions and the military; a group that provided over-sampling of disadvantaged white people, and black and Hispanic people; and people in the military. Intelligence was tested when the sample ranged between ages 16 and 23, and they took 10 subtests of the Armed Forces Qualification Test. There were follow-up studies every year from 1979 to 1994, and every two years from 1994 to 2004. The data include social and medical factors. Also, children of the women in the National Longitudinal Survey of Youth are examined, including cognitive assessments using the Peabody Individual Achievement Test.

Data from the National Longitudinal Survey of Youth have been used to examine the intelligence-mortality association.

There were 360 deaths among 11,321 individuals with cognitive and other relevant data. Even adjusting for health problems at baseline and parental education, a standard deviation advantage in intelligence at baseline was associated with a 22% reduction in the risk of mortality to 2004 (Jokela et al., 2009). This was the first U.S.-based study of the intelligence-mortality association with early life intelligence and in a representative sample; the results concern mortality up to early mid-life. Marital status and household income accounted for almost all of the effect. Also, there was little evidence of the effect in people whose parents had low education. Moreover, the influence of education and socioeconomic status on mortality was not accounted for by intelligence, a finding also reported in analyses of the Wisconsin Longitudinal Study and the Health and Retirement Survey (Link et al., 2008).

Data from the National Longitudinal Survey of Youth 1979 found that lower early life intelligence is significantly associated with greater occurrence of a large number of illnesses – to about age 40 years (Der et al., 2009). This included physician diagnoses of chronic lung disease, hypertension, diabetes, and arthritis, rheumatism. It also included self-reported eye problems, ulcers, severe tooth or gum troubles (also found in the NHANES-III study; Stewart et al., 2008), epilepsy or fits, stomach or intestinal ulcers, lameness/paralysis/polio, frequent trouble sleeping, frequent headaches/dizziness/fainting, chest pain/palpitations, anemia, leg pain/bursitis, foot and leg problems, asthma, depression/anxiety, and kidney or bladder problems. People with higher intelligence at baseline were more prone to report high cholesterol, thyroid trouble or goiter, and tumor/growth/cyst. These latter findings are not necessarily contradictory to the direction of the majority of the results: It is possible that people with higher intelligence are more likely to be tested for cholesterol levels, to take part in screening and self-examination for tumors, and to understand the meaning of the thyroid gland and its functions.

The fact that the female participants' children were followed up in this study has been used to make a novel contribution to cognitive epidemiology. Birth weight, breast-feeding, and maternal smoking in pregnancy are all variables that are related to children's intelligence; are considered as environmental exposures; and are thought to affect later health. Therefore, these could act as partial explanations of the association between intelligence and later health. However, after controlling for mother's intelligence, the association between birth weight (Deary et al., 2005), breast-feeding (Der, Batty, & Deary, 2006), and maternal smoking in pregnancy (Batty, Der, & Deary, 2006) were all very substantially attenuated, typically to nonsignificant levels. These results indicated that the associations in the children were largely spurious and might be traced back to the causes of mother's intelligence level, which is highly influenced – though not solely – by genetic factors.

Other Cohort Studies

A number of other cohorts have been used in fewer cognitive epidemiology studies. These include the Aberdeen (Scotland) Children of the 1950s study, the Danish Metropolit Study, the Dunedin Birth Cohort, the USA's "Termites" study, and the Newcastle (England) Thousand Families study.

Aberdeen Children of the 1950s Study

The sample and its original and follow-up data were described in detail by Batty et al. (2004). The baseline subjects were about 15,000 children who were attending primary schools in Aberdeen (Scotland) in 1962. From childhood there are birth-related data, intelligence tests, and socioeconomic information. From 1998, 98.5% were traced and follow-up information was gathered on health, lifestyle, and other factors at mid-life (on over 7,000 individuals), and links were made to databases containing information on deaths and hospital admissions.

Data from the Aberdeen Children of the 1950s study were used to examine the links between childhood intelligence and mortality between 15 and 57 years. A standard deviation advantage in intelligence at age 7 was associated with a 20% reduced risk of mortality (Leon et al., 2009). The study had unusually rich childhood data – perinatal factors, father's occupational social class at birth, number of siblings, childhood height and weight – but adjustment for all of these together barely altered the association. The associations were similar for men and women and for deaths before and after 40 years; were found across the range of intelligence; were strongest for the external causes of death (26% reduced risk of mortality in the follow-up period per standard deviation of childhood intelligence); and also were significant for cancer deaths (19% reduced risk). In the same sample there was a 48% reduction in the risk of coronary heart disease and stroke (defined as a combined outcome) per standard deviation advantage in intelligence at age 11 for women, and a 22% reduced risk for men (Lawlor et al, 2008).

Data from the Aberdeen Children of the 1950s study were used to examine the links between childhood intelligence and later health behaviors and physiological risk factors for health. A standard deviation advantage in childhood intelligence was associated with the following in adulthood (percentage reduction in odds ratio): regular smoking (23%); heavy alcohol consumption (11%); obesity (22%); and being overweight (14%). A standard deviation advantage in intelligence at age 11 years was associated with a 20% lower prevalence of alcohol-related hangovers in middle age, a marker of binge drinking (Batty, Deary, & Macintyre, 2006).

Danish Metropolit 1953 Male Birth Cohort

This is a study of over 11,500 males born in Copenhagen in 1953. There are intelligence data on almost 8,000 of them at age 12 years, and most had intelligence tested at conscription at about age 18 years. Data on deaths and hospital admissions from 1978 have been collected from national registers (e.g., see Osler et al., 2007). One standard deviation disadvantage in childhood intelligence (a combination of spatial, inductive, and verbal subtests) was significantly associated with a 42% increase in the risk of coronary heart disease (fatal or nonfatal; Batty, Mortensen, et al., 2005). Adjusting for childhood social class and birth weight had little attenuating influence. One standard deviation advantage in intelligence at 12 years was associated with an 18% reduced risk of any form of fatal or nonfatal unintentional injury in adulthood (Osler et al., 2007). The risks were especially strong for falls (23% reduced risk per standard deviation advantage in childhood intelligence) and poisoning (36%). These predate and support the findings in the Swedish Conscripts Study for these specific outcomes. As with other findings in this chapter, statistically adjusting for education attenuated these findings, but the appropriateness of this adjustment and its meaning are unclear.

Dunedin Birth Cohort

This is a representative sample of around one thousand births in the years 1972–1973 from Dunedin, New Zealand. They are still, therefore, only in young adulthood. In this sample, a standard deviation of intelligence tested in childhood using the Wechsler scales was significantly associated with the following by age 32 years: 32% reduced odds of schizophrenia spectrum disorder, 23% reduced odds of depression, and 26% reduction in the odds of anxiety disorder (Koenen et al., 2009). These data are in accord with findings in the Swedish Conscripts Study (Gale, Batty, et al., 2010) and with findings from the Vietnam Experience Study (Gale et al., 2008). The authors speculated that this might be a reflection of people with lower intelligence having less cognitive reserve, with the possible mechanisms as follows: lower intelligence reflecting neuroanatomical deficits, less resistance to psychosocial stress, less mental or health knowledge, or intelligence sharing etiology – genetic and /or environmental – with mental disorders. These suggested mechanisms should be compared with the framework in Figure 34.1.

Newcastle Thousand Families Study

This study from England was based upon 1,142 births from May and June 1947 in the city of Newcastle. The subjects took tests of intelligence, English, and arithmetic at age 11, and 717 were followed up for mortality to the end of 2003. A standard deviation advantage in childhood intelligence in men was significantly associated with a 43% reduced risk of death in the follow-up period (Pearce et al., 2006). The reduced odds in women was 21%; this reduction was not significant, but there were few female deaths, and the effect was similar to effect sizes seen in other, larger samples.

Terman Life Cycle Study

In perhaps the most unusual study, the participants in the Terman Life Cycle study – sometimes referred to as the "Termites" – were recruited in 1922 and all participants had an IQ of 135 or higher (Martin & Kubzansky, 2005). In a report of almost 900 people, a standard deviation advantage in intelligence in childhood was associated with a 32% reduced risk of mortality – in those with IQ scores up to 163 – over a 64-year period of follow-up (Martin & Kubzansky, 2005). This suggests that the dose-response effect of intelligence on health progresses well above the average level, and that higher intelligence continues to add increments to health even into what is sometimes called genius levels.

Conclusion

After about a decade of consistent work in cognitive epidemiology, associations have been established between lower early life intelligence and mortality from all causes taken together, specific causes of death, incident illnesses, chronic disease risk factors, and illness behaviors. It is as yet unclear if the impact of intelligence on mortality and specific diseases is mediated by health behaviors and physiological risk factors. Similarly, the role of education, income, and adult social class – which often attenuate the apparent influence of intelligence when they are adjusted statistically in multivariate models – is a point of much debate.

Intelligence now has a seat at the table of epidemiology. However, there are times when it is still in people's blind spot when it comes to epidemiologists' thinking about the causes of health inequalities. For example, studies of education and health and mortality often fail to consider the possible role of intelligence as a prior partial cause of both (e.g., Lleras-Muney, 2005). Therefore, it is important to continue to engage with the various branches of science that contribute to the field of health inequalities.

With associations having been established convincingly, the field of cognitive epidemiology must now move into more mechanistically oriented studies. Twin and adoption studies, and genome-wide association and genetic sequencing studies, might be helpful in discovering shared genetic and environmental etiology between intelligence and health. More studies are required that have early life intelligence data, and then health-relevant variables assessed across the life course, and then follow-up to mortality. As the participants grow older, the British cohort studies of 1946, 1958, and 1970 will be especially well placed in this regard. Theoretical suggestions, such as the system integrity hypothesis, and various mediating hypotheses, need to be tested more thoroughly and with better delineation of the constructs. More studies are required that include women and nonwhite ethnic groups, although there are no strong reasons yet to anticipate differential intelligence-health effects in these groups.

Acknowledgments

Work on this chapter was undertaken by the University of Edinburgh Centre for Cognitive Ageing and Cognitive Epidemiology, part of the cross-council Lifelong

Health and Wellbeing Initiative. Funding from the Biotechnology and Biological Sciences Research Council (BBSRC), Engineering and Physical Sciences Research Council (EPSRC), Economic and Social Research Council (ESRC) and Medical Research Council (MRC) is gratefully acknowledged (G0700704/84698). David Batty is supported by the Wellcome Trust.

References

Arden, R., Gottfredson, L. S., & Miller, G. (2009). Does a fitness factor contribute to the association between intelligence and health outcomes? Evidence from medical abnormality counts among 3654 US Veterans. *Intelligence*, 37, 581–591.

Batty, G. D., Deary, I. J., Benzeval, M.,& Der, G. (2010). Does IQ predict cardiovascular disease mortality as strongly as established risk factors? Comparison of effect estimates using the west of Scotland "Twenty-07" cohort study. *European Journal of Cardiovascular Prevention and Rehabilitation*, 17, 24–27.

Batty, G. D., Deary, I. J., & Gottfredson, L. S. (2007). Premorbid (early life) IQ and later mortality risk: Systematic review. *Annals of Epidemiology*, 17, 278–288.

Batty, G. D., Deary, I. J., & Macintyre, S. (2006). Low childhood IQ and life course socio-economic disadvantage as predictors of alcohol hangover in adulthood: The Aberdeen Children of the 1950s Study. *Journal of Epidemiology and Community Health*, 60, 872–874.

Batty, G. D., Deary, I. J., Schoon, I., & Gale, C. R. (2007a). Childhood mental ability in relation to food intake and physical activity in adulthood: The 1970 British Cohort Study. *Pediatrics*, 119, e38–e45.

Batty, G. D., Deary, I. J., Schoon, I., & Gale, C. R. (2007b). Mental ability across childhood in relation to risk factors for premature mortality in adult life: The 1970 British Cohort Study. *Journal of Epidemiology and Community Health*, 61, 997–1003.

Batty, G. D., Deary, I. J., Schoon, I., Emslie, C., Hunt, K., & Gale, C. R. (2008a). Childhood mental ability and adult alcohol intake and alcohol problems: The 1970 British Cohort Study. *American Journal of Public Health*, 98, 2237–2243.

Batty, G. D., Deary, I. J., Tengstrom, A., & Rasmussen, F. (2008b). IQ in early adulthood and risk of death by homicide: Cohort study of one million men. *British Journal of Psychiatry*, 193, 461–465.

Batty, G. D., Der, G., & Deary, I. J. (2006). Effect of maternal smoking during pregnancy on offspring's cognitive ability: Empirical evidence for complete confounding in the US National Longitudinal Survey of Youth. *Pediatrics*, 118, 943–950.

Batty, G. D., Der, G., Macintyre, S., & Deary, I. J. (2006). Does IQ explain socio-economic inequalities in health? Evidence from a population-based cohort study in the west of Scotland. *British Medical Journal*, 332, 580–584.

Batty, G. D., Gale, C. R., Mortensen, L. H., Langenberg, C., Shipley, M., & Deary, I. J. (2008). Pre-morbid IQ, the metabolic syndrome and mortality: The Vietnam Experience Study. *Diabetologia*, 51, 436–443.

Batty, G. D., Gale, C. R., Tynelius, P., Deary, I. J., & Rasmussen, F. (2009). IQ in early adulthood, socio-economic position, and unintentional injury mortality by middle-age: Cohort study of over one million Swedish men. *American Journal of Epidemiology*, 169, 606–615.

Batty, G. D., Mortensen, L. H., Gale, C. R., & Deary, I. J. (2008). Is low IQ related to risk of death by homicide? Testing an hypothesis using data from the Vietnam Experience Study. *Psychiatry Research*, 161, 112–115.

Batty, G. D., Mortensen, E. L., Nybo Andersen, A.-M., & Osler, M. (2005). Childhood intelligence in relation to adult coronary heart disease and stroke risk: Evidence from a Danish birth cohort study. *Paediatric and Perinatal Epidemiology*, 19, 452–459.

Batty, G. D., Mortensen, L. H., Gale, C. R., Shipley, M., Roberts, B., & Deary, I. J. (2009). IQ in early adulthood, risk factors in middle age, and later cancer mortality in men: The Vietnam Experience Study. *Psycho-Oncology*, 18, 1122–1126.

Batty, G. D., Morton, S. M. B., Campbell, D., Clark, H., Davey Smith, G., Hall, M., Macintyre, S., & Leon, D. A. (2004). The Aberdeen Children of the 1950s cohort study: Background, methods and follow-up information on a new resource for the study of life course intergenerational influences on health. *Paediatric and Perinatal Epidemiology*, 18, 221–239.

Batty, G. D., Shipley, M. J., Dundas, R., Macintyre, S., Der, G., Mortensen, L. H., & Deary, I. J. (2009). Does IQ explain socioeconomic differentials in total and cardiovascular disease mortality? Comparison with the explanatory power of traditional cardiovascular disease risk factors in the Vietnam Experience Study. *European Heart Journal*, 30, 1903–1909.

Batty, G. D., Shipley, M. J., Mortensen, L. H., Boyle, S. H., Barefoot, J., Gronbaek, M., Gale, C. R., & Deary, I. J. (2008a). IQ in late adolescence/early adulthood, risk factors in middle age and later all-cause mortality in men: The Vietnam Experience Study. *Journal of Epidemiology and Community Health*, *62*, 522–531.

Batty, G. D., Shipley, M. J., Mortensen, L. H., Gale, C. R., & Deary, I. J. (2008b). IQ in late adolescence/early adulthood, risk factors in middle age, and later coronary heart disease mortality in men: The Vietnam Experience Study. *European Journal of Cardiovascular Prevention and Rehabilitation*, *15*, 359–361.

Batty, G. D., Shipley, M. J., Gale, C. R., Mortensen, L. H., & Deary, I. J. (2008c). Does IQ predict total and cardiovascular disease mortality as strongly as other risk factors? Comparison of effect estimates using the Vietnam Experience Study. *Heart*, *94*, 1541–1544.

Batty, G. D., Wennerstad, K. M., Davey Smith, G., Gunnell, G., Deary, I. J., Tynelius, P., & Rasmussen, F. (2007). IQ in early adulthood and later cancer risk: Cohort study of 1 million Swedish men. *Annals of Oncology*, *18*, 21–28.

Batty, G. D., Wennerstad, K. M., Davey Smith, G., Gunnell, D., Deary, I. J., Tylenius, P., & Rasmussen, F. (2009). IQ in early adulthood and mortality by middle age: Cohort study of one million Swedish men. *Epidemiology*, *20*, 100–109.

Chandola, T., Deary, I. J., Blane, D., & Batty, G. D. (2006). Childhood intelligence in relation to obesity and weight gain in adult life: Findings from the National Child Development (1958) Study. *International Journal of Obesity*, 30, 1422–1432.

Cox, B. D. (1987). *The Health and Lifestyle Survey*. London, UK: Health Promotion Research Trust.

Cox, B. D., Huppert, F. A., & Whichelow, M. J. (1993). *The Health and Lifestyle Survey: Seven years on*. Aldershot, UK: Dartmouth.

Cox, D. R. (1972). Regression models and life tables. *Journal of the Royal Statistical Society (Series B)*, *34*, 187–220.

Deary, I. J. (2008). Why do intelligent people live longer? *Nature*, *456*, 175–176.

Deary, I. J. (2009). Introduction to the special issue on cognitive epidemiology. *Intelligence*, *37*, 573–580.

Deary, I. J., Bastin, M. E., Pattie, A., Clayden, J. D., Whalley, L. J., Starr, J. M., & Wardlaw, J. M. (2006). White matter integrity and cognition in childhood and old age. *Neurology*, *66*, 505–512.

Deary, I. J., & Batty, G. D. (2007). Cognitive epidemiology: A glossary. *Journal of Epidemiology and Community Health*, *61*, 378–384.

Deary, I. J., Batty, G. D., Pattie, A., & Gale, C. G. (2008). More intelligent, more dependable children live longer: A 55-year longitudinal study of a representative sample of the Scottish nation. *Psychological Science*, *19*, 874–880.

Deary, I. J., & Der, G. (2005). Reaction time explains IQ's association with death. *Psychological Science*, *16*, 64–69.

Deary, I. J., Der, G., & Shenkin, S. D. (2005). Does mother's IQ explain the association between birth weight and cognitive ability in childhood? *Intelligence*, *33*, 445–454.

Deary, I. J., Gow, A. J., Taylor, M. D., Corley, J., Brett, C., Wilson, V., Campbell, H., Whalley, L. J., Porteous, D. J., & Starr, J. M. (2007). The Lothian Birth Cohort 1936: A study to examine influences on cognitive ageing from age 11 to age 70 and beyond. *BMC Geriatrics*, *7*, 28.

Deary, I. J., Whalley, L. J., Batty, G. D., & Starr, J. M. (2006). Physical fitness and lifetime cognitive change. *Neurology*, *67*, 1195–1200.

Deary, I. J., Whalley, L. J., & Starr, J. M. (2009). *A lifetime of intelligence: Follow-up studies of the Scottish Mental Surveys of 1932 and 1947*. Washington, DC: American Psychological Association.

Deary, I. J., Whiteman, M. C., Starr, J. M., Whalley, L. J., & Fox, H. C. (2004). The impact of childhood intelligence on later life: Following up the Scottish Mental Surveys of 1932 and 1947. *Journal of Personality and Social Psychology*, *86*, 130–147.

Der, G., Batty, G. D., & Deary, I. J. (2006). The effect of breastfeeding on offspring intelligence: Prospective study, sibling pairs analysis and meta-analysis. *British Medical Journal*, *333*, 945–948.

Der, G., Batty, G. D., & Deary, I. J. (2009). The association between IQ in adolescence and a range of health outcomes at 40 in the 1979 US National Longitudinal Study of Youth. *Intelligence*, *37*, 573–580.

Elliott, J., & Shepherd, P. (2006). Cohort profile: 1970 British Birth Cohort (BCS70). *International Journal of Epidemiology*, *35*, 836–843.

Ford, G., Ecob, R., Hunt, K., Macintyre, S., & West, P. (1994). Patterns of class inequality throughout the lifespan: Class gradients at 15, 35 and 55 in the West of Scotland. *Social Science and Medicine*, *39*, 1037–1050.

Furu, M., Lingarde, F., & Ljung, B.-O., et al. (1984). *Premature death, cognitive ability and socioeconomic background*. Stockholm: AVEBE Grafiska.

Gale, C. R., Batty, G. D., Cooper, C., & Deary, I. J. (2009). Psychomotor co-ordination and intelligence in childhood and health in adulthood: Testing the system integrity hypothesis. *Psychosomatic Medicine*, *71*, 675–681.

Gale, C. R., Batty, G. D., Tynelius, P., Deary, I. J., & Rasmussen, F. (2010). Intelligence in early adulthood and subsequent hospitalisation and admission rates for the whole range of mental disorders: Longitudinal study of 1,049,663 men. *Epidemiology*, *21*, 70–77.

Gale, C. R., Deary, I. J., Schoon, I., & Batty, G. D. (2007). IQ in childhood and vegetarianism in adulthood: 1970 British cohort study. *British Medical Journal*, *334*, 245–248.

Gale, C. R., Deary, I. J., Boyle, S. H., Barefoot, J., Mortensen, L. H., & Batty, G. D. (2008). Cognitive ability in early adulthood and risk of five specific psychiatric disorders in mid life: The Vietnam Experience Study. *Archives of General Psychiatry*, *65*, 1410–1418.

Gale, C. R., Hatch, S. L., Batty, G. D., & Deary, I. J. (2009). Intelligence in childhood and risk of psychological distress in adulthood: The 1958 National Child Development Survey and the 1970 British Cohort Study. *Intelligence*, *37*, 592–599.

Gale, C. R., Johnson. W., Deary, I. J., Schoon, I., & Batty, G. D. (2009). Intelligence in girls and their subsequent smoking behaviours as mothers: The 1958 National Child Development Study and the 1970 British Cohort Study. *International Journal of Epidemiology*, *38*, 173–181.

Gottfredson, L. S. (2004). Intelligence: Is it the epidemiologists' elusive "fundamental cause" of social class inequalities in health? *Journal of Personality and Social Psychology*, *86*, 174–199.

Gunnell, D., Magnusson, P. K. E., & Rasmussen, F. (2005). Low intelligence test scores in 18 year old men and risk of suicide: Cohort study. *British Medical Journal*, *330*, 167.

Hart, C. L., Deary, I. J., Taylor, M. D., MacKinnon, P. L., Davey Smith, G., Whalley, L. J., Wilson, V., Hole, D. J., & Starr, J. M. (2003). The Scottish Mental Survey 1932 linked to the Midspan studies: A prospective investigation of childhood intelligence and future health. *Public Health*, *117*, 187–195.

Hart, C. L., MacKinnon, P. L., Watt, G. C. M., Upton, M. N., McConnachie, A., Hole, D. J., Davey Smith, G., Gillis, C. R., & Hawthorne, V. M. (2005). The Midspan studies. *International Journal of Epidemiology*, *34*, 28–34.

Hart, C. L., Taylor, M. D., Davey Smith, G., Whalley, L. J., Starr, J. M., Hole, D. J., Wilson, V., & Deary, I. J. (2005). Childhood IQ and all cause mortality before and after age 65: Prospective observational study linking the Scottish Mental Survey 1932 and the Midspan studies. *British Journal of Health Psychology*, *10*, 153–165.

Hart, C. L., Taylor, M. D., Davey Smith, G., Whalley, L. J., Starr, J. M., Hole, D. J., Wilson, V., & Deary, I. J. (2003). Childhood IQ, social class, deprivation and their relationships with mortality and morbidity risk in later life: Prospective observational study linking the Scottish Mental Survey 1932 and the Midspan studies. *Psychosomatic Medicine*, *65*, 877–883.

Hart, C. L., Taylor, M. D., Davey Smith, G., Whalley, L. J., Starr, J. M., Hole, D. J., Wilson, V., & Deary, I. J. (2004). Childhood IQ and cardiovascular disease in adulthood: Prospective observational study linking the Scottish Mental Survey 1932 and the Midspan studies. *Social Science and Medicine*, *59*, 2131–2138.

Hemmingsson, T., Kriebel, D., Melin, B., Allebeck, P., & Lundberg, I. (2008). How does IQ affect onset of smoking and vessation of smoking – linking the Swedish 1969 Conscription Cohort to the Swedish Survey of Living Conditions. *Psychosomatic Medicine*, *70*, 805–810.

Jokela, M., Batty, G. D., Deary, I. J., Gale, C. R., & Kivimaki, M. (2009). Low childhood IQ as a predictor of early adult mortality: The role of explanatory factors in a 35-year follow-up of the 1958 British birth cohort. *Pediatrics*, *124*, E380–E388.

Jokela, M., Elovainio, M., Singh-Manoux, A., & Kivimaki, M. (2009). IQ, socioeconomic status, and early death: The US National Longitudinal Survey of Youth. *Psychosomatic Medicine*, *71*, 322–328.

Koenen, K. C., Moffitt, T. E., Roberts, A. L., Martin, L. T., Kubzansky, L., Harrington, H.,

Poulton, R., & Caspi, A. (2009). Childhood IQ and adult mental disorders: A test of the cognitive reserve hypothesis. *American Journal of Psychiatry*, *166*, 50–57.

Luciano, M., Marioni, R. E., Gow, A. J., Starr, J. M., & Deary, I. J. (2009). Reverse causation in the association between C reactive protein and fibrinogen levels and cognitive abilities in an aging sample. *Psychosomatic Medicine*, *71*, 404–409.

Kuh, D., Richards, M., Hardy, R., Butterworth, S., & Wadsworth, M. E. J. (2004). Childhood cognitive ability and deaths until middle age: A post-war birth cohort study. *International Journal of Epidemiology*, *33*, 408–413.

Kuh, D., Shah, I., Richards, M., Mishra, G., Wadsworth, M., & Hardy, R. (2009). Do childhood cognitive ability or smoking behaviour explain the influence of lifetime socioeconomic conditions in premature adult mortality in a British post war birth cohort? *Social Science and Medicine*, *68*, 1565–1573.

Lawlor, D. A., Batty, G. D., Clark, H., McIntyre, S., & Leon, D. A. (2008). Association of childhood intelligence with risk of coronary heart disease and stroke: Findings from the Aberdeen Children of the 1950s cohort study. *European Journal of Epidemiology*, *23*, 695–706.

Leon, D. A., Lawlor, D. A., Clark, H., Batty, G. D., & Macintyre, S. (2009). The association of childhood intelligence with mortality risk from adolescence to middle age: Findings from the Aberdeen Children of the 1950s cohort study. *Intelligence*, *37*, 520–528.

Link, B. G., Phelan, J. C., Miech, R., & Westin, E. L. (2008). The resources that matter: Fundamental social causes of health disparities and the challenge of intelligence. *Journal of Health and Social Behavior*, *49*, 72–91.

Lleras-Muney, A. (2005). The relationship between education and adult mortality in the United States. *Review of Economic Studies*, *72*, 189–221.

Maller, J. B. (1933). Vital indices and their relation to psychological and social factors. *Human Biology*, *5*, 94–121.

Marmot, M., & Brunner, E. (2005). Cohort profile: The Whitehall II Study. *International Journal of Epidemiology*, *34*, 251–256.

Martin, L. T., & Kubzansky, L. D. (2005). Childhood cognitive performance and risk of mortality: A prospective cohort study. *American Journal of Epidemiology*, *162*, 887–890.

Martin, L. T., Kubzansky, L. D., LeWinn, K. Z., Lipsitt, L. P., Satz, P., & Buka, S. L. (2007). Childhood cognitive performance and risk of generalized anxiety disorder. *International Journal of Epidemiology*, *36*, 769–775.

McGurn, B., Deary, I. J., & Starr, J. M. (2008). Childhood cognitive ability and risk of late-onset Alzheimer and vascular dementia. *Neurology*, *71*, 1051–1056.

Osler, M., Nybo Andersen, A.-M., Laursen, B., & Lawlor, D. A. (2007). Cognitive function in childhood and early adulthood and injuries later in life: The Metropolit 1953 male birth cohort. *International Journal of Epidemiology*, *36*, 212–219.

O'Toole, B. I., & Stankov, L. (1992). Ultimate validity of psychological tests. *Personality and Individual Differences*, *13*, 699–716.

Pearce, M. S., Deary, I. J., Young, A. H., & Parker, L. (2006). Childhood IQ and deaths up to middle age: The Newcastle Thousand Families Study. *Public Health*, *120*, 1020–1026.

Power, C., & Elliot, J. (2006). Cohort profile: 1958 British Birth Cohort (National Child Development Study). *International Journal of Epidemiology*, *35*, 34–41.

Power, C., Li, L., & Hertzman, C. (2008). Cognitive development and cortisol patterns in mid-life: Findings from a British birth cohort. *Psychoneuroendocrinology*, *33*, 530–539.

Richards, M., Black, S., Mishra, G., Gale, C. R., Deary, I. J., & Batty, G. D. (2009). IQ in childhood and the metabolic syndrome in middle age: Extended follow-up of the 1946 British Birth Cohort Study. *Intelligence*, *37*, 567–572.

Richards, M., Strachan, D., Hardy, R., Kuh, D., & Wadsworth, M. (2005). Lung function and cognitive ability in a longitudinal birth cohort study. *Psychosomatic Medicine*, *67*, 602–608.

Roberts, B. A., Der, G., Deary, I. J., & Batty, G. D. (2009). Reaction time and established risk factors for total and cardiovascular disease mortality: Comparison of effect estimates in the follow-up of a large, UK-wide, general-population based survey. *Intelligence*, *37*, 561–566.

Sabia, S., Gueguen, A., Marmot, M. G., Shipley, M. J., Ankri, J., & Singh-Manoux, A. (2010). Does cognition predict mortality in midlife? Results from the Whitehall II cohort study. *Neurobiology of Aging*, *31*, 688–695.

Shenkin, S. D., Bastin, M. E., MacGillivray, T. J., Deary, I. J., Starr, J. M., & Wardlaw, J. M. (2003). Childhood and current cognitive function in healthy 80-year-olds: A DT-MRI study. *NeuroReport*, *14*, 345–349.

Shipley, B. A., Der, G., Taylor, M. D., & Deary, I. J. (2006). Cognition and all-cause mortality across the entire adult age range: Health and Lifestyle Survey. *Psychosomatic Medicine, 68*, 17–24.

Shipley, B. A., Der, G., Taylor, M. D., & Deary, I. J. (2007). Association between mortality and cognitive change over 7 years in a large representative sample of UK residents. *Psychosomatic Medicine, 69*, 640–650.

Shipley, B. A., Der, G., Taylor, M. D., & Deary, I. J. (2008). Cognition and mortality from the major causes of death: The Health and Lifestyle Survey. *Journal of Psychosomatic Research, 65*, 142–152.

Silventoinen, K., Modig-Wennerstad, K., Tynelius, P., & Rasmussen, F. (2007). Association between intelligence and coronary heart disease mortality: A population-based cohort study of 682,361 Swedish men. *European Journal of Cardiovascular Prevention and Rehabilitation, 14*, 555–560.

Singh-Manoux, A., Ferrie, J. E., Lynch, J. W., & Marmot, M. (2005). The role of cognitive ability (intelligence) in explaining the association between socioeconomic position and health: Evidence from the Whitehall II Prospective Cohort Study. *American Journal of Epidemiology, 161*, 831–839.

Singh-Manoux, A., Sabia, S., Kivimaki, M., Shipley, M. J., Ferrie, J. E., & Marmot, M. G. (2009). Cognition and incident coronary heart disease in late midlife: The Whitehall II study. *Intelligence, 37*, 529–534.

Starr, J. M., Taylor, M. D., Hart, C. L., Davey Smith, G., Whalley, L. J., Hole, D, J., Wilson, V., & Deary, I. J. (2004). Childhood mental ability and blood pressure at midlife: Linking the Scottish Mental Survey 1932 and the Midspan studies. *Journal of Hypertension, 22*, 893–897.

Stewart, R., Sabbah, W., Tsakos, G., D'Aaiuto, F., & Watt, R. G. (2008). Oral health and cognitive function in the Third National Health and Nutrition Examination Survey (NHANES III). *Psychosomatic Medicine, 70*, 936–941.

Taylor, M. D., Hart, C. L., Davey Smith, G., Starr, J. M., Hole, D. J., Whalley, L. J., Wilson, V., & Deary, I. J. (2003). Childhood mental ability and smoking cessation in adulthood: Prospective observational study linking the Scottish Mental Survey 1932 and the Midspan studies. *Journal of Epidemiology and Community Health, 57*, 464–465.

The Centres for Disease Control Vietnam Experience Study. (2004). Postservice mortality among Vietnam veterans. *Journal of the American Medical Association, 257*, 790–795.

Wadsworth, M., Kuh, D., Richards, M., & Hardy, R. (2006). Cohort profile: The 1946 National Birth Cohort (MRC National Survey of Health and Development). *International Journal of Epidemiology, 35*, 49–54.

Walker, N. P., McConville, P. M., Hunter, D., Deary, I. J., & Whalley, L. J. (2002). Childhood mental ability and lifetime psychiatric contact: A 66-year follow-up study of the 1932 Scottish Mental Survey. *Intelligence, 30*, 233–245.

Weiss, A., Gale, C. R., Batty, G. D., & Deary, I. J. (2009). Emotionally stable, intelligent men live longer: The Vietnam Experience Study. *Psychosomatic Medicine, 71*, 385–394.

Whalley, L. J., & Deary, I. J. (2001). Longitudinal cohort study of childhood IQ and survival up to age 76. *British Medical Journal, 322*, 819–822.

Whalley, L. J., Starr, J. M., Athawes, R., Hunter, D., Pattie, A., & Deary I. J. (2000). Childhood mental ability and dementia. *Neurology, 55*, 1455–1459.

Part VIII

INTELLIGENCE IN RELATION TO ALLIED CONSTRUCTS

CHAPTER 35

Intelligence and Personality

Colin G. DeYoung

One purpose of this chapter is to explore the conceptual relation of intelligence to personality. Another is to review empirical research on the relation of intelligence to other traits. Personality and intelligence have often been viewed as distinct domains that intersect only to a very limited degree. However, research on both personality and intelligence over the last three decades suggests the possibility that, both conceptually and empirically, intelligence could be integrated with larger models of personality. Such an integration may allow a more unified conception of the structure and sources of individual differences.

Following presentation of working definitions for intelligence and personality, the chapter reviews arguments for and against three of the most common distinctions that are drawn between intelligence and personality. These three dichotomies provide an overview of the major conceptual issues at stake. Given the amount of thought that has been devoted to the conceptual relation of intelligence to personality, this chapter cannot hope to be comprehensive. Additional perspectives can be found in three excellent edited collections (Collis & Messick, 2001; Saklofske & Zeidner, 1995; Sternberg & Ruzgis, 1994). Additionally, the chapter discusses whether intelligence can be located within the Big Five model (John, Naumann, & Soto, 2008). Finally, the Big Five personality dimensions serve to organize a review of empirical associations of intelligence with various personality traits, with a separate section at the end for associations with sociopolitical orientation.

Definition of Intelligence

In 1994, a group of 52 experts in the study of intelligence and related fields endorsed the following definition of intelligence (Gottfredson, 1997a, p. 13):

> *Intelligence is a very general mental capability that, among other things, involves the ability to reason, plan, solve problems, think abstractly, comprehend complex ideas, learn quickly and learn from experience. It is not merely book learning, a narrow academic skill, or test-taking smarts. Rather it reflects a broader*

and deeper capability for comprehending our surroundings – "catching on," "making sense" of things, or "figuring out" what to do.

This definition emphasizes that intelligence represents the ability to solve problems (including problems of comprehension) by thinking. Intelligence is widely considered to occupy the apex of a hierarchy of more specific abilities that are all related to each other (Carroll, 1993). Indeed, the concept of a general intelligence, or "*g*," was first elaborated in psychology because of the so-called positive manifold, the tendency for performance on all cognitive tests to be positively correlated, regardless of their content (Jensen, 1998; Spearman, 1904). Intelligence is posited as the general ability that accounts for the covariation of the many specific abilities. However, specific abilities covary to different degrees, and *g* cannot account for all of the shared variance among them. Thus, below *g* in the hierarchy are a number of more specific but still fairly general abilities; below these are the many specific abilities, and below these are various different instances or measures of those specific abilities (Carroll, 1993; Johnson & Bouchard, 2005a, 2005b).

The most widely used distinction between abilities, at the level of the hierarchy immediately below *g*, is between *fluid* and *crystallized* intelligence (Horn & Cattell, 1966), though other factors may also be identified at this level (Carroll, 1993). Fluid intelligence describes abilities that are innate and not dependent on prior education or experience (and thus, in theory, cannot be modified by experience), whereas crystallized intelligence describes abilities that rely on knowledge or skill acquired from experience. Traditional measures of fluid and crystallized intelligence are differentially related to various other traits, and this finding has led to the incorporation of these concepts in many theories regarding the relation of intelligence to personality. However, recent evidence from factor analysis suggests that individual differences in ability do not, in fact, covary according to whether they are fluid or crystallized, but rather according to whether they are verbal or nonverbal (Johnson & Bouchard, 2005a, 2005b).[1]

Most tests traditionally considered to measure crystallized intelligence are verbal, whereas most tests traditionally considered to measure fluid intelligence are nonverbal. Thus, most past findings regarding fluid and crystallized intelligence and personality can be translated cleanly into a verbal-nonverbal framework, simply by replacing terms, and this chapter will primarily discuss *verbal* and *nonverbal intelligence* rather than *crystallized* and *fluid intelligence*. "Crystallized" and "fluid" are not good labels for the two commonly used types of test, not only because of the verbal-nonverbal factor structure identified by Johnson and Bouchard (2005a, 2005b), but also because both verbal and nonverbal intelligence are determined by a combination of innate ability and acquired knowledge and skills. Verbal intelligence cannot be entirely crystallized (dependent on experience), given that it is just as heritable (genetically influenced) as nonverbal intelligence, even when controlling for *g* (Johnson & Bouchard, 2007; Johnson et al., 2007). And nonverbal intelligence cannot be entirely fluid (independent of experience), both because it is influenced by environmental factors in studies of heritability (Johnson & Bouchard, 2007; Johnson et al., 2007) and because it may be improved by schooling (Ceci, 1991) and by training on video games (Feng, Spence, & Pratt, 2007), working memory tasks (Jaeggi, Buschkuehl, Jonides, & Perrig, 2008; but see Moody, 2009), and other mentally stimulating activities (Tranter & Koutstal, 2008). On average, nonverbal intelligence declines with age after the mid-20s whereas verbal intelligence increases or remains stable until very old age (Berg, 2000), but this does not provide sufficient evidence to claim that

1 Johnson and Bouchard (2005a, 2005b distinguished between "verbal" and "perceptual" abilities, but nonverbal memory and reasoning tasks were encompassed by the perceptual factor, and "nonverbal" seems a more adequately inclusive label. They also identified a small, third factor representing the ability to rotate images mentally.

verbal intelligence is exclusively crystallized whereas nonverbal intelligence is exclusively fluid. The underlying brain systems responsible for these two types of intelligence are at least partially distinct (Choi et al., 2008) and may age differently, even though both incorporate fluid and crystallized processes.

Definition of Personality

Personality is a broader concept than intelligence, as can be seen in the following definition by McAdams and Pals (2006, p. 212):

> *Personality is an individual's unique variation on the general evolutionary design for human nature, expressed as a developing pattern of dispositional traits, characteristic adaptations, and integrative life stories, complexly and differentially situated in culture.*

This definition highlights three distinct levels at which personality can be described: traits, characteristic adaptations, and life stories. Characteristic adaptations and life stories both describe the individual's adaptation to his or her particular sociocultural context (e.g., as a lawyer). Traits describe relatively stable patterns of behavior, motivation, emotion, and cognition (Pytlik Zillig, Hemenover, & Dienstbier, 2002; Wilt & Revelle, 2009) that are not bound to a particular sociocultural context but could be observed in any such context (e.g., argumentativeness). This is not to say that all traits will be evident to the same extent or with identical manifestations in all cultures, nor that all traits can be observed in any situation, but rather that any trait can be observed in a subset of situations in any culture. Traits will be the primary level of focus in this chapter. For this reason, vocational interests will not be discussed, despite their relevance to intelligence and related personality traits (Ackerman & Heggestad, 1997), as they are more like characteristic adaptations than traits, in their cultural specificity.

A central project in personality psychology has been the development of a comprehensive taxonomy of traits. To develop such a taxonomy, one needs a reasonably comprehensive set of traits to be classified. The *lexical hypothesis* states that natural language (as represented in dictionaries) provides a reasonably comprehensive pool of trait descriptors, which can be used to determine the general factors that underlie the covariation among many specific traits (Saucier & Goldberg, 2001). Another promisingly large and broad pool of traits in which to locate general factors can be found in existing personality questionnaires. Lexical and questionnaire research have both provided evidence for a five-factor solution, leading to a taxonomy known as the Five Factor Model or Big Five, which includes the broad trait domains of Extraversion, Neuroticism, Agreeableness, Conscientiousness, and Openness/Intellect (Digman, 1990; Goldberg, 1990; John et al., 2008; Markon, Krueger, & Watson, 2005). The Big Five are strongly genetically influenced (Rieman, Angleitner, & Strelau, 1997), and the genetic factor structure of the Big Five appears to be invariant across European, North American, and East Asian samples, suggesting the biological universality of this model (Yamagata et al., 2006).

Personality traits are hierarchically organized, with more specific traits (e.g., talkativeness, sociability, enthusiasm) varying together, such that one can deduce the presence of broader traits (e.g., Extraversion, for the three traits just mentioned) that account for their covariance. Higher order traits may exist above the Big Five (DeYoung, 2006; Digman, 1997), but they do not appear to be related to intelligence (DeYoung, Peterson, Séguin, & Tremblay, 2008). For the present purpose, therefore, they are of less interest than levels of trait structure below the Big Five. Each Big Five domain comprises a large number of lower level traits, called *facets*, with no consensus as to how many facets exist for each domain. Additionally, research suggests the existence of a level of personality structure between the Big Five and their facets. In two samples, two genetic factors were necessary to account for the shared genetic variance among the facets within each of the

Big Five (Jang, Livesley, Angleitner, Riemann, & Vernon, 2002). If the Big Five were the next level above the facets, only one genetic factor should have been necessary for each domain. In factor analysis of phenotypic data, using 15 facets for each domain, two factors similar to the genetic factors were found for each of the Big Five (DeYoung, Quilty, & Peterson, 2007). These factors were then characterized empirically by their correlations with over 2,000 items from the International Personality Item Pool (Goldberg, 1999). Of particular relevance for intelligence, the two factors in the Openness/Intellect domain clearly differentiated between Openness to Experience and Intellect, with Openness reflecting aesthetically oriented traits related to engagement in sensation and perception (e.g., "Believe in the importance of art"; "See beauty in things that others might not notice") and Intellect reflecting intellectual interest or engagement (e.g., "Avoid philosophical discussions"–reversed) and perceived intelligence (e.g., "Am quick to understand things").

Importantly, traits are probabilistic entities. Each of the Big Five encompasses many subtraits, and a high score on a Big Five trait indicates an increased likelihood of high scores on its various subtraits but is not deterministic. This means that people scoring high in Intellect will, on average, score higher in Openness than people scoring low in Intellect. However, the correlation between Openness and Intellect is far from perfect, which means that some people will score high in Intellect but only moderate or low in Openness, and vice versa. One must remember, when interpreting correlations among traits, that a significant correlation does not indicate a pattern of necessary co-occurrence in every individual, but rather a general trend in the population. The fact that Openness and Intellect are two subtraits within a single Big Five dimension suggests that they share some of their sources, but the fact that they are psychometrically separable means that each additionally has unique sources that differentiates it from the other.

The Conceptual Relation of Intelligence to Personality

Given a broad definition of personality, like the one presented above, the possibility of describing intelligence as a personality trait seems clear. Indeed, some early theorists considered personality to include intelligence (Cattell, 1950; Guilford, 1959). However, most theorists have not considered intelligence to be part of personality, instead asserting either that intelligence (as defined above) is unrelated to personality (e.g., Eysenck, 1994) or that intelligence and personality are related but nonetheless categorically distinct (e.g., Chamorro-Premuzic & Furnham, 2005a). The large body of empirical evidence reviewed in the latter half of this chapter rules out the possibility that intelligence is unrelated to personality. A number of personality traits show consistent and meaningful relations to intelligence. Thus, the important contrast is between the view that intelligence is a personality trait and the more common view that intelligence is fundamentally different from personality traits.

Three dichotomies seem to be largely responsible for the view that intelligence and personality may be related but must be considered as categorically distinct. (Because many researchers have advanced similar dichotomies, with slight variations, what follows represents a distillation of many viewpoints.) First, a distinction is often made between cognitive and noncognitive traits, with intelligence considered to be cognitive and personality considered to be noncognitive. Second, intelligence and personality differ in their typical methods of measurement: Intelligence is usually assessed using ability tests, whereas personality is usually assessed by questionnaire. Third, the difference in typical measurement corresponds to a conceptual distinction in which intelligence is often considered to reflect "maximal performance" (i.e., performance when individuals are trying their hardest), whereas personality is considered to reflect "typical behavior" (Cronbach, 1949). The following section reviews arguments for and against the validity of these dichotomies.

The cognitive/noncognitive dichotomy is widely used, but the evidence against it is strong enough that even some psychologists who utilize it acknowledge that it is flawed and a "misnomer" (Duckworth, 2009, p. 279). The distinction between cognitive and noncognitive fails because almost all traits have cognitive attributes, though these are more prominent in some traits than others. In a study of common Big Five questionnaires, items describing cognitive traits were found in all five domains, with Openness/Intellect containing the most such items and Extraversion and Neuroticism containing the fewest (Pytlik Zillig, Hemenover, & Dienstbier, 2002). Examples of cognitive attributes are easily provided, even for traits that might be considered relatively less cognitive: Neuroticism is associated with rumination, compulsive thinking about possible threats (Nolan, Roberts, & Gotlib, 1998); Agreeableness is associated with "social-cognitive theory of mind," understanding and considering the mental states of others (Nettle & Liddle, 2008). Personality includes stable patterns of cognition, in addition to behavior, motivation, and emotion. Duckworth (2009) suggests that psychologists may continue to employ this problematic dichotomy because "cognitive" is a convenient shorthand for "cognitive ability." "Noncognitive," therefore, is used as shorthand to indicate all variables other than cognitive ability or intelligence, even though many of those other variables have cognitive attributes. Thus, the existence of the cognitive/noncognitive dichotomy may reflect imprecise use of language rather than a strong theoretical assertion that intelligence is categorically distinct from personality.

The second dichotomy involves methods of measurement. Historically, research on intelligence has been separated from research on personality because personality has typically been assessed by questionnaire, whereas intelligence has typically been assessed by ability tests. These two research traditions thus represent two *paradigms*, in Kuhn's (1970) original sense, separated from each other by differing sets of conventional scientific practices. Nonetheless, most psychologists would not assert that different methods of measurement, in and of themselves, justifiy a categorical distinction between the constructs that have been measured. (Whether the differences in measurement are necessary because of an underlying conceptual distinction is a separate question and the focus of the third dichotomy, discussed later.) Psychometricians warn against confusing constructs with measures (Jensen, 1998; Loevinger, 1957). Personality traits are not identical to scores on personality questionnaires, just as intelligence is not identical to an IQ score. In both cases, the measures merely provide estimates of what researchers typically want to investigate – namely, latent traits, actual patterns of human functioning that persist over time – and these cannot be measured without error. (Some researchers may be interested exclusively in the manner in which people represent or describe personality traits, without reference to actual patterns of functioning, but they are in the minority.) Multiple methods can be used to measure a single latent trait; each method may incorporate different sources of error or bias, and one method may be better than another for the purposes intended, but nonetheless each can be said to measure the same trait. For example, given our working definition of intelligence as "a general mental capability," one should expect it to be best measured by ability tests, but one could also measure it, albeit less accurately, using questionnaires that require self-, peer, or observer ratings of subjects' mental ability (this approach is discussed in more detail later in the chapter). Differences in typical methods of measurement, therefore, would not usually be seen as sufficient to rule out the possibility that intelligence is part of personality.

What makes the issue of measurement more complicated, however, is the possibility that the different types of measures typically used for intelligence and personality correspond to a valid dichotomy between maximal performance and typical behavior. If intelligence really involves only maximal performance, and if personality really involves only typical behavior, then one would be forced to conclude that intelligence and personality are categorically distinct. The working definition of intelligence given earlier can be read to imply that maximal performance is what matters. However, some theorists have questioned the sharpness of the distinction between maximal performance and typical behavior (e.g., Ackerman, 1996). This distinction becomes blurred because ability can affect typical behavior, illustrated by the fact that IQ scores are good predictors of outcomes that depend on typical behavior – including job success, academic performance, and health (Gottfredson, 2002; Gottfredson & Deary, 2004). If being intelligent did not typically entail often using one's intelligence, IQ would be unlikely to predict real-world outcomes. Because the complexity of the world always outstrips our simplified mental models (Peterson & Flanders, 2002), intelligence will often be expressed in typical behavior (Gottfredson, 1997b). Even idle thoughts seem likely to be different for those high as opposed to low in intelligence. Any ability for which there is frequent demand or possibility for application will influence typical behavior, and tests of that ability will provide indices of both maximal performance and typical behavior. This is not to say that maximal performance is identical to typical behavior – underachievers who fail to make the best use of their abilities are a clear counterexample – but a case can be made that intelligence, as a trait, entails typical behavior as well as maximal performance.

The idea that personality involves only typical behavior has also been contested. The personality research framework provided by the lexical hypothesis has generally not excluded abilities. Traits that describe ability have been included in all selections of personality descriptors from natural languages (though more in some than others; John Naumann, & Soto, 2008), and these have not fallen exclusively within the Openness/Intellect domain in factor analysis. For example, empathy is a component of Agreeableness that involves the ability to detect the mental states of others. Many components of Conscientiousness, such as self-discipline and patience, can be considered abilities (Mischel, Shoda, & Rodriguez, 1989). For example, large differences in outcome may be evident when people are trying their hardest to be patient, rather than not attempting to restrain themselves, and some people may be more successful in the attempt than others. Abilities thus appear to be relatively common within the Big Five.

One complement to the observation that numerous personality traits involve abilities is the idea that ability tests could be used to measure traits other than intelligence (Ackerman, 2009; Cattell & Birkett, 1980; Cattell & Warburton, 1967; Wallace, 1966; Willerman, Turner, & Peterson, 1976). For example, tests of the ability to detect and understand others' mental and emotional states might be good measures of Agreeableness (Nettle & Liddle, 2008). Tests of the ability to delay gratification or resist distraction might be good measures of Conscientiousness (Mischel et al., 1989). And tests of the ability to remain calm under stress might be good measures of Neuroticism. Personality includes many abilities that could potentially be measured by tests of maximal performance. Past attempts at ability tests for traits other than intelligence have not been very successful (Kline, 1995). However, better progress may be made if such tests are designed to reflect theories regarding the key underlying processes involved in different personality traits (DeYoung & Gray, 2009; Van Egeren, 2009) and if the field recognizes that, because of the differences in method, correlations between questionnaires and tests measuring the same trait are unlikely to be very high, even if the tests are valid (correcting correlations for attenuation due to unreliability and using multiple measures with latent variable models are important strategies for dealing with this problem).

Having reviewed arguments for and against the three dichotomies commonly used to separate intelligence from personality, one can conclude that viewing intelligence as a personality trait is a viable, if relatively uncommon, conceptual strategy. Many personality traits appear to involve both cognitive processes and abilities, which have sometimes been considered exclusive to intelligence. One might argue that maximal performance (relative to typical behavior) is more important in intelligence than in other traits, but this could suggest a difference of degree between intelligence and other traits, rather than a qualitative or categorical difference. The question of whether intelligence should be considered a personality trait remains open.

Intelligence in the Big Five

The previous section raised the question of whether intelligence can be considered part of personality. Given the potential viability of an affirmative answer, another important question is whether intelligence can be integrated with models of personality, like the Big Five, that are derived from trait descriptors and attempt to provide comprehensive taxonomies of traits. Any trait model that would claim comprehensiveness should presumably include intelligence. In considering evidence related to this question, method is an important consideration: One must differentiate between descriptors of intelligence (as in lexical and questionnaire research) and ability tests of intelligence.

Based on lexical and questionnaire studies, a natural home for descriptors of intelligence, in the Big Five taxonomy, appears to be within the Intellect aspect of the Openness/Intellect domain. The compound label "Openness/Intellect" reflects a history of debate about how best to characterize the content of this domain, with some researchers preferring "Openness to Experience" (e.g., Costa & McCrae, 1992a) and others "Intellect" (e.g., Goldberg, 1990). This debate was largely resolved conceptually by the observation that "Openness" and "Intellect" describe two central aspects of the larger domain (DeYoung et al., 2007; Johnson, 1994; Saucier, 1992). Lexical studies made it clear that both aspects are represented in natural language and appear within a single Big Five factor (e.g., Goldberg, 1990; Saucier, 1992). Many words describe Intellect – *intellectual, intelligent, philosophical, erudite, clever* – and many words describe Openness – *artistic, perceptive, poetic, fantasy-prone*. Additionally, many words could characterize people high in Intellect or Openness or both – *imaginative, original, innovative*. In fact, Saucier (1992, 1994) proposed that "Imagination" might be a better single label for the domain as a whole, given the existence of both intellectual and aesthetic forms of imagination. This broad sense of "imagination" is appropriate for a trait domain that has, as its central characteristic, the disposition to detect, explore, and utilize abstract and sensory information (DeYoung, Peterson, & Higgins, 2005; DeYoung et al., 2009). Importantly, general measures of Openness/Intellect (such as the Revised NEO Personality Inventory; NEO PI-R; Costa & McCrae, 1992b; the Trait Descriptive Adjectives; Goldberg, 1992; or the Big Five Inventory; John et al., 2008) contain content reflecting both Openness and Intellect, and they predict other variables very similarly, no matter which label their authors prefer (DeYoung et al., 2005).

In studies of the Big Five in languages other than English, less agreement about the nature of the factor corresponding to Openness/Intellect has emerged, relative to the other four factors. In a Dutch study, for example, this factor was most strongly characterized by descriptors of unconventionality (Hofstee, Kiers, De Raad, & Goldberg, 1997). (Content related to unconventionality also appears in the English Openness/Intellect factor, but less centrally.) However, these differences between languages appear to be related primarily to criteria for variable selection. In Dutch and Italian lexical studies, for example, descriptors related to abilities were undersampled, leading to the exclusion of many terms that might reflect intellectual ability (John, Naumann,

& Soto, 2008). Additionally, in a six-factor lexical solution that has been proposed as a slight modification of the Big Five (dividing Agreeableness into two factors), the content of Openness/Intellect was more consistent across all languages (Ashton et al., 2004). Thus, the relative lack of consensus about the content of Openness/Intellect appears to have been due to methodological issues. The current state of lexical research suggests that Openness/Intellect encompasses a range of trait descriptors related to intellectual and aesthetic curiosity, imagination, and ability – including descriptors of intelligence.

As measured by questionnaires, therefore, intelligence can be located within the Big Five. Despite this semantic fit, objections have been raised because intelligence tests do not behave quite like descriptors of intelligence. If multiple intelligence tests are factor analyzed with personality questionnaires, they tend to form a sixth factor, rather than grouping with questionnaire variables reflecting Openness/Intellect (McCrae & Costa, 1997). However, this result may be due to one or two method artifacts, the first of which is the presence of two distinct sources of method variance in these factor analyses. In addition to substantive trait variance, all of the ability tests share method variance that they do not share with any questionnaire variables, and vice versa. This shared variance inflates the intercorrelations within each type of measure, relative to their correlations with the other type, and inclines the two types of measure to form separate factors, regardless of what they share substantively.

A second possible artifact resembles what Cattell (1978) called a "bloated specific factor," which could result from the inclusion of many intelligence tests in factor analysis of broad personality questionnaires. A bloated specific factor appears when measures of a single lower level trait are overrepresented in the pool of variables to be factor analyzed. Their large number will tend to cause them to form a separate factor, even when the other factors recovered are at a higher level of the trait hierarchy and one of them should subsume the lower level trait in question. As an analogy, consider what would happen if one included 10 scales measuring different types of anxiety in a factor analysis with the 30 facets of the Big Five measured by the NEO PI-R. One would be likely to find a sixth factor for anxiety, in addition to the usual Neuroticism factor encompassing traits like depression, vulnerability, and self-consciousness. This would be considered a bloated specific factor because the location of anxiety as a lower level trait within Neuroticism is well established (John et al., 2008, Markon et al., 2005).

The existence of distinct method variance for intelligence tests and questionnaires, plus the possibility of bloated specific factors, makes interpretation ambiguous for results of joint factor analyses of tests and questionnaires. The factor-analytic results summarized by McCrae and Costa (1997) can be taken to indicate that intelligence falls outside of the Big Five (which would imply that descriptors of intelligence do not measure intelligence as much as they measure some other construct), or they can be challenged by the argument that an adequate factor analysis would need to model method variance explicitly and test a model in which the intelligence tests marked a lower level factor below Openness/Intellect. The question of whether intelligence can be located within the Big Five thus remains open.

The idea that intelligence could be a lower level trait in the personality hierarchy might strike some as odd, given the obvious importance of intelligence in human functioning and the number of cognitive abilities that make up the hierarchy below *g*. Nonetheless, the location of descriptors of intelligence within the Big Five seems clear. As noted above, the existence of Openness and Intellect as two correlated but separable aspects of Openness/Intellect was supported by factor analysis of 15 facet scales in this domain, and empirical characterization of the Intellect factor by correlations with thousands of personality items indicated that it includes at least two facets, intellectual engagement and perceived intelligence (DeYoung et al., 2007). In the Big

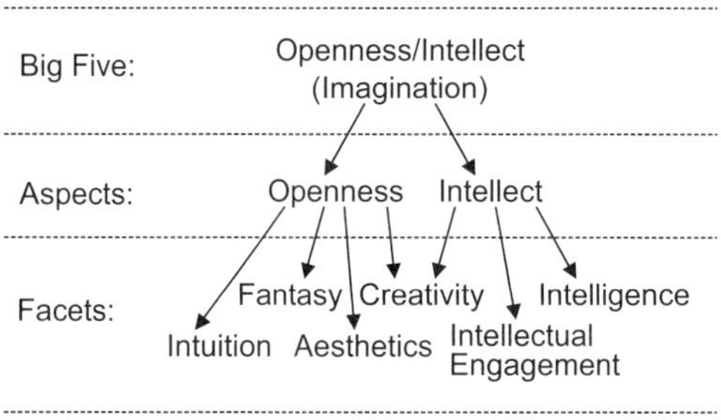

Figure 35.1. Hierarchical structure of personality descriptions within the Openness/Intellect dimension of the Big Five ("Imagination" is an alternative label for this dimension; Saucier, 1992, 1994). Levels of the hierarchy are labeled at left. Note that the number and identity of facets remains speculative. However, item analysis suggests that both intelligence and intellectual engagement are subsumed by Intellect (DeYoung et al., 2007). Creativity receives arrows from both Openness and Intellect to suggest that it is likely to be jointly influenced by both traits.

Five personality hierarchy, therefore, intelligence appears to be at a relatively low level: one facet out of at least two within Intellect, which is itself one of two aspects of the broader Openness/Intellect domain (see Figure 35.1). This structural finding highlights the great complexity of the personality hierarchy, in terms of how many different patterns of emotion, motivation, cognition, and behavior it encompasses. Intelligence is by no means unique in being an extremely important and multifaceted construct that is, nonetheless, relatively narrow when compared to traits like the Big Five that represent very broad regularities in personality. Anxiety, for example, appears to be one facet of the Withdrawal aspect of Neuroticism (DeYoung et al., 2007) and thus exists at the same level of the personality hierarchy as intelligence. The relative breadth of a trait places no limitation on its importance to human beings and seems to place little limitation on the extent to which it may be further subdivided.

Having located intelligence within the personality hierarchy conceptually, we can turn to the question of how it relates empirically to the Big Five and their lower order traits. Its putative position within Intellect suggests that it should be most strongly related to other measures of Intellect and to general measures of the Openness/Intellect domain, but less strongly to specific measures of Openness and to other Big Five domains. Having suggested earlier that ability tests are likely to be better measures of intelligence than questionnaires, this chapter will continue to focus on these tests, and when "intelligence" is discussed, in relation to empirical work, it has been measured by ability tests, unless otherwise noted.

Openness/Intellect

Several thorough reviews of associations between intelligence and personality have been published (Ackerman, 2009; Chamorro-Premuzic & Furnham, 2005a; Eysenck, 1994; Zeidner & Matthews, 2000), but only one has been meta-analytic (Ackerman & Heggestad, 1997). This meta-analysis included only three studies reporting the correlation of Openness/Intellect with *g*, and they indicated a correlation of .33. (Other Big Five traits showed correlations of around .1 or lower.) The last decade has seen a surge of research on this topic, especially research utilizing the Big Five, which consistently replicates the finding that, of the Big Five, Openness/Intellect shows by far the strongest association with intelligence. A comprehensive meta-analysis is beyond the scope of this chapter, but the *N*-weighted average of correlations from 9 studies ($N = 2220$) not included in Ackerman and Heggestad's meta-analysis was $r = .30$ (range = .06 to .42; Ashton, Lee, Vernon, & Jang, 2000; Austin, Deary, & Gibson, 1997; Austin et al., 2002; Chamorro-Premuzic & Furnham, 2008; DeYoung et al., 2005, 2009; Furnham & Chamorro-Premuzic, 2004; Holland, Dollinger, Holland, & MacDonald, 1995).[2]

2 Two large studies ($N = 1507$) were excluded from this calculation because they were collected in business and military recruiting and assessment contexts, which are likely to induce impression management strategies that reduce the validity of self-report questionnaires (Moutafi, Furnham, &

In these studies, mean weighted correlations of intelligence with the other Big Five traits were all very close to those reported by Ackerman and Heggestad, with the exception of Conscientiousness, which showed a correlation of –.12, whereas Ackerman and Heggestad reported .02 (across 3 studies). Although the correlation of about .3 between intelligence and Openness/Intellect is moderate (though tending toward large for variables that do not share method; Hemphill, 2003), it is consistent with the possibility of including intelligence as a facet of Openness/Intellect, given the lack of shared method. Note that the average correlation between facets of Openness/Intellect in the NEO PI-R is only .28 (Costa & McCrae, 1992b).

In studies that have examined verbal and nonverbal intelligence separately, Openness/Intellect consistently shows a stronger correlation with verbal than nonverbal intelligence (Ackerman & Heggestad, 1997; Ashton et al., 2000; Austin et al., 1997; Baker & Bichsel, 2006; Bates & Shieles, 2003; Beauducell, Liepmann, Felfe, Nettelnstroth, 2007; DeYoung et al., 2005; Holland et al., 1995), which has led many researchers to hypothesize that Openness/Intellect causes increased crystallized intelligence through increased motivation to learn (e.g., Chamorro-Premuzic & Furnham, 2005a). The problem with this interpretation is that, as discussed earlier, verbal intelligence cannot be equated conceptually to crystallized intelligence (Johnson & Bouchard, 2005a, 2005b). Because both verbal and nonverbal intelligence are influenced by a mix of genetic and environmental forces, their differential associations with Openness/Intellect are uninformative regarding the causal relation between Openness/Intellect and intelligence.

Although a great deal of speculation has gone into the question of how Openness/Intellect might influence the development of intelligence, thus far little evidence has been provided that is not correlational and cross-sectional (i.e., assessing people of different ages at one point in time). Longitudinal studies are necessary to make any strong claims about causal influence. One such study found no support for the idea that Openness/Intellect is related to change in intelligence over time, using IQ at ages 11 and 79 years (Gow, Whiteman, Pattie, & Deary, 2005). Although Openness/Intellect, assessed at 79, was correlated with IQ at both ages (r = .32 at age 11 and .22 at age 79), it ceased to predict IQ at age 79 after controlling for IQ at age 11. Consistent with the argument of this chapter that intelligence is a facet of Openness/Intellect, Gow and colleagues concluded that the variance shared between Openness/Intellect and intelligence simply reflects the same stable trait of intelligence across the life span. In addition to developing models positing effects of Openness/Intellect on intelligence, or vice versa, it may be that researchers should be looking for shared psychological and biological substrates (DeYoung et al., 2005, 2009).

Thus far, this section has considered total Openness/Intellect scores. Considering Intellect and Openness separately is additionally informative. No instrument other than the Big Five Aspect Scales (BFAS; DeYoung et al., 2007) has been explicitly designed to measure Intellect and Openness as distinct constructs using single scales. However, many older questionnaires tap core components of these two traits. Most measures of Intellect can be categorized according to whether they measure intellectual engagement or perceived intelligence. Commonly used scales measuring intellectual engagement include Typical Intellectual Engagement (TIE; Goff & Ackerman, 1992), Need for Cognition (NFC; Cacioppo, Petty, Feinstein, & Jarvis, 1996), and the Ideas facet of the NEO PI-R (Costa & McCrae, 1992b). The Ideas facet is much more strongly correlated with TIE (r = .77; Ackerman & Goff, 1994) and NFC (r = .78; Cacioppo et al., 1996) than with any of the other NEO PI-R facets (Costa & McCrae, 1992b). Like Ideas,

Crump, 2003; Perkins & Corr, 2006). As one would expect, they found that Openness/Intellect was the only Big Five trait significantly positively associated with intelligence, but with attenuated correlations relative to most other studies (r = .15 and .12).

TIE and NFC have been found to be associated with intelligence (Ackerman & Heggestad, 1997; Cacioppo et al., 1996; Espejo, Day, & Scott, 2005; Frederick, 2005; Gow et al., 2005).

Whereas Ideas is the only NEO PI-R facet that is a good marker of Intellect (DeYoung et al., 2007), four NEO PI-R facets are good markers of Openness; listed from largest to smallest loading, they are Aesthetics, Fantasy, Feelings, and Actions.[3] (The sixth Openness/Intellect facet, Values, does not mark either Openness or Intellect strongly and is discussed later in the section on sociopolitical orientation.) In studies that consider the NEO PI-R facets individually, Ideas typically predicts intelligence (whether general, verbal, or nonverbal) more strongly than do the four Openness facets (DeYoung et al., 2005, 2009; Furnham, Dissou, Sloan, & Chamorro-Premuzic, 2007; Holland et al., 1995; McCrae, 1993; Moutafi, Furnham, & Crump, 2003, 2006).

From the few studies that not only examined the NEO PI-R facets but also separated verbal and nonverbal intelligence, it appears that the stronger association of Intellect (Ideas) than Openness with intelligence may be especially pronounced for nonverbal intelligence (DeYoung et al., 2005; McCrae, 1993; Moutafi et al., 2006; but see Holland et al., 1995). The Openness facets appear more likely to be associated with verbal intelligence than with nonverbal intelligence, whereas Ideas is often associated with both forms of intelligence about equally. This pattern suggests one reason that total Openness/Intellect scores might be associated more strongly with verbal than nonverbal intelligence: Intellect may be associated with both verbal and nonverbal intelligence, whereas Openness may be associated primarily with verbal intelligence. This possibility requires more investigation, as does the more general question of which cognitive abilities are and are not associated with Openness, as opposed to Intellect. Studies of these questions should distinguish unique variance in Openness from variance shared with Intellect, using partial correlations or structural equation modeling.

Measures of perceived intelligence (or *subjectively assessed intelligence*; Chamorro-Premuzic & Furnham, 2005a, 2005b) are not as widely used or standardized as measures of intellectual engagement. Furthermore, items reflecting perceived intelligence rather than intellectual engagement are rarely incorporated into standard Big Five questionnaires (with the important exception of questionnaires derived from the International Personality Item Pool; DeYoung et al., 2007; Goldberg, 1999). Nonetheless, enough studies have assessed perceived intelligence to conclude (1) that perceived intelligence is correlated with Ideas more strongly than with the four Openness facets of the NEO PI-R (Chamorro-Premuzic, Moutafi, & Furnham, 2005; DeYoung et al., 2007), and (2) that correlations of self-reported intelligence with tested intelligence are similar in magnitude to correlations discussed above for Openness/Intellect and intellectual engagement – typically in the range of .20 to .35 (Chamorro-Premuzic & Furnham, 2005a, 2005b; Chamorro-Premuzic et al., 2005; Paulhus et al., 1998). These effect sizes are consistent with the location of intelligence within the personality hierarchy but imply that self-reported intelligence should not be used as a proxy for tested intelligence (Paulhus et al., 1998). Other-ratings of intelligence fare somewhat better, though they have been less well studied. Teacher-ratings of intelligence strongly predict student IQ, with correlations ranging from about .45 all the way up to .80 (Alvidrez & Weinstein, 1999; Brickenkamp, 1975, cited in Ostendorf & Angleitner, 1994; Pedulla, Airasian, & Madaus, 1980). Additional research is necessary to learn how well intelligence can

3 That the NEO PI-R contains only one Intellect facet and four Openness facets is an idiosyncrasy of that instrument and does not constitute evidence that Intellect is not central to the larger Openness/Intellect domain. The facets of the NEO PI-R were derived rationally, rather than empirically, and its authors have often argued against Intellect as a valid interpretation of content in this domain (Costa & McCrae, 1992a; McCrae & Costa, 1997). As noted earlier, however, considerable evidence in both lexical and questionnaire research indicates that Intellect is just as central to the larger domain as Openness.

be rated by others who are not teachers, such as friends or family members.

The relative lack of accuracy for self-ratings of intelligence suggests the utility of studying discrepancies between self-rated and tested intelligence (Ackerman, Beier, & Bown, 2002; Paulhus & John, 1998). Self-reported intelligence may reflect a combination of actual intelligence and inaccurate self-perception that could be due to over- or underconfidence. Indeed, self-esteem predicts the tendency to rate one's intelligence more highly than is warranted by one's tested intelligence (Gabriel, Critelli, & Ee, 1994). It is also possible that when individuals rate their own intelligence they are taking into account abilities that are not strongly tested by typical intelligence tests (such as divergent or creative thinking). This supposition is supported by the observation that the accuracy of self-ratings in predicting ability tests appears to be higher when individuals are tested and rate themselves on more specific abilities, below *g* in the intelligence hierarchy, such as verbal, mathematical, or spatial ability (Ackerman et al., 2002). Asking individuals to rate their own general intelligence may make it harder for people to form accurate self-perceptions (because they are required to consider a large and poorly specified range of their own experience) and may also make it easier for them to base their responses on wishful thinking or insecurity or on conceptions of intelligence that differ from the one operationalized in most intelligence tests (Saucier, 2009). Note that the last point raises a possibility that should be further explored empirically: In relation to abilities that are not well tested by typical intelligence tests, self-reports might be more accurate reflections of ability than the typical tests.

The link between intelligence and Openness/Intellect is reinforced by studies of working memory and brain function. Intelligence is very strongly associated with working memory, the ability to maintain and manipulate information in short-term memory, despite distraction (Conway, Kane, & Engle, 2003). Further, the brain systems in the prefrontal cortex (PFC) and parietal cortex that support both working memory and intelligence overlap substantially, indicating that working memory may be one of the primary cognitive substrates of intelligence (Gray & Thompson, 2004). Openness/Intellect, and especially its Intellect aspect, are also associated with working memory (DeYoung et al., 2005, 2009), and a recent study investigated associations of Intellect, Openness, and intelligence with brain activity during a difficult working memory task ($N = 104$; DeYoung et al., 2009). Intellect was measured using the Ideas scale, which was the only facet of Openness/Intellect that was associated with working memory-related brain activity. In the left frontal pole of prefrontal cortex, Ideas was associated with brain activity that predicted better working memory performance; however, this association was attenuated when controlling for intelligence, suggesting that this brain region is a shared substrate of both intelligence and intellectual engagement. The brain's frontal pole is particularly involved in the abstract integration of multiple cognitive operations and in drawing abstract analogies (Gilbert et al., 2006; Green, Fugelsang, Kraemer, Shamosh, & Dunbar, 2006; Ramnani & Owen, 2004). Ideas was also associated with working memory-related brain activity in a posterior region of the medial frontal cortex, which is known to be involved in monitoring goal-directed performance and detecting likelihood of error (Brown & Braver, 2005; Ridderinkhof, Ullsperger, Crone, & Nieuwenhuis, 2004). In this region, Ideas remained significantly related to neural activity even after controlling for intelligence, suggesting that this region and its functions may be involved in intellectual engagement, independently of intelligence. Intellectual engagement suggests a motivation to succeed at cognitive tasks, which is plausibly associated with greater monitoring of cognitive performance. Intelligence and intellectual engagement are conceptually distinct facets of Intellect (though each seems likely to support the other), and this study is relevant to the important question of the extent to which their sources are shared versus distinct.

Another trait that falls within Openness/Intellect in lexical studies is creativity (Saucier, 1992), and both Openness/Intellect and intelligence are consistently associated with creativity, whether the latter is measured by trait-descriptive questionnaires, by real-world achievement, or by measures of creative production in the laboratory, such as divergent thinking (Carson, Peterson, & Higgins, 2005; Feist, 1998; McCrae, 1987). Another chapter in this volume (see Chapter 38, Intelligence and Creativity) provides an in-depth review of the association of intelligence with creativity. Creativity has often been considered a personality trait, and some other mental capacities could also potentially be considered personality traits. Psychologists have studied a variety of individual differences in the ways that people reason – for example, through logic, heuristics, and intuition (e.g., Stanovich & West, 2000). If these were considered personality traits, they too might fall within Openness/Intellect in the Big Five hierarchy.

Extraversion

Extraversion comprises a set of lower level traits related to approach behavior and positive affect, including assertiveness, talkativeness, sociability, and positive emotionality. Extraversion appears to represent the manifestation in personality of sensitivity to rewards, both anticipated and received (Depue & Collins, 1999; DeYoung & Gray, 2009). Across 35 studies, Ackerman and Heggestad (1997) reported a very small, but statistically significant, positive correlation of Extraversion with g, $r = .08$. An updated meta-analysis for Extraversion (Wolf & Ackerman, 2005), including 50 new studies, found a similar effect size overall, $r = .05$, but noted that different measures of Extraversion and different subtraits within Extraversion yielded significantly different, though all weak, effects (an example of moderation), and that in studies published since 2000 the correlation was, in fact, significantly negative, $r = -.04$. In any case, any weak positive association of intelligence with Extraversion might be artifactual, simply reflecting Extraversion's positive correlation with Openness/Intellect (DeYoung, 2006; Digman, 1997) rather than a real association with intelligence specifically. Studies assessing the association of Extraversion and intelligence while controlling for Openness/Intellect could help to resolve this question.

Another possibility is that weak associations of Extraversion with intelligence reflect individual differences in low-level cognitive processes. For example, Extraversion has been found to predict better short-term memory (Zeidner & Matthews, 2000), although it does not typically predict working memory, in which information in short-term memory must be manipulated or maintained despite distraction (DeYoung et al., 2005, 2009). Extraversion may be related to some aspects of intelligence test taking rather than to actual intelligence. Faster speed of test taking and a lack of persistence during tests have been associated with Extraversion, but results are equivocal (Chamorro-Premuzic, & Furnham, 2005a). In general, the cognitive correlates of Extraversion are moderated by contextual factors, such as sensory stimulation and incentives (Eysenck, 1994; Zeidner & Matthews, 2000). Perhaps because it primarily reflects basic positive emotional and motivational tendencies, Extraversion appears to be related to the stylistic ways in which people solve problems that require intelligence, while affecting their ability to solve them correctly only slightly, if at all.

Neuroticism

Neuroticism encompasses a variety of traits reflecting the tendency to experience negative emotion, including anxiety, depression, irritability, and insecurity. It appears to reflect the primary manifestation in personality of sensitivity to threat and punishment (DeYoung & Gray, 2009; Gray & McNaughton, 2000). Neuroticism exhibits a small but reliable negative correlation with intelligence, $r = -.15$ across 30 studies (Ackerman & Heggestad, 1997). This correlation is likely to be due to the facts that negative emotion typically interferes with higher cognition, in part by interrupting the functions of PFC (Fales et al., 2008; Keightley et al., 2003), and that neurotic individuals are more likely to experience anxiety under the pressures of testing situations (Ackerman & Heggestad, 1997). Measures specifically designed to assess test anxiety are negatively correlated with intelligence, $r = -.33$ (Ackerman & Heggestad, 1997). The most likely reason that this correlation is considerably stronger than the correlation of intelligence with Neuroticism is that trait and state anxiety are not identical. Individuals who are high in Neuroticism and generally anxious may nonetheless be non-anxious while taking tests because of their particular histories and characteristic adaptations. (Similarly, individuals scoring low in Neuroticism, who are not generally anxious, may nonetheless be anxious about taking tests for reasons related to their personal histories.) Neuroticism is not inevitably associated with test anxiety, but the substantial correlation between the two ($r \approx .5$; Ackerman & Heggestad, 1997) means that high levels of Neuroticism increase the probability of anxiety during tests, which presumably leads to the small negative correlation between Neuroticism and intelligence.

That the association of Neuroticism with intelligence is mediated by test anxiety (Moutafi, Furnham, & Tsaousis, 2006) raises the question of whether this association should be considered substantive. Is Neuroticism really associated with intelligence, or is it merely associated with performance on intelligence tests? One's answer to this question will depend on one's view regarding the distinction between maximal performance and typical behavior. If one limits intelligence to maximal performance, then presumably test performance is diagnostic of intelligence only to the extent that test anxiety has not impaired performance. If, however, one takes seriously the argument, presented earlier, that intelligence entails typical behavior as well as maximal performance, then the situation becomes more complicated. Intelligence involves solving problems, and problems are often a source of stress in daily life. Thus, given the likelihood that a neurotic person's mental function will be impaired by anxiety precisely when intelligence would be most useful, perhaps the association between Neuroticism and intelligence should indeed be considered substantive. Additional evidence for the possibility of a substantive nature of this association comes from a longitudinal study that found a small negative correlation ($r = -.18$) of Neuroticism with change in IQ over 68 years (Gow et al., 2005), suggesting either that Neuroticism influences the development of intelligence or that it influences age-related declines in intelligence. Investigations of how Neuroticism and negative emotion influence the development and ongoing function of cognitive processes and brain systems involved in intelligence may usefully expand our understanding of the way intelligence is integrated with the rest of an individual's personality.

Another possibility to consider is that intelligence may influence the effects of Neuroticism, as suggested by studies of interactions between Neuroticism and intelligence in predicting various outcomes. One such study found that leadership performance was predicted by the interaction of Neuroticism and intelligence (Perkins & Corr, 2006). For individuals high in Neuroticism, intelligence was positively associated with performance, whereas for those low in Neuroticism, intelligence was unrelated to performance. Another study found a similar effect for the interaction of Neuroticism and intelligence, among military conscripts, in predicting performance, physical health, and adjustment to military life (Leikas, Mäkinen, Lönnqvist, & Verkasalo, 2009). Those high in Neuroticism showed poor performance, health, and adjustment only if they were low in intelligence. Intelligence, therefore, may act as a buffer for neurotic individuals, allowing them to cope with stressors despite heightened sensitivity to negative affect.

Agreeableness (Versus Aggression)

Agreeableness reflects traits related to altruism (DeYoung & Gray, 2009; Nettle, 2006), contrasting empathy, politeness, and cooperation with callousness, rudeness, and aggression. Ackerman and Heggestad's (1997) meta-analysis, and the subsequent studies mentioned earlier, indicate that Agreeableness is not associated with intelligence. However, aggression is negatively associated with intelligence, on average, with correlations around –.20 (Ackerman & Heggestad, 1997; DeYoung et al., 2008; Huesmann, Eron, & Yarmel, 1987; Seguin, Boulerice, Harden, Tremblay, & Pihl, 1999), and aggression clearly marks the negative pole of Agreeableness (Markon et al., 2005). What might explain this paradox? One likely explanation is that measures of Agreeableness rarely include direct assessment of the tendency toward aggression, often assessing rudeness and callousness but stopping short of outright aggression and other extreme antisocial behaviors. Aggression typically has a skewed distribution, with high levels being relatively rare in the general population. Low levels of aggression might indicate moderate but not necessarily high levels of Agreeableness. An association of intelligence with aggression, in the absence of any association with Agreeableness as typically measured, suggests the possibility that the association between Agreeableness and intelligence may be nonlinear, remaining relatively flat until the lower range of Agreeableness. The possibility of nonlinear relations between intelligence and other traits has rarely been investigated (but see Austin et al., 1997, 2002). One study failed to find any nonlinear association between Agreeableness and intelligence (Austin et al., 2002), but this may suggest that the researchers' measure of Agreeableness did not cover the full range of the Agreeableness dimension.

As well as with aggression, intelligence is also negatively associated with the broader trait of externalizing behavior (DeYoung et al., 2008; Seguin et al., 1999), which includes antisocial behavior, impulsivity, and drug abuse, in addition to aggression (Krueger et al., 2002, 2007). Among the Big Five, Agreeableness and Conscientiousness show the strongest (negative) correlations with externalizing behavior (Miller & Lynam, 2001). Behavioral and molecular genetic studies indicate that the association between externalizing behavior and intelligence is genetically based (Koenen, Caspi, Moffitt, Rijsdijk, & Taylor, 2006) and moderated by variation in a gene that produces a receptor for the neurotransmitter dopamine (DeYoung et al., 2006). Such studies may begin to shed light on the question of the causal relation of intelligence and externalizing behavior. Past theories have highlighted the possibility that unintelligent people may experience more frustration, leading to aggression and other externalizing behavior, or that intelligent people may be better able to understand the consequences of their actions, disinclining them from such behavior (e.g., Lynam, Moffitt, & Stouthamer-Loeber, 1993). It is also possible that externalizing behavior and intelligence are both influenced by a shared biological substrate (DeYoung et al., 2006).

Aggression and antisocial behavior may not be the only components of Agreeableness that are associated with intelligence. When components of Agreeableness such as detecting the emotional states of others or facilitating harmonious social relations are measured by ability tests rather than questionnaires, they are correlated with intelligence (Mayer, Salovey, & Caruso, 2004; Mayer, Roberts, & Barsade, 2008; Roberts, Schulze, & MacCann, 2008). This finding has emerged primarily from work on emotional intelligence, which has been defined as "the ability to engage in sophisticated information processing about one's own and others' emotions and the ability to use this information as a guide to thinking and behavior" (Mayer, Salovey, & Caruso, 2008, p. 503). Many questionnaires have been developed to assess emotional intelligence, but they reflect a diverse and rather incoherent collection of different conceptualizations of the construct (Mayer, Salovey, & Caruso, 2008; Roberts et al.,

2008). Of more interest are ability tests that have been developed to assess emotional intelligence, most prominently the Mayer-Salovey-Caruso Emotional Intelligence Test (MSCEIT), which comprises a battery of subtests that involve tasks like identifying emotions in facial expressions or judging how best to manage others' emotions in social situations. Despite psychometric limitations (Barchard, 2003; Brody, 2004), the MSCEIT can be considered an encouraging example of the assessment of personality using ability tests rather than questionnaires. Scores on the MSCEIT are consistently associated with intelligence, with a correlation of about .3 (Mayer et al., 2004; Roberts et al., 2008). Like Openness/Intellect, the MSCEIT appears to be more strongly associated with verbal intelligence than with nonverbal intelligence (Mayer et al., 2004; Roberts et al., 2008).

Despite the fact that the MSCEIT is at least moderately related to intelligence, the term "emotional ability" is currently preferable to the term "emotional intelligence" for two reasons. First, use of the word "intelligence" implies that emotional intelligence is on par with constructs like verbal and nonverbal intelligence, in the hierarchy below *g*. This possibility appears remote but cannot yet be ruled out; latent structural modeling, using extensive batteries of emotional ability tests in conjunction with standard intelligence tests would be necessary to test it properly. Second, in relation to the Big Five, the emotional abilities tested by the MSCEIT have their primary association with Agreeableness, whereas intelligence, both as tested and as perceived, has its primary association with Openness/Intellect.

Across a number of studies, scores on the MSCEIT have been found to be correlated with Agreeableness in the range of .20 to .30 (Mayer et al., 2008; Roberts et al., 2008). They are also correlated with Openness/Intellect, but more weakly, in the range of .10 to .20. Correlations with Extraversion, Neuroticism, and Conscientiousness are lower still (Mayer et al., 2004, 2008; Roberts et al., 2008). Thus, emotional ability shows roughly the same magnitude of relation to Agreeableness that intelligence shows to Openness/Intellect and self-reported intelligence. The ability to recognize and manage emotions effectively in social situations can be considered an important component of Agreeableness (cf. Ode, Robinson, & Wilkowski, 2008) and one that appears to be positively associated with intelligence.

If the emotional abilities measured by the MSCEIT can be considered features of Agreeableness, how might one understand the contribution made to them by intelligence? Understanding emotions and their uses certainly constitutes a potential problem for the individual, but to what extent can this problem be solved by thinking? One study found that the combination of intelligence, Agreeableness, and gender predicted MSCEIT scores with a multiple correlation of .81 (corrected for unreliability), with each predictor contributing independently (Schulte, Ree, & Carretta, 2004). Emotional intelligence tests may simply measure the conjunction of two independent traits, the ability to empathize (a component of Agreeableness) and the ability to solve problems by thinking (intelligence), or it is possible that individual differences in empathy are substantively associated with intelligence (despite the fact that Agreeableness questionnaires are not). Many questions remain regarding the relation of Agreeableness and its various components to intelligence.

Conscientiousness (Versus Impulsivity)

Conscientiousness contrasts traits like self-discipline, industriousness, and orderliness with carelessness, distractibility, and disorganization. It appears to reflect the ability and tendency to constrain immediate impulses and to exert effort, in order to pursue nonimmediate goals or follow rules. The association of Conscientiousness with intelligence is as complicated and uncertain as that of Agreeableness. Ackerman and Heggestad's (1997) meta-analysis and the subsequent studies reviewed earlier suggest either no correlation or a weak negative correlation between Conscientiousness and intelligence. Chamorro-Premuzic and Furnham (2005a) have hypothesized that higher Conscientiousness in those with lower intelligence might be a compensatory mechanism. People who are unintelligent may be more orderly, in order to avoid complexity that they find difficult to manage because of their low intelligence. Similarly, they may tend to work extra hard so as to accomplish tasks that could be performed more quickly or easily by someone more intelligent. Conscientiousness and intelligence are the two best trait predictors of academic and occupational performance, and they predict performance independently (Barchard, 2003; Higgins, Peterson, Pihl, & Lee, 2007; Mount, Barrick, & Strauss, 1999). Thus, increasing one might indeed compensate for a deficiency in the other.

However, although the idea of Conscientiousness as a compensation for low intelligence is plausible, a number of reasons exist to hypothesize that Conscientiousness should be positively associated with intelligence instead. As noted earlier, externalizing behavior is negatively correlated with both intelligence and Conscientiousness, and impulsivity is an important component of externalizing behavior. Impulsivity marks the negative pole of Conscientiousness[4] (Markon et al., 2005) and has been found to correlate negatively with intelligence (Kuntsi et al., 2004; Lynam et al., 1993; Vigil-Colet & Morales-Vives, 2005).

Conceptually, Conscientiousness is clearly linked to the tendency to forgo immediate rewards in favor of longer term goals. Normatively, people discount rewards that are delayed (Frederick, Loewenstein, & O'Donoghue, 2002), but the strength of this *delay discounting* shows considerable variability and has the characteristics of a stable personality trait (Kirby, 2009). Delay discounting is typically measured through a series of choices between smaller, more immediate rewards and larger, delayed rewards, with similar outcomes obtained whether these choices are hypothetical or actually result in reward (Shamosh & Gray, 2008). A large literature demonstrates that delay discounting is negatively associated with intelligence, with a meta-analysis of 24 studies indicating a correlation of −.23 (Shamosh & Gray, 2008). In one study, this association was partially mediated by working memory capacity and by neural activity in the same fronto-polar brain region discussed earlier in relation to Intellect (Shamosh et al., 2008). Delay discounting is positively correlated with questionnaire measures of impulsivity (Hinson, Jameson, & Whitney, 2003; Ostaszewski, 1996; Richards, Zhang, Mitchell, & de Wit, 1999; Swann, Bjork, Moeller, & Dougherty, 2002), but whether it is correlated with standard questionnaire measures of Conscientiousness is not yet clear.

Finally, in both childhood and adulthood, descriptions of intelligence and Intellect in questionnaires are related positively to descriptions of Conscientiousness (Costa & McCrae, 1992a; DeYoung et al., 2007). In adults, this association does not prevent Intellect descriptors from loading primarily on a broader Openness/Intellect factor. In preschool-age children, however, this association appears to be strong enough that traits reflecting Intellect may group with Conscientiousness in factor analysis rather than with traits that reflect Openness (De Pauw, Mervielde, & Van Leeuwen, 2009; Shiner & DeYoung, in press).

A link between Intellect and Conscientiousness may reflect their related biological substrates in the PFC (Shamosh et al., 2008). The lateral PFC is responsible for carrying out plans and inhibiting impulsive responses (Bunge & Zelazo, 2006), functions associated with Conscientiousness, but it is also responsible for manipulating information in working memory and forming abstract

4 Some forms of impulsivity may be more strongly associated with Neuroticism or Extraversion than with Conscientiousness (Whiteside & Lynam, 2001), and impulsivity might best be conceived as a compound trait that reflects variation in multiple, more basic traits (Depue & Collins, 1999). However, low Conscientiousness is a key element of any such compound. Nonetheless, different forms of impulsivity may be differently associated with intelligence.

analogies, functions associated with Intellect and intelligence (DeYoung et al., 2005, 2009). These two classes of PFC function, one more stabilizing and the other more exploratory, may be in tension, though both have been described as "executive function." As the PFC is developing rapidly in young children, differences in overall state of development might cause Intellect and Conscientiousness to co-vary (Shiner & DeYoung, in press). After the PFC is more fully developed, however, the functional similarity of Intellect and Openness, as forms of exploratory cognition, may link Intellect more strongly with Openness than with Conscientiousness. At biological, behavioral, and psychometric levels of analysis, the relation of intelligence to Conscientiousness and related traits is a pressing topic for investigation in personality psychology.

Sociopolitical Orientation

Although culturally specific social and political attitudes are clearly characteristic adaptations rather than traits, a general tendency toward conservativism versus liberalism is a trait that might be found in any culture and that has been studied along with related traits like right-wing authoritarianism (Bouchard et al., 2003; Koenig & Bouchard, 2006). Sociopolitical orientation receives a separate section here because it cannot easily be categorized within any one of the Big Five. Conservativism and authoritarianism are associated negatively with Openness/Intellect but also positively with Conscientiousness (Carney, Jost, Gosling, & Potter, 2008; Hirsh, DeYoung, Xu, & Peterson, 2010; Goldberg & Rosolack, 1994). Additionally, conservativism is associated negatively with the aspect of Agreeableness labeled *Compassion*, which includes empathy, but it is associated positively with the other aspect of Agreeableness, *Politeness* (Hirsh et al., 2010). Sociopolitical orientation thus appears to reflect a complex blend of multiple basic traits, and this blend is consistent with the characterization of the core of conservativism as dislike of change and uncertainty, plus tolerance of inequality, and the core of liberalism as openness to change, plus egalitarianism (Jost et al., 2007).

In keeping with their negative association with Openness/Intellect, conservativism and authoritarianism are negatively associated with intelligence, with correlations in the range of –.20 to –.35 (Block & Block, 2006; Bouchard et al., 2003; Deary, Batty, & Gale, 2008; Koenig & Bouchard, 2006). In the NEO PI-R, the Values facet of Openness/Intellect assesses liberal versus conservative sociopolitical attitudes, and an alternative measure of this facet has been labeled "Liberalism" (Goldberg, 1999). The Values facet seems to behave most like the Ideas facet in its association with intelligence, often showing stronger correlations than the four Openness facets (DeYoung et al., 2005, 2009; Chamorro-Premuzic et al., 2005). However, Values does not clearly mark either the Intellect or Openness aspect of Openness/Intellect, presumably because it represents a compound of Openness/Intellect with Conscientiousness (DeYoung et al., 2007). In the study of brain function discussed above (DeYoung et al., 2009), Values, like Ideas, was associated with intelligence and working memory, but it was not associated with neural activity, suggesting a less clear link between sociopolitical orientation and brain function than that which exists for Intellect (but see Amodio, Jost, Master, & Yee, 2007).

Liberalism is characterized by appreciation of diverse points of view and embrace of change, which may be facilitated by intelligence and working memory in part because change and consideration of diverse perspectives produce higher levels of complexity in one's ongoing experience. Such complexity may be difficult to manage for those of lesser intelligence (note the similarity of this argument to the one described above regarding the possible negative correlation between Conscientiousness and intelligence; Chamorro-Premuzic & Furnham, 2005a).

Conclusions and Future Directions

Intelligence can be viewed either as a construct that is categorically distinct from personality, or as one construct within the larger domain of personality. Neither viewpoint is supported by incontrovertible evidence. However, I believe that psychology would benefit from the conceptual integration of intelligence and personality. The mandate of personality psychology is to understand the whole person as a coherent entity (McAdams & Pals, 2006), and this goal can be furthered by consideration of intelligence as a personality trait. In discussing the relation of intelligence to Openness/Intellect, Saucier (1994, p. 294) wrote, "Intelligence is prone to suck in, or perturb the orbit of, any construct that comes near it." This assertion evokes an image of personality traits as small planets orbiting a massive sun of intelligence. Framed grandiosely, one purpose of this chapter is to propose a Copernican revolution, whereby intelligence is now simply one trait among many, orbiting the central concept of personality. (As mentioned above, this proposal is not entirely novel, but similar proposals in the past have not been much heeded.) Our understanding of personality generally and intelligence specifically will be enriched by considering how the psychological functions and biological systems that underlie intelligence are related to and interact with those that underlie other personality traits.

The major conceptual barrier to integrating intelligence and personality is the old distinction between maximal performance and typical behavior. I suggested above that this dichotomy, although intuitively appealing, may ultimately fail, both because individual differences in intelligence entail individual differences in typical behavior and because many personality traits encompass abilities other than intelligence. Broad personality traits reflect pervasive regularities in human functioning, and such regularities are likely to reflect types of challenge that are common in everyday life (Nettle, 2006, Van Egeren, 2009). Any such challenge provides an opportunity, or even a demand, for the application of relevant ability, ensuring that ability will be intimately tied to typical behavior.

A full integration of intelligence with personality would require locating intelligence within hierarchical trait taxonomies, like the Big Five model. In the Big Five, descriptors of intelligence are located within the Intellect aspect of the broader domain of Openness/Intellect. As reviewed above, this location is reasonably consistent with the patterns of correlation of intelligence tests with trait questionnaires. Having located intelligence within Intellect, one can address what is perhaps a more interesting question: Are there personality traits *other* than Intellect that are associated with intelligence, and if so, why? Utilizing the Big Five framework, this chapter reviewed what is known about these associations and highlighted a number of empirical questions that should be addressed in future research.

One set of questions to be addressed in the future surrounds the differential relations of intelligence tests to different subtraits within Openness/Intellect. Intellect, not surprisingly, appears to relate more strongly than Openness to general intelligence. But do verbal and nonverbal intelligence show different patterns of relation to Openness? Can this explain why Openness/Intellect, as a whole, is more strongly related to verbal than nonverbal intelligence? Given that individual differences in the intelligence hierarchy below *g* appear to group according to whether they involve verbal or nonverbal operations, rather than according to whether they are crystallized or fluid (Johnson & Bouchard, 2005a, 2005b), new causal theories regarding the causal and developmental links between Openness, imagination, intellectual engagement, and intelligence probably need to be developed. Clearly, innate versus experience-dependent aspects of intelligence are still of interest, but investigating them will be more challenging now that one cannot simply assume that verbal tests assess crystallized intelligence while nonverbal tests assess fluid intelligence. One promising approach to experience-dependent abilities is to investigate domain-specific knowledge, while controlling for verbal and nonverbal intelligence (e.g., Ackerman, 2000).

Another set of questions involves the mystery of the relations of Agreeableness and Conscientiousness to intelligence. As typically measured in Big Five questionnaires, they show little or no association. However, some of their components and related measures do show significant associations with intelligence. Agreeableness reflects the mechanisms by which we are able to cooperate with others, and Conscientiousness reflects the mechanisms by which we are able to follow rules and work toward distant goals; understanding exactly how intelligence relates to these sophisticated psychological functions is of paramount importance for understanding personality as a coherent system.

A biological layer can be added to all of the questions raised in this chapter. In each case, we know relatively little about how the biological systems that underlie intelligence relate to the biological systems that underlie other personality traits. Pinpointing specific genetic and neurobiological mechanisms involved in the association of intelligence with other traits is an important project that has barely begun.

In pursuing research on intelligence and personality, one methodological advance should be adopted as often as possible, namely, the use of large samples and structural equation modeling to perform analyses of latent, rather than observed, variables. Failure to analyze latent variables ensures that most of the effect sizes reviewed above are likely to be underestimated. Almost none of them were based on latent modeling, and most were not corrected for unreliability. When error variance is removed, by modeling latent variables, the relations between questionnaire measures and ability tests may reach more impressive magnitudes (e.g., Deary et al., 2008; DeYoung et al., 2005, 2008). Another methodological advance would be to diversify the kinds of association that are investigated between intelligence and other traits. Very few studies have examined nonlinear relations or interactions. Many factors may moderate the association of intelligence with other personality traits.

Research on intelligence and personality appears to have reached a point of critical mass, at which we know a sufficient amount to locate intelligence within larger theories of personality but still know little enough that a great number of questions cry out to be researched. This chapter has raised some of those questions, but, perhaps more important, it has also attempted to provide a sound basis for integrative theory. Although the Big Five model began as a purely descriptive taxonomy, theories are being developed to explain the sources and functions of the Big Five (DeYoung & Gray, 2009; Nettle, 2006; Van Egeren, 2009). Van Egeren (2009) has proposed a functional role for each of the Big Five that unifies them within the psychological system by which individuals pursue their goals. The function of Openness/Intellect he described as "perceiving dynamic possibilities of the environment" through imaginative exploration of its causal structure (Van Egeren, 2009, p. 101). With this in mind, one can understand intelligence – a "capability for comprehending our surroundings" (Gottfredson, 1997a, p. 13) – as one important mechanism for analysis of structure and perception of possibilities, one that is complemented by intellectual engagement and by the aesthetic interests and abilities encompassed by Openness.

Acknowledgment

My thanks to everyone who read drafts of this chapter and provided thoughtful and useful feedback: Tom Bouchard, Wendy Johnson, Niels Waller, Auke Tellegen, Aldo Rustichini, Raymond Mar, and Jacob Hirsh. Any remaining errors or infelicities are my own.

References

Ackerman, P. L. (1996). A theory of adult intellectual development: Process, personality, interests, and knowledge. *Intelligence*, **22**, 229–259.

Ackerman, P. L. (2000). Domain-specific knowledge as the "dark matter" of adult intelligence: Gf/Gc, personality, and interest correlates. *Journal of Gerontology: Psychological Sciences*, ***55B***, 69–84.

Ackerman, P. L. (2009). Personality and intelligence. In P. J. Corr & G. Matthews (Eds.), *The Cambridge handbook of personality psychology* (pp. 162–174). New York, NY: Cambridge University Press.

Ackerman, P. L., Beier, M. E., & Bowen, K. R. (2002). What we really know about our abilities and our knowledge. *Personality and Individual Differences*, **34**, 587–605.

Ackerman, P. L., & Goff, M. (1994). Typical intellectual engagement and personality: Reply to Rocklin (1994). *Journal of Educational Psychology*, 86, 150–153.

Ackerman, P. L., & Heggestad, E. D. (1997). Intelligence, personality, and interests: Evidence for overlapping traits. *Psychological Bulletin*, **121**, 219–245.

Alvidrez, J., & Weinstein, R. S. (1999). Early teacher perceptions and later student academic achievement. *Journal of Educational Psychology*, **91**, 731–746.

Amodio, D. M., Jost, J. T., Master, S. L., & Yee, C. M. (2007). Neurocognitive correlates of liberalism and conservatism. *Nature Neuroscience*, **10**, 1246–1247.

Ashton, M. C., Lee, K., Perugini, M., Szarota, P., de Vries, R. E., Blas, L. D., Boies, K., & De Raad, B. (2004). A six-factor structure of personality descriptive adjectives: Solutions from psycholexical studies in seven languages. *Journal of Personality and Social Psychology, 86*, 356–366.

Ashton, M. C., Lee. K., Vernon, P. A., & Jang, K. L. (2000). Fluid intelligence, crystallized intelligence, and the Openness/Intellect factor. *Journal of Research in Personality*, **34**, 197–207.

Austin, E. J., Deary, I. J., & Gibson, G. J. (1997). Relationship between ability and personality: Three hypotheses tested. *Intelligence*, 25, 49–70.

Austin, A. J., Deary, I. J., Whiteman, M. C., Fowkes, F. G. R., Padersen, N. L., Rabbitt, P., Bent, N., & McInnes, L. (2002). Relationships between ability and personality: Does intelligence contribute positively to personal and social adjustment? *Personality and Individual Differences*, **32**, 1391–1411.

Baker, T. J., & Bichsel, J. (2006). Personality predictors of intelligence: Differences between young and cognitively healthy older adults. *Personality and Individual Differences*, **41**, 861–871.

Barchard, K. A. (2003). Does emotional intelligence assist in the prediction of academic success? *Educational and Psychological Measurement*, 63, 840–858.

Bates, T. C., & Shieles, A. (2003). Crystallized intelligence as a product of speed and drive for experience: The relationship of inspection time and openness to g and Gc. *Intelligence*, **31**, 275–287.

Berg, C. A. (2000). Intellectual development in adulthood. In R. J. Sternberg (Ed.), *Handbook of intelligence* (pp. 117–140). New York, NY: Cambridge University Press.

Beauducel, A., Liepmann, D., Felfe, J., & Nettelnstroth, W. (2007). The impact of different measurement models for fluid and crystallized intelligence on the correlation with personality traits. *European Journal of Psychological Assessment*, **23**, 71–78.

Block, J., & Block, J. H. (2006). Nursery school personality and political orientation two decades later, *Journal of Research in Personality*, **40**, 734–749.

Bouchard, T., Segal, N., Tellegen, A., McGue, M., Keyes, M., & Krueger, R. (2003). Evidence for the construct validity and heritability of the Wilson–Patterson conservatism scale: A reared-apart twins study of social attitudes. *Personality and Individual Differences*, **34**, 959–969.

Brickenkamp, R. (1975). *Handbuch psychologischer und padagogischer Tests. [Handbook of Psychological and Educational Tests]*. Gottingen, Germany: Hogrefe.

Brody, N. (2004). What cognitive intelligence is and what emotional intelligence is not. *Psychological Inquiry*, **15**, 234–238.

Brown, J. W., & Braver, T. S. (2005). Learned predictions of error likelihood in the anterior cingulate cortex. *Science*, **307**, 1118–1121.

Bunge, S. A., & Zelazo, P. D. (2006). A brain-based account of the development of rule use in childhood. *Current Directions in Psychological Science*, **15**, 118–121.

Cacioppo, J. T., Petty, R. E., Feinstein, J. A., & Jarvis, W. B. G (1996). Dispositional differences in cognitive motivation: The life and times of individuals differing in need for cognition. *Psychological Bulletin*, *119*, 197–253.

Carney, D., Jost, J., Gosling, S., & Potter, J. (2008). The secret lives of liberals and conservatives: Personality profiles, interaction styles, and the things they leave behind. *Political Psychology*, *29*(6), 807–840.

Carroll, J. B. (1993). *Human cognitive abilities*. New York, NY: Cambridge University Press.

Carson, S., Peterson, J. B., & Higgins, D. (2005). Reliability, validity, and factor structure of the Creative Achievement Questionnaire. *Creativity Research Journal*, *17*, 37–50.

Cattell, R. B. (1950). *Personality*. New York, NY: McGraw-Hill.

Cattell, R. B. (1978). *Scientific use of factor analysis in behavioral and life sciences*. New York, NY: Plenum Press.

Cattell, R. B., & Birkett, H. (1980). The known personality factors found aligned between first order T-data and second order Q-data factors, with new evidence on the inhibitory control, independence and regression traits. *Personality and Individual Differences*, *1*, 229–238.

Cattell, R. B., & Warburton, F. W. (1967). *Objective personality and motivation tests: A theoretical introduction and practical compendium*. Champaign: University of Illinois Press.

Ceci, S. J. (1991). How much does school influence general intelligence and its cognitive components: A reassessment of the evidence. *Developmental Psychology*, *27*, 703–722.

Chamorro-Premuzic, T., & Furnham, A. (2005a). *Personality and intellectual competence*. Mahwah, NJ: Erlbaum.

Chamorro-Premuzic, T., & Furnham, A. (2005b). The relationship between personality traits, subjectively-assessed and fluid intelligence. *Personality and Individual Differences*, *38*, 1517–1528.

Chamorro-Premuzic, T., & Furnham, A. (2008). Personality, intelligence and approaches to learning as predictors of academic performance. *Personality and Individual Differences*, *44*, 1596–1603.

Choi, Y. Y., Shamosh, N. A., Cho, S. H., DeYoung, C. G., Lee, M. J., Lee, J.-M., Kim, S. I., Cho, Z.-H., Kim, K., Gray, J. R., & Lee, K. H. (2008). Multiple bases of human intelligence revealed by cortical thickness and neural activation. *Journal of Neuroscience*, *28*, 10323–10329.

Collis, J. M., & Messick, S. (Eds.). (2001). *Intelligence and personality: Bridging the gap in theory and measurement*. Mahwah, NJ: Erlbaum.

Conway, A. R., Kane, M. J., & Engle, R. W. (2003). Working memory capacity and its relation to general intelligence. *Trends in Cognitive Sciences*, *7*, 547–552.

Costa, P. T., & McCrae, R. R. (1992a). Four ways five factors are basic. *Personality and Individual Differences*, *13*, 653–665.

Costa, P. T., & McCrae, R. R. (1992b). *NEO PI-R Professional Manual*. Odessa, FL: Psychological Assessment Resources.

Cronbach, L. J. (1949). *Essentials of psychological testing*. New York, NY: Harper & Row.

De Pauw, S. S. W., Mervielde, I., & Van Leeuwen, K. G. (2009). How are traits related to problem behavior in preschoolers? Similarities and contrasts between temperament and personality. *Journal of Abnormal Child Psychology*, *37*, 309–325.

Deary, I. J., Batty, G. D., & Gale, C. R. (2008). Bright children become enlightened adults. *Psychological Science*, *19*, 1–6.

Depue, R. A., & Collins, P. F. (1999). Neurobiology of the structure of personality: Dopamine, facilitation of incentive motivation, and extraversion. *Behavioral and Brain Sciences*, *22*, 491–569.

DeYoung, C. G. (2006). Higher-order factors of the Big Five in a multi-informant sample. *Journal of Personality and Social Psychology*, *91*, 1138–1151.

DeYoung, C. G., & Gray, J. R. (2009). Personality neuroscience: Explaining individual differences in affect, behavior, and cognition. In P. J. Corr & G. Matthews (Eds.), *The Cambridge handbook of personality psychology* (pp. 323–346). New York, NY: Cambridge University Press.

DeYoung, C. G., Peterson, J. B., & Higgins, D. M. (2005). Sources of Openness/Intellect: Cognitive and neuropsychological correlates of the fifth factor of personality. *Journal of Personality*, *73*, 825–858.

DeYoung, C. G., Peterson, J. B., Séguin, J. R., Mejia, J. M., Pihl, R. O., Beitchman, J. H., Jain, U., Tremblay, R. E., Kennedy, J. L., & Palmour, R. M. (2006). The dopamine D4 receptor gene and moderation of the association between externalizing behavior and IQ. *Archives of General Psychiatry*, *63*, 1410–1416.

DeYoung, C. G., Peterson, J. B., Séguin, J. R., Pihl, R. O., & Tremblay, R. E. (2008). Externalizing behavior and the higher-order factors of the Big Five. *Journal of Abnormal Psychology, 117*, 947–953.

DeYoung, C. G., Quilty, L. C., & Peterson, J. B. (2007). Between facets and domains: 10 aspects of the Big Five. *Journal of Personality and Social Psychology, 93*, 880–896.

DeYoung, C. G., Shamosh, N. A., Green, A. E., Braver, T. S., & Gray, J. R. (2009). Intellect as distinct from Openness: Differences revealed by fMRI of working memory. *Journal of Personality and Social Psychology, 97*, 883–892.

Digman, J. M. (1990). Personality structure: Emergence of the five-factor model. *Annual Review of Psychology, 41*, 417–440.

Digman, J. M. (1997). Higher-order factors of the Big Five. *Journal of Personality and Social Psychology, 73*, 1246–1256.

Duckworth, A. L. (2009). (Over and) beyond high-stakes testing. *American Psychologist, 64*, 279–280.

Espejo, J., Day, E. A., & Scott, G. (2005). Performance evaluations, need for cognition, and the acquisition of a complex skill: An attribute–treatment interaction. *Personality and Individual Differences, 38*, 1867–1877.

Eysenck, H. J. (1994). Personality and intelligence: Psychometric and experimental approaches. In R. J. Sternberg & P. Ruzgis (Eds.), *Personality and intelligence* (pp. 3–31). New York, NY: Cambridge University Press.

Fales, C. L., Barch, D. M., Burgess, G. C., Schaefer, A., Mennin, D. S., Braver, T. S., & Gray, J. R. (2008). Anxiety and cognitive efficiency: Differential modulation of transient and sustained neural activity during a working memory task. *Cognitive, Affective, and Behavioral Neuroscience, 8*, 239–253.

Feist, G. J. (1998). A meta-analysis of personality in scientific and artistic creativity. *Personality & Social Psychology Review, 2*, 290–309.

Feng, J., Spence, I., & Pratt, J. (2007). Playing an action video games reduces gender differences in spatial cognition. *Psychological Science, 18*, 850–855.

Frederick, S., Loewenstein, G., & O'Donoghue, T. (2002). Time discounting and time preference: A critical review. *Journal of Economic Literature, 40*, 351–401.

Furnham, A., & Chamorro-Premuzic, T. (2004). Personality, intelligence, and art. *Personality and Individual Differences, 36*, 705–715.

Furnham, A., Dissou, G., Sloan, P., & Chamorro-Premuzic, T. (2007). Personality and intelligence in business people: A study of two personality and two intelligence measures. *Journal of Business and Psychology, 22*, 99–109.

Gabriel, M. T., Critelli, J. W., & Ee, J. S. (1994). Narcissistic illusions in self-evaluations of intelligence and attractiveness. *Journal of Personality, 62*, 143–155.

Gilbert, S. J., Spengler, S., Simons, J. S., Steele, J. D., Lawrie, S. M., Frith, C. D., & Burgess, P. W. (2006). Functional specialization within rostral prefrontal cortex (area 10): A meta-analysis. *Journal of Cognitive Neuroscience, 18*(6), 932–948.

Goff, M., & Ackerman, P. L. (1992). Personality–intelligence relations: Assessment of typical intellectual engagement. *Journal of Educational Psychology, 84*, 537–552.

Goldberg, L. R. (1990). An alternative "description of personality": The Big-Five factor structure. *Journal of Personality and Social Psychology, 59*, 1216–1229.

Goldberg, L. R. (1992). The development of markers for the big-five factor structure. *Psychological Assessment, 4*, 26–42.

Goldberg, L. R. (1999). A broad-bandwidth, public domain, personality inventory measuring the lower-level facets of several five-factor models. In I. Mervielde, I. Deary, F. De Fruyt, & F. Ostendorf (Eds.), *Personality psychology in Europe* (Vol. 7, pp. 7–28). Tilburg, the Netherlands: Tilburg University Press.

Goldberg, L. R., & Rosolack, T. K. (1994) The big five factor structure as an integrative framework: An empirical comparison with Eysenck's P-E-N model. In C. F. Halverson, Jr., G. A. Kohnstamm, & R. P. Martin (Eds.), *The developing structure of temperament and personality from infancy to adulthood* (pp. 7–35). Hillsdale, NJ: Erlbaum.

Gottfredson, L. S. (1997a). Mainstream science on intelligence: An editorial with 52 signatories, history, and bibliography. *Intelligence, 24*, 13–23.

Gottfredson, L. S. (1997b). Why *g* matters: The complexity of everyday life. *Intelligence, 24*, 79–132.

Gottfredson, L. S. (2002). g: Highly general and highly practical. In R. J. Sternberg & E. L. Grigorenko (Eds.), *The general factor of intelligence: How general is it?* (pp. 331–380). Mahwah, NJ: Erlbaum.

Gottfredson, L. S., & Deary, I. J. (2004). Intelligence predicts health and longevity, but why? *Current Directions in Psychological Science, 13*, 1–4.

Gow, A. J., Whiteman, M. C., Pattie, A., & Deary, I. J. (2005). The personality–intelligence interface: Insights from an ageing cohort. *Personality and Individual Differences*, 39, 751–761.

Gray, J. A., & McNaughton, N. (2000). *The neuropsychology of anxiety: An enquiry into the functions of the septo-hippocampal system* (2nd ed.). New York, NY: Oxford University Press.

Gray, J. R., & Thompson, P. M. (2004). Neurobiology of intelligence: Science and ethics. *Nature Reviews Neuroscience*, 5, 471–482.

Green, A. E., Fugelsang, J. A., Kraemer, D. J., Shamosh, N. A., & Dunbar, K. N. (2006). Frontopolar cortex mediates abstract integration in analogy. *Brain Research*, **1096**, 125–137.

Guilford, J. P. (1959). *Personality*. New York, NY: McGraw-Hill.

Hemphill, J. F. (2003). Interpreting the magnitudes of correlation coefficients. *American Psychologist*, 58, 78–80.

Higgins, D. M., Peterson, J. B., Pihl, R. O., & Lee, A. G. M. (2007). Prefrontal cognitive ability, intelligence, Big Five personality, and the prediction of advanced academic and workplace performance. *Journal of Personality and Social Psychology*, 93, 298–319.

Hinson, J. M., Jameson, T. L., & Whitney, P. (2003). Impulsive decision making and working memory. *Journal of Experimental Psychology: Learning, Memory, & Cognition*, 29, 298–306.

Hirsh, J. B., DeYoung, C. G., Xu, X., & Peterson, J. B. (2010). Compassionate liberals and polite conservatives: Associations of Agreeableness with political ideology and values. *Personality and Social Psychology Bulletin*, 36, 655–664.

Hofstee, W. K. B., Kiers, H. A., De Raad, B., & Goldberg, L. R. (1997). A comparison of Big Five structures of personality traits in Dutch, English, and German. *European Journal of Personality*, **11**, 15–31.

Holland, D. C., Dollinger, S. J., Holland, C. J., & MacDonald, D. A. (1995). The relationship between psychometric intelligence and the five-factor model of personality in a rehabilitation sample. *Journal of Clinical Psychology*, **51**, 79–88.

Horn, J. L., & Cattell, R. B, (1966). Refinement and test of the theory of fluid and crystallized general intelligences. *Journal of Educational Psychology*, 57, 253–270.

Huesmann, L. R., Eron, L. D., & Yarmel, P. W. (1987). Intellectual functioning and aggression. *Journal of Personality and Social Psychology*, 52, 232–240.

Jaeggi, S. M., Buschkuehl, M., Jonides, J., & Perrig,W. J. (2008). Improving fluid intelligence with training on working memory. *Proceedings of the National Academy of Sciences of the United States of America*, **105**, 6829–6833.

Jang, K. L., Hu, S., Livesley, W. J., Angleitner, A., Riemann, R., & Vernon, P. A. (2002). Genetic and environmental influences on the covariance of facets defining the domains of the five-factor model of personality. *Personality and Individual Differences*, 33, 83–101.

Jensen, A. R. (1998). *The g factor: The science of mental ability*. Westport, CT: Praeger.

John, O. P., Naumann, L. P., & Soto, C. J. (2008). Paradigm shift to the integrative Big Five trait taxonomy: History: Measurement, and conceptual issue. In O. P. John, R. W. Robins, & L. A. Pervin (Eds.), *Handbook of personality: Theory and research* (pp. 114–158). New York, NY: Guilford Press.

Johnson, J. A. (1994). Clarification of factor five with the help of the AB5C model. *European Journal of Personality*, 8, 311–334.

Johnson, W., & Bouchard, T. J., Jr. (2005a). The structure of human intelligence: It's verbal, perceptual, and image rotation (VPR), not fluid crystallized. *Intelligence*, 33, 393–416.

Johnson, W., & Bouchard, T. J., Jr. (2005b). Constructive replication of the visual–perceptual-image rotation model in Thurstone's (1941) battery of 60 tests of mental ability, *Intelligence*, 33, 417–430.

Johnson, W., & Bouchard, T. J., Jr. (2007). Sex differences in mental abilities: g masks the dimensions on which they lie. *Intelligence*, 35, 23–39.

Johnson, W., Bouchard, T. J., Jr., McGue, M., Segal, N. L., Tellegen, A., Keyes, M., & Gottesman, I. I. (2007). Genetic and environmental influences on the Verbal-Perceptual-Image Rotation (VPR) model of the structure of mental abilities in the Minnesota study of twins reared apart. *Intelligence*, 35, 542–562.

Jost, J. T., Napier, J. L., Thorisdottir, H., Gosling, S. D., Palfai, T. P., & Ostafin, B. (2007). Are needs to manage uncertainty and threat associated with political conservatism or ideological extremity? *Personality and Social Psychology Bulletin*, 33(7), 989.

Keightley, M. L., Seminowicz, D. A., Bagby, R. M., Costa, P. T., Fossati, P., & Mayberg, H. S. (2003). Personality influences limbic-cortical interactions during sad mood. *NeuroImage, 20,* 2031–2039.

Kirby, K. N. (2009). One-year temporal stability of delay-discount rates. *Psychonomic Bulletin & Review, 16,* 457–462.

Kline, P. (1995). A critical review of the measurement of personality and intelligence. In D. H. Saklofske & M. Zeidner (Eds.), *International handbook of personality and intelligence* (pp. 505–524). New York, NY: Plenum Press.

Koenen, K. C., Caspi, A., Moffitt, T. E., Rijsdijk, F., & Taylor, A. (2006). Genetic influences on the overlap between low IQ and antisocial behavior in young children. *Journal of Abnormal Psychology, 115,* 787–797.

Koenig, L. B., & Bouchard, T. J., Jr. (2006). Genetic and environmental influences on the Traditional Moral Values Triad – Authoritarianism, Conservatism and Religiousness – as assessed by quantitative behavior genetic methods. In P. McNamara (Ed.), *Where God and science meet: How brain and evolutionary studies alter our understanding of religion: Vol. 1. Evolution, genes, and the religious brain.* Westport, CN: Praeger.

Krueger, R. F., Hicks, B. M., Patrick, C. J., Carlson, S. R., Iacono, W. G., & McGue, M. (2002). Etiologic connections among substance dependence, antisocial behavior, and personality: Modeling the externalizing spectrum. *Journal of Abnormal Psychology, 111,* 411–424.

Krueger, R. F., Markon, K. E., Patrick, C. J., Benning, S. D., & Kramer, M. D. (2007). Linking antisocial behavior, substance use, and personality: An integrative quantitative model of the adult externalizing spectrum. *Journal of Abnormal Psychology, 116,* 645–666.

Kuhn, T. (1970). *The structure of scientific revolution* (2nd ed.). Chicago: University of Chicago Press.

Kuntsi, J., Eley, T. C., Taylor, A., Hughes, C., Asherson, P., Caspi, A., et al. (2004). Co-occurrence of ADHD and low IQ has genetic origins. *American Journal of Medical Genetics, 124,* 41–47.

Leikas, S., Mäkinen, S., Lönnqvist, J.-E., & Verkasalo, M. (2009). Cognitive ability × Emotional stability interactions on adjustment. *European Journal of Personality, 23,* 329–342.

Loevinger, J. (1957). Objective tests as instruments of psychological theory. *Psychological Reports, 3,* 635–694.

Lynam, D. R., Moffitt, T. E., & Stouthamer-Loeber, M. (1993). Explaining the relation between IQ and delinquency: Class, race, test motivation, school failure, or self-control? *Journal of Abnormal Psychology, 102,* 187–196.

Markon, K. E., Krueger, R. F., & Watson, D. (2005). Delineating the structure of normal and abnormal personality: An integrative hierarchical approach. *Journal of Personality and Social Psychology, 88,* 139–157.

Mayer, J. D., Roberts, R. D., & Barsade, S. G. (2008). Human abilities: Emotional intelligence. *Annual Review of Psychology, 59,* 507–536.

Mayer, J. D., Salovey, P., & Caruso, D. R. (2004). Emotional intelligence: Theory, findings, and implications. *Psychological Inquiry, 60,* 197–215.

Mayer, J. D., Salovey, P., & Caruso, D. R. (2008). Emotional intelligence: New ability or eclectic traits? *American Psychologist, 63,* 503–517.

McAdams, D. P., & Pals, J. L. (2006). A new Big Five: Fundamental principles for an integrative science of personality. *American Psychologist, 61,* 204–217.

McCrae, R. R. (1987). Creativity, divergent thinking, and openness to experience. *Journal of Personality and Social Psychology, 52,* 1258–1265.

McCrae, R. R. (1993). Openness to Experience as a basic dimension of personality. *Imagination, Cognition, and Personality, 13,* 39–55.

McCrae, R. R., & Costa, P. T., Jr. (1997). Conceptions and correlates of Openness to Experience. In R. Hogan, J. Johnson, & S. Briggs (Eds.), *Handbook of personality psychology* (pp. 825–847). Boston, MA: Academic Press.

Miller, J. D., & Lynam, D. R. (2001). Structural models of personality and their relation to antisocial behavior: A meta-analytic review. *Criminology, 39,* 765–798.

Mischel, W., Shoda, Y., & Rodriguez, M. I. (1989). Delay of gratification in children. *Science, 244,* 933–938.

Moody, D. E. (2009). Can intelligence be increased by training on a task of working memory? *Intelligence, 37,* 327–328.

Mount, M. K., Barrick, M. R., & Strauss, J. P. (1999). The joint relationship of conscientiousness and ability with performance: Test of the interaction hypothesis. *Journal of Management, 25,* 707–721.

Moutafi, J., Furnham, A., & Crump, J. (2003). Demographic and personality predictors of intelligence: A study using the NEO Personality Inventory and the Myers-Briggs Type Indicator. *European Journal of Personality, 17,* 79–94.

Moutafi, J., Furnham, A., & Crump, J. (2006). What facets of openness and conscientiousness predict fluid intelligence score? *Learning and Individual Differences*, 16, 31–42.

Moutafi, J., Furnham, A., & Paltiel, L. (2004). Why is Conscientiousness negatively correlated with intelligence? *Personality and Individual Differences*, 37, 1013–1022.

Moutafi, J., Furnham, A., & Tsaousis, I. (2006). Is the relationship between intelligence and trait neuroticism mediated by test anxiety? *Personality and Individual Differences*, 40, 587–597.

Nettle, D. (2006). The evolution of personality variation in humans and other animals. *American Psychologist*, 61, 622–631.

Nettle, D., & Liddle, B. (2008). Agreeableness is related to social-cognitive, but not social-perceptual, theory of mind. *European Journal of Personality*, 22, 323–335.

Nolan, S. A., Roberts, J. E., & Gotlib, I. H. (1998). Neuroticism and ruminative response style as predictors of change in depressive symptomatology. *Cognitive Therapy and Research*, 22, 445–455.

Ode, S., Robinson, M. D., & Wilkowski, B. M. (2008). Can one's temper be cooled? A role for agreeableness in moderating neuroticism's influence on anger and aggression. *Journal of Research in Personality*, 42, 295–311.

Ostaszewski, P. (1996). The relation between temperament and rate of temporal discounting. *European Journal of Personality*, 10, 161–172.

Ostendorf, F., & Angleitner, A. (1994). Reflections on different labels for Factor V. *European Journal of Personality*, 8, 341–349.

Paulhus, D. L., & John, O. P. (1998). Egoistic and moralistic biases in self-perception: The interplay of self-deceptive styles with basic traits and motives. *Journal of Personality*, 66, 1025–1060.

Paulhus, D. L., Lysy, D. C., & Yik, M. S. M. (1998). Self-report measures of intelligence: Are they useful as proxy IQ tests? *Journal of Personality*, 66, 525–554.

Pedulla, J. J., Airasian, P. W., & Madaus, G. F. (1980). Do teacher ratings and standardized test results of students yield the same information? *American Educational Research Journal*, 17, 303–307.

Perkins, A. M., & Corr, P. J. (2006). Cognitive ability as a buffer to neuroticism: Churchill's secret weapon? *Personality and Individual Differences*, 40, 39–51.

Peterson, J. B., & Flanders, J. L. (2002). Complexity management theory: Motivation for ideological rigidity and social conflict. *Cortex*, 38, 429–458.

Pytlik Zillig, L. M., Hemenover, S. H., & Dienstbier, R. A. (2002). What do we assess when we assess a Big 5 trait? A content analysis of the affective, behavioral and cognitive processes represented in the Big 5 personality inventories. *Personality & Social Psychology Bulletin*, 28, 847–858.

Ramnani, N., & Owen, A. M. (2004). Anterior prefrontal cortex: Insights into function from anatomy and neuroimaging. *Nature Reviews Neuroscience*, 5, 184–194.

Richards, J. B., Zhang, L., Mitchell, S., & de Wit, H. (1999). Delay and probability discounting in a model of impulsive behavior: Effect of alcohol. *Journal of the Experimental Analysis of Behavior*, 71, 121–143.

Riemann, R., Angleitner, A., & Strelau, J. (1997). Genetic and environmental influences on personality: A study of twins reared together using the self- and peer report NEO-FFI scales. *Journal of Personality*, 65, 449–476.

Ridderinkhof, K. R., Ullsperger, M., Crone, E. A., & Nieuwenhuis, S. (2004). The role of the medial frontal cortex in cognitive control. *Science*, 306, 443–447.

Roberts, R. D., Schulze, R., & MacCann, C. (2008). The measurement of emotional intelligence: A decade of progress? In G. Boyle, G. Matthews, & D. H. Saklofske (Eds.), *The Sage handbook of personality theory and assessment* (Vol. 2). Los Angeles, CA: Sage.

Saklofske, D. H., & Zeidner, M. (Eds.). (1995). *International handbook of personality and intelligence*. New York, NY: Plenum Press.

Saucier, G. (1992). Openness versus intellect: Much ado about nothing? *European Journal of Personality*, 6, 381–386.

Saucier, G. (1994). Trapnell versus the lexical factor: More ado about nothing? *European Journal of Personality*, 8, 291–298.

Saucier, G. (2009). Semantic and linguistic aspects of personality. In P. J. Corr & G. Matthews (Eds.), *The Cambridge handbook of personality psychology* (pp. 379–399). New York, NY: Cambridge University Press.

Saucier, G., & Goldberg, L. R. (2001). Lexical studies of indigenous personality factors: Premises, products, and prospects. *Journal of Personality*, 69, 847–879.

Schulte, M. J., Ree, M. J., & Carretta, T. (2004). Emotional intelligence: Not much more than *g* and personality. *Personality and Individual Differences*, 37, 1059–1068.

Séguin, J. R., Boulerice, B., Harden, P., Tremblay, R. E., & Pihl, R. O. (1999). Executive functions and physical aggression after controlling for attention deficit hyperactivity disorder, general memory, and IQ. *Journal of Child Psychology and Psychiatry*, *40*, 1197–1208.

Shamosh, N. A., DeYoung, C. G., Green, A. E., Reis, D. L., Johnson, M. R., Conway, A. R. A., Engle, R. W., Braver, T. S., & Gray, J. R. (2008). Individual differences in delay discounting: Relation to intelligence, working memory, and anterior prefrontal cortex. *Psychological Science*, *19*, 904–911.

Shamosh, N. A., & Gray, J. R. (2008). Delay discounting and intelligence: A meta-analysis. *Intelligence*, *38*, 289–305.

Shiner, R. L., & DeYoung, C. G. (in press). The structure of temperament and personality traits: A developmental perspective. In P. D. Zelazo (Ed.), *The Oxford handbook of developmental psychology*. New York, NY: Oxford University Press.

Spearman, C. (1904). "General intelligence," objectively determined and measured. *American Journal of Psychology*, *15*, 201–293.

Stanovich, K. E., & West, R.F. (2000). Individual differences in reasoning: Implications for the rationality debate? *Behavioral and Brain Sciences*, *23*, 645–726.

Sternberg, R. J., & Ruzgis, P. (Eds.). (1994). *Personality and intelligence*. New York, NY: Cambridge University Press.

Swann, A. C., Bjork, J. M., Moeller, F. G., & Dougherty, D. M. (2002). Two models of impulsivity: Relationship to personality traits and psychopathology. *Biological Psychiatry*, *51*, 988–994.

Tranter, L. J., & Koutstaal, W. (2008). Age and flexible thinking: An experimental demonstration of the beneficial effects of increased cognitively stimulating activity on fluid intelligence in healthy older adults. *Aging, Neuropsychology, and Cognition*, *15*, 184–207.

Van Egeren, L. F. (2009). A cybernetic model of global personality traits. *Personality and Social Psychology Review*, *13*, 92–108.

Vigil-Colet, A., & Morales-Vives, F. (2005). How impulsivity is related to intelligence and academic achievement. *Spanish Journal of Psychology*, *8*, 199–204.

Wallace, J. (1966). An abilities conception of personality: Some implications for personality measurement. *American Psychologist*, *21*, 132–138.

Whiteside, S. P., & Lynam, R. W. (2001). The Five Factor Model and impulsivity: Using a structural model of personality to understand impulsivity. *Personality and Individual Differences*, *30*, 669–689.

Willerman, L., Turner, R. G., & Peterson, M. (1976). A comparison of the predictive validity of typical and maximal personality measures. *Journal of Research in Personality*, *10*, 482–492.

Wilt, J., & Revelle, W. (2009). Extraversion. In M. Leary & R. Hoyle (Eds.), *Handbook of individual differences in social behavior* (pp. 27–45). New York, NY: Guilford.

Wolf, M. B., & Ackerman, P. L. (2005). Extraversion and intelligence: A meta-analytic investigation. *Personality and Individual Differences*, *39*, 531–542.

Yamagata, S., Suzuki, A., Ando, J., Ono, Y., Kijima, N., Yoshimura, K., Ostendorf, F., Angleitner, A., Riemann, R., Spinath, F. M., Livesley, W. J., & Jang, K. L. (2006). Is the genetic structure of human personality universal? A cross-cultural twin study from North America, Europe, and Asia. *Journal of Personality and Social Psychology*, *90*, 987–998.

Zeidner, M., & Matthews, G. (2000). Intelligence and personality. In R. Sternberg (Ed.), *Handbook of intelligence* (pp. 581–610). New York, NY: Cambridge University Press.

CHAPTER 36

Intelligence and Achievement

Richard E. Mayer

This chapter examines the reciprocal relation between intelligence and achievement, particularly within academic domains such as verbal ability and mathematical ability. In particular, the chapter examines the specific knowledge needed for successful performance on tests of verbal ability that focus on decoding or reading comprehension, and tests of mathematical ability that focus on solving arithmetic computation problems or arithmetic word problems.

Three Episodes in the History of Intelligence and Achievement

In the waning years of the 19th century, the world's first educational psychologist, E. L. Thorndike, undertook his first major experimental study of how learning works (Mayer, 2003a). Working in the attic of his advisor's house in Cambridge, Massachusetts, in a typical study, he put a hungry cat into a crate with a bowl of food just outside. If the cat pulled on a loop of string hanging overhead, a trap door would open and the cat could get out and eat the food. According to Thorndike the cat began with a family of responses each linked to the situation in varying strengths based on past experience. Furthermore, Thorndike proposed that the cat learned by trial and error – unsuccessful responses were weakened each time they failed and successful responses were strengthened each time they worked. Thorndike called this learning principle *the law of effect,* and it went on to become one of the fundamental pillars of learning theory and educational practice. Eventually, Thorndike reported his research in a book that he chose to call, *Animal Intelligence* (Thorndike, 1911). Why did he claim to be studying intelligence? Thorndike sought to study the ability to learn, which he saw as "the most important of all original abilities" (p. 278). As you can see, from the very start, psychologists saw intellectual ability as the ability to learn and noted that it was based on prior learning experiences.

Next, let's shift the scene to Paris in the early 1900s where officials of the Paris school system were looking for ways to predict school success so they could identify students who might need special help before they got too far behind. They called upon Alfred Binet, who is credited with inventing the world's first intelligence test (Wolf, 1973). Rather than viewing intelligence as a single monolithic ability, he posited that intelligence – or the ability to learn – was reflected in many smaller components. His test measured the many pieces of knowledge that children at various ages had acquired – what can be called achievement – such as the names of the colors of rainbow or the counting numbers from 1 to 10. Children who could answer factual questions customarily known by older children were considered above average in intelligence because they had learned more from the same experiences as their peers. Similarly, children who could not answer factual questions customarily answered by their peers were considered below average because they learned less based on the same experiences. His test was effective in predicting school success and became the basis for many subsequent intelligence tests. As you can see, Binet was the first to popularize the idea that intelligence, viewed as someone's ability to learn, is reflected in achievement, viewed as what someone has learned.

Finally, for our third historical scenario, let's consider the saga of college entrance examinations produced by the Educational Testing Service (ETS) – America's largest testing organization, founded in 1947 in Princeton, New Jersey (Zwick, 2002). The SAT-1 is a well-known college entrance exam intended to predict college success by measuring verbal and mathematical abilities. Originally, the test was called the "Scholastic Aptitude Test," which was later changed to "Scholastic Assessment Test," and eventually to simply "SAT." What does the ambiguity over naming tell us about the relation between intelligence and achievement? It appears that that the test was originally intended to measure aptitude, the ability to learn, but seems to have wound up measuring achievement, what students had learned. For example, mathematical test items include solving arithmetic word problems and the verbal test items include reading comprehension items. The newer SAT-II (formerly called "Achievement Tests") was designed to focus on the content of specific school subjects, reflecting the growing focus on past achievement as an indication of future learning ability. As you can see, the line between ability and achievement becomes blurred when tests originally intended to measure ability (e.g., the ability to learn) actually measure achievement (e.g., solving word problems and comprehending text). Thus, the SAT saga provides our third example of how intellectual ability, such as the ability to learn in school, appears to be intimately tied to achievement, such as what has already been learned in school.

One More Historic Clue: The Search for Attribute x Treatment Interactions

Are certain instructional methods better for one kind of learner and other methods better for a different kind of learner? If so, you would have evidence for an *attribute x treatment interaction* (or ATI). The modern search for ATIs dates back to Cronbach and Snow's (1977) heroic efforts, documented in their classic book, *Aptitudes and Instructional Methods*, and continues today on many fronts (Massa & Mayer, 2006; Pashler, McDaniel, Rohrer, & Bjork, in press; Sternberg & Zhang, 2001). The overwhelming consensus is that well-documented cases of ATIs are somewhat rare.

Does that mean that individual differences should not be taken into account when designing instruction? One important exception is that ATIs have been found when the individual differences dimension is the learner's prior knowledge. For example, Kalyuga (2005) has summarized evidence for the *expertise reversal effect* – the finding that instructional methods that are effective for low-knowledge learners are not effective and may even be harmful for high-knowledge learners and vice versa. In general, low-knowledge learners perform best with well-structured instructional methods whereas high-knowledge learners perform best with less-structured instructional

Table 36.1. An Educational Approach to Intelligence and Achievement

Name	*Definition*	*Example*
intelligence	the ability to learn	Performance on an intelligence test intended to measure someone's ability to acquire knowledge from experience.
achievement	what is learned	Performance on an achievement test intended to measure someone's knowledge gained from experience.

methods (Mayer, in press). This work suggests that if you are interested in designing instruction for a learner, perhaps the single most important individual differences dimension for you to consider is the learner's prior knowledge (Mayer, in press). The expertise reversal effect has important implications for the relation between achievement and intelligence – showing that your past learning influences your ability to learn under different instructional methods. In short, the history of research on learning is studded with clues concerning the reciprocal relation between intelligence and achievement, which is the theme of this chapter.

What Is the Relation Between Intelligence and Achievement?

Taking an educational perspective, let's define academic intelligence as the ability to learn (e.g., performing a cognitive task) and let's define academic achievement as what is learned (e.g., specific knowledge). As shown in the top row of Table 36.1, academic intelligence can be measured by a person's performance on a cognitive ability test in which someone must accomplish an academic task such as comprehending printed text (verbal ability) or solving a story problem (mathematical ability). As shown in the bottom row of Table 31.1, academic achievement can be measured by a person's performance on a knowledge test aimed at assessing specific knowledge components (including facts, concepts, procedures, strategies, and beliefs).

The unifying theme of this chapter is that there is a reciprocal relation between intelligence and achievement. First, intelligence (which is the ability to learn) helps you to acquire knowledge (which is the outcome of learning). In short, intelligence enables learning. Second, the knowledge that you have (i.e., achievement) improves your ability to learn (i.e., intelligence). In short, achievement enables intelligence. This reciprocal relation is illustrated in Figure 36.1.

How does the reciprocal relation between intelligence and achievement work? Consider the cognitive model of learning shown in Figure 36.2. Based on your experiences in the outside world, sounds and images enter your cognitive system through your ears and eyes and are briefly held in your sensory memory. If you pay attention to this fleeting incoming material in sensory memory (indicated by the *selecting* arrow), some of the incoming material enters working memory where you mentally organize it (indicated by the *organizing* arrow) and integrate it with existing knowledge activated from long-term memory (indicated by the *integrating* arrow). Long-term memory is your large-capacity, permanent storehouse of knowledge and working memory

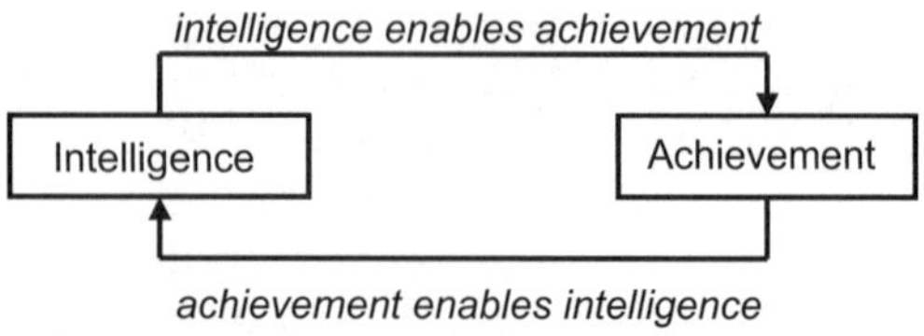

Figure 36.1. The reciprocal relation between intelligence and achievement.

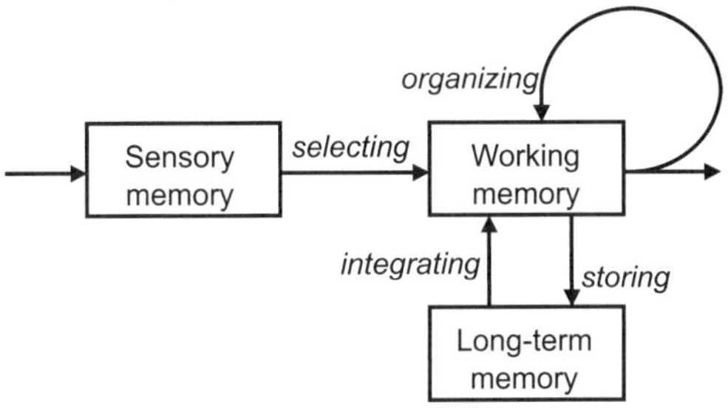

Figure 36.2. Four cognitive processes in learning.

is your limited-capacity, temporary store for processing a small amount of material. Achievement is represented as knowledge in long-term memory, and intelligence is represented as the appropriate use of cognitive processes during learning to acquire new knowledge in working memory (such as selecting, organizing, and integrating). These learning processes can be enhanced and guided by prior knowledge activated from long-term memory.

What Causes Task Performance?

An important goal of education is to equip learners with what they need to know for accomplishing challenging tasks. Figure 36.3 shows a model of the factors involved in task performance – that is, performance on an academic task such as comprehending a passage or solving a mathematics problem (Mayer, 2003b). As you can see, task performance is indicated by the box on the right side of the figure. What are the determinants of the learner's task performance? The rightmost arrow in Figure 36.3 shows that the learner's knowledge – including facts, concepts, procedures, strategies, and beliefs – determines task performance. Where does the learner's knowledge come from? As shown in the left side of Figure 36.3, knowledge is the result of the combination of intelligence and experience, that is, knowledge depends on the learner having appropriate learning experiences (i.e., such as provided by appropriate instruction) and the ability to benefit from learning experiences.

The model presented in Figure 36.3 is based on research on the development of expert performance on cognitive tasks (Ericsson, 2003; Sternberg & Grigorenko, 2003). Let's consider three examples of relevant research findings.

First, when people begin to learn how to perform a cognitive task, their task performance is most strongly correlated with their general ability; but as they progress from novice to expert, their task performance becomes increasingly more strongly correlated with their specialized knowledge (Ackerman & Beier, 2003; Krampe & Baltes, 2003). In short, as a learner gains expertise on a cognitive task, it appears that specialized knowledge comes to compensate for general ability. However, it is important to note that general ability is not completely out of the loop because it may have enabled the creation of specialized knowledge, which in turn can be used to help learners to be even more effective in using their general ability for new learning.

Second, consider the Flynn effect. The Flynn effect refers to the finding that IQ scores have been rising throughout the 20th century at a rate of about five points per decade in each of 20 industrialized countries for which data are available (Flynn, 1998; Martinez, 2000). Martinez (2000) interprets this finding as showing that improvements in access to education serve not only to increase knowledge (what is learned) but also to improve intelligence (the ability to learn). Similarly, Ceci, Barnett, and Kanaya (2003) interpret the Flynn effect as evidence that intelligence and experience interact

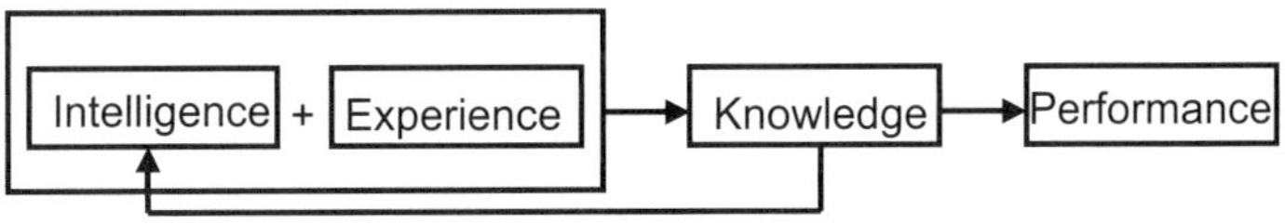

Figure 36.3. What causes task performance?

Table 36.2. Performance Tasks and Supporting Knowledge for Components of Verbal and Mathematical Ability

Name	*Performance Task*	*Supporting Knowledge*
verbal ability		
decoding	pronounce printed words or pseudowords	phonemes
reading comprehension	answer questions after reading a prose passage	prose schemas
mathematical ability		
arithmetic	solve arithmetic computation problems	number sense
problem solving	solve arithmetic word problems	problem schemas

(as indicated in the left side of Figure 36.3) to produce improvements in the learner's knowledge. Ceci et al. propose a multiplier mechanism in which general ability may predispose a learner to seek certain experiences, which result in specialized knowledge that enables the learner to use his or her general ability to learn even more effectively in that domain, resulting in more specialized knowledge that in turns increases the effectiveness of learning in the domain, and so on. The multiplier mechanism is consistent with viewing "ability + experience" (in the left side of Figure 36.3) as an interactive process, rather than one in which ability or experience dominates (Mayer, 2003b).

As a third example, consider the finding that deliberate practice can greatly enhance task performance (Ericsson, 2003). Deliberate practice occurs when a learner continually devotes considerable time and effort to practicing tasks that are challenging – that is, somewhat beyond the learner's current level of performance – until reaching mastery. For example, Ericsson (2003) describes case studies in which people who engaged in concentrated practice in remembering number lists showed impressive improvements in their digit span – from about 7 digits without practice to 20 digits after 50 hours of practice, to 80 digits after 400 hours of practice. Based on numerous examples of how specialized practice can improve cognitive performance, Ericsson (2003) concludes that expert performance depends on acquiring specialized knowledge, as indicated in the right side of Figure 36.3. Importantly, the learner's willingness to engage in large amounts of deliberate practice may be dependent on the learner's ability (Mayer, 2003b).

What Is Academic Ability?

Academic ability is a kind of intelligence most relevant to academic domains, such as the verbal domain and the mathematical domain. In particular, verbal ability refers to a person's ability to learn and perform verbal tasks, whereas mathematical ability refers to a person's ability to learn and perform mathematical tasks. Table 36.2 lists examples of several kinds of tasks related to verbal ability and mathematical ability. As shown in the top of Table 36.2, two important components of verbal ability are decoding and reading comprehension, whereas two important components of mathematical ability are arithmetic computation and problem solving. The knowledge underlying these aspects of academic ability are explored in the following two sections.

What Is the Relation Between Intelligence and Achievement in the Verbal Domain?

Verbal ability is widely recognized as an important component of intelligence

(Carroll, 1993). Verbal ability refers to learning and performing on tasks that involve words. Within verbal ability, two important factors are reading decoding (being able to pronounce printed words) and reading comprehension (being able to understand the meaning of a printed passage). In this section, let's examine the relation between intelligence and achievement for each of these two important types of verbal tasks.

First, consider the task of reading decoding – when given printed words, reading them out loud. For example, given the printed word, CAT, you have to blend the sounds /c/ and /a/ and /t/ into the spoken word, /cat/. Helping students develop decoding skill is perhaps the central mission of language arts instruction in the primary grades, and it is an essential skill for lifelong learning. As shown in the first row of Table 36.2, a common test of decoding is a word recognition test, which consists of asking students to pronounce a set of printed words, or a word attack test, which consist of asking students to pronounce a set of pseudowords (such as BLUD). Strong performance on such tests is an indication that the test taker has high verbal ability.

What knowledge is needed to perform well on a word recognition or word attack test? Research on early reading shows that a particular kind of knowledge called *phonological awareness* is strongly related to decoding performance (Bradley & Bryant, 1983; Ehri et al., 2001; Goswami & Bryant, 1990). Phonological awareness refers to someone's knowledge of the sound units of their language – including knowing how to produce each of the sounds and knowing how to recognize each sound. In English, there are approximately 42 sound units. For example, one test of phonological awareness involves substitution of the first phoneme, such as when the tester says, "Ball. Instead of /b/ begin the word with /p/." Students who enter primary school with high levels of phonological awareness tend to learn to read more easily, and students who lack phonological awareness tend to have difficulty in learning to read (Bradley & Bryant, 1985; Juel, Griffin, & Gough, 1986; Wagner & Torgesen, 1987). Similarly, students who receive training in phonological awareness tend to show later improvements in reading (Bradley & Bryant, 1983; Ehri, Nunes, Stahl, & Willows, 2001; Fuchs et al., 2001). Overall, research on phonological awareness is an example of the relation between knowledge (i.e., knowing the 42 phonemes of English) and verbal ability (i.e., decoding performance).

Second, consider the task of reading comprehension – that is, given a printed passage, be able to read for understanding so you can remember important information and answer questions about the content of the passage. As shown in the second row of Table 36.2, a common reading comprehension test involves being able to answer integrative questions, such as summarizing the passage or answering a question about the passage content in which you have to make an inference. Performance on reading comprehension tests can be considered a measure of verbal ability (Carroll, 1993).

What knowledge is needed for success on a reading comprehension task? Research on reading comprehension shows that people perform better if they have domain knowledge, including schemas, that allow them to focus on important material (Bartlett, 1932; Lipson, 1983; Marr & Gormley, 1982; Pearson, Hansen, & Gordon, 1979). Importantly, teaching students about the schemas – or structures – for a given kind of prose material serves to improve their reading comprehension performance (Cook & Mayer, 1988; Taylor & Beach, 1984). Overall, research shows that domain-specific schemas are prerequisites for reading comprehension performance.

What Is the Relation Between Intelligence and Achievement in the Mathematical Domain?

Mathematical ability is widely recognized as an important component of intelligence

(Carroll, 1993). Mathematical ability refers to learning and performing on tasks that involve numbers. Within mathematical ability, two important tasks are arithmetic computation (being able to solve computational problems involving addition, subtraction, multiplication, and/or division) and problem solving (being able to solve arithmetic word problems). These are summarized in the bottom of Table 36.2. In this section, we examine the relation between intelligence and achievement for each of these two important types of mathematical tasks.

First, consider the task of solving arithmetic problems – for example, given a printed problem such as 5 − 2 = ___, you compute a numerical answer. Solving computation problems is a fundamental component in mathematical ability and is part of tests intended to measure mathematical ability (Carroll, 1993).

What do you need to know to perform well on numerical computation problems? Research on arithmetic learning shows that an important prerequisite for computational performance is a form of conceptual knowledge that can be called *number sense* – the ability to represent numbers along a mental number line (Case & Okamoto, 1996; Griffin, Case, & Siegler, 1994). For example, number sense is indicated when a student determines which of two numbers is smaller or correctly moves a token along a path in a board game for a certain number of steps. Students who enter the primary grades without number sense tend to have more difficulty in learning arithmetic, and students who are given direct instruction in how to use a mental number line tend to learn arithmetic more easily (Case & Okamoto, 1996; Griffin, Case, & Siegler, 1994; Moreno & Mayer, 1999). Overall, there is convincing evidence of a strong relation between computational ability and knowledge of the mental number line (i.e., number sense).

Second, consider word problems in which you are given a verbal statement of a quantitative situation and must find an answer, such as the following:

> *A car traveling at a speed of 30 miles per hour left a certain place at 10:00* A.M. *At 11:30* A.M., *another car departed from the same place traveling at 40 miles per hour and traveled the same route. At what time will the second car overtake the first car?*

Performance on solving word problems such as this one is an indication of mathematical ability (Mayer, 2008; Reed, 1999).

What knowledge is needed for success on this test of mathematical ability? Research on mathematical problem solving shows that students perform better when they possess appropriate problem schemas – mental categories for each kind of situation described in the problem (Hinsley, Hayes, & Simon, 1977; Riley, Greeno, & Heller, 1982). For example, the car problem fits within the category of a time-rate-distance problem involving overtaking (Mayer, 1981). Problem solvers are better able to mentally represent word problems when they can organize them based on a preexisting problem schema. This work is another example of how a form of academic ability is highly related to the student's domain-specific knowledge. Determining the relation between ability and knowledge as it develops in specific domains is an important challenge for cognitive theory and educational practice.

Discussion

The theme of this chapter is that there is a reciprocal relation between intelligence and achievement, particularly within academic domains such as verbal ability and mathematical ability. In examining this theme, it is useful to consider the classic distinction between *fluid intelligence* (cognitive ability that is independent of specific knowledge) and *crystallized intelligence* (cognitive ability that depends on specific knowledge; Carroll, 1993; Sternberg, 1990). In this chapter, my focus has been on crystallized intelligence, because of its importance for education. Crystallized intelligence is important for education because it can be changed

Table 36.3. Five Kinds of Knowledge in Academic Tasks

Name	*Definition*	*Example*
facts	characteristics of elements	knowing the definitions of words; knowing that cars drive on roads
concepts	categories, principles, models, schemas	phonemes, prose schema, mental number line, problem schema
procedures	step-by-step processes	sound production algorithm, addition algorithm
strategies	general methods	comprehension monitoring strategy, self-evaluation strategy
beliefs	thoughts about one's learning	thinking that success depends on effort

through appropriate opportunities for learning. In short, the theme of this chapter is that specific kinds of knowledge that are the result of learning (i.e., achievement) can promote the ability to succeed in new learning (i.e., intelligence), and the ability to learn (intelligence) can help to enhance a learner's storehouse of relevant kinds of knowledge (i.e., achievement).

This analysis places knowledge at the center of the story. Table 36.3 summarizes five important kinds of knowledge and provides examples of each (Anderson et al., 2001; Mayer, 2008) – facts, concepts, procedures, strategies, and beliefs. An important goal of educational research is to pinpoint specific knowledge that enhances new learning, as suggested in the right column of Table 36.3. As you can see, the examples focus mainly on specific kinds of concepts that are useful for performing verbal tasks (namely, categorical knowledge of phonemes and schemas for prose structures) and specific kinds of concepts that are useful for performing mathematical tasks (namely, the concept of a mental number line and schemas for arithmetic word problems). This chapter has provided a glimpse into successful past research on the kinds of knowledge that enhance new learning and encourages a continuation of this fruitful line of research for the future.

Acknowledgment

Preparation of this chapter was supported by a grant from the Office of Naval Research. The author's address is Richard E. Mayer, Department of Psychology, University of California, Santa Barbara, CA 93106. E-mail: mayer@psych.ucsb.edu.

References

Ackerman, P., & Beier, M. E. (2003). Trait complexes, cognitive investment, and domain knowledge. In R. J. Sternberg & E. L. Grigorenko (Eds.), *The psychology of abilities, competencies, and expertise* (pp. 1–30). New York, NY: Cambridge University Press.

Anderson, L. W., Krathwohl, D. R., Airasian, P. W., Cruikshank, K. A., Mayer, R. E., Pintrich, P. R., Raths, J., & Wittrock, M. C. (2001). *A taxonomy for learning, teaching, and assessing: A revision of Bloom's taxonomy of educational objectives*. New York, NY: Longman.

Bartlett, F. C. (1932). *Remembering*. London, UK: Cambridge University Press.

Bradley, L., & Bryant, P. (1983). Categorizing sounds and learning to read – a causal connection. *Nature*, *301*, 419–421.

Bradley, L., & Bryant, P. (1985). *Rhyme and reason in reading and spelling*. Ann Arbor: University of Michigan Press.

Carroll, J. B. (1993). *Human cognitive abilities*. New York, NY: Cambridge University Press.

Case, R., & Okamoto, Y. (1996). The role of central conceptual structures in the development of children's thought. *Monographs of the Society for Research in Child Development*, 61(1 & 2), No. 246.

Ceci, S. J., Barnett, S. M., & Kanaya, T. (2003). Developing childhood proclivities into adult competencies: The overlooked multiplier effect. In R. J. Sternberg & E. L. Grigorenko (Eds.), *The psychology of abilities, competencies, and expertise* (pp. 70–93). New York, NY: Cambridge University Press.

Cronbach, L. J., & Snow, R. E. (1977). *Aptitudes and instructional methods*. New York, NY: Wiley.

Cook, L. K., & Mayer, R. E. (1988). Teaching readers about the structure of scientific text. *Journal of Educational Psychology, 80*, 448–456.

Ehri, L. C., Nunes, S. R., Stahl, S. A., & Willows, D. M. (2001). Systematic phonics instruction helps students learn to read: Evidence from the National Reading Panel's meta-analysis. *Review of Educational Research, 71*, 393–447.

Ericsson, K. A. (2003). The search for general abilities and basic capacities: Theoretical implications from the modifiability and complexity of mechanisms mediating expert performance. In R. J. Sternberg & E. L. Grigorenko (Eds.), *The psychology of abilities, competencies, and expertise* (pp. 93–125). New York, NY: Cambridge University Press.

Flynn, J. R. (1998). IQ gains over time: Toward finding the causes. In U. Neisser (Ed.), *The rising curve: Long-term gains in IQ and related measures* (pp. 25–66). Washington, DC: American Psychological Association.

Fuchs, D., Fuchs, L. S., Thompson, A., Al Otaiba, A., Yen, L., Yang, N. J., Braun, M., & O'Connor, R. E. (2001). Is reading in reading readiness programs? A randomized field trial with teachers as program implementers. *Journal of Educational Psychology, 93*, 251–267.

Goswami, U., & Bryant, P. (1990). *Phonological skills and learning to read*. Hillsdale, NJ: Erlbaum.

Griffin, S. A., Case, R., & Siegler, R. S. (1994). Rightstart: Providing the central conceptual prerequisites for first formal learning of arithmetic to students at risk for school failure. In K. McGilly (Ed.), *Classroom lessons: Integrating cognitive theory and classroom practice*. Cambridge, MA: MIT Press.

Hinsley, D., Hayes, J. R., & Simon, H. A. (1977). From words to equations. In P. Carpenter & M. Just (Eds.), *Cognitive processes in comprehension*. Hillsdale, NJ: Erlbaum.

Juel, C., Griffith, P. L., & Gough, P. B. (1986). Acquisition of literacy: A longitudinal study of children in first and second grade. *Journal of Educational Psychology, 78*, 243–255.

Kalyuga, S. (2005). Prior knowledge principle in multimedia learning. In R. E. Mayer (Ed.), *The Cambridge handbook of multimedia learning* (pp. 325–338). New York, NY: Cambridge University Press.

Krampe, R. T., & Baltes, P. B. (2003). Intelligence as adaptive resource development and resource allocation: A new look through the lenses of SOC and Expertise. In R. J. Sternberg, & E. L. Grigorenko (Eds.), *The psychology of abilities, competencies, and expertise* (pp. 31–70). New York, NY: Cambridge University Press.

Lipson, M. Y. (1983). The influence of religious affiliation on children's memory for text information. *Reading Research Quarterly, 18*, 448–457.

Marr, M. B., & Gormley, K. (1982). Children's recall of familiar and unfamiliar text. *Reading Research Quarterly, 18*, 89–104.

Martinez, M. E. (2000). *Education as the cultivation of intelligence*. Mahwah, NJ: Erlbaum.

Massa, L. J., & Mayer, R. E. (2006). Testing the ATI hypothesis: Should multimedia instruction accommodate verbalizer-visualizer cognitive style? *Learning and Individual Differences, 16*, 321–336.

Mayer, R. E. (1981). Frequency norms and structural analysis of algebra story problems into families, categories, and templates. *Instructional Science, 10*, 135–175.

Mayer, R. E. (2003a). E. L. Thorndike's enduring contributions to educational psychology. In B. J. Zimmerman & D. H. Schunk (Eds.), *Educational psychology: A century of contributions* (pp. 113–154). Washington, DC: American Psychology Association.

Mayer, R. E. (2003b). What causes individual differences in cognitive performance? In R. J. Sternberg & E. L. Grigorenko (Eds.), *The psychology of abilities, competencies, and expertise* (pp. 263–274). New York, NY: Cambridge University Press.

Mayer, R. E. (2008). *Learning and instruction* (2nd ed.). Upper Saddle River, NJ: Pearson Merrill Prentice-Hall.

Mayer, R. E. (in press). *Applying the science of learning*. Upper Saddle River, NJ: Pearson Merrill Prentice-Hall.

Moreno, R., & Mayer, R. E. (1999). Multimedia supported metaphors for meaning making in mathematics. *Journal of Educational Psychology, 92*, 724–733.

Pashler, H., McDaniel, M., Rohrer, D., & Bjork, R. (in press). Learning styles: Concepts and evidence. *Psychological science in the public interest.*

Pearson, P. D., Hanson, J., & Gordon, C. (1979). The effect of background knowledge on young children's comprehension of explicit and implicit information. *Journal of Reading Behavior, 11*, 201–209.

Reed, S. K. (1999). *Word problems.* Mahwah, NJ: Erlbaum.

Riley, M., Greeno, J. G., & Heller, J. (1982). The development of children's problem solving ability in arithmetic. In H. Ginsburg (Ed.), *The development of mathematical thinking.* New York, NY: Academic Press.

Sternberg, R. J. (1990). *Metaphors of mind.* New York, NY: Cambridge University Press.

Sternberg, R. J., & Grigorenko, E. L. (Eds.). (2003). *The psychology of abilities, competencies, and expertise.* New York, NY: Cambridge University Press.

Sternberg, R. J., & Zhang, L-F. (Eds.). (2001). *Perspectives on thinking, learning, and cognitive styles.* Mahwah, NJ: Erlbaum.

Taylor, B. M., & Beach, R. W. (1984). The effects of text structure instruction on middle-grade students' comprehension and production of expository text. *Reading Research Quarterly, 19*, 134–146.

Thorndike, E. L. (1911). *Animal intelligence.* New York: Hafner.

Wagner, R. K., & Torgesen, J. K. (1987). The nature of phonological processing and its causal role in the acquisition of reading skills. *Psychological Bulletin, 101*, 192–212.

Wolf, T. H. (1973). *Alfred Binet.* Chicago: University of Chicago Press.

Zwick, R. (2002). *Fair game: The use of standardized admissions tests in higher education.* New York: Routledge Falmer.

CHAPTER 37

Intelligence and Motivation

Priyanka B. Carr and Carol S. Dweck

Intelligence and Motivation

To understand intelligence one must understand motivation. In the past, intelligence was often cast as an entity unto itself, relatively unaffected by motivation. The prevailing view in the study of cognition and intelligence was that intellectual ability and intellectual performance were simply a function of the individual's cognitive apparatus (as noted by Dai & Sternberg, 2004). As far as motivation was concerned, everyone agreed, of course, that the "motor" had to be turned on, but beyond that there was no well-articulated view of how motivational factors ignited and shaped intellectual performance. In this chapter, we attempt to articulate such a view.

What do we mean by motivation? Motivational factors – which can include beliefs, nonintellectual skills, and affect – are those factors that influence the pursuit of goals. In the present case, these goals are related to the acquisition and display of intellectual skills. In our chapter, we spell out how motivational factors determine (1) whether individuals initiate goals relating to the acquisition and display of intellectual skills, (2) how persistently they pursue those goals, and (3) how effectively they pursue those goals, that is, how effectively they learn and perform in the intellectual arena. As will be seen, motivational factors have a consistent and profound effect on such indices of intellectual ability as grades, achievement test scores, IQ test scores, and outstanding professional accomplishment.

Background

For many years, the focus in the study of intelligence was on documenting stable individual differences in intelligence (e.g., Conley, 1984; Galton, 1883; Jensen, 1998; Terman, 1926) rather than understanding the factors that shape it. Where did this notion of pure intelligence, unaffected by context, experience, or motivation, come from? Much of the impetus for this view came from implications of Darwinian theory, in particular the ideas of variation within species and the survival of the fittest (Darwin, 1859). These implications were developed by Sir Francis Galton, Darwin's cousin, who had a passion for measuring human variation in all its forms, and whose studies of eminent men and twins led him to conclude that nature rather than nurture was the primary factor behind intelligence (Galton, 1883, 1892; Jensen, 2002).

Inspired in part by Galton, Lewis Terman (1916) adopted the view of intelligence as a heritable trait, reflecting differences in "original mental endowment" (p. 4), and as more or less unchanged by other factors inside or outside of the individual. He wrote, "practically all of the investigations which have been made of the influence of nature and nurture on mental performance agree in attributing far more to original endowment . . . children from successful and cultured parents test higher than children from wretched and ignorant homes for the simple reason that their heredity is better" (p. 115). Terman believed that with the intelligence test he adapted for the American population (the Stanford-Binet) he could uncover a child's level of fixed intelligence and then ascertain the position that that child should occupy in society later in life (Terman, 1916, p. 18). In this view, motivation had little role either in intelligence or in long-term achievement.

However, this was not the only view. Alfred Binet, the co-creator with Theodore Simon of the intelligence test (Binet & Simon, 1913) that Terman later revised, conceptualized intelligence very differently. He saw it, within limits, as malleable and trainable through education (Siegler, 1992). In fact, Binet did not believe his test tapped fixed intelligence at all. He emphasized that intelligence manifested itself differently in different children and was developed at different rates through teaching (Siegler, 1992). Indeed, Binet expressed his alarm at the emerging view of intelligence as a fixed entity that could be measured by his test: "A few modern philosophers . . . assert that an individual's intelligence is a fixed quantity, a quantity which cannot be increased. We must protest and react against this brute pessimism. . . . With practice, training, and above all, method, we manage to increase our attention, our memory, our judgment and literally to become more intelligent than we were before" (Binet, 1909/1975, pp. 106–107). Interestingly, even Terman, after 35 years of following children he classified as intellectually gifted, began to change his mind. He saw that many of his high-IQ participants achieved relatively little in life. In an effort to understand how this could be, he was led to conclude that motivational variables such as "persistence in the accomplishment of ends" and "integration toward goals" played a role in intellectual performance and life achievement (Terman & Oden, 1959, p. 149).

Certainly, people may have different genetic endowments and aptitudes to begin with. However, it is becoming increasingly clear that intelligence is greatly affected by nongenetic factors and is not static (see Sternberg, 2005; Sternberg & Gigorenko, 2001). Indeed, recent research with college students (Jaeggi, Buschkuel, Jonides, & Perrig, 2008) has found that fluid intelligence – the ability to reason and solve novel problems independent of previously acquired knowledge – is plastic even in adulthood (see Chapter 20, Working Memory and Intelligence, this volume, for a more detailed discussion of changes in fluid intelligence). In this research, scores on a test of fluid intelligence were raised through training on an entirely different task that involved working memory. Given the emerging evidence about the dynamic nature of intelligence and its components (see also Diamond, Barnett, Thomas, & Munro, 2007; Rueda, Rothbart, McCandliss, Saccomanno, & Posner, 2005), one is led away from questions about how to measure and classify people and toward questions about the factors that foster or inhibit the growth of intelligence: What can lead us to be more (or less) intelligent than we were before?

Our perspective is that motivational factors offer an answer to this question. As suggested earlier, we conceptualize motivational factors as variables that foster or interfere with effective goal pursuit and, in the case of intelligence, the effective pursuit of intellectual goals. We argue that motivation is much more than simply a motor that turns actions on or off and more than simply a desire to do well. Motivation, importantly, also involves beliefs (for example, beliefs about the nature of one's intelligence), nonintellectual skills (for example, the ability to enforce self-discipline to achieve one's goals), and affect (for example, how much one enjoys learning in a particular area) – all of which influence people's ability to pursue intellectual goals effectively. There are several important implications of this approach. One is that context can have a strong, consistent impact on the motivation-relevant beliefs and affects that are activated and hence on intellectual performance. The second is that motivation-relevant beliefs, skills, and affect can be changed. That is, once one pinpoints the specific factors that play a role in intellectual performance, one can take steps to foster them and thereby enhance intellectual performance.[1] While people may be born with certain temperaments, proclivities, interests, and motivations, the research we review suggests that the context exerts great influence and can change motivation.

We present evidence from laboratory studies, field studies, and interventions showing that beliefs, nonintellectual skills, and affective factors play a key role in intellectual performance. For example, we show that individuals' beliefs about intelligence, beliefs about stereotypes, and beliefs about "belonging" in a setting can transform intellectual performance, and that training that speaks to these beliefs can improve intellectual performance. We also discuss how the emerging view of intelligence as dynamic and as influenced by motivation is changing the field's view of giftedness and talent. It is changing the conception of giftedness from an endowment that needs only to be measured to emerging abilities that need to be cultivated and nurtured. We turn now to motivational factors that have been shown to influence intellectual performance.

Beliefs About the Nature of Intelligence

Research has found that people differ in how they view their intelligence. Some people believe that intelligence is fixed (an *entity theory* of intelligence) and others believe that intelligence is malleable and affected by training and effort (an *incremental theory* of intelligence). These different beliefs about intelligence lead to very different motivational frameworks and to differences in performance on intellectual tasks (e.g., Dweck, 1999; Dweck, Chiu, & Hong 1995; Dweck & Leggett, 1988; Mueller & Dweck, 1998).

An entity theory of intelligence orients people to see intellectual performances as tests of their fixed level of intellectual ability. People endorsing this theory thus tend to adopt *performance* goals more often than people with an incremental theory, striving to validate their intelligence through their performance. An incremental theory of intelligence, on the other hand, is more likely than an entity theory to give rise to *learning* goals. Incremental theorists, because they believe intelligence can be improved and changed through effort, tend to see intellectual performances as opportunities to cultivate ability rather than simply as opportunities to impress through performance (Blackwell, Trzesniewski, & Dweck, 2007; Dweck & Leggett, 1988; Robins & Pals, 2002).

Motivation, as we have defined it, is about the pursuit of goals. And the theory of intelligence one holds can affect not only which goal – performance or learning – is pursued, but also how persistently it is pursued. While both performance and learning goals can be important for intellectual performance, a predominant focus on performance goals rather than learning goals can have detrimental effects on intellectual ability and its growth over time. We present evidence that an entity theory and the

1 We define intellectual performance as not just scores on IQ tests but more broadly as performance in a variety of intellectual tasks and domains. This includes performance in school, on achievement tests, and in professional arenas.

performance goals it engenders can actually lead to lowered intellectual performance, as indexed by grades, achievement test scores, and even IQ scores. We also present evidence that possessing an entity theory and performance goals, compared to an incremental theory and learning goals, results in exposing oneself to fewer opportunities for learning and thus can interfere with intellectual growth. As we present the research below, it is important to remember that while a person's theory of intelligence can remain relatively stable over time, these theories are amenable to change and can be influenced through targeted interventions.

Theories of Intelligence and Intellectual Performance

Across different ways of assessing intellectual performance – grades, academic achievement tests, and even IQ tests – there is increasing evidence that the lay theory of intelligence one holds affects intellectual performance. The evidence also indicates that theories of intelligence affect intellectual performance through a motivational pathway, that is, through their effects on goals.

Academic performance: Grades and achievement tests. First, we consider two studies (Blackwell et al., 2007; Henderson & Dweck, 1990) that examined intellectual performance (grades) across a difficult academic transition period – the transition to junior high school. In these studies, researchers assessed students' theories of intelligence through the students' agreement with items such as "You have a certain amount of intelligence and you really can't do much to change it" (with higher agreement indicating a more entity belief about intelligence) and "You can always greatly change how intelligent you are" (with higher agreement indicating a more incremental belief about intelligence). Both of these studies found that theories of intelligence and their associated (performance or learning) goals were significant predictors of grades, above and beyond prior achievement. For example, in the Blackwell et al. (2007) study, although entity and incremental theorists entered junior high at the same level of prior math achievement, incremental theorists saw their math grades steadily increase while entity theorists showed no improvement. Blackwell and colleagues (2007) also demonstrated that students' goals and motivations mediated the effects of beliefs about intelligence on improved intellectual performance. Possessing an incremental theory of intelligence, compared with an entity theory, led to increased endorsement of learning goals and increased belief in the importance of effort. These motivational factors and their downstream effects (e.g., positive, effort-based study strategies in response to difficulty) mediated the positive effect of a belief that intelligence is malleable on intellectual growth. Motivation triggered by theories of intelligence and not prior ability level was critical in determining intellectual growth.

In their second study, Blackwell et al. (2007) demonstrated that students' beliefs about intelligence are malleable and that changing these beliefs could produce substantial effects on intellectual performance. In this research, seventh-graders with declining math grades were assigned to receive either training in study skills (control group) or an intervention that combined study skills with an incremental theory of intelligence. The incremental theory part of the intervention taught students that intelligence was malleable (that their brains formed new connections every time they stretched themselves to learn something new) and that one could become smarter over time through effort. Whereas the control group continued their decline in grades after the intervention, the incremental theory group did not: The intervention stopped the decline in grades and students in this group tended to show an actual rebound in grades following the intervention. In addition, teachers, who did not know which group students were in, were three times more likely to spontaneously report increased motivation for the students who were taught that intelligence is malleable than for the control students. It is essential to note that the control group received eight sessions of training in important study skills, skills that are key to intellectual performance. Moreover, they learned these skills quite well. Nonetheless, without the motivation to put them into practice, the skills remained relatively inert and did not express themselves in improved grades.

In another powerful study, Aronson, Fried, and Good (2002) found that the effect of changing theories of intelligence on intellectual performance extend as late as college. An intervention affirming that intelligence is malleable significantly improved the enjoyment of academic work, the perceived importance of academic work, and the GPAs of college students one quarter later. The two control groups, one of which learned that intelligence was multifaceted and one of which received no treatment, showed no change in their academic enjoyment, values, or performance.

Another important intervention examined the impact of theories of intelligence on achievement test performance. Good, Aronson, and Inzlicht (2003) assigned adolescents to receive an incremental theory intervention (teaching them to view intelligence as malleable) or antidrug training at the start of seventh grade. At the end of the school year, students were administered standardized tests of reading achievement. Those who had received the incremental theory training scored significantly higher on the test than did those in the control condition. The studies, then, demonstrate that changing students' beliefs about their intelligence can change their academic performance significantly and meaningfully.

IQ test performance. Recent studies (Cury, Da Fonseca, Zahn, & Elliot, 2008; Cury, Elliot, Da Fonseca, & Moller, 2006) are also showing that people's beliefs about intelligence can affect not only grades or achievement test scores but also performance on an IQ test – an area that many might have considered a motivation-free assessment of cognitive abilities. In one of these studies (Cury et al., 2006), adolescents in France were administered a portion of an intelligence test (the Coding Test of the WISC-III; Wechsler, 1996). Then, they were taught either that intelligence was fixed (entity theory condition) or that intelligence was malleable through effort (incremental theory condition). After this, all participants completed another portion of the same IQ test. The two groups in the experiment did not differ in their performance on the first portion of the IQ test, before their beliefs were influenced. However, they differed significantly on the second portion of the test. Those in the entity theory condition performed significantly worse than those in the incremental theory condition. It was as if being given an entity motivational framework made the students suddenly less intelligent. Moreover, the researchers found that adoption of performance goals mediated the relationship between theories of intelligence and intellectual performance. An entity framework created a goal of avoiding performance failure, which, in turn, led to hampered intellectual performance.

Mueller and Dweck (1998) found similar effects of motivational frameworks on IQ test performance after an experience of difficulty. In their studies, students were given a set of moderately difficult items from a nonverbal IQ test (Raven's Progressive Matrices; Raven, Styles, & Raven, 1998), were told that they had performed well, and were praised for their performance. Some were given praise for being intelligent (intelligence praise), some for working hard (effort praise), and some were given no additional praise (control). These different types of praise oriented students toward different theories of intelligence, with intelligence praise leading to more of an entity belief about intelligence compared with effort praise, which led to more of an incremental belief. The students then experienced difficulty on a second, very challenging set of problems from the same IQ test, after which they received a third set of problems that was matched in difficulty to the first set. We might expect that the students would do better on this third set (given the practice they had accumulated) or at least just as well as the first time around. However, how students performed depended on the motivational framework toward which they had been oriented. Those in the control group slightly improved their performance. Those given the effort praise improved their performance significantly. But, importantly, those who were given intelligence praise performed significantly *worse* on the third trial than the first trial and significantly worse than the other two groups on this third set of problems. The change in performance from the first trial to the third trial was significantly different across the three conditions, with those in the intelligence praise condition showing significantly less (actually negative) improvement than those in the effort praise and control conditions.

Summary. There is consistent evidence from laboratory studies and from real-world field studies that beliefs about intelligence and their concomitant goals affect intellectual performance as reflected in grades (e.g., Aronson et al., 2002; Blackwell et al., 2007; Henderson & Dweck, 1990), achievement test scores (e.g., Good et al., 2003), and IQ scores (e.g., Cury et al. 2008; Cury et al., 2006; Mueller & Dweck, 1998). These effects are particularly striking for groups of people who are facing challenges, whether it is a difficult school transition or the experience of failure (e.g., Blackwell et al., 2007; Mueller & Dweck, 1998). When concerns about one's level of fixed intelligence predominate and the motivation to learn remains in the background, intellectual performance can suffer. The research suggests that differences among people that may have been assumed to arise from differences in underlying intelligence may instead arise from differences in motivation. Furthermore, it is critical to note that theories of intelligence and the associated motivations can be changed, and interventions that promote an incremental theory of intelligence are an effective way to increase intellectual performance.

Theories of Intelligence and Opportunities for Intellectual Growth

In this section, we propose that theories of intelligence may also affect intelligence in the longer term by changing people's reactions to opportunities for intellectual growth. With their belief that intelligence is immutable and their goal of proving their intelligence, entity theorists might give themselves fewer opportunities to experience challenges and intellectual growth than those who hold an incremental theory.

In the Blackwell et al. (2007) research described earlier, students with an incremental theory expressed a greater preference for difficult tasks they could learn from than did entity theorists, who tended to prefer tasks that would allow them to perform well. A study by Dweck and Leggett (1988) examined whether theories of intelligence also translated to actual behavioral choices about challenging tasks. Adolescents were given a choice between tasks that were either within their comfort zone or not. They could choose to do tasks that were "fairly easy, so I'll do well," "problems that are hard enough to show I'm smart," or "problems that are hard, new and different so that I could learn." The first two task options allowed students to remain in or near their comfort zone – at a level at which they knew they could succeed. The last task, however, presented a novel challenge with opportunity to stretch themselves in the service of learning. While 61% percent of incremental theorists chose the novel, challenging task, only about 18% of entity theorists did so (see also Mueller & Dweck, 1998). Thus, the vast majority of those with a belief that intelligence was fixed denied themselves an opportunity to experience intellectual growth through novel tasks that pushed them out of their comfort zone.

Hong, Chiu, Dweck, Lin, and Wan (1999) found that entity theorists were less likely than incremental theorists to take steps to improve their performance. They manipulated people's theories of intelligence and gave them an intelligence test. Some participants were then told that their performance had been unsatisfactory and were offered a choice between an unrelated task or a task that would help them improve their performance on intelligence tests. Of those given the incremental theory, 73% chose the remedial task that would allow them to grow and improve. However, only 13% of those in the entity theory condition chose this remedial task.

There is also electrophysiological evidence that people holding an entity theory are more affected by information about their performance and that they less effectively process information that might help them learn. In this research, Mangels, Butterfield, Lamb, Good, and Dweck (2006) used electroencephalography (EEG) to determine how people with different theories of intelligence process performance-relevant and learning-relevant information. Each participant took a long and difficult test of general knowledge. After the participants answered each question (e.g., What is the capital of Nepal?), participants learned whether they got the question right or wrong and then a short time later what the right answer was. Analysis of the EEG brain waves indicated that entity and incremental theorists differed in how they appraised negative feedback (i.e., you got the answer wrong). Entity theorists, compared with incremental theorists, found the negative performance information to be more affectively significant, perhaps viewing it more as a threat to their adequacy than as a simple indication of where they needed to improve.

Mangels et al. (2006) also found brainwave patterns indicating that entity and incremental theorists responded very differently to learning-relevant information (e.g., "The correct answer is Kathmandu"). Entity theorists, compared with incremental theorists, processed the correct answer in a less sustained and deep manner, thus encoding it less well. Moreover, the more sustained and deeper processing of the incremental theorists predicted better performance for them than for entity theorists on a subsequent surprise test of questions that they had answered incorrectly.

Summary. Research supports the idea that entity theorists compared to incremental theorists expose themselves to fewer challenging learning environments (e.g., Blackwell et al., 2007; Dweck & Leggett, 1988; Hong et al., 1999; Mueller & Dweck, 1998). Their appraisal of performance feedback as an indicator of their fixed intelligence appears to interfere with their ability to attend to and take advantage of learning opportunities, resulting in poorer learning (Mangels et al., 2006). There is additional evidence that performance goals (predominant for entity theorists), compared with learning goals, lead to engaging with material at a less nuanced and deep level and can therefore also create a less effective learning experience (Grant & Dweck, 2003). Through their avoidance of opportunities for challenging learning and their less effective processing of learning material, entity theorists might experience less intellectual growth and lose ground to incremental theorists over time.

Beliefs About Being Viewed Through the Lens of a Stereotype

Believing that you may be judged through the lens of a negative stereotype, one that questions your underlying ability, can also dramatically affect intellectual performance. Many stereotypes cast groups of people – Blacks, Latinos, those of lower socioeconomic status, and women – as inherently lacking in intelligence or particular kinds of intellectual ability. However, much research finds that group differences in intellectual performance are far from fixed. Perhaps the most striking example of this type of research is the research on stereotype threat (Steele, 1997; Steele & Aronson, 1995). Stereotype threat is triggered when people believe that their performance may fulfill a negative stereotype about their group's ability, and it has been shown repeatedly to hamper intellectual performance (e.g., Aronson, Lustina, Good, Keough, Steele, & Brown, 1999; Brown & Josephs, 1999; Croizet & Claire, 1998; Davies, Spencer, Quinn, &

Gerhardstein, 2002; Gonzales, Blanton, & Williams, 2002; O'Brien & Crandall, 2003; Spencer, Steele, & Quinn, 1999; Steele & Aronson, 1995; for meta-analyses see Nguyen & Ryan, 2008; Walton & Cohen, 2003; Walton & Spencer, 2009). We describe the effects of stereotype threat and review evidence that these effects occur for motivational reasons.

Understanding Stereotype Threat

In the original study on stereotype threat, Steele and Aronson (1995) administered a measure of intellectual performance, the Graduate Record Exam (GRE), to Black and White college students. Half of the students were told that the test was diagnostic of intellectual ability (diagnostic condition) and the other that the experimenters were not interested in diagnosing ability (nondiagnostic condition). The instructions that the test was diagnostic of intellectual ability made the negative stereotype of intellectual inferiority relevant for Black participants, leading them to believe they could be judged through the lens of that stereotype. The effects of this minor manipulation on performance were striking. In the diagnostic condition, that is, when stereotype threat was present for the Black participants, a race gap in performance appeared: The Black participants underperformed relative to the White participants. However, when this threat was lifted and the test was described as nondiagnostic, the race gap disappeared: The performance of the Black participants rose to the level of the White participants, eliminating any group differences. This means that simply changing the instructions in a way that made people believe stereotypes were relevant or not relevant significantly changed intellectual performance. There have been many other studies demonstrating the same phenomenon for multiple groups, such as those of lower socioeconomic status (e.g., Croizet & Clare, 1998), Latinos (e.g., Gonzales et al., 2002), women in math and science (e.g., Spencer et al., 1999), and the elderly (e.g., Andreoletti & Lachman, 2004). Effects have been found not only for standardized tests of performance but also for other markers of intelligence such as working memory, cognitive flexibility, and speed of processing (e.g., Carr & Steele, 2009; Schmader & Johns, 2003; Seibt & Förster, 2004).

Does not require a history of stigmatization. Stereotype threat effects do not arise simply because a group has been chronically stereotyped. It is a threat cued by the situation. Even groups who have no history of stigmatization can be made to believe that they could be viewed as inherently inferior to others, and when they are, they display lowered intellectual performance (Aronson et al., 1999). White men are typically unburdened by negative stereotypes impugning their academic abilities. Yet, when told they are participating in a study examining why Asians are superior to Whites in math, White male math majors then underperform on a test of math ability. The situation cuing the belief that your performance could confirm the notion that your group is inferior subverts intellectual performance.

Does not arise merely from knowledge of a group difference. Women are stereotyped as less able in math compared to men, and they typically experience stereotype threat and exhibit underperformance on math tests when told that there are gender differences on the math test they will take. This underperformance does not manifest itself when they are told that there are no gender differences (e.g., Spencer et al., 1999).

However, stereotype threat is also not always triggered from just being reminded that there are group differences in performance and that you belong to the disadvantaged group. It is more reliably triggered when there is an implication about your underlying capacity for success. Dar-Nimrod and Heine (2006) found that women who were told that gender differences in math performance were due to experiential causes, such as treatment by teachers, did not experience stereotype threat, and they performed at the same high level as women who were told there were no gender differences. In contrast, women who were told that sex differences in math were due to genetic differences between males and females experienced stereotype threat and performed substantially worse. Thus, it is not just knowing or being reminded that gender differences exist that creates underperformance; it is the threat of your inherent capacity being questioned.

Summary. We have presented evidence that stereotype threat interferes with intellectual performance (e.g., Steele & Aronson, 1995). Stereotype threat is created in a situation that signals that you might be judged through the lens of a negative stereotype and does not require a history of stigmatization (e.g., Aronson et al., 1999). It is, moreover, not triggered simply by the knowledge that your group may have underperformed in the past (e.g., Dar-Nimrod & Heine, 2006). It stems from the indication that your group may be viewed as inherently deficient and that your performance may confirm this deficiency. We will argue that stereotype threat affects intellectual functioning through its impact on motivational frameworks and resources.

The Motivational Argument

Much research has tried to understand exactly how and why stereotype threat undermines intellectual performance (e.g., Ben-Zeev, Fein, & Inzlicht, 2005; Bosson, Haymovitz, & Pinel, 2004; Cadinu, Maass, Frigerio, Impagliazzo, & Latinotti, 2003; Davies et al., 2002; Krendl, Richeson, Kelley, & Heatherton, 2008; Schmader & Johns, 2003). We propose that one can understand the process through a motivational lens. Stereotype threat triggers evaluative concerns, that is, concern that poor performance will confirm a stereotype that questions underlying ability. These concerns lead to a goal of proving your intelligence to others (a performance goal) and can sap the mental resources needed for effective goal-pursuit and achievement of high performance.

Under the burden of a stereotype about their group's innate intellectual inferiority, people can be expected to become preoccupied not with maximizing learning and absorbing information but rather with negative stereotypes and their performance. We propose that while experiencing stereotype threat, a person's principal focus is not to grow and cultivate ability (a learning goal) but to perform and disprove the stereotype (a performance goal). Preliminary evidence discussed later supports this hypothesis, finding that when they experience stereotype threat, people become focused on the stereotype and do not focus on learning (e.g., Davies et al., 2002; Krendl et al., 2008). In addition, research finds that changing motivational frameworks – orienting people toward an incremental theory and the associated learning goals – reduces stereotype threat and its negative effects on intellectual performance (Aronson et al., 2002; Good et al., 2003).

Preoccupation with stereotypes and performance. Studies have found that after experiencing stereotype threat, the self-relevant negative stereotype becomes activated and salient for the targets of the stereotype. One such study (Steele & Aronson, 1995) found that Black participants in the stereotype threat condition compared to all other unthreatened participants completed more word-stems (e.g., d_ _ b) with words related to the negative stereotype questioning their ability, such as "dumb" and "inferior," indicating that they were thinking of the negative stereotype more. In another study, women's level of activation of such stereotype-relevant words predicted their underperformance on a math test (Davies et al., 2002), suggesting that thinking about the stereotype that questions your ability actually hampers your ability to perform intellectually.

There is also some direct evidence that stereotype threat triggers preoccupation with performance and ability. Stereotype threat has been found to result in a prevention-focus, a state focused on avoiding failure (Seibt & Forster, 2004). Moreover, Cadinu, Maass, Rosabianca, and Kiesner (2005) found that those experiencing stereotype threat have more negative thoughts about their performance and ability in math (e.g., I am not good at math) and that these thoughts mediated the effects of stereotype threat on underperformance.

This research, which finds a preoccupation with stereotypes that indict ability and with poor performance under stereotype threat, suggests a shift to a motivational framework driven by performance goals. Indeed, recent neuroimaging data also support the idea that burdened by stereotype threat, people become focused on evaluation and rejection and not on learning and deep processing. Krendl and colleagues (2008) used functional magnetic resonance imaging (fMRI) to investigate brain activation during stereotype threat. In their study, women took a math test in the fMRI scanner and were then either reminded of the negative stereotype about women's abilities in math (threat condition) or not (no threat condition). They then took another math test. On the second test, those who had not experienced stereotype threat increased recruitment and engagement of brain areas associated with processing mathematical information and mathematical learning (such as the left prefrontal cortex). They appeared to be increasing their engagement with and learning of the math material. In contrast, those reminded about the negative stereotype did not increasingly recruit these mathematical learning areas. They, instead, increased recruitment of the area of the brain that processes social and emotional information such as stereotypes and social rejection, the ventral anterior cingulate cortex. Those not reminded of the stereotype did not increase activation of this area. Thus, it appears that under stereotype threat, concerns about how others might view you and your performance become salient, and learning and deep processing have to take a back seat. In this way, preoccupation with thoughts about stereotypes, evaluation, and ability may create intellectual underperformance.

Changing motivational frameworks reduces stereotype threat. Perhaps the most striking evidence that motivational frameworks are important in the effects of stereotype threat on intellectual performance come from interventions designed to reduce the impact of stereotype threat on intellectual performance. Good et al. (2003) conducted an intervention to eliminate achievement gaps created by stereotype threat, specifically, a gender gap in math scores in junior high school. One group in their study received an intervention that taught them an incremental theory of intelligence, which, as discussed earlier, is typically associated with a greater focus on learning rather than performance goals. The control group simply received antidrug training. In the control group, girls underperformed relative to boys on the standardized math test administered at the end of the year. In the incremental theory group, however, the gender difference in performance was substantially reduced. Although boys also tended to experience an improvement in performance in the incremental group compared with the control, the positive effect was even stronger for the stereotype-threatened participants – the girls. Drawing the focus away from performance as an index of intelligence and putting it on brain growth and learning was especially beneficial for the group burdened by the stereotype.

In another study, Aronson et al. (2002) also found that stereotype threat effects for Black college students could be reduced through an intervention that changed theories of intelligence. White and Black college students were assigned to one of three conditions. In the incremental intelligence condition, they were taught about the malleability of intelligence and wrote letters to pen pals affirming that intelligence was "like a muscle" that could be strengthened through effort. In the control pen pal condition they wrote letters about intelligence that did not contain a malleability message, instead explaining that that there were many kinds of intelligence. The third condition was a no-treatment control. There was an achievement gap in the control conditions, with Black students underperforming compared with White students. Though the White students in the incremental intelligence condition tended to improve their GPA nine weeks later, this effect was only marginally significant. However, the intervention significantly increased the performance of Black students, rendering it not significantly different from that of Whites. An incremental belief about intelligence significantly increased stereotyped students' GPA and helped eliminate an achievement gap created by stereotype threat.

Other factors compromising effective goal-pursuit. The belief that your group is viewed as inherently deficient can also lead to difficulty in pursuing intellectual goals by creating strategic inefficiency and depletion of self-control resources.

Several lines of research suggest that stereotype threat may prevent achievement of intellectual goals because it leads to strategic inefficiency. It has been found that individuals experiencing stereotype threat have difficulty generating problem-solving strategies (Quinn & Spencer, 2001), tend to become more formulaic in their processing of information (Seibt & Forster, 2004), and become more rigid in the strategies they use (Carr & Steele, 2009). Such inefficiency can greatly hamper their performance, as most complex intellectual tasks require a certain degree of flexibility and agility with information processing and cognitive strategies.

Furthermore, research indicates that stereotype threat exhausts self-control resources. An important part of successful goal pursuit is the ability to direct and control oneself – to be able to persist when challenged or frustrated and to direct attention to the task when other thoughts or impulses intrude. However, this self-control ability may be drawn from a limited resource that can be exhausted (Baumeister, Bratslavsky, Muraven, & Tice, 1998). Preoccupation with performance and stereotypes is taxing and as individuals over-monitor their performance and suppress negative stereotypes, their self-control resources may become depleted: Inzlicht, McKay, and Aronson (2006) found that stereotype threat leads to greater difficulty on the Stroop task, a task that requires one to exert self-control to suppress the dominant response. Because of this depletion of self-regulatory resources, targets of stereotype threat may be impaired in their pursuit of intellectual performance goals.

Summary. Stereotype threat subverts intellectual performance on standardized tests (e.g., Steele & Aronson, 1995), on tests of working memory (e.g., Schmader & Johns, 2003), and on tests of cognitive speed (e.g., Seibt & Förster, 2004), and likely does so because of its motivational effects. The burden of contending with stereotypes that characterize your group as inherently deficient shifts people to a performance-focused motivational framework and interferes with the ability to effectively pursue intellectual goals. As they become preoccupied with proving their ability, it becomes more difficult to focus on and engage with learning (e.g., Krendl et al., 2008), cognitive resources are sapped (e.g., Schmader & Johns, 2003), strategies become more inflexible (e.g., Carr & Steele, 2009), and people become less able to control their responses and attention (e.g., Inzlicht et al., 2006). This shift in motivational framework and the sapping of goal-pursuit resources likely combine to create the significant depression of intellectual performance seen in the targets of stereotypes.

A Note on Stereotype Lift

While we have focused on how the motivational effects of negative stereotypes interfere with intellectual performance, positive stereotypes can also affect intellectual performance. Negative stereotypes that cast doubt on the ability of one group (e.g., of women in math) also indicate that another group (e.g., men) is considered superior. Moreover, as the negatively stereotyped group experiences stereotype threat, those in the positively stereotyped group experience stereotype lift – a boost in intellectual performance on the stereotyped task (e.g., a math test) (Walton & Cohen, 2003).

Stereotype lift has recently been found to be one case in which a motivational framework based on an entity theory of intelligence leads to *better* intellectual performance (Mendoza-Denton, Kahn, & Chan, 2008). Individuals who were viewed favorably through the lens of a stereotype (males in math), when told that ability was determined by innate factors (an entity view) rather than effort (an incremental view), performed better on a subsequent math test. In other words, knowing that the ability was fixed, and that they had it, made performance easier and better. However, given that an entity theory does not serve people as well in the face of setbacks (cf. also the effects of intelligence praise; Mueller & Dweck, 1998), given that an entity theory does not promote the growth of intellectual skills over time (e.g., Hong et al., 1999), and given the cost of entity beliefs for those who are negatively stereotyped (e.g., Aronson et al., 2002), we believe that an incremental motivational framework is overall more beneficial for intellectual performance.

Beliefs About Belonging

The need to belong is a powerful human motivator (Baumeister & Leary, 1995). As social animals evolved in small groups that worked cooperatively, humans are driven to fit in and belong in their social settings. In this context, it is not surprising that when people are not certain about whether they belong in an academic setting, their motivation and ability to learn can be compromised.

We present evidence that uncertainty about belonging, perhaps by causing a shift in motivational frameworks, can make people "less intelligent than they were before." The research we review shows that people's beliefs about their belonging can affect performance on an IQ test and that interventions and procedures that heighten an individual's sense of belonging affect intellectual performance and effort.

Lack of Belonging Subverts Intellectual Performance

Baumeister, Twenge, and Nuss (2002) examined whether social rejection, which calls belonging into question, could actually lower IQ. Participants in their study took a personality test and received experimentally manipulated feedback. In the social belonging condition, participants were told they would have many friends. In the social exclusion condition, they were told that they might lose friends. The control condition provided negative information to participants that wasn't social in nature. All participants then took an IQ test (General Mental Abilities Test; Janda, 1996). The social exclusion condition significantly reduced intellectual performance compared with the social belonging or control conditions. Those in the social exclusion condition got 25% fewer answers correct than those in the social belonging condition. Concern about social fit made participants appear substantially less intelligent.

Creating Belonging Improves Intellectual Performance

Walton and Cohen (2007) asked the flip side of the question that Baumeister and colleagues (2002) asked: What would happen to intellectual performance if you bolstered a sense of belonging for students who are typically stereotyped in intellectual settings? These students (e.g., Black students) may be particularly vulnerable to worrying about whether people fully accept them in school; that is, they may experience uncertainty about their belonging in academic settings. Walton and Cohen (2007) developed an intervention to alleviate students' uncertainty about their belonging. In it, they taught university freshmen that uncertainty about belonging is very common across all ethnic groups and that such worries dissipate over time. Students in the control condition were taught that social and political views become more sophisticated over time. The researchers followed these students throughout their college career and recorded the effects of their intervention on intellectual performance. The effects were striking.

The White students, who were not expected to be experiencing concerns about belonging in an academic setting, did not benefit from the intervention, as predicted. However, the Black students did benefit greatly. One semester after the intervention,

Black students in the control condition and campuswide saw their grades decline. In contrast, Black students who received the belonging intervention actually saw their grades significantly improve. Moreover, these effects persisted over the next three years of college. At the end of college, the Black-White achievement gap (the discrepancy in grades) decreased by almost 70% in the treatment condition.

Why does a boost in belonging increase intellectual achievement? It may do so because it frees students from concerns about proving themselves (a performance goal) and allows them to engage with learning. In fact, Black students in the intervention group were more far likely to exhibit learning-motivated behavior, such as going to office hours, attending review sessions, and asking questions in class. Walton, Cohen, and colleagues are currently finding similar effects of a belonging intervention for women in male-dominated fields and for middle-schoolers from stereotyped groups as well (Walton, Cohen, Garcia, Apfel, & Master, 2009; Walton, Logel, Peach, & Spencer, 2009)

Belonging Is Beneficial Not Just for Stereotyped Groups

Can increasing feelings of belonging sometimes benefit nonstereotyped groups? Although stigmatized groups may be particularly susceptible to belonging concerns in academic and intellectual settings, almost everyone questions whether he or she belongs or fits in some settings. Anyone may feel uncertainty about belonging when switching to a different major, moving to a new country, or confronting a novel task in a psychology study. Can feelings of belonging increase intellectual performance for nonstereotyped groups? Research suggests that they can. Walton, Cohen, Cwir, and Spencer (2009) found that even minimal indicators of belonging increase intellectual persistence and effort. Participants for whom belonging was induced through minimal means – learning that a math major shared their birthday – worked harder and longer on a math puzzle than participants who were not given a heightened sense of belonging. The puzzle, in this case, was insoluble but one can expect that on other tasks the extra effort might pay off in improved intellectual performance.

Summary

Research supports the idea that beliefs about belonging affect intelligence. Uncertainty about belonging can hamper performance on an IQ test and adversely affect grades in college (Baumeister et al., 2002; Walton & Cohen, 2007). Being freed from this uncertainty, it appears, allows individuals to focus on learning, increase their intellectual effort, and improve their intellectual performance.

The Skill of Self-Regulation

To this point we have discussed how different motivation-relevant beliefs – about intelligence, about stereotypes, and about one's belonging – change intellectual performance. Now, we turn to another critical component of motivation – people's skill at self-regulation – and its impact on intellectual performance.

Self-regulation is the executive function process that directs cognitions, attention, and behaviors toward the attainment of an individual's goals in the face of other information (internal or external) that competes for the individual's attention (Baumeister & Heatherton, 1996, Baumeister et al., 1998; Engle, 2002; Kane, Conway, Hambrick, & Engle, 2007). It is the resource we use when we undertake a challenging goal, when we choose to study instead of going out with friends, when we keep working when tired, and when we tune out an exciting conversation to stay focused on our work. It is a resource necessary for effective goal-pursuit.

In self-regulation, we see the intertwining of intelligence and motivation. Attention-regulation and response-inhibition are considered to be part of executive function, but executive function also includes working memory (Engle, 2002), a more purely intellectual factor. In this section, we will focus on people's self-control skills to highlight the role they play in intellectual performance. These skills – specifically, delay of gratification, self-discipline, and behavioral control abilities – have powerful and enduring effects on intellectual outcomes, affecting standardized test scores, academic success, professional success, and intellectual growth and learning.

Delay of Gratification and Self-Discipline

One of the most striking examples of self-regulation affecting long-term intellectual performance comes from the research of Walter Mischel and his colleagues. In their classic studies of delay of gratification (Mischel, Shoda, & Rodriguez, 1989), preschool children were offered a choice by the experimenter. They could choose to have one marshmallow now, or if they waited the full time the experimenter was out of the room, they could have two marshmallows when the experimenter returned. The experimenter placed the tempting marshmallows in front of the children and stepped out, but the children were given a bell to ring. If the children rang this bell, they were told, the experimenter would rush back and give them one marshmallow, but they would have to forfeit the second. The experimenters measured how long each child waited before ringing the bell and whether the child waited until the experimenter returned some 15 minutes later – a measure of how able they were to control their urges, resist temptation, and stay focused on their goal of the larger prize. On average, children waited less than three minutes, but, strikingly, the length of time they waited predicted their scores on a measure of intellectual performance, the SAT, more than a decade later. The child who waited the entire 15 minutes as a preschooler, on average, scored 210 points higher on the SAT as a teenager than the child who waited 30 seconds (Shoda, Mischel, & Peake, 1990). Thus the ability to regulate oneself in service of one's goal appears to be a strong predictor of intellectual performance over time.

More recently, Duckworth and Seligman (2005) reexamined the effects of self-discipline and delay of gratification with eighth-graders. Using self-report, teacher reports, parent reports, and delay of gratification tasks (e.g., "Would you like $1 now or $2 next week?"), the researchers derived a self-discipline score for each student in the fall of the school year. These students were also administered an IQ test. The researchers then tracked students' grades, their scores on standardized achievement tests, and their selection into a rigorous and competitive high school program – all intellectual performance variables – through the spring of that school year. They found that even after controlling for prior achievement, highly self-disciplined adolescents had higher grades than their less disciplined counterparts. In addition, they outperformed those lower in self-discipline on every other measure of intellectual performance. What was particularly impressive was that self-discipline predicted more variance in these intellectual outcomes than did the adolescents' IQ scores. What many people would consider a measure of pure intellectual ability – the IQ test – was not as effective in predicting intellectual success as was a motivational variable like self-discipline (see also Tangney, Baumeister, & Boone, 2004; Wolfe & Johnson, 1995).

It makes sense that self-discipline and delay of gratification would be so important for intellectual success. Even the most gifted children may not get very far if they do not spend time learning. Ericsson, Krampe and Tesch-Römer (1993) made this very point not only for academic success but also for professional success across domains. Ericsson and his colleagues determined that what distinguished the great – the highly gifted – in a field from those who were just good was disciplined hard work and hours of dedicated, deliberate practice. The greats, like Mozart, Einstein, or even Bill Gates, spent at least 10,000 hours honing their skill before they became great. The good may spend only 6,000 hours engaged in self-disciplined practice and thus never reach the pinnacle in their professions. After people had a minimum amount of requisite ability, Ericsson concluded, self-discipline and dedication to learning seemed to carry the weight in determining performance.

Behavioral Regulation and Effortful Control

A closely related construct that has received a lot of attention recently is that of behavioral regulation and effortful control – the ability to follow instructions and inhibit inappropriate responses (Blair & Razza, 2007; McCelland et al., 2007). Behavioral regulation and effortful control, as well, have been found to affect intellectual performance. In one study, researchers (McClelland et al., 2007) measured preschooler's behavioral regulation ability in the fall and spring of their pre-kindergarten year using a "Head-to-Toes" game in which the children have to do the opposite of what the experimenter asks them to do (e.g., touch their toes when asked to touch their head). This task demands self-regulatory skill, as it requires the child to inhibit the dominant, inappropriate response and keep the task goal and rules salient in the face of distraction. Researchers also measured the children's math, vocabulary, and literacy abilities at both times. They found that children's behavioral control predicted their intellectual performance at both points in time. Furthermore, growth in a child's behavioral regulation ability predicted improvement in intellectual performance: Making great gains in behavioral regulation from fall to spring predicted making great gains in math, vocabulary, and literacy, even after controlling for prior achievement. In a similar study, Blair and Razza (2007) found that a teacher's reports of a child's effortful control ability in preschool (how able a child is to stay focused on activities, control responses when asked to, and not become frustrated) predicted math performance in kindergarten, even after controlling for IQ as measured by Raven's Progressive Matrices (Raven et al., 1998). Thus the degree to which a child can inhibit inappropriate responses and not succumb to distractions – can effectively self-regulate in the pursuit of his or her goals – predicts intellectual performance and intellectual growth (see also Bull & Scerif, 2001; Espy et al., 2004; Howse, Calkins, Anastopoulos, Keane, & Shelton, 2003; Ponitz, McClelland, Matthews, & Morrison, 2009; St Clair-Thompson & Gathercole, 2006; Valiente, Lemery-Chalfant, Swanson, & Reiser, 2008).

Improving Self-Regulation

It is clear that self-regulation skill measured early in life can have an impact on intellectual outcomes even much later in life. However, that does not mean that self-regulation abilities are unchangeable or simply proxies for intelligence. In fact, research has shown that they can be trained. In one study (Diamond et al., 2007), researchers used the "Tools of the Mind" materials (which included training in inhibiting responses, sustaining attention, and keeping information in mind over time) to teach executive function to one group of preschool children. It was woven into the standard curriculum and the "Tools of the Mind" group was later compared to a similar group of children who received only the standard curriculum. At the end of one to two years of such training, their executive function abilities were measured on self-regulation tasks that were not familiar to any of the children. On these tasks that measured ability to tune out distracters and inhibit natural responses, the children who had received the "Tools of the Mind" training significantly outperformed the children who had received the standard curriculum. Thus, a curriculum focused on self-regulation had successfully increased self-regulation (executive function) capacity in young children (see also Dowsett & Livesey, 2000; Rueda et al., 2005). Moreover, as we have discussed, performance on tasks demanding self-regulation are predictive of academic achievement.

Summary

The evidence is clear in showing that self-regulation – people's skill at setting and maintaining their focus on their goals – is critical to short- and long-term intellectual performance (e.g., Duckworth & Seligman, 2005; McClelland et al., 2007; Mischel et al., 1989). The effects of self-regulation on intellectual performance are long-lasting, sizable, and above and beyond the effects of prior achievement and IQ scores. Taken together with the recent success in training self-regulation (e.g., Diamond et al., 2007), these findings again support the idea that intelligence is molded by motivation.

Feelings of Intrinsic Motivation

We last consider the effects of affective components of motivation on intellectual performance. We first describe research that finds that the affective states of pleasure, enjoyment, and interest (that accompany and constitute "intrinsic" motivation for an activity) enhance intellectual performance, leading to higher grades and test scores. We then turn to a related definition of intrinsic motivation – engaging in an activity for its own sake rather than simply because of external demands and pressures (Sansone & Harackiewicz, 2000). Research finds that such internally driven motivation enhances intellectual performance.

Researchers have examined whether creating learning environments that enhance interest leads to better intellectual performance. In one study (Cordova & Lepper, 1996), researchers used several strategies to increase elementary school students' intrinsic interest in a game that taught arithmetic operations. The instructional content was identical in all conditions, but in some conditions, the researchers increased intrinsic motivation and interest by adding an element of fantasy (e.g., participants would advance a spaceship through solving math operations), creating personalization (e.g., participant's name and birthday was included in the game), or allowing participants choice (e.g., naming their character and the opponent's character). One to two weeks after the game was played, participants were given a written test of equations. Compared to the control condition, which was not designed to increase intrinsic interest, these strategies significantly improved performance on the math test. Thus, although all students received the same instruction, students who experienced greater intrinsic interest during the instruction exhibited better intellectual performance (see also Cordova, Atkins, & Lepper, 2009).

Another study investigated the effects of goals that were intrinsic in nature and contexts that were supportive of autonomy. Self-determination theory proposes and research finds that tasks that satisfy a need for autonomy are more intrinsically motivating (Deci, Koestner, & Ryan, 1999; Deci & Ryan, 1985; Ryan & Deci, 2000). Vansteenkiste, Simons, Lens, Sheldon, and Deci (2004) found that people performed significantly better on a test of new material when the material was framed in terms of intrinsic goals (e.g., material allowing personal growth) and not extrinsic goals (e.g., material allowing you to earn more) and when people were made to feel autonomous and volitional (for example, by using phrases such as "you can" and "if you choose" in instructions) rather than controlled (for example, by using phrases such as "you must" and "you have to" in instructions).

Iyengar and Lepper (1999) found that providing choice (by allowing students to pick which puzzles to work on) in contrast to not providing choice (by assigning students puzzles picked by authority figures) increased motivation for European American students. For the more interdependent, Asian American students, choices made by valued and trusted others (such as their mother or their in-group) produced high intrinsic motivation, but choices made by lesser valued others (such as the out-group) undermined their motivation. And across all cultures, situations that enhanced intrinsic motivation led to improved task performance. Thus, it appears that contexts that facilitate intrinsic motivation lead to better learning, comprehension, and intellectual performance.

We now turn to intrinsic motivation defined in a different, but very related way – engaging in a task for its own sake or on your own terms. Of course, engaging in tasks for such reasons may also be accompanied by greater interest and enjoyment, and the findings we discuss later may be mediated by such affective states. Several longitudinal studies have investigated whether children who possess higher intrinsic motivation for academics and learning – desire to learn for learning's sake – actually perform better academically in school. In one such study (Lepper, Corpus, & Iyengar, 2005), students' intrinsic motivation was measured through agreement with items such as "I work on problems to learn how to solve them." The researchers found that higher intrinsic motivation for academics predicted higher grades and higher standardized test scores months later. In contrast, higher extrinsic motivation, motivation arising from external rewards or pressure (assessed by agreement with items such as "I work on problems because I'm supposed to"), was negatively correlated with future grades and standardized test scores. Many other studies have found similar effects. Being intrinsically motivated for academics correlates with increased academic achievement (e.g., Harter, 1981; Gottfried, 1985; Gottfried, 1990; Gottfried, Fleming, & Gottfried, 2001). Though both extrinsic and intrinsic motivation may reflect a desire to do well, pursuing academic activities for their own sake is associated with better intellectual performance.

Moreover, research also finds that interference with this desire to engage in an activity for its own sake through superfluous extrinsic rewards leads to worse performance (Lepper, Greene, & Nisbett, 1973). Researchers recruited children in a nursery school who had shown existing intrinsic interest in a drawing activity. They then either asked the children to simply engage in the drawing activity or asked them to engage in it in exchange for an extrinsic reward (a certificate with a gold star). Researchers found that the "over-justification" for the drawing activity created through the extrinsic reward actually lowered children's future interest in the activity and led to drawings of a lower quality.

Extrinsic rewards and extrinsic motivation may certainly "turn on the motor." However, as noted, research finds that intrinsic motivation – defined either as an affective state of interest and enjoyment or an internally driven motivation to engage with the material – is associated with greater academic achievement as reflected in grades and standardized test performance. In addition, creating intrinsic motivation creates better learning and intellectual performance.

It is important to note that extrinsic rewards may not always be detrimental to performance, especially if there was no intrinsic interest to begin with. There has been a recent push to pay students for academic performance and it is possible that such programs could jump-start engagement with academic work for some students. However, these programs must be seen in light of the decades of research on the benefits of intrinsic motivation and in the context of extensive research on the beneficial impact of interventions that teach an incremental theory of intelligence and those that create a sense of belonging for these same groups of lower achieving or negatively stereotyped students. The implication is that such programs might be supplemented by or replaced by programs in which students are motivated to learn in order to grow their brains and because school is a place where they belong and are valued.

Conclusion

In this chapter, we have presented research conducted in the laboratory and in field settings demonstrating the powerful effects of motivational variables on intellectual outcomes as varied as grades, achievement on standardized tests, IQ test scores, and professional accomplishment (e.g., Blackwell et al., 2007; Cury et al., 2006; Ericsson et al., 1993; Steele & Aronson, 1995). And the research indicates that these dynamic motivational variables – individually and taken together – may be more important than traditional measures of intellectual ability, like IQ, in predicting and shaping intellectual performance (e.g., Duckworth & Seligman, 2005). The effects of motivation on intelligence emerge among individuals of equal cognitive ability and at equal levels of prior intellectual accomplishment (e.g., Duckworth & Seligman, 2005). They emerge early in childhood and persist into adulthood (e.g., Mischel et al., 1989), for struggling and stigmatized individuals (e.g., Aronson et al., 2002), and for individuals unburdened by stereotypes (e.g., Cury et al., 2006).

Importantly, this research suggests motivational routes to enhancing intellectual accomplishment and has deep implications for our understanding of giftedness and intelligence, as it draws our attention to the importance of educational environments and cultures. Indeed, highlighting the point that motivation is amenable to change, we have described several empirically tested avenues for enhancing intellectual performance through affecting motivation (e.g., Aronson et al., 2002; Blackwell et al., 2007; Cordova & Lepper, 1996; Diamond et al., 2007; Good et al., 2003; Jaeggi et al., 2008; Walton & Cohen, 2007).

The ability to change motivation and thereby change intellectual performance also pushes us to alter the focus of intelligence and giftedness research. The focus in intelligence and giftedness research has long been on identifying those who are highly intelligent or gifted and tracking and supporting them (e.g., Colombo, Shaddy, Blaga, Anderson, & Kannass, 2009; Gagné, 2009; Jensen, 1998; Simonton, 2005; Terman, 1926). The research we have presented makes it evident that while we may come into the world with different aptitudes, our changeable beliefs, goals, skills, and interests dramatically shape the expression of intelligence. Given this evidence, it is no longer satisfactory to merely identify levels of intelligence – to test performance at one point in time, label children as gifted or not, or place them into enduring categories. In light of the research, the boundary between gifted and not gifted becomes fluid and fuzzy, something that can change with time and environments. Thus, instead of focusing on measurement and categorization, we are pushed to examine the factors that interfere with and that enhance intellectual accomplishment (e.g., Claxton & Meadows, 2009; Dweck, 2009a, b; Hymer, 2009; Subotnik, 2009).

The research we have reviewed also gives us a different understanding of what it *means* to be "intelligent" or "gifted." Being intelligent or gifted over the long run seems to require not just initial ability but also the right motivation – a focus on learning and not performance, freedom from stereotypes and belonging concerns, ability to pursue goals in a disciplined manner, and a pursuit of intrinsic goals. As Ericsson and colleagues (1993) noted, even the talented, without hard work and discipline to enhance their skills and address their weaknesses, lose the giftedness race. Such hard work and accomplishment can be facilitated by environments that help build self-regulatory skills, that pique intrinsic interest, and that draw the focus on learning and not on performing or disproving stereotypes.

In conclusion, the research we have reviewed changes our understanding of intelligence and brings to light avenues through which motivation can enhance intellectual performance. While we are not arguing that motivation is a substitute for the learning of content and skills, we argue that it is the vehicle through which intellectual knowledge and skills are successfully acquired, expressed, and built upon.

References

Andreoletti, C., & Lachman, M. E. (2004). Susceptibility and resilience to memory aging stereotypes: Education matters more than age. *Experimental Aging Research*, 30(2), 129–148.

Aronson, J., Fried, C. B., & Good, C. (2002). Reducing the effects of stereotype threat on African American college students by shaping theories of intelligence. *Journal of Experimental Social Psychology*, 38(2), 113–125.

Aronson, J., Lustina, M. J., Good, C., Keough, K., Steele, C. M., & Brown, J. (1999). When White men can't do math: Necessary and sufficient factors in stereotype threat. *Journal of Experimental Social Psychology*, 35(1), 29–46.

Baumeister, R. F., Bratslavsky, E., Muraven, M., & Tice, D. M. (1998). Ego depletion: Is the active self a limited resource? *Journal of Personality and Social Psychology*, 74(5), 1252–1265.

Baumeister, R. F., & Heatherton, T. F. (1996). Self-regulation failure: An overview. *Psychological Inquiry*, 7(1), 1–15.

Baumeister, R. F., & Leary, M. R. (1995). The need to belong: Desire for interpersonal attachments as a fundamental human motivation. *Psychological Bulletin*, 117(3), 497–529.

Baumeister, R. F., Twenge, J. M., & Nuss, C. K. (2002). Effects of social exclusion on cognitive processes: Anticipated aloneness reduces intelligent thought. *Journal of Personality and Social Psychology*, 83(4), 817–827.

Ben-Zeev, T., Fein, S., & Inzlicht, M. (2005). Arousal and stereotype threat. *Journal of Experimental Social Psychology*, 41(2), 174–181.

Binet, A., & Simon, T. (1913). *A method of measuring the development of the intelligence of young children* (C. H. Town, Trans.). Lincoln, IL: Courier.

Binet, A. (1975). *Modern ideas about children.* (S. Heisler, Trans.). Menlo Park, CA: Suzanne Heisler. (Original work published 1909)

Blackwell, L. S., Trzesniewski, K. H., & Dweck, C. S. (2007). Implicit theories of intelligence predict achievement across an adolescent transition: A longitudinal study and an intervention. *Child Development*, 78(1), 246–263.

Blair, C., & Razza, R. P. (2007). Relating effortful control, executive function, and false belief understanding to emerging math and literacy ability in kindergarten. *Child Development*, 78(2), 647–663.

Bosson, J. K., Haymovitz, E. L., & Pinel, E. C. (2004). When saying and doing diverge: The effects of stereotype threat on self-reported versus non-verbal anxiety. *Journal of Experimental Social Psychology*, 40(2), 247–255.

Brown, R. P., & Josephs, R. A. (1999). A burden of proof: Stereotype relevance and gender differences in math performance. *Journal of Personality and Social Psychology*, 76(2), 246–257.

Bull, R., & Scerif, G. (2001). Executive functioning as a predictor of children's mathematics ability: Inhibition, switching, and working memory. *Developmental Neuropsychology*, 19(3), 273–293.

Cadinu, M., Maass, A., Frigerio, S., Impagliazzo, L., & Latinotti, S. (2003). Stereotype threat: The effect of expectancy on performance. *European Journal of Social Psychology*, 33(2), 267–285.

Cadinu, M., Maass, A., Rosabianca, A., & Kiesner, J. (2005). Why do women underperform under stereotype threat? Evidence for the role of negative thinking. *Psychological Science*, 16(7), 572–578.

Carr, P. B., & Steele, C. M. (2009). Stereotype threat and inflexible perseverance in problem solving. *Journal of Experimental Social Psychology*, 45(4), 853–859.

Claxton, G., & Meadows, S. (2009). Brightening up: How children learn to be gifted. In T. Balchin, B. Hymer, & D. J. Matthews (Eds.), *The Routledge international companion to gifted education* (pp. 3–9). New York, NY: Routledge.

Colombo, J., Shaddy, D. J., Blaga, O. M., Anderson, C. J., & Kannass, K. N. (2009). High cognitive ability in infancy and early childhood. In F. D. Horowitz, R. F. Subotnik, & D. Matthews (Eds.), *The development of giftedness and talent across the life-span* (pp. 23–42). Washington, DC: American Psychological Association.

Conley, J. J. (1984). The hierarchy of consistency: A review and model of longitudinal findings on adult individual differences in intelligence, personality and self-opinion. *Personality and Individual Differences*, 5(1), 11–25.

Cordova, D. I., Atkins, D., & Lepper, M. R. (2009). *The effects of intrinsic versus extrinsic rewards on the process of learning.* Manuscript in preparation, Stanford University, Stanford, CA.

Cordova, D. I., & Lepper, M. R. (1996). Intrinsic motivation and the process of learning: Beneficial effects of contextualization, personalization, and choice. *Journal of Educational Psychology*, 88(4), 715–730.

Croizet, J., & Claire, T. (1998). Extending the concept of stereotype and threat to social class: The intellectual underperformance of students from low socioeconomic backgrounds. *Personality and Social Psychology Bulletin, 24*(6), 588–594.

Cury, F., Da Fonseca, D., Zahn, I., & Elliot, A. (2008). Implicit theories and IQ test performance: A sequential mediational analysis. *Journal of Experimental Social Psychology, 44*(3), 783–791.

Cury, F., Elliot, A. J., Da Fonseca, D., & Moller, A. C. (2006). The social-cognitive model of achievement motivation and the 2 × 2 achievement goal framework. *Journal of Personality and Social Psychology, 90*(4), 666–679.

Dai, D. Y., & Sternberg, R. J. (2004). Beyond cognitivism: Toward an integrated understanding of intellectual functioning and development. In D.Y. Dai & R. J. Sternberg (Eds.), *Motivation, emotion, and cognition: Integrative perspectives on intellectual functioning and development* (pp. 3–40). Mahwah, NJ: Erlbaum.

Dar-Nimrod, I., & Heine, S. J. (2006). Exposure to scientific theories affects women's math performance. *Science, 314*(5798), 435–435.

Darwin, C. (1859). *On the origin of species by means of natural selection, or the preservation of favoured races in the struggle for life*. London, UK: John Murray.

Davies, P. G., Spencer, S. J., Quinn, D. M., & Gerhardstein, R. (2002). Consuming images: How television commercials that elicit stereotype threat can restrain women academically and professionally. *Personality and Social Psychology Bulletin, 28*(12), 1615–1628.

Deci, E. L., Koestner, R., & Ryan, R. M. (1999). A meta-analytic review of experiments examining the effects of extrinsic rewards on intrinsic motivation. *Psychological Bulletin, 125*(6), 627–668.

Deci, E. L., & Ryan, R. M. (1985). The general causality orientations scale: Self-determination in personality. *Journal of Research in Personality, 19*(2), 109–134.

Diamond, A., Barnett, W. S., Thomas, J., & Munro, S. (2007). Preschool program improves cognitive control. *Science, 318*(5855), 1387–1388.

Dowsett, S. M., & Livesey, D. J. (2000). The development of inhibitory control in preschool children: Effects of "executive skills" training. *Developmental Psychobiology, 36*(2), 161–174.

Duckworth, A. L., & Seligman, M. E. P. (2005). Self-discipline outdoes IQ in predicting academic performance of adolescents. *Psychological Science, 16*(12), 939–944.

Dweck, C. S. (1999). *Self-theories: Their role in motivation, personality, and development*. New York, NY: Psychology Press.

Dweck, C. S., Chiu, C., & Hong, Y. (1995). Implicit theories and their role in judgments and reactions: A world from two perspectives. *Psychological Inquiry, 6*(4), 267–285.

Dweck, C. S., & Leggett, E. L. (1988). A social-cognitive approach to motivation and personality. *Psychological Review, 95*(2), 256–273.

Dweck, C. S. (2009a). Foreword. In F. D. Horowitz, R. F. Subotnik, & D. Matthews (Eds.), *The development of giftedness and talent across the life-span* (pp. xi–xiv). Washington, DC: American Psychological Association.

Dweck, C. S. (2009b). Self-theories and giftedness: A reflective conversation. In T. Balchin, B. Hymer, & D. J. Matthews (Eds.), *The Routledge international companion to gifted education* (pp. 308–316). New York, NY: Routledge.

Engle, R. W. (2002). Working memory capacity as executive attention. *Current Directions in Psychological Science, 11*(1), 19–23.

Ericsson, K. A., Krampe, R. T., & Tesch-Römer, C. (1993). The role of deliberate practice in the acquisition of expert performance. *Psychological Review, 100*(3), 363–406.

Espy, K. A., McDiarmid, M. M., Cwik, M. F., Stalets, M. M., Hamby, A., & Senn, T. E. (2004). The contribution of executive functions to emergent mathematic skills in preschool children. *Developmental Neuropsychology, 26*(1), 465–486.

Gagné, F. (2009). Talent development as seen through the differentiated model of talent and giftedness. In T. Balchin, B. Hymer, & D. J. Matthews (Eds.), *The Routledge international companion to gifted education* (pp. 32–41). New York, NY: Routledge.

Galton, F. (1883). *Inquiries into human faculty and its development*. London, UK: Macmillan.

Galton, F. (1892). *Hereditary genius: An inquiry into its laws and consequences*. London, UK: Macmillan.

Gonzales, P. M., Blanton, H., & Williams, K. J. (2002). The effects of stereotype threat and double-minority status on the test performance of Latino women. *Personality and Social Psychology Bulletin, 28*(5), 659–670.

Good, C., Aronson, J., & Inzlicht, M. (2003). Improving adolescents' standardized test performance: An intervention to reduce the effects of stereotype threat. *Journal of Applied Developmental Psychology*, 24(6), 645–662.

Gottfried, A. E. (1985). Academic intrinsic motivation in elementary and junior high school students. *Journal of Educational Psychology*, 77(6), 631–645.

Gottfried, A. E. (1990). Academic intrinsic motivation in young elementary school children. *Journal of Educational Psychology*, 82(3), 525–538.

Gottfried, A. E., Fleming, J. S., & Gottfried, A. W. (2001). Continuity of academic intrinsic motivation from childhood through late adolescence: A longitudinal study. *Journal of Educational Psychology*, 93(1), 3–13.

Grant, H., & Dweck, C. S. (2003). Clarifying achievement goals and their impact. *Journal of Personality and Social Psychology*, 85(3), 541–553.

Harter, S. (1981). A new self-report scale of intrinsic versus extrinsic orientation in the classroom: Motivational and informational components. *Developmental Psychology*, 17(3), 300–312.

Henderson, V. L., & Dweck, C. S. (1990). Motivation and achievement. In S. S. Feldman, & G. R. Elliott (Eds.), *At the threshold: The developing adolescent* (pp. 308–329). Cambridge, MA: Harvard University Press.

Hong, Y., Chiu, C., Dweck, C. S., Lin, D. M., & Wan, W. (1999). Implicit theories, attributions, and coping: A meaning system approach. *Journal of Personality and Social Psychology*, 77(3), 588–599.

Howse, R. B., Calkins, S. D., Anastopoulos, A. D., Keane, S. P., & Shelton, T. L. (2003). Regulatory contributors to children's kindergarten achievement. *Early Education and Development*, 14(1), 101–119.

Hymer, B. J. (2009). Beyond compare? Thoughts towards an inclusional, fluid and non-normative understanding of giftedness. In T. Balchin, B. Hymer, & D. J. Matthews (Eds.), *The Routledge international companion to gifted education* (pp. 299–307). New York, NY: Routledge.

Inzlicht, M., McKay, L., & Aronson, J. (2006). Stigma as ego depletion: How being the target of prejudice affects self-control. *Psychological Science*, 17(3), 262–269.

Iyengar, S. S., & Lepper, M. R. (1999). Rethinking the value of choice: A cultural perspective on intrinsic motivation. *Journal of Personality and Social Psychology*, 76(3), 349–366.

Jaeggi, S. M., Buschkuehl, M., Jonides, J., & Perrig, W. J. (2008). Improving fluid intelligence with training on working memory. *Proceedings of the National Academy of Sciences*, 105(19), 6829–6833.

Janda, L. (1996). *The psychologists' book of self-tests*. New York, NY: Berkley.

Jensen, A. R. (1998). *The g factor: The science of mental ability*. Westport, CT: Praeger Publishers/Greenwood Publishing Group.

Jensen, A. R. (2002). Galton's legacy to research on intelligence. *Journal of Biosocial Science*, 34, 145–172.

Kane, M. J., Conway, A. R. A., Hambrick, D. Z., & Engle, R. W. (2007). Variation in working memory capacity as variation in executive attention and control. In A. R. A. Conway, C. Jarrold, M. J. Kane, A. Miyake, & J. N. Towse (Eds.), *Variation in working memory* (pp. 21–46). New York, NY: Oxford University Press.

Krendl, A. C., Richeson, J. A., Kelley, W. M., & Heatherton, T. F. (2008). The negative consequences of threat: A functional magnetic resonance imaging investigation of the neural mechanisms underlying women's underperformance in math. *Psychological Science*, 19(2), 168–175.

Lepper, M. R., Corpus, J. H., & Iyengar, S. S. (2005). Intrinsic and extrinsic motivational orientations in the classroom: Age differences and academic correlates. *Journal of Educational Psychology*, 97(2), 184–196.

Lepper, M. R., Greene, D., & Nisbett, R. E. (1973). Undermining children's intrinsic interest with extrinsic reward: A test of the "overjustification" hypothesis. *Journal of Personality and Social Psychology*, 28(1), 129–137.

Mangels, J. A., Butterfield, B., Lamb, J., Good, C., & Dweck, C. S. (2006). Why do beliefs about intelligence influence learning success? A social cognitive neuroscience model. *Social Cognitive and Affective Neuroscience*, 1(2), 75–86.

McClelland, M. M., Cameron, C. E., Connor, C. M., Farris, C. L., Jewkes, A. M., & Morrison, F. J. (2007). Links between behavioral regulation and preschoolers' literacy, vocabulary, and math skills. *Developmental Psychology*, 43(4), 947–959.

Mendoza-Denton, R., Kahn, K., & Chan, W. (2008). Can fixed views of ability boost performance in the context of favorable stereotypes? *Journal of Experimental Social Psychology*, 44(4), 1187–1193.

Mischel, W., Shoda, Y., & Rodriguez, M. L. (1989). Delay of gratification in children. *Science*, 244(4907), 933–938.

Mueller, C. M., & Dweck, C. S. (1998). Praise for intelligence can undermine children's motivation and performance. *Journal of Personality and Social Psychology*, 75(1), 33–52.

Nguyen, H. D., & Ryan, A. M. (2008). Does stereotype threat affect test performance of minorities and women? A meta-analysis of experimental evidence. *Journal of Applied Psychology*, 93(6), 1314–1334.

O'Brien, L. T., & Crandall, C. S. (2003). Stereotype threat and arousal: Effects on women's math performance. *Personality and Social Psychology Bulletin*, 29(6), 782–789.

Ponitz, C. C., McClelland, M. M., Matthews, J. S., & Morrison, F. J. (2009). A structured observation of behavioral self-regulation and its contribution to kindergarten outcomes. *Developmental Psychology*, 45(3), 605–619.

Quinn, D. M., & Spencer, S. J. (2001). The interference of stereotype threat with women's generation of mathematical problem-solving strategies. *Journal of Social Issues. Special Issue: Stigma: An Insider's Perspective*, 57(1), 55–71.

Raven, J. C., Styles, I., & Raven, M. A. (1998). *Raven's Progressive Matrices: SPM plus test booklet*. Oxford, UK: Oxford Psychologists Press.

Robins, R. W., & Pals, J. L. (2002). Implicit self-theories in the academic domain: Implications for goal orientation, attributions, affect, and self-esteem change. *Self and Identity*, 1(4), 313–336.

Rueda, M. R., Posner, M. I., & Rothbart, M. K. (2005). The development of executive attention: Contributions to the emergence of self-regulation. *Developmental Neuropsychology*, 28(2), 573–594.

Ryan, R. M., & Deci, E. L. (2000). Self-determination theory and the facilitation of intrinsic motivation, social development, and well-being. *American Psychologist*, 55(1), 68–78.

Sansone, C., & Harackiewicz, J. M. (2000). Looking beyond rewards: The problem and promise of intrinsic motivation. In C. Sansone & J. M. Harackiewicz (Eds.), *Intrinsic and extrinsic motivation: The search for optimal motivation and performance* (pp. 1–13). San Diego, CA: Academic Press.

Schmader, T., & Johns, M. (2003). Converging evidence that stereotype threat reduces working memory capacity. *Journal of Personality and Social Psychology*, 85(3), 440–452.

Seibt, B., & Förster, J. (2004). Stereotype threat and performance: How self-stereotypes influence processing by inducing regulatory foci. *Journal of Personality and Social Psychology*, 87(1), 38–56.

Shoda, Y., Mischel, W., & Peake, P. K. (1990). Predicting adolescent cognitive and self-regulatory competencies from preschool delay of gratification: Identifying diagnostic conditions. *Developmental Psychology*, 26(6), 978–986.

Siegler, R. S. (1992). The other Alfred Binet. *Developmental Psychology*, 28(2), 179–190.

Simonton, D. K. (2005). Giftedness and genetics: The emergenic-epigenetic mode and its implications. *Journal for the Education of the Gifted*, 28, 270–286.

Spencer, S. J., Steele, C. M., & Quinn, D. M. (1999). Stereotype threat and women's math performance. *Journal of Experimental Social Psychology*, 35(1), 4–28.

St. Clair-Thompson, H. L., & Gathercole, S. E. (2006). Executive functions and achievements in school: Shifting, updating, inhibition, and working memory. *Quarterly Journal of Experimental Psychology*, 59(4), 745–759.

Steele, C. M. (1997). A threat in the air: How stereotypes shape intellectual identity and performance. *American Psychologist*, 52(6), 613–629.

Steele, C. M., & Aronson, J. (1995). Stereotype threat and the intellectual test performance of African Americans. *Journal of Personality and Social Psychology*, 69(5), 797–811.

Sternberg, R. J. (2005). Intelligence, competence and expertise. In A. J. Elliot & C. S. Dweck (Eds.), *Handbook of competence and motivation* (pp. 15–30). New York, NY: Guilford Press

Sternberg, R. J., & Grigorenko, E. L. (Eds.). (2001). *Environmental effects on cognitive abilities*. Mahwah, NJ: Erlbaum.

Subotnik, R. F. (2009). Developmental transitions in giftedness and talent: Adolescence into adulthood. In F. D. Horowitz, R. F. Subotnik, & D. Matthews (Eds.), *The development of giftedness and talent across the life-span* (pp. 155–170). Washington, DC: American Psychological Association.

Tangney, J. P., Baumeister, R. F., & Boone, A. L. (2004). High self-control predicts good adjustment, less pathology, better grades, and interpersonal success. *Journal of Personality, 72*(2), 271–322.

Terman, L. M. (1916). *The measurement of intelligence: An explanation of and a complete guide for the use of the Stanford revision and extension of the Binet-Simon intelligence scale.* Boston, MA: Houghton Mifflin.

Terman, L. M. (1926). *Genetic studies of genius* (Vol. 1). Stanford, CA: Stanford University Press.

Terman, L. M., & Oden, M. H. (1959). *Genetic studies of genius: The gifted group at mid-life* (Vol. 5). Oxford, UK: Stanford University Press.

Valiente, C., Lemery-Chalfant, K., Swanson, J., & Reiser, M. (2008). Prediction of children's academic competence from their effortful control, relationships, and classroom participation. *Journal of Educational Psychology, 100*(1), 67–77.

Vansteenkiste, M., Simons, J., Lens, W., Sheldon, K. M., & Deci, E. L. (2004). Motivating learning, performance, and persistence: The synergistic effects of intrinsic goal contents and autonomy-supportive contexts. *Journal of Personality and Social Psychology, 87*(2), 246–260.

Walton, G. M., & Cohen, G. L. (2003). Stereotype lift. *Journal of Experimental Social Psychology, 39*(5), 456–467.

Walton, G. M., & Cohen, G. L. (2007). A question of belonging: Race, social fit, and achievement. *Journal of Personality and Social Psychology, 92*(1), 82–96.

Walton, G. M., Cohen, G. L., Cwir, D., & Spencer, S. J. (2009). *Mere belonging: The power of social connections.* Manuscript submitted for publication, Stanford University, Stanford, CA.

Walton, G. M., Cohen, G. L., Garcia, J., Apfel, N., & Master A. (2009). *A brief intervention to buttress middle school students' sense of social-belonging: Effects by race and gender.* Manuscript in preparation, Stanford University, Stanford, CA.

Walton, G. M., Logel, C., Peach, J., & Spencer, S. J. (2009). *Two interventions to boost women's achievement in engineering; Social-belonging and affirmation-training.* Manuscript in preparation, Stanford University, Stanford, CA.

Walton, G. M., & Spencer, S. J. (2009). Latent ability: Grades and test scores systematically underestimate the intellectual ability of negatively stereotyped students. *Psychological Science, 20*(9), 1132–1139.

Wechsler, D. (1996) *Eschelle d'Intelligence de Wechsler pour enfants Troisieme Edition* (Wechsler Intelligence Scale for Children–III). Paris: ECPA (Original work published 1971).

Wolfe, R. N., & Johnson, S. D. (1995). Personality as a predictor of college performance. *Educational and Psychological Measurement, 55*(2), 177–185.

CHAPTER 38

Intelligence and Creativity

James C. Kaufman and Jonathan A. Plucker

How are intelligence and creativity related? The question is of great interest because, in our schools and tests, we seem to value intelligence over creativity. In life, however, creativity is at least as important because it involves adapting to the novel situations that can lead people either to great success or stunning failure. Sternberg and O'Hara (1999) have argued that the relationship between creativity and intelligence "is theoretically important, and its answer probably affects the lives of countless children and adults" (p. 269).

Their point is well taken: Psychologists and educators frequently address issues related to either creativity *or* intelligence, but they often ignore the interplay between the two – or worse, they feel that intelligence and creativity are inversely related. This may explain why research has consistently shown that teachers prefer intelligent students over creative students (e.g., Westby & Dawson, 1995), as though students are unlikely to exhibit evidence of high (or low) levels of both constructs. In addition, the nature of the relationship could help identify aspects of each construct that are ignored in traditional classroom settings.

For example, Wallach and Kogan (1965) suggested that students with high creativity but low intelligence are more disadvantaged in the traditional classroom setting than students with low creativity and low intelligence. If accurate, this observation has considerable implications for how instruction, the curriculum, and assessment are differentiated in classroom settings. Subsequent research has largely supported Wallach and Kogan's observations (e.g., Beghetto, 2006, 2007; Brandau et al., 2007).

Plucker and Renzulli (1999) conclude that it is now a matter of uncovering not *whether* but *how* the two are related. Certainly, creativity has been an important part of many major theories of intelligence. For example, divergent thinking was an integral part of Guilford's (1967) Structure of the Intellect model. But in general, the research on this topic is murky if not seemingly in outright conflict. As an example of research and theories that seem to contradict each other, the threshold theory suggests that intelligence is a necessary but not a sufficient condition of creativity (Barron, 1969; Yamamoto, 1964), certification theory proposes that there are environmental factors that allow people to display both creativity and intelligence (Hayes, 1989), and the interference hypothesis suggests that very high levels of intelligence may interfere with creativity (Simonton, 1994; Sternberg, 1996).

The lack of clear conclusions about the nature of creativity-intelligence relationships is due, at least in part, to the dynamic yet at times underdeveloped constructs being studied. After all, we should not be surprised if conflicting results are observed when a notoriously ill-defined, complex construct (Plucker, Beghetto, & Dow, 2004), measured similarly for decades (Kaufman, Plucker, & Baer, 2008), is compared to another complex construct that has seen rapid theoretical and psychometric development (A. S. Kaufman, 2009). Researchers have often been aiming at two moving targets at the same time.

From an assessment perspective, the relationship of creativity to intelligence is of particular interest. First, the overlap (or lack thereof) between intelligence and creativity is an issue enduringly popular, controversial, and heavily dependent on psychometric issues. Second, creativity plays a major role in several theories of giftedness, and school districts struggle with the development of systems to identify gifted students, especially those with above-average creative abilities.

Roots of Creativity

The roots of creativity as a scientific discipline are planted in the intelligence literature. Many of the earlier scholars (such as Francis Galton, Lewis Terman, Alfred Binet, and Charles Spearman) who considered and discussed creativity were more primarily focused on intelligence. Indeed, it was an intelligence researcher, J. P. Guilford, who first publicly recognized the need for an independent study of creativity.

Guilford (1950, 1967) placed creativity into a larger framework of intelligence in his Structure of Intellect (SOI) model. He attempted to organize all of human cognition along three dimensions. The first dimension was called "operations," and simply meant the mental processes needed to complete almost any kind of task, such as cognition. The second dimension, "content," referred to the general subject matter, such as words. The third dimension, "product," represented the actual products that might result from different kinds of thinking in different kinds of subject matters, such as writing. With five operations, four contents, and six products, Guilford's (1967) model had 120 different possible mental abilities. Indeed, he later expanded the model to include 180 different abilities (Guilford, 1988), although the 120 abilities model is the one more often studied. This model was influential in educational circles (Meeker, 1969), and Renzulli (1973) developed an entire creativity curriculum based on the aspects of the SOI Model involving divergent thinking.

One of Guilford's operations (or thought processes) was divergent thinking – analyzing one's response to questions with no obvious, singular answer. Such questions might include "What would happen if we didn't need sleep?" This work, followed up by other researchers (most notably Torrance, 1974a), has often been used as a measure of creativity. Two of the most common ways of scoring these tests are fluency (the total number of responses given) and originality (how unique are the responses).

A Framework for Exploring the Research

Sternberg (1999) has provided a framework for examining the research on this topic. We find this framework to be helpful because it emphasizes that one's conclusions about the creativity-intelligence relationship will largely be determined by one's theoretical conceptualization of each construct. The Sternberg framework includes five possible intelligence-creativity relationships:

creativity as a subset of intelligence; intelligence as a subset of creativity; creativity and intelligence as overlapping sets; creativity and intelligence as coincident sets; and creativity and intelligence as disjoint sets. In the following sections, we provide examples of each type of relationship.[1]

Theories of Intelligence Which Encompass Creativity

As already discussed, Guilford placed creativity within the context of an intellectual framework. In doing so, he was the first of many to consider creativity to be part of intelligence. Some theories of intelligence include creativity as a subcomponent. Undoubtedly, the theory of intelligence that is most often applied to IQ tests is the CHC (Cattell-Horn-Carroll) theory, a combination of two earlier theories. The Cattell-Horn theory (e.g., Horn & Cattell, 1966) initially proposed two types of intelligence, crystallized (G_c) and fluid (G_f). G_c signifies what a person knows and has learned, and G_f represents how a person handles a new and different situation (i.e., problem solving). Horn expanded the theory to include more dimensions (known as Broad Abilities). Carroll's (1993) theory proposed a hierarchy of intellectual abilities. At the top of the hierarchy is general ability; in the middle of the hierarchy are various broad abilities (including learning and memory processes and the effortless production of many ideas). At the bottom of the hierarchy are many narrow, specific abilities such as spelling ability and reasoning speed.

The combined CHC theory incorporates both the concept of a general intelligence (all of the different aspects of intelligence are considered to be related to a common "*g*," although this aspect is not often emphasized; see Flanagan & Ortiz, 2002) and the concept of many different aspects of intelligence. Ten different broad factors of intelligence are proposed. These include G_f and G_c from the initial Cattell-Horn theory. They also include G_q (quantitative knowledge, typically math-related), G_{rw} (reading and writing), G_{sm} (short-term memory), G_v (visual processing), G_a (auditory processing), G_{lr} (long-term storage and retrieval), G_s (processing speed), and G_t (decision speed/reaction time). Of these 10, only 7 are directly measured by today's intelligence tests: G_q and G_{rw} are in the domain of academic achievement, and, therefore, are measured by achievement tests, and G_t is not measured by any major standardized test. Intelligence tests may indirectly measure some of these other skills, however. In addition, some of the components of each broad factor may not be well measured by either ability or achievement tests.

The Stanford-Binet 5 (SB5, Roid, 2003) and the Woodcock-Johnson-Revised (WJ-III; Woodcock, McGrew, & Mather, 2001) were the first intelligence tests to be built on Gf-Gc theory. Today, nearly every major intelligence test is founded either explicitly or implicitly on the current version of the theory, namely, CHC. In addition, largely because of the influence of CHC theory, all current IQ tests (including the Wechsler Intelligence Scale for Children – Fourth Edition; WISC-IV, Wechsler, 2003) have shifted the historical focus from a small number of part scores to a contemporary emphasis on anywhere from four to seven cognitive abilities (Sternberg, Kaufman, & Grigorenko, 2008).

Although in the early stages of the Cattell-Horn G_f-G_c theory, G_f (fluid intelligence) was hypothesized to be strongly linked to creativity (Cattell & Butcher, 1968), such a relationship is no longer explicitly part of the CHC theory. The current model, based on factor analytic studies by Carroll (1993) and others, includes originality/creativity as a component of long-term storage and retrieval (G_{lr}). According to the most recent presentation of CHC (McGrew, 2009), "Some G_{lr} narrow abilities have been prominent in creativity research (e.g., production, ideational fluency, or associative fluency)" (p. 6). In the detailed description

1 We do not include discussion of the coincident set and disjoint set categories, which in our view are much less common compared to the other categories and do not reflect current, major lines of inquiry within the field.

of the model, this sentence is the only mention of creativity, originality, or divergent thinking. Fluid intelligence (G_f) is discussed in terms of its relationship to problem-solving and coping with novel problems (both considered to be highly related to creativity), yet the emphasis is on G_{lr}.

Martindale (1999) proposed a differential relationship between G_s (processing speed) and creativity. According to Martindale's theory, people who are creative are selective with their speed of information processing. Early in the creative problem-solving stage, they widen their breadth of attention, allowing a larger amount of information to be processed (and thereby lowering their speediness). Later, when the problem is better understood, their attention span is shortened and their reaction time is quicker. This theory is reminiscent of Sternberg's (1981) distinction between global and local planning: Brighter people spend more time in initial global planning so that later they do not have to spend as much time in local planning.

Some have argued that the current CHC model shortchanges creativity (J. C. Kaufman, 2009). Placing all references to creativity and originality under G_{lr} seems quite narrow. The ability to draw selectively on past experiences is essential for creating something new. But the connection between fluid intelligence and creativity is minimized in new conceptions of the model.

An intriguing and fairly recent perspective in this category is Sternberg's (1996, 1997, 1999; Sternberg et al., 2008) theory of successful intelligence. This theory comprises three "subtheories": a *componential subtheory*, which relates intelligence to the internal world of the individual; an *experiential subtheory*, which relates intelligence to both the external and the internal worlds of the individual; and a *contextual subtheory*, which relates intelligence to the external world of the individual. The componential subtheory specifies the mental mechanisms responsible for planning, carrying out, and evaluating intelligent behavior. The experiential subtheory expands on this definition by focusing on those important behaviors that involve either adjustment to relative novelty, automatization of information processing, or both. The contextual subtheory defines intelligent behavior as involving purposeful adaptation to, selection of, and shaping of real-world environments relevant to one's life (Sternberg et al., 2008).

The experiential subtheory is directly related to creativity. Sternberg's application of creativity assessments to admissions data increased prediction of college success beyond that obtained with standard admissions tests; in addition, ethnic-group differences were significantly reduced (Sternberg, 2006; Sternberg & the Rainbow Project Collaborators, 2006). Gardner's well-known theory of multiple intelligences (1999) does not specifically address creativity. However, his eight intelligences (interpersonal, intrapersonal, spatial, naturalistic, linguistic, logical-mathematical, bodily-kinesthetic, and musical) certainly seem to apply to creativity. Gardner (1993) used case studies of eminent creative individuals to argue that creative people can shine as a function of embodying different intelligences. For example, he selected Freud as an example of intrapersonal intelligence; Einstein to represent logical-mathematical intelligence; Picasso, spatial intelligence; Stravinsky, musical intelligence; T. S. Eliot, linguistic intelligence; Martha Graham, bodily-kinesthetic intelligence; and Gandhi, interpersonal intelligence (naturalistic intelligence had not been added at this time).

Theories of Creativity That Encompass Intelligence

Systems Theories

In recent years, there has been an emphasis on creativity theories that incorporate factors that are interrelated (Kozbelt, Beghetto, & Runco, 2010). Some of these theories emphasize issues such as the environment or evolution and are less relevant here. Other theories emphasize a confluence of different elements and include intellectual and cognitive abilities in the equation. One such theory is Sternberg and Lubart's (1996) "investment" theory of creativity, in which the key to being creative is to buy low and sell high in the world of ideas. In this model, a creative person is like a talented Wall Street investor. A successful creator will generate ideas that may be initially unpopular or underappreciated (as in buying stocks with low price-earnings ratios) yet will persist and convince others of the ideas' merits. The creator will then know when to move on to pursue other ideas (as in selling high, when one divests oneself of stocks).

According to this model, six main elements contribute to creativity: intelligence, knowledge, thinking styles, personality, motivation, and the environment. Intelligence contributes using three elements drawn from Sternberg's triarchic theory (1988, 1996; later expanded into the theory of successful intelligence).

The first element is synthetic ability, which is the ability to generate ideas that are novel, high in quality, and high in task appropriateness. Because creativity is viewed as an interaction between a person, a task, and an environment, what is novel, high in quality, or task appropriate may vary from one person, task, or environment to another. Central to this ability is being able to redefine problems. Creative people may take problems that other people see, or they themselves may previously have seen, in one way, and redefine the problems in a different way. This synthetic ability includes three knowledge-acquisition components. The first, selective encoding, involves distinguishing relevant from irrelevant information. Selective combination, the second, involves combining bits of relevant information in novel ways. Finally, selective comparison involves relating new information to old information in a novel way.

The second element, practical ability, is needed to communicate creative ideas to other people (i.e., "selling" an idea). Good ideas do not always sell themselves – the creative person needs to devise strategies for and expend effort in selling those ideas.

The third component, analytical ability, is often measured by traditional intelligence tests. Yet this component is also related to creativity, as a successful creator must be able to judge the value of his or her own ideas and decide which ones to pursue. Such analytical ability can be used to evaluate the strengths and weaknesses of the idea and determine the best steps to improve upon the idea. People who are high in synthetic ability but low in analytical ability may need someone else to evaluate and judge their work for them. People who are able incisively to evaluate their own work may be said to be high in metacognition (which is related to planning, a key component of Luria's model).

There has been some empirical work on the role of metacognitive abilities in creativity. Runco and colleagues (Runco & Dow, 2004; Runco & Smith, 1992) found that people who tended to produce more original responses also were better at rating their most original responses to a divergent-thinking task. Silvia (2008a) asked people to pick their best responses to a similar divergent-thinking task, and then examined whether they were more likely to choose responses that outside raters considered creative. Silvia found that people were able to discern their more creative responses – and that people who were more open to experience were more likely to choose accurately. Researching the extremely creative end of the spectrum, Kozbelt (2007) analyzed Beethoven's self-critiques and found that the great composer was a reasonably accurate rater of his own work.

Another theory that views creativity as a mix of different abilities is Amabile's (1982, 1996) componential model of creativity. She argued that three variables were needed for creativity to occur: domain-relevant skills, creativity-relevant skills, and task motivation. Domain-relevant skills include knowledge, technical skills, and specialized talent (i.e., a creative mathematician should know basic algebra and geometry). Creativity-relevant skills are personal factors that are associated with creativity. These skills include tolerance for ambiguity, self-discipline, and risk-taking. Finally, Amabile singles out one's motivation toward the task at hand. Intelligence would primarily occur at the domain-relevant skill level.

A third theory that accounts for multiple variables and also takes a domain-specific approach is the Amusement Park theory (Baer & Kaufman, 2005a, 2005b; Kaufman & Baer, 2005). In an amusement park there are *initial requirements* (e.g., a ticket) that apply to all areas of the park. Similarly, there are initial requirements that, to varying degrees, are necessary to creative performance in all domains. One such key initial requirement is intelligence. Amusement parks also have *general thematic areas* (e.g., at Disney World one might select among EPCOT or Disney-MGM Studios), just as there are several different general areas in which someone could be creative (e.g., the arts, science). Once in one type of park, there are sections (e.g., Fantasyland and Adventureland are all found in the Magic Kingdom), just as there are *domains* of creativity within larger *general thematic areas* (e.g., physics and biology are domains in the *general thematic area* of science). These domains in turn can be subdivided into *micro-domains* (e.g., in Fantasyland one might visit Cinderella's Castle or It's a Small World; in the domain of psychology, one might specialize in cognitive psychology or social psychology).

Cognitive Theories of Creativity

The other group of theories that includes intellectual abilities as a key component is the set of cognitive theories of creativity. Guilford, as discussed earlier, pioneered these ideas, and his convergent versus divergent thinking dichotomy is still a key idea in creativity. Even before Guilford, however, Wallas (1926) proposed a model of the cognitive creative process. According to his five-stage model, you first use *preparation* to begin work on a problem. Next, there is *incubation*, in which you may work on other things while your mind thinks about the problem. In *intimation*, you realize you are about to have a breakthrough (this phase is sometimes dropped from the model), and then you actually have the insight in the *illumination* phase. Finally, with *verification*, you actually test, develop, and use your ideas.

More recently, the Geneplore model has two phases, generative and explorative, that are comparable to Guilford's convergent and divergent thinking distinction. In the generative phase, someone constructs a preinventive structure, or a mental representation of a possible creative solution (Finke, Ward, & Smith, 1992). For example, Elias Howe was working on his invention of the modern sewing machine. He couldn't quite get the needle correctly designed. Howe had an odd dream in which he was chased by savages who threw spears at him. The spears had a circle loop at the end – and Howe realized that adding the circle (or an "eye") to the end of the needle was the solution he needed (Hartman, 2000). The image of a spear with a circle at the end – the image that preceded Howe's insight – would be an example of one of these preinventive structures. They don't need to be as dramatic or sudden as the realization based on Howe's dream. Indeed, the generation of preinventive structures is only one part of the creative process, according to the Geneplore model. The thinker must then explore these different preinventive structures within the constraints of the final goal. There may be several cycles before a creative work is produced.

Although the model focuses on the creative process, most tests of the model have actually measured the creative product. In an experiment testing the model, people were shown parts of objects (such as a circle or a cube). They were then asked to combine these parts together to produce a practical object or device. The creativity (and practicality) of the items was then assessed (e.g., Finke, 1990; Finke & Slayton, 1988). Interestingly, people produced more creative objects when they were told which parts had to be combined than when they could pick the parts to be combined.

Other theories have also focused on cognitive-oriented components of the creative process. Michael Mumford and his colleagues (Blair & Mumford, 2007; Mumford, Longergan, & Scott, 2002; Mumford,

Mobley, Uhlman, Reiter-Palmon, & Doares, 1991) have argued for an eight-part model, focusing on problem construction, information encoding, category selection, category combination and reorganization, idea generation, idea evaluation, implementation planning, and solution monitoring. Basadur, Runco, and Vega (2000) offer a simplified model centered around finding good problems, solving these problems, and then implementing these solutions. Mednick (1962, 1968) proposed the idea that creativity occurs when different elements are associated together to form new combinations. Creative individuals are assumed to be able to make meaningful, useful associations between disparate concepts and ideas to a greater extent than a relatively uncreative individual. The Remote Associates Test was developed based on this idea (Mednick & Mednick, 1967).

Overlapping Sets

The third category of theories includes conceptualizations in which the constructs of intelligence and creativity overlap but remain distinct, with one not subsuming the other. For example, Renzulli's (1978) three-ring conception of giftedness theorizes that giftedness – implicitly cast as high-level creative production – is caused by the overlap of high intellectual ability, creativity, and task commitment. From this perspective, creativity and intelligence are distinct constructs but overlap considerably under the right conditions. Renzulli distinguishes between two types of giftedness: schoolhouse (i.e., what would be measured by an ability or achievement test) and creative-production. Examples of his components of creativity include Guilford's divergent thinking components (fluency, flexibility, and originality), and being open to new experiences, curious, willing to take risks, and sensitive to aesthetic characteristics (Renzulli, 2002).

Another theory of intelligence that incorporates creativity is the PASS (Planning, Attention, Simultaneous, and Successive) cognitive processing theory based on the works of Luria (see Das, Naglieri, & Kirby, 1994, for an overview). Like the CHC model, Luria's model is frequently applied to intelligence tests. Luria's (1966, 1970, 1973) original neuropsychological model featured three Blocks or functional units. The first unit is responsible for focused and sustained attention. The second functional unit receives and stores information with both simultaneous and successive (or sequential) processing. Simultaneous processing involves integrating chunks of information together, largely in parallel; chunks are synthesized together simultaneously, much as one might appreciate a painting all at once. Successive processing is interpreting chunks of information separately, in sequential fashion, much as when one listens to a news broadcast reporting successive stories.

The third functional unit is responsible for planning, decision making, and self-monitoring behavior. It is this last ability, planning, that has been hypothesized to be related to creativity (Naglieri & Kaufman, 2001). For example, in a study of cognitive styles and creativity, the cognitive style emphasizing planning (called, appropriately enough, "the planner") was strongly linked to creative productivity (Guastello, Shissler, Driscoll, & Hyde, 1998). Also, people who spent time planning and replanning a project were more productive and more creative (Redmund, Mumford, & Teach, 1993).

Theories on How Intelligence and Creativity Are Related

The threshold theory argues that intelligence is a necessary but not a sufficient condition of creativity (Barron, 1969; Yamamoto, 1964). According to this view, creativity and intelligence are positively correlated up until an IQ of approximately 120; in people with higher IQs, the two constructs are said to show little relationship (e.g., Barron, 1963; Getzels & Jackson, 1962; Richards, 1976). The interference hypothesis suggests that very high levels of intelligence may interfere with creativity (Simonton, 1994; Sternberg, 1996).

Runco (2007) offers an interesting, alternative view of the threshold concept. He argues that traditional investigations of the creativity-intelligence relationship may be ignoring the presence of heteroscedasticity – the idea that levels of creativity may vary considerably at different levels of intelligence. Acknowledging that a minimal level of intelligence is probably necessary for optimal creative contributions, Runco notes research (e.g., Hollingworth, 1942) suggesting that people with extremely high IQs often exhibit low levels of creativity.

Empirical Work on Intelligence and Creativity

Most studies that investigate creativity and intelligence use divergent-thinking tests (such as the TTCT) or other related paper-and-pencil tests also scored for fluency, originality, or other divergent thinking-related methods of scoring (e.g., Plucker, 1999). The studies have generally found that creativity is significantly associated with psychometric measures of intelligence (especially verbally oriented measures, regardless of the type of creativity measured). This relationship is typically not a particularly strong one (Barron & Harrington, 1981; Kim, 2005; Wallach & Kogan, 1965), although Silvia (2008a, 2008b) argued that the relationship between the latent constructs of creativity and intelligence is underestimated because the analyses only look at observable scores (i.e., performance on an intelligence test). If it were possible to get a "true" measure of the constructs, there might be a higher relationship.

Most of these studies reinforce the threshold theory discussed earlier (e.g., Fuchs-Beauchamp, Karnes, & Johnson, 1993; Getzels & Jackson, 1962), but the threshold theory has come under fire. Runco and Albert (1986) found that the nature of the relationship was dependent on the measures used and the populations tested. Preckel, Holling, and Weise (2006) looked at measures of fluid intelligence and creativity (as measured through divergent thinking tests) and found modest correlations across all levels of intellectual abilities. Wai, Lubinski, and Benbow (2005), in a longitudinal study of gifted (top 1%) 13-year-olds, found that differences in SAT scores – even within such an elite group – predicted creative accomplishments 20 years later. Park, Lubinski, and Benbow (2007) examined intellectual patterns of ability and eventual creativity in different domains. Using math and verbal SAT scores of people at age 13, they then tracked the accomplishments of these same people 25 years later. Unsurprisingly, early prowess was associated with eventual success. However, a person's specific strengths (in this case, math vs. verbal) predicted patents (math) and literary publications (verbal). Park, Lubinski, and Benbow (2008) further extended their findings to demonstrate this link in the fields of science and technology. Kim (2005), in a meta-analysis of 21 studies, found virtually no support for the threshold theory, with small positive correlations found at all levels of ability between several different measures of intelligence and creativity.

It is notable, however, that nearly all of these studies do not use traditional, individually administered intelligence tests. In Kim's (2005) meta-analysis, many of the studies were more than 30 years old and, therefore, were conducted using intelligence tests that do not reflect current theories of intelligence. In addition, most of the studies used group intelligence tests. Although group intelligence tests serve a strong purpose in research studies, they are not used by most school psychologists for psychoeducational assessment (A. S. Kaufman & Lichtenberger, 2006).

One of the few research studies to use an individually administered, modern IQ test was Sligh, Conners, and Roskos-Ewoldsen (2005), who used the Kaufman Adolescent and Adult Intelligence Scale (Kaufman & Kaufman, 1993) and a creative invention task (in which people would use shapes to create a possible object, and then name and describe their invention; see Finke, 1990). Sligh et al. (2005) delved deeper into the intelligence-creativity relationship by specifically examining the relationship between Gf (novel problem solving) and

Gc (acquired knowledge) and a measure of actual creative innovation. Gc showed the same moderate and positive relationship to creativity as past studies, mentioned previously; in contrast, Gf showed the opposite pattern. Measured intelligence and creativity were significantly correlated for the high IQ group, but they were not significantly correlated for people with average IQs. This finding implies that students who receive high Gf scores may be more likely to be creative than students who receive high Gc scores.

The Sligh et al. study also addresses a second major weakness in this line of research: the overreliance on divergent thinking measures as the sole assessment of creativity. Few studies have been conducted that include measures of creative personality, creative products, and creative processes (other than divergent thinking).

An interesting suggestion posed by Batey and Furnham (2006) is that the role of Gf and Gc in creativity may shift across the life span of a creative person. Gf, they argue, might be more important in early stages of a career. Conversely, a later-career creator may rely more on Gc – and, we might postulate, Glr.

Given the existing studies, what do all of these results mean? Few studies contradict the idea that creative people tend to be fairly smart, and smart people are usually somewhat creative. But some of the tested-and-true ideas about the specific relationship are still unclear. If the threshold theory is correct, then there may be a certain point at which being smart stops helping creativity; recent psychometric studies, however, call the existence of the threshold effect into question. Given all of the weaknesses of this area of study, the threshold theory may be best viewed as largely untested.

Conclusion

Intelligence is strongly valued in schools, and extensive and popular measures are often used to measure it. There are usually hundreds of empirical studies about each intelligence test. Creativity may be theoretically desired in school, but it is often considered less important than intelligence; some teachers may even dislike creative students (Westby & Dawson, 1995). Creativity assessment is murkier than intellectual assessment. The Torrance Tests remain the most-used creativity tests despite extensive critiques (Kaufman et al., 2008).

Each of the five possible relationships in Sternberg's framework enjoys at least some empirical support (Sternberg & O'Hara, 1999), but the difficulty in interpreting empirical results illustrates the problems associated with reaching a consensus on the validity of any of these five relations (see Hattie & Rogers, 1986). For example, Haensly and Reynolds (1989) believe that Mednick's (1962) association theory supports the creativity as a subset of intelligence position, yet Sternberg and O'Hara (1999) feel that this body of work supports the overlapping sets position. In another example, if Gardner's work with creativity had come before his work with MI theory, we would be tempted to argue that his efforts fall within the intelligence as a subset of creativity category.

From our perspective, the complexity of possible intelligence-creativity relationships is not surprising. Whenever one compares two constructs, the way in which each construct is conceptualized and assessed will have a significant impact on any empirical results. Researchers and theorists do not believe that intelligence and creativity are completely orthogonal, but beyond that, the exact nature of that relationship remains an open question. The basic need for both creativity and intelligence, however, remains undisputed.

References

Amabile, T. M. (1982). Social psychology of creativity: A consensual assessment technique. *Journal of Personality and Social Psychology, 43*, 997–1013.

Amabile, T. M. (1996). *Creativity in context: Update to "The Social Psychology of Creativity."* Boulder, CO: Westview Press.

Baer, J., & Kaufman, J. C. (2005a). Bridging generality and specificity: The Amusement Park Theoretical (APT) model of creativity. *Roeper Review*, 27, 158–163.

Baer, J., & Kaufman, J. C. (2005b). Whence creativity? Overlapping and dual aspect skills and traits. In J. C. Kaufman & J. Baer (Eds.), *Creativity across domains: Faces of the muse* (pp. 313–320). Hillsdale, NJ: Erlbaum.

Batey, M., & Furnham, A. (2006). Creativity, intelligence and personality: A critical review of the scattered literature. *Genetic, Social, and General Psychology Monographs*, 132, 355–429.

Barron, F. (1963). *Creativity and psychological health*. Princeton, NJ: D. Van Nostrand.

Barron, F. (1969). *Creative person and creative process*. New York, NY: Holt, Rinehart & Winston.

Barron, F., & Harrington, D. M. (1981). Creativity, intelligence, and personality. *Annual Review of Psychology*, 32, 439–476.

Basadur, M. S., Runco, M. A., & Vega, L. A. (2000). Understanding how creative thinking skills, attitudes and behaviors work together: A causal process model. *Journal of Creative Behavior*, 34, 77–100.

Beghetto, R. A. (2006). Creative justice? The relationship between prospective teachers' prior schooling experiences and perceived importance of promoting student creativity. *Journal of Creative Behavior*, 40, 149–162.

Beghetto, R. A. (2007). Does creativity have a place in classroom discussions? Prospective teachers' response preferences. *Thinking Skills and Creativity*, 2, 1–9. doi:10.1016/j.tsc.2006.09.002.

Blair, C. S., & Mumford, M. D. (2007). Errors in idea evaluation: Preference for the unoriginal? *Journal of Creative Behavior*, 41, 197–222.

Brandau, H., Daghofer, F., Hollerer, L., Kaschnitz, W., Kirchmair, G., Krammer, I., & Schlagbauer, A. (2007). The relationship between creativity, teacher ratings on behavior, age, and gender in pupils from seven to ten years. *Journal of Creative Behavior*, 41, 91–113.

Cattell, R. B., & Butcher, H. (1968). *The prediction of achievement and creativity*. Indianapolis, IN: Bobbs-Merrill.

Carroll, J. B. (1993). *Human cognitive abilities: A survey of factor-analytic studies*. New York, NY: Cambridge University Press.

Das, J. P., Naglieri, J. A., & Kirby, J. R. (1994). *Assessment of cognitive processes: The PASS theory of intelligence*. Boston: Allyn & Bacon.

Finke, R. (1990). *Creative imagery: Discoveries and inventions in visualization*. Hillsdale, NJ: Erlbaum.

Finke, R. A., & Slayton, K. (1988). Explorations of creative visual synthesis in mental imagery. *Memory & Cognition*, 16, 252–257.

Finke, R. A., Ward T. B., & Smith, S. M. (1992). *Creative cognition: Theory, research, and applications*. Cambridge, MA: MIT Press.

Flanagan, D. P., & Ortiz, S. O. (2002). Best practices in intellectual assessment: Future directions. In A. Thomas & J. Grimes (Eds.), *Best practices in school psychology IV* (pp. 1351–1372).Washington, DC: National Association of School Psychologists.

Fuchs-Beauchamp, K. D., Karnes, M. B., & Johnson, L. J. (1993). Creativity and intelligence in preschoolers. *Gifted Child Quarterly*, 37, 113–117.

Gardner, H. (1993). *Creating minds*. New York, NY: Basic Books.

Gardner, H. (1999). *Intelligence reframed: Multiple intelligences for the 21st century*. New York, NY: Basic Books.

Getzels, J. W., & Jackson, P. W. (1962). *Creativity and intelligence: Explorations with gifted students*. New York, NY: Wiley.

Guilford, J. P. (1950). Creativity. *American Psychologist*, 5, 444–454.

Guilford, J. P. (1967). *The nature of human intelligence*. New York, NY: McGraw-Hill.

Guilford, J. P. (1988). Some changes in the Structure-of-Intellect Model. *Educational and Psychological Measurements*, 48, 1–4.

Guastello, S. J., Shissler, J., Driscoll, J., & Hyde, T. (1998). Are some cognitive styles more creatively productive than others? *Journal of Creative Behavior*, 32, 77–91.

Hartman, E. (2000). *Dreams and nightmares: The origin and meaning of dreams*. New York, NY: Perseus.

Haensly, P. A., & Reynolds, C. R. (1989). Creativity and intelligence. In J. A. Glover, R. R. Ronning, & C. R. Reynolds (Eds.), *Handbook of creativity* (pp. 111–132). New York: Plenum Press.

Hattie, J., & Rogers, H. J. (1986). Factor models for assessing the relation between creativity and intelligence. *Journal of Educational Psychology*, 78, 482–485.

Hayes, J. R. (1989). Cognitive processes in creativity. In J. A. Glover, R. R. Ronning, & C. R. Reynolds (Eds.), *Handbook of creativity* (pp. 135–145). New York: Plenum Press.

Hollingworth, L. S. (1942). *Children above 180 IQ (Stanford-Binet): Origin and development.* Yonkers-on-Hudson, NY: World Book.

Horn, J. L., & Cattell, R. B. (1966). Refinement and test of theory of fluid and crystallized intelligence. *Journal of Educational Psychology, 57*, 253–270.

Kaufman, A. S. (2009). *IQ Testing 101.* New York, NY: Springer.

Kaufman, J. C. (2009). *Creativity 101.* New York, NY: Springer.

Kaufman, A. S., & Kaufman, N. L. (1993). *Kaufman Adolescent and Adult Intelligence Test (KAIT).* Circle Pines, MN: American Guidance Service.

Kaufman, A. S., & Lichtenberger, E. O. (2006). *Assessing adolescent and adult intelligence* (3rd ed.). New York, NY: Wiley.

Kaufman, J. C., & Baer, J. (2005). The amusement park theory of creativity. In J. C. Kaufman & J. Baer (Eds.), *Creativity across domains: Faces of the muse* (pp. 321–328). Hillsdale, NJ: Erlbaum.

Kaufman, J. C., Plucker, J. A., & Baer, J. (2008). *Essentials of creativity assessment.* New York, NY: Wiley.

Kim, K. H. (2005). Can only intelligent people be creative? *Journal of Secondary Gifted Education, 16*, 57–66.

Kozbelt, A. (2007). A quantitative analysis of Beethoven as self-critic: Implications for psychological theories of musical creativity. *Psychology of Music, 35*, 147–172.

Kozbelt, A., Beghetto, R. A., & Runco, M. A. (2010). Theories of creativity. In J. C. Kaufman & R. J. Sternberg (Eds.), *Cambridge handbook of creativity* (pp. 20–47). Cambridge, NY: Cambridge University Press.

Luria, A. R. (1966). *Human brain and psychological processes.* New York, NY: Harper & Row.

Luria, A. R. (1970). The functional organization of the brain. *Scientific American, 222*, 66–78.

Luria, A. R. (1973). *The working brain: An introduction to neuropsychology.* London, UK: Penguin.

Martindale, C. (1999). Biological bases of creativity. In R. J. Sternberg (Ed.), *Handbook of creativity* (pp. 137–152). New York, NY: Cambridge University Press.

McGrew, K. S. (2009). CHC theory and the human cognitive abilities project: Standing on the shoulders of the giants of psychometric intelligence research. *Intelligence, 37*, 1–10.

Mednick, S. A. (1962). The associative basis of the creative process. *Psychological Review, 69*, 220–232.

Mednick, S. A. (1968). The Remote Associates Test. *Journal of Creative Behavior, 2*, 213–214.

Mednick, S. A., & Mednick, M. T. (1967). *Examiner's manual: Remote Associates Test.* Boston, MA: Houghton Mifflin.

Meeker, M. N. (1969). *The structure of intellect: Its interpretation and uses.* Columbus, OH: Merrill.

Mumford, M. D., Lonergan, D. C., & Scott, G. M. (2002). Evaluating creative ideas: Processes, standards, and context. *Inquiry: Critical Thinking Across the Disciplines, 22*, 21–30.

Mumford, M. D., Mobley, M. I., Uhlman, C. E., Reiter-Palmon, R., & Doares, L. M. (1991). Process analytic models of creative capacities. *Creativity Research Journal, 4*, 91–122.

Naglieri, J. A., & Kaufman, J. C. (2001). Understanding intelligence, giftedness, and creativity using PASS theory. *Roeper Review, 23*, 151–156.

Park, G., Lubinski, D., & Benbow, C. P. (2007). Contrasting intellectual patterns predict creativity in the arts and sciences. *Psychological Science, 18*, 948–952.

Park, G., Lubinski, D., & Benbow, C. P. (2008). Ability differences among people who have commensurate degrees matter for scientific creativity. *Psychological Science, 19*, 957–961.

Plucker, J. A. (1999). Is the proof in the pudding? Reanalyses of Torrance's (1958 to present) longitudinal study data. *Creativity Research Journal, 12*, 103–114.

Plucker, J. A., Beghetto, R. A., & Dow, G. (2004). Why isn't creativity more important to educational psychologists? Potential, pitfalls, and future directions in creativity research. *Educational Psychologist, 39*, 83–96.

Plucker, J. A., & Renzulli, J. S. (1999). Psychometric approaches to the study of human creativity. In R. J. Sternberg (Ed.), *Handbook of creativity* (pp. 35–60). New York, NY: Cambridge University Press.

Preckel, F., Holling, H., & Wiese, M. (2006). Relationship of intelligence and creativity in gifted and non-gifted students: An investigation of threshold theory. *Personality and Individual Differences, 40*, 159–170.

Renzulli, J. S. (1973). *New directions in creativity.* New York: Harper & Row.

Renzulli, J. S. (1978). What makes giftedness? Reexamining a definition. *Phi Delta Kappan, 60*, 180–261.

Renzulli, J. S. (1986). The three-ring conception of giftedness: A developmental model for creative productivity. In R. J. Sternberg & J. Davidson (Eds.), *Conceptions of giftedness* (pp. 53–92). New York, NY: Cambridge University Press.

Renzulli, J. S. (2002). Expanding the conception of giftedness to include co-cognitive traits and to promote social capital. *Phi Delta Kappan, 84*, 33–58.

Redmond, M. R., Mumford, M. D., & Teach, R. (1993). Putting creativity to work: Effects of leader behavior on subordinate creativity. *Organizational Behavior and Human Decision Processes, 55*, 120–151.

Richards, R. L. (1976). A comparison of selected Guilford and Wallach Kogan creative thinking tests in conjunction with measures of intelligence. *Journal of Creative Behavior, 10*, 151–164.

Roid, G. H. (2003). *Stanford-Binet Intelligence Scales, Fifth Edition: Technical manual*. Itasca, IL: Riverside.

Runco, M. A. (2007). *Creativity. Theories and themes: Research, development, and practice*. San Diego, CA: Elsevier Academic Press.

Runco, M. A., & Albert, R. S. (1986). The threshold theory regarding creativity and intelligence: An empirical test with gifted and nongifted children. *Creative Child & Adult Quarterly, 11*, 212–218.

Runco, M. A., & Dow, G. T. (2004). Assessing the accuracy of judgments of originality on three divergent thinking tests. *Korean Journal of Thinking & Problem Solving, 14*, 5–14.

Runco, M. A., & Smith, W. R. (1992). Interpersonal and intrapersonal evaluations of creative ideas. *Personality and Individual Differences, 13*, 295–302.

Silvia, P. J. (2008a). Another look at creativity and intelligence: Exploring higher-order models and probable confounds. *Personality and Individual Differences, 44*, 1012–1021.

Silvia, P. J. (2008b). Creativity and intelligence revisited: A latent variable analysis of Wallach and Kogan (1965). *Creativity Research Journal, 20*, 34–39.

Simonton, D. K. (1994). *Greatness: Who makes history and why*. New York, NY: Guilford Press.

Sligh, A. C., Conners, F. A., & Roskos-Ewoldsen, B. (2005). Relation of creativity to fluid and crystallized intelligence. *Journal of Creative Behavior, 39*, 123–136.

Sternberg, R. J. (1981). Intelligence and nonentrenchment. *Journal of Educational Psychology, 73*, 1–16.

Sternberg, R. J. (1988). A three-facet model of creativity. In R. J. Sternberg (Ed.), *The nature of creativity* (pp. 125–147). New York, NY: Cambridge University Press.

Sternberg, R. J. (1996). *Successful intelligence*. New York, NY: Simon & Schuster.

Sternberg, R. J. (1997). *Successful intelligence*, NY. New York: Plume.

Sternberg, R. J. (1999). The theory of successful intelligence. *Review of General Psychology, 3*, 292–316.

Sternberg, R. J. (2003). *WICS: Wisdom, intelligence, and creativity, synthesized*. Cambridge, UK: Cambridge University Press.

Sternberg, R. J. (2006). Creating a vision of creativity: The first 25 years. *Psychology of Aesthetics, Creativity, and the Arts, S*, 2–12.

Sternberg, R. J. (2008). Applying psychological theories to educational practice. *American Educational Research Journal, 45*, 150–165.

Sternberg, R. J., Kaufman, J. C., & Grigorenko, E. L. (2008). *Applied intelligence*. Cambridge, UK: Cambridge University Press.

Sternberg, R. J., & Lubart, T. I. (1996). *Defying the crowd*. New York, NY: Free Press.

Sternberg, R. J., & O'Hara, L. A. (1999). Creativity and intelligence. In R. J. Sternberg (Ed.), *Handbook of creativity* (pp. 251–272). Cambridge, UK: Cambridge University Press.

Sternberg, R. J., & the Rainbow Project Collaborators. (2006). The Rainbow Project: Enhancing the SAT through assessment of analytical, practical and creative skills. *Intelligence, 34*, 321–350.

Torrance, E. P. (1974a). *Torrance Test of Creative Thinking: Directions manual and scoring guide*. Verbal test booklet A. Bensenville, IL: Scholastic Testing Service.

Torrance, E. P. (1974b). *Torrance Test of Creative Thinking: Norms-technical manual*. Bensenville, IL: Scholastic Testing Service.

Wai, J., Lubinski, D., & Benbow, C. P. (2005). Creativity and occupational accomplishments among intellectually precocious youths: An age 13 to age 33 longitudinal study. *Journal of Educational Psychology, 97*, 484–492.

Wallach, M. A., & Kogan, N. (1965). *Modes of thinking in young children: A study of the creativity-intelligence distinction*. New York, NY: Holt, Rinehart and Winston.

Wallas, G. (1926). *The art of thought*. New York, NY: Harcourt Brace.

Westby, E. L., & Dawson, V. L. (1995). Creativity: Asset or burden in the classroom? *Creativity Research Journal, 8*, 1–10.

Woodcock, R. W., McGrew, K. S., & Mather, N. (2001). *Woodcock-Johnson III*. Itasca, IL: Riverside.

Yamamoto, K. (1964). Creativity and sociometric choice among adolescents. *Journal of Social Psychology, 64*, 249–261.

CHAPTER 39

Intelligence and Rationality

Keith E. Stanovich, Richard F. West, and Maggie E. Toplak

Intelligence tests are often treated as if they encompassed all cognitive abilities. Our goal in this chapter is to challenge this assumption by showing that an important class of cognitive skills is missing from commonly used intelligence tests. We accomplish this by showing that intelligence, narrowly defined by what intelligence tests measure, fails to encompass rational thinking. In this chapter we will (1) define the concept of rational thought; (2) show how its components could be measured; (3) show how its components are not assessed on traditional tests of intelligence; and (4) demonstrate why intelligence is a very imperfect correlate of rational thought.

One way of understanding the difference between rationality and intelligence is to do a little analysis of a phenomenon we have all observed: smart people acting stupidly. In analyzing this phenomenon, we need first to ask ourselves whether this expression makes any sense. For example, Robert Sternberg once edited a book titled *Why Smart People Can Be So Stupid* (2002b), considered the logic of the title of his volume, and found it wanting! A typical dictionary definition of the adjectival form of the word smart is "characterized by sharp quick thought; bright" or "having or showing quick intelligence or ready mental capacity." Thus, being smart seems much like being intelligent, according to the dictionary. Sternberg (2002a) points out that the same dictionaries tell us that a stupid person is "slow to learn or understand; lacking or marked by lack of intelligence." Thus, if a smart person is intelligent and stupid means a lack of intelligence and, by the law of contradiction, someone cannot be intelligent and not intelligent, then the "smart people being stupid" phrase seems to make no sense.

But if we look at the secondary definitions of the term, we see what is motivating the phrase "smart but acting stupid." The second definition of the word stupid in Dictionary.com is "tending to make poor decisions or careless mistakes" – a phrase that attenuates the sense of contradiction. A similar thing happens if we analyze the word dumb to see if the phrase, "smart but acting dumb," makes sense. The primary definition describes dumb as the antonym of intelligent, again leading to a contradiction. But in phrases referring to decisions or actions such as "what a dumb thing to do!" we see a secondary definition similar to that of stupid: tending to make poor decisions. These phrases pick out a particular meaning of "stupid" or "dumb" – albeit not the primary one.

For this reason, Sternberg (2002a) suggested that a better phrasing for these examples is that they represent smart people acting foolishly. Perkins (1995, 2002) likewise prefers the term "folly" to characterize what is being described in these examples. A foolish person is a person "lacking good sense or judgment; showing a lack of sense; unwise; without judgment or discretion." This definition picks out the aspect of "stupid" and "dumb" that we wish to focus on here – the aspect that refers not to intelligence (general mental "brightness"), but instead to the tendency to make judicious decisions (or, rather, injudicious ones).

We are not at all concerned with arguing about the terminology here. However we phrase it – "smart but acting dumb," "smart but acting foolish," or whatever – it is only essential that the phrase pick out the phenomenon that we are discussing: intelligent people taking injudicious actions or holding unjustified beliefs. But there is one more problem here. Some conceptualizations of intelligence define it, at least in part, as the ability to adapt to one's environment by making judicious decisions (Neisser et al., 1996; Sternberg & Detterman, 1986). Thus, we are right back at the problem of contradiction again. If we are concerned with cases where intelligent people make foolish decisions (decisions that do not serve their goals), and intelligence is in part the tendency to make decisions that serve one's goals, then we have a contradiction – smart people can't *possibly* have the (general) tendency to act foolishly. We should stress here that we are speaking of a *systematic* pattern of irrational actions – not a single, isolated instance of irrational thought or action.

What is happening here is that we are bumping up against an old controversy in the study of cognitive ability – the distinction between broad and narrow theories of intelligence. Broad theories include aspects of functioning that are captured by the *vernacular* term intelligence (adaptation to the environment, showing wisdom and creativity, etc.) whether or not these aspects are actually measured by existing tests of intelligence. Narrow theories, in contrast, confine the concept of intelligence to the set of mental abilities actually tested on extant IQ tests. Narrow theories adopt the operationalization of the term that is used in psychometric studies of intelligence, neurophysiological studies using brain imaging, and studies of brain disorder. This definition involves a statistical abstraction from performance on established tests and cognitive ability indicators. It yields a scientific concept of general intelligence usually symbolized by *g* or, in cases where the fluid/crystallized theory is adopted, Gf and Gc. The latter theory is sometimes termed the Cattell/Horn/Carroll (CHC) theory of intelligence (Carroll, 1993; Cattell, 1963, 1998; Horn & Cattell, 1967). The theory posits that tests of mental ability tap a small number of broad factors, of which two are dominant. Fluid intelligence (Gf) reflects reasoning abilities operating across a variety of domains – including novel ones. It is measured by tests of abstract thinking such as figural analogies, Raven Matrices, and series completion. Crystallized intelligence (Gc) reflects declarative knowledge acquired from acculturated learning experiences. It is measured by vocabulary tasks, verbal comprehension, and general knowledge assessments. Ackerman (1996) discusses how the two dominant factors in the CHC theory reflect a long history of considering two aspects of intelligence: intelligence-as-process (Gf) and intelligence-as-knowledge (Gc).

The narrow view of intelligence then takes these operationally defined constructs – *g*, Gf, Gc – and validates them in studies of brain injury, educational attainment, cognitive neuroscience, developmental trends, and information processing. These constructs of the narrow theory are grounded in the types of mental abilities measured on traditional tests of intelligence. Critics of intelligence tests are eager to point out that the tests ignore important parts of mental life – many largely noncognitive domains such as socioemotional abilities, empathy, and interpersonal skills, for example. However, a tacit assumption in such critiques is that although intelligence tests miss certain key noncognitive areas, they do encompass most of what is important in the cognitive domain. It is just this unstated assumption that we wish to challenge. Instead, we wish to argue that intelligence tests are radically incomplete as measures of *cognitive* functioning – in addition to whatever they fail to assess in noncognitive domains.

When laypeople think of individual differences in reasoning they think of IQ tests. It is quite natural that this is their primary associate, because IQ tests are among the most publicized products of psychological research. This association is not entirely inaccurate either, because intelligence – as measured using IQ-like instruments – is correlated with performance on a host of reasoning tasks (Ackerman, Kyllonen, & Roberts, 1999; Carroll, 1993; Deary, 2000, 2001; Flynn, 2007; Lohman, 2000; Lubinski, 2004; Sternberg, 1977, 1985). Nonetheless, a major theme of this chapter will be that certain very important classes of individual differences in thinking are ignored if only intelligence-related variance is the primary focus. A number of these ignored classes of individual differences are those relating to rational thought. Thus, in our cognitive framework, which employs the narrow view of intelligence, the notion of smart people acting stupidly becomes completely explicable.

In this chapter we will argue that intelligence-related individual differences in thinking are largely the result of differences at the algorithmic level of cognitive control. Intelligence tests thus largely fail to tap processes at the reflective level of cognitive control. Because understanding rational behavior necessitates understanding processes operating at both levels, an exclusive focus on intelligence-related individual differences will tend to obscure important differences in human thinking. We will begin by explicating the difference between the algorithmic and reflective level of processing as they are understood in contemporary dual-process theories of cognition.

Dual Process Models of Cognition

Evidence from cognitive neuroscience and cognitive psychology is converging on the conclusion that the functioning of the brain can be characterized by two different types of cognition having somewhat different functions and different strengths and weaknesses (Evans, 1984, 2006, 2008; Evans & Frankish, 2009; Kahneman & Frederick, 2002; Sloman, 1996, 2002; Stanovich, 2004, 2009). The wide variety of converging evidence for this conclusion is indicated by the fact that theorists in a diverse set of specialty areas (including cognitive psychology, social psychology, cognitive neuroscience, and decision theory) have proposed that there are both Type 1 and Type 2 processes in the brain (e.g., Brainerd & Reyna, 2001; Feldman Barrett, Tugade, & Engle, 2004; Frank, Cohen, & Sanfey, 2009; Haidt, 2001; McClure, Laibson, Loewenstein, & Cohen, 2004; Metcalfe & Mischel, 1999; Prado & Noveck, 2007; Smith & Decoster, 2000). Type 1 processing is fast and automatic heuristic processing. Type 2 is, slow, analytic, and computationally expensive.

There are many such theories (over 20 dual-process theories are presented in a table in Stanovich, 2004) and they have some subtle differences, but they are similar in that all distinguish autonomous from nonautonomous processing. The two types of processing were termed systems in earlier writings, but theorists have been moving toward more atheoretical characterizations, so we shall follow Evans (2009) in using the terms Type 1 and Type 2 processing.

The defining feature of Type 1 processing is its autonomy. Type 1 processes are termed autonomous because (1) their execution is rapid, (2) their execution is mandatory when the triggering stimuli are encountered, (3) they do not put a heavy load on central processing capacity (i.e., they do not require conscious attention), (4) they are not dependent on input from high-level control systems, and (5) they can operate in parallel without interfering with themselves or with Type 2 processing. Type 1 processing would include behavioral regulation by the emotions; the encapsulated modules for solving specific adaptive problems that have been posited by evolutionary psychologists; processes of implicit learning; and the automatic firing of overlearned associations (see Evans, 2007, 2008; Stanovich, 2004, 2009). Type 1 processing, because of its computational ease, is a common processing default.

In contrast, Type 2 processing is relatively slow and computationally expensive – it is the focus of our awareness. And what we can attend to – be aware of – is limited. We call it "*paying* attention" for a reason: Attention is a limited resource and it has costs in terms of available computational power. Many Type 1 processes can operate at once in parallel, but only one (or a very few) Type 2 thoughts can be executed at once. Type 2 processing is thus serial processing, and it is what psychologists call controlled processing. It is the type of processing going on when we talk of things like "conscious problem solving."

Although either Type 1 or Type 2 processing can lead to rational behavior, most individual differences in rational thought result from variation in Type 2 processing. In fact, one of the most critical functions of Type 2 processing is to override Type 1 processing. Type 1 processing (processes of emotional regulation, Darwinian modules, associative and implicit learning processes) can be overgeneralized and produce responses that are irrational in a particular context if not overridden. In order to override Type 1 processing, Type 2 processing must display at least two (possibly related) capabilities. One is the capability of interrupting Type 1 processing and suppressing its response tendencies. Type 2 processing thus involves inhibitory mechanisms of the type that have been the focus of work on executive functioning (e.g., Hasher, Lustig, & Zacks, 2007; Kane & Engle, 2003; Miyake, Friedman, Emerson, & Witzki, 2000; Salthouse, Atkinson, & Berish, 2003; Zelazo, 2004).

However, the ability to suppress Type 1 processing gets the job only half done. Suppressing one response is not helpful unless a better response is available to substitute for it. Where do these better responses come from? One answer is that they come from processes of hypothetical reasoning and cognitive simulation that are a unique aspect of Type 2 processing (Evans, 2007; Evans & Over, 2004; Kahneman & Tversky, 1982; Nichols & Stich, 2003; Suddendorf & Corballis, 2007). When we reason hypothetically, we create temporary models of the world and test out actions (or alternative causes) in that simulated world. In order to reason hypothetically we must, however, have one critical cognitive capability – the ability to distinguish our representations of the real world from representations of imaginary situations. For example, when considering an alternative goal state different from the one we currently have, we must be able to represent our current goal and the alternative goal and to keep straight which is which. Likewise, we need to be able to differentiate the representation of an action about to be taken from representations of potential *alternative* actions we are considering. The latter must not infect the former while the mental simulation is being carried out.

In a much-cited article, Leslie (1987) modeled pretense by positing a so-called secondary representation (see Perner, 1991) that was a copy of the primary representation but that was decoupled from the world so that it could be manipulated – that is, be a mechanism for simulation. The important issue for our purposes is that decoupling secondary representations from the world and then maintaining the decoupling while simulation is carried out is a Type 2 processing operation. It is computationally taxing and greatly restricts the ability to conduct any other Type 2 operation simultaneously. In fact, decoupling operations might well be a major contributor to a distinctive Type 2 property – its seriality.

Figure 39.1 represents a preliminary model of mind, based on what we have outlined thus far. We have said that by taking offline early representations triggered by

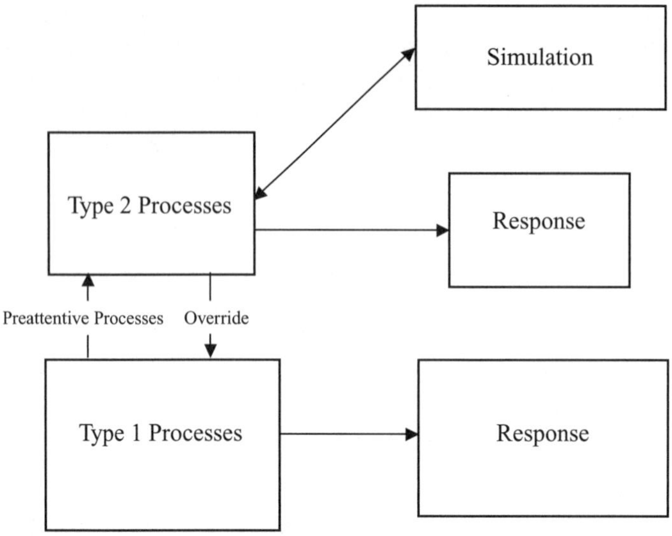

Figure 39.1. A preliminary dual-process model. Reprinted from *What Intelligence Tests Miss: The Psychology of Rational Thought* by Keith E. Stanovich, courtesy of Yale University Press.

Type 1 processing, we can often optimize our actions. Type 2 processing (slow, serial, computationally expensive) is needed to inhibit Type 1 processing and to sustain the cognitive decoupling needed to carry out processes of imagination whereby alternative responses are simulated in temporary models of the world. The figure shows the override function we have been discussing, as well as the Type 2 process of simulation. Also rendered in the figure is an arrow indicating that Type 2 processes receive inputs from Type 1 computations. These so-called preattentive processes fix the content of most Type 2 processing (see Evans, 2009).

Three Kinds of Minds and Two Kinds of Individual Differences

In 1996, philosopher Daniel Dennett wrote a book about how some aspects of the human mind were like the minds of other animals and how other aspects were not. He titled the book *Kinds of Minds* to suggest that within the brains of humans are control systems of very different types – different kinds of minds. In the spirit of Dennett, we will here make a "kinds of minds" distinction between aspects of Type 2 processing in terms of levels of control. The distinction is best understood by analogy to the different levels of explanation in two imaginary stories:

> *Both stories involve a lady walking on a cliff. The stories are both sad – the lady dies in each. The purpose of this exercise is to get us to think about how we explain the death in each story. In incident A, a woman is walking on a cliffside by the ocean and goes to step on a large rock, but the rock is not a rock at all. Instead, it is actually the side of a crevice and she falls down the crevice and dies. In incident B, a woman attempts suicide by jumping off an ocean cliff and dies when she is crushed on the rocks below.*

In both cases, at the most basic level, when we ask ourselves for an explanation of why the woman died, we might say that the answer is the same. The same laws of physics in operation in incident A (the gravitational laws that describe why the woman will be crushed upon impact) are also operative in incident B. However, we feel that the laws of gravity and force somehow do not provide a complete explanation of what has happened in either incident. Further, when we attempt a more fine-grained explanation, incidents A and B seem to call for a different level of explanation if we wish to zero in on the *essential* cause of death.

In analyzing incident A, a psychologist would be prone to say that when processing a stimulus (the crevice that looked somewhat like a rock) the woman's information-processing system malfunctioned – sending the wrong information to response decision mechanisms which then resulted in a disastrous motor response. Cognitive scientists refer to this level of analysis as the algorithmic level (Anderson, 1990; Marr, 1982; Stanovich, 1999). In the realm of machine intelligence, this would be the level of the instructions in the abstract computer language used to program the computer (BASIC, C, etc.). The cognitive psychologist works largely at this level by showing that human performance can be explained by positing certain information-processing mechanisms in the brain (input coding mechanisms, perceptual registration mechanisms, short- and long-term memory storage systems, etc.). For example, a simple letter pronunciation task might entail encoding the letter, storing it in short-term memory, comparing it with information stored in long-term memory, if a match occurs making a response decision, and then executing a motor response. In the case of the woman in incident A, the algorithmic level is the right level to explain her unfortunate demise. Her perceptual registration and classification mechanisms malfunctioned by providing incorrect information to response decision mechanisms, causing her to step into the crevice.

Incident B, on the other hand, does not involve such an algorithmic-level information-processing error. The woman's perceptual apparatus accurately recognized the edge of the cliff and her motor command centers quite accurately programmed her body to jump off the cliff. The computational processes posited at the algorithmic level of analysis executed quite perfectly. No error at this level of analysis explains why the woman is dead in incident B. Instead, this woman died because of her overall goals and how these goals interacted with her beliefs about the world in which she lived.

In the terms of Stanovich (2009), the woman in incident A had a problem with the algorithmic mind and the woman in incident B had a problem with the reflective mind.[1] This terminology captures the fact that we turn to an analysis of goals, desires, and beliefs to understand a case such as B. The algorithmic level provides an incomplete explanation of behavior in cases like incident B because it provides an information-processing explanation of how the brain is carrying out a particular task (in this case, jumping off a cliff) but no explanation of *why* the brain is carrying out this particular task. We turn to the level of the reflective mind where we ask questions about the *goals* of the system's computations (*what* the system is attempting to compute and *why*). In short, the reflective mind is concerned with the goals of the system, beliefs relevant to those goals, and the choice of action that is optimal given the system's goals and beliefs. All of these characteristics (e.g., choice of action that is optimal given the system's goals and beliefs) implicate the reflective mind in many issues of rationality. Assessing the reflective mind means assessing rational thought and rational action. The algorithmic mind can be evaluated in terms of efficiency, but high computational efficiency in the algorithmic mind is not a sufficient condition for rationality.

This concern for the efficiency of information processing as opposed to its rationality is mirrored in the status of intelligence tests. They are measures of computational efficiency but not rationality – a point made clear by considering a distinction that is very old in the field of psychometrics. Psychometricians have long distinguished typical performance situations from optimal

1 This example also helps to contextualize our use of the term *reflective*. Obviously, given this example involving suicide, we do not wish to imply that goals associated with the reflective mind necessarily exemplify wisdom or prudence. In fact, as in this example, sometimes the reflective mind is not *well* reflective. Our use of the term refers only to the necessity of employing intentional-level goal states (and belief states) to describe behavior. Those goals and beliefs can lead to irrational as well as rational outcomes.

(sometimes termed maximal) performance situations (see Ackerman, 1994, 1996; Ackerman & Heggestad, 1997; Ackerman & Kanfer, 2004; Cronbach, 1949; Matthews, Zeidner, & Roberts, 2002; Sternberg, Grigorenko, & Zhang, 2008). Typical performance situations are unconstrained in that no overt instructions to maximize performance are given, and the task interpretation is determined to some extent by the participant. The goals to be pursued in the task are left somewhat open. The issue is what a person would typically do in such a situation, given few constraints. Typical performance measures are measures of the reflective mind – they assess in part goal prioritization and epistemic regulation. In contrast, optimal performance situations are those in which the task interpretation is determined externally.[2] The person performing the task is instructed to maximize performance. Thus, optimal performance measures examine questions of efficiency of goal pursuit – they capture the processing efficiency of the algorithmic mind. All conventional tests of cognitive aptitude are optimal performance assessments, whereas measures of critical or rational thinking are often assessed under typical performance conditions.

The difference between the algorithmic mind and the reflective mind is captured in another well-established distinction in the measurement of individual differences – the distinction between cognitive ability and thinking dispositions. The former are, as just mentioned, measures of the efficiency of the algorithmic mind. The latter travel under a variety of names in psychology – thinking dispositions or cognitive styles being the two most popular. Many thinking dispositions concern beliefs, belief structure, and, importantly, attitudes toward forming and changing beliefs. Other thinking dispositions that have been identified concern a person's goals and goal hierarchy. Examples of thinking dispositions that have been investigated by psychologists are actively open-minded thinking, need for cognition (the tendency to think a lot), consideration of future consequences, need for closure, superstitious thinking, and dogmatism (Cacioppo et al., 1996; Kruglanski & Webster, 1996; Norris & Ennis, 1989; Schommer-Aikins, 2004; Stanovich, 1999, 2009; Sternberg, 2003; Sternberg & Grigorenko, 1997; Strathman et al., 1994).

The literature on these types of thinking dispositions is vast and our purpose is not to review that literature here. It is only necessary to note that the types of cognitive propensities that these thinking disposition measures reflect are the tendency to collect information before making up one's mind, the tendency to seek various points of view before coming to a conclusion, the disposition to think extensively about a problem before responding, the tendency to calibrate the degree of strength of one's opinion to the degree of evidence available, the tendency to think about future consequences before taking action, the tendency to explicitly weigh pluses and minuses of situations before making a decision, and the tendency to seek nuance and avoid absolutism. In short, individual differences in thinking dispositions are assessing variation in people's goal management, epistemic values, and epistemic self-regulation – differences in the operation of the reflective mind. They are all psychological characteristics of the reflective mind that underpin rational thought and action.

The cognitive abilities assessed on intelligence tests are not of this type. They are not about high-level personal goals and their regulation, or about the tendency to change beliefs in the face of contrary evidence, or about how knowledge acquisition is internally regulated when not externally directed. People have indeed come up with *definitions* of intelligence that encompass such things. Theorists often define intelligence in ways that encompass rational action and belief but, nevertheless, *the actual measures of intelligence in use assess only algorithmic-level cognitive capacity*. No current intelligence test that is even moderately

2 The exception of course is cross-cultural uses of intelligence tests, a situation that is beyond the scope of our argument. We restrict our discussion here to individual difference comparisons *within* a culture.

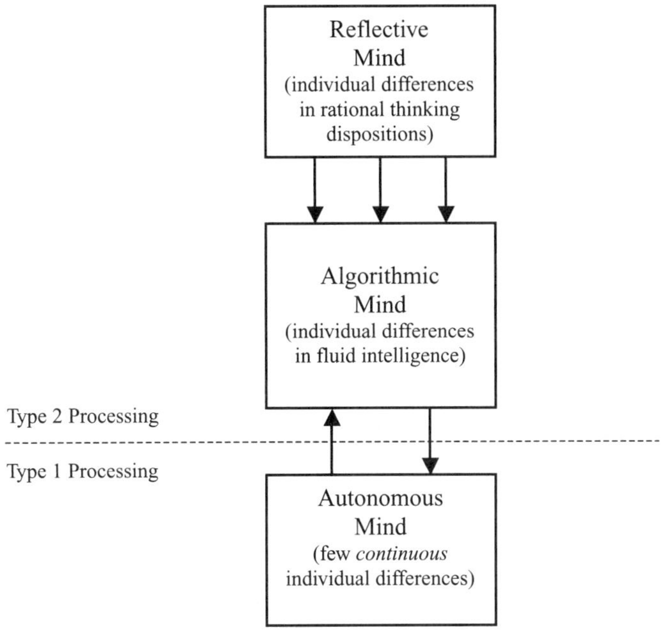

Figure 39.2. Individual differences in the tripartite structure. Reprinted from *What Intelligence Tests Miss: The Psychology of Rational Thought* by Keith E. Stanovich, courtesy of Yale University Press.

used in practice assesses rational thought or behavior.

We now have the distinctions needed to identify three kinds of minds. Figure 39.2 represents the classification of individual differences in the tripartite view presented in this chapter. The part of the mind that carries out Type 1 processing we will call the autonomous mind. The broken horizontal line represents the location of the key distinction in older, dual-process views. The figure identifies variation in fluid intelligence (Gf) with individual differences in the efficiency of processing of what we will call the algorithmic mind. In contrast, thinking dispositions index individual differences in what will be termed the reflective mind. In terms of individual differences, the reflective and algorithmic minds are characterized by continuous variation. Disruptions to the autonomous mind often reflect damage to cognitive modules that results in very discontinuous cognitive dysfunction such as autism or the agnosias and alexias (Anderson, 2005; Bermudez, 2001; Murphy & Stich, 2000).

Figure 39.2 highlights an important sense in which rationality is a more encompassing construct than intelligence. To be rational, a person must have well-calibrated beliefs and must act appropriately on those beliefs to achieve goals – both properties of the reflective mind. The person must, of course, have the algorithmic-level machinery that enables him or her to carry out the actions and to process the environment in a way that enables the correct beliefs to be fixed and the correct actions to be taken. Thus, individual differences in rational thought and action can arise because of individual differences in intelligence (the algorithmic mind) or because of individual differences in thinking dispositions (the reflective mind). To put it simply, the concept of rationality encompasses two things (thinking dispositions of the reflective mind and algorithmic-level efficiency) whereas the concept of intelligence – at least as it is commonly operationalized – is largely confined to algorithmic-level efficiency.

The conceptualization in Figure 39.2 has two great advantages. First, it conceptualizes intelligence in terms of what intelligence tests actually measure. That is, all current tests assess various aspects of algorithmic efficiency. But that is all that they assess. None attempt to measure directly an aspect of epistemic or instrumental rationality, nor do they examine any thinking dispositions that relate to rationality. To think rationally means adopting appropriate goals, taking the appropriate action given one's goals and beliefs, and holding beliefs that are commensurate with available evidence. Standard intelligence tests do not assess such functions (Perkins, 1995, 2002; Stanovich, 2002, 2009; Sternberg, 2003, 2006). For example, although intelligence tests do assess the ability to focus on an immediate goal in the face of distraction, they do not assess whether a person has the tendency to develop goals that are rational in the first place. Likewise, intelligence tests are good measures of how well a person can hold beliefs in short-term memory and manipulate those beliefs, but they do not assess whether a person has the tendency to *form* beliefs rationally when presented with evidence. Finally, intelligence tests are good measures of how efficiently a person processes information that has been provided, but they do not at all assess whether the person is a *critical assessor* of information as it is gathered in the natural environment.

It is clear from Figure 39.2 why rationality and intelligence can become dissociated. As long as variation in thinking dispositions is not perfectly correlated with fluid intelligence, there is the statistical possibility of dissociations between rationality and intelligence. Substantial empirical evidence indicates that individual differences in thinking dispositions and intelligence are far from perfectly correlated. Many different studies involving thousands of subjects (e.g., Ackerman & Heggestad, 1997; Austin & Deary, 2002; Baron, 1982; Bates & Shieles, 2003; Cacioppo et al., 1996; Eysenck, 1994; Goff & Ackerman, 1992; Kanazawa, 2004; Kokis et al., 2002; Zeidner & Matthews, 2000) have indicated that measures of intelligence display only moderate to weak correlations (usually less than .30) with some thinking dispositions (e.g., actively open-minded thinking, need for cognition) and near zero correlations with others (e.g., conscientiousness, curiosity, diligence).

Other important evidence supports the conceptual distinction made here between algorithmic cognitive capacity and thinking dispositions. For example, across a variety of tasks from the heuristics and biases literature, it has consistently been found that rational thinking dispositions will predict variance after the effects of general intelligence have been controlled (Bruine de Bruin, Parker, & Fischhoff, 2007; Klaczynski, Gordon, & Fauth, 1997; Klaczynski & Lavallee, 2005; Klaczynski & Robinson, 2000; Kokis et al., 2002; Newstead, Handley, Harley, Wright, & Farrelly, 2004; Macpherson & Stanovich, 2007; Parker & Fischhoff, 2005; Sá & Stanovich, 2001; Stanovich & West, 1997, 1998a, 2000; Toplak, Liu, Macpherson, Toneatto, & Stanovich, 2007; Toplak & Stanovich, 2002). These empirical studies indicate that different types of cognitive predictors are tapping separable variance, and the reason that this is to be expected is because cognitive capacity measures such as intelligence and thinking dispositions map on to different levels in the tripartite model.

The functions of the different levels of control are illustrated more completely in Figure 39.3. There, it is clear that the override capacity itself is a property of the algorithmic mind and it is indicated by the arrow labeled A. However, previous dual-process theories have tended to ignore the higher level cognitive function that initiates the override function in the first place. This is a dispositional property of the reflective mind that is related to rationality. In the model in Figure 39.3, it is represented by arrow B which represents, in machine intelligence terms, the call to the algorithmic mind to override the Type 1 response by taking it offline. This is a different mental function from the override function itself (arrow A), and we have presented evidence indicating that the two functions are indexed by different types of individual differences – the ability to sustain the inhibition of the Type

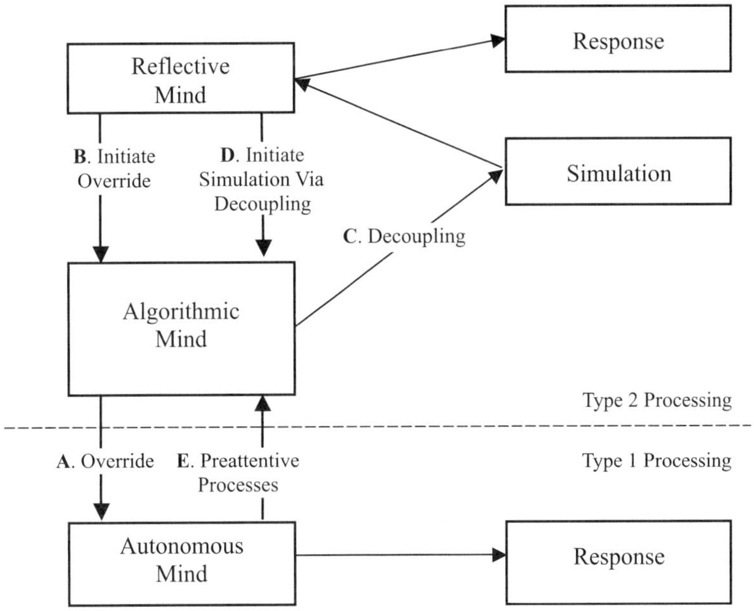

Figure 39.3. A more complete model of the tripartite framework. Reprinted from *What Intelligence Tests Miss: The Psychology of Rational Thought* by Keith E. Stanovich, courtesy of Yale University Press.

1 response is indexed by measures of fluid intelligence, and the tendency to initiate override operations is indexed by thinking dispositions such as reflectiveness and need for cognition.

Figure 39.3 represents another aspect of cognition somewhat neglected by previous dual-process theories. Specifically, the override function has loomed large in dual-process theory but less so the simulation process that computes the alternative response that makes the override worthwhile. Figure 39.3 explicitly represents the simulation function as well as the fact that the call to initiate simulation originates in the reflective mind. The decoupling operation (indicated by arrow C) itself is carried out by the algorithmic mind and the call to initiate simulation (indicated by arrow D) by the reflective mind. Again, two different types of individual differences are associated with the initiation call and the decoupling operator – specifically, rational thinking dispositions with the former and fluid intelligence with the latter. Finally, the algorithmic mind receives inputs from the computations of the autonomous mind (arrow E) via so-called preattentive processes (Evans, 2006, 2007, 2008, 2009).

Mindware in the Tripartite Model

Knowledge bases, both innate and derived from experience, also importantly bear on rationality. We have used the term mindware to refer to these knowledge bases. The term mindware was coined by Perkins (1995) to refer to the rules, knowledge, procedures, and strategies that a person can retrieve from memory to aid decision making and problem solving. Each of the levels in the tripartite model of mind has to access knowledge to carry out its operations, as illustrated in Figure 39.4. As the figure indicates, the reflective mind not only accesses general knowledge structures but, importantly, also accesses the person's opinions, beliefs, and reflectively acquired goal structure. The algorithmic mind accesses microstrategies for cognitive operations and production system rules for sequencing behaviors and thoughts. Finally, the autonomous mind accesses not only evolutionarily compiled encapsulated

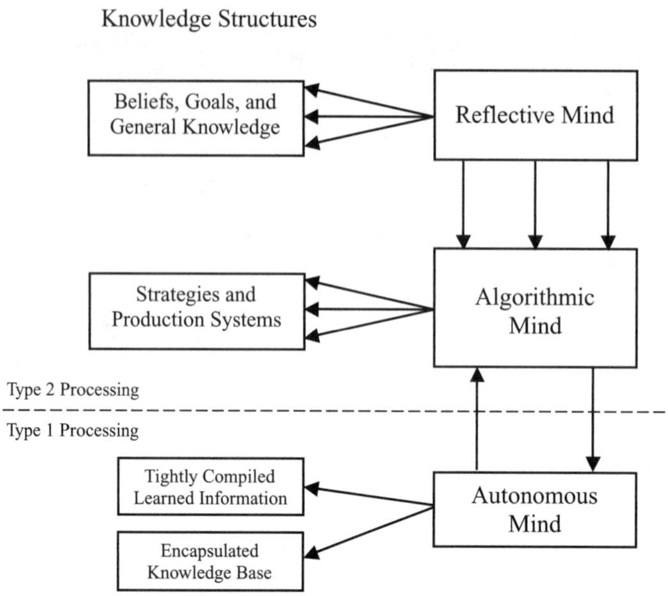

Figure 39.4. Knowledge structures in the tripartite framework.

knowledge bases, but also retrieves information that has become tightly compiled and available to the autonomous mind due to overlearning and practice.

It is important to note that what is displayed in Figure 39.4 is the knowledge bases that are *unique* to each mind. Algorithmic- and reflective-level processes also receive inputs from the computations of the autonomous mind (see arrow E in Figure 39.3). The mindware available for retrieval, particularly that available to the reflective mind, is in part the product of past learning experiences. The knowledge structures available for retrieval by the reflective mind represent Gc, crystallized intelligence. Recall that Gf, fluid intelligence (intelligence-as-process), is already represented in Figure 39.3. It is the general computational power of the algorithmic mind – importantly exemplified by the ability to sustain cognitive decoupling.

It is important to see how both of the major components of Gf/Gc theory miss critical aspects of rational thought. Fluid intelligence will, of course, have some relation to rationality because it indexes the computational power of the algorithmic mind to sustain decoupling. Because override and simulation are important operations for rational thought, Gf will definitely facilitate rational action in some situations. Nevertheless, the tendency to initiate override (arrow B in Figure 39.3) and to initiate simulation activities (arrow D in Figure 39.2) are both aspects of the reflective mind unassessed by intelligence tests, so the tests will miss these components of rationality.

The situation with respect to Gc is a little different. It is true that much of the mindware of rational thought would be classified as crystallized intelligence in the abstract. But is it the kind of crystallized knowledge that is specifically assessed on the tests? The answer is no. The mindware of rational thought is somewhat specialized mindware (it clusters in the domains of probabilistic reasoning, causal reasoning, and scientific reasoning; see Stanovich, 2009). In contrast, the crystallized knowledge assessed on IQ tests is deliberately designed to be nonspecialized. The designers of the tests, to make sure the sampling of Gc is fair and unbiased, explicitly attempt to *broadly* sample vocabulary, verbal comprehension domains, and general knowledge. The broad sampling ensures elimination of bias in the test, but it inevitably means that the specific knowledge bases critical to rationality will not be assessed. In short, Gc, as traditionally measured, does not assess individual differences in rationality, and Gf will do so only indirectly and to a mild extent.

Rational Thought and Its Operationalizations in Cognitive Science

To this point we have established that rationality is a more encompassing construct than intelligence, narrowly defined. We have seen conceptually the components of rationality that IQ tests miss. What if we were to attempt to assess the larger concept – rational thought? As psychologists, we would turn to how the concept of rationality has been operationalized within cognitive science. This avoids a number of pitfalls. First, dictionary definitions of rationality ("the state or quality of being in accord with reason") tend to be weak and not specific enough to be testable. Additionally, some theorists have wished to downplay the importance of rationality and have promulgated a caricature of rationality. Such caricatures are exemplified in discussions that seem to restrict its definition to the ability to do the syllogistic reasoning problems that are encountered in Philosophy 101. The meaning of rationality in modern cognitive science is, in contrast, much more robust and important.

Cognitive scientists recognize two types of rationality: instrumental and epistemic. In its simplest definition, *instrumental rationality* is behaving in the world so that you get exactly what you most want, given the resources (physical and mental) available to you. Somewhat more technically, we could characterize instrumental rationality as the optimization of the individual's goal fulfillment. Economists and cognitive scientists have refined the notion of optimization of goal fulfillment into the technical notion of expected utility. The model of rational judgment used by decision scientists is one in which a person chooses options based on which option has the largest expected utility (see Baron, 2008; Dawes, 1998; Hastie & Dawes, 2001; Wu, Zhang, & Gonzalez, 2004).

The other aspect of rationality studied by cognitive scientists is termed *epistemic rationality*. This aspect of rationality concerns how well beliefs map onto the actual structure of the world. Epistemic rationality is sometimes called theoretical rationality or evidential rationality (see Audi, 1993, 2001; Foley, 1987; Harman, 1995; Manktelow, 2004; Over, 2004). Instrumental and epistemic rationality are related. In order to take actions that fulfill our goals, we need to base those actions on beliefs that are properly calibrated to the world.

Although many people feel (mistakenly or not) that they could do without the ability to solve textbook logic problems (which is why the caricatured view of rationality works to undercut its status), virtually no person wishes to eschew epistemic rationality and instrumental rationality, properly defined. Virtually all people want their beliefs to be in some correspondence with reality, and they also want to act to maximize the achievement of their goals. Manktelow (2004) has emphasized the practicality of both types of rationality by noting that they concern two critical things: what is true and what to do. Epistemic rationality is about what is true and instrumental rationality is about what to do. For our beliefs to be rational they must correspond to the way the world is – they must be true. For our actions to be rational, they must be the best means toward our goals – they must be the best things to do.

The literature of cognitive science contains many examples of advantages of epistemic rationality and the disadvantages of epistemic irrationality. People who lack epistemic rationality tend to get many surprises in life – they think they know things that they do not. They have poor knowledge calibration, to use the technical term. In a knowledge calibration paradigm, for example, they tend to say that they are 99% certain of things that they actually know with only 70% accuracy (Fischhoff, Slovic, & Lichtenstein, 1977). Likewise, research has demonstrated the many practical consequences of failing to follow the strictures of instrumental rationality. For example, in the domains of personal finance and investing it has been found that people who violate the principles of instrumentally rational thought suffer more financial misfortune and make less money from investments (Camerer, 2000; Fenton-O'Creevy, et al., 2003; Hilton, 2003).

One of the fundamental advances in the history of modern decision science was the demonstration that if people's preferences follow certain patterns (the so-called axioms of choice – things like transitivity and freedom from certain kinds of context effects) then they are behaving as if they are maximizing utility – they are acting to get what they most want (Edwards, 1954; Jeffrey, 1983; Luce & Raiffa, 1957; Savage, 1954; von Neumann & Morgenstern, 1944). This is what makes people's degrees of rationality measurable by the experimental methods of cognitive science. Although it is difficult to assess utility directly, it is much easier to assess whether one of the axioms of rational choice is being violated. This has been the logic of the seminal heuristics and biases research program inaugurated in the much-cited studies of Kahneman and Tversky (1972, 1973, 1979; Tversky & Kahneman, 1974, 1981, 1983, 1986).

Researchers in the heuristics and biases tradition have demonstrated, in a host of empirical studies, that people violate many of the strictures of rationality and that the magnitude of these violations can be measured experimentally. For example, people display confirmation bias, they test hypotheses inefficiently, they display preference inconsistencies, they do not properly calibrate degrees of belief, they overproject their own opinions onto others, they combine probabilities incoherently, and they allow prior knowledge to become implicated in deductive reasoning (for summaries of the large literature, see Baron, 2008; Evans, 1989, 2007; Gilovich, Griffin, & Kahneman, 2002; Kahneman & Tversky, 2000; Shafir & LeBoeuf, 2002; Stanovich, 1999, 2004, 2009). These are caused by many well-known cognitive biases: base-rate neglect, framing effects, representativeness biases, anchoring biases, availability bias, outcome bias, and vividness effects, to name just a few. Degrees of rationality can be assessed in terms of the number and severity of such cognitive biases that individuals display.[3] Failure to display a bias becomes a measure of rational thought.

The Requirements of Rational Thinking

Within the tripartite framework, rationality requires mental characteristics of three different types. First, algorithmic-level cognitive capacity (intelligence) is needed in order that override and simulation activities can be sustained. Second, the reflective mind must be characterized by the tendency to initiate the override of suboptimal responses generated by the autonomous mind and to initiate simulation activities that will result in a better response (these might be termed the fluid aspects of rational thought). Finally, the mindware that allows the computation of rational responses needs to be available and accessible during simulation activities (this mindware might be described as the crystallized aspect of rational thought). Intelligence tests assess only the first of these three characteristics that determine rational thought and action. As measures of rational thinking, IQ tests are radically incomplete.

Problems in rational thinking arise when cognitive capacity is insufficient to sustain autonomous system override, when the necessity of override is not recognized, or when simulation processes do not have access to the mindware necessary

3 There of course has been considerable debate about the extent to which people display rational thinking errors both in the lab and in real life (Cohen, 1981; Gigerenzer, 1996, 2007; Kahneman & Tversky, 1996; Stanovich, 1999, 2004, 2009; Stein, 1996). Most (but perhaps not all) of these debates are orthogonal to the arguments made in this chapter because of our focus on individual differences. That is, virtually all commentators in these disputes acknowledge that there are substantial individual differences displayed on rational thinking tasks (see Stanovich, 1999; Stanovich & West, 2000).

for the synthesis of a better response. The source of these problems, and their relation to intelligence, helps to explain one data trend that has been uncovered – that some rational thinking problems show surprising degrees of dissociation from cognitive ability (Stanovich, 2009; Stanovich & West, 2007, 2008a, 2008b; West, Toplak, & Stanovich, 2008). Myside bias, for example, is virtually independent of intelligence (Macpherson & Stanovich, 2007; Sá, Kelley, Ho, & Stanovich, 2005; Stanovich & West, 2007, 2008a, 2008b; Toplak & Stanovich, 2003). For example, individuals with higher IQs in a university sample are no less likely to process information from an egocentric perspective than are individuals with relatively lower IQs.

Irrational behavior can occur because the right mindware (cognitive rules, strategies, knowledge, and belief systems) is not available to use in decision making. We would expect to see a correlation with intelligence here because mindware gaps most often arise because of lack of education or experience. Nevertheless, while it is true that more intelligent individuals learn more things than less intelligent individuals, much knowledge (and many thinking dispositions) relevant to rationality are picked up rather late in life. Explicit teaching of this mindware is not uniform in the school curriculum at any level. That such principles are taught very inconsistently means that some intelligent people may fail to learn these important aspects of critical thinking. In university samples, correlations with cognitive ability have been found to be roughly (in absolute magnitude) in the range of .20–.35 for probabilistic reasoning tasks and scientific reasoning tasks measuring a variety of rational principles (Bruine de Bruin, Parker, & Fischhoff, 2007; Kokis et al., 2002; Parker & Fischhoff, 2005; Sá, West, & Stanovich, 1999; Stanovich & West, 1997, 1998a, 1998b, 1999, 2000; Toplak & Stanovich, 2002). This is again a magnitude of correlation that allows for substantial discrepancies between intelligence and rationality. Intelligence is thus no inoculation against many of the sources of irrational thought. None of these sources of rational thought are directly assessed on intelligence tests, and the processes that *are* tapped by IQ tests are not highly overlapping with the processes and knowledge that explain variation in rational thinking ability.

In fact, there is enough important cognition missing from IQ tests in this domain that we can easily conceive of the need for a rational thinking test. Indeed, perhaps assessing rationality more explicitly is what is needed in order to both draw more attention toward rational thinking skills and to highlight the limitations of what intelligence tests assess. At present, of course, there is no IQ-type test for rationality – that is, a test that results in an RQ (rationality quotient). Of course, such instruments are not constructed on the back of an envelope – it would instead take an effort costing millions of dollars. Nevertheless, there is nothing *conceptually* or *theoretically* preventing us from developing such a test. We know the types of thinking processes that would be assessed on such an instrument, and we have in hand prototypes of the kinds of tasks that would be used in the domains of both instrumental rationality and epistemic rationality. In the next section we illustrate what the cognitive science of rationality suggests such a test would look like.

What Would Rationality Assessment Look Like?

A Framework for the Assessment of Rational Thinking

Rationality is a multifarious concept – not a single mental quality. Cognitive scientists have developed ways to test both epistemic rationality and instrumental rationality as they were defined earlier. For example, psychologists have studied aspects of epistemic rationality such as the ability to avoid the following: the tendency toward overconfidence in knowledge judgments; the tendency to ignore base-rates; the tendency not to seek to falsify hypotheses; the tendency to try to explain chance events; the tendency toward self-serving personal judgments; the tendency to evaluate evidence with a myside bias; and the tendency to ignore the alternative hypothesis.

Additionally, psychologists have studied aspects of instrumental rationality such as the ability to avoid these biases: the tendency to show inconsistent preferences because of framing effects; the tendency to show a default bias; the tendency to substitute affect for difficult evaluations; the tendency to over-weight short-term rewards at the expense of long-term well-being; the tendency to have choices overly affected by vivid stimuli; and the tendency for decisions to be affected by irrelevant context.

In terms of concepts discussed in the tripartite model presented in this chapter, Figure 39.5 shows what we propose as the conceptual structure of rational thought. The first partition in the figure indicates that rational thought can be partitioned into fluid and crystallized components by analogy to the Gf and Gc of the Cattell/Horn/Carroll fluid-crystallized theory of intelligence (Carroll, 1993; Cattell, 1963, 1998; Horn & Cattell, 1967). Fluid rationality encompasses the process part of rational thought – the thinking dispositions of the reflective mind that lead to rational thought and action. The top part of the figure illustrates that unlike the case of fluid intelligence, fluid rationality is likely to be multifarious – composed of a variety of cognitive styles and dispositions. Some of these styles and dispositions will be related (for instance, actively open-minded thinking and objective reasoning styles) but others probably not – research on the interrelationships among these thinking dispositions is in its infancy (Bruin de Bruine et al., 2007; Klaczynski, 2001; Parker & Fischhoff, 2005; Stanovich & West, 1998a; West et al., 2008). As a multifarious concept, fluid rationality cannot be assessed with a single type of item in the manner that the homogeneous Raven Progressive Matrices, for example, provides a measure of Gf.

Crystallized rationality is likewise multifarious. However, the bottom part of Figure 39.5 illustrates that the concept of crystallized rationality introduces another complication. Problems with rational thinking in the domain of mindware come in two types – mindware gaps and contaminated mindware (Stanovich, 2009). Mindware gaps occur because people lack declarative knowledge that can facilitate rational thought – they lack crystallized facilitators as indicated in Figure 39.5. A different type of mindware problem arises because not all mindware is helpful – either to attaining our goals (instrumental rationality) or to having accurate beliefs (epistemic rationality). In fact, some acquired mindware can be the direct cause of irrational actions that thwart our goals. This type of problem has been termed contaminated mindware (Stanovich, 2009; Stanovich, Toplak, & West, 2008). It occurs when a person has acquired one (or more) of the crystallized inhibitors listed in Figure 39.5.

Figure 39.5 presents components of rationality that are of all three types – components of fluid rationality as well as some of the most common crystallized facilitators and crystallized inhibitors. Figure 39.5 should not be mistaken for the kind of list of "good thinking styles" that appears in textbooks on critical thinking, however. In terms of providing a basis for a system of rational thinking assessment, it goes considerably beyond such lists in a number of ways. First, unlike the many committee-like attempts to develop feature-lists of critical thinking skills (e.g., Facione, 1990), our conceptual components are grounded in paradigms that have been extensively researched within the literature of cognitive science. This will be illustrated more concretely when we discuss Table 39.1. Second, many textbook attempts at lists of "good thinking styles" deal only with aspects of fluid rationality and give short shrift to the crystallized knowledge bases that are necessary supports for rational thought and action. In contrast, our framework for rationality assessment emphasizes that crystallized knowledge underlies much rational responding (crystallized facilitators) and that crystallized knowledge can also be the direct cause of irrational behavior (crystallized inhibitors).

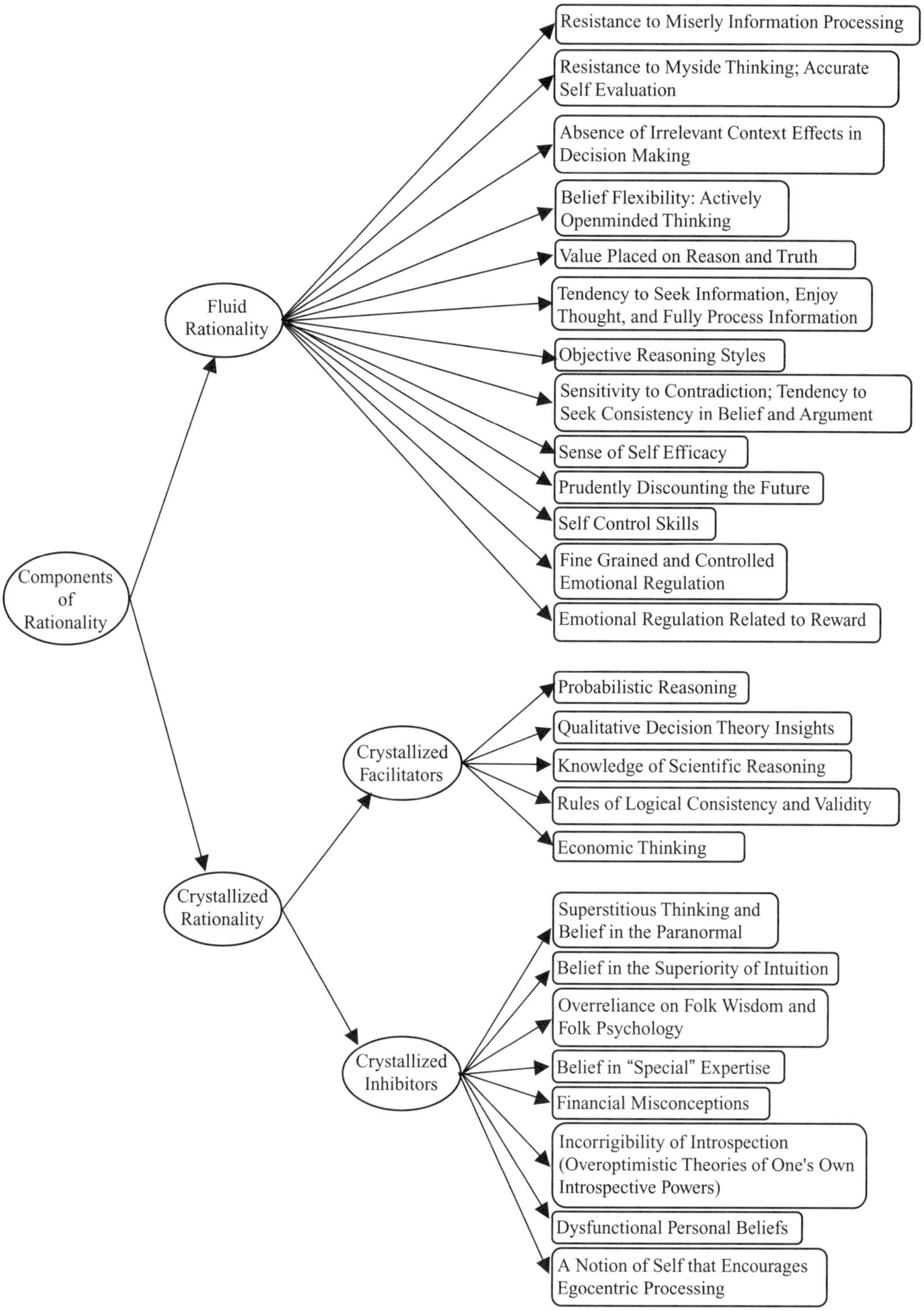

Figure 39.5. The conceptual structure of rational thought.

Table 39.1

Components of Rational Thought			
Fluid Rationality			
Major Dimensions	*Measurement Paradigms*	*Source for Paradigm*	*Example Item*
Resistance to Miserly Information Processing	Belief Bias Paradigms	Evans, Barston, & Pollard (1983) or Markovits & Nantel (1989)	Decide if the conclusion follows logically from the premises, assuming the premises are absolutely true: All flowers have petals; roses have petals; therefore, roses are flowers.
	Attribute Substitution (i.e., Vividness Substitution; Affect Substitution; Denominator Neglect)	Kahneman & Frederick (2002); Slovic et al. (2002); Denes-Raj & Epstein (1994)	Assume that you are presented with two trays of marbles that are spread in a single layer in each tray. You must draw out one marble (without peeking, of course) from either tray. If you draw a black marble you win $100. Consider a condition in which the small tray contains 1 black marble and 9 white marbles, and the large tray contains 8 black marbles and 92 white marbles. From which tray would you prefer to select a marble?
	Cognitive Reflection Test	Frederick (2005)	A bat and a ball cost $1.10 in total. The bat costs a dollar more than the ball. How much does the ball cost?
	Disjunctive Reasoning Tasks	Toplak & Stanovich (2002)	Jack is looking at Ann but Ann is looking at George. Jack is married but George is not. Is a married person looking at an unmarried person? A) Yes B) No C) Cannot be determined
	Accurate Perception of Risks and Benefits	Finucane, Alhakami, Slovic, & Johnson (2000)	Judgments of risks and benefits should be independent. For example, information about the benefits of nuclear energy should not reduce the risk estimate for this source of energy.
	Resistance to Baserate Neglect	Tversky & Kahneman (1982)	A cab was involved in a hit-and-run accident at night. Two cab companies, the Green and the Blue, operate in the city in which the accident occurred. You are given the following fact: 85% of the cabs in the city are Green and 15% are Blue. A witness reported that the cab in the accident was blue. The court tested the reliability of the witness under the same circumstances that existed on the night of the accident and concluded that the witness called about 80% of the Blue cabs blue, but called 20% of the Blue cabs green. The witness also called about 80% of the Green cabs green, but called 20% of the Green cabs blue. What is the probability (expressed as a percentage ranging from 0 to 100%) that the cab involved in the accident was Blue?

Components of Rational Thought			
		Fluid Rationality	
Major Dimensions	*Measurement Paradigms*	*Source for Paradigm*	*Example Item*
	Outcome Bias Paradigms; Status Quo Bias; Endowment Effects	Baron & Hershey (1988); Kahneman, Knetsch, & Thaler (1990, 1991)	A 55-year-old man had a heart condition. He had to stop working because of chest pain. He enjoyed his work and did not want to stop. His pain also interfered with other things, such as travel and recreation. A type of bypass operation would relieve his pain and increase his life expectancy by 5 [15] years. However, 8% [2%] of the people who have this operation die from the operation itself. His physician decided to go ahead with the operation. The operation succeeded [failed, and the man died]. Evaluate the physician's decision to go ahead with the operation.
	Hindsight Bias Paradigms	Fischhoff (1975) or Pohl (2004)	An immigrant arriving at Ellis Island in 1900 was most likely to be from (a) England or Ireland; (b) Scandinavia; (c) Latin America; *(d) Eastern Europe The correct answer to the item is indicated by an asterisk. Please indicate on the scale provided the probability that you would have answered this item correctly.
	Diagnostic Hypothesis Testing	Doherty et al. (1979) or Stanovich (2010a)	Four-card selection task: If there is a vowel on one side of the card, then there is an even number on the other. Your task is to decide which card or cards must be turned over to find out whether the rule is true or false.
	Accuracy of Affective Forecasting	Kermer, Driver-Linn, Wilson, & Gilbert (2006)	Part 1: How happy/sad do you think you will be if you win/lose this coin toss? Part 2: Now that you have won/lost the coin toss, how happy/sad are you right now?
Resistance to Myside Thinking; Accurate Self-Evaluation	Overconfidence Paradigms; Fairness Paradigms; Argument Evaluation Test	Fischhoff, Slovic, & Lichtenstein (1977); Messick & Sentis (1979); Stanovich & West (1997)	Select the correct answer: Absinthe is (a) a precious stone or (b) a liqueur. What is the probability that the alternative you selected is correct?
	Unbiased Processing of Evidence	Klaczynski (2000) or Taber & Lodge (2006)	In this part of the task, we will ask you to read a set of arguments on gun control and tell us how weak or strong you believe each argument is.

(continued)

Table 39.1 (*continued*)

Components of Rational Thought			
Fluid Rationality			
Major Dimensions	*Measurement Paradigms*	*Source for Paradigm*	*Example Item*
Absence of Irrelevant Context Effects in Decision Making	Framing Effects; Preference Reversals	Frisch (1993); Lichtenstein & Slovic (2006)	Decision 1. Imagine that the United States is preparing for the outbreak of a disease which is expected to kill 600 people. If Program A is adopted, 200 people will be saved. If Program B is adopted, there is a one-third probability that 600 people will be saved and a two-thirds probability that no people will be saved. Which of the two programs would you favor? Decision 2. Imagine that the United States is preparing for the outbreak of a disease which is expected to kill 600 people. If Program C is adopted, 400 people will die. If Program D is adopted, there is a one-third probability that nobody will die and a two-thirds probability that 600 people will die. Which of the two programs would you favor?
	Avoidance of Irrelevant Anchoring	Jacowitz & Kahneman (1995) or Epley & Gilovich (2004)	Is the length of the Mississippi River greater than 3,000 [less than 200] miles? What is the length of the Mississippi River?
Belief Flexibility: Actively Open-minded Thinking	Actively Open-minded Thinking Scale; Need for Closure; Dogmatism; Belief Identification; Epistemological Understanding	Stanovich & West (2008a); Kruglanski & Webster (1996); Christie (1991); Sá, West, & Stanovich (1999); Kuhn et al. (2000)	Agree or disagree: Changing your mind is a sign of weakness (reflected item)
Value Placed on Reason and Truth	The Master Rationality Motive Scale	Stanovich (2008)	Agree or disagree: I like to think that my actions are motivated by sound reasons.
Tendency to Seek Information, Enjoy Thought, and Fully Process Information	Measures of Need for Cognition and Typical Intellectual Engagement	Cacioppo et al. (1996); Goff & Ackerman (1992)	Agree or disagree: I like the responsibility of handling a situation that requires a lot of thinking.
	Disjunctive Reasoning Tasks	Toplak & Stanovich (2002)	There are 5 blocks in a stack pictured in the figure below. Block 1 is on the bottom and Block 5 is on the top. Block 4 (the second from the top) is green, and Block 2 (the second from the bottom) is not green. Is there a green block *directly* on top of a non-green block? (a) Yes (b) No (c) Cannot be determined

Components of Rational Thought			
		Fluid Rationality	
Major Dimensions	*Measurement Paradigms*	*Source for Paradigm*	*Example Item*
Objective Reasoning Styles	Separating Fact from Opinion and Theory from Evidence; Recognizing the Validity and Invalidity of Informal Arguments; Argument Evaluation Test	Kuhn (1991); Watson & Glaser (1980) or Ricco (2007); Stanovich & West (1997)	Dale states: Seat belts should always be worn to make traveling by car safer. A critic's counterargument is: There are times when your life may be saved by your being thrown free of a car during an accident (assume statement factually correct); Dale's rebuttal is: You are several times more likely to be killed if you are thrown from a car (assume statement factually correct). Indicate the strength of Dale's rebuttal to the critic's counterargument.
Sensitivity to Contradiction; Tendency to Seek Consistency in Belief and Argument	Informal Reasoning and Argument Evaluation Paradigms	Baron (1995) or Perkins (1985) or Toplak & Stanovich (2003) or Halpern (2008)	Subsequent to rating their level of agreement with positions expressed in a series of statements (e.g., The cost of gasoline should be doubled to discourage people from driving), participants were asked to write down arguments both for and against the position.
Sense of Self-Efficacy	Locus of Control Scales	Lefcourt (1991)	Agree or disagree: When bad things happen, they were just going to happen no matter what you did. (reflected)
Prudently Discounting the Future	Temporal Discounting of Reward	Kirby (2009); Shamosh et al. (2008)	Would you prefer $55 today, or $75 in 60 days?
Self-Control Skills	Delay of Gratification Paradigms; Time Preference; Future Orientation	Rodriguez, Mischel, & Shoda (1989); Steinberg et al. (2009); Strathman et al. (1994)	Which description best describes you: Some people would rather be happy today than take their chances on what might happen in the future, but other people will give up their happiness now so that they can get what they want in the future.
Fine-Grained and Controlled Emotional Regulation	Measures of Alexithymia	Bagby, Parker, & Taylor (1994)	Agree or disagree: I am often confused about what emotion I am feeling.
Emotional Regulation Related to Reward	Iowa Gambling Task	Bechara, Damasio, Damasio, & Anderson (1994)	Participants choose from four decks of cards, each of which is associated with a different potential payoff. They must learn to avoid decks that produce high immediate gains but larger future losses.

(*continued*)

Table 39.1 (*continued*)

Crystallized Rationality: Crystallized Facilitators			
Major Dimensions	*Measurement Paradigms*	*Source for Paradigm*	*Example Item*
Probabilistic Reasoning	Importance of Sample Size	Tversky & Kahneman (1974) or Griffin & Tversky (1992) or Fong et al. (1986)	A certain town is served by two hospitals. In the larger hospital about 45 babies are born each day, and in the smaller hospital about 15 babies are born each day. As you know, about 50% of all babies are boys. The exact percentage of baby boys, however, varies from day to day. Sometimes it may be higher than 50%, sometimes lower. For a period of one year, each hospital recorded the days on which more than 60% of the babies born were boys. Which hospital do you think recorded more such days? (a) The larger hospital will have more days with more than 60% boys (b) The smaller hospital will have more days with more than 60% boys (c) About the same for both hospitals
	Consistent Probability Judgments	Bruine de Bruin et al. (2007); Peters et al. (2006)	In each time frame, some item pairs present nested subset and superset events (e.g., dying in a terrorist attack is a subset of the superset dying from any cause). To be scored as correct, the probability of a subset event should not exceed that of its superset event.
	Resistance to Baserate Neglect	Sloman et al. (2003); Jepson et al. (1983)	Imagine that disease X occurs in one in every 1,000 people. A test has been developed to detect the disease. Every time the test is given to a person who has the disease, the test comes out positive. But sometimes the test also comes out positive when it is given to a person who is completely healthy. Specifically, 5% of all people who are perfectly healthy test positive for the disease. Imagine that we have given this test to a random sample of Americans. They were selected by a lottery. Those who conducted the lottery had no information about the health status of any of these people. What is the chance that a person found to have a positive result actually has the disease?

Crystallized Rationality: Crystallized Facilitators			
Major Dimensions	*Measurement Paradigms*	*Source for Paradigm*	*Example Item*
	Resistance to Gambler's Fallacy	Ayton & Fischer (2004) or Burns & Corpus (2004) or Toplak et al., (2007)	When playing slot machines, people win something about 1 in every 10 times. Lori, however, has just won on her first three plays. What are her chances of winning the next time she plays?
	Use of Chance in Explanatory Frameworks; Understanding Random Processes	Fenton-O'Creevy et al. (2003); Towse & Neil (1998)	Simulate the random outcome of tossing a fair coin 150 times in succession.
	Understanding Regression Effects	Nisbett et al. (1983); Fong et al. (1986)	After the first two weeks of the major league baseball season, newspapers begin to print the top 10 batting averages. Typically, after two weeks, the leading batter often has an average of about .450. However, no batter in major league history has ever averaged .450 at the end of the season. Why do you think this is?
	Recognizing Biased and Unbiased Samples	Nisbett et al. (1983); Fong et al. (1986)	An economist was arguing in favor of a guaranteed minimum income for everyone. He cited a recent study of several hundred people in the United States with inherited wealth. Nearly 92% of those people, he said, worked at some job that provided earned income sufficient to provide at least a middle-class lifestyle. The study showed, he said, that contrary to popular opinion, people will work in preference to being idle. Thus a guaranteed income policy would result in little or no increase in the number of people unwilling to work. Comment on the economist's reasoning.
	Diagnostic Hypothesis Testing	Doherty & Mynatt (1990); Mynatt et al. (1993)	Imagine you are a doctor. A patient comes to you with a red rash on his fingers. What information would you want in order to diagnose whether the patient has the disease "Digirosa." Which of the following pieces of information are necessary to make the diagnosis? (a) percentage of people without Digirosa who have a red rash; (b) percentage of people with Digirosa; (c) percentage of people without Digirosa; (d) and percentage of people with Digirosa who have a red rash.
	Accurate Perception of Risks	Lichtenstein et al. (1978)	Consider all the people now living in the United States – children, adults, everyone. Which cause of death is more likely? (a) dying in a tornado; (b) dying of tuberculosis

(continued)

Table 39.1 (*continued*)

Crystallized Rationality: Crystallized Facilitators			
Major Dimensions	*Measurement Paradigms*	*Source for Paradigm*	*Example Item*
Qualitative Decision Theory Insights	Stable Preferences; Adherence to Basic Probability/Utility Trade-offs in SEU Theory; Preferences in Line with SEU Axioms	Moore (1999) or Lichtenstein & Slovic (1971, 1973); Frederick (2005) or Benjamin & Shapiro (2005); Birnbaum (1999)	Choose A or B: A. You get \$0.40 for sure. B. If a die comes up 1, 2, or 3, you get \$1.58. If a die comes up 4, 5, or 6, you get nothing.
Knowledge of Scientific Reasoning	Scientific Control Concepts; Causal Variable Isolation; Control Group Necessity; Understanding Placebo and Selection Effects	Greenhoot et al. (2004); Tschirgi (1980); Lehman et al. (1988); Lehman & Nisbett (1990)	The city of Middletown has had an unpopular police chief for the past 2 years. He is a political appointee who is a crony of the mayor and he had little previous experience in police administration when he was appointed. The mayor has recently defended the police chief in public, announcing that in the time since he took office, crime rates had decreased by 12%. What evidence would most refute the mayor's claim and instead show that the police chief may not be doing a good job?
	Avoidance of Confirmation Bias	Taber & Lodge (2006)	Search for pro or con information about a highly valenced issue (affirmative action, gun control, etc.)
	Diagnostic Covariation Judgment	Wasserman, Dörner, & Kao (1990)	Imagine that you are a research chemist for a pharmaceutical company. You want to assess how well a certain experimental drug works on psoriasis, a severe skin rash. In your experiment, you will give some rats the drug and others a placebo, which is known to have no effect on psoriasis. After the experiment, there will be four types of rats: Those who did not receive the drug and whose psoriasis did not improve . . . etc. Was the treatment effective?
	Covariation Detection Free of Belief Bias; Avoidance of Illusory Correlations	Stanovich & West (1998b); Fiedler (2004)	As the cell above except for an issue with valence and/or prior belief, such as: Do couples who live together before marriage have more successful marriages?

Crystallized Rationality: Crystallized Facilitators			
Major Dimensions	*Measurement Paradigms*	*Source for Paradigm*	*Example Item*
	Difference Between Correlation and Causation; Recognizing Spurious Correlation	Halpern (2008); Burns (1997)	A recent report in a magazine for parents and teachers showed that adolescents who smoke cigarettes also tend to get low grades in school. As the number of cigarettes smoked each day increased, grade-point averages decreased. One suggestion made in this report was that we could improve school achievement by preventing adolescents from smoking. Based on this information, would you support this idea as a way of improving the school achievement of adolescents who smoke?
	Understanding Falsifiability as a Context for Confirmation; Thinking of the Alternative Hypothesis	Oswald & Grosjean (2004) or Gale & Ball (2006) or Tweney et al. (1980)	I have made up a rule for the construction of sequences of numbers. For instance, the three numbers 2–4–6 satisfy this rule. To find out what the rule is, you may construct other sets of three numbers to test your assumption about what the rule is. I will give you feedback about whether your set satisfies my rule or not. If you are sure you have the solution, you may stop testing and tell me what you believe the rule to be. [the rule is "increasing numbers"]
	Differentiating Theory from Evidence	Kuhn (1991, 1992)	"How do you know that this is the cause?" "If you were trying to convince someone else that your view, [focal theory repeated here], is right, what evidence would you give to try to show this?"
	Appreciation of Converging Evidence	Stanovich (2010b)	The principle of converging evidence urges us to base conclusions on data that arise from a number of slightly different experimental sources.
	Appreciating the Limits of Personal Observation, Testimonials, and Single-Case Evidence	Jepson et al. (1983) and Halpern (2008)	The Caldwells looked in *Consumer Reports* and there they found that the consensus of the experts was that the Volvo was superior to the Saab. Mr. Caldwell called up friends. One Volvo owner hated his car. Which car do you think the Caldwells should buy?

(*continued*)

Table 39.1 (*continued*)

Crystallized Rationality: Crystallized Facilitators			
Major Dimensions	*Measurement Paradigms*	*Source for Paradigm*	*Example Item*
Rules of Logical Consistency and Validity	Logical Validity Judgment Tasks	Evans, Handley, Harper, & Johnson-Laird (1999)	For "All A are B" evaluate logically: 1. No A are B 2. Some A are B 3. Some A are not B 4. All B are A 5. No B are A 6. Some B are A 7. Some B are not A Answer: conclusions 2 and 6 are necessary; 4 and 7 are possible (but not necessary); and 1, 3, and 5 are impossible.
Economic Thinking	Cost/Benefit Reasoning; Limited Resource Reasoning	Larrick, et al. (1993) or NCEE (2005); Larrick, et al. (1990)	When a person rents an apartment, who benefits from the transaction?
	Recognizing Opportunity Costs	Larrick, et al. (1990); Thaler (1985, 1987)	What are the costs involved in attending university. List all of the costs you can.
	Avoiding Sunk Costs	Arkes & Blumer (1985)	You are staying in a hotel room on vacation. You paid $6.95 to see a movie on pay TV. After 5 minutes you are bored and the movie seems pretty bad. Would you continue to watch the movie or not?
	Understanding Externalities	Heath (2001)	A customer walks into a small convenience store and gives the store's owner $8 for a six-pack of beer. The owner of the store hands over the six-pack. After this transaction is complete, describe the gains and losses to everyone affected by this transaction.
	Awareness of the Logic of Exponential Growth and Compounding	Wagenaar & Sagaria (1975); Dorner (1996)	Pollution Index: 1970 – 3; 1971 – 7; 1972 – 20; 1973 – 55; 1974 – 148; 1975 – ?
	Understanding Commons Dilemmas, Zero-sum, and Nonzero-sum Games	Komorita & Parks (1994); Shafir & Tversky (1992)	Two players must choose to either cooperate or compete with the other player while being blind to the other's choice.

Crystallized Rationality: Crystallized Facilitators			
Major Dimensions	*Measurement Paradigms*	*Source for Paradigm*	*Example Item*
	Recognizing Regression Effects that Encourage Buying High and Selling Low	Nisbett et al. (1983)	Harold, a boys' football coach, says the following of his experience: "Every year we add 10–20 younger boys to the team on the basis of their performance at the try-out practice. Usually the staff and I are extremely excited about two or three of these kids – but they usually turn out to be no better than the rest." Why do you suppose that the coach usually has to revise downward his opinion of players that he originally thought were brilliant?
	Appropriate Mental Accounting and Understanding of Fungibility	Thaler (1980, 1985, 1987)	Imagine that you go to purchase a calculator for $30. The salesperson informs you that the calculator you wish to buy is on sale for $20 at the other branch of the store which is 10 minutes away by car. Would you drive to the other store? Option A: Yes, Option B: No Imagine that you go to purchase a jacket for $250. The salesperson informs you that the jacket you wish to buy is on sale for $240 at the other branch of the store which is 10 minutes away by car. Would you drive to the other store? Option C: Yes, Option B: No

Crystallized Rationality: Crystallized Inhibitors			
Superstitious Thinking and Belief in the Paranormal	Paranormal, Superstitious Thinking, and Luck scales; Illusion of Control	Stanovich (1989) or Tobacyk & Milford (1983); Fenton-O'Creevy et al. (2003) or Thompson (2004)	Agree or disagree: If you break a mirror, you will have bad luck.
Belief in the Superiority of Intuition	Faith in Intuition Scale	Epstein et al. (1996)	Agree or disagree: My initial impressions of people are almost always right.
Overreliance on Folk Wisdom and Folk Psychology	Bias Blind Spot Test	Pronin, Lin, & Ross (2002)	Psychologists have claimed that people show a "self-serving" tendency in that they take credit for success but deny responsibility for failure. Questions to participants: A. To what extent do you believe that *you* show this effect or tendency? B. To what extent do you believe the *average American* shows this effect or tendency?

(*continued*)

Table 39.1 (*continued*)

Crystallized Rationality: Crystallized Facilitators			
Major Dimensions	*Measurement Paradigms*	*Source for Paradigm*	*Example Item*
Belief in "Special" Expertise	High Value Placed on Nongrounded Knowledge Sources	Eckblad & Chapman (1983)	Agree or disagree: Horoscopes are right too often for it to be a coincidence.
Financial Misconceptions	Financial Literacy/Illiteracy Scales	Chen & Volpe (1998); Mandell (2009); NCEE (2005)	What is the best way to minimize the dollar amount in finance charges on a credit card?
Incorrigibility of Introspection (Overoptimistic Theories of One's Own Introspective Powers)	Accuracy of Affective Forecasting	Kermer, Driver-Linn, Wilson, & Gilbert (2006)	Part 1: How happy/sad do you think you will be if you win/lose this coin toss? Part 2: Now that you have won/lost the coin toss, how happy/sad are you right now?
	Bias Blind Spot Test	Pronin, Lin, & Ross (2002)	Psychologists have shown that people tend not to trust media sources that contradict their views. Questions to participants: A. To what extent do you believe that *you* show this effect or tendency? B. To what extent do you believe the *average American* shows this effect or tendency?
Dysfunctional Personal Beliefs	Measures of Irrational Personal Beliefs	Terjesen, Salhany, & Sciutto (2009) or Lindner et al. (1999)	Agree or disagree: If important people dislike me, it is because I am an unlikable, bad person
A Notion of Self that Encourages Egocentric Processing	Unbiased Processing of Evidence	Klaczynski & Gordon (1996)	Belief-consistent conclusions were drawn from those experiments which yielded results that cast participants' religions in a positive light. Belief-inconsistent conclusions were drawn from research that yielded results casting participants' religions in a negative light. Unbiasedness is defined as rating the quality of the experiment independent of its level of belief consistency.
	Self-Perception Biases and Unrealistic Optimism	Weinstein (1980)	Compared to other students – same sex as you – what do you think are the chances that the following events will happen to you: You will get a good job before graduation.

Even more important than these points, however, is that unlike many such lists of thinking skills in textbooks, the fluid characteristics and crystallized knowledge bases listed in Figure 39.5 are each grounded in a task or paradigm in the literature of cognitive science. That is, they are not just potentially measurable, but in fact have been operationalized and measured at least once in the scientific literature – and in many cases (e.g., context effects in decision making; tendency to enjoy thought; probabilistic reasoning) they have generated enormous empirical literatures.

Table 39.1 shows some of the paradigms that ground the component concepts and that could be used as the basis for constructing test items. There are many paradigms that have been used to measure the resistance to miserly information processing, the first major dimension of fluid rationality in Table 39.1. Many of these paradigms have been extensively investigated and have yielded tasks that could be used to devise assessment items. The study of belief bias – that people have difficulty processing data pointing toward conclusions that conflict with what they think they know about the world – has yielded many such items (Balcetis & Dunning, 2006; Dias, Roazzi, & Harris, 2005; Evans, Barston, & Pollard, 1983; Evans & Curtis-Holmes, 2005; Handley, Capon, Beveridge, Dennis, & Evans, 2004; Klaczynski & Lavallee, 2005; Klauer, Musch, & Naumer, 2000; Markovits & Nantel, 1989; Sá, West, & Stanovich, 1999).

Likewise, good decision making is in part defined by decisions that are not unduly affected by irrelevant context (the third major dimension of fluid rationality in Table 39.1). Two paradigms that assess the latter tendency have each generated enormous literatures. Resistance to framing has been measured with countless tasks (Epley, Mak, & Chen Idson, 2006; Friedrich, Lucas, & Hodell, 2005; Kahneman & Tversky, 1984, 2000; Levin et al., 2002; Maule & Villejoubert, 2007; Schneider, Burke, Solomonson, & Laurion, 2005; Tversky & Kahneman, 1981, 1986), as has the resistance to irrelevant anchoring in decisions (Brewer & Chapman, 2002; Epley & Gilovich, 2004, 2006; Jacowitz & Kahneman, 1995; LeBoeuf & Shafir, 2006; Mussweiler & Englich, 2005; Tversky & Kahneman, 1974).

As a final example of an area of rational thinking with a history dense with empirical research and with paradigms that could serve as assessment devices, consider the tendency to conform, qualitatively, to the insights of normative decision theory – the second major dimension of crystallized rationality facilitators in Table 39.1. Since the early 1950s (see Edwards, 1954), psychologists have studied the tendency to adhere to the axioms of expected utility theory with a variety of tasks and paradigms (Baron, 2008; Dawes, 1998; Kahneman & Tversky, 2000; Koehler & Harvey, 2004; Nickerson, 2004, 2008; Shafir & LeBoeuf, 2002; Tversky, 2003; Wu et al., 2004).

Not all of the concepts of rational thought listed in Table 39.1 have potential measurement paradigms with as much background research on them as those discussed here, but in fact *most* of them do. For the reader not as conversant with the literature of cognitive psychology as the last several paragraphs have presumed, we have listed in Table 39.1 a source for each of the potential measurement paradigms. That is, Table 39.1 points the reader to specific studies or review papers in the research literature that contain examples of tasks that could be adapted to serve as actual test items. In most cases, the citations in Table 39.1 will allow the reader to uncover an extensive literature on such tasks (as in the examples in the previous paragraphs). At a minimum, the citations provide clear guidance on how such task items might be developed.

The citations in Table 39.1 are to papers that will lead the reader to empirical studies containing measurement paradigms that would make a good source of assessment items. The citation is *not* intended as a reference to the classic introduction to the effect, or to the paper with priority of discovery, or to the most historic or most cited paper. This is because often the best source for test items is not the paper in which the effect/task was introduced. For example, for framing effects (the first measurement paradigm from the top under fluid rationality) we have listed Frisch (1993) as the pointer citation because it contains a large number of framing items (we could equally have cited Levin et al., 1998, 2002) rather than the classic Tversky and Kahneman (1981) paper where framing was introduced with the now-famous Asian Disease problem.

In the far right column of Table 39.1 is an example of an item type from each of the measurement paradigms. The reader is warned that because of the size of the table (i.e., number of different paradigms), many of these items have been truncated, abridged, or paraphrased so that they would fit into a reasonable space. They are not meant to be literal exemplars that could be immediately inserted into a test but are there merely to give the reader unfamiliar with the measurement paradigm a flavor of what is being measured. Items of that type are explicated in detail in the citations given.

Some measurement paradigms appear in Table 39.1 more than once. For example, diagnostic hypothesis testing appears as a measure of resistance to miserly processing and as a measure of probabilistic reasoning. Likewise, the accuracy of affective forecasting appears as a measure of resistance to miserly processing and as a measure of contaminated mindware (belief in absolutely accurate introspection). These measurement paradigms are complex in this manner simply because some tasks measure more than one rationality dimension.

Table 39.1 illustrates the basis for our statement that there is no *conceptual* barrier to creating a test of rational thinking. However, this does not mean that it would be *logistically* easy. Quite the contrary, we have stressed that both fluid and crystallized rationality are likely to be more multifarious than their analogous intelligence constructs. Likewise, we are not claiming that there exist comprehensive assessment devices for each of these components with adequate psychometric properties. However, in virtually every case, laboratory tasks that have appeared in the published literature give us, at a minimum, a hint at what comprehensive assessment of the particular component would look like. In fact, in some cases, there do exist fully developed measures with adequate psychometric properties (for example, measures of self efficacy, see Lefcourt, 1991).

Thus, Table 39.1 displays, in visual form, what we mean by claiming that the measurement of rational thought is conceptually possible with the use of currently available instruments. Nonetheless, the complexity of the table illustrates that measuring rational thought could be logistically daunting. For example, the factor structure of the table is still undetermined. We do not know the correlational relationships between the major dimensions or the measurement paradigms. This means that we do not know whether it might be possible to measure several features by measuring one with high multicollinearity.

Work on the structure of rational thought is nascent, but there are indications that there may be considerable separability in these components (Bruine de Bruin et al., 2007; Klaczynski, 2001; Parker & Fischhoff, 2005; Slugoski, Shields, & Dawson, 1993; Stanovich & West, 1998a, West et al., 2008). It may be that to get reasonable coverage of the domains listed in Table 39.1 each of the domains would have to be assessed separately. It might be that a comprehensive assessment of rational thought could not be accomplished in a single sitting. Although this represents a logistical problem, a diffuse factor structure does not negate the importance of assessing individual differences in rational thought. Rational thought does not require a *g* factor in order to justify its measurement. More important will be research linking these rational thinking tendencies to real-life decision making, and a reasonable amount of such research has already been conducted (Baron, Bazerman, & Shonk, 2006; Camerer, 2000; Fenton-O'Creevy, et al., 2003; Groopman, 2007; Hilton, 2003; Milkman, Rogers, & Bazerman, 2008; Thaler & Sunstein, 2008)

In short, the assessment of rational thought will be determined by the importance of the content domains listed in

Table 39.1 and by the fact that they fit within extant conceptual models of reasoning and judgment. Their importance, and hence the necessity for assessment, stands or falls on the conceptual model, not on any future psychometric finding. An oversimplified example will illustrate the point. Imagine that highway safety researchers found that braking skill was causally associated with lifetime automobile accident frequency, that knowledge of the road rules was causally associated with lifetime automobile accident frequency, that city driving skill was causally associated with lifetime automobile accident frequency, that cornering skill was causally associated with lifetime automobile accident frequency, that defensive driving was causally associated with lifetime automobile accident frequency, and a host of other relationships. In short, these skills, collectively, define a construct called "overall driver skill." Now we could in fact ask of these studies whether driving skill is a *g* factor or whether it is really 50 little separate skills. But the point is that the outcome of the investigation of the structure of individual differences in driving skill would have no effect on the conceptual definition of what driving skill is. It may have logistical implications for measurement, however. Skills that are highly correlated might not all have to be assessed to get a good individual difference metric. But if they were all causally related to accident frequency, they would remain part of the conceptual definition of overall driver skill.

It is likewise with rational thinking. There is independent evidence in the literature of cognitive science that the cognitive components in Table 39.1 form part of the conceptual definition of rational thought. If several components or measurement paradigms turn out to be highly correlated, that will make assessment more efficient and logistically easier, but it will not enhance or diminish the status of these components as aspects of rational thought. Conversely, finding that many of the components or measurement paradigms are separable in individual difference analyses in no way detracts from the importance of any component. It would, however, have logistical implications by making the assessment of rational thought time-consuming and unwieldy. In short, the point is that psychometric findings do not trump what cognitive scientists have found are the conceptually essential features of rational thought and action.

All of this is not to deny that it would obviously be useful to really know the structure of rational thinking skills, from a psychometric point of view. Our research group has contributed to clarifying that structure. We have found that certain rational thinking tasks consistently correlate with each other even after cognitive ability has been partialed out. For example, we have found that the ability to avoid belief bias in syllogistic reasoning is related to the ability to reason statistically in the face of conflicting case evidence – and that this relationship is maintained after intelligence is partialed out (Stanovich & West, 1998a; West et al., 2008). Additionally, our group has consistently found rational tasks that are predicted by thinking dispositions after cognitive ability has been partialed – particularly tasks involving statistical reasoning and informal argumentation (Kokis et al., 2002; Stanovich & West, 1997, 1998a; West et al., 2008).

Our point here, though, is to emphasize that the importance of assessing rational thought is not contingent on any empirical outcome – and it especially is not contingent on any type of psychometric outcome. We want to spur efforts at assessing components of rational thought, and thus in this early stage of the endeavor we do not want the effort to be impeded by unthoughtful protests that it cannot be measured because its psychometric structure is uncertain. That structure will become clarified once our call for greater attention to the measurement of this domain is heeded. We do not fail to measure something because of lack of knowledge of the full structure of its domain. We would not fail to measure braking skill if we were ignorant of its relationship to cornering ability or knowledge of road rules.

If neither the fluid nor the crystallized components of rational thought cluster in the manner of a *g* factor (which we suspect), then rational thought will be a difficult concept to practically assess in its entirety. But again, we should not shirk from measuring something just because it is logistically difficult – particularly if the domain is important. Economists and public policy experts measured the size of their country's GDP in 1935 despite (by present standards) primitive statistical tools and data gathering technology. The myriad components of the GDP (wheat, corn, ingots produced, heavy machinery produced, clothing, financial services, etc.) were each an important component of GDP in and of themselves, and it was not an argument against measuring them that they were hard to measure, that there were myriad components, and that we did not know how all of the components hung together statistically. In 1935, economists measured what they could with the tools they had, and they simply hoped that better knowledge via better tools lay in the future. We are at a similar juncture in the measurement of the multifarious concept of rational thought.

The Rationality Concept Is Superordinate to Critical Thinking as Well as Intelligence

We saw in a previous discussion that the concept of rationality – in encompassing both the reflective mind and the algorithmic mind – can be said to be a superordinate construct to intelligence. Like the study of wisdom (Sternberg, 2001, 2003; Sternberg & Jordan, 2005), the study of rational thinking is a normative/evaluative endeavor (Lee, 2008). Specifically, if one's goal is to *aid* people in their thinking, then it is essential that one have some way of *evaluating* thinking. The admonition to educators to "teach thinking skills" contains implicit evaluative assumptions. The students *already* think. Educators are charged with getting them to think *better* (Adams, 1993; Baron, 1993). This of course implies a normative model of what we mean by better thinking (Baron, 1993, 2008).

A somewhat analogous issue arises when thinking dispositions are discussed in the educational literature of critical thinking. Why do we want people to think in an actively open-minded fashion? Why do we want to foster multiplist and evaluative thinking (Kuhn, 1993, 2001, 2005; Kuhn & Udell, 2007) rather than absolutist thinking? Why do we want people to be reflective? It can be argued that the superordinate goal we are actually trying to foster is that of rationality (Stanovich, 2004, 2009). We value certain thinking dispositions because we think that they will at least aid in bringing belief in line with the world and in achieving our goals. By a parallel argument, we could equally well claim that the superordinate goal is to educate for wisdom (Sternberg, 2001, 2002a, 2003).

We can see that it is rationality, and not critical thinking per se, that is the higher level goal by conducting some simple thought experiments or imaginative hypotheticals. For example, we could imagine a person with excellent epistemic rationality (his or her degree of confidence in propositions being well calibrated to the available evidence relevant to the proposition) and optimal practical rationality (the person optimally satisfies desires) who was *not* actively open-minded – that is, who was not a good critical thinker under standard assumptions. Of course, we would still want to mold such an individual's dispositions in the direction of open-mindedness for the sake of society as a whole. But the essential point for the present discussion is that, from a purely *individual* perspective, we would now be hard-pressed to find reasons for *wanting* to change such a person's thinking dispositions if – whatever they were – they had led to rational thought and action in the past.

In short, a large part of the rationale for educational interventions to change thinking dispositions derives from a tacit assumption that actively open-minded critical-thinking dispositions make the individual a more rational person – or as Sternberg (2001, 2005) argues, a wiser, less foolish person. Our view is consistent with that of many other theorists who have moved toward conceptualizing critical thinking as a subspecies of rational thinking or at least as closely related to rational thinking (Kuhn, 2005; Moshman, 2004, 2010; Reyna, 2004; Siegel, 1988, 1997). Grounding critical thinking within the concept of rationality in this manner has an advantage because the concept of rationality is deeply intertwined with the data and theory of modern cognitive science (see LeBoeuf & Shafir, 2005; Over, 2004; Samuels & Stich, 2004; Stanovich, 2004, 2009) in a way that the concept of critical thinking is not.

In short, our theoretical argument seeks to "tame" the concept of critical thinking by pointing out that it does not trump the concept of rationality. Likewise, we hope in this chapter to open up some space for rationality in the lexicon of the mental and, in doing so, tame the intelligence concept. Our goal is to prevent the intelligence concept from absorbing the concept of rationality – something that IQ tests do not measure. Restricting the term *intelligence* to what the tests actually measure has the advantage of getting usage in line with the real world of measurement and testing. We have coherent and well-operationalized concepts of rational action and belief formation. We have a coherent and well-operationalized concept of intelligence. No scientific purpose is served by fusing these concepts, because they are very different. To the contrary, scientific progress is made by *differentiating* concepts.

The tripartite model of mind presented in this chapter explains why rationality is a more encompassing construct than intelligence. Rationality requires the proper functioning of both the reflective and the algorithmic mind. In contrast, intelligence tests index the computational power of the algorithmic mind. Likewise, the construct of critical thinking is subsumed under the construct of rationality. For example, the processes of critical thinking are often summarized as a set of thinking dispositions that must be developed or inhibited: need for cognition, actively open-minded thinking, belief identification, consideration of future consequences, reflectivity/impulsivity, rational/experiential orientation, need for closure, openness, conscientiousness, and so on. These thinking dispositions are the individual difference constructs that capture fluid rationality in the tripartite model (see Figure 39.5 and Table 39.1).

It is important to note that the thinking dispositions of the reflective mind are the psychological mechanisms that underlie rational thought. *Maximizing* these dispositions is *not* the criterion of rational thought itself. Rationality involves instead the maximization of goal achievement via judicious decision making and optimizing the fit of belief to evidence. The thinking dispositions of the reflective mind are a *means* to these ends. Certainly high levels of such commonly studied dispositions as reflectivity and belief flexibility are needed for rational thought and action. But high levels do not necessarily mean the maximal level. One does not maximize the reflectivity dimension, for example, because such a person might get lost in interminable pondering and never make a decision. Likewise, one does not maximize the thinking disposition of belief flexibility either, because such a person might end up with a pathologically unstable personality. Reflectivity and belief flexibility are "good" cognitive styles (in that most people are not high enough on these dimensions, so that more would be better), but they are not meant to be maximized.

In the context of this model (see Figures 39.3 and 39.4), rationality requires three things: the propensity to override suboptimal responses from the autonomous mind; the algorithmic capacity to inhibit the suboptimal response and to simulate an alternative; and finally the presence of the mindware that allows the computation of an alternative response. The propensity to override suboptimal responses from the autonomous mind – a property of the reflective mind – captures virtually all of the propensities of critical thinking that have been discussed in the traditional literature on that construct. The algorithmic capacity to inhibit the suboptimal response and to simulate an alternative is captured in standard tests of fluid intelligence such as the Raven Matrices.

We can further tame the intelligence concept in folk psychology by pointing out that there are legitimate scientific terms for the other valued parts of cognitive life and that some of these are measurable. This strategy uses to advantage a fact of life that many IQ-test critics have lamented – that intelligence tests are not going to change any time soon. The tests have the label "intelligence" and thus what they measure will always be dominant in the folk psychology of intelligence. We would argue that it is mistake to ignore this fact. The tests do not measure rationality, and thus the ability to think rationality will be a subordinate consideration in our schools, in our employment selection devices, and in our society as a whole as long as we conflate it with intelligence. We have tried to separate the two here by showing that they are conceptually different and by showing that rationality is in principle measurable in ways very much like intelligence is measured by IQ tests.

References

Ackerman, P. L. (1994). Intelligence, attention, and learning: Maximal and typical performance. In D. K. Detterman (Ed.), *Current topics in human intelligence* (Vol. 4, pp. 1–27). Norwood, NJ: Ablex.

Ackerman, P. L. (1996). A theory of adult development: Process, personality, interests, and knowledge. *Intelligence*, **22**, 227–257.

Ackerman, P. L., & Heggestad, E. D. (1997). Intelligence, personality, and interests: Evidence for overlapping traits. *Psychological Bulletin*, **121**, 219–245.

Ackerman, P. L., & Kanfer, R. (2004). Cognitive, affective, and conative aspects of adult intellect within a typical and maximal performance framework. In D. Y. Dai & R. J. Sternberg (Eds.), *Motivation, emotion, and cognition: Integrative perspectives on intellectual functioning and development* (pp. 119–141). Mahwah, NJ: Erlbaum.

Ackerman, P., Kyllonen, P., & Richards, R. (Eds.). (1999). *Learning and individual differences: Process, trait, and content determinants*. Washington, DC: American Psychological Association.

Adams, M. J. (1993). Towards making it happen. *Applied Psychology: An International Review*, **42**, 214–218.

Anderson, J. R. (1990). *The adaptive character of thought*. Hillsdale, NJ: Erlbaum.

Anderson, M. (2005). Marrying intelligence and cognition: A developmental view. In R. J. Sternberg & J. E. Pretz (Eds.), *Cognition and intelligence* (pp. 268–287). New York, NY: Cambridge University Press.

Arkes, H. R., & Blumer, C. (1985). The psychology of sunk cost. *Organizational Behavior and Human Decision Processes*, **35**, 124–140.

Audi, R. (1993). *The structure of justification*. Cambridge, UK: Cambridge University Press.

Audi, R. (2001). *The architecture of reason: The structure and substance of rationality*. Oxford. UK: Oxford University Press.

Austin, E. J., & Deary, I. J. (2002). Personality dispositions. In R. J. Sternberg (Ed.), *Why smart people can be so stupid* (pp. 187–211). New Haven, CT: Yale University Press.

Ayton, P., & Fischer, I. (2004). The hot hand fallacy and the gambler's fallacy: Two faces of subjective randomness? *Memory & Cognition*, **32**, 1369–1378.

Bagby, R. M., Parker, J. D. A., & Taylor, G. J. (1994). The twenty-item Toronto Alexithymia Scale-I. Item selection and cross-validation of the factor structure. *Journal of Psychosomatic Research*, 38, 23–32.

Balcetis, E., & Dunning, D. (2006). See what you want to see: Motivational influences on visual perception. *Journal of Personality and Social Psychology*, **91**, 612–625.

Baron, J. (1982). Personality and intelligence. In R. J. Sternberg (Ed.), *Handbook of human intelligence* (308–351). Cambridge, UK: Cambridge University Press.

Baron, J. (1993). Why teach thinking?–An essay. *Applied Psychology: An International Review*, **42**, 191–214.

Baron, J. (1995). Myside bias in thinking about abortion. *Thinking and Reasoning*, **1**, 221–235.

Baron, J. (2008). *Thinking and deciding* (4th ed.). New York, NY: Cambridge University Press.

Baron, J., & Hershey, J. C. (1988). Outcome bias in decision evaluation. *Journal of Personality and Social Psychology*, **54**, 569–579.

Bates, T. C., & Shieles, A. (2003). Crystallized intelligence as a product of speed and drive for experience: The relationship of inspection

time and openness to g and Gc. *Intelligence*, *31*, 275–287.
Baron, J., Bazerman, M. H., & Shonk, K. (2006). Enlarging the societal pie through wise legislation. A psychological perspective. *Perspectives on Psychological Science*, *1*, 123–132.
Bechara, A., Damasio, A. R., Damasio, H., & Anderson, S. (1994). Insensitivity to future consequences following damage to human prefrontal cortex. *Cognition*, *50*, 7–15.
Benjamin, D., & Shapiro, J. (2005, February 25). Does cognitive ability reduce psychological bias? *Journal of Economic Literature*, *J24*, *D14*, C91.
Bermudez, J. L. (2001). Normativity and rationality in delusional psychiatric disorders. *Mind & Language*, *16*, 457–493.
Birnbaum, M. H. (1999). Testing critical properties of decision making on the internet. *Psychological Science*, *10*, 399–407.
Brainerd, C. J., & Reyna, V. F. (2001). Fuzzy-trace theory: Dual processes in memory, reasoning, and cognitive neuroscience. In H. W. Reese & R. Kail (Eds.), *Advances in child development and behavior* (Vol. 28, pp. 41–100). San Diego, CA: Academic Press.
Brewer, N. T., & Chapman, G. (2002). The fragile basic anchoring effect. *Journal of Behavioral Decision Making*, *15*, 65–77.
Bruine de Bruin, W., Parker, A. M., & Fischhoff, B. (2007). Individual differences in adult decision-making competence. *Journal of Personality and Social Psychology*, *92*, 938–956.
Burns, B. D., & Corpus, B. (2004). Randomness and inductions from streaks: "Gambler's fallacy" versus "hot hand." *Psychonomic Bulletin & Review*, *11*, 179–184.
Burns, W. C. (1997). *Spurious correlations*. Accessed July 29, 2009, from http://www.burns.com/wcbspurcorl.htm.
Cacioppo, J. T., Petty, R. E., Feinstein, J., & Jarvis, W. (1996). Dispositional differences in cognitive motivation: The life and times of individuals varying in need for cognition. *Psychological Bulletin*, *119*, 197–253.
Camerer, C. F. (2000). Prospect theory in the wild: Evidence from the field. In D. Kahneman & A. Tversky (Eds.), *Choices, values, and frames* (pp. 288–300). Cambridge, UK: Cambridge University Press.
Carroll, J. B. (1993). *Human cognitive abilities: A survey of factor-analytic studies*. Cambridge, UK: Cambridge University Press.
Cattell, R. B. (1963). Theory for fluid and crystallized intelligence: A critical experiment. *Journal of Educational Psychology*, *54*, 1–22.
Cattell, R. B. (1998). Where is intelligence? Some answers from the triadic theory. In J. J. McArdle & R. W. Woodcock (Eds.), *Human cognitive abilities in theory and practice* (pp. 29–38). Mahwah, NJ: Erlbaum.
Chen, H., & Volpe, R. P. (1998). An analysis of personal financial literacy among college students. *Financial Services Review*, *7*, 107–128.
Christie, R. (1991). Authoritarianism and related constructs. In J. P. Robinson, P. Shaver, & L. S. Wrightsman (Eds.), *Measures of personality and social psychological attitudes* (pp. 501–571). San Diego, CA: Academic Press.
Cohen, L. J. (1981). Can human irrationality be experimentally demonstrated? *Behavioral and Brain Sciences*, *4*, 317–370.
Cronbach, L. J. (1949). *Essentials of psychological testing*. New York, NY: Harper.
Dawes, R. M. (1998). Behavioral decision making and judgment. In D. T. Gilbert, S. T. Fiske, & G. Lindzey (Eds.), *The handbook of social psychology* (Vol. 1, pp. 497–548). Boston, MA: McGraw-Hill.
Deary, I. J. (2000). *Looking down on human intelligence: From psychometrics to the brain*. Oxford, UK: Oxford University Press.
Deary, I. J. (2001). *Intelligence: A very short introduction*. Oxford, UK: Oxford University Press.
Denes-Raj, V., & Epstein, S. (1994). Conflict between intuitive and rational processing: When people behave against their better judgment. *Journal of Personality and Social Psychology*, *66*, 819–829.
Dennett, D. C. (1996). *Kinds of minds: Toward an understanding of consciousness*. New York, NY: Basic Books.
Dias, M., Roazzi, A., & Harris, P. L. (2005). Reasoning from unfamiliar premises: A study with unschooled adults. *Psychological Science*, *16*, 550–554.
Doherty, M. E., & Mynatt, C. (1990). Inattention to P(H) and to P(D/~H): A converging operation. *Acta Psychologica*, *75*, 1–11.
Doherty, M. E., Mynatt, C., Tweney, R., & Schiavo, M. (1979). Pseudodiagnositicity. *Acta Psychologica*, *43*, 111–121.
Dörner, D. (1996). *The logic of failure: Why things go wrong and what we can do to make them right*. New York, NY: Metropolitan Books.
Eckblad, M., & Chapman, L. J. (1983). Magical ideation as an indicator of schizotypy. *Journal*

of Consulting and Clinical Psychology, 51, 215–225.

Edwards, W. (1954). The theory of decision making. *Psychological Bulletin, 51*, 380–417.

Epley, N., & Gilovich, T. (2004). Are adjustments insufficient? *Personality and Social Psychology Bulletin, 30*, 447–460.

Epley, N., & Gilovich, T. (2006). The anchoring-and-adjustment heuristic: Why the adjustments are insufficient. *Psychological Science, 17*, 311–318.

Epley, N., Mak, D., & Chen Idson, L. (2006). Bonus or rebate? The impact of income framing on spending and saving. *Journal of Behavioral Decision Making, 19*, 213–227.

Epstein, S., Pacini, R., Denes-Raj, V., & Heier, H. (1996). Individual differences in intuitive-experiential and analytical-rational thinking styles. *Journal of Personality and Social Psychology, 71*, 390–405.

Evans, J. St. B. T. (1984). Heuristic and analytic processes in reasoning. *British Journal of Psychology, 75*, 451–468.

Evans, J. St. B. T. (1989). *Bias in human reasoning: Causes and consequences*. Hove, UK: Erlbaum.

Evans, J. St. B. T. (2006). The heuristic-analytic theory of reasoning: Extension and evaluation. *Psychonomic Bulletin and Review, 13*, 378–395.

Evans, J. St. B. T. (2007). *Hypothetical thinking: Dual processes in reasoning and judgment*. New York, NY: Psychology Press.

Evans, J. St. B. T. (2008). Dual-processing accounts of reasoning, judgment and social cognition. *Annual Review of Psychology, 59*, 255–278.

Evans, J. St. B. T. (2009). How many dual-process theories do we need? One, two, or many? In J. Evans & K. Frankish (Eds.), *In two minds: Dual processes and beyond* (pp. 33–54). Oxford, UK: Oxford University Press.

Evans, J. St. B. T., Barston, J., & Pollard, P. (1983). On the conflict between logic and belief in syllogistic reasoning. *Memory & Cognition, 11*, 295–306.

Evans, J. St. B. T., & Curtis-Holmes, J. (2005). Rapid responding increases belief bias: Evidence for the dual-process theory of reasoning. *Thinking and Reasoning, 11*, 382–389.

Evans, J. S. B. T., & Frankish, K. (Eds.). (2009). *In two minds: Dual processes and beyond*. Oxford, UK: Oxford University Press.

Evans, J. St. B. T., Handley, S. J., Harper, C., & Johnson-Laird, P. N. (1999). Reasoning about necessity and possibility: A test of the mental model theory of deduction. *Journal of Experimental Psychology: Learning, Memory, and Cognition, 25*, 1495–1513.

Evans, J. St. B. T., Newstead, S. E., & Byrne, R. M. J. (1993). *Human reasoning: The psychology of deduction*. Hove, UK: Erlbaum.

Evans, J. St. B. T., & Over, D. E. (2004). *If*. Oxford, UK: Oxford University Press.

Eysenck, H. J. (1994). Personality and intelligence: Psychometric and experimental approaches. In R. J. Sternberg & P. Ruzgis (Eds.), *Personality and intelligence* (pp. 3–31). Cambridge, UK: Cambridge University Press.

Facione, P. (1990). *Critical thinking: A statement of expert consensus for purposes of educational assessment and instruction (Executive Summary of the Delphi Report)*. La Cruz, CA: California Academic Press.

Feehrer, C. E., & Adams, M. J. (1986). *Odyssey: A curriculum for thinking*. Watertown, MA: Charlesbridge.

Feldman Barrett, L. F., Tugade, M. M., & Engle, R. W. (2004). Individual differences in working memory capacity and dual-process theories of the mind. *Psychological Bulletin, 130*, 553–573.

Fenton-O'Creevy, M., Nicholson, N., Soane, E., & Willman, P. (2003). Trading on illusions: Unrealistic perceptions of control and trading performance. *Journal of Occupational and Organizational Psychology, 76*, 53–68.

Fiedler, K. (2004). Illusory correlation. In R. Pohl (Ed.), *Cognitive illusions: A handbook on fallacies and biases in thinking, judgment and memory* (pp. 97–114). Hove, UK: Psychology Press.

Finucane, M. L., Alhakami, A., Slovic, P., & Johnson, S. M. (2000). The affect heuristic in judgments of risks and benefits. *Journal of Behavioral Decision Making, 13*, 1–17.

Fischhoff, B. (1975). Hindsight ≠ foresight: The effect of outcome knowledge on judgment under uncertainty. *Journal of Experimental Psychology: Human Perception and Performance, 1*, 288–299.

Fischhoff, B., Slovic, P., & Lichtenstein, S. (1977). Knowing with certainty: The appropriateness of extreme confidence. *Journal of Experimental Psychology: Human Perception and Performance, 3*, 552–564.

Fisk, J. E. (2004). Conjunction fallacy. In R. Pohl (Ed.), *Cognitive illusions: A handbook on fallacies and biases in thinking, judgment and memory* (pp. 23–42). Hove, UK: Psychology Press.

Flynn, J. R. (2007). *What is intelligence?* Cambridge, UK: Cambridge University Press.
Foley, R. (1987). *The theory of epistemic rationality*. Cambridge, MA: Harvard University Press.
Fong, G. T., Krantz, D. H., & Nisbett, R. E. (1986). The effects of statistical training on thinking about everyday problems. *Cognitive Psychology*, *18*, 253–292.
Frank, M. J., Cohen, M., & Sanfey, A. G. (2009). Multiple systems in decision making. *Current Direction in Psychological Science*, *18*, 73–77.
Frederick, S. (2005). Cognitive reflection and decision making. *Journal of Economic Perspectives*, *19*, 25–42.
Friedrich, J., Lucas, G., & Hodell, E. (2005). Proportional reasoning, framing effects, and affirmative action: Is six of one really half a dozen of another in university admissions? *Organizational Behavior and Human Decision Processes*, 98, 195–215.
Frisch, D. (1993). Reasons for framing effects. *Organizational Behavior and Human Decision Processes*, *54*, 399–429.
Gale, M., & Ball, L. J. (2006). Dual-goal facilitation in Wason's 2–4–6 task: What mediates successful rule discovery? *Quarterly Journal of Experimental Psychology*, *59*, 873–885.
Gigerenzer, G. (1996). On narrow norms and vague heuristics: A reply to Kahneman and Tversky (1996). *Psychological Review*, *103*, 592–596.
Gigerenzer, G. (2007). *Gut feelings: The intelligence of the unconscious*. New York, NY: Viking Penguin.
Gilovich, T., Griffin, D., & Kahneman, D. (Eds.). (2002). *Heuristics and biases: The psychology of intuitive judgment*. New York, NY: Cambridge University Press.
Goff, M., & Ackerman, P. L. (1992). Personality-intelligence relations: Assessment of typical intellectual engagement. *Journal of Educational Psychology*, 84, 537–552.
Greenhoot, A. F., Semb, G., Colombo, J., & Schreiber, T. (2004). Prior beliefs and methodological concepts in scientific reasoning. *Applied Cognitive Psychology*, *18*, 203–221.
Griffin, D., & Tversky, A. (1992). The weighing of evidence and the determinants of confidence. *Cognitive Psychology*, *24*, 411–435.
Groopman, J. (2007). *How doctors think*. Boston, MA: Houghton Mifflin.
Haidt, J. (2001). The emotional dog and its rational tail: A social intuitionist approach to moral judgment. *Psychological Review*, *108*, 814–834.
Halpern, D. (2008). *Halpern Critical Thinking Assessment: Background and scoring standards*. Unpublished manuscript. Claremont, CA: Claremont McKenna College.
Handley, S. J., Capon, A., Beveridge, M., Dennis, I., & Evans, J. S. B. T. (2004). Working memory, inhibitory control and the development of children's reasoning. *Thinking and Reasoning*, *10*, 175–195.
Harman, G. (1995). Rationality. In E. E. Smith & D. N. Osherson (Eds.), *Thinking* (Vol. 3, pp. 175–211). Cambridge, MA: MIT Press.
Hasher, L., Lustig, C., & Zacks, R. (2007). Inhibitory mechanisms and the control of attention. In A. Conway, C. Jarrold, M. Kane, A. Miyake, & J. Towse (Eds.), *Variation in working memory* (pp. 227–249). New York, NY: Oxford University Press.
Hastie, R., & Dawes, R. M. (2001). *Rational choice in an uncertain world*. Thousand Oaks, CA: Sage.
Heath, C., Larrick, R. P., & Wu, G. (1999). Goals as reference points. *Cognitive Psychology*, *38*, 79–109.
Heath, J. (2001). *The efficient society*. Toronto, Canada: Penguin Books.
Hilton, D. J. (2003). Psychology and the financial markets: Applications to understanding and remedying irrational decision-making. In I. Brocas & J. D. Carrillo (Eds.), *The psychology of economic decisions: Vol. 1, Rationality and well-being* (pp. 273–297). Oxford, UK: Oxford University Press.
Horn, J. L., & Cattell, R. B. (1967). Age differences in fluid and crystallized intelligence. *Acta Psychologica*, *26*, 1–23.
Hsee, C. K., & Zhang, J. (2004). Distinction bias: Misprediction and mischoice due to joint evaluation. *Journal of Personality and Social Psychology*, 86, 680–695.
Jacowitz, K. E., & Kahneman, D. (1995). Measures of anchoring in estimation tasks. *Personality and Social Psychology Bulletin*, *21*, 1161–1167.
Jeffrey, R. C. (1983). *The logic of decision* (2nd ed.). Chicago, IL: University of Chicago Press.
Jepson, C., Krantz, D., & Nisbett, R. (1983). Inductive reasoning: Competence or skill? *Behavioral and Brain Sciences*, *6*, 494–501.
Kahneman, D., & Frederick, S. (2002). Representativeness revisited: Attribute substitution in intuitive judgment. In T. Gilovich, D. Griffin, & D. Kahneman (Eds.), *Heuristics and biases: The psychology of intuitive judgment*

(pp. 49–81). New York, NY: Cambridge University Press.

Kahneman, D., Knetsch, J. L., & Thaler, R. H. (1990). Experimental tests of the endowment effect and the Coase theorem. *Journal of Political Economy*, 98, 1325–1348.

Kahneman, D., Knetsch, J. L., & Thaler, R. H. (1991). The endowment effect, loss aversion, and status quo bias. *Journal of Economic Perspectives*, 5, 193–206.

Kahneman, D., & Tversky, A. (1972). Subjective probability: A judgment of representativeness. *Cognitive Psychology*, 3, 430–454.

Kahneman, D., & Tversky, A. (1973). On the psychology of prediction. *Psychological Review*, 80, 237–251.

Kahneman, D., & Tversky, A. (1979). Prospect theory: An analysis of decision under risk. *Econometrica*, 47, 263–291.

Kahneman, D., & Tversky, A. (1982). The simulation heuristic. In D. Kahneman, P. Slovic, & A. Tversky (Eds.), *Judgment under uncertainty: Heuristics and biases* (pp. 201–208). Cambridge, UK: Cambridge University Press.

Kahneman, D., & Tversky, A. (1984). Choices, values, and frames. *American Psychologist*, 39, 341–350.

Kahneman, D., & Tversky, A. (1996). On the reality of cognitive illusions. *Psychological Review*, 103, 582–591.

Kahneman, D., & Tversky, A. (Eds.). (2000). *Choices, values, and frames*. Cambridge, UK: Cambridge University Press.

Kanazawa, S. (2004). General intelligence as a domain-specific adaptation. *Psychological Review*, 111, 512–523.

Kane, M. J., & Engle, R. W. (2003). Working-memory capacity and the control of attention: The contributions of goal neglect, response competition, and task set to Stroop interference. *Journal of Experimental Psychology: General*, 132, 47–70.

Kermer, D. A., Driver-Linn, E., Wilson, T. D., & Gilbert, D. T. (2006). Loss aversion is an affective forecasting error. *Psychological Science*, 17, 649–653.

Kirby, K. N. (2009). One-year temporal stability of delay-discount rates. *Psychonomic Bulletin & Review*, 16, 457–462.

Klaczynski, P. A. (2000). Motivated scientific reasoning biases, epistemological beliefs, and theory polarization: A two-process approach to adolescent cognition. *Child Development*, 71, 1347–1366.

Klaczynski, P. A. (2001). Analytic and heuristic processing influences on adolescent reasoning and decision making. *Child Development*, 72, 844–861.

Klaczynski, P. A., & Gordon, D. H. (1996). Everyday statistical reasoning during adolescence and young adulthood: Motivational, general ability, and developmental influences. *Child Development*, 67, 2873–2891.

Klaczynski, P. A., Gordon, D. H., & Fauth, J. (1997). Goal-oriented critical reasoning and individual differences in critical reasoning biases. *Journal of Educational Psychology*, 89, 470–485.

Klaczynski, P. A., & Lavallee, K. L. (2005). Domain-specific identity, epistemic regulation, and intellectual ability as predictors of belief-based reasoning: A dual-process perspective. *Journal of Experimental Child Psychology*, 92, 1–24.

Klaczynski, P. A., & Robinson, B. (2000). Personal theories, intellectual ability, and epistemological beliefs: Adult age differences in everyday reasoning tasks. *Psychology and Aging*, 15, 400–416.

Klauer, K. C., Musch, J., & Naumer, B. (2000). On belief bias in syllogistic reasoning. *Psychological Review*, 107, 852–884.

Koehler, D. J., & Harvey, N. (Eds.). (2004). *Blackwell handbook of judgment and decision making*. Oxford, UK: Blackwell.

Kokis, J., Macpherson, R., Toplak, M., West, R. F., & Stanovich, K. E. (2002). Heuristic and analytic processing: Age trends and associations with cognitive ability and cognitive styles. *Journal of Experimental Child Psychology*, 83, 26–52.

Komorita, S. S., & Parks, C. D. (1994). *Social dilemmas*. Boulder, CO: Westview Press.

Kruglanski, A. W., & Webster, D. M. (1996). Motivated closing the mind: "Seizing" and "freezing." *Psychological Review*, 103, 263–283.

Kuhn, D. (1991). *The skills of argument*. Cambridge, UK: Cambridge University Press.

Kuhn, D. (1992). Thinking as argument. *Harvard Educational Review*, 62, 155–178.

Kuhn, D. (1993). Connecting scientific and informal reasoning. *Merrill-Palmer Quarterly*, 38, 74–103.

Kuhn, D. (2001). How do people know? *Psychological Science*, 12, 1–8.

Kuhn, D. (2005). *Education for thinking*. Cambridge, MA: Harvard University Press.

Kuhn, D. (2007, February/March). Jumping to conclusions: Can people be counted on to make sound judgments? *Scientific American Mind*, 44–51.

Kuhn, D., Cheney, R., & Weinstock, M. (2000). The development of epistemological understanding. *Cognitive Development*, 15, 309–328.

Kuhn, D., & Udell, W. (2007). Coordinating own and other perspectives in argument. *Thinking & Reasoning*, 13, 90–104.

Larrick, R. P. (2004). Debiasing. In D. J. Koehler & N. Harvey (Eds.), *Blackwell handbook of judgment and decision making* (pp. 316–337). Malden, MA: Blackwell.

Larrick, R. P., Morgan, J. N., & Nisbett, R. E. (1990). Teaching the use of cost-benefit reasoning in everyday life. *Psychological Science*, 1, 362–370.

Larrick, R. P., Nisbett, R. E., & Morgan, J. N. (1993). Who uses the cost-benefit rules of choice? Implications for the normative status of microeconomic theory. *Organizational Behavior and Human Decision Processes*, 56, 331–347.

LeBoeuf, R. A., & Shafir, E. (2005). Decision making. In K. J. Holyoak & R. G. Morrison (Eds.), *The Cambridge handbook of thinking and reasoning* (pp. 243–265). New York, NY: Cambridge University Press.

LeBoeuf, R. A., & Shafir, E. (2006). The long and short of it: Physical anchoring effects. *Journal of Behavioral Decision Making*, 19, 393–406.

Lee, C. J. (2008). Applied cognitive psychology and the "strong replacement" of epistemology by normative psychology. *Philosophy of the Social Sciences*, 38, 55–75.

Lefcourt, H. M. (1991). Locus of control. In J. P. Robinson, P. Shaver, & L. S. Wrightsman (Eds.), *Measures of personality and social psychological attitudes* (pp. 413–499). San Diego, CA: Academic Press.

Lehman, D. R., Lempert, R. O., & Nisbett, R. E. (1988). The effect of graduate training on reasoning. *American Psychologist*, 43, 431–442.

Lehman, D. R., & Nisbett, R. E. (1990). A longitudinal study of the effects of undergraduate training on reasoning. *Developmental Psychology*, 26, 952–960.

Leslie, A. M. (1987). Pretense and representation: The origins of "Theory of Mind." *Psychological Review*, 94, 412–426.

Levin, I. P., Schneider, S. L., & Gaeth, G. J. (1998). All frames are not created equal: A typology and critical analysis of framing effects. *Organizational Behavior and Human Decision Processes*, 76, 149–188.

Levin, I. P., Gaeth, G. J., Schreiber, J., & Lauriola, M. (2002). A new look at framing effects: Distribution of effect sizes, individual differences, and independence of types of effects. *Organizational Behavior and Human Decision Processes*, 88, 411–429.

Lichtenstein, S., & Slovic, P. (1971). Reversal of preferences between bids and choices in gambling decisions. *Journal of Experimental Psychology*, 89, 46–55.

Lichtenstein, S., & Slovic, P. (1973). Response-induced reversals of preference in gambling: An extended replication in Las Vegas. *Journal of Experimental Psychology*, 101, 16–20.

Lichtenstein, S., & Slovic, P. (Eds.). (2006). *The construction of preference*. Cambridge, UK: Cambridge University Press.

Lichtenstein, S., Slovic, P., Fischhoff, B., Layman, M., & Combs, B. (1978). Judged frequency of lethal events. *Journal of Experimental Psychology: Human Learning and Memory*, 4, 551–578.

Lindner, H., Kirkby, R., Wertheim, E., & Birch, P. (1999). A brief assessment of irrational thinking: The Shortened General Attitude and Belief Scale. *Cognitive Therapy and Research*, 23, 651–663.

Lohman, D. F. (2000). Complex information processing and intelligence. In R. J. Sternberg (Ed.), *Handbook of intelligence* (pp. 285–340). Cambridge, UK: Cambridge University Press.

Lubinski, D. (2004). Introduction to the special section on cognitive abilities: 100 years after Spearman's (1904) "General Intelligence, Objectively Determined and Measured." *Journal of Personality and Social Psychology*, 86, 96–111.

Luce, R. D., & Raiffa, H. (1957). *Games and decisions*. New York, NY: Wiley.

Macpherson, R., & Stanovich, K. E. (2007). Cognitive ability, thinking dispositions, and instructional set as predictors of critical thinking. *Learning and Individual Differences*, 17, 115–127.

Mandell, L. (2009). *The financial literacy of young American adults*. Washington, DC: Jump-Start Coalition for Personal Financial Literacy. Items at http://www.jumpstart.org/upload/2009_FinLit-Mandell.pdf.

Manktelow, K. I. (2004). Reasoning and rationality: The pure and the practical. In K. I. Manktelow & M. C. Chung (Eds.), *Psychology of reasoning: Theoretical and historical perspectives* (pp. 157–177). Hove, UK: Psychology Press.

Markovits, H., & Nantel, G. (1989). The belief-bias effect in the production and evaluation of logical conclusions. *Memory & Cognition, 17*, 11–17.

Marr, D. (1982). *Vision*. San Francisco, CA: W. H. Freeman.

Matthews, G., Zeidner, M., & Roberts, R. D. (2002). *Emotional intelligence: Science and myth*. Cambridge, MA: MIT Press.

Maule, J., & Villejoubert, G. (2007). What lies beneath: Reframing framing effects. *Thinking and Reasoning, 13*, 25–44.

McClure, S. M., Laibson, D. I., Loewenstein, G., & Cohen, J. D. (2004). Separate neural systems value immediate and delayed monetary rewards. *Science, 306*, 503–507.

Messick, D. M., & Sentis, K. P. (1979). Fairness and preference. *Journal of Experimental Social Psychology, 15*, 418–434.

Metcalfe, J., & Mischel, W. (1999). A hot/cool-system analysis of delay of gratification: Dynamics of will power. *Psychological Review, 106*, 3–19.

Milkman, K. L., Rogers, T., & Bazerman, M. H. (2008). Harnessing our inner angels and demons. *Perspectives on Psychological Science, 3*, 324–338.

Miyake, A., Friedman, N., Emerson, M. J., & Witzki, A. H. (2000). The utility and diversity of executive functions and their contributions to complex "frontal lobe" tasks: A latent variable analysis. *Cognitive Psychology, 41*, 49–100.

Moore, D. A. (1999). Order effects in preference judgments: Evidence for context dependence in the generation of preferences. *Organizational Behavior and Human Decision Processes, 78*, 146–165.

Moshman, D. (2004). From inference to reasoning: The construction of rationality. *Thinking and Reasoning, 10*, 221–239.

Moshman, D. (2010). The development of rationality. In H. Siegel (Ed.), *Oxford handbook of philosophy of education* (pp. 145–161). Oxford, UK: Oxford University Press.

Murphy, D., & Stich, S. (2000). Darwin in the madhouse: Evolutionary psychology and the classification of mental disorders. In P. Carruthers & A. Chamberlain (Eds.), *Evolution and the human mind: Modularity, language and meta-cognition* (pp. 62–92). Cambridge, UK: Cambridge University Press.

Mussweiler, T., & Englich, B. (2005). Subliminal anchoring: Judgmental consequences and underlying mechanisms. *Organizational Behavior and Human Decision Processes, 98*, 133–143.

Mussweiler, T., Strack, F., & Pfeiffer, T. (2000). Overcoming the inevitable anchoring effect: Considering the opposite compensates for selective accessibility. *Personality and Social Psychology Bulletin, 9*, 1142–1150.

Mynatt, C. R., Doherty, M. E., & Dragan, W. (1993). Information relevance, working memory, and the consideration of alternatives. *Quarterly Journal of Experimental Psychology, 46A*, 759–778.

NCEE (National Council for Economic Education). (2005), *What American teens and adults know about economics*. Accessed July 28, 2009, from http://www.ncee.net/cel/WhatAmericansKnowAboutEconomics_042605-3.pdf.

Neisser, U., Boodoo, G., Bouchard, T., Boykin, A. W., Brody, N., Ceci, S. J., Halpern, D., Loehlin, J., Perloff, R., Sternberg, R., & Urbina, S. (1996). Intelligence: Knowns and unknowns. *American Psychologist, 51*, 77–101.

Newstead, S. E., Handley, S. J., Harley, C., Wright, H., & Farrelly, D. (2004). Individual differences in deductive reasoning. *Quarterly Journal of Experimental Psychology, 57A*, 33–60.

Nichols, S., & Stich, S. P. (2003). *Mindreading: An integrated account of pretence, self-awareness, and understanding other minds*. Oxford, UK: Oxford University Press.

Nickerson, R. S. (2004). *Cognition and chance: The psychology of probabilistic reasoning*. Mahwah, NJ: Erlbaum.

Nickerson, R. S. (2008). *Aspects of rationality*. New York, NY: Psychology Press.

Nisbett, R. E., Krantz, D. H., Jepson, C., & Kunda, Z. (1983). The use of statistical heuristics in everyday inductive reasoning. *Psychological Review, 90*, 339–363.

Norris, S. P., & Ennis, R. H. (1989). *Evaluating critical thinking*. Pacific Grove, CA: Midwest.

Oswald, M. E., & Grosjean, S. (2004). Confirmation bias. In R. Pohl (Ed.), *Cognitive illusions: A handbook on fallacies and biases in thinking, judgment and memory* (pp. 81–96). Hove, UK: Psychology Press.

Over, D. E. (2004). Rationality and the normative/descriptive distinction. In D. J. Koehler & N. Harvey (Eds.), *Blackwell handbook of judgment and decision making* (pp. 3–18). Malden, MA: Blackwell.

Parker, A. M., & Fischhoff, B. (2005). Decision-making competence: External validation through an individual differences approach.

Journal of Behavioral Decision Making, 18, 1–27.

Perkins, D. N. (1985). Postprimary education has little impact on informal reasoning. *Journal of Educational Psychology, 77*, 562–571.

Perkins, D. N. (1995). *Outsmarting IQ: The emerging science of learnable intelligence*. New York, NY: Free Press.

Perkins, D. N. (2002). The engine of folly. In R. J. Sternberg (Ed.), *Why smart people can be so stupid* (pp. 64–85). New Haven, CT: Yale University Press.

Perner, J. (1991). *Understanding the representational mind*. Cambridge, MA: MIT Press.

Peters, E., Vastfjall, D., Slovic, P., Mertz, C. K., Mazzocco, K., & Dickert, S. (2006). Numeracy and decision making. *Psychological Science, 17*, 407–413.

Pohl, R. (2004). Hindsight bias. In R. Pohl (Ed.), *Cognitive illusions: A handbook on fallacies and biases in thinking, judgment and memory* (pp. 363–378). Hove, UK: Psychology Press.

Poulton, E. C. (1994). *Behavioral decision theory: A new approach*. Cambridge, UK: Cambridge University Press.

Prado, J., & Noveck, I. A. (2007). Overcoming perceptual features in logical reasoning: A parametric functional magnetic resonance imaging study. *Journal of Cognitive Neuroscience, 19*, 642–657.

Pronin, E., Lin, D. Y., & Ross, L. (2002). The bias blind spot: Perceptions of bias in self versus others. *Journal of Personality and Social Psychology Bulletin, 28*, 369–381.

Reyna, V. F. (2004). How people make decisions that involve risk. *Current Directions in Psychological Science, 13*, 60–66.

Ricco, R. B. (2007). Individual differences in the analysis of informal reasoning fallacies. *Contemporary Educational Psychology, 32*, 459–484.

Rodriguez, M. L., Mischel, W., & Shoda, Y. (1989). Cognitive person variables in delay of gratification of older children at risk. *Journal of Personality and Social Psychology, 57*, 358–367.

Sá, W., Kelley, C., Ho, C., & Stanovich, K. E. (2005). Thinking about personal theories: Individual differences in the coordination of theory and evidence. *Personality and Individual Differences, 38*, 1149–1161.

Sá, W., & Stanovich, K. E. (2001). The domain specificity and generality of mental contamination: Accuracy and projection in judgments of mental content. *British Journal of Psychology, 92*, 281–302.

Sá, W., West, R. F., & Stanovich, K. E. (1999). The domain specificity and generality of belief bias: Searching for a generalizable critical thinking skill. *Journal of Educational Psychology, 91*, 497–510.

Salthouse, T. A., Atkinson, T. M., & Berish, D. E. (2003). Executive functioning as a potential mediator of age-related cognitive decline in normal adults. *Journal of Experimental Psychology: General, 132*, 566–594.

Samuels, R., & Stich, S. P. (2004). Rationality and psychology. In A. R. Mele & P. Rawling (Eds.), *The Oxford handbook of rationality* (pp. 279–300). Oxford, UK: Oxford University Press.

Savage, L. J. (1954). *The foundations of statistics*. New York, NY: Wiley.

Schneider, S. L., Burke, M. D., Solomonson, A. L., & Laurion, S. K. (2005). Incidental framing effects and associative processes: A study of attribute frames in broadcast news stories. *Journal of Behavioral Decision Making, 18*, 261–280.

Schommer-Aikins, M. (2004). Explaining the epistemological belief system: Introducing the embedded systemic model and coordinated research approach. *Educational Psychologist, 39*, 19–30.

Shafir, E., & LeBoeuf, R. A. (2002). Rationality. *Annual Review of Psychology, 53*, 491–517.

Shafir, E., & Tversky, A. (1992). Thinking through uncertainty: Nonconsequential reasoning and choice. *Cognitive Psychology, 24*, 449–474.

Shamosh, N. A., et al. (2008). Individual differences in delay discounting. *Psychological Science, 19*, 904–911.

Siegel, H. (1988). *Educating reason*. New York, NY: Routledge.

Siegel, H. (1997). *Rationality redeemed? Further dialogues on an educational ideal*. New York, NY: Routledge.

Sloman, S. A. (1996). The empirical case for two systems of reasoning. *Psychological Bulletin, 119*, 3–22.

Sloman, S. A. (2002). Two systems of reasoning. In T. Gilovich, D. Griffin, & D. Kahneman (Eds.), *Heuristics and biases: The psychology of intuitive judgment* (pp. 379–396). New York, NY: Cambridge University Press.

Sloman, S. A., Over, D., Slovak, L., & Stibel, J. M. (2003). Frequency illusions and other fallacies. *Organizational Behavior and Human Decision Processes, 91*, 296–309.

Slovic, P., Finucane, M. L., Peters, E., & MacGregor, D. G. (2002). The affect heuristic. In T. Gilovich, D. Griffin, & D. Kahneman (Eds.),

Heuristics and biases: The psychology of intuitive judgment (pp. 397–420). New York: Cambridge University Press.
Slugoski, B. R., Shields, H. A., & Dawson, K. A. (1993). Relation of conditional reasoning to heuristic processing. *Personality and Social Psychology Bulletin*, 19, 158–166.
Smith, E. R., & DeCoster, J. (2000). Dual-process models in social and cognitive psychology: Conceptual integration and links to underlying memory systems. *Personality and Social Psychology Review*, 4, 108–131.
Stanovich, K. E. (1989). Implicit philosophies of mind: The dualism scale and its relation to religiosity and belief in extrasensory perception. *Journal of Psychology*, 123, 5–23.
Stanovich, K. E. (1999). *Who is rational? Studies of individual differences in reasoning*. Mahwah, NJ: Erlbaum.
Stanovich, K. E. (2002). Rationality, intelligence, and levels of analysis in cognitive science: Is dysrationalia possible? In R. J. Sternberg (Ed.), *Why smart people can be so stupid* (pp. 124–158). New Haven, CT: Yale University Press.
Stanovich, K. E. (2004). *The robot's rebellion: Finding meaning in the age of Darwin*. Chicago, IL: University of Chicago Press.
Stanovich, K. E. (2008). Higher-order preferences and the Master Rationality Motive. *Thinking & Reasoning*, 14, 111–127.
Stanovich, K. E. (2009). *What intelligence tests miss: The psychology of rational thought*. New Haven, CT: Yale University Press.
Stanovich, K. E. (2010a). *Decision making and rationality in the modern world*. New York, NY: Oxford University Press.
Stanovich, K. E. (2010b). *How to think straight about psychology* (9th ed.). Boston: Allyn & Bacon.
Stanovich, K. E., Toplak, M. E., & West, R. F. (2008). The development of rational thought: A taxonomy of heuristics and biases. *Advances in child development and behavior*, 36, 251–285.
Stanovich, K. E., & West, R. F. (1997). Reasoning independently of prior belief and individual differences in actively open-minded thinking. *Journal of Educational Psychology*, 89, 342–357. Items at http://web.mac.com/kstanovich/iWeb/Site/Argument%20Evaluation%20Test%20%28AET%29.html.
Stanovich, K. E., & West, R. F. (1998a). Individual differences in rational thought. *Journal of Experimental Psychology: General*, 127, 161–188.
Stanovich, K. E., & West, R. F. (1998b). Who uses base rates and P(D/~H)? An analysis of individual differences. *Memory & Cognition*, 26, 161–179.
Stanovich, K. E., & West, R. F. (1999). Discrepancies between normative and descriptive models of decision making and the understanding/acceptance principle. *Cognitive Psychology*, 38, 349–385.
Stanovich, K. E., & West, R. F. (2000). Individual differences in reasoning: Implications for the rationality debate? *Behavioral and Brain Sciences*, 23, 645–726.
Stanovich, K. E., & West, R. F. (2007). Natural myside bias is independent of cognitive ability. *Thinking & Reasoning*, 13, 225–247.
Stanovich, K. E., & West, R. F. (2008a). On the failure of intelligence to predict myside bias and one-sided bias. *Thinking & Reasoning*, 14, 129–167.
Stanovich, K. E., & West, R. F. (2008b). On the relative independence of thinking biases and cognitive ability. *Journal of Personality and Social Psychology*, 94, 672–695.
Stein, E. (1996). *Without good reason: The rationality debate in philosophy and cognitive science*. Oxford, UK: Oxford University Press.
Steinberg, L., Graham, S., O'Brien, L., Woolard, J., Cauffman, E., & Banich, M. (2009). Age differences in future orientation and delay discounting. *Child Development*, 80, 28–44.
Sternberg, R. J. (1977). *Intelligence, information processing, and analogical reasoning*. Hillsdale, NJ: Erlbaum.
Sternberg, R. J. (1985). *Beyond IQ: A triarchic theory of human intelligence*. New York: Cambridge University Press.
Sternberg, R. J. (2001). Why schools should teach for wisdom: The balance theory of wisdom in educational settings. *Educational Psychologist*, 36, 227–245.
Sternberg, R. J. (2002a). Smart people are not stupid, but they sure can be foolish: The imbalance theory of foolishness. In R. J. Sternberg (Ed.), *Why smart people can be so stupid* (pp. 232–242). New Haven, CT: Yale University Press.
Sternberg, R. J. (Ed.). (2002b). *Why smart people can be so stupid*. New Haven, CT: Yale University Press.
Sternberg, R. J. (2003). *Wisdom, intelligence, and creativity synthesized*. Cambridge, UK: Cambridge University Press.
Sternberg, R. J. (2005). Foolishness. In R. J. Sternberg & J. Jordan (Eds.), *A handbook of wisdom: Psychological perspectives* (pp. 331–352). New York, NY: Cambridge University Press.

Sternberg, R. J. (2006). The Rainbow Project: Enhancing the SAT through assessments of analytical, practical, and creative skills. *Intelligence, 34*, 321–350.

Sternberg, R. J., & Detterman, D. K. (Eds.). (1986). *What is intelligence?* Norwood, NJ: Ablex.

Sternberg, R. J., & Grigorenko, E. L. (1997). Are cognitive styles still in style? *American Psychologist, 52*, 700–712.

Sternberg, R. J., Grigorenko, E. L., & Zhang, L. (2008). Styles of learning and thinking matter in instruction and assessment. *Perspectives on Psychological Science, 3*, 486–506.

Sternberg, R. J., & Jordan, J. (Eds.). (2005). *A handbook of wisdom: Psychological perspectives*. New York, NY: Cambridge University Press.

Strathman, A., Gleicher, F., Boninger, D. S., & Scott Edwards, C. (1994). The consideration of future consequences: Weighing immediate and distant outcomes of behavior. *Journal of Personality and Social Psychology, 66*, 742–752.

Suddendorf, T., & Corballis, M. C. (2007). The evolution of foresight: What is mental time travel and is it unique to humans? *Behavioral and Brain Sciences, 30*, 299–351.

Taber, C. S., & Lodge, M. (2006). Motivated skepticism in the evaluation of political beliefs. *American Journal of Political Science, 50*, 755–769.

Terjesen, M. D., Salhany, J., & Sciutto, M. J. (2009). A psychometric review of measures of irrational beliefs: Implications for psychotherapy. *Journal of Rational-Emotive & Cognitive-Behavior Therapy, 27*, 83–96.

Thaler, R. H. (1980). Toward a positive theory of consumer choice. *Journal of Economic Behavior and Organization, 1*, 39–60.

Thaler, R. H. (1985). Mental accounting and consumer choice. *Marketing Science, 4*, 199–214.

Thaler, R. H. (1987). The psychology and economics conference handbook: Comments on Simon, on Einhorn and Hogarth, and on Tversky and Kahneman. In R. M. Hogarth & M. Reder (Eds.), *Rational choice: The contrast between economics and psychology* (pp. 95–100). Chicago, IL: University of Chicago Press.

Thaler, R. H., & Sunstein, C. R. (2008). *Nudge: Improving decisions about health, wealth, and happiness*. New Haven, CT: Yale University Press.

Thompson, S. C. (2004). Illusions of control. In R. Pohl (Ed.), *Cognitive illusions: A handbook on fallacies and biases in thinking, judgment and memory* (pp. 115–126). Hove, UK: Psychology Press.

Tobacyk, J., & Milford, G. (1983). Belief in paranormal phenomena. *Journal of Personality and Social Psychology, 44*, 1029–1037.

Toplak, M., Liu, E., Macpherson, R., Toneatto, T., & Stanovich, K. E. (2007). The reasoning skills and thinking dispositions of problem gamblers: A dual-process taxonomy. *Journal of Behavioral Decision Making, 20*, 103–124.

Toplak, M. E., & Stanovich, K. E. (2002). The domain specificity and generality of disjunctive reasoning: Searching for a generalizable critical thinking skill. *Journal of Educational Psychology, 94*, 197–209.

Toplak, M. E., & Stanovich, K. E. (2003). Associations between myside bias on an informal reasoning task and amount of post-secondary education. *Applied Cognitive Psychology, 17*, 851–860.

Towse, J. N., & Neil, D. (1998). Analyzing human random generation behavior: A review of methods used and a computer program for describing performance. *Behavior Research Methods, Instruments & Computers, 30*, 583–591.

Tschirgi, J. E. (1980). Sensible reasoning: A hypothesis about hypotheses. *Child Development, 51*, 1–10.

Tversky. A. (2003). *Preference, belief, and similarity: Selected writings of Amos Tversky*. Shafir, E. (Ed.). Cambridge, MA: MIT Press.

Tversky, A., & Kahneman, D. (1974). Judgment under uncertainty: Heuristics and biases. *Science, 185*, 1124–1131.

Tversky, A., & Kahneman, D. (1981). The framing of decisions and the psychology of choice. *Science, 211*, 453–458.

Tversky, A., & Kahneman, D. (1982). Evidential impact of base rates. In D. Kahneman, P. Slovic, & A. Tversky (Eds.), *Judgment under uncertainty: Heuristics and biases* (pp. 153–160). Cambridge, UK: Cambridge University Press.

Tversky, A., & Kahneman, D. (1983). Extensional versus intuitive reasoning: The conjunction fallacy in probability judgment. *Psychological Review, 90*, 293–315.

Tversky, A., & Kahneman, D. (1986). Rational choice and the framing of decisions. *Journal of Business, 59*, 251–278.

Tweney, R. D., Doherty, M. E., Warner, W. J., & Pliske, D. (1980). Strategies of rule discovery in an inference task. *Quarterly Journal of Experimental Psychology, 32*, 109–124.

von Neumann, J., & Morgenstern, O. (1944). *The theory of games and economic behavior*. Princeton, NJ: Princeton University Press.

Wagenaar, W. A., & Sagaria, S. D. (1975). Misperception of exponential growth. *Perception and Psychophysics, 18*, 416–422.

Wasserman, E. A., Dorner, W. W., & Kao, S. F. (1990). Contributions of specific cell information to judgments of interevent contingency. *Journal of Experimental Psychology: Learning, Memory, and Cognition, 16*, 509–521.

Watson, G., & Glaser, E. M. (1980). *Watson-Glaser Critical Thinking Appraisal*. New York, NY: Psychological Corporation.

Weinstein, N. (1980). Unrealistic optimism about future life events. *Journal of Personality and Social Psychology, 39*, 806–820.

West, R. F., Toplak, M. E., & Stanovich, K. E. (2008). Heuristics and biases as measures of critical thinking: Associations with cognitive ability and thinking dispositions. *Journal of Educational Psychology, 100*, 930–941.

Wu, G., Zhang, J., & Gonzalez, R. (2004). Decision under risk. In D. J. Koehler & N. Harvey (Eds.), *Blackwell handbook of judgment and decision making* (pp. 399–423). Malden, MA: Blackwell.

Zeidner, M., & Matthews, G. (2000). Intelligence and personality. In R. J. Sternberg (Ed.), *Handbook of intelligence* (pp. 581–610). New York, NY: Cambridge University Press.

Zelazo, P. D. (2004). The development of conscious control in childhood. *Trends in Cognitive Sciences, 8*, 12–17.

CHAPTER 40

Intelligence and Wisdom

Ursula M. Staudinger and Judith Glück

Wisdom is a construct characterized by a rich cultural history and complex associations. Across cultures and history, wisdom has been discussed as the prototypical ideal of human knowledge and character. Starting from the dictionary definition of wisdom as "good judgment and advice in difficult and uncertain matters of life," psychologists have described wisdom as the search for the moderate course between extremes, a dynamic between knowledge and doubt, a sufficient detachment from the problem at hand, and a well-balanced coordination of emotion, motivation, and thought. This implies that wisdom shows overlap with the construct of intelligence but clearly extends beyond it. Most wisdom researchers probably agree that a certain level of intelligence is necessary but not sufficient for wisdom to be displayed. Within psychological research on wisdom, two kinds of approaches can be distinguished. One is the study of lay conceptions of wisdom and the other is the attempt to measure expressions of wisdom. With regard to expressions, personal and general wisdom have been distinguished. Age trajectories, antecedents, and plasticity of general and personal wisdom are discussed with a focus on the relationship between wisdom and intelligence.

Historical Background

Since the beginnings of human culture, wisdom has been viewed as an ideal end point of human development. Indeed, the idea of wisdom as one of the highest forms of knowledge and skill is evident in the very definition of the historical grand master of all scholarship, philosophy (philosophia): "The love/pursuit of wisdom." Historically, wisdom was conceptualized in terms of a state of idealized being (such as Lady Wisdom), as a process of perfect knowing and judgment as in King Solomon's judgments, or as an oral or written product such as wisdom-related proverbs and the so-called wisdom literature. Important to recognize is that the identification of wisdom with individuals (such as wise persons), the predominant approach in psychology, is but one of the ways by which wisdom is instantiated. In fact, in the historical literature on wisdom, the identification of wisdom with the mind and character of individuals is not the preferred mode of analysis. Rather, wisdom is conceptualized as a characteristic of texts or other bodies of knowledge. Wisdom is considered an ideal that is difficult to be fully represented in the isolated individual.

Throughout history, interest in the topic of wisdom has waxed and waned. In general, two main lines of argument were pivotal in the historical evolution of the concept of wisdom: the distinction between philosophical and practical wisdom – often attributed to Aristotle's differentiation between sophia and phronesis – and the question of whether wisdom is divine or human. In the Western world, these two issues (philosophical vs. practical; divine vs. human) were at the center of heated discourse during the Renaissance, with many important works written on these wisdom topics during the 15th through the 17th centuries. An initial conclusion of this debate was reached during the later phases of the Enlightenment. Wisdom was still critical, for instance, to the thinking of Kant and Hegel. Both understood wisdom as being based on the coordination of the world of science and the practical world of humankind. However, the 18th-century French *Encyclopedia* of Diderot (and others), despite its more than 50 volumes, barely mentioned the topic. During the Enlightenment and the process of secularization, wisdom lost its salience as one of the fundamental categories guiding human thought and conduct.

Nevertheless, from time to time, scholars in such fields as philosophy, political science, theology, and cultural anthropology continue to attend to wisdom, although in our view, less in a cumulative sense of theory building than in rejuvenating and revisiting its meaning, historical roots, and implications for raising human awareness about the complexities and uncertainties of life. During the last decade, for example, some philosophers have struggled with the definition of wisdom, including the polarization between practical and philosophical wisdom, the integration of different forms of knowledge into one overarching whole, and the search for orientation in life (e.g., Kekes, 1995; Welsch, 2001). The last issue has gained special importance in relation to the advent of postmodernity. Finally, there is archaeological-cultural work dealing with the origins of religious and secular bodies of wisdom-related texts in China, India, Egypt, Old Mesopotamia, and other sites of ancient civilizations. Proverbs, maxims, and tales constitute a great part of the materials underlying such efforts. It is impressive to realize how wisdom-related proverbs and tales evince a high degree of cultural and historical invariance. This relative invariance gives rise to the assumption that concepts such as wisdom, with its related body of knowledge and skills, have been selected in the course of cultural development because of their adaptive value for humankind.

The psychological study of wisdom emerged around the late 1970s and early 1980 in the general context of a search for the potentials of aging or, more specifically, the search for domains or types of intellectual functioning that would not show age-related decline. While earlier investigations of cognitive aging had largely focused on losses in fluid intelligence, later the focus shifted to include the crystallized, experience-based dimension of intelligence that was found to grow until mid-life and remain stable into old age. It was suggested that with age, experience is able to compensate for the declines in fluid intelligence (Baltes, Dittmann-Kohli, & Dixon, 1984). In this vein, life experience and wisdom as well as professional expertise, everyday problem solving, or practical intelligence were selected as topics of investigation from the 1980s on (e.g., Sternberg & Jordan, 2005).

Psychological Approaches to the Definition of Wisdom

A first approach to the definition of wisdom from a psychological perspective is its treatment in dictionaries. The major German historical dictionary, for instance, defined wisdom as "insight and knowledge about oneself and the world...and sound judgment in the case of difficult life problems" (Grimm & Grimm, 1854/1984). Similarly, the *Oxford English Dictionary* includes in its definition of wisdom "Good judgment and advice in difficult and uncertain matters of life" (Fowler & Fowler, 1964). These definitions differ from the notion of intelligence in that they define a certain problem domain – that is, difficult life problems – which asks for the application of knowledge and intelligence. Furthermore, good judgment and advice in difficult life matters not only ask for intelligence. They also require one to deal with emotional, social, and moral aspects.

When psychologists approach the definition of wisdom, like philosophers, they are confronted with the need to specify the content and formal properties of wisdom-related thought, judgment, and advice in terms of psychological categories. Another important goal of wisdom research has been to describe characteristics of persons who have approached a state of wisdom and who are capable of transmitting wisdom to others. Initial efforts by psychologists in this direction were for the most part theoretical and speculative. In his pioneering piece on senescence, G. Stanley Hall (1922), for example, associated wisdom with the emergence of a meditative attitude, philosophic calmness, impartiality, and the desire to draw moral lessons that emerge in later adulthood. Furthermore, other writers have emphasized that wisdom involves the search for the moderate course between extremes, a dynamic between knowledge and doubt, a sufficient detachment from the problem at hand, and a well-balanced coordination of emotion, motivation, and thought. In line with dictionary definitions, writings by psychologists typically refer to wisdom as knowledge about the human condition at its frontier, knowledge about the most difficult questions of the meaning and conduct of life, and knowledge about the uncertainties of life, about what cannot be known, and how to deal with that limited knowledge. Thus, much of wisdom is meta-knowledge, knowledge about the limitations of knowledge and about when to apply which strategy of problem solution or self-regulation.

Most of the empirical psychological research on wisdom to date falls into one of two categories (Sternberg, 1998): studies of so-called implicit theories, that is, what "laypeople" think wisdom is, and studies based on theoretical conceptions of wisdom that psychologists have developed. In the following, we first review the literature on implicit theories of wisdom and then give an overview of explicit theories and related empirical findings.

Implicit (Subjective) Theories About Wisdom

Most empirical research on wisdom in psychology so far has focused on further elaboration of the definition of wisdom. Moving beyond dictionary definitions of wisdom, research explored the nature of everyday beliefs, folk conceptions, or implicit (subjective) theories of wisdom. The pursuit of answers to questions such as "What is wisdom?" "How is wisdom different from intelligence or creativity?" "Which situations require wisdom?" "What is a wise act?" and "What are the characteristics of wise people?" has been an important focus of psychological wisdom research since the 1980s. These studies in principle built on research initiated by Clayton and colleagues (e.g., Clayton, 1975; Clayton & Birren, 1980), whose methodology to identify lay conceptions of wisdom has become fairly common among wisdom researchers (overview in Bluck & Glück, 2005): First, a sample of laypersons or experts (e.g., professors from different fields; Sternberg, 1985) are asked to generate a list of wisdom-related characteristics or vignettes. The resulting pool of items – or, at least, a subgroup of items that is left after terms have been screened for synonyms and redundancies – in turn, is rated by another group of individuals in terms of its wisdom-relatedness or typicality. Subsequently, statistical procedures such as factor analysis or multidimensional scaling are frequently used to identify underlying dimensions of items. In Clayton and Birren's study, this procedure yielded three dimensions found to be prototypical of wise people: (1) *affective characteristics* such as empathy and compassion, (2) *reflective processes* such as intuition and introspection, and (3) *cognitive capacities* such as experience and intelligence. The dimensions found by Clayton and Birren (1980) pertain until today (e.g., Ardelt, 2003).

Recently, new dimensions have been added, and characteristics have been ordered differently (see Table 40.1). For example, in their review of implicit theories Bluck and Glück (2005) draw more heavily on the distinction between real-world skills and interpersonal skills ("concern for others") as opposed to capacities with a less interactive emphasis, such as cognitive ability, insight, and reflective attitude. Notably, results of studies on implicit notions of wisdom are heavily influenced by the initial pool of items. For example, a study by Hershey and Farrell (1997), comprising – in contrast to most other studies – also characteristics assumed *not* to be associated with wisdom yielded one dimension labeled "egotism" comprising only attributes deemed as unwise. In the same vein, another study including items referring to *protection of the environment* or *religion* resulted in two additional factors that had not been identified by previous studies (Jason et al., 2001; see Table 40.1).

Additional dimensions of a contextual and interactive nature emerge when individuals are asked about their own experiences with wisdom (rather than describing a wise person in general), as is the case, for example, in studies on wisdom nominees or when asking participants about their own wisdom. In studies of wisdom nominees, typically, individuals are asked to name persons they consider wise, and potential commonalities are identified among the nominees. The most general finding of these studies is that most wisdom nominees are *relatively old* (e.g., around 60 years in the studies by Jason et al., 2001 or Baltes, Staudinger, Maercker, & Smith, 1995). Further criteria ascribed to wise people emerging from the nominee approach – next to those mentioned earlier – were, most of all, *guidance*, and *moral principles*.

Finally one may ask, What is the function of wisdom in everyday life? Drawing on autobiographical memories of events in which individuals retrospectively viewed themselves as wise, three forms of wisdom were identified (Glück, Bluck, Baron, & McAdams, 2005): *empathy and support*, *self-determination and assertion*, and *knowledge and flexibility*. *Self-determination and assertion*, as opposed to the other two facets, may be recognized as an aspect of wisdom primarily when people are asked about their own life, that is, when interviewees also have access to their inner thoughts, feelings, and motivations. A similar result, that is, a focus on inner motives or the relationship between intentions and external circumstances, was found when analyzing wise acts. According to studies by Oser and colleagues (1999), wise acts seem to be characterized by the following seven features: (1) *paradoxical, unexpected*; (2) of *moral integrity*; (3) *selfless*; (4) *overcoming internal and external dictates*; (5) *striving toward equilibrium*; (6) *implying a risk*; (7) *striving toward improving the human condition*. Hence, different approaches to the study of implicit notions of wisdom yield findings that supplement and enrich the results from other studies.

From this research on implicit theories of wisdom and wise persons, it is evident that people in Western samples hold fairly clear-cut images of the essential characteristics of wisdom. There are also interesting individual differences in individual conceptions, however. Using an exploratory approach, Glück and Bluck (in press) found two distinct types of conceptions of wisdom in a large German-speaking sample. About one-third of the participants viewed wisdom as largely a property of the *mind:* they judged knowledge and life experience, insight, and cognitive complexity as the most important characteristics of wisdom. The other two-thirds viewed wisdom as an integration of *mind and virtue:* They also endorsed the cognitive aspects but viewed tolerance, empathy, an orientation to the greater good, and love for humanity as equally central

Table 40.1. Implicit Theories of Wisdom: A Comparison of Findings from Five Studies with Sample Items[a]

Clayton (1975)	*Sternberg (1985)*	*Holliday & Chandler (1986)*	*Hershey & Farrell (1997)*	*Jason et al. (2001)*
Affective (1) – Empathy – Compassion	Sagacity (2) – Concern for others – Considers advice	Interpersonal skills (4) – Sensitive – Sociable	Egotism, inverse (2) – Extravagant – Presumptuous	Warmth (2) – Compassion and warmth for others – Kindness
	Perspicacity (6) – Intuition – Offers right and true solutions	Judgment and communication skills (2) – Is a good source of advice – Understands life	Perceptive Judgment (1) Sincere – Fair – Thoughtful	
Reflective (2) – Intuition – Introspection	Judgment (4) – Acts within own limitations – Is sensible	Social unobtrusiveness (5) – Discreet – Nonjudgmental	Basic Temperament (3) – Withdrawn – Reflective	Harmony (1) – Good judgment – Experiences an underlying unity in life
	Learning from ideas and environment (3) – Perceptive – Learns from mistakes	Exceptional understanding as based on ordinary experience (1) – Has learned from experience – Sees things in a larger context		
Cognitive (3) – Experience – Intelligence	Reasoning ability (1) – Good problem-solving ability – Logical mind	General competence (3) – Intelligent – Educated		Intelligence (3) – Intelligence – Problem-solving ability Connecting to nature (4) – Reverence for nature – Childlike wonder and awe Spirituality (5) – Feels love, fellowship, or union with god – Living a spiritual life
	Expeditious use of information (5) – Experienced – Seeks out information			

Note: Sequence of factors or dimensions obtained in original research is given in parentheses. Studies are based on different methodologies (factor analysis, multidimensional scaling).

[a] Modified after Staudinger and Baltes, 1994.

components of wisdom. Thus, the two clusters differ in the importance they assign to intelligence-related components within the concept of wisdom: The first group seems to view wisdom as a form of intelligence, while the second group views intelligence as but one necessary component of wisdom. The noncognitive components seem to become more important to people in the course of young adulthood: While most individuals under age 30 viewed wisdom as a property of the mind, the majority of those over 30 shared the mind-and-virtue view.

Interestingly, gender differences in conceptions of wisdom are mostly small to nonexistent: men and women differ only marginally in the characteristics they associate with wisdom (Glück, Strasser, & Bluck, 2009). This picture changes somewhat when participants think about concrete instances of wisdom in their own lives: Men are more often nominated as wise than women, and this is particularly so with male nominators (e.g., Glück, Bischof, & Siebenhüner, 2009; Jason et al., 2001). When asked about events in which they were wise in their own life, men mostly report professional situations whereas women tend to report family or relationship-related events (Glück et al., 2009).

What about other cultures? Are similar conceptions of wisdom found in non-Western cultures? Several studies have reported cultural differences in conceptions of wisdom (Takahashi, 2000; Takahashi & Bordia, 2000; Takahashi & Overton, 2002, 2005; Yang, 2001). Takahashi and Bordia (2000), for instance, compared implicit definitions of wisdom among young adults from the United States, Australia, India, and Japan. They found that the association between wisdom and cognitive variables pervasive in Western samples is less important in East-Asian cultures, in which characteristics such as being aged, experienced, and discreet are perceived as pivotal for wisdom. Additionally, the association of wisdom with experience and practical knowledge was found to be stronger in Asian than in Western samples. Integrating these findings with psychological models of wisdom, Takahashi and Overton (2005) distinguished two broad modes of wisdom: an analytic (Western) mode that emphasizes knowledge and cognitive complexity, and a synthetic (Eastern) mode that focuses on the integration of cognition, reflection, and affect. Thus, according to these authors, the analytic conception assigns intelligence a much more prominent role for wisdom than the synthetic conception. Takahashi and Overton identified these two modes of wisdom in both theoretical models of wisdom and cross-cultural studies of Eastern and Western wisdom conceptions. They linked the analytic conception of wisdom to the developmental idea of wisdom as highly complex life expertise developed through learning. The synthetic notion of wisdom was viewed as developing through transformation of the individual through existential experiences.

Despite differences, five features can be identified that are common to how people across different cultures view wisdom, wise people, and wise acts: First, in the minds of people, wisdom seems to be closely related to wise persons and their acts as "carriers" of wisdom. Second, wise people are expected to combine features of mind and character (even though the mind may have be assigned varying importance), and to balance multiple interests and choices. Third, wisdom carries a strong interpersonal and social aspect with regard both to its application (advice) and the consensual recognition of its occurrence. Fourth, wisdom exhibits overlap with other related concepts, such as intelligence; but in aspects like sagacity, prudence, and the integration of cognition, emotion, and motivation, it also carries unique variance. Fifth, it seems to make a difference whether I conceive of my own wisdom or describe that of another prototypical person.

"Explicit" Theories and the Assessment of Wisdom

A more recent line of empirical psychological inquiry on wisdom addresses the question of how to define wisdom conceptually ("explicit," as compared to laypeople's more implicit conceptions of wisdom) and measure behavioral expressions of wisdom based on scientific definitions. Researchers of wisdom are usually quite aware that it is a courageous undertaking to try to study wisdom empirically. Wisdom is a complex and content-rich phenomenon, and, as many scholars have claimed, it defies attempts at scientific identification. However, research on explicit theories of wisdom has made remarkable progress at measuring wisdom in terms of personality characteristics (standardized or open-ended), characteristics of adult thought, and performance (judgment, advice) on difficult life tasks.

The Distinction Between General and Personal Wisdom

The various lines of work can be subsumed under two main headings, namely, *personal* wisdom, on the one hand, and *general* wisdom, on the other. This distinction is loosely related to the philosophical separation between the ontology of the first and the third person (Searle, 1992). The ontology of the first person indicates insight into life based on personal experience. In contrast, the ontology of the third person refers to the view on life that is based on an observer's perspective. In loose analogy to Searle's first-person perspective, *personal wisdom* refers to a person's insight into his or her own life: What does a person know about himself or herself, his or her life? Analogous to the third-person perspective, *general wisdom* is concerned with insights into life in general. What does an individual know about life from an observer's point of view, that is, when she or he is not personally concerned? For instance, your general wisdom is tapped if a friend comes to you because *his or her* marriage is in a deep crisis and he or she is considering divorce. But it takes your personal wisdom if you search for a solution because your *own* marriage is in a deep crisis and you are considering divorce.

The distinction between general and personal wisdom may be helpful when trying to settle some of the ongoing debates in the field of wisdom research. For heuristic purposes, Table 40.2 assigns many of the extant approaches in research on wisdom to either a personal-wisdom or a general-wisdom perspective. Note that this categorization is sometimes difficult to make because the original authors do not describe their notion of wisdom along the distinction between personal and general wisdom. Consequently, the assignment is based on inferences on our behalf and is made according to the relative emphasis placed on either personal or general wisdom. Another way of ordering could also be to classify the different approaches on a multifaceted continuum from highly personal, experience-based, intuitive wisdom to wisdom as an abstract characteristic of writings or problem solutions.

The two types of wisdom do not necessarily have to coincide in a person. A person can be wise with regard to the life and problems of other people and can be sought out for advice from others because of her wisdom but the very same person does not necessarily have to be wise about her own life and her own problems. To test this contention, the two types of wisdom need to be conceptualized and measured independently of each other.

Different research traditions have led to interest in one or the other type of wisdom. The approaches primarily geared toward personal wisdom are usually based in the tradition of personality research and personality development. Wisdom in this perspective describes the mature personality or an ideal end point of personality growth (e.g., Erikson or Ryff). Intelligence is not explicitly mentioned in these conceptions of wisdom but one may infer that it is at most viewed as a necessary precondition of wisdom. When one thinks about wisdom from this vantage point, clearly there is also a close link to research on personality growth and learning from traumatic events (e.g., stress-related growth, Park, Cohen, & Murch, 1996; post-traumatic growth, Tedeschi & Calhoun, 2004). The approaches primarily investigating general wisdom typically have a stronger connection with the historical wisdom

Table 40.2. Tentative Assignment of Extant Wisdom Approaches to Personal or General Wisdom[a]

Wisdom Approach	*Personal Wisdom*	*General Wisdom*
Explicit Theories		
Self-report Questionnaires		
Erikson: Integrity	X	
Loevinger: Ego level	X	
Helson & Wink: . . .	X	
Orwoll & Perlmutter: . . .	X	
Ardelt: Reflection – Cognition – Affect	X	
Webster: Five-component model	X	
Ryff, Whitbourne	X	
Performance Measures e.g., Arlin, Kitchener, Kramer		X
Berlin Paradigm: Expertise in the Fundamental Pragmatics of Life		X
Sternberg: Balance Theory		X
Labouvie-Vief: Integration of Affect and Cognition	X	
Bremen Paradigm of Personal Wisdom	X	
Self-concept Maturity	X	
Implicit Theories		
Holliday & Chandler	X	X
Clayton & Birren	X	X
Hershey & Farrell		X
Jason et al.		X

[a] Modified after Staudinger, Dörner, & Mickler, 2005.

literature (i.e., wisdom as sound advice or life insight independent of individuals) and an expertise approach to the study of wisdom (e.g., Berlin wisdom paradigm, e.g., Baltes & Staudinger, 2000; Sternberg's balance theory of wisdom, e.g., Sternberg, 1998).

The distinction between personal and general wisdom is also relevant when exploring the ontogenesis of wisdom. First, there is reason to assume that it is the dynamic between personal and general life insight that is at the heart of eventually attaining wisdom. Decades of research on self-regulation as well as research on the therapeutical process have demonstrated that it is much more difficult to obtain insight into one's own life (let alone apply it) than into the difficulties and problems of others (e.g., Greenwald & Pratkanis, 1984). Thus, general wisdom might be less difficult to attain than personal wisdom (first empirical evidence for that claim has been ascertained: Mickler & Staudinger, 2008) and therefore the final attainment of the former may precede that of the latter in ontogenesis. Certainly, in the *course* of ontogeny, that is, in working toward general and/or personal wisdom, both types may alternate in taking the lead. Generally, the development of wisdom is a dynamic process in which cognitive, affective, and motivational resources develop interactively through the reflection of experience. We do know, however, from research on the development of the self-concept that the infant appropriates general knowledge about the world before she or he is able to acknowledge the self. From research on the self later in ontogeny, we have learned that self-related information is processed differently from general information. On the one hand, under certain conditions we do have better memory for self-related information. However, threatening or inconsistent self-related information is often suppressed or modified, which may hinder the development of personal wisdom. On the other hand, it is conceivable that even individuals who have been able to overcome perceptual and cognitive biases and have attained personal wisdom, which involves the ability to be critical of oneself, do not have the ability and/or the motivation to think about life problems beyond their own specific circumstances or to give advice to others. As a consequence, the coincidence of personal and general wisdom in one person is probably very rare (Staudinger, Mickler, & Dörner, 2005).

Psychological Conceptions of General Wisdom

Various approaches to general wisdom can be distinguished, one of which is the cultural-historical analysis of wisdom mentioned above. Cultural-historical work concerning the origins of religious and secular bodies of wisdom-related texts has revealed a common core of defining features of wisdom that seems to reflect the notion of general wisdom more than that of personal wisdom. According to an analysis conducted by Paul Baltes, the common core of general wisdom is this: (1) Wisdom comprises knowledge with extraordinary scope, depth, measure, and balance; (2) it addresses important and difficult questions and strategies about the conduct and meaning of life; (3) it includes knowledge about the limits of knowledge and the uncertainties of the world; (4) it represents a truly superior level of knowledge, judgment, and advice; (5) it is easily recognized when manifested, but difficult to achieve and to specify. Note that in this analysis personality characteristics are not mentioned as a defining feature common to wisdom across cultures and historical time.

Wisdom as postformal operations. Within psychology, different approaches to general wisdom include wisdom as postformal thought in the neo-Piagetian tradition (Riegel, 1975; Labouvie-Vief, 1990), Sternberg's balance theory of wisdom (Sternberg, 1998, 2001), and the notion of wisdom as expert knowledge in the Berlin wisdom paradigm (e.g., Baltes & Staudinger, 2000). In the following, these conceptions of general wisdom are discussed in more detail.

Informed by the Piagetian tradition of studying cognitive development, several investigators proposed a postformal stage of adult thinking and related this stage to mature thought or wisdom. In theories of postformal thought, wisdom is conceptualized as increasingly complex and dialectical thinking (Riegel, 1975). Criteria of postformal thinking include awareness of multiple causes and solutions; awareness of paradoxes and contradictions; and the ability to deal with uncertainty, inconsistency, imperfection, and compromise. Pivotal for postformal thinking is the transcendence of the universal truth criterion that characterizes formal logic – a tolerance of ambiguity created by an acceptance of multiple truths. (In this approach, little attention has been paid to the need for setting boundaries of relativity.) Thus, conceptions of wisdom as a postformal stage of cognitive development obviously view wisdom as the adult form of intelligence characterized by particularly high tolerance of complexity and ambiguity, which renders its assessment through classical, linear, intelligence tasks highly difficult.

Empirical research in the field of *neo-Piagetian conceptions* of wisdom has addressed, for example, the relationship of postformal stages of cognitive development with social cognition (e.g., Arlin, 1990; Kitchener & Brenner, 1990; Kramer, 1983; Labouvie-Vief, 1990, Pascual-Leone, 1990). For example, postformal thinkers demonstrated a tendency to show less of an actor-observer effect (in which situational causes are held responsible for one's own behavior and dispositional factors for others' behavior) and higher levels of moral reasoning than nonpostformal thinkers. It was also found that positive mood induction and relaxation improved postformal thinking, whereas focusing attention had detrimental effects. In sum, it might be concluded that "wise thinking" in the neo-Piagetian sense is related to a tolerant and open-minded attitude, which is also characteristic of the Big Five personality dimension "openness to experience," a frequent correlate of general and personal wisdom in empirical studies. Plus, it seems easier to think "wisely" when relaxed and in a positive mood.

Sternberg's (1998, 2001) balance theory. Sternberg relates wisdom to both practical and academic intelligence. Academic intelligence, in the sense of fluid intelligence, provides a necessary but by no means sufficient basis to wisdom-related functioning. But wisdom also involves the application of tacit knowledge, which is the key aspect of practical intelligence. Tacit knowledge is action-oriented (procedural) knowledge that is usually implicit and acquired without direct help from others (rather by role modeling) and that allows individuals to achieve goals that they personally value. In contrast to practical intelligence, however, wisdom is by definition oriented toward a balance between self-interest, the interests of others, and external contextual interests in order to achieve a common good. This balancing is the key aspect of Sternberg's theory of wisdom. The output of wisdom typically is a piece of advice. Wisdom is assessed by presenting people with problems whose best solution integrates several intrapersonal, interpersonal, and extrapersonal interests (Sternberg, 2001).

A wise person in this sense is comfortable with ambiguity, in contrast to a conventionally intelligent person, who considers ambiguity as something to be resolved, and in contrast to a creative person who can tolerate ambiguity but is uncomfortable with it (Sternberg, 1998). Also, when faced with obstacles, the wise person tries to understand the problem and its implications for self and others. The wise person endorses a judicial thinking style, that is, she or he likes to analyze and evaluate ideas and procedures and not only pass judgment on them (Sternberg, 1997). Also related to the area of personality is the assumption that a wise person is highly motivated to seek the common good.

The Berlin wisdom paradigm (e.g., Baltes & Smith, 1990; Baltes & Staudinger, 2000). Here, wisdom is defined as expertise in the fundamental pragmatics of life. The fundamental pragmatics of life refer to deep knowledge and sound judgment about the essence of the human condition and the ways and means of planning, managing, and understanding a good life. Expert knowledge in fundamental pragmatics of life can be described according to five criteria. The first criterion, *factual knowledge*, concerns knowledge about such topics as human nature, life span development, variations in developmental processes and outcomes, interpersonal relations, and social norms. The second criterion, *procedural knowledge*, involves strategies and heuristics for dealing with the meaning and conduct of life – for example, heuristics for giving advice, ways to handle life conflicts. Additionally, a wise person should show *life span contextualism*, that is, to consider life problems in relation to the domains of life (e.g., education, family, work, friends, leisure, the public good of society, etc.), their interrelations, and to put these in a lifetime perspective (i.e., past, present, future). *Relativism of values and life priorities* is another criterion of wisdom. It means to acknowledge and tolerate interindividual differences in values while at the same time being geared toward optimizing and balancing the individual and the common good. Finally, the last criterion, the *recognition and management of uncertainty*, is based on the idea that human beings can never know everything that is necessary to determine the best decision in the present, to predict the future perfectly, or to be 100% sure about why things happened the way they did in the past. A wise person is aware of this uncertainty and has developed ways to manage it.

Measurement. To elicit and measure general wisdom-related knowledge and skills, the Berlin group of wisdom researchers has presented participants with difficult life dilemmas such as the following: "Imagine a good friend of yours calls you up and tells you that he/she can't go on anymore and has decided to commit suicide. What would one/you be thinking about, how would one/you deal with this situation?" Participants are then asked to "think aloud" about the dilemma. Their responses are recorded on tape and later transcribed. To quantify performance quality, a select panel of judges, who are extensively trained and calibrated to apply the five wisdom criteria defined above, evaluates the protocols of the respondents using 7-point scales. Every rater only evaluates one criterion in order to avoid halo affects. Two raters were assigned to each criterion to allow calculation of interrater reliabilities, which, across many studies, were consistently in the 70s and 80s per criterion and even above .9 for the overall wisdom score, which averages across the five criteria. The obtained scores provide an approximation of the quantity and quality of wisdom-related knowledge and skills of a given person. When using this wisdom paradigm to study people who were nominated as wise according to nominators' subjective beliefs about wisdom, wisdom nominees received higher wisdom scores than comparable control samples of various ages and professional backgrounds (Baltes, Staudinger, Maercker, & Smith, 1995).

Ontogenetic model. In the context of the Berlin paradigm, a general framework was developed that outlines the conditions for the development of wisdom as it is instantiated in persons. The model presents a set of factors and processes that need to "cooperate" for wisdom to develop. First, there are general individual characteristics such as intelligence and personality. Second, the model presumes that the development of wisdom is advanced by certain expertise-specific factors, such as a strong motivation to learn about life, practice with difficult life situations, and guidance by a mentor. Third, the model implies the operation of macro-level facilitative experiential contexts. For example, certain professions and historical periods are more conducive to the development of wisdom than others. Given such experiences, certain social-cognitive processes (life planning, life management, and life review) are assumed to be critical for the development of wisdom-related knowledge and judgment.

Empirical work testing this ontogenetic model confirmed that crystallized and fluid intelligence are a necessary but by no means a sufficient condition for wisdom. In line with the historical wisdom literature, which portrays wisdom as the ideal combination of mind and virtue, it was found that wisdom-related performance is best predicted by measures located at the interface of cognition and personality, such as social intelligence, creativity, and moral reasoning (Staudinger, Lopez, & Baltes, 1997; Pasupathi & Staudinger, 2001). Neither intelligence nor personality, as measured by standard tests, independently of each other made a significant contribution to wisdom-related knowledge and judgment. Interestingly, a very different predictive pattern is found when wisdom-related performance in adolescence is considered, where cognitive development seems to be a crucial basis for the emergence of wisdom-related knowledge (Staudinger & Pasupathi, 2003). While general wisdom as measured according to the Berlin wisdom paradigm is unrelated to subjective well-being, Kunzmann and Baltes (2003) found that it is related to experiencing positive and negative affect. Wise individuals reported experiencing both positive (e.g., happy, cheerful) and negative affect (e.g., angry, afraid) less frequently than other individuals, but they reported a higher degree of affective involvement (e.g., interested, inspired) than the rest of the sample. According to the authors, this pattern suggests that wisdom might go along with a more realistic, less self-enhancing and less positively biased view of life, but at the same time with better skills of regulating negative emotions. A further finding of this study was that wise individuals tended to endorse values referring to personal growth, life insight, societal engagement, the well-being of friends, and ecological protection more than other individuals did.

Age trajectories and plasticity. Contrary to work on the fluid mechanics of cognitive aging, older adults perform as well as younger adults (> 25 yrs.) in the Berlin wisdom paradigm (overview in Staudinger, 1999a). It seems that wisdom-related knowledge and judgment emerges between the ages of 14 and 25 years (Pasupathi, Staudinger, & Baltes, 2001). Furthermore, when advanced age was combined with wisdom-related experiential contexts, such as professional specializations involving training and experience in matters of life (e.g., clinical psychology), higher levels of performance were observed (Smith, Staudinger, & Baltes, 1994; Staudinger, Smith, & Baltes, 1994). Wisdom-related knowledge and judgment have also been found to demonstrate plasticity. In two intervention studies, Staudinger and coworkers found that by either providing for a certain type of social performance context (Staudinger & Baltes, 1996) or by teaching a certain knowledge search strategy (Böhmig-Krumhaar, Staudinger, & Baltes, 2002), wisdom-related performance was significantly increased. Thus, interventions that support individuals to trace their memory and construct relevant insights can enhance wisdom-related performance. However, activation of their abstract knowledge about wisdom (by means of the instruction to "try to give a wise response") does not lead to increases in performance (Glück & Baltes, 2006).

Psychological Conceptions of Personal Wisdom

As explained earlier, personal wisdom is asked for when problems in one's own life (rather than those of other people) are at stake. Models of personal wisdom differ in whether they put special emphasis on difficult, negative events (e.g., Ardelt, 2005a; Kramer, 2000), as is central in related conceptions such as post-traumatic or stress-related growth, but they agree that learning from the socioemotional changes and challenges of an individual's personal life experience is necessary for making progress on the path toward personal wisdom. In this vein, two other notions come to mind: "maturity" and "personal growth." Influential conceptions of personal wisdom can be found in clinical, personality, and developmental psychology.

Since the space is far too limited to provide a complete overview here, only a selection can be discussed. In this area of wisdom research two large strands can be distinguished based on their respective ways of assessing personal wisdom: (1) approaches that use self-report questionnaires (e.g., Ardelt, 1997, 2003; Ryff & Keyes, 1995; Webster, 2003, 2007), and (2) approaches that use various kinds of performance measures (Loevinger & Wessler, 1978; (Labouvie-Vief & Medler, 2002; Mickler & Staudinger, 2008; Dörner & Staudinger, 2009).

PERSONAL WISDOM AS MEASURED BY SELF-REPORT QUESTIONNAIRES

(i) Ardelt's three-dimensional model of wisdom as a personality characteristic (e.g., Ardelt, 1997, 2003). This model proposes that wisdom is a personality characteristic rather than a body of knowledge and that it has three broad components based on Clayton and Birren's (1980) work on implicit wisdom theories. The *cognitive* component is based on a constant desire to understand the truth about the human condition, especially intra- and interpersonal matters, and includes the knowledge resulting from this desire. The *reflective* component refers to the ability to take multiple perspectives, which also implies self-examination and self-insight. The *affective* component is defined as "sympathetic and compassionate love for others," that is, a positive, empathetic attitude toward other persons. Following the classical traditions of personality assessment, Ardelt (2003) has developed a self-report scale (Three-Dimensional Wisdom Scale, 3DWS) to measure the three dimensions of wisdom. The 3DWS shows significant and positive correlations with mastery, subjective well-being, purpose in life, and subjective health and negative relations with depressive symptoms, death avoidance, fear of death, and feelings of economic pressure. Education

and occupation both showed significant and positive correlations with 3DWS.

(ii) Ryff and Whitbourne's Eriksonian approach. Based on the theory of personality development proposed by Erikson (1959), *Ryff* and also *Whitbourne* characterized a wise person as integrating rather than ignoring or repressing self-related information, by having coordinated opposites, and by having transcended personal agendas and turned to collective or universal issues. Ryff (Ryff & Heincke, 1983) and Whitbourne (e.g., Walaskay, Whitbourne, & Nehrke, 1983–84), for example, have undertaken the effort to develop self-report questionnaires based on the Eriksonian notions of personality development, especially integrity or wisdom. More recently, Carol Ryff integrated her earlier work on personal wisdom in the development of a questionnaire assessing psychological well-being (PWB). In particular, one of the six scales of the PWB questionnaire aims at personal growth. In cross-sectional work to date, slightly negative age trends were found for this scale (Ryff & Keyes, 1995). Also working with Erikson's theory, Orwoll (1988) investigated people who had been nominated as wise according to subjective beliefs about wisdom. She found that wise nominees were indeed characterized by high scores on questionnaire measures of Erikson's notion of ego integrity and showed a greater concern for the world state or humanity as a whole than the comparison group.

(iii) Webster's self-assessment wisdom scale (SAWS; 2003, 2007). SAWS was developed based on components that were identified in a review of the psychological wisdom literature. The SAWS assesses five components of wisdom: emotional regulation, reminiscence and reflectiveness, openness, humor, and experience. In line with expectations, the SAWS scores have been shown to correlate with measures of generativity and ego integrity. Furthermore, the scores were not significantly correlated with the age of the respondents.

Measuring wisdom is generally difficult because of the complexity of the construct; it becomes even more difficult when personal wisdom, as opposed to general wisdom, is the focus, as the notion of personal wisdom entails a focus on individual experiences, emotion, and reflection. Self-report measures of personal wisdom may constitute a particularly difficult instance of some general problems of self-report assessment: If wise individuals are assumed to be more reflective and critical of themselves than less wise individuals, then one could actually predict a negative correlation between wisdom and favorable self-presentation in questionnaires (see also Aldwin, 2009).

PERSONAL WISDOM AS ASSESSED BY PERFORMANCE MEASURES

(i) Loevinger's ego levels. In contrast, Loevinger's ego level (Loevinger & Wessler, 1978) is measured by qualitative coding of standardized self-descriptions. It was Loevinger's goal to capture character development in a stage model similar to the Piagetian model of cognitive development. She conceived the stages of ego development as a successive progression toward psychological maturity, unfolding along the four dimensions of impulse control, interpersonal style, conscious preoccupations, and cognitive styles. The model comprises eight stages (impulsive, self-protective, conformist, self-aware, conscientious, individualistic, autonomous, integrated) that are characterized by increasingly mature forms of those four dimensions. Most people are categorized in the third to fifth stages, that is, the conformist, self-aware, and conscientious stages. The self-aware stage is the modal stage in late adolescence and adult life. The eighth stage, the integrated stage, is rarely observed in random samples.

Ego level has been found to be positively related with ego-resiliency, interpersonal integrity, and regulation of needs, or mastery of socioemotional tasks and impulse-control, as well as indicators of mental health (for a review of associations between ego level and other relevant constructs, see Cohn & Westenberg, 2004 and Manners & Durkin, 2001). Interestingly, ego level is also positively correlated with number of lifetime psychiatric visits and regular psychotherapeutic sessions. It is unclear, however, whether psychotherapy helped subjects to advance developmentally or whether later stage capacity to see ambiguities in life increased their willingness to seek psychotherapy (see Dörner, 2006). The latter interpretation is in line with the positive quadratic relation between neuroticism and ego level (i.e., *higher* neuroticism at low *and* high ego level) and a negative quadratic relation between conscientiousness and ego level (i.e., *lower* conscientiousness at low *and* high ego level). Openness to experience, extraversion, and agreeableness show positive linear relations with ego level. Finally, chronological age is unrelated to ego development.

In sum, this pattern of results around Loevinger's measure of ego development suggests that central features of (general and personal) wisdom such as moving beyond the given, seeing reality more clearly, transcending extant social norms, do not come without costs. It seems that being faced with the complexities of one's own life in the way it is true for a person at high levels of ego development does not always lead to greater happiness but also to greater concern and doubt as well as the insight that further self-development is needed ("I know that I don't know").

(ii) Labouvie-Vief's theory of the life span development of affect. Combining Piaget's cognitive theory with psychoanalytic notions and ideas from adult attachment theory, Gisela Labouvie-Vief designed developmental models of self as well as emotional understanding (e.g., Labouvie-Vief, 1982; Labouvie-Vief, Hakim-Larson et al., 1989). Building on this earlier work, her most recent publications have focused on the development and/or maturation of self- and affect-regulation. In this latest approach, she has developed a notion of growth or maturity that combines Affect Optimization (AO), "the tendency to constrain affect to positive values," with Affect Complexity (AC), "the amplification of affect in the search for differentiation and objectivity." In this notion of maturity, it is crucial that the search for complexity and differentiation is combined with, or rather, constrained by, a search for optimizing positive affect in any given situation. But at the same time, the search for positive affect is guarded by the ability to experience events and other persons in an open and differentiated fashion. Combining the two (dichotomized) dimensions of AC and AO results in four "personality" types, Labouvie-Vief and Medler (2002) expected individuals with high levels on both dimensions to function best also in other aspects of psychological adjustment. And, indeed, high ego levels, high fluid intelligence, and adaptive coping patterns, excluding repressive or regressive strategies, characterize this group.

(iii) The Bremen measure of personal wisdom. Another performance measure of personal wisdom has been developed by the first author and her coworkers starting from the Berlin general wisdom paradigm (Mickler & Staudinger, 2008). Thus, five criteria have been defined, based on the literature about personality development, to index personal wisdom. The first criterion is *rich self-knowledge*, that is, deep insight into oneself. A self-wise person should be aware of his or her own competencies, emotions, and goals and should have a sense of meaning in life. The second criterion requires a self-wise person to have available *heuristics for growth and self-regulation* (e.g., how to express and regulate emotions or how to develop and maintain deep social relations). Humor is an example of an important heuristic that helps one cope with various difficult and challenging situations. *Interrelating the self*, the third criterion, refers to the ability to reflect on and have insight in the possible causes of one's behavior and/or feelings. Such causes can be age-related or situational or linked to personal characteristics. Interrelating the self also implies that there is an awareness about one's own dependency on others. The fourth criterion is called *self-relativism*. People high in self-relativism are able to evaluate themselves as well as others with a distanced view. They critically appraise their own behavior but at the same time display a basic acceptance of themselves. They also show tolerance for others' values and

lifestyles – as long as they are not damaging to self or others. Finally, *tolerance of ambiguity* involves the ability to recognize and manage the uncertainties in one's own life and one's own development. It is reflected in the awareness that life is full of uncontrollable and unpredictable events, including death and illness. At the same time, tolerance for ambiguity includes the availability of strategies to manage this uncertainty through openness to experience, basic trust, and the development of flexible solutions. Personal wisdom is measured by first using a thinking-aloud and subsequently a rating procedure.

Age trajectory and validity. In a first study, the new measure of personal wisdom showed good convergent validity (Mickler & Staudinger, 2008). It was positively correlated with other measures of personality growth, such as Ryff's personal growth and purpose in life, and Loevinger's ego development, as well as with benevolent personal values. With regard to discriminant validity, personal wisdom, as to be expected for a measure of personal maturity, was uncorrelated with notions of well-being and adaptation, such as life satisfaction, negative or positive emotions, and adaptive motives such as power, achievement, and hedonism. Also, personal wisdom is not preempted by knowing a person's intelligence. Interestingly, the relationship between personal wisdom and fluid intelligence followed an inverted u-shape, implying that among highly intelligent persons there is a significant negative correlation of fluid intelligence with personal wisdom. Follow-up analyses suggested that this may be due to differences in the value system, in particular, lower scores in the value domain "universalism." Extremely intelligent people may tend to be rather egotistical and focused on achievement, such as career, as opposed to interpersonal or social issues. As far as the relationship with personality variables is concerned, openness to experience was the most important predictor; of the other Big Five variables, none showed significant correlations with personal wisdom. Psychological mindedness, a concept measuring interest in thoughts and feelings of other people, however, was positively correlated with personal wisdom.

(iv) Finally, the last performance measure of personal wisdom, *self-concept maturity*, is based on the self-concept literature. Five self-concept facets were identified as theoretically meaningful indicators of personal wisdom, namely, complexity of content, self-concept integration, affect balance, self-esteem, and value orientation. It was hypothesized that only by combining these five components an appropriate operationalization of personal wisdom was obtained. That is, a profile of the five self-concept facets was established that should serve as a prototype of a mature personality as reflected in the self-concept or *self-concept maturity* (SCM).

Validity, age trends, and plasticity. As hypothesized, SCM correlated strongly and significantly with other measures of personal wisdom, especially with Loevinger's ego development and the newly developed personal-wisdom task presented earlier, whereas no significant associations existed with chronological age and fluid as well as crystallized intelligence (Dörner & Staudinger, 2009). This lack of a significant relationship with the two components of intelligence is most likely due to the measurement paradigm that does not have a problem-solving component like the other performance measures of personal wisdom discussed previously.

Also, in a first intervention study using SCM and the Bremen measure of personal wisdom, in contrast to findings for general wisdom (see earlier discussion; Staudinger & Baltes, 1996), personal wisdom was not facilitated by the opportunity to exchange ideas with a familiar person before responding. Rather, it was found that receiving instruction about how to infer insight from personal experiences (Staudinger, 2001) increased personal wisdom ratings (Staudinger, Kessler, & Dörner, 2006). The authors provided the following interpretation for this finding: In the case of personal wisdom, the exchange with a well-known other person may be less helpful as partners often learn to get along well without touching upon sensitive issues. Thus, for personal wisdom to be facilitated, it seems more useful to seek support from a "stranger." However, as strangers usually are not inclined to provide that kind of support, it may be better to seek support from a professional, that is, a psychotherapist.

Conclusion and Future Directions

Research over the last decades has demonstrated that the concept of wisdom represents a fruitful topic for psychological investigations for several reasons. First, the study of wisdom emphasizes the search for continued optimization and the further evolution of the human condition, and second, it allows, in a prototypical fashion, for the study of collaboration between cognitive, emotional, and motivational processes. Currently, there has been a notable increase of psychological work on the topic of wisdom (Ardelt, 2005b), a development that may be related to a general interest in features of a positive psychology as well as an ever increasing uncertainty of individuals about how to lead their lives. We expect that future research on wisdom will be expanded in at least three ways.

1. *The further identification of social and personality factors and life processes relevant for the ontogeny of wisdom*: Why do some individuals develop further than others on the road to wisdom in the course of their life? Is it possible to distinguish societies according to how much they facilitate the development of wisdom? Wisdom theorists agree that the development of wisdom is a complex interaction of intraindividual, interindividual, and external factors that dynamically interact over the course of an individual life (e.g., Baltes & Staudinger, 2000; Brugman, 2006; Kramer, 2000; Sternberg, 1998). To date, however, no longitudinal data are yet available to trace these interactions and possibly identify different types of developmental trajectories leading toward wisdom. These investigations into the ontogenesis of wisdom will also help to clarify the developmental dynamics between personal and general wisdom.
2. *The exploration of wisdom as a meta-heuristic aimed at orchestrating mind and virtue toward human excellence*: As mentioned at the beginning of this chapter, wisdom does not necessarily need to be viewed as a characteristic of individuals. It can also be a characteristic of problem solutions in a very general sense, for example, political or legal decisions. Understanding characteristics of wise strategies of information processing and decision making may be highly fruitful beyond the boundaries of psychology.
3. *The differentiation between personal and general wisdom and their ontogenetic dynamics*: The controversy among wisdom researchers about the definition of wisdom will probably never be resolved unequivocally. The question may not be which model is "right," but how much can be learned about wisdom by integrating the findings from different conceptualizations and operationalizations of wisdom, as well as what can be learned for designing the best interventions to facilitate wisdom.

All these approaches might contribute to building a psychological art of living based on life insight and life composition and integrating the analytic, aesthetic, and moral aspects of human life (Staudinger, 1999b), and improving societal ways of fostering wisdom and of dealing wisely with difficult problems of today's world (e.g., Ferrari & Potworowski, 2008).

Bibliography

Aldwin, C. (2009). Gender and wisdom: A brief overview. *Research in Human Development, 6*, 1–8.

Alexander, C. N., & Langer, E. J. (Eds.). (1990). *Higher stages of human development. Perspectives on adult growth*. New York, NY: Oxford University Press.

Ardelt, M. (1997). Wisdom and life satisfaction in old age. *Journals of Gerontology: Psychological Sciences*, *52B*, P15–P27.

Ardelt, M. (2003). Development and empirical assessment of a three-dimensional wisdom scale. *Research on Aging*, *25*, 275–324.

Ardelt, M. (2005a). How wise people cope with crises and obstacles in life. *ReVision*, *28*, 7–19.

Ardelt, M. (2005b). *Foreword*. In R. J. Sternberg & J. Jordan (Eds.), *A Handbook of wisdom: Psychological perspectives* (pp. xi–xvii). Cambridge, UK: Cambridge University Press.

Arlin, P. K. (1990). Wisdom: The art of problem finding. In R. J. Sternberg (Ed.), *Wisdom: Its nature, origins, and development* (pp. 230–243). New York, NY: Cambridge University Press.

Baltes, P. B., Dittmann-Kohli, F., & Dixon, R. A. (1984). New perspectives on the development of intelligence in adulthood: Toward a dual-process conception and a model of selective optimization with compensation. In P. B. Baltes & O. G. Brim Jr. (Eds.), *Life-span development and behavior* (Vol. 6, pp. 33–76). New York, NY: Academic Press.

Baltes, P. B., & Smith, J. (1990). Toward a psychology of wisdom and its ontogenesis. In R. J. Sternberg (Ed.), *Wisdom: Its nature, origins, and development* (pp. 87–120). New York, NY: Cambridge University Press.

Baltes, P. B., Smith, J., & Staudinger, U. M. (1992). Wisdom and successful aging. In T. B. Sonderegger (Ed.), *Nebraska symposium on motivation* (Vol. 39, pp. 123–167). Lincoln: University of Nebraska Press.

Baltes, P. B., & Staudinger, U. M. (2000). Wisdom: A metaheuristic to orchestrate mind and virtue toward excellence. *American Psychologist*, *55*, 122–136.

Baltes, P. B., Staudinger, U. M., Maercker, A., & Smith, J. (1995). People nominated as wise: A comparative study of wisdom-related knowledge. *Psychology and Aging*, *10*, 155–166.

Bluck, S., & Glück, J. (2005). From the inside out: People's implicit theories of wisdom. In R. J. Sternberg & J. Jordan (Eds.), *A handbook of wisdom. Psychological perspectives* (pp. 84–109). New York, NY: Cambridge University Press.

Böhmig-Krumhaar, S. A., Staudinger, U. M., & Baltes, P. B. (2002). Mehr Toleranz tut Not: Lässt sich wert-relativierendes Wissen und Urteilen mit Hilfe einer wissensaktivierenden Gedächtnisstrategie verbessern? [More tolerance is needed: Can value-relativistic knowledge and judgement be enhanced by means of a knowledge-activating memory strategy?]. *Zeitschrift für Entwicklungspsychologie und Pädagogische Psychologie*, *34*, 30–43.

Brugman, G. (2006). Wisdom and aging. In J. E. Birren, K. W. Schaie, & R. P. Abeles (Eds.), *Handbook of the psychology of aging* (6th ed., pp. 445–476). San Diego, CA: Academic Press.

Clayton, V. P. (1975). Erikson's theory of human development as it applies to the aged: wisdom as contradictive cognition. *Human Development*, *18*, 119–28.

Clayton, V. P., & Birren, J. E. (1980). The development of wisdom across the lifespan: A re-examination of an ancient topic. In P. B. Baltes & O. G. Brim (Eds.), *Life-span development and behavior* (Vol. 3, pp. 103–135). San Diego, CA: Academic Press.

Cohn, L. D., & Westenberg, P. M. (2004). Intelligence and maturity: Meta-analytic evidence for the incremental and discriminant validity of Leovinger's measure of Ego Development. *Journal of Personality and Social Psychology*, *86*, 760–782.

Dörner, J. (2006). *A self-concept measure of personality growth*. (http://www.jacobs-university.de/phd/files/1149071132.pdf) Bremen, Germany: Jacobs University.

Dörner, J., & Staudinger, U. M. (2009). *A self-concept measure of personality maturity*. Unpublished manuscript. Bremen, Germany: Jacobs University.

Erikson, E. H. (1959). *Identity and the life cycle*. New York, NY: International University Press.

Ferrari, M., & Potworowski, G. (Eds.). (2008). *Teaching for wisdom*. New York, NY: Springer.

Fowler, H. W., & Fowler, F. G. (1964). *The concise Oxford dictionary of current English*. Oxford, UK: Clarendon Press.

Glück, J., & Baltes, P. B. (2006). Using the concept of wisdom to enhance the expression of wisdom knowledge: Not the philosopher's dream, but differential effects of developmental preparedness. *Psychology and Aging*, *21*, 679–690.

Glück, J., Bischof, B., & Siebenhüner, L. (2009). "Knows what is good and bad," "Can teach you things," "Does lots of crosswords:" *Children's knowledge about wisdom*. Unpublished manuscript. Klagenfurt, Austria: Klagenfurt University.

Glück, J., & Bluck, S. (in press). Laypeople's conceptions of wisdom and its development: Cognitive and integrative views. *Journal of Gerontology: Psychological Sciences*.

Glück, J., Bluck, S., Baron, J., & McAdams, D. (2005). The wisdom of experience: Autobiographical narratives across adulthood. *International Journal of Behavioral Development*, *29*, 197–208.

Glück, J., Strasser, I., & Bluck, S. (2009). Gender differences in implicit theories of wisdom. *Research in Human Development*, *6*, 27–44.

Greenwald, A. G., & Pratkanis, A. R. (1984). The self. In R. W. Wyer & T. K. Srull (Eds.), *Handbook of social cognition* (Vol. 3, pp. 129–178). Hillsdale, NJ: Erlbaum.

Grimm, J., & Grimm, W. (1984). *Deutsches Wörterbuch* (original 1854). München, Germany: Deutscher Taschenbuch-Verlag.

Hall, G. S. (1922). *Senescence, the last half of life*. New York, NY: Appleton. Reprint edition, New York, NY: Arno Press, 1972.

Hershey, D. A., & Farrell, A. H. (1997). Perceptions of wisdom associated with selected occupations and personality characteristics. *Current Psychology: Developmental, Learning, Personality, Social*, *16*, 115–130.

Holliday, S. G., & Chandler, M. J. (1986). *Wisdom: Explorations in adult competence*. New York, NY: Karger.

Jason, L. A., Reichler, A., King, C., Madsen, D., Camacho, J., & Marchese, W. (2001). The measurement of wisdom: A preliminary effort. *Journal of Community Psychology*, *29*, 585–598.

Kekes, J. (1995). *Moral wisdom and good lives*. Ithaca, NY: Cornell University Press.

Kitchener, K. S., & Brenner, H. G. (1990). Wisdom and reflective judgement: Knowing in the face of uncertainty. In R. J. Sternberg (Ed.), *Wisdom. Its nature, origins, and development* (pp. 212–229). New York, NY: Cambridge University Press.

Kramer, D. A. (1983). Postformal operations? A need for further conceptualization. *Human Development*, *26*, 91–105.

Kramer, D. A. (2000). Wisdom as a classical source of human strength: Conceptualization and empirical inquiry. *Journal of Social and Clinical Psychology*, *19*, 83–101.

Kunzmann, U., & Baltes, P. B. (2003). Wisdom-related knowledge: Affective, motivational, and interpersonal correlates. *Personality & Social Psychology Bulletin*, *29*, 1104–1119.

Labouvie-Vief, G. (1982). Dynamic development and mature autonomy: A theoretical prologue. *Human Development*, *25*, 161–191.

Labouvie-Vief, G. (1990). Wisdom as integrated thought: Historical and developmental perspectives. In R. J. Sternberg (Ed.), *Wisdom: Its nature, origins, and development* (pp. 52–83). New York, NY: Cambridge University Press.

Labouvie-Vief, G., & Medler, M. (2002). Affect optimization and affect complexity: Modes and styles of regulation in adulthood. *Psychology & Aging*, *17*, 571–587.

Labouvie-Vief, G., Hakim-Larson, J., DeVoe, M., & Schoeberlein, S. (1989). Emotions and self-regulation. A life-span view. *Human Development*, *32*, 279–299.

Loevinger, J., & Wessler, R. (1978). *Measuring ego development I: Construction and use of a sentence completion task*. San Francisco, CA: Jossey-Bass.

Manners, J., & Durkin, K. (2000). Processes involved in adult ego development: A conceptual framework. *Developmental Review*, *20*(4), 475–513.

Mickler, C., & Staudinger, U. M. (2008). Personal wisdom: Validation and age-related differences of a performance measure. *Psychology and Aging*, *23*(4), 787–799.

Orwoll, L. (1988). *Wisdom in late adulthood: Personality and life history correlates*. Unpublished doctoral dissertation, Boston University.

Oser, F. K., Schenker, C., & Spychiger, M. (1999). Wisdom: An action-oriented approach. In K. H. Reich, F. K. Oser, & W. G. Scarlett (Eds.), *Psychological studies on spiritual and religious development*. Lengerich, Germany: Pabst.

Park, C. L., Cohen, L. H., & Murch, R. (1996). Assessment and prediction of stress-related growth. *Journal of Personality*, *64*, 71–105.

Pascual-Leone, J. (1990). An essay on wisdom: Toward organismic processes that make it possible. In R. J. Sternberg (Ed.), *Wisdom: Its nature, origins, and development* (pp. 224–278). New York, NY: Cambridge University Press.

Pasupathi, M., & Staudinger, U. M. (2001). Do advanced moral reasoners also show wisdom? Linking moral reasoning and wisdom-related knowledge and judgment. *International Journal of Behavioral Development*, *25*/5, 401–415.

Pasupathi, M., Staudinger, U. M., & Baltes, P. B. (2001). Seeds of wisdom: Adolescents' knowledge and judgment about difficult life problems. *Developmental Psychology*, *37*, 351–361.

Riegel, K. F. (1975). The development of dialectical operations. *Human Development*, *18*, 1–3.

Ryff, C. D. (1989). Happiness is everything, or is it? Explorations on the meaning of psychological well-being. *Journal of Personality & Social Psychology*, *57*, 1069–1081.

Ryff, C. D., & Heincke, S. G. (1983). Subjective organization of personality in adulthood and aging. *Journal of Personality & Social Psychology*, *44*, 807–816.

Ryff, C. D., & Keyes, C. L. M. (1995). The structure of psychological well-being revisited. *Journal of Personality and Social Psychology*, 69(4), 719–727.

Searle, J. R. (1992). *The rediscovery of the mind*. Cambridge, UK: Cambridge University Press.

Smith, J., Staudinger, U. M., & Baltes, P. B. (1994). Occupational settings facilitative of wisdom-related knowledge: The sample case of clinical psychologists. *Journal of Consulting and Clinical Psychology*, *62*, 989–1000.

Staudinger, U. M. (1999a). Older and wiser? Integrating results on the relationship between age and wisdom-related performance. *International Journal of Behavioral Development*, *23*, 641–664.

Staudinger, U. M. (1999b). Social cognition and a psychological approach to an art of life. In F. Blanchard-Fields & T. Hess (Eds.), *Social cognition, adult development and aging* (pp. 343–375). New York, NY: Academic Press.

Staudinger, U. M. (2001). Life reflection: A social-cognitive analysis of life review. *Review of General Psychology*, *5*, 148–160.

Staudinger, U. M., & Baltes, P. B. (1994). The psychology of wisdom. In R. J. Sternberg (Ed.), *Encyclopedia of human intelligence* (pp. 1143–1152). New York, NY: Macmillan.

Staudinger, U. M., & Baltes, P. B. (1996). Interactive minds: A facilitative setting for wisdom-related performance? *Journal of Personality and Social Psychology*, *71*, 746–762.

Staudinger, U. M., Dörner, J., & Mickler, C. (2005). Wisdom and personality. In R. J. Sternberg & J. Jordan (Eds.), *A handbook of wisdom: Psychological perspectives* (pp. 191–219). New York, NY: Cambridge University Press.

Staudinger, U. M., Kessler, E.-M., & Dörner, J. (2006). Wisdom in social context. In K. W. Schaie & L. Carstensen (Eds.), *Social structures, aging, and self-regulation in the elderly* (pp. 33–54). New York, NY: Springer.

Staudinger, U. M., Lopez, D., & Baltes, P. B. (1997). The psychometric location of wisdom-related performance: Intelligence, personality, and more? *Personality and Social Psychology Bulletin*, *23*, 1200–1214.

Staudinger, U. M., & Pasupathi, M. (2003). Correlates of wisdom-related performance in adolescence and adulthood: Age-graded differences in "paths" toward desirable development. *Journal of Research on Adolescence*, *13*, 239–268.

Staudinger, U. M., Smith, J., & Baltes, P. B. (1994). Wisdom-related knowledge in a life review task: Age differences and the role of professional specialization. *Psychology and Aging*, *7*, 271–281.

Sternberg, R. J. (1985). Implicit theories of intelligence, creativity, and wisdom. *Journal of Personality and Social Psychology*, *49*, 607–627.

Sternberg, R. J. (Ed.). (1990). *Wisdom: Its nature, origins, and development*. New York, NY: Cambridge University Press.

Sternberg, R. J. (1997). *Thinking styles*. Cambridge, UK: Cambridge University Press.

Sternberg, R. J. (1998). A balance theory of wisdom. *Review of General Psychology*, *2*, 347–365.

Sternberg, R. J. (2001). Why schools should teach for wisdom: The balance theory of wisdom in educational settings. *Educational Psychologist*, *36*, 227–245.

Sternberg, R., & Jordan, J. (Eds.). (2005). *Handbook of wisdom*. New York, NY: Cambridge University Press.

Takahashi, M. (2000). Toward a culturally inclusive understanding of wisdom: Historical roots in the East and West. *International Journal of Aging and Human Development*, *51*, 217–230.

Takahashi, M., & Bordia, P. (2000). The concept of wisdom: A cross-cultural comparison. *International Journal of Psychology*, *35*, 1–9.

Takahashi, M., & Overton, W. F. (2002). Wisdom: A culturally inclusive developmental perspective. *International Journal of Behavioral Development*, *26*, 269–277.

Takahashi, M., & Overton, W. F. (2005). Cultural foundations of wisdom: An integrated developmental approach. In R. J. Sternberg & J. Jordan (Eds.), *A handbook of wisdom: Psychological perspectives* (pp. 32–60). New York, NY: Cambridge University Press.

Tedeschi, R. G., & Calhoun, L. G. (2004). Posttraumatic growth: Conceptual foundations and empirical evidence. *Psychological Inquiry*, *15*, 1–18.

Walaskay, M., Whitbourne, S. K., & Nehrke, M. F. (1983–1984). Construction and validation of an ego integrity status interview. *International Journal of Aging and Human Development*, *18*, 61–72.

Webster, J. D. (2003). An exploratory analysis of a self-assessed wisdom scale. *Journal of Adult Development*, *10*, 13–22.

Webster, J. D. (2007). Measuring the character strength of wisdom. *International Journal of Aging &. Human Development*, 65, 163–183.
Welsch, W. (2001). Wisdom, philosophical aspects. In N. Smelser & P. B. Baltes (Eds.), *International encyclopedia of the social and behavioral sciences*. London, UK: Elsevier.
Yang, S.-Y. (2001). Conceptions of wisdom among Taiwanese Chinese. *Journal of Cross-Cultural Psychology*, 32, 662–680.

CHAPTER 41

Intelligence and Expertise

Phillip L. Ackerman

Defining Terms

One traditional approach to starting a discussion of the relations between two constructs is to attempt to define one's terms. Various methods are often used for providing such a foundation for discussion, but the two most common, and central to the current purposes are the "lexical" and "stipulative" forms of definition (see Robinson, 1950). Lexical definitions are those that are essentially "dictionary" definitions. They are historically documented and based on current and prior usage. The truthvalue of a lexical definition is one that can be determined in a straightforward fashion, merely by reference to original source material. Stipulative definitions are those that are proposed by the individual who chooses to use a word to mean a particular concept. As such, there is no way to determine the truthvalue of a stipulative definition. The value of the stipulative definition is instead determined by other indicators, such as its consistency in a wider network of other constructs. Why provide a short discourse on definition here? The answer lies in the need to relate two different concepts that rely on different kinds of definitions. For expertise, we can rely on a lexical definition, but for intelligence, it is largely impossible to provide a coherent discussion without a stipulative definition.

Expertise

The lexical definition of expertise is both straightforward and useful for the current discussion. "Expertise" refers to having the skill of an expert. An expert, according to the *Oxford English Dictionary* (Oxford University Press, 1971), is someone who is experienced, and who has been "trained by experience or practice, skilled" (p. 930). The term "expert" has been used since Chaucer's time, and current usage is generally consistent with usage over the past 600 years. The foundation for expertise, then, is the notion that one has a skill or skills, and that they are obtained through practice or other experiences. The one addition that should be provided here is that in modern usage, expertise need not be limited to skills that involve a significant physical component (such as playing the violin or performing heart bypass surgery), but they may also involve "knowledge" in a more general sense.

In psychology and education, three forms of knowledge have been articulated. One kind of knowledge is called "procedural knowledge" or "knowing how" (Ryle, 1949/2000). Skills that involve physical components generally fall into this category of knowledge. Such skills range in complexity from carpentry and bricklaying to neurosurgery and world-class musical performances. The second kind of knowledge is called "declarative knowledge" or "knowing that" (Ryle, 1949/2000). Declarative knowledge is essentially factual knowledge, whether it is the knowledge of a lawyer, novelist, physicist, psychologist, or a member of many other "knowledge-worker" professions. A third kind of knowledge, has been called "tacit knowledge" (Polanyi, 1966/1983, Wagner & Sternberg, 1985), or "knowing with" (Broudy, 1977). This kind of knowledge is less well understood than the other two forms of knowledge. This kind of knowledge is called "tacit" because it is not usually spontaneously articulated nor is it often easily accessible to verbal reports. It is thought to develop through one's educational and cultural experiences, but it is something that is not directly trained or practiced. Nonetheless, such knowledge is especially important when an individual is faced with problem solving that is outside of his or her normal areas of declarative or procedural expertise.

From a practical perspective, declarative knowledge can be categorized into a variety of different topic domains, and procedural knowledge can be categorized by particular skills. Tacit knowledge as conceptualized by Polanyi and Broudy, cannot be easily categorized and thus is quite difficult to study. In a later section, these categories of knowledge will be discussed in greater detail.

Intelligence

Lexical definitions of intelligence are especially problematic because there have been literally hundreds of different definitions offered for the concept over the past several hundred years. Psychologists have several times attempted to come to a consensus over how to define intelligence (e.g., *Journal of Educational Psychology*, 1921; Sternberg & Detterman, 1986), without much success. One can surely find a wide variation in how intelligence is defined by the different chapter authors in this book.

In order to have a coherent discussion of intelligence and expertise here, I will propose a stipulative definition – one that allows for consideration of how aspects of intelligence relate to different kinds of expertise. The definition is based on theories initially articulated by Hebb (1942), and by Cattell and Horn (Cattell, 1943, 1957, 1971; Horn, 1968, 1989; Horn & Cattell, 1966). Although their theories are more nuanced than is represented here, the fundamental property of the theories is that there are two central components of intelligence – one that is associated with "process" and the other associated with "knowledge." The component of intelligence that is associated with "process" is typically called "General Fluid Intelligence" (Gf) and the other component is associated with "knowledge" and is typically called "General Crystallized Intelligence (Gc) (see Cattell, 1943). Gf refers to abstract reasoning, short-term memory and working memory. Gf is most often involved in the solution of novel problems, or keeping track of decontextualized information in one's head for brief periods of time (e.g., letters, numbers, or random words). Gf also plays an important role in learning, especially for young children. Cattell's conceptualization of Gf is that it is essentially innate, that is, one is born with a certain level of Gf that determines one's success in later learning and intellectual development – a conceptualization that is consistent with Spearman's notion of general intelligence or *g* (Spearman, 1904).

In contrast to Gf, Gc is developed through education and experience. It represents the individual's knowledge that he or she acquires throughout the life span. Language, such as vocabulary and reading comprehension, reasoning, and problem solving in context-dependent domains (math, science, arts and humanities, law, business, etc.) all make up an individual's Gc. In practice, however, assessments of individual differences in Gc focus on broad knowledge but almost always only at a surface level rather than a deep level. For adults, this brings us to a distinction between what Cattell (1957) referred to as "historical" Gc and "current" Gc.

Historical and Current Gc

Because Gc represents the entire repertoire of knowledge and skill that an individual has, it does not directly translate to "expert" levels of performance in any single domain. Cattell suggested that as individuals reach adolescence and adulthood, Gc becomes more diverse and differentiated, especially as young adults acquire direct experience in occupational and avocational domains. The problem of assessment is that to assess an adult's Gc, one must develop tests of every possible domain of knowledge, both declarative and procedural. Without such a wide array of tests, for example, a master carpenter is given no credit for his or her knowledge/skills at carpentry, a dentist is given no credit for his or her skills at filling cavities, a psychologist is given no credit for knowing the current and historical theories of the field, and no credit for being able to design experiments, and so on. The alternative to this impossible task of developing hundreds of tests for expert knowledge, according to Cattell, was to assess only what the individual had learned prior to receiving specialized training or practice, namely, one's "historical" Gc.

Historical Gc

The assessment of historical Gc is in essence how Gc is usually assessed for adolescents and adults. The quantitative sections of the SAT examination, for example, contain only algebra and geometry problems, even though students take the examination in their junior and senior years of high school, when some of the students have proceeded to trigonometry and a smaller set of students has moved even further to calculus courses. Four years later, when college/university students want to apply for graduate study, they often take the Graduate Record Examination (GRE). Although some students have majored in mathematics or related fields, the math section of the GRE General test is made up of algebra and geometry problems – even though it may have been six or more years since the student had completed a course in these topic domains. Such assessments are one example of testing for historical Gc rather than current Gc.

Current Gc

For adults, assessments of current Gc are frequently narrow occupational and professional tests designed to measure a particular domain of expert knowledge and skills. That is, they don't attempt to determine the individual's entire repertoire of knowledge; rather, they attempt to determine whether the individual has acquired an acceptable level of expertise to be licensed to practice in a particular profession. These assessments can be a grueling ordeal as they often require extensive education, experience, and months of study and preparation. In addition, the tests themselves can last for several days.

For example, among people seeking to pursue a law career, admission to the Bar (the professional certification process for lawyers in the United States) requires an examination that typically involves two to three consecutive days of testing, with six hours a day or more of tests, depending on the state. Similarly, the U.S. medical licensing examination (Step 3, from the Federation of State Medical Boards) requires two eight-hour days of testing. Sonographers seeking board certification with the Physicians' Vascular Interpretation examination must complete a four-hour test (American Registry for Diagnostic Sonography, 2008), and each year nearly 175,000 people worldwide take one of the three, eight-hour tests conducted over a single 10-hour period to achieve the status of Chartered Financial Analyst (CFA Institute, 2008; *The Economist*, 2008). Individuals who seek state licensure to practice psychology typically take a four-hour, 15-minute examination (Association of State and Provincial Psychology Boards, 2008), which is often supplemented by a state-specific examination taken on the same day. These tests are aimed at measuring individual differences in expertise, but they are also measuring one aspect of current Gc.

Summary

To this point, we have established that expertise is defined as knowledge and skills that have been acquired through experience/practice. In addition, we have stipulated that there are two broad components of intelligence; Gf is associated with abstract reasoning and short-term memory, and Gc is associated with knowledge and skills. Within Gc, we have distinguished between historical Gc (knowledge/skills common to a culture) and current Gc (both common knowledge and specialized knowledge/skills). Expertise is most highly identified with current Gc in adults. However, we have not addressed the relationship between the components of intelligence and the acquisition of expertise – that is, answering the question of what are the roles of Gf and Gc in determining who develops expertise and whether an individual's level of Gf and Gc relates to the domain of expertise that is developed. The next section focuses on how expertise is developed and the role that intelligence plays in the development of expertise. First, however, a review of the difficulties in researching individual differences in expertise is provided.

Methods for the Study of Individual Differences in Expertise

The study of individual differences in the acquisition of expertise is fraught with difficulties. First, most scholars of expertise agree that it takes several years of study or "deliberate practice" (e.g., see Ericsson, Krampe, & Tesch-Römer, 1993; Simonton, 1988) to develop high levels of expertise within a single domain. Although one can study early acquisition curves for knowledge and skill development in the laboratory, because of the substantial time and effort investment, it is simply not feasible to randomly assign individuals of a wide range of intelligence levels the task of acquiring expertise in nearly any domain. Moreover, to take a group of individuals who are at the beginning of their study and follow them long enough to determine whether they ultimately develop higher or lower levels of expertise is difficult.

Most researchers rely on one of two different methods for studying individual differences in expertise. The first method employs intact groups of individuals who have already acquired a high level of expertise in a field. These individuals are compared to one another, and sometimes to a group of individuals who are not expert in the field. Both kinds of comparisons have limited utility. Looking for individual differences in intelligence among a group of Ph.D.-level physicists, for example, who have already been the subject of repeated selections (at college entry, at graduate school entry, and through exams in graduate school) is likely to reveal very little useful information, because correlations are severely attenuated (i.e., close to zero) when the range of talent is very small. By way of analogy, consider that even though one could reasonably assert that height is a critical requirement for expert performance in basketball, the correlation between player height and performance in the National Basketball League (NBA) is attenuated because the *average* height of NBA players in the 2007–2008 season is 6′7″ inches, and the shortest NBA player was 5′9″ (NBA, 2009).

The second method, that is, comparing a group of experts with a group of nonexperts (e.g., master bridge players vs. non–master bridge players who have been playing for a similar amount of time), may be informative, but such a method suffers from the classic problem of unknown third variables that may also contribute to the differences between those individuals who acquire high levels of expertise and those who do not. Other variables may also differentiate the experts from the population at large, including individual differences in intelligence, but without random assignment to practice/training, one cannot know the amount of influence these other variables might have on the development of expertise. Finding an appropriate group of nonexpert individuals for comparison purposes is a nearly impossible task. One may well ask, for example, if board-certified neurosurgeons are, as a group, more intelligent than non-board-certified neurosurgeons, or more intelligent than doctors without surgical specialties, or college graduates, or the at-large population, and so on. Such comparisons *suggest* that there are many domains of expertise that are associated with higher levels of intelligence, but they do not definitively indicate whether high levels of intelligence are necessary for the development of expertise, partly because people who are lower in intellectual abilities are less likely to be encouraged to, or allowed to, pursue these professions. For additional details, see Ackerman and Beier (2006).

Professions or hobbies that allow for the development of expertise but do not have strict educational gatekeepers, such as betting at the racetrack (Ceci & Liker, 1986a) or playing Scrabble (Halpern & Wai, 2007), bridge, and chess, (Gobet & Charness, 2006) or having other skills (see Ericsson & Charness, 1994 for a review) are more amenable to expert/novice comparisons with respect to differences in intellectual abilities. However, individuals who acquire expertise in these domains are likely to have done so with vastly different experiences from those of professionals in medicine (e.g., see Norman, Eva, Brooks, & Hamstra, 2006), who have gone through very structured educational/training programs. Nonetheless, existing studies of these other domains often do not find striking differences in the intellectual levels of experts and others who have not developed high levels of expertise, despite extensive experience (e.g., see Tuffiash, Roring, & Ericsson, 2007).

Acquiring Expertise

Closed Skills

For some kinds of expertise, the domain of knowledge or procedural skill to be acquired is relatively fixed and finite. In a narrow sense, becoming an expert typist represents a "closed" skill, as the number of keys to be used on the computer keyboard is fixed, and no changes are made to their arrangement. Increasing levels of deliberate practice lead to increasing performance, though after the initial phase of practice, performance improvements show diminishing returns with additional practice. Newell and Rosenbloom (1981) called this the "power law of practice." In essence, an equal amount of improvement in speed of performance is found for the first 10 trials, the next 100 trials, the next 1,000 trials, and so on. Performance keeps improving with practice, but the increments in improvement become smaller and smaller over time. The literature on closed procedural skills suggests that intellectual abilities may be influential in the first phase of skill acquisition, when learners are still figuring out strategies for completing the task. With high levels of practice, there is a reduction in both the range of differences between individuals in performance and a concomitant reduction in the influence of intellectual abilities on individual differences in performance (e.g., see Ackerman, 1987, 1988). Thus, acquiring expertise on relatively straightforward closed skills is within the capabilities of much of the population. Once learned, these tasks are often "automatic," in that it requires little or no effort on the part of the individual to perform them at a high level of expertise. This is not to say that such skills are at a world-class level. To reach that level, more extensive practice is necessary, even for text messaging, driving a car, or mental multiplication. In addition, to achieve truly exceptional performance in such domains, the individual has to focus his or her attention on the task while it is being performed (e.g., think of the difference in your driving performance when you turn off the radio and other distractions in comparison to when you are driving and thinking about your grocery shopping list at the same time).

Open Skills

Most domains of expertise that depend on declarative knowledge rather than procedural knowledge are open, in the sense that more knowledge brings about improved performance, and in the sense that once one component of the skill is acquired, another, more complex component of the skill is yet to be learned. Becoming an expert at mathematics has this characteristic: Once the learner acquires arithmetic skills at addition and subtraction, he or she is presented multiplication/division, then algebra, geometry, trigonometry, derivative and integral calculus, and so on. Although each separate component of the skill may be "closed" – with a fixed set of rules, facts, and procedures to be learned – to become an expert requires that one acquire knowledge and skill at each of the more complex components of the task. Acquiring expertise in such domains is a lifelong task and one that depends on intellectual abilities because these abilities are integral in acquiring expertise when faced with each increasingly complex component of the skill to be learned. At some level, the individual may choose to "specialize," in which case the challenges to acquire more complex task components *might* be diminished, depending on how rapidly the domain changes. Any time there is a change in the field of expertise, such as the introduction of new technology (whether it be, for example, new equipment for surgical procedures or diagnostic tools in medicine, or new computer systems for the solution of technical problems or design), the challenge to stay up-to-date is one that will make demands on the individual's intellectual abilities. (The decline in Gf associated with increasing age in middle-aged and older adults tends to make such new learning more difficult than it is for younger adults – see Kubeck, Delp, Haslett, & McDaniel, 1996.)

Expert Short-Term/Working Memory

There have been a few notable studies that have attempted to develop expertise in short-term and working memory capabilities. The general framework proposed by Miller (1956) is that humans have a capacity of keeping about 7 +/−2 items active in short-term memory at any one time. Individuals differ in their short-term memory capacity, and such differences are considered to be an integral part of fluid intellectual abilities. Strategies for memorizing new information in a more efficient and effective manner have been common since the time of the Greeks (e.g., the Method of Loci; see Yates, 1966). These strategies, along with "chunking" – that is, combining new information into larger units – are not aimed at creating expertise in memory per se, but rather they are aimed at more effective use of one's limited attentional resources. In the normal day-to-day environment, having expert memory appears to be a matter of Gf abilities, allocation of effort to memorize information and to the use of effective strategies. Remembering phone numbers or names of people at a party, for example, is dependent mainly on those three factors.

However, in one research program (Chase & Ericsson, 1981), the authors were able to train *some* individuals to keep track of much more information. In one noteworthy case, with 250 hours of practice over the course of two years, one learner was able to develop the skill of keeping track of over 80 random digits read aloud at a rate of 1 per second (where the typical individual can keep track of no more than 7 digits). This individual was able to use his extensive long-term memory of running speeds (e.g., world records for various distance races) as reference tags for chunks of numbers and then to retrieve the numbers on a recall test. Attempts to train other individuals without such deep knowledge of numerically based information, or to train the same individual to recall long sequences of letters instead of numbers, were largely unsuccessful. Being able to recall over 80 random digits when presented only once at a rapid rate, is clearly an example of expertise, but whether it represents skilled short-term or working memory (which would make it a Gf ability) or a unique use of a highly organized long-term memory (which would make it more of a Gc ability) is debatable.

Is Gf a Limiting Factor?

One of the most contentious issues in the study of individual differences in expertise is the question of whether Gf is a limiting factor in the development of expertise. There are, in essence, two related questions. The first question is whether there is a *threshold* of Gf needed for developing expertise. The second question is whether higher levels of Gf lead to higher levels of expertise or a faster development of expertise, ceteris paribus (that is, all other things being equal). Each of these issues is treated in turn.

Gf as Threshold

One conceptualization of the acquisition of expertise is that there is a threshold level of Gf or general intelligence, below which, an individual is unlikely to develop expertise in a particular domain (e.g., Gibson & Light, 1992). In the limit, this is surely true. For example, moderately or profoundly retarded individuals are highly unlikely to develop expertise in nuclear physics, compared to individuals who have high levels of Gf. However, there is no "fixed" threshold for the development of expertise in most areas. Indeed, early studies of the relationship between intelligence and occupational status (e.g., Stewart, 1947) showed that there is a wide range of intelligence levels for nearly all occupations, even though mean levels of intelligence for the occupations of doctor, lawyer, and scientist are well above average. There are two likely explanations for these findings. First, standard group measures of intellectual abilities (both Gf and Gc) – the kind most frequently administered to large groups of job and school applicants – are not comprehensive, in that they may miss some important components of intelligence that are relevant to educational and occupational success (such as spatial abilities; see, e.g., Webb, Lubinski, and Benbow, 2007). Second, because the acquisition of expertise depends on the investment of practice and study over an extended period of time, individuals with relatively lower levels of intellectual abilities may sometimes compensate for their abilities by working harder and longer to acquire the knowledge/skills necessary to develop expertise. In practice, however, the overwhelming majority of regressions between ability and job performance is found to be linear (Coward & Sackett, 1990), suggesting that the intelligence threshold conceptualization is not particularly viable, and that higher levels of intelligence lead generally to higher levels of occupational performance.

Impact of Higher Gf – Declarative Knowledge

Even though there may not be a fixed threshold for Gf in determining the acquisition of expertise, extant data suggest that, ceteris paribus, higher levels of Gf will result in a higher likelihood of developing expertise in a variety of academic and other declarative knowledge-dependent domains. Studies of individuals who have extremely high levels of intellectual abilities indicate a much higher representation of experts in such fields (e.g., see Lubinski & Benbow, 2006). At some point in the acquisition of expertise, however, the role of Gf appears to be diminished in favor of an increasing influence from Gc, in the form of transfer.

Impact of Higher Gf – Procedural Knowledge

Gf is, however, not as important in the development of many procedural skills. For expertise that depends on procedural skills, especially when initial performance on such tasks is within the capabilities of most individuals (even if slow and error prone), Gf has a much diminished association with acquisition of expertise. For this to happen, though, the procedural skill to be learned needs to be "closed" rather than "open" (for discussions, see Ceci & Liker, 1986b, Ericsson & Lehmann, 1996). If the skill has increasingly complex procedures that must be learned, then, it can be expected that intellectual abilities will have an increased effect on individual differences in performance, at each higher level of complexity required by the skill to be acquired.

Gc and Transfer

Earlier, when a stipulative definition of intelligence was provided, the two main components of intelligence were denoted Gf and Gc. If current Gc represents acquired knowledge and skills, then domain-specific expertise represents a subset of an individual's intellectual repertoire. By definition, then, expertise is closely related to intelligence. But this assertion does not address the role of Gc in the acquisition of expertise. Gf has been shown to be instrumental in reasoning and problem solving in the absence of prior context, a critical component when one attempts to acquire knowledge and skill in a novel domain. But as people begin to learn about a particular domain, new knowledge and skill are developed partly on the foundation of earlier learning and skills. Ferguson (1956) offered a strong thesis along these lines. He suggested that learning of only a newborn child occurs in the absence of transfer – that is, building new knowledge on existing knowledge. In that sense, individual differences in existing knowledge are the most important determinant of acquiring new knowledge in the same domain. As learners attempt to acquire expertise, what they already "know" is the main limiting factor for new learning.

If Ferguson's assertion is true, then current Gc, in that it represents the individual's repertoire of knowledge and skill, should be more highly related to an individual's current level of expertise than is Gf, and Gc should be more highly related to the acquisition of new knowledge in the same general domain. Scientifically evaluating this assertion is difficult, for some of the same reasons that comparisons of individual differences among experts or contrasts between experts and novices is problematic. One can evaluate the individual's current domain-specific knowledge with tests that allow for assessment of deep domain knowledge, but people cannot be randomly assigned to control and experimental groups for domain-learning situations that require years of experience to develop high levels of expertise.

Although there have not been extensive studies that have related historical Gc to domain-specific expertise, assessments of adult knowledge in the physical sciences, technology, social sciences, humanities, business/law, health and nutrition, and current events illustrate a consistent pattern of correlations (e.g., Ackerman, 2000; Ackerman & Rolfhus, 1999, Beier & Ackerman, 2001, 2003). For all of these knowledge domains, measures of Gc show substantial correlations with individual differences in the depth of knowledge (correlations in the range of $r = .48$ to $.80$). Correlations between Gf and domain knowledge are usually much smaller (in the range of $r = .33$ to $.49$) for most domains, with the exception of physical sciences and technology, where both Gc and Gf abilities are both highly correlated with domain knowledge. These studies do not necessarily point to direct transfer of knowledge from historical Gc to domain-specific expertise, especially because a third variable could account for both high Gc and high levels of domain-specific expertise. However, they are consistent with Ferguson's conceptualization that transfer is a key ingredient to intellectual development and to the development of expertise.

Expertise Transfer and Intelligence

Just as individual differences in intellectual abilities and skills can be expected to transfer to the development of expertise, the development of expertise can be expected to transfer to intellectual abilities. The problem in assessing the degree of transfer from domain knowledge and skills, or even memory skills to intellectual abilities, lies in determining how best to assess the transfer. On the one hand, because standardized intelligence tests, as discussed earlier, tend to sample broadly, but at a surface level, developing expertise in, say, medicine, might have a small beneficial effect on a vocabulary subscale but little effect on digit-span or reading comprehension. Developing expert memory skills, on the other hand, might have much larger effects on standard intelligence measures, especially those that depend on short-term and working memory (for a discussion of these issues, see Chapter 6, Developing Intelligence Through Instruction, this volume). Other researchers have suggested that the challenges of complex jobs through adulthood lead to better maintenance of intellectual abilities (Kohn & Schooler, 1978; Schooler, 2001; Willis & Tosti-Vasey, 1990).

Another issue to be considered is whether intelligence, per se, represents "developing expertise" (e.g., see Sternberg, 1999), or is a form of expertise. Certainly one general aim of education is the development of knowledge and skills that make up a significant portion of what is considered to be intellectual, especially in the basic skills in literacy and foundations of science, math, and other areas (e.g., see Alexander & Murphy, 1999; Snow, 1996; Stanovich & West, 1989). These are important aspects of the development and expression of intelligence, but they relate more to a view of "expertise" that is much more general than we have discussed to this point, and they probably fall into the tacit/knowing with kinds of knowledge proposed by Polanyi (1966/1983) and discussed by Broudy (1977).

An Alternate Viewpoint

Several researchers and theorists, often identified with the "deliberate practice" framework offered by Ericsson and his colleagues (e.g., Ericsson, 2006; Ericsson et al., 1993, but also see, for example, the seminal work by Chi, Glaser, & Rees, 1982) have proposed that intellectual abilities are largely irrelevant to the development of expertise and that individual differences in the depth and extent of focused practice are the main determinants of expertise. Most of the sources of expertise studied by these researchers include tasks like playing chess, typing, performing music, and playing sports. Comparison groups are typically those individuals who have practiced a task for similar amounts of time as the expert group but have not achieved high levels of expert performance. The lack of a substantial difference between these groups on standard ability tests is taken as evidence that intellectual abilities are not relevant for distinguishing between experts and nonexperts. The professional basketball player height analogy mentioned earlier applies to these comparisons. That is, when one is dealing with a group of individuals who are severely limited in range-of-talent (because even those individuals deemed "nonexperts" perform many levels higher than the at-large population), one expects that even if an individual-differences variable is related to success in a random sample of people, it will not be revealed in a group that has a severe restriction in range-of-talent. Such studies do not inform one about the role that intellectual abilities plays at the various stages of entry to the domain, the speed with which one develops expertise, or the level of expertise ultimately attained. However, if a group of experts was found to have average intelligence (e.g., IQ = 100), or below-average intelligence, one could reasonably assert that individual differences in intelligence do not serve as a major threshold variable for the development of expertise (at least, within whatever range of intelligence scores are exhibited by the experts).

Maintenance of Expertise

One of the interesting aspects of expertise that provides an additional basis for aligning it closer to Gc than to Gf is the pattern of growth and decline of expertise that occurs during middle age and older adulthood. Both theory and extant data indicate that Gf reaches a peak for most people in early adulthood, generally between 18 and the mid-20s (see, e.g., Horn, 1989; Salthouse, 1996). In contrast, both historical and current Gc is maintained well into middle age, and some studies have suggested that current Gc also shows growth into middle age (e.g., see Ackerman, 2000; Horn, 1989; Horn & Masunaga, 2006). Domain-specific expertise in many areas is also well preserved into middle age and beyond, in reviews that have been conducted on this issue (e.g., Simonton, 1988). In the first longitudinal study of intelligence of adults, Owens (1953) found that on an information test first administered 31 years earlier when participants were 19, a group of adults performed much better on a test of general information. The average score was nearly one standard deviation higher than at initial testing. In a more extensive longitudinal study, Schaie (1996, 2005) found that general verbal knowledge grows and is maintained up to about age 60, then it shows declines as people reach their 70s and 80s.

For narrower areas of domain knowledge, other studies have indicated that knowledge and skills are well preserved, *if it has been well learned to begin with*, even if the individuals do not actively use the knowledge in the intervening years. Studies of Spanish language knowledge by Bahrick (1984), and algebra and geometry knowledge (Bahrick and Hall, 1991) acquired first in high school and college, found high levels of recall over periods of up to 50 years, though "A" students performed much better at recall than did "C" students.

Procedural knowledge and skills, once acquired, have also been shown to be well preserved over long periods of time. The old adage about retaining skill in riding a bicycle, even after many years of nonuse is consistent with the extant data. For juggling, when an individual was trained for 42 daily sessions at initial acquisition, performance assessed six years later was nearly as good as the last performance during initial acquisition (Swift, 1910). In a remarkable study of typewriting skill retention, Hill, a novice typist, acquired expertise at typing over five months of daily practice (Hill, Rejall, & Thorndike, 1913). In two follow-up assessments, he assessed his retained typing skill first after a 25-year period during which he did not use the typewriter (Hill, 1934), and then after a total of 50 years after the initial training, again without using the typewriter (Hill, 1957), when he was 80 years old. After 25 years of nonuse, he performed at a level that he had only achieved after 27 days of initial practice. After 50 years, even though his perceptual/motor abilities had surely declined with age, he was able to achieve the same level of performance after only eight days of retraining.

It should be emphasized that the important finding is that when the procedural skills are well developed to begin with, the retention period can be very long indeed, even when the skill is not regularly exercised. Of course, continued use of the skill can be expected to lead to even better maintenance or improvement, up to the limits of a person's perceptual and motor abilities, as was exemplified in the skills of Michael DeBakey, the pioneering heart surgeon. By the time he finally retired from practice at age 90, he had performed more than 60,000 cardiovascular procedures and was still considered one of the best surgeons in the field (see Nuland, 2007). Similarly, several world-class classical musicians have performed well into their 70s and 80s (e.g., Isaac Stern, Arthur Rubinstein, Vladimir Horowitz). At advanced ages, these musicians are more likely to perform the standard repertoire pieces, yet their skills are exceptionally well maintained.

Tacit Knowledge Expertise

Determining the relationship between intelligence and tacit knowledge expertise is even more of a challenge than it is for declarative and procedural knowledge. Where declarative knowledge can be reasonably well measured with tests designed to assess knowledge that can be verbally reported and procedural knowledge can be measured by asking the individual to perform the skill in question, tacit knowledge is by definition not spontaneously articulated nor is it often easily accessible to verbal reports. A few studies have been conducted to assess tacit knowledge by providing scenarios in the domain to examinees (e.g., in-basket management problems; see Wagner, 2000) and then evaluating the quality of the responses. Under these circumstances, good or excellent performance is determined not by evaluating the difference between optimal strategies and the individual's response, but rather by determining the similarity of the individual's response and a consensus response by experts (e.g., see Wagner & Sternberg, 1987). To date, studies in this area have suggested relatively low correlations between tacit knowledge and standard tests of intellectual abilities, although the comparisons between experts and novices made in these studies are subject to the same limitations noted earlier about evaluating individual differences in samples where there is a restriction in range-of-talent (e.g., see Cianciolo, Matthew, Sternberg, & Wagner, 2006).

Summary and Conclusions

The study of intelligence and expertise is a much more recent focus for researchers than is the study of, say, intelligence and academic performance. Nonetheless, based on research from experimental psychology that has focused on understanding the development and expression of expertise, and a small number of studies that have examined individual differences in expertise, a relatively consistent pattern of results has been found. Individual differences in expertise are not directly measured by historical Gc assessments. Most current Gc measures do not involve the kind of depth in assessment necessary to probe an individual's expertise, in contrast to measures of professional competency or professional certification tests.

Experts in domains that are highly dependent on declarative knowledge, most often acquired through extensive education and experience (e.g., in law, medicine, science), will have higher levels of intellectual abilities (both Gf and Gc) than the lay public. Whether higher intellectual abilities are *necessary* for acquisition of such levels of expertise is not directly known, because gatekeepers to entry for these occupations depend on intellectual ability tests for selection into the educational or occupational programs. However, intellectual abilities are not *sufficient* for the development of expertise; other factors, such as motivation and effort for learning and task practice over long periods of time, play an important role in determining who becomes an expert.

Studies of experts in domains that are more highly dependent on procedural knowledge show mixed results in the correlations with intellectual abilities. In several studies, researchers have claimed that there is essentially a zero correlation between expertise in these domains and intellectual abilities, though such inferences are dependent on the interpretation of data from individuals who are already restricted in range-of-talent, or nonexpert comparison groups that may or not be equivalent to the expert groups.

For experts in the domain of tacit knowledge, it is as yet difficult to draw conclusions regarding the role of intellectual abilities. Improved measurement techniques for assessing tacit knowledge may ultimately help address these issues. In addition, a better understanding of how tacit knowledge is acquired can be expected to provide additional insights into the relationships between Gf, Gc, and tacit knowledge.

In the final analysis, higher levels of intellectual abilities appear to give the learner a head start or an overall advantage in the acquisition of expertise over learners with lower levels of intelligence. For closed tasks, especially those that are mostly dependent on procedural skills, the influence of intellectual abilities diminishes with increasing practice, as motivation, effort, and persistence increase in influence. For open tasks, especially those that are mostly dependent on declarative knowledge, intellectual abilities, and especially Gc, appear to be important determinants of higher levels of expertise.

References

Ackerman, P. L. (1987). Individual differences in skill learning: An integration of psychometric and information processing perspectives. *Psychological Bulletin*, **102**, 3–27.

Ackerman, P. L. (1988). Determinants of individual differences during skill acquisition: Cognitive abilities and information processing. *Journal of Experimental Psychology: General*, **117**, 288–318.

Ackerman, P. L. (2000). Domain-specific knowledge as the "dark matter" of adult intelligence: gf/gc, personality and interest correlates. *Journal of Gerontology: Psychological Sciences*, **55B**(2), P69–P84.

Ackerman, P. L., & Beier, M. E. (2006). Methods for studying the structure of expertise: Psychometric approaches. In A. Ericsson, P. Feltovich, N. Charness, & R. R. Hoffman (Eds.), *Cambridge handbook on expertise and expert performance* (pp. 147–166). New York, NY: Cambridge University Press.

Ackerman, P. L., & Rolfhus, E. L. (1999). The locus of adult intelligence: Knowledge, abilities, and non-ability traits. *Psychology and Aging*, **14**, 314–330.

Alexander, P. A., & Murphy, P. K. (1999). Learner profiles: Valuing individual differences within classroom communities. In P. L. Ackerman, P. C. Kyllonen, & R. D. Roberts (Eds.), *Learning and individual differences: Process, trait, and content determinants* (pp. 413–436). Washington, DC: American Psychological Association.

American Registry for Diagnostic Sonography. http://www.ardms.org (retrieved 7/20/2008).

Association of State and Provincial Psychology Boards. http://www.asppb.org/epppExam/test/test.aspx (retrieved 7/20/2008).

Bahrick, H. P. (1984). Fifty years of second language attrition: Implications for programmatic research. *Modern Language Journal*, 68(2), 105–118.

Bahrick, H. P., & Hall, L. K. (1991). Lifetime maintenance of high school mathematics content. *Journal of Experimental Psychology: General*, **120**(1), 20–33.

Beier, M. E., & Ackerman, P. L. (2001). Current events knowledge in adults: An investigation of age, intelligence and non-ability determinants. *Psychology and Aging*, **16**, 615–628.

Beier, M. E., & Ackerman, P. L. (2003). Determinants of health knowledge: An investigation of age, gender, abilities, personality, and interests. *Journal of Personality and Social Psychology*, 84(2), 439–448.

Broudy, H. S. (1977). Types of knowledge and purposes of education. In R. C. Anderson, R. J. Spiro, & W. E. Montague (Eds.), *Schooling and the acquisition of knowledge* (pp. 1–17). Hillsdale, NJ: Erlbaum.

Cattell, R. B. (1943). The measurement of adult intelligence. *Psychological Bulletin*, **40**, 153–193.

Cattell, R. B. (1957). *Personality and motivation structure and measurement*. Yonkers-on-Hudson, NY: World Book.

Cattell, R. B. (1971). *Abilities: Their structure, growth, and action*. New York, NY: Houghton Mifflin.

Ceci, S. J., & Liker, J. K. (1986a). A day at the races: A study of IQ, expertise, and cognitive complexity. *Journal of Experimental Psychology: General*, **115**, 255–266.

Ceci, S. J., & Liker, J. (1986b). Academic and nonacademic intelligence: An experimental separation. In R. J. Sternberg & R. K. Wagner (Eds.), *Practical intelligence: Nature and origins of competence in the everyday world* (pp. 119–142). New York, NY: Cambridge University Press.

Chartered Financial Analyst Institute (CFA). http://www.cfainstitute.org/cfaprogr/resources/examdetails (retrieved 7/20/2008).

Chase, W. G., & Ericsson, K. A. (1981). Skilled memory. In J. R. Anderson (Ed.), *Cognitive skills and their acquisition* (pp. 141–189). Hillsdale, NJ: Erlbaum.

Chi, M. T. H., Glaser, R., & Rees, E. (1982). Expertise in problem solving. In R. J. Sternberg (Ed.), *Advances in the psychology of human intelligence* (Vol. **1**, pp. 7–76). Hillsdale, NJ: Erlbaum.

Cianciolo, A. T., Matthew, C., Sternberg, R. J., & Wagner, R. K. (2006). In A. Ericsson, P. Feltovich, N. Charness, & R. R. Hoffman (Eds.), *Cambridge handbook on expertise and expert performance* (pp. 613–632). New York, NY: Cambridge University Press.

Coward, W. M., & Sackett, P. R. (1990). Linearity of ability-performance relationships: A reconfirmation. *Journal of Applied Psychology*, 75, 297–300.

Economist. (2008, June 5). Charter School. Retrieved from the Web 7/20/2008.

Ericsson, K. A. (2006). The influence of experience and deliberate practice on the development of superior expert performance. In A. Ericsson, P. Feltovich, N. Charness, & R. R. Hoffman (Eds.), *Cambridge handbook on expertise and expert performance* (pp. 683–703). New York, NY: Cambridge University Press.

Ericsson, K. A., & Charness, N. (1994). Expert performance: Its structure and acquisition. *American Psychologist*, *49*, 725–747.

Ericsson, K. A., Krampe, R. T., & Tesch-Römer, C. (1993). The role of deliberate practice in the acquisition of expert performance. *Psychological Review*, **100**(3), 363–406.

Ericsson, K. A., & Lehmann, A. C. (1996). Expert and exceptional performance: Evidence of maximal adaptation to task constraints. *Annual Review of Psychology*, *47*, 273–305.

Ferguson, G. A. (1956). On transfer and the abilities of man. *Canadian Journal of Psychology*, **10**, 121–131.

Gibson, J., & Light, P. (1992). Intelligence among university scientists. In R. S. Albert (Ed.), *Genius and eminence* (2nd ed.). *International series in experimental social psychology*, **22**, 109–111. Elmsford, NY: Pergamon Press.

Gobet, F., & Charness, N. (2006). In A. Ericsson, P. Feltovich, N. Charness, & R. R. Hoffman (Eds.), *Cambridge handbook on expertise and expert performance* (pp. 523–538). New York, NY: Cambridge University Press.

Halpern, D. F., & Wai, J. (2007). The world of competitive Scrabble: Novice and expert differences in visuospatial and verbal abilities. *Journal of Experimental Psychology: Applied*, **13**, 79–94.

Hebb, D. O. (1942). The effect of early and late brain injury upon test scores, and the nature of normal adult intelligence. *Proceedings of the American Philosophical Society*, 85(3), 275–292.

Hill, L. B. (1934). A quarter century of delayed recall. *Journal of Genetic Psychology*, *44*, 231–238.

Hill, L. B. (1957). A second quarter century of delayed recall, or relearning at eighty. *Journal of Educational Psychology*, 48, 65–69.

Hill, L. B., Rejall, A. E., & Thorndike, E. L. (1913). Practice in the case of typewriting. *Pedagogical Seminary*, **20**, 516–529.

Horn, J. L. (1968). Organization of abilities and the development of intelligence. *Psychological Review*, *75*, 242–259.

Horn, J. L. (1989). Cognitive diversity: A framework of learning. In P. L. Ackerman, R. J. Sternberg, & R. Glaser (Eds.), *Learning and individual differences. Advances in theory and research* (pp. 61–116). New York, NY: W. H. Freeman.

Horn, J. L., & Cattell, R. B. (1966). Refinement and test of the theory of fluid and crystallized general intelligences. *Journal of Educational Psychology*, *57*, 253–270.

Horn, J., & Masunaga, H. (2006). A merging theory of expertise and intelligence. In A. Ericsson, P. Feltovich, N. Charness, & R. R. Hoffman (Eds.), *Cambridge handbook on expertise and expert performance* (pp. 147–166). New York, NY: Cambridge University Press.

Journal of Educational Psychology. (1921). Intelligence and its measurement: A symposium. *Journal of Educational Psychology*, **12**, 123–275.

Kohn, M. L., & Schooler, C. (1978). The reciprocal effects of the substantive complexity of work and intellectual flexibility: A longitudinal assessment. *American Journal of Sociology*, *84*, 24–52.

Kubeck, J. E., Delp, N. D., Haslett, T. K., & McDaniel, M. A. (1996). Does job-related training performance decline with age? *Psychology and Aging*, **11**(1), 92–107.

Lubinski, D., & Benbow, C. P. (2006). Study of mathematically precocious youth after 35 years: Uncovering antecedents for the development of math-science expertise. *Perspectives on Psychological Science*, **14**, 316–345.

Miller, G. A. (1956). The magical number seven, plus or minus two: Some limits on our capacity for processing information. *Psychological Review*, 63, 81–97.

National Basketball Association (NBA). http://www.nba.com/news/survey_height_2007.html (retrieved 8/8/09).

Newell, A., & Rosenbloom, P. S. (1981). Mechanisms of skill acquisition and the law of practice. In J. R. Anderson (Ed.), *Cognitive skills and their acquisition* (pp. 1–55). Hillsdale, NJ: Erlbaum.

Norman, G., Eva, K., Brooks, L., & Hamstra, S. (2006). Expertise in medicine and surgery. In A. Ericsson, P. Feltovich, N. Charness, & R. R. Hoffman (Eds.), *Cambridge handbook on expertise and expert performance* (pp. 339–353). New York, NY: Cambridge University Press.

Nuland, S. B. (2007). *The art of aging: A doctor's prescription for well-being.* New York, NY: Random House.

Owens, W. A., Jr. (1953). Age and mental abilities: A longitudinal study. *Genetic Psychology Monograph*, 48, 3–54.

Oxford University Press. (1971). *The compact edition of the Oxford English dictionary*. New York: Author.

Polanyi, M. (1966/1983). *The tacit dimension*. Gloucester, MA: Peter Smith.

Robinson, R. (1950). *Definition*. London, UK: Oxford University Press.

Ryle, G. (1949/2000). *The concept of mind*. Chicago, IL: University of Chicago Press.

Salthouse, T. A. (1996). The processing-speed theory of adult age differences in cognition. *Psychological Review*, 103(3), 403–428.

Schaie, K. W. (1996). *Intellectual development in adulthood: The Seattle longitudinal study*. New York, NY: Cambridge University Press.

Schaie, K. W. (2005). *Developmental influences on adult intelligence: The Seattle Longitudinal Study*. New York, NY: Oxford University Press.

Schooler, C. (2001). The intellectual effects of the demands of the work environment. In R. J. Sternberg & E. L. Gigorenko (Eds.), *Environmental effects on cognitive abilities* (pp. 363–380). Mahwah, NJ: Erlbaum.

Simonton, D. K. (1988). *Scientific genius: A psychology of science*. New York, NY: Cambridge University Press.

Snow, R. E. (1996). Aptitude development and education. *Psychology, Public Policy, and Law*, 2, 536–560.

Stanovich, K. E., & West, R. F. (1989). Exposure to print and orthographic processing. *Reading Research Quarterly*, 24, 403–433.

Sternberg, R. J. (1999). Intelligence as developing expertise. *Contemporary Educational Psychology*, 24, 359–375.

Sternberg, R. J., & Detterman, D. K. (1986). *What is intelligence? Contemporary viewpoints on its nature and definition*. Norwood, NJ: Ablex.

Stewart, N. (1947). A.G.C.T. scores of army personnel grouped by occupation. *Occupations*, 26, 5–41.

Swift, E. J. (1910). Relearning a skillful act: An experimental study in neuro-muscular memory. *Psychological Bulletin*, 7, 17–19.

Tuffiash, M., Roring, R. W., & Ericsson, K. A. (2007). Expert performance in Scrabble: Implications for the study of the structure and acquisition of complex skills. *Journal of Experimental Psychology: Applied*, 13, 124–134.

Wagner, R. K. (2000). Practical intelligence. In R. J. Sternberg (Ed.), *Handbook of intelligence* (pp. 380–395). New York, NY: Cambridge University Press.

Wagner, R. K., & Sternberg, R. J. (1985). Practical intelligence in real-world pursuits: The role of tacit knowledge. *Journal of Personality and Social Psychology*, 49, 436–458.

Wagner, R. K., & Sternberg, R. J. (1987). Tacit knowledge in managerial success. *Journal of Business and Psychology*, 1, 301–312.

Webb, R. M., Lubinski, D., & Benbow, C. P. (2007). Spatial ability: A neglected dimension in talent searches for intellectually precocious youth. *Journal of Educational Psychology*, 99, 397–420.

Willis, S., & Tosti-Vasey, J. L. (1990). How adult development, intelligence, and motivation affect competence. In S. L. Willis & S. S. Dubin (Eds.), *Maintaining professional competence: Approaches to career enhancement, vitality, and success throughout a work life* (pp. 64–84). San Francisco, CA: Jossey-Bass.

Yates, F. (1966). *The art of memory*. London, UK: Routledge & Kegan Paul.

Part IX

MOVING FORWARD

CHAPTER 42

Where Are We? Where Are We Going? Reflections on the Current and Future State of Research on Intelligence

Earl Hunt

Where are we? Where are we going? These are good questions for most people, and the people who study intelligence are no exceptions.

Some form of cognitive skill is used in everything we do. Different lives require different but overlapping sets of skills. The cognitive skills required by a surgeon are not the same as those required by a lawyer, nor are the skills required by modern, urbanized postindustrial life precisely the same as the cognitive skills required by Paleolithic hunter-gatherers. On the other hand, every society insists that its members learn the society's language adequately, although only a few become admired speakers and writers. Some numerical skill is required in all modern societies, but only a few people become mathematicians. The same thing is true across settings; ordering in a restaurant and driving on a freeway call upon some situation-general and some situation-unique skills. In a highly differentiated society such as ours, there can be considerable variation in situation-unique cognitive skills.

Intelligence tests measure three different types of cognitive skills: skills that are unique to the testing situation (like how to take a multiple-choice examination), skills that are unique to the industrial and postindustrial societies (largely tests of knowledge and some forms of reasoning), and skills that are common to all humanity (memory, spatial-visual reasoning). After a century of test development, it is not surprising that the tests provide good measures of those cognitive skills relevant to the society that created them (the urban-oriented industrial society) and not irrelevant, but less accurate, measures of skills required by other societies. What has been discovered about measuring the mind?

There is no unanimously agreed upon answer to this question. The views expressed here are a summarization of a more detailed review and argument, which literally took a book to state (Hunt, 2011). That is not surprising, considering that very intelligent people have mused about individual differences in thought for thousands of years and that the modern, scientifically oriented approach is now over a century old. Nor is it surprising, considering the complexity of the topic, that different observers have come to somewhat different conclusions. These range from the belief that there are many varieties of intelligence, and everyone has at least one of them (Gardner 1983, 1993) to the conclusion that there is basically just one general dimension of cognitive competence (Jensen, 1998).

Certain themes will appear and reappear throughout the discussion. The first, and most important, is the necessity of distinguishing between intelligence in the conceptual sense, which I take to mean individual differences in cognitive competence, and intelligence in the much narrower sense of the trait that is measured by conventional cognitive tests. Arguments over this distinction date back to the early days of mental testing (Boring, 1923; Lippmann, 1922a,b) and are alive today. Test scores are seldom important in themselves; they are important only as an indicator of intelligence in the conceptual sense. On the other hand, science depends on measurement. This sets up an inevitable tension between often reasonable claims that the tests do not measure this or that aspect of conceptual intelligence and the equally reasonable claim that scientific models are intended to account for data, and that the data we obtain is always the result of measurement. Therefore those who chastise our present measures of intelligence have an obligation to say how the trait should be measured.

The second theme that will run through the chapter can be understood by an analogy to gold mining in California. Mining gold in California was a sensible thing to do in the 1850s. The gold that was mined is as good as it ever was; most of it is hanging around in jewelry (and maybe teeth) today. By 1860 there were still a few nuggets in the ground, but it was time to move to new fields. I will argue that the same thing is true of research on intelligence. A great deal has been learned using the testing techniques that are ubiquitous today. Forgetting or denigrating this information would be silly; science progresses by building on the past. But it is time to move on to new techniques of measurement if we want to obtain any major breakthrough.

This chapter is divided into four sections. The first three discuss developments in the measurement of intelligence, the causes of intelligence, and the implications of having or not having intelligence. The final section deals with demographic issues. Throughout I focus on intelligence within the normal and superior range. There will be no discussion of mental disabilities severe enough to keep a person from participating as an independent member of society.

Measuring Intelligence

Present Psychometric Models

Psychometrics is very largely a technology for analyzing the data that come out of the structured interview that we call a test. Hundreds of different topics can go into this structured interview: vocabulary, paragraph comprehension, analyzing block designs, doing arithmetic, and so on. Psychometric models summarize the variation in test scores in terms of latent traits presumed to be descriptive of basic psychological processes underlying the various ways that cognitive skills have been assessed.

After a century of debate, two models of psychometric data have emerged as "'more or less" triumphant. The first model, which traces its origins to Charles Spearman, early in the 20th century (Spearman, 1904, 1927), is the general intelligence (*g*) plus special "group factors" model. The idea is that there is a general reasoning factor, which applies almost everywhere, augmented by broad, but not completely general, talents for language analysis, visual-spatial reasoning, and the like.

The best developed form of this model (I would hesitate to say "final" about any theory) is the *g*-VPR model developed by Wendy Johnson and Tom Bouchard (Johnson & Bouchard 2005a,b; Johnson, te Nijenhuis & Bouchard, 2007). In this model *g* stands for general reasoning, and the V, P, and R terms for three broad factors; language skill, perceptual-analytic (the ability to recognize and pick out details of visual stimuli) and "rotation" (the ability to manipulate images "in the mind's eye"). Johnson and Bouchard's model subsumes a great deal of research on similar models emphasizing general intelligence across the span of the 20th century.

The second model is the fluid-crystallized model, which is based on a distinction between a talent for solving new problems using general reasoning skills (fluid intelligence, Gf) and the ability to apply previously acquired knowledge and problem-solving methods to the current problem (Gc). These abilities are correlated, so a general reasoning factor *g* can be extracted from them. The basic idea can be traced back to the writings of the 16th-century Spanish philosopher/physician Juan Huarte de San Juan, but its modern incarnation is clearly due to Raymond Cattell, with subsequent major modifications by John Horn (1986) and then Robert Sternberg (2003, and many other references).

Placing Sternberg's work in the Cattell-Horn line may surprise some, for he has never described his work this way. Therefore I should justify the statement. Sternberg has proposed a model of intelligence that contains three broad abilities: analytic, creative, and practical intelligence. His version of analytic ability is, by his own description, quite similar to general reasoning, as derived from the *g*-VPR model and the Gf-Gc model. His method of evaluating creativity relies on presenting people with unusual "toy problems," such as writing a short story with the title *The Octopus's Sneakers*. While one can argue over whether such efforts are "real" creativity, they do extend intelligence testing and are highly similar to previous attempts to evaluate creativity. They also challenge the examinee with a new problem; dealing with such problems is the definition of fluid intelligence.

Sternberg's third dimension, practical intelligence, is evaluated by presenting people with problems that are appropriate to their background, and thus differ over backgrounds. For instance, Inuit hunters were asked questions about hunting in sub-Arctic regions, children in a rural village in Kenya were asked about traditional medical practices, and U.S. military officers were asked how they would handle a variety of military leadership problems (Sternberg et al., 2000). Cattell (1971) emphasized that Gc involved the use of previously acquired knowledge, which is the sort of information Sternberg evaluates in his tests of practical intelligence. Thus Cattell placed Sternberg's work squarely in the Gf-Gc tradition before the work was accomplished.

As a practical matter, though, the tests of crystallized intelligence that were actually created to evaluate Gc were intended for use in the general population, with an emphasis on the United States. Therefore the tests that became associated with the latent trait of crystallized ability were tests of the lowest common denominator of cultural knowledge in industrial and postindustrial societies– roughly what you would expect a high school senior to know. This is a much narrower definition of intelligence than Cattell (or Huarte!) intended. Sternberg has made the important pragmatic contribution of extending intelligence testing to take into account a person's particular social situation.

Similar extensions have been made, outside the intelligence testing area, by industrial-organizational (I-O) psychologists. I-O psychologists deal with narrowly focused segments of society – the company or industry they are studying. Some of their methods for personnel evaluation in these specialized situations, such as situational judgment tests, closely resemble the tests that Sternberg and his colleagues have proposed to evaluate practical intelligence. There appears to be a convergence of ideas here, which is good, for independent developments coming to the same conclusion strengthen our evaluation of the conclusion.

Which of these models is best? Standard theory of science says that knowledge advances by the clash of new ideas, but in this case a competition between theories may not be the best approach. The theory that you want depends upon why you want it. One reason for measuring intelligence is to connect individual differences in cognitive skills to individual differences in physiological or genetic makeup. Here the advantage clearly goes to the *g*-VPR model, for the behavioral distinctions it makes map onto studies of the biological origins of general reasoning, verbal, and perceptual capacities.

A second and equally scientific reason for measuring individual differences in cognitive skills is to further our understanding of how intelligence is used in society. Such understanding can guide the development of intelligence, through education, and guide the use of intelligence in the workplace. Here a good deal can be said for a model that stresses the difference between intelligence-as-knowledge and intelligence-as-an-ability-to-deal-with-novelty: Gc and Gf. Ackerman (2000) has pointed out that intelligence-as-knowledge is tremendously important when we are dealing with adult behavior. Much of Sternberg's work on practical intelligence addresses this issue, for if a person is going to work in a particular domain, then it is important that he or she know the rules for that domain.

It is likely that we will see a good deal of future research along these lines, for two reasons. One is that as we move more and more into research on adult cognition during the working years, there will be a greater research need for tests that evaluate specialized capabilities. The other reason is more pragmatic. Specialized tests that reflect a particular segment of the workplace are easier to defend in court than general tests, devoid of content related to the particular situation involved.

All-in-all, psychometric approaches have given us two reasonably good models, each useful for different purposes. I do not expect to see great progress beyond the present models, for the analogy of gold in California applies. Over the last 100 years some very smart people have thought quite a bit about what sort of model characterizes the observations that can be made within the conventional testing paradigm. It is not likely that major theoretical advances will be made by continued examination of such observations. Major advances are going to come from observations of how people apply their cognitive skills outside the testing session, over extended periods of time. We need a new measurement paradigm that goes beyond the structured interview.

The structured interview is not a good forum for evaluating a person's talent for reflecting upon difficult problems or for being able to deal with problems that can be seen from several different perspectives. Even if a test is "untimed," everyone knows that testing cannot last for days. Rapid thinking is stressed, mulling over problems is not. Skills in setting goals, establishing priorities for action, and resisting distractions – all part of intelligence in any conceptual sense – can only be evaluated indirectly. The measurement of creative thought has been a consistently problematical topic. We ask people to respond to silly problems, such as suggesting different uses for a brick. Creativity in life involves extended reflection and the seeking out and examining of relevant evidence, still more activities that do not fit into the standard testing situation. In cross-cultural applications, we have to remember that the test setting is itself is a social situation, and it brings with it procedures that simply do not work in some societies.

This brings me to my first and perhaps most important speculation. Any major advance in our understanding of intelligence will depend upon the development of techniques for monitoring behavior "in life," outside of structured interviews. Such records exist today – medical records, credit card purchases, cell-phone use, employment records, and tax returns contain a tremendous amount of information that could be analyzed to reveal a great deal about a person's intelligence. And I have not yet mentioned use of the Internet or the rapidly developing field of social media!

Accessing these sources of information raises substantial issues concerning privacy and personal independence. The issues are not unresolvable. Numerous longitudinal studies have been conducted in which volunteers provide researchers a great deal of personal information. It is now physically possible to extend such studies by arranging for access to the electronic footprints a person leaves as he or she goes through life. Assuming that participation is voluntary and that privacy concerns are met, I see no reason that such information cannot be used to further scientific understanding of the use and development of intelligence.

How Is Intelligence Produced?

Biological Causes

In Richard Dresser's 1997 play *Below the Belt*, one character explains the actions of another by saying "Merkin's brain has a mind of its own." Dresser was right; every mental action is, eventually, the result of brain processes.

Again the gold in California analogy applies. For the first 75 years of modern research on intelligence, psychologists had a meager set of instruments for analyzing brain-behavior relationships. Considerable reliance was placed on the analysis of the behavioral effects of fortuitous events, largely nonfatal injuries to the brain (*neuropsychology*). A great deal was learned, for example, about the location of language centers, but theory testing was constrained by limitations on our ability to relate behavioral measures, such as test scores, and biological measurements. Then, in the last quarter of the 20th century, a new source of data appeared; brain imaging. The effect on intelligence research was like the opening of the Australian and Alaskan goldfields after the California fields had petered out.

We have and now are learning a tremendous amount about the relation between brain structures and intelligence. We know that general reasoning is associated with circuits involving the dorso-lateral prefrontal cortex and the cingulate cortex. We know that the hippocampus is involved in two things: storage of explicit memories and (along with the parietal cortex) spatial orientation. We have known for years that the left anterior parietal and left posterior frontal regions were involved in language, with some involvement of homologous areas in the right hemisphere. In general, we have a good idea of the location of brain activities. There is certainly more to know, but we have learned a lot.

Intelligence depends upon computations in the brain. By using modern imaging technologies we have obtained a much better picture than we had previously of where these computations take place. We have a much fuzzier picture of what these computations are, and how the brain realizes them. This becomes important when we are interested in individual differences. Imaging studies have suggested that intelligent individuals have more efficient brains, in the sense that they expend less metabolic energy in solving a given problem than do the less intelligent. We also know that metabolic efficiency can be produced in two ways: by genetic differences or by learning – the better learned an activity, the lower the required metabolic expenditure. There may also be a shift of highly learned activities away from the involvement of the frontal-cingulate cortex circuits. Understanding the computational processes behind human cognition is essential for understanding how individual differences in cognitive power relate to brain processes. Right now we know that there is a moderate correlation between brain size and intelligence (McDaniel, 2005), but that is far too global a parameter. We do not understand why it is that people who score high on intelligence tests learn more rapidly than others, because we do not have a good picture of the neural basis for learning concepts. (We do have a good idea of the neural basis for Pavlovian learning, but there is a long way to go between Pavlovian conditioning and learning calculus.) We hope the next 20 years will move from speculation to data on the relation between intelligence and individual variation in brain processes. There is every reason to be optimistic, for new biomedical technologies are opening up new sources of data, and that is bound to produce new insights on brain-behavior relations in all fields of psychology, including research on intelligence.

Within the major postindustrial societies there is a substantial genetic component to intelligence. Note that the statement is limited to a particular population. I did this for two reasons. First, virtually all the data we have on the genetic basis of intelligence comes from these societies, and even more narrowly, samples of the middle and upper socioeconomic (SES) sectors of those societies. Second, the genetic component to intelligence, h, is by definition the percentage of variance in test scores that can be associated with variation in genetic heritage. (There are refinements to this statement, such as "broad sense" and "narrow sense" heritability, but for the purposes of this summary they can be ignored.) This percentage can vary over time and place, which brings me to a major point that is too often lost in discussions of heritability.

No one inherits an IQ. What is inherited is a genetic potential for intelligence, the *reaction range*. Actual intelligence (along with its accessory, the IQ score) is determined by what the individual learns, and how well the individual benefits from physical factors, such as diet, during a lifetime of interactions with the environment. It follows that on a population basis, the value of h depends upon the extent of genetic variation in the population with regard to those genes that are relevant to cognition, and upon the extent of variation in environmental factors that are relevant to intelligence. Within the middle and upper SES segments of the major industrial/postindustrial societies, it appears that at least 50% of the variation is a result of genetic background, and the figure may be somewhat higher (Plomin et al., 2008). There is evidence that the figure is substantially smaller in the lower SES sectors of these societies (Turkheimer et al., 2003).

Why such differences might appear can be clarified by a thought experiment. What has happened to the heritability coefficient in England since Galton wrote *Hereditary Genius* (Galton, 1869)? To make the question easier, restrict consideration only to those living Englishmen and Englishwomen whose ancestors resided in England in 1865. THINK ABOUT IT before reading the next paragraph.

I am quite sure that the heritability coefficient has gone up. Why? Read a few of Charles Dickens's novels. In the mid-19th century there were huge environmental differences between social classes in health, education, nutrition, and virtually any other variable that you care to mention that has been associated with intelligence. Modern-day England provides schooling for everyone, has a national health plan, and on and on. One hundred and fifty years (roughly five human generations) is not enough time to produce substantial changes in the genetic variation in a large human population, but it is quite enough time to reduce the environmental variation. The heritability coefficient went up.

There is also a tricky logical problem. Genetic effects may be either *proximal* or *distal*. If genetic variation produces individual differences in the size or efficiency of a brain structure associated with cognition, that is a proximal effect. If genetic variation influences a behavior that, itself, influences intelligence, that is a distal effect. Let us take an example: parenting practice. *I stress that this is an illustrative example only*.

Dealing with young children can be extremely frustrating to an adult. Suppose, solely for the sake of argumentation, that a temperament for tolerating or not tolerating frustration is partly under genetic control. This may lead to less than optimal parental behavior on the part of the parent and, since the child shares genes with the parent, less than optimal behavior on the child's part. However, the adult has inherited a reaction range, so the parent's behavior can be influenced by training or social pressures. This could include going to parenting classes (hopefully beneficial) or having to deal with children while also dealing with financial stresses (probably not beneficial). We have a genetic potential that can be influenced by environmental variation. Picking apart the genetic and environmental contributions to the development of the child's intelligence will not be an easy task!

There is a substantial genetic component to intelligence in industrial/postindustrial societies. The exact value does not matter. The finding has been replicated so often that we do not need another study directed to this point. The important finding is that that a relevant genetic mechanism exists. But what is it? The answer to this question is outside of quantitative behavior genetics. We must turn to molecular genetics.

There are a number of known genetic anomalies that produce striking deficiencies in intelligence. We have not identified one or even a few genetic variations that account for variations of intelligence in the normal range. Furthermore, the methods that have been used to search for such genes are quite sensitive enough to pick up, say, three or four variations that accounted for 40% of the variance. Combining this negative finding with the positive findings about the heritability coefficient leads to an important conclusion. The genetic component to intelligence, in the normal range, must depend upon the combined contribution of many genes, no one of which contributes very much (Plomin, Kennedy, & Craig, 2006).

Tracing down the genetic mechanisms for intelligence is an important goal. Given modern techniques for genetic analysis it is a doable project and should be done. It is likely that the project will be characterized by many small findings, not by a major breakthrough.

The Information Processing Underpinnings of Intelligence

Suppose that we knew exactly where in the brain intelligence resided. We would still need to know what the implications are for behavior. Behavior can be characterized either by its information-processing characteristics or by its knowledge-level characteristics. To illustrate, showing the circumstances under which people can recite 10 digits, or letters, or words is a demonstration of information-processing capacity; showing the circumstances under which people can recall telephone numbers, acronyms, or sentences is a demonstration of knowledge-level capacity. The existence of knowledge-level capacity implies some information-processing capacity. In research on intelligence, one of the issues is the extent to which variations in complicated cognitive behaviors, such as solving mathematical equations or playing chess, are constrained by individual differences at the information-processing level or individual differences at the knowledge level. To offer an easily imagined example, consider the task of playing blindfold chess. Some chess masters can do this and can even play blindfolded against several opponents at once. Playing blindfold chess requires a substantial information-processing ability to keep track of the information on one or more boards. You also have to know a lot about chess.

We now know that general intelligence, the *g* component of intelligence, is related to two information-processing capacities. One is the ability to control attention and keep information in mind while working on a problem. This was first demonstrated by Kyllonen and Christal (1990) in a study of Air Force enlistees, and since then the finding has been confirmed in many other studies. See Hunt (2011, Chapter 6) for the principal references. This is often referred to as working memory capacity (Baddeley, 1986) although the ability to control attention is certainly part of the capacity. The other is simply speed of information processing (Jensen, 2006). The working memory-control of attention aspect of intelligence is supported by the dorso-lateral prefrontal cortex (DLPFC)-cingulate cortex system (Jung & Haier, 2007). We are not certain what brain processes determine neural processing speed, although we do know that the extent to which a person is practiced in a task makes a major contribution to processing speed.

There has been a spate of research trying to fractionate the working memory-attention control system into its components, such as the ability store information (storage capacity), the ability to process information rapidly to avoid overloading storage (processing capacity, somewhat loosely defined), and the ability to resist distractions while working on a problem (control of attention). The goal of the studies has been to see whether just one of these components is crucial for intelligence. Most of this research has been directed toward establishing separate roles for the storage function (how many things can be kept in mind) and the attention control function (how is attention focused on the right thing at the right time?) of working memory. These attempts at fractionation have not worked out particularly well. I believe the reason is that intelligent action depends jointly upon the ability to store information for short periods of time, the ability to process that information, and the ability to focus on relevant information, with all three abilities working together as a system. Treating the various components of working memory on their own is a bit like trying to understand the maneuvering abilities of an automobile by independent analyses of the power, transmission, and suspension systems.

The extent to which processing speed constrains intelligence depends upon the population you are talking about. In healthy, reasonably bright young adults (college students!) the constraint is modest, so the processing speed-test score correlations are modest. However, if we look over the entire age span, or if we move to a broader population, we find that processing speed is an important constraint, and that it is a very important constraint in old age (Salthouse 1996). This finding is important in itself and illustrates a broader principle – what is constraining in one population may not be constraining in another.

What big questions are left concerning the relation between information processing and intelligence? Outside of research on special populations, I do not think there are any. The gold in California analogy applies again. Understanding information-processing constraints on intelligence was an important thing to do. As was the case in establishing the range of the heritability coefficient, it has been done. There will be important situations in which we want to understand how information-processing constraints apply in a particular situation. The basic research issue does not need to be revisited.

Environmental Causes

Test scores have risen throughout most of the 20th century. The effect was brought to widespread attention by analyses presented by Jim Flynn (2007), in a series of papers starting in 1990. Thanks to his influential writings, the rise in test scores is often referred to as the "Flynn effect," although several other investigators had observed it as early as the 1940s and it had been extensively documented by gerontologists in the 1970s and 1980s (Schaie, 2005). I will refer to it, more neutrally, as the cohort effect.

The cohort effect is large. It has to be environmental, for the time involved (roughly three human generations) is too short for there to be simultaneous genetic shifts in large, largely endogamous populations. Many hypothetical causes have been proposed, ranging from better health practices to the spread of video games that stress visual-spatial reasoning. A good case can be made that we will never know what the cause is, because any time-linked phenomenon will be collinear with other contemporary phenomena. For example, improvements in education over the 20th century were accompanied by improvements in health and nutrition, and (in the industrial world) reductions in family size. These variables have all been shown to have positive effects on intelligence. Also, just as there is no one gene for intelligence, there is probably no single cause for the cohort effect. It is possible that more refined studies of the cohort effect, in which the size of the effect is compared across different segments of the population, may narrow the list of suspected causes, but it is unlikely that a complete explanation will ever be found. What we do know, though, is that there are environmental effects that can have a considerable effect upon intelligence. But, as was the case for the genes, we do not know what these effects are. Let us look at some of the candidates.

The Physical Environment

We know a good deal about the influence of some of the physical aspects of the environment upon intelligence. Discouragingly, most of what we know is how to destroy intelligence rather than how to create it. Environmental lead is a bad thing, excessive alcohol use is a bad thing (especially for pregnant women and their fetuses), and prolonged nutritional deficiency in childhood can cause lags in neural development and, hence, intelligence. Obviously there should be continual searches for environmental contaminants, including agents that lead to prolonged illnesses that may damage the brain.

We do not have a "smart pill" for improving intelligence. There are some pharmacological agents, such as Ritalin, that improve the working-memory control of the attentional system on a temporary basis. These agents were originally used to counteract attention deficit disorders but are increasingly being used (somewhat illegally) by college students and others to enhance cognitive skills on a temporary basis. For that purpose, the drugs do have some effect, although one suspects that behavioral training might do as well. An open question is what these drugs do to intelligence as a trait, on a long-term basis. They could be helpful, harmful, or benign. Investigating this issue is fraught with difficulty for legal and ethical reasons. However, the drugs are being used to enhance performance, so it would be well to understand the issues involved.

The Social Environment

What about the social environment? Diane Halpern (Halpern et al., 2007) has offered a simple principle, which she refers to as the psychological equivalent of the law of gravity. People learn to do what they practice doing. Educational systems more or less force students to do things such as arithmetic word problems that they would seldom do on their own, and the students thereby learn cognitive skills. And the more you practice, the more you learn. This is clear in international comparisons. One of the striking differences between industrial/postindustrial countries whose students post high scores on international examinations (Japan, South Korea, Finland) and countries where students often do not meet expectations commensurate with financial investments in the schools (United States) is that in the high-scoring countries children simply spend more time in school. The more you practice a skill, the greater your learning, a law that works as well in cognition as in sports.

The psychological law of gravity applies to learning outside the classroom as well. It is clear that children's abilities prior to entering school, that is, school readiness, has a major impact on how much they learn during their school careers (Phillips, Crouse, & Ralph, 1998). Children who come from families with fairly high socioeconomic status (SES) tend to have been exposed to more situations in which they have to pick up cognitive skills than have children from low SES families (Nisbett, 2009). Peer group attitudes toward learning differ in various racial/social/ethnic groups in direct relation to performance in school (Steinberg, 1996). The more people practice cognitive skills, the better they get at using these skills, that is, the more intelligent they become. If social support encourages such practice, intelligence will be facilitated. If it works against such practice, intelligence will be hurt.

Except for extreme cases, such as assignment to special education classes and, to a much lesser extent, assignment to gifted programs, there has been a tendency to keep the results of intelligence testing separate from the selection of curricula. This is unfortunate. The work of Sternberg and his colleagues represents an exception to this, for they have investigated incorporating test scores into the selection of educational programs for individual students (Sternberg, Grigorenko, & Zhang, 2008). Similar research was done earlier by Cronbach and Snow (1977) but their ideas were not picked up by the educational establishment. Whether Sternberg's particular approach will prove to be a useful one in education remains to be seen. The goal of developing programs that combine testing with the planning of individual curricula and/or styles of education is clearly an important one and ought to receive further investigation.

Research on environmental effects upon intelligence and, more generally, cognitive accomplishment has been plagued by failures to consider the difference between a laboratory demonstration of a problem that could affect cognitive assessments and an ecological demonstration that the relevant variables actually do exert a major influence outside of the laboratory. Studies of the *stereotype threat* phenomenon provide a good example, although not the only one. A person experiences stereotype threat if he or she believes (or is reminded) that he or she belongs to a group that typically does not do well on certain problems. This reminder then reduces problem-solving performance. For instance, *in the laboratory*, reminding women of their gender, and then confronting them with mathematics problems, results, on average, in lower performance than is observed in a control group (Shih, Pittinsky, & Ambady, 1999). Similar demonstrations have been made using reminders of racial and ethnic membership.

Is stereotype threat important outside the laboratory? The evidence here is not so strong. Stereotype threat operates by lowering people's motivation to work hard. When high-stakes tests (e.g., college entrance examinations, final examinations in a course) are involved, motivation may be sufficient to override stereotype threat. The evidence is that this is so, but the evidence is far from definitive (Sackett, Hardison, & Cullen, 2004; Strickler & Ward, 2004).

The stereotype threat studies provide a good illustration of an area where much more research is needed. Environmental effects, and especially social effects, are typically demonstrated in the laboratory. As is the case for laboratory studies in the biomedical sciences, laboratory studies in psychology show what could happen to intelligence (and many other behaviors). In doing so, variables other than the ones being studied are either randomized or controlled – good experimental design! When we want to generalize to the world outside the laboratory we have to consider the relative strength of the effects that we studied in the laboratory, compared to the effects of the variables that were controlled or randomized in the laboratory but are free to roam in the normal world. What we lack is an analog of medicine's epidemiological studies, which show what variables influence behavior in the world at large.

The converse effect may also occur. There may be variables that are extremely important outside the laboratory, such as the effects of social stressors that exert their pressure over the course of years but are extremely hard to study inside the laboratory. Much more research is needed on such variables, and most of it will *not* be on college students! Or for that matter, students at all! A good deal of life occurs between leaving high school and entering a senior citizen residence. We need to explore how variations in the adult working world affect variations in intelligence. At present there is a paucity of research on this issue.

There is, however, a good deal of research on a related question: How do variations in intelligence influence variations in life?

What Good Is Intelligence?

Intelligence, as evaluated by the tests, is certainly not a perfect indicator of future success in the society. On the other hand, it is the best indicator we have of such success, both in academia and in the general society. We know that test scores obtained in early adolescence correlate positively, and substantially, with later success in academia, future socioeconomic status, performance in the workplace, health status, marital social adjustment, mortality rates (smart people live longer), and a tendency toward liberal rather than conventional views on social and political issues. (See Hunt, 2011, Chapter 10, for extensive documentation, and Deary, Whalley, & Starr, 2009, for an account of the life history of Scottish children who were tested at age 11, and then had their lives traced when the survivors had reached their 80s.) Let us provide a few numbers.

1. A very large study of English schoolchildren found that there was a correlation of .8 between general academic ability, evaluated at age 16, and cognitive test scores obtained at age 11 (Deary et al., 2007.)
2. The predictive correlation between college entrance examination scores (such as the SAT) and first year grades is approximately .5 This is not because of the relation between test scores and family socioeconomic status (Sackett et al., 2009). Note that predictive correlations, which apply to the applicant population and are the appropriate correlation for use in personnel decisions, will be somewhat higher than the correlation between test scores and grades in the population of people accepted into college, due to restriction in range within the population of candidates selected.
3. The predictive correlation of .5 also applies very widely to job performance measures, such as supervisor ratings and (in military studies) objective measures of a person's ability to do his or her job (Campbell & Knapp, 2001; Schmidt & Hunter, 1998; Sackett, Borneman, & Connelly, 2008). Not surprisingly, the correlation is highest for those jobs, and aspects of jobs, that stress cognitive performance, and lowest for jobs and measures that stress physical performance or social interactions. However, it is important to note that intelligence measures are almost always better predictors of performance than personality measures.

We also know that these tendencies appear at the extremes. Terman's studies in the first half of the 20th century should have dispelled the picture of the sickly nerd forever (Terman & Oden, 1959). Various critics have deconstructed Terman because of his use of recruiting methods that (the critics believed) were biased toward his recruiting people with relatively high SES. Subsequent studies of people with high test scores have replicated Terman's basic finding; high test scores are statistically associated with very impressive success in life, on a group basis (Benbow & Lubinski, 1996). The relation between test scores and success extends into the very high ranges of test scores. It is simply not true that beyond a certain level intelligence no longer predicts success (Lubinski et al., 2006).

It is worth contrasting studies of the gifted to (largely military) studies of people with low-normal test scores. The impression one gets is of people who can "make it" in society, but who lag behind average performance. Category IV soldiers, recruits who are in 10th to 30th percentile in terms of scores on the Armed Services Qualifying test (the lowest acceptable recruiting category for the United States Armed Services), fail basic training at a somewhat higher rate (but still less than 10%) than better qualified recruits, have slightly more disciplinary problems, and are promoted at a slower rate than their comrades with higher test scores. They are not drags on society, but they are not major contributors either (Sticht et al., 1987).

These findings, which are very well established, are not in agreement with many lay perceptions that intelligence tests either do not predict well, or that they are useful only in predicting academic success. Why is there this discrepancy between well-established facts and common perceptions? I think there are two reasons for the disagreement.

The first reason is that these are statistical trends. The predictive correlations between test scores and indices of social success, after various statistical corrections have been applied, are on the order of .5. This is a hard value to understand without considerable knowledge of statistics. Nonstatisticians tend to confuse "positively correlated with" with $r \sim .95$, and point to exceptions (which are certainly allowed with r = .5) as proof that there is no correlation. Such reasoning is spurious, but understandable.

A related point is that it is not realistic to expect any measure of a personal trait to be a terribly accurate predictor of success 20 years later, simply because success and failure will be determined by the many things that can happen in the test – evaluation interval (e.g., disease, economic booms and busts, automobile accidents, lottery winnings) that have nothing to do with personal characteristics.

Finally, there is a statistical point. You cannot obtain good measurement with unreliable measures. Cognitive tests generally have reliabilities in excess of .8. This is not the case for many of our various measures of success. Grades assigned in classrooms are not likely to have reliabilities over .6. Furthermore, grading standards vary markedly over disciplines, especially at the postsecondary level. An A in physics is not the same as an A in communication arts. Unless supervisors are carefully trained, ratings of job performance are variable across raters. Unreliability in our measures of the criteria for success sharply limits the accuracy of any predictor, including but not limited to intelligence tests.

The second reason for the disagreement between statistical evaluations and popular perception is that the society of the postindustrial world is, to a great extent, segregated by level of cognitive skills. This is true of our workplaces, our neighborhoods, and our social groups. The people we meet and know are roughly as intelligent as we are. Therefore our personal experiences only allow us to observe people whose intelligence varies over a limited range. As a result, intelligence is not a major predictor of the behaviors that we observe personally, and we erroneously generalize our personal experiences to the much wider social world.

In order to gain a better understanding of how intelligence is used in the world we need to go beyond correlations, and especially beyond correlations with gross variables, such as socioeconomic status. We need to develop an in-depth understanding of how intellectual skills are nurtured, developed, and then used at all levels of intelligence. The sorts of studies I am thinking of will involve monitoring people's daily lives in schools and the workplace for extended periods of time, the same sorts of studies that we need to expand our notions of what intelligence is, will be needed to understand what intelligence does.

Achieving this goal will require a confluence of efforts by industrial-organizational psychologists, whose work has proceeded surprisingly independently of research on intelligence, educators, and researchers interested in intelligence per se. Both the industrial-organizational psychologists and the educators have, of course, conducted extensive studies of performance variables in both the workplace and the school. In many ways these efforts mimic the work on intelligence; explicit assessments taken using the conventional structured interview paradigm, variously named intelligence or aptitude tests, are related to other explicit performance measures, such as grades, supervisor ratings, or promotion records.

What I am calling for here is something different. I want to see an evaluation, over time, of the relation between intelligence measures and demonstrations of cognition on a daily basis. The evaluations should be extended enough to evaluate the ability to reflect, to organize one's time, and to evaluate the strategies used to acquire new information. Going back to the gold in California analogy, it is time to move from the field provided by the standard paradigm – in intelligence research, industrial-organizational psychology, and in education – to the new fields afforded by our increased ability to monitor people's behavior outside of a traditional testing situation. Such a research program would have to be done carefully, for monitoring raises serious issues of privacy. These issues can be resolved, and should be, in order to further our understanding of how intelligence is used and is developed over the life span.

The Epidemiology of Intelligence

Intelligence is not distributed uniformly across all demographic groups. Changes in intelligence with age, differences between men and women, and differences across racial/ethnic groups all raise scientific and social policy issues. Discussing these topics raises a great many emotions. In an ideal world, social-policy concerns would be guided by scientific findings but not determined by them. Science would be used, dispassionately, to decide what could be done and how much it might cost. Policy makers would then choose between well-understood programs, consistent with their goals and resources.

In practice, things do not work quite that way. While scientific findings do receive rational analysis, they may also be used as bargaining chips to justify particular social policies. Facts can also be thought of as "negative bargaining chips"; people who want society to accept a certain goal may not welcome findings suggesting that the goal will be difficult to achieve. The automotive industry did not welcome research on the deleterious effects of atmospheric lead, and it is understandable that they did not, for the decision to ban lead in gasoline cost the industry billions of dollars (Kovarik, 2005). Questions about group differences in intelligence raise even deeper passions.

Before discussing particular demographic variables, a general problem has to be considered: recruitment effects (Hunt & Madhyastha, 2008). In a typical "'epidemiological' study, participants from two or more groups are recruited from an accessible population." The results of a comparison between the recruited groups are then frequently generalized to a population much larger than the accessible population. For instance, many studies of male-female differences have contrasted the behaviors of male and female college students. If differences are observed, they may be generalized to men and women, or young adult men and women, in general. However, if there has been differential recruitment from the general population into the accessible population, generalization has to be carefully limited.

Let us take a specific example. Since the 1980s a higher percentage of women than men have applied to U.S. colleges. Suppose, as has been observed, that men have higher overall SAT scores than women. Can we assume that men are smarter than women? No, because we are comparing (to take a crude model) roughly the top 55% of female academic talent to the top 45% of male talent. More sophisticated modeling is required in practice, but the point should be clear. When contrasting the performance of members of defined demographic groups, some consideration has to be given to differential recruitment of the groups from the general population into the accessible population.

The reader should keep this caution in mind when considering the following discussion of trends, or when reviewing other studies that may be subject to recruitment effects.

Aging. Intelligence, in the general sense of cognitive skills, changes with age throughout the adult years. Processing speed begins to decrease quite early in adult life. The working memory-attention complex weakens somewhat later. Experiences pile up, and in some cases experiences produce knowledge. In a highly differentiated society such as ours, experiences also produce specialization. We need to know a great deal more about both the physiological and social changes that are associated with, and to some extent dependent on, changes in cognitive skills with age.

The study of adult cognition (by which I mean people who have reached the age of roughly 40 and beyond) requires a substantial rethinking of the way intelligence is measured. Reliance on standard tests, appropriate for high school and college students, is no longer appropriate. Evaluating older people by their ability to do novel problems, such as those posed by progressive matrix tests, fails to capture the fact that most adults cope with society, most of the time, by using crystallized rather than fluid intelligence. But the crystallized intelligence they use is specialized. If you want to make an estimate of how well a person can deal with our cognitively oriented society it is not appropriate to give plumbers, physicians, lawyers, police officers, and information technology support personnel the same test. The fluid-crystallized distinction, coupled with Sternberg's (and the industrial-organization psychologists') emphasis upon practical intelligence and job knowledge assume more relevance in the investigation of adult cognition than in the investigation of intelligence in schools and colleges.

The distinction is also relevant to techniques used widely by industrial-organizational psychologists to predict job performance. These include work samples, job knowledge tests, and situational judgment tests in which people are asked to role-play the participants in a job-related scenario. All such tests evaluate specific knowledge of work situations in addition to drawing on general reasoning powers. Taken alone, general reasoning tests turn out to be slightly better predictors of workplace performance than are the specialized measures, but the specialized measures do add to the validity of the prediction (Schmidt & Hunter, 1998).

These results suggest that both general reasoning and situation-specific knowledge are important. We need a better understanding of how they interact, for on a worldwide basis, there are interesting differences in the way the age distributions of different societies are changing.

In the postindustrial societies, the population is growing older at such a rate that retirement policies are being changed. This will force changes in the cognitive resources available to the workplace (Hunt, 1995). In general, we can expect that the workforce as a whole will show an increase in accumulated knowledge but somewhat decreased abilities to learn new methods of working. This trend has to be balanced against the cohort effect discussed earlier, which suggests that general intelligence is increasing (but possibly not at the top!). How will these conflicting trends influence the potential for both technological and social changes in our society?

In developing societies, exactly the opposite is happening. Reductions in infant mortality have produced an excess of young people while, tragically, the ravages of war and diseases such as HIV-AIDS have produced a shortage of middle-aged adults. The picture is one of a society whose workforce is capable of learning, but possibly detached from the knowledge possessed by people who normally pass on the social and technological basis of the culture. How will this affect the cognitive resources of populations in developing countries?

No one knows the answers to these questions. What we can foresee is that all societies will have to deal with the changes in the supply of cognitive resources that accompany distortions of what has been the typical human age distribution across populations. The questions raised have implications for both biological and social research.

Male-female differences. Male-female differences are both a matter of gender (the social distinction) and sex (the biological distinction). When dealing with male-female differences the *g*-VPR model is more useful than the Gf-Gc model, because the *g*-VPR model maps more closely onto established physiological differences than the Gf-Gc model (Johnson & Bouchard, 2007a,b). However, when dealing with differences between men and women in the working years and beyond there will be cases when specialized tests of knowledge are more useful than the ubiquitous standardized tests.

Three facts about male-female differences have been very well established. With respect to the important general intelligence dimension (*g*), there is at most a trivial mean difference between men and women. However men are more variable, which results in high male to female ratios in both remedial education and gifted programs. On average, men have a marked advantage over women in certain aspects of spatial/visual reasoning, especially when the task involves dealing with real or imagined movement or orientation in space. For some reason that is not clearly understood, these abilities are related to performance in mathematics. Because mathematics is central to performance in the science and engineering fields, many people have suggested that this may be the reason that there is a high male to female ratio in those fields. However, even among highly talented young men and women, there are more men than women in the science and technology fields, suggesting that interests rather than abilities may be the most important factor in determining male-female differences in career choices (Lubinski et al., 2006; Robertson et al., 2010).

There are considerably smaller differences between men and women in verbal functioning (in favor of women) and in perceptual tasks that require focusing on small details in static displays.

Are male-female differences due to social or biological factors? The answer is quite clear: Both are implicated to some degree. There are differences between male and female brains, and certainly differences in hormonal balances that influence brain development and processes.

There are also differences in social roles and learning opportunities. These vary considerably across societies. The influence of male-female disparities in opportunity can be seen in international comparisons of schoolchildren's facility with mathematics. In almost all countries tested, by high school, males outperform females. However, the size of the male-female difference, across countries, is related to international indices of gender equality in social roles. This effect can be considerable. Females in the high-performing countries outperform males in the low-performing countries – something that is true when one confines one's attention to the industrially developed countries. There may be some biological basis for male-female differences in mathematics performance, but clearly biology is not destiny. Halpern's psychological law of gravity wins again; girls and boys will learn to do what they practice doing.

The biomedical aspects of male-female differences in cognition will continue to receive a great deal of attention. Progress can be expected, simply because progress in the biomedical sciences will produce sources of data that are unavailable to us today.

Studies of the social aspects of male-female differences will continue but will be difficult because we are shooting at a moving target. For instance, in the developed countries, over the 20th century there was a substantial shift toward gender equality in social roles, especially in employment. Historically, this has been accompanied by the growth of a huge fashion and advertising industry that emphasizes sexuality and sexual differences. (The same thing is true of aging. As the population ages, more emphasis has been placed on appearing to retain the physical attributes of youth.) International differences in gender roles are so marked that one country, the Netherlands, includes in its compulsory orientations for immigrants a discussion of the differences between gender roles in the Netherlands and in many of the immigrants' home countries. Studying the effects of the substantial changes in social roles upon male and female cognitive skills may shed a good deal of light on a complex topic. The necessary research might look at historical differences, international differences, and changes as people emigrate from one country to another.

Racial/ethnic differences. We now come to what is possibly the most explosive topic in psychology – the discussion of racial/ethnic differences in intelligence. Some people who have looked at the topic have claimed that there are substantial differences that are genetic in origin (Rushton & Jensen, 2005); others have argued that there are differences but that they have no genetic component (Nisbett, 2009). Others claim that biological races do not exist, so whatever differences one encounters, they are not a result of biological race because there is no such thing (Sternberg, Grigorenko, & Kidd, 2005). They point out, for example, that the average genetic differences among various "Black" groups in Africa are greater than the average differences between "White" and "Black" groups in the United States. Hence they argue that, genetically, there is no more basis for distinguishing between White and Black "races" than there is for distinguishing among various "Black" races.

Given these very strongly held differences of opinion, the following intermediate remarks are unlikely to satisfy anyone.

As Sternberg, Grigorenko, and Kidd made the most extreme statement, that races do not exist, I examine that point first. This is logical, because if their statement is correct, there is no point in discussing the issue further.

Socially, people identify with recognized racial/ethnic groups. In the United States, where most of the data have been gathered, the major groups are "Whites," African Americans, Asians, and Latinos, now the largest minority group, and the much smaller group of Native Americans. People also self-identify as Irish Americans, Italian Americans, Jewish Americans, and so on. Such identifications do have practical social and genetic consequences. For instance, people derived from settlers from Britain are more prone to skin cancer than people derived from Mediterranean populations. The smaller distinctions will be ignored, for virtually all the debates over psychological characteristics concern the four major groups.

Racial/ethnic identifications do not refer to highly homogeneous groups, either culturally or biologically. "Whites" can be the descendants of the North European groups that settled North America in the early 17th century, or people who arrived from Lebanon only a few years ago. Latinos, and to a greater extent, Asians, include peoples with very different cultures, biological heritage, and circumstances of immigration. While the typical image of a "Latino" is of a fairly recent immigrant group, there are Latino populations in the Southwestern states who have resided there since before the American Revolution. Similar distinctions between internally heterogeneous groups exist in Europe, where the relative frequency of minority group members is increasingly rapidly due to immigration and low birth rates among the historic European populations.

Within the framework of the general American European culture these different groups also vary in socioeconomic status and in a variety of cultural practices, including parenting practices, family solidarity, and emphasis upon children's achievement in, for instance, mathematics or sports. All of these social practices could affect the development of intelligence, both in the important conceptual sense and in the side result of achieving high test scores. However, as is also undisputed, the distinctions are gradations rather than absolute. African American household incomes are lower than White household incomes on the average, but there are some African Americans who earn far more than a substantial majority of Whites. The same thing is true of education, health status, or virtually any other variable you care to name.

When we discuss social and cultural distinctions such as these, we generally speak of ethnic groups, and there is little dispute over statistical differences in the frequency of cultural practice. The dispute comes when we begin to make a genetically determined biological distinction. At that point we are more likely to use the term racial rather than ethnic differences.

Sternberg, Grigorenko, and Zhang are correct in saying that there is more genetic variation within groups than between groups. But how relevant is this to the issue of racial identification on a genetic basis?

Internationally, it has been estimated that about 5% of the permissible genetic variation in humans (i.e., variation within the genetic variation of the species, not considering genes shared across species) is associated with continent of ancestry (Rosenberg et al., 2002). However this amount of genetic variation is quite enough to make accurate racial identification, using multivariate techniques based upon the co-occurrence of alleles of several genes (Edwards, 2003).

Bamshad et al. (2004) offer some interesting statistics that illustrate the issue. Consider three randomly chosen individuals, an African, a European, and an Asian. For each of these individuals choose, randomly, a shadow partner from the same population, that is, a shadow for the African, the European, and the Asian. We can compute the genetic similarity between each pair and for the shadow pairs. What is the likelihood that the African's genotype resembles the African shadow partner to a greater degree than it resembles the genotype of the randomly chosen European, or Asian? The answer is .64 for the European and .65 for the Asian. A European Asian contrast has a probability of .62 (Bamshad et al., Figure 2b). These are comparisons between individuals and do not preferentially weight the genes whose allele frequencies vary across continent of ancestral origin. When such weightings are used the distinctions become much sharper. Within the U.S. population, identification of ancestral origin from genetic clustering is a highly accurate predictor of self-identification as a European-derived, African-derived, or Asian-derived American (Bamshad et al., 2004, Figure 1; Tang et al., 2005).

The conclusion is clear. Within the mixed populations of North America and Europe, ancestrally derived groupings can be identified by both social practices and genetic analysis. The nonexistence of such groups simply cannot be maintained. The term "race" has, in some quarters, acquired a pejorative connotation. So perhaps we need another word. But until one is found, I suggest that "race" be used when the intent is to emphasize biological differences between groups of different ancestry, and that "ethnicity" be used when the intent is to emphasize social/cultural differences.

Both race and ethnicity are "fuzzy" concepts, in the sense that membership is held in them to some degree. This does not make the distinctions between groups any less real, just a bit more complex.

Having concluded that racial and ethnic groups do, indeed, exist, do they have different cognitive competencies, and if so, why?

Scores on cognitive tests do differ across racial/ethnic groups. The order of group means differs somewhat depending upon the test used. If the comparison is made on the basis of a general intelligence (*g*) measure in the United States the ordering is Asians Americans, Whites (slightly behind), Latinos, and African Americans, with the gap between Whites and African Americans being about one standard deviation (see Hunt, 2011, Chapter 11) for reports of several such comparisons. Two of the better studies, based upon samples representative of the United States are the National Longitudinal Study of Youth, 1979, extensively analyzed by Herrnstein and Murray (1994), and the standardization of the Woodcock-Johnson intelligence test, analyzed for racial differences by Murray (2007). There is evidence that the gap between Whites and African Americans decreased during the latter part of the 20th century, but it appears to have stabilized at somewhere between .8 and 1 standard deviation units for cohorts born after the 1970s (Hedges & Nowell, 1998; Murray, 2007).

Studies of selected subpopulations, such as comparisons of the SAT scores of applicants to college, show similar results. For instance, the 2009 overall SAT scores were 1623 for self-identified Asian American, 1581 for Whites, 1364 for Latinos, and 1276 for African Americans (College Board, 2009). These scores represent information about an important subpopulation, better educated youth, but cannot be generalized to the overall population due to recruitment effects.

A slightly different picture applies when we look at the type of test. Using the 2009 SAT as an example, for the critical reading part of the examination the scores were White 528, Asian American 516, Latino 453, African American 429. For the mathematics part of the examination the scores were Asian American 587, White 536, Latinos 461 (averaged across different Latino groups), and African American 426. Based on an approximate standard deviation of 100 for each test, the White- African American gap in standard deviation units was .99 for the reading part of the examination and 1.12 for the mathematics part (data from the College Board Report *College Bound Seniors: 2009*). Due to the recruitment effect mentioned earlier, the exact numbers presented here should not be taken as representative of ethnic group comparisons across the entire U.S. population. The important thing is that the pattern is similar to the pattern found in many studies. On the average, Asian Americans score slightly lower than Whites on language-related tests and markedly higher than Whites on tests emphasizing mathematics. African Americans score markedly lower than Whites on both types of tests. A pattern similar to the mathematics pattern is found on the Raven's Matrices tests, which are considered one of the best markers for *g* (Raven, 2008). In spite of the wide variety in groups tested and type of test, the same general pattern appears over and over again. Depending upon the test used (and again, with the warning about recruitment effects) the gap seems to have stabilized at somewhere between .8 and 1.0, in standard deviation units, for the cohorts born in the late 1970s and afterward.

It has been claimed that similar trends appear internationally, including the claim that test scores are startlingly low in sub-Saharan Africa (Lynn & Vanhanen, 2002, 2006). However, the latter claim is based on selective citation of studies that contained very low estimates of IQ scores in some of the sub-Saharan nations, including cases where the score for a nation was based on studies of groups that were not remotely representative of the nation in question, or where the relevance of the test used was highly questionable. A much higher quality review of the evidence suggests that mean IQs in the sub-Saharan African nations are about five IQ points below values typically reported for African-derived groups in the United States and Europe (Wicherts, Dolan, & Van der Maas, 2010).

The claim is sometimes made that the test scores are unfair to minority groups. The answer to this question depends upon the definition of "unfair." A test could be unfair to a group in the sense that it does not accurately predict their performance on a criterion, or it could be unfair in the sense that, compared to other examinees, members of the affected group have not had adequate opportunity to acquire the skills evaluated by the test. Various academic aptitude tests, such as the SAT, generally overpredict the academic achievements of African Americans, and underpredict the achievements of Asian Americans (Mattern et al., 2008). A similar pattern appears in the workplace. A recent analysis of work sample tests provides a good illustration. Recall that the predictive validity between cognitive test scores and workplace performance is about .5, averaged over all groups. If there is a one standard deviation difference between workplace performance and test scores, it follows that there should be *not more than* a .5 standard deviation unit difference on work sample tests, assuming that these tests are an accurate and reliable measure of workplace performance. This is not the case. The difference between groups on work sample tests is from .6 to .8, depending upon the extent to which the test evaluates cognitive skills (Roth et al., 2008).

Neither the academic nor the industrial data support the contention that the tests are unfair because they underpredict the performance of African Americans, the group for which most of the data has been gathered.

The second charge, that minority group members do not have adequate opportunities to acquire the skills required both to score well on the tests and to do well in academia and the workplace is not a criticism of the test, for a test can only be expected to evaluate current skills. But it does raise an important question. Why do these group differences appear?

The short answer is that we do not know. A longer answer is that although we know something relevant to the topic, we do not know enough to answer the question definitively.

Certain environmental variables affecting group differences have been identified. Some concern aspects of the environment over which the affected individuals have relatively little control. Latino and African American families tend to be of lower SES than Whites and thus to live in more impoverished neighborhoods. This may result in greater exposure to atmospheric toxins, including atmospheric lead. Minority children tend to be born at lower birth weights, which is an indicator of risk for lower test scores. Other negative indices of maternal health during pregnancy are high in low-SES groups and thus are statistically associated with minority group status, because Latino and African American families are more likely than White families to be in an economically stressed SES group (Nisbett, 2009).

Some studies have identified social practices that appear to injure cognitive growth. Children from low SES families, in general, are less prepared for schooling, upon entering, than are children from middle and high SES families. This deficiency appears to influence the rate of learning throughout a child's school career (Phillips, Crouse, & Ralph, 1998). Because minority group children tend to come from families with relatively low SES, African American and Latino children will be differentially affected by deficiencies in the home environment. Once in the school system, peer group pressures for studying (or not studying) differ across minority groups, in a way that could influence the observed gaps in educational performance (Steinberg, 1996).

Abstractly, deleterious social processes could be changed by variables such as parenting classes or advertising campaigns aimed at convincing high school students that studying is socially desirable. In practice, social customs may be embedded in other customs and/or situational constraints, such as economic stressors. Deleterious behaviors can be changed, but doing so is not easy.

Many, although not all, of the studies that support these statements have been isolated controlled or semicontrolled, "natural" experiments. As such, they show that certain variables associated with minority group status could have an influence on racial/ethnic differences in performance. However, the studies are not sufficiently widespread to make an "epidemiological" statement about how much of the gap actually is associated with various environmental variables. Therefore, statements that the gap is entirely due to environmental variables (Nisbett, 2009) are not warranted.

On the other hand, statements that assign large portions of the gap to genetic variation (Rushton & Jensen, 2005) are equally unwarranted. The latter statements are carried forward entirely by analogy to genetic variation within the White group. Because the genes that separate racial/ethnic groups are only a small part of the total genome, and because we do not know what genes are involved in variations in normal intelligence, speculating about the size of the genetic contribution to the gap goes far beyond the evidence.

What is the future for studies of racial/ethnic differences in intelligence? Some may feel that the subject does not warrant investigation, either because the situation is so complicated that clear answers cannot be obtained or because finding low scores among minority group members could then be used to justify cessation of various affirmative action and equal opportunity programs.

The second objection is a specific example of the argument that some knowledge is too dangerous to have. Discussing this argument fully would raise issues of ethics and social policy that go far beyond the study of intelligence. However, I do want to close this section with two comments that are related to the objection.

A case can be made for studying group differences per se because the groups do exist as important segments of our society. It is important to determine the cognitive resources within different groups in order to make informed decisions about programs intended to promote equality of opportunity, including programs intended to increase those resources. Otherwise, relevant policy decisions will be made on the basis of what different policy makers think the situation is, rather than what it actually is. Understanding group differences would not dicate policy decisions, but it could inform them. In the words of a widely cited comment on politics, "Everyone is entitled to his own opinion, but not to his own facts."[1] The second point is that research on group differences in intelligence

1 Usually attributed to U.S. Senator Daniel Patrick Moynihan (1927–2005), but at times to other political figures.

certainly should not stop at documenting differences. We need to know what causes them. Research on the causes of cognitive competence is important in its own right. Inhibiting such research because it might reveal group differences is both inimical to the scientific ideal of free inquiry into the natural world and, as a practical matter, isolates policy makers from information that can be relevant to them in many important situations. So the research should be done.

But, given the understandable emotions aroused by reports of group differences, special care should be taken to maintain the highest scientific standards when discussing racial/ethnic differences in intelligence (Hunt & Carlson, 2007).

Summary

I have attempted to lay out the current status and future research questions relevant to several fields of intelligence. To close I briefly remind the reader of what these questions are.

The biggest challenge (and opportunity) will be to expand research on intelligence from observations within the conventional testing paradigm to observations of behavior in everyday life. This will assist us in expanding our notions of intelligence, coordinating research on intelligence and personality, and understanding how intelligence is used in the workplace and in everyday life. We need a far better picture of the role of intelligence in adult behavior than we now have.

Advances in brain imaging have made possible great advances in our understanding of the relation between brain structures and intelligence. The next step will be to understand the relation between brain processes and intelligence. One of the most important issues will be to provide a physiological explanation for individual differences in processing speed. Understanding why there are marked changes in processing speed across the adult years will be particularly important.

Questions relating to the genetics of intelligence will move from studies showing the value of h (something we do not need to investigate further!) to the identification of the genes that produce individual differences in cognitive power, within the normal range. This is likely to be a slow process, as we may be looking at many small effects.

Epidemiological and demographic studies of intelligence will, we hope, move from demonstrations of differences in test scores and demonstrations of potential environmental influences to a more constructive analysis of the quantitative contribution of various causes of intelligence to the gap between different racial/ethnic groups, and to the much smaller, more specialized differences in cognition between men and women. These studies should be conducted in the tradition of detached analysis that characterizes science at its best. Given the emotionally charged nature of the topic, this may be too much to hope for.

Much has been learned; much remains to be learned.

References

Ackerman, P. L. (2000). Domain-specific knowledge as the "dark matter" of adult intelligence: Gf/Gc, personality, and interest correlates. *Journal of Gerontology: Psychological Sciences, 55B*, 69–84.

Baddeley, A. D. (1986). *Working memory*. Oxford, UK: Oxford University Press.

Bamshad, M., Woodling, S., Salisbury, B. A., & Stephens, J. C. (2004, August). Deconstructing the relationship between genetics and race. *Nature Reviews: Genetics, 5*, 598–609.

Benbow, C. P., & Lubinski, D. (Eds.). (1996). *Intellectual talent: Psychometric and social issues*. Baltimore, MD: Johns Hopkins University Press.

Boring, E. G. (1923, June 6). Intelligence as the tests test it. *New Republic, 35*, 35–37.

Campbell, J. P., & Knapp, D. (Eds.). (2001). *Exploring the limits in personnel selection and classification*. Mahwah, NJ: Erlbaum.

Cattell, R. B. (1971). *Abilities: Their structure, growth, and action*. Boston, MA: Houghton Mifflin.

College Board. (2009). *College Bound Seniors, 2009*. New York, NY: Author.

Cronbach, L. J., & Snow, R. E. (1977). *Aptitudes and instructional methods: A handbook for research on interactions*. New York, NY: Irvington.

Deary, I. J., Strand, S., Smith, P., & Fernandes, C. (2007), Intelligence and educational achievement. *Intelligence*, 35(1), 13–21.

Deary, I. J., Whalley, L. J., & Starr, J. M. (2009). *A lifetime of intelligence: Follow-up studies of the Scottish Mental Surveys of 1932 and 1947*. Washington, DC: American Psychological Association.

Edwards, A. W. F. (2003). Human genetic diversity: Lewontin's fallacy. *BioEssays*, 25(8), 798–801.

Flynn, J. R. (2007). *What is intelligence?* Cambridge, UK: Cambridge University Press.

Gardner, H. (1983). *Frames of mind: The theory of multiple intelligences*. New York, NY: Basic Books.

Gardner, H. (1993). *Multiple intelligences: The theory in practice*. New York, NY: Basic Books.

Halpern, D. F., Benbow, C. P., Geary, D. C., Gur, R. C., Hyde, J. S., & Gernsbacher, M. A. (2007). The science of sex differences in science and mathematics. *Psychological Science in the Public Interest*, 6(1), 1–51.

Hedges, L. V., & Nowell, A. (1998). Black-White test score convergence since 1965. In C. Jenks & M. Phillips (Eds.), *The black-white test score gap* (pp. 129–181). Washington, DC: Brookings Institution.

Horn, J. L. (1986). Intellectual ability concepts. In R. L. Sternberg (Ed.), *Advances in the psychology of human intelligence* (Vol. 3, pp. 35–78). Hillsdale, NJ: Erlbaum.

Hunt, E. (1995). *Will we be smart enough? A cognitive analysis of the coming workforce*. New York, NY: Russell Sage.

Hunt, E. (2011). *Human intelligence*. Cambridge, UK: Cambridge University Press.

Hunt, E., & Carlson, J. (2007). Considerations relating to the study of group differences in intelligence. *Perspectives in Psychological Science*, 2(2), 194–213.

Hunt, E., & Madhyastha, T. M. (2008). Recruitment modeling: An analysis and application to the study of male-female differences in intelligence. *Intelligence*, 36(6), 653–663.

Jensen, A. R. (1998). *The g factor: The science of mental ability*. Westport, CT: Praeger Publishers/Greenwood.

Jensen, A. R. (2006). *Clocking the mind: Mental chronometry and individual differences*. Amsterdam, the Netherlands: Elsevier.

Johnson, W., & Bouchard, T. J., Jr. (2005a). The structure of human intelligence: It is verbal, perceptual, and image rotation (VPR), not fluid and crystallized. *Intelligence*, 33(4), 393–416.

Johnson, W., & Bouchard, T. J., Jr. (2005b). Constructive replication of the visual perceptual image-rotation model in Thurstone's (1941) battery of 60 tests of mental ability. *Intelligence*, 33(4), 417–430.

Johnson, W., & Bouchard, T.J., Jr. (2007a). Sex differences in mental abilities: *g* masks the dimensions on which they lie. *Intelligence*, 35(1), 23–39.

Johnson, W., & Bouchard, T. J., Jr. (2007b). Sex differences in mental ability: A proposed means to link them to brain structure and functioning. *Intelligence*, 35(3), 197–209.

Johnson, W., te Nijenhuis, J., & Bouchard, T. J., Jr. (2007). Replication of the hierarchical visual-perception-rotation model in De Wolff and Buiten's (1963) battery of 46 tests of mental ability. *Intelligence*, 35(3), 69–81.

Jung, R. E., & Haier, R. J. (2007). The parieto-frontal integration theory (P-FIT) of intelligence. Converging neuroimaging evidence. *Behavioral and Brain Sciences*, 30, 135–187.

Kovarik, W. (2005). Ethyl leaded gasoline: How a classic occupational disease became an international public health disaster. *International Journal of Occupational Health*, 11(4), 384–397.

Kyllonen, P. C., & Christal, R. E. (1990). Reasoning ability is (little more than) working memory capacity?! *Intelligence*, 14, 389–433.

Lippmann, W. (1922a, October 25). The mental age of Americans. *New Republic* 32(412), 213–215.

Lippmann, W. (1922b, November 1). The mental age of Americans. *New Republic*, 32(413), 246–248.

Lubinski, D., Benbow, C. P., Webb, R. M., & Bleske-Rechek, A. (2006). Tracking exceptional human capital over two decades. *Psychological Science*, 17(3), 194–199.

Lynn, R., & Vanhanen, T. (2002). *IQ and the wealth of nations*. Westport, CT: Praeger.

Lynn, R., & Vanhanen, T. (2006). *IQ and global inequality*. Augusta, GA: Washington Summit.

Mattern, K. D., Pattern, B. F., Shaw, E. J., Kobrin, J. F., & Barbuti, S. M. (2008). Differential validity and prediction of the SAT.

College Board Research Report 2008–4. New York, NY: College Entrance Examination Board.

McDaniel, M. A. (2005). Big-brained people are smarter: A meta-analysis of the relationship between in vivo brain volume and intelligence. *Intelligence*, 33(4), 337–346.

Murray, C. (2007). The magnitude and components of change in the black-white IQ difference from 1920 to 1991: A birth cohort analysis of the Woodcock-Johnson standardizations. *Intelligence*, 35, 305–318.

Nisbett, R. E. (2009). *Intelligence and how to get it*. New York, NY: Norton.

Phillips, M., Crouse, J., & Ralph, J. (1998). Does the black-white test score gap widen after children enter school? In C. Jenks & M. Phillips (Eds.), *The black-white test score gap* (pp. 229–272).Washington, DC: Brookings Institution.

Plomin, R., DeFries, J. C., McClearn, G. E., & McGuffin, P. (2008). *Behavioral genetics* (5th ed.). New York, NY: Worth.

Plomin, R., Kennedy, J. K. J., & Craig, I. W. (2006). The quest for quantitative trait loci associated with intelligence. *Intelligence*, 34(6), 513–526.

Robertson, K. F., Smeets, S., Lubinski, D., & Benbow, C. P. (2010) Beyond the threshold hypothesis. Even among the gifted and top math/science graduate students cognitive abilities, vocational interests, and lifestyle preferences matter for career choice, performance, and persistence. *Current Directions in Psychological Science*, 19(6), 346–351.

Roth, P., Borko, P., McFaurland, L., & Bauster, M. (2008). Work sample tests in personnel selection: A meta-analysis of black-white differences in overall and exercise scores. *Personnel Psychology*, 61(3), 637–662.

Rosenberg, N. A., Pritchard, J. K., Weber, J. L., Cann, H. M., Field, K. K., Zhivotovsky, L. A., & Feldman, M. A. (2002, December 20). Genetic structure of human populations. *Science*, 298, 2381–2385.

Rushton, J. P., & Jensen, A. R. (2005). Thirty years of research on race differences in cognitive ability. *Psychology, Public Policy, and Law*, 11(2), 235–294.

Sackett, P. R., Borneman, M. J., & Connelly, B. S. (2008). High-stakes testing in higher education and employment. *American Psychologist*, 6(4), 215–227.

Sackett, P. R., Kuncel, N. R., Arenson, J. J., Cooper, S. R., & Waters, S. D. (2009). Does socioeconomic status explain the relationship between admissions tests and post-secondary academic performance? *Psychological Bulletin*, 135(1), 1–22.

Sackett, P. R., Hardison, C. M., & Cullen, M. J. (2004). On interpreting stereotype threat as accounting for African American-White differences on cognitive tests. *American Psychologist*, 59(1),7–13.

Salthouse, T. A. (1996). The processing-speed theory of adult age differences in cognition. *Psychological Review*, 103(3), 403–428.

Schaie, K. W. (2005). *Developmental influences on adult intelligence*. Oxford, UK: Oxford University Press.

Schmidt, F. L., & Hunter, J. E. (1998). The validity and utility of selection methods in personnel psychology: Practical and theoretical implications of 85 years of research findings. *Psychological Bulletin*, 124(2), 262–274.

Shih, M., Pittinsky, T. L., & Ambady, N. (1999). Stereotype susceptibility: Identity salience and shifts in quantitative performance. *Psychological Science*, 10(1), 80–83.

Spearman, C. (1904). General intelligence, objectively determined and measured. *American Journal of Psychology*, 15, 201–293.

Spearman, C. (1923). *The nature of "intelligence" and the principles of cognition*. London, UK: Methuen.

Spearman, C. (1927). *The abilities of man*. London, UK: Macmillan.

Steinberg, R., with Brown, B. B., & Dornbusch, S. M. (1996). *Beyond the classroom: Why school reform has failed and what parents need to do*. New York, NY: Simon & Schuster.

Sternberg, R. J. (2003). *Wisdom, intelligence, and creativity synthesized*. Cambridge, UK: Cambridge University Press.

Sternberg, R. J., Forsythe, G. B., Hedlund, J., Horvath, J. A., Wagner, R. K., Williams, W. M., Snook, S. A., & Grigorenko, E. L. (2000). *Practical intelligence in everyday life*. New York, NY: Cambridge University Press.

Sternberg, R. J., Grigorenko, E. L., & Kidd, K. K. (2005). Intelligence, race, and genetics. *American Psychologist*, 60(1), 46–59.

Sternberg, R. J., Grigorenko, E. L.,Zhang, L-F. (2008) Styles of learning and thinking matter in instruction and assessment. *Perspectives on Psychological Science*, 3(6), 486–506.

Sticht, T. G., Armstrong, W. B., Hickey, D. T., & Caylor, J. S. (1987). *Cast-off youth: Policy and training methods from the military experience*. New York, NY: Praeger.

Strickler, L. J., & Ward, W. C. (2004). Stereotype threat, inquiring about test takers' ethnicity and gender, and standardized test performance. *Journal of Applied Social Psychology*, 34(4), 665–693.

Tang, H., Quertermous, T., Rodriguez, B., Kardia, S. L. R., Zhu, X., Brown, A., Pankow, J. S., Province, M. A., Hunt, S. C., Boerwinkle, E., Schork, N. J., & Risch, N. J. (2005). Genetic structure, self-identified race/ethnicity, and confounding in case-control association studies. *American Journal of Human Genetics*, 76, 268–275.

Terman, L. M., & Oden, M. H. (1959). *The gifted group at mid-life. Thirty five years' follow-up of the superior child*. Palo Alto, CA: Stanford University Press.

Turkheimer, E., Haley, A., Waldron, M., D'Onofrio, B., & Gottesman, I. (2003). Socioeconomic status modifies heritability of IQ in young children. *Psychological Science*, 14(6), 623–628.

Wicherts, J. M., Dolan, C. V., & Van Der Maas, H. L. J. (2010). A systematic literature review of the average IQ of Africans. *Intelligence*, 38(1), 1–20.

Author Index

Subject Index